Fifth Edition
Blue Book of
Tactical Firearms Values

by S.P. Fjestad
Edited by John B. Allen and David Kosowski

$29.95
Publisher's Softcover
Suggested List Price

Publisher's Limited Edition Hardcover
Suggested List Price - $49.95 (limited quantities)

Fifth Edition *Blue Book of Tactical Firearms Values*
by S.P. Fjestad

Publisher's Note:

This book is the result of nonstop and continuous firearms research obtained by attending and/or participating in trade shows, gun shows, auctions, and also communicating with contributing editors, gun dealers, collectors, company historians, and other knowledgeable industry professionals worldwide each year. This book represents an analysis of prices for which tactical firearms have actually been selling during that period at an average retail level. Although every reasonable effort has been made to compile an accurate and reliable guide, gun prices may vary significantly (especially auction prices) depending on such factors as the locality of the sale, the number of sales we were able to consider, and economic conditions. Accordingly, no representation can be made that the guns listed may be bought or sold at prices indicated, nor shall the author or publisher be responsible for any error made in compiling and recording such prices and related information.

All Rights Reserved
Copyright 2014
Blue Book Publications, Inc.
8009 34th Avenue South, Suite 250
Minneapolis, MN 55425 U.S.A.

Customer Service: 800-877-4867, ext. 3 (domestic only)
Phone No.: 952-854-5229
Fax No.: 952-853-1486
General Email: support@bluebookinc.com
Web site: www.bluebookofgunvalues.com

Published and printed in the United States of America

ISBN 10: 1-936120-53-4
ISBN 13: 978-1-936120-53-6

Distributed in part to the book trade by Ingram Book Company and Baker & Taylor.
Distributed throughout Europe by:

Visier GmbH
Wipsch 1
Bad Ems, Germany D-56130
www.vsmedien.de

Deutsches Waffen Journal
Rudolf-Diesel-Strasse 46
Blaufelden, D-74572 Germany
Website: www.dwj.de

ABOUT THE FRONT COVER

This year's front cover features Sturm Ruger's Model 77-GS Gunsite Scout bolt action rifle in .308 Win. cal. It features an 18 inch stainless steel barrel with flash suppressor, 10 shot box mag., alloy steel receiver, matte black finish, forward mounted Picatinny rail, checkered grey laminate stock, recoil pad, sling swivels, protected front sight and adj. ghost ring rear sight, Gunsite engraved logo grip cap, non-rotating Mauser type controlled round feed extractor, and comes in right or left-hand action.

ABOUT THE BACK COVER

Featuring the Patriot Ordnance Factory USA Gen4 semi-auto pistol - this pistol has a 12 ½ in. barrel and includes POF's new E² chamber design along with a fully ambidextrous lower complemented with the Phase 5 pistol buffer tube to provide comfort for the operator. The lower includes POF's 4 ½ lb. single stage drop-in trigger, and the upper has a nickel boron plated carrier with patented roller cam pin.

CREDITS

Art Department – Clint H. Schmidt
Printing – Forms & Systems Minnetonka, MN
Manuscript Supervision – Cassandra Faulkner
Proofing – David Kosowski, John Allen, Kelsey Fjestad, Cassandra Faulkner, and Lisa Beuning

TABLE OF CONTENTS

GENERAL INFORMATION

While many of you have probably dealt with our company for years, it may be helpful for you to know a little bit more about our operation, including information on how to contact us regarding our various titles and other informational services.

Blue Book Publications, Inc.
8009 34th Avenue South, Suite 250
Minneapolis, MN 55425 USA
GPS Coordinates: N44° 51 28.44, W93° 13.1709
Phone No.: 952-854-5229 • Customer Service (domestic and Canada): 800-877-4867
Fax No.: 952-853-1486 (available 24 hours a day)
Web site: www.bluebookofgunvalues.com

General Email: support@bluebookinc.com - we check our email at 9am, 12pm, and 4pm M - F (excluding major U.S. holidays). Please refer to individual email addresses listed below with phone extension numbers.

To find out the latest information on our products, including availability and pricing, consumer related services, and up-to-date industry information (blogs, trade show recaps with photos/captions, upcoming events, feature articles, etc.), please check our website, as it is updated on a regular basis. Surf us - you'll have fun!

Since our phone system is equipped with voice mail, you may also wish to know extension numbers, which have been provided below:

Ext. 10 - Beth Schreiber	(beths@bluebookinc.com)	Ext. 17 - Zachary R. Fjestad	(zachf@bluebookinc.com)
Ext. 11 - Katie Sandin	(katies@bluebookinc.com)	Ext. 18 - Tom Stock	(toms@bluebookinc.com)
Ext. 13 - S.P. Fjestad	(stevef@bluebookinc.com)	Ext. 19 - Cassandra Faulkner	(cassandraf@bluebookinc.com)
Ext. 14 - Kelsey Fjestad	(kelseyf@bluebookinc.com)	Ext. 20 - Adam Burt	(adamb@bluebookinc.com)
Ext. 15 - Clint H. Schmidt	(clints@bluebookinc.com)	Ext. 22 – Kate Steffenson	(kates@bluebookinc.com)
Ext. 16 - John B. Allen	(johna@bluebookinc.com)		

Office hours are: 8:30am - 5:00pm CST, Monday - Friday.

Additionally, an after-hours message service is available for ordering. All orders are processed within 24 hours of receiving them, assuming payment and order information is correct. Depending on the product, we typically ship Fed Ex, UPS, Media Mail, or Priority Mail. Expedited shipping services are also available domestically for an additional charge. Please contact us directly for an expedited shipping quotation.

All correspondence regarding technical information/values on guns or guitars is answered in a FIFO (first in, first out) system. That means that letters, faxes, and email are answered in the order in which they are received, even though some people think that their emails take preference over everything else.

Online subscriptions and informational services are available for the *Blue Book of Gun Values, Blue Book of Tactical Firearms Values, Blue Book of Modern Black Powder Arms, American Gunsmiths, Blue Book of Airguns, Ammo Encyclopedia, Blue Book of Pool Cues, Blue Book of Electric Guitars, Blue Book of Acoustic Guitars,* and the *Blue Book of Guitar Amplifiers.*

As this edition goes to press, the following titles/products are currently available, unless otherwise specified:

35th Anniversary Edition *Blue Book of Gun Values* by S.P. Fjestad

5th Edition *Blue Book of Tactical Firearms Values* by S.P. Fjestad

Ammo Encyclopedia, 4th Edition by Michael Bussard

Blue Book Pocket Guide for Beretta Firearms & Values by S.P. Fjestad

Blue Book Pocket Guide for Browning/FN Firearms & Values
2nd Edition by S.P. Fjestad

Blue Book Pocket Guide for Colt Dates of Manufacture, 2nd Edition by R.L. Wilson

Blue Book Pocket Guide for Colt Firearms & Values 2nd Edition by S.P. Fjestad

Blue Book Pocket Guide for Remington Firearms & Values
2nd Edition by S.P. Fjestad

Blue Book Pocket Guide for Smith & Wesson Firearms & Values
2nd Edition by S.P. Fjestad

Blue Book Pocket Guide for Sturm Ruger Firearms & Values
2nd Edition by S.P. Fjestad

Blue Book Pocket Guide for Winchester Firearms & Values 2nd Edition by S.P. Fjestad

11th Edition *Blue Book of Airguns* by Dr. Robert D. Beeman & John B. Allen

8th Edition *Blue Book of Modern Black Powder Arms* by John Allen

Black Powder Revolvers - Reproductions & Replicas by Dennis Adler

Black Powder Long Arms & Pistols - Reproductions & Replicas by Dennis Adler

John Bianchi – An American Legend – 50 Years of Gunleather by Dennis Adler

3rd Edition *The Book of Colt Firearms* by R.L. Wilson

Book of Colt Paper 1834-2011 by John Ogle

L.C. Smith Production Records by Jim Stubbendieck

American Engravers – The 21st Century by C. Roger Bleile

Mario Terzi – Master Engraver by Elena Micheli-Lamboy & Stephen Lamboy

Firmo & Francesca Fracassi – Master Engravers by Elena Micheli-Lamboy & Stephen Lamboy

Giancarlo & Stefano Pedretti – Master Engravers by Elena Micheli-Lamboy & Stephen Lamboy

American Gunsmiths, 2nd Edition by Frank Sellers

Parker Gun Identification & Serialization, compiled by Charlie Price and edited by S.P. Fjestad

Blue Book of Electric Guitars, 14th Edition, by Zachary R. Fjestad

Blue Book of Acoustic Guitars, 14th Edition, by Zachary R. Fjestad

Blue Book of Guitar Amplifiers, 4th Edition, by Zachary R. Fjestad

Blue Book of Guitars 14th Edition DVD-ROM

Blue Book of Guitar Amplifiers 4th Edition CD-ROM

Gibson Flying V 2nd Edition by Larry Meiners & Zachary R. Fjestad

Gibson Amplifiers 1933-2008 – 75 Years of the Gold Tone by Wallace Marx Jr.

The Marshall Bluesbreaker – The Story of Marshall's First Combo by John R. Wiley

B.B. King's Lucille and the Loves Before Her by Eric E. Dahl

If you would like to get more information about any of the above publications/products, simply check our web sites: www.bluebookofgunvalues.com and www.bluebookofguitarvalues.com

We would like to thank all of you for your business in the past – you are the reason we are successful. Our goal remains the same – to give you the best products, the most accurate and up-to-date information for the money, and the highest level of customer service available in today's marketplace. If something's right, tell the world over time. If something's wrong, please tell us immediately – we'll make it right.

FOREWORD
by S.P. Fjestad

Nobody does tactical better than FNH USA's booth at the SHOT Show. Author/Publisher S.P. Fjestad is shown with an FN M3M .50 BMG cal. belt-fed machine gun, which cycles at 1,100 RPM!

Welcome to the new and significantly expanded 5th Edition of the *Blue Book of Tactical Firearms Values*. Having just attended the SHOT (Shooting, Hunting, Outdoor Trade) Show in Las Vegas and its European equivalent, IWA (International Trade Fair for Hunting and Sporting Arms and Accessories), in Nuremberg, Germany, tactical firearms in a wide variety of configurations will continue to be a factor for domestic consumer sales. Now with over 250 AR-15 and AK-47 manufacturers/trademarks included, most of which have complete model listings with detailed descriptions, this newest 5th Edition remains your only source for tactical information and up-to-date values.

Barack Obama
The World's Greatest Tactical Gun Salesman!

2013 will go down in the annals of history as the year U.S. firearms consumers shattered all previous records on the staggering gross dollar amount spent on guns and ammo purchases, with the lion's share of this astronomical figure expended on the ever expanding variations of tactical firearms – especially AR-15s and high-cap semi-auto pistols. One long-time gun dealer summed up 2013 during the SHOT Show by commenting, "I've never seen consumers for tactical firearms this desperate before. A lot of them didn't buy their first or second choice, they bought whatever was left."

Are We Headed Down From the Summit?

So what's changed in the past year as this edition goes to press? A lot. This time last year, the AR-15 marketplace was still on fire, mostly due to the fear, greed, and speculation about what Obama and Congress might do after the Sandy Hook tragedy. Despite threats and promises from many congressional leaders determined to pass some type of new firearms legislation, not one new federal gun law was enacted. Sensing nothing threatening was on the horizon for potential AR-15 restrictions and high cap magazines (both pistol and rifle), consumer demand started falling off in late summer, and by Thanksgiving most of the back orders had either been cancelled or fulfilled. The buffalo herd (American AR-15 buyers) had finally stopped stampeding after being on almost a non-stop run for five years. How has it affected pricing? With a few exceptions, most new AR-15 values are now below their suggested retails, and more importantly, they're not selling that well. AR-15 demand is now concentrated on the lower, entry-level $500-$600 price point.

So What's Hot This Year?

- Tactical bolt action rifles. Twenty-five years ago, this configuration was commonly referred to as sniper rifles, and Steyr's legendary SSG led the way with most of the sales going to SWAT teams and law enforcement with little consumer interest. It amazes me that despite a proliferation of expensive, high-quality makes and models, this segment of the marketplace is flourishing.

- Today, consumer interest in the expensive sport of long range shooting and hunting has never been greater, no doubt aided by all the new precision optics, high tech software, and smart phone/tablet apps. A 15 inch group at 1,000 yards used to be obtainable only by Camp Perry level of shooters. With today's advances in electronics, optics, and precision machining technology, even a beginner with the right equipment can put 1,000-yard shots on the paper with a little coaching. The best example of this is what TrackingPoint has been able to accomplish in a couple of years.

- .22 LR ammo – still hard to get with $35-$50 per brick pricing now the norm. No, it won't get any better the rest of this year, and I doubt if it will ever be cheap again. The .22 cal. segment of the AR-15 marketplace continues to suffer as a result – why buy the hardware if the software isn't available or too expensive? Plinking has been replaced by plunking!

- High cap pistols remain back ordered regardless of caliber or finish. Buzz words for finishes this year are Muddy Girl, Kryptek, Cerakote, and FDE (flat dark earth).

- Conceal carry anything.

Predictions for 2014

Many gun manufacturers and experienced dealers have told me they would be satisfied if 2014 will be as good as 2012. Nobody is expecting another 2013 anytime in the near future. This will be the year that store owners and managers will really have to manage their inventory carefully. Many dealers who didn't cancel their AR-15 back orders during the last quarter of 2013 are now receiving their shipments, with little consumer interest unless deep discounting is used to sell the product. This is a major problem because as these AR-15 bills become due, dealers are squeezed for cash flow, and even worse, cannot afford to buy the inventory that is still in demand.

In closing, I would like to thank our entire staff for its dedication, perseverance, and commitment to both quality products and services. All of the contributing editors and firearms industry personnel also deserve a large thank you for all the help and support they have provided over the years. And finally, you, the consumer/reader are the reason this book has become the firearms industry's most recognized and accepted reference source on tactical firearms and up-to-date values. We will continue to expand it, and make certain this publication stays the best value for your money.

Sincerely,

S.P. Fjestad

Author and Publisher – *Blue Book of Tactical Firearms Values*

GUN QUESTIONS/APPRAISALS POLICY

Whether we wanted it or not, Blue Book Publications, Inc. has ended up in the driver's seat as the clearing house for gun information. Because the volume of gun questions now requires full-time attention, we have developed a standardized policy that will enable us to provide you with the service you have come to expect from Blue Book Publications, Inc. To that end, we have extended all of these services to our website (www.bluebookofgunvalues.com).

To ensure that the research department can answer every gun question with an equal degree of thoroughness, a massive firearms library of well over 1,300 reference books, thousands of both new and old factory brochures, price sheets, most major auction catalogs, and dealer inventory listings are maintained and constantly updated. It's a huge job, and we answer every question like we could go to court on it.

POLICY FOR GUN QUESTIONS

The charge is $10 per gun value question ($15 per if the firearm make and/or model needs to be identified first) payable by a major credit card. All gun questions are answered on a first-come, first-served basis. All pricing requests will be answered with a value range only. Gun question telephone hours are 1:00 p.m. to 5:00 p.m., M-F, CST, no exceptions please. You must provide us with all the necessary gun information if you want an accurate answer. Our goal is to answer most telephone gun questions in less than 5 business days, unless we're away attending trade/gun shows.

APPRAISAL INFORMATION

Written appraisals will be performed only if the following criteria are met:

We must have good quality photos with a complete description, including manufacturer's name, model, gauge or caliber, barrel length, and other pertinent information. On some firearms (depending on the trademark and model), a factory letter may be necessary. Our charge for a written is 2% of the appraised value with a minimum of $30 per gun. For email appraisals please refer to www.bluebookofgunvalues.com. Please allow 2-3 weeks response time per appraisal request.

ADDITIONAL SERVICES

Individuals requesting a photocopy of a particular page or section from any edition for insurance or reference purposes will be billed at $5 per page, up to 5 pages, and $3.50 per page thereafter. Please direct all gun questions and appraisals to:

Blue Book Publications, Inc.
Attn: Research Dept.
8009 34th Ave. S., Suite 250
Minneapolis, MN 55425 USA
Phone: 952-854-5229, ext. 16 • Fax: 952-853-1486 • www.bluebookofgunvalues.com
Email: guns@bluebookinc.com
Use "Firearm Inquiry" in the subject line or it may get deleted.

ACKNOWLEDGEMENTS

The publisher would like to express his thanks to the following people and companies:

David Kosowski	Eyck Pflaumer – Umarex	Paul Pluff – Smith & Wesson
John B. Allen	Dr. Leonardo M. Antaris	McMillian Group International
G. Brad Sullivan	Michael Tenny – Cheaper Than Dirt	DSA, Inc.
Linda Powell - Mossberg	Midway USA	PTR 91, Inc.
Bud Fini – SIG Arms	Brownells	Olympic Arms
"Uncle" Randy Luth	Stanley Ruselowski	FNH USA
DPMS Firearms (LLC)	Terry Carter	Richard Churchill – Colt
Mark Eliason – Windham Weaponry	Richard Fitzpatrick – Magpul Industries	Chad Hiddleson
Mark Westrom – Armalite	Steve Hornady	Rick Nahas
Jeff Swisher & Angela Harrell – H&K USA	Jay Portz – RWC Group LLC	

MEET THE STAFF

Many of you may want to know what the person on the other end of the telephone/fax/email looks like, so here are the faces that go with the voices and emails.

S.P. Fjestad
Author/Publisher

Co-editors John B. Allen (l), and David Kosowski (r), contemplate yet another iron sight image.

Lisa Beuning
Manuscript Editor

Cassandra Faulkner
Executive Editor

Adam Burt
President

Tom Stock
CFO

Clint H. Schmidt
Art Director

Kelsey Fjestad
Web Media Manager/Proofreader

Beth Schreiber
Operations Manager

Kate Steffenson
Operations

Katie Sandin
Operations

Zachary R. Fjestad
Author/Editor Guitar & Amp Division

DEFINITIONS OF TACTICAL FIREARMS
For Revolvers, Rifles, Semi-Auto Pistols, and Shotguns

Like beauty, the descriptive adjective "tactical" as applied to firearms lies in the eyes of the beholder. That said, determining if a specific firearm is a tactical weapon is more often than not a subjective and emotional process. But that process also depends upon several generally accepted criteria, i.e. the firearm's finish, design, specific components, and/or accessories. Whether a firearm is "tactical" may also depend upon the circumstances associated with how or when that firearm is utilized. The author and editors have devoted a considerable amount of effort in defining "tactical", and determining the criteria for a firearm's inclusion in this book. We could be neither all-inclusive, nor overly restrictive, as that would diminish this book's utility. But we believe those criteria have been fairly and equitably applied. We recognize that you may not find a specific firearm(s), which you consider to be tactical, within these pages. We also expect that you will question why some firearms were included. Your comments, critiques, and suggestions are always welcome, as this newest 5th Edition of the *Blue Book of Tactical Firearms Values* remains a work-in-progress.

Author's Note: Original military contract firearms, including variations of rifles, shotguns, and pistols, are NOT included in this text (i.e., M1 Carbines, M1 Garands, Enfields, Trench Guns, etc.). Please refer to the *Blue Book of Gun Values* for current listings and values of these firearms (www.bluebookofgunvalues.com). Fully auto military contract firearms (and/or variations) that have been converted, modified, or redesigned by military arsenals and/or contracts for semi-auto operation only are included.

TACTICAL REVOLVERS

Tactical revolvers have at least three of the following factory/manufacturer standard features or options:

Non-glare finish (generally but there may be exceptions)

Mil Std 1913 Picatinny or equivalent rail(s)

Combat style grips (wood or synthetic)

Fixed or adjustable low profile primary sights

Auxiliary aiming/sighting/illumination equipment

Compensators or barrel porting

Combat triggers and hammers

Note: In addition to the above, open or iron sights for tactical revolvers may be tritium illuminated "night sights", fiber optic, "three dot" (which are now essentially "factory standard" for most handguns), or other visually- enhanced types. The benefits of attaching a suppressor to a revolver's barrel are negated as it is impossible to suppress the noise and flash which emanates from the barrel/cylinder gap.

TACTICAL RIFLES/CARBINES

Tactical rifles and carbines (semi-auto, bolt action, or slide action) have at least two of the following factory/manufacturer standard features or options:

Magazine capacity over ten rounds

Non-glare finish (generally, but there may be exceptions)

Mil Std 1913 Picatinny or equivalent rail(s)

Mostly synthetic stocks which may be fixed, folding, collapsible, adjustable, or with/without pistol grip

Some "Assault Weapon" Ban characteristics, such as flash suppressors, detachable magazines, bayonet lugs, or threaded barrels

Note: In addition to the above, tactical rifles normally have attachments for single-, traditional two-, or three-point slings. Open or iron sights may be tritium illuminated "night sights", fiber optic, or other visually-enhanced types. The capability to attach a suppressor is not by itself sufficient to include a firearm in this book.

For Revolvers, Rifles, Semi-Auto Pistols, and Shotguns

TACTICAL SEMI-AUTO PISTOLS

Tactical semi-auto pistols have at least three of the following factory/manufacturer standard features or options:
Magazine capacity over ten rounds if caliber is less than .45 ACP cal.

Non-glare finish (generally, but there may be exceptions)

Mil Std 1913 Picatinny or equivalent rail(s)

Combat style grips (wood or synthetic)

Fixed or adjustable low profile primary sights, or high profile sights for use with a suppressor

Auxiliary aiming/sighting/illumination equipment

Compensators, barrel porting, or threaded muzzles

Note: In addition to the above, tactical semi-auto pistols may have a lanyard attachment device. Open or iron sights may be tritium illuminated "night sights", fiber optic, "three dot" types (which are now essentially "factory standard" for most handguns) or other visually-enhanced types. The capability to attach a suppressor is not by itself sufficient to include a firearm in this book.

TACTICAL SHOTGUNS

Tactical shotguns (semi-auto or slide action) have at least two of the following factory/manufacturer standard features or options:
Higher capacity (than sporting/hunting shotguns) magazines, or magazine extensions

Non-glare finish (generally, but there may be exceptions)

Mil Std 1913 Picatinny or equivalent rail(s)

Mostly synthetic stocks which may be fixed, folding, collapsible, adjustable, or with/without pistol grip

Some "Assault Weapon" Ban characteristics, such as bayonet lugs, or detachable "high capacity" magazines

Rifle or ghost ring sights (usually adjustable)

Short (18-20 inches) barrel with a fixed cylinder choke, or a breaching/stand-off device

Note: In addition to the above, tactical shotguns normally have attachments for single-, traditional two-, or three-point slings. Open or iron sights may be tritium illuminated "night sights", fiber optic, "three dot", or other visually-enhanced types.

HOW TO USE THIS BOOK

The values listed in this Fifth Edition of the *Blue Book of Tactical Firearms Values* are based on the national average retail prices gathered from gun shows, dealers, and auction sites. This is not a wholesale pricing guide (there is no such thing). More importantly, do not expect to walk into a gun/pawn shop or trade/gun show and think that the proprietor/dealer should pay you the retail price listed within this text for your gun(s). Resale offers on most models could be anywhere from close to retail to up to 50% less than the values listed, depending on condition, availability and overall supply/demand economics. Prices paid by dealers will be dependent upon locality, desirability, dealer inventory, and potential profitability. In other words, if you want to receive 100% of the price (retail value), then you have to do 100% of the work (become the retailer, which also includes assuming 100% of the risk).

Percentages of original finish, (condition factors with corresponding prices/values, if applicable) are listed between 60% and 100%. Please consult the Photo Percentage Grading System (PPGS), available at no charge online at www.www.bluebookofgunvalues.com and also included in the *Blue Book of Gun Values.*

Included in this Fifth Edition is the most extensive Glossary ever compiled for tactical firearms, sights, and optics. Combined with the Anatomy illustrations, this will help you out immensely in determining correct terminology on the wide variety of tactical firearms available in today's marketplace. Also see Abbreviations for more detailed information about both nomenclature and terminology abbreviations.

This book contains three unique Trademark Indexes – one for current tactical firearms manufacturers, importers, and distributors, one for accessories, and another for ammunition. These Trademark Indexes are actually a source book unto themselves, and include the most recent emails, websites, and other pertinent contact information for these companies. No other publication has anything like it, and you could research online for days before getting this much up-to-date information!

The Index might be the fastest way to find the make/model you are looking for. To find a model in this text, first look under the name of the manufacturer, trademark, brand name, and in some cases, the importer. Next, find the correct category name (if any), which are typically Pistols, Revolvers, Rifles and Shotguns. In some cases, models will appear with MSRs only after the heading/category description.

Once you find the correct model or sub-model, determine the specimen's percentage of original condition, and find the corresponding percentage column showing the value of a currently manufactured model or the value on a discontinued model.

For the sake of simplicity, the following organizational framework has been adopted throughout this publication.

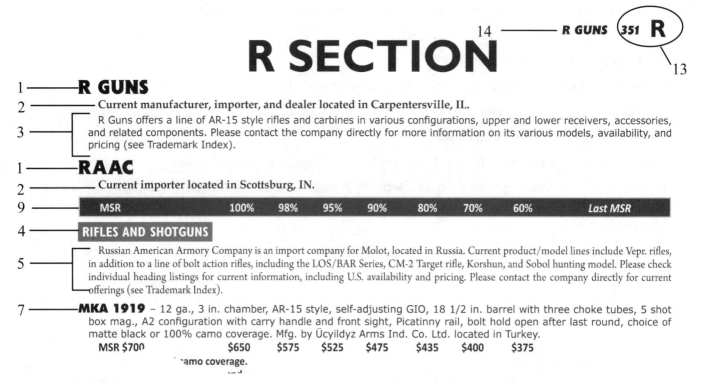

1. **Manufacturer Name or Trademark** – brand name, importer, trademark or manufacturer is listed alphabetically in uppercase bold face type.

2. **Manufacturer Status** – This information is listed directly beneath the manufacturer/trademark heading, providing current status and location along with importer information for foreign trademarks.

3. **Manufacturer Description** – These notes may appear next under individual heading descriptions and can be differentiated by the typeface. This will be specific information relating to the trademark or models.

4. **Category Name** – (normally, in alphabetical sequence) in upper case (inside a screened gray box), referring to various tactical configurations, including Pistols, Revolvers, Rifles, and Shotguns.

5. **Category Note** – May follow a category name to help explain the category, and/or provide limited information on models and current MSRs.

6. **Value Additions/Subtractions** – Value add ons or subtractions may be encountered directly under individual price lines or in some cases, category names, and are typically listed in either dollar amounts or percentages. These individual lines appear bolder than other descriptive typeface. On many guns less than 15 years old, these add/subtract adjustments will reflect the last

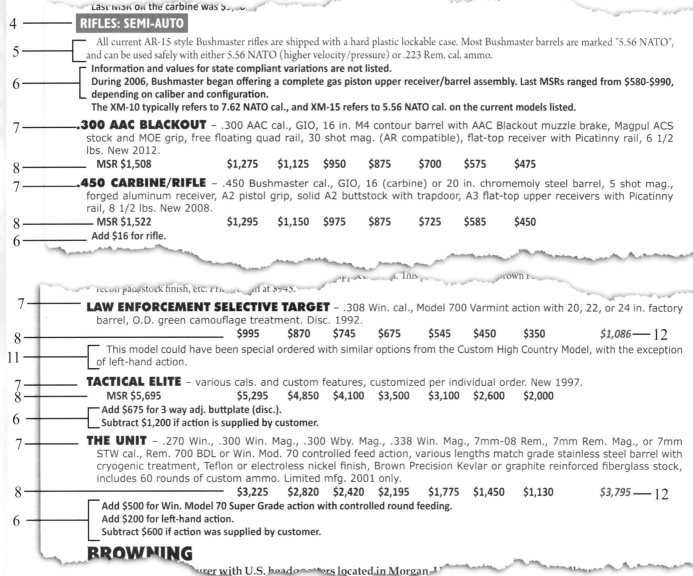

4 — **RIFLES: SEMI-AUTO**

5 — All current AR-15 style Bushmaster rifles are shipped with a hard plastic lockable case. Most Bushmaster barrels are marked "5.56 NATO", and can be used safely with either 5.56 NATO (higher velocity/pressure) or .223 Rem. cal. ammo.

6 — Information and values for state compliant variations are not listed.
During 2006, Bushmaster began offering a complete gas piston upper receiver/barrel assembly. Last MSRs ranged from $580-$990, depending on caliber and configuration.
The XM-10 typically refers to 7.62 NATO cal., and XM-15 refers to 5.56 NATO cal. on the current models listed.

7 — **.300 AAC BLACKOUT** – .300 AAC cal., GIO, 16 in. M4 contour barrel with AAC Blackout muzzle brake, Magpul ACS stock and MOE grip, free floating quad rail, 30 shot mag. (AR compatible), flat-top receiver with Picatinny rail, 6 1/2 lbs. New 2012.

8 — MSR $1,508 $1,275 $1,125 $950 $875 $700 $575 $475

7 — **.450 CARBINE/RIFLE** – .450 Bushmaster cal., GIO, 16 (carbine) or 20 in. chromemoly steel barrel, 5 shot mag., forged aluminum receiver, A2 pistol grip, solid A2 buttstock with trapdoor, A3 flat-top upper receivers with Picatinny rail, 8 1/2 lbs. New 2008.

8 — MSR $1,522 $1,295 $1,150 $975 $875 $725 $585 $450

6 — Add $16 for rifle.

7 — **LAW ENFORCEMENT SELECTIVE TARGET** – .308 Win. cal., Model 700 Varmint action with 20, 22, or 24 in. factory barrel, O.D. green camouflage treatment. Disc. 1992.

8 — $995 $870 $745 $675 $545 $450 $350   *$1,086* — 12

11 — This model could have been special ordered with similar options from the Custom High Country Model, with the exception of left-hand action.

7 — **TACTICAL ELITE** – various cals. and custom features, customized per individual order. New 1997.

8 — MSR $5,695 $5,295 $4,850 $4,100 $3,500 $3,100 $2,600 $2,000

6 — Add $675 for 3 way adj. buttplate (disc.).
Subtract $1,200 if action is supplied by customer.

7 — **THE UNIT** – .270 Win., .300 Win. Mag., .300 Wby. Mag., .338 Win. Mag., 7mm-08 Rem., 7mm Rem. Mag., or 7mm STW cal., Rem. 700 BDL or Win. Mod. 70 controlled feed action, various lengths match grade stainless steel barrel with cryogenic treatment, Teflon or electroless nickel finish, Brown Precision Kevlar or graphite reinforced fiberglass stock, includes 60 rounds of custom ammo. Limited mfg. 2001 only.

8 — $3,225 $2,820 $2,420 $2,195 $1,775 $1,450 $1,130   *$3,795* — 12

6 — Add $500 for Win. Model 70 Super Grade action with controlled round feeding.
Add $200 for left-hand action.
Subtract $600 if action was supplied by customer.

BROWNING

...rer with U.S. headquarters located in Morgan...

---

factory MSRs (manufacturer's suggested retail price) for that option, and need to be either added or subtracted to ascertain the original MSR.

7. Model Name and Description – Model Name appears flush left, is bold faced in all upper-case letters, either in chronological order (normally) or alphabetical order (sometimes, the previous model name and/or close sub variation will appear at the end in parentheses). Model descriptions follow and usually start out with caliber/gauge, type of action, barrel length, important features, weight, and year(s) of manufacture/importation.

8. Value line – This pricing information will follow directly below the model name and description. The information appears in descending order from left to right with the values corresponding to a condition factor shown in the Grading Line near the top of the page. A pricing line with an MSR automatically indicates the gun is currently manufactured, and the MSR (Manufacturer's Suggested Retail) is shown left of the 100% column. 100% price on a currently manufactured gun also assumes not previously sold at retail. In some cases, N/As (Not Applicable) are listed and indicate that either there is no MSR on this particular model or the condition factor is not frequently encountered, and the value is not predictable. On a currently manufactured gun, the lower condition specimens will bottom out at a value, and a lesser condition gun value will approximate the lowest value listed. Recently manufactured 100% specimens without boxes, warranties, etc., that are currently manufactured must be discounted slightly (5%-20%, depending on the desirability of make and model).

9. Grading Line – The 100%-60% grading line will normally appear at or near the top of each page.

10. Sub-model Name and Description – Variations within a model appear as sub-models, and they are differentiated from model names because they are preceded by a bullet, indented, and are in upper and lower case type, and are usually followed by a short description.

11. Model Note – Model notes and other pertinent information may follow price lines and value additions/subtractions. These appear in different type, and should be read since they contain both important and other critical, up-to-date information.

12. On many discontinued models and sub-models, an italicized value may appear at the end of the price line, indicating the last manufacturer's suggested retail price (LAST MSR).

13. Alphabetical Designator/Page Number – Capital letter indicating which alphabetical section you are in and the page number you are on.

14. Manufacturer Heading/Continued Heading – Continued Headings may appear at the top of the page, indicating a continuation of information for the manufacturer/trademarks from the previous page.

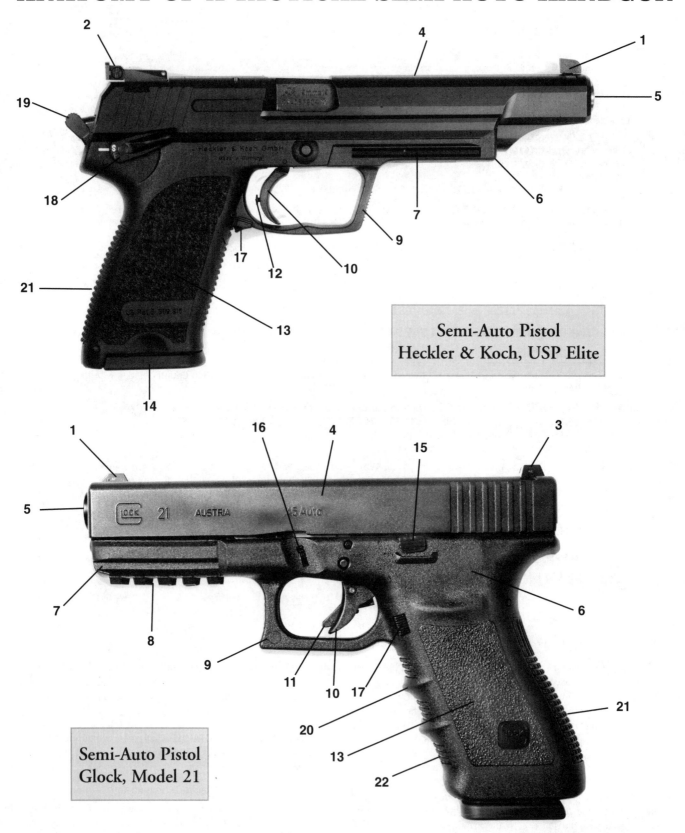

Semi-Auto Pistol
Heckler & Koch, USP Elite

Semi-Auto Pistol
Glock, Model 21

1.	Fixed blade front sight	9.	Trigger guard	17.	Magazine release
2.	Adj. rear sight	10.	Trigger	18.	Safety/decocking lever
3.	Fixed rear sight	11.	Trigger safety	19.	Hammer
4.	Slide	12.	Trigger overtravel stop	20.	Contoured finger grooves
5.	Barrel muzzle	13.	Grip frame	21.	Checkered rear grip frame
6.	Frame	14.	Magazine	22.	Checkered front grip frame
7.	Accessory/equipment rail	15.	Slide stop		
8.	Picatinny rail	16.	Takedown lever		

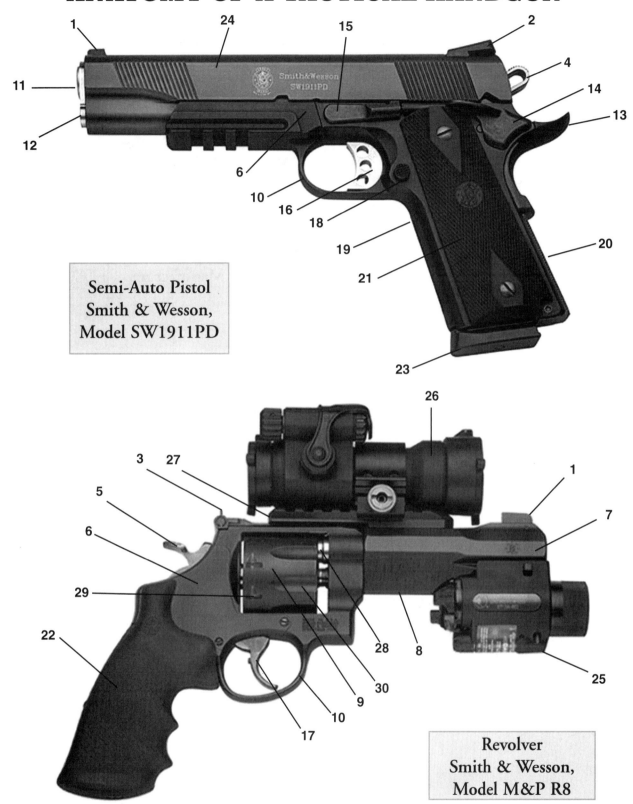

Semi-Auto Pistol
Smith & Wesson,
Model SW1911PD

Revolver
Smith & Wesson,
Model M&P R8

1.	Fixed blade front sight	11.	Barrel muzzle	21.	Grip
2.	Low profile combat rear sight	12.	Recoil spring guide rod	22.	Finger grooved grip
3.	Adj. blade rear sight	13.	Beavertail grip safety	23.	Magazine
4.	Skeletonized hammer	14.	Safety lever	24.	Slide with front and rear serrations
5.	Hammer with full spur	15.	Slide stop lever	25.	Flashlight (accessory)
6.	Frame	16.	Skeletonized trigger	26.	Reflex sight
7.	Barrel	17.	Trigger with over tactel stop	27.	Picatinny rail
8.	Barrel lug	18.	Magazine release	28.	Breech end of barrel
9.	Cylinder	19.	Checkered front grip strap	29.	Cylinder stop notch
10.	Trigger guard	20.	Checkered rear grip strap	30.	Cylinder flute

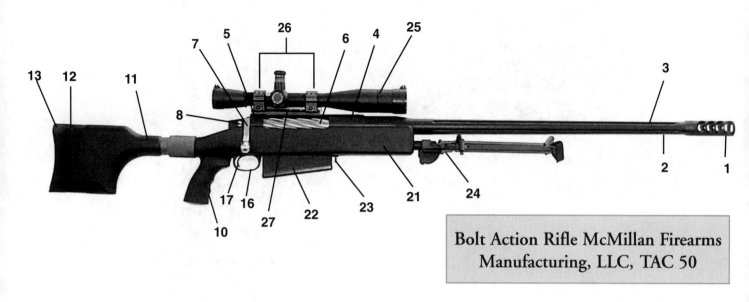

Bolt Action Rifle McMillan Firearms Manufacturing, LLC, TAC 50

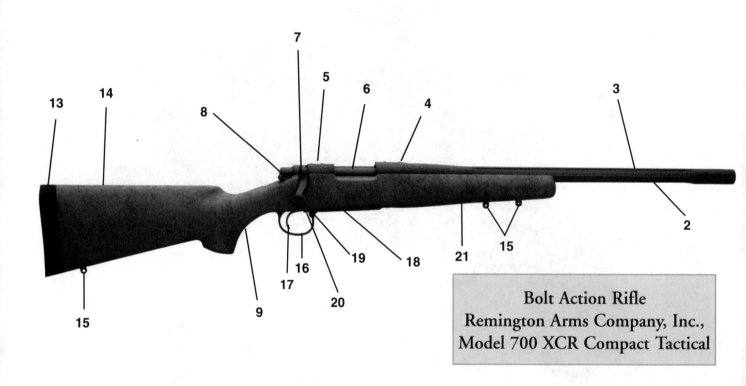

Bolt Action Rifle Remington Arms Company, Inc., Model 700 XCR Compact Tactical

1.	Muzzle brake	10.	Full pistol grip	19.	Floorplate release
2.	Barrel	11.	Takedown buttstock	20.	Bolt release lever
3.	Barrel fluting	12.	Buttstock spacers	21.	Forend
4.	Front receiver ring	13.	Buttpad	22.	Detachable box magazine
5.	Rear receiver bridge	14.	Buttstock	23.	Magazine release
6.	Bolt	15.	Sling swivel stud	24.	Detachable military style bipod
7.	Bolt handle	16.	Trigger guard	25.	Variable power scope w/target turrets
8.	Safety	17.	Trigger	26.	Scope rings
9.	Semi-pistol grip	18.	Hinged floorplate	27.	Picatinny rail (scope base)

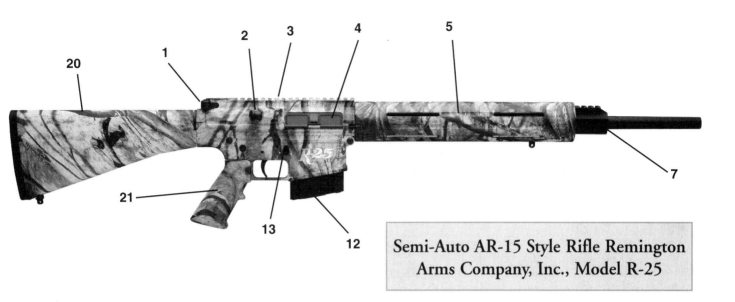

Semi-Auto AR-15 Style Rifle Remington
Arms Company, Inc., Model R-25

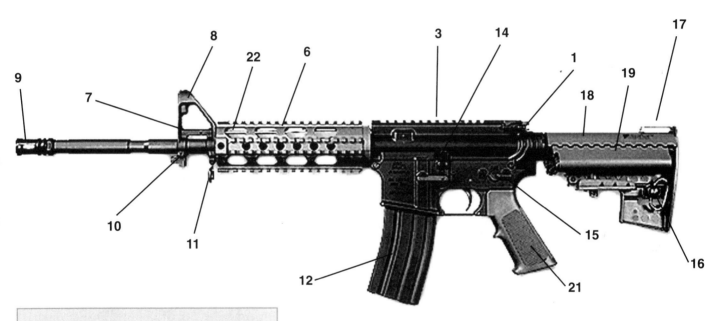

Semi-Auto AR-15/M4 Style Rifle
DSA Inc., ZM-4 Carbine

1. Charging handle	9. Flash suppressor	17. Single point sling attachment
2. Forward bolt assist	10. Bayonet mounting lug	18. Collapsible stock
3. Flat-top upper w/Picatinny rail	11. Front sling swivel	19. Cheekpiece
4. Ejection port dust cover	12. Detachable box magazine	20. Fixed buttstock
5. Free floating forearm	13. Magazine release button	21. Pistol grip
6. Quad rail forearm	14. Bolt release lever	22. Gas tube
7. Gas block w/Picatinny rail	15. Safety lever	
8. A2 style front sight	16. Rear sling swivel	

ANATOMY OF A TACTICAL SEMI-AUTO RIFLE

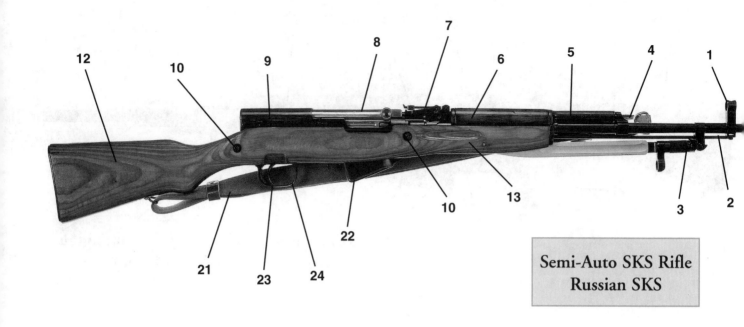

Semi-Auto SKS Rifle
Russian SKS

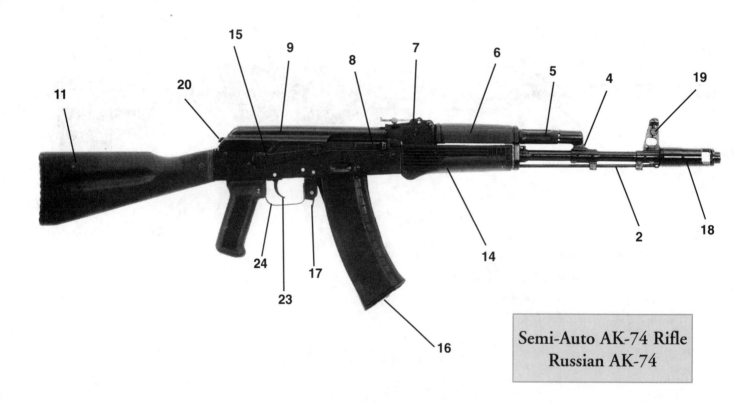

Semi-Auto AK-74 Rifle
Russian AK-74

1.	Hooded adjustable front sight	9.	Receiver cover	17.	Magazine release lever
2.	Cleaning rod	10.	Stock reinforcing cross bolts	18.	Flash suppressor
3.	Non-detachable folding bayonet	11.	Fixed buttstock	19.	Adjustable front sight
4.	Gas block	12.	Buttstock	20.	Takedown button
5.	Gas tube	13.	Forend	21.	Sling
6.	Handguard	14.	Forearm	22.	Non-detachable box magazine
7.	Rear tangent adjustable sight	15.	Safety lever	23.	Trigger
8.	Bolt	16.	Detachable box magazine	24.	Trigger Guard

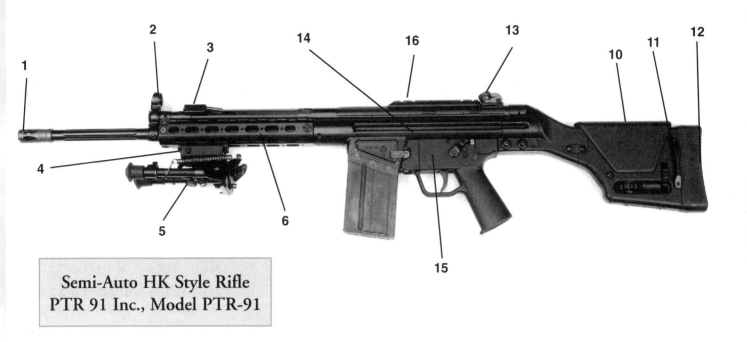

Semi-Auto HK Style Rifle
PTR 91 Inc., Model PTR-91

Semi-Auto AR-15 Style Rifle
Olympic Arms Inc., OA-93 Carbine

1.	Flash suppressor	7.	Free floating forearm	13.	Adjustable diopter rear sight
2.	Hooded front sight	8.	Shell deflector	14.	Stamped sheet metal receiver
3.	Charging handle	9.	Skeleton side folding stock	15.	Fire control group
4.	Bipod mounting adapter	10.	Adjustable cheekpiece	16.	Accessory and optics rail
5.	Bipod	11.	Sling attachment bar		
6.	Ventilated forearm	12.	Adjustable LOP (length of pull) buttpad		

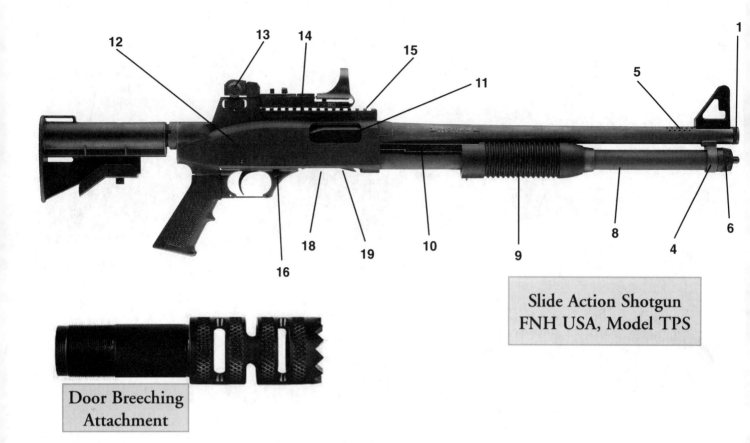

**Slide Action Shotgun
FNH USA, Model TPS**

**Door Breeching
Attachment**

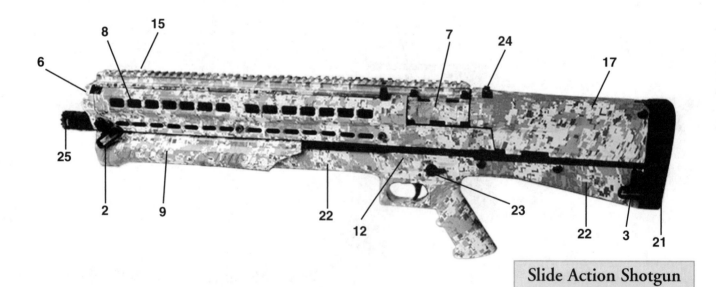

**Slide Action Shotgun
Utas - USA
Model UTS-15**

1.	Removable choke tube	10.	Action bar	19.	Carrier
2.	Front sling swivel	11.	Bolt	20.	Recoil absorbing pistol grip
3.	Rear sling swivel	12.	Receiver	21.	Recoil pad
4.	Forward magazine tube barrel band	13.	Back up iron sights	22.	Lower stock
5.	Barrel porting	14.	Reflex sight	23.	Safety lever
6.	Magazine end cap	15.	Picatinny rail	24.	Shell stop/mag. selector
7.	Left loading port door	16.	Safety button	25.	Tactical choke tube
8.	Magazine tube	17.	Upper stock		
9.	Forearm	18.	Loading port		

ANATOMY OF A TACTICAL SEMI-AUTO SHOTGUN

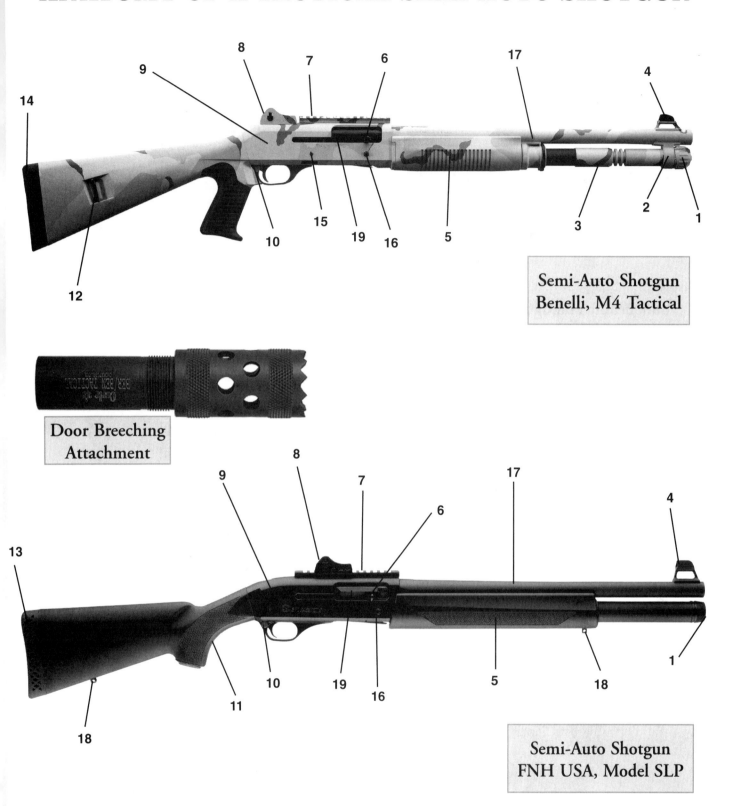

Semi-Auto Shotgun
Benelli, M4 Tactical

Door Breeching
Attachment

Semi-Auto Shotgun
FNH USA, Model SLP

1.	Magazine end cap	8.	Adjustable ghost-ring rear sight
2.	Forward magazine tube barrel band	9.	Receiver
3.	Magazine tube extension	10.	Safety
4.	Elevated front sight	11.	Semi-pistol grip
5.	Forearm	12.	Side mount sling bar
6.	Charging handle	13.	Ventilated recoil pad
7.	Picatinny rail	14.	Solid recoil pad

15.	Takedown pin
16.	Action release button
17.	Fixed choke barrel
18.	Sling swivel stud
19.	Ejection port w/charging handle slot

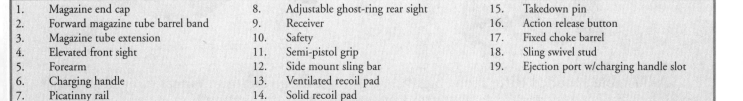

OPEN SIGHT ILLUSTRATIONS

Low Profile Handgun Combat Sights

Flip-Up Aperture Rear Sight

AR-15 Style Front Sight

AK Style Tangent Rear Sight

Adjustable Hooded Rifle Front Sight

Rifle or Shotgun Ghost Ring Rear Sight

OPEN SIGHT ILLUSTRATIONS

Elevated Rifle or Shotgun Front Sight

Tactical Shotgun Sight

Rail Mounted Laser Sight

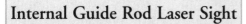

Internal Guide Rod Laser Sight

Grip Mounted Laser Sight

OPTICAL SIGHT ILLUSTRATIONS

Compact Fixed Power Scope

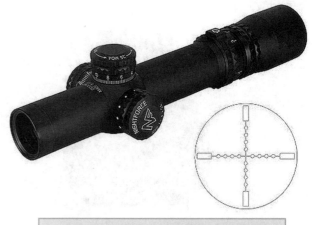

Compact Adjustable Power Scope with Mil-Dot Reticle

Full Size Fixed Power Scope with Mil-Dot Reticle and Target Turrets

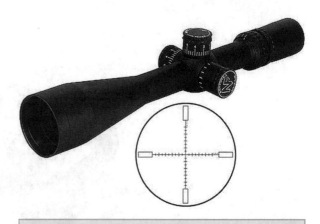

Full Size Adjustable Power Scope with Duplex Reticle and Target Turrets

Tube Style Reflex Dot Sight

Tubeless Style Reflex Dot Sight

Compact Reflex Dot Sight

GLOSSARY

1989 BUSH BAN

Refers to the U.S. Federal executive branch study and resulting regulations which banned the importation of firearms which did not meet sporting criteria , i.e. certain paramilitary semi-auto only rifles and shotguns. The study was undertaken in response to the Stockton, CA tragedy in which an AK-47 type rifle was criminally used by a so-called mass murderer. The Federal regulation, U.S.C. Title 18, Section 922r, applies to imported firearms and to firearms assembled in the U.S. using imported components. It is important to note that even though the Assault Weapon Ban (which applied to U.S. manufactured firearms, not imports) has expired, Section 922r remains in effect, and has the force of U.S. Federal law, regardless of its executive branch origin as opposed to U.S. Senate and House of Representatives legislation. Also see Section 922r.

5R

Five groove rifling developed in Russia. Instead of conventional six groove rifling with opposing lands and sharp edged transitions between lands and grooves, 5R lands oppose grooves and the sides of lands are cut at a sixty-five degree angle. Claimed benefits are: decreased bullet deformation, less jacket fouling, increased velocity, and greater accuracy.

A1 STYLE

Refers to an AR style rifle in A1 configuration, or A1 specific components (triangular handguard, short fixed buttstock, receiver with integral carry handle, four slot bird cage flash hider, smooth pistol grip, rear flip sight with short and long range apertures, lighter weight 1:14 twist barrel).

A2 STYLE

Refers to an AR style rifle in A2 configuration, or A2 specific components (circular bi-lateral handguard, longer fixed buttstock, receiver with integral carry handle and spent case deflector, five slot bird cage flash hider, finger rib pistol grip, windage and elevation adjustable rear flip sight with small day and large low light apertures, heavier weight 1:7 twist barrel).

A3 STYLE

Refers to an AR style rifle in A3 configuration, or A3 specific components (circular bi-lateral handguard, collapsible buttstock, receiver with flat top Picatinny rail and detachable carry handle, A2 flash hider/pistol grip/rear sight/barrel).

A4 STYLE

Refers to an AR style rifle in A4 configuration, or A4 specific components (same as A2 except for Modular Weapons System handguard).

ACCOUTREMENT

All equipment carried by soldiers on the outside of their uniform, such as buckles, belts, or canteens, but not weapons.

ACTION

An assembly consisting of the receiver or frame and the mechanism by which a firearm is loaded, fired, and unloaded. See ACTION TYPES for the various kinds of actions.

ACTION BAR FLATS

See WATER TABLE.

ACTION TYPES

Actions are broadly classified as either manual or self-loading. Manual actions may be single shot or repeater. Single shot actions include dropping block (tilting, falling, and rolling), break, hinged, and bolt. Repeater actions include revolver, bolt, lever, pump, and dropping block. Self-loading actions may be semiautomatic or automatic. Semi-auto and automatic actions by sub-type are:

  a. blowback: simple, lever delayed, roller delayed, gas delayed, toggle delayed, hesitation locked, and chamber-ring delayed.

  b. blow-forward.

  c. recoil: short, long, and inertia.

  d. gas: short stroke piston, long stroke piston, direct impingement, and gas trap.

ADJUSTABLE CHOKE

A device built into the muzzle of a shotgun enabling changes from one choke to another.

ADJUSTABLE FRONT SIGHT

A front sight which can be moved, relative to the barrel's axis, vertically for elevation and/or horizontally for windage adjustments.

ADJUSTABLE REAR SIGHT

A rear sight which can be moved, relative to the barrel's axis, vertically for elevation and/or horizontally for windage adjustments.

ADJUSTABLE SIGHT

A firearm sight which can be adjusted so that the shooter's point of aim and the projectile's point of impact coincide at a desired target distance. On a majority of firearms only the rear sight is adjustable, but front sights may also be adjustable.

AIRGUN

A gun that utilizes compressed air or gas to launch the projectile.

AK/AKM STYLE ACTION

A gas operated rifle action with a long-stroke gas piston, a tilting breechblock locking design, and a heavy milled (early versions) or lighter sheet metal (later versions) receiver. No regulator is used; the overall design, machining, tolerances, ease of maintenance, and component durability assure reliable function in all circumstances.

ANY OTHER WEAPON

Any other firearm which is not an NFA defined machine gun, short barrel rifle, short barrel shotgun, modern shoulder stocked pistol, suppressor (BATFE uses the term "silencer"), or destructive device. An AOW is: a device capable of being concealed on a person from which a shot can be discharged through the energy of an explosive; a smooth bore barrel pistol or revolver designed or redesigned to fire a fixed shotgun shell; a weapon with combination shotgun and rifle barrels twelve inches or more but less than eighteen inches in length, from which only a single discharge can be made from either barrel without manual reloading; and any such weapon which may be readily restored to fire. AOW examples: H&R Handyguns, Ithaca Auto-Burglar guns, cane guns, and guns modified/disguised so as to be unrecognizable as firearms.

APERTURE SIGHT

An iron rear sight which has a hole or aperture in a disc or semi-circular blade instead of a rectangular or "vee" notch of an open sight. May also be a front sight, or adjustable for windage/elevation, or have adjustable/interchangeable apertures.

AR-15 STYLE ACTION

A gas operated rifle action with a direct gas impingement system (i.e. no gas piston, no regulator, no moving parts), a bolt carrier enclosing a multi-lugged rotating bolt locking design, and a two-part light-weight receiver. Propellant gas flows through a gas tube, acts directly upon the bolt carrier to cycle the action, and vents into the receiver. AR-15 style actions have fewer parts, are more adaptable/modifiable, and are significantly lighter than AK, FAL, or HK91 style actions. However, more maintenance, cleaning, and lubrication are absolutely required for reliability, in contrast to other gas operated actions.

ASSAULT RIFLE

Definition usually depends on if you're pro-gun or anti-gun. If you're pro-gun, it generally refers to a military styled, short to immediate range battle rifle capable of selective fire (semi-auto or full auto). If you're anti-gun, it can include almost anything, including sporter rifles from the turn of the 20th century.

ASSAULT SHOTGUN

Refers to a shotgun manufactured by contract for the military or law enforcement with a barrel shorter than 18 inches, usually a semi-auto or slide action configuration.

ASSAULT WEAPONS BAN

Popular title for the Violent Crime Control and Law Enforcement Act of 1994, Public Law 103-322. See VIOLENT CRIME...LAW 103-322.

AUTO LOADING/LOADER

See SEMI-AUTO ACTION.

AUTOMATIC ACTION

An action design which continuously fires and performs all steps in the operating cycle if the trigger remains fully depressed and ammunition is present in the firearm's magazine or feeding system. Also known as full auto or fully automatic. Machine guns utilize automatic actions, which may be recoil, gas, or externally powered.

AUTOMATIC EJECTOR

See SELECTIVE AUTOMATIC EJECTOR.

BACK BORE/BACK-BORED

A shotgun barrel which has been bored to a diameter greater than normal for its gauge, but not greater than SAAMI specs for that gauge. The advantages of this are: higher shot velocity, more uniform and denser patterns and fewer deformed pellets.

BACK UP IRON SIGHTS

Flip up or fixed iron sights which are not the primary sight system. They are used if the primary optical sight system fails and usually co-witness (optic sight picture and back up sight picture share the same zero).

BACKSTRAP

Those parts of the revolver or pistol frame which are exposed at the rear of the grip.

BARREL

The steel tube (may be wrapped in a sleeve of synthetic material) which a projectile travels through. May or may not be rifled.

BARREL BAND

A metal band, either fixed or adjustable, around the forend of a gun that holds the barrel to the stock.

BARREL FLATS

The lower flat surfaces under the chambers of side-by-side shotgun barrels which contact the corresponding flat areas of the shotgun's receiver. Also see WATER TABLE.

BARREL LUG

A projection which extends from a barrel and performs a locating, supporting, or energy transfer function. Lugs may be separate components, or integral to barrels.

BARREL THROAT

At the breech end of a barrel, the segment of the bore which tapers from a non-rifled projectile diameter to a fully rifled dimension. Also known as a forcing cone, leade, lede, or throat.

BATFE 922r COMPLIANT

A semi-auto paramilitary rifle (assembled with U.S. and foreign manufactured parts) which meets the statutory requirements of Section 922r of the United States code. Also refers to U.S. made parts which bring the rifle into compliance.

BATTUE

A ramped fixed rear sight assembly located on the back of the barrel, allowing quick target acquisition.

BEAVERTAIL FOREND

A wider than normal forend.

BENCH REST STOCK

A rifle stock specifically designed for a "bench rest" competition rifle which is fired from a table or bench, but supported only by sandbags or other devices. Optimized for stability, it often has a very wide flat-bottomed forend.

BESPOKE

A British term for a firearm custom-made to the purchaser's specifications. From the verb "bespeak", which means "to give order for it to be made".

BIRD'S HEAD

Refers to curved grip configuration on revolvers which resembles the outline of a bird's head, usually with 3 1/2 - 5 1/2 in. barrel lengths. Patterned after the grips on Colt's 1877 Thunderer revolver.

BLIND MAGAZINE

A box magazine which is completely concealed within the action and stock.

BLOWBACK ACTION

A semi-automatic or automatic firearm operating design which uses expanding propellant gasses to push a heavy unlocked breech bolt open, and which relies upon the inertia of its moving parts to keep the action closed until the bullet has exited the muzzle and pressure has decreased to a safe level.

BLUING

The chemical process of artificial oxidation (rusting) applied to gun parts so that the metal attains a dark blue or nearly black appearance.

BOLT

An assembly which reciprocates along the axis of a firearm's bore; it supports the cartridge case head and locks the action. Also see BOLT ACTION.

BOLT (REVOLVER)

The lug or projection which rises from a revolver's frame in order to immobilize the cylinder and align a charge hole with the bore of the barrel. Also called a cylinder stop.

BOLT ACTION

A manual action with a bolt body (usually including locking, firing pin, extractor, and ejector components) enclosed by and moving within the firearm's receiver.

BORE

Internal dimensions of a barrel (smooth or rifled) that can be measured using the Metric system (i.e. millimeters), English system (i.e. inches), or by the Gauge system (see GAUGE). On a rifled barrel, the bore is measured across the lands. Also, it is a traditional English term used when referring to the diameter of a shotgun muzzle (gauge in U.S. measure).

BOX MAGAZINE

A boxlike feed device for a firearm, which allows cartridges to be stacked one on top of the other. Most box magazines are removable for reloading.

BOXLOCK ACTION

Typified by Parker shotguns in U.S. and Westley Richards in England. Generally considered inferior in strength to the sidelock. Developed by Anson & Deeley, the boxlock is hammerless. It has two disadvantages. First, the hammer pin must be placed directly below knee of action, which is its weakest spot. Second, action walls must be thinned out to receive locks. These are inserted from below into large slots in the action body, which is then closed with a plate. If a correctly made Greener crossbolt is used, many of the boxlock's weaknesses can be negated. Also see CROSSBOLT.

BRADY ACT/BILL

See BRADY HANDGUN VIOLENCE PREVENTION ACT.

BRADY HANDGUN VIOLENCE PREVENTION ACT

1998 Federal legislation which established the National Instant Criminal Background Check System (NICS). Also commonly known as the Brady Bill, or the Brady Act. See NATIONAL INSTANT CRIMINAL BACKGROUND CHECK SYSTEM.

BREAK BARREL ACTION

A type of action where the barrels pivot on a hinge pin, allowing access to the chamber(s) in the breech. Configurations include: single shot, SxS, O/U, combination guns, drillings, and vierlings.

BREAK OPEN ACTION

See BREAK BARREL ACTION

BREECH

The rear end of a barrel where a cartridge is chambered. Also commonly used in reference to the entire chamber, breech, and receiver of long guns.

BREVETTE

French word which, in gun terminology, refers to a European copy (usually English, French, or Belgian) or patterned after a more famous design (i.e., Brevette Remington O/U derringer refers to a copy of the Remington O/U .41 cal. derringer).

BROWNING

An acid oxidation method of applying a rust-resistant finish to steel; so named because of the resultant surface color of the finished metal surface.

BUCKHORN SIGHT

Open metallic rear sight with sides that curl upward and inward.

BULL BARREL

A heavier, thicker than normal barrel with little or no taper.

BULLET BUTTON

A magazine locking device for AR-15 style rifles. It transforms a rifle with a standard manually operable magazine release and detachable magazine functionality into a fixed magazine rifle in order to comply with the State of California's firearm statutes. Depressing the "button" with a tool, e.g. bullet tip, small screwdriver, etc., is the only way to remove the magazine (which cannot hold more than ten rounds).

BUTT SPIKE

A fixed or adjustable monopod mounted near the rear on the bottom of a rifle's buttstock that, when used with forearm support of the rifle, enables the user to observe the target area for extended periods with minimal fatigue.

BUTTPAD

A rubber or synthetic composition part attached to the buttstock's end; intended to absorb recoil energy, prevent damage to the buttstock, and vary length of pull. May be fixed, solid, ventilated, or adjustable (horizontally, vertically, cant).

BUTTPLATE

A protective plate, usually steel, attached to the back of the buttstock.

BUTTSTOCK

The portion of a stock which is positioned against the user's shoulder; also known as the butt. On AR-15/M16 style or similar long guns, the separate component which is attached to the rear of the receiver. Also see STOCK.

CALIBER

The diameter of the bore (measured from land to land), usually measured in either inches or millimeters/centimeters. It does not designate bullet diameter.

CAMO (CAMOUFLAGE) FINISH

Refers to a patterned treatment using a variety of different colors/ patterns that enables a gun to blend into a particular outdoors environment. In most cases, this involves a film or additional finish applied on top of a gun's wood and/or metal parts (i.e. Mossy Oak Break-Up, Mossy Oak Brush, Advantage Timber, Realtree Hardwoods, Realtree Max-4, Muddy Girl, etc.). Mossberg introduced camo finishes on its shotguns in the mid-1980s.

CARTOUCHE

Generally refers to a manufacturer's inspector marking impressed into the wood of a military gun, usually in the form of initials inside a circle or oval.

CASE COLORS

See COLOR CASE HARDENING.

CAST OFF

The distance that a buttplate is offset to the right of the line of sight for a right-handed shooter. Especially important in shotgun stocks.

CAST ON

The same as Cast Off, except that the buttplate is offset to the left of the line of sight for a left-handed shooter.

CENTERFIRE

Refers to ammunition with primers centrally positioned in the cartridge case head; or to a firearm which is chambered for centerfire ammunition.

CERAKOTE

A ceramic based firearms coating with improved performance and reliability compared to traditional firearms finishes. Offers abrasion, corrosion, and solvent protection, in many colors and designs.

CHAMBER

Rear part of the barrel which has been reamed out so that it will contain a cartridge. When the breech is closed, the cartridge is supported in the chamber, and the chamber must align the primer with the firing pin, and the bullet with the bore.

CHAMBER THROAT

See BARREL THROAT.

CHARGE HOLE

The hole bored completely through a revolver's cylinder in which cartridges are loaded.

CHARGING HANDLE

A semi-auto firearm component which is manipulated to cycle the action, but which does not fire the cartridge. Also called cocking handle, cocking knob, or operating handle.

CHECKERING

A functional decoration consisting of pointed pyramids cut into the wood or metal surfaces of a firearm. Generally applied to the pistol grip and forend/forearm areas, affording better handling and control.

CHEEKPIECE

An elevated section of the upper buttstock on which the shooter's cheek rests when holding a rifle or shotgun in firing position. It may be integral to the buttstock, or a separate component. Adjustable cheekpieces may be moved in one or more ways: up, down, fore, aft, or side-to-side.

CHOKE

The muzzle constriction on a shotgun which controls the spread of the shot.

CHOKE TUBES

Interchangeable screw-in devices allowing different choke configurations (i.e., cylinder, improved cylinder, improved modified, modified, full). While most choke tubes fit flush with the end of the barrel, some choke tubes now also protrude from the end of the barrel. Most recently made shotguns usually include three to five choke tubes with the shotgun.

CHOPPER LUMP

A method of construction of barrels for double barreled, SxS shotguns in which the "lump" extending beneath the breech of the barrel is forged as an integral part of the barrel. When the barrels are assembled, the two lumps are carefully fitted on their mating surfaces and brazed solidly together into a single unit, into which locking and other functional recesses are cut.

CLIP

A metal or synthetic material formed/shaped to hold cartridges in readiness to be loaded into a magazine or chamber. A clip is NOT a magazine (i.e., stripper clips for most variations of the Mauser Broomhandle). Also known as a stripper or cartridge clip.

COCKING INDICATOR

Any device for which the act of cocking a gun moves it into a position where it may be seen or felt, in order to notify the shooter that the gun is cocked. Typical examples are the pins found on some high-grade hammerless shotguns, which protrude slightly when they are cocked, and also the exposed cocking knobs on bolt-action rifles. Exposed hammers found on some rifles and pistols are also considered cocking indicators.

COIN FINISH

Older definition referring to a metal finish, typically on a rifle or shotgun, which resembles the finish of an old silver coin. Most coin finishes are based on nickel plating (not chrome) and are generally high polish.

COLLAPSIBLE STOCK

Mostly used in reference to a buttstock which can be shortened or lengthened along its fore to aft axis. Also applies in theory to top-folding, under-folding, and side folding buttstocks; all of which when folded reduce the weapon's length.

COLOR CASE HARDENING

A method of hardening steel and iron while imparting colorful swirls as well as surface figure. Traditional color case hardening using charcoal and bone meal is achieved by putting the desired metal parts in a crucible packed with a mixture of charcoal and finely ground animal bone to temperatures in the 800°C – 900°C range, after which they are slowly cooled. Then they are submerged into cold water, leaving a thin, colorful protective finish. Can also be achieved by treating the necessary metal parts with a cyanide liquid, which helps harden the metal surface, and can be denoted from charcoal color case hardening by a more layered color appearance.

COMB

The portion of the stock on which the shooter's cheek rests.

COMBINATION GUN

Generally, a break-open shotgun-type configuration that is fitted with at least one shotgun barrel and one rifle barrel. Such guns may be encountered with either two or three barrels, and less frequently with as many as four or five, and have been known to chamber as many as four different calibers.

COMPENSATOR

Slots, vents, or ports machined into a firearm's barrel near its muzzle, or a muzzle device, which allow propellant gasses to escape upwards and partially reduce muzzle jump.

CONTROLLED ROUND FEEDING

A bolt action rifle design in which the cartridge is mechanically secured by the extractor and bolt during all parts of the operating cycle.

CRANE

In a modern solid-frame, swing-out cylinder revolver, the U-shaped yoke on which the cylinder rotates, and which holds the cylinder in the frame. The crane/yoke is the weakest part of a revolver's mechanism.

CRIME BILL

Popular title for the Violent Crime Control and Law Enforcement Act of 1994, Public Law 103-322. See VIOLENT CRIME...LAW 103-322.

CRIMP

A turning in of the case mouth to affect a closure or to prevent the projectile(s) from slipping out of the case mouth. Various crimps include: roll, pie, star or folded, rose, stab, and taper.

CROSSBOLT

A transverse locking rod/bar used in many SxS boxlock shotguns and a few rifles, which locks the standing breech and barrels to each other. Originally designed by W.W. Greener, this term is also referred to as the Greener crossbolt. Also a transverse metal bolt which reinforces and prevents damage to the stock from recoil or abusive handling.

CROWNING

The rounding or chamfering normally done to a barrel muzzle to ensure that the mouth of the bore is square with the bore axis and that its edges are countersunk below the surface to protect it from impact damage. Traditionally, crowning was accomplished by spinning an abrasive-coated brass ball against the muzzle while moving it in a figure-eight pattern, until the abrasive had cut away any irregularities and produced a uniform and square mouth.

CRYOGENIC TEMPERING

Computer controlled cooling process that relieves barrel stress by subjecting the barrel to a temperature of -310 degrees Fahrenheit for 22 hours.

CURIO/RELIC

Firearms which are of special interest to collectors by reason of some quality other than that which is normally associated with firearms intended for sporting use or as offensive or defensive weapons. Must be older than 50 years.

CYLINDER

A rotating cartridge holder in a revolver. The cartridges are held in chambers and the cylinder turns, either to the left or the right, depending on the gun maker's design, as the hammer is cocked.

CYLINDER ARM

See CRANE.

DA/SA

A semi-auto pistol fire control design which allows an initial shot to be fired in double action mode, and subsequent shots in single action mode until the magazine is empty or the user decocks the pistol. For most modern semi-auto pistols, the cocking is either manual or automatic; and in both instances the trigger and hammer/striker are returned to their respective double action states. See also DOUBLE ACTION and SINGLE ACTION.

DAMASCENE

The decorating of metal with another metal, either by inlaying or attaching in some fashion.

DAMASCUS BARREL

A barrel made by twisting, forming, and welding thin strips of steel around a mandrel.

DE-HORNING

The removal of all sharp edges from a firearm that would cut or pinch the shooter, the shooter's clothing, and/or holster, but still maintains the nice clean lines of the firearm.

DELAYED IMPINGEMENT GAS SYSTEM

A trademarked gas operating system for AR-15 style carbines, designed by Allan Zitta. Similar to a gas piston action in concept, it has instead an operating rod and recoil spring which run through the receiver, over the barrel, and sleeve the gas tube at the gas block. The gas tube does not enter the receiver, and the recoil spring replaces the buffer and spring in the AR-15 buttstock.

DEMI-BLOC/DEMI-BLOCK

See CHOPPER LUMP.

DERRINGER

Usually refers to a small, concealable pistol with one or two short barrels.

DETACHABLE MILITARY STYLE BIPOD

A bipod designed for severe/heavy use and greater durability, with a Picatinny rail or other type of quick attach/detach mounting system.

DIRECT IMPINGEMENT GAS SYSTEM

A gas operating system in which high pressure and temperature propellant gas is routed into the firearm receiver to make contact with and move action components. There are no "moving parts" (e.g. piston, return spring, operating rod, tappet) in a direct impingement gas sytem. A typical direct impingement gas system has a gas block surrounding the barrel and covering the gas port, and a gas tube.

DOUBLE ACTION

The principle in a revolver or auto-loading pistol wherein the hammer can be cocked and dropped by a single pull of the trigger. Most of these actions also provide capability for single action fire. In auto loading pistols, double action normally applies only to the first shot of any series, the hammer being cocked by the slide for subsequent shots.

DOUBLE ACTION ONLY

A firearm action which cannot be operated in single action mode. Many newer DAO firearms are either hammerless, or their hammers and triggers cannot be positioned in a single action status.

DOUBLE UNDERLUGS

The two underlugs on the lower barrel of an over/under double barrel shotgun or rifle.

DOUBLE-BARREL(ED)
A gun which has two barrels joined either side-by-side or one over the other.

DOUBLE-SET TRIGGER
A device that consists of two triggers - one to cock the mechanism that spring-assists the other trigger, substantially lightening the other trigger's pull weight.

DOVETAIL
A flaring machined or hand-cut slot that is also slightly tapered toward one end. Cut into the upper surface of barrels and sometimes actions, the dovetail accepts a corresponding part on which a sight is mounted. Dovetail slot blanks are used to cover the dovetail when the original sight has been removed or lost; this gives the barrel a more pleasing appearance and configuration.

DRILLED & TAPPED
Refers to holes drilled into the top of a receiver/frame and threaded, which allow scope bases, blocks, rings, or other sighting devices to be rigidly attached to the gun.

DRILLING
German for triple, which is their designation for a three-barrel gun, usually two shotgun barrels and one rifle barrel.

EJECTOR
A firearm component which propels an extracted cartridge or fired case out of the receiver or chamber. Ejectors may be fixed or movable, spring loaded or manually activated. Also see SELECTIVE AUTOMATIC EJECTOR.

ELASTOMER
A synthetic elastic polymer, soft and compressible like natural rubber, used for seals, grip and stock inlays, and other molded firearm components.

ELECTROCIBLE
Unique reusable target designed like an aircraft propeller that causes it to spin and go in different directions. In competition, electrocibles come out of one of five boxes located 25 meters from the shooter, who must hit it before it crosses over the ring at 21 meters.

ELECTRO-OPTICAL SIGHT
An optical sight (see definition) with the addition of electronic battery powered components which illuminate a reticle (least complex), or which generate a reticle/optional reticles. Electro-optical sights may be: magnifying, non-magnifying, full-tube traditional optical design , or reflex types (see REFLEX SIGHT).

ELEVATION
A firearm sight's vertical distance above the barrel's bore axis; also the adjustment of a sight to compensate for the effect of gravity on a projectile's exterior ballistic path.

ENGINE TURNING
Machined circular polishing on metal, creating a unique overlapping pattern.

ENGLISH STOCK
A straight, slender-gripped stock.

ENGRAVING
The art of engraving metal in decorative patterns. Scroll engraving is the most common type of hand engraving encountered. Much of today's factory engraving is rolled on which is done mechanically. Hand engraving requires artistry and knowledge of metals and related materials.

ERGO SUREGRIP
A Falcon Industries Inc. right hand or ambidextrous replacement pistol grip for AR-15/M-16 style rifles. The grip has finger grooves, upper rear extension to support the web of the shooter's hand, is oil and solvent resistant, and a non-slip textured overmolded rubber surface.

ETCHING
A method of decorating metal gun parts, usually done by acid etching or photo engraving.

EXTRACTOR
A device which partially pulls a cartridge or fired hull/case/casing(s) from the chamber, allowing it to be removed manually.

FALLING BLOCK
A single shot action where the breechblock drops straight down when a lever is actuated.

FARQUHARSON ACTION
A single shot hammerless falling block rifle action patented in 1872 by John Farquharson.

FENCES
The hemispherical formations on a side-by-side shotgun's receiver which are adjacent to the barrel breeches. Originally fences were the curving metal flanges surrounding a percussion ignition firearm's nipple, or a flintlock ignition firearm's priming pan, which protected the shooter from sparks, smoke, and escaping gas.

FIBER OPTIC SIGHT
An iron sight with fiber optic light gathering rods or cylinders; the rod ends are perceived as glowing dots and enhance sight visibility and contrast.

FIT AND FINISH
Terms used to describe over-all firearm workmanship.

FIRE CONTROL GROUP
All components necessary to cause a cartridge to be fired; may be a self-contained assembly, easily disassembled or not user-serviceable, detachable, modular/interchangeable, and may or may not include a safety, bolt release, or other parts.

FIRING PIN
That part of a firearm which strikes the cartridge primer, causing detonation.

FLASH SUPPRESSOR/HIDER
A muzzle attachment which mechanically disrupts and reduces muzzle flash. It does not reduce muzzle blast or recoil.

FLAT-TOP UPPER
An AR-15/M16 style or other tactical semi-auto rifle with a literally flat receiver top. The majority of flat-top uppers have an extended Picatinny rail for mounting iron sights, optical sights, and other accessories, which provides much more versatility than the original "carry handle" receiver design.

FLOATING BARREL
A barrel bedded to avoid contact with any point on the stock.

FLOOR PLATE
Usually, a removable/hinged plate at the bottom of the receiver covering the magazine well.

FN FAL STYLE ACTION
A gas operated rifle action with a short-stroke spring-loaded gas piston, a tilting breechblock locking design, and a heavy receiver. A regulator valve allows the user to increase the volume of gas entering the system in order to ensure reliable operation in adverse conditions. Unlike direct gas impingement or delayed blowback operating systems, propellant gas does not vent into the receiver and fire control components.

FOLDING STOCK
Usually a buttstock hinged at or near the receiver so that it can be "folded" towards the muzzle, reducing the firearm's overall length. Not an adjustable stock as defined above, and usually does not prevent operating/firing when in its folded position.

FORCING CONE
The segment of a shotgun barrel immediately forward of the chamber where its internal diameter is reduced from chamber to bore diameter. The forcing cone aids the passage of shot into the barrel. For revolvers, the tapering portion of the barrel bore from the breech to the rifling.

FOREARM
In this text, a separate piece of wood in front of the receiver and under the barrel used for hand placement when shooting.

FOREARM/FOREND CAP

A separate piece attached to the muzzle end of a forearm; often with a colored spacer, and usually in a contrasting color/material.

FOREND/FORE-END

Usually the forward portion of a one-piece rifle or shotgun stock (in this text), but
can also refer to a separate piece of wood.

FORWARD BOLT ASSIST

A button, usually found on AR-15 type rifles, which may be pushed or struck to move the bolt carrier fully forward so that the extractor has completely engaged the cartridge rim and the bolt has locked. Mainly used to close/lock the bolt when the rifle's chamber and receiver are excessively fouled or dirty.

FRAME

The part of a firearm to which the action (lock work), barrel, and stock/grip are connected. Most of the time used when referring to a handgun or hinged frame long gun.

FREE FLOATING FOREARM

A forearm which does not contact the barrel at any point, as it attaches and places mechanical stress only on the receiver. An accuracy enhancement for AR-15/M16 style rifles, which by their modular design, are not able to have a conventionally free floated barrel in a one-piece stock.

FREE RIFLE

A rifle designed for international-type target shooting. The only restriction on design is a weight maximum 8 kilograms (17.6 lbs.).

FRONT STRAP

That part of the revolver or pistol grip frame which faces forward and often joins with the trigger guard. In target guns, notably the .45 ACP, the front strap is often stippled to give shooter's hand a slip-proof surface.

FULL AUTO

See AUTOMATIC ACTION

GAS IMPINGEMENT OPERATING SYSTEM

An action in which high pressure propellant gas is diverted from the barrel to supply the energy required to unlock the breech, extract/eject the fired case, load a cartridge, and lock the breech. This type of system generates a large amount of heat and also a considerable amount of fouling directly back into the action.

GAS PISTON OPERATING SYSTEM

A gas operation design in which a piston is used to transfer propellant gas energy to the action components. No gas enters the receiver or makes contact with other action components. Consequently, less heat is absorbed by, and less fouling accumulates in the receiver. This system also has a much different recoil pulse or "feel".

GAS PORT

A small opening in the barrel of a gas operated firearm which allows high pressure gas to flow into the gas system's components. Also an escape vent in a firearm's receiver, a safety feature.

GAUGE/GA.

A unit of measure used to determine a shotgun's bore. Determined by the amount of pure lead balls equaling the bore diameter needed to equal one pound (i.e., a 12 ga. means that 12 lead balls exactly the diameter of the bore weigh one pound). In this text, .410 is referenced as a bore (if it was a gauge, it would be a 68 ga.).

GAUGE VS. BORE DIAMETER

10-Gauge = Bore Diameter of .775 inches or 19.3mm
12-Gauge = Bore Diameter of .729 inches or 18.2mm
16-Gauge = Bore Diameter of .662 inches or 16.8mm
20-Gauge = Bore Diameter of .615 inches or 15.7mm
28-Gauge = Bore Diameter of .550 inches or 13.8mm
68-Gauge = Bore Diameter of .410 inches or 12.6mm

GCA

The Gun Control Act of 1968, 18 USC Chapter 44.

GLACIERGUARDS

AR-15/M-16 carbine length replacement handguard (two-piece) which has fifteen internal heat dispersing fins rather than the standard heat shield. The fins provide greater strength and rigidity; fiber-reinforced polymer shells resist heat and reduce weight. A DPMS product.

GRIP

The handle used to hold a handgun, or the area of a stock directly behind and attached to the frame/receiver of a long gun.

GRIPS

Can be part of the frame or components attached to the frame used to assist in accuracy, handling, control, and safety of a handgun. Many currently manufactured semi-auto handguns have grips that are molded w/checkering as part of the synthetic frame.

GRIPSTRAP(S)

Typically refers to the front and back metal attached to a handgun frame which supports the grips/stocks. Also known as the front strap and back strap.

GROOVES

The spiral depressions of the rifling in a barrel bore; created by cutting, swaging, broaching, hammering, cation action, or other methods. Also see LANDS and RIFLING.

HALF COCK

A position of the hammer in a hammer activated firing mechanism that serves as a manual safety.

HAMMER

A part of a gun's mechanism which applies force to the firing pin or other components, which in turn fires the gun.

HAMMERLESS

Some "hammerless" firearms do in fact have hidden hammers, which are located in the action housing. Truly hammerless guns, such as the Savage M99, have a firing mechanism based on a spring-powered striker.

HANDGUARD

A wooden, synthetic, or ventilated metal part attached above the barrel and ahead of the receiver to protect the shooter's hand from the heat generated during semi-auto rapid firing.

HEEL

Back end of the upper edge of the butt stock at the upper edge of the buttplate or recoil pad.

HK91/G3 STYLE ACTION

A roller locked delayed blowback rifle action. There is no gas system per se; gas pressure in the cartridge case pushes the case against the bolt and bolt carrier. Spring-loaded rollers in the bolt resist unlocking and carrier/bolt movement until chamber pressure has dropped to a safe level. Components are heavier, recoil (actual and perceived) is greater, chambers must be fluted to assure extraction, and cocking effort is much greater than direct gas or gas piston weapons.

ILAFLON

Industrielack AG trademarked ceramic reinforced enamel firearms finish coating; highly resistant to abrasion, corrosion, and chemicals/solvent.

INTEGRAL LOCKING SYSTEM

A North American Arms safety system; a key allows the user to internally lock the hammer in place, which prevents discharging the firearm.

INTRAFUSE

A trademarked system of synthetic stocks and accessories designed for tactical firearms.

IN-THE-WHITE

Refers to a gun's finish w/o bluing, nickel, case colors, gold, etc. Since all metal surfaces are normally polished, the steel appears white, hence, "in-the-white" terminology.

IRON SIGHTS

A generic term for metallic front or rear sights which do not use optical lens (magnifying or non-magnifying) components.

JUXTAPOSED

See SIDE-BY-SIDE.

KRYPTEK

A proprietary camo finish utilizing a multi-directional design to affectively conceal in a multitude of terrains that have either a lateral or vertical flow. The bi-level layering of the patterns incorporate background transitional shading and sharp random geometrical foregrounds to create a three dimensional effect that ensures the utmost in concealment at both close and long ranges. Patterns include Highlander, Typhon, and Raid.

LAMINATED STOCK

A gunstock made of many layers of wood glued together under pressure. The laminations become very strong, preventing damage from moisture or heat, and warping.

LANDS

Portions of the bore left between the grooves of the rifling in the bore of a firearm. In rifling, the grooves are usually twice the width of the land. Land diameter is measured across the bore, from land to land.

LASER SIGHT

An aiming system which projects a beam of laser light onto the target. Usually mounted so the beam is parallel to the barrel bore but not a "traditional" front or rear sight as the shooter does not look through the laser apparatus.

LENS COATINGS

Metallic coatings on optic surfaces which increase light transmission, image brightness, and color rendition. Also used to improve abrasion resistance and filter out unwanted or harmful light.

LEVER ACTION

A manual repeating action operated by an external lever.

LUMP

An English term for an underlug.

M1913 PICATINNY RAIL

Original designation for a Picatinny rail. Also see PICATINNY RAIL.

M4 STYLE

Refers to an AR style rifle in M4 carbine configuration (A2 configuration but with short handguard, short barrel, and relocated gas block).

MACHINE GUN

National Firearms Act and Gun Control Act of 1968 definition:

Any weapon which shoots, is designed to shoot, or can be readily restored to shoot, automatically more than one shot, without manual reloading, by a single function of the trigger. The term shall also include the frame or receiver of any such weapon, any part designed and intended solely and exclusively, or combination of parts designed and intended, for use in converting a weapon into a machine gun, and any combination of parts from which a machine gun can be assembled if such parts are in the possession or control of a person.

MAGAZINE (MAG.)

The container (may be detachable) which holds cartridges under spring pressure to be fed into the gun's chamber. A clip is NOT a magazine. May be a single or double or multiple column, rotary, helical, drum, or other design. The term "high capacity" denotes a magazine capable of holding more than ten rounds.

MAGNUM (MAG.)/MAGNUM AMMUNITION

A term first used by Holland & Holland in 1912 for their .375 H&H Magnum cartridge. The term has now been applied to rimfire, centerfire, or shotshell cartridges having a larger cartridge case, heavier shot charge, or higher muzzle velocity than standard cartridges or shotshells of a given caliber or gauge. Most Magnum rifle cartridges are belted designs.

MAINSPRING

The spring that delivers energy to the hammer or striker.

MANNLICHER STOCK

A full-length slender stock with slender forend extending to the muzzle (full stock) affording better barrel protection.

MICROMETER SIGHT

A windage and elevation adjustable sight with very precise and small increments of adjustment.

MICRO SLICK

A firearms finish coating which creates a permanently lubricated surface; it impedes galling and seizing of firearm components.

MIL

See MILRADIAN

MIL SPEC

A series of quality control standards used by manufacturers to guarantee machine tolerances ensuring the consistency and interchangeability of parts.

MIL-DOT

A reticle with dots spaced center-to-center one milradian apart; the distance to an object of known dimension may be calculated based upon the number of milradians which are subtended by the target's known dimension.

MILRADIAN

The horizontal angle subtended by one unit of measurement at 1,000 units distance. Also called a "mil".

MINUTE OF ANGLE (MOA)

1/60 of a degree of circular angle; at 100 yards it subtends 1.047 inches. Also commonly used to describe a firearm's accuracy and precision capability, i.e. a rifle which shoots under one minute of angle. Abbreviated MOA.

MODERN SPORTING RIFLE

A National Shooting Sports Foundation term for civilian legal semiautomatic AR-15 style rifles. The NSSF promotes its usage to counter the negative anti-gun connotations, confusion, and misunderstandings which have become associated with the term "AR15". A modern sporting rifle is not an automatic or assault rifle, not a regulated NFA weapon, not a military/law enforcement M16 despite its similar cosmetic appearance, and no more powerful than other traditional configuration sporting/hunting/ competition rifles of the same caliber. Sometimes called Sport Utility Rifle or SUR. Note: the letters "AR" stand for Armalite Rifle.

MODULAR WEAPONS SYSTEM

A generic term of military origin for quick attach/detach components/systems which allow flexibility and adaptability for using various sighting, illumination, and other accessories, etc. on a weapon. Also see PICATINNY RAIL.

MONOBLOC

A form of construction and assembly for double barreled shotguns wherein the breeching and locking surfaces are cut into a single separate housing or "bloc" into which the breeches of the barrels are brazed or threaded. Compare to CHOPPER LUMP.

MONTE CARLO STOCK

A stock with an elevated comb used primarily for scoped rifles.

MUZZLE

The forward end of the barrel where the projectile exits.

MUZZLE BRAKE

A muzzle device (permanent or removable) or barrel modification which reduces muzzle jump and recoil by diverting propellant gasses sideways or to the rear. Not to be confused with a flash hider or a flash suppressor. Also see COMPENSATOR.

NATIONAL INSTANT CRIMINAL BACKGROUND CHECK SYSTEM (NICS)

A U. S. federal government system which an FFL must, with limited exceptions, contact for information on whether receipt of a firearm by a person who is not licensed under 18 U.S.C. 923 would violate Federal or state law.

NEEDLE GUN

Ignition system invented by Johan Nikolas von Dreyse in 1829. This ignition system used a paper cartridge and became obsolete with the invention of the metallic cartridge.

NFA

The National Firearms Act, 26 USC Chapter 53.

NFA FIREARM

A firearm which must be registered in the National Firearm Registration and Transfer Record, as defined in the NFA and 27 CFR, Part 479. Included are: machine guns, frames or receivers of machine guns, any combination of parts designed and intended for use in converting weapons into machine guns, any combination of parts from which a machine gun can be assembled if the parts are in the possession or under control of a person, silencers and any part designed or intended for fabricating a silencer, short-barreled rifles, short-barreled shotguns, destructive devices, and "any other weapon". NFA semi-auto carbines with less than 16 in. barrels are not listed in this book.

NICS CHECK

See NATIONAL INSTANT CRIMINAL BACKGROUND CHECK SYSTEM.

NIGHT SIGHTS

Iron sights with radioactive tritium gas capsules; the capsules are inserted into recesses in the sight body with their ends facing the shooter. The tritium glow provides sight alignment and aiming references in lowlight/no-light conditions.

NON-DETACHABLE BOX MAGAZINE

A rectangular magazine which is never removed during normal use or maintenance of the firearm. It may extend beyond/below the receiver or stock, may be high capacity, and generally is loaded from its top (single cartridges or stripper clips).

NON-DETACHABLE FOLDING BAYONET

An articulated bayonet which cannot be removed from the firearm by the end user. Normally locked into its fully folded or extended position.

NP3/NP3 PLUS

An electroless plated nickel-phosphorus alloy firearms finish which offers uniform thickness, lubricity, and hardness equivalent to hard chromium plating.

OBJECTIVE LENS

A telescopic sight's front, usually larger lens which may be adjustable to reduce parallax error.

OCULAR LENS

The rear lens of a telescopic sight, normally adjustable by rotation to focus the sight image.

OPEN SIGHT

A simple rear iron sight with a notch – the shooter aims by looking through the notch at the front sight and the target.

OPTICAL SIGHT

A generic term for a sight which has one or more optical lenses through which the weapon is aimed. Optical sights usually magnify the target image, but there are many non- magnifying optical sights.

OVER-UNDER (O/U)

A double-barrel gun in which the barrels are stacked one on top of the other. Also called Superposed.

PARALLAX

Occurs in telescopic sights when the primary image of the objective lens does not coincide with the reticle. In practice, parallax is detected in the scope when, as the viewing eye is moved laterally, the image and the reticle appear to move in relation to each other.

PARAMILITARY

Typically refers to a firearm configured or styled to resemble a military weapon with one or more of the military weapon's configurations or features, EXCEPT FOR automatic or selective fire capability. Paramilitary firearms may be slide action (primarily shotguns), bolt action, or semi-automatic (most handguns and rifles).

PARKERIZING

Matte rust-resistant oxide finish, usually dull gray or black in color, found on military guns.

PEEP SIGHT

A rear sight consisting of a disc or blade with a hole or aperture through which the front sight and target are aligned.

PEPPERBOX

An early form of revolving repeating pistol, in which a number of barrels were bored in a circle in a single piece of metal resembling the cylinder of a modern revolver. Functioning was the same as a revolver, the entire cylinder being revolved to bring successive barrels under the hammer for firing. Though occurring as far back as the 16th century, the pepperbox did not become practical until the advent of the percussion cap in the early 1800s. Pepperboxes were made in a wide variety of sizes and styles, and reached their popularity peak during the percussion period. Few were made after the advent of practical metallic cartridges. Both single and double action pepperboxes were made. Single-barreled revolvers after the 1840s were more accurate and easier to handle and soon displaced the rather clumsy and muzzle-heavy pepperbox.

PERCH BELLY

Refers to a rifle's stock configuration where the bottom portion is curved rather than straight between the buttplate and pistol grip.

PICATINNY RAIL

A serrated flat rail typically located on the top of a frame/slide/receiver, but may also be located on the sides and bottom, allowing different optics/sights/accessories to be used on the gun. Developed at the U.S. Army's Picatinny Arsenal.

PINFIRE

An obsolete ignition system; a pinfire cartridge had an internal primer and a small firing pin protruding from the rear sidewall of its metallic case.

POLYGONAL

Rifling w/o sharp edged lands and grooves. Advantages include a slight increase in muzzle velocity, less bullet deformation, and reduced lead fouling since there are no traditional lands and grooves. See RIFLING.

POPE RIB

A rib integral with the barrel. Designed by Harry M. Pope, famed barrel maker and shooter, the rib made it possible to mount a target scope low over the barrel.

PORTED BARREL

A barrel with multiple holes or slots drilled near the muzzle. See PORTING.

PORTING

Multiple holes or slots drilled into a firearm barrel near the muzzle. Porting reduces felt/perceived recoil, and if located on the upper half of the barrel reduces muzzle jump. Disadvantages are increased muzzle blast and noise.

POST-BAN

See 1989 BUSH BAN, and SECTION 922r.

PRE-BAN

See 1989 BUSH BAN, and SECTION 922r.

PRIMER

A percussion device designed to ignite the propellant charge of a centerfire cartridge or shotshell by generating flame and high temperature expanding gasses.

PRIMER RING

Refers to a visible dark ring around the firing pin hole in a breech or bolt face, created by the impact of centerfire ammunition primer cups when a cartridge is fired.

PROOFMARK

Proofmarks are usually applied to all parts actually tested, but normally appear on the barrel (and possibly frame), usually indicating the country of origin and time-frame of proof (especially on European firearms). In the U.S., there is no federalized or government proof house, only the manufacturer's in-house proofmark indicating that a firearm has passed its manufacturer's quality control standards per government specifications.

PUMP ACTION
See SLIDE ACTION.

QUAD RAIL FOREARM
A rifle forearm with upper, lower, and lateral Picatinny rails which allow attachment of multiple accessories.

QUARTER RIB
A short raised portion of a ribbed barrel, which forms a base for a rear metallic or optical sight.

RATE OF TWIST
The distance in which rifling makes one complete revolution; normally expressed as one turn in a specific number of inches or millimeters. Also called rifling pitch, or merely twist.

RECEIVER
That part of a rifle or shotgun (excluding hinged frame guns) which houses the bolt, firing pin, mainspring, trigger group, and magazine or ammunition feed system. The barrel is threaded or pressed into the somewhat enlarged forward part of the receiver, called the receiver ring. At the rear of the receiver, the butt or stock is fastened. In semiautomatic pistols, the frame or housing is sometimes referred to as the receiver.

RECOIL
The rearward motion of a firearm when a shot is fired (i.e. the gun recoiled); the term for the energy or force transferred into the firearm as it discharges a projectile.

RECOIL ACTION/OPERATION
A selfloading or automatic action which uses recoil energy to unlock, extract, eject, cock the firing mechanism, and reload the chamber.

RECOIL SPRING GUIDE ROD
A metal or synthetic rod which positions the recoil spring within the firearm's receiver or slide, and prevents binding/dislocation of the spring during its compression or expansion.

RED DOT SIGHT
See REFLEX SIGHT.

REFLEX SIGHT
An optical sight which generates reticle image upon a partially curved objective lens; the reticle appears superimposed in the field of view and focused at infinity. Most reflex sights are non-magnifying and battery powered. Fiber optic light collectors or tritium may also be used to generate the reticle. Reflex sights are adjustable and virtually parallax free. Popularly known as "red dot" sights; they are NOT laser sights.

RELEASE TRIGGER
A trap shooting trigger which fires the gun when the trigger is released.

RELIC
See CURIO/RELIC.

REPEATER/REPEATING ACTION
An manual action with a magazine or cylinder loaded with more than one cartridge; all cartridges
may be fired without reloading.

RETICLE
The shapes, lines, marks, etc. which provide an aiming reference when using an optical sight. Reticles may be illuminated electronically, with tritium, or with fiber optics, and are available in a multitude of designs for many differing requirements.

REVOLVER/REVOLVING ACTION
A manual repeating action so named for its multi-chambered cylinder which rotates on an axis parallel to the barrel bore. Primarily a handgun action, but there have been long gun examples (e.g. Colt Model 1855 Revolving Rifle).

RIB
A raised sighting plane affixed to the top of a barrel.

RIFLING
The spirally cut grooves in the bore of a rifle or handgun barrel. The rifling causes the bullet to spin, stabilizing the bullet in flight. Rifling may rotate to the left or the right, the higher parts of the bore being called lands, the cuts or lower parts being called the grooves. Many types exist, such as oval, polygonal, button, Newton, Newton-Pope gain twist, parabolic, Haddan, Enfield, segmental rifling, etc. Most U.S.-made barrels have a right-hand twist, while British gun makers prefer a left-hand twist. In practice, there seems to be little difference in accuracy or barrel longevity.

RIMFIRE
Self contained metallic cartridge where the priming compound is evenly distributed within the cartridge head, but only on the outer circumference of the rim. Detonated by the firing pin(s) striking the outer edge of the case head.

RINGS
See SCOPE RINGS.

ROLLING BLOCK ACTION
A single shot action, designed in the U.S. and widely used in early Remington arms. Also known as the Remington-Rider action, the breechblock, actuated by a lever, rotates down and back from the chamber. The firing pin is contained within the block and is activated by hammer fall.

ROUND ACTION
A transitional action design, between the boxlock and sidelock, which has its lock assembly attached to the action's lower rearward projecting trigger bar. Also called a trigger plate action.

SAFETY
A mechanism(s) in/on a gun which prevents it from firing. There are many different types and variations.

SAAMI
The Sporting Arms and Ammunition Manufacturers' Institute; a branch of the National Shooting Sports Foundation.

SAW HANDLE
A distinctive squared off pistol grip design which literally is shaped like a saw handle.

SCHNABEL FOREND/FOREARM
The curved/carved flared end of the forend/forearm that resembles the beak of a bird (Schnabel in German). This type of forend is common on Austrian and German guns. In the U.S., the popularity of the Schnabel forend/forearm comes and goes with the seasons. A Schnabel forend is often seen on custom stocks and rifles.

SCOPE RINGS (BLOCKS/BASES)
Metal mounts used to attach a scope to the top of a gun's frame/receiver.

SEAR
The pivoting part in the firing or lock mechanism of a gun. The sear is linked to the trigger, and may engage the cocking piece, striker, or the firing pin.

SECTION 922r
A 1989 Federal regulation which established sporting criteria for centerfire weapons, either imported, or assembled from imported and domestic components. Firearms which do not meet the criteria are "banned", i.e. non-importable as of the regulation's effective date. Also the source of the popular terms "pre-ban" and post-ban". Due to the complexity of this regulation readers are advised to refer to the actual text of the regulation and contact the BATFE. See 1989 BUSH BAN.

SELECTIVE AUTOMATIC EJECTOR
An ejector which propels only fired cases out of a break open action firearm; and only extracts unfired cartridges. Very often found in double barrel shotguns, and also called an automatic Southgate, Holland & Holland, or Baker ejector.

SELECTIVE FIRE

Describes a firearm which has more than one firing mode; which is controlled, or "selected", by the user. Most often used in reference to firearms which can fire in semi-auto, burst, or full auto mode.

SEMI-AUTO ACTION/SEMI-AUTOMATIC/SELFLOADING/AUTOLOADING

A pistol, rifle, or shotgun that is loaded manually for the first round. Upon pulling the trigger, the gun fires, ejects the fired round, cocks the firing mechanism, and feeds a fresh round from the magazine. The trigger must be released after each shot and pulled again to fire the next round.

SHELL DEFLECTOR

A protrusion of the receiver near the ejection port which is positioned and shaped to deflect an ejected case away from the shooter's body. Especially appreciated by left-handed shooters when firing a semi-auto with right side ejection.

SHORT ACTION

A rifle action designed for short overall length cartridges.

SHORT BARREL RIFLE

Any rifle having one or more barrels less than sixteen inches in length and any weapon made from a rifle (whether by alteration, modification, or otherwise) if such weapon, as modified, has an overall length of less than twenty-six inches.

SHORT BARREL SHOTGUN

Any shotgun, which was originally equipped with a shoulder stock, with a barrel or barrels less than eighteen inches long and any weapon made from a shotgun (whether by alteration, modification, or otherwise) if such weapon as modified has an overall length of less than twenty-six inches.

SHOTSHELL

An assembly consisting of a rimmed metal head, paper or plastic base wad, 209 battery cup primer, and paper or plastic body. A shotshell cartridge is a shotshell loaded with propellant, wad column, and shot charge or a single large diameter slug.

SIDE-BY-SIDE (Sx)

A two-barrel rifle or shotgun where the barrels are horizontally arranged side-by-side. Also called juxtaposed.

SIDE FOLDING STOCK

A folding stock variation which has its buttstock rotate horizontally, usually to the right side of the firearm's receiver. See FOLDING STOCK.

SIDE LEVER

Refers to opening mechanism lever on either left or right side of receiver/frame.

SIDELOCK

A type of action, usually long gun, where the moving parts are located on the inside of the lock plates, which in turn are inlet in the sides of the stock. Usually found only on better quality shotguns and rifles.

SIDEPLATES

Ornamental metal panels normally attached to a boxlock action to simulate a sidelock.

SIGHT(S)

Any part or device which allows a firearm to be aimed, versus merely pointed, at a target. There are two main systems: "iron" and optical. Iron sights, also known as "open" sights, are now made of other substances than metal and in many variations. Optical sights have a lens, or lenses, which may or may not magnify the target image.

SINGLE ACTION

A firearms design which requires the hammer to be manually cocked for each shot. Also an auto loading pistol design which requires manual cocking of its mechanism for the first shot only.

SINGLE SHOT ACTION

An action which limits storing or loading only a single cartridge, and is manually operated.

SLIDE ACTION

A manual repeating action with a reciprocating forearm. Sliding the forearm towards the receiver opens the action and extracts/ejects the fired case; forward motion chambers a cartridge and locks the action. Also known as a pump action.

SINGLE TRIGGER

One trigger on a double-barrel gun. It fires each barrel individually by successive pulls, or may be selective, i.e., the barrel to be fired first can be selected via a control button or lever.

SLING SWIVELS

Metal loops affixed to the gun to which a carrying strap is attached.

SOUND SUPPRESSOR

See SUPPRESSOR.

SPECIAL IMPACT MUNITIONS

A class or type of firearm ammunition loaded with one or more projectiles; when fired at a human target the projectiles have a low probability of causing serious injury or death. For example: bean bag, baton, tear gas, and rubber ball rounds. A sub-class of SIMs is known as SPLLAT, or special purpose less lethal anti terrorist munitions.

SPORT UTILITY RIFLE

See MODERN SPORTING RIFLE.

SPUR TRIGGER

A firearm design which housed the trigger in an extension of the frame in some older guns. The trigger projected only slightly from the front of the extension or spur, and there was no trigger guard.

SQUARE BRIDGE ACTION

A bolt action design which has an enlarged rectangular shaped rear receiver bridge. If the front receiver bridge is also in an enlarged square, the action is termed a double square bridge.

SQUIB LOAD

A cartridge with no propellant, or so little propellant, that when fired in a semi-auto the action does not cycle; and in any type of firearm a squib load most likely results in the projectile remaining in and completely obstructing the barrel's bore.

STAMPED SHEET METAL RECEIVER

A receiver manufactured out of sheet metal which has been cut, stamped into a three-dimensional shape, and welded. An economical alternative to milling a receiver from a solid block of metal.

STANDOFF/BREACHING BARREL

Refers to a barrel that has a jagged muzzle to assist in the physical entry of a door and allows no slipping.

STATE COMPLIANT

Firearms whose features have been changed to comply with state laws/regulations such as CA, MA, MD, NJ, NY, HI, etc. are not listed in this text, as there are almost endless variations. Values of state compliant guns in the secondary marketplace will not be as high as the standard non-compliant models from which they are derived.

STOCK

Usually refers to the buttstock of a long gun, or that portion of a rifle or shotgun that comes in contact with the shooter's shoulder, and is attached to the frame/receiver.

STOCKS

Older terminology used to describe handgun grips. See GRIPS.

STRIKER

An elongated firing pin, or a separate component which imparts energy to a firing pin. Most commonly found in hammerless semi-auto pistols.

SUICIDE SPECIAL

A mass-produced inexpensive single action revolver or derringer, usually with a spur trigger. Produced under a variety of trade names, these guns earned their nickname by being almost as dangerous to shoot as to be shot at.

SUPERPOSED
Refers to an O/U barrel configuration.

SUPPRESSOR
A mechanical device, usually cylindrical and detachable, which alters and decreases muzzle blast and noise. Commonly referred to, in error, as a silencer, it acts only on the sound of the firearms discharge. It does not have any effect on the sounds generated by: the firearm's moving parts, a supersonic bullet in flight, or the bullet's impact. Legality varies per state.

TACTICAL
An imprecise term referring to certain features on handguns, rifles, and shotguns. Before 2000, a tactical gun generally referred to a rifle or carbine designed for military or law enforcement. In today's marketplace, tactical refers to certain features of both handguns and long arms.

TACTICAL REVOLVERS
Tactical revolvers have at least three of the following factory/manufacturer options or features: non-glare finish (generally but there may be exceptions), Mil Std 1913Picatinny or equivalent rail(s), combat style grips (wood or synthetic), fixed or adjustable low profile primary sights (most often night sights), auxiliary aiming/sighting/illumination equipment, compensators or barrel porting, as well as combat triggers and hammers.

TACTICAL RIFLES
Semi-auto, bolt action, or slide action rifles which have at least two of the following factory/manufacturer options or features: magazine capacity over ten rounds, nonglare finish (generally but there may be exceptions), Mil Std 1913 Picatinny or equivalent rail(s), mostly synthetic stocks which may be fixed, folding, collapsible, adjustable, or with/without pistol grip, most have sling attachments for single, traditional two, or three point slings, tritium night sights, and some Assault Weapon Ban characteristics, such as flash suppressors, detachable magazines, bayonet lugs, etc.

TACTICAL SEMI-AUTO PISTOLS
Tactical semi-auto pistols have at least three of the following factory/manufacturer options or features: magazine capacity over ten rounds, non-glare finish (generally but there may be exceptions), Mil Std 1913 Picatinny or equivalent rail(s), combat style grips (wood or synthetic), fixed or adjustable low profile primary sights (most often night sights), auxiliary aiming/sighting/illumination equipment, and compensators or barrel porting.

TACTICAL SHOTGUNS
Semi-auto or slide action shotguns which have at least two of the following factory/manufacturer options or features: higher capacity (than sporting/hunting shotguns) magazines, or magazine extensions, non-glare finish (generally but there may be exceptions), Mil Std 1913 Picatinny or equivalent rail(s), mostly synthetic stocks which may be fixed, folding, collapsible, adjustable, or with/without pistol grip, most have sling attachments for single, traditional two, or three point slings, some Assault Weapon Ban characteristics, such as bayonet lugs, or detachable high capacity magazines, rifle or night or ghost ring sights (usually adjustable), and short (18-20 inches) barrels with fixed cylinder choke.

TAKE DOWN
A gun which can be easily disassembled into two sections for carrying or shipping.

TANG(S)
Usually refers to the extension straps (upper and lower) of a rifle or shotgun receiver/frame to which the stock or grip is attached.

TARGET STOCK
A stock optimized for accuracy, consistency, ergonomics, and reliability; for firearms used primarily in formal known-distance competition shooting. Rifle versions may have many adjustment options (e.g.length of pull, cast, comb/cheek piece, buttplate, palm rest, hand stop, accessory attachment); handgun versions may have thumb or palm rests, spacers, inserts, etc.

THUMBHOLE STOCK (CRIME BILL)
An adaptation of the sporter thumbhole stock design which removed a weapon from semi-auto assault weapon legal status. The thumbhole was/is very large and provides the functionality of a true pistol grip stock.

THUMBHOLE STOCK (SPORTER)
A sporter/hunting stock with an ergonomic hole in the grip; the thumb of the shooter's trigger hand fits into the hole which provides for a steadier hold.

TOP BREAK
See BREAK BARREL ACTION.

TOP BREAK ACTION
See BREAK BARREL ACTION.

TOP FOLDING STOCK
A folding stock variation; the buttstock pivots upwards and over the top of the frame/receiver. See FOLDING STOCK.

TOP LEVER
Refers to the opening lever mechanism on top of the upper frame/tang.

TOP STRAP
The upper part of a revolver frame, which often is either slightly grooved - the groove serving as rear sight - or which carries at its rearward end a sight (which may or may not be adjustable).

TORQUE
The force which causes a rifled firearm to counter-rotate when a projectile travels down its bore.

TRACER
A type of military bullet that emits a colored flame from its base when fired allowing the gunner to adjust his fire onto a target.

TRAJECTORY
The curved flight path of a bullet from muzzle to target; resembling but not a true parabolic arc.

TRAJECTORY TABLE
A numerical table of computed data summarizing the down range trajectory of a projectile.

TRAP STOCK
A shotgun stock with greater length and less comb drop (Monte Carlo, in many cases) used for trap shooting, enabling a built-in height lead when shooting.

TRIGGER
Refers to a release device (mechanical or electrical) in the firing system that starts the ignition process. Usually a curved, grooved, or serrated piece of metal which is pulled rearward by the shooter's finger, and which releases the sear or hammer.

TRIGGER GUARD
Usually a circular or oval band of metal, horn, or plastic that goes around the trigger to provide both protection and safety in shooting circumstances.

TRIGGER SAFETY
A trigger assembly component which must be depressed or otherwise moved before the trigger can be pulled completely through to fire the weapon. Most often a pivoting blade in the center of a trigger which protrudes from the face of the trigger when it is engaged/"on" and automatically resets itself.

TURRETS
Cylinders on an optical sight's main tube which hold adjustment knobs or screws. A turret is dedicated to one of several functions: windage, elevation, parallax, reticle type, reticle illumination, or ranging.

TWIST BARRELS
A process in which a steel rod (called a mandrel) was wrapped with skelps - ribbons of iron. The skelps were then welded in a charcoal fire to form one piece of metal, after which the rod was driven out to be used again. The interior of the resulting tube then had to be laboriously bored out by hand to remove the roughness. Once polished, the outside was smoothed on big grinding wheels, usually turned by waterpower.

TWIST RATE

Refers to the distance required for one complete turn of rifling, usually expressed as a ratio such as 1:12 in. twist, which refers to one complete twist of rifling within 12 inches of barrel. Typically, the heavier the bullet, the faster the twist rate needs to be.

UNDER-LEVER

Action opening lever that is usually located below or in the trigger guard, can also be side pivoting from forearm.

UNDERLUG

On a break open action firearm, the lug on the chamber end of the barrel which locates the barrel in the receiver, and which locks the barrel into battery when intercepted by the bolt/underbolt. Also called a lump.

UNDER FOLDING STOCK

A folding stock variation; the buttstock rotates downwards and underneath the frame/receiver. See FOLDING STOCK.

UNLOAD

To remove all ammunition/cartridges from a firearm or magazine.

UNSERVICEABLE FIREARM

A firearm that is damaged and cannot be made functional in a minimal amount of time.

UPPER ASSEMBLY

For a semi-auto pistol this includes the barrel and slide assembly, for AR style rifles it includes the barrel, bolt and receiver housing.

VARIABLE POWER OPTICAL SIGHT

A optical sight with a multiple magnification levels, most common are 3-9 power general purpose scopes.

VENTILATED

Denotes a component with holes, slots, gaps, or other voids which reduce weight, promote cooling, have a structural purpose, or are decorative.

VENTILATED RIB

A sighting plane affixed along the length of a shotgun barrel with gaps or slots milled for cooling and lightweight handling.

VERNIER

Typically used in reference to a rear aperture (peep) sight. Usually upper tang mounted, and is adj. for elevation by means of a highly accurate finely threaded screw.

VIERLING

A German word designating a four-barrel gun.

VIOLENT CRIME CONTROL AND LAW ENFORCEMENT ACT OF 1994, PUBLIC LAW 103-322

On September 13, 1994, Congress passed the Violent Crime Control and Law Enforcement Act of 1994, Public Law 103-322. Title IX, Subtitle A, Section 110105 of this Act generally made it unlawful to manufacture, transfer, and possess semiautomatic assault weapons (SAWs) and to transfer and possess large capacity ammunition feeding devices (LCAFDs). The law also required importers and manufacturers to place certain markings on SAWs and LCAFDs, designating they were for export or law enforcement/government use. Significantly, the law provided that it would expire 10 years from the date of enactment. Accordingly, effective 12:01 am on September 13, 2004, the provisions of the law ceased to apply and the following provisions of the regulations in Part 478 no longer apply:

- Section 478.11- Definitions of the terms "semiautomatic assault weapon" and "large capacity ammunition feeding device"
- Section 478.40- Entire section
- Section 478.40a- Entire section
- Section 478.57- Paragraphs (b) and (c)
- Section 478.92- Paragraph (a)(3) – [NOTE: Renumbered from paragraph (a)(2) to paragraph (a)(3) by TD ATF – 461 (66 FR 40596) on August 3, 2001]
- Section 478.92- Paragraph (c)
- Section 478.119- Entire section- [NOTE: An import permit is still needed pursuant to the Arms Export Control Act- see 27 CFR 447.41(a)]
- Section 478.132- Entire section
- Section 478.153- Entire section

NOTE: The references to "ammunition feeding device" in section 478.116 are not applicable on or after September 13, 2004.

NOTE: The references to "semiautomatic assault weapons" in section 478.171 are not applicable on or after September 13, 2004.

Information from BATFE Online - Bureau of Alcohol, Tobacco and Firearms, and Explosives an official site of the U.S. Department of Justice.

WAD

A shotshell component in front of the powder charge and has a cup or flat surface that the shot charge rests on. Various types of wads exist with the most common being a column of plastic.

WADCUTTER BULLET

A lead target bullet for revolvers having a flat nose and a sharp outer edge or shoulder which will cut clean holes in paper targets to aid in spotting and scoring.

WATER TABLE

The flat surfaces forward of the standing breech of a side-by-side shotgun. Also called action bar flats or action flats.

WEAVER-STYLE RAIL

A mounting rail system similar in dimensions and use as the Picatinny Rail. Weaver-style grooves are .180 wide and do not always have consistent center-to-center widths. Most Weaver-style accessories will fit the Picatinny system, however Picatinny accessories will not fit the Weaver-style system. Also see PICATINNY RAIL.

WILDCAT CARTRIDGE

An experimental or non-standard cartridge, not commercially manufactured, often using a standard cartridge case which has been significantly modified.

WINDAGE

The deflection of a projectile from its trajectory due to wind. Also, adjustment of a firearm's sight(s) to compensate for the deflection.

WING SAFETY

A bolt action rifle safety which has a horizontally rotating lever located on the rear of the bolt assembly. Also known as a Mauser safety, after its designer, Peter Paul Mauser.

WUNDHAMMER GRIP/SWELL

Originally attributed to custom gunsmith Louis Wundhammer, it consists of a bulge on the right side of the pistol grip that ergonomically fills the palm of a right-handed shooter.

YOKE

See CRANE.

YOUTH DIMENSIONS

Usually refers to shorter stock dimensions and/or lighter weight enabling youth/women to shoot and carry a firearm.

ZERO

The procedure of adjusting a firearm's sight(s) so that the point of aim coincides with the bullet's point of impact at a selected range.

Abbreviation	Definition
*	Banned due to 1994-2004 Crime Bill (may be current again)
5R	Five (groove) Rifling
A	Standard Grade Walnut
A.R.M.S.	Atlantic Research Marketing Systems
A2	AR-15 Style/Configuration w/ fixed carry handle
A3	AR-15 Style/Configuration w/ detachable carry handle
AA	Extra Grade Walnut
AAA	Best Quality Walnut
ACB	Advanced Combat Bolt (LWRC)
ACP	Automatic Colt Pistol
ACR	Adaptive Combat Rifle
ACS	MAGPUL Adaptable Carbine/ Storage (stock)
adj.	Adjustable
AE	Automatic Ejectors or Action Express
AECA	Arms Export Control Act
AFG	MAGPUL Angled Fore Grip
AK	Avtomat Kalashnikova rifle
AMU	Army Marksman Unit
AOW	Any Other Weapon (NFA)
appts.	Appointments
AR	Armalite Rifle
ASAP	MAGPUL Ambi Sling Attachment Point
ATR	All Terrain Rifle (Mossberg)
ATS	All Terrain Shotgun (Mossberg)
AWB	Assault Weapons Ban
AWR	Alaskan/African Wilderness Rifle
B	Blue
BAC	Browning Arms Company
BAD	MAGPUL Battery Assist Device (bolt catch lever)
BAN/CRIME BILL ERA	Mfg. between Nov. 1989 - Sept. 12, 2004
BAR	Browning Automatic Rifle
BASR	Bolt Action Sniper Rifle (H&K)
BB	Brass Backstrap
BBL	Barrel
BLR	Browning Lever Rifle
BMG	Browning Machine Gun
BOSS	Ballistic Optimizing Shooting System
BOSS-CR	BOSS w/o Muzzle Brake
BP	Buttplate or Black Powder
BPE	Black Power Express
BPS	Browning Pump Shotgun
BR	Bench Rest
BT	Beavertail
BT	Browning Trap shotgun
BUIS	Back-Up Iron Sight(s)
c.	Circa
C/B 1994	Introduced Because of 1994 Crime Bill
CAD	Computer Assisted Design
cal.	Caliber
CAR	Colt Automatic Rifle or Carbine
CAWS	Close Assault Weapons System
CB	Crescent Buttplate
CC	Case Colors
CCA	Colt Collectors Association
CF	Centerfire
CFR	Code of Federal Regulations
CH	Cross Hair
CLMR	Colt Lightning Magazine Rifle
CMV	Chrome Moly Vanadium Steel
CNC	Computer Numeric Controlled (machining/machinery)
COMM.	Commemorative
COMP	Compensated/Competition
CQB	Close Quarter Battle
CQC	Close Quarter Combat
C-R	Curio-Relic
CRF	Controlled Round Feed
CRPF	Controlled Round Push Feed
CSAT	Combat Shooting & Tactics (accessories)
CTF	Copper/Tin Frangible (bullet)
CTG/CTGE	Cartridge
CTR	MAGPUL Compact/Type Restricted (stock)
CYL/C	Cylinder
DA	Double Action
DA/SA	Double Action/Single Action
DAGR	Dual aperture Gunsite rifle scope
DAK	Double Action Kellerman Trigger (SIG)
DAO	Double Action Only
DB	Double Barrel
DBM	Detachable Box Magazine
DCM	Director of Civilian Marksmanship
DI	Direct Impingement Gas System, see Glossary
DIGS	Delayed Impingement Gas System, see Glossary
DISC or disc.	Discontinued
DMR	Designated Marksman Rifle (U.S Army, LWRC)
DPMS	Defense Procurement Manufacturing Services
DSL	Detachable Side Locks
DST	Double Set Triggers
DT	Double Triggers
DWM	DeutscheWaffen and Munitions Fabriken
EGLM	Enhanced Grenade Launcher Module (FNH)
EJT	Ejector or Ejectors
EMAG	MAGPUL Export MAGazine
EMP	Enhanced Micro Pistol (Springfield Inc.)
EXC	Excellent
EXT	Extractor or Extractors
F	Full Choke
F&M	Full & Modified
FA	Forearm
FAL	Fusil Automatique Leger
FBT	Full Beavertail Forearm
FDE	Flat Dark Earth (finish color)
FDL	Fleur-de-lis
FE	Forend/Fore End
FFL	Federal Firearms License
FIRSH	Free Floating Integrated Rail System Handguard
FK	Flat Knob
FKLT	Flat Knob Long Tang
FM	Full Mag
FMJ	Full Metal Jacket
FN CAL	FN Carabine Automatique Leger
FN GP	FN Grande Puissance (pistol)
FN LAR	Fabrique Nationale Light Automatic Rifle
FN	Fabrique Nationale
FNAR	FN Automatic Rifle
FNC	Fabrique Nationale Carabine
FNH USA	Fabrique Nationale Herstal (U.S. sales and marketing)
FNH	Fabrique Nationale Herstal
FOL	Foliage (finish)
FPS	Feet Per Second
g.	Gram
ga.	Gauge
GCA	Gun Control Act
GIO	Gas Impingement Operation
G-LAD	Green Laser Aiming Device
GOVT	Government
GPO	Gas Piston Operation
gr.	Grain
H&H	Holland & Holland
HAMR	High accuracy multi-range rifle scope
HB	Heavy Barrel
H-BAR	H(eavy)-BARrel, AR-15/M16
HC	Hard Case
HK	Heckler und Koch
HMR	Hornady Magnum Rimfire
HP	High Power (FN/Browning pistol)
HP	Hollow Point
HPJ	High Performance Jacket
I	Improved
IAR	Infantry Automatic Rifle (LWRC)
IC	Improved Cylinder
ICORE	International Confederation of Revolver Enthusiasts
ILS	Integral Locking System (North American Arms)
IM	Improved Modified
IMI	Israel Military Industries
in.	Inch
intro.	Introduced
IOM	Individual Officer Model (FNH model suffix)
IPSC	International Practical Shooting Confederation
ISSF	International Shooting Sports Federation
ITAR	International Traffic (in) Arms Regulation
IVT	Italian Value-Added Tax
JCP	Joint Combat Pistol
KAC	Knight's Armament Co.
KMC	Knight's Manufacturing Co.
KSG	Kel Tec Shotgun
L	Long
LBA	Lightning Bolt Action (Mossberg)
LBC	Les Baer Custom (Inc.)
lbs.	Pounds
LC	Long Colt
LCW	Lauer Custom Weaponry
LDA	Light Double Action (PARA USA INC.)
LEM	Law Enforcement Model or Modification
LEO	Law Enforcement Only
LMT	Lewis Machine and Tool (Company)
LOP	Length of Pull
LPA	Lightning Pump Action (Mossberg)
LPI	Lines Per Inch
LR	Long Rifle
LT	Long Tang or Light
LTR	Light Tactical Rifle (Rem.)
LTRK	Long Tang Round Knob
LWRC	Land Warfare Resources Corporation
LWRC	Leitner-Wise Rifle Company, Inc.
M (MOD.)	Modified Choke
M&P	Military & Police
M-4	Newer AR-15/M16 Carbine Style/ Configuration
Mag.	Magnum Caliber
mag.	Magazine
MARS	Modular Accessory Rail System
MBUS	MAGPUL Back-Up Sight
MC	Monte Carlo
MCS	Modular Combat System (Rem.)
MFG or Mfg.	Manufactured/manufacture
MIAD	MAGPUL Mission Adaptable (grip, other)
mil	see Glossary
mil-dot	See Glossary
MIL SPEC	Mfg. to Military Specifications
MK	Mark
mm	Millimeter
MOA	Minute of Angle
MOE	MAGPUL Original Equipment
MOUT	Military Operations (on) Urbanized Terrain
MR	Matted Rib
MS2	MAGPUL Multi Mission Sling System
MSR	Manufacturer's Suggested Retail

MVG	MAGPUL MOE Vertical Grip
MWS	Modular Weapons System
N	Nickel
N/A	Not Applicable or Not Available
NATO	North Atlantic Treaty Org.
NE	Nitro Express
NFA	National Firearms Act (U.S. 1934)
NIB	New in Box
NM	National Match
no.	Number
NP	New Police
NP3/NP3 Plus	Nickel-Phosphorus (firearm coating)
NSST	Non Selective Single Trigger
NVD	Night Vision Device
O/U	Over and Under
OA	Overall
OAL	Overall Length
OB	Octagon Barrel
OBFM	Octagon Barrel w/full mag.
OBO	Or Best Offer
OCT	Octagon
ODG	Olive Drab Green (finish color)
ORC	Optics Ready Carbine
oz.	Ounce
P	Police (Rem. rifle/shotgun)
P99AS	Pistol 99 Anti Stress (trigger, Walther)
PAD	Personal Anti-recoil Device (Savage)
Para.	Parabellum
PBR	Patrol Bolt Rifle (FNH)
PDA	Personal Defense Assistant (PARA USA INC.)
PFFR	Percantage of factory finish remaining
PG	Pistol Grip
PGF	Precision Guided Firearm
PK	Pistol Kompact (Walther)
PMAG	MAGPUL Polymer MAGazine
POR/P.O.R.	Price on Request
POST-'89	Paramilitary mfg. after Federal legislation in Nov. 1989
POST-BAN	Refers to production after Sept. 12, 2004
PPC	Pindell Palmisano Cartridge
PPD	Post Paid
PPK	Police Pistol Kriminal (Walther 1931 design)
PPKs	Police Pistol Kriminal (Walther 1968 design)
PPQ	Police Pistol Quick (defense trigger, Walther)
PRE-'89	Paramilitary mfg. before Federal legislation in Nov. 1989
PRE-BAN	Mfg. before September 13, 1994 per C/B or before Nov. 1989.
PRS/PRS2	MAGPUL Precision Rifle/Sniper (stock)
PSD	Personal Security Detail rifle (LWRC)
PSG	PrazisionSchutzenGewehr (H&K rifle)
PSR	Precision Shooting Rifle (FNH)
PXT	Power Extractor Technology (PARA USA INC.)
QD	Quick Detachable
RACS	Remington Arms Chassis System
RAS	Rail Adapter System
RB	Round Barrel/Round Butt
RCM	Ruger Compact Magnum
RCMP	Royal Canadian Mounted Police
RDS	Rapid Deployment Stock
REC	Receiver
REM	Remington
REM. MAG.	Remington Magnum
REPR	Rapid Engagement Precision Rifle (LWRC)
RF	Rimfire
RFB	Rifle Forward (ejection) Bullpup
RFM	Rim Fire Magnum

RIS	Rail Interface system
RK	Round Knob
RKLT	Round Knob Long Tang
RKST	Round Knob Short Tang
RMEF	Rocky Mt. Elk. Foundation
RMR	Rimfire Magnum Rifle (Kel Tec)
RPD	Ruchnoy Pulemyot Degtyaryova (machine gun)
RR	Red Ramp
RSA	MAGPUL Rail Sling Attachment
RSUM	Remington Short-Action Ultra Magnum
RUM	Remington Ultra Magnum
RVG	MAGPUL Rail Vertical Grip
S	Short
S&W	Smith & Wesson
S/N	Serial Number
SA	Single Action
SAA	Single Action Army
SAAMI	Sporting Arms and Ammunition Manufacturers' Institute
SABR	Sniper/Assaulter Battle Rifle (LWRC)
SAE	Selective Automatic Ejectors
SAS	SIG Anti Snag (pistol models)
SASS	Single Action Shooting Society or (U.S. Army) Semi Automatic Sniper System
SAUM	Short Action Ultra Magnum
SAW	Semiautomatic Assault Weapon
SAW	Squad Automatic Weapon
SB	Shotgun butt or Steel backstrap
SBR	Short Barrel Rifle
SCAR	Special (Operations Forces) Combat Assault Rifle (FNH)
SCW	Sub Compact Weapon (Colt)
SDT	Super Dynamic Technology (PARA USA INC.)
ser.	serial
SFO	Striker Fire Operation
SG	Straight Grip
SIG	Schweizerische Industriegesellschaft
SIM	Special Impact Munition
SK	Skeet
SLP	Self Loading Police (FNH shotgun)
SMG	Submachine Gun
SMLE	Short Magazine Lee Enfield Rifle
SNT	Single Non-Selective Trigger
SOCOM	Special Operations Command
SOPMOD	Special Operations Peculiar Modification
SP	Special Purpose
SPC	Special Purpose Cartridge
SPEC	Special
SPEC-OPS	Special Operations
SPG	Semi-Pistol Grip
Spl.	Special
SPLLAT	Special Purpose Low Lethality Anti Terrorist (Munition)
SPR	Special Police Rifle (FNH), Special Purpose Rifle
SPS	Special Purpose Synthetic (Remington)
SPS	Superalloy Piston System (LWRC)
sq.	Square
SR	Solid Rib
SRC	Saddle Ring Carbine
SRT	Short Reset Trigger
SS	Single Shot or Stainless Steel
SSA	Super Short Action
SSR	Sniper Support Rifle (FNH)
SST	Single Selective Trigger
ST	Single Trigger
SUR	Sport Utility Rifle - see Glossary
SWAT	Special Weapons Assault Team
SWAT	Special Weapons and Tactics
SxS	Side by Side
TB	Threaded Barrel
TBA	To be Announced

TBM	Tactical Box Magazine
TD	Take Down
TDR	Target Deployment Rifle (Rem.)
TGT	Target
TH	Target Hammer
TIR	Target Interdiction Rifle (Rem.)
TPS	Tactical Police Shotgun (FNH)
TRP	Tactical Response Pistol (Springfield Inc.)
TRPAFD	Take Red Pen Away From Dave!
TS	Target Stocks
TSOB	Scope Mount Rail Weaver Type
TSR XP USA	Tactical Sport Rifle - Extreme Performance Ultra Short Action (FNH)
TSR XP	Tactical Sport Rifle - Extreme Performance (FNH)
TT	Target Trigger
TTR	Tactical Target Rifle (PARA USA INC.)
TWS	Tactical Weapons System (Rem.)
UBR	MAGPUL Utility/Battle Rifle (stock)
UCIW	Ultra Compact Individual Weapon (LWRC)
UCP	Universal Combat Pistol (H&K)
UIT	Union Internationale de Tir
UMC	Union Metallic Cartridge Co.
UMP	Universal Machine Pistol (H&K)
USA	Ultra Safety Assurance (Springfield Inc.)
USAMU	U.S. Army Marksmanship Unit
USC	Universal Self-Loading Carbine (H&K)
USG	United States Government (FNH model suffix)
USP	Universal Self-Loading Pistol (H&K)
USPSA	United States Practical Shooting Association
USR	Urban Sniper Rifle (Rem.)
USSOCOM	U.S. Special Operations Command
VAT	Value Added Tax
Vent.	Ventilated
VG	Very Good
VR	Ventilated Rib
VTAC	Viking Tactics, Inc. (accessories)
VTR	Varmint Triangular Profile Barrel (Remington)
w/	With
w/o	Without
WBY	Weatherby
WC	Wad Cutter
WCF	Winchester Center Fire
WD	Wood
WFF	Watch For Fakes
WIN	Winchester
WMR	Winchester Magnum Rimfire
WO	White Outline
WRA	Winchester Repeating Arms Co.
WRF	Winchester Rim Fire
WRM	Winchester Rimfire Magnum
WSL	Winchester Self-Loading
WSM	Winchester Short Magnum
WSSM	Winchester Super Short Magnum
WW	World War
X (1X)	1X Wood Upgrade or Extra Full Choke Tube
XD	Extreme Duty (Springfield Inc.)
XDM	Extreme Duty M Factor (Springfield Inc.)
XX (2X)	2X Wood Upgrade or Extra Extra Full Choke Tube
XXX (3x)	3X Wood Upgrade
YHM	Yankee Hill Machine

GRADING CRITERIA

The old, NRA method of firearms grading – relying upon adjectives such as "Excellent" or "Fair" – has served the firearms community for a many years. Today's dealers/collectors, especially those who deal in modern guns, have turned away from the older subjective system. There is too much variance within some of the older subjective grades, therefore making accurate grading difficult.

Most dealers and collectors are now utilizing what is essentially an objective method for deciding the condition of a gun: THE PERCENTAGE OF ORIGINAL FACTORY FINISH(ES) REMAINING ON THE GUN. After looking critically at a variety of firearms and carefully studying the Photo Percentage Grading System™ (available free of charge on our website: www.bluebookofgunvalues.com, it will soon become evident if a specific a gun has 98%, 90%, 70% or less finish remaining. Remember, sometimes an older gun described as NIB can actually be 98% or less condition, simply because of the wear accumulated by taking it in and out of the box and handling it too many times. Every gun's unique condition factor – and therefore the price – is best determined by the percentage of original finish(es) remaining, with the key consideration being the overall frame/receiver finish. The key word here is "original", for if anyone other than the factory has refinished the gun, its value as a collector's item has been diminished, with the exception of rare and historical pieces that have been properly restored. Every year, top quality restorations have become more accepted, and prices have gone up proportionately with the quality of the workmanship. Also popular now are antique finishes, and a new question has come up, "what is 100% antique finish on new reproductions?" Answer – a gun that started out as new, and then has been aged to a lower condition factor to duplicate natural wear and tear.

It is important to remember that most tactical firearms have either a parkerized, phosphated, matte black, or camouflaged finish which is very durable and resistant to wear and extreme weather conditions. Because of this, observing wear on the breech block, internal firing mechanism, and in the barrel may be the only way to accurately determine condition as these black/camo wonders get used, since most of them are all going to look 98% or better from the outside!

Every gun's unique condition factor – and therefore the price – is best determined by the percentage of original finish(es) remaining, with the key consideration being the overall frame/receiver finish. The key word here is "original", for if anyone other than the factory has refinished the gun, its value as a collector's item has been diminished, with the exception of rare and historical pieces that have been properly restored.

Note where the finishes of a firearm typically wear off first. These are usually places where the gun accumulates wear from holster/case rubbing, and contact with the hands or body over an extended period of time. A variety of firearms have been shown in four-color to guarantee that your "sampling size" for observing finishes with their correct colors is as diversified as possible.

It should be noted that the older a collectible firearm is, the smaller the percentage of original finish one can expect to find. Some very old and/or very rare firearms are sought by collectors in almost any condition!

For your convenience, NRA Condition Standards are listed on page 39. Converting from this grading system to percentages can now be done accurately. Remember the price is wrong if the condition factor isn't right!

GRADING SYSTEM CONVERSION GUIDELINES

New/Perfect	100% condition with or without box. 100% on currently manufactured firearms assumes NIB (New In Box) condition and not sold previously at retail.
Mint	typically 98%-99% condition, depending on the age of the firearm. Probably sold previously at retail, and may have been shot occasionally.
Excellent	95%+ - 98% condition (typically).
Very Good	80% - 95% condition (all parts/finish should be original).
Good	60% - 80% condition (all parts/finish should be original).
Fair	20% - 60% condition (all parts/finish may or may not be original, but must function properly and shoot).
Poor	under 20% condition (shooting not a factor).

NRA CONDITION STANDARDS

The NRA conditions listed below have been provided as guidelines to assist the reader in converting and comparing condition factors. In order to use this book correctly, the reader is urged to examine these images of NRA condition standards. Once the gun's condition has been accurately assessed, only then can values be accurately ascertained.

NRA MODERN CONDITION DESCRIPTIONS

New - not previously sold at retail, in same condition as current factory production.

Perfect - in new condition in every respect.

Excellent - new condition, used but little wear, no noticeable marring of wood or metal, bluing near perfect (except at muzzle or sharp edges).

Very Good - in perfect working condition, no appreciable wear on working surfaces, no corrosion or pitting, only minor surface dents or scratches.

Good - in safe working condition, minor wear on working surfaces, no broken parts, no corrosion or pitting that will interfere with proper functioning.

Fair - in safe working condition, but well worn, perhaps requiring replacement of minor parts or adjustments which should be indicated in advertisement, no rust, but may have corrosion pits which do not render article unsafe or inoperable.

NRA ANTIQUE CONDITION DESCRIPTIONS

Factory New - all original parts; 100% original finish; in perfect condition in every respect, inside and out.

Excellent - all original parts; over 80% original finish; sharp lettering, numerals and design on metal and wood; unmarred wood; fine bore.

Fine - all original parts; over 30% original finish; sharp lettering, numerals and design on metal and wood; minor marks in wood; good bore.

Very Good - all original parts; none to 30% original finish; original metal surfaces smooth with all edges sharp; clear lettering, numerals and design on metal; wood slightly scratched or bruised; bore disregarded for collectors firearms.

Good – less than 20% original finish, some minor replacement parts; metal smoothly rusted or lightly pitted in places, cleaned or reblued; principal lettering, numerals and design on metal legible; wood refinished, scratched, bruised or minor cracks repaired; in good working order.

Fair – less than 10% original finish, some major parts replaced; minor replacement parts may be required; metal rusted, may be lightly pitted all over, vigorously cleaned or reblued; rounded edges of metal and wood; principal lettering, numerals and design on metal partly obliterated; wood scratched, bruised, cracked or repaired where broken; in fair working order or can be easily repaired and placed in working order.

Poor – little or no original finish remaining, major and minor parts replaced; major replacement parts required and extensive restoration needed; metal deeply pitted; principal lettering, numerals and design obliterated, wood badly scratched, bruised, cracked or broken; mechanically inoperative, generally undesirable as a collector's firearm.

PPGS – FIREARMS GRADING MADE EASY

The Photo Percentage Grading System™ (PPGS) is included free of charge on our website at www. bluebookofgunvalues.com. If you carefully study all the images, and thoroughly read the accompanying captions, the color images will help you accurately determine condition better than anything that's ever been published or posted online. This revised Photo Percentage Grading System™ (PPGS) includes images of both NRA new and antique condition factors, in addition to all the 100%-10% percentage conditions for revolvers, pistols, rifles, and shotguns.

After more than 23 editions, the Photo Percentage Grading System™ has now become the industry standard for visibly ascertaining various condition factors based on a percentage system. The PPGS also retains the "PPGS-o-meters" whenever possible, so you can get a quick fix on condition factors.

Condition factors pictured (indicated by PPGS-o-meters), unless otherwise noted, refer to the percentage of a gun's remaining finish(es), including blue, case colors, nickel, or another type of original finish remaining on the frame/receiver. On older guns, describing the receiver/frame finish accurately is absolutely critical to ascertain an accurate grade, which will determine the correct value.

Additional percentages of condition may be used to describe other specific parts of a gun (i.e. barrel, wood finish, plating, magazine tube, etc.). Percentages of patina/brown or other finish discoloration factors must also be explained separately when necessary, and likewise be interpolated accurately. With antiques, the overall percentage within this text is NOT an average of the various condition factors, but again, refers to the overall original condition of the frame/receiver. Being able to spot original condition has never been more important, especially when the prices get into four, five, and six figures. Remember, the price is wrong if the condition factor isn't right!

Now, more than ever, it takes well-trained senses of sight, hearing, touch, and smell, with a direct connection to the most powerful computer ever built, a trained human brain, to accurately fingerprint a gun's correct condition factor. Regardless of how much knowledge you've accumulated from books, websites, auction catalogs, dealer listings, etc., you're still in potential danger as a buyer if you can't figure out a gun's condition factor(s) accurately. More than anything else, an older gun's overall condition must "add up" (i.e., an AR-15 with visible barrel wear should not have a bright blue magazine tube, and a Model 1911 Colt with 98% frame finish should not have an 80% slide).

While the Photo Percentage Grading System™ certainly isn't meant to be the Last Testament on firearms grading, it hopefully goes a lot further than anything else that's been published or posted on the web on the subject. Once you've accumulated the experience necessary to grade guns accurately, a ten-second "CAT scan" is usually all the time that is needed to zero in on each gun's unique condition factor.

In closing, the publisher wishes to express his thanks and gratitude to Pat Hogan, Judy Voss, and Matt Parise at Rock Island Auctions, and Dr. Leonardo Antaris, M.D. for authorizing the use of their digital images for the Photo Percentage Grading System™ (PPGS).

Sincerely,

S.P. Fjestad
Author & Publisher - *Blue Book of Tactical Firearms Values*

2 VETS ARMS CO., LLC

Current custom rifle manufacturer located in Eufaula, OK.

2 Vets Arms Co., LLC is a female Service-connected Disabled Veteran Owned Business (SDVOB) that specializes in building high performance custom rifles for American patriots with an emphasis on serving the U.S. Military Veteran and those actively serving in the U.S. Armed Forces. A portion of the proceeds from each sale goes to support honored military veterans and veteran support organizations.

MSR	100%	98%	95%	90%	80%	70%	60%	Last MSR

RIFLES: SEMI-AUTO

.300 BLACKOUT – .300 Blackout cal., GIO, 16 in. free floating stainless steel barrel, low profile gas block, carbine length free float quad rail, optional lightweight free float tube, or PRI carbone fiber free float forend, side charging upper receiver, 2VA lower receiver and parts kit, Magpul MOE grip and trigger guard, and CTR mil-spec (standard or five optional style) buttstock.

	100%	98%	95%	90%	80%	70%	60%	Last MSR
	$1,475	$1,300	$1,100	$1,000	$825	$675	$525	*$1,650*

5.56 mm RIFLE – 5.56 NATO cal., GIO, 16 in. free floating M4 profile stainless barrel, option of A2 front sight or low pro gas block, side charging upper receiver, 2 VA lower receiver and parts kit, Magpul MOE grip, trigger guard, and CTR mil-spec buttstock.

	100%	98%	95%	90%	80%	70%	60%	Last MSR
	$1,075	$950	$800	$725	$600	$500	$425	*$1,199*

6.8 SPC II – 6.8 SPC cal., GIO, match grade 16, 18, or 20 in. free floating stainless steel barrel, low profile gas block, standard rifle length free float quad rail, or optional lightweight quad rail, free float tube, or PRI carbon fiber tube, side charging upper receiver, 2 Vets Arms lower receiver and parts kit, Magpul MOE grip and trigger guard, Magpul CTR mil-spec (standard or five optional) buttstock.

	100%	98%	95%	90%	80%	70%	60%	Last MSR
	$1,475	$1,300	$1,100	$1,000	$825	$675	$525	*$1,650*

2VA LRRP – 5.56 NATO or .300 Blackout cal., GIO, 16 in. stainless steel barrel with mid-length gas system, 10 in. tactical lightweight Evolution rail and Texas Custom Guns micro gas block, B5 Systems SOPMOD Alpha buttstock, Bravo Company Mfg. Gunfighter grip, LAR side charged upper receiver, 2VA forged lower receiver.

	100%	98%	95%	90%	80%	70%	60%	Last MSR
MSR $1,650	$1,475	$1,300	$1,100	$1,000	$825	$675	$525	

Add $25 for .300 Blackout cal.

2VA SOPMOD – 5.56 NATO or .300 Blackout cal., GIO, 16 in. stainless steel barrel, mid-length gas system, 10 in. Spectre quad rail covering Texas Custom Guns micro gas block, B5 SOPMOD Alpha buttstock, Bravo Company Mfg. Gunfighter grip, LAR side charged upper receiver, 2VA lower receiver.

	100%	98%	95%	90%	80%	70%	60%	Last MSR
MSR $1,525	$1,375	$1,200	$1,025	$935	$750	$625	$475	

2VA 5.56 BRAVO – 5.56 NATO cal., GIO, billet side charged upper receiver, forged lower receiver, 16 in. chromemoly barrel, A2 front sight base, B5 bravo stock and forend, Umbrella Corp. grip, G.I. five controls, Phase 5 enhanced side charged compatible BAD lever. New 2014.

	100%	98%	95%	90%	80%	70%	60%	Last MSR
MSR $1,300	$1,175	$1,050	$875	$800	$650	$550	$425	

2VA 5.56 ALPHA – 5.56 NATO cal., mid-length GIO, billet side charged upper receiver, forged lower receiver, 16 in. stainless steel match barrel with full flutes, B5 SOPMOD Alpha stock, BCM gunfighter grip, KNS anti-rotation pins, Geissele SAA fire controls, Battle Arms Development ambi selector, Phase 5 enhanced side charged compatible BAD lever, 13 in. Keymod compatible free float rail. New 2014.

	100%	98%	95%	90%	80%	70%	60%	Last MSR
MSR $1,825	$1,650	$1,450	$1,250	$1,125	$925	$750	$600	

2VA 6.8 DMR – 6.8 SPC cal., intermediate length GIO, billet side charged upper receiver, forged lower receiver, 20 in. stainless steel match barrel, Battle Comp BABC compensator, B5 SOPMOD Alpha stock, BCM gunfighter grip, 15 in. tactical Evo rail, adj. two-stage trigger. New 2014.

	100%	98%	95%	90%	80%	70%	60%	Last MSR
MSR $1,849	$1,660	$1,450	$1,250	$1,125	$925	$750	$600	

A.A. ARMS INC.

Previous manufacturer located in Monroe, NC until 1999.

CARBINES: SEMI-AUTO

AR9 CARBINE – 9mm Para. cal., similar action to AP9, except has carbine length barrel and side-folding metal stock. Banned 1994.

	100%	98%	95%	90%	80%	70%	60%
	$750	$625	$550	$475	$425	$375	$325

MSR	100%	98%	95%	90%	80%	70%	60%	Last MSR

PISTOLS: SEMI-AUTO

AP9 MINI-SERIES PISTOL – 9mm Para. cal., semi-auto blowback design, phosphate/blue or nickel finish, 2 barrel lengths, 10 (C/B 1994) or 20* shot mag. Disc. 1999, parts cleanup during 2000.

	$425	$375	$325	$275	$225	$200	$175	$245

Add $20 for nickel finish.

Add $200 for AP9 long barrel Target Model (banned 1994).

A & B HIGH PERFORMANCE FIREARMS

Previous competition pistol manufacturer located in Arvin, CA.

PISTOLS: SEMI-AUTO

OPEN CLASS – 9mm Para. or .38 Super cal., single action, competition M1911-styled action, STI frame, Ultimatch or Hybrid compensated barrel, Caspian slide, C-More scope, blue or chrome finish.

	$2,800	$2,300	$1,875	$1,600	$1,375	$1,000	$750	$2,800

A.R. SALES

Previous manufacturer located in South El Monte, CA, circa 1968-1977.

RIFLES: SEMI-AUTO

MARK IV SPORTER – .308 Win. cal., semi-auto, M-14 style action, adj. sights. Approx. 200 mfg.

	$725	$650	$575	$500	$450	$400	$350	

AK-47 DESIGN CARBINES, RIFLES, & PISTOLS

Select-fire military design rifle originally designed in Russia (initials refer to Avtomat Kalashnikova, 1947). The AK-47 was officially adopted by Russia in 1949. Russian-manufactured select fire AK-47s have not been manufactured since the mid-1950s. Semi-auto AK-47 and AKM clones are currently manufactured by several arsenals in China including Norinco and Poly Technologies, Inc. (currently illegal to import), in addition to being manufactured in other countries including the Czech Republic, Bulgaria, Russia, Egypt, and Hungary. On April 6th, 1998, recent "sporterized" variations (imported 1994-1998) with thumbhole stocks were banned by presidential order. Beginning in 2000, AK-47s were being assembled in the U.S., using both newly manufactured and older original military parts and components.

AK-47s and variations are not rare - approximately 75 million AK-47s and over 100 million AK-74 design carbine/rifles have been manufactured since 1947.

AK-47/AK-74/AKM HISTORY

Since the early 1950s, the AK-47/AK-74/AKM series of select fire rifles has been the standard issue military rifle of the former Soviet Union and its satellites. It continues to fulfill that role reliably today. The AK series of rifles, from the early variants of the AK-47 through the AKM and AK-74, is undoubtedly the most widely used military small arms design in the world. Developed by Mikhail Kalashnikov (the AK stands for Avtomat Kalashnikova) in 1946, the AK went into full production in 1947 in Izhevsk, Russia. In 1953, the milled receiver was put into mass production. Since then, variants of the original AK-47 have been manufactured by almost every former Soviet bloc country and some free world nations, including Egypt. The AK action is the basis for numerous other weapons, including the RPK (Ruchnoy Pulemyot Kalashnikova).

The AK-47 was replaced in 1959 by the AKM, and retained the same basic design. The rifle was simply updated to incorporate easier and more efficient production methods, using a stamped, sheet metal receiver that was pinned and riveted in place, rather than a milled receiver. Other changes included a beavertail forearm, muzzle compensator, and an anti-bounce device intended to improve controllability and increase accuracy.

The AK was designed to be, and always has been, a "peasant-proof" military weapon. It is a robust firearm, both in design and function. Its record on the battlefields around the world is impressive, rivaled only by the great M1 Garand of the U.S. or bolt rifles such as the English Mark III Enfield. The original AK-47 prototypes are on display in the Red Army Museum in Moscow.

All of the current semi-auto AK "clones" are copies of the AKM's basic receiver design and internal components minus the full-auto parts. The Saiga rifle (see separate listing), manufactured by the Izhevsk Machining Plant, in Izhevsk, Russia, is the sole Russian entry into this market. It is available in the standard 7.62x39 mm, 5.45x39 mm (disc.) and 20 gauge or .410 bore. Molot (hammer) JSC also exports semi-automatic AKs to the U.S. under the trade name Vepr. (see separate listing). Saiga is imported by RWC (Russian Weapon Company), and the Vepr. is imported by Robinson Armaments. Molot was the home of the PPSh-41 sub-machine gun during WWII, and also manufactured the RPK and the RPK-74. Other AK European manufacturers include companies in the Czech Republic, Bulgaria, and the former Yugoslavia. The Egyptian-made Maahdi AK clones were also available in the U.S. market.

Interest in the Kalashnikov design is at an all-time high due to the availability of high quality military AK-74, AKS-74, AKS-74U, and RPK-74 parts kits. Some models, such as those produced by Marc Krebs, are of very high quality. Currently, it is hard to go to a gun show or page through a buy/sell firearms magazine and not see a variety of parts, accessories, and high capacity magazines available for many of the AK

MSR	100%	98%	95%	90%	80%	70%	60%	*Last MSR*

variants. For shooters, the value represented by these guns is undeniable for the price point.

Values for almost all of the imported AK clones are based solely on their use as sporting or target rifles. Fit and finish varies by country and importer. Most fall on the "low" side. Interest peaked prior to the passage of the 1994 Crime Bill and both AK clones and their "high capacity" magazines were bringing a premium for a short period of time in 1993 and 1994. However, interest waned during 1995-97, and the reduced demand lowered prices. In November of 1997, the Clinton Administration instituted an "administrative suspension" on all import licenses for these types of firearms in order to do a study on their use as "sporting firearms."

On April 6th, 1998, the Clinton Administration, in the political wake of the Jonesboro tragedy, banned the further import of 58 "assault-type" rifles, claiming that these semi-automatics could not be classified as sporting weapons - the AK-47 and most related configurations were included. During 1997, firearms importers obtained permits to import almost 600,000 reconfigured rifles - approximately only 20,000 had entered the country when this ban took effect. When the ban began, applications were pending to import an additional 1,000,000 guns. Previously, thumbhole-stocked AK Sporters were still legal for import, and recent exporters included the Czech Republic, Russia, and Egypt.

AK-47 DESIGN CARBINES, RIFLES, & PISTOLS: RECENT/CURRENT MFG. & IMPORTATION

The following is a listing of both current and recent manufacturers and importers that offer/have offered AK-47 design carbines, rifles, and pistols for sale domestically. Please look under each current company, importer, or brand name/trademark heading for up-to-date information and values on current makes and models that are offered.

These companies include: AKS (AK-47, AK-74, & AKM Copies), American Arms, Inc., American Tactical Imports, Armory USA LLC, Armscor, Arsenal 2000 JSCo., Arsenal Inc., Arsenal USA LLC, B-West, Baikal, Bingham, Blackheart International, Bulgaria Arsenal, Bushmaster, CZ (Ceska Zbrojovka), Century International Arms, Inc., Czechpoint Inc., E.D.M. Arms, E.M.F. Co. Inc., European American Armory Corp., Feather Industries, Inc., Federal Ordnance, FEG, German Sport Guns GmbH, Hakim, Hesse Arms, I.O., Inc., Inter Ordnance of America, LP, Interarms Arsenal, Intrac Arms International, K.B.I., K-VAR Corp., Liberty Arms International, LLC, M+M, Inc., Mitchell Arms, Inc., Molot JSCo., Navy Arms Company, Norinco, Ohio Ordnance Works, Poly Technologies, Inc., Rasheed (Rashid), Robinson Armament Co., Russian American Armory Company, Russian Weapon Company, SAIGA, Samco Global Arms, Inc., Sarco, Inc., Sentinel Arms, TG International, Valmet, Vector Arms Inc., Vepr, Vulcan Armament, and ZDF Import/Export.

CARBINES/RIFLES: SEMI-AUTO, AK-47, AK-74, & AKM MODELS

"AK-47" stands for Automatic Kalashnikov Rifle, 1947 Model, first developed in the former Soviet Union by Mikhail Kalashnikov, who passed away in 2013. This gas-operated military rifle was originally designed for select-fire operation, and quickly gained acceptance within the Soviet Union's military forces. While very early military production used stamped receivers, problems in the manufacturing process forced the adoption of milled receivers, which took more time, but solved all of the earlier production problems. The arsenals of Soviet satellite countries, as well as China also began producing AK-47s for military use, but later also began producing semi-auto variations for commercial sales. In 1959, the AKM (M designates modernized or upgraded) was developed with a stamped receiver and also featured a slanted muzzle brake - it was also approximately 33% lighter than the earlier milled AK-47s. There are far more AKMs available in the American marketplace for sale than semi-auto AK-47s. Chinese importation stopped during late 1990.

AK-47/AKM – 7.62x39mm (most common cal., former Russian M43 military), 5.45x39mm (Romanian mfg. or Saiga/MAK - recent mfg. only), or .223 Rem. cal., semi-auto Kalashnikov action, stamped (most common) or milled (pre-1959) receiver, typically 16 1/2 in. barrel, 5, 10, or 30* (C/B 1994) shot curved mag., wood or synthetic stock and forearm except on folding stock model, 1994-early 1998 importation typically had newer "sporterized" fixed stocks with thumbholes, may be supplied with bayonet, sling, cleaning kit, patterned after former military production rifle of China and Russia.

* **AK-47/AKM Post-WWII-Pre-1994 Mfg./Importation** – 7.62x39mm (most common cal., former Russian M43 military), 5.45x39mm (Romanian mfg. or Saiga/MAK - recent mfg. only), or .223 Rem. cal., semi-auto Kalashnikov action, stamped (most common) or milled receiver, typically 16 1/2 in. barrel, 5, 10, or 30* (C/B 1994) shot mag., wood or synthetic stock and forearm except on folding stock model, may be supplied with bayonet, sling, cleaning kit, patterned after former military production rifle of Russia and China. Check markings and/or proofs on gun for country of origin and possible importer.

	100%	98%	95%	90%	80%	70%	60%
Romanian mfg.	$450	$395	$350	$325	$295	$275	$250
Yugoslavian mfg.	$795	$725	$675	$575	$450	$425	$400
Hungarian mfg.	$795	$725	$675	$575	$450	$425	$400
Czech mfg.	$795	$725	$675	$575	$450	$425	$400
Bulgarian mfg.	$795	$725	$675	$575	$450	$425	$400
Egyptian mfg.	$650	$600	$550	$450	$400	$365	$335

Add 20% for milled receiver.
Add 10% for chrome-lined barrel.
Add 10% for older folding stock variations.
Add 10%-15% for 5.45x39 mm cal. on Eastern European mfg. (non-recent import).
Values are for original guns completely manufactured in the countries listed above and will have various import markings stamped on the receiver or barrel.

MSR	100%	98%	95%	90%	80%	70%	60%	Last MSR

* ***AK-47/AKM 1994-2004 Mfg.*** – most feature "sporterized" fixed stocks with thumbholes to avoid the GCA of 1994.

| | $550 | $450 | $395 | $350 | $325 | $295 | $265 | |

* ***AK-47/AKM Post 2004 Mfg./Importation*** – most AK-47/AKMs manufactured/imported after 1998 utilize plastic/synthetic furniture, stamped receivers, and folding/telescoping stocks which have different components and construction from those rifles/carbines produced before 1998. Recent U.S. assembly refers to an original stamped European (mostly FEG) or milled receiver with U.S. assembly, using either new parts or matched, older unused original Eastern European-manufactured parts (BATFE 922.R compliant). This newest generation of AK-47/AKMs typically have features as described above, and cannot be sold in several states. Check city and state laws regarding high capacity magazine compliance.

| | $450 | $395 | $350 | $325 | $295 | $265 | $235 | |

The most desirable configuration of these recently assembled rifles/carbines has a folding/collapsible stock, high capacity mag., barrel compensator, and a bayonet lug.

These post-2004 AK-47/AKM variations typically do not have import markings, and indicate they have been made up as "parts guns" assembled from various manufacturers, and have usually been put together in the U.S. recently. Additional AK-47 listings can be found under current individual manufacturers and importers listed separately in this text (i.e., Arsenal Inc., Century International, Interarms, etc.).

AK-74/AKM – 5.45x39mm cal., semi-auto action based on the AKM, imported from Bulgaria and other previous Eastern bloc countries, in addition to recent assembly in the U.S., using FEG receivers, Bulgarian parts sets, and additional U.S.-made components.

	100%	98%	95%	90%	80%	70%	60%
Bulgarian mfg.	$700	$650	$600	$525	$450	$400	$350
Recent U.S. assembly	$650	$575	$500	$425	$350	$300	$275

PISTOLS: SEMI-AUTO, AK-47 VARIATIONS

AK-47 PISTOLS – 7.62x39mm, or .223 Rem. cal., patterned after the AK-47 rifle/carbine, barrel length approx. 12 1/4, but can vary according to mfg., typically wood furniture, 5 to 30 shot mag. (depends on configuration), adj. rear sight, pistol grip, parkerized finish most common, recent Romanian mfg., approx. 5 lbs.

| | $375 | $325 | $295 | $275 | $250 | $225 | $200 | |

AMAC

See the "Iver Johnson" section in the I section. AMAC stands for American Military Arms Corporation. Manufactured in Jacksonville, AR. AMAC ceased operations in early 1993.

A.M.S.D. (ADVANCED MILITARY SYSTEM DESIGN)

Current manufacturer located in Geneva, Switzerland. No current U.S. importation. Previously distributed 2010-2012 by Loki Weapon Systems, located in Coalgate, OK.

RIFLES: BOLT ACTION

TACTEN RIFLE – .338 Lapua cal., tactical stock, bipod, two 10 shot mags., muzzle brake, two-stage trigger, includes cleaning kit and case.

Prices on this model are P.O.R. Please contact the company directly for pricing and U.S. availability (see Trademark Index).

OM 50 NEMESIS – various cals., 27 1/2 in. barrel, high performance muzzle brake, box mag., Picatinny top and side rails, adj. folding stock, adj. two-stage trigger, extended forend, adj. ground spike, scope rings, includes bipod, field cleaning kit, tool kit and fitted storage case. Disc. 2010.

In 2010, AMSD sold the rights to the OM 50 Nemesis to the Swiss company San Swiss Arms AG (SAN). The model is now called the SAN 511. Rifles sold by AMSD before December 2010 are covered by AMSD's 25 year warranty. Please refer to the San Swiss listing in the S section for current listings.

AMP TECHNICAL SERVICE GmbH

Previous manufacturer located in Puchheim, Germany. Previously imported and distributed 2001-2004 by CQB Products, located in Tustin, CA.

RIFLES: BOLT ACTION

DSR-1 – .300 Win. Mag., .308 Win., or .338 Lapua cal., bolt action, bull pup design with in-line stock, receiver is made from aluminum, titanium, and polymers, internal parts are stainless steel, two-stage adj. trigger, 4 or 5 shot mag., 25.6 in. Lothar Walther fluted barrel with muzzle brake and vent. shroud, includes bipod, ambidextrous 3-position safety, 13 lbs. Imported 2002-2004.

| | $7,295 | $6,300 | $5,200 | $4,100 | $3,000 | $2,500 | $2,000 | $7,795 |

Add $100 for .300 Win. Mag. cal.
Add $300 for .338 Lapua cal.

MSR	100%	98%	95%	90%	80%	70%	60%	*Last MSR*

AR 57 LLC (57CENTER LLC)

Current AR-15 style rifle manufacturer located in Bellevue, WA, and previously located in Redmond, WA.

CARBINES: SEMI-AUTO

AR57A1 - PDW – 5.7x28mm cal., 16 in. barrel, flash suppressor, black matte finish, ergonomic design custom grip with battery and accessory compartment, 50 shot box magazine runs horizontally over barrel and can be inserted from top or side of weapon, mil spec fire control group, M-4 carbine six position stock with forged aluminum stock tube, front and rear upper Picatinny rails between mag., lower accessory rails, includes four 50 shot mags. Mfg. 2010-2013.

	100%	98%	95%	90%	80%	70%	60%	Last MSR
	$1,100	$975	$825	$750	$600	$500	$400	*$1,099*

AR57 GEN II/LEM – 5.7x28mm cal., 16 in. fluted barrel, ambidextrous mag. release and charging handle, carbine buffer, extended rear quad rail, includes two 50 shot mags. New 2013.

	100%	98%	95%	90%	80%	70%	60%	
MSR $1,099	$975	$850	$725	$675	$550	$450	$350	

AR-7 INDUSTRIES, LLC

Previous manufacturer 1998-2004, and located in Geneseo, IL. Previously located in Meriden, CT, from 1998 to early 2004.

In February 2004, AR-7 Industries LLC was purchased by ArmaLite, Inc., and recent manufacture was in Geneseo, IL.

RIFLES: BOLT ACTION

AR-7 TAKEDOWN – .22 LR cal., bolt action variation of the AR-7 Explorer rifle, similar takedown/storage configuration, 2 1/2 lbs. Advertised 2002 only.

While advertised during 2002, this model was never manufactured.

RIFLES: SEMI-AUTO

AR-7 EXPLORER RIFLE – .22 LR cal., takedown barrelled action stores in synthetic stock which floats, 8 shot mag., aperture rear sight, 16 in. barrel (synthetic sleeve with steel liner), black matte finish on AR-7, silvertone on AR-7S (disc. 2000), camouflage finish on AR-7C, two-tone (silver receiver with black stock and barrel) on AR-7T (disc. 2000), walnut finish on AR-W (mfg. 2001-2002), stowed length 16 1/2 in., 2 1/2 lbs. Mfg. late 1998-2004.

	100%	98%	95%	90%	80%	70%	60%	Last MSR
	$175	$150	$125	$110	$100	$90	$80	*$200*

Add $15 for camouflage or walnut finish.

This model was also previously manufactured by Survival Arms, Inc. and Charter Arms - see individual listings for information.

AR-7 SPORTER (AR-20) – .22 LR cal., 16 1/2 in. steel barrel with vent. aluminum shroud, metal skeleton fixed stock with pistol grip, 8 (new 2001) or 16 shot "flip clip" (optional) mag., 3.85 lbs. Mfg. late 1998-2004.

	100%	98%	95%	90%	80%	70%	60%	Last MSR
	$175	$150	$125	$110	$100	$90	$80	*$200*

Add $100 for sporter conversion kit (includes aluminum shrouded barrel, pistol grip stock, and 16 shot flip clip).

This model was also previously manufactured by Survival Arms, Inc. - see individual listing for information.

AR-7 TARGET – .22 LR cal., 16 in. bull barrel with 7/8 in. cantilever scope mount, tube stock with pistol grip, 8 shot mag., 3-9x40mm compact rubber armored scope was optional, 5.65 lbs. Mfg. 2002-2004.

	100%	98%	95%	90%	80%	70%	60%	Last MSR
	$195	$175	$150	$125	$105	$95	$80	*$210*

Add $60 for compact scope.

AR-15 STYLE CARBINES, RIFLES, AND PISTOLS

AR-15 HISTORY

AR-15 refers to the model nomenclature originally given to the select-fire, gas-operated carbine/rifle featuring synthetic furniture and chambered in 5.56 NATO cal., and developed by Eugene Stoner in 1957. At the time, he was under contract by the Armalite division of the Fairchild Aircraft Corp. In 1958, this new AR-15 lost out in military competition to the select-fire M-14 manufactured by Springfield Armory. After losing this competition, Fairchild Aircraft Corp. thought their new carbine/rifle design would never prove to be successful or obtain a military contract. As a result, during 1959 it sold the design and all future manufacturing rights to Colt. In 1962, the U.S. Department of Defense Advanced Research Projects Agency (ARPA) purchased 1,000 AR-15 rifles from Colt which were immediately sent to South Vietnam for field trials. In 1963, Colt was awarded an 85,000 rifle contract for the U.S. Army (designated XM16E1), and another 19,000 for the U.S. Armed Forces (designated M-16). This new select-fire M-16 was a direct variation of Stoner's original AR-15 design, but had U.S. ordnance markings. In 1963, a presidential order given to the U.S. Army made the M-16 its official service rifle.

In 1966, because of the U.S. involvement in the escalating war in Vietnam, the U.S. government submitted an order for 840,000 M-16s to be delivered to the U.S. Armed Forces at a cost of $92 million. The rest like they say is history.

MSR	100%	98%	95%	90%	80%	70%	60%	Last MSR

AR-15 INFORMATION AND RECENT/CURRENT MANUFACTURERS & IMPORTERS

Because of the consumer popularity and resulting proliferation of the semi-auto AR-15 style carbines/rifles over the past twenty years, there are many companies who now offer the AR-15 style platform for sale with their brand name or trademark stamped on the guns. However, there are only four primary domestic manufacturers which currently produce the majority of lower receivers for the AR marketplace. The following listing includes those manufacturers of AR-15 lower receivers, in addition to those brand names, trademarks, and private labels for other companies.

Lewis Machine & Tool = LMT, Lauer (disc.), DS Arms, PWA, Eagle, Knights Armament, Barrett, Bushmaster (possibly).

Continental Machine & Tool = Stag, RRA, High Standard, Noveske (disc.), Century, Global Tactical, CLE, S&W, MGI (1st variation), Wilson Tactical (not all models), Colt, Ratworx.

LAR = Grizzly, Bushmaster (L Prefix), Ameetech, DPMS (possibly), CMMG, Double Star, Fulton, Spike's Tactical, Noveske.

Mega Machine Shop = Mega, Gunsmoke, Dalphon, POF (forged), Alexander Arms, Singer, Spike's Tactical (disc.).

Additional smaller AR-15 lower receiver manufacturers include JV Precision (Double Star, LRB), Olympic (Olympic, SGW, Tromix, Palmetto, Dalphon, Frankford, Century (disc.), Superior (Superior Arms, Lauer), Grenadier Precision, and Sabre Defense (disc.).

Some companies also manufacture custom cut lower receivers out of solid billets, and they include MGI, Cobb, JP, Socom, Sun Devil, POF, and S&W (Performance Center).

The following is a listing of both current and recent manufacturers and importers that offer/have offered complete AR-15 style carbines, rifles, and pistols for sale domestically. Please look under each current company, importer, or brand name/trademark heading for up-to-date information and values on the makes and models that are offered.

These companies include: 2 Vets Arms Co. LLC, Accurate Tool & Mfg. Co., Adams Arms, Adcor Defense, Adeq Firearms Co., Advanced Armament Corp., Alaska Magnum AR's, Alberta Tactical Supply, Alexander Arms LLC, Ambush Firearms, American Precision Arms, American Spirit Arms, American Spirit Arms Corp., American Tactical Imports, AM-TAC Precision, Anderson Manufacturing, AR57 LLC (57Center LLC), Ares Defense, Armalite Inc., Arizona Armory, Arms LLC, The Arms Room, Arms Tech Ltd., Astra Arms S.A., Australian Automatic Arms Pty. Ltd., Aztek Arms, Barnes Precision Machine, Inc., Barrett Firearms Manufacturing, Inc., Battle Rifle Company, Black Dawn Industries, Black Forge, Blackheart International LLC, BlackOps Technologies, Black Rain Ordnance, Black Rifle Company, Black Weapons Armory, BlueGrass Armory, Bobcat Weapons Inc., Bohica, Bravo Company Mfg. Inc., Budischowsky, Bushmaster Firearms International LLC, C3 Defense, Inc., CMMG, Inc., Carbon 15, Cavalry Arms Corporation, Chattahoochee Gun Works, LLC, Christian Armory Works, Christensen Arms, Century International Arms, Inc., Cobb Manufacturing, Inc., Colt's Manufacturing Company, Inc., Controlled Chaos Arms, Coronado Arms, Core 15, Crossfire LLC, Crusader Weaponry, DAR GmbH, DPMS Firearms, LLC, DSA Inc., Daewoo, Charles Daly (1976-2010), Dane Armory, Daniel Defense, Del-Ton Incorporated, Desert Ordnance, Desert Tech, DEZ Tactical Arms, Dlask Arms Corp., Double Star Corp., Dreadnaught Industries LLC, E.M.F. Company, Inc., Eagle Arms, Inc., East Ridge Gun Co., Edward Arms Company, Entreprise Arms Inc., Evolution USA, Firebird Precision, Fulton Armory, G-A Precision, G.A.R. Arms, The Gun Room Co., LLC, Gunsmoke Enterprises, GWACS Armory, Halo Arms, LLC, Hatcher Gun Company, Head Down Products LLC, Hera Arms, Hesse Arms, High Standard Manufacturing Co., Hogan Manufacturing LLC, Houston Firearms, Houlding Precision Firearms, Huldra Arms, Integrity Arms & Survival, Interarms Arsenal, Intercontinental Arms Inc., Iron Ridge Arms Co., Israel Military Industries (Galil), J.B. Custom Inc., JP Enterprises, Inc., JR Carbines LLC, Jard, Inc., K.B.I. Inc., King's Arsenal, Knight's Armament Company, L.A.R. Manufacturing, Inc., LRB Arms, LWRC International, Inc., Larue Tactical, Lauer Custom Weaponry, Leitner-Wise Defense, Inc., Leitner-Wise Rifle Co. Inc., Legion Firearms, Les Baer Custom, Inc., Lewis Machine & Tool Company (LMT), Liberty Arms International LLC, Loki Weapon Systems, Inc., Lone Star Armament, Inc., Lone Star Tactical Supply, MBA Associates, MG Arms Incorporated, MGI, Maunz, McDuffee Arms, Microtech Small Arms Research Inc. (MSAR), Miller Precision Arms, Miltac Industries, LLC, Mossberg, O.F. & Sons., Inc., Mohawk Armory, Nemesis Arms, New Evolution Military Ordnance (NEMO), Newtown Firearms, Next Generation Arms, Northern Competition, Nosler, Inc., Noveske Rifleworks, LLC, Oberland Arms, Ohio Ordnance Works, Inc., Olympic Arms, Inc., Palmetto State Defense, Patriot Ordnance Factory (POF), Peace River Classics, Precision Firearms, Precision Reflex, Inc., Predator Custom Shop, Primary Weapons Systems (PWS), Pro Arms Armory, Professional Ordnance, Inc., Proof Research, Quality Arms, Quality Parts Co., R Guns, R.I.P. Tactical, RND Manufacturing, Red X Arms, Remington Arms Company, Inc., Rhino Arms, Robinson Armament Co., Rock River Arms, Inc., Rocky Mountain Arms, Inc., Russian American Armory Company, SI Defense, SOG Armory, STI International, S.W.A.T. Firearms, Sabre, Sabre Defence Industries LLC, Scorpion Tactical, Seekins Precision, Sharps Milspec, Sharps Rifle Company, Sig Sauer, Sionics Weapon Systems, Southern Gun Company, Specialized Dynamics, Specialized Tactical Systems, Spike's Tactical, LLC, Smith & Wesson, Spirit Gun Manufacturing Company LLC, Stag Arms, Sterling Arsenal, Stoner Rifle, Sturm, Ruger & Co., Inc., Superior Arms, Tactical Arms Manufacturing, Tactical Armz, Tactical Rifles, Tactical Weapons Solutions, Templar Consulting, LLC, Templar Tactical Arms LLC, Templar Tactical Firearms, Thureon Defense, TNW, Inc., Tromix Corporation, Troy Defense, USA Tactical Firearms, Uselton Arms, VM Hy-Tech LLC, Valor Arms, Victor Arms Corporation, Vltor Weapon Systems, Volquartsen Custom, Ltd., Vulcan Armament, Inc., Wilson Combat, Windham Weaponry, Xtreme Machining, Yankee Hill Machine Co., Inc. (YHM), Z-M Weapons, Zombie Defense.

ACCU-MATCH INTERNATIONAL INC.

Previous handgun and pistol parts manufacturer located in Mesa, AZ circa 1996.

PISTOLS: SEMI-AUTO

ACCU-MATCH PISTOL – .45 ACP cal., patterned after the Colt Govt. 1911, SA, competition pistol features stainless steel construction with 5 1/2 in. match grade barrel with 3 ports, recoil reduction system, 8 shot mag., 3-dot sight system. Approx. 160 mfg. 1996 only.

MSR	100%	98%	95%	90%	80%	70%	60%	Last MSR
	$795	$700	$625	$550	$450	$375	$325	$840

MSR	100%	98%	95%	90%	80%	70%	60%	Last MSR

ACCURACY INTERNATIONAL LTD.

Current rifle manufacturer located in Hampshire, England since 1978, with offices in Fredericksburg, VA. Currently distributed by Mile High Shooting Accessories, located in Broomfield, CO, SRT Supply, located in St. Petersburg, FL, and Tac Pro Shooting Center, located in Mingus, TX. Previously imported by Accuracy International North America, located in Orchard Park, NY until circa 2005, and 1998-2005 in Oak Ridge, TN. Also previously imported until 1998 by Gunsite Training Center, located in Paulden, AZ.

RIFLES: BOLT ACTION

In addition to the models listed, Accuracy International also makes military and law enforcement rifles, including the SR98 Australian, G22 German, and the Dutch SLA. On Models AE, AW, AWP, and AWM listed in this section, many options and configurations are available which will add to the base prices listed.

Add $255 for Picatinny rail on all currently manufactured rifles (standard on Model AE and AW50).

AE MODEL – .243 Win., .260 Rem., .308 Win., or 6.5 Creedmoor cal., similar to AWP Model, 5 shot mag., 20 or 24 in. stainless barrel, Harris bipod attachment point, four sling attachment points, Picatinny rail, black, green, or dark earth finish, approx. 8 1/2 lbs. Importation began 2002.

MSR $3,600	$3,325	$2,775	$2,400	$2,000	$1,700	$1,425	$1,200	

Add $307 for adj. cheekpiece (disc. 2012) or $422 for folding stock.
Add $213 for standard muzzle brake.
Add $357 for butt spike.
Add $454 for 26 in. barrel.

AW MODEL – .243 Win. (new 2000), .260 Rem., .300 Win. Mag., .308 Win., .338 Lapua (disc. 2012), or 6.5 Creedmoor cal., precision bolt action featuring 20, 24, 26, or 27 (disc.) in. 1:12 twist stainless steel barrel with or w/o muzzle brake, 3-lug bolt, 10 shot detachable mag., green synthetic folding (military/LE only) thumbhole adj. stock, AI bipod, 14 lbs. Importation began 1995.

MSR $6,050	$5,500	$4,650	$4,000	$3,400	$2,850	$2,200	$1,800	

Add $203 for fluted barrel.
Add $257 for Picatinny rail or $422 for folding stock.
Add $342 for threaded barrel with muzzle brake.
Add $357 for butt spike.
Add $797 for .300 Win. Mag. cal. with 20 or 26 in. fluted and threaded barrel.
Add $376 for AW-F Model (disc. 2002).

AWP MODEL – similar to AW Model, except has 20 or 24 in. barrel w/o muzzle brake, 15 lbs. Imported 1995-2007.

	$4,250	$3,650	$3,150	$2,650	$2,150	$1,800	$1,500	$4,600

Add $310 for AWP-F Model (disc. 2002).

AW50 – .50 BMG, advanced ergonomic design, features built-in anti-recoil system, 5 shot mag., adj. third supporting leg, folding stock, 27 in. fluted barrel with muzzle brake, Picatinny rail, approx. 30 lbs. Mfg. 1998-2012.

	$12,500	$10,500	$8,750	$7,500	$6,250	$4,950	$3,750	$13,096

AWM MODEL (SUPER MAGNUM) – .300 Win. Mag. or .338 Lapua cal., 6-lug bolt, 26 or 27 in. 1:9/1:10 twist stainless steel fluted barrel with muzzle brake, 5 shot mag., 15 1/2 lbs. Imported 1995-2009.

	$5,600	$5,100	$4,675	$3,800	$2,950	$2,500	$1,750	$5,900

Add $100 for .338 Lapua cal. Add $324 for AWM-F Model (disc. 2002).

AX MODEL – .243 Win., .260 Rem., .308 Win., .338 Lapua, or 6.5 Creedmoor cal., 10 shot mag., 20, 24, 26, or 27 in. barrel with or w/o muzzle brake, Picatinny rail included, pistol grip with adj. cheekpiece, fixed butt pad with additional spacers, choice of green, black, or dark earth finished hardware, folding chassis.

MSR $6,500	$6,000	$5,200	$4,600	$4,000	$3,350	$2,750	$2,250	

Add $226 for muzzle brake. Add $959 for .338 Lapua cal.

* AX50 – .50 BMG cal., 27 in. stainless match grade barrel with muzzle brake, includes Picatinny rail, black folding chassis with adj. cheekpiece, butt pad, and butt spike (optional), accessory rails, choice of green, black, or dark earth finished hardware, 27 1/2 lbs.

MSR $10,610	$9,650	$8,750	$8,000	$7,250	$6,500	$5,750	$4,950	

Add $243 for butt spike.

AXMC (MULTI CALIBER) – .308 Win., .300 Win. Mag., or .338 Lapua Mag. cal., sniper configuration, solid steel, flat bottomed action, bolted to combat tested AI chassis, Quickloc match grade stainless steel barrel with muzzle brake, side cutaway magwell, detachable 10 shot double stack mag, 6 lug, 60 degree bolt with leaf spring extractor, two-stage trigger, right folding stock with adj. cheekpiece and LOP, configurable pistol grip, 3 position safety, black, green, or pale brown finish, KeySlot accessory mounting systems with full length top rail and three accessory side rails. New 2014.

As this edition went to press, U.S. retail pricing was not available on this model.

MSR	100%	98%	95%	90%	80%	70%	60%	Last MSR

AX308 – .308 Win. cal., similar to AXMC, except is only available in .308 Win. cal. New 2014.

As this edition went to press, U.S. retail pricing was not available on this model.

PALMAMASTER – .308 Win. cal., available with either NRA prone or UIT style stock, 30 in. stainless steel fluted barrel, designed for competition shooting, laminated stock. Disc. 2002.

| | $2,600 | $2,350 | $2,100 | $1,900 | $1,700 | $1,500 | $1,250 | $2,850 |

CISMMASTER – .22 BR, 6mm BR, .243 Win., .308 Win., 6.5x55mm, or 7.5x55mm cal., designed for slow and rapid fire international and military shooting competition, 10 shot mag., 2-stage trigger. Disc. 2002.

| | $3,175 | $2,850 | $2,600 | $2,350 | $2,100 | $1,900 | $1,700 | $3,480 |

VARMINT RIFLE – .22 Middlested, .22 BR, .22-250 Rem., .223 Rem., 6mm BR, .243 Win., .308 Win., or 7mm-08 Rem. cal., features 26 in. fluted stainless steel barrel. Mfg. 1997-2002.

| | $3,200 | $2,725 | $2,350 | $1,950 | $1,675 | $1,475 | $1,300 | $3,650 |

ACCURATE TOOL & MFG. CO.

Current custom manufacturer located in Lexington, KY.

RIFLES: SEMI-AUTO

Accurate Tool & Mfg. Co. builds custom AR-15 rifles/carbines. Current models include: Classic Carbine - MSR $1,020, LE Carbine - MSR $1,290, and LE Light - MSR $1,191. Please contact the company directly for more information including options, pricing, and availability (see Trademark Index).

ACTION ARMS LTD.

Previous firearms importer and distributor until 1994, located in Philadelphia, PA.

Only Action Arms Models AT-84S, AT-88S, and the Model B Sporter will be listed under this heading. Galil, Timberwolf, and Uzi trademarks can be located in their respective sections.

CARBINES: SEMI-AUTO

MODEL B SPORTER – 9mm Para. cal., patterned after the original Uzi Model B Sporter, 16.1 in. barrel, fires from closed bolt, thumbhole stock with recoil pad, 10 shot mag., adj. rear sight, 8.8 lbs. Limited importation from China 1994 only.

| | $695 | $625 | $550 | $475 | $435 | $385 | $335 | $595 |

ACTION LEGENDS MFG., INC.

Previous manufacturer, importer, and distributor until circa 2006 and located in Houston, TX.

RIFLES

MODEL 888 M1 CARBINE – .22 LR or .30 Carbine cal., 18 in. barrel, mfg. from new original M1 parts and stock and unused GI parts, 10, 15, or 30 shot mag., choice of birch or walnut stock, parkerized finish, metal or wood handguard, 5 1/2 lbs.

| | $675 | $625 | $550 | $495 | $425 | $375 | $325 | $650 |

Add $11 for .22 LR cal.

Add $31 for walnut/metal forearm or $47 for walnut/wood forearm.

ADAMS ARMS

Current rifle manufacturer located in Palm Harbor, FL. Adams Arms also manufactures a complete line of accessories for the AR-15 platform, in addition to barrels, upper assemblies, and free floating rails.

Please also refer to the Huldra Arms section for AR-15s manufactured by Adams under the Huldra trademark, and the Korstog section for the AR-15s manufactured under the Korstog trademark.

RIFLES: SEMI-AUTO

Adams Arms manufactures a complete line of AR-15 platform rifles. For more information on options, availability, and delivery time, please contact the company directly (see Trademark Index).

Adams Arms also manufactures the Huldra line of AR-15 style rifles/carbines exclusively for Fleet Farm. Please refer to the H section for a current listing.

MID BASE – 5.56 NATO cal., GPO, 16 in. Government Contour melonited barrel with A2 flash hider, Mil Spec 6-position retractable stock, 30 shot GI aluminum magazine, Mil-Spec forged upper and lower receiver with Picatinny rail, hard coat anodized finish, ribbed mid-length M-4 style molded polymer handguards.

| MSR $1,331 | $1,200 | $1,050 | $900 | $825 | $650 | $550 | $425 | |

MSR	100%	98%	95%	90%	80%	70%	60%	Last MSR

CARBINE BASE – .223 Rem. cal., GPO, similar to Mid Base model, except has 16 in. M4 Profile 4150 CM melonited barrel, and short forearm.

MSR $1,317	$1,195	$1,050	$900	$825	$650	$550	$425	

MID TACTICAL EVO – 5.56 NATO cal., GPO, 14 1/2 (law enforcement only) or 16 in. Government Contour 4150 CM melonited barrel with A2 flash hider, VLTOR IMOD collapsible stock, Ergo grip, 30 shot GI aluminum magazine, Samson free float light weight modular rail system, Mil-Spec forged upper and lower receiver, hard coat anodized finish, Picatinny flat-top rail with dry lube internal finish and laser engraved.

MSR $1,725	$1,550	$1,375	$1,175	$1,050	$850	$700	$550	

CARBINE TACTICAL EVO – 5.56 NATO cal., GPO, similar to Mid Tactical Evo model, except has 16 in. M4 Profile melonited barrel.

MSR $1,691	$1,525	$1,350	$1,150	$1,025	$825	$675	$525	

MID TACTICAL ELITE – 5.56 NATO cal., GPO, 14 1/2 (law enforcement only) or 16 in. Government Contour melonited barrel with A2 flash hider, VLTOR IMOD collapsible stock, Ergo grip, 30 shot GI aluminum magazine, Samson free float light weight modular quad rail system, Mil-Spec forged upper and lower receiver, hard coat anodized finish, Picatinny flat-top rail with dry lube internal finish and laser engraved.

MSR $1,991	$1,750	$1,525	$1,325	$1,195	$975	$800	$625	

CARBINE TACTICAL ELITE – 5.56 NATO cal., GPO, similar to Mid Tactical Elite, except has 16 in. M4 Contour melonited barrel.

MSR $1,952	$1,725	$1,515	$1,325	$1,195	$975	$800	$625	

ADCO ARMS INC. (ADCO SALES INC.)

Adco Sales Inc. was a previous importer of Diamond shotguns circa 2007-2012 manufactured by Vega in Istanbul, Turkey. Adco Arms Inc. currently imports accessories only and is located in Woburn, MA. During 2012, the name Adco Sales Inc. was changed to Adco Arms Inc.

SHOTGUNS: SLIDE ACTION

All Adco slide action shotguns were manufactured in Turkey.

MARINER MODEL – 12 ga., 3 in. chamber, choice of 18 1/2 plain or 22 in. VR barrel with chokes, 5 shot mag., black synthetic stock and forearm. Imported 2003-2006.

	$250	$225	$200	$175	$150	$135	$110	*$319*

ADCOR DEFENSE

Current manufacturer located in Baltimore, MD.

RIFLES/CARBINES

A-556 ELITE – 5.56 NATO cal., GPO, 16, 18, or 20 in. chrome lined free floating barrel, forward placed reversible/ambidextrous charging handle, multi-purpose regulator, optics ready, ejection port dust wiper, two-piece keyed quad rail system, tool-less field strip design, custom rifle stock, custom ergonomic rifle grip with aggressive texturing. New 2013.

MSR $2,295	$2,295	$2,025	$1,725	$1,550	$1,250	$1,050	$800	

A-556 ELITE GI – 5.56 NATO cal., GIO, 16, 18, or 20 in. chrome lined barrel with or without ambidextrous forward charging handle, multi-position gas regulator with removable gas tube, ejection port dust wiper, key-locked, highly rigid rail system mounts to upper receiver, upper and lower rails separate with push of a button, no tools needed, custom rifle stock, custom ergonomic rifle grip with aggressive texturing, 6.9 lbs. New 2013.

MSR $2,295	$2,295	$2,025	$1,725	$1,550	$1,250	$1,050	$800	

B.E.A.R. – 5.56 NATO cal., GPO with multi-position regulator, 16, or 18 in. free floating chrome-lined barrel, forward placed reversible/ambidextrous charging handle, ejection port dust wiper, two-piece keyed quad rail system, aluminum alloy receivers and rail systems, configured with sights or optics ready, 6.45-7.6 lbs. Disc. 2013.

	$1,885	$1,650	$1,425	$1,275	$1,050	$850	$650	*$2,092*

* B.E.A.R. Elite – 5.56 NATO cal., GPO, similar to B.E.A.R., except has hammer forged chrome-lined barrels, comes with sights or optics ready, also features Magpul MOE rifle stock, Magpul MOE ergonomic rifle grip with aggressive texturing, 6.45-7.6 lbs.

As this edition went to press, prices could not be ascertained for this model.

B.E.A.R. GI – 5.56 NATO cal., GIO with multi-position gas regulator and removable gas tube, 16 or 18 in. chrome-lined barrel, with or w/o ambidextrous forward placed charging handle, ejection port dust wiper, key-locked, highly rigid rail system mounts to upper receiver, upper and lower rails separate with the push of a button, no special tools needed, approx. 6.8 lbs.

	$1,750	$1,525	$1,325	$1,195	$975	$795	$625	

MSR	100%	98%	95%	90%	80%	70%	60%	Last MSR

* B.E.A.R. GI Elite – 5.56 NATO cal., GIO, similar to B.E.A.R. GI, except also features hammer forged chrome-lined barrels, Magpul MOE rifle stock, Magpul MOE ergonomic rifle grip with aggressive texturing, approx. 6.8 lbs.

As this edition went to press, values could not be ascertained for this model.

B.E.A.R. LIMITED EDITION SIGNATURE SERIES – 5.56 NATO cal., 18 or 20 in. hammer forged, chrome-lined barrel, full billet upper and lower receiver, Magpul pistol grip and buttstock, AMBI Products ambidextrous fire selector switch, matte black finish, hand built and signed by Michael Brown. Mfg. mid-2013.

	100%	98%	95%	90%	80%	70%	60%	Last MSR
	$2,040	$1,785	$1,525	N/A	N/A	N/A	N/A	$2,399

ADEQ FIREARMS COMPANY

Current manufacturer established in 2010 and located in Tampa, FL.

Adeq Firearms Company manufactures custom and standard production AR platform weapons, sniper rifles, 1911 pistols, and firearm suppression systems. Alongside the civilian sales, the company handles custom built firearms for law enforcement and government agencies, as well as security contract operating companies. In addition, the company makes a limited number of custom arsenal rebuilds of classic vintage military weapons based on parts availability.

PISTOLS: SEMI-AUTO

VIGILUM 1911 STYLE TACTICAL PISTOL – 9mm Para., .40 S&W, or .45 ACP cal., full sized 1911-style, GIO, match grade barrel, trigger, hammer, and sear, G-10 grip, with or w/o rail, parkerized finish, 3-dot Novak low profile sights, 2.6 lbs. Mfg. 2011-2013.

	100%	98%	95%	90%	80%	70%	60%	Last MSR
	$1,950	$1,700	$1,465	$1,325	$1,075	$880	$685	$2,300

CK 6 – .45 ACP cal., limited production gun utilizing custom production frames and slides. New 2014.

MSR $3,000	$2,550	$2,225	$1,915	$1,735	$1,400	$1,150	$895	

PALADIN DAGGER – .22 LR (special order by request) or 5.56 NATO cal., AR-style, custom built with Paladin lower receiver. New 2012.

MSR $1,200	$1,025	$895	$775	$695	$565	$460	$360	

RIFLES: BOLT ACTION

INTERCEPTOR – .308 Win. or .300 Win. Mag. cal., Rem. 700 action, Lilja barrel, APO chassis, tactical and hunter variations. New 2014.

MSR $3,200	$2,725	$2,385	$2,050	$1,850	$1,500	$1,225	$950	

Add $300 for tactical variation.

RIFLES: SEMI-AUTO

L-TAC (LIGHTWEIGHT TACTICAL RIFLE) – 5.56 NATO cal., GIO, available in three configurations: standard forged lower receiver with ultralight barrel and furniture (weighs 5.2 lbs.), the Gen 2 with ultralight lower receiver (weighs less than 5 lbs.), or the L-Tac SBR with 11 1/2 in. barrel and ultralight alloy lower receiver (approx. 5 lbs.), optional Gen 3 with both ultralight upper and lower receivers. Mfg. 2013.

	100%	98%	95%	90%	80%	70%	60%	Last MSR
	$1,450	$1,275	$1,100	$975	$800	$650	$525	$1,600

PALADIN PATROL CARBINE – 5.56 NATO, 6.8 SPC, 7.62x39mm (disc.) or .300 AAC Blackout cal., rotary bolt GIO, available in semi-auto, auto, or 3-round bursts (NFA rules apply), 16 or 18 in. chrome-lined barrel, A2 front and quick detach A2 rear sights, Mil-Spec forged aluminum upper and lower receivers with anodized finish, Manganese phosphate barrel finish, standard A2 round mid-length handguards, GI pistol grip, Rogers 6-position adj. commercial tube buttstock, SST, includes cable lock, sling, and owner's manual, 5.8 lbs. New 2011.

MSR $1,082	$925	$810	$695	$625	$525	$450	$395	

Add $218 for Magpul MOE stock (Carbine 02).

Add $318 for Troy free-float forearm, Magpul stock, and BUIS (Carbine 03).

PALADIN ULTRALIGHT – 5.56 NATO cal., Magtech magnesium infused lower receiver, 16 in. Voodoo Tactical barrel, Magpul stock, pistol grip. Mfg. 2013-2014.

	100%	98%	95%	90%	80%	70%	60%	Last MSR
	$1,500	$1,315	$1,125	$1,025	$825	$675	$525	$1,776

PRECISION LONG RANGE RIFLE – 7.62 NATO cal., GIO, 18 in. fluted bull barrel with Gogun flash hider, anodized receiver and Manganese phosphate barrel finish, PRi Gen3 carbon fiber forearm handguards, Magpul PRS buttstock, SST, includes Leupold Mark IV ER/T optics, pelican case, sniper data book, and cleaning kit, 11.6 lbs. Mfg. 2011-2013.

	100%	98%	95%	90%	80%	70%	60%	Last MSR
	$1,950	$1,700	$1,465	$1,325	$1,075	$880	$685	$2,300

VENATOR BATTLE RIFLE – 7.62 NATO cal., rotary bolt GIO, AR-15 style, 16, 18, or 20 in. chrome-lined barrel with GO-GUN Talon muzzle brake, A2 front and quick detach A2 rear sights, Mil-Spec anodized receiver finish and Manganese phosphate barrel finish, free float aluminum handguard with Troy Alpha rail system, 6-position adj. commercial tube buttstock, SST, 20 shot detachable box mag., 8.1 lbs. New 2011.

MSR $1,800	$1,625	$1,425	$1,225	$1,100	$900	$725	$575	

MSR	100%	98%	95%	90%	80%	70%	60%	Last MSR

RECON – 5.56 or 7.62 NATO cal., 16 (5.56 NATO cal.) in. nitride or 18 (7.62 NATO cal.) in. SASS fluted barrel, LanTac flash hider, Dueck offset sights (18 in. barrel only), Magpul ACS stock, Troy MRF handguard, ERGO pistol grip. New 2014.

	100%	98%	95%	90%	80%	70%	60%	
MSR $2,200	$1,875	$1,640	$1,400	$1,275	$1,025	$850	$650	

Add $300 for 7.62 NATO cal.

ADVANCED ARMAMENT CORP.

Current manufacturer of AR-15 style rifles, barrels, upper receivers, silencers, muzzle brakes, flash hiders and accessories located in Lawrenceville, GA. Advanced Armament Corp. is part of the Freedom Group.

RIFLES: BOLT ACTION

.300 AAC BLACKOUT MODEL 7 – .300 AAC Blackout cal., Rem. Model 7 bolt action, 16 in. threaded black nitride barrel, black glass filled polymer stock with adj. cheek riser, X-Mark Pro trigger, includes 20 MOA scope rail, 6 lbs. 8 oz.

MSR $899	$815	$715	$610	$555	$450	$365	$285	

RIFLES: SEMI-AUTO

.300 AAC BLACKOUT MPW – .300 AAC Blackout cal., GIO, 16 in. barrel with AAC 51T Blackout flash hider, nickel boron coated bolt carrier and cam pin, free floating quad rail sized to match length of barrel, 6-position Magpul CTR stock, Magpul MOE grip, Geissele two stage trigger.

MSR $1,600	$1,450	$1,275	$1,095	$985	$800	$650	$515	

RIFLES: SINGLE SHOT

.300 AAC BLACKOUT HANDI-RIFLE – .300 AAC Blackout cal., single shot, H&R Handi-Rifle break action, 16.2 in. threaded barrel, black glass filled polymer stock and furniture, H&R transfer bar trigger, 6.9 lbs. New 2012.

MSR $360	$325	$285	$245	$220	$180	$145	$115	

ALASKA MAGNUM AR'S

Current manufacturer located in Fairbanks, AK.

RIFLES: SEMI-AUTO

KODIAK – 6.9 AR Long, .300 RCM, .338 RCM, or .375 GrizzinatAR cal., 20 in. match grade stainless steel barrel with muzzle brake, adj. rifle length gas system, flat-top upper with Picatinny rail handguard, alum. upper and lower receivers, nickel bolt carrier group, synthetic butt stock, non-slip ergonomic ambidextrous grip, free float forend, Cerakote finish.

MSR $3,999	$3,595	$3,150	$2,695	$2,450	$1,975	$1,625	$1,250	

GRIZZLY – 6.9 AR Short or .460 GrizzinatAR cal., 18 in. match grade stainless steel barrel with muzzle brake, adj. rifle length gas system, flat-top upper with Picatinny rail handguard, alum. upper and lower receivers, synthetic stock, non-slip ergonomic ambidextrous grip, free float forend, nickel bolt carrier group, stainless steel firing pin, Cerakote finish.

MSR $3,999	$3,595	$3,150	$2,695	$2,450	$1,975	$1,625	$1,250	

WOLVERINE – .450 Bushmaster cal., 18 in. match grade stainless steel barrel with muzzle brake, adj. rifle length gas system, flat-top upper with Picatinny rail handguard, synthetic buttstock, free float forend, non-slip ergonomic ambidextrous grip, Cerakote finish.

MSR $2,999	$2,695	$2,350	$2,025	$1,850	$1,475	$1,225	$950	

ALBERTA TACTICAL RIFLE SUPPLY

Current manufacturer located in Calgary, Alberta, Canada.

RIFLES

Alberta Tactical Rifle Supply builds custom made bolt action and AR-15 style carbines and rifles in a variety of configurations and calibers, including .50 BMG. Each gun is built per customer's specifications, and the possibilities are unlimited. Please contact the company directly for a listing of available options, delivery time, and an individualized price quotation (see Trademark Index).

ALCHEMY ARMS COMPANY

Previous manufacturer located in Auburn, WA, 1999-circa 2006.

PISTOLS: SEMI-AUTO

SPECTRE STANDARD ISSUE (SI) – 9mm Para., .40 S&W, or .45 ACP cal., SA, SFO, full size design, hammerless firing mechanism, linear action trigger, keyed internal locking device, aluminum receiver with 4 1/2 in. match grade stainless steel barrel and slide, tactical rail, various silver/black finishes, lowered ejection port, 10 shot double column mag, 32 oz. Mfg. 2000-2006.

	$675	$585	$525	$465	$415	$350	$300	*$749*

MSR	100%	98%	95%	90%	80%	70%	60%	Last MSR

SPECTRE SERVICE GRADE (SG & SGC) – similar to Spectre Standard Issue, except does not have tactical rail and rounded trigger guard, SGC is Commander style with 4 in. barrel and weighs 27 oz. Mfg. 2000-2006, SGC mfg. 2001-2006.

	$675	$585	$525	$465	$415	$350	$300	$749

SPECTRE TITANIUM EDITION (TI/TIC) – similar to Spectre Series, except features a titanium slide with aluminum receiver, 22 (TIC is Commander style) or 24 oz. Mfg. 2000-2006.

	$895	$775	$675	$575	$500	$450	$395	$999

ALEXANDER ARMS LLC

Current manufacturer of AR-15 style rifles located in Radford, VA. Law enforcement, military, dealer, and consumer sales.

RIFLES: SEMI-AUTO

Add $130 for Shilen barrel.

.50 BEOWULF – .50 Beowulf cal., AR-15 style, GIO, shoots 300-400 grain bullet at approx. 1,800 feet per second, forged upper and lower receiver, 7 shot mag., rotary locking bolt and gas delay mechanism, various configurations include Entry, Over Match kit, Over Match Plus kit, Over Match Tactical kit, Precision Entry, Precision kit, AWS, and Law Enforcement (POR). New 2002.

* *Beowulf Overwatch .50* – similar to .50 Beowulf, GIO, except has 24 in. stainless steel barrel, extended range model, shoots 334 grain bullet at approx. 2,000 feet per second, 9 1/4 lbs. Mfg. 2004-2005.

	$1,550	$1,355	$1,160	$1,055	$850	$695	$540	$1,789

* *Beowulf Entry 16* – .50 Beowulf cal., GIO, 16 1/2 in. chromemoly barrel, mid length hand guard, Picatinny rail, 7 shot mag., flat-top receiver, Black or Coyote Brown stock.

MSR $1,375	$1,225	$1,075	$925	$850	$675	$550	$425	

* *Beowulf Precision 16* – .50 Beowulf cal., GIO, 16 1/2 in. chromemoly barrel, composite free float hand guards, Picatinny rail, low profile gas block, 7 shot mag., black furniture standard or optional camo upgrades available.

MSR $1,485	$1,325	$1,150	$1,000	$900	$725	$600	$475	

* *Beowulf AWS 16 (Advanced Weapons System)* – .50 Beowulf cal., GIO, 16 1/2 in. chromemoly barrel, low profile gas block, four rail handguard system, Picatinny rail, black stock, 7 shot mag., includes soft carry bag.

MSR $1,595	$1,425	$1,250	$1,075	$975	$775	$650	$500	

* *Beowulf Overmatch Plus* – .50 Beowulf cal., GIO, 16 1/2 in. chromemoly barrel, flat-top receiver, detachable iron sights, mid-length hand guard, Picatinny rail, 7 shot mag., rear carry handle, black stock.

MSR $1,595	$1,425	$1,250	$1,075	$975	$775	$650	$500	

* *Beowulf 24 Overwatch* – .50 Beowulf cal., GIO, 24 in. barrel, full length free float handguard, standard trigger and buttstock, Picatinny rail. Disc. 2009.

	$1,775	$1,555	$1,330	$1,200	$975	$800	$620	$1,789

* *Beowulf Piston Rifle* – .50 Beowulf cal., GPO, 10 shot mag., 16 1/2 in. threaded barrel with no standard muzzle device, Picatinny rail receiver, M4 stock, Samson EX handguard, includes soft carry bag. Mfg. 2012-2013.

	$2,000	$1,750	$1,500	$1,375	$1,100	$900	$700	$2,000

GENGHIS – 5.45x39mm cal., GIO, M-4 styling with 16 in. stainless steel barrel, forged upper and lower receiver, 10 shot mag., various configurations included Entry ($1,066 last MSR), Over Match kit ($1,158 last MSR), Over Match Plus kit ($1,267 last MSR), and Over Match Tactical kit ($1,372 last MSR). Mfg. 2002-2005.

6.5 GRENDEL – 6.5 Grendel cal., GIO, M-4 styling with 18 1/2, 19, 20, or 24 in. stainless steel barrel, 10 shot mag. New 2004.

* *Grendel Overwatch 6.5* – 6.5 Grendel cal., GIO, 24 in. stainless steel barrel with match chamber, extremely accurate, forged and hard anodized upper and lower receiver. Mfg. 2004-disc.

	$1,375	$1,200	$1,030	$935	$755	$620	$480	$1,499

* *Grendel 20 (19.5) Entry* – 6.5 Grendel cal., GIO, 19 1/2 (disc.) or 20 in. stainless steel fully lapped threaded barrel with A2 flash hider, A2 buttstock, Ergo grip, G10 composite free float hand guard, flat-top receiver with Picatinny rail, 10 shot mag., black stock.

MSR $1,540	$1,375	$1,200	$1,025	$950	$750	$625	$500	

* *Grendel 24 Overwatch* – 6.5 Grendel cal., GIO, 24 in. stainless steel fully lapped threaded barrel with A2 flash hider, A2 buttstock, Ergo grip, composite free float hand guard, flat-top receiver with Picatinny rail, low profile gas block, black hardware.

MSR $1,628	$1,450	$1,275	$1,100	$975	$800	$650	$525	

MSR	100%	98%	95%	90%	80%	70%	60%	Last MSR

* **Grendel AWS** – 6.5 Grendel cal., GIO, 20 or 24 in. stainless steel fully lapped threaded barrel with A2 flash hider, four rail hand guard, Picatinny rail, 10 shot mag., black furniture.

| MSR $1,649 | $1,475 | $1,300 | $1,100 | $1,000 | $825 | $675 | $525 | |

Add $55 for 24 in. barrel.

* **Grendel Hunter** – 6.5 Grendel cal., GIO, 19 1/2 in. stainless steel fully lapped threaded barrel, flat-top receiver, full length military hand guard, Picatinny rail, black or coyote brown stock, 10 shot mag., standard trigger. Disc. 2012.

| | $1,300 | $1,125 | $975 | $875 | $700 | $595 | $450 | *$1,370* |

* **Grendel Tactical 16** – 6.5 Grendel cal., GIO, 16 in. threaded barrel with or w/o flutes, A2 flash hider, M4 style or folding stock, with or w/o rail, mid-length handguard, 10 shot mag., fixed or folding sights, includes soft carry bag.

| MSR $1,650 | $1,475 | $1,300 | $1,100 | $1,000 | $825 | $675 | $525 | |

This model is also available with a 14 1/2 in. barrel for law enforcement only (Tactical 14).

* **Grendel Ultralight** – 6.5 Grendel cal., GIO, 16, 18, or 20 in. unthreaded free floating 5R cut rifled barrel with six straight flutes, integral three prong flash hider (16 or 18 in. barrel only), vented composite hand guard, M4 collapsible stock, Enedine buffer. Disc. 2012.

| | $1,975 | $1,730 | $1,480 | $1,345 | $1,085 | $890 | $690 | *$2,100* |

* **GDMR** – 6.5 Grendel cal., GIO, 10 shot mag., 16 (disc.), 20, or 24 in. barrel, Magpul PRS OD Green or black stock, Ergo grip, full tactical model, LaRue four rail hand guard, sight base, bipod mount, Magpul rail covers, tactical single stage trigger, Troy fold up front and rear back up iron sights. Disc. 2013.

| | $3,500 | $3,075 | $2,625 | $2,375 | $1,925 | $1,575 | $1,225 | *$3,500* |

* **Grendel Sniper Rifle** – 6.5 Grendel cal., GIO, 10 shot mag., 16 in. fluted barrel, side charger loading, Magpul PRS stock, SST, MK10 vented composite handguard, LaRue SPR mount and Ergo deluxe grip, includes soft carry bag. New 2012.

| MSR $3,410 | $3,075 | $2,700 | $2,300 | $2,200 | $1,700 | $1,375 | $1,075 | |

* **Grendel MK3 Gas Piston** – 6.5 Grendel cal., GPO, 16, 18, or 24 in. button rifled and fluted Lite series barrel with AAC flash hider, 10 shot mag., black or tactical dark earth furniture, includes soft carry bag. Mfg. 2012-2013.

| | $2,150 | $1,875 | $1,625 | $1,475 | $1,185 | $975 | $750 | *$2,150* |

* **Grendel Lightweight Rifle** – 6.5 Grendel cal., GIO, lightweight 16, 18, 20, or 24 (new 2014) in. button rifled stainless steel barrel with A2 flash hider, 10 shot mag., M4 folding stock, composite free floating handguard, black furniture, includes soft carry bag. New 2012.

| MSR $1,540 | $1,375 | $1,200 | $1,025 | $950 | $750 | $625 | $475 | |

Add $88 for 24 in. barrel.

* **GSR** – 6.5 Grendel cal., GIO, 10 shot mag., 20, 24, or 28 (disc.) in. threaded (except 28 in.) barrel with A2 flash hider, Magpul PRS stock, Ergo deluxe pistol grip, blade style single stage tactical trigger, composite vented hand guard system, side charging handle, black or Dark Earth stock, long range precision rifle. Disc. 2012.

| | $3,100 | $2,710 | $2,325 | $2,110 | $1,700 | $1,395 | $1,085 | *$3,100* |

.17 HMR – .17 HMR cal., GIO, 18 in. stainless steel button rifled barrel with spiral flutes, 10 shot mag., black or camo finish, flat-top receiver with Picatinny rail, six vent A1 flash hider, G10 composite handguard, non-vented mid-length free float tube, includes two mags. New 2011.

| MSR $1,210 | $1,075 | $950 | $800 | $725 | $600 | $475 | $375 | |

5.56 NATO RIFLE – 5.56 NATO cal., GIO, two 30 shot mags., 16 or 20 in. fluted barrel with A2 flash hider, flat-top receiver with Picatinny rail, free-floated G10 composite handguard, M4 stock, black furniture, includes soft carry bag. New 2012.

| MSR $1,760 | $1,575 | $1,375 | $1,175 | $1,075 | $875 | $725 | $550 | |

Add $88 for 20 in. barrel.

.300 AAC RIFLE – .300 AAC cal., GIO, 16 in. fluted stainless steel barrel with AAC Blackout flash hider, 30 shot mag., G10 free floated composite handguard, M4 stock, black furniture, includes soft carry bag. New 2012.

| MSR $1,980 | $1,775 | $1,550 | $1,325 | $1,200 | $975 | $800 | $625 | |

ULFBERHT – .338 Lapua cal., based on the Russian DP 28 machine gun, adj. gas piston operating system, 27 1/2 in. chromemoly steel barrel with flash hider, a wide variety of additional accessories such as slings and bipods are available on this model, includes four 10 shot mags., Magpul PRS stock, hard case. New 2014.

| MSR $6,850 | $6,175 | $5,400 | $4,625 | $4,200 | $3,395 | $2,775 | $2,150 | |

The name Ulfberht comes from Norse legend - it was a unique type of sword made and carried by the Vikings over 1,000 years ago.

MSR	100%	98%	95%	90%	80%	70%	60%	Last MSR

ALPINE INDUSTRIES

Previous manufacturer located in Los Angeles, CA.

Alpine Industries was a commercial M1 carbine manufacturer which produced approximately 17,000 guns between 1962-1965. Guns were made with newly manufactured cast receivers and military surplus parts, including some from England.

AMBUSH FIREARMS

Current AR-15 style semi-auto rifle manufacturer located in Black Creek, GA.

CARBINES: SEMI-AUTO

AMBUSH A11 6.8/5.56 – 5.56 NATO (new 2012), or 6.8 SPC cal., AR-15 configuration, featuring 18 in. barrel with Magpul MOE adj. stock, free floating full length Picatinny modular rail, with two smaller rails on bottom and front, Black, standard (disc. 2013), Pink (mfg. 2013), Mossy Oak Break-Up Infinity (mfg. 2012-2013), or Realtree AP camo coverage, pistol grip, 5 shot mag., Geissele super semi-auto trigger, 6 lbs. New 2011.

MSR $1,799	$1,795	$1,575	$1,350	$1,225	$985	$800	$625	

AMBUSH 300 AAC BLACKOUT – .300 AAC Blackout (7.62x35mm) cal., otherwise similar to Ambush 6.8/5.56, 6 1/2 lbs. New 2012.

MSR $1,799	$1,795	$1,575	$1,350	$1,225	$985	$800	$625	

AMERICAN ARMS, INC.

Previous importer and manufacturer located in North Kansas City, MO, until 2000. American Arms imported various Spanish shotguns (Indesal, Lanber, Norica, and Zabala Hermanos), Italian shotguns including F. Stefano, several European pistols and rifles, and Sites handguns (1990-2000) mfg. in Torino, Italy. This company also manufactured several pistols in North Kansas City, MO. For more information and pricing on Norica airguns previously imported by American Arms, please refer to the *Blue Book of Airguns* by Dr. Robert Beeman & John Allen (also available online).

In late 2000, TriStar Sporting Arms, Ltd. acquired the parts inventory for some models previously imported by American Arms, Inc. Original warranties from American Arms do not apply to TriStar Sporting Arms, Ltd.

RIFLES: SEMI-AUTO

MODEL ZCY 308 – .308 Win. cal., gas operated semi-auto AK-47 type action, Yugoslavian mfg. Imported 1988 only.

	$775	$650	$550	$450	$400	$375	$350	*$825*

MODEL AKY 39 – 7.62x39mm cal., gas operated semi-auto AK-47 type action, teakwood fixed stock and grip, flip up Tritium front and rear night sights, Yugoslavian mfg. Imported 1988-1989 only.

	$650	$550	$495	$440	$395	$350	$300	*$559*

This model was supplied with sling and cleaning kit.

* ***Model AKF 39 Folding Stock*** – 7.62x39mm cal., folding stock variation of the Model AKY-39. Imported 1988-89 only.

	$725	$625	$550	$475	$425	$375	$325	*$589*

EXP-64 SURVIVAL RIFLE – .22 LR cal., semi-auto, takedown rifle stores in oversize synthetic stock compartment, 21 in. barrel, 10 shot mag., open sights, receiver grooved for scope mounting, cross bolt safety, 40 in. overall length, 7 lbs. Imported 1989-90 only.

	$150	$135	$125	$115	$105	$95	$85	*$169*

AMERICAN INTERNATIONAL CORP.

Previous manufacturer and importer located in Salt Lake City, UT, circa 1972-1984. American International was a wholly owned subsidiary of ARDCO (American Research & Development). ARDCO's previous name was American Mining & Development. American International imported firearms from Voere, located in Kufstein, Austria. American Arms International (AAI) was another subsidiary of ARDCO.

In 1979, after American International Corp. had dissolved, AAI resumed production using mostly Voere parts. After running out of Voere parts, late production featured U.S. mfg. receivers (can be recognized by not having a pivoting barrel retainer slotted on the bottom of the receiver). American Arms International declared bankruptcy in 1984.

CARBINES: SEMI-AUTO

AMERICAN 180 AUTO CARBINE (M-1) – .22 LR cal., a specialized design for military use, 177 round drum mag., 16 1/2 in. barrel, aperture sight, high impact plastic stock and forearm, aluminum alloy receiver with black finish. Semi-auto variation mfg. 1979-c.1984. Total Voere production (denoted by A prefix serial number) between 1972 and 1979

MSR	100%	98%	95%	90%	80%	70%	60%	Last MSR

was 2,300 carbines (includes both full and semi-auto versions). Later mfg. was marked either M-1 (semi-auto) or M-2 (fully auto). "B" serial number prefix was introduced in 1980, and barrel markings were changed to "Amer Arms Intl, SLC, UT."

	$725	$600	$475	$375	$350	$325	$295	

Add $550 for Laser Lok System - first commercially available laser sighting system.
Add approx. $300 for extra drum mag. and winder (fragile and subject to breakage).

AMERICAN PRECISION ARMS

Current manufacturer established in 2001, and located in Jefferson, GA.

In addition to rifles, American Precision Arms offered a shotgun modification service on customer supplied Remington 870s. Prices began at $1,395. Please contact the company directly for more information on the wide lineup of available options and configurations (see Trademark Index).

RIFLES: BOLT ACTION

Previously, the company offered the .308 Raven (disc. 2011, last MSR was $3,395), and the Revelation Tactical Rifle (disc. 2011, last MSR was $3,995), Genesis Tactical Rifle (disc. 2010, last MSR was $2,450). Hunting models were also available, and previous models included the Revelation Hunter (disc. 2010, last MSR was $3,450), and the Genesis Hunter (disc. 2010, last MSR was $2,450). All MSRs are considered base price. Many options and custom services are also available.

CRITTER GET'R – .300 Win. Mag. cal., APA Genesis Hunting action, 24 in. stainless steel barrel, corrosion resistant finish, APA tactical knob and bipod stud, Timney trigger, one piece fluted bolt, M16 style extractor, side bolt release, McMillan stock.

MSR $5,160	$4,395	$3,850	$3,300	$3,000	$2,425	$1,975	$1,550

DO IT ALL APR – .308 Win. cal., APA Genesis action with pinned recoil, 22 in. contour barrel, McMillan HTG stock, spiral fluted bolt, mini-16 extractor, APA bolt knob, Timney trigger, Sage finish, two flush cups on left side of stock, includes one 10 shot mag. and royal gun case, 9 1/4 lbs.

MSR $4,950	$4,225	$3,700	$3,175	$2,875	$2,325	$1,900	$1,475

MEAT STICK – .300 Win. Mag. cal., APA Genesis Hunting action, one-piece bolt body, 25 in. match grade stainless barrel, fluted bolt, pinned recoil lug, side bolt release, Williams steel trigger guard, McMillan HTG stock with adj. cheek piece, APA tactical bipod stud, corrosion resistant finish, 20 in. MOA rail, M16 style extractor. New 2013.

MSR $5,615	$4,800	$4,200	$3,600	$3,275	$2,650	$2,175	$1,675

PARAGON – .223 Rem. or .308 Win. cal., APA Genesis receiver includes side bolt release, M16 style extractor, one-piece bolt, 20 (.223 Rem.) or 22 (.308 Win.) in. stainless steel match grade barrel, uses A1 or AW mags., Manners TF1 folding stock, two side flush cups, APA tactical bipod stud, 13 1/2 LOP with decelerator pad, Huber trigger, Cerakote coating, tan finish. New 2013.

MSR $6,640	$5,675	$4,975	$4,250	$3,850	$3,125	$2,550	$1,995

RIFLES: SEMI-AUTO

Previous AR-15 style models included the Lycan (disc. 2011, last MSR was $3,450), the Urban Sniper .223 (disc. 2011, last MSR was $2,450), and the Urban Sniper .308 (disc. 2011, last MSR was $3,098). All MSRs reflected base pricing. Many options and custom services were also available.

RIFLES: TARGET

American Precision Arms also builds custom target rifles per customer's specifications. All models are POR, and a wide variety of options are available.

AMERICAN SPIRIT ARMS

Current manufacturer established circa 1995, and located in Scottsdale, AZ.

PISTOLS: SEMI-AUTO

American Spirit Arms previously offered a 5.56 NATO cal. AR-15 style pistol with A2 fixed carry handle (last MSR was $1,199, disc. 2012).

A2 PISTOL – 5.56 NATO cal., 7 1/2 in. chromemoly barrel, forged lower receiver and forged A2 upper with fixed carry handle, 30 shot mag., includes hard case.

MSR $1,390	$1,175	$1,025	$885	$780	$650	$525	$450

AR-15 PISTOL WITH HANDGUARD – 5.56 NATO cal., 7 1/2 in. chromemoly barrel, forged A3 flat-top upper receiver, Picatinny rail, carbine-length free float handguard, 30 shot mag., includes hard carry case.

MSR $1,350	$1,150	$1,000	$875	$775	$650	$525	$450

MSR	100%	98%	95%	90%	80%	70%	60%	Last MSR

AR-15 PISTOL WITH QUAD RAIL – 5.56 NATO cal., 7 1/2 in. chromemoly barrel, forged A3 flat-top upper receiver, Picatinny rail, quad rail with gas block, 30 shot mag., includes hard carry case.

	100%	98%	95%	90%	80%	70%	60%	Last MSR
MSR $1,350	$1,150	$1,000	$875	$775	$650	$525	$450	

9MM PISTOL – 9mm Para. cal., 7 1/2 in. chromemoly barrel, 25 shot mag., forged lower and forged upper receiver with fixed carry handle, fixed front iron sight base, includes hard carry case.

MSR $1,525	$1,250	$1,100	$950	$850	$700	$575	$500	

FLAT TOP 9MM PISTOL – 9mm Para. cal., 7 1/2 in. chromemoly barrel, 25 shot, forged lower and forged A3 flat-top upper receiver, Picatinny rail, fixed front iron sight base, includes hard carry case.

MSR $1,485	$1,265	$1,100	$950	$850	$700	$575	$450	

RIFLES/CARBINES: SEMI-AUTO

American Spirit Arms manufactures a wide variety of AR-15 style semi-auto carbines and rifles based on the AR-15, M16, and the M4 in 5.56 NATO, .223 Rem., 9mm Para., and .308 Win. cal. A complete line of options, accessories, and parts are available. Base models are listed. Additionally, ASA has a Custom Shop for custom order rifles only built to customer specifications. Please contact the company directly regarding pricing for options and accessories (see Trademark Index).

ASA-A2 RIFLE – 5.56 NATO cal., GIO, 20 in. Govt. profile barrel, 30 shot, fixed carry handle, M4 feed ramps, fixed (A2) buttstock, includes hard carrying case.

MSR $1,296	$1,100	$975	$825	$750	$600	$500	$400	

ASA-A320(G) RIFLE – 5.56 NATO cal., GIO, 20 in. barrel, choice of flat-top or fixed carry handle, gas rifle length handguard and A2 stock, choice of A2 sight or gas block.

MSR $1,260	$1,075	$950	$800	$725	$600	$500	$400	

ASA-M4A2 CARBINE – 5.56 NATO cal., GIO, 16 in. barrel, 30 shot mag., fixed carry handle, 6-pos. M4 collapsible stock, includes hard carrying case.

MSR $1,296	$1,100	$975	$825	$750	$600	$500	$400	

ASA-M4A3 CARBINE – 5.56 NATO cal., GIO, flat-top with 16 in. barrel, 6-position collapsible stock, with (ASA-M4A3G) or without gas block.

MSR $1,250	$1,075	$950	$800	$725	$600	$500	$400	

Add $20 for mid-length handguard.

ASA-M4CS1 CARBINE – 5.56 NATO cal., GIO, 16 in. M4 profile barrel, flat-top receiver, 10 in. Samson Evo Rail, low profile gas block, Ergo grip, MagPul MOE stock and trigger guard, Black or Flat Dark Earth furniture. New 2013.

MSR $1,476	$1,255	$1,100	$950	$850	$700	$575	$450	

ASA-M4CS2 CARBINE – 5.56 NATO cal., GIO, 16 in. M4 profile barrel with A2 flash hider, flat-top receiver, MI Gen 2 drop in rail, MagPul MOE stock, grip, and trigger guard, choice of A2 front sight or gas block, choice of FDE or OD Green furniture. New 2013.

MSR $1,476	$1,255	$1,100	$950	$850	$700	$575	$450	

ASA-MID-LENGTH A3 M16 RIFLE – 5.56 NATO cal., 16 in. nitrided mid-length barrel, 30 shot mag., M4 feed ramps, forged lower and flat-top upper receiver with Picatinny rail, CAR-length gas system, gas block with 1913 rail, front and rear sling swivels, 6-pos. buttstock, includes hard carrying case.

MSR $1,278	$1,085	$955	$800	$725	$600	$500	$400	

ASA-DISSIPATOR A2 CARBINE – 5.56 NATO cal., GIO, 16 in. M4 barrel, forged A2 upper receiver with fixed carry handle, 30 shot mag., adj. open rear sights, M4 feed ramps, A2 fixed buttstock, dissipator CAR length gas system, front and rear sling swivels, includes hard carrying case.

MSR $1,386	$1,200	$1,050	$900	$825	$675	$550	$450	

ASA-DISSIPATOR A3G CARBINE – 5.56 NATO cal., GIO, 16 in. barrel, gas block, flat-top receiver with Picatinny rail, Magpul MOE handguard and six position stock, dissipator CAR length gas system, 30 shot mag.

MSR $1,350	$1,150	$1,000	$875	$775	$650	$525	$425	

ASA-SPR – 5.56 NATO cal., GIO, 18 in. stainless steel heavy profile barrel with A2 flash hider, flat-top receiver, low profile gas block, 12 in. Samson Evo rail, two stage trigger, Ergo grip, MOE trigger guard, VLTOR Emod stock. New 2013.

MSR $1,700	$1,450	$1,275	$1,100	$975	$800	$675	$550	

ASA-9mm CARBINE – 9mm Para. cal., GIO, 16 in. lightweight barrel, 25 shot mag., front and rear sling swivels, fixed front sight base, drop-in magwell adapter, 4-pos. collapsible CAR stock, fixed carry handle, includes hard carrying case.

MSR $1,476	$1,255	$1,100	$950	$850	$700	$575	$450	

ASA-9mm A3G CARBINE – 9mm Para. cal., GIO, 16 in. barrel, flat-top, gas block, collapsible stock.

MSR $1,440	$1,225	$1,075	$925	$835	$675	$550	$450	

MSR	100%	98%	95%	90%	80%	70%	60%	*Last MSR*

ASA-BULL A3 CARBINE – 5.56 NATO cal., GIO, 16 in. bull barrel, flat-top, choice of six position or A2 stock.

| MSR $1,600 | $1,375 | $1,200 | $1,025 | $950 | $750 | $625 | $525 | |

ASA-BULL A3 RIFLE – 5.56 NATO cal., GIO, 24 in. bull barrel, fixed buttstock. Disc. 2012.

| | $1,300 | $1,150 | $1,000 | $875 | $750 | $625 | $500 | *$1,475* |

ASA-BULL BARREL FLAT TOP RIFLE – .223 Rem. cal., 24 in. stainless steel bull barrel, forged A3 flat-top upper receiver with Picatinny rail, free float handguard with gas block, 30 shot mag., M4 feed ramps, A2 buttstock, includes hard carrying case.

| MSR $1,800 | $1,525 | $1,350 | $1,150 | $1,050 | $850 | $700 | $600 | |

ASA-BULL SIDE CHARGER CARBINE – 5.56 NATO cal., 24 in. stainless steel bull barrel, 30 shot mag., aluminum flat-top side charge upper receiver, Picatinny rail, forged lower receiver, front and rear sling swivels, M4 feed ramps, standard A2 buttstock, includes hard carrying case.

| MSR $2,000 | $1,700 | $1,500 | $1,275 | $1,150 | $950 | $775 | $650 | |

ASA-BULL SIDE CHARGER CARBINE/RIFLE – .223 Rem. cal., GIO, 16 (carbine) or 24 (rifle) in. bull stainless steel barrel, features left side charger, Magpul PRS stock with circular free floating handguard with gas block. Disc. 2012.

| | $1,550 | $1,375 | $1,175 | $1,000 | $875 | $775 | $675 | *$1,725* |

ASA-308 SIDE CHARGER CARBINE/RIFLE – .308 Win. cal., GIO, flat-top receiver with Picatinny rail, 16 (standard-disc. 2012 or bull - new 2013), 20 (bull) or 24 (disc. 2011) in. bull barrel, full length quad rail became standard 2012, Hogue grip, two-stage trigger, MagPul CTR stock, includes two 20 shot AR-10 mags.

| MSR $2,600 | $2,600 | $2,275 | $1,950 | $1,775 | $1,425 | $1,175 | $925 | |

Add $450 for 20 in. bull barrel.

Subtract approx. $600 if without full length quad rail.

AMERICAN SPIRIT ARMS CORP.

Previous rifle and components manufacturer 1998-2005, and located in Tempe, AZ. Previously located in Scottsdale, AZ.

RIFLES: SEMI-AUTO

Add $25 for green furniture, $65 for black barrel finish, $75 for fluted barrel, $125 for porting, $119 for two-stage match trigger, and $55 for National Match sights on .223 cal. models listed below.

ASA 24 IN. BULL BARREL FLAT-TOP RIFLE – .223 Rem. cal., patterned after AR-15, GIO, forged steel lower receiver, forged aluminum flat-top upper receiver, 24 in. stainless steel bull barrel, free floating aluminum handguard, includes Harris bipod. Mfg. 1999-2005.

| | $850 | $700 | $625 | $550 | $500 | $450 | $400 | *$950* |

ASA 24 IN. BULL BARREL A2 RIFLE – .223 Rem. cal., similar to ASA Bull Barrel Flat-top, except features A2 upper receiver with carrying handle and sights. Mfg. 1999-2005.

| | $875 | $725 | $650 | $565 | $500 | $450 | $400 | *$980* |

OPEN MATCH RIFLE – .223 Rem. cal., GIO, 16 in. fluted and ported stainless steel match barrel with round shroud, flat-top without sights, forged upper and lower receiver, two-stage match trigger, upgraded pistol grip, individually tested, USPSA/IPSC open class legal. Mfg. 2001-2005.

| | $1,350 | $1,100 | $950 | $825 | $725 | $650 | $525 | *$1,500* |

LIMITED MATCH RIFLE – .223 Rem. cal., GIO, 16 in. fluted stainless steel match barrel with round shroud with staggered hand grip, National Match front and rear sights, two-stage match trigger, upgraded pistol grip, individually tested, USPSA/IPSC open class legal. Mfg. 2001-2005.

| | $1,175 | $975 | $825 | $725 | $650 | $525 | $475 | *$1,300* |

DCM SERVICE RIFLE – .223 Rem. cal., GIO, 20 in. stainless steel match barrel with ribbed free floating shroud, National Match front and rear sights, two-stage match trigger, pistol grip, individually tested. Mfg. 2001-2005.

| | $1,175 | $975 | $825 | $725 | $650 | $525 | $475 | *$1,300* |

ASA 16 IN. M4 RIFLE – .223 Rem. cal., GIO, features non-collapsible stock and M4 handguard, 16 in. barrel with muzzle brake, aluminum flat-top upper receiver. Mfg. 2002-2005.

| | $795 | $700 | $625 | $525 | $450 | $400 | $350 | *$905* |

ASA 20 IN. A2 RIFLE – .223 Rem. cal., GIO, features A2 receiver and 20 in. National Match barrel. Mfg. 1999-2005.

| | $765 | $640 | $565 | $500 | $425 | $350 | $300 | *$820* |

MSR	100%	98%	95%	90%	80%	70%	60%	Last MSR

ASA CARBINE WITH SIDE CHARGING RECEIVER – .223 Rem. cal., GIO, features aluminum side charging flat-top upper receiver, M4 handguard, 16 in. NM barrel with slotted muzzle brake. Mfg. 2002-2004.

	$865	$750	$650	$565	$500	$450	$400	$970

C.A.R. POST-BAN 16 IN. CARBINE – .223 Rem. cal., GIO, non-collapsible stock, Wilson 16 in. National Match barrel. Mfg. 1999-2005.

	$775	$650	$575	$500	$450	$400	$350	$830

ASA 16 IN. BULL BARREL A2 INVADER – .223 Rem. cal., similar to ASA 24 in. Bull Barrel rifle, except has 16 in. stainless steel barrel. Mfg. 1999-2005.

	$860	$725	$630	$550	$500	$450	$400	$955

ASA 9MM A2 CAR CARBINE – 9mm Para. cal., GIO, forged upper and lower receiver, non-collapsible CAR stock, 16 in. Wilson heavy barrel w/o muzzle brake, with birdcage flash hider (pre-ban) or muzzle brake (post-ban), includes 9mm conversion block, 25 shot modified Uzi mag. Mfg. 2002-2005.

	$860	$725	$630	$550	$500	$450	$400	$950

Add $550 per extra 25 shot mag.

ASA 9MM FLAT-TOP CAR RIFLE – 9mm Para. cal., similar to A2 CAR Rifle, except has flat-top w/o sights. Mfg. 2002-2005.

	$860	$725	$630	$550	$500	$450	$400	$950

ASA 16 IN. TACTICAL RIFLE – .308 Win. cal., GIO, 16 in. stainless steel air gauged regular or match barrel, side charging handle, Hogue pistol grip, guaranteed 1/2 in. MOA accuracy, individually tested, 8 3/4 lbs. Mfg. 2002-2005.

	$1,475	$1,200	$995	$850	$750	$650	$525	$1,675

Add $515 for Match Rifle (includes fluted and ported barrel, 2 stage trigger, and hard chromed bolt and carrier).

ASA 24 IN. MATCH RIFLE – .308 Win. cal., GIO, 24 in. stainless steel air gauged match barrel with or w/o fluting/porting, side charging handle, Hogue pistol grip, guaranteed 1/2 in. MOA accuracy, individually tested, approx. 12 lbs. Mfg. 2002-2005.

	$1,475	$1,200	$995	$850	$750	$650	$525	$1,675

Add $515 for Match Rifle (includes fluted and ported barrel, 2 stage trigger, and hard chromed bolt and carrier).

AMERICAN TACTICAL IMPORTS (ATI)

Current importer located in Summerville, SC. Previously located in Rochester, NY.

American Tactical Imports imports a wide variety of firearms and products, including pistols, AR-15 style and AK-47 design semi-auto rifles, and shotguns. Trademarks, imports, and private labels currently include American Tactical Imports (ATI), Cavalry O/Us (new 2013), FMK (disc. 2013), German Sport Guns (GSG), Head Down Products (mfg. 2012-2013), Masterpiece Arms (MPA, disc. 2011), Ottoman Shotguns (disc. 2011), Tisas (imported 2008-2011), and Xtreme Rifles (disc. 2012). Please see individual listings for current model information and pricing (see Trademark Index).

CARBINES/RIFLES: SEMI-AUTO

AT-15 – 5.56 NATO cal., AR-15 style, GIO, 16 in. barrel with muzzle brake, flat-top receiver with mid-length quad rail, post front sight, collapsible stock, 30 shot mag. Limited importation 2011 only.

	$650	$595	$525	$465	$435	$400	$375	$719

AT-47 – 5.56x45 cal., AK-47 design, 16 in. M4 barrel, blued finish, A3 flat-top, 10 shot mag., 6-position original under-folding stock, original wood furniture, includes hard case, unissued M70 Yugo parts kit. New 2014.

MSR $950	$850	$750	$650	$575	$475	$375	$325	

AT-47 MILLED – 7.62x39mm cal., AK-47 design, 16 1/2 in. match ER Shaw barrel, blue finish, mfg. from unissued Bulgarian parts kit, wood furniture, 30 shot mag., milled receiver, includes hard case. Disc. 2013.

	$725	$675	$600	$550	$450	$350	$275	$790

Add $120-$150 for Strikeforce Elite package with adj. polymer stock, pistol grip, recoil system, removable cheekpiece and three Picatinny rails (new 2012).

AT-47 STAMPED – 7.62x39mm cal., AK-47 design, similar to AT47 Milled, except has stamped receiver and is mfg. in the US. Mfg. 2011-2013.

	$525	$450	$410	$325	$275	$225	$200	$600

Add $120-$150 for Strikeforce Elite package with adj. polymer stock, pistol grip, recoil system, removable cheekpiece and three Picatinny rails (new 2012).

OMNI 22 (VK22 STANDARD) – .22 LR cal., AR-15 style, GIO, 16 in. barrel, fixed or tele-stock, black finish, flat-top receiver with Picatinny rail, 10 or 28 shot mag. Disc. 2013.

	$425	$375	$325	$275	$250	$225	$200	$470

MSR	100%	98%	95%	90%	80%	70%	60%	Last MSR

OMNI 22 OPS (VK22 TACTICAL) – .22 LR cal., AR-15 style, GIO, 16 in. barrel, fixed or tele-stock, black finish, flat-top receiver, 10 or 28 shot mag., quad rail, vertical foregrip, tactical rear sight. Disc. 2013.

	$465	$425	$385	$335	$295	$250	$225	*$520*

OMNI 556 – 5.56 NATO cal., GIO, 10 or 30 shot mag., 16 in. M4 style barrel, fixed or telescoping stock, flat-top receiver with Picatinny rail, Omni polymer lower receiver, black furniture. New 2013.

MSR $600	$525	$475	$425	$395	$375	$350	$325	

Add $45 for 7 in. quad rail.

OMNI HYBRID – 5.56 NATO cal., 16 in. barrel, 10 or 30 shot mag., flat-top, polymer lower receiver, inter-lock hammer and trigger pin retainment system, enhanced trigger guard, bevelled mag. well, includes AR15 parts kit, 7 lbs. New 2014.

MSR $145	$130	$115	$100	$90	$75	$60	$50	

MILSPORT M4 CARBINE – 5.56 NATO cal., GIO, 10 or 30 shot mag., 16 in. barrel, A3 flat-top receiver with Picatinny rail, tubular ribbed handguard, six position stock, black hardware and finish, includes hard case. New 2012.

MSR $740	$650	$550	$500	$425	$395	$375	$350	

HDH16 CARBINE – 5.56 NATO cal., GIO, 10 or 30 shot mag., 16 in. Hbar barrel, A3 flat-top receiver with Picatinny rail, six position stock, black hardware and finish, includes hard case. Mfg. 2012-2013.

	$650	$575	$525	$475	$425	$395	$325	*$750*

V916/VX916 CARBINE – 5.56 NATO cal., GIO, 10 or 30 shot mag., 16 in. heavy barrel, flat-top receiver with Picatinny rail, 9 or 13 in. quad rail, six position stock, black hardware and finish, includes hard case. Mfg. 2012-2013.

	$775	$675	$575	$500	$450	$400	$350	*$889*

Add $20 for 13 in. quad rail (Model VX916).

.300 AAC CARBINE – .300 AAC cal., GIO, 10 or 30 shot mag., 16 in. heavy barrel with muzzle brake, six position stock, flat-top receiver with Picatinny rail, 9 in. quad rail, black hardware and finish. Mfg. 2012-2013.

	$875	$750	$675	$575	$475	$400	$350	*$999*

PISTOLS: SEMI-AUTO

FX 45K – .45 ACP cal., features 5 in. threaded barrel with cap, SA, 8 shot, lower front Picatinny rail, bobbed hammer, beavertail safety, extended ambidextrous safety lock, skeletonized aluminum trigger, checkered mahogany grips, low profile rear sight, blued or Flat Dark Earth (new 2014) finish. New 2013.

MSR $740	$635	$550	$495	$450	$400	$350	$300	

Add $50 for Flat Dark Earth finish (new 2014).

FX FAT BOY – .45 ACP cal., 3.2 in. barrel, SA, blue finish, 10 or 12 shot double stack mag., all steel serrated grips, lightweight configuration became standard 2013, mfg. by Shooters Arms Manufacturing in the Phillipines. New mid-2010.

MSR $720	$610	$525	$450	$400	$350	$300	$250	

FX G.I. – .45 ACP cal., 1911 style frame, 4 1/4 in. barrel, SA, blue finish, 8 shot mag., double diamond checkered wood grips, military style rear slide serrations, slide stop, safety lock, matte black trigger, round hammer, beavertail grip safety, mfg. by Shooters Arms Manufacturing in the Phillipines. New mid-2010.

MSR $520	$440	$375	$325	$295	$250	$225	$195	

* FX G.I. Enhanced – .45 ACP cal., similar to G.I. model, except has Novak sights. New mid-2010.

MSR $565	$475	$415	$350	$315	$260	$225	$195	

FX MILITARY – .45 ACP cal., 1911 style frame, 5 in. barrel, SA, blue finish, 8 shot mag., double diamond checkered wood grips, military style rear slide serrations, slide stop, safety lock and trigger, mfg. by Shooters Arms Manufacturing in the Phillipines. New mid-2010.

MSR $520	$440	$375	$325	$295	$250	$225	$195	

FX TITAN – .45 ACP cal., 1911 style frame, 3 5/8 in. bull barrel, blue (Titan), SA, NiBX (new 2013) finish or stainless steel (Titan SS, disc. 2012), 7 shot mag., double diamond checkered wood grips, low profile rear sights, stainless steel slide, rear slide serrations, military style slide stop, safety lock, skeletonized aluminum trigger, mfg. by Shooters Arms Manufacturing in the Phillipines. New mid-2010.

MSR $590	$495	$435	$365	$315	$275	$235	$195	

Add $80 for NiBX finish (new 2013).

Add $100 for Titan SS (stainless steel), disc. 2012.

* FX Titan Lightweight – .45 ACP cal., similar to Titan, except has 3 1/8 in. bull barrel, NIBX finish only. New 2013.

MSR $610	$500	$440	$365	$315	$275	$235	$195	

MSR	100%	98%	95%	90%	80%	70%	60%	Last MSR

FX THUNDERBOLT – .45 ACP cal., 1911 style frame, 5 in. non-ported or ported (new 2012) barrel, SA, blue finish or stainless steel (mfg. 2012 only), 8 shot mag., lower Picatinny rail standard, matte chrome round hammer and extended safety, beavertail safety grip, dovetail front sight, Champion rear sight, aluminum trigger, double diamond checkered wood grips, wide front and rear slide serrations, mfg. by Shooters Arms Manufacturing in the Phillipines. New mid-2010.

	100%	98%	95%	90%	80%	70%	60%	Last MSR
MSR $858	$740	$625	$550	$475	$400	$350	$295	

Add $42 for FX Thunderbolt E with ported slide (new 2012) or $40 for FX Thunderbolt SS with stainless construction (mfg. 2012 only).

AT CS9 SERIES – 9mm Para. cal., 4 in. barrel, SA/DA, Picatinny rail, ported slide, 18 shot mag., blue, chrome, or two tone finish, mfg. in Turkey. Limited importation 2010-2011 only.

	$335	$295	$250	$230	$185	$150	$115	*$380*

Add $60 for chrome finish.

AT CS40 SERIES – .40 S&W cal., 4 in. barrel, DA/SA, Picatinny rail, 12 shot mag., blue, chrome, or two tone finish, mfg. in Turkey. Limited importation 2010-2011 only.

	$360	$315	$270	$245	$200	$160	$125	*$406*

Add $15 for two tone or $40 for chrome finish.

AT C45 SERIES – .45 ACP cal., 4.6 in. barrel, DA/SA, Picatinny rail, ported slide, 9 shot mag., blue, chrome, or two tone finish, mfg. in Turkey. Limited importation 2010-2011 only.

	$325	$285	$245	$220	$180	$145	$115	*$370*

Add $36 for chrome finish.

AT FS9 SERIES – 9mm Para. cal., 5 in. barrel, DA/SA, Picatinny rail, ported slide, 18 shot mag., blue, chrome, or two tone finish, mfg. in Turkey. Limited importation 2010-2011 only.

	$335	$295	$250	$230	$185	$150	$115	*$380*

Add $60 for chrome finish.

AT FS40 SERIES – .40 S&W cal., 5 in. barrel, DA/SA, Picatinny rail, 12 shot mag., blue, chrome, or two tone finish, mfg. in Turkey. Limited importation 2010-2011 only.

	$360	$315	$270	$245	$200	$160	$125	*$406*

Add $14 for two tone or $40 for chrome finish.

AT HP9 SERIES – 9mm Para. cal., 5 in. barrel, DA/SA, 18 shot mag., blue, chrome, or two tone finish, mfg. in Turkey. Limited importation 2010-2011 only.

	$335	$295	$250	$230	$185	$150	$115	*$380*

Add $31 for chrome finish.

AT MS380 SERIES – .380 ACP cal., 3.9 in. barrel, DA/SA, 12 shot mag., black, chrome, or two tone finish, mfg. in Turkey. Disc. 2011.

	$335	$295	$250	$230	$185	$150	$115	*$380*

Add $20 for chrome or black finish.

SHOTGUNS: O/U

CAVALRY SX – 12, 20, 28 ga. or .410 bore, 3 in. chambers, 26 or 28 (12 ga. only) in. chromemoly steel barrels, blue finish, oil finished checkered Turkish walnut pistol grip stock and forearm, brass bead front sight, alloy receiver with light game scene engraving, five interchangeable chokes, SST, with extractors. Importation began mid-2013.

MSR $500	$425	$375	$325	$295	$235	$190	$150	

Add $360 for Cavalry SX Combo model with extra 28 ga. barrel.

* **Cavalry SX Youth** – 20 ga. or .410 bore, 26 in. barrel, youth configuration, otherwise similar to Cavalry SX. New 2014.

MSR $500	$425	$375	$325	$295	$235	$190	$150	

CAVALRY SXE – 12, 20 ga. or .410 bore, 3 in. chambers, 26 or 28 (12 ga. only) in. chromemoly steel barrels, blue finish, oil finished checkered Turkish walnut pistol grip stock and forearm, brass bead front sight, alloy receiver with light game scene engraving, five interchangeable chokes, SST, with ejectors. Importation began mid-2013.

MSR $560	$475	$425	$350	$325	$250	$215	$175	

SHOTGUNS: SEMI-AUTO

TAC-S – 12 ga., 3 in. chamber, 18 1/2 in. barrel, blue finish, matte black synthetic pistol grip stock and forearm.

MSR $380	$325	$285	$245	$220	$180	$145	$115	

* **TAC-S Combo** – 12 ga., similar to TAC-S, except is two barrel set, features 18 1/2 in. cyl. barrel and 28 in. vented ribbed barrel with 3 choke tubes. New 2014.

MSR $500	$450	$400	$350	$300	$250	$200	$160	

MSR	100%	98%	95%	90%	80%	70%	60%	Last MSR

SHOTGUNS: SLIDE ACTION

TAC-P – 12 ga., 3 in. chamber, 18 1/2 in. barrel, 5 shot, matte black finish, fixed synthetic stock with pistol grip, trigger guard mounted safety, ramped front sight, rubber recoil pad, 7 lbs. 1 oz. New 2013.

MSR $300	$250	$225	$195	$175	$140	$115	$90

* **TAC-P Combo** – 12 ga., similar to TAC-P, except includes extra barrel and choke tubes. New 2014.

MSR $400	$335	$285	$245	$220	$180	$145	$115

AM-TAC PRECISION

Current manufacturer of AR-15 style carbines/rifles located in Garden City, ID beginning 2009.

AM-TAC Precision produces firearms, components, and tactical products for the professional and recreational user.

RIFLES: SEMI-AUTO

LTC RIFLE – 5.56 NATO or .300 Blackout cal., 16 in. stainless steel match grade barrel, "Jake Brake" muzzle device, Keymod Rail System V2 handguard with Qik System, 30 shot mag., forged receivers, MBUS front and flip-up rear sights, ALG Act combat trigger, BCM Mod 4 charging handle, QD end plate, enhanced trigger guard, Magpul MOE grip, MOE milspec 6-position stock, Black finish.

MSR $1,969	$1,750	$1,525	$1,325	$1,200	$975	$795	$625

Add $30 for .300 Blackout cal.

PREDITOR ELITE RIFLE – 5.56 NATO or .300 Blackout cal., 16 in. stainless steel match grade barrel, thread protector, 13 in. Keymod rail system handguard, forged receivers, Magpul MOE grip, fixed A2 rifle stock, ALG Act combat trigger, BCM Mod 4 charging handle, QD end plate, enhanced trigger guard, 10 or 20 shot mag., two-color cerakote camo finish.

MSR $2,049	$1,825	$1,600	$1,375	$1,250	$1,000	$825	$700

AMTEC 2000, INC.

Previous trademark incorporating Erma Werke (German) and H & R 1871 (U.S.) companies located in Gardner, MA until 1999. Amtec 2000, Inc. previously imported the Erma SR 100 rifle (see listing in Erma Suhl section).

REVOLVERS

5 SHOT REVOLVER – .38 S&W cal., 5 shot double action, swing-out cylinder, 2 or 3 in. barrel, transfer bar safety, Pachmayr composition grips, high polish blue, matte electroless nickel, or stainless steel construction, fixed sights, approx. 25 oz., 200 mfg. 1996-99, all were distributed and sold in Europe only (no U.S. pricing).

ANDERSON MANUFACTURING

Current rifle manufacturer established during 2010 and located in Hebron, KY. Distributor and dealer sales.

Anderson Manufacturing utilizes a proprietary metal treatment for all its rifles and carbines called RF-85. This metal treatment reduces friction on steel surfaces by 85%, and RF-85 treated weapons do not require any wet lubricants, which also result in less dirt and carbon fouling in the action.

CARBINES/RIFLES: SEMI-AUTO

Anderson Manufacturing is currently producing AR-15 style rifles and carbines in various configurations. Calibers include .223 Rem./5.56 NATO or 6.8 SPC. Previously Anderson Manufacturing also produced the following models until 2011: M15M4 6.8 SPC (last MSR was $1,519), AM15M416LE (last MSR was $1,392), AM15AORNZ (was POR), AM15M416ZE (last MSR was $1,392), AM10-BD (last MSR was $1,617), or AM10-MSR (last MSR was $1,555). The preceding models have either forged receivers (standard) made from 7075-T6 steel, or can be milled from solid billets.

AM10-BD – .308 Win. cal., GIO, 18 in. heavy barrel with flash hider, free float forearm, Magpul MOE buttstock and pistol grip, Picatinny rail and elevated modular rail, black furniture, 8.5 lbs.

MSR $1,365	$1,225	$1,075	$925	$850	$675	$550	$450

AM10-MSR – .308 Win. cal., GIO, 22 in. fluted barrel with crowned muzzle, low profile gas block, 14 1/4 in. free float forearm, A2 buttstock and pistol grip, black furniture, 9 lbs.

MSR $1,319	$1,195	$1,050	$895	$815	$650	$550	$425

AM15-AOR (HEAVY BARREL CARBINE) – .223 Rem. cal., GIO, 16 in. heavy barrel with A2 flash hider and Picatinny rail, front mounted low profile gas block, hard anodized finish with a forged aluminum flat-top receiver, ribbed oval M4 handguard, optic ready front sight, 6-position collapsible butt stock, includes two 30-shot MagPul magazines and hard case, 6.4 lbs.

MSR $886	$775	$675	$575	$525	$450	$375	$300

Add $210 for AM15-AOR16 Billet model (disc. 2012).

MSR	100%	98%	95%	90%	80%	70%	60%	Last MSR

AM15-HBOR16/AM15-HBOR20 – .223 Rem. cal., GIO, 16 or 20 in. heavy barrel with target crown and flash suppressor, Wilson target trigger, Magpul PRS adj. stock, Magpul MIAD grip, front mounted low profile gas block, free floated hand guard with upper and lower Picatinny rails, tactical charging handle, featuring hard anodized finish and aluminum flat-top receiver, includes two-30 shot magazines and hard black case, 9.44 lbs.

| MSR $1,411 | $1,275 | $1,125 | $950 | $875 | $700 | $575 | $450 | |

Add $50 for 20 in. barrel.

Add $210 for AM-15HBOR16-Billet or AM-15HBOR20-Billet models (disc. 2012).

AM15-M416 (M4 CARBINE) – .223 Rem. or 6.8 SPC cal., GIO, 16 in. M4 heavy barrel with Phantom flash hider, front mounted low profile gas block, MagPul MOE 6-position adj. stock with pistol grip and quad-rail forend with upper and lower Picatinny rails, 8 in. free float modular forearm, hard anodized finish with aluminum flat-top receiver, includes two 30 shot MagPul magazines and hard black case, 6.3 lbs.

| MSR $1,038 | $925 | $825 | $700 | $625 | $515 | $425 | $325 | |

Add $50 for 6.8 SPC cal.

Add $210 for AM15M416-Billet model in .223 Rem. cal. (disc. 2012), or $337 for AM15M416-Billet model in 6.8 SPC cal. (disc. 2012).

* **AM15-M416 Camo** – .223 Rem. cal., similar to AM15-M416, except features 8 in. free float CAMO forearm, A2 pistol grip, tactical intent buttstock, and Digital Camo coverage. New 2013.

| MSR $1,152 | $1,025 | $900 | $775 | $700 | $575 | $475 | $375 | |

* **AM15-M416 LE** – .223 Rem. cal., similar to AM15-M416, except features A2 front sight post, 6 in. free float modular forearm.

| MSR $1,070 | $950 | $825 | $715 | $650 | $525 | $425 | $350 | |

* **AM15-M416 Tiger** – .223 Rem.cal., similar to AM15-M416, except features 8 in. free float TIGER forearm. New 2013.

| MSR $1,152 | $1,025 | $900 | $775 | $700 | $575 | $475 | $375 | |

* **AM15-M416 ZE** – .223 Rem. cal., similar to AM15-M416, except features 8 in. free float ZOMBIE forearm.

| MSR $1,078 | $950 | $825 | $715 | $650 | $525 | $425 | $350 | |

AM15-VS24 (HEAVY BARREL VARMINTER) – .223 Rem. cal., GIO, 24 in. stainless steel fluted bull barrel with target crown, flat-top receiver, 14 in. free float modular forearm tube, Magpul PRS butt stock, Ergo tactical deluxe palm shelf pistol grip, two-30 shot magazines, low profile gas block, tactical charging handle, Timney trigger, black furniture, includes Harris bipod and hard black case, 9.44 lbs.

| MSR $1,681 | $1,525 | $1,350 | $1,150 | $1,025 | $850 | $675 | $550 | |

Add $210 for AM-15VS24-Billet model (disc. 2012).

ANSCHÜTZ

Current manufacturer (J. G. Anschütz, GmbH & Co. KG) established in 1856 and currently located in Ulm, Germany. Sporting rifles are currently being imported beginning 2010 by Steyr Arms, Inc. located in Bessemer, AL. Previously located in Trussville, AL until 2013. Merkel USA imported Anschutz from 2006-2010, until the company was purchased by Steyr Arms, Inc.

Target/competition rifles are currently being imported by Champion's Choice, Inc. located in La Vergne, TN, Champion Shooters Supply located in New Albany, OH, and Altius Handcrafted Firearms located in West Yellowstone, MT.

Sporting rifles were imported 1996-2003 by Tristar Sporting Arms. Ltd., located in N. Kansas City, MO. Previously distributed until 2000 by Go Sportsmens Supply, located in Billings, MT. Previously imported and distributed through 1995 in the U.S. by Precision Sales International Inc., located in Westfield, MA.

Anschütz was founded by Julius Gottfried Anschütz in 1856, and located in Zella-Mehlis, Germany until 1945. WWII nearly ended the company. Members of the Anschütz family were evacuated to West Germany after the war, while the company's possesions were expropriated and dismantled. Brothers Max & Rudolf Anschütz, grandsons of Julius, re-established the company in Ulm after WWII. In 1968, Max Anschütz turned over general management to his son Dieter (4th generation), who retired on March 31, 2008. The family business is now managed by Dieter's two sons, Jochen (President) and Uwe.

For more information and current pricing on both new and used Anschütz airguns, please refer to the *Blue Book of Airguns* by Dr. Robert Beeman & John Allen (now online also).

RIFLES: SEMI-AUTO

RX 22 – .22 LR cal., GIO, blowback action, 16 1/2 in. plain barrel, full length Picatinny rail with integrated quad rail in forend, folding iron sights, forward cocking lever, folding adj. stock, pistol grip, 10 shot mag., choice of black or desert tan finish, ambidextrous safety, adj. trigger, approx. 7 lbs. New 2012.

| MSR $895 | $795 | $725 | $650 | $575 | $500 | $450 | $400 | |

RX PRECISION – .22 LR cal., GIO, blowback action, 16 1/2 in. plain barrel, full length Picatinny rail with folding iron

MSR	100%	98%	95%	90%	80%	70%	60%	Last MSR

sights, forward cocking lever, skeletonized non-folding wood buttstock painted grey, pistol grip, 8 shot mag., choice of aluminum anodized or flat black receiver, ambidextrous safety, adj. trigger, approx. 7 lbs. New 2012.

| MSR $995 | $875 | $775 | $675 | $575 | $500 | $450 | $400 | |

ANZIO IRONWORKS CORP.

Current manufacturer established during 2000, and located in St. Petersburg, FL. Anzio Ironworks has been making gun parts and accessories since 1994. Dealer and consumer sales.

RIFLES: BOLT ACTION

.50 BMG SINGLE SHOT TAKEDOWN MODEL – .50 BMG cal., modified bullpup configuration, tube stock with 2 in. buttpad, 17 in. barrel with match or military chambering and muzzle brake, automatic ambidextrous safety and decocking mechanism, takedown action allowing disassembly in under 25 seconds, adj. target trigger, inclined sight mounting rail, cased, 25 lbs. Mfg. 2000-2002.

| | $4,200 | $4,000 | $3,500 | $2,350 | $2,000 | $1,800 | $1,600 | *$2,500* |

Add $150 for 29 in. barrel or $1,050 for 29 in. barrel assembly.

.50 BMG SINGLE SHOT TITANIUM TAKEDOWN MODEL – .50 BMG cal., modified bullpup configuration, tube stock, 16 in. barrel with match or military chambering and muzzle brake, automatic ambidextrous safety and decocking mechanism, interrupted thread lockup, takedown action allowing disassembly in under 12 seconds, adj. target trigger, Picatinny rail mount, cased, 11 lbs. Limited mfg. 2002 only.

| | $5,700 | $5,000 | $4,000 | $3,500 | $3,500 | $3,000 | $2,500 | *$3,200* |

Add $250 for 29 in. barrel, $350 for custom barrel length to 45 in., or $1,050 for 29 in. barrel assembly.

.50 BMG SINGLE SHOT MODEL LTD. – .50 BMG cal., laminated wood stock, butter knife bolt handle, bolt complete with ejector and extractor, parkerized finish, inclined sight mounting rail, 17 in. barrel with match or military chambering and muzzle brake, 21 lbs. Limited mfg. 2002 only.

| | $2,500 | $2,200 | $1,950 | $1,675 | $1,400 | $1,200 | $1,000 | *$2,750* |

Add $150 for 29 in. barrel or $250 for custom barrel length to 45 in.

.50 BMG SINGLE SHOT MODEL – .50 BMG cal., 29 1/2 in. Lothar Walther match grade barrel, AR-15 trigger and safety, fixed metal buttstock with shrouded barrel and optional muzzle brake, 22 lbs. Mfg. 2003-2006.

| | $1,800 | $1,625 | $1,400 | $1,200 | $1,000 | $900 | $800 | *$1,995* |

.50 BMG TAKEDOWN COMPETITION RIFLE – .50 BMG cal., 30 in. free floating match grade stainless steel takedown barrel with clamshell muzzle brake, 20 minute inclined sight mounting rail, all steel receiver, hand polished trigger, knurled steel handguard, titanium firing pin, .49 MOA guaranteed, black or green duracoat finish, includes fitted pelican case. New 2005.

| MSR $4,200 | $3,675 | $3,150 | $2,750 | $2,400 | $2,100 | $1,900 | $1,700 | |

.338 LAPUA TAKEDOWN RIFLE – .338 Lapua cal., 26 or 29 in. Supermatch chromemoly free floated barrel or stainless heavy target free floated barrel, all steel receiver, hand polished trigger, titanium firing pin, solid or vented steel handguard, 5 shot detachable box mag., black or green duracoat finish, includes fitted pelican case.

| MSR $4,700 | $4,225 | $3,695 | $3,175 | $2,875 | $2,325 | $1,900 | $1,475 | |

Please call the manufacturer directly for more info. on custom camo patterns and colors, as well as other options available on this model.

.50 BMG SUPER LIGHTWEIGHT REPEATER MODEL – .50 BMG cal., lightweight model with 18 in. Lothar Walther fluted target barrel with 3 (standard) or 5 shot detachable mag., titanium muzzle brake, scope rail, bipod, and sling, includes fitted case, 13 1/2 lbs. New 2003.

| MSR $4,995 | $4,500 | $3,950 | $3,300 | $2,775 | $2,350 | $2,125 | $1,850 | |

Add $250 for bipod.

Add $250 for 22 or 26 in. Lothar Walther fluted barrel.

.50 BMG TAKEDOWN LIGHTWEIGHT RIFLE – .50 BMG cal., lightweight model with 30 in. Supermatch chromemoly free floated takedown barrel with clamshell muzzle brake, 20 minute incline scope rail, all steel receiver, hand polished trigger, 3 (standard) or 5 (optional) shot round detachable box mag., knurled steel handguard, titanium firing pin, Cryo treated barrel, Black or Green Duracoat finish, fitted Pelican case.

| MSR $5,700 | $5,125 | $4,495 | $3,850 | $3,495 | $2,825 | $2,300 | $1,800 | |

ANZIO .50 BMG STANDARD REPEATER – .50 BMG cal., 18 or 26 in. Lothar Walther free floated stainless match grade barrel, 3 shot mag., Pachmayr Magnum recoil pad, 3 lug steel bolt, all steel receiver, guaranteed 1 MOA, Black Duracoat, Tiger Stripe Desert, Winter camo, or Urban Digital camo finish, fitted Pelican case, 18-24 lbs. New 2004.

| MSR $3,995 | $3,475 | $2,850 | $2,400 | $2,000 | $1,750 | $1,500 | $1,350 | |

Add $300 for left-hand action.

Add $350 for Tiger Stripe Desert or Winter camo finish.

Add $425 for Urban Digital camo finish.

MSR	100%	98%	95%	90%	80%	70%	60%	Last MSR

ANZIO 20/50 RIFLE – 20mm or .50 BMG cal., single shot or mag fed configuration, 36, 40 (standard), or 45 in. takedown barrel, Black or camo patterned finish, includes fitted Pelican case. New 2013.

MSR $7,500	$6,750	$5,900	$5,075	$4,595	$3,725	$3,050	$2,375	

Add $300 for 45 in. barrel.
Add $300 for camo pattern finish.
Add $1,000 for mag. fed configuration.

ANZIO SINGLE SHOT 50 – .50 BMG cal., 21 in. free floating target barrel, all steel and alloy receiver, Pachmayr white line recoil pad, Black, Tiger Stripe, Desert, Winter camo, or Urban Digital camo finish, 21 lbs. New 2012.

MSR $2,500	$2,250	$1,975	$1,695	$1,525	$1,250	$1,025	$800	

Add $300 for left-hand action.
Add $350 for Tiger Stripe, Desert, or Winter camo finish.
Add $425 for Urban Digital camo finish.

MAG. FED RIFLE – 14.5x114mm, 20mm Vulcan (requires $200 transfer tax in states where legal), or Anzio .20-50 cal., single shot or repeater, 49 in. match grade fluted take down barrel with heavy duty clamshell brake, detachable 3 shot box mag., fully adj. rear monopod, titanium firing pin, bipod, scope rail, customer choice of Duracoat color finish, oversized bolt handle. New 2008.

MSR $11,900	$11,900	$9,950	$8,750	$8,000	$7,250	$6,500	$5,750	

Add $1,100 for handguard, free floating barrel, and adj. bipod.
Add $3,200 for suppressor.
Subtract $2,100 for single shot.
Subtract $4,400 for Anzio .20-50 cal. (single shot) or $3,400 for mag. fed .20-50 cal.

ARES DEFENSE SYSTEMS INC.

Current manufacturer established in 1997, located in Melbourne, FL.

RIFLES: SEMI-AUTO

Ares Defense Systems manufactures quality firearms and firearm accessories for military, law enforcement, and the sporting market. Current mission configurable weapons include: ARES-16 MCR, ARES-16 AMG-1, and the ARES-16 AMG-2. For more information including options, availability, and pricing, please contact the company directly (see Trademark Index).

ARIZONA ARMORY

Current AR-15 style rifle manufacturer located in Phoenix, AZ since 2007.

RIFLES: SEMI-AUTO

All rifles can be customized per individual specifications with a wide variety of upgrades and options.

AA-15 CARBINE – 5.56 NATO cal., GIO, 16 in. M4 chromemoly barrel, AZA billet lower, AZA billet A3 flat-top slick side upper, CAR 4-position stock, CAR handguard, 30 shot mag.

MSR $775	$685	$600	$525	$475	$375	$325	$250	

AA-15 M4A3 BASIC – 5.56 NATO cal., GIO, 16 in. M4 chromemoly barrel, AZA billet lower and A3 flat-top upper with forward assist, M4 handguards, M4 6-position stock, 30 shot mag.

MSR $875	$775	$675	$575	$525	$425	$350	$275	

AA-15 M4A3 OPERATOR – 5.56 NATO cal., GIO, 16 in. M4 chrome lined barrel with M4 feed ramp, A2 flash suppressor, M4 double heatshield handguards, AZA billet lower and A3 flat-top upper with forward assist, 2 stage National Match trigger, M4 6-position stock, 30 shot mag.

MSR $985	$885	$775	$675	$600	$475	$400	$325	

AA-15 18 SPR – .223 Rem. cal., GIO, 18 in. stainless steel 1x8 SPR barrel, rifle length YHM lightweight railed free float handguards, low pro gas block, AZA billet lower and slick side A3 upper, 2-stage match trigger, A2 stock, YHM QDS folding back-up iron sights, 20 shot mag.

MSR $1,075	$950	$825	$715	$650	$525	$425	$350	

AA-15 20V/T – .223 Rem./5.56 NATO (.223 Wylde chamber) cal., GIO, Walther 20 in. stainless steel target crown barrel, aluminum free float tube, AZA billet lower and A3 billet slick side upper, adj. JP trigger, A2 stock, single Picatinny rail gas block, optic ready no sights, 5 shot mag.

MSR $1,025	$925	$825	$700	$625	$525	$425	$325	

AA-15 20M – GIO, 20 in. stainless steel match barrel with A2 flash suppressor, AZA billet lower, A2 forged upper with national match A2 rear sight assembly, national match front sight, A2 free float handguards, adj. trigger, anti-rotation trigger/hammer pins, 30 shot mag.

This model is available as a special order and is POR.

MSR	100%	98%	95%	90%	80%	70%	60%	*Last MSR*

AA-15 9MM – 9mm Para. cal., GIO, 16 in. chromemoly barrel with A2 flash suppressor, AZA billet lower, A3 billet smooth side upper with 9mm door kit, standard trigger group, CAR 4-position stock with 9mm buffer, CAR handguards, 9mm mag. block adapter with last round bolt hold open, 32 shot mag.

MSR $975	$875	$775	$650	$600	$475	$400	$300	

ARLINGTON ORDNANCE

Previous importer located in Westport, CT until 1996. Formerly located in Weston, CT.

CARBINES/RIFLES: SEMI-AUTO

M1 GARAND RIFLE – .30-06 cal., imported from Korea in used condition, various manufacturers, with import stamp. Imported 1991-96.

	$825	$750	$675	$550	$500	$475	$450	

Add $40 for stock upgrade (better wood).

* Arsenal Restored M1 Garand Rifle – .30-06 or .308 Win. cal., featured new barrel, rebuilt gas system, and reinspected components. Imported 1994-1996.

	$850	$700	$650	$600	$575	$550	$500	

Add 5% for .308 Win. cal.

TROPHY GARAND – .308 Win. cal. only, action was original mil spec., included new barrel and checkered walnut stock and forend, recoil pad. Imported 1994-1996.

	$925	$825	$725	$675	$575	$525	$475	*$695*

T26 TANKER – .30-06 or .308 Win. cal., included new barrel and other key components, updated stock finish. Imported 1994-1996.

	$850	$700	$650	$600	$575	$550	$500	

.30 CAL. CARBINE – .30 Carbine cal., 18 in. barrel, imported from Korea in used condition, various manufacturers, with import stamp. Imported 1991-1996.

	$725	$650	$575	$525	$475	$425	$400	

Add approximately $55 for stock upgrade (better wood).

MODEL FIVE CARBINE – while advertised, this model never went into production.

ARMALITE

Previous manufacturer located in Costa Mesa, CA, approx. 1959-1973.

RIFLES: SEMI-AUTO

AR-7 EXPLORER – .22 LR cal., 16 in. aluminum barrel with steel liner, aperture rear sight, take down action and barrel store in hollow plastic stock in either brown (rare), black, or multi-color, gun will float, designed by Gene Stoner, mfg. 1959-73 by Armalite, 1973-90 by Charter Arms, 1990-97 by Survival Arms located in Cocoa, FL, and by AR-7 Industries, LLC, located in Meriden, CT, 1998-2004. Current mfg. beginning 1997 by Henry Repeating Arms Co. located in NJ.

Black/Multi-color stock	$400	$375	$325	$275	$250	$215	$190	
Brown stock	$550	$500	$450	$375	$325	$260	$220	

Some unusual early Costa Mesa AR-7 variations have been observed with ported barrels, extendable wire stock, hooded front sight, and hollow pistol grip containing a cleaning kit, perhaps indicating a special military contract survival weapon.

AR-7 CUSTOM – similar to AR-7 Explorer, only with custom walnut stock including cheekpiece, pistol grip. Mfg. 1964-70.

	$325	$300	$265	$235	$200	$190	$180	

AR-180 – .223 Rem. cal., semi-auto, GPO, 18 1/4 in. barrel, folding stock. Manufactured by Armalite in Costa Mesa, CA, 1969-1972, Howa Machinery Ltd., Nagoya, Japan, 1972 and 1973, and by Sterling Armament Co. Ltd., Dagenham, Essex, England.

Sterling Mfg.	$1,750	$1,600	$1,450	$1,300	$1,225	$1,125	$1,050	
Howa Mfg.	$2,100	$1,900	$1,800	$1,650	$1,500	$1,300	$1,150	
Costa Mesa Mfg.	$2,100	$1,900	$1,800	$1,650	$1,500	$1,300	$1,150	

ARMALITE, INC.

Current manufacturer located in Geneseo, IL. New manufacture began in 1995 after Eagle Arms, Inc. purchased the ArmaLite trademarks. The ArmaLite trademark was originally used by Armalite (no relation to ArmaLite, Inc.) during mfg. in Costa Mesa, CA, approx. 1959-1973 (see Armalite listing above). Dealer and distributor sales.

MSR	100%	98%	95%	90%	80%	70%	60%	Last MSR

PISTOLS: SEMI-AUTO

MODEL AR-24 (ULTIMATE) – 9mm Para. cal., full size (AR-24-15 w/4.67 in. barrel) or compact (AR-24K-13 w/3.89 in. barrel) frame, DA/SA, blowback operation, 10, 13 (compact only), or 15 shot mag., 3-dot sights with fixed or adj. rear sight, black parkerized finish, checkered polymer grips, includes case and two magazines, 35 oz. Mfg. by Sarzsilmaz in Turkey. Imported 2007-2013.

	$475	$415	$355	$325	$260	$215	$165	$550

Add $81 for Model AR-24-10C/15C Combat/Tactical Custom pistol with C-suffix (full or compact size), adj. rear sight and checkered grip straps.

MODEL AR-24-15 – 9mm Para. cal., DA/SA, full size frame, 4.67 in. barrel, blowback operation, all steel construction, 15 shot mag., 3-dot sights with fixed or adj. rear sight, black parkerized finish, checkered polymer grips, serrated front and back strap, includes case and two magazines, 35 oz. Mfg. by Sarzsilmaz in Turkey. Imported 2007-2013.

	$475	$415	$355	$325	$260	$215	$165	$550

* Model AR-24-15C Combat Custom – 9mm Para. cal., similar to AR-24-15, except has fully adj. rear sight, checkered front and back strap. Mfg. by Sarzsilmaz in Turkey. Imported 2007-2013.

	$550	$480	$415	$375	$305	$250	$195	$631

MODEL AR-24K-13 COMPACT – 9mm Para. cal., similar to AR-24-15, except has 3.89 in. barrel and 13 shot mag., approx. 31 oz. Mfg. by Sarzsilmaz in Turkey. Imported 2007-2013.

	$475	$415	$355	$325	$260	$215	$165	$550

Add $81 for Model AR-24-10C/15C Combat/Tactical Custom pistol with C-suffix (full or compact size), adj. rear sight and checkered grip straps.

* Model AR-24K-13C Combat Custom Compact – 9mm Para. cal., similar to AR-24K-13, except has fully adj. rear sight, checkered front and back strap, 13 shot mag., 32 oz. Mfg. by Sarzsilmaz in Turkey. Imported 2007-2013.

	$550	$480	$415	$375	$305	$250	$195	$631

RIFLES: BOLT ACTION

AR-30(M) – .300 Win. Mag., .308 Win., or .338 Lapua cal., scaled down AR-50, repeater, Shilen modified single stage trigger, w/o muzzle brake, 5 shot detachable mag., 26 in. chromemoly barrel, 12 lbs. Mfg. 2003-2012.

	$1,850	$1,575	$1,350	$1,125	$1,000	$900	$800	$2,021

Add $140 for .338 Lapua cal.

AR-30A1 STANDARD – .300 Win. Mag. or .338 Lapua cal., 24 or 26 in. chromemoly barrel with muzzle brake, modified octagonal receiver, metal standard fixed stock, SST, 12.8-13.4 lbs. New 2013.

MSR $3,264	$2,900	$2,550	$2,175	$1,975	$1,600	$1,300	$1,025	

Add $140 for .338 Lapua cal.

* AR-30A1 Target – .300 Win. Mag. or .338 Lapua cal., similar to AR-30A1 Standard, except is Target configuration and features metal adjustable fixed stock, 14 1/2 lbs. New 2013.

MSR $3,460	$3,100	$2,725	$2,325	$2,125	$1,700	$1,400	$1,075	

Add $139 for .338 Lapua cal.

AR-31 – .308 Win. cal., 24 in. double lapped chromemoly barrel with muzzle brake, 10 shot mag. (accepts AR-10B double stack mags.), detachable sight rail and accessory rails, adj. stock, pistol grip. matte black finish, 14 lbs. New 2014.

MSR $3,460	$3,125	$2,735	$2,350	$2,125	$1,725	$1,400	$1,095	

AR-50A1 (AR-50) – .50 BMG or .416 Barrett (new 2013, AR-50A1B-416) cal., single shot bolt action with octagonal receiver integrated into a skeletonized aluminum stock with adj. cheekpiece and recoil pad, 30 in. tapered barrel w/o sights and sophisticated muzzle brake (reduces felt recoil to approx. .243 Win. cal.), removable buttstock, right or left-hand action, single stage trigger, approx. 34 lbs. New 1999.

MSR $3,359	$3,195	$2,925	$2,600	$2,400	$2,175	$2,000	$1,875	

Add $420 for left-hand action (disc. 2013).

During 2004, this model was produced with a special commemorative stamp notation on the left side of the receiver.

AR-50A1BNM – .50 BMG cal., similar to AR-50A1, except features 33 in. chromemoly fluted National Match barrel, right or left-hand action, also includes ArmaLite Skid System, 33.6 lbs. New 2013.

MSR $4,230	$3,800	$3,325	$2,850	$2,575	$2,100	$1,725	$1,325	

RIFLES: SEMI-AUTO

All ArmaLite AR-15 style semi-auto rifles have a limited lifetime warranty. Some previously manufactured models had stainless steel barrels and NM triggers at an additional charge. Descriptions and pricing are for currently manufactured models.

MSR	100%	98%	95%	90%	80%	70%	60%	Last MSR

Beginning 2009, a forward bolt assist became standard on all AR-10A4 upper receivers.

Add $99-$228 for A4 carry handle assembly.

Add $150 for 100% Realtree Hardwoods or Advantage Classic camo finish (disc.).

AR-10 SERIES – various configurations, GIO, with or w/o sights and carry handle, choice of standard green, black (new 1999), or camo finish, supplied with two 10 shot mags. (until 2004), current mfg. typically ships with one 10 round and one 20 round mag., during 2014, several variations of the AR-10 Series now accepts third party polymer mags., two-stage NM trigger became standard during 2008. New late 1995.

* **AR-10A2 Rifle (Infantry)** – .243 Win. (disc. 2003) or .308 Win. cal., features GIO, 20 in. chrome-lined barrel, fixed stock, A2 front sight, flash suppressor, tactical two-stage trigger, forged lower receiver, carry handle, Black or Green finish, includes one 10 shot mag., one 20 shot mag., sling, and hard case, 9.2 lbs. Disc. 2013.

| | $1,400 | $1,225 | $1,050 | $950 | $775 | $625 | $500 | $1,583 |

* **AR-10A2 Carbine** – 7.62 NATO cal., similar to AR-10A2 Rifle, except has 16 in. barrel and six-position collapsible stock with extended tube, includes one 10 shot mag., one 20 shot mag., sling, and hard case, 8 lbs. Disc. 2013.

| | $1,400 | $1,225 | $1,050 | $950 | $775 | $625 | $500 | $1,583 |

Add $74 for 4-way quad rail on front of forearm (mfg. 2004-2008).

* **AR-10A4 Rifle SPR - Special Purpose Rifle** – .243 Win. (disc. 2003, re-introduced 2011, Black only) or 7.62 NATO cal., features GIO, 20 in. chrome-lined barrel with flash suppressor, forged flat-top receiver with Picatinny rail, forward assist, and gas block with rail, forged lower with tactical two-stage trigger, removable front sight, Black or Green furniture, w/o carry handle, includes one 10 shot mag., one 20 shot mag., sling, and hard case, 8.9 lbs. Disc. 2013.

| | $1,400 | $1,225 | $1,050 | $950 | $775 | $625 | $500 | $1,571 |

* **AR-10A4 Carbine** – 7.62 NATO cal., similar to AR-10A4 SPR Rifle, except has 16 in. barrel, mid-length handguard, and 6-position collapsible stock with G.I. Diameter extension tube, 7.8 lbs.

| MSR $1,571 | $1,400 | $1,225 | $1,050 | $950 | $775 | $625 | $500 | |

Add $414 for SIR System (Selective Integrated Rail System, mfg. 2004-2006).

* **AR-10A4 Mod 1** – .308 Win. cal., GIO, 16 in. barrel with flash suppressor, forged one-piece upper receiver/rail system with detachable side and bottom rails, two-stage tactical trigger, collapsible tube stock with pistol grip, black finish and furniture.

While this model was advertised during 2012, it never went into production.

* **AR10A4 Tactical Carbine (CBA2F)** – .308 Win. cal., GIO, 16 in. double lapped chrome lined chromemoly barrel with flash suppressor, two-stage tactical trigger, anodized aluminum receiver, forged aluminum A4 flat-top upper receiver with Picatinny rail and permanent carry handle, A2 front sight, 20 shot Magpul PMAG, aluminum handguard tube, adj. stock, 9 lbs. New 2014.

| MSR $1,571 | $1,425 | $1,245 | $1,070 | $970 | $785 | $640 | $500 | |

* **AR10A4 Low Profile Carbine (CBFX)** – .308 Win. cal., 16 in. double lapped chrome line chromemoly barrel with flash suppressor, anodized aluminum receiver, forged aluminum upper receiver with free float quadrail handguards, low profile gas block, 20 shot Magpul PMAG, adj. stock, two-stage tactical trigger, 8.8 lbs. New 2014.

| MSR $1,850 | $1,675 | $1,475 | $1,250 | $1,150 | $925 | $750 | $595 | |

* **AR10A4243BF** – .243 Win. cal., 20 in. match grade chromemoly barrel, two-stage tactical trigger, anodized aluminum lower receiver, forged flat-top upper receiver with Picatinny gas block, forward assist, fixed polymer stock, includes one 5 shot and one 10 shot mag., sling 9 lbs. Disc. 2013.

| | $1,425 | $1,245 | $1,070 | $970 | $785 | $640 | $500 | $1,571 |

* **A10TBNF** – .308 Win. cal., 20 in. triple lapped stainless steel match grade barrel, forged flat-top receiver, NM two-stage trigger, Picatinny gas block, fixed polymer stock, free float handguard, pistol grip, 10 shot mag., hard anodized matte black (BNF) or green (NF, disc. 2013) finish, 10.3 lbs.

| MSR $1,914 | $1,725 | $1,525 | $1,295 | $1,175 | $950 | $775 | $600 | |

* **AR-10B Rifle** – .308 Win. cal., patterned after the early Armalite AR-10 rifle, GIO, featuring tapered M16 handguards, pistol grip, distinctive charging lever on top inside of carry handle (cannot be used to mount sighting devices), original brown color, 20 in. barrel, 9 1/2 lbs. Mfg. 1999-2008.

| | $1,495 | $1,300 | $1,125 | $1,025 | $825 | $675 | $525 | $1,698 |

* **AR10A4BF/F** – .308 Win. cal., 20 in. double lapped chrome lined chromemoly barrel with flash suppressor, two-stage tactical trigger, anodized aluminum forged flat-top upper and lower receiver, Picatinny rail gas block, 20 shot mag., adj. stock, matte black (BF) or green (F) finish, includes sling, 9 lbs. New 2013.

| MSR $1,571 | $1,425 | $1,245 | $1,070 | $970 | $785 | $640 | $500 | |

MSR	100%	98%	95%	90%	80%	70%	60%	*Last MSR*

* **AR10A4CBF/CF** – .308 Win. cal., 16 in. double lapped chrome lined chromemoly threaded barrel with flash suppressor, two-stage tactical trigger, anodized aluminum lower receiver, forged flat-top upper receiver with Picatinny rail and forward assist, adj. tactical stock, 20 shot mag., matte black (CBF) or green (CF) finish, 7 3/4 lbs. New 2013.

MSR $1,571	$1,425	$1,245	$1,070	$970	$785	$640	$500	

* **AR-10 National Match** – 7.62 NATO cal., GIO, 20 in. stainless steel match barrel with stainless A2 flash suppressor, forged flat-top receiver with Picatinny rail and forward assist, NM quad rail free float handguard, carry handle, forged lower with two-stage NM trigger, 10 shot mag., Mil Std. 1913 rail handguard, extended elevation NM sights, includes two 20 shot mags., USMC sling, black hard case, 11 1/2 lbs. Mfg. 2009-2013.

	$2,125	$1,860	$1,595	$1,445	$1,170	$955	$745	*$2,365*

AR-10SOF (SPECIAL OPERATION FORCES) CARBINE – .308 Win. cal., GIO, available in either A2 or A4 configurations, fixed tube stock, 16 in. barrel, black finish only. Mfg. 2003-2004.

	$1,250	$1,095	$940	$850	$690	$565	$440	*$1,503*

Add $52 for A2 configuration (includes Picatinny rail).

* **AR-10T Carbine (Navy Model)** – 7.62 NATO cal., similar to AR-10T Rifle, except has 16 in. stainless barrel with A2 flash suppressor, recent mfg. has flat-top receiver and Picatinny rail and round mid-length free floating handguard, Black finish, includes two 10 shot mags. and hard case, 8 1/2 lbs. Mfg. 2004-2012.

	$1,725	$1,510	$1,295	$1,175	$950	$775	$605	*$1,914*

* **AR-10T Rifle (10TCBNF)** – .243 Win. (mfg. 1995-2003, and 2009-2010), .260 Rem. (new 2009), .300 RSUM (mfg. 2004-2008, Ultra Mag Model), 7mm-08 Rem. (mfg. 2009-2010), .338 Federal (new 2009), or 7.62 NATO cal., GIO, features 20 (7.62 NATO), 22 (.338 Federal or .260 Rem.), or 24 (disc. 2008) in. stainless steel heavy match barrel, two-stage NM trigger, smooth green or black finish, black fiberglass (disc. 2008) or aluminum handguard tube, stock, and pistol grip, flat-top receiver with Picatinny rail, w/o sights or carry handle, forward bolt assist became standard in 2009, includes two 10 shot mags. and hard case, 9 1/2 - 10 1/2 lbs. Disc. 2013.

	$1,725	$1,510	$1,295	$1,175	$950	$775	$605	*$1,914*

Add $80 for .338 Federal cal.

Add $214 for .300 RSUM cal. (disc. 2008).

Add $250 for Lothar Walther barrel (disc.).

* **AR10B Target (10TBNF/NF)** – .308 Win. cal., 20 in. triple lapped stainless steel match grade barrel, forged flat-top receiver, NM two-stage trigger, Picatinny gas block, fixed polymer stock, free float handguard, pistol grip, 10 shot mag., hard anodized matte black (BNF) or green (NF, disc. 2013) finish, 10.3 lbs.

MSR $1,914	$1,725	$1,525	$1,295	$1,175	$950	$775	$600	

AR-10 SUPER SASS RIFLE (10SBF) – 7.62 NATO cal., GIO, AAC suppressor (military or law enforcement), mock AAC (disc.) or A2 flash suppressor, 20 in. triple lapped ceramic coated stainless steel threaded barrel, forged flat-top receiver with Picatinny rail, SuperSASS quad rail free floating handguard with rail covers, forged lower receiver, 20 shot mag., Magpul adj. buttstock, black finish, two-stage NM trigger, available with various accessories, includes one 10 shot mag., one 20 shot mag., USMC quick adjust sling, and sling swivel mount, 11.8 lbs.

MSR $3,100	$2,625	$2,300	$1,975	$1,785	$1,450	$1,175	$925	

* **AR-10A Super SASS Rifle (A10SBF)** – .308 Win. cal., similar to AR-10 Super SASS, except is shipped with Magpul 20 shot PMAG, 11.8 lbs. New 2012.

MSR $3,078	$2,625	$2,300	$1,975	$1,785	$1,450	$1,175	$925	

This model has magazine interchangeability with the AR-10B.

» **AR-10A Super SASS Carbine (A10SCBF)** – .308 Win. cal., similar to AR-10 Super SASS Rifle, except has 16 in. barrel, 9.1 lbs. New 2014.

MSR $3,078	$2,625	$2,300	$1,975	$1,785	$1,450	$1,175	$925	

This model has magazine interchangeability with the AR-10B.

M4A1C CARBINE – features GIO, 16 in. chrome-lined 1:9 twist heavy barrel with National Match sights and detachable carrying handle, grooved barrel shroud, 7 lbs. Disc. 1997.

	$795	$700	$600	$550	$450	$375	$275	*$935*

M4C CARBINE – similar to M4A1C Carbine, except has non-removable carrying handle and fixed sights, 7 lbs. Disc. 1997.

	$725	$650	$550	$500	$400	$325	$250	*$870*

M15 RIFLE/CARBINE VARIATIONS – .223 Rem. cal. standard unless otherwise noted, GIO, various configurations, barrel lengths, sights, and other features.

* **M15 22 LR Carbine** – .22 LR cal., GIO, 16 in. barrel with A2 flash suppressor, standard .223 lower with .22 LR upper receiver, forward assist, 6 in. handguard, Picatinny gas block. Mfg. 2011 only.

	$625	$550	$475	$425	$350	$275	$225	*$749*

MSR	100%	98%	95%	90%	80%	70%	60%	Last MSR

* **M15A4 SPR Mod 1 (15SPR1CB)** – 5.56 NATO, 6.8 SPC (mfg. 2012-2013), or 7.62x39mm (mfg. 2012-2013) cal., GIO, 16 in. chrome-lined threaded barrel with flash hider, gas block with rail, forged flat-top receiver with Picatinny rail and laser engraved rail numbering, three extra detachable rails, collapsible stock, tactical two-stage trigger, aluminum lower receiver, ARMS polymer (disc. 2013) or flip up front and rear sights, black furniture, includes one 30 shot mag., sling, and hard case, 6 1/2 lbs. New mid-2010.

| MSR $1,589 | $1,350 | $1,175 | $1,015 | $925 | $750 | $610 | $475 | |

Add $35 for mid-length free floating quad rail (disc. 2013).

Add $160 for 7.62x39mm cal. (disc. 2013).

Add $190 for 6.8 SPC cal. (disc. 2013).

* **M15A2/A4 National Match Rifle** – .223 Rem. cal., features GIO, 20 in. stainless steel NM sleeved 1:8 twist barrel with flash suppressor, forged A2 receiver with NM hooded rear sights and A2 NM clamp on front sight, forged lower with NM two-stage trigger, grooved barrel shroud, Black or Green furniture, with or w/o detachable carrying handle, includes one 30 shot mag., USMC quick adjust sling, and hard case, 9 lbs. Disc. 2013.

| | $1,195 | $1,050 | $900 | $825 | $650 | $550 | $425 | *$1,422* |

* **M15A2 Golden Eagle** – .223 Rem. cal., similiar to M15A2 National Match Rifle, except has 20 in. heavy barrel, 9.4 lbs. Limited mfg. 1998 only.

| | $1,150 | $1,000 | $875 | $775 | $650 | $525 | $400 | *$1,350* |

* **M15A2 Service Rifle** – 5.56 NATO cal., GIO, includes 20 in. chrome-lined 1:9 twist barrel, green or black furniture, forged A2 receiver, fixed stock, A2 front sight, tactical two-stage trigger, flash suppressor, carrying handle, includes one 30 shot mag., sling, and hard case, 8.2 lbs. Disc. 2013.

| | $995 | $875 | $750 | $675 | $550 | $450 | $350 | *$1,174* |

* **M15A2 Carbine** – 5.56 NATO cal., similar to M15A2 Service Rifle, except has 16 in. barrel, six-position collapsible stock with G.I. diameter extension tube, includes one 30 shot mag., sling, and hard case, 7 lbs. Disc. 2013.

| | $995 | $875 | $750 | $675 | $550 | $450 | $350 | *$1,174* |

* **M15A4 National Match SPR** – .223 Rem. cal., similar to M15A2 National Match, except has forged flat-top receiver with Picatinny rail and NM detachable carry handle, includes one 30 shot mag., USMC quick adjust sling, and hard case, 9.8 lbs. Disc. 2013.

| | $1,195 | $1,050 | $900 | $815 | $650 | $550 | $425 | *$1,435* |

* **M15A4 SPR (Special Purpose Rifle, 15A4/15A4B)** – 5.56 NATO cal., GIO, includes 20 in. chrome-lined H-Bar 1:9 twist barrel, green (15A4) or black (15A4B) finish, gas block with rail, forged flat-top receiver with Picatinny rail, tactical two-stage trigger, flash suppressor, includes one 30 shot mag., sling, and hard case, 7.8 lbs.

| MSR $1,073 | $900 | $785 | $675 | $600 | $500 | $400 | $300 | |

* **M15A4 SPR II National Match (Special Purpose Rifle)** – 5.56 NATO cal., similar to M15A4 SPR, except has triple lapped rifled barrel, strengthened free floating barrel sleeve and two-stage match trigger, green or black furniture. Mfg. 2003-2005.

| | $1,250 | $1,100 | $950 | $850 | $700 | $575 | $450 | *$1,472* |

* **M15A4 Carbine** – 5.56 NATO, 6.8 SPC (mfg. 2009-2013), or 7.62x39mm (mfg. 2009-2013) cal., similar to M15A4 Special Purpose Rifle, except has 16 in. barrel and six-position collapsible stock with G.I. diameter extension tube, green (15A4C) or black (15A4CB) furniture, includes one 10 shot mag., one 20 shot mag., sling, and hard case, 7 lbs.

| MSR $1,073 | $900 | $785 | $675 | $600 | $500 | $400 | $300 | |

Add $42 for 6.8 SPC or 7.62x39mm cal. (disc. 2013).

Subtract $60 for fixed front sight w/detachable carry handle (disc.).

* **M15A4 CBA2K** – 5.56 NATO cal., features GIO, 16 in. double lapped chrome lined barrel, flash suppressor, two-stage tactical trigger, forged flat-top receiver with Picatinny rail, A2 front sight, 8 in. mid-length handguard, forged lower receiver, six-position collapsible stock with G.I. diameter extension tube, includes one 30 shot mag., sling, and hard case, 6 1/2 lbs. Mfg. 2008-2013.

| | $875 | $775 | $650 | $600 | $475 | $400 | $300 | *$1,031* |

* **M15ARTN** – .223 Rem. cal., GIO, 20 in. stainless steel barrel, National Match trigger, green or black finish. Mfg. 2004-2007.

| | $1,095 | $950 | $825 | $750 | $600 | $500 | $385 | *$1,322* |

* **M-15T Target (15A4TBN Rifle Eagle Eye)** – .223 Rem. cal. w/Wylde chamber, GIO, 20 or 24 (disc. 2009) in. stainless steel 1:8 twist heavy barrel, two-stage NM trigger, smooth green or black fiberglass (disc. 2008) or lightweight aluminum hand guard, Picatinny front sight rail but w/o sights and carrying handle, black or green furniture, includes one 10 shot mag. and hard case, 8.6 lbs. Disc. 2005, reintroduced 2007.

| MSR $1,318 | $1,095 | $950 | $825 | $750 | $600 | $500 | $385 | |

MSR	100%	98%	95%	90%	80%	70%	60%	Last MSR

* **M-15TBN** – .223 Rem. cal., GIO, 18 in. triple lapped stainless steel match barrel, free float quad rail handguards, includes one 10 shot mag., collapsible stock, two-stage NM trigger, pistol grip, matte black finish, 7.9 lbs. New 2014.

| MSR $1,449 | $1,195 | $1,050 | $900 | $825 | $650 | $550 | $425 | |

* **M15A4T Carbine (Eagle Eye)** – features GIO, 16 in. stainless steel 1:9 twist heavy barrel, picatinny rail, smooth fiberglass handguard tube, two-stage trigger, 7.1 lbs. Mfg. 1997-2004.

| | $1,175 | $1,025 | $875 | $800 | $650 | $525 | $400 | $1,383 |

* **M15A4 Predator** – similar to M15A4T Eagle Eye, except has 1:12 twist barrel. Disc. 1996.

| | $1,125 | $985 | $845 | $765 | $625 | $500 | $400 | $1,350 |

* **M15A4 Action Master** – GIO, includes 20 in. stainless steel 1:9 twist barrel, two-stage trigger, muzzle brake, Picatinny flat-top design w/o sights or carrying handle, 9 lbs. Disc. 1997.

| | $995 | $875 | $750 | $675 | $550 | $450 | $350 | $1,175 |

* **M15SOF (Special Operation Forces) Carbine** – .223 Rem. cal., GIO, available in either A2 or A4 configurations, fixed tube stock, 16 in. barrel, black finish only. Mfg. 2003-2004.

| | $895 | $785 | $675 | $600 | $500 | $400 | $300 | $1,084 |

Add $69 for A2 configuration (includes Picatinny rail).

LEC15A4CBK (LAW ENFORCEMENT CARBINE) – 5.56 NATO cal., GIO, 16 in. double lapped chrome lined threaded barrel, forged flat-top receiver with Picatinny rail, flash suppressor, A2 front sight, 6 in. handguard, tactical two-stage trigger, six position collapsible stock with G.I. diameter extension tube, includes one 30 shot mag., sling, and hard case, 6 1/2 lbs. New 2009.

| MSR $989 | $825 | $725 | $625 | $575 | $450 | $375 | $300 | |

AR-180B – .223 Rem. cal., GPO, polymer lower receiver with formed sheet metal upper, standard AR-15 trigger group/magazine, incorporates the best features of the M15 (lower group with trigger and mag. well) and early AR-180 (gas system, which keeps propellant gas outside of the receiver) rifles, 19.8 in. barrel with integral muzzle brake, 6 lbs. Mfg. 2003-2007.

| | $625 | $550 | $475 | $425 | $350 | $275 | $225 | $750 |

For more information on the original ArmaLite AR-180 and variations, please refer to the previous ArmaLite listing.

ARMAMENT TECHNOLOGY

Previous firearms manufacturer located in Halifax, Nova Scotia, Canada 1988-2003.

Armament Technology discontinued making bolt action rifles in 2003. Currently, the company is distributing optical rifle sights only.

RIFLES: BOLT-ACTION

AT1-C24 TACTICAL RIFLE – .308 Win. or .300 Win. Mag. (disc. 2000) cal., similar to AT1-M24, except has detachable mag., adj. cheekpiece, and buttstock adj. for LOP, includes 3.5-10x30mm tactical scope and mil spec shipping case, 1/2" MOA guaranteed, available in left-hand action, 14.9 lbs. Mfg. 1998-2003.

| | $4,095 | $3,650 | $2,775 | $2,250 | $1,825 | $1,500 | $1,275 | $4,195 |

AT1-C24B TACTICAL RIFLE – .308 Win. cal., similar to AT1-C24, except is not available in left-hand, 15.9 lbs. Mfg. 2001-2003.

| | $4,250 | $3,750 | $2,850 | $2,300 | $1,850 | $1,525 | $1,300 | $4,695 |

AT1-M24 TACTICAL RIFLE – .223 Rem. (new 1998), .308 Win., or .300 Win. Mag. (disc. 2000) cal., bolt action, tactical rifle with competition tuned right-hand or left-hand Rem. 700 action, stainless steel barrel, Kevlar reinforced fiberglass stock, Harris bipod, matte black finish, competition trigger, 1/2" MOA guaranteed, 14.9 lbs. Disc. 2003.

| | $4,350 | $3,850 | $2,850 | $2,350 | $1,900 | $1,600 | $1,350 | $4,495 |

ARMAMENT TECHNOLOGY CORP.

Previous manufacturer located in Las Vegas, NV between 1972 and 1978.

RIFLES: SEMI-AUTO

In addition to the models listed below, ATC also manufactured the "Firefly II", a select fire pistol.

M-2 FIREFLY – 9mm Para. cal., unique gas delayed blowback action, collapsible stock, very limited mfg., 4 3/4 lbs.

| | $695 | $625 | $550 | $475 | $395 | $350 | $295 | |

ARMITAGE INTERNATIONAL, LTD.

Previous manufacturer until 1990 located in Seneca, SC.

MSR	100%	98%	95%	90%	80%	70%	60%	Last MSR

PISTOLS: SEMI-AUTO

SCARAB SKORPION – 9mm Para. cal., design patterned after the Czech Model 61, blowback operation, SFO, 4.63 in. barrel, matte black finish, 12 shot (standard) or 32 shot (optional) mag., 3 1/2 lbs. Mfg. in U.S. 1989-1990 only.

	$695	$625	$550	$500	$425	$375	$325	$400

Add $45 for threaded flash hider or imitation suppressor.

Only 602 Scarab Skorpions were manufactured during 1989-1990.

ARMORY USA L.L.C.

Previous manufacturer/importer until 2008, and located in Houston, TX. Previous company name was Arsenal USA LLC.

RIFLES: SEMI-AUTO

Armory USA, LLC produced a variety of AK-47/AKM/AK-74 semi-auto rifles. Early rifles used Bulgarian milled receivers, later versions were built using sheet metal receivers made in Hungary by FEG.

During 2004, Armory USA began production of 1.6 mm thick U.S. made AK receivers, which were sold as both receivers and complete rifles. Production of 1 mm thick receivers began in Jan. 2005. Models not listed here may have been assembled by other manufacturers using these receivers. During 2004, Armory USA began assembling rifles at a new factory in Kazanlak, Bulgaria. Some components were made in the U.S., in compliance with the BATFE.

Please refer to the Arsenal USA listing for pre-2004 manufactured/imported rifles.

MODEL SSR-56-2 – 7.62x39mm cal., Armory USA made 1.6mm receiver wall thickness, Poly-Tec barrel assembly, Bulgarian internal parts. Approx. 400 mfg. during 2004.

	$750	$700	$675	$650	$600	$500	$475	$500

MODEL AMD-63-2 UP – 7.62x39mm cal., Armory USA made 1.6mm receiver wall thickness, Hungarian parts, underfolding buttstock. Approx. 125 mfg. 2004.

	$950	$900	$850	$800	$700	$650	$600	$600

Add $200 for milled receiver.

MODEL SSR-85C-2 – 7.62x39mm cal., assembled in Bulgaria, marked "ISD Ltd", blonde wood and black polymer furniture. Imported 2004-2006.

	$795	$750	$700	$650	$600	$525	$475	$550

Add $100 for sidefolding buttstock (Model SSR-85C-2 SF).

MODEL SSR-74-2 – 5.45x39mm cal., assembled in Bulgaria, marked "ISD Ltd", blonde wood and black polymer furniture. Imported 2005-2008.

	$775	$725	$695	$625	$600	$525	$475	$550

ARMS LLC

Current manufacturer located in Oregon since 2008.

Arms LLC is a custom manufacturing company, dealer, and custom shop. They specialize in AR-15 and MP5 style pistols, short barrel rifles, and personal defense rifles.

PISTOLS: SEMI-AUTO

Arms LLC currently manufactures the ARMS-5 and ARMS-15 pistols. Each model is built to customer specifications. Please contact the company directly for more information including options, pricing, and availability (see Trademark Index).

RIFLES: SEMI-AUTO

Arms LLC currently manufactures the following models: ARMS-15 Classic, ARMS-15 Elite Custom, ARMS-15 Quadrail, ARMS-15 Long Range, ARMS-5 SBR, and the ARMS-5 rifle. Each model is built to customer specifications. Please contact the company directly for more information including options, pricing, and availability (see Trademark Index).

ARMS RESEARCH ASSOCIATES

Previous manufacturer until 1991, located in Stone Park, IL.

CARBINES: SEMI-AUTO

KF SYSTEM – 9mm Para. cal., 18 1/2 in. barrel, vent. barrel shroud, 20 or 36 shot mag., matte black finish, 7 1/2 lbs., select-fire NFA class III transferable only.

	$395	$350	$300	$275	$250	$230	$210	$379

MSR	100%	98%	95%	90%	80%	70%	60%	Last MSR

ARMS ROOM LLC

Current manufacturer of pistols and AR-15 style carbines/rifles located in Orlando, FL.

CARBINES: SEMI-AUTO

All rifles are 100% American made and include a custom presentation box, mil-spec cleaning kit, Magpul 30 shot mag., gun lock, operator's manual and a lifetime warranty.

TAR-15 BOOT CARBINE – 5.56 NATO cal., carbine length GIO, 16 in. chromemoly barrel, M4 barrel profile, fixed front sight base, black anodized finish, A2 flash hider, double heat shield handguards, M16 bolt carrier group, flat-top upper with M4 cuts, Magpul Gen 2 rear flip up sight, mil-spec upper and lower parts, M4 stock and buffer tube.

| MSR $995 | $850 | $750 | $650 | $575 | $475 | $385 | $300 | |

TAR-15 GRUNT CARBINE – 5.56 NATO cal., GIO, 16 in. chromemoly barrel, M4 barrel profile, fixed front sight base, black anodized finish, A2 flash hider, two-piece drop in quad rail, M16 bolt carrier group, flat-top upper with M4 cuts, Magpul Gen 2 rear flip up sight, Arms Room lower receiver, mil-spec upper and lower parts, Rogers Super stock and buffer tube, Magpul MOE Plus grip.

| MSR $1,135 | $975 | $850 | $725 | $665 | $535 | $440 | $340 | |

TAR-15 SAPPER CARBINE – 5.56 NATO cal., GIO, 16 in. chromemoly barrel, M4 barrel profile, Magpul MBUS folding front and rear sights, black anodized finish, Phantom flash hider, free float quad rail, M16 bolt carrier group, flat-top upper with M4 cuts, Arms Room lower receiver, mil-spec upper and lower parts, M4 stock and buffer tube, M4 grip, front sight adj. tool.

| MSR $1,125 | $950 | $825 | $725 | $650 | $525 | $430 | $335 | |

TAR-15 SCOUT CARBINE – 5.56 NATO cal., GIO, 16 in. chromemoly barrel, M4 barrel profile, Magpul MBUS folding front and rear sights, black anodized finish, twisted Phantom flash hider, free float quad rail, M16 bolt carrier group, flat-top upper with M4 cuts, Arms Room lower receiver, mil-spec upper and lower parts, Rogers Super stock and mil-spec buffer tube, ERGO or Magpul MOE grip, front sight adj. tool.

| MSR $1,215 | $1,025 | $895 | $775 | $695 | $565 | $460 | $360 | |

ZMB-02 ZOMBIE KILLER CARBINE – 5.56 NATO cal., GIO, 16 in. chromemoly barrel, black and green two-tone finish, Phantom flash hider, OD or BLK quad rail, front and rear sights, pistol grip and magazine, M16 bolt carrier group, M4 cut, mil-spec upper and lower parts, Rogers Super stock and mil-spec buffer tube, laser etched ejection port door, Zombie engraved logo with color fill, "LIVE - DEAD - UNDEAD" selector designations, includes soft case.

| MSR $1,324 | $1,125 | $985 | $850 | $775 | $625 | $500 | $395 | |

PISTOLS: SEMI-AUTO

SPIKE'S TACTICAL PISTOL – .22 LR cal., GIO, SA, mil spec parkerized finish, 16 in. barrel, chromemoly match grade air gauged Lothar Walther M4 upper, Arms Room or Spike's Tactical lower, receiver end cap, no rear sight or optional MBUS Magpul or Daniel Defense rear sight, heat treated bolt, M4 or Magpul AFG handguard w/Ergo bolt-on rail.

| MSR $775 | $660 | $580 | $495 | $450 | $365 | $295 | $230 | |

Add $50 for MBUS Magpul or $60 for Daniel Defense rear sight.
Add $25 for Spike's Tactical lower.
Add $35 for Magpul AFG handguard.

ARMS TECH LTD.

Current manufacturer established in 1987, and located in Phoenix, AZ.

RIFLES: BOLT ACTION

Current models include the SMIR ($9,000 MSR), TTR-50 ($9,000 MSR), TTR-700 ($4,500 MSR), USR ($3,000 MSR), Voyager ($3,000 MSR), and the Overwatch ($3,500 MSR). The SBA 2000 model was offered until 2012. Arms Tech Ltd. also offers a wide variety of options and accessories. Please contact the company directly for more information, including options and availability (see Trademark Index).

RIFLES: SEMI-AUTO

Current models include several models available for military/law enforcement, including the Compak-16 and the Recon Rifle. Previously, the company offered the Urban Support Rifle for the civilian marketplace. Please contact the company directly for more information, including pricing and availability for law enforcement and military models (see Trademark Index).

SUPER MATCH INTERDICTION POLICE MODEL – .243 Win., .300 Win. Mag., or .308 Win. (standard) cal., GIO, features 22 in. free floating Schnieder or Douglas air gauged stainless steel barrel, McMillan stock, updated trigger group, detachable box mag., 13 1/4 lbs. Limited mfg. 1996-98.

| | $3,950 | $3,650 | $3,300 | $3,000 | $2,750 | $2,350 | $2,000 | $4,800 |

MSR	100%	98%	95%	90%	80%	70%	60%	Last MSR

SHOTGUNS: SLIDE ACTION

Currently, Arms Tech Ltd. offers the Alpha Entry, utilizing the Rem. 870 action, with a folding stock. Previously, the company offered another folding stock model called the Hammer. Please contact the company directly regarding pricing and availability (see Trademark Index).

ARMSCOR

Current trademark of firearms manufactured by Arms Corporation of the Philippines (manufacturing began 1952) established in 1985 (Armscor Precision - API). Currently imported and distributed beginning 1999 by Armscor Precision International (full line), located in Pahrump, NV. Previously imported 1995-1999 by K.B.I., Inc. located in Harrisburg, PA, by Ruko located in Buffalo, NY until 1995 and by Armscorp Precision Inc. located in San Mateo, CA until 1991.

In 1991, the importation of Arms Corporation of the Philippines firearms was changed to Ruko Products, Inc., located in Buffalo, NY. Barrel markings on firearms imported by Ruko Products, Inc. state "Ruko-Armscor" instead of the older "Armscorp Precision" barrel markings. All Armscorp Precision, Inc. models were discontinued in 1991.

The models listed also provide cross-referencing for older Armscorp Precision and Ruko imported models.

PISTOLS: SEMI-AUTO

All semi-auto pistols were discontinued during 2008, and currently Armscor manufactured pistols can be found under the Rock Island Armory trademark.

M-1911-A1 FS (FULL SIZE STANDARD) – .45 ACP cal., patterned after the Colt Govt. Model, SA, 7 shot mag. (2 provided), 5 in. barrel, parkerized (disc. 2001), blue (new 2002), two-tone (new 2002), or stainless steel (new 2002), skeletonized combat hammer and trigger, front and rear slide serrations, hard rubber grips, 38 oz. Imported 1996-97, reintroduced 2001-2008.

	100%	98%	95%	90%	80%	70%	60%	Last MSR
	$350	$300	$280	$260	$240	$220	$200	*$399*

Add $31 for two-tone finish.
Add $75 for stainless steel.

This model was also available in a high capacity configuration (Model 1911-A2 HC, 13 shot mag., $519 last MSR).

M-1911-A1 MS (COMMANDER) – .45 ACP cal., SA, Commander configuration with 4 in. barrel, otherwise similar to M-1911 A1 Standard, rear slide serrations only. Imported 2001-2008.

	100%	98%	95%	90%	80%	70%	60%	Last MSR
	$360	$300	$280	$260	$240	$220	$200	*$408*

Add $37 for two-tone finish.
Add $90 for stainless steel.

M-1911-A1 CS (OFFICER) – .45 ACP cal., SA, officer's configuration with 3 1/2 in. barrel, checkered hardwood grips, 2.16 lbs. Imported 2002-2008.

	100%	98%	95%	90%	80%	70%	60%	Last MSR
	$370	$310	$285	$265	$245	$220	$200	*$423*

Add $52 for two-tone finish.
Add $105 for stainless steel.

M-1911-A1 MEDALLION SERIES – 9mm Para., .40 S&W, or .45 ACP cal., 5 in. barrel, SA, customized model including many shooting enhancements, match barrel, hand fitted slide and frame, choice of checkered wood or Pachmayr grips, available in either Standard or Tactical variation, blue, two-tone or chrome finish. Imported 2002-2008.

	100%	98%	95%	90%	80%	70%	60%	Last MSR
	$445	$350	$310	$285	$260	$240	$220	*$539*

Add $129 for Tactical Model, add $198 for Tactical Model two-tone, or $203 for Tactical Model chrome.

RIFLES: SEMI-AUTO

M-1600 – .22 LR cal., GIO, 10 or 15 (disc.) shot mag., 18 in. barrel, copy of the Armalite M16, ebony stock, 5 1/4 lbs.

	100%	98%	95%	90%	80%	70%	60%	Last MSR
No MSR	$180	$150	$130	$110	$100	$80	$70	

* **M-1600R** – similar to M-1600, except has stainless steel retractable buttstock and vent. barrel hood, 7 1/4 lbs. Importation disc. 1995, reintroduced 2008-2011.

	100%	98%	95%	90%	80%	70%	60%	Last MSR
	$155	$135	$115	$105	$85	$70	$55	

M-AK22(S) – .22 LR cal., copy of the famous Russian Kalashnikov AK-47 rifle, 18 1/2 in. barrel, 10 or 15 (disc.) shot mag., mahogany stock and forearm, 7 lbs.

	100%	98%	95%	90%	80%	70%	60%	Last MSR
No MSR	$185	$160	$140	$125	$100	$85	$65	

* **M-AK22(F)** – similar to M-AK22, except has metal folding stock, and 30 shot mag. Disc. 1995.

	100%	98%	95%	90%	80%	70%	60%	Last MSR
	$275	$240	$205	$185	$150	$125	$95	*$299*

MIG 22 STANDARD – .22 LR cal., GIO, 18 in. barrel, blowback action, 15 shot detachable box mag., matte black finish, fixed synthetic stock, top Picatinny rail. New mid-2012.

As this edition went to press, pricing was not available on this model.

MSR	100%	98%	95%	90%	80%	70%	60%	Last MSR

MIG 22 TARGET – .22 LR cal., GIO, 18 in. heavy barrel, blowback action, 15 shot detachable box mag., matte black finish, skeletonized aluminum stock, top Picatinny rail, 8 lbs. New mid-2012.

As this edition went to press, pricing was not available on this model.

SHOTGUNS: SLIDE ACTION

M-30 DG (DEER GUN) – 12 ga. only, law enforcement version of M-30, 20 in. plain barrel, iron sights, 7 shot mag., approx. 7 lbs. Importation disc. 1999, resumed during 2001.

	$165	$140	$120	$100	$85	$75	$70	$195

M-30SAS1 – 12 ga. only, riot configuration with 20 in. barrel and vent. barrel shroud, and Speedfeed 4 shot (disc.) or 6 shot mag., regular synthetic buttstock and forearm, matte finish, 8 lbs. Imported 1996-1999 and 2001-2008.

	$180	$155	$130	$110	$95	$85	$75	$211

Add $56 for Speedfeed stock (new 2002).

M-30 R6/R8 (RIOT) – 12 ga. only, similar to M-30DG, except has front bead sight only, 5 or 7 shot mag., cyl. bore. Importation disc. 1999, reintroduced 2001-2008.

	$155	$135	$110	$90	$80	$75	$70	$181

Add $7 for 7 shot mag.

M-30BG – 12 ga. only, 18 1/2 in. barrel, 5 shot mag., polymer pistol grip and forearm. New 2004.

This model is currently not being imported into the United States.

M-30F/FS – similar to M-30BG, except has additional folding metal stock unit. Disc. 2008.

	$180	$155	$130	$110	$95	$85	$75	$211

M30 C (COMBO) – 12 ga., 20 in. barrel, 5 shot mag., unique detachable black synthetic buttstock which allows pistol grip only operation. Disc. 1995.

	$210	$175	$145	$120	$100	$90	$80	$289

M30 RP (COMBO) – 12 ga. only, same action as M-30 DG, interchangeable black pistol grip, 18 1/4 in. plain barrel w/front bead sight, 6 1/4 lbs. Disc. 1995.

	$210	$175	$145	$120	$100	$90	$80	$289

ARMSCORP USA, INC.

Previous manufacturer and importer located in Baltimore, MD. Currently Armscorp USA deals in parts only.

PISTOLS: SEMI-AUTO

HI POWER – 9mm Para. cal., patterned after Browning design, 4 2/3 in. barrel, DA/SA, military finish, 13 shot mag., synthetic checkered grips, spur hammer, 2 lbs. mfg. in Argentina, imported 1989-90 only.

	$395	$350	$295	$275	$250	$225	$200	$450

Add $15 for round hammer.
Add $50 for hard chrome finish w/combat grips (disc. 1989).

RIFLES: SEMI-AUTO

M-14 RIFLE (NORINCO PARTS) – .308 Win. cal., 20 shot mag., mfg. M-14 using Norinco parts, wood stock. Mfg. 1991-92 only.

	$1,225	$1,150	$1,050	$975	$875	$775	$675	$688

M-14R RIFLE (USGI PARTS) – .308 Win. cal., 10 (C/B 1994) or 20* shot mag., newly manufactured M-14 using original excellent condition forged G.I. parts including USGI fiberglass stock with rubber recoil pad. Mfg. 1986-2006.

	$1,925	$1,675	$1,400	$1,275	$1,125	$1,000	$850	$1,895

Add $80 for medium weight National Match walnut stock (M-14RNS).
Add $25 for G.I. buttplate (disc.).
Add $45 for USGI birch stock (M-14RNSB, disc.).

M-14 BEGINNING NATIONAL MATCH – .308 Win. cal., mfg. from hand selected older USGI parts, except for new receiver and new USGI air gauged premium barrel, guaranteed to shoot 1 1/4 in. group at 100 yards. Mfg. 1993-96.

	$2,050	$1,650	$1,350	$1,225	$1,125	$1,025	$925	$1,950

M-14 NMR (NATIONAL MATCH) – .308 Win. cal., built in accordance with USAMU mil spec standards, 3 different barrel weights to choose from, NM rear sight system, calibrated mag., leather sling, guaranteed 1 MOA. Mfg. 1987-2006.

	$2,675	$2,125	$1,750	$1,400	$1,200	$1,075	$950	$2,850

M-21 MATCH RIFLE – .308 Win. cal., NM rear lugged receiver, choice of McMillan fiberglass or laminated wood stock, guaranteed 1 MOA accuracy.

	$3,475	$2,900	$2,325	$2,000	$1,650	$1,350	$1,175	$3,595

MSR	100%	98%	95%	90%	80%	70%	60%	Last MSR

T-48 FAL ISRAELI PATTERN RIFLE – .308 Win. cal., mfg. in the U.S. to precise original metric dimensions (parts are interchangeable with original Belgium FAL), forged receiver, hammer forged chrome lined mil spec. 21 in. barrel (standard or heavy) with flash suppressor, adj. front sight, aperture rear sight, 10 lbs. Imported 1990-92.

| | $1,650 | $1,475 | $1,300 | $1,150 | $1,075 | $975 | $875 | $1,244 |

This model was guaranteed to shoot within 2.5 MOA with match ammunition.

* ***T-48 FAL L1A1 Pattern*** – .308 Win. cal., fully enclosed forend with vents, 10 lbs. Imported 1992 only.

| | $1,675 | $1,500 | $1,325 | $1,175 | $1,100 | $1,000 | $900 | $1,181 |

Add $122 for wood handguard sporter model (limited supply).

* ***T-48 Bush Model*** – similar to T-48 FAL, except has 18 in. barrel, 9 3/4 lbs. Mfg. 1990 only.

| | $1,625 | $1,450 | $1,325 | $1,175 | $1,025 | $925 | $850 | $1,250 |

FRHB – .308 Win. cal., Israeli mfg. with heavy barrel and bipod. Imported 1990 only.

| | $2,175 | $1,900 | $1,600 | $1,425 | $1,325 | $1,225 | $1,175 | $1,895 |

FAL – .308 Win. cal., Armscorp forged receiver, 21 in. Argentinian rebuilt barrel, manufactured to military specs., supplied with one military 20 shot mag., aperture rear sight, 10 lbs. Mfg. 1987-89.

| | $1,800 | $1,575 | $1,425 | $1,250 | $1,125 | $1,025 | $925 | $875 |

Subtract $55 if without flash hider.
Add $75 for heavy barrel with bipod (14 lbs.).
Add $400 (last retail) for .22 LR conversion kit.

This model was guaranteed to shoot within 2.5 MOA with match ammunition.

* ***FAL Bush Model*** – similar to FAL, except has 18 in. barrel with flash suppressor, 9 3/4 lbs. Mfg. 1989 only.

| | $2,200 | $2,050 | $1,925 | $1,825 | $1,750 | $1,500 | $1,250 | $900 |

* ***FAL Para Model*** – similar to FAL Bush Model, except has metal folding stock, leaf rear sight. Mfg. 1989 only.

| | $2,400 | $2,150 | $1,050 | $1,950 | $1,750 | $1,650 | $1,550 | $930 |

* ***FAL Factory Rebuilt*** – factory (Argentine) rebuilt FAL without flash suppressor in excellent condition with Armscorp forged receiver, 9 lbs. 10 oz. Disc. 1989.

| | $1,675 | $1,450 | $1,195 | $1,025 | $950 | $775 | $695 | $675 |

Add 20% for heavy barrel variation manufactured in Argentina under license from F.N.

M36 ISRAELI SNIPER RIFLE – .308 Win. cal., gas operated semi-auto, bullpup configuration, 22 in. free floating barrel, Armscorp M14 receiver, 20 shot mag., includes flash suppressor and bipod, 10 lbs. Civilian offering 1989 only.

| | $3,050 | $2,650 | $2,425 | $2,200 | $2,050 | $1,925 | $1,750 | $3,000 |

ARSENAL, BULGARIA

Current manufacturer located in Kazanlack, Bulgaria. Currently imported by Arsenal, Inc., located in Las Vegas, NV. Previously imported exclusively in 1994-1996 by Sentinel Arms located in Detroit, MI. For currently imported models, please refer to the Arsenal, Inc. listing.

The artillery arsenal in Rousse began operating in 1878, and was managed by Russian officers until 1884, when a Bulgarian was appointed the director. In 1891, the factory was transferred to Sofia, and was renamed the Sofia Artillery Arsenal until the entire facility was moved to Kazanlak in 1924. At that point, the name was changed to the State Military Factory. After WWII, the arsenal diversified into civilian production, and its Cold War security name was "Factory 10". In 1958, the first AK-47 design under Russian license came off the assembly line, and in 1982, the one millionth AK-47 had been manufactured.

RIFLES: SEMI-AUTO

BULGARIAN SA-93 – 7.62x39mm cal., Kalashnikov with hardwood thumbhole stock, 16.3 in. barrel, 5 shot detachable mag., 9 lbs. Disc. 1996.

| | $800 | $715 | $625 | $550 | $600 | $475 | $450 | |

* ***Bulgarian SA-93L*** – 7.62x39mm cal., similar to Bulgarian SA-93 except has 20 in. barrel, with or without optics, 9 lbs. Disc. 1996.

| | $795 | $725 | $650 | $595 | $550 | $495 | $450 | |

Add $145 with optics.

BULGARIAN SS-94 – 7.62x39mm cal., Kalashnikov action, thumbhole hardwood stock, 5 shot detachable mag., 9 lbs. Disc. 1996.

| | $625 | $550 | $475 | $425 | $375 | $350 | $325 | |

MSR		100%	98%	95%	90%	80%	70%	60%	*Last MSR*

ARSENAL FIREARMS

Current pistol manufacturer located in Gardone, Italy. Currently imported beginning late 2013 by EAA Corp., located in Rockledge, FL. Previously distributed by Apex International, located in Middletown, CT.

PISTOLS: SEMI-AUTO

AF2011-DOUBLE BARREL PISTOL – .38 Super or .45 ACP cal., unique design allows side by side 4.92 in. barrels, double hammer with single spur, double independent or single trigger uses two single 8 shot magazines paired together with single floorplate, choice of blue steel with walnut grips and fixed sights, or stainless steel with rubber grips and adj. sights, approx. 51 oz. New 2012.

	MSR $4,400	$3,995	$3,550	$3,100	$2,750	$2,300	$2,100	$1,950	

Add $700 for stainless steel construction with rubber grips and adj. sights.

STRIKE ONE – 9mm Para. cal., 5 in. barrel, 17 shot mag., matte black finish, lower accessory rail, fully guided, non-tilting barrel locking system, beveled magwell, ambidextrous mag. release, short travel trigger, approx. 27 oz. New 2013.

As this edition went to press, prices had yet to be established on this model.

ARSENAL INC.

Current importer of non-military Arsenal 2000 JSCo (Bulgarian Arsenal), established during 2001 and located in Las Vegas, NV. Dealer and distributor sales.

PISTOLS: SEMI-AUTO

SAM7K – 7.62x39mm cal., GPO, 10 1/2 in. chrome lined cold hammer forged barrel, SA, milled receiver, short gas system, front sight block/gas block combination, 5 shot mag., black polymer furniture, original pistol grip with ambidextrous safety lever, aperture rear sight, AK scope rail, includes sling and cleaning kit. Limited importation 2013.

		$1,025	$895	$775	$695	$565	$460	$360	*$1,199*

SLR-106U/UR – 5.56 NATO cal., GIO, 10 1/2 in. chrome lined hammer forged barrel, SA, front sight block, gas block combination, faux flash hider, 5 shot mag., stamped receiver, black polymer furniture, includes sling and cleaning kit, 5 1/2 lbs. Imported 2013.

		$875	$775	$650	$595	$475	$395	$300	*$1,025*

RIFLES: SEMI-AUTO

Arsenal Inc. is the exclusive licensed manufacturer of various Arsenal Bulgaria AK-47 design rifles which conform 100% to Arsenal Bulgaria specifications and manufacturing procedures. Models are built on forged and milled receivers with CNC technology, and feature solid, under-folding or side-folding stock.

Additionally, Arsenal Inc. has also imported AK-47 design configurations with a thumbhole stock design (pre-2004). Values for these earlier models will be slightly less than current models with fixed or collapsible stocks.

SA M-5 SERIES – .223 Rem. cal., patterned after the AK-47, 16.3 in. barrel, black (SA M-5) or green (SA M-5G, disc. 2005) synthetic furniture with pistol grip, approx. 8.1 lbs. Mfg. 2003-2009.

		$710	$620	$530	$480	$390	$320	$250	*$800*

Add $75 for SA M-5 R with scope rail (new 2007).
Add $10 for SA M-5G (disc. 2005).
Add $75 for SA M-5S with scope rail (limited edition, disc. 2005).
Add $80 for SA M-5SG (disc. 2005).

SA M-7 S – 7.62x39mm cal., milled receiver, also available in carbine, otherwise similar to SA M-5, R Series with scope rail became standard 2009. Mfg. 2003-2011.

		$1,395	$1,295	$1,050	$850	$750	$650	$550	*$1,550*

Add $35 for SA M-7S with scope rail (disc.).
Add $5 for SA M-7G with OD green furniture (disc.)
Add $40 for SA M-7SG with scope rail (disc.)
Subtract approx. 15% if w/o scope rail (disc.)

SA M-7 CLASSIC – 7.62x39mm cal., features blonde wood stock, pistol grip and forearm, double stack magazine, heavy barrel and slanted gas block, Warsaw Pact buttstock, less than 200 mfg. 2001-2002, reintroduced 2007.

	MSR $1,995	$1,750	$1,500	$1,250	$1,125	$900	$775	$650	

SA M-7 A1/SA M-7 A1 R – 7.62x39mm cal., milled receiver, front sight gas block w/bayonet lug, 24mm flash hider, cleaning rod, accessory lug, black polymer furniture, NATO buttstock. Mfg. 2007-2009.

		$850	$745	$635	$580	$465	$380	$295	*$960*

Add $75 for SA M-7 A1 R w/scope rail.

MSR	100%	98%	95%	90%	80%	70%	60%	Last MSR

SA M-7 R – 7.62x39mm cal., 14mm muzzle threads, muzzle nut, cleaning rod, bayonet lug, black polymer furniture, NATO buttstock, scope rail. New 2012.

| MSR $2,000 | $1,750 | $1,500 | $1,250 | $1,125 | $900 | $775 | $650 | |

SA M-7 SF – 7.62x39mm cal., U.S. mfg., 16.3 in. cold hammer forged barrel, milled receiver, front sight gas block with bayonet lug, 24mm flash hider, cleaning rod, accessory lug, black polymer furniture, right hand side folding stock, ambidextrous safety, scope rail. Mfg. 2007-2009, reintroduced 2013.

| MSR $1,650 | $1,400 | $1,225 | $1,050 | $950 | $775 | $650 | $495 | |

SA M-7 SFC/SA M-7 SFK – 7.62x39mm cal., U.S. mfg., milled receiver, front sight/gas block combination with 24mm thread protector, cleaning rod, black polymer furniture, right hand side folding tubular buttstock, ambidextrous safety, scope rail, SA M-7 SFK model with short gas system and laminated wood Krinkov handguards became standard 2009. Mfg. 2007-2011, limited production SFK SBR model reintroduced 2013.

| MSR $3,200 | $2,725 | $2,395 | $2,050 | $1,850 | $1,500 | $1,225 | $950 | |

SA RPK-3R – 5.45x39mm, milled receiver, RPK heavy barrel, removable flash hider, folding bipod, blonde wood furniture or black polymer, paddle style buttstock, scope rail, one 45 shot mag., sling, oil bottle, and cleaning kit. Mfg. 2011 only.

| | $2,250 | $1,950 | $1,750 | $1,500 | $1,250 | $1,000 | $850 | $2,500 |

SA RPK-5 (S) – .223 Rem. cal., features blonde wood stock, RPK heavy barrel, 14mm muzzle threads, pistol grip and forearm, 23 1/4 in. barrel with folding tripod, approx. 11 lbs. Limited edition 2003-2005, reintroduced 2007-2011, SA RPK-5 R model with scope rail reintroduced 2013.

| MSR $2,500 | $2,125 | $1,875 | $1,595 | $1,450 | $1,175 | $950 | $750 | |

SA RPK-7 – 7.62x39mm cal., paddle style buttstock, folding bipod, no scope rail, otherwise similar to SA RPK-5 (S). Limited edition 2003-2005, reintroduced 2007-2009.

| | $995 | $870 | $745 | $675 | $545 | $450 | $350 | $1,250 |

Add $75 for SA RPK-7 R with scope rail.

SAS M-7 – 7.62x39mm cal., U.S. mfg., authentic semi-auto version of Bulgarian model AR M1F with vertical gas block and BATFE-approved fixed metal underfolding-style stock. Mfg. 2004-2007.

| | $1,075 | $940 | $800 | $730 | $590 | $485 | $375 | $1,250 |

SAS M-7 CLASSIC – 7.62x39mm cal., U.S. mfg., authentic semi-auto version of Russian 1953 Model AKS-47 with slant gas block and BATFE-approved fixed metal underfolding-style stock, blonde furniture, heavy barrel. Limited edition 2001-2002, reintroduced 2007.

| MSR $1,995 | $1,750 | $1,500 | $1,250 | $1,125 | $900 | $775 | $650 | |

SLR 101 S – 7.62x39mm cal., similar to SA M-7, except has thumbhole synthetic stock, available in black (SLR 101SB1) or OD Green (SLR 101SG1). Mfg. 2003-2005.

| | $595 | $550 | $500 | $450 | $400 | $350 | $325 | $410 |

Add $100 for SLR 101SB1.
Add $110 for SLR 101SG1.

* **SLR-101S (Recent Importation)** – 7.62x39mm cal., 16 1/4 in. chrome lined hammer forged barrel, milled receiver, 14mm muzzle threads, muzzle brake, cleaning rod, black polymer furniture, intermediate length buttstock, scope rail, 10 shot mag., includes sling and cleaning kit. Imported 2013.

| | $875 | $775 | $650 | $595 | $475 | $395 | $300 | $1,019 |

SLR 101SB/SG – 7.62x39mm cal., double stack mag., side mount scope rail, 16 in. barrel, standard military stock configuration. Mfg. 2004-2005.

| | $725 | $635 | $545 | $495 | $400 | $325 | $255 | $655 |

Add $45 for SG Model with green polymer stock.

SLR-104 SERIES – 5.45x39mm cal., 16 1/4 in. chrome lined hammer forged barrel with removable muzzle brake, bayonet lug, accessory lug, black left-side folding stock, stamped receiver, stainless steel heat shield, scope rail, 30 shot mag., two-stage trigger. Importation began late 2013.

| MSR $1,099 | $950 | $825 | $715 | $650 | $525 | $450 | $400 | |

Add $150 for SLR-104 UR model with front sight block and gas block combination (imported 2013 only).

SLR-105 SERIES – 5.45x39.5mm cal., stamped receiver, cleaning rod, black polymer furniture, NATO buttstock. Mfg. 2007-2009.

| | $695 | $650 | $600 | $550 | $475 | $425 | $350 | $475 |

Add $50 for SLR-105 R with scope rail.
Add $150 for SLR-105 A1 model with front sight gas block, bayonet lug, and 24mm muzzle brake.
Add $200 for SLR-105 A1 R model with scope rail.

MSR		100%	98%	95%	90%	80%	70%	60%	Last MSR

SLR-106 SERIES – 5.56 NATO cal., stamped receiver, left-side wire (disc. 2011) or solid black polymer (new 2012) folding stock, 24mm muzzle brake, gas block with bayonet lug, accessory lug (optional), stainless steel heat shield, two-stage trigger, Black or Desert Sand. Imported 2007-2013.

		100%	98%	95%	90%	80%	70%	60%	Last MSR
		$900	$795	$675	$615	$495	$400	$315	*$1,080*

Add $30 for Desert Sand finish and side scope rail.
Add $50 for SLR-106 CR with front sight and gas block combined (new 2012).
Add $50 for SLR-106 FR with scope and forend rails.
Subtract approx. $250 if with wire folding stock (disc. 2011).
Add $205 for SLR-106 UR Model with scope rail.
Add $199 for SLR-106 U Model with combination short-stroke gas block and front sight system and black furniture.
Add $179 for SLR-106 Model with removable muzzle attachment (disc.).
The SLR-106 UR Model is also available as a short barreled rifle.

SLR-107 SERIES – 7.62x39mm cal., stamped receiver, left-side wire (disc. 2011) folding solid polymer (new 2012) stock, 24mm flash hider, gas block with bayonet lug, accessory lug, stainless steel heat shield, two-stage trigger, Black or Desert Sand finish. New 2008.

MSR $1,099		100%	98%	95%	90%	80%	70%	60%	
		$950	$825	$715	$650	$525	$450	$400	

Add $110 for forend rail.
Add $6 for Desert Sand finish.
Subtract $149 for left-side folding stock (Model SLR-107F).
Subtract $149 for SLR-107 FR Model with scope rail.
Subtract $149 for SLR-107 UR Model with combination short-stroke gas block and front sight system and black furniture and scope rail.
The SLR-107 UR Model is also available as a short barreled rifle.

ARSENAL USA LLC

Previous manufacturer/importer from 1999-2004, and located in Houston, TX. During September 2004, Arsenal USA LLC changed its name to Armory USA L.L.C. Please refer to the Armory USA L.L.C. listing for recently manufactured rifles.

RIFLES: SEMI-AUTO

MODEL SSR-99 – 7.62x39mm cal., Bulgarian milled receiver and parts, black polymer furniture. Less than 300 mfg. 1999-2000.

		$825	$750	$700	$650	$600	$550	$500	*$600*

MODEL K-101 – .223 Rem. cal., Bulgarian milled receiver and parts, black polymer furniture. Less than 200 mfg. 1999-2000.

		$875	$775	$700	$650	$600	$550	$500	*$600*

MODEL SSR-99P – 7.62x39mm cal., Bulgarian milled receiver and parts, with rare Polish grenade launching variant parts, Polish wood furniture. Less than 500 mfg. 1999-2001.

		$875	$775	$700	$650	$600	$550	$500	*$600*

MODEL SSR-85B – 7.62x39mm cal., Hungarian FEG receiver and Polish AKM parts, blond Hungarian wood furniture, small number produced using ITM U.S. made receiver. Approx. 1,200 mfg. 2000-2003.

		$875	$775	$700	$650	$600	$550	$500	*$450*

MODEL AMD-63 – 7.62x39mm cal., Hungarian FEG receiver and Polish AKM parts, unique metal lower handguard with pistol grip. 200 mfg. 2000-2003.

		$875	$775	$700	$650	$600	$550	$500	*$600*

MODEL SSR-56 – 7.62x39mm cal., Hungarian FEG receiver, Poly-Tec barrel assembly and Bulgarian internal parts. Approx. 500 mfg. 2002-2003.

		$775	$700	$650	$600	$550	$500	$450	*$450*

ASHBURY PRECISION ORDNANCE

Current manufacturer established in 1995 and located in Charlottesville, VA. APO is a division of the Ashbury International Group, Inc. Consumer direct sales.

RIFLES: BOLT ACTION

Ashbury Precision Ordnance (APO) makes a high quality line of precision tactical rifles called the Asymmetric Warrior Series (ASW) and a Tactical Competition Rifle Series (TCR). Specifications, features, and options vary from model to model, so please contact the manufacturer directly for more information and current availability (see Trademark Index).

MSR	100%	98%	95%	90%	80%	70%	60%	Last MSR

ASW50 – .50 BMG cal., McMillan bolt action repeater, Pinnacle Series 27 in. stainless steel barrel with integrated muzzle brake and suppressor system, ambidextrous paddle lever magazine release, 5 shot detachable box mag., Huber Tactical two stage trigger, Quattro carbon fiber heat/Mirage Mitigating Ergonomic forend, fully adj. PBA-H shoulder stock, Limbsaver recoil pad and grip, ErgoGrip Magpul M1AD grip set, Picatinny bottom accessory rail, Black, Flat Dark Earth, OD Green, or Nordic Gray finish, 25 3/4 lbs.

	100%	98%	95%	90%	80%	70%	60%	Last MSR
MSR $12,575	$11,250	$10,000	$9,200	$8,000	$6,750	$5,500	$4,500	

ASW338LM – .338 Lapua Mag. cal., Surgeon XL-II bolt action repeater, similar to ASW50 except has Pinnacle Series 20 or 27 in. stainless steel barrel, target crown with AAC Blackout muzzle brake, and detachable 5 or 10 shot box mag. 14 lbs.

MSR $8,550	$7,850	$7,100	$6,400	$5,500	$4,600	$3,700	$2,850	

Add $200 for 10 shot mag.

ASW300 – .300 Win. Mag. cal., similar to ASW338, except has 24 in. stainless steel barrel.

MSR $8,500	$7,825	$7,100	$6,400	$5,500	$4,600	$3,700	$2,850	

Add $250 for 10 shot detachable box mag.

ASW308 – .308 Win. Mag. cal., similar to ASW338, except has 20 in. stainless steel barrel, and 10 shot detachable box mag. only, approx. 12 1/2 lbs.

MSR $7,700	$7,000	$6,200	$5,500	$4,700	$4,000	$3,250	$2,550	

ASW223 – .223 Rem. cal., otherwise similar to ASW308. New 2012.

MSR $7,700	$7,000	$6,200	$5,500	$4,700	$4,000	$3,250	$2,550	

TCR338 – .338 Norma Mag. cal., Surgeon bolt action repeater, Pinnacle Series 27 in. stainless steel barrel with Badger FTE muzzle brake, ambidextrous paddle lever magazine release, 5 shot detachable box mag., Huber Tactical two stage trigger, integral scope rail, Quattro carbon fiber heat/Mirage Mitigating Ergonomic forend, hand tool adj. (HTA) shoulder stock, Limbsaver recoil pad and grip, ErgoGrip Magpul M1AD grip set, 4 in. Picatinny top and bottom accessory rail, Black, Flat Dark Earth, OD Green, or Nordic Gray finish.

MSR $7,295	$6,650	$5,750	$5,000	$4,200	$3,500	$2,850	$2,300	

TCR223 – .223. Rem. cal., similar to TCR338, except has 20 in. barrel, and 10 shot detachable box mag. New 2012.

MSR $6,325	$5,650	$5,100	$4,500	$3,900	$3,300	$2,700	$2,100	

TCR260 – .260 Rem. cal., similar to TCR338, except has 24 in. barrel and 10 shot detachable box mag.

MSR $6,325	$5,650	$5,100	$4,500	$3,900	$3,300	$2,700	$2,100	

TCR300 – .300 Win. Mag. cal., similar to TCR338, except has a 24 in. barrel.

MSR $7,295	$6,650	$5,750	$5,000	$4,200	$3,500	$2,850	$2,300	

TCR308 – .308 Win. Mag. cal., similar to TCR338, except has 20 in. barrel with muzzle target crown, and 10 shot detachable box mag.

MSR $6,325	$5,650	$5,100	$4,500	$3,900	$3,300	$2,700	$2,100	

TCR6.5 – 6.5 Creedmore cal., similar to TCR338, except has 24 in. barrel, and 10 shot detachable box mag. New 2012.

MSR $6,325	$5,650	$5,100	$4,500	$3,900	$3,300	$2,700	$2,100	

SUPERSPORT .375CT-XLR – .375 CheyTac cal., 28 in. match grade stainless steel barrel, 7 shot detachable box mag., Arclight muzzle brake, 40-MOA monolithic rail, two-stage trigger, Desert Tan finish, ergonomic adj. folding stock, pistol grip, oversized bolt handle, 22 lbs., 8 oz. Mfg. 2013 only.

	$7,225	$6,325	$5,425	$4,915	$3,975	$3,250	$2,525	*$8,500*

ASP

Previously manufactured customized variation of a S&W Model 39-2 semi-auto pistol (or related variations) manufactured by Armament Systems and Procedures located in Appleton, WI.

PISTOLS: SEMI-AUTO

ASP – 9mm Para. cal., compact, DA/SA, see-through grips with cut-away mag. making cartridges visible, Teflon coated, re-contoured lightened slide, combat trigger guard, spurless hammer, and mostly painted Guttersnipe rear sight (no front sight), supplied with 3 mags., 24 oz. loaded. Approx. 3,000 mfg. until 1981.

	$2,800	$1,500	$1,275	$1,050	$875	$775	$695	

Add $200 for Tritium filled Guttersnipe sight.

This pistol is marked "ASP" on the magazine extension.

ASTRA ARMS S.A.

Current manufacturer established in 2008 and located in Sion, Switzerland. No current U.S. importation.

MSR	100%	98%	95%	90%	80%	70%	60%	Last MSR

Astra Arms manufactures a line of AR-15 style tactical rifles called the Sturmgewehr 4 Series. Current models include the Carbine and Commando. These models are not currently imported into the U.S. Please contact the company directly for more information, including availability and pricing (see Trademark Index).

AUSTRALIAN AUTOMATIC ARMS PTY. LTD.

Previous manufacturer located in Tasmania, Australia. Previously imported and distributed by California Armory, Inc. located in San Bruno, CA.

PISTOLS: SEMI-AUTO

SAP – .223 Rem. cal., GIO, 10 1/2 in. barrel, SA, 20 shot mag., fiberglass stock and forearm, 5.9 lbs. Imported 1986-1993.

	100%	98%	95%	90%	80%	70%	60%	Last MSR
	$795	$700	$600	$550	$500	$475	$450	$799

RIFLES: SEMI-AUTO

SAR – .223 Rem. cal., GIO, 16 1/4 or 20 in. (new 1989) barrel, 5 or 20 shot M-16 style mag., fiberglass stock and forearm, 7 1/2 lbs. Imported 1986-89.

	100%	98%	95%	90%	80%	70%	60%	Last MSR
	$1,250	$1,000	$900	$800	$775	$750	$700	$663

Add $25 for 20 in. barrel.

This model was also available in a fully automatic version (AR).

SAC – .223 Rem. cal., GIo, 10 1/2 in. barrel, 20 shot mag., fiberglass stock and forearm, 6.9 lbs. New 1986.

This model was available to NFA class III dealers and law enforcement agencies only.

SP – .223 Rem. cal., GIO, sporting configuration, 16 1/4 or 20 in. barrel, wood stock and forearm, 5 or 20 shot M-16 style mag., 7 1/4 lbs. Imported late 1991-93.

	100%	98%	95%	90%	80%	70%	60%	Last MSR
	$850	$750	$650	$600	$550	$500	$475	$879

Add $40 for wood stock.

AUSTRALIAN INTERNATIONAL ARMS

Previous manufacturer and exporter located in Brisbane, Australia until circa 2009. Previously, Australian International Arms worked in cooperation with ADI Limited Lithgow, formerly Small Arms Factory, known for its SMLE No. I MKIII and L1A1 rifles. AIA outsourced the manufacture of its designs and specifications. Previously imported in North America by Marstar Canada, located in Ontario, Canada, and imported and distributed until 2004 by Tristar Sporting Arms, Ltd., located in N. Kansas City, MO.

RIFLES: BOLT ACTION, ENFIELD SERIES

M10-A1 – 7.62x39mm cal., redesigned and improved No. 4 MK2 action, parkerized finish, all new components, teak furniture with No. 5 Jungle Carbine style stock with steel or brass buttplate, 20 in. chrome lined barrel with muzzle brake, adj. front sight, 10 shot mag., Picatinny rail, 8.3 lbs.

While advertised in 2007, this model never went into production.

* **M10-A2** – 7.62x39mm cal., similar to M10A2, except has No. 8 style forend, Monte Carlo stock, and 16.1 in. chrome lined barrel. Limited importation 2003-2004 by Tristar.

	100%	98%	95%	90%	80%	70%	60%	Last MSR
	$750	$700	$600	$525	$450	$375	$300	$659

M10-B1 – .308 Win. cal., redesigned and improved No. 4 MK2 action, matte blue finish, all new components, teak furniture with sporter carbine style stock and steel buttplate, 22 in. barrel, adj. front sight, 10 shot mag., Picatinny rail, 8.3 lbs. Imported 2006-disc.

	100%	98%	95%	90%	80%	70%	60%	Last MSR
	$575	$500	$425	$350	$300	$275	$250	$675

* **M10-B2** – .308 Win. cal., similar to M10-B1, except has brass buttplate, gloss blue finish, 25 in. chrome lined bull barrel, and bipod stud, 10 1/2 lbs. Imported 2006-disc.

	100%	98%	95%	90%	80%	70%	60%	Last MSR
	$650	$525	$425	$350	$300	$275	$225	$760

* **M10-B3** – .308 Win. cal., similar to M10-B1, except has chrome steel buttplate, gloss blue finish, and 22 in. lightweight barrel, 7 1/2 lbs. Limited importation 2006-disc.

	100%	98%	95%	90%	80%	70%	60%	Last MSR
	$900	$800	$700	$600	$500	$425	$350	$1,000

NO.4 MK IV – .308 Win. cal., parkerized finish, 25.2 in. chrome lined medium weight barrel, teak furniture with steel buttplate, 9.1 lbs. Prototype only imported by Tristar. Limited importation beginning 2006.

	100%	98%	95%	90%	80%	70%	60%	Last MSR
	$575	$500	$425	$350	$300	$275	$250	$675

Add $440 for walnut stock, glass bedding, target barrel, elevated Picatinny rail, and accessories (disc.).

MSR	100%	98%	95%	90%	80%	70%	60%	Last MSR

M 42 – .308 Win. cal., 27.6 in. barrel with mahogany stock and extra cheekpiece, blue printed action, bright metal/barrel finish, includes Picatinny rail, 8.2 lbs. Imported 2003-2004.

	$1,125	$950	$800	$650	$550	$450	$350	$1,295

AUTO-ORDNANCE CORP.

Current manufacturer with facilities located in Worcester, MA, and corporate offices in Blauvelt, NY. Auto-Ordnance Corp. became a division of Kahr Arms in 1999. Auto-Ordnance Corp. was a division of Gun Parts Corp. until 1999. Previously located in West Hurley, NY. Consumer, dealer, and distributor sales.

CARBINES: SEMI-AUTO

For Thompson semi-auto carbine models, please refer to the Thompson listing.

AUTO-ORDNANCE M1-CARBINE (.30 CAL.) – .30 Carbine cal., birch (disc.) or walnut (standard beginning 2008) stock, 18 in. barrel, all new parts, parkerized receiver, metal handguard, aperture rear sight, and bayonet lug, 10 (new 2005) or 15 shot mag., 5.4 lbs. New 2004.

MSR $816	$700	$600	$500	$425	$375	$325	$275	

* **Auto-Ordnance M1 Carbine Paratrooper (AOM150)** – .30 Carbine cal., similar to .30 cal. M1 Carbine, except has folding stock, walnut handguard, parkerized finish, 15 shot mag. New 2008.

MSR $903	$775	$675	$575	$475	$375	$325	$295	

* **Auto-Ordnance M1 Carbine Tactical** – .30 Carbine cal., similar to .30 cal. M1 carbine, except has black polymer folding stock, metal handguard, 15 shot mag. Mfg. 2008-2012.

	$650	$575	$475	$375	$325	$300	$275	$792

AUTO-ORDNANCE 1927 A-1 STANDARD – .45 ACP cal., 16 in. plain barrel, solid steel construction, standard military sight, walnut stock and horizontal forearm. Disc. 1986.

	$570	$490	$430	$360	$315	$290	$270	$575

PISTOLS: SEMI-AUTO

During 1997, Auto Ordnance discontinued all calibers on the pistols listed below, except for .45 ACP cal. or 9mm Para. Slide kits were available for $179. Also, conversion units (converting .45 ACP to .38 Super or 9mm Para.) were available for $195.

All current Auto Ordnance 1911 Models include a spent cartridge case, plastic carrying case, and cable lock.

1911 COMPETITION – .38 Super (1996 only) or .45 ACP cal., SA, competition features included compensated barrel, commander hammer, flat mainspring housing, white 3-dot sighting system, beavertail grip safety, black textured wraparound grips. Mfg. 1993-1996.

	$530	$415	$375	$330	$300	$285	$270	$636

Add $10 for .38 Super cal.

* **1911 A1 WWII Parkerized** – .45 ACP cal., no frills variation of the 1911 A1, military parkerizing, G.I. detailing with military style roll stamp, plastic or checkered walnut (disc. 2001, reintroduced 2007) grips, and lanyard loop. New 1992.

MSR $668	$525	$425	$325	$275	$235	$225	$215	

Add $17 for wood grips with U.S. logo (new 2007).

AZTEK ARMS

Current rifle manufacturer located in Mapleton, UT.

RIFLES: BOLT ACTION

H 1200 LONG RANGE HUNTER – 7mm Rem. Mag., 7mm Ultra, .300 Win., .300 WSM, 300 Ultra, or .338 Ultra cal., 25 or 27 in. match grade Schneider fluted barrel with muzzle brake, Picatinny rail, Black CORAL stock, hinged trigger guard, extended box mag., Shilen match trigger, Cerakote coating on all metal surfaces, 6 3/4 - 7 1/2 lbs.

MSR $4,295	$3,850	$3,375	$2,900	$2,625	$2,125	$1,750	$1,350	

H 1500 LONG RANGE HUNTER – 7mm Rem. Mag., 7mm Ultra, .300 Win. Mag., .300 Ultra, or .338 Edge cal., 26 (7mm Rem or .300 Win. only) or 28 in. fluted match grade Schneider LRC barrel with muzzle brake, Picatinny rail, Shilen match trigger, includes one 5 shot detachable mag., Cerakote coating, 9-10 1/2 lbs.

MSR $4,395	$3,950	$3,450	$2,925	$2,650	$2,125	$1,750	$1,350	

H 2000 LONG RANGE HUNTER – 7mm Rem. Mag., 7mm Ultra, .300 Win. Mag., .300 Ultra, .338 Ultra, or .338 Edge cal., 28 or 30 in. match grade heavy contour fluted barrel with muzzle brake, Black MOMBA stock with adj. LOP and cheek piece, Picatinny rail, Shilen match trigger, detachable magazine trigger guard, includes one 5 shot mag., Cerakote coating, 11 1/2-12 lbs.

MSR $4,795	$4,325	$3,785	$3,250	$2,950	$2,375	$1,950	$1,525	

MSR		100%	98%	95%	90%	80%	70%	60%	*Last MSR*

T1200 TACTICAL URBAN – .243 Win., .260 Rem., .308 Win. Mag., and 6.5 Creedmoor cal., 20, 24, or 26 in. match grade heavy contour barrel, Tan ALPHA stock, Picatinny rail, one 5 shot mag., detachable magazine trigger guard, Shilen match trigger, Cerakote coating, 10 1/2-12 lbs.

| MSR $4,095 | | $3,685 | $3,225 | $2,775 | $2,500 | $2,025 | $1,675 | $1,300 | |

T 1500 TACTICAL RANGER – 7mm Rem. Mag. or .300 Win. Mag. cal., 26 in. match grade heavy contour barrel, Picatinny rail, McMillan adj. A5 stock in Black, OD Green, or Tan, one 5 shot mag., detachable magazine trigger, Shilen match trigger, Cerakote coating, 10 1/2-12 lbs.

| MSR $4,295 | | $3,850 | $3,375 | $2,900 | $2,625 | $2,125 | $1,750 | $1,350 | |

T 2000 TACTICAL MAXRANGE – .338 Norma or .338 Lapua cal., 27 in. match grade Schneider body guard contour barrel with muzzle brake, Picatinny rail, Shilen match trigger, one 5 shot mag., detachable magazine trigger, McMilland adj. A5 stock in Black, OD Green, or Tan, Cerakote coating, 10 1/2-12 lbs.

| MSR $4,795 | | $4,325 | $3,785 | $3,250 | $2,950 | $2,375 | $1,950 | $1,525 | |

RIFLES: SEMI-AUTO

Aztek Arms makes AR-15 style rifles in various configurations. Please contact the company directly for more information on pricing, availability, and options (see Trademark Index).

NOTES

B SECTION

BCM EUROPEARMS

Current manufacturer located in Torino, Italy. No current U.S. importation.

BCM Europearms manufactures high quality bolt action competiton, hunting, and tactical/Law Enforcement rifles; the Storm semi-auto pistol (in 9x21mm and .40 S&W); and customized Remington 700 rifles. The "Barrel Block" competition rifle features a monolithic stock with integrally machined bedding (no separate bedding components) which allows both action and barrel to free float. The barrel and action are held in the stock by a "cap" which clamps over the barrel's chamber and is attached to the stock, not the action, by eight screws.

Currently these models are not being imported into the U.S. Please contact the company directly for more information, U.S. availability, and pricing (see Trademark Index).

BWE FIREARMS

Current rifle manufacturer and customizer with gunsmithing services established during 2002, and located in Longwood, FL.

BWE Firearms is a full service custom gunsmith shop specializing in NFA (Class III) firearms. It is also a Class II manufacturer. Please contact the company directly for more information on their models and services (see Trademark Index).

RIFLES: BOLT ACTION

BWE Firearms manufactured a bolt action rifle based on the Remington Model 700 long action. It was chambered for the .300 Blackout/Whisper, .338 Thumper, or .50 Thumper caliber, and features included blue printed actions, fully adjustable Bell and Carlson tactical stock, and Picatinny rail. Finishes included bead blast, polished blue, or parkerizing.

BAIKAL

Current trademark of products manufactured by the Russian Federal State Unitary Plant "Izhevsky Mechanichesky Zavod" (FSUP IMZ), located in Izhevsk, Russia. Currently imported by U.S. Sporting Goods, Inc. located in Rockledge, FL beginning 2011. Previously imported from late 1998 until 2004 by European American Armory Corp., located in Sharpes, FL, and from 1993-1996 by Big Bear, located in Dallas, TX.

Baikal SxS and O/U hunting guns (including air guns) were imported and distributed exclusively 2005-2009 by U.S. Sporting Goods (USSG), located in Rockledge, FL. Many Baikal shotguns and rifles were marketed domestically by Remington under the Spartan Gunworks trademark until 2008. See listings under Spartan Gunworks for more information.

Please contact the importer directly for more information and availability on Baikal firearms (see Trademark Index).

Baikal (the name of a lake in Siberia) was one of the key holding companies from the former Soviet Union, specializing in the production of firearms, and science intensive, complex electronic equipment.

The company was founded in 1942 as part of the Russian National Defense Industry. At that time, the plant produced world renowned Tokarev TT pistols. Upon conclusion of WWII, the company expanded its operation to include non-military firearms (O/U, SxS, and single barrel shotguns). FSUP IMZ is one of the world's largest manufacturers of military and non-military firearms. The total amount of guns produced by the FSUP IMZ is 680,000 units per year. The products range from various smoothbore guns, including slide action and self-loading models, rifled and combination guns, to a full array of sporting, civil, and combat pistols, including the internationally famous Makarov pistol. Since 2000, Baikal has produced a new pistol for the Russian Army which was developed by the enterprise designers and named after the group's leader - the Yarygin pistol.

FSUP IMZ features efficient manufacturing capacity and the unique intellectual potential of its qualified engineers-and-technicians staff. The FSUP IMZ is also undertaking the task of reintroducing the world to the "Russian Custom Gunsmith". There is a gunsmith school at the factory area for custom, one-of-a-kind hand engraved shotguns and rifles. The guns produced by the school feature high-quality assembly, attractive appearance, and high functional quality according to the best traditions of Russian gunmakers.

In the past, Baikal shotguns have had limited importation into the U.S. 1993 marked the first year that Baikals were officially (and legally) imported into the U.S. because of Russia's previous export restrictions. In prior years, however, a few O/Us have been seen for sale and have no doubt been imported into this country one at a time. Currently produced Baikals are noted for their good quality at low-level costs.

MSR	100%	98%	95%	90%	80%	70%	60%	Last MSR

RIFLES: SEMI-AUTO

MP161K – .17 HMR (disc. 2010), .22 LR, or .22 WMR (disc. 2010) cal., 19 1/2 in. accurized barrel, grey polymer thumbhole pistol grip stock with adj. LOP and cheekpiece height, 10 shot mag., integral Picatinny rail, adj. open sight, loaded chamber indicator, trigger guard mounted bottom safety, blue recoil pad and inserts in the forend. Importation began 2009.

MSR $437	$375	$325	$275	$250	$200	$175	$140

Add 20% for .17 HMR or .22 WMR cal. (disc. 2010).

MSR		100%	98%	95%	90%	80%	70%	60%	Last MSR

BARNES PRECISION MACHINE, INC.

Current semi-auto rifle manufacturer located in Apex, NC. Dealer and consumer direct sales.

RIFLES: SEMI-AUTO

Barnes manufactures a complete line of AR-15 style rifles, as well as parts and accessories. Many options are available for each rifle. Please contact the company directly for a complete list and pricing (see Trademark Index). All rifles include a plastic hard case and one Magpul PMAG.

Add $272 for Basic Robar NP3 coating rifle upgrade.

Add $433 for Maritime Robar NP3 coating rifle upgrade.

CQB PATROLMAN'S CARBINE – 5.56 NATO cal., ,223 Wylde chambered, GOP. 16 or 18 (new 2014) in. BPM stainless steel match barrel, stainless steel low profile gas block, A2-style flash hider, Black or FDE finish, 12 in. Ultralite XT modular free-float rail system, optional sling swivels, Magpul MBUS Gen2 sights, six position MOE adj. stock, Picatinny rail, breaching tip, includes hard plastic Patriot AR case.

MSR $1,309		$1,175	$1,050	$875	$800	$650	$525	$415	

Add $28 for FDE finish.

Add $11 for 18 in. barrel (new 2014).

Add $54 for Magpul MOE package or $88 for Magpul MOE package with 18 in. barrel.

This model is also available in 11 1/2 or 14 1/2 in. barrel configuration for law enforcement/military.

> * ***CQB Patrolman's Carbine .300 Blackout*** – .300 AAC Blackout cal., GIO, carbine length adj. gas system, 16 in. stainless steel barrel with BPMA2 style flash hider, breaching tip, MagPul MOE stock and pistol grip, MagPul MBUS sights, flat-top Picatinny rail receiver with 12 in. quad rail, includes plastic hard case, black finish/furniture. New 2013.
>
> | | | | | | | | | |
> |---|---|---|---|---|---|---|---|---|
> | MSR $1,609 | | $1,450 | $1,275 | $1,095 | $975 | $800 | $650 | $525 |

DESIGNATED MARKSMAN RIFLE – 5.56 NATO cal., GIO, 18 in. BPM stainless steel match barrel, Black finish, 12 in. Ultralite XT modular free-float rail system, optional sling swivels, A2 fixed (disc. 2013), Magpul PRS or MOE stock, Picatinny rail, Miculek muzzle break, Hiperfire match trigger.

MSR $1,612		$1,450	$1,275	$1,095	$995	$800	$650	$510

THREE GUN MATCH CARBINE – 5.56 NATO cal., .223 Wylde chambered, GIO, 16 or 18 in. BPM stainless steel match barrel, adj. gas system, Robar NP3 electroless nickel or black finish, 12 in. Ultralite PSFFRS hand guard with optional sling swivels, Magpul MOE or ACE SOCOM rifle length stock, Picatinny rail, Miculek muzzle compensator, Hiperfire match trigger.

MSR $1,571		$1,400	$1,225	$1,050	$950	$775	$625	$500

Add $11 for 18 in. barrel.

BARRETT FIREARMS MANUFACTURING, INC.

Current rifle manufacturer established in 1982, and located in Murfreesboro, TN. Dealer direct sales.

RIFLES: BOLT ACTION

MODEL 90 – .50 BMG cal., 29 in. match grade barrel with muzzle brake, 5 shot detachable box mag., includes extendible bipod legs, scope optional, 22 lbs. Mfg. 1990-1995.

		100%	98%	95%	90%	80%	70%	60%	Last MSR
		$3,450	$2,950	$2,400	$2,150	$1,875	$1,600	$1,500	*$3,650*

Add $1,150 for Swarovski 10X scope and rings.

MODEL 95(M) – .50 BMG cal., 29 in. match grade barrel with high efficiency muzzle brake, 5 shot detachable box mag., includes extendible bipod legs, full length M1913 receiver optics rail, scope optional, includes carrying case, 22 1/2 lbs. New 1995.

MSR $6,500		$6,150	$5,600	$5,000	$4,250	$3,500	$2,750	$2,200

Add $1,370 for Leupold scope and Barrett ultra high rings (new 2012).

Add $2,769 for rifle system including Leupold scope, BORS ultra high rings, 120 rounds of XM33 ammo, Pelican case, and bipod (new 2011).

Add $2,900 for QDL suppressor (new 2013).

MODEL 98B – .338 Lapua cal., 20 in. heavy unfluted, 26 (new 2013), or 27 (disc. 2012) in. fluted barrel, includes two 10 shot detachable mags. with muzzle brake, adj. stock, Harris bipod, monopod, full length M1913 optics receiver rail with 3 accessory rails on shroud, two sling loops, adj. trigger, ergonomic bolt handle, black finish, air/watertight case, 13 1/2 lbs. New 2009.

MSR $4,699		$4,300	$3,925	$3,550	$3,100	$2,800	$2,500	$2,150

Add $150 for 26 in. fluted barrel (new 2013).

Add $1,300 for Leupold scope and cleaning kit (disc. 2012).

Add $1,370 for Leupold scope and Barrett ultra high rings (new 2012).

Add $2,769 for Leupold scope, BORS, and Barrett ultra high rings.

MSR	100%	98%	95%	90%	80%	70%	60%	*Last MSR*

MODEL 99 – .416 Barrett (32 in. barrel only) or .50 BMG cal., single shot bolt action, 25 (disc.) or 29 in. (.50 BMG cal. only) lightweight fluted, or 32 in. heavy barrel with muzzle brake, straight through design with pistol grip and bipod, full length M1913 receiver optics rail, Black, Brown (disc.), Silver (disc.), or Flat Dark Earth (new 2012) finish, 23-25 lbs. New 1999.

| MSR $3,999 | $3,650 | $3,275 | $2,850 | $2,500 | $2,175 | $1,775 | $1,400 | |

Add $100 for .50 BMG cal. with flat dark earth finish.
Subtract $150 for .416 Barret cal. in black finish or $150 for .50 BMG cal. with 32 in. heavy barrel.
Add $1,370 for Leupold scope and Barrett Ultra high rings (new 2012).
Add $2,789 for Leupold scope, BORS, and Barrett Ultra high rings (new 2012).
Add $2,900 QDL suppressor (new 2013).
Add $251 for Bushnell Elite 10x scope (disc.).

MODEL MRAD – .300 Win. Mag. (new 2014) or .338 Lapua cal., 20 (new 2012), 24 (new 2013), 24 1/2 (disc. 2013), 26 (new 2013) or 27 (mfg. 2012 only) in. fluted or heavy barrel with muzzle brake, features aluminum receiver with modular construction including user-changeable barrel system, match grade trigger, thumb operated safety, ambidextrous mag. release, 21 3/4 in. M1913 optics rail plus side rails on vent forend, folding stock with adj. cheekpiece, Barret Multi-Role Brown, Black anodized (new 2013), Grey Cerakote (new 2014), OD Green Cerakote (new 2014), or Tan Cerakote (new 2014) finish, includes two 10 shot mags., two sling loops, three accessory rails, and Pelican case, 14.8 lbs. New mid-2011.

| MSR $6,000 | $5,750 | $5,350 | $4,800 | $4,300 | $3,750 | $3,150 | $2,600 | |

Subtract $150 for 20, 24, or 26 in. fluted barrel.
Add $1,370 for Leupold scope and Barret ultra high rings (new 2012).
Add $2,769 for Leupold scope, BORS, and ultra high rings (new 2012).
Add $1,522 for barrel conversion kit (includes complete barrel assembly, bolt, case, and one 10 shot mag. - new 2014).

RIFLES: SEMI-AUTO

MODEL 82 RIFLE – .50 BMG cal., semi-auto recoil operation, 33-37 in. barrel, 11 shot mag., 2,850 FPS muzzle velocity, scope sight only, parkerized finish, 35 lbs. Mfg. 1982-1987.

| | $5,000 | $4,350 | $3,950 | $3,450 | $2,700 | $2,150 | $1,800 | |

Last MSR for consumers was $3,180 in 1985

This model underwent design changes after initial production. Only 115 were mfg. starting with ser. no. 100.

MODEL 82A1 – .416 Barrett (new 2010) or .50 BMG cal., short recoil operating system, variant of the original Model 82, back-up iron sights, fitted hard case, 20, 29 (new late 1989), or 33 (disc. 1989) in. fluted (current mfg.) or unfluted (disc.) barrel, current mfg. has muzzle brake, 10 shot detachable or fixed (.416 Barrett cal. only) mag., Black anodized or Tan Cerakote (new 2013) finish, 32 1/2 lbs. for 1989 and older mfg., approx. 30 lbs. for 1990 mfg. and newer. Current mfg. includes elevated M1913 optics rail, watertight case, and cleaning kit.

| MSR $8,900 | $8,900 | $7,800 | $6,675 | $6,050 | $4,900 | $4,000 | $3,125 | |

Add $200 for Tan Cerakote finish (new 2013).
Add $1,370 for Leupold scope, Barrett ultra high rings, and Monopod (new 2012).
Add $2,769 for Leupold scope, BORS, Barrett ultra high rings, and Monopod (new 2012).
Add $375 for pack-mat backpack case (new 1999).
Add $2,800 for rifle system including Leupold scope, ultra high rings, Pelican case, and detachable bipod (new 2011).
Add approx. $4,900 per upper conversion kit.
Add $1,500 for Leupold Mark IV 4.5-14x50mm scope (disc. 2011).
Add $275 for camo backpack carrying case (disc.).
Add $1,325 for Swarovski 10X scope and rings (disc.).

This model boasts official U.S. military rifle (M107) status following government procurement during Operation Desert Storm. In 1992, a new "arrowhead" shaped muzzle brake was introduced to reduce recoil.

MODEL 98 – .338 Lapua Mag. cal., 10 shot box mag., 24 in. match grade barrel with muzzle brake, bipod, 15 1/2 lbs. While advertised during mid-1999, this model was never produced.

MODEL 107A1 – .50 BMG cal., 20 (new 2012) or 29 in. fluted barrel with four port titanium muzzle brake, integrated M1913 full length receiver optics rail including flip up iron sights, features new bolt carrier group and aluminum recoil buffer system, Black (new 2013), Multi-Role Brown Cerakote (new 2014), Grey Cerakote (new 2014), OD Green Cerakote (new 2014), Olive Drab Cerakote (new 2014), or Tan Cerakote finish, detachable adj. lightweight bipod, monopod on buttstock, 10 shot mag., 30.9 lbs. New mid-2011.

| MSR $12,000 | $12,000 | $10,500 | $9,000 | $8,175 | $6,600 | $5,400 | $4,200 | |

Add $1,370 for Leupold scope and Barrett ultra high rings (new 2012, Black Cerakote finish only).
Add $2,769 for Leupold scope, BORS, and Barrett ultra high rings (new 2012, Black Cerakote finish only).
Add $2,900 for QDL suppressor (new 2013).

MSR	100%	98%	95%	90%	80%	70%	60%	Last MSR

MODEL M468 – 6.8 SPC cal., aluminum upper and lower receiver, 16 in. barrel with muzzle brake, 5, 10, or 30 shot mag., dual spring extractor system, folding front and rear sight, gas block, two-stage trigger, integrated rail system, choice of full or telescoping 4-position stock, 8 lbs. Mfg. 2005-2008.

| | $2,400 | $2,050 | $1,675 | $1,375 | $1,175 | $995 | $875 | *$2,700* |

Add $1,590 for Model M468 upper conversion kit.

MODEL REC7 – 5.56 NATO or 6.8 SPC cal., AR-15 style, GPO, aluminum upper and lower receiver, 16 in. chrome lined barrel with A-2 flash hider, 30 shot mag., folding front and ARMS rear sight, single stage trigger, ARMS selective integrated rail system (disc.) or Omega X rail (current mfg.), 6-position MOE stock, includes tactical soft case and two mags., 7.62 lbs. Mfg. 2008-2013.

| | $1,950 | $1,700 | $1,475 | $1,325 | $1,075 | $875 | $675 | *$1,950* |

Add $1,650 per individual upper conversion kit.

Add $676 for Aimpoint Micro T-1 optics (mfg. 2011-2012).

MODEL REC7 GEN II – 5.56 NATO or 6.8 SPC cal., 16 in. barrel, Magpul MOE pistol grip stock, PWS Triad flash suppressor, flip-up iron sights, Geissele trigger, Barrett handguard with KeyMod, available in Black, Grey, Flat Dark Earth, or OD Green finish, 30 shot mag., includes one keymod rail attachment and soft carrying case. New 2014.

| MSR $2,759 | $2,750 | $2,500 | $2,200 | $2,000 | $1,850 | $1,700 | $1,550 | |

BATTLE RIFLE COMPANY

Current manufacturer of AR-15 style rifles located in Houston, TX. Previously located in Seabrook, TX.

RIFLES: SEMI-AUTO

BR308 WARHAMMER – 7.62 NATO cal., GIO, 16, 18, or 20 in. barrel with disintegrator flash suppressor, combat trigger system, enhanced combat stock system w/sling swivel attachment and easy grip adjustments, cheek weld designed finish w/Battle Rifle logo, Harris style bipod (18 or 20 in. only), forearm grip (16 in. only), 6-position buffer tube, ambi charging handle, Magpul front and rear MBUS sights, custom ambi pistol grip, heavy buffer, low profile gas block, additional rails for lights/optics, ambi fire control selector switch (option), includes one mag. and tactical bag.

| MSR $2,895 | $2,450 | $2,125 | $1,800 | $1,625 | $1,300 | $1,075 | $830 | |

Add $100 for 18 in. barrel or $200 for 20 in. barrel.

Add $200 for ambidextrous fire controls.

Add $100 for two-stage trigger.

BR4 LIT-CARBINE – 5.56 NATO or .300 Blackout cal., 16 in. SOCOM profile barrel with flash suppressor, 12 or 15 in. free float Gen. 2 SS rail, SST, sling adaptor, enhanced combat stock with Battle Rifle logo, Black furniture, available with KEYMOD rail.

| MSR $1,495 | $1,325 | $1,175 | $1,000 | $900 | $750 | $600 | $475 | |

Add $100 for KEYMOD option with 12 in. rail. or $100 for 15 in. rail.

Add $200 for .300 Blackout cal. or $200 for KEYMOD option with 15 in. rail.

BR4 SPECTRE – 5.56 NATO, 6.8 SPC, or .300 Blackout cal., 16 in. HBar or SOCOM profile barrel with flash suppressor, 12 in. free float quad rail, flip-up front and rear sight, Ergo pistol grip, buttstock pad, micro gas block under quad rail, SST, custom stock from Choate, Black furniture.

| MSR $1,395 | $1,250 | $1,095 | $950 | $850 | $700 | $575 | $450 | |

Add $100 for 6.8 SPC or .300 Blackout cal.

BR4 SPARTAN – 5.56 NATO, 6.8mmSPC, 7.62x6mm (new 2014), or .300 Blackout (disc. 2013) cal., GIO, choice of 16 in. Hbar profile or SOCOM profile barrel with flash suppressor, gas block with A2 front sight tower, collapsible stock, forged aluminum flat-top upper receiver with Picatinny rail and laser engraved, and lower receiver with matching 2-piece quad rail, polished trigger, black furniture, Ergo pistol grip, buttstock pad, includes one 30 shot mag. and black case, 6 1/2 lbs.

| MSR $1,195 | $1,075 | $950 | $825 | $725 | $600 | $500 | $375 | |

Add $100 for 6.8mmSPC or 7.62x6mm (new 2014) cal.

Add $246 for .300 Blackout cal. (disc. 2013).

BR4 STRYKER – 5.56 NATO cal., 16 in. M4 or SOCOM profile barrel with flash suppressor, flip-up front sight, quad rail with continuous top rail, Ergo pistol grip, buttstock pad, SST, single point sling adapter.

| MSR $1,395 | $1,250 | $1,095 | $950 | $850 | $700 | $575 | $450 | |

BR4 TROOPER – 5.56 NATO cal., 16 in. M4 profile barrel with A2 flash hider, 30 shot mag., carbine or mid-length, optional quad rail, carry handle with sights, collapsible or MOE stock, Black furniture.

| MSR $995 | $875 | $775 | $650 | $600 | $475 | $400 | $300 | |

Add $100 for mid-length, quad rail or MOE stock.

Add $154 for mid-length MOE Trooper model.

MSR	100%	98%	95%	90%	80%	70%	60%	Last MSR

BR4 WOLVERINE – .300 Blackout cal., 16 in. M4 profile barrel, 5 1/2 in. simulated suppressor, 15 1/2 in. KEYMOD rail, front and rear flip-up sights, Ergo pistol grip, Mission First tactical stock, single point sling adaptor, Black furniture. New 2014.

| MSR $1,595 | $1,425 | $1,250 | $1,075 | $975 | $795 | $650 | $500 | |

Add $100 for .300 Blackout cal.

BR15 DMR – 5.56 NATO cal., 20 in. heavy barrel with flash suppressor, rifle length quad rail, Harris style bipod, SST or 2-stage trigger, Ergo pistol grip, standard, ECS, or Magpul PRS stock, Black furniture.

| MSR $1,595 | $1,425 | $1,250 | $1,075 | $975 | $795 | $650 | $500 | |

Add $200 for Magpul PRS stock.

BR15 LIT-RIFLE – 5.56 NATO or .300 Blackout cal., GIO, light infantry tactical rifle, 16 (disc. 2013) or 20 in. threaded, chrome lined barrel with flash suppressor, Magpul MBUS front and rear sights, M16 bolt carrier with nickel finish, forged flat-top upper receiver with Picatinny rail and laser and free float 12 in. rail (16 in. barrel, disc. 2013) or 15 in. rail (20 in. barrel), forged aluminum lower receiver, polished trigger, ECS stock, single point sling endplate, includes one 30 shot mag. and black case, 6.7-7.9 lbs.

| MSR $1,695 | $1,525 | $1,325 | $1,150 | $1,025 | $850 | $675 | $550 | |

Add $100 for 2-stage trigger option.

BR15 STANDARD – 5.56 NATO cal., 20 in. barrel with A2 flash suppressor, 30 shot mag., rifle length polymer handguards, carry handle rear sight, standard A2 fixed stock and pistol grip, SST, Black furniture.

| MSR $1,295 | $1,150 | $1,000 | $850 | $750 | $625 | $500 | $375 | |

BR15 PATROLMAN – 5.56 NATO cal., similar to BR4, except features 16 in. steel straight profile barrel with flash suppressor, available with carbine or mid-length forearm, 7 1/2 lbs. Disc. 2013.

| | $1,235 | $1,080 | $925 | $840 | $680 | $550 | $430 | *$1,449* |

BR15 VARMITEER – 5.56 NATO cal., 18 or 20 in. heavy barrel, low profile gas block, 10 shot mag., rifle length forend tube, optics ready, Ergo pistol grip, Magpul stock, available in Black, Desert Tan pattern, or Woodland pattern finish.

| MSR $1,295 | $1,150 | $1,000 | $850 | $725 | $600 | $500 | $375 | |

BR15 6mmx45 – 6mmx45 cal., AR-15 style, 18 or 20 in. barrel, mid (18 in.) or rifle (20 in.) length gas sytem, KEYMOD 15 1/2 in. rail, ECS stock, Black furniture, includes bipod.

| MSR $1,595 | $1,425 | $1,250 | $1,075 | $975 | $795 | $650 | $500 | |

Add $100 for 20 in. barrel.

BR16 PRECISION TACTICAL RIFLE – 5.56 NATO cal., GIO, 20 in. heavy threaded barrel with flash suppressor, gas block with A2 front sight tower, forged aluminum flat-top upper with Picatinny rail and laser engraved, two-piece quad rail, forged alum. lower receiver, polished trigger, black furniture, fixed or adj. stock, includes one 30 shot mag., bipod match 600 meter sights, and black case. Disc. 2013.

| | $1,450 | $1,275 | $1,095 | $985 | $800 | $650 | $510 | *$1,695* |

Add $100 for Magpul PRS or CAA Ansl adj. stock.

BENELLI

Current manufacturer established in 1967, and located in Urbino, Italy. Benelli USA was formed during late 1997, and is currently importing all Benelli shotguns and rifles. Benelli pistols (and air pistols) are currently imported by Larry's Guns, located in Gray, ME beginning 2003. Company headquarters are located in Accokeek, MD. Shotguns were previously imported 1983-1997 by Heckler & Koch, Inc., located in Sterling, VA. Handguns were previously imported until 1997 by European American Armory, located in Sharpes, FL, in addition to Sile Distributors, Inc., until 1995, located in New York, NY, and Saco, located in Arlington, VA.

For more information on Benelli air pistols, please refer to the *Blue Book of Airguns* by Dr. Robert Beeman and John Allen (also available online).

RIFLES: SEMI-AUTO

MR1 CARBINE/RIFLE – 5.56 NATO cal., self-adjusting gas operation (similar to the Benelli M4 shotgun used by the Marines) with rotating bolt head featuring three lugs, accepts 5 shot AR-15 style mags., 12 1/2 (law enforcement only), 16, or 20 (Europe only) in. barrel, regular or pistol grip (12 1/2 or 16 in. barrel only), rifle sights, includes Picatinny rail with ghost ring sights, push button safety on trigger guard, black finish, approx. 8 lbs. New late 2009.

| MSR $1,339 | $1,175 | $1,000 | $875 | $750 | $650 | $550 | $450 | |

* **MR1 ComforTech Carbine** – 5.56 NATO, 16 in. barrel features black pistol grip ComforTech stock, otherwise similar to MR1 Carbine/Rifle. New 2011.

| MSR $1,469 | $1,275 | $1,075 | $925 | $775 | $675 | $575 | $475 | |

MSR	100%	98%	95%	90%	80%	70%	60%	Last MSR

SHOTGUNS: SEMI-AUTO, 1985-OLDER

Benelli semi-auto 3rd generation (inertia recoil) shotguns were imported starting in the late 1960s. The receivers were mfg. of light aluminum alloy - the SL-80 Model 121 had a semi-gloss, anodized black finish, the Model 123 had an ornate photo-engraved receiver, the Model Special 80 had a brushed, white nickel-plated receiver, and the Model 121 M1 had a matte finish receiver, barrel, and stock. All 12 ga. SL-80 Series shotguns will accept 2 3/4 or 3 in. shells, and all SL-80 Series 12 ga. Models have interchangeable barrels (except the 121 M1) with 4 different model receivers (121, 121 M1, 123, and Special 80). All 4 models had fixed choke barrels.

The SL-80 Series shotguns were disc. during 1985, and neither H&K nor Benelli USA has parts for these guns. Some misc. parts still available for the 12 ga. from Gun Parts Corp. (see Trademark Index for more information).

Approx. 50,000 SL-80 series shotguns were mfg. before discontinuance - choke markings (located on the side or bottom of the barrel) are as follows: * full choke, ** imp. mod., *** mod., **** imp. cyl. SL-80 series guns used the same action (much different than current mfg.) and all had the split receiver design. Be aware of possible wood cracking where the barrel rests on the thin area of the forend and also on the underside of the buttstock behind trigger guard.

The marketplace for older Benelli semi-auto shotguns has changed recently, with more interest being shown on these older models as they represent a value compared to Benelli's new offerings. As a result of this additional interest and demand, values have gone up, after being dormant for many years.

100% values within this section assume NIB condition.

Subtract 5% for "SACO" importation (Saco was located in Arlington, VA).

SL-80 SERIES MODEL 121 M1 POLICE/MILITARY – 12 ga. only, similar in appearance to the Super 90 M1, hardwood stock, 7 shot mag., matte metal and wood finish, most stocks had adj. lateral sling attachment inside of buttstock, 18 3/4 in. barrel. Disc. 1985.

	$600	$525	$450	$400	$325	$250	$225	

Since many of this model were sold to the police and military, used specimens should be checked carefully for excessive wear and/or possible damage. Since these guns usually saw extensive use, they are much less desirable than other SL-80 listed in this section, It is also difficult to find commonly needed parts for these guns. These models are not rare, but fewer have been traded, most likely due to poor sales history.

SHOTGUNS: SEMI-AUTO, 1986-NEWER

Unless indicated otherwise, all currently manufactured Benelli shotguns utilize a red fiber optic sight, and are equipped with a patented Benelli keyed chamber lock. As of 2011, Benelli had manufactured well over 2 million shotguns in many configurations.

M1 DEFENSE (SUPER 90) – similar to Super 90 Slug, except has pistol grip stock, 7.1 lbs. Disc. 1998.

	$700	$560	$425	$325	$300	$270	$250	$851

Add $41 for ghost-ring sighting system.

M1 PRACTICAL (SUPER 90) – 12 ga. only, 3 in. chamber, 26 in. plain barrel with muzzle brake, designed for IPSC events, extended 8 shot mag. tube, oversized safety, speed loader, larger bolt handle, mil spec adj. ghost ring sight and Picatinny rail, black regular synthetic stock and forearm, matte metal finish, includes 3 choke tubes, 7.6 lbs. Mfg. 1998-2004.

	$925	$785	$675	$575	$450	$350	$300	$1,285

M1 TACTICAL (SUPER 90) – 12 ga. only, 3 in. chamber, 18 1/2 in. barrel, fixed rifle or ghost ring sighting system, available with synthetic pistol grip or standard buttstock, includes 3 choke tubes, 5 shot mag., 6.7 - 7 lbs. Mfg. 1993-2004.

	$725	$600	$525	$425	$335	$275	$250	$975

Add $50 for ghost ring sighting system.

Add $50-$65 for pistol grip stock.

* M1 Tactical M – similar to M1 Tactical, except has military ghost ring sights and standard synthetic stock, 7.1 lbs. Mfg. 1999-2000.

	$725	$600	$525	$425	$335	$275	$250	$960

Add $10 for pistol grip stock.

M1 ENTRY (SUPER 90) – 12 ga. only, 14 in. barrel, choice of synthetic pistol grip or standard stock, choice of rifle or ghost ring sights, 5 shot mag. (2 shot extension), approx. 6.7 lbs. Mfg. 1992-2006.

	$810	$675	$585	$450	$395	$340	$310	

Add $15 for synthetic pistol grip stock.

Add $65 for ghost ring sighting system.

This model required special licensing (special tax stamp) for civilians, and was normally available to law enforcement/military only.

M2 – 12 ga., 2 3/4 or 3 in. chamber, 18 1/2 in. barrel, open or ghost ring sights, matte black finish, pistol grip or straight grip stock, includes three choke tubes, 6.7 lbs. New 2013.

MSR $1,549		$1,300	$1,125	$975	$885	$715	$585	$450

MSR	100%	98%	95%	90%	80%	70%	60%	Last MSR

M2 THREE GUN – 12 ga., 3 in. chamber, 21 in. VR barrel with Crio chokes, 3 shot mag., HiViz sights, black synthetic ComforTech stock, designed for 3 gun competition, 7.3 lbs. New 2012.

| MSR $2,499 | $2,225 | $1,875 | $1,550 | $1,200 | $950 | $800 | $700 | |

M2 PRACTICAL – 12 ga. only, 3 in. chamber, 26 in. compensated barrel with ghost ring sights, designed for IPSC competition, 8 shot mag., Picatinny rail. Limited importation 2005.

| | $1,135 | $965 | $825 | $650 | $550 | $475 | $425 | $1,335 |

M2 TACTICAL – 12 ga. only, 3 in. chamber, Inertia Driven system, 18 1/2 in. barrel with choice of pistol grip, regular stock, or ComforTech stock configuration, matte finish, 5 shot mag., AirTouch checkering pattern on stock and forearm, open rifle or ghost ring sights, 6.7-7 lbs. New 2005.

| MSR $1,359 | $1,225 | $1,025 | $875 | $750 | $600 | $500 | $400 | |

Add $110 for ghost ring sights w/ComforTech stock.
Subtract $110 for tactical open rifle sights.

M3 CONVERTIBLE AUTO/PUMP (SUPER 90) – 12 ga. only, 3 in. chamber, defense configuration incorporating convertible (fingertip activated) pump or semi-auto action, 19 3/4 in. cyl. bore barrel with ghost ring or rifle (disc. 2007) sights, 5 shot mag., choice of standard black polymer stock or integral pistol grip (disc. 1996, reintroduced 1999), approx. 7.3 lbs. New 1989.

| MSR $1,589 | $1,375 | $1,175 | $1,025 | $900 | $800 | $700 | $600 | |

Add $110 for folding stock (mfg. 1990-disc.) - only available as a complete gun.
Add $340 for Model 200 Laser Sight System with bracket (disc.).
Subtract approx. 10% for rifle sights (disc. 2007).

M4 TACTICAL – 12 ga. only, 3 in. chamber, consumer version of the U.S. Military M4, includes Auto Regulating Gas Operating (ARGO) system, dual stainless self cleaning pistons, 4 shot mag., matte black phosphated metal standard, H2O coating (mfg. 2012, then 2014), or 100% Desert camo coverage (except for pistol grip, mfg. 2007-2012), 18 1/2 in. barrel with ghost ring sights, pistol grip, tactical (new 2012), telescoping (new 2012), or non-collapsible (disc. 2004) stock and forearm, Picatinny rail, approx. 7.8 lbs. Importation began late 2003.

| MSR $1,899 | $1,675 | $1,450 | $1,225 | $1,050 | $925 | $850 | $750 | |

Add $300 for ATI Raven stock (mfg. 2013 only).
Add $100 for 100% Desert camo coverage (mfg. 2007-2012).
Add $500 for pistol grip or tactical stock with H20 coating (new 2014).
Add $370 for tactical stock with H2O coating (mfg. 2012 only) or $500 for telescoping stock with H2O coating (mfg. 2012 only).

M1014 LIMITED EDITION – similar to M4, except only available with non-collapsible stock, U.S. flag engraved on receiver, 8 lbs. Limited edition of 2,500 mfg. 2003-2004.

| | $1,375 | $1,100 | $950 | $825 | $725 | $650 | $600 | $1,575 |

* **Super Black Eagle II Slug** – 12 ga. only, 3 in. chamber, 24 in. barrel with rifled bore and adj. sights, includes Picatinny rail, choice of satin walnut (disc. 2012) stock and forearm or black synthetic stock, ComforTech became standard 2007, or 100% camo coverage of Timber HD (disc. 2008) or Realtree APG HD, approx. 7.4 lbs. New 2004.

| MSR $1,899 | $1,750 | $1,475 | $1,175 | $950 | $725 | $625 | $525 | |

Add $100 for 100% camo treatment.
Subtract approx. $100 if with satin walnut stock and forearm.

SHOTGUNS: SLIDE-ACTION

All currently manufactured Benelli shotguns are equipped with a patented Benelli keyed chamber lock.

* **Nova Tactical (Special Purpose Smooth Bore)** – 12 ga. only, 3 1/2 in. chamber, similar action to Nova, features 18 1/2 in. cyl. bore barrel with choice of rifle or ghost ring (new 2000) sights, black synthetic stock and forearm only, 7.2 lbs. New 1999.

| MSR $419 | $350 | $285 | $260 | $230 | $210 | $200 | $190 | |

Add $40 for ghost ring sights.

* **Nova Entry** – 12 ga. only, 14 in. barrel, choice of ghost ring or open rifle sights, black synthetic stock and forearm, 4 shot mag., approx. 6.9 lbs. Importation began 2003.

This model is available to law enforcement or military only.

* **SuperNova Tactical** – 12 ga., features 18 or 18 1/2 (disc.) in. barrel with choice of ComforTech or pistol grip synthetic stock, matte finish or Desert camo (mfg. 2007-2012, pistol grip only), choice of rifle or ghost ring sights. New 2006.

| MSR $499 | $450 | $350 | $300 | $250 | $225 | $200 | $185 | |

Add $60 for ghost ring sights.
Add $170 for Desert camo w/pistol grip and ghost ring sights (mfg. 2007-2012).

MSR		100%	98%	95%	90%	80%	70%	60%	Last MSR

* **SuperNova Slug** – 12 ga., 3 in. chamber, features 24 in. rifled bore drilled and tapped barrel with adj. rifle sights, black synthetic ComforTech or 100% coverage Realtree APG HD camo stock and forearm, 8.1 lbs. New 2007.

MSR $829	$700	$575	$450	$375	$325	$275	$250

Add $100 for 100% camo coverage. Add $10 for Field & Slug combo with extra 26 in. Field barrel (mfg. 2007 only).

BERETTA

Current manufacturer located in Brescia, Italy since 1526. The company name in Italy is Fabbrica d'Armi Pietro Beretta. Beretta U.S.A. Corp. was formed in 1977 and is located in Accokeek, MD. Beretta U.S.A. Corp. has been importing Beretta Firearms exclusively since 1980. 1970-1977 manufacture was imported exclusively by Garcia. Distributor and dealer direct sales.

Beretta is one of the world's oldest family owned industrial firms, having started business in 1526. In addition to Beretta owning Benelli, Stoeger, and Franchi, the company also purchased Sako and Tikka Companies in late 1999, Aldo Uberti & Co. in 2000, Burris Optics in 2002, and Steiner International Optics. Beretta continues to be a leader in firearms development and safety, and shooters attest to the reliability of their guns worldwide.

For more information and current pricing on both new and used Beretta precision airguns, please refer to the *Blue Book of Airguns* by Dr. Robert Beeman & John Allen (also available online).

PISTOLS: SEMI-AUTO, POST WWII MFG.

On Beretta's large frame pistols, alphabetical suffixes refer to the following: F Model - double/single action system with external safety decocking lever, G Model - double/single action system with external decocking only lever, D Model - double action only without safety lever, DS Model - double action only with external safety lever. Pistols have been manufactured in both Italy and America, and country of origin can be determined on the slide legend.

Information and values for state compliant variations are not listed.

The models in this section appear in numerical sequence.

MODEL PX4 STORM – 9mm Para., .40 S&W, or .45 ACP (new 2007) cal., single/double action, 3.2 (Compact model) or 4 in. barrel, polymer frame, locked breech with rotating barrel system, matte black finish with plastic grips, Pronox (disc.) or Super Luminova 3-dot night sights, 9 (.45 ACP only), 10, 14, or 17 shot mag. (varies due to caliber), accessory rail on lower frame, approx. 27 1/2 oz. New mid-2005.

MSR $575	$485	$435	$380	$330	$275	$250	$225

Add $75 for .45 ACP cal. (new 2007).

The trigger mechanism of this gun can be customized to four different configurations: Type F (single/double action decocker and manual safety), Type D (DAO with spurless hammer, LE only), Type G (single/double action decocker with no manual safety, LE only), or Type C (constant action, spurless hammer). Values are for Type C and Type F variations.

* **Model PX4 Storm Inox** – 9mm Para. or .40 S&W cal., similar to Model PX4 Storm, except has stainless steel construction, and 10, 14, or 17 shot only. New 2012.

MSR $650	$545	$485	$410	$360	$300	$275	$250

* **Model PX4 Storm Special Duty** – .45 ACP cal. only, 4.6 in. extended barrel, Type F action only, dark earth polymer frame and matte black slide, includes one 9 shot flush and two 10 shot extended mags., two additional backstraps and waterproof case, 28.6 oz.

MSR $1,145	$975	$825	$700	$600	$500	$425	$350

* **Model PX4 Storm Compact** – 9mm Para. or .40 S&W (new 2012) cal., similar to Model PX4 Storm, except has compact frame and 3.2 in. barrel, 10, 12 (.40 S&W only, new 2012) or 15 (9mm Para. cal. only) shot mag., 27.3 oz. New late 2010.

MSR $575	$485	$435	$380	$330	$275	$250	$225

* **Model PX4 Storm Sub-Compact** – 9mm Para. or .40 S&W cal., similar to Model PX4 Storm, except has 10 or 13 (9mm Para. cal. only) shot mag., has sub-compact frame with 3 in. barrel, includes three backstraps, 26 oz. New 2007.

MSR $575	$485	$435	$380	$330	$275	$250	$225

ARX 160 – .22 LR cal., 9 in. barrel with flash suppressor, 20 shot STANAG Type mag., matte black finish, Mil-Std. 1913 upper and lower rails, polymer flip-up sights, adj. folding stock, pistol grip, ambidextrous mag. release, 5.7 lbs. New 2013.

MSR $545	$475	$425	$375	$325	$275	$250	$225

Pistols: Semi-Auto, Model 92 & Variations - 4.9 in. barrel

MODEL 90-TWO TYPE F – 9mm Para. or .40 S&W cal., 4.9 in. barrel, DA/SA, matte metal finish, removable single piece wraparound grip in two sizes, internal recoil buffer and captive recoil spring guide assembly, low profile fixed sights, 10, 12 (.40 S&W cal.), or 17 (9mm Para. cal.) shot mag., lower accessories rail with cover, 32 1/2 oz. Mfg. 2006-2009.

	$600	$525	$450	$375	$330	$300	$275	$700

MSR	100%	98%	95%	90%	80%	70%	60%	*Last MSR*

MODEL 92FS VERTEC – 9mm Para. cal., DA/SA, straight backstrap grip, special short reach trigger, thin dual textured grip panels, and integral accessory rail on lower frame, removable front sight, beveled magwell, 10 shot mag., Bruniton finish, 32.2 oz. Mfg. 2002-2005.

	$635	$495	$440	$385	$340	$300	$275	*$760*

Add $25 for B-Lok safety system using key lock (mfg. 2003).

* Model 92FS Vertec Stainless (Inox) – stainless variation of the Model 92FS Vertec. Mfg. 2002-2005.

	$670	$525	$425	$360	$315	$260	$225	*$825*

Add $170 for laser grips (new 2004).
Add $25 for B-Lok safety system using key lock (mfg. 2003).

MODEL 92F WITH U.S. M9 MARKED SLIDE/FRAME – 9mm Para. cal., 100 mfg. with special serial no. range, "BER" prefix, government assembly numbers on frame, slide, hammer, mag. etc., includes plastic case and cleaning brush. Mfg. for the Armed Forces Reserve shooters, identical to military M9, except for serial number.

	$1,750	$1,525	$1,350	$1,100	$950	$825	$700	

MODEL 92A1 – 9mm Para. cal., DA/SA, similar to Model 92FS/F, except includes three 10 or 17 shot mags., has removable front sight, frame accessory rail, internal recoil buffer, rounded trigger guard, and captive recoil spring assembly, black Bruniton finish, plastic grips, 34.4 oz, mfg. in Italy. New 2010.

MSR $745	$635	$550	$475	$425	$350	$285	$250	

M9A1 – 9mm Para. cal., DA/SA, features accessory rail on lower frame and checkered grip straps, 10 or 15 shot mag., 3-dot sights, beveled mag. well, 35.3 oz. New 2006.

MSR $745	$635	$550	$475	$425	$350	$285	$250	

Pistols: Semi-Auto, Model 92 & Variations - 4.7 in. barrel

MODEL 92FS INOX TACTICAL – 9mm Para. cal., 4.7 in. barrel, DA/SA, features satin matte finished stainless steel slide and alloy frame, rubber grips, Tritium sights. Mfg. 1999-2000.

	$695	$560	$480	$425	$375	$325	$295	*$822*

MODEL 92G ELITE IA (BRIGADIER) – 9mm Para. cal., similar to Model 92FS Brigadier, DAO, except has 4.7 in. stainless barrel and many standard I.D.P.A. competition features including front and rear serrated slide, skeletonized hammer, and removable three-dot sighting system, plastic grips, includes Elite engraving on slide, 35.3 oz. Mfg. 1999-2005.

	$725	$585	$495	$425	$360	$300	$275	*$875*

* Model 92G Elite II (Brigadier) – similar to Model 92G Elite, except has stainless steel slide with black "Elite II" markings, target barrel crown, extended mag. release, optimized trigger mechanism, front and back strap checkering, low profile Novak rear sight, 35 oz. Mfg. mid-2000-2005.

	$815	$635	$530	$450	$385	$325	$295	*$985*

Pistols: Semi-Auto, Model 92 & Variations - 4.3 in. barrel

MODEL 92F/92FS COMPACT – similar to Model 92F, except has 4.3 in. barrel, DA/SA, 13 shot mag., plastic or wood grips, 31 1/2 oz. While temporarily suspended in 1986, production was resumed 1989-1993.

	$550	$450	$415	$375	$335	$300	$275	*$625*

Add $20 for checkered walnut grips (Model 92F Wood).
Add $65 for Trijicon sight system.

MODEL 92F & 92FS CENTURION – 9mm Para. cal., similar to Model 92F, except has compact barrel slide unit with full size frame, 4.3 in. barrel, choice of plastic or wood grips, 3 dot sight system, same length as Model 92F Compact, 10 (C/B 1994) or 15* shot mag., 33.2 oz. Mfg. 1992-98.

	$525	$435	$395	$365	$335	$300	$275	*$613*

Add approx. $20 for checkered walnut grips (Model 92F Wood).
Add $90 for Tritium sight system (mfg. 1994-98).
Add 10% for Trijicon sights (disc).

MODEL 92FS COMPACT RAIL STAINLESS (INOX) – 9mm Para. cal., aluminum alloy frame, stainless steel slide, 10 or 13 shot mag., 1913 style lower accessory rail, combat trigger guard, ambidextrous safety, 32 oz. New 2013.

MSR $775	$650	$575	$495	$440	$360	$295	$225	

Pistols: Semi-Auto, Model 96 & Variations, Recent Mfg.

The models in this section appear in approximate chronological sequence.

MODEL 96A1 – .40 S&W, DA/SA, similar to Model 96F/FS, except includes three 10 or 12 shot mags., has removable front sight, frame accessory rail, internal recoil buffer, rounded trigger guard, and captive recoil spring assembly, black Bruniton finish, plastic grips, 34.4 oz, mfg. in Italy. New 2010.

MSR $745	$640	$535	$450	$400	$350	$300	$285	

MSR		100%	98%	95%	90%	80%	70%	60%	Last MSR

RIFLES: SEMI-AUTO, RECENT MFG.

BM-59 M-1 GARAND – with original Beretta M1 receiver, M-14 style detachable mag., only 200 imported into the U.S.

		$3,200	$2,900	$2,400	$1,800	$1,500	$1,300	$1,175	$2,080

BM-62 – similar to BM-59, except has flash suppressor and is Italian marked.

		$3,200	$2,900	$2,400	$1,800	$1,500	$1,300	$1,175	

AR-70 – .222 Rem. or .223 Rem. cal., 5, 8, or 30 shot mag., diopter sights, epoxy finish, 17.72 in. barrel, 8.3 lbs.

		$1,925	$1,675	$1,375	$1,150	$1,025	$850	$750	$1,065

1989 Federal legislation banned the importation of this model into U.S.

ARX 100 – 5.56 NATO cal., lightweight techno-polymer receiver, no pins, matte black finish, 16 in. quick change cold hammer forged barrel with flash suppressor, can be removed and replaced with various lengths and calibers in a matter of seconds, 30 shot mag., ambidextrous magazine release, accepts AR magazines, case projection can be switched from right to left with a simple push of a button, telescoping folding stock, ambidextrous safety selector, all critical controls are ambidextrous, quad Picatinny rails with full-length upper. New mid-2013.

MSR $1,950		$1,725	$1,525	$1,275	$1,125	$915	$750	$575	

ARX 160 – .22 LR cal., 18.1 in. barrel with flash suppressor, 10 (new 2014), 14 (mfg. 2013 only), or 20 (new 2014) shot STANAG-Type mag., matte black finish, quad Picatinny rails with full-length upper, polymer flip-up sights, adj. folding stock, pistol grip, ambidextrous safety lever and mag. release, 6 lbs. 6 oz. New 2013.

MSR $595		$525	$440	$375	$335	$315	$285	$250	

CX4 STORM CARBINE – 9mm Para. (92 Carbine), .40 S&W (96 Carbine) or .45 ACP (8045 Carbine, disc. 2013.) cal., blowback single action, Giugiaro design featuring tactical styling with one-piece matte black synthetic stock with thumbhole, rubber recoil pad and stock cheekpiece, quad Picatinny rails, ghost ring sights, 16.6 in. hammer forged barrel, reversible crossbolt safety, mag. button, bolt handle, and ejection port, mag. capacities vary depending on caliber, current mfg. has 8 (.45 ACP cal.), 14 (.40 S&W cal., Px4 Storm mag.), 15 (9mm Para. with high cap Model 92 mag.), or 17 (high cap PX4 Storm mag.) shot mag., (this series also accepts Models 96, 8000, 8040, and 8045 pistol mags.), 29.7 in. overall length, 5 3/4 lbs. New mid-2003.

MSR $915		$795	$625	$550	$495	$450	$395	$350	

Add $95 for 92 Carbine package (includes scope, 9mm Para. (disc. 2005) or .40 S&W cal.). Disc.

Add $50 for top rail (only available in 9mm Para. or .40 S&W cal., mfg. 2006-2007).

This model has been available in many variations - 8045 (.45 ACP), 92 Carbine (8000, 9mm Para.), 92 Carbine package (w/scope), and 96 Carbine (8040, .40 S&W).

RX4 STORM CARBINE – .223 Rem. cal., ARGO, gas operating system, available in collapsible five position telescoping stock or sporter style stock with optional pistol grip, black matte finish, ghost ring sights, includes 5 and 10 shot AR-15 style magazines. Limited importation 2007-2008.

		$1,100	$925	$800	$700	$600	$525	$450	$1,100

While advertised, only a few samples were brought into the U.S.

SHOTGUNS: SEMI-AUTO

It is possible on some of the following models to have production variances occur including different engraving motifs, stock configurations and specifications, finishes, etc. These have occurred when Beretta changed from production of one model to another. Also, some European and English distributors have sold their excess inventory through Beretta U.S.A., creating additional variations/configurations that are not normally imported domestically. While sometimes rare, these specimens typically do not command premiums over Beretta's domestic models.

The following Beretta semi-auto models have been listed in numerical sequence, if possible, disregarding any alphabetical suffix or prefix.

Note: values are for unaltered guns.

Subtract 10% on the following factory multi-choke models if w/o newer Beretta Optima-chokes (12 ga. only, became standard 2003).

* **Model 1200 Riot** – 12 ga. only, 2 3/4 or 3 in. chamber, 20 in. cyl. bore barrel with iron sights, extended mag. Imported 1989-90 only.

		$400	$375	$350	$295	$250	$225	$200	$660

* **Model 1201 FP (Riot)** – 12 ga., riot configuration featuring 18 (new 1997) or 20 (disc. 1996) in. cylinder bore barrel, 5 shot mag, choice of adj. rifle sights (disc.), Tritium sights (disc. 1998) or ghost ring (new 1999, Tritium front sight insert) sights, matte wood (disc.) or black synthetic stock and forearm, matte metal finish (disc.), 6.3 lbs. Mfg. 1991-2004.

		$725	$595	$500	$400	$300	$250	$200	$890

Add $80 for Tritium sights (mfg. 1997-98).

Add $45 for pistol grip configuration (Model 1201 FPG3 - mfg. 1994 only).

MSR	100%	98%	95%	90%	80%	70%	60%	*Last MSR*

TX4 STORM – 12 ga., 3 in. chamber, gas operated, dual lug action with rotating bolt, 18 in. OptimaBore barrel with OptimaChoke HP cylinder tube, optional TX4 Stand Off Device, 5 shot mag., matte black finish, alloy receiver with integral Picatinny rail, black synthetic stock, ghost ring rear sight, elevated post front sight, includes plastic case, approx. 6.4 lbs. Mfg. 2010-2011.

	$1,200	$995	$850	$725	$625	$525	$450	*$1,450*

BERGARA

Current rifle and barrel manufacturer located in Bergara, Spain. Barrels and Apex rifles imported by Connecticut Valley Arms, located in Duluth, GA, bolt action rifles are currently imported by Black Powder Products, located in Duluth, GA.

Bergara manufactures high quality rifle barrels, in addition to bolt action rifles and single shot Apex rifles imported by Connecticut Valley Arms. Please refer to the Connecticut Valley Arms section for current single shot rifle information and pricing (see Trademark Index).

RIFLES: BOLT ACTION

Add $200 for KDF muzzle brake.

MEDIUM TACTICAL BCR17 – .308 Win. cal., 22 in. nitride finished stainless steel contoured barrel, Timney or Shilen trigger, pillar bedded with Marine Tex steel filled epoxy, custom machined 20 MOA Picatinny rail, Badger M-4 bottom metal, McMillan A1-3 stock, olive finish with tan and black marbling, 9.9 lbs. New 2013.

MSR $4,000	$3,800	$3,400	$2,975	$2,550	$2,310	$1,870	$1,525	

HEAVY TACTICAL BCR19 – .308 Win. or .300 Win. Mag. cal., 26 in. nitride finished stainless steel contoured barrel, 5 shot detachable mag., Timney or Shilen trigger, pillar bedded with Marine Tex steel filled epoxy, custom machined 20 MOA Picatinny rail, Badger M-5 bottom metal, six flush cups, bipod mounting stud, McMillan A-4 stock with adj. butt and comb., OD Green finish, 12 1/2 lbs. New 2013.

MSR $4,500	$4,200	$3,825	$3,350	$2,875	$2,600	$2,100	$1,725	

HEAVY TACTICAL CHASSIS STOCK – .308 Win. cal., Bergara custom action, 24 in. stainless steel barrel, nitride barrel finish, 10 shot detachable mag., Timney trigger, full length unitized Monolithic rail, tubular aluminum forend with accessory rails and flush cups, APO Mod-1 Chassis folding stock, adj. comb height, rear mono pod, 10 1/2 lbs. New 2014.

MSR $5,000	$4,600	$4,025	$3,450	$3,125	$2,525	$2,075	$1,625	

BERSA

Current manufacturer established circa 1958 and located in Ramos Mejia, Argentina. Currently distributed exclusively by Eagle Imports, Inc. located in Wanamassa, NJ. Previously imported and distributed before 1988 by Rock Island Armory located in Geneseo, IL, Outdoor Sports Headquarters, Inc. located in Dayton, OH, and R.S.A. Enterprises, Inc. located in Ocean, NJ. Distributor sales only.

PISTOLS: SEMI-AUTO

THUNDER PRO HC 9/40 – 9mm Para. or .40 S&W cal., DA/SA, 4 1/4 in. barrel with interchangeable Sig Sauer type 3 dot sights, alloy frame/steel slide, 17 (9mm Para. cal.), or 13 (.40 S&W cal.) shot mag., checkered black polymer grips, integral locking system, Picatinny lower rail, polygonal rifling, loaded chamber indicator, ambidextrous releases, matte black or duo-tone finish, 30.7 oz.

MSR $550	$465	$400	$350	$315	$250	$210	$165	

Add $8 for duo-tone finish.

BP9/BP40CC – 9mm Para. or .40 S&W (disc. 2011) cal., 3.3 in. barrel, DAO, striker fired, 8 shot mag., interchangeable Sig Sauer type front and Glock type rear sights, loaded chamber indicator, black or Olive Drab (new 2014) polymer frame with integral grips and front Picatinny rail, matte black or duo-tone finish, ambidextrous mag. release, steel slide, 21.5 oz. New 2010.

MSR $475	$400	$350	$300	$275	$225	$175	$150	

Add $10 for duo-tone finish.

BINGHAM, LTD.

Previous manufacturer located in Norcross, GA circa 1976-1985.

Information regarding this manufacturer is available online free of charge at www.bluebookofgunvalues.com.

BLACK DAWN INDUSTRIES

Current manufacturer of semi-auto rifles located in Sedalia, MO since 2010.

Black Dawn Industries currently manufactures a complete line of AR-15 style rifles as well as designing their own parts. Their Pro-Shop offers accessories geared toward the AR market, and they also have their own in-house Custom Shop that offers a wide range of services and finish options.

MSR	100%	98%	95%	90%	80%	70%	60%	Last MSR

RIFLES: SEMI-AUTO

Please contact the company directly regarding models that do not have current retail pricing (see Trademark Index).

BDR-10 – .308 Win. cal., GIO, 16 or 20 in. M4 profile barrel, Magpul MOE collapsible stock, Magpul MOE grip, flared magwell, free floating handguard, Magpul 20 shot PMag., Black anodized finish, includes hard case. New 2012.

BDR-15A – 5.56 NATO/.223 Rem. cal., GIO, 16 in. M4 profile barrel with A2 flash hider, A2 front sight, MBUS rear sight, 30 shot mag., Magpul MOE collapsible stock, Magpul MOE grip, enhanced trigger guard, flared mag. well, ambi. sling mount, M4 feed ramp, carbine length MFR rail, available in Black, Flat Dark Earth, or OD Green finish, includes hard case and one 30 shot PMag., 6 lbs. 10 oz. New 2012.

MSR $1,499	$1,350	$1,175	$1,025	$925	$750	$625	$475	

* **BDR-15AP** – 5.56 NATO/.223 Rem. cal., similar to BDR-15A, except features GPO. New 2012.

BDR-15B – 5.56 NATO/.223 Rem. cal., GIO, 16 in. M4 profile barrel with A2 flash hider, MBUS front and rear sights, 30 shot mag., Magpul MOE collapsible stock, Magpul MOE grip, enhanced trigger guard, flared mag. well, ambi. sling mount, M4 feed ramp, mid-length MFR rail, available in Black, Flat Dark Earth, or OD Green finish, includes hard case and one 30 shot PMag., 6 lbs. 15 oz.

* **BDR-15BP** – 5.56 NATO/.223 Rem. cal., similar to BDR-15B, except features GPO.

BDR-15BLK – .300 AAC Blackout cal., GIO, 16 in. M4 profile barrel with A2 flash hider, no sights, 30 shot mag., Magpul MOE collapsible stock, Magpul MOE grip, enhanced trigger guard, flared mag. well, ambi. sling mount, M4 feed ramp, mid-length MFR rail, available in Black, Flat Dark Earth, or OD Green finish, includes hard case and one 30 shot PMag., 6 lbs. 11 oz. New 2012.

BDR-15E – 5.56 NATO/.223 Rem. cal., AR-15 style, GIO, 20 in. M4 profile heavy barrel with target crown, no sights, 30 shot mag., fixed A2 stock, Ergo pistol grip, free-floating handguard, black anodized finish, 8 lbs. 9 oz.

BDR-15M – 5.56 NATO/.223 Rem. cal., GIO, 16 in. M4 profile barrel with A2 flash hider, A2 front sight, MBUS rear sight, 30 shot mag., Magpul MOE collapsible stock, Magpul MOE grip, enhanced trigger guard, flared mag. well, ambi. sling mount, M4 feed ramp, carbine length MFR rail, available in Black, Flat Dark Earth, or OD Green finish, includes hard case and one 30 shot PMag., 7 lbs.

* **BDR-15MP** – 5.56 NATO/.223 Rem. cal., similar to BDR-15M, except features GPO. New 2012.

ALPHA – 5.56 NATO cal., GIO, custom built model featuring 16 in. M4 profile barrel with A2 muzzle brake and M4 extensions, fixed A2 front sight, forged aluminum upper and lower receivers, flat-top upper receiver w/M4 feed ramp, enhanced flared mag. well, standard A2 grip, six-position collapsible stock, black anodized finish, accessories include Black Dawn rear flip sight, two 30 shot mags., and a case, 9 lbs.

BRAVO – 5.56 NATO cal., GIO, custom built model similar to Alpha, except accessories include extended Black Dawn MFR free float rail enclosing a low profile gas block, Black Dawn front and rear flip up sights, two 30 shot mags., and hard case.

CHARLIE EDITION – 5.56 NATO cal., custom built model similar to Alpha, except features GPO, accessories include a Black Dawn rear flip up sight, two 30 shot mags., hard case.

DELTA EDITION – 5.56 NATO cal., custom built model featuring GPO, 16 in. M4 profile barrel and M4 extensions, forged aluminum upper and lower receivers, flat-top upper receiver w/M4 feed ramps, enhanced flared mag. well, standard A2 grip, 6-position collapsible stock, black anodized finish, accessories include Black Dawn MFR free float rail enclosing a Black Dawn low profile gas block, front and rear flip up sights, two 30 shot mags., and hard case, 9 lbs.

ECHO EDITION – 5.56 NATO cal., GIO, custom built model featuring 20 in. H-Bar profile barrel with M4 extensions and 11 in. target crown, fluted and vented free float tube forend with sling swivel stud, 4 rail Picatinny gas block, flat-top upper receiver with M4 feed ramp, enhanced flared mag. well, A2 fixed stock, Hogue overmolded pistol grip, Black anodized finish, accessories include two 20 shot mags. and hard case.

MOE EDITION – 5.56 NATO cal., GIO, custom built model featuring 16 in. M4 profile barrel with A2 muzzle brake and M4 extensions, fixed A2 front and Magpul MBUS rear sights, forged aluminum upper and lower receivers, flat-top upper receiver w/M4 feed ramps, enhanced flared mag. well, Magpul MOE carbine length handguard, Magpul MOE pistol grip and Magpul MOE 6-position collapsible stock, black anodized finish, includes one 30 shot mag. and hard case, 9 lbs.

ZOMBIE SLAYER – 5.56 NATO cal., GIO, custom built model similar to Alpha, except accessories included are one 30 shot Zombie magazine and hard case.

BLACK FORGE

Current manufacturer of semi-auto rifles located in Florida.

RIFLES: SEMI-AUTO

A3 FLAT-TOP CARBINE – 5.45x39mm or 5.56 NATO cal., GIO, 16 1/2 in. chromemoly steel barrel with A2 bird cage flash hider, A3 flat-top removable carry handle, A2 front sight post gas block, adj. rear sights, 6-position collapsible

MSR	100%	98%	95%	90%	80%	70%	60%	Last MSR

stock and poly grip with Milspec size buffer tube, double shield M4 handguard, black furniture.

MSR $899 $810 $710 $610 $550 $450 $375 $275

Add $100 for 5.45x39mm cal.

BADGER – .223 Rem., 5.45x39mm, or 7.62x39mm cal., AK-47 design, GIO, 16 1/2 in. hammer forged heavy chrome-lined barrel with Phantom muzzle brake and internal recoil reducer, factory integrated adj. sights, M4 Magpul MOE collapsible stock and ACE sidefolder, 4-way adj. milled Red Star Arms trigger system, high grade polymer Scorpion grip, 4-rail Picatinny adapter system, black finish.

MSR $1,550 $1,395 $1,225 $1,050 $950 $775 $625 $500

BF-15 TIER 1 – 5.56 NATO cal., AR-15 style, GIO, 16 1/2 in. M4 barrel with A2 bird cage flash suppressor, 30 shot mag., aluminum flat-top A3 upper receiver w/Picatinny rail, Magpul MBUS Gen2 rear flip-up sight, double shield M4 handguard, alum. forged lower receiver w/Black Forge logo, SST, Magpul trigger guard, 6-position collapsible stock w/ buffer tube, Magpul MOE grip, black furniture.

MSR $1,099 $990 $875 $750 $675 $550 $450 $350

* **BF-15 Tier 2** – 5.56 NATO or 5.45x39mm cal., GIO, similar to BF-15 Tier 1, except built with standard M4 accessories.

MSR $999 $900 $795 $675 $625 $500 $400 $325

Add $100 for 5.45x39mm cal.

KALASHNIKOV – 7.62x54R cal., AK-47 design, GIO, 23 in. hammer forged heavy chrome-lined barrel, Mojo MicroClick rear peep sight and factory front sight, RPK front trunnion, quick detach Advanced Armament Corps. Blackout muzzle brake with suppressor, spring-loaded UTG bipod in the front, and a monopod grip attached to the Magpul PRS adj. stock via a Picatinny rail underneath, Surefire SGM handguard, 4-way adj. milled Red Star Arms trigger guard, Magpul MOE pistol gip, black finish.

MSR $1,975 $1,775 $1,550 $1,325 $1,200 $975 $800 $625

OPERATOR – .308 Win. cal., GIO, 16 1/2 in. barrel, Tromix charging handle and shark muzzle brake, 6-position Magpul MOE stock and ACE Pig Nose adapter, one-piece milled Texas Weapons Systems dog leg rail w/Picatinny rail, flip-up Magpul MBUS sights, Magpul MOE grip, 4-rail Midwest Rail adapter system, black furniture.

MSR $1,725 $1,550 $1,350 $1,175 $1,050 $850 $700 $550

OPERATOR GEN 2 – 5.45x39mm cal., GIO, 16 1/2 in. barrel, built on Russian Vepr receiver, includes one 30 shot mag.

MSR $1,495 $1,350 $1,175 $1,015 $925 $750 $625 $475

RPK – 5.45x39mm cal., GIO, AK-47 design, 23 in. hammer forged heavy chrome-lined barrel, built on Russian Vepr 5.45 receiver, Russian red birch laminate original club foot style stock, pistol grip, and handguard, AK Cage Brake, UTG Dragon Claw clamp-on bipod, adj. sights, black finish.

MSR $1,650 $1,485 $1,300 $1,115 $1,010 $815 $675 $525

STINGER – 5.45x39mm cal., GIO, 16 in. barrel, 30 shot mag., Vepr RBK receiver, black furniture.

MSR $1,625 $1,475 $1,300 $1,100 $1,000 $825 $675 $525

TACTICAL BLACK POLY – .223 Rem., 5.45x39mm, or 7.62x39mm cal., AK-47 design, GIO, 16 1/2 in. hammer forged heavy chrome-lined barrel with Afghan era AK-74 style muzzle brake, black polymer stock, adj. sights, 4-way adj. milled Red Star Arms trigger system, integrated bullet guide, internal recoil reducer, adapter block, black finish.

MSR $1,350 $1,225 $1,075 $925 $850 $675 $550 $425

Add $75 for .223 Rem. cal.

* **Tactical Plum Poly** – .223 Rem., 5.45x39mm, or 7.62x39mm cal., GIO, similar to Tactical Black Poly, except features an ACE 8 1/2 in. skeleton stock with a sidefolder adapter, and comes with a Phantom muzzle brake, factory plum colored pistol grip and two-piece handguard.

MSR $1,475 $1,325 $1,150 $995 $900 $725 $600 $475

Add $75 for .223 Rem. cal.

WA-SPr 74 – 5.45x39mm cal., AK-47 design, GIO, 16 1/2 in. hammer forged heavy chrome-lined barrel, ACE lightweight stock braided in paracord for comfort and design matched with an Ace sidefolder adapter, 30 shot mag., 4-way adj. milled Red Star Arms trigger system and one-piece recoil reducer, Cerakote firearm coatings in Burnt Bronze with Cerakote Ceramic Micro Clear finish, includes matching Para Patriot Single Point Sling set.

MSR $2,375 $2,125 $1,875 $1,600 $1,450 $1,175 $950 $750

WOLVERINE – .223 Rem., 5.45x39mm, or 7.62x39mm cal., AK-47 design, GIO, 16 1/2 in. hammer forged heavy chrome-lined barrel, factory integrated adj. sights, Russian red birch laminate stock, 2-piece handguard and slant muzzle brake with crush washer, bullet guide, 4-way adj. milled Red Star Arms trigger system, black finish.

MSR $1,350 $1,225 $1,075 $925 $850 $675 $550 $425

Add $75 for .223 Rem. cal.

MSR	100%	98%	95%	90%	80%	70%	60%	Last MSR

VEPR TACTICAL 308 – .308 Win. cal., GIO, 16 1/2 in. barrel with Razr muzzle brake and internal recoil reducer, 10 or 20 shot mag., 4-way adj. milled trigger intrafuse handguard, ACE skeleton stock, Vepr adapter block, Hogue polymer grip, HK front and rear sights, black furniture.

MSR $1,650	$1,485	$1,300	$1,100	$1,000	$825	$675	$525	

SHOTGUNS: SEMI-AUTO

Modified Izhmash, Saiga, and Vepr shotguns are also available in various configurations -prices range from $699-$1,295.

SAIGA 12 CHAOS – 12 ga., 18.1 in. smooth bore barrel with Tromix Mini-Monster muzzle brake, 12 shot mag., Chaos Titan quad rail system, monolithic Picatinny rail, iron sights, Ergo F93 AR-15 side folding stock, Red Star Arms 4-way adj. milled fire control group, TAC-47 gas plug, black finish.

MSR $1,695	$1,525	$1,350	$1,150	$1,050	$850	$675	$550	

VEPR 12 TROMIX SF – 12 ga., threaded, chrome-lined barrel, Tromix side-folding stock, Demon brake and Red Star Arms adj. milled trigger, hinged dust cover w/Picatinny rail, Molot polymer pistol grip, upper and lower handguard, Tromix charging handle, 5 shot mag., adj. rear sight, black furniture.

MSR $1,899	$1,725	$1,525	$1,300	$1,175	$950	$775	$600	

BLACKHEART INTERNATIONAL LLC

Current manufacturer located in Philippi, WV. The company also manufactures separate components for AR-15 style carbines/rifles, in addition to custom bolt actions and barreled actions.

PISTOLS: SEMI-AUTO

BHI manufactured a line of AR-15 style pistols in 5.56 NATO cal. including the BHI-15 with various options. MSRs started at $1,050.

BHI-15 S2 AR57 PISTOL – 5.7x28mm cal.,12 in. free float barrel, aluminum upper and lower receiver, Geissele Super Dynamic Combat trigger, Wolff trigger springs, Stark SE-1 pistol grip, black anodized finish.

MSR $1,304	$1,100	$965	$825	$750	$600	$495	$385	

RIFLES: BOLT ACTION

BHI also offers a line of tactical and sport bolt action models. They include the BBG Light Sniper - MSR is $4,054, BBG Hunter - MSR is $3,321, BBG F-Class - MSR is $3,324, and BBG Tactical - MSR is $4,579. Please contact the company directly for more information, including pricing for available options (see Trademark Index).

RIFLES: SEMI-AUTO

Blackheart International also makes a variety of NFA carbines for military and law enforcement.

BHI-15 (A) – 5.56 NATO cal., AR-15 style, GIO, 16 in. chrome lined barrel, 30 shot mag., manganese phosphate barrel finish, A2 flash hider, standard collapsible stock, polycarbonate hand guard, A3 flat-top upper and aluminum lower, hard coat black anodized finish, standard charging handle, front post sight, rear aperture sight, Mil-Spec trigger group, Wolff springs, detachable carry handle.

MSR $1,245	$1,025	$900	$775	$700	$575	$450	$350	

BHI-15 MIL-SPEC2 AR57 RIFLE – 5.7x28mm cal., semi-auto, 16 in. free float fluted barrel and Gen 2 receiver, alum. upper and lower receivers, Mil-Spec trigger group, A2 pistol grip, black hard-coat anodized finish, 5.91 lbs.

MSR $1,411	$1,175	$1,030	$875	$800	$650	$525	$425	

This model also comes with a short barrel configuration (BHI-15 Mil-Spec AR57 SBR).

BHI-15 S2 – 5.56 NATO cal., AR-15 style, GIO, 16 in. chrome lined barrel with Surefire flash hider/suppressor adaptor, flat-top receiver with Picatinny rail, 30 shot mag., manganese phosphate barrel finish, Magpul CTR collapsible stock, aluminum free float tube, mid-length hand guard, hard coat black anodized finish, PRI Gasbuster charging handle, Geissele SSA 2-stage trigger, Wolff springs, Stark SE-1 pistol grip, Titanium firing pin.

MSR $2,095	$1,775	$1,550	$1,325	$1,200	$975	$800	$625	

Add $1,800 for BHI-15 S Executive Package - a complete tactical support system for your rifle including Harris bipod and adapter, Magpul flip-up front and rear sights, Aimpoint Micro-H1 with QD mount and lens covers, Insight M3X tactical illuminator light, J. Dewey field cleaning kit, hard travel case with padded nylon case, and more.

This model is also available in a Short Barrel Rifle configuration (BHI-15 SBR2) with an 11 in. barrel for military/law enforcement.

BHI-15 S2 AR57 RIFLE – 5.7x28mm cal., semi-auto, 16 in. free float fluted barrel, milled aluminum lightweight AR57 upper receiver, and BHI-15 S2 lower receiver, Geissele Super Dynamic Combat trigger, Wolff trigger springs, Stark SE-1 pistol grip, hard-coat black anodized finish, 6.15 lbs.

MSR $1,721	$1,450	$1,275	$1,100	$985	$800	$650	$500	

This model is also available in a Short Barrel Rifle configuration (BHI-15 S2 AR57 SBR).

MSR	100%	98%	95%	90%	80%	70%	60%	Last MSR

BHI-15 SPR2 (SPECIAL PURPOSE RIFLE) – 5.56 NATO cal., AR-15 style, GIO, 20 in. chrome lined barrel with Surefire flash hider/suppressor adaptor, flat-top receiver with Picatinny rail, 20 shot mag., manganese phosphate barrel finish, Magpul PRS adj. stock, aluminum free float tube, rifle length hand guard, hard coat black anodized finish, PRI Gasbuster charging handle, Geissele SSA 2-stage trigger, Mil-Spec A3 flat-top upper, aluminum lower, hard chromed titanium firing pin, adj. DPMS Panther Tactical grip, oversized magwell.

MSR $2,475	$2,100	$1,850	$1,575	$1,425	$1,150	$950	$750	

Add $1,600 for BHI-15 SPR Executive Package - a complete tactical support system for your rifle including Leupold Mark-AR 3x9 scope, Harris bipod and adapter, Magpul flip-up front and rear sights, Freedom Reaper Scope mount, J. Dewey field cleaning kit, hard travel case with padded nylon case, and more.

BHI SOPMOD AK – 7.62x39mm cal., semi-auto AK-47 design, hammer forged chrome lined barrel, 30 shot polymer mag., Magpul CTR collapsible or folding stock, SAW style pistol grip, black finish, widened mag. release lever, CCA aluminum quad rail forend, AK-103 muzzle brake, tritium front and rear sights, offset vertical grip, quick attach scope mount, enhanced selector lever, black furniture, includes AKARS sight mounting system, 8.7 lbs.

MSR $1,850	$1,525	$1,335	$1,150	$1,025	$850	$685	$525	

SHOTGUNS: SLIDE ACTION

BH-870-4 – 12 ga., 2 3/4 or 3 in. chamber, Rem. 870 action, 18 1/2 in. barrel, matte black finish, 7 shot, collapsible adj. pistol grip tactical stock, Picatinny rails on the magazine clamp and saddle rail. New 2013.
   Please contact the company directly for pricing and available options for this model (see Trademark Index).

BLACKOPS TECHNOLOGIES
Current manufacturer located in Columbia Falls, MT.

PISTOLS: SEMI-AUTO

CLASSIC 1911 – 9mm Para., 10mm, .40 S&W, or .45 ACP cal., Government or Commander frame, 5 in. KART National Match barrel, SA, precision tuned trigger, custom made VZ grips, fixed sights with tritium inserts optional. New 2013.

MSR $3,195	$2,875	$2,525	$2,150	$1,950	$1,575	$1,300	$1,000	

RECON 1911 – 9mm, 10mm, .40 S&W, or .45 ACP cal., Government or Commander frame, 4 1/4 in. KART National Match barrel, SA, precision tuned trigger, custom made VZ grips, full perimeter precision TiG magwell, max bevel MSH, fixed sights with tritium inserts optional. New 2013.

MSR $3,295	$2,950	$2,575	$2,225	$2,000	$1,625	$1,325	$1,050	

RIFLES: BOLT ACTION

JAEGER – .300 Win. Mag., or .338 LM cal., Model 911 action, 20 or 22 in. barrel with Surefire muzzle brake/suppressor adapter, pinned recoil lug, Manners MCS-T4A or T6 A stock, Timney trigger, embedded front rail night vision mount, Picatinny rail, Cerakote finish, shipped in fitted Pelican case.

MSR $5,995	$5,100	$4,475	$3,825	$3,475	$2,800	$2,300	$1,775	

KUKRI – .260 Rem. or .308 Win. cal., Model 911 action, 18 in. Bartlein Kukri contour barrel, Manners MCS-T or T3 stock, Timney trigger, black finish, shipped in fitted Pelican case.

MSR $4,725	$4,250	$3,725	$3,200	$2,900	$2,350	$1,925	$1,500	

PERSEUS – .308 Win. cal., Model 911 action, 19 in. RECON contour barrel, Timney trigger, Manners MCS-T4A or T6A stock, embedded front rail night vision mount, shipped in fitted Pelican case.

MSR $5,725	$5,150	$4,500	$3,875	$3,500	$2,825	$2,325	$1,800	

RANCH RIFLE – .223 Rem. or .308 Win. cal., Model 911 action, 16 1/2 in. Bartlein Specter contour stainless steel barrel, BlackOps Precision Ranch rifle stock, Timney trigger, Picatinny rail, M16 style extractor and plunger ejector, black finish.

MSR $4,725	$4,250	$3,725	$3,200	$2,900	$2,350	$1,925	$1,500	

RECON – .308 Win. cal., Model 911 action, 18 in. Bartlein Kukri contour stainless steel barrel with Surefire muzzle brake and suppressor adapter, Manners MCS-T6 or T6-A stock, EFR night vision mount, Timney trigger, nitride or cerakote finish, precision Pillar system, enhanced heavy duty DBM, ground recoil lug, shipped in custom fitted Pelican case.

MSR $5,525	$4,975	$4,350	$3,725	$3,375	$2,750	$2,250	$1,750	

SPECTER-BABR – .308 Win. cal., Model 911 action, 18 in. Bartlein Specter contour barrel, Manners MCS Series of stocks, integral back-up iron sight system, EFR or Specter night vision mount, Timney trigger, black finish, shipped in custom fitted Pelican case.

MSR $6,625	$5,975	$5,225	$4,475	$4,075	$3,275	$2,700	$2,100	

MSR	100%	98%	95%	90%	80%	70%	60%	Last MSR

BLACK RAIN ORDNANCE, INC.

Current rifle manufacturer established in 2008 and located in Neosho, MO. Dealer and distributor sales.

RIFLES: SEMI-AUTO

PG1 – .223 Rem. cal., GPO or GIO, 20 shot mag., 16 in. slim blast stainless steel barrel with flash suppressor, detachable folding sights, flat-top Picatinny rail with 7 in. black barrel quad rail, black pistol grip and collapsible MOE stock, Pink Splash receiver finish.

MSR $2,039	$1,725	$1,525	$1,300	$1,175	$950	$775	$600	

Add $350 for PG1 with gas piston operation.

PG2 – .223 Rem. cal., GIO or GPO, 20 shot mag., 16 in. partially fluted black barrel with flash suppressor, flat-top Picatinny rail with 7 in. FDE quad rail, FDE (flat dark earth) UBR stock, Digital Tan receiver finish, detachable folding sights.

MSR $2,439	$2,050	$1,795	$1,550	$1,400	$1,125	$925	$725	

Add $360 for PG2 with gas piston operation.

PG3 – .223 Rem. cal., GIO or GPO, 20 shot mag., 16 in. black/white finished partially spiral fluted barrel with flash suppressor, flat-top Picatinny rail with 7 in. black quad rail, black UBR stock, Silver Skulls receiver finish, detachable folding sights.

MSR $2,379	$1,995	$1,750	$1,500	$1,350	$1,100	$900	$700	

Add $400 for PG3 with gas piston operation.

PG4 – .223 Rem. cal., GIO, 20 shot mag., 24 in. partially fluted black bull barrel, flat-top Picatinny rail with 12 in. black or FDE (disc. 2012) quad rail, black PRS stock, black or flat dark earth (disc. 2012) finish.

MSR $2,239	$1,895	$1,650	$1,425	$1,300	$1,050	$850	$675	

Add $30 for FDE finish (disc. 2012).

PG5 – .223 Rem. cal., GIO or GPO, 20 shot mag., 16 in. partially fluted black barrel with flash suppressor, flat-top Picatinny rail with 7 in. black quad rail, black MOE stock, black finish, detachable folding sights.

MSR $2,109	$1,775	$1,550	$1,325	$1,200	$975	$800	$625	

Add $330 for PG5 with gas piston operation.

PG6 – .223 Rem. cal., GIO or GPO, 20 shot mag., 16 in. partially fluted black barrel with flash suppressor, flat-top Picatinny rail with 7 in. FDE quad rail, FDE MOE stock, black receiver finish, detachable folding sights.

MSR $2,109	$1,775	$1,550	$1,325	$1,200	$975	$800	$625	

Add $360 for PG6 with gas piston operation.

PG7 – Disc. 2011.

	$1,675	$1,465	$1,250	$1,150	$925	$750	$585	*$1,989*

PG8 – Disc. 2011.

	$1,675	$1,465	$1,250	$1,150	$925	$750	$585	*$1,989*

PG9 – .223 Rem. cal., GIO or GPO, 20 shot mag., 16 in. M4 partially fluted MACH barrel with flash suppressor, flat-top Norguard finished receiver with 7 in. black quad rail, black pistol grip and MOE stock, detachable folding sights.

MSR $2,109	$1,775	$1,550	$1,325	$1,200	$975	$800	$625	

Add $350 for PG9 with gas piston operation.

PG10

More research is underway for current values on this discontinued model.

PG11 – .223 Rem. cal., GIO, 20 shot mag., 18 or 20 in. partially fluted black barrel with compensator, no sights, flat-top Picatinny rail with 12 in. black or flat dark earth modular rail, black or FDE UBR stock, Black, Digital Tan, Flat Dark Earth, Norguard, Pink Splash, or Silver Skulls receiver finish.

MSR $2,689	$2,275	$1,995	$1,700	$1,550	$1,250	$1,025	$800	

Add $40 for Digital Tan, Flat Dark Earth, Norguard, Pink Splash, or Silver Skulls finish.

PG12 – .308 Win. cal., GIO, 20 shot mag., 18 or 20 in. partially fluted black or stainless finished barrel with compensator, flat-top Picatinny rail with 12 in. Black or Flat Dark Earth modular rail, Black or FDE PRS stock, Black, Digital Tan, Flat Dark Earth, Norguard, Pink Splash, or Silver Skulls finish.

MSR $3,189	$2,695	$2,350	$2,025	$1,850	$1,475	$1,225	$950	

Add $40 for Digital Tan, Flat Dark Earth, Norguard, Pink Splash, or Silver Skulls finish.

PG13 – .308 Win. cal., GIO, 20 shot mag., 18 in. partially spiral fluted black/white finished barrel with flash suppressor, no sights, Silver Skull finished receiver with flat-top Picatinny rail and 9 in. black modular rail, black pistol grip and UBR stock.

MSR $3,049	$2,575	$2,250	$1,925	$1,750	$1,425	$1,150	$900	

	MSR	100%	98%	95%	90%	80%	70%	60%	Last MSR

PG14 – .308 Win. cal., GIO, 20 shot mag., 18 in. partially fluted stainless barrel with flash suppressor, Norguard finished receiver with Picatinny rail and 9 in. Black modular rail, Black pistol grip and MOE stock, no sights.

| | MSR $2,699 | $2,295 | $2,000 | $1,725 | $1,550 | $1,250 | $1,050 | $800 | |

PG15 – .308 Win. cal., GIO, 20 shot mag., 18 or 20 in. partially fluted black barrel with compensator, flat-top Picatinny rail with 9 in. Black modular rail, Black MOE stock, Black or FDE receiver finish. New 2013.

| | MSR $2,809 | $2,375 | $2,075 | $1,775 | $1,625 | $1,300 | $1,075 | $825 | |

Add $50 for FDE (flat dark earth) finish.

PG16 – .308 Win. cal., GIO, 20 shot mag., 24 in. partially fluted black bull barrel, flat-top Picatinny rail with 12 in. Black or FDE modular rail, Black or FDE pistol grip and PRS stock, Black or FDE finish, no sights.

| | MSR $2,869 | $2,425 | $2,125 | $1,825 | $1,650 | $1,350 | $1,100 | $850 | |

Add $30 for FDE (flat dark earth) finish.

PG17 – .223 Rem. cal., GIO, 20 shot mag., 18 or 24 in. partially fluted black bull barrel, no sights, flat-top Picatinny rail with 9 or 12 in. black or FDE modular rail, black or FDE pistol grip and UBR stock, black or FDE finish. Disc. 2013.

| | | $2,150 | $1,875 | $1,625 | $1,450 | $1,185 | $975 | $750 | *$2,359* |

Add $30 for FDE (flat dark earth) finish.

BLACK RIFLE COMPANY LLC

Current rifle and accessories manufacturer located in Clackamas, OR.

RIFLES: SEMI-AUTO

BRC FORGED RECEIVER MOE CARBINE – AR-15 style, GIO, stainless steel low profile gas block, 16 in. M4 Isonite barrel with Victory compensator/flash hider, Magpul MOE stock and grip, tactical trigger, forged upper and lower receiver, CNC machined quad rail, hard coat anodized cerakote ceramic coating, Black or Flat Dark Earth finish.

As this edition went to press, prices could not be ascertained on this model. Please call the company directly for pricing and other options.

BRC FORGED RECEIVER MID-LENGTH CARBINE – AR-15 style, GIO, similar to BRC Forged Receiver MOE Carbine, except has 16 in. mid-length gas medium contour isonite barrel, Black, Dark Earth, Olive Drab, Sniper Gray, or White finish.

As this edition went to press, prices could not be ascertained on this model. Please call the company directly for pricing and other options.

BRC BILLET MID-LENGTH CARBINE – AR-15 style, GIO, similar to BRC Forged MOE Carbine, except has 16 in. gas medium contour barrel, billet mid-length receiver, Magpul MOE stock and grip standard, other stock options are available, choice of Black, Dark Earth, Olive Drab, Sniper Gray, or White finish.

| | MSR $1,490 | $1,350 | $1,175 | $1,015 | $925 | $750 | $610 | $475 | |

BRC SASS RIFLE – 6.8 SPC cal., AR-15 style, GIO, billet receivers, 18 in. match barrel with Victory compensator, 13 in. MQR rail, Magpul PRS stock, ergo grip, tactical latch, stainless steel polished carrier with MP tested bolt.

| | MSR $1,799 | $1,625 | $1,425 | $1,225 | $1,100 | $895 | $725 | $575 | |

BLACK WEAPONS ARMORY

Current custom manufacturer located in Tucson, AZ.

Black Weapons Armory specializes in custom gun orders and gunsmithing as well as AR-15 parts and accessories.

RIFLES: SEMI-AUTO

Black Weapons Armory manufactures custom AR-15 rifles built to customer specifications. Current models include the PUG (Practical Ugly Gun) - MSR $2,050. Please contact the company directly for more information including options, pricing, and availabilty (see Trademark Index).

BLASER

Currently manufactured by Blaser Jagdwaffen GmbH in Isny im Allgäu, Germany. Currently imported and distributed beginning late 2006 by Blaser USA, located in San Antonio, TX. Previously located in Stevensville, MD. Previously imported and distributed 2002-2006 by SIG Arms located in Exeter, NH, and circa 1988-2002 by Autumn Sales Inc. located in Fort Worth, TX. Dealer sales.

The Blaser Company was founded in 1963 by Horst Blaser. In 1986, the company was taken over by Gerhard Blenk. During 1997, the company was sold to SIG. In late 2000, SIG Arms AG, the firearms portion of SIG, was purchased by two Germans, Michael Lüke and Thomas Ortmeier, who have a background in textiles. Today the Lüke & Ortmeier group (L&O Group) includes independently operational companies such as Blaser Jadgwaffen GmbH, Mauser Jagdwaffen GmbH, J.P. Sauer & Sohn GmbH, SIG-Sauer Inc., SIG-Sauer GmbH and SAN Swiss Arms AG.

Blaser currently makes approximately 20,000 rifles and shotguns annually, with most being sold in Europe.

MSR	100%	98%	95%	90%	80%	70%	60%	Last MSR

RIFLES: BOLT ACTION

The R-93 rifle system's biggest advantage is its component interchangeability. Both barrels and bolt heads/assemblies can be quickly changed making the R-93 a very versatile rifle platform. Many special orders and features are available; please contact Blaser USA directly for additional information, including pricing and availability (see Trademark Index).

Add $415 for saddle scope mount on all current Blaser rifles.

Add $355 for left-hand stock available on currently manufactured R-8 and R-93 models.

Add $242 for Kickstop recoil pad on currently manufactured Blaser rifles.

Beginning late 2006, Blaser began offering graded wood between grades 3-11 on most models. Please refer to these listings under each current model.

R-93 TACTICAL 2 – please refer to listing in the Sig Sauer section under the Rifles: Bolt Action category.

This model is distributed by Sig Sauer Inc., located in Exeter, NH.

BLUEGRASS ARMORY

Current rifle manufacturer located in Ocala, FL. Previously located in Richmond, KY. Consumer direct sales.

During 2010, Bluegrass Armory was purchased by Good Times Outdoors.

RIFLES: BOLT ACTION

VIPER XL 50 – .50 BMG cal., single shot action with 3-lug bolt, 29 in. chromemoly steel barrel with muzzle brake, one-piece frame with aluminum stock (choice of gray, OD green, or black), incorporates Picatinny rail, includes detachable bipod, right or left hand, approx. 24 lbs. New 2003.

MSR $4,200	$3,895	$3,675	$3,150	$2,850	$2,310	$1,900	$1,475

Add $100 for OD Green or Grey finish.

MOONSHINER – .308 Win., .300 Win. Mag., or .338 Lapua cal., Bullpup configuration with twin lugs, 21, 24, or 26 in. barrel with muzzle brake, 8 in. Picatinny rail on top of receiver plus 3 on forearm, detachable mag., soft contoured recoil pad with storage compartment in stock, available in Desert Tan, OD Green, or Tactical Black finish, 11 lbs. New 2011.

MSR $2,995	$2,750	$2,400	$2,100	$1,750	$1,475	$1,125	$975

BOBCAT WEAPONS INC.

Previous manufacturer from April, 2003-circa 2006 and located in Mesa, AZ. During late 2006, the company name was changed to Red Rock Arms. Please refer to the R section for current information and pricing.

RIFLES: SEMI-AUTO

BW-5 MODEL – 9mm Para. cal., stamped steel or polymer (Model BW-5 FS) lower receiver, roller locked delayed blowback operating system, 16 1/2 in. stainless steel barrel, choice of black, desert tan, OD green, or camo stock, pistol grip, and forearm, Model BW-5 FS has fake suppressor, paddle mag. release and 8 7/8 in. barrel, 10 shot mag., approx. 6.4 lbs. Mfg. 2003-2006.

	$1,175	$995	$875	$800	$725	$650	$575	$1,350

Add $275 for Model BW-5 FS.

BOHICA

Previous manufacturer and customizer located in Sedalia, CO, circa 1993-1994.

RIFLES: SEMI-AUTO

M16-SA – .223 Rem., .50 AE, or various custom cals., AR-15 style, GIO, 16 or 20 in. barrel, A-2 sights, standard handguard, approx. 950 were mfg. through September 1994.

	$1,375	$1,225	$1,000	$850	$725	$600	$525	

Add $100 for flat-top receiver with scope rail.

Add $65 for two-piece, free floating handguard.

In addition to the rifles listed, Bohica also manufactured a M16-SA Match variation (retail was $2,295, approx. 10 mfg.), a pistol version of the M16-SA in both 7 and 10 in. barrel (retail was $1,995, approx. 50 mfg.), and a limited run of M16-SA in .50 AE cal. (retail was $1,695, approx. 25 mfg.).

BRAVO COMPANY MFG. INC.

Current rifle manufacturer located in Hartland, WI.

CARBINES/RIFLES: SEMI-AUTO

Bravo Company Mfg., Inc. manufactures a line of AR-15 style rifles with many available options and accessories. The company is also a dealer/distributor for other companies that specialize in tactical gear.

MSR	100%	98%	95%	90%	80%	70%	60%	Last MSR

CAR-16LW MOD 0 CARBINE – 5.56 NATO cal., GIO, 16 in. lightweight barrel, basic rifle with double heat shield handguards, no rear sight, black hardcoat anodized finish, adj. Magpul stock, mil spec F-marked forged front sight, M4 flat-top receiver, upper Picatinny rail, Mod 4 charging handle, chrome lined bore and chamber.

| MSR $1,099 | $925 | $810 | $700 | $625 | $500 | $400 | $325 | |

CAR-16LW MOD 1 CARBINE – 5.56 NATO cal., similar to CAR-16LW, except has detachable carry handle with windage and elevation adj. 600m rear sight.

| MSR $1,219 | $1,025 | $895 | $775 | $700 | $575 | $450 | $350 | |

M4 MOD 0 CARBINE – 5.56 NATO cal., GIO, 16 in. barrel, basic rifle with double heat shield handguards, no rear sight, black hardcoat anodized finish, adj. Magpul stock, mil spec F-marked forged front sight, M4 flat-top receiver, upper Picatinny rail, Mod 4 charging handle, chrome lined bore and chamber, MOE enhanced trigger guard, M4 feed ramp barrel extension.

| MSR $1,099 | $925 | $810 | $700 | $625 | $500 | $400 | $325 | |

M4 MOD 1 CARBINE – 5.56 NATO cal., GIO, 16 in. barrel, double heat shield handguards, detachable carry handle with windage and elevation adj. 600m rear sight, black hardcoat anodized finish, adj. Magpul stock, mil spec F-marked forged front sight, M4 flat-top receiver, Mod 4 charging handle, chrome lined bore and chamber, MOE enhanced trigger guard, M4 feed ramp barrel extension.

| MSR $1,219 | $1,025 | $895 | $775 | $700 | $575 | $450 | $350 | |

M4 MOD 2 CARBINE – 5.56 NATO cal., GIO, 16 in. barrel, drop in tactical handguard, folding rear battle sight, black hardcoat anodized finish, adj. Magpul stock, mil spec F-marked forged front sight, M4 flat-top receiver, quad rail, Mod 4 charging handle, chrome lined bore and chamber, MOE enhanced trigger guard, M4 feed ramp barrel extension.

| MSR $1,379 | $1,150 | $1,000 | $875 | $775 | $650 | $525 | $400 | |

MID-16 MOD 0 CARBINE – 5.56 NATO cal., GIO, 16 in. barrel, basic rifle with Magpul MOE handguards, no rear sight, black hardcoat anodized finish, adj. Magpul stock, mil spec F-marked forged front sight, M4 flat-top receiver, upper Picatinny rail, Mod 4 charging handle, chrome lined bore and chamber, M4 feed ramp barrel extension.

| MSR $1,119 | $950 | $825 | $725 | $650 | $525 | $425 | $350 | |

MID-16 MOD 2 CARBINE – 5.56 NATO cal., GIO, 16 in. barrel, drop in tactical handguard, folding rear battle sight, black hardcoat anodized finish, adj. Magpul stock, mil spec F-marked forged front sight, M4 flat-top receiver, quad rail, Mod 4 charging handle, chrome lined bore and chamber, MOE enhanced trigger guard, M4 feed ramp barrel extension.

| MSR $1,395 | $1,175 | $1,025 | $875 | $800 | $650 | $525 | $425 | |

MID-16LW MOD 0 CARBINE – 5.56 NATO cal., GIO, 16 in. lightweight barrel, M4 flat-top receiver, black hardcoat anodized finish, adj. Magpul stock, mil spec F-marked forged front sights, Mod 4 charging handle, chrome lined bore and chamber, Magpul MOE enhanced trigger guard. New 2011.

| MSR $1,119 | $950 | $825 | $725 | $650 | $525 | $425 | $350 | |

RECCE-16 CARBINE – 5.56 NATO cal., GIO, 16 in. barrel, Magpul MOE handguards, black hardcoat anodized finish, adj. Magpul stock, M4 flat-top receiver, full length quad rail, Mod 4 charging handle, chrome lined bore and chamber, M4 feed ramp barrel extension, MOE enhanced trigger guard.

| MSR $1,299 | $1,095 | $960 | $825 | $750 | $600 | $500 | $375 | |

Add $100 for Precision model configuration.

This model is also available with a 14 1/2 in. barrel for law enforcement/military.

A4 RIFLE – 5.56 NATO cal., GIO, polymer handguards, detachable carry handle with windage and elevation adj. 600m rear sight, black hardcoat anodized finish, fixed buttstock, mil spec F-marked forged front sights, M4 flat-top receiver, Mod 4 charging handle, chrome lined bore and chamber, MOE enhanced trigger guard, M4 feed ramp barrel extension.

| MSR $1,219 | $1,025 | $895 | $775 | $700 | $575 | $450 | $350 | |

BREN 10 (PREVIOUS MFG.)

Previous trademark manufactured 1983-1986 by Dornaus & Dixon Ent., Inc., located in Huntington Beach, CA.

Bren 10 magazines played an important part in the failure of these pistols to be accepted by consumers. Originally, Bren magazines were not shipped in some cases until a year after the customer received his gun. The complications arising around manufacturing a reliable dual caliber magazine domestically led to the downfall of this company. For this reason, original Bren 10 magazines are currently selling for $150-$175 if new (watch for fakes).

PISTOLS: SEMI-AUTO

Note: the Bren 10 shoots a Norma factory loaded 10mm auto. cartridge. Ballistically, it is very close to a .41 Mag. Bren pistols also have unique power seal rifling, with five lands and grooves. While in production, Bren pistols underwent four engineering changes, the most important probably being re-designing the floorplate of the magazine to prevent the magazine from dislocating as the pistol recoiled.

100% values in this section assume NIB condition. Add 5% for extra original factory mag. Subtract 10% without box/manual.

MSR	100%	98%	95%	90%	80%	70%	60%	Last MSR

BREN 10 MILITARY/POLICE MODEL – 10mm cal. only, DA/SA, identical to standard model, except has all black finish, 5 in. barrel, "83MP" ser. no. prefix. Mfg. 1984-1986.

	100%	98%	95%	90%	80%	70%	60%	Last MSR
	$2,650	$2,300	$2,100	$1,850	$1,250	$900	$700	*$550*

BREN 10 SPECIAL FORCES MODEL – 10mm cal. only, DA/SA, 4 in. barrel, commercial version of the military pistol submitted to the U.S. gov't. Model D has dark finish. Model L has light finish, "SFD" ser. no. prefix on Model D, "SFL" ser. no. prefix on Model L. Disc. 1986.

	100%	98%	95%	90%	80%	70%	60%	Last MSR
Dark finish - Model D	$2,675	$2,250	$2,100	$1,850	$1,450	$975	$600	
Light finish - Model L	$3,675	$2,975	$2,750	$2,100	$1,650	$1,050	$675	*$600*

BREN 10 (RECENT MFG.)

Previous trademark manufactured in limited quantities from 2010-2011 by Vltor Mfg., located in Tucson, AZ. Previously distributed exclusively until early 2011 by Sporting Products, LLC, located in W. Palm Beach, FL.

PISTOLS: SEMI-AUTO

SM SERIES – 10mm or .45 ACP cal., 5 in. barrel, DA/SA, stainless steel frame with blue slide, 10 (SM45) or 15 (SM10) shot mag., two-tone finish, synthetic grips, approx. 500 (SM10) or 300 (SM45) were scheduled to be mfg., but very few were produced mid-2010-2011.

	100%	98%	95%	90%	80%	70%	60%	Last MSR
	$1,095	$995	$875	$750	$650	$550	$450	*$1,200*

SMV SERIES – 10mm or .45 ACP cal., 5 in. barrel, DA/SA, stainless steel frame, hard chrome slide, 10 (SMV10) or 15 (SMV15) shot mag., black synthetic grips, approx. 500 (SMV10) or 300 (SMV45) were scheduled to be produced, but very few were mfg. mid-2010-2011.

	100%	98%	95%	90%	80%	70%	60%	Last MSR
	$1,175	$1,050	$925	$800	$700	$600	$495	*$1,299*

SFD45 – .45 ACP cal., 4 in. barrel, DA/SA, matte black finished frame and slide, synthetic grips, 10 shot mag., approx. 500 were scheduled to be produced, but very few were mfg. mid-2010-2011.

	100%	98%	95%	90%	80%	70%	60%	Last MSR
	$995	$895	$800	$700	$600	$500	$425	*$1,100*

SFL45 – .45 ACP cal., 4 in. barrel, DA/SA, matte finished stainless steel frame, hard chrome slide, 10 shot mag., synthetic grips, two-tone finish, approx. 200 were scheduled to be produced, but very few were mfg. mid-2010-2011.

	100%	98%	95%	90%	80%	70%	60%	Last MSR
	$1,095	$995	$875	$750	$650	$550	$450	*$1,200*

BRILEY

Current trademark of pistols and rimfire semi-auto rifles with choke tubes currently manufactured in Houston, TX. Current pistol and rifle manufacture is sub-contracted to other manufacturers using the Briley trademark. Briley has previously produced both pistols and rifles, including those listed, in addition to manufacturing a complete line of top quality shotgun barrel tubes and chokes since 1976. Additionally, beginning late March, 2006-2007 Briley Manufacturing imported and distributed Mauser Models 98 and 03 bolt action rifles from Germany.

PISTOLS: SEMI-AUTO

Briley still has some new old stock pistols remaining. Please check their website for availability and pricing (see Trademark Index).
Add $30 for ambidextrous safety. Add $225 for custom mag well. Add $175 for hard chrome finish. Add $157 for tritium night sights.

PLATE MASTER – 9mm Para. or .38 Super cal., SA, features 1911 Govt. length frame, Briley TCII titanium barrel compensator, Briley scope mount, and other competition features, hot blue finish. Mfg. 1998-2004.

	100%	98%	95%	90%	80%	70%	60%	Last MSR
	$1,675	$1,325	$1,075	$895	$775	$625	$575	*$1,895*

Add $175 for hard chrome finish.

EL PRESIDENTE – 9mm Para. or .38 Super cal., SA, top-of-the-line competition model with Briley quad compensator with side ports, checkered synthetic grips and front grip strap, squared off trigger guard. Mfg. 1998-2004.

	100%	98%	95%	90%	80%	70%	60%	Last MSR
	$2,250	$1,925	$1,625	$1,325	$1,075	$875	$750	*$2,550*

Add $175 for hard chrome finish.

BROLIN ARMS, INC.

Previous importer of handguns (FEG mfg.), rifles (older Mauser military, see Mauser listing), shotguns (Chinese mfg.), and airguns from 1995 to 1999. Previously located in Pomona, CA, until 1999, and in La Verne, CA until 1997.

PISTOLS: SEMI-AUTO, SINGLE ACTION

PATRIOT SERIES MODEL P45 COMP – .45 ACP cal., similar to Legend Series Model L45, except has one-piece match 4 in. barrel with integral dual port compensator, 7 shot mag., Millett or Novak combat sights (new 1997), test target provided, choice of blue or satin (frame only) finish, 38 oz. Mfg. 1996-97 only.

	100%	98%	95%	90%	80%	70%	60%	Last MSR
	$585	$475	$415	$365	$325	$285	$250	*$649*

MSR	100%	98%	95%	90%	80%	70%	60%	Last MSR

Add $70 for Novak combat sights (new 1997). Add $20 for T-tone finish (frame only).

* ***Patriot Series Model P45C (Compact)*** – .45 ACP cal., similar to Model P45 Comp, except has 3 1/4 in. barrel with integral conical lock-up system, 34 1/2 oz. Mfg. 1996-97.

| | $610 | $495 | $425 | $375 | $325 | $285 | $250 | *$689* |

Add $70 for Novak combat sights.
Add $20 for T-tone finish (frame only).

* ***Patriot Series Model P45T*** – features standard frame with compact slide, 3 1/4 in. barrel, 35 1/2 oz. Mfg. 1997 only.

| | $620 | $500 | $425 | $375 | $325 | $285 | $250 | *$699* |

Add $60 for Novak combat sights (new 1997).
Add $10 for T-tone finish (frame only).

TAC 11 – .45 ACP cal., 5 in. conical barrel w/o bushing, beavertail grip safety, 8 shot mag., T-tone or blue finish, Novak low profile combat or Tritium sights, black rubber contour grips, 37 oz. Mfg. 1997-98.

| | $595 | $485 | $425 | $365 | $325 | $285 | $250 | *$670* |

Add $90 for Tritium sights (disc. 1997).

* ***Tac 11 Compact*** – similar to Tac 11, except has shorter barrel. Mfg. 1998 only.

| | $610 | $495 | $435 | $365 | $325 | $285 | $250 | *$690* |

Add $60 for hard-chrome finish.

PISTOLS: SEMI-AUTO, DOUBLE ACTION

The following models had limited manufacture 1998 only.

TAC SERIES SERVICE MODEL – .45 ACP cal., full sized service pistol, DA/SA, 8 shot single column mag., front and rear slide serrations, combat style trigger guard, royal or satin blue finish, low profile 3-dot sights. Mfg. 1998 only.

| | $360 | $315 | $285 | $260 | $240 | $220 | $200 | *$400* |

Add $20 for royal blue finish.

TAC SERIES FULL SIZE MODEL – 9mm Para., .40 S&W, or .45 ACP cal., DA/SA, similar to Tac Series Service Model, except longer barrel, checkered walnut or plastic grips, 8 (.45 ACP only) or 10 shot mag. Mfg. 1998 only.

| | $360 | $315 | $285 | $260 | $240 | $220 | $200 | *$400* |

Add $20 for royal blue finish.

TAC SERIES COMPACT MODEL – 9mm Para. or .40 S&W cal., DA/SA, shortened barrel/slide with full size frame, 10 shot mag. Mfg. 1998 only.

| | $360 | $315 | $285 | $260 | $240 | $220 | $200 | *$400* |

Add $20 for royal blue finish.

TAC SERIES BANTAM MODEL – 9mm Para. or .40 S&W cal., super compact size, DA/SA, with concealed hammer, all steel construction, 3-dot sights. Mfg. 1998 only.

| | $360 | $315 | $285 | $260 | $240 | $220 | $200 | *$399* |

BANTAM MODEL – 9mm Para. or .40 S&W cal., DA/SA, super compact size, concealed hammer, all steel construction, 3-dot sights, royal blue or matte finish. Limited mfg. by FEG 1999 only.

| | $360 | $315 | $285 | $260 | $240 | $220 | $200 | *$399* |

SHOTGUNS: SEMI-AUTO

MODEL SAS-12 – 12 ga. only, 2 3/4 in. chamber, 24 in. barrel with IC choke tube, 3 (standard) or 5 shot (disc. late 1998) detachable box mag., synthetic stock and forearm, gas operated. Mfg. 1998-99.

| | $445 | $385 | $335 | $300 | $280 | $260 | $240 | *$499* |

Add $39 for extra 3 or 5 (disc.) shot mag.

SHOTGUNS: SLIDE ACTION

Brolin shotguns were manufactured in China by Hawk Industries, and were unauthorized copies of the Remington Model 870. Most of these slide action models were distributed by Interstate Arms, and it is thought that Norinco or China North Industries were connected to the manufacturer during the importation of these shotguns.

LAWMAN MODEL – 12 ga. only, 3 in. chamber, action patterned after the Rem. Model 870 (disc. 1998) or the Ithaca Model 37 (new 1999) 18 1/2 in. barrel, choice of bead, rifle (disc. 1998), or ghost ring (disc. 1998) sights, matte (disc. 1998), nickel (disc. 1997), royal blue (new 1998), satin blue (new 1998) or hard chrome finish, black synthetic or hardwood stock and forearm, 7 lbs. Mfg. in China 1997-99.

| | $165 | $155 | $145 | $135 | $125 | $115 | $105 | *$189* |

Add $20 for nickel finish (disc. 1997).
Add $20 for hard chrome finish.
Add $20 for ghost ring sights.

MSR	100%	98%	95%	90%	80%	70%	60%	Last MSR

BROWN PRECISION, INC.

Current manufacturer established in 1968, and located in Los Molinos, CA. Previously manufactured in San Jose, CA. Consumer direct sales.

Brown Precision Inc. manufactures rifles primarily using Remington or Winchester actions and restocks them using a combination of Kevlar, fiberglass, and graphite (wrinkle finish) to save weight. Stock colors are green, brown, grey, black, camo brown, camo green, or camo grey. Chet Brown pioneered the concept of the fiberglass rifle stock in 1965. He started blueprinting actions and using stainless steel match grade barrels on hunting rifles in 1968, and became the first custom gunmaker to use high tech weather-proof metal finishes on hunting rifles during 1977.

RIFLES: BOLT ACTION

Brown Precision will also stock a rifle from a customer supplied action. This process includes a Brown Precision stock, custom glass bedding, recoil pad, stock finish, etc. Prices begin at $945.

LAW ENFORCEMENT SELECTIVE TARGET – .308 Win. cal., Model 700 Varmint action with 20, 22, or 24 in. factory barrel, O.D. green camouflage treatment. Disc. 1992.

	$995	$870	$745	$675	$545	$450	$350	$1,086

This model could have been special ordered with similar options from the Custom High Country Model, with the exception of left-hand action.

TACTICAL ELITE – various cals. and custom features, customized per individual order. New 1997.

MSR $5,695	$5,295	$4,850	$4,100	$3,500	$3,100	$2,600	$2,000	

Add $675 for 3 way adj. buttplate (disc.).
Subtract $1,200 if action is supplied by customer.

THE UNIT – .270 Win., .300 Win. Mag., .300 Wby. Mag., .338 Win. Mag., 7mm-08 Rem., 7mm Rem. Mag., or 7mm STW cal., Rem. 700 BDL or Win. Mod. 70 controlled feed action, various lengths match grade stainless steel barrel with cryogenic treatment, Teflon or electroless nickel finish, Brown Precision Kevlar or graphite reinforced fiberglass stock, includes 60 rounds of custom ammo. Limited mfg. 2001 only.

	$3,225	$2,820	$2,420	$2,195	$1,775	$1,450	$1,130	$3,795

Add $500 for Win. Model 70 Super Grade action with controlled round feeding.
Add $200 for left-hand action.
Subtract $600 if action was supplied by customer.

BROWNING

Current manufacturer with U.S. headquarters located in Morgan, UT. Browning guns originally were manufactured in Ogden, UT, circa 1880. Browning firearms are manufactured by Fabrique Nationale in Herstal and Liège, Belgium. Beginning 1976, Browning also contracted with Miroku of Japan and A.T.I. in Salt Lake City, UT to manufacture both long arms and handguns. In 1992, Browning (including F.N.) was acquired by GIAT of France. During late 1997, the French government received $82 million for the sale of F.N. Herstal from the Walloon business region surrounding Fabrique Nationale in Belgium.

The author would like to express his sincere thanks to the Browning Collector's Association, including members Rodney Herrmann, Richard Spurzem, Jim King, Bert O'Neill, Jr., Anthony Vanderlinden, Richard Desira, Gary Chatham, Bruce Hart, and Glen Nilson for continuing to make their important contributions to the Browning section.

In addition to the models listed within this section, Browning also offered various models/variations that were available only at the annual SHOT SHOW beginning 2004. More research is underway to identify these models, in addition to their original MSRs (if listed).

PISTOLS: SEMI-AUTO, CENTERFIRE, F.N. PRODUCTION UNLESS OTHERWISE NOTED

HI-POWER: POST-1954 MFG. – 9mm Para. or .40 S&W (mfg. 1995-2010) cal.,SA, similar to FN Model 1935, has BAC slide marking, 10 (C/B 1994) or 13* shot mag., 4 5/8 in. barrel, polished blue finish, checkered walnut grips, fixed sights, molded grips were introduced in 1986 (disc. in 2000), ambidextrous safety was added to all models in 1989, approx. 32 (9mm Para.) or 35 (.40 S&W) oz., mfg. by FN in Belgium, imported 1954-2000, reintroduced 2002.

* **Hi-Power Standard - Polished Blue Finish (Imported 1954-2000)** – 9mm Para. or .40 S&W (new 1995-) cal., includes fixed front and lateral adj. rear sight, 32 or 35 oz.

	$875	$700	$550	$475	$425	$350	$325	

Add 50% for ring hammer and internal extractor.
Add 20% for ring hammer and external extractor (post 1962 mfg.).
Add 30% for thumb print feature.
Add 15% for T-prefix serial number.
Older specimens in original dark green, maroon, or red/black plastic boxes were mfg. 1954-1965 and are scarce - add $100+ in value.
Black pouches (circa 1965-1968, especially with gold metal zipper) will also command a $25-$50 premium, depending on condition.

MSR	100%	98%	95%	90%	80%	70%	60%	*Last MSR*

Major identifying factors of the Hi-Power are as follows: the "Thumb-Print" feature was mfg. from the beginning through 1958. Old style internal extractor was mfg. from the beginning through 1962, the "T" SN prefix (T-Series start visible extractor) was mfg. 1963-mid-1970s for all U.S. imports by BAC, 69C through 77C S/N prefixes were mfg. 1969-1977. Rounded type Ring Hammers with new external extractor were mfg. from 1962-1972 (for U.S. imports by BAC, much later on FN marked pistols). Spur Hammers have been mfg. 1972-present, and the "245" S/N prefix has been mfg. 1977-present. During 2010, all Hi-Powers featured a 75th Anniversary logo etched onto the top of the slide.

* ***Hi-Power Standard with Adj. Rear Sight*** – 9mm Para. or .40 S&W cal. (disc. 2010), similar to Hi-Power Standard blue, except has adj. rear sight.

MSR	100%	98%	95%	90%	80%	70%	60%	Last MSR
MSR $1,160	$900	$715	$585	$485	$425	$385	$350	

* ***Hi-Power Mark III*** – 9mm Para. or .40 S&W (mfg. 1994-2000, reintroduced 2003-2010) cal., non-glare matte blue (disc. 2005) or black epoxy (new 2006) finish, ambidextrous safety, tapered dovetail rear fixed sight, two-piece molded grips, Mark III designation became standard in 1994, approx. 35 oz. Imported 1985-2000, reintroduced 2002.

MSR	100%	98%	95%	90%	80%	70%	60%	Last MSR
MSR $1,070	$845	$585	$485	$425	$365	$335	$300	

This model's finish may be confused with some other recent imports which have a "black" painted finish. These black finish guns are painted rather than blue, and some parties have been selling them as original military FNs.

* ***Hi-Power Practical Model*** – 9mm Para. or .40 S&W (new 1995) cal., features blue (disc. 2005) or black epoxy slide, silver-chromed frame finish, wraparound Pachmayr rubber grips, round style serrated hammer, and choice of adj. sights (mfg. 1993-2000) or removable front sight, 36 (9mm Para.) or 39 (.40 S&W) oz. Imported 1990-2000, reintroduced 2002-2006.

MSR	100%	98%	95%	90%	80%	70%	60%	Last MSR
	$725	$600	$525	$450	$425	$400	$375	*$863*

Add $58 for adj. sights (disc. 2000).

* ***Hi-Power GP Competition*** – 9mm Para. cal., competition model with 6 in. barrel, detent adj. rear sight, rubber wraparound grips, front counterweight, improved barrel bushing, decreased trigger pull, approx. 36 1/2 oz.

MSR	100%	98%	95%	90%	80%	70%	60%	Last MSR
	$995	$895	$725	$600	$550	$500	$450	

The original GP Competition came in a black plastic case w/accessories and is more desirable than later imported specimens which were computer serial numbered and came in a styrofoam box. Above prices are for older models - subtract 10% if newer model (computer serial numbered). This model was never cataloged for sale by BAC in the U.S., and it is not serviced by Browning.

* ***Hi-Power Tangent Rear Sight & Slotted*** – 9mm Para. cal., variation with grip strap slotted to accommodate shoulder stock. Early pistols had "T" prefixes. Later pistols had spur hammers and are in the serial range 73CXXXX-74CXXXX.

MSR	100%	98%	95%	90%	80%	70%	60%	Last MSR
	$1,550	$1,300	$1,100	$900	$775	$650	$525	

Add $200 if with "T" prefix.
Add $50 for original pouch and instruction booklet.

This variation will command a premium; beware of fakes, however (carefully examine slot milling and look for ser. no. in 3 places).

Vektor Arms in N. Salt Lake, UT, imported this model again in limited quantities circa 2004 with both the "245" and seldom seen "511" (includes wide trigger, loaded chamber indicator and external extractor) ser. no. prefixes. These guns are not arsenal refinished or refurbished, and were sold in NIB condition, with two 13 shot mags. Original pricing was $895 for the "245" prefix, and $995 for the "511" prefix.

PRO-9/PRO-40 – 9mm Para. or .40 S&W cal., DA/SA, 4 in. barrel, 10, 14 (.40 S&W cal. only), or 16 (9mm Para. cal. only) shot mag., ambidextrous decocking and safety, black polymer frame with satin stainless steel slide, under barrel accessory rail, interchangeable backstrap inserts, fixed sights only, 30 (9mm Para.) or 33 oz. Mfg. in the U.S. by FNH USA 2003-2006.

MSR	100%	98%	95%	90%	80%	70%	60%	Last MSR
	$525	$430	$370	$350	$315	$295	$260	*$641*

Please refer to FNH USA handgun listing for current manufacture.

SHOTGUNS: SEMI-AUTO, A-5 1903-1998, 2012-CURRENT MFG.

BROWNING CHOKES AND THEIR CODES (ON REAR LEFT-SIDE OF BARREL)

* designates full choke (F).

*- designates improved modified choke (IM).

** designates modified choke (M).

**- designates improved cylinder choke (IC).

**$ designates skeet (SK).

*** designates cylinder bore (CYL).

INV. designates barrel is threaded for Browning Invector choke tube system.

INV. PLUS designates back-bored barrels.

MSR	100%	98%	95%	90%	80%	70%	60%	Last MSR

Miroku manufactured A-5s can be determined by year of manufacture in the following manner: RV suffix - 1975, RT - 1976, RR - 1977, RP - 1978, RN - 1979, PM - 1980, PZ - 1981, PY - 1982, PX - 1983, PW - 1984, PV - 1985, PT - 1986, PR - 1987, PP - 1988, PN - 1989, NM - 1990, NZ - 1991, NY - 1992, NX - 1993, NW - 1994, NV - 1995, NT - 1996, NR - 1997, NP - 1998, ZY - 2012, ZX - 2013, ZW - 2014, ZV - 2015.

Browning resumed importation from F.N. in 1946. On November 26, 1997, Browning announced that the venerable Auto-5 would finally be discontinued. Final shipments were made in February, 1998. Over 3 million A-5s were manufactured by Fabrique Nationale in all configurations between 1903-1976. 1976-1998 manufacture was by Miroku in Japan. The A-5 was reintroduced in 2012 with a Kinematic Drive System, aluminum receiver, and a fixed barrel.

NOTE: Barrels are interchangeable between older Belgian A-5 models and recent Japanese A-5s manufactured by Miroku, if the gauge and chamber length are the same. A different barrel ring design and thicker barrel wall design might necessitate some minor sanding of the inner forearm on the older model, but otherwise, these barrels are fully interchangeable.

NOTE: The use of steel shot is recommended ONLY in those recent models manufactured in Japan - NOT in the older Belgian variations.

The "humpback" design on the Auto-5 (both Belgian and Japanese mfg.) features recoil operation with a scroll engraved steel receiver. During 1909, Browning introduced the magazine cutoff, and moved the safety from inside to the front of the triggerguard. 1946-1951 mfg. has a safety in front of triggerguard. 1951-1976 mfg. has crossbolt safety behind the trigger. Post-war 16 ga. imports by Browning are chambered for 2 3/4 in., and have either a horn (disc. 1964) or plastic (1962-1976) buttplate, high luster wood finish (disc. 1962) or glossy lacquer (1962-1976) finish. Walnut buttstock has either round knob pistol grip (disc. 1967) or flat knob (new 1967). In today's Auto-5 marketplace, all gauges of the A-5 have become extremely collectible. Obviously, the Belgian A-5s are the most desirable. However, the pre-1998 Miroku guns are gaining in collectible popularity. It also has become very apparent that the demand for the FN lightweight 20 ga. has superceded the Sweet 16 due to availablilty. Both the lightweight 20 ga. and the Sweet 16 are the most desirable and have seen a dramatic increase in collectibility. Rarity of configurations such as choke designations, and barrel lengths are very important factors in determinging value. Older rare barrels such as the solid rib and the 16 and 20 ga. guns with shorter barrels and open chokes are more desirable than a 30 in. 12 ga. gun with full choke barrel.

The publisher would like to thank Mr. Richard "Doc" Desira for his recent contributions to the Auto-5/A-5 section.

Add 15% for NIB condition on Belgian mfg. Auto-5 models only, depending on desirability. Beware of reproduced boxes and labels, especially on the more desirable configurations.

Add 15% for the round knob (rounded pistol grip knob on stock, pre-1967 mfg.) variation on FN models only, depending on desirability.

Add $250-$500 per additional barrel, depending on the gauge, barrel length, choke, condition, and rarity (smaller gauge open chokes are the most desirable).

Add 20% for reddish stock and forearm configurations (Belgian mfg. - pre 1962).

Add 15% on FN models with blonde stock and forearm - mfg. mid-1960s.

AUTO-5 POLICE CONTRACT – 12 ga. only, 5 or 8 (factory extended) shot mag., black enamel finish on receiver and barrel, can be recognized by the European "POL" police markings below serial number, 24 in. barrel. Imported in limited quantities during 1999.

	MSR	100%	98%	95%	90%	80%	70%	60%
5 shot mag.	N/A	$700	$650	$625	$575	$525	$500	
8 shot mag.	N/A	$1,300	$1,095	$995	$895	$850	$750	

BRÜGGER & THOMET

Current manufacturer located in Thun, Switzerland. Currently imported by D.S.A., located in Barrington, IL. Brügger and Thomet also manufactures a wide variety of high quality tactical style and select-fire rifles and pistols. During 2004, the company purchased all rights to the TMP pistol, and SMG from Steyr Arms in Austria. After many design improvements the TP-9 pistol platform was released.

PISTOLS: SEMI-AUTO

TP-9 – 9mm Para. or .45 ACP (new late 2011) cal., 5.1 in. barrel, SA, short recoil delayed blowback, features ambidextrous and trigger safeties, polymer frame construction in choice of Black, OD Green, or Desert Tan finish, full length upper integrated Picatinny rail with partial lower rail in front of trigger guard, 10 or 30 shot mag., adj. rear sight with post front sight, includes hard case, 44 oz. Importation disc. 2011.

100%	98%	95%	90%	80%	70%	60%	Last MSR
$1,650	$1,475	$1,300	$1,125	$900	$800	$700	*$1,795*

This model is also available in a select-fire variation available to law enforcement and government agencies.

BUDISCHOWSKY

Previous trade name of firearms designed by Edgar Budischowsky, initially manufactured in Ulm, Germany by Korriphila GmbH, and subsequently by Norton Armament Corporation (NORARMCO) in Mt. Clemens, MI.

PISTOLS: SEMI-AUTO

SEMI-AUTO PISTOL – .223 Rem. cal., 11 5/8 in. barrel, 20 or 30 shot mag., fixed sights, a novel tactical designed type pistol.

100%	98%	95%	90%	80%	70%	60%
$470	$415	$385	$360	$305	$250	$220

MSR	100%	98%	95%	90%	80%	70%	60%	*Last MSR*

RIFLES: SEMI-AUTO

TACTICAL DESIGN RIFLE – .223 Rem. cal., semi-auto, 18 in. barrel, wood tactical stock.

	$500	$440	$415	$385	$330	$275	$250	

TACTICAL DESIGN RIFLE W/FOLDING STOCK – .223 Rem. cal., semi-auto, 18 in. barrel, folding stock.

	$575	$500	$450	$425	$395	$360	$330	

BULLSEYE GUN WORKS

Previous manufacturer located in Miami, FL circa 1954-1959.

CARBINES: SEMI-AUTO

Bullseye Gun Works initially started as a gun shop circa 1954, and several years later, they started manufacturing M1 carbines using their own receivers and barrels. Approx. 2,000 - 2,500 were manufactured with their name on the receiver side until the company was reorganized as Universal Firearms Corporation circa late 1950s. Values are typically in the $200 - $350 range, depending on originality and condition.

BUL LTD. (TRANSMARK)

Current manufacturer located in Tel Aviv, Israel. Bul M1911 parts are currently being imported by All America Sales, Inc. located in Piggot, AR. Previously imported 2003-early 2010 by K.B.I., located in Harrisburg, PA. Previously imported and distributed in North America during 2009 by Legacy Sports International, located in Reno, NV, and during 2002 by EAA Corp., located in Sharpes, FL. Previously imported and distributed 1997-2001 by International Security Academy (ISA) located in Los Angeles, CA, and from 1996-1997 by All America Sales, Inc. located in Memphis, TN. Dealer sales only.

PISTOLS: SEMI-AUTO

Please refer to the Charles Daly section in this text for most recent information and prices on Charles Daly imported Bul Transmark pistols (domestic imports were marked Charles Daly 2004-early 2010). Non-domestic Bul Pistols are typically marked Bul M-5 on left side of slide except for the Cherokee and Storm models. M-5 frame kits were previously available at $399 retail.

BUL CHEROKEE – 9mm Para. cal., DA/SA, full size black polymer frame finger groove grips, integral Picatinny rail, DA, exposed hammer, double stack 17 shot mag., squared off trigger guard, includes hard case, cleaning kit and two mags. Imported 2009.

	$495	$435	$370	$335	$270	$225	$175	*$575*

* *Bul Cherokee Compact* – 9mm Para. cal., similar to the Cherokee, except has compact polymer frame. Imported 2009.

	$495	$435	$370	$335	$270	$225	$175	*$575*

BUSHMASTER FIREARMS INTERNATIONAL

Current trademark of carbines, rifles, and pistols established in 1978, and currently manufactured in Ilion, NY beginning late 2011 and company headquarters located in Madison, NC. Previously located in Windham, ME until 2011. On March 31, 2011, Freedom Group Inc. announced that Bushmaster's manufacturing facility in Windham, ME would be closing, and new Bushmaster products would be produced in other Freedom Group facilities. The previous company name was Bushmaster Firearms, and the name changed after the company was sold on April 13, 2006 to Cerberus, and became part of the Freedom Group Inc. Older mfg. was by Gwinn Arms Co. located in Winston-Salem, NC 1972-1974. The Quality Parts Co. gained control in 1986. Distributor, dealer, or consumer direct sales.

During 2003, Bushmaster purchased Professional Ordnance, previous maker of the Carbon 15 Series of semi-auto pistols and rifles/carbines. Carbon 15s are still made in Lake Havasu City, AZ, but are now marked with the Bushmaster logo. For pre-2003 Carbon 15 mfg., please refer to the Professional Ordnance section in this text.

Bushmaster formed a custom shop during 2009, and many configurations are now available by special order only. Please contact Bushmaster directly for more information and availability on these special order guns.

PISTOLS: SEMI-AUTO

BUSHMASTER PISTOL – .223 Rem. cal., AK-47 design, top (older models with aluminum receivers) or side mounted charging handle (most recent mfg.), steel frame on later mfg., 11 1/2 in. barrel, parkerized finish, adj. sights, 5 1/4 lbs.

	$625	$550	$450	$400	$375	$350	$300	*$375*

Add $40 for electroless nickel finish (disc. 1988).

Add $200 for matte nickel finish (mfg. circa 1986-1988).

This model uses a 30 shot M-16 mag. and the AK-47 gas piston operating system.

During 1985-1986, a procurement officer for the U.S. Air Force ordered 2,100 of this model for pilot use with a matte nickel finish. Eventually, this officer was retired or transferred, and the replacement officer turned down the first batch, saying they were "too reflective". Bushmaster then sold these models commercially circa 1986-1988.

MSR	100%	98%	95%	90%	80%	70%	60%	Last MSR

CARBON-15 TYPE P21S/TYPE 21 – 5.56 NATO cal., GIO, ultra lightweight carbon fiber upper and lower receivers, 7 1/4 in. "Profile" stainless steel barrel, quick detachable muzzle compensator, ghost ring sights, 10 or 30 (new late 2004) shot mag., A2 pistol grip, also accepts AR-15 type mags., Stoner type operating sytem, tool steel bolt, extractor and carrier, 40 oz. Mfg. 2003-2012 (Bushmaster mfg.).

	$725	$625	$550	$475	$400	$325	$295	$871

Subtract approx. $200 if without full-length barrel shroud and Picatinny rail (Type 21, disc. 2005).

CARBON-15 TYPE 97/TYPE P97S – GIO, similar to Professional Ordnance Carbon 15 Type 20, except has fluted barrel, Hogue overmolded pistol grip and chrome plated bolt carrier, Type 97S has full length barrel shroud, upper and lower Picatinny rail, 46 oz. Mfg. 2003-2012 (Bushmaster mfg.).

	$695	$600	$525	$450	$375	$300	$285	$825

Add $78 for Model P97S with full length barrel shroud and lower Picatinny rail.
Subtract approx. $100 if w/o full length barrel shroud and lower Picatinny rail (disc.)

CARBON-15 9MM – 9mm Para. cal., GIO, blow-back operation, carbon fiber composite receivers, 7 1/2 in. steel barrel with A1 birdcage flash hider, A2 front sight, full-length Picatinny optics rail, Neoprene foam sleeve over buffer tube, 10 or 30 shot mag., 4.6 lbs. Mfg. 2006-2012.

	$785	$710	$625	$550	$475	$400	$325	$871

PIT VIPER AP-21 – 5.56 NATO cal., GIO, features 7 1/4 in. barrel with birdcage flash suppressor, visible upper gas transfer tube, receiver Picatinny rail, approx. 3 1/2 lbs. Limited mfg. 2011 only.

	$725	$625	$550	$475	$400	$325	$295	$873

XM-15 PATROLMAN'S AR PISTOL – 5.56 NATO cal., GIO, 7 or 10 1/2 in. stainless steel barrel with A2 flash hider, knurled free float tubular handguard, flat-top receiver with Picatinny rail, Phase 5 ambi single point sling attachment, A2 pistol grip and standard trigger guard, aluminum pistol buffer tube with foam featuring laser engraved Bushmaster logo, 30 shot mag. New 2013.

MSR $973	$825	$700	$600	$525	$450	$375	$325	

XM-15 ENHANCED PATROLMAN'S AR PISTOL – 5.56 NATO cal., GIO, 7 or 10 1/2 in. stainless steel barrel with AAC 3 prong flash hider, free float lightweight quad rail handguard, Phase 5 ambi single point sling attachment, Magpul MOE pistol grip and trigger guard, aluminum pistol buffer tube with foam featuring laser engraved Bushmaster logo, 30 shot mag. New 2013.

MSR $1,229	$995	$875	$750	$675	$550	$450	$350	

RIFLES: BOLT ACTION

BA50 CARBINE/RIFLE – .50 BMG cal., 22 (carbine, disc. 2011) or 30 (rifle) in. Lothar Walther free floating barrel with vent. forend, AAC Cyclops muzzle brake/silencer adapter (new 2014), 10 shot mag., left side bolt handle, full length receiver Picatinny rail, Magpul PRS adj. buttstock with LimbSavr recoil pad, high efficiency recoil reducing muzzle brake, steel bipod with folding legs, ErgoGrip deluxe tactical pistol grip, aluminum lower receiver, manganese phosphate finish on steel parts, hard anodized black finish on aluminum parts, includes Storm hardcase and two mags., 20 or 27 lbs. New 2009.

MSR $5,657	$4,995	$4,500	$4,000	$3,500	$3,000	$2,650	$2,300	

Last MSR on the carbine was $5,261.

RIFLES: SEMI-AUTO

All current AR-15 style Bushmaster rifles are shipped with a hard plastic lockable case. Most Bushmaster barrels are marked "5.56 NATO", and can be used safely with either 5.56 NATO (higher velocity/pressure) or .223 Rem. cal. ammo.

Information and values for state compliant variations are not listed.

During 2006, Bushmaster began offering a complete gas piston upper receiver/barrel assembly. Last MSRs ranged from $580-$990, depending on caliber and configuration.

The XM-10 typically refers to 7.62 NATO cal., and XM-15 refers to 5.56 NATO cal. on the current models listed.

.300 AAC BLACKOUT – .300 AAC cal., GIO, 16 in. M4 contour barrel with AAC Blackout muzzle brake, Magpul ACS stock and MOE grip, free floating quad rail, 30 shot mag. (AR compatible), flat-top receiver with Picatinny rail, 6 1/2 lbs. New 2012.

MSR $1,508	$1,275	$1,125	$950	$875	$700	$575	$475	

.450 CARBINE/RIFLE – .450 Bushmaster cal., GIO, 16 (carbine) or 20 in. chromemoly steel barrel, 5 shot mag., forged aluminum receiver, A2 pistol grip, solid A2 buttstock with trapdoor, A3 flat-top upper receivers with Picatinny rail, 8 1/2 lbs. New 2008.

MSR $1,522	$1,295	$1,150	$975	$875	$725	$585	$450	

Add $16 for rifle.

MSR	100%	98%	95%	90%	80%	70%	60%	Last MSR

6.8mm SPC/7.62x39mm CARBINE – 6.8mm SPC or 7.62x39mm (new 2010) cal., GIO, 16 in. M4 profile barrel with Izzy muzzle brake, six-position telescoping stock, available in A2 (disc. 2012) or A3 configuration, 26 shot mag., includes black web sling, extra mag. and lockable carrying case, approx. 7 lbs. Mfg. late 2006-late 2013.

| | $1,225 | $1,075 | $925 | $850 | $675 | $550 | $450 | *$1,402* |

Add $100 for A3 configuration (disc. 2010).

BUSHMASTER RIFLE – 5.56 NATO cal., GPO, top (older models with aluminum receivers) or side mounted charging handle (current mfg.), steel receiver (current mfg.), 18 1/2 in. barrel, parkerized finish, adj. sights, wood stock, 6 1/4 lbs., base values are for folding stock model.

| | $695 | $625 | $550 | $500 | $475 | $425 | $400 | *$350* |

Add $40 for electroless nickel finish (disc. 1988).

Add $65 for fixed rock maple wood stock.

This model uses a 30 shot M-16 mag. and the AK-47 gas piston system.

* **Bushmaster Rifle Combination System** – GPO, includes rifle with both metal folding stock and wood stock with pistol grip.

| | $750 | $675 | $625 | $575 | $525 | $475 | $450 | *$450* |

TARGET/COMPETITION A-2/A-3 RIFLE (XM15-E2S) – 5.56 NATO cal., GIO, patterned after the Colt AR-15, 20, 24 (disc. 2012), or 26 (disc. 2002) in. Govt. spec. match grade chrome lined or stainless steel (new 2002) barrel, 10 or 30 shot mag., manganese phosphate or Realtree Camo (20 in. barrel only, mfg. 2004 - late 2006) barrel finish, rear sight adj. for windage and elevation, cage flash suppressor (disc. 1994), approx. 8.3 lbs. Mfg. began 1989 in U.S.

| MSR $1,179 | $995 | $870 | $750 | $675 | $550 | $450 | $400 | |

Add $24 for A-3 removable carry handle.

Add $88 for stainless steel barrel with A-3 removable carry handle.

Add $194 for heavy 1 in. diameter competition barrel (disc. 2011).

Add $50 for fluted barrel or $40 for stainless steel barrel (mfg. 2002-2009).

Add $10 for 24 in. (disc. 2012) or $25 for 26 in. (disc. 2002) barrel.

Add $60 for Realtree Camo finish (disc.).

HEAVY BARREL CARBINE A-2/A-3 (XM15-E2S, SHORTY CARBINE) – 5.56 NATO cal., GIO, fixed (disc.) or telescoping buttstock, 11 1/2 (LE only, disc. 1995), 14 (LE only, disc. 1994), or 16 in. heavy barrel with birdcage flash suppressor, 30 shot mag., choice of A2 or A3 configuration, approx. 7.4 lbs. Mfg. began 1989.

| MSR $1,211 | $1,050 | $925 | $825 | $675 | $550 | $475 | $425 | |

Add $15 for A-3 removable carry handle.

This model does not have the target rear sight system of the XM15-E2S rifle.

* **M4 Post-Ban Carbine (XM15-E2S)** – 5.56 NATO cal., GIO, 16 in. barrel, features fixed or telestock (new late 2004) tubular stock, pistol grip, black, Flat Dark Earth, OD Green, phosphate (disc.), A-TACS camo, or Desert Camo (stock, pistol grip, and forearm only, disc. 2005) finish, M4 carbine configuration with permanently attached Izzy muzzle brake, 30 shot mag. became standard in late 2004. New 2003.

| MSR $1,331 | $1,125 | $985 | $850 | $775 | $625 | $500 | $400 | |

Add $107 for A-TACS camo.

Add $35 for desert camo finish (disc. 2005).

Add $85 for A3 removable carrying handle (disc. 2012).

* **XM-15 Limited Edition 20th Anniversary Rifle** – GIO, 20 in. barrel, features 20th Anniversary engraving on upper and lower receiver, special medallion in buttstock, includes hardwood presentation case. Limited mfg. 1998-99.

| | $1,450 | $1,275 | $1,095 | $985 | $800 | $650 | $525 | |

* **XM-15 Limited Edition 25th Anniversary Carbine** – GIO, features skeletonized tubular stock, pistol grip, A-3 type flat-top with flip-up sights, laser engraved 25th anniversary crest on lower magwell, nickel plated ejection port cover. Limited mfg. of 1,500 during 2003.

| | $1,450 | $1,275 | $1,095 | $985 | $800 | $650 | $525 | *$1,695* |

* **E2 Carbine** – 5.56 NATO cal., GIO, features 16 in. match chrome lined barrel with new M16A2 handguard and short suppressor, choice of A1 or E2 sights. Mfg. 1994-95.

| | $850 | $775 | $675 | $575 | $475 | $425 | $400 | |

Add approx. $50 for E2 sighting system.

AK CARBINE – 5.56 NATO cal., 17 in. barrel featuring AK-47 style muzzle brake, tele-stock standard, choice of A2 or A3 configuration, ribbed oval forearm, approx. 7 1/2 lbs. Mfg. 2008-2010.

| | $995 | $875 | $750 | $675 | $550 | $450 | $400 | *$1,215* |

Add $85 for A3 removable carry handle.

MSR	100%	98%	95%	90%	80%	70%	60%	Last MSR

DISSIPATOR CARBINE – 5.56 NATO cal., GIO, 16 in. heavy barrel with full length forearm and special gas block placement (gas block system is located behind the front sight base and under the rifle length handguard), A2 or A3 style with choice of solid buttstock or six-position telestock, 30 shot mag., lockable carrying case. Mfg. 2004-2010.

	100%	98%	95%	90%	80%	70%	60%	Last MSR
	$995	$875	$750	$675	$550	$450	$395	*$1,246*

Add $25 for tele-stock.
Add $50 for fluted barrel (disc. 2005).
Add $115 for A3 removable carrying handle.

MOE DISSIPATOR CARBINE – 5.56 NATO cal., GIO, 16 in. heavy barrel with muzzle brake, flat-top with Picatinny rail, pistol grip stock, features Magpul Original Equipment (MOE) accessories such as ACS adj. stock, MBUS rear flip sight, mid-length handguard, Black, OD Green, or Flat Dark Earth finish, 6.42 lbs. New 2011.

MSR $1,331	$1,125	$985	$850	$775	$625	$500	$400	

MOE .223 MID-LENGTH – 5.56 NATO cal., GIO, similar to MOE Dissipator, except has standard barrel and half-length handguard, available in black or flat dark earth finish. New 2011.

MSR $1,331	$1,125	$985	$850	$775	$625	$500	$400	

MOE 308 MID-LENGTH – .308 Win. cal., GIO, otherwise similar to MOE .223 Mid-length, except has 10 shot mag., Black, OD Green or FDE finish, 6.1 lbs. New 2011.

MSR $1,546	$1,295	$1,150	$975	$875	$725	$585	$450	

M4 A.R.M.S. CARBINE – 5.56 NATO cal., GIO, 14 1/2 (law enforcement only) or 16 in. chromemoly vanadium steel barrel with chrome lined bore and chamber, 30 shot mag., features A3 removable carry handle, black, foliage green (new 2010), or flat dark earth (new 2010) anodized finish, Magpul adj. buttstock with optional MOE (new 2010), Hogue pistol grip, optional Troy four rail handguard and front sights or A.R.M.S. 41-B front and rear flip-up sights (new 2010, became standard 2011), 6.2 lbs. Mfg. 2009-2011.

	100%	98%	95%	90%	80%	70%	60%	Last MSR
	$995	$875	$750	$675	$550	$450	$400	*$1,247*

Subtract approx. 10% if without A.R.M.S. front and rear flip up sights.

PATROLMAN'S CARBINE – 5.56 NATO, 6.8 SPC or 7.62x39mm NATO cal., GIO, 16 in. standard barrel, choice of A2 (bullet button) or A3 configuration, two piece tubular handguard, six position adj. stock, black finish only, approx. 6 1/2 lbs. Disc. 2013.

	100%	98%	95%	90%	80%	70%	60%	Last MSR
	$1,075	$950	$800	$725	$600	$485	$400	*$1,275*

Add $116 for 6.8 Rem. SPC or 7.62x39 NATO cal. (A3 configuration only).

M4 PATROLMAN'S CARBINE – 5.56 NATO cal., GIO, 16 in. chromemoly vanadium steel barrel with chrome lined bore and chamber, 30 shot mag., A2 birdcage suppressor, six position telestock, with or w/o quad rail, Black anodized finish, approx. 6 1/2 lbs. New 2009.

MSR $1,227	$1,050	$925	$800	$725	$575	$475	$400	

Add $199 for quad rail (new 2011).

M4 A3 PATROLMAN'S CARBINE CERAKOTE – 5.56 NATO cal., GIO, 16 in. M4 barrel with A2 flash hider, A3 upper with removable carry handle, A2 carbine two-piece handguard, six position stock, 30 shot mag., choice of OD Green or FDE Cerakote finished receiver, 6.7 lbs. New 2013.

MSR $1,321	$1,125	$985	$850	$775	$625	$500	$400	

M4 MOE/A-TACS CARBINE – 5.56 NATO cal., GIO, includes Magpul adj. A-frame buttstock, 16 in. barrel with muzzle brake, available in Black, OD Green, FDE or A-TACS camo (disc. 2012) finish (does not have Magpul features and 6-position telestock), 6.42 lbs. New 2011.

MSR $1,321	$1,125	$985	$850	$775	$625	$500	$400	

Add $104 for A-TACS camo w/o MOE features (disc. 2012).

M17S BULLPUP – 5.56 NATO cal., GIO, semi-auto bullpup configuration featuring gas operated rotating bolt, 10 (C/B 1994) or 30* shot mag., 21 1/2 plain or 22 (disc.) in. barrel with flash suppressor (disc.), glass composites and aluminum construction, phosphate coating, 8 1/4 lbs. Mfg. 1992-2005.

	100%	98%	95%	90%	80%	70%	60%	Last MSR
	$750	$650	$525	$475	$425	$400	$385	*$765*

MODULAR CARBINE – 5.56 NATO cal., GIO, 16 in. barrel with flash suppressor, includes many Bushmaster modular accessories, such as skeleton telestock and four-rail free floating tubular forearm, detachable folding front and rear sights, 10 or 30 (new late 2004) shot mag., 6.3 lbs. New 2004.

MSR $1,793	$1,495	$1,3125	$1,125	$1,025	$825	$675	$525	

SUPERLIGHT CARBINE – 5.56 NATO cal., GIO, 16 in. lightweight barrel, choice of fixed (disc.), 6-position telestock, or stub (disc.) stock with finger groove pistol grip, A2 or A3 type configuration, 30 shot mag., black finish, 5.8 - 6 1/4 lbs. New 2004.

MSR $1,291	$1,095	$950	$825	$750	$600	$500	$400	

Subtract 5% if without telestock. Subtract approx. $75 if without A-3 removable carry handle.

MSR	100%	98%	95%	90%	80%	70%	60%	Last MSR

ACR BASIC A-TACS CARBINE – 5.56 NATO cal., GPO, similar to ACR Enhanced, except has fixed A-frame stock with rubber butt pad and sling mounts, Black (disc. 2013), Coyote Brown (disc. 2010), or A-TACS camo finish, 8.2 lbs.

| MSR $2,604 | $2,195 | $1,925 | $1,650 | $1,500 | $1,200 | $1,000 | $775 | |

ACR BASIC FOLDER – 5.56 NATO or 6.8 SPC (new 2013) cal., GPO, 16 1/2 in. barrel, similar to ACR Basic, except has side folding, six-position telescoping stock, rubber buttpad, sling mounts, Magpul MBUS front, black or Coyote Brown finish, rear flip up sights, 8.2 lbs. New mid-2011.

| MSR $2,552 | $2,100 | $1,850 | $1,575 | $1,425 | $1,150 | $950 | $750 | |

ACR BASIC ORC CARBINE – 5.56 NATO cal., GPO, 16 1/2 in. barrel with muzzle brake, features full-length top Picatinny rail w/o sights and fixed stock, 30 shot mag., Black or Coyote Brown finish, 8.2 lbs. Mfg. 2011-2013.

| | $1,975 | $1,725 | $1,475 | $1,350 | $1,085 | $895 | $695 | *$2,343* |

ACR DMR – 5.56 NATO cal., 18 1/2 in. stainless melonite barrel, AAC51T Blackout flash hider, Geissele trigger, ACR railed handguard, Magpul PRS style stock, 8 3/4 lbs. New 2014.

| MSR $2,799 | $2,375 | $2,075 | $1,775 | $1,625 | $1,300 | $1,075 | $850 | |

ACR ENHANCED – 5.56 NATO or 6.8mm SPC (while advertised in 2010, this caliber hasn't been mfg. to date) cal., Bushmaster proprietary GPO, modular design allows caliber interchangeability by changing the barrel, magazine, and bolt head, 16 1/2 in. chromemoly steel barrel with Melonite coating, AAC Blackout NSM flash hider, ambidextrous controls, adj. two-position GPO, 30 shot mag., folding or six position telestock, black or Coyote Brown finish, three sided aluminum handguard, Magpul MBUS front/rear flip-up sights, upper and lower accessory rails, includes sling, hardcase and extra mag., 8.2 lbs. New 2010.

| MSR $2,766 | $2,350 | $2,075 | $1,775 | $1,625 | $1,300 | $1,075 | $850 | |

ACR PATROL CARBINE – 5.56 NATO or 6.8mm SPC cal., GPO, 16 1/2 in. chromemoly steel barrel with Melonite coating, AAC Blackout flash hider, ratchet-style suppressor mounting, 30 shot mag., fixed stock, adj. cheekpiece, Picatinny rail, includes sling and three mags, 8.2 lbs. New 2010.

| MSR $2,490 | $2,095 | $1,850 | $1,575 | $1,425 | $1,150 | $950 | $750 | |

ACR SPECIAL PURPOSE CARBINE – 5.56 NATO cal., GPO, similar to ACR Patrolman's Carbine, except has 6-position telescoping polymer stock, quad Picatinny rails, and includes three 30 shot PMAG magazines and soft nylon case, Black finish only, 8.3 lbs. New 2011.

| MSR $2,799 | $2,375 | $2,075 | $1,775 | $1,625 | $1,300 | $1,075 | $850 | |

ORC (OPTICS READY CARBINE) ACR – 5.56 NATO or .308 Win. (mfg. 2010-2012) cal., GPO, 16 in. barrel with A2 birdcage flash suppressor, receiver length Picatinny rail with risers ready for optical sights, six position telestock, 30 shot mag., oval M4 type forearm, 6 lbs. Mfg. 2008-2013.

| | $925 | $825 | $700 | $625 | $525 | $425 | $400 | *$1,112* |

Add $239 for .308 Win. cal. (mfg. 2010-2012).

ORC BASIC FOLDER CARBINE – 5.56 NATO cal., GPO, 16 1/2 in. barrel with muzzle brake, similar to ACR Enhanced Carbine, except does not have 3-sided aluminum handguard with Picatinny rails, Black or Coyote Brown finish, 8.2 lbs. Mfg. 2011 only.

| | $2,075 | $1,825 | $1,550 | $1,425 | $1,150 | $950 | $725 | *$2,490* |

ORC – 5.56 NATO or 7.62 NATO cal., GPO, 16 or 18 (disc.) in. heavy profile barrel with flash suppressor, full-length receiver Picatinny rail, heavy oval handguard, 6-position telescoping stock, 10 or 30 shot mag., Black finish, 7 3/4 lbs. New 2011.

| MSR $1,083 | $895 | $785 | $675 | $625 | $500 | $425 | $375 | |

Add $355 for 7.62 NATO cal.

MOE/ORC GAS PISTON CARBINE – 5.56 NATO cal., GPO, 16 in. barrel, MOE carbine features many Magpul accessories, is available in Black, OD Green, or Flat Dark Earth finish, ORC model does not have MOE features, but 6-position tactical stock and receiver length Picatinny rail with risers for optics, approx. 6.3 lbs. Mfg. 2011-2012.

| | $1,050 | $925 | $800 | $725 | $575 | $475 | $400 | *$1,247* |

Add $89 for ORC model.

Add $100-$149 for extra Magpul features on MOE model.

GAS PISTON CARBINE – 5.56 NATO cal., features GPO, similar to AK-47s and FALs, 16 in. M4 profile barrel with flash suppressor, telestock, ribbed oval forearm with flip-up sight. Mfg. 2008-2010.

| | $1,495 | $1,325 | $1,125 | $1,025 | $825 | $675 | $525 | *$1,850* |

PREDATOR – 5.56 NATO cal., GIO, includes DCM (disc.) 20 in. extra fluted, or stainless steel (disc. 2006) varmint barrel, two-stage competition trigger, rubberized pistol grip, flat-top receiver with mini-risers (adds 1/2 in. height for

MSR	100%	98%	95%	90%	80%	70%	60%	Last MSR

scope mounting), free floating vented tube forearm, 10 shot mag., controlled ejection path, choice of black or A-TACS Digital Camo (new 2011, compliant configuration only) finish, 8 lbs. Mfg. 2006-2013.

	$1,195	$1,045	$900	$825	$650	$550	$425	$1,415

Add $104 for A-TACS Digital Camo finish (compliant configuration only).

The stainless variation included an adj. ergonomic pistol grip.

HUNTER – .308 Win. cal., GIO, 20 in. fluted barrel, features vented free floating aluminum forearm tube, 10 shot mag., Hogue rubberized pistol grip (Hunter) or A2 grip (Vista, disc. late 2011), Grey/Green or camo finish, 8.2 lbs. Mfg. 2011-2013.

	$1,395	$1,225	$1,050	$950	$775	$650	$500	$1,685

Add $100 for Vista Hunter model (disc. late 2011).

DCM COMPETITION RIFLE – 5.56 NATO cal., GIO, includes DCM competition features such as modified A2 rear sight, 20 in. extra heavy 1 in. diameter competition barrel, custom trigger job, and free-floating handguard. Mfg. 1998-2005.

	$1,250	$1,095	$950	$850	$700	$575	$450	$1,495

DCM-XR COMPETITION RIFLE – 5.56 NATO cal., GIO, features dual aperture rear sight and competition ground for clarity front sight, 20 in. extra heavy competition barrel, free-floating ribbed forearm, competition trigger, choice of A2 solid or A3 removable carry handle, 13 1/2 lbs. Mfg. 2008-2010.

	$975	$850	$725	$675	$550	$450	$400	$1,150

Add $100 for A3 removable carry handle.

CARBINE-15 COMPETITION – 5.56 NATO cal., GIO, various configurations, choice of extra heavy or heavy barrel in 20 or 24 in. with or w/o muzzle brake, A2 or A3 configuration, various type of sights, 8.5-13.85 lbs. Mfg. 2011 only.

	$925	$825	$700	$650	$525	$425	$375	$1,112

Add approx. $75 for A3 removeable carry handle.

Add $194 for heavy 1 in. diameter competition barrel.

CARBON-15 R21 – 5.56 NATO cal., GIO, ultra lightweight carbon fiber upper and lower receivers, 16 in. "Profile" stainless steel barrel, quick detachable muzzle compensator, Stoner type operating system, tool steel bolt, extractor and carrier, optics mounting base, fixed tube stock, 10 or 30 (new late 2004) shot mag., also accepts AR-15 type mags., 3.9 lbs. Mfg. 2003-2009 (Bushmaster mfg.).

	$825	$725	$625	$550	$450	$375	$300	$990

* Carbon-15 Lady – 5.56 NATO cal., GIO, 16 in. barrel, includes overall tan finish (except for barrel) and webbed tube stock with recoil pad, chrome/nickel plating on small parts, supplied with soft case, 4 lbs. Mfg. 2004-2006.

	$825	$725	$625	$550	$450	$375	$300	$989

CARBON-15 (R97/97S) – 5.56 NATO cal., AR-15 style, GIO, ultra lightweight carbon fiber upper and lower receivers, hard chromed tool steel bolt, extractor and carrier, 16 in. fluted stainless steel barrel, quick detachable muzzle compensator, optics mounting base, 10 or 30 (new late 2004) shot mag., quick detachable stock, also accepts AR-15 type mags., 3.9 or 4.3 (Model 97S) lbs. Mfg. 2003-2010.

	$1,075	$950	$800	$725	$600	$475	$400	$1,300

Subtract approx. $175 without Picatinny rail and "Scout" extension, double walled heat shield foregrip, ambidextrous safety, and multi-carry silent sling (Model Type 97, disc. 2005).

CARBON-15 .22 LR – .22 LR cal., GIO, similar to Carbon-15 R21, 16 in. barrel, Picatinny rail, 10 shot mag., fixed stock, approx. 4.4 lbs. Disc. 2009.

	$650	$575	$500	$450	$375	$300	$250	$790

Bushmaster also made a Carbon-15 .22 rimfire upper receiver/barrel assembly, which is exclusively designed for Bushmaster lower receivers - last MSR was $387 (new 2005).

CARBON-15 9MM – 9mm Para. cal., blow-back operation, carbon fiber composite receiver, 16 in. steel barrel with A1 birdcage flash suppressor, A2 front sight and dual aperture rear sight, Picatinny optics rail, collapsible stock, 10 or 30 shot mag., 5.7 lbs. Mfg. 2006-2012.

	$775	$675	$575	$525	$425	$350	$275	$933

CARBON-15 TOP LOADING RIFLE – 5.56 NATO cal., GIO, carbon fiber composite receiver, 16 in. M4 profile barrel with Izzy suppressor, A2 front sight and dual aperture rear sight, Picatinny optics rail, collapsible stock, 10 shot top-loading internal mag., 5.8 lbs. Mfg. 2006-2010.

	$875	$765	$650	$600	$475	$400	$325	$1,100

CARBON-15 MODEL 4 CARBINE – 5.56 NATO cal., GIO, features carbon composite receiver, collapsible tube stock, 14 1/2 (LE only), or 16 (disc. 2012) in. barrel with compensator, 30 shot mag., semi-auto design styled after the military M4, 5 1/2 lbs. Mfg. 2005-2013.

	$795	$700	$600	$550	$450	$375	$300	$956

MSR	100%	98%	95%	90%	80%	70%	60%	Last MSR

CARBON-15 FLAT-TOP CARBINE – 5.56 NATO cal., GIO, similar to Carbon-15 Model 4 Carbine except has receiver length Picatinny rail with dual aperture flip-up rear sight, 5 1/2 lbs. New 2006.

	100%	98%	95%	90%	80%	70%	60%	
MSR $956	$795	$700	$600	$550	$450	$350	$300	

CARBON-15 ORC – 5.56 NATO cal., GIO, 16 in. barrel with Izzy flash suppressor, 10 (disc. 2013) or 30 shot mag., features red dot optics. New 2012.

MSR $866	$725	$650	$550	$500	$400	$325	$275	

CARBON-15 M4 QUAD RAIL – 5.56 NATO cal., GIO, similar to Carbon-15 Flat-top, except has quad rail handguard. New 2013.

MSR $866	$725	$650	$550	$500	$400	$325	$275	

CARBON-15 C22 COMBO – .22 LR and 5.56 NATO cals., GIO, includes two barrels chambered for .22 LR and 5.56 NATO cals., flat-top receiver with Picatinny rail, 16 in. M4 style barrels with A2 flash hiders, Mission First Tactical polymer quad rail with rail covers, 4-position stock, supplied with 25 shot (.22 LR cal.) and 30 shot (5.56 NATO) magazines. New 2013.

MSR $1,222	$995	$875	$750	$675	$550	$450	$375	

CARBON 22 – .22 LR cal., 16 in. barrel. New 2014.

MSR $499	$450	$395	$350	$300	$275	$250	$225	

V-MATCH COMPETITION RIFLE – 5.56 NATO cal., GIO, top-of-the line match/competition rifle, flat-top receiver with extended aluminum barrel shroud, choice of 20, 24, or 26 (disc. 2002) in. barrel, 8.3 lbs. Mfg. 1994-2010.

	$925	$825	$700	$650	$525	$425	$325	$1,115

Add $50 for fluted barrel.
Add $10 for 24 in. or $25 for 26 (disc. 2002) in. barrel.
Add $117 for A-3 removable carry handle.

* V-Match Commando Carbine – similar to V-Match Competition Rifle, except has 16 in. barrel. Mfg. 1997-2010.

	$925	$825	$700	$650	$525	$425	$325	$1,105

Add $50 for fluted barrel. Add $117 for A-3 removable carry handle.

VARMINTER – 5.56 NATO cal., GIO, includes DCM 24 in. extra heavy fluted or stainless steel varmint barrel, competition trigger, rubberized pistol grip, flat-top receiver with mini-risers (adds 1/2 in. height for scope mounting), free floating vented tube forearm, 5 shot mag., controlled ejection path, choice of Black or A-TACS Digital camo (new 2011, compliant configuration only) finish. Mfg. 2002-2013.

	$1,195	$1,045	$900	$825	$650	$550	$425	$1,430

Add $71 for stainless steel barrel (compliant variation only). Add $105 for A-TACS Digital camo coverage (compliant configuration only).
The stainless variation includes an adj., ergonomic pistol grip.

BUSHMASTER .308 SERIES – .308 Win. cal., 16 or 20 in. phosphate coated heavy alloy steel barrel with Izzy compensator, 20 shot mag., solid buttstock or skeletonized stock, available in A2 or A3 style with a variety of configurations, including muzzle brakes, flash suppressors, and sighting options. Mfg. late 2004-2005.

	$1,425	$1,250	$1,075	$975	$785	$650	$500	$1,750

Add $25 for A3 removable carry handle.
Add $10 for 20 in. barrel.
Add $50 (16 in. barrel) or $60 (20 in. barrel) for skeletonized stock.
Add approx. $100 for free-floating foream.

XM-10 .308 ENHANCED ORC – .308 Win. cal., 16 in. chrome lined barrel, Troy modular free-floating handguard, Magpul MOE stock, MOE grip, two-stage trigger, 9 lbs. New 2014.

MSR $1,599	$1,275	$1,125	$950	$875	$700	$575	$450	

XM-10 DMR – 7.62 NATO cal., 18 1/2 in. stainless Cerakote bull barrel, Troy free-floating handguard, Magpul PRS stock, MIAD grip and trigger guard, AAC 51T Blackout brake, Gieselle trigger, 10 1/2 lbs. New 2014.

MSR $1,999	$1,595	$1,395	$1,195	$1,085	$875	$725	$575	

XM-15 BASIC TACTICAL CARBINE – 5.56 NATO cal., 16 in. mid-length stainless steel barrel with AAC 51T Blackout flash hider, 15 in. Barnes Precision modular free-float handguard, Magpul MOE grip, Magpul MOE stock, two-stage match trigger, enhanced trigger guard, 7 3/4 lbs. New 2014.

MSR $1,350	$1,125	$985	$850	$775	$625	$500	$400	

XM-15 3-GUN ENHANCED CARBINE – 5.56 NATO cal., 16 in. mid-length stainless steel barrel, Rolling Thunder compensator, 15 in. AP Custom carbon fiber handguard, Timney trigger, Magpul MIAD grip, Magpul MOE stock, PVD bolt carrier group, crimson anodized receiver, Bravo Company charging handle, ambi selector switch, Arrendondo mag. release, Black finish, 7 3/4 lbs. New 2014.

MSR $1,750	$1,450	$1,275	$1,095	$985	$800	$650	$525	

NOTES

C3 DEFENSE, INC.
Previous manufacturer until 2013 of AR-15 style rifles, upper/lower receivers, and related components located in Hiram, GA.

MSR	100%	98%	95%	90%	80%	70%	60%	Last MSR

RIFLES: SEMI-AUTO

C3 Defense discontinued all manufacture of complete firearms in 2013. C3 Defense also offered the short barrel C315 Clandestine Series for military/law enforcement.

C315 RANGER – .223 Rem. cal., GIO, 16 in. barrel, matte black finish, forged upper and lower, flared magwell, M4 feed ramps, mil-spec trigger group, A2 front post sight, 30 shot mag., six-position retractable stock, A2 grip, M16 bolt carrier group, Magpul rear MBUS.

	100%	98%	95%	90%	80%	70%	60%	Last MSR
	$895	$775	$650	$525	$450	$400	$350	$995

This model was also available with 10 1/2, 11 1/2 or 14 1/2 in. barrels for military/law enforcement.

C315 RECON – .223 Rem. cal., GIO, 16 in. barrel, matte black finish, forged upper and lower, flared magwell, M4 feed ramps, mil-spec trigger group, A2 front sight, 30 shot mag., Magpul MOE stock and grip, M16 bolt carrier group, Magpul MBUS and polymer extended trigger guard.

	100%	98%	95%	90%	80%	70%	60%	Last MSR
	$995	$850	$700	$575	$500	$450	$400	$1,112

This model was also available with 10 1/2, 11 1/2 or 14 1/2 in. barrels for military/law enforcement.

C315 SFR (STANDARD FULL RIFLE) – .223 Rem. cal., GIO, 16 in. barrel, matte black finish, billet upper and lower, flared magwell, tension screw, front textured grip, M4 feed ramps, mil-spec trigger group, A2 front sight, 30 shot mag., Magpul MOE stock, A2 grip, Magpul extended trigger guard, carbine length handguard with rail.

	100%	98%	95%	90%	80%	70%	60%	Last MSR
	$1,195	$1,000	$875	$775	$675	$575	$475	$1,349

This model was also available with 10 1/2, 11 1/2 or 14 1/2 in. barrels for military/law enforcement.

C315 EFR (ENHANCED FULL RIFLE) – .223 Rem. or .300 BLK cal., GIO, 16 in. barrel, matte black finish, enhanced billet upper and lower, flared magwell, tension screw, front textured grip, M4 feed ramps, mil-spec trigger group, 13 in. free float handguard with rail, 30 shot mag., Magpul MOE stock and grip, Magpul front and rear MBUS, Triad flash suppressor, M16 bolt carrier group.

	100%	98%	95%	90%	80%	70%	60%	Last MSR
	$1,395	$1,175	$1,000	$875	$750	$625	$525	$1,579

This model was also available with 10 1/2, 11 1/2 or 14 1/2 in. barrels for military/law enforcement.

C315 EFR OW (OVERWATCH) – .223 Rem. or 6.8 SPC cal., GIO, 18 in. stainless steel barrel with fitted bolt, matte black finish, enhanced billet upper and lower, flared magwell, tension screw, front textured grip, M4 feed ramps, two-stage match trigger, 13 in. free float handguard with rail, chromed NM bolt carrier, 20 shot mag., Magpul UBR stock and MIAD grip, Magpul front and rear MBUS, Triad flash suppressor.

	100%	98%	95%	90%	80%	70%	60%	Last MSR
	$2,175	$1,995	$1,775	$1,525	$1,300	$1,150	$875	$2,539

CETME
Previous manufacturer located in Madrid, Spain. CETME is an abbreviation for Centro Estudios Technicos de Materiales Especiales.

RIFLES: SEMI-AUTO

AUTOLOADING RIFLE – 7.62x51mm NATO cal., 17 3/4 in. barrel, roller locked delayed blowback action, similar to HK-91 in appearance, wood military style stock, aperture rear sight.

	100%	98%	95%	90%	80%	70%	60%	Last MSR
	$2,950	$2,650	$2,350	$2,000	$1,725	$1,500	$1,350	

The H&K G3 is the next generation of this rifle, and many parts are interchangeable between the CETME and the G3.

CMMG, INC.
Current manufacturer of AR-15 style carbines/rifles and related components and accessories established in 2002, and located in Fayette, MO.

RIFLES: SEMI-AUTO

.22 LR SERIES

* **M4 Profile Model 22A7C3D** – .22 LR cal., AR-15 style, GIO, 16 in. WASP treated chromemoly steel M4 barrel, phosphated bolt group, 6-position stock, 25 shot grey mag., optics ready with railed gas block or low profile railed gas block, Black finish. Disc. 2013.

	100%	98%	95%	90%	80%	70%	60%	Last MSR
	$675	$600	$500	$475	$375	$300	$250	$750

MSR		100%	98%	95%	90%	80%	70%	60%	Last MSR

* **Lightweight Model 22A1CF6** – .22 LR cal., AR-15 style, GIO, 16 in. WASP treated chromemoly steel M4 lightweight barrel, stainless steel bolt group with BHOA and forward assist adapter, M4 handguard, 6-position stock, 25 shot Evolution mag., "F" marked front sight base and Magpul MBUS rear sight, Black finish. Disc. 2013.

		$750	$650	$575	$525	$425	$350	$275	$830

.300 AAC BLACKOUT SERIES

* **Model 30AF8A6** – .300 AAC Blackout cal., GIO, 16 in. M300 profile WASP treated chromemoly steel barrel, optics ready with low profile gas block, K9 quad rail, mid-length free float tube, 6-position stock, 30 shot Magpul PMag., Black finish. Disc. 2013.

		$900	$795	$675	$625	$500	$400	$325	$1,000

* **Model 30A77E1 Stainless** – .300 AAC Blackout cal., GIO, 16 in. M300 profile stainless steel barrel, mid-length handguard, carbine low pro gas block, 6-position stock, 30 shot Magpul PMag., "F" marked front sight base and Magpul MBUS rear sight, Black finish. Disc. 2013.

		$950	$825	$725	$650	$525	$425	$350	$1,050

* **Model 30AF8DF** – .300 AAC Blackout cal., GIO, 16 in. M300 profile WASP treated chromemoly barrel, Revolution handguard with 5 slot rails and Revolution modular handguard panels, "F" marked front sight base and Magpul MBUS rear sight, 6-position stock, 30 shot PMag., Black finish. Disc. 2013.

		$950	$825	$725	$650	$525	$425	$350	$1,050

.308 MK3 SERIES – .308 Win./7.62 NATO cal., GIO, standard barrel options include 16 or 18 in. stainless steel medium contour or a hammer forged chrome lined barrel, aluminum upper and lower receivers, uses SR25 or LR308 mags., and can be configured with Magpul MOE stocks, MOE pistol grips, and CMMG two-stage triggers. Disc. 2013.

* **Model 38A20FB** – .308 Win. cal., GIO, 18 in. medium contour stainless steel threaded barrel, low profile gas block, 10 in. modular free float tube, 4-slot rail, Mil-Spec 6-position stock, standard trigger, 20 shot PMag., black finish. Disc. 2013.

		$1,300	$1,150	$975	$875	$715	$575	$450	$1,450

* **Model 38AB136** – .308 Win. cal., GIO, 16 in. medium contour cold hammer forged stainless steel barrel, low profile gas block, 10 in. mod. free float tube, three 4-slot rails, Mil-Spec 6-position Magpul MOE stock and grip, 2-stage trigger, 20 shot PMag., black finish. Disc. 2013.

		$1,450	$1,275	$1,100	$975	$800	$650	$525	$1,600

* **Model 38A6DFO** – .308 Win. cal., GIO, 16 in. hammer forged barrel, low profile gas block, mod. free float tube, 4-slot rail, Magpul MOE stock and grip, 2-stage trigger, 20 shot PMag., Black finish. Disc. 2013.

		$1,675	$1,475	$1,250	$1,150	$925	$750	$575	$1,850

* **Model 38AF432** – .308 Win. cal., GIO, 18 in. threaded hammer forged barrel, low profile gas block, 10 in. modular free float tube, 4-slot rail, 6-position stock, 20 shot PMag., Black finish. Disc. 2013.

		$1,525	$1,325	$1,150	$1,050	$850	$675	$550	$1,700

5.56 HAMMER FORGED SERIES – 5.56 NATO cal., GIO, 16 in. hammer forged chrome-lined M4, M10, or Government profile barrel, 30 shot Magpul PMag., "F" marked front sight base, with or w/o Magpul MBUS rear sight, Black or FDE finish, other options available. Disc. 2013.

* **Model 55AD33B** – 5.56 NATO cal., GIO, 16 in. hammer forged chrome-lined barrel, mid-length low profile gas block, "F" marked front sight base and Magpul MBUS rear sight, Magpul MOE rifle length handguard, Mil-Spec 6-position Magpul MOE stock and grip, 30 shot Magpul PMag., Black finish. Disc. 2013.

		$1,125	$975	$850	$775	$625	$500	$400	$1,250

* **Model 55AD3A1** – 5.56 NATO cal., GIO, 16 in. M10 profile cold hammer forged chrome-lined barrel, mid-length handguard, "F" marked front sight base and Magpul MBUS rear sight, 6-position stock, 30 shot PMag., Black finish. Disc. 2013.

		$1,050	$925	$800	$725	$575	$475	$375	$1,180

* **Model 55AD37C** – 5.56 NATO cal., GIO, 16 in. M10 profile hammer forged chrome-lined barrel, "F" marked front sight base and Magpul MBUS rear sight, mid-length low pro gas block, Magpul MOE rifle length handguard in Flat Dark Earth, Mil-Spec 6-position Magpul MOE stock and grip in Flat Dark Earth, 30 shot Magpul PMag. in FDE finish. Disc. 2013.

		$1,125	$975	$850	$775	$625	$500	$400	$1,250

* **Model 55AD3B2** – 5.56 NATO cal., GIO, 16 in. M10 profile hammer forged chrome-lined barrel, "F" marked front sight base and rear sight, mid-length low pro gas block, Mil-Spec 6-position stock, 30 shot Magpul PMag., Black finish. Disc. 2013.

		$1,050	$925	$800	$725	$575	$475	$375	$1,200

MSR	100%	98%	95%	90%	80%	70%	60%	Last MSR

* **Model 55A8433** – 5.56 NATO cal., GIO, 16 in. M4 profile hammer forged chrome-lined barrel, "F" marked front sight base and rear sight, Mil-Spec 6-position stock, 30 shot Magpul PMag., Black finish. Disc. 2013.

| | $1,025 | $900 | $775 | $700 | $575 | $475 | $350 | *$1,150* |

* **Model 55A5252** – 5.56 NATO cal., GIO, 16 in. Government profile hammer forged chrome-lined barrel, "F" marked front sight base and Magpul MBUS rear sight, Magpul MOE mid-length handguard, Mil-Spec 6-position Magpul MOE stock and grip, 30 shot Magpul PMag., Black finish. Disc. 2013.

| | $1,125 | $975 | $850 | $775 | $625 | $500 | $400 | *$1,250* |

* **Model 55A5244** – 5.56 NATO cal., GIO, 16 in. Government profile hammer forged chrome-lined barrel, "F" marked front sight base and Magpul MBUS rear sight, Magpul MOE mid-length handguard, Mil-Spec 6-position Magpul MOE stock and grip, 30 shot Magpul PMag., Flat Dark Earth furniture. Disc. 2013.

| | $1,125 | $975 | $850 | $775 | $625 | $500 | $400 | *$1,250* |

* **Model 55A526D** – 5.56 NATO cal., GIO, 16 in. Government profile hammer forged chrome-lined barrel, "F" marked front sight base and rear sight, Mil-Spec 6-position stock, 30 shot Magpul PMag., Black finish. Disc. 2013.

| | $1,050 | $925 | $800 | $725 | $575 | $475 | $375 | *$1,200* |

5.56 LE SERIES – 5.56 NATO cal., GIO or GPO, features WASP (Weapon Armament Surface Protection) finish, the nitriding conversion is applied to the barrel inside and out, along with the front sight base and uppers, 16 in. chromemoly M4 or Bull barrel, 30 shot Magpul PMag., LE rifles use "T" marked upper receivers with M4 feed ramps and forged lower receivers with Mil-Spec components, Black or FDE finish. Disc. 2013.

* **Model 55AE1AD** – 5.56 NATO cal., GIO or GPO, 16 in. WASP treated M4 profile chromemoly steel barrel, "T" marked front sight base, rear sight, M4 handguard, Mil-Spec 6-position stock, A2 pistol grip, 30 shot Magpul PMag., Flat Dark Earth furniture. Disc. 2013.

| | $850 | $750 | $650 | $575 | $475 | $375 | $300 | *$950* |

* **Model 55AE1BB** – 5.56 NATO cal., GPO or GIO, 16 in. WASP treated M4 profile chromemoly steel barrel, optics ready with piston system, Mil-Spec 6-position stock, 30 shot Magpul PMag., Black finish. Disc. 2013.

| | $950 | $825 | $725 | $650 | $525 | $425 | $350 | *$1,050* |

* **Model 55AED49** – 5.56 NATO cal., GIO or GPO, 16 in. WASP treated chromemoly steel Bull barrel, optics ready with low profile gas block, carbine length round free float tube, Mil-Spec 6-position stock, 30 shot Magpul PMag., Black finish. Disc. 2013.

| | $750 | $650 | $575 | $525 | $425 | $350 | $275 | *$850* |

* **Model 55AEDA5** – 5.56 NATO cal., GIO or GPO, 16 in. WASP treated chromemoly steel Bull barrel, optics ready with piston system, Revolution handguard with 5 slot rails, Mil-Spec 6-position stock, 30 shot Magpul PMag., Black finish. Disc. 2013.

| | $1,050 | $925 | $800 | $725 | $575 | $475 | $375 | *$1,200* |

5.56 STAINLESS STEEL SERIES – 5.56 NATO cal., GIO, 16, 18, 22, or 24 in. stainless steel M4 profile or Bull barrel, with or w/o fluting, low profile gas block, A1 or 6-position stock, 30 shot Magpul PMag., free float tube, Black finish. Disc. 2013.

* **Model 55ABB89** – 5.56 NATO cal., GIO, 16 in. stainless steel Bull barrel, carbine length round free float handguard tube, low profile gas block, 6-position stock, 30 shot Magpul PMag., Black finish. Disc. 2013.

| | $800 | $700 | $600 | $550 | $450 | $375 | $275 | *$900* |

* **Model 55A3C9E** – 5.56 NATO cal., GIO, 18 in. stainless steel Bull barrel, optics ready with low profile gas block, mid-length round free float tube, Mil-Spec 6-position stock, 30 shot Magpul PMag., Black finish. Disc. 2013.

| | $825 | $725 | $625 | $575 | $450 | $375 | $300 | *$930* |

* **Model 55A8EDC** – 5.56 NATO cal., GIO, 22 in. stainless steel Bull barrel, optics ready low profile gas block, rifle length round free float tube, A1 stock, 30 shot Magpul PMag., Black finish. Disc .2013.

| | $875 | $775 | $650 | $600 | $475 | $400 | $300 | *$980* |

* **Model 55AE392** – 5.56 NATO cal., GIO, 25 in. stainless steel fluted barrel, optics ready with low profile gas block, rifle length round free float tube, A1 stock, 30 shot Magpul PMag., Black finish. Disc. 2013.

| | $975 | $850 | $725 | $675 | $550 | $450 | $350 | *$1,100* |

* **Model 55A3866** – 5.56 NATO cal., GIO, 16 in. stainless steel M4 profile barrel, optics ready with railed gas block, Mil-Spec 6-position stock, 30 shot Magpul PMag., Black finish. Disc. 2013.

| | $850 | $750 | $650 | $575 | $475 | $375 | $300 | *$950* |

MK3 – .308 Win. cal., 18 in. stainless steel heavy taper barrel with A2 compensator, RKM15 Keymod free float handguard, billet aluminum receiver, SST, A2 pistol grip, A1 buttstock, 20 shot PMag., 9.3 lbs. New 2014.

| MSR $1,600 | $1,375 | $1,200 | $1,025 | $950 | $750 | $625 | $475 | |

MSR	100%	98%	95%	90%	80%	70%	60%	Last MSR

MK3 3GR – .308 Win. cal., 18 in. stainless steel heavy taper barrel with CMMG SV muzzle brake, RKM15 Keymod free float handguard, Billet aluminum receiver, Geissele automatics SSA trigger, Magpul MOE pistol grip, trigger guard, buttstock, 9.4 lbs. New 2014.

MSR $1,850 $1,575 $1,375 $1,175 $1,075 $875 $725 $550

MK3 CBR (CARBINE BATTLE RIFLE) – .308 Win. cal., GIO, 16 in. nitrided stainless steel match barrel, Surefire SOCOM suppressor adapter muzzle break, full length free float Revo KeyMod handguard and KeyMod accessory attachment system, one 5-slot rail, Magpul MOE pistol grip and ACS-L buttstock, Geissele Super semi-auto 2-stage trigger, 20 shot PMag., Black finish.

MSR $2,000 $1,700 $1,500 $1,275 $1,150 $950 $775 $600

MK3 D – .308 Win. cal., GIO, 16 in. chrome-lined hammer forged barrel with A2 compensator, RKM15 Keymod free float handguard, BIllet alum. receiver, SST, 20 shot PMag., Magpul MOE pistol grip and stock, Black furniture, 8.2 lbs. New 2014.

MSR $2,000 $1,700 $1,500 $1,275 $1,150 $950 $775 $600

MK3 T – .308 Win. cal., 16.1 in. medium taper profile barrel with A2 compensator, RKM15 Keymod free float handguard, Billet alum. receiver, SST, A2 pistol grip, M4 buttstock, Black furniture, 8.1 lbs. New 2014.

MSR $1,650 $1,400 $1,225 $1,050 $950 $775 $625 $500

MK4 3GR – 5.56 NATO cal., 18 in. stainless steel medium taper profile barrel with CMMG SV muzzle brake, RKM14 Keymod free float handguard, Geissele SSA two-stage trigger, Magpul MOE pistol grip, trigger guard, rifle buttstock, Black furniture, 7 lbs. New 2014.

MSR $1,400 $1,200 $1,050 $900 $815 $650 $550 $425

MK4 A4 (GOVERNMENT PROFILE MODEL 22A6A1F) – .22 LR or 5.56 NATO (new 2014) cal., AR-15 style, GIO, 20 in. WASP treated chromemoly steel Government profile barrel with A2 compensator, stainless steel bolt group with BHOA and forward assist adapter, "F" marked front sight base and Magpul MBUS rear sight, A2 two-piece handguard, A1 (disc.) or M4 butt stock with A2 pistol grip, 25 shot Evolution mag., Black finish, 6 1/2 lbs.

MSR $925 $795 $695 $595 $550 $450 $350 $300

Add $175 for 5.56 NATO cal.

MK4 D – 5.56 NATO cal., 16.1 in. medium taper hammer forged barrel, RKM14 KEymod free float handguard, forged aluminum receiver, SST, Magpul MOE pistol grip, trigger guard, and buttstock, 6.4 lbs.

MSR $1,400 $1,200 $1,050 $900 $815 $650 $550 $425

MK4 HT – .22 LR, 5.56 NATO, or .300 Blackout cal., GIO or GPO (5.56 NATO cal. only), 16.1 in. heavy taper chromemoly or stainless steel barrel with castellated thread protector, RKM Keymod free float handguard, forged aluminum receiver, ST, A2 pistol grip and M4 buttstock, Black furniture, 7 lbs. New 2014.

MSR $925 $785 $685 $600 $550 $450 $350 $275

Add $125 for stainless steel barrel.

Add $175 for 5.56 NATO or .300 Blackout cal.

Add $425 for GPO (gas piston operation).

MK4LE – 9mm Para., .22 LR, 5.56 NATO, or .300 AAC Blackout cal., AR-15-style, GIO, 16 in. WASP treated chromemoly steel M4 profile barrel or M300 multi-role profile barrel (.300 AAC Blackout cal. only) with A2 compensator, M4 two-piece handguard, M4 buttstock with A2 pistol grip, 30 shot, forged aluminum receiver, SST, Black furniture, "F" marked front sight base and MBUS rear sight, 6.2 lbs.

MSR $850 $725 $650 $550 $500 $400 $325 $250

Add $75 for 5.56 NATO cal., $100 for .300 AAC Blackout, or $250 for 9mm Para. cal.

* MK4LE Optics Ready – 9mm Para., .22 LR, 5.56 NATO, or .300 AAC Blackout cal., similar to MK4LE, except has railed gas block and no sights.

MSR $825 $785 $685 $595 $535 $425 $350 $275

Add $75 for 5.56 NATO cal., $100 for .300 Blackout cal., or $250 for 9mm Para. cal.

MK4LEM – 5.56 NATO cal., GIO, 16 in. chromemoly steel medium taper profile barrel with A2 compensator, mid-length two-piece handguard, forged aluminum receiver, SST, M4 buttstock with A2 pistol grip, Black furniture, 6 1/2 lbs. New 2014.

MSR $950 $825 $725 $625 $550 $450 $375 $300

MK4 RCE – 5.56 NATO or .300 Blackout cal., 16 in. stainless steel medium taper profile barrel with CMMG SV brake, RKM14 Keymod free-float handguard, Geissele two-stage trigger, Magpul MOE pistol grip, MOE trigger guard, CTR buttstock, 6.7 lbs. New 2014.

MSR $1,400 $1,200 $1,050 $900 $815 $650 $550 $425

MK4 S – 5.56 NATO cal., 18 in. stainless steel medium taper barrel with A2 compensator, RKM14 Keymod free float handguard, forged aluminum receiver, SST, A2 pistol grip, M4 buttstock, Black furniture, 6.7 lbs.

MSR $1,100 $950 $825 $725 $650 $525 $425 $350

MSR	100%	98%	95%	90%	80%	70%	60%	Last MSR

MK4 V – 5.56 NATO cal., 24 in. fluted medium contour stainless steel barrel, RKM14 Keymod free float handguard, forged alum. receiver, SST, A2 pistol grip, A1 fixed buttstock, 7 1/2 lbs. New 2014.

MSR $1,250	$1,075	$950	$800	$725	$600	$485	$375	

MK4 T – 9mm Para., .22 LR, .300 Blackout, or 5.56 NATO cal., 16.1 in. medium taper chromemoly or stainless steel barrel with A2 compensator, RKM11 Keymod free float handguard, forged aluminum receiver, SST, A2 pistol grip, M4 buttstock, 6.3 lbs. New 2014.

MSR $900	$775	$675	$575	$525	$425	$350	$275	

Add $100 for stainless steel barrel.

Add $150 for 5.56 NATO or .300 Blackout cal. or $250 for 9mm Para. cal.

C Z (CESKÁ ZBROJOVKA)

Current manufacturer located in Uhersky Brod, Czech Republic since 1936. Previous manufacture was in Strakonice, Czechoslovakia circa 1923-late 1950s. Newly manufactured CZ firearms are currently imported exclusively by CZ USA located in Kansas City, KS. Previously imported by Magnum Research, Inc. located in Minneapolis, MN until mid-1994. Previously imported before 1994 by Action Arms Ltd. located in Philadelphia, PA. Dealer and distributor sales.

For CZ manufactured airguns, please refer to the *Blue Book of Airguns* by Dr. Robert Beeman and John Allen (now online also).

CZ USA currently has four product lines, which include CZ (pistols, rifles, and shotguns), Safari Classics (best quality bolt action rifles), Dan Wesson (semi-auto pistols), and Brno (combination guns and rifles). Please refer to the individual listings for more information and current values.

PISTOLS: SEMI-AUTO, RECENT MFG.

CZ P-01 – 9mm Para. cal., based on CZ-75 design, but with metallurgical improvements, DA/SA, aluminum alloy frame, hammer forged 3.8 in. barrel, 10 or 14 (new 2005) shot mag., decocker, includes M3 rail on bottom of frame, checkered rubber grips, matte black polycoat finish, 27.2 oz. Importation began 2003.

MSR $627	$545	$480	$420	$365	$315	$275	$250	

Add $99 for tactical block with bayonet (mfg. 2006-2012).

Add $67 for Crimson Trace laser grips (mfg. 2007-2010).

CZ P-06 – .40 S&W cal., 10 shot mag., otherwise similar to CZ P-01. Mfg. 2008-2009, re-introduced 2011.

MSR $680	$575	$485	$415	$350	$300	$275	$250	

Add $99 for tactical block with bayonet (disc. 2012).

CZ P-07 DUTY – 9mm Para. or .40 S&W cal., DA/SA, 3.8 in. standard or threaded (new 2012) barrel, black polycoat or OD Green (new 2012) polymer frame with black slide, squared off trigger guard, 10 (9mm only),12 (.40 S&W only) or 16 shot mag., fixed sights, decocking lever, Omega trigger system, 27 oz. Mfg. 2009-2013.

	$435	$370	$325	$280	$260	$240	$220	*$483*

Add $13 for .40 S&W cal.

Add $6 for OD Green frame in 9mm Para. cal. with 16 shot mag. (new 2012).

Add $45 for threaded barrel (9mm Para. cal. only) with black finish (new 2012).

CZ P-09 DUTY – 9mm Para. or .40 S&W cal., full size variation of the P-07 Duty, 4 1/2 in. barrel, 15 (.40 S&W) or 19 (9mm Para.) shot staggered mag., includes lower Picatinny rail and low profile sights, Omega SA/DA trigger, black polymer frame and black steel slide, approx. 30 oz. New 2013.

MSR $530	$475	$400	$350	$315	$285	$250	$225	

Add $14 for .40 S&W cal.

Add $47 for suppressor ready (9mm Para. only), 19 shot mag. New 2014.

CZ-40B/CZ-40P – .40 S&W cal. only, CZ-75B operating mechanism in alloy (CZ-40B) or polymer (CZ-40P) M1911 style frame, DA/SA, black polycoat finish, 10 shot double column mag., fixed sights, firing pin block safety. Limited importation 2002 only, reintroduced 2007 only.

	$425	$365	$325	$290	$275	$250	$225	*$499*

* CZ-40 P Compact – .40 S&W cal., 1,500 imported 2004, reimported 2006.

	$325	$285	$265	$245	$225	$200	$175	*$370*

CZ-75 SERIES – 9mm Para. or .40 S&W (disc. 1997, reintroduced 1999) cal., Poldi steel, selective double action, double action only, or single action only, frame safety, 4 3/4 in. barrel, 10 (C/B 1994, standard for .40 S&W cal.), 15* (disc.), or 16 (9mm Para. cal. only) shot mag., currently available in black polycoat/polymer (standard, DA and SA only), matte blue (disc. 1994), high polish (disc. 1994), glossy blue (mfg. 1999-2010), dual tone (mfg. 1998-2012), satin nickel (mfg. 1994-2012), high polished stainless steel, or matte stainless steel (new 2006) finish, black plastic grips, non-suffix early guns did not have a firing pin block safety, reversible mag. release, or ambidextrous safety, and were usually shipped with two mags., B suffix model nomenclature was added 1998, and designated some internal mechanism changes, BD suffix indicates decocker mechanism, 34.3 oz. New 1975.

MSR		100%	98%	95%	90%	80%	70%	60%	Last MSR

Add 10% with lanyard loop.

These early pistols sell for $1,200 if NIB condition, chrome engraved $1,650 (NIB), factory competition $1,500 (NIB).

"First Model" variations, mostly imported by Pragotrade of Canada, are identifiable by short slide rails, no half-cock feature, and were mostly available in high polish blue only. Current values range from $275-$595, depending on original condition.

* CZ-75 Semi-Compact – 9mm Para. cal. only, 13 shot mag., choice of black polymer, matte, or high polish blue finish. Imported 1994 only.

		$350	$300	$275	$250	$230	$250	$200	$519

Add $20 for matte blue finish.

Add $40 for high polish blue finish.

* CZ-75 B Military – 9mm Para. cal. Importation 2000-2002.

		$365	$315	$270	$250	$225	$210	$195	$429

* CZ-75 B Tactical – similar to CZ-75 B, except has OD green frame and matte black slide, includes CZ knife. Limited importation during 2003.

		$425	$355	$305	$270	$225	$210	$195	$499

CZ-75 COMPACT – 9mm Para. or .40 S&W (mfg. 2005-2010) cal. only, otherwise similiar to CZ-75, full-size frame, except has 3.9 in. barrel, 10 (C/B 1994) or 13* (disc.), or 14 shot mag., checkered walnut grips, 33 oz. New 1993.

MSR $544		$485	$425	$375	$325	$275	$250	$225	

Add $37 for 10 shot mag. (new 2014).

Add $41 for glossy blue (disc. 2006), dual tone (disc. 2012), or satin nickel (disc. 2012) finish.

Add $41 for .40 S&W cal. (disc. 2010).

Add $99 for tactical block with bayonet (.40 S&W cal. only) mfg. 2006-2012.

Add $391 for CZ Kadet .22 LR adapter I or II (includes .22 LR upper slide assembly and mag., mfg. 1998-disc.).

* CZ-75 D PCR Compact – 9mm Para. cal., similar to CZ-75 Compact, except has black polymer alloy frame, decocker, PCR stands for Police of Czech Republic, 1.7 lbs. Importation began 2000.

MSR $599		$515	$465	$400	$350	$300	$265	$235	

* CZ-75 Compact SDP – 9mm Para. cal., DA/SA, 3.7 in. barrel, black alloy frame with black aluminum grips, lower Picatinny rail, low profile Tritium two-dot night sights, 14 shot mag., front and rear slide serrations, bobbed hammer, 28 1/2 oz. New 2013.

MSR $1,420		$1,250	$1,075	$925	$800	$700	$600	$500	

CZ-75 KADET – .22 LR cal., black polymer finish, 10 shot mag, 4.7 in. barrel, 37.9 oz. Mfg. 1999-2004, reintroduced 2006-2012.

		$560	$500	$450	$400	$350	$300	$275	$690

CZ-75 SHADOW – 9mm Para. cal., DA/SA or SAO (new 2013), black or dual-tone finish, competition hammer/trigger with beavertail frame, stainless steel guide rod, ambidextrous extended manual safety, new style 85 combat trigger, includes two 16 (SAO, new 2013), or 18 shot mags. and test target, fiber optic front sight and shadow rear sight, checkered black plastic grips, 39 oz. Mfg. in Czech Republic, assembled in USA. Mfg. 2011-2013.

		$915	$800	$725	$650	$575	$500	$425	$1,053

Subtract $74 for SAO (new 2013, includes two 16 shot mags.).

* CZ-75 Shadow T – 9mm Para. cal., similar to CZ-75 Shadow, except is DA/SA, and has black rubber grips and full adj. rear sight. Mfg. 2011-2013.

		$1,075	$940	$815	$725	$650	$575	$500	$1,180

CZ-75 SHADOW CTS LS-P – 9mm Para. cal., DA/SA, black polycoat frame/grips, satin nickel long slide, adj. sights. Mfg. by Custom Shop. Mfg. 2012-2013.

		$1,300	$1,150	$1,025	$875	$775	$675	$550	$1,521

CZ-75 TS CZECHMATE – 9mm Para. cal., includes 2 barrels and all accessories necessary to shoot in IPSC open or limited division, aluminum grips, competition hammer, undercut trigger guard, three 20 shot mags. and one 26 shot mag., black polycoat finish. Custom Shop mfg. New 2011.

MSR $3,317		$2,850	$2,475	$2,150	$1,825	$1,500	$1,250	$1,000	

CZ-75 SP-01 – 9mm Para. cal., 4 3/4 in. barrel, includes lower Picatinny rail, ambidextrous thumb safety, adj. tritium sights, matte black polycoat finish, decocker, checkered black rubber grips, two 10 or 18 shot mags, 38 oz. New 2006.

MSR $680		$575	$485	$410	$350	$300	$275	$250	

* CZ-75 SP-01 Phantom – 9mm Para. cal., SA/DA, polymer frame with accessory rail, steel slide, fixed sights, two interchangable grip inserts, decocking lever, 19 shot mag. (also fits standard CZ-75 models), black polycoat finish, squared off trigger guard, 28.2 oz. Mfg. 2009-2013.

		$520	$440	$375	$325	$275	$250	$225	$595

MSR	100%	98%	95%	90%	80%	70%	60%	Last MSR

* CZ-75 SP-01 Accu-Shadow – 9mm Para. cal., 4.6 in. barrel, features Accu-Bushing system enabling precise barrel placement and better accuracy, competition hammer, lighter springs, short reset disconnector, fiber optic front and Hajo serrated target rear sight, lower Picatinny rail, black finish, 38 1/2 oz. New 2013.

MSR $1,715 $1,475 $1,295 $1,075 $925 $800 $700 $600

* CZ-75 SP-01 Shadow Custom – 9mm Para. cal., features adj. competition rear and fiber optic front sight, 19 shot mag., custom tuned action and trigger, competition hammer, reduced power springs, stainless guide rod, and thin black aluminum grips, dual tone finish, Custom Shop mfg. Mfg. 2011 only.

    $1,050 $900 $750 $600 $500 $400 $325   *$1,199*

* CZ-75 SP-01 Shadow Target – 9mm Para. cal., similar to SP-01 Series, except has custom shop target features, including Champion style hammer, fiber optic front sight and competition rear sight, extended mag. release, fully beveled magwell, 19 shot mag., rubber grips, 2.6 lbs., Custom Shop mfg. New 2010.

MSR $1,361 $1,175 $995 $825 $700 $600 $500 $425

CZ-75 SP-01 TACTICAL – 9mm Para. or .40 S&W cal., lower Picatinny rail, decocker, 10 or 19 shot mag., tritium sights, black polycoat finish.

MSR $680 $575 $485 $410 $350 $300 $275 $250

Add $79 for .40 S&W cal.

Add $99 for tactical block with bayonet (disc. 2012).

CZ-83 – .32 ACP (disc. 1994, reintroduced 1999-2002 and 2006) or .380 ACP (new 1986), or 9mm Makarov (mfg. 1999-2001) cal., modern design, 3-dot sights, 3.8 in. barrel, DA/SA, choice of carry models, blue (disc. 1994), glossy blue (new 1998), satin nickel (new 1999, not available in .32 ACP), or black polymer (disc. 1997) finish, black synthetic grips, 10 (C/B 1994), 12* (.380 ACP) or 15* (.32 ACP) shot mag., 26.2 oz. Mfg. began 1985, but U.S. importation started in 1992. Importation disc. 2012.

    $375 $315 $265 $235 $200 $175 $160   *$452*

Add $36 for satin nickel.

CZ-85, CZ-85 B – 9mm Para. or 9x21mm (imported 1993-94 only) cal., DA/SA, variation of the CZ-75 with ambidextrous controls, new plastic grip design, sight rib, available in black polymer, matte blue (disc. 1994), glossy blue (mfg. 2001 only), or high-gloss blue (9mm Para. only, disc. 1994) finish, includes firing pin block and finger rest trigger, plastic grips, 10, 15 (disc.), or 16 shot mag. New 2005, B suffix model nomenclature was added during 1998, approx. 2.2 lbs.

MSR $628 $525 $465 $410 $375 $330 $295 $275

Add $391 for CZ Kadet .22 LR adapter (includes .22 LR upper slide assembly and mag., mfg. 1998 only).

* CZ-85 Combat – similar to CZ-85B, except has fully adj. rear sight, available in black polymer, matte blue (disc. 1994), glossy blue (mfg. 2001-2010), dual-tone (disc. 2012), satin nickel (disc. 2012), or high-gloss blue (disc. 2010) finish, walnut (disc. 1994) or black plastic (new 1994) grips, extended mag. release, drop free 15 (mfg. 1995-2011), or 16 shot mag. Importation began 1992.

MSR $664 $550 $465 $425 $375 $350 $325 $295

Add $26 for glossy blue (disc. 2010) satin nickel (disc. 2012), or dual-tone (disc. 2012) finish.

Add $291 for CZ Kadet .22 LR adapter (includes .22 LR upper slide assembly and mag., mfg. 1998 only).

CZ-2075 RAMI – 9mm Para. or .40 S&W cal., DA/SA, 3 in. barrel, double stack 7 (.40 S&W cal. new 2012), 8 (.40 S&W cal.), 10 (9mm Para. cal., flush fit) or 14 (9mm Para. cal., disc. 2013) shot mag. with finger extension, snag free sights, black polycoat finish with black checkered grips, alloy or polymer (mfg. 2006-2011) frame, 25 oz. New 2005.

MSR $614 $510 $445 $375 $325 $300 $250 $225

Add $19 for .40 S&W with 7 shot mag. (new 2012).

Subtract approx. $100 for polymer frame with black polycoat finish (disc. 2011).

* CZ-2075 RAMI BD – 9mm Para. cal., DA/SA, 3 in. barrel, 10 or 14 shot mag., similar to CZ-2075 RAMI, except has decocking lever, weight reduction scallop on slide, tritium 3-dot night sights, 23 1/2 oz. New 2009.

MSR $680 $590 $480 $425 $385 $350 $325 $295

CZ VZ 61 SKORPION – imported by CZ 2009-2010. Please refer to this model listing in the Skorpion section.

RIFLES: BOLT ACTION, CENTERFIRE, COMMERCIAL MFG.

Ceská Zbrojovka began manufacturing rifles circa 1936. Long gun production was discontinued between 1948-1964, with the exception of the massive military contracts during that time period.

* CZ 527 M1 American – .223 Rem. cal., styling similar to U.S. military M1 carbine featuring 3 shot flush detachable mag., no sights, walnut (disc. 2013) or black polymer stock, approx. 6 lbs. New 2008.

MSR $665 $555 $475 $420 $365 $335 $295 $250

Add $66 for walnut stock (disc. 2013).

MSR	100%	98%	95%	90%	80%	70%	60%	Last MSR

CZ 550 MAGNUM H.E.T. (HIGH ENERGY TACTICAL) – .300 Win. Mag. (disc. 2013), .300 Rem. Ultra Mag. (disc. 2013), or .338 Lapua cal., 28 in. barrel, flat black finish, Kevlar tactical (disc. 2013) or Manners composite camo (new 2014) stock, 4 to 6 shot fixed (disc. 2013) or detachable A1 (new 2014) mag., SST, muzzle brake, oversized bolt handle, 13 lbs. New 2009.

| MSR $3,929 | $3,500 | $3,125 | $2,625 | $2,250 | $1,950 | $1,575 | $1,325 | |

CZ 550 URBAN COUNTER SNIPER – .308 Win. cal., 16 in. barrel with SureFire muzzle brake, OD Green Kevlar stock, 10 shot mag. Mfg. 2010-2013.

| | $2,275 | $2,000 | $1,750 | $1,500 | $1,250 | $1,000 | $825 | $2,530 |

CZ 700 SNIPER – .308 Win. cal., sniper design features forged billet receiver with permanently attached Weaver rail, 25.6 in. heavy barrel w/o sights, 10 shot detachable mag., black synthetic thumbhole stock with adj. cheekpiece and buttplate, large bolt handle, fully adj. trigger, 11.9 lbs. Limited importation 2001 only.

| | $1,875 | $1,575 | $1,250 | $1,025 | $895 | $775 | $650 | $2,097 |

CZ 700M1 SNIPER – .308 Win. cal., similar to CZ 700 Sniper, except has laminated stock, limited importation 2001 only.

| | $1,875 | $1,575 | $1,250 | $1,025 | $895 | $775 | $650 | |

CZ 750 SNIPER – .308 Win. cal., sniper design, black synthetic thumbhole stock w/adj. comb, scope mounting via detachable Weaver rail or integral CZ 19mm dovetail, 26 in. barrel w/muzzle brake, includes two 10 shot mags., thread protector, and mirage shield, 11.9 lbs. Limited mfg. beginning 2006.

| MSR $1,999 | $1,775 | $1,550 | $1,250 | $1,050 | $925 | $775 | $675 | |

RIFLES: SEMI-AUTO

CZ-M52 (1952) – 7.62x45mm Czech cal., semi-auto, 20 2/3 in. barrel, 10 shot detachable mag., tangent rear sight, this model was also imported briefly by Samco Global Arms, Inc. located in Miami, FL.

| | $550 | $450 | $350 | $300 | $250 | $200 | $150 | |

CZ-M52/57 (1957) – 7.62x39mm cal., later variation of the CZ-M52.

| | $425 | $375 | $325 | $300 | $250 | $200 | $150 | |

VZ 58 MILITARY/TACTICAL SPORTER – 7.62x39mm cal., gas operated, AK-47 design, milled receiver, 16.14 in. barrel, tilting breech block, choice of Zytel skeletonized (Tactical) or plastic impregnated wood (Military) stock, alloy 30 shot mag., 7.32 lbs. Mfg. 2008-2011.

| | $925 | $850 | $750 | $650 | $550 | $450 | $350 | $999 |

Add $30 for Tactical Sporter model (available with synthetic or folding (new 2010) stock).

SHOTGUNS: SEMI-AUTO

CZ-712 PRACTICAL – 12 ga., 22 in. barrel with 5 choke tubes, 9 shot extended mag., 6-position M4 style adj. stock, matte black finish, 8.1 lbs. New 2014.

| MSR $699 | $595 | $550 | $495 | $450 | $415 | $385 | $335 | |

SHOTGUNS: SLIDE ACTION

CZ 612 HC-P – 12 ga., 20 in. barrel with cyl. choke tube, tactical configuration features black polymer pistol grip stock and grooved forearm, ghost ring sights with fiber dots, matte black metal finish, 6 1/2 lbs. New 2013.

| MSR $366 | $310 | $285 | $250 | $225 | $200 | $185 | $170 | |

CZ 612 HOME DEFENSE – 12 ga., 18 1/2 in. barrel with fixed cyl. choke and front bead sight, black synthetic stock and forearm, matte black metal finish, 6 lbs. New 2013.

| MSR $304 | $265 | $235 | $210 | $190 | $170 | $150 | $135 | |

Add $105 for Home Defense Combo two barrel set with extra 26 in. barrel (new 2014).

CZ (STRAKONICE)

Current manufacturer established in 1919 and located in Strakonice, Czech Republic. No current U.S. importation. Previously imported by Adco Sales, Inc., located in Woburn, MA.

PISTOLS: SEMI-AUTO

Older Strakonice manufacture can be found in the CZ (Ceska Zbrojovka) section.

CZ-TT – 9mm Para., .40 S&W, or .45 ACP cal., DA/SA, polymer frame, 3.77 in. ported or unported barrel, matte finish, 10 shot mag., 26.1 oz. Imported 2004-2006.

| | $450 | $415 | $375 | $325 | $295 | $275 | $250 | $479 |

Add $30 for ported barrel (disc.).
Add $40 for ported barrel and slide serrations (disc.).
Add $399 for conversion kit with one mag.

MSR	100%	98%	95%	90%	80%	70%	60%	*Last MSR*

CZ-T POLYMER COMPACT – similar to CZ-TT, except has shorter barrel. Limited importation 2004 only.

	$475	$425	$375	$325	$295	$275	$225	*$559*

CZ ST9 – 9mm Para. cal., 5 in. barrel, 16 shot mag., DA/SA, manual safety lever, matte blue finish, checkered wood grips.

This model has not been imported into the U.S.

CALICO LIGHT WEAPONS SYSTEMS

Current manufacturer established during 1986, and located in Cornelius, OR, previously located in Hillsboro, OR from 2002-2010, located in Sparks, NV 1998-2001, and in Bakersfield, CA.

CARBINES: SEMI-AUTO

Extra magazines are currently priced as follows: $141 for 100 shot 9mm Para. cal., $118 for 50 shot 9mm Para. cal., or $125 for 100 shot .22 LR cal.

LIBERTY I/II & LIBERTY 50-100 – 9mm Para. cal., 16.1 in. barrel, downward ejection, retarded blowback CETME type action, aluminum alloy receiver, synthetic stock with pistol grip (some early post-ban specimens had full wood stocks with thumbhole cutouts), 50 or 100 shot helical feed mag., ambidextrous safety, 7 lbs. Mfg. 1995-2001, reintroduced late 2007.

MSR $710	$625	$550	$500	$450	$400	$350	$300	

Add $70 for Liberty 50 Tactical with quad rails (new 2010).
Add $189 for Liberty I Tactical with quad rails (new 2010), or $197 for Liberty II Tactical with quad rails (new 2010).
Add $119 for Liberty I with skeletal adj. stock, or $137 for Liberty II with fixed stock.
Add $46 for Liberty 100 (100 shot mag.), or $116 for Liberty 100 Tactical with quad rails (new 2010).
Current MSR is for the Liberty 50 Model.

M-100 – .22 LR cal., blowback action, folding buttstock, 100 shot helical feed mag., alloy frame, aluminum receiver, ambidextrous safety, 16.1 in. shrouded barrel with flash suppressor/muzzle brake, adj. sights, 4.2 lbs. empty. Mfg. 1986-1994, reintroduced late 2007.

MSR $573	$515	$450	$400	$350	$300	$275	$250	

* ***M-100 Tactical*** – similar to M-100, except has quad Picatinny rails. New 2010.

MSR $643	$550	$475	$425	$375	$325	$300	$275	

* ***M-100 FS*** – similar to M-100, except has solid stock and barrel does not have flash suppressor. Mfg. 1996-2001, reintroduced late 2007.

MSR $573	$515	$450	$400	$350	$300	$275	$250	

* ***M-100 FS Tactical*** – similar to M-100 FS, except has quad Picatinny rail. New 2010.

MSR $643	$550	$475	$425	$375	$325	$300	$275	

M-101 – while advertised, this model never went into production.

M-105 SPORTER – similar to M-100, except has walnut distinctively styled buttstock and forend, 4 3/4 lbs. empty. Mfg. 1989-1994.

	$650	$550	$495	$450	$350	$295	$250	*$335*

M-106 – while advertised, this model never went into production.

M-900 – 9mm Para. cal., retarded blowback action, wood (disc.) or collapsible buttstock (current mfg.), cast aluminum receiver with stainless steel bolt, static cocking handle, 16 in. barrel, fixed rear sight with adj. post front, 50 (standard) or 100 shot helical feed mag., ambidextrous safety, black polymer pistol grip and forend, approx. 3.7 lbs. Mfg. 1989-1990, reintroduced 1992-1993, again during 2007-2010.

	$775	$700	$650	$600	$500	$450	$400	*$875*

Add $157 for 100 shot mag.

* ***M-900S*** – similar to M-900, except has non-collapsible shoulder stock. Disc. 1993.

	$650	$550	$475	$400	$350	$300	$275	*$632*

* ***M-901 Canada Carbine*** – 9mm Para. cal., similar to M-900, except has 18 1/2 in. barrel and sliding stock. Disc. 1992.

	$675	$595	$550	$475	$350	$300	$285	*$643*

This model was also available with solid fixed stock (Model 901S).

M-951 TACTICAL CARBINE – 9mm Para. cal., 16.1 in. barrel, similar appearance to M-900 Carbine, except has muzzle brake and extra pistol grip on front of forearm, 4 3/4 lbs. Mfg. 1990-94.

	$750	$700	$675	$650	$600	$475	$450	*$556*

MSR	100%	98%	95%	90%	80%	70%	60%	Last MSR

* M-951S – similar to M-951, except has synthetic buttstock. Mfg. 1991-94.

	100%	98%	95%	90%	80%	70%	60%	Last MSR
	$650	$595	$525	$450	$400	$350	$300	$567

PISTOLS: SEMI-AUTO

LIBERTY III – 9mm Para. cal., 6 in. ported barrel, choice of 50 or 100 shot mag., ribbed forend, 2 1/4 lbs. w/o mag. New 2010.

MSR $783	$700	$625	$550	$500	$450	$400	$350

Add $70 for Liberty III Tactical with quad rails (new 2011).

M-110 – .22 LR cal., blowback action, 6 in. barrel with muzzle brake, 100 round helical feed mag., includes notched rear sight and adj. windage front sight, 10 1/2 in. sight radius, ambidextrous safety, pistol grip storage compartment, 2.21 lbs. empty. Mfg. 1989-2001, reintroduced 2007.

MSR $619	$550	$475	$375	$325	$275	$225	$200

M-950 – 9mm Para. cal., same operating mechanism as the M-900 Carbine, 6 in. barrel, 50 (standard) or 100 shot helical feed mag., 2 1/4 lbs. empty. Mfg. 1989-1994, mfg. late 2007-2010.

	100%	98%	95%	90%	80%	70%	60%	Last MSR
	$775	$700	$650	$600	$500	$450	$400	$872

CANIK55

Current trademark of pistols manufactured by Samsun Domestic Defence and Industry Corporation (a subsidiary of Aral Industry Corporation), established in 1997 and located in Samsun, Turkey. Currently imported beginning 2013 by Tristar, located in N. Kansas City, MO. Previously imported circa mid-2010-2011 by Canik-USA, located in Pueblo West, CO.

PISTOLS: SEMI-AUTO

Canik55 is a line of good quality semi-auto 1911-style pistols, including the Shark Series, Stingray Series, TP-9 Series (new 2012, SFO), Piranha Series, LSC Series, S-FC 100 Series, MKEK Series, and Dolphin Series. Currently, only some of these models are being imported into the U.S. Please contact the importer directly for more information, including pricing and U.S. availability (see Trademark Index).

CARACAL

Current manufacturer of semi-auto pistols established in 2006, and located in the Abu Dhabi, United Arab Emirates. Currently imported beginning 2011 by Caracal USA, located in Trussville, AL. Previously located in Knoxville, TN. Currently distributed in Italy exclusively by Fratelli Tanfoglio Snc, located in Brescia, Italy.

PISTOLS: SEMI-AUTO

MODEL C – 9mm Para., 9x21mm, .357 SIG, or .40 S&W cal., modified Browning-type blowback design, double action, SFO, 3.66 in. barrel, 14 shot mag., ribbed black polymer frame with colored inserts and Picatinny rail in front of trigger guard, matte black slide with rear slide serrations and integral sights (fiber optic front sight), Glock style trigger safety, cocking indicator, approx. 25 oz.

	100%	98%	95%	90%	80%	70%	60%	Last MSR
	$550	$450	$415	$375	$335	$300	$275	$625

Caracal has issued a recall on all of its Model C pistols following an incident where one gun suffered a catastrophic slide failure. The company advises owners not to load or use any Model C pistol and to contact Caracal immediately at 205-655-7050. Caracal is offering a full refund of the purchase price on all C Model pistols.

MODEL F – similar to Model C, except has 4.1 in. barrel and 18 shot mag., 26 1/2 oz.

MSR $625	$550	$450	$415	$375	$335	$300	$275

MODEL SC – 9mm Para. or 9x21mm cal., similar to Model C, except is compact variation with 3.38 in. barrel and 13 shot mag., approx. 23 oz. Limited mfg. 2009-2011.

	100%	98%	95%	90%	80%	70%	60%	Last MSR
	$550	$450	$415	$375	$335	$300	$275	$625

MODEL CAL .40 – .40 S&W cal., 4.1 in. barrel, 14 shot mag., SFO, lightweight polymer frame, lower accessory rail, corrosion resistant matte black finish, low profile slide, short trigger pull, ambidextrous mag. release, approx. 27 oz. New 2013.

U.S. retail pricing has yet to be determined on this model.

RIFLES: BOLT ACTION

MODEL CSR – .308 Win. cal., 20 or 32 in. hammer forged threaded barrel, folding adj. skeletonized stock, pistol grip, quad rail, 10 shot mag., adj. match grade trigger, black finish, approx. 11 lbs. New 2012.

Please contact Caracal USA directly for current pricing on this model.

RIFLES: SEMI-AUTO

MODEL CC10 – 9mm Para. cal., modern bull pup design with skeletonized stock with grip safety, full length Picatinny rail, sights integrated into the frame, 18 shot detachable mag., right hand ejection with bolt lever on left side, black

MSR	100%	98%	95%	90%	80%	70%	60%	Last MSR

finish, choice of 9.3 (CC10-SB, LE only) or 16.1 (CC10 LB) in. barrel. New 2012.

Please contact Caracal USA directly for current pricing on this model.

CARBON 15

Please refer to the Professional Ordnance (discontinued mfg.) and Bushmaster (current mfg.) listings for more information on this trademark.

CAVALRY ARMS CORPORATION

Previous manufacturer located in Gilbert, AZ until 2010 and previously located in Mesa, AZ.

CARBINES/RIFLES: SEMI-AUTO

Cavalry Arms Corporation manufactured the CAV-15 Series, pattern after the AR-15 style carbine/rifle. Cavalry Arms also made conversions for select slide action shotguns.

CAV-15 SCOUT CARBINE – .223 Rem. cal., GIO, 16 in. chrome lined barrel, A2 flash hider, A3 flat-top upper receiver, longer sight radius, stand alone rear sight, Black, Green, or Coyote Brown finish, C6 handguards. Disc. 2010.

	$765	$675	$575	$525	$425	$350	$275	$850

Add $199 for drop in rail system.
Add $259 for free float system.
Add $92 for YHM flip up front or rear sight.

CAV-15 RIFLEMAN – .223 Rem. cal., GIO, 20 in. chrome lined Govt. profile barrel, A2 flash hider, A3 flat-top upper receiver, stand alone rear sight, Black, Green, or Coyote Brown finish, A2 handguard. Disc. 2010.

	$765	$675	$575	$525	$425	$350	$275	$850

Add $279 mid-length free float system.
Add $310 for rifle length free float system.
Add $92 for YHM flip up front or rear sight.

CENTURION ORDNANCE, INC.

Previous importer located in Helotes, TX. Centurion Ordnance also imported Aguila ammunition.

SHOTGUNS: SLIDE ACTION

POSEIDON – 12 ga., 1 3/4 in. chamber (shoots "mini-shells" and slugs), 18 1/4 in. smoothbore barrel, 13 in. LOP, black synthetic stock and forearm, 6 shot mag., adj. rear sight, 5 lbs., 5 oz. Limited importation 2001.

	$285	$250	$225	$200	$185	$170	$155	

While prototypes of this model were imported briefly during 2001, this gun never made it into the consumer marketplace.

Mini-shells retailed for $12.60 for a box of 20 (shot sizes include 7, #4 & #1 buckshot).

CENTURY INTERNATIONAL ARMS, INC.

Current importer and distributor founded in 1961 with current corporate offices located in Delray Beach, FL. Century International Arms, Inc. was previously headquartered in St. Albans, VT until 1997, and Boca Raton, FL from 1997-2004.

Century International Arms, Inc. imports a large variety of used military rifles, shotguns, and pistols. Because inventory changes daily, especially on tactical style rifles, carbines and pistols, please contact the company directly for the most recent offerings and pricing (see Trademark Index).

Additionally, Century International Arms imports a wide range of accessories, including bayonets, holsters, stocks, magazines, grips, mounts, scopes, misc. parts, new and surplus ammunition, etc., and should be contacted directly (see Trademark Index) for a copy of their most recent catalog, or check their web site for current offerings.

PISTOLS: SEMI-AUTO

Century International Arms Inc. also imports Arcus pistols from Bulgaria and Daewoo pistols from South Korea. Please refer to the individual sections for more information.

M-1911 STYLE PISTOLS – .45 ACP cal., SA, patterned after the Colt Govt. Model 1911, choice of 4 1/4 (Blue Thunder Commodore, Commodore 1911, or GI-Officer's Model) or 5 (SAM Elite/SAM Standard, Military, or SAM Chief/Falcon or Scout) ported (disc. 2002) or unported barrel, 7 or 8 shot mag., various configurations and finishes, target features are available on select models, approx. 41 oz. Imported from the Phillipines beginning 2001, current mfg. is from Shooter's Arms.

No MSR	$500	$450	$375	$350	$275	$225	$175	

Add $35 for Commodore Blue Thunder Model with squared off trigger guard (disc. 2013).

MSR	100%	98%	95%	90%	80%	70%	60%	Last MSR

C93 PISTOL – 5.56 NATO or 7.62x39mm (new 2013) cal., patterned after the H&K MP-5 using the roller lock bolt system and fluted chamber, 8 1/2 in. barrel with flash suppressor, adj. rear sight, includes two 40 shot mags., 6.4 lbs. Importation began 2012.

| No MSR | $900 | $795 | $675 | $625 | $495 | $400 | $315 | |

DRACO – 7.62x39mm cal., blonde wood forend, 12 1/4 in. barrel, 30 shot mag., approx. 5 1/2 lbs. Imported 2010-2012.

| | $395 | $350 | $300 | $265 | $235 | $200 | $185 | *$450* |

CENTURION 39 AK PISTOL – 7.62x39mm cal., AK-47 design, features 11 3/8 in. barrel with M16 style birdcage muzzle brake, machined receiver, quad Picatinny rails, Tapco G2 trigger, ergonomic pistol grip, black polymer furniture, optional Shark Fin front sight, 5.4 lbs. Mfg. in the U.S. beginning 2011.

| No MSR | $800 | $700 | $600 | $550 | $450 | $375 | $295 | |

CZ 999/CZ 999 COMPACT – 9mm Para. cal., 3 1/2 (Compact) or 4 1/4 in. barrel, DA/SA, 15 shot double column mag., ambidextrous controls, white dot sights, inertial firing pin, loaded chamber indicator, decocking lever, mfg. by Zastava. Importation began 2013.

| No MSR | $470 | $410 | $350 | $325 | $260 | $210 | $175 | |

PAP M92 PV – 7.62x39mm cal., GPO, AK design, 10 in. cold hammer forged barrel, 30 shot mag., dual aperture Krinkov style rear sight, bolt hold-open notch on selector, steel alloy bolt and barrel, stamped receiver, hinged top cover, 6.6 lbs., mfg. by Zastava. Importation began 2013.

| No MSR | $520 | $450 | $395 | $350 | $285 | $235 | $180 | |

Add $30 for Krinkov muzzle brake.

PAP M85 PV – .223 Rem. cal., GPO, AK design, 10 in. cold hammer forged barrel, 30 shot mag., dual aperture Krinkov style rear sight, bolt hold-open notch on selector, steel alloy bolt and barrel, stamped receiver, hinged top cover, 6.4 lbs., mfg. by Zastava. Importation began 2013.

| No MSR | $620 | $550 | $475 | $425 | $350 | $275 | $215 | |

Add $30 for Krinkov muzzle brake.

COLEFIRE MAGNUM – 7.62 Tokarev cal., styled after the Sterling Mk7 pistol, manganese phosphate finish coated with black wrinkle paint, enlarged and knurled charging handle, 4 1/2 in. barrel, SA, optional accessory rail. Imported 2013.

| | $250 | $225 | $195 | $175 | $140 | $115 | $90 | |

This model did not include a magazine (sold separately).

P1 Mk 7 – 9mm Para. cal., 3.7 in. stainless steel barrel, polymer frame, integral Picatinny rail, fully ambidextrous, four interchangeable grip backstraps, matte black finish, includes two 15 shot mags., 24 oz. Mfg. by Grand Power, importation began mid-2013.

| No MSR | $500 | $440 | $375 | $340 | $275 | $225 | $175 | |

RIFLES/CARBINES: SEMI-AUTO

G-3 SPORTER – .308 Win. cal., mfg. from genuine G3 parts, and American made receiver with integrated scope rail, includes 20 shot mag., 19 in. barrel, pistol grip stock, matte black finish, refinished condition only, 9.3 lbs. Imported 1999-2006.

| | $785 | $685 | $590 | $535 | $430 | $355 | $275 | |

FAL SPORTER – .308 Win. cal., U.S. mfg., new barrel receiver, synthetic furniture, 20 shot mag. Imported 2004-2006.

| | $850 | $745 | $635 | $580 | $465 | $380 | $295 | |

CETME SPORTER – .308 Win. cal., new mfg. Cetme action, 19 1/2 in. barrel, 20 shot mag., choice of blue or Mossy Oak Break-Up camo (disc.) metal finish, wood (disc.) or synthetic stock, pistol grip, and vent. forearm, refinished condition only, 9.7 lbs. Imported 2002-2011.

| | $550 | $475 | $400 | $350 | $300 | $275 | $250 | *$635* |

S.A.R. 1 – 7.62x39mm cal., AK-47 styling, 16 1/2 in. barrel, wood stock and forearm, scope rail mounted on receiver, includes one 10 and two 30 shot double stack mags., 7.08 lbs. Mfg. by Romarm of Romania. Importation disc. 2003.

| | $750 | $655 | $560 | $510 | $410 | $335 | $260 | |

S.A.R. 2 – 5.45x39mm cal., AK-47 styling, 16 in. barrel, wood stock and forearm, includes one 10 and one 30 shot double stack mags., 8 lbs. Mfg. by Romarm of Romania. Importation disc. 2003.

| | $750 | $655 | $560 | $510 | $410 | $335 | $260 | |

S.A.R. 3 – .223 Rem. cal., AK-47 styling, 16 in. barrel, wood stock and forearm, includes one 10 and one 30 shot double stack mags., 8 lbs. Mfg. by Romarm of Romania. Importation disc. 2003.

| | $750 | $655 | $560 | $510 | $410 | $335 | $260 | |

MSR	100%	98%	95%	90%	80%	70%	60%	Last MSR

GP WASR-10 LO-CAP – 7.62x39mm cal., AK-47 design, 16 1/4 in. barrel, wood stock and forearm, includes one 5 and one 10 shot single stack mags., 7 1/2 lbs. Mfg. by Romarm of Romania. Importation disc. 2011.

	$400	$350	$315	$275	$250	$225	$200	$450

GP WASR-10 HIGH-CAP SERIES – 7.62x39mm cal., AK-47 styling, 16 1/4 in. barrel, various configurations, includes two 30 shot double stack mags., 7 1/2 lbs. Mfg. by Romarm of Romania.

No MSR	$600	$525	$450	$410	$350	$275	$210	

Add $10 for bayonet.
Add $133 for 100 shot drum mag.
Add $250 for factory installed slide fire stock (new 2014).
Add $67 for recoilless buttstock with gun (new 2012).
Add $60 for 50th Anniversary model with Century Arms logo on back right of receiver (only 50 mfg. during 2012).

AK-74 BULLPUP – 5.45x39mm cal., AK-47 design, 16 1/4 in. barrel with muzzle brake, vent. handguard, top Picatinny rail, two 30 shot mags., 7.35 lbs. Limited importation 2010-2011.

	$575	$500	$425	$365	$335	$295	$275	$650

AK-74 SPORTER – 5.45x39mm cal., AK-47 design, 16 1/4 in. barrel with muzzle brake, side mount rail, bayonet lug, fixed wood stock, includes two 30 shot mags., sling, mag. pouch, cleaning rod and oil bottle, 7.6 lbs. Importation began 2014.

No MSR	$790	$695	$595	$535	$435	$350	$275	

AKMS – 7.62x39mm cal., AK-47 design, 16 1/4 in. barrel with muzzle brake, features laminate wood handguards, pistol grip, and steel folding buttstock with skeleton buttplate, includes two 30 shot mags., 7.8 lbs. Imported 2011-2013.

	$625	$550	$500	$425	$350	$275	$225	$700

L1A1/R1A1 SPORTER – .308 Win. cal., current mfg. receiver patterned after the British L1A1, includes carrying handle, synthetic furniture, 20 shot mag., 22 1/2 in. barrel, fold over aperture rear sight, 9 1/2 lbs. Mfg. in U.S., disc. 2010.

	$975	$850	$750	$650	$575	$500	$450	

Subtract approx. $200 for L1A1 Sporter.

DRAGUNOV – 7.62x54R cal., new CNC milled receiver, Dragunov configuration, thumbhole stock, 26 1/2 in. barrel, supplied with scope and cleaning kit. Mfg. in Romania. Disc. 2010.

	$975	$855	$730	$665	$535	$440	$340	

GOLANI SPORTER – .223 Rem. cal., 21 in. barrel, 35 shot mag., folding stock, optional bayonet lug, approx. 8 lbs., mfg. in Israel.

	$625	$550	$500	$425	$350	$275	$225	$700

Add $30 for bayonet lug (disc.).

TANTAL SPORTER – 5.45x39mm cal., 18 in. barrel, parkerized finish, side folding wire stock, flash hider, includes extra mag., 8 lbs.

	$475	$400	$350	$300	$275	$250	$225	$550

GORIUNOV SG43 – 7.62x54R cal., copy of Soviet model, gas operated, 28.3 in. barrel, 250 shot belt-fed, charging handle, spade grips, includes wooden crate, folding carriage, 3 ammo belts, 96 lbs. Importation disc. 2011.

	$4,750	$4,200	$3,750	$3,250	$2,650	$2,100	$1,850	$5,325

VZ2008 SPORTER – 7.62x39mm cal., copy of the Czech VZ58, 16 1/4 in. barrel, steel receiver, dull matte finish, bead blasted metal parts, wood or plastic (disc. 2011) buttstock, CA compliant, 7 lbs. Importation disc. 2011, resumed 2014.

No MSR	$600	$525	$450	$410	$325	$275	$210	

M-76 SNIPER/SPORTER MODEL – 8mm Mauser cal., semi-auto version of the Yugoslav M76, new U.S. receiver and 21 1/2 in. barrel, includes original scope, mount, and 10 shot mag., 11.3 lbs. Importation disc. 2011.

	$1,495	$1,200	$1,000	$875	$750	$650	$550	$1,725

GP 1975 – 7.62x39mm cal., AK-47 design, 16 1/4 in. barrel, black synthetic furniture, new U.S. receiver and barrel, includes two 30 shot mags., approx. 7.4 lbs. Importation disc. 2011.

	$595	$425	$375	$325	$275	$250	$225	$675

Add approx. $140 for collapsible stock and Picatinny rail forearm.

DEGTYAREV MODEL – top mounted magazine, semi-auto version of the Soviet model, available in three variations.

* **DP 28** – 7.62x54R cal., 23.8 in. barrel, gas operated, 47 shot drum mag., full shoulder stock.

	$3,500	$3,060	$2,625	$2,380	$1,925	$1,575	$1,225	

* **DPM 28** – 7.62x54R cal., 23.8 in. barrel, gas operated, 47 shot drum mag., pistol grip stock.

	$3,500	$3,060	$2,625	$2,380	$1,925	$1,575	$1,225	

MSR	100%	98%	95%	90%	80%	70%	60%	Last MSR

* DTX Tank Model – 7.62x54R cal., 23.8 in. barrel, 50 shot drum mag., collapsible stock, approx. 10 lbs.

| | $3,500 | $3,060 | $2,625 | $2,380 | $1,925 | $1,575 | $1,225 | |

STERLING SA – 9mm Para. cal., blowback action, semi-auto version of the Sterling submachine gun, 16 1/4 in. barrel, American made receiver and barrel, original style crinkle painted finish, folding stock, includes two 34 shot mags., available in Type I (disc.) or Type II, L sight with 100 and 200 yard apertures, front post sight, full length heat shield, unique port feed angle, 9.2 lbs.

| No MSR | $550 | $475 | $415 | $375 | $300 | $250 | $195 | |

C15A1 SPORTER – 5.56 NATO cal., AR-15 style, based on M16A1, GIO, triangular "Vietnam era" style handguard, 16 in. barrel with muzzle brake, fixed stock, includes two original Colt 30 shot mags. (disc. 2011) or fixed 10 shot mag. (current mfg.), choice of green polymer or walnut wood furniture, A3 carry handle and sights. Importation began mid-2010.

This model is POR.

Add 15% for High Cap Mag. model

C15 M4 – 5.56 NATO cal., AR-15 style, 16 in. barrel with birdcage muzzle brake, flat-top receiver with detachable carry handle, adj. T6 stock, one 30 shot mag. Importation began 2014.

| No MSR | $700 | $615 | $525 | $475 | $385 | $315 | $250 | |

CENTURION 39 – 7.62x39mm cal., 16 1/2 in. barrel, V-shape Chevron compensator, available in Tactical (fixed black synthetic stock), Sporter (black synthetic stock, or Classic (laminated wood furniture) configurations. black finish, fixed buttstock with pistol grip, four Picatinny rails, includes two 30 shot mags., 8.2 lbs. All parts mfg. in U.S. beginning mid-2010.

| No MSR | $800 | $700 | $600 | $550 | $450 | $360 | $295 | |

AES10-B RPK STYLE – 7.62x39mm cal., 23 1/8 in. heavy barrel with folding bipod, laminated stock and forend, includes two AK style 40 shot mags., 10.9 lbs. Imported 2012.

| | $575 | $500 | $450 | $400 | $375 | $350 | $325 | *$675* |

DPM – 7.62x54R cal., semi-auto closed bolt copy of the WWII Soviet machine gun, 47 shot pan magazine mounted on top of receiver, 23.8 in. barrel, includes upper bipod, adj. sights, wood furniture, blued metal, 18 1/2 lbs. w/out mag. Imported 2011-2012.

| | $1,775 | $1,575 | $1,350 | $1,150 | $950 | $750 | $675 | *$2,000* |

CENTURION UC-9 CARBINE – 9mm Para. cal., patterned after the Israeli sub-machine gun, straight blowback action, 16 in. barrel, blue finish, closed bolt, folding steel stock, includes two 32 shot all steel double column mag., approx. 9 lbs. Importation began mid-2012.

| No MSR | $900 | $795 | $675 | $610 | $495 | $400 | $315 | |

M70 SERIES – 7.62x39mm cal., based on Yugoslavian Paratrooper model, 16 1/4 in. barrel, includes two 30 shot double stack mags., classic wood furniture (disc.) or black polymer upper and lower handguards, black under folding stock (AB2) or fixed synthetic stock (B1), slant brake, bayonet lug, approx. 7 1/2 lbs. Limited importation beginning 2013.

| No MSR | $660 | $575 | $495 | $450 | $365 | $295 | $230 | |

Add $40 for AB2 Model.

PAP SERIES – 7.62x39 or 7.62x51mm cal., 16 1/4 in. cold hammer forged barrel, choice of classic wood stock with pistol grip, black thumbhole stock with polymer handguard, or T6 collapsible stock with plastic handguard, 10 or 30 shot mag., accessory rail, 7.7-8 lbs. Mfg. by Zastava. Importation began 2013.

| No MSR | $580 | $510 | $435 | $395 | $325 | $260 | $200 | |

Add $80 for Hi-Cap Model with fixed wood buttstock, handguard, and two 30 shot mags (new 2014).

Add $120 for DF Model with T6 collapsible stock.

PAP M77 PS – .308 Win. cal., 16 1/4 in. cold hammer forged barrel, 30 shot mag., black polymer thumbhole stock with upper and lower handguard, Picatinny rail, dust cover, mfg. by Zastava. Importation began 2013.

| No MSR | $650 | $575 | $495 | $440 | $360 | $295 | $250 | |

SAIGA SERIES – 5.45x39mm or 7.62x39mm cal., 16 1/4 (Hi-Cap) or 16 1/2 in. chrome lined barrel, 10 or 30 (Hi-Cap) shot mag., iron sights, fixed plastic straight grip stock with pistol grip or checkered synthetic pistol grip stock, side mount rail, matte black finish, approx. 8 lbs. Importation began 2014.

| No MSR | $650 | $575 | $495 | $450 | $375 | $295 | $250 | |

Add $310 for Hi-Cap Model.

MEXSAR – .22 LR cal., 21 1/4 in. barrel, 16 shot mag., fiber optic front sight, uncheckered pistol grip hardwood stock, dovetailed for scope mounts, blue finish, 6.2 lbs. Importation began 2014.

| No MSR | $230 | $200 | $175 | $150 | $125 | $100 | $80 | |

MSR	100%	98%	95%	90%	80%	70%	60%	Last MSR

RIFLES: SLIDE ACTION

PAR 1 OR 3 – 7.62x39mm (PAR 1) or .223 Rem. (PAR 3) cal., AK receiver styling, 10 shot mag., accepts double stack AK magazines, wood stock, pistol grip, and forearm, 20.9 in. barrel, 7.6 lbs. Mfg. by PAR, and imported 2002-2009.

| | $360 | $300 | $275 | $250 | $225 | $200 | $175 | |

SHOTGUNS

SAS-12 SEMI-AUTO – 12 ga. only, 2 3/4 in. chamber, detachable 3 (Type II) or 5 shot mag., black synthetic stock and forearm, 22 or 23 1/2 in. barrel. Mfg. by PRC in China.

| | $225 | $195 | $170 | $155 | $125 | $100 | $80 | |

Add approx. $25 for ghost ring rear with blade front or bead sight.

CATAMOUNT FURY I SEMI-AUTO – 12 ga., 3 in. chamber, 5 shot detachable box mag., adj. gas system, top optics rail, AK-style safety lever, 20.1 in. barrel, matte black finish, fixed black synthetic stock with pistol grip, 8 lbs., 11 oz. New 2013.

| No MSR | $565 | $495 | $425 | $385 | $310 | $250 | $200 | |

MODEL IJ2 SLIDE ACTION – 12 ga. only, 2 3/4 or 3 in. chamber, 19 in. barrel with ghost ring sights or fiber optic front sights, fixed choke only, 7.2 lbs. Mfg. in China.

| | $200 | $175 | $150 | $135 | $110 | $90 | $70 | |

ULTRA 87 SLIDE ACTION – 12 ga., 3 in. chamber, 19 in. barrel with iron sights, optional pistol grip, metal heatshield (disc.), fixed black synthetic (current mfg.) or side folding (disc.) stock, 8.2 lbs.

| | $185 | $160 | $145 | $130 | $115 | $100 | $90 | *$200* |

Add $65 for extra 28 in. barrel.

MKA 1919 – 12 ga., AR-15 style, gas operation, aluminum alloy upper, one piece polymer lower receiver, pistol grip fixed stock, matte black or 100% camo finish, right side magwell mag. release, bolt stop, 5 shot detachable mag., removable carry handle, three internal chokes, integral Picatinny rail, approx. 6 1/2 lbs. Imported from Turkey beginning mid-2012.

| No MSR | $850 | $750 | $640 | $575 | $475 | $385 | $300 | |

CHARLES DALY: 1976-2010

Previous manufactured trademark imported late 1996-early 2010 by KBI, Inc. located in Harrisburg, PA. Previously imported by Outdoor Sports Headquarters, Inc. located in Dayton, OH until 1995.

In 1976, Sloan's Sporting Goods sold the Daly division to Outdoor Sports Headquarters, Inc., a sporting goods wholesaler located in Dayton, OH. OSHI continued the importation of high-grade Daly shotguns, primarily from Italy and Spain. By the mid-1980s, the Charles Daly brand was transformed into a broad consumer line of excellent firearms and hunting accessories.

In 1996, OSHI was sold to Jerry's Sports Center, Inc. of Forest City, PA, a major wholesaler of firearms and hunting supplies. Within a few months of Jerry's acquisition of OSHI, K.B.I., Inc. of Harrisburg, PA, purchased the Charles Daly trademark from JSC. As it turned out, Michael Kassnar, president of K.B.I., Inc., had produced almost all of the Charles Daly products for OSHI from 1976-1985 in his capacity of president of Kassnar Imports, Inc. K.B.I., Inc. resurrected the complete line of O/U and SxS shotguns in early 1997.

In 1998, the line expanded to include rimfire rifles and the first pistol produced under the Daly name, a Model 1911-A1 in .45 ACP cal. In 1999, semi-auto and slide action shotguns were also reintroduced. In 2000, the additions included 3 1/2 in. slide actions and semi-autos, Country Squire .410 bore shotguns, bolt action centerfire rifles, and the DDA 10-45, the first double action pistol produced under the Charles Daly name.

During 2004, Charles Daly began importing Bul Transmark pistols from Israel. In 2007, the Little Sharps single shot rifles were introduced.

In 2008, a Charles Daly Defense line was established, which includes AR-15 style semi-auto rifles.

On Jan. 29, 2010, K.B.I. announced it was shutting its doors and discontinued importation of all models.

COMBINATION GUNS

SUPERIOR COMBINATION MODEL – 12 ga. (multi-chokes became standard in 2001) over choice of .22 Hornet, .22-250 Rem. (disc. 1998), .223 Rem., .243 Win. (disc. 1998), .270 Win. (disc. 1998), .30-06, or .308 Win. (disc. 1998) cal., boxlock action with dovetailed receiver (accepts scope mounts and iron sights), 23 1/2 in. barrels with iron sights, approx. 7 5/8 lbs. Mfg. by Sabatti in Italy. Imported 1997-2005.

| | $1,260 | $1,105 | $945 | $855 | $695 | $565 | $440 | *$1,479* |

EMPIRE COMBINATION MODEL – 12 ga. (multi-chokes became standard in 2001) over choice of .22 Hornet, .22-250 Rem. (disc. 1998), .223 Rem., .243 Win. (disc. 1998), .270 Win. (disc. 1998), .30-06, or .308 Win. (disc. 1998) cal., boxlock action, 23 1/2 in. barrels, engraved with choice checkered walnut stock and forearm. Mfg. by Sabatti in Italy. Imported 1997-2005.

| | $1,800 | $1,575 | $1,350 | $1,225 | $990 | $810 | $630 | *$2,189* |

MSR	100%	98%	95%	90%	80%	70%	60%	Last MSR

HANDGUNS: LEVER ACTION

MODEL 1892 – .357 Mag. or .45 LC cal., similar to Model 1892 rifle, except has 12 in. blue barrel, color case hardened finish, walnut stock. Mfg. 2009.

	100%	98%	95%	90%	80%	70%	60%	Last MSR
	$1,195	$1,050	$900	$775	$675	$575	$475	*$1,309*

PISTOLS: SEMI-AUTO

During 2001, the nomenclature on these 1911 models was changed to include a new "E" prefix. The "E" stands for enhanced, and features included extended high-rise beavertail grip safety, combat trigger, combat hammer, beveled magwell, flared and lowered ejection port, dovetailed front and low profile rear sights, and hand checkered double diamond grips. The Enhanced pistols were manufactured by Armscor of the Philipines. M-5 pistols are manufactured by Bul Transmark in Israel.

GOVERNMENT 1911-A1 FIELD EFS/FS – .38 Super (mfg. 2005-2007), .40 S&W (mfg. 2005-2007), .45 ACP cal., steel frame, single action, skeletonized combat hammer and trigger, ambidextrous safety, 8 or 10 shot mag., extended slide release and beavertail grip safety, oversized and lowered ejection port, 5 in. barrel with solid barrel bushing, matte blue (Field FS), stainless slide/blue frame (Superior FS, mfg. 1999-2002), or all stainless (Empire EFS, new 1999) finish, includes two 8 or 10 shot mags. and lockable carrying case, 39 1/2 oz. Mfg. 1998-2008.

	100%	98%	95%	90%	80%	70%	60%	Last MSR
	$475	$415	$355	$325	$260	$215	$165	*$589*

Add $50 for Superior EFS Model (disc. 2002).

Add $199 for .22 LR conversion kit with adj. sight (disc. 1999).

* ***Government 1911A1 Field EFS Stainless Empire*** – .45 ACP cal. only, similar to Field FS, except is stainless steel. Disc. 2007.

	100%	98%	95%	90%	80%	70%	60%	Last MSR
	$575	$505	$430	$390	$315	$260	$200	*$709*

GOVERNMENT 1911-A1 TARGET EFST/FST – similar to Government 1911-A1 Field FS, except has target sights. Imported 2000-2007.

	100%	98%	95%	90%	80%	70%	60%	Last MSR
	$550	$480	$415	$375	$305	$250	$195	*$679*

Add $40 for Superior FST Model (disc. 2000).

Add $65 for Empire FST Model (disc. 2000).

* ***Government 1911-A1 Target EFST Stainless Empire*** – .45 ACP cal. only, similar to Target EFST, except is stainless steel. Mfg. 2001-2007.

	100%	98%	95%	90%	80%	70%	60%	Last MSR
	$650	$570	$490	$440	$360	$295	$230	*$789*

* ***Government 1911-A1 Target Field EFST*** – .45 ACP cal., 5 3/4 in. compensated barrel with 3 ports, blue or stainless steel, 44.5 oz. Limited importation 2001 only.

	100%	98%	95%	90%	80%	70%	60%	Last MSR
	$550	$480	$415	$375	$305	$250	$195	*$679*

Add $100 for stainless steel (Empire EFSTC).

EMPIRE ECMT CUSTOM MATCH – .45 ACP cal., 5 in. barrel, match features, high polish stainless steel, 38 1/2 oz. Imported 2001-2007.

	100%	98%	95%	90%	80%	70%	60%	Last MSR
	$750	$650	$575	$500	$425	$350	$275	*$895*

COMMANDER 1911-A1 FIELD EMS/MS – similar to Government 1911-A1, except has 4 in. Commander barrel and features, 37 oz. Imported 1999-2008.

	100%	98%	95%	90%	80%	70%	60%	Last MSR
	$475	$415	$355	$325	$260	$215	$165	*$589*

Add $40 for Superior MS Model (includes stainless steel slide and blue frame, disc. 2000).

* ***Commander 1911-A1 Field EMS Stainless Empire*** – .45 ACP cal. only, similar to Field EMS/MS, except is stainless steel. Imported 1999-2007.

	100%	98%	95%	90%	80%	70%	60%	Last MSR
	$575	$505	$430	$390	$315	$260	$200	*$709*

* ***Commander 1911-A1 Field EMSCC*** – carry comp., similar to Commander Field EMS, except has single port compensator, blue or stainless. Imported 2001 only.

	100%	98%	95%	90%	80%	70%	60%	Last MSR
	$540	$475	$405	$365	$295	$245	$190	*$619*

OFFICER'S 1911-A1 FIELD ECS/CS – similar to Commander, except has 3 1/2 in. barrel and Officer's Model features, 34 1/2 oz. Imported 1999-2008.

	100%	98%	95%	90%	80%	70%	60%	Last MSR
	$475	$415	$355	$325	$260	$215	$165	*$589*

Add $40 for Superior CS Model (includes stainless steel slide and blue frame, disc. 2000).

* ***Officer's 1911-A1 Field ECS Stainless Empire*** – .45 ACP cal. only, similar to Field ECS/CS, except is stainless steel. Imported 1999-2008.

	100%	98%	95%	90%	80%	70%	60%	Last MSR
	$575	$505	$430	$390	$315	$260	$200	*$709*

* ***Officer's 1911-A1 Field ECSCC*** – carry comp., similar to Officer's Field ECS, except has single port compensator, blue or stainless. Importation began 2001.

	100%	98%	95%	90%	80%	70%	60%	Last MSR
	$540	$475	$405	$365	$295	$245	$190	*$619*

Add $100 for Empire ECS Model (full stainless steel construction).

MSR	100%	98%	95%	90%	80%	70%	60%	Last MSR

COMMANDER 1911-A1 POLYMER FRAME PC – .45 ACP only, features polymer frame, 4 in. barrel, available in matte blue (Field PC) or stainless slide/blue frame (Superior PC). Imported 1999-2000.

| | $460 | $405 | $345 | $315 | $255 | $205 | $160 | $530 |

Add $25 for Superior PC Model (includes stainless steel slide and blue frame).

GOVERNMENT 1911-A2 FIELD EFS HC – .40 S&W or .45 ACP cal., 5 in. barrel, SA, similar to Government 1911 A-1 Field EFS, 13 (.45 ACP cal.), or 15 (.40 S&W cal.) shot mag., blue finish only. Imported 2005-2007.

| | $595 | $520 | $445 | $405 | $325 | $270 | $210 | $725 |

Add $124 for Target Model (.45 ACP cal. only, new 2005).

MODEL DDA 10-45 FS (DOUBLE ACTION) – .40 S&W (disc. 2001) or .45 ACP cal., DA/SA, 4 3/8 in. barrel, polymer frame with checkering, double stack 10 shot mag. with interchangeable base plate (allowing for extra grip length), matte black or two-tone (new 2001) finish, 28 1/2 oz. Imported 2000-2002.

| | $450 | $395 | $340 | $305 | $250 | $205 | $160 | $519 |

Add $40 for two-tone finish.

*   **Model DDA 10-45 CS** – similar to Model DDA 10-45 FS, except has 3 5/8 in. barrel, 26 oz. Imported 2000-2002.

| | $450 | $395 | $340 | $305 | $250 | $205 | $160 | $519 |

Add approx. $10 for colored frame (yellow, OD green, or fuschia, new 2001) and compensated barrel.

FIELD HP HI-POWER – 9mm Para. cal., SA, 4 3/4 in. barrel, patterned after the Browning Hi-Power, blue or hard chrome (mfg. 2005) finish, 10 or 13 shot mag., XS Express sight system, mfg. in U.S. Mfg. late 2003-2006.

| | $385 | $335 | $290 | $260 | $210 | $175 | $135 | $458 |

Add $120 for hard chrome finish (mfg. 2005).

This model has been produced both by Dan Wesson (2003-2004) and Magnum Research (2005-2006).

CD9 – 9mm Para. cal., 4.46 in. barrel, SA, SFO, black polymer frame and finish, striker fired, adj. sights, trigger safety, forward/lower accessory rail, 10 or 15 shot mag., three grip inserts. Imported 2009 only.

| | $375 | $330 | $280 | $255 | $205 | $170 | $130 | $437 |

G4 1911 SERIES – .45 ACP cal., 5 in. barrel, 7 shot, black finish or stainless steel, beveled mag well, flared and lowered ejection port, beavertail grip safety, internal extractor, Novak sights, three slot aluminum trigger, available in Standard, Target, and Tactical configurations, mfg. in Israel. Imported 2009 only.

| | $750 | $655 | $565 | $510 | $415 | $340 | $265 | $867 |

Add $96 for either Tactical or Target model.
Add $96 for stainless steel.
Add $354 for .22 LR conversion kit.

M-5 FS STANDARD (BUL 1911 GOVERNMENT) – 9mm Para. (new 2010), .40 S&W or .45 ACP cal., 5 in. barrel, polymer double column frame, SA, steel slide, aluminum speed trigger, checkered front and rear grip straps, blue or chrome finished slide, 10, 14, or 17 (9mm Para. cal.) shot staggered mag., 31-33 oz. Mfg. by Bul Transmark in Israel. Imported 2004-2009.

| | $665 | $580 | $500 | $450 | $365 | $300 | $235 | $803 |

*   **M-5 MS Standard Commander** – .40 S&W or .45 ACP cal., similar to M-5 FS Standard, except has 4 1/3 in. barrel, 29-30 oz. Imported 2004-2009.

| | $665 | $580 | $500 | $450 | $365 | $300 | $235 | $803 |

*   **M-5 Ultra-X** – 9mm Para. or .45 ACP cal., 10 or 12 (9mm Para. cal. only) shot mag., compact variation with 3.15 in. barrel. Imported 2005-2009.

| | $665 | $580 | $500 | $450 | $365 | $300 | $235 | $803 |

M-5 IPSC – .40 S&W, or .45 ACP cal., configured for IPSC competition, 5 in. barrel, with custom slide to frame fit and match grade barrel bushing. Mfg. by Bul Transmark in Israel. Imported 2004-2007.

| | $1,250 | $1,095 | $940 | $850 | $690 | $565 | $440 | $1,439 |

JERICHO SERIES – 9mm Para., .40 S&W, or .45 ACP cal., 3 1/2 (Compact), 3.82 (Mid-Size), or 4.41 (Full Size) in. barrel, DA/SA, 10, 12, 13, or 15 shot mag., polymer or steel frame with black or chrome (Mid-size .45 ACP cal. only) finish, combat style trigger guard, slide mounted thumb decocker, two slot accessory rail (except Compact), ergonomic grips, mfg. by IWI, Ltd. (formerly IMI) in Israel. Limited importation 2009.

| | $595 | $520 | $445 | $405 | $325 | $270 | $210 | $699 |

Add $198 for steel frame and chrome finish (Full or Mid-size only).

ZDA MODEL – 9mm Para. or .40 S&W cal., DA/SA, 4 1/8 in. barrel, 12 (.40 S&W cal.) or 15 (9mm Para. cal.) shot mag., mfg. by Zastava. Limited importation 2005 only.

| | $490 | $430 | $370 | $335 | $270 | $220 | $170 | $589 |

MSR		100%	98%	95%	90%	80%	70%	60%	Last MSR

REVOLVERS: DA

S222/S224/S226 SERIES – .22 LR cal., 2 (S222), 4 (S224) or 6 (S226) in. barrel, blue finish, 9 shot, rubber grips, fixed (S222) or adj. (S224 or S226) sights, steel construction. While advertised during 2006, this Series was never imported.

		$265	$230	$200	$180	$160	$140	$120	$321

S352/S354/S356 SERIES – .357 Mag. cal., 2 (S352), 4 (S354), or 6 (S356) in. barrel, blue finish, 6 shot, fixed (S382) or adj. (S384 or S386) sights, rubber grips, steel construction. While advertised during 2006, this Series was never imported.

		$300	$265	$240	$215	$185	$165	$145	$350

S382/S384/S386 SERIES – .38 Spl. cal., 2 (S382), 4 (S384), or 6 (S386) in. barrel, blue finish, 6 shot, fixed (S382) or adj. (S384 or S386) sights, rubber grips, steel construction. While advertised during 2006, this Series was never imported.

		$265	$230	$200	$180	$160	$140	$120	$321

Z222/Z224/Z226 SERIES – .22 LR cal., 2 (Z222), 4 (Z224) or 6 (Z226) in. barrel, blue finish, 9 shot, rubber grips, fixed (Z222) or adj. (Z224 or Z226) sights. While advertised during 2006, this Series was never imported.

		$200	$180	$160	$140	$120	$100	$80	$244

Z382 – .38 Spl. cal., 2 in. barrel, blue finish, 6 shot, fixed sights, rubber grips. While advertised during 2006, this Series was never imported.

		$210	$185	$160	$140	$125	$110	$95	$249

REVOLVERS: SA

Models were manufactured by Flli. Pietta in Italy.

MODEL 1873 CLASSIC – .357 Mag. or .45 LC cal., 4 3/4, 5 1/2, or 7 1/2 in. barrel, case hardened frame, blue finish, choice of brass (.45 LC only) or steel backstrap and trigger guard. Imported 2004-2007.

		$415	$365	$310	$280	$230	$185	$145	$485

Add $20 for steel backstrap and trigger guard.

* **Model 1873 Classic Stainless** – similar to Model 1873, except has matte finish, stainless construction with steel backstrap and trigger guard. Imported 2004-2006.

		$515	$450	$385	$350	$285	$230	$180	$587

MODEL 1873 SONORA – similar to Model 1873 Classic, except has matte blue finish, and not available with steel backstrap and trigger guard. Imported 2006-2007.

		$325	$285	$245	$220	$180	$145	$115	$399

MODEL 1873 BIRDSHEAD – .45 LC cal. only, 4 3/4 in. barrel, color case hardened finish, steel backstrap and trigger guard. Imported 2006-2007.

		$445	$390	$335	$305	$245	$200	$155	$549

* **Model 1873 Birdshead Sheriff** – .45 LC cal. only, 3 in. barrel, color case hardened finish, steel backstrap and trigger guard. Imported 2006-2007.

		$445	$390	$335	$305	$245	$200	$155	$549

MODEL 1873 LIGHTNING – .45 LC cal. only, 4 3/4 in. barrel, color case hardened finish, steel backstrap and trigger guard. Imported 2006-2007.

		$445	$390	$335	$305	$245	$200	$155	$549

* **Model 1873 Lightning Sheriff** – .45 LC cal. only, 3 in. barrel, color case hardened finish, steel backstrap and trigger guard. Imported 2006-2007.

		$445	$390	$335	$305	$245	$200	$155	$549

MODEL 1874 RUSSIAN – .44 Russian or .45 LC cal., 6 1/2 in. barrel, blue finish. Limited importation 2006.

		$800	$700	$600	$545	$440	$360	$280	$931

RIFLES: BOLT ACTION

K.B.I. also imported a wide variety of Mauser and Mini-Mauser actions until 2006. MSRs ranged between $319-$659.

MAUSER 98 – various cals., Mauser 98 action, 22 (new 2001) or 23 (disc.) in. barrel, 3-5 shot, hinged floorplate, fiberglass/graphite composite (Field Grade) or checkered European walnut (Superior Grade) stock, open sights, drilled and tapped receiver, side safety. Mfg. by Zastava. Importation began 1998, and resumed 2001-2005.

* **Mauser 98 Field Grade** – features fiberglass/graphite composite stock, matte blue finish or matte stainless steel.

		$395	$345	$295	$270	$215	$180	$140	$459

MSR	100%	98%	95%	90%	80%	70%	60%	Last MSR

Add $90 for stainless steel.
Add $30 for Mag. cals. (.300 Win. Mag. or 7mm Rem. Mag.).
Add 50% for .375 H&H or .458 Win. Mag. cal. (disc.).

* ***Mauser 98 Superior Grade*** – features checkered European walnut stock and high polish blue finish.

| | $525 | $460 | $395 | $355 | $290 | $235 | $185 | *$599* |

Add $190 for .375 H&H or .458 Win. Mag. cal.
Add $30 for Mag. cals. (.300 Win. Mag. or 7mm Rem. Mag.).
Add $30 for left-hand action (.30-06 cal. only).

MINI-MAUSER 98 – .22 Hornet, .22-250 Rem. (disc.), .223 Rem., or 7.62x39mm cal., similar to Mauser 98, except has 18.1 (new 2001) or 19 1/4 (disc.) in. barrel, 5 shot.

* ***Mini-Mauser 98 Field Grade*** – features fiberglass/graphite composite stock.

| | $345 | $300 | $260 | $235 | $190 | $155 | $120 | *$399* |

* ***Mini-Mauser 98 Superior Grade*** – features checkered European walnut stock.

| | $525 | $460 | $395 | $355 | $290 | $235 | $185 | *$599* |

Add $30 for left-hand action (.223 Rem. cal. only).

FIELD HUNTER – .22 Hornet, .223 Rem., .243 Win., .270 Win., .30-06, .308 Win., .300 Rem. Ultra Mag., .300 Win. Mag., .338 Win. Mag., or 7mm Rem. Mag. cal., 22 or 24 (Mag. cals. only) in. barrel w/o sights, detachable mag. on short action cals. (.22 Hornet, .223 Rem., or .243 Win.), high polish bluing, checkered walnut stock and forend, right or left-hand action, gold trigger, approx. 7 1/3 lbs. Imported 2000 only.

| | $475 | $415 | $355 | $325 | $260 | $215 | $165 | *$565* |

Add approx. $31 for left-hand action (.223 Rem., .243 Win., .270 Win., .30-06, .300 Rem. Ultra Mag., or 7mm Rem. Mag.).

* ***Field Hunter Stainless/Polymer*** – similar to Field Hunter, except has stainless steel barrel and action, black polymer stock with checkering. Imported 2000 only.

| | $495 | $435 | $370 | $335 | $270 | $225 | $175 | *$580* |

FIELD GRADE .22 LR CAL. – .22 LR cal., 16 1/4 (True Youth Standard), 17 1/2 (Youth), or 22 5/8 (Standard) in. barrel, single shot (True Youth Standard) or 6 shot mag., all steel shrouded action, grooved receiver, walnut finished hardwood stock. Imported 1998-2002.

| | $110 | $95 | $85 | $75 | $60 | $50 | $40 | *$135* |

Add $14 for repeater Youth Model (6 shot, new 2000).
Add $20 for single shot True Youth Standard with shortened dimensions.

* ***Field Grade .22 LR Cal. Polymer/Hardwood*** – similar to Field Grade, except has stainless steel action and barrel with black polymer (disc.) or hardwood (new 2001) checkered stock, 6 1/3 lbs. Imported 2000-2002.

| | $120 | $105 | $90 | $80 | $65 | $55 | $40 | *$149* |

* ***Field Grade .22 LR Cal. Superior Grade*** – .22 LR (disc. 2001), .22 WMR, or .22 Hornet cal., 22 5/8 in. barrel, 5 or 6 shot mag., features checkered walnut finished stock with adj. rear sight. Imported 1998-2002.

| | $175 | $155 | $130 | $120 | $95 | $80 | $60 | *$209* |

Add $160 for .22 Hornet cal.
Subtract $20 for .22 LR cal. (disc. 2001).

* ***Field Grade .22 LR Cal. Empire Grade*** – similar to Superior Grade, except has checkered California walnut stock with rosewood grip and forend caps, high polish bluing and damascened bolt. Imported 1998-2001.

| | $290 | $255 | $220 | $195 | $160 | $130 | $100 | *$349* |

Add $20 for .22 WMR cal.
Add $130 for .22 Hornet cal.

SUPERIOR II RIMFIRE – .17 HMR, .22 LR, or .22 WMR cal., 22 in. barrel, walnut stock. Limited importation 2005 only.

| | $215 | $190 | $160 | $145 | $120 | $95 | $75 | *$259* |

Add $40 for .22 WMR or $75 for .17 HMR cal.

RIFLES: LEVER ACTION, REPRODUCTIONS

MODEL 1866 – .38 Spl., .357 Mag., or .45 LC cal., brass or case colored blue (rifle, .357 Mag. cal. only) frame, choice of 19 (carbine), 20 (short rifle), or 24 1/4 (rifle) in. barrel, patterned after the Winchester Model 1866, mfg. by Chapparal. Limited importation 2008.

| | $725 | $635 | $545 | $495 | $400 | $325 | $255 | *$849* |

MODEL 1873 – .357 Mag. or .45 LC cal., case colored frame, choice of 18 (Trapper), 19 (carbine), 20 (short rifle), or 24 1/4 (rifle) in. barrel, patterned after the Winchester Model 1873, mfg. by Chapparal. Limited importation 2008.

| | $740 | $660 | $550 | $475 | $400 | $350 | $295 | *$875* |

Add $40 for half-round, half-octagon rifle or for Triwood stock.

MSR	100%	98%	95%	90%	80%	70%	60%	Last MSR

MODEL 1876 – .45-60 WCF or .45-75 WCF cal., case colored or blue (NWMP short rifle) frame, choice of 22 (short rifle or musket), 26, or 28 in. barrel, patterned after the Winchester Model 1876, mfg. by Chapparal. Limited importation 2008.

	$875	$765	$655	$595	$480	$395	$305	$1,019

Add $250 for NWMP short rifle or musket.

Add $90 for short rifle or $46 for Triwood stock.

1892 RIFLE/CARBINE – .357 Mag. or .45 LC cal., color case hardened frame, 20 (Carbine) or 24 1/4 (Rifle) in. barrel, patterned after the Winchester Model 1892, mfg. by Armi Sport. Disc. 2009.

	$925	$810	$695	$630	$510	$415	$325	$1,094

* **1892 Rifle/Carbine Takedown** – .357 Mag. or .45 LC cal., color case hardened receiver, 20 (Carbine) or 24 1/4 (Rifle) in. barrel, takedown action. Disc. 2009.

	$1,075	$940	$805	$730	$590	$485	$375	$1,249

RIFLES: O/U

SUPERIOR EXPRESS – .30-06 cal., 23 1/2 in. barrels with quarter rib and leaf sights, dovetailed receiver for scope mounting, silver finished boxlock receiver, gold SST, checkered walnut stock and forearm, 7 3/4 lbs. Imported 2000-2005.

	$1,900	$1,665	$1,425	$1,290	$1,045	$855	$665	$2,259

EMPIRE EXPRESS – .30-06, .375 H&H (new 2005), or .416 Rigby (new 2005) cal., 23 1/2 in. barrels with quarter rib and leaf sights, dovetailed receiver for scope mounting, silver finished boxlock receiver with shoulders, gold SST, checkered European style walnut stock with Bavarian cheekpiece and forearm, 7 3/4 lbs. Imported 2000-2005.

	$2,525	$2,210	$1,895	$1,715	$1,390	$1,135	$885	$2,949

Add $710 for .375 H&H or .416 Rigby cal.

RIFLES/CARBINES: SEMI-AUTO

All recently manufactured semi-auto rifles have forged aluminum alloy receivers that are hard coat milspec anodized and Teflon coated, manganese phosphate barrel (except stainless), radiused aluminum magazine release button, aluminum trigger guard, safety selector position on right side of receiver, dust cover, brass deflector, forward assist, and include one magazine and hard plastic carrying case. All recently manufactured rifles were covered by a lifetime repair policy.

SEMI-AUTO RIFLE – .22 LR cal., steel receiver, 20 3/4 in. barrel with adj. rear sight, 10 shot mag. Mfg. 1998-2002.

* **Semi-Auto Rifle Field Grade** – features uncheckered walnut finished hardwood stock.

	$110	$95	$85	$75	$60	$50	$40	$135

* **Semi-Auto Rifle Field Grade Polymer/Hardwood** – similar to Field Grade, except has stainless steel action and barrel with black polymer (disc.) or hardwood checkered stock, 6 1/8 lbs. Mfg. 2000-2002.

	$120	$105	$90	$80	$65	$55	$40	$149

* **Semi-Auto Rifle Superior Grade** – features checkered walnut finished stock. Disc. 2001.

	$175	$155	$130	$120	$95	$80	$60	$209

* **Semi-Auto Rifle Empire Grade** – features checkered California walnut stock. Disc. 2001.

	$275	$240	$205	$185	$150	$125	$95	$334

D-M4/D-M4P CARBINE – 5.56 NATO cal., GIO, 16 in. chromemoly match barrel with M-203 mounting groove, 10, 20, or 30 shot mag., forged "F" front sight base with bayonet lug and rubber coated sling swivel, A3 detachable carry handle, T-Marked flat-top upper, six-position telestock, A2 birdcage flash hider, oval double heat shield M4 forend. Mfg. 2008-2009.

	$925	$810	$695	$630	$510	$415	$325	$1,143

Add $90 for M4 feed ramp (Model DM-4).

D-M4LE CARBINE – 5.56 NATO cal., GIO, similar to D-M4 carbine, except has mil spec diameter receiver extension with "H" buffer. Mfg. 2008-2009.

	$1,275	$1,115	$955	$865	$700	$575	$445	$1,373

D-M4S CARBINE – GIO, similar to D-M4 carbine, except has two Picatinny riser blocks, oval double heat shield M4 forend with QD sling swivel and swivel/bipod stud installed, Magpul enhanced trigger guard. Mfg. 2008-2009.

	$1,025	$895	$770	$695	$565	$460	$360	$1,189

D-M4LX CARBINE – 5.56 NATO cal., GIO, 16 in. chromemoly H-bar fluted match barrel, M4 feed ramps, T-Marked flat-top upper, flip up rear sight, folding front gas block with bayonet lug, aluminum free floating quad rail forend with swiveling sling stud, nine 5-slot low profile ladder style quad rail covers, Ace M4 SOCOM standard length telestock with half buttpad, Phantom flash suppressor, Ergo Ambi AR grip. Mfg. 2008-2009.

	$1,650	$1,445	$1,240	$1,120	$910	$745	$580	$1,783

MSR	100%	98%	95%	90%	80%	70%	60%	Last MSR

D-M4LT CARBINE – 5.56 NATO cal., GIO, Milspec diameter receiver extension with "H" buffer, chrome lined lightweight A1 barrel, permanently attached Phantom suppressor, slim carbine type forend, 30 shot Magpul PMAG black mag. Limited mfg. 2009.

	$1,275	$1,115	$955	$865	$700	$575	$445	*$1,373*

Add $890 for permanently attached Smith Vortex flash suppressor, Magpul CTR stock with buttpad, and Daniel Defense light rail (Model D-M4LTD, mfg. 2009 only).

Add $1,050 for Vltor Modstock, mid-length gas system, Smith Vortex suppressor, Daniel Defense light rail, and Magpul grip (Model D-M4MG, mfg. 2009 only).

Add $150 for A2 birdcage flash hider, full length hand guard, Troy flip up BUIS (Model D-M4MLL, mfg. 2009 only).

D-MCA4 RIFLE – .223 Rem. cal., 20 in. chrome lined govt. profile barrel, A3 detachable carry handle, A2 buttstock, A2 birdcage flash hider, A2 hand guard, forged front sight base, 30 shot mil spec mag. Limited mfg. 2009.

	$1,175	$1,030	$880	$800	$645	$530	$410	*$1,317*

Add $622 for KAC M5 quad rail with KAC panels (Model D-MCA4-M5).

D-M4LED CARBINE – 5.56 NATO cal., GIO, 16 in. chrome lined govt. profile barrel, flat Dark Earth finish, Magpul CTR mil spec buttstock, A2 birdcage flash hider, M4 feedramp, Daniel Defense light rail, Magpul MIAD grip, Troy rear BUIS. Limited mfg. 2009.

	$1,925	$1,675	$1,500	$1,250	$1,050	$875	$725	*$2,209*

D-MR20 RIFLE – 5.56 NATO cal., GIO, 20 in. Wilson Arms stainless steel fluted bull barrel, Magpul PRS II stock, three slot riser blocks, Daniel Defense light rail forearm with Picatinny rail gas block, two-stage match trigger, Phantom suppressor, 20 shot mag. Mfg. 2009.

	$1,825	$1,595	$1,370	$1,240	$1,005	$820	$640	*$1,979*

DR-15 TARGET – 5.56 NATO cal., GIO, 20 in. chromemoly match H-bar barrel, A2 upper with carry handle, fixed A2 buttstock, A2 birdcage flash hider, forged front sight tower with bayonet lug and rubber coated sling swivel. Limited mfg. 2008.

	$895	$785	$670	$610	$490	$405	$315	*$1,089*

DV-24 MATCH TARGET/VARMINT – 5.56 NATO cal., GIO, 24 in. free float match stainless steel bull barrel, T-Marked flat-top upper, two Picatinny half riser blocks, ported aluminum tube forend with swivel/bipod stud installed, Ace skeletonized butt stock, Picatinny rail milled gas block, two-stage match trigger. Mfg. 2008-2009.

	$1,250	$1,095	$940	$850	$690	$565	$440	*$1,389*

JR CARBINE – 9mm Para. (JR9), .40 S&W (JR40), or .45 ACP (JR45) cal., GIO, 16 1/4 in. triangular contoured barrel, 13 (.45 ACP), 15 (.40 S&W), or 17 (9mm) shot mag., features unique magwell interchangability, allowing the owner to use handgun magazine of choice, matte black synthetic six-position telescoping AR stock, anodized aluminum receiver, Picatinny rail, free float quad rail forearm, ergonomic AR grip, includes two mags., approx. 6 1/2 lbs. Disc. 2009.

	$875	$775	$700	$625	$550	$475	$400	*$987*

RIFLES: SINGLE SHOT

FIELD GRADE – .22 Hornet, .223 Rem., .243 Win., or .270 Win. cal., single shot break open action, 22 in. barrel with mount base, drilled and tapped, adj. or no sights, checkered hardwood stock and forearm. Limited importation 2001 only.

	$165	$145	$125	$110	$90	$75	$60	*$189*

Add $10 for adj. sights.

This model was also available in a Youth configuration at no extra charge.

MODEL 1874 LITTLE SHARPS – .17 HMR, .218 Bee, .22 LR (new 2008), .22 Hornet, .22 WMR (new 2009), .357 Mag., .30-30 Win., .38-55 WCF (new 2008), .44-40 WCF (new 2008), or .45 LC cal., 24 (rimfire only) or 26 in. tapered octagon barrel, case colored frame, straight grip uncheckered walnut stock and forearm, mfg. by Armi Sport. Mfg. 2007-2009.

	$1,075	$940	$805	$730	$590	$485	$375	*$1,249*

SHOTGUNS: O/U

Recent O/U production was from Italy and Turkey.

PRESENTATION MODEL – 12 or 20 ga., with choke tubes, Purdey double underlug locking action with decorative engraved sideplates, French walnut, single trigger, ejectors. Disc. 1986.

	$995	$870	$745	$675	$545	$450	$350	*$1,165*

COUNTRY SQUIRE MODEL – .410 bore only, 3 in. chambers, case colored boxlock action, gold DT, 25 1/2 in. vent. barrels with VR and F/F chokes, checkered straight grip stock and Schnabel forearm, approx. 6 lbs. Disc. 2002.

	$640	$560	$480	$435	$350	$290	$225	*$715*

MSR	100%	98%	95%	90%	80%	70%	60%	Last MSR

FIELD II HUNTER – 12, 16 (new 2001), 20, 28 ga., or .410 bore, similar to DeLuxe Model except has fixed chokes, extractors, machine-cut stock checkering, and blue receiver, 5 1/2 - 7 lbs., depending on ga./barrel lengths. Imported 1989-2005.

	$850	$745	$640	$580	$470	$385	$300	$1,029

Add $100 for 28 ga. or .410 bore.

* **Field II Hunter with Ejectors** – similar to Field II Hunter, except has ejectors and multi-chokes (not available on 28 ga. or .410 bore), Monte Carlo stock. Imported 1997-2005.

	$1,065	$900	$800	$675	$575	$475	$375	$1,279

* **Field II Hunter Ultra-Light** – 12 or 20 ga., alloy frame, 26 in. VR barrels only with fixed IC/M (disc. 2000) or multi-chokes (new 2001), thin forearm, approx. 5 1/2 lbs. Imported 1999-2005.

	$965	$840	$725	$625	$525	$425	$325	$1,199

DELUXE MODEL – 12, 20, 28 ga. (disc. 1995), or .410 bore (disc. 1995), boxlock with self adj. crossbolt, 26 or 28 in. chrome lined VR barrels with internal choke tubes, SST, ejectors, antique silver finish on receiver, deluxe hand checkered walnut stock and forearm. Imported 1989-96.

	$650	$570	$490	$440	$360	$295	$230	$770

SPORTING CLAYS MODEL – 12 ga. only, SST, ejectors, silver engraved receiver, checkered walnut stock and forearm, screw-in chokes, 28 (disc.) or 30 (new 1996) in. VR ported barrels. Imported 1995-96.

	$775	$680	$580	$525	$425	$350	$270	$895

SUPERIOR II – 12 or 20 ga., various chokes, boxlock action, single trigger, ejectors, engraved. Disc. 1988.

	$675	$590	$505	$460	$370	$305	$235	$875

Add $35 for 12 ga. Mag. (disc. 1987).

FIELD III – 12 or 20 ga., various chokes, boxlock action, single trigger. Disc. 1989.

	$395	$345	$295	$270	$215	$180	$140	$450

SUPERIOR II HUNTER – 12, 20, 28 ga. (new 1998), or .410 bore, 3 in. chambers (except 28 ga.), boxlock action, ejectors, 26, 28, or 30 in. VR barrels with multi-chokes (except 28 ga. and .410 bore), barrel porting became standard during 2000, select checkered walnut stock and forearm, 6 1/8-7 lbs. Imported 1997-2005.

	$1,325	$1,160	$995	$900	$730	$595	$465	$1,519

Subtract $70 for 28 ga. or .410 bore.

* **Superior II Hunter Sporting** – 12 or 20 ga. (disc. 1998), 26 (disc. 1998), 28, or 30 (12 ga. only) in. 10mm VR barrels with multi-chokes and ported barrels. Imported 1997-2005.

	$1,400	$1,225	$1,050	$950	$770	$630	$490	$1,659

* **Superior II Hunter Trap** – 12 ga. only, 30 or 32 (disc. 2001) in. VR barrels with choice of fixed chokes or multi-chokes, regular or Monte Carlo stock. Imported 1997-2005.

	$1,450	$1,270	$1,090	$985	$800	$655	$510	$1,699

Subtract 10% if w/o multi-chokes with Monte Carlo stock.

* **Superior II Hunter Skeet** – 12 or 20 ga., 26 in. VR barrels with choice of Skeet fixed chokes or multi-chokes, regular or Monte Carlo stock. Imported 1997-98.

	$935	$820	$700	$635	$515	$420	$325	$1,039

Add $120 for multi-chokes with Monte Carlo stock.

EMPIRE DL HUNTER – 12, 20, 28 ga., or .410 bore, boxlock action, silver receiver with game scene engraving, ejectors, SST, 26 or 28 (12 or 20 ga. only) in. VR barrels with multi-chokes (except 28 ga. and .410 bore). Imported 1997-98.

	$1,025	$875	$750	$650	$550	$475	$395	$1,159

Add $65 for 28 ga. or $110 for .410 bore.

EMPIRE II EDL HUNTER – similar to Empire DL Hunter, except has engraved sideplates featuring game scenes. Imported 1998-2005.

	$1,675	$1,465	$1,255	$1,140	$920	$755	$585	$2,029

Subtract $10 for 28 ga. or .410 bore.

* **Empire II EDL Hunter Sporting** – 12 or 20 ga. (disc. 1999), 26 (disc. 1999), 28, or 30 (12 ga. only) in. VR barrels with multi-chokes. Imported 1997-2005.

	$1,675	$1,465	$1,255	$1,140	$920	$755	$585	$2,049

* **Empire II EDL Hunter Trap** – 12 ga. only, 30 or 32 (disc. 2000) in. VR barrels with choice of fixed chokes (32 in. barrel only) or multi-chokes, regular (disc. 1998) or Monte Carlo stock. Imported 1997-2005.

	$1,700	$1,490	$1,275	$1,155	$935	$765	$595	$2,099

Subtract 10% if w/o multi-chokes.

MSR	100%	98%	95%	90%	80%	70%	60%	Last MSR

* Empire II EDL Hunter Mono Trap – features 30 or 32 in. single top barrel, standard or adj. Monte Carlo stock. Imported 1999-2005.

| | $2,825 | $2,400 | $2,150 | $1,800 | $1,425 | $1,150 | $925 | $3,249 |

Subtract approx. 20% if w/o adj. Monte Carlo stock.

* Empire II EDL Hunter Trap Combo – includes mono 32 in. barrel and extra set of 30 in. O/U barrels, standard or adj. Monte Carlo stock. Imported 1999-2005.

| | $3,500 | $3,150 | $2,700 | $2,250 | $1,925 | $1,625 | $1,375 | $3,919 |

Subtract approx. 20% if w/o adj. Monte Carlo stock.

* Empire II EDL Hunter Skeet – 12 or 20 ga., 26 in. VR barrels with choice of Skeet fixed chokes or multi-chokes, regular or Monte Carlo stock. Imported 1997-98.

| | $1,050 | $920 | $790 | $715 | $580 | $475 | $370 | $1,189 |

Add $125 for multi-chokes with Monte Carlo stock.

DIAMOND FIELD – 12 or 20 ga. (disc. 1986) Mag., with choke tubes. Same action as Presentation Model without sideplates, engraved, select walnut, single trigger, ejectors. Disc. 1986.

| | $695 | $610 | $520 | $475 | $380 | $315 | $245 | $895 |

* Diamond Field Trap or Skeet – 12 ga. only, 26 or 30 in. barrels only. Disc. 1986.

| | $850 | $745 | $640 | $580 | $470 | $385 | $300 | $1,050 |

Subtract $50 for Skeet Model.

DIAMOND GTX DL HUNTER – 12, 20, 28 ga., or .410 bore, sidelock action, ejectors, SST, elaborate engraving with select checkered walnut stock and forearm, 26, 28 (12 or 20 ga. only), or 30 (12 ga. only) in. VR barrels with multi-chokes (except 28 ga. and .410 bore). Imported 1997 only.

| | $11,250 | $9,845 | $8,440 | $7,650 | $6,190 | $5,065 | $3,940 | $12,399 |

* Diamond GTX EDL Hunter – more elaborate variation of the Diamond GTX DL Hunter. Imported 1997 only.

| | $13,750 | $12,030 | $10,315 | $9,350 | $7,565 | $6,190 | $4,815 | $15,999 |

DIAMOND GTX SPORTING – 12 or 20 (disc. 1998) ga., boxlock Boss action with light perimeter engraving, 28 or 30 (12 ga. only) in. VR barrels with multi-chokes and porting. Imported 1997-2001.

| | $5,260 | $4,605 | $3,945 | $3,575 | $2,895 | $2,365 | $1,840 | $5,849 |

DIAMOND GTX TRAP – 12 ga. only, boxlock Boss action with light perimeter engraving, 30 in. VR barrels with choice of fixed (disc. 1999) or multi-chokes with barrel porting, regular or adj. (new 1999) Monte Carlo stock. Imported 1997-2001.

| | $5,865 | $4,900 | $4,400 | $3,825 | $3,175 | $2,750 | $2,175 | $6,699 |

Subtract 10% w/o fixed chokes.

DIAMOND GTX MONO TRAP – features single top barrel, adj. Monte Carlo stock. Imported 1999-2001.

| | $5,795 | $4,850 | $4,400 | $3,825 | $3,150 | $2,750 | $2,175 | $6,619 |

* Diamond GTX Mono Trap Combo – includes 32 in. mono barrel and extra set of 30 in. O/U barrels, adj. Monte Carlo stock. Imported 1999-2001.

| | $6,775 | $5,930 | $5,080 | $4,605 | $3,725 | $3,050 | $2,370 | $7,419 |

DIAMOND GTX SKEET – 12 or 20 ga., 26 or 28 (20 ga. only with Monte Carlo stock) in. VR barrels with choice of Skeet fixed chokes or multi-chokes, regular or Monte Carlo stock. Imported 1997-98.

| | $4,700 | $4,115 | $3,525 | $3,195 | $2,585 | $2,115 | $1,645 | $5,149 |

Add $140 for multi-chokes with Monte Carlo stock.

DIAMOND REGENT GTX DL HUNTER – 12, 20, 28 ga., or .410 bore, sidelock action, ejectors, SST, best quality engraving with premium checkered walnut stock and forearm, 26, 28 (12 or 20 ga. only), or 30 (12 ga. only) in. VR barrels with multi-chokes (except 28 ga. and .410 bore). Imported 1997 only.

| | $19,750 | $17,280 | $14,815 | $13,430 | $10,865 | $8,890 | $6,915 | $22,299 |

* Diamond Regent GTX EDL Hunter – top-of-the-line model incorporating best quality engraving and premium walnut. Imported 1997 only.

| | $23,000 | $20,125 | $17,250 | $15,640 | $12,650 | $10,350 | $8,050 | $26,429 |

MODEL 105 – 12 ga., 26 or 28 in. barrels, fixed chokes, extractors, DT, silver engraved receiver, Turkish walnut stock, mfg. in Turkey. Imported 2006-2007.

| | $355 | $310 | $265 | $240 | $195 | $160 | $125 | $409 |

MODEL 106 – 12, 20, 28 ga. or .410 bore, 26 or 28 in. barrels, SST, extractors, fixed (.410 bore) or multi-chokes, inlaid blue receiver, mfg. in Turkey. Imported 2006-2007.

| | $525 | $460 | $395 | $355 | $290 | $235 | $185 | $599 |

MSR	100%	98%	95%	90%	80%	70%	60%	Last MSR

MODEL 206 – 12 ga., 3 in. chambers, extractors or ejectors, 26 or 28 in. VR barrels with three multichokes, SST, silver receiver, select Turkish Monte Carlo walnut stock, mfg. in Turkey. Imported 2007-2009.

| | $685 | $600 | $515 | $465 | $375 | $310 | $240 | $793 |

Add $126 for auto ejectors.

* Model 206 Sporting – 12 ga., 28 or 30 in. VR barrels with 5 multichokes, ejectors, SST. Imported 2007-2009.

| | $925 | $800 | $700 | $600 | $500 | $400 | $350 | $1,059 |

Add $240 for adj. comb.

* Model 206 Trap – 12 ga., 30 in. VR barrels with 5 multichokes, ejectors. Imported 2007-2009.

| | $975 | $850 | $750 | $650 | $550 | $450 | $375 | $1,123 |

Add $240 for adj. comb.

DALY UL – 12 ga., aluminum receiver, SST, ejectors, 26 in. barrels with five multi-chokes. Imported 2007 only.

| | $525 | $460 | $395 | $355 | $290 | $235 | $185 | $599 |

MAXI-MAG – 12 ga., 3 1/2 in. chambers, boxlock action, 26 or 28 in. VR barrels with three choke tubes, SST, extractors, checkered walnut stock and forearm. Imported 2007 only.

| | $485 | $425 | $365 | $330 | $265 | $220 | $170 | $559 |

Add $60 for Advantage Max-4 or Realtree HD camo finish.

SHOTGUNS: SXS

FIELD III – 12 or 20 ga., various chokes, boxlock action, single trigger. Disc.

| | $350 | $305 | $265 | $240 | $195 | $160 | $125 | |

COUNTRY SQUIRE MODEL – .28 ga. or .410 bore, 3 in. chambers, case colored boxlock action, gold DT, 26 in. barrels with fixed chokes, checkered stock and splinter forearm, approx. 6 lbs. Disc. 2000.

| | $600 | $525 | $450 | $410 | $330 | $270 | $210 | $680 |

FIELD II HUNTER MODEL – 10 (disc. 2002), 12, 16 (new 2005), 20, 28 ga., or .410 bore, boxlock action, 26, 28, 30 (12 ga. only), or 32 (10 ga. only) in. barrels, fixed (disc. 2000) or multi-chokes (12 or 20 ga. only), 6-7 3/8 lbs., or 11 1/4 (10 ga.) lbs. Imported 1997-2005.

| | $975 | $875 | $750 | $650 | $550 | $450 | $375 | $1,189 |

Subtract $90 for 16 ga., 28 ga. or .410 bore (extractors only).

Subtract approx. 15% if w/o ejectors and multi-chokes (not available in 28 ga. or .410 bore).

SUPERIOR – 12 or 20 ga., boxlock action, various chokes, single trigger. Disc. 1985.

| | $550 | $480 | $415 | $375 | $305 | $250 | $195 | $624 |

SUPERIOR HUNTER – 12, 20, or 28 (new 1999) ga., or .410 bore (new 2000), 26 or 28 in. barrels with fixed (disc. 2000) or multi-chokes (new 2001, 12 or 20 ga. only), 5 7/8-6 3/4 lbs. Imported 1997-2005.

| | $1,395 | $1,220 | $1,045 | $950 | $765 | $630 | $490 | $1,659 |

Subtract $30 for 28 ga. or .410 bore.

LUXE MODEL – 12 (disc. 1991) or 20 ga., boxlock action, SST, ejectors, 26 in. barrels with choke tubes, checkered pistol grip walnut stock with semi-beavertail forearm, recoil pad. Imported 1990-94.

| | $575 | $505 | $430 | $390 | $315 | $260 | $200 | $650 |

This model was manufactured by Hermanos located in Spain.

EMPIRE HUNTER – 12, 20, or 28 (disc. 1998) ga., 26 or 28 in. barrels with fixed or multi-chokes (new 2001), 6-6 7/8 lbs. Imported 1997-2005.

| | $1,700 | $1,490 | $1,275 | $1,155 | $935 | $765 | $595 | $2,119 |

DIAMOND DL – 12, 20, 28 ga., or .410 bore, case colored sidelock action with 3rd lever fastener, scroll engraving, select checkered walnut stock and splinter forearm, 26 or 28 in. barrels with fixed chokes. Importation began 1997.

| | $6,060 | $5,305 | $4,545 | $4,120 | $3,335 | $2,725 | $2,120 | $6,999 |

DIAMOND REGENT DL – 12, 20, 28 ga., or .410 bore, sidelock action with best quality engraving and premium checkered walnut stock and forearm, 26 or 28 in. barrels with fixed chokes. Imported 1997 only.

| | $18,950 | $16,580 | $14,215 | $12,885 | $10,425 | $8,530 | $6,635 | $21,659 |

MODEL 306 – 12 or 20 (new 2007) ga., 3 in. chambers, engraved boxlock action, 26 or 28 in. barrels with three multichokes, gold SST, extractors, checkered Turkish walnut stock and forearm, 6 1/2 - 7 lbs. Importation from Turkey 2006-2007.

| | $580 | $510 | $435 | $395 | $320 | $260 | $205 | $649 |

CLASSIC COACH GUN – 12 ga., 3 in. chambers, engraved boxlock action, 20 in. barrels with three multichokes, gold SST, extractors, checkered Turkish walnut stock and forearm, 6.3 lbs. Imported 2007.

| | $550 | $480 | $415 | $375 | $305 | $250 | $195 | $635 |

MSR	100%	98%	95%	90%	80%	70%	60%	*Last MSR*

SHOTGUNS: LEVER ACTION

MODEL 1887 – 12 ga., patterned after the Winchester Model 1887, case-colored frame, 22 or 28 in. barrel. Imported 2007-2009.

| | $1,100 | $950 | $800 | $700 | $600 | $500 | $450 | *$1,279* |

Add $60 for 28 in. barrel.

SHOTGUNS: SEMI-AUTO

The Charles Daly "Novamatic" shotguns were produced in 1968 by Breda in Italy. The Novamatic series was not imported by Outdoor Sport Headquarters, Inc.

NOVAMATIC LIGHTWEIGHT MODEL – 12 ga., 26 or 28 in. barrel, various chokes, available with quick choke interchangeable tubes, checkered pistol grip stock, similar to the Breda shotgun. Mfg. 1968 only.

| | $305 | $265 | $230 | $205 | $170 | $135 | $105 | |

Add $25 for vent. rib.
Add $15 for quick choke.

NOVAMATIC SUPER LIGHTWEIGHT – 12 or 20 ga., similar to Lightweight, except approx. 1/2 lb. lighter.

| | $330 | $290 | $250 | $225 | $180 | $150 | $115 | |

Add $25 for vent. rib.
Add $15 for quick choke.

NOVAMATIC MAGNUM – 12 or 20 ga. with 3 in. chambers, similar to Lightweight, 28 or 30 in. vent rib barrel, full choke.

| | $330 | $290 | $250 | $225 | $180 | $150 | $115 | |

NOVAMATIC TRAP – similar to Lightweight, with 30 in. full vent. rib barrel, Monte Carlo stock.

| | $360 | $315 | $270 | $245 | $200 | $160 | $125 | |

MULTI-XII – 12 ga. only, 3 in. chamber, 27 in. VR multichoke barrel, self-adjusting gas operation, deluxe checkered walnut stock with recoil pad and forearm. Imported 1987-88 only.

| | $425 | $370 | $320 | $290 | $235 | $190 | $150 | *$498* |

CHARLES DALY AUTOMATIC – 12 ga., 2 3/4 or 3 in. chambers, gas operation, alloy frame, pistol grip (high gloss) or English stock, vent. rib, 5 shot mag. Also available as slug gun with iron sights. Invector chokes became standard in 1986. Disc. 1988.

| | $320 | $280 | $240 | $220 | $175 | $145 | $110 | *$365* |

Add $15 for oil finished English stock.

FIELD GRADE ERCT – 12 or 20 ga., 22 in. barrel, adj. sight or cantilever scope mount, blue finish or RealTree Hardwoods camo coverage, extended rifle choke tube, deer variation, mfg. in Turkey. Imported 2006-2007.

| | $340 | $300 | $255 | $230 | $185 | $155 | $120 | *$399* |

Add $70 for Youth Model.
Add $10 for cantilever scope mount.
Add $60 for 100% camo coverage.

FIELD GRADE FRB – 12 ga., 22 in. fully rifled barrel with choice of fiber optic sights or cantilever scope mount, blue or camo finish, mfg. in Turkey. Imported 2007-2008.

| | $385 | $335 | $290 | $260 | $210 | $175 | $135 | *$449* |

Add $70 for 100% camo coverage.
Add $180 for combo variation with cantilever mount barrel and extra 28 in. multi-choke barrel.
Add $16 for cantilever scope mount.

FIELD IV (FIELD HUNTER) – 12, 20 (new 2002), or 28 (new 2002) ga., 3 in. chamber (12 or 20 ga.), gas operated, aluminum receiver, 22 (Youth or smoothbore slug), 24-30 in. VR barrel with multi-chokes, choice of standard wood/black metal or 100% Next (new 2009), Advantage (disc. 2001), Advantage Timber HD (mfg. 2002-2008), Realtree (disc. 2001), RealTree Hardwoods HD (disc. 2009), Advantage Max-4 HD (12 ga. only, mfg. 2004-2009), Realtree APG (mfg. 2008-2009), Advantage Wetlands (mfg. 2001-2003), or Advantage Classic (disc. 2001) camo coverage, synthetic stock and forearm, 6 7/8-7 1/8 lbs. Imported 1999-2009.

| | $440 | $385 | $330 | $300 | $240 | $200 | $155 | *$509* |

Add $74 for 100% camo coverage.
Add $20 for 28 ga.
Add $124 for Turkey Model with 24 in. barrel, pistol grip stock, and camo coverage (new 2009).
Add $28 for left-hand action (12 ga. only).
Add $20 for Advantage Timber HD camo (20 ga. only, disc. 2008).

MSR	100%	98%	95%	90%	80%	70%	60%	Last MSR

* *Field Hunter Slug* – 12 ga. only, 22 in. cyl. bore barrel with adj. sights, black synthetic stock and forearm, nickel (disc. 2002) or black chrome finish, adj. open sights. Imported 1999-2003.

| | $355 | $310 | $265 | $240 | $195 | $160 | $125 | $409 |

Add $20 for satin nickel finish (disc. 2002).
Add $40 for fully rifled barrel with adj. sights (new 2002).

FIELD HUNTER MAXI-MAG – 12 ga. only, 3 1/2 in. chamber, 24, 26 (new 2001), or 28 in. VR barrel with multi-choke, 7mm VR rib, choice of wood/metal or 100% camo coverage similar to Field Hunter, 6 7/8-7 1/8 lbs. Importation began 2000.

| | $440 | $385 | $330 | $300 | $240 | $200 | $155 | $499 |

Add $75 for 100% camo coverage.

* *Field Hunter Maxi-Mag Turkey* – 12 ga. only, includes 24 in. barrel, Hi/TriViz fiber optic sights and XX full ported turkey choke tube, Advantage Timber or Realtree Hardwoods HD camo treatment, Uncle Mike's camo sling and sling swivels. Mfg. 2002-2009.

| | $550 | $480 | $415 | $375 | $305 | $250 | $195 | $639 |

SUPERIOR II/IV HUNTER – similar to Field Hunter, except has 20 LPI checkered Turkish walnut stock and forearm, gold highlights and trigger. Imported 1999-2009.

| | $565 | $495 | $425 | $385 | $310 | $255 | $200 | $675 |

Add $32 for 28 ga.
Add $100 for left-hand action (12 ga. only, disc. 2006).

Model nomenclature was changed from Superior II Hunter to Superior IV Hunter during 2009.

* *Superior II/IV Hunter Sporting* – 12, 20, or 28 ga., similar to Superior Hunter, except has 28 or 30 in. ported 10mm VR barrels. Imported 1999-2009.

| | $625 | $525 | $450 | $410 | $330 | $270 | $210 | $739 |

Add $236 for adj. comb.
Add $30 for 28 ga.

* *Superior II/IV Hunter Trap* – 12 ga. only, 30 or 32 (disc. 2007) in. ported barrel with front and mid bead sights. Imported 1999-2009.

| | $640 | $540 | $460 | $420 | $340 | $275 | $215 | $769 |

Add $230 for adj. comb.

TACTICAL – 12 ga., 18 1/2 in. barrel, matte black synthetic pistol grip stock, Picatinny rail, ghost ring sights, extended tactical choke tube. Limited mfg. 2009.

| | $495 | $435 | $370 | $335 | $270 | $225 | $175 | $587 |

Add $80 for 100% A-Tacs camo finish (new 2010).

SHOTGUNS: SLIDE ACTION

FIELD ERCT – 12 or 20 ga., 22 in. barrel with rifled choke tubes, blue or RealTree Hardwoods HD camo finish, available with either adj. sights or cantilevered scope mount, also available in Youth Model (20 ga. only), deer variation. Imported 2006-2007.

| | $220 | $195 | $165 | $150 | $120 | $100 | $75 | $259 |

Add $10 for cantilevered scope mount.
Add $60 for 100% camo coverage.
Add $6 for Youth Model (20 ga. only).

FIELD HUNTER – 12 or 20 (new 2001) ga., 3 in. chamber, 22 (Youth, 20 ga. only), 24, 26, 28, or 30 in. VR barrel with multi-choke, black or pink (Youth only) synthetic stock and forearm, choice of standard wood/metal, chrome (Youth only) or 100% Next (new 2009), Advantage Timber HD (mfg. 2002-2008), Realtree APG (mfg. 2008-2009), Realtree AP HD (mfg. 2008-2009), Realtree Hardwoods HD 12 ga. only, (mfg. 2002-2008) or Advantage Classic (disc. 2001) camo coverage, 5 5/8-6 7/8 lbs. Imported 1999-2009.

| | $240 | $210 | $180 | $165 | $130 | $110 | $85 | $299 |

Add $14 for Youth model with pink synthetic stock (new 2009).
Add $80 for camo.
Add $124 for Turkey Model with pistol grip stock and camo (new 2009).

* *Field Hunter Slug* – 12 ga. only, 18 1/2 in. cyl. bore or 22 in. fully rifled (new 2002) barrel with adj. sights, black synthetic stock and forearm, black chrome or dull nickel finish. Imported 1999-2003.

| | $210 | $185 | $160 | $145 | $115 | $95 | $75 | $229 |

Subtract 15% for 18 1/2 in. barrel.

MSR	100%	98%	95%	90%	80%	70%	60%	Last MSR

FIELD HUNTER MAXI-MAG – 12 ga. only, 3 1/2 in. chamber, 24, 26 (new 2001), or 28 in. VR barrel with multi-choke, 7mm VR rib, choice of wood/metal or 100% camo coverage similar to Field Hunter, approx. 6 3/4 lbs. Imported 2000-2009.

| | $270 | $235 | $205 | $185 | $150 | $120 | $95 | *$339* |

Add $80 for camo.
Add $114 for Turkey Model with camo, Hi/TriViz fiber optic sights and XX full ported turkey choke tube - also includes sling and sling swivels (new 2002).

TACTICAL – 12 ga. or 20 (new 2009), 3 in. chamber, 18 1/2 in. cyl. bore barrel with front sight, black synthetic stock and forearm or 100% camo coverage (new 2009), matte blue metal or chrome finish, 6 lbs. Imported 2000-2009.

| | $250 | $220 | $190 | $170 | $140 | $115 | $90 | *$289* |

Add $24 for Field Tactical AW with chrome finish and adj. sights.
Add $74 for pistol grip stock, ghost ring sights, and MC1 multichoke.
Add $134 for pistol grip stock, ghost ring sights, Picatinny rail, and extended choke tube.
Add $124 for camo with ghost ring and fiber optic sights (new 2009).

CHARLES DALY: 2011-PRESENT

Current registered trademark of shotguns imported by Samco Global Arms located in Miami, FL.

During Sept. 2012, Samco Global Arms, Inc. purchased the Charles Daly trademarks from the Kassnar family. On Akkar and Charles Daly shotguns imported by Samco during 2011-2012, service can be provided directly by Samco. Samco can also supply service parts and accessories for Charles Daly semi-auto, pump, and O/U shoguns imported by K.B.I., Inc. and made by the Akkar factory in Turkey, from 1999 through 2010. These models are identifiable by the serial number. Samco cannot provide direct service and/or parts for any other firearms imported by K.B.I. Inc. or others, that were sold under the Charles Daly name. Parts for other Charles Daly firearms imported by K.B.I., Inc., such as 1911 pistols made in the Phillipines - contact Armscor. Shotguns made in Italy, contact Sabatti, or Fausti. For Miroku shotguns made in Japan, contact Browning, etc.

SHOTGUNS: SEMI-AUTO

MODEL 600 HD (HOME DEFENSE) – 12 ga., 3 in. chamber, 18 1/2 in. chromemoly steel barrel, cyl. choke, bead sight, Black synthetic stock, blue finish. New 2012.

| MSR $509 | $450 | $395 | $340 | $300 | $250 | $200 | $150 | |

* *Model 600 HD-LH (Left Hand)* – 12 ga., similar to Model 600 HD, except features camo stock and left-hand action. New 2013.

| MSR $541 | $485 | $425 | $375 | $325 | $275 | $225 | $175 | |

MODEL 600 THD (TACTICAL) – 12 ga., 3 in. chamber, 18 1/2 in. chromemoly steel barrel, MC chokes, ghost ring sights, Picatinny rail, Black synthetic pistol grip stock with blue finish or full digital camo. New 2012.

| MSR $613 | $540 | $475 | $400 | $375 | $300 | $250 | $200 | |

Add $94 for full digital camo stock and finish.

CHARTER ARMS

Previously manufactured by Charco, Inc. located in Ansonia, CT 1992-1996. Previously manufactured by Charter Arms located in Stratford, CT 1964-1991.

The company's first model was the Undercover.

PISTOLS: SEMI-AUTO

EXPLORER II & S II PISTOL – .22 LR cal., semi-auto survival pistol, barrel unscrews, SA, 8 shot mag., black, gold (disc.), silvertone, or camouflage finish, 6, 8, or 10 in. barrels, simulated walnut grips. Disc. 1986.

| | $90 | $80 | $70 | $60 | $55 | $50 | $45 | *$109* |

This model uses a modified AR-7 action.

Manufacture of this model was by Survival Arms located in Cocoa, FL.

RIFLES: SEMI-AUTO

AR-7 EXPLORER RIFLE – .22 LR cal., takedown, barreled action stores in Cycolac synthetic stock, 8 shot mag., adj. sights, 16 in. barrel, black finish on AR-7, silvertone on AR-7S. Camouflage finish new 1986 (AR-7C). Mfg. until 1990.

| | $125 | $100 | $85 | $75 | $65 | $55 | $50 | *$146* |

In 1990, the manufacturing of this model was taken over by Survival Arms located in Cocoa, FL. Current mfg. AR-7 rifles will be found under the Henry Repeating Arms Company.

MSR	100%	98%	95%	90%	80%	70%	60%	Last MSR

CHATTAHOOCHEE GUN WORKS, LLC

Current custom rifle manufacturer located in Phenix City, AL.

PISTOLS: SEMI-AUTO

Chattahoochee Gun Works currently manufactures the CGW-15 AR-15 style pistol in 5.56 NATO cal. For more information on this model including pricing, options, and availability, please contact the company directly (see Trademark Index).

RIFLES: SEMI-AUTO

Chattahoochee Gun Works currently manufactures custom AR-15 style rifles in several calibers and configurations. Current models include: 16 in. Gen. III Switchblock - MSR $2,930, 18 in. Gen. III - MSR $2,595, Recce Basic - MSR $1,730, 16 in. Gen. III - MSR $2,575, Rogue Hunter - MSR $1,825-$1,845, 16 in. Infantry - MSR $2,365, CGW-7.62 - MSR $2,399, 300 Blackout 16T - MSR $1,550, 300 Blackout SPR 16 - MSR $1,950, CGW-15 Series includes: 20-DMR-3G - MSR $1,950, 18-FSM-1 - MSR $1,850, 16-NSS-1 - MSR $1,850, 16-DOSS-1 - MSR $1,750, 16-Y1 - MSR $1,700, B 16 M1 - MSR $1,550, B 16-RU2 - MSR $1,350, NT 16 - MSR $1,850, T 16 - MSR $1,750, AS-16 - MSR $1,250, B 16-R1 - MSR $1,695, SM-16 - MSR $1,225, 3 Gun 16 - MSR $1,775, 3 Gun 18 - MSR $1,800, B 16 R1V - MSR $1,695, G 16 - 2013 MSR was $1,825, G18 SPR - 2013 MSR was $1,850, BDM 20 - 2013 MSR was $1,725, G DMR 20 - MSR $1,799, and Pred II CF-DE - 2013 MSR was $2,000. Please contact the company directly for more information including options, pricing, and availability (see Trademark Index).

CHEYTAC

Current manufacturer located in Arco, ID. Previously distributed by SPA Defense, located in Ft. Lauderdale, FL, and by Knesek Guns, Inc., located in Van Buren, AR. Dealer sales.

RIFLES: BOLT ACTION

Cheytac currently manufactures an advanced 5 shot bolt action design in .375 or .408 Cheyenne Tactical cal. The Intervention Model 200 Military weighs 27 lbs., and includes an advanced ballistic computer to help with accuracy. The M-325 model is also offered. Cheytac also builds an Intervention Model M310 Target Model. Please contact the company directly for more information, including pricing and commercial availability (see Trademark Index).

CHIAPPA FIREARMS LTD.

Current manufacturer established during 2008 and located in Dayton, OH. Marketed by MKS Supply, located in Dayton, OH with sales through various domestic distributors. Chiappa Firearms Ltd. is one division of the Chiappa Group, which includes Armi Sport (replica firearms manufacturer established in 1958), Chiappa Firearms Ltd. (firearms manufacturer), Kimar Srl (firearms manufacturer), Costa Srl (metal surface finish treatment), ACP (laser training system), and AIM (video/target simulations).

Chiappa Firearms Ltd. manufacturers a wide variety of firearms including reproductions and replicas. The models listed in this section are marketed exclusively by MKS Supply, Inc., and are marked Chiappa Firearms on the guns. Chiappa also manufactures private label guns for Cimarron Firearms, Legacy Sports, and Taylor's and Company. Please refer to these sections for more information on those Chiappa mfg. models.

PISTOLS: SEMI AUTO

M FOUR-22 – .22 LR cal., GIO, replica of the M4 carbine, 6 in. steel barrel, blue finish, fire control group, finger groove pistol grip, dust cover, adj. sights, 10 or 28 shot mag., faux flash hider, machined quad rail forearm, includes two mags. Mfg. 2011-2013.

	$450	$395	$350	$300	$265	$250	$230	$515

Add $27 for red dot scope.

RIFLES: SEMI-AUTO

M-22 SERIES – While a Carbine, National Match, and Precision Match were advertised during 2011, this series never went into production and was not imported.

M FOUR-22 – .22 LR cal., GIO, 5, 10 or 28 shot, 16 in. barrel with flash hider, forward assist and bolt release, Black or Tan finish, fixed tube stock, ribbed tube-type forearm, A-4 adj. sights, Picatinny flat-top, detachable carry handle, accepts Mil Spec handguards, 5 1/2 lbs. Disc. 2012.

	$360	$325	$300	$265	$230	$200	$180	$419

Add $30 for red dot scope.

M1 CARBINE – please refer to listing under Citadel.

M FOUR-22 GEN II PRO CARBINE/RIFLE – .22 LR cal., blowback action, 16 in. heavy match threaded barrel, 10 or 28 shot mag., 7.8 (Carbine) or 11.8 (Rifle) in. free floating aluminum quad rail with 8-position Picatinny rail, pistol grip, 6-position collapsible stock, parkerized finish. New 2013.

MSR $538	$450	$400	$360	$325	$285	$260	$240	

Add $21 for 11.8 in. quad rail.

MSR	100%	98%	95%	90%	80%	70%	60%	Last MSR

Chiappa also offers an M Four-22 conversion unit (upper only) - current MSR is $361-$377, depending on forend length (new 2012).

M FOUR-22 RIFLE PRO – .22 LR cal., blowback action, 16 in. heavy match threaded barrel, 10 or 28 shot mag., 7.8 or 11.8 in. free floating aluminum quad rail with 8-position Picatinny rail, pistol grip, fixed stock, Muddy Girl camo finish. New 2014.

| MSR $569 | $485 | $425 | $365 | $330 | $285 | $260 | $240 | |

Add $40 for 11.8 in. quad rail.

AK-22 RIFLE – .22 LR cal., blued steel receiver, 17 1/4 in. blue barrel, synthetic or wood stock, includes two 10 shot mags., 6-6.7 lbs. New 2014.

| MSR $429 | $365 | $325 | $275 | $250 | $200 | $165 | $130 | |

Add $35 for wood stock.

SHOTGUNS: SLIDE ACTION

C6 SERIES – 12 ga., 3 in. chamber, 18 1/2 in. barrel with fixed front sight and one Rem. choke, 5 shot mag., choice of black synthetic stock with pistol grip or pistol grip only, or four-position adj. stock (black finish only), matte black or satin nickel finish. New 2013.

| MSR $335 | $285 | $250 | $230 | $195 | $175 | $160 | $150 | |

Add $9 for field stock with pistol grip.
Add $29 for satin nickel finish.
Add $39 for 20 ga. Youth model with Next G1 camo stock and forend.

C9 SERIES – 12 ga. only, 3 in. chamber, 22 in. barrel, black synthetic stock with pistol grip, 8 shot mag., fixed or fiber optic front, ghost ring Picatinny rear sight, matte black or satin nickel finish. New 2013.

| MSR $349 | $295 | $260 | $225 | $200 | $175 | $160 | $140 | |

Add $28 for satin nickel finish.
Add $35 for full length pistol grip stock, ghost ring sights and rail, and breecher tube.

CHRISTENSEN ARMS

Current rifle manufacturer established in 1995, and currently located in Gunnison, UT. Previously located in Fayette, UT during 2000-2010, and in St. George, UT during 1995-99. Direct sales only.

PISTOLS: SEMI-AUTO

Add $50 for Cerakote slide. Add $75 for Cerakote frame or $60 for Cerakote hardware. Add $140 for carbon grips. Add $40 for ambi-safety. Add $1,400 for damascus slide. Add $70 for threaded barrel.

* ***Tactical Government (Tactical Lite)*** – .45 ACP cal., similar to Government model, except has Picatinny rail, and flared magazine well. New 2011.

| MSR $3,250 | $2,825 | $2,350 | $2,050 | $1,775 | $1,500 | $1,250 | $1,050 | |

Add $1,000 for titanium frame.

RIFLES: BOLT ACTION

In addition to the models listed below, Christensen Arms also offers the Carbon One Custom barrel installed on a customer action (any caliber) for $1,100 ($875 if short chambered by competent gunsmith), as well as providing a Carbon Wrap conversion to an existing steel barrel ($675). Additionally, a Custom Long Range Package is available for $6,695, as well as an Extreme Long Range Package for $4,650.

Add $1,200 for titanium action, $195 for titanium muzzle brake, $275 for Jewell trigger, $150 for Teflon coated action, $150 for Realtree (disc. 2013), Mossy Oak (disc. 2013), King's Desert (mfg. 2011-2013), King's Snow (mfg. 2011-2013) or Natural Gear (disc. 2010) camo stock. Add $200 for Camo stock dip (new 2014), $250 for lightened action (disc. 2013), $150 for Black Nitride action, $200 for natural graphite stock finish on the models listed below.

CARBON ONE EXTREME – various cals., 18-26 in. carbon wrap free floating barrel, choice of carbon classic or thumbhole Christensen Arms stock, Teflon coated and lightened action, 3 lb. trigger pull, 5 1/2-7 lbs. Mfg. 2007-2012.

| | $2,875 | $2,400 | $1,900 | $1,500 | $1,200 | $975 | $800 | *$3,295* |

CARBON ONE RANGER (CONQUEST) – .50 BMG cal., single shot (disc. 2010) or repeater (5 shot), McMillan stainless steel bolt action, max barrel length is 32 in. with muzzle brake, Christensen composite stock with bipod, approx. 16 (single shot) - 24 lbs. New 2001.

| MSR $8,995 | $8,200 | $6,700 | $5,450 | $4,500 | $3,750 | $2,850 | $2,500 | |

Add $300 for Tac-50 stock.
Add $240 for Atlas Bipod BT10.
Add $200 for camo stock dip.
Subtract 20% for a single shot action (disc. 2010).

MSR	100%	98%	95%	90%	80%	70%	60%	Last MSR

CARBON ONE TACTICAL – various cals., grey synthetic stock, various barrel lengths, stainless steel free floating Shilen barrel with muzzle brake, glass bedded barrel assembly, precision trigger, many options available per customer request, 5.5-7 lbs. Mfg. 2010-2012.

| | $4,150 | $3,650 | $3,250 | $1,825 | $2,300 | $1,950 | $1,700 | $4,595 |

CARBON RANGER – .50 BMG cal., large diameter graphite barrel casing (up to 36 in. long), no stock or forearm, twin rails extending from frame sides are attached to recoil pad, Omni Wind Runner action, bipod and choice of scope are included, 25-32 lbs. Limited mfg. 1998-2000 only.

| | $9,950 | $8,900 | $8,000 | $7,100 | $6,200 | $5,300 | $4,400 | $10,625 |

RIFLES: SEMI-AUTO

Christensen Arms also offered a Carbon One Challenge drop-in barrel (16 oz.) for the Ruger Model 10/22. Last MSR was $499 (disc. 2010).

CARBON ONE CHALLENGE (CUSTOM) – .17 HMR, .22 LR, or .22 WMR cal., features Ruger 10/22 Model 1103 action with modified bolt release, synthetic bull barrel with precision stainless steel liner, 2 lb. Volquartsen trigger, Fajen brown laminated wood (disc.) or black synthetic stock with thumbhole, approx. 3.5-4 lbs. Mfg. 1996-2010.

| | $1,500 | $1,250 | $1,050 | $875 | $750 | $600 | $500 | $1,750 |

Add $350 for .17 HMR or .22 WMR cal.

The 100% price represents the base model, with no options.

CARBON CHALLENGE II – similar to Carbon Challenge I, except has AMT stainless receiver and trigger, black synthetic stock, approx. 4 1/2 lbs. Limited mfg. 1997-1998 only.

| | $1,150 | $975 | $875 | $800 | $725 | $650 | $525 | $1,299 |

CA-10 RECON – .243 Win., 6.8 Creedmoor, .308 Win., or .338 Federal cal., GIO, features 16-24 in. carbon fiber match grade barrel, various stock configurations, flat-top receiver with Picatinny rail, adj. Timney trigger, carbon handguard, 20 shot mag., black carbon fiber or camo forearm finish, 6-8 lbs. Mfg. 2011-2013.

| | $2,995 | $2,650 | $2,250 | $2,035 | $1,650 | $1,350 | $1,050 | $3,575 |

Subtract $200 for steel barrel.

CARBON ONE CA-15 SERIES (AR-15) – .223 Rem. cal., GIO, forged aluminum upper and lower receiver, choice of round shroud with quad rails or integrated forearm with full Picatinny rail on top, adj. stock, carbon fiber wrapped stainless steel barrel, ambidextrous charging handle, Timney adj. drop-in trigger, 30 shot detachable AR-15 style mag., 5.5 - 7 lbs. Mfg. 2009-2010.

| | $2,500 | $2,195 | $1,875 | $1,700 | $1,375 | $1,125 | $875 | $2,950 |

* **CA-15 Predator** – .223 Rem., .204 Ruger, 6.8 Spc., or 6.5 Grendel, GIO, 20 or 24 in. carbon fiber match grade barrel, collapsible stock, flat-top receiver with Picatinny rail, ambidextrous controls, adj. Timney trigger, 20 shot mag., Hogue pistol grip, black, King's Desert Shadow, or King's Snow Shadow finish, 5.5-7 lbs. Mfg. 2011-2012.

| | $2,550 | $2,235 | $1,925 | $1,750 | $1,400 | $1,150 | $900 | $2,995 |

* **CA-15 Recon** – .204 Ruger, .223 Rem./5.56 NATO (.223 Wylde chamber), 6.5 Grendel, 6.8 SPC or .300 AAC cal., GPO, 16 or 20 in. match grade carbon fiber barrel, carbon fiber handguard with built-in Picatinny rails, choice of adj. stock, adj. Timney trigger, piston drive, titanium birdcage flash suppressor, 30 shot mag., Hogue pistol grip, factory black synthetic, Digital Desert Brown, King's Desert Shadow, or King's Snow Shadow finish, 5.5-7 lbs. New 2011.

| MSR $3,395 | $3,000 | $2,625 | $2,250 | $2,040 | $1,650 | $1,350 | $1,050 | |

CHRISTIAN ARMORY WORKS

Current custom rifle manufacturer located in Rock Spring, GA.

RIFLES: SEMI-AUTO

Christian Armory Works currently manufactures rifles in several calibers and configurations. Current A2 standard models start at $1,289, Standard NP3 Tactical rifles start at $1,897, Precision Target System models start at $1,649, and Standard Tactical Defense models start at $1,399. Please contact the company directly for more information on options, pricing, and availability (see Trademark Index).

CIMARRON F.A. CO.

Current importer, distributor, and retailer located in Fredericksburg, TX. Cimarron is currently importing A. Uberti, D. Pedersoli, Chiappa Firearms, Pietta, and Armi-Sport firearms and black powder reproductions and replicas. Previous company name was Old-West Co. of Texas. Dealer sales only.

Please refer to the *Blue Book of Modern Black Powder Arms* by John Allen (also online) for more information and prices on Cimarron's lineup of modern black powder models.

Black Powder Revolvers - Reproductions & Replicas and *Black Powder Long Arms & Pistols - Reproductions & Replicas* by Dennis Adler are also invaluable sources for most black powder reproductions and replicas, and they include hundreds of color images on most popular makes/models, provide manufacturer/trademark histories, and up-to-date information on

MSR	100%	98%	95%	90%	80%	70%	60%	*Last MSR*

related items/accessories for black powder shooting - www.bluebookofgunvalues.com

PISTOLS: SEMI-AUTO

M4-22 – .22 LR cal., AR-15 style, GIO, 6 in. barrel with muzzle brake, quad rail, includes A2 carry handle, black finish, 5, 10, or 28 shot Atchison style conversion mag., cased with cleaning kit, 3.9 lbs. Mfg. by Armi Chiappa in Italy. Imported 2011-2012.

	100%	98%	95%	90%	80%	70%	60%	Last MSR
	$485	$430	$385	$350	$325	$300	$275	*$587*

CITADEL

Current trademark imported beginning 2009 by Legacy Sports International, located in Reno, NV.

CARBINES: SEMI-AUTO

M1 CARBINE – 22 LR cal., M1 design, 18 in. threaded (new 2013) barrel with fixed front sight and adj. rear sight, black synthetic, Harvest Moon camo (new 2013), Muddy Girl camo (new 2013), Outshine camo (new 2013), or wood (new 2012) stock, 10 shot mag., blued finish, 4.8 lbs. Mfg. by Chiappa in Italy, importation began 2011.

MSR $316	$265	$235	$200	$185	$170	$160	$150	

Add $52 for Harvest Moon, Muddy Girl, or Outshine camo (new 2013) stock.
Add $84 for wood stock (new 2012).

PISTOLS: SEMI-AUTO

M-1911 – .45 ACP cal., full size 1911 style frame, 5 in. barrel, SA, matte black, brushed nickel (new 2010), or polished nickel (new 2010), steel slide, 8 shot, skeletonized hammer and trigger, Novak sights, lowered and flared ejection port, extended ambidextrous safety, checkered wood or Hogue wraparound (available in Black, Green, or Sand, new 2010) grips, includes two magazines and lockable plastic case, 2.3 lbs. New 2009.

MSR $592	$495	$425	$395	$365	$325	$275	$250	

Add $38 for Hogue wraparound grips in Black, Green, or Sand.
Add $89 for brushed nickel or $108 for polished nickel.
Add $250 for Wounded Warrior Project configuration with matte black finish.

* **M-1911 Compact** – .45 ACP cal., 3 1/2 in. barrel, 6 shot, similar to Citadel M-1911 FS, except has compact frame, not available in polished nickel, 2.1 lbs. New 2009.

MSR $592	$495	$425	$395	$365	$325	$275	$250	

Add $38 for Hogue grips. Add $89 for brushed nickel.

SHOTGUNS: SLIDE ACTION

CITADEL LE TACTICAL – 12 ga., 20 (disc. 2011) or 22 (new 2012) in. barrel, 7 shot mag., matte black finish, available in Standard, Spec-Ops (features Blackhawk Spec-Ops stock with recoil reduction), Talon (features thumbhole stock with Blackhawk recoil reduction), or Pistol grip w/heat shield (features interchangeable stock and removeable pistol grip) configuration, approx. 5.8-7 lbs. Mfg. in the U.S. 2010-2012.

	100%	98%	95%	90%	80%	70%	60%	Last MSR
	$385	$335	$285	$240	$210	$180	$150	*$466*

Add $41 for Pistol grip w/heat shield or $166 for either Spec-Ops or Talon configuration.

CLARIDGE HI-TEC INC.

Previous manufacturer located in Northridge, CA 1990-1993. In 1990, Claridge Hi-Tec, Inc. was created and took over Goncz Armament, Inc.

All Claridge Hi-Tec firearms utilized match barrels mfg. in-house, which were button-rifled. The Claridge action is an original design and does not copy other actions. Claridge Hi-Tec models can be altered (Law Enforcement Companion Series) to accept Beretta 92F or Sig Model 226 magazines.

PISTOLS: SEMI-AUTO

Add $40 for polished stainless steel frame construction.

L-9 PISTOL – 9mm Para., .40 S&W, or .45 ACP cal., blowback telescoping bolt operation, SA, 7 1/2 (new 1992) or 9 1/2 (disc. 1991) in. shrouded barrel, aluminum receiver, choice of black matte, matte silver, or polished silver finish, one-piece grip, safety locks firing pin in place, 10 (disc.), 17 or 30 shot double row mag., adj. sights, 3 3/4 lbs. Mfg. 1991-1993.

	100%	98%	95%	90%	80%	70%	60%	Last MSR
	$595	$525	$375	$300	$265	$225	$200	*$598*

Add $395 for a trigger activated laser sight available in Models M, L, C, and T new mfg.

S-9 PISTOL – similar to L-9, except has 5 in. non-shrouded threaded barrel, 3 lbs. 9 oz. Disc. 1993.

	100%	98%	95%	90%	80%	70%	60%	Last MSR
	$695	$625	$550	$475	$350	$280	$250	*$535*

MSR	100%	98%	95%	90%	80%	70%	60%	Last MSR

T-9 PISTOL – similar to L-9, except has 9 1/2 in. barrel. Mfg. 1992-93.

	$550	$495	$375	$300	$265	$225	$200	$598

M PISTOL – similar to L Model, except has 7 1/2 in. barrel, 3 lbs. Disc. 1991.

	$575	$515	$375	$300	$265	$225	$200	$720

CARBINES: SEMI-AUTO

C-9 CARBINE – same cals. as L and S Model pistols, 16.1 in. shrouded barrel, choice of black graphite composite or uncheckered walnut stock and forearm, 5 lbs. 12 oz. Mfg. 1991-1993.

	$650	$595	$525	$450	$395	$350	$300	$675

Add $74 for black graphite composite stock.
Add $474 for integral laser model (with graphite stock).

This model was available with either gloss walnut, dull walnut, or black graphite composite stock.

LAW ENFORCEMENT COMPANION (LEC) – 9mm Para., .40 S&W, or .45 ACP cal., 16 1/4 in. button rifled barrel, black graphite composition buttstock and foregrip, buttstock also provides space for an extra mag., available in either aluminum or stainless steel frame, matte black finish, available with full integral laser sighting system. Limited mfg. 1992-93.

	$750	$650	$575	$495	$425	$375	$325	$749

Add $400 for integral laser sighting system.

CLARK CUSTOM GUNS, INC.

Current custom gun maker and gunsmith located in Princeton, LA. Clark Custom Guns, Inc. has been customizing various configurations of handguns, rifles, and shotguns since 1950. It would be impossible to list within the confines of this text the many conversions this company has performed. Please contact the company directly (see Trademark Index) for an up-to-date price sheet and catalog on their extensive line-up of high quality competition pistols and related components. Custom revolvers, rifles, and shotguns are also available in addition to various handgun competition parts, related gunsmithing services, and a firearms training facility called The Shootout.

The legendary James E. Clark, Sr. passed away during 2000. In 1958, he became the first and only full-time civilian to win the National Pistol Championships.

PISTOLS: SEMI-AUTO

Clark Custom Guns manufactures a wide variety of M1911 style handguns, including the Bullseye Pistols (MSR $1,695-$3,100), the Custom Combat (MSR $1,925-$2,900), the Meltdown (MSR $1,995-$2,295), Millennium Meltdown (damascus slide, only 50 mfg. during 2000 - MSR was $3,795), .460 Rowland Hunter LS (last MSR $2,640), and the Unlimited (last MSR $3,395-$3,790). Clark will also build the above configurations on a customer supplied gun - prices are less. Please contact the company directly regarding more information on its wide variety of pistols, including availability and pricing (see Trademark Index).

CLIFTON ARMS

Previous manufacturer of custom rifles from 1992-1997 located in Medina, TX. Clifton Arms specialized in composite stocks (with or without integral, retractable bipod).

Clifton Arms manufactured composite, hand laminated stocks, which were patterned after the Dakota 76 stock configuration.

RIFLES: BOLT ACTION

CLIFTON SCOUT RIFLE – .243 Win. (disc. 1993), .30-06, .308 Win., .350 Rem. Mag., .35 Whelen, 7mm-08 Rem. (disc. 1993), or .416 Rem. Mag. cal., choice of Dakota 76, pre-64 Winchester Model 70, or Ruger 77 MK II (standard) stainless action with bolt face altered to controlled round feeding, Shilen stainless premium match grade barrel, Clifton synthetic stock with bipod, many other special orders were available. Mfg. 1992-97.

$3,000	$2,350	$1,650	$$1,455	$1,195	$1,010	$835

This model was available as a Standard Scout (.308 Win. cal. with 19 in. barrel), Pseudo Scout (.30-06 cal. with 19 1/2 in. barrel), Super Scout (.35 Whelen or .350 Rem. Mag. with 20 in. barrel), or African Scout (.416 Rem. Mag. with 22 in. barrel).

COBB MANUFACTURING, INC.

Previous rifle manufacturer located in Dallas, GA until 2007.

On Aug. 20, 2007, Cobb Manufacturing was purchased by Bushmaster, and manufacture was moved to Bushmaster's Maine facility. Please refer to the Bushmaster section for current information.

RIFLES: BOLT ACTION

MODEL FA50 (T) – .50 BMG cal., straight pull bolt action, lightweight tactical rifle, standard A2 style stock, ergonomic

MSR	100%	98%	95%	90%	80%	70%	60%	*Last MSR*

pistol grip, parkerized finish, Lothar Walther 22 or 30 in. barrel, recoil reducing Armalite muzzle brake, padded Mil-spec sling, includes two 10 shot mags., detachable M60 bipod, watertight case, 29 lbs. Disc. 2007.

	$6,275	$5,300	$4,500	$3,900	$2,700	$2,300	$2,100	*$6,995*

Add $300 for 22 in. barrel.

Add $1,000 for Ultra Light model with lightweight 22 or 30 in. barrel.

Add $89 for additional 10 shot mag.

RIFLES: SEMI-AUTO

MCR (MULTI-CALIBER RIFLE) SERIES – available in a variety of calibers from 9mm Para. to .338 Lapua, offered in MCR 100, MCR 200, MCR 300, and MCR 400 configurations, variety of stock, barrel and finish options. Mfg. 2005-2007.

Prices on this series started at $3,000, and went up according to options chosen by customer.

COBRAY INDUSTRIES

See listing under S.W.D. in the S section of this text.

COLT'S MANUFACTURING COMPANY, LLC

Current manufacturer with headquarters located in West Hartford, CT.

Manufactured from 1836-1842 in Paterson, NJ; 1847-1848 in Whitneyville, CT; 1854-1864 in London, England; and from 1848-date in Hartford, CT. Colt Firearms became a division of Colt Industries in 1964. In March 1990, the Colt Firearms Division was sold to C.F. Holding Corp. located in Hartford, CT, and the new company was called Colt's Manufacturing Company, Inc. The original Hartford plant was closed during 1994, the same year the company was sold again to a new investor group headed by Zilkha Co., located in New York, NY. During 1999, Colt Archive Properties LLC, the historical research division, became its own entity.

In late 1999, Colt discontinued many of their consumer revolvers, but reintroduced both the Anaconda and Python Elite through the Custom Shop. Production on both models is now suspended. The semi-auto pistols remaining in production are now referred to as Model "O" Series.

In November 2003, Colt was divided into two separate companies, Colt Defense LLC (military/law enforcement) and Colt's Manufacturing Company LLC (handguns and match target rifles). The largest portion of Colt Defense's business is now in sporting rifles, a line of business the company got back into during 2011. Military orders have been on the decline since 2009.

During 2013, Colt Defense LLC acquired Colt's Manufacturing LLC for $60.5 million and reunited Colt's military and civilian handgun businesses. By combining the two companies after a decade long split, Colt Defense has eliminated the risk that its contract with Colt's Manufacturing to sell commercial firearms to civilian sportsmen and hunters under its namesake brand wouldn't be extended beyond March 2014. The company plans to remain in West Hartford.

For more information and current pricing on both new and used Colt airguns, please refer to the *Blue Book of Airguns* by Dr. Robert Beeman & John Allen (also available online). For more information and current pricing on both new and used Colt black powder reproductions and replicas, please refer to the *Blue Book of Modern Black Powder Arms* by John Allen (also available online).

Black Powder Revolvers - Reproductions & Replicas and *Black Powder Long Arms & Pistols - Reproductions & Replicas* by Dennis Adler are also invaluable sources for most 2nd and 3rd Generation black powder reproductions and replicas, and include hundreds of color images on most popular makes/models, provide manufacturer/trademark histories, and up-to-date information on related items/accessories for black powder shooting - www.bluebookofgunvalues.com

PISTOLS: SEMI-AUTO, SINGLE ACTION, RECENT MFG.

Factory Colt abbreviations used on its price sheets are as follows: F-H - Front Heinie sight, CC/B - colored case/blue, L/W - lightweight, BSTS - bright polished stainless steel, CCBS - Colt Champion Bo-Mar style sight, BRS - Bo-Mar rear sights, NNS - Novak night sights, WDS - white dot sights, FXS - fixed sights, HBAR - heavy barrel, HC - hard chrome, CCES - Colt Champion Elliason style sights, BPF - black powder frame, B - blue, STS - stainless steel, TT - two-tone, WDC - white dot carry, M - matte, and WDCN - white dot carry Novak sights.

Some Series 80 pistols, including Gold Cups and Defenders with slanted slide serrations, polished ejection port, and beavertail safety are more desirable than standard models without these features. See individual models for pricing.

SPECIAL COMBAT GOVERNMENT (CARRY MODEL) SERIES 80 – .45 ACP cal., similar to Special Combat Government, except has blue or royal blue (disc.), hard chrome, or two-tone finish, bar-dot-bar (disc. 2000) or Novak (new 2009) night sights, and ambidextrous safety. Mfg. 1992-2000, reintroduced 2009.

MSR $2,095	$1,775	$1,450	$1,125	$950	$775	$675	$575	

SPECIAL COMBAT GOVERNMENT CMC MARINE PISTOL – .45 ACP cal., full size with 5 in. National Match barrel, front and rear slide serrations, features Desert Tan cerakote finish, stainless steel receiver and slide, Novak 3-dot sights, serrated grip straps with lanyard loop, aluminum trigger, unique patterned grips, lower Picatinny rail, includes Pelican case with two 7 shot mags, cleaning kit, and test target. New 2013.

MSR $2,158	$1,875	$1,550	$1,125	$950	$775	$675	$575	

MSR	100%	98%	95%	90%	80%	70%	60%	Last MSR

DEFENDER SERIES MODEL O – 9mm Para., .40 S&W (mfg. 1999 only) or .45 ACP cal., 3 in. barrel with 3-dot (disc.) or white dot carry Novak sights, 7 shot mag., rubber wrap-around grips with finger grooves, lightweight perforated trigger, stainless steel slide and frame - frame finished in matte stainless, firing pin safety, 22 1/2 oz. New 1998.

MSR $1,098	$950	$795	$675	$575	$475	$425	$375	

Note: Colt has issued a factory recall on the safety for this model sold after March 2007 in the following ser. no. range: DR33036 - DR35948 X. Colt will send you a new recoil spring assembly kit that includes the Guide Pad to replace in your pistol.

* **Defender Plus** – .45 ACP cal., similar to Defender Model O, except has aluminum frame and 8 shot mag. Mfg. 2002-2003.

	$875	$775	$700	$625	$575	$550	$475	*$876*

* **XSE Series Model O Rail Gun** – .45 ACP cal., 5 in. barrel, 8 shot mag., stainless, two-tone (disc.), or Cerakote (new 2011) finish, similar to Government Stainless model, except has Picatinny rail underneath frame in front of trigger guard. New 2009.

MSR $1,198	$1,025	$895	$725	$625	$525	$450	$395	

Add $86 for Cerakote finish (new 2011).

NEW AGENT SA MODEL O – 9mm Para. (disc. 2012) or .45 ACP cal., 3 in. barrel, Series 80 firing pin safety system, hammerless, 7 shot mag., double diamond slim fit or Crimson Trace (new 2012) grips, black anodized aluminum frame, blue finish, beveled mag. well, skeletonized trigger, snag free trench style sights, front strap serrations, captive recoil spring system. New 2008.

MSR $1,078	$925	$795	$650	$550	$450	$400	$350	

Add $288 for Crimson Trace laser grips (new 2012).

Note: Colt has issued a factory recall on the safety for this model sold after March 2007 in the following ser. no. range: GT01001-GT04505 XX. These pistols must be returned to Colt's factory for part(s) replacement.

GOVERNMENT MODEL 1911A1 .22 CAL. RAIL GUN – .22 LR cal., similar to Government Model 1911 .22 cal., except has lower Picatinny rail on frame, double slide serrations, skeleton trigger, low mount 3-dot combat style sights, beavertail grip safety and Commander style hammer, black or FDE (new 2013) finish, 36 oz. Mfg. by Umarex in Germany beginning 2011, and distributed by Umarex USA, located in Fort Smith, AR.

MSR $449	$385	$325	$285	$240	$215	$195	$185	

Add $50 for FDE finish (new 2013).

This model is also available in a Gold Cup variation - please refer to the listing in the Pistols: Semi-Auto, National Match Models - WWII & Post-WWII category.

RIFLES: BOLT ACTION, CENTERFIRE

COLT PRECISION RIFLE (M2012SA308) – .308 Win. cal., tactical configuration featuring 22 in. heavy match grade spiral fluted stainless steel barrel with muzzle brake, skeletonized adj. forged aluminum stock, pistol grip, vent. aluminum handguard with 2/3 length Picatinny rail, 5 or 10 shot mag., black finish, Timney single stage adj. trigger, 13.2 lbs. Mfg. by Cooper Firearms of Montana. New 2013.

MSR $3,796	$3,300	$2,950	$2,600	$2,300	$2,000	$1,850	$1,625	

RIFLES: SEMI-AUTO, CENTERFIRE, AR-15 & VARIATIONS

The AR-15 rifle and variations are the civilian versions of the U.S. armed forces M-16 model, which was initially ordered by the U.S. Army in 1963. Colt's obtained the exclusive manufacturing and marketing rights to the AR-15 from the Armalite division of the Fairchild Engine and Airplane Corporation in 1961.

Factory Colt AR-15 receivers are stamped with the model names only (Sporter II, Government Model, Colt Carbine, Sporter Match H-Bar, Match Target), but are not stamped with the model numbers (R6500, R6550, R6521, MT6430, CR6724). Because of this, if an AR-15 rifle/carbine does not have its original box, the only way to determine whether the gun is pre-ban or not is to look at the serial number and see if the configuration matches the features listed below within the two pre-ban subcategories.

AR-15 production included transition models, which were made up of obsolete and old stock parts. These transition models include: blue label box models having large front takedown pins, no internal sear block, 20 in. barrel models having bayonet lugs, misstamped nomenclature on receivers, or green label bolt assemblies.

Rifling twists on the Colt AR-15 have changed throughout the years, and barrel twists are stamped at the end of the barrel on top. They started with a 1:12 in. twist, changed to a 1:7 in. twist (to match with the new, longer .223 Rem./5.56mm SS109-type bullet), and finally changed to a 1:9 in. twist in combination with 1:7 in. twist models as a compromise for bullets in the 50-68 grain range. Current mfg. AR-15s/Match Targets have rifling twists/turns incorporated into the model descriptions.

Colt's never sold pre-ban lower receivers individually. It only sold completely assembled rifles.

A Colt letter of provenance for the following AR-15 models is $100 per gun.

MSR	100%	98%	95%	90%	80%	70%	60%	Last MSR

AR-15, Pre-Ban, 1963-1989 Mfg. w/Green Label Box

Common features of 1963-1989 mfg. AR-15s are bayonet lug, flash hider, large front takedown pin, no internal sear block, and w/o reinforcement around the magazine release button.

AR-15 boxes during this period of mfg. had a green label with serial number affixed on a white sticker. Box is taped in two places with brown masking tape. NIB consists of the rifle with barrel stick down the barrel, plastic muzzle cap on flash hider, factory tag hanging from front sight post, rifle in plastic bag with ser. no. on white sticker attached to bag, cardboard insert, accessory bag with two 20 round mags., manual, sling, and cleaning brushes. Cleaning rods are in separate bag.

Pre-ban parts rifles are rifles, which are not assembled in their proper factory configuration. Counterfeit pre-ban rifles are rifles using post-ban receivers and assembled into a pre-ban configuration (it is a felony to assemble or alter a post-ban rifle into a pre-ban configuration).

Add $100 for NIB condition.

Add $300 for early green label box models with reinforced lower receiver.

SP-1 (R6000) – .223 Rem. cal., GIO, original Colt tactical configuration without forward bolt assist, 20 in. barrel with 1:12 in. twist, identifiable by the triangular shaped handguards/forearm, no case deflector, A1 sights, finishes included parkerizing and electroless nickel, approx. 6 3/4 lbs. Ser. no. range SP00001-SP5301 (1976). Mfg. 1963-1984.

| | $2,100 | $1,975 | $1,850 | $1,725 | $1,600 | $1,500 | $1,200 | |

Add 40%-60% for mint original models with early two and three digit serial numbers.

Pre-ban serialization is ser. no. SP360,200 and lower.

Early SP-1s were packaged differently than later standard green box label guns.

* **SP-1 Carbine (R6001)** – .223 Rem. cal., similar to SP-1, except has 16 in. barrel, ribbed handguards, collapsible buttstock, high gloss finish.

| | $2,900 | $2,700 | $2,425 | $2,225 | $2,075 | $1,900 | $1,650 | |

Mint original condition models with early two and three digit serial numbers are selling in the $3,250 - $3,500 range.

Pre-ban serialization is ser. no. SP360200 and lower.

Early SP-1s were packaged differently than later standard green box label guns.

SPORTER II (R6500) – .223 Rem. cal., GIO, various configurations, receiver stamped "Sporter II", 20 in. barrel, 1:7 twist, A1 sights and forward assist, disc.

| | $1,875 | $1,650 | $1,475 | $1,300 | $1,175 | $1,075 | $995 | |

Serial numbers SP360200 and below are pre-ban.

* **Sporter II Carbine (R6420)** – .223 Rem. cal., similar to Sporter II, except has 16 in. barrel, A1 sights and collapsible buttstock.

| | $2,225 | $2,000 | $1,850 | $1,675 | $1,525 | $1,425 | $1,275 | |

Serial numbers SP360200 and below are pre-ban.

GOVERNMENT MODEL (R6550) – .223 Rem. cal., GIO, receiver is stamped Government Model, 20 in. barrel with 1:7 in. twist and bayonet lug, A2 sights, forward assist and brass deflector, very desirable because this model has the closest configurations to what the U.S. military is currently using.

| | $2,250 | $2,100 | $1,950 | $1,800 | $1,650 | $1,400 | $1,200 | |

In 1987, Colt replaced the AR-15A2 Sporter II Rifle with the AR-15A2 Govt. Model. This new model has the 800 meter rear sighting system housed in the receiver's carrying handle (similar to the M-16 A2).

Serial numbers GS008000 and below with GS prefix are pre-ban.

* **Government Model (6550K)** – .223 Rem. cal., similar to R6550, except does not have bayonet lug, originally supplied with .22 L.R. cal. conversion kit.

| | $2,050 | $1,900 | $1,750 | $1,600 | $1,450 | $1,250 | $1,100 | |

Subtract $300 w/o conversion kit.

Serial numbers GS008000 and below with GS prefix are pre-ban.

* **Government Model (R6550CC)** – .223 Rem. cal., similar to R6550, except has Z-Cote tiger striped camo finish, very scarce (watch for cheap imitation paint jobs).

| | $3,500 | $3,350 | $3,100 | $2,800 | $2,600 | $2,400 | $2,000 | |

Serial numbers GS008000 and below with GS prefix are pre-ban.

H-BAR MODEL (R6600) – GIO, H-Bar model with 20 in heavy barrel, 1:7 twist, forward assist, A2 sights, brass deflector, 8 lbs. New 1986.

| | $2,050 | $1,900 | $1,750 | $1,600 | $1,400 | $1,200 | $1,000 | |

Serial numbers SP360200 and below are pre-ban.

MSR	100%	98%	95%	90%	80%	70%	60%	Last MSR

* **H-Bar (R6600K)** – similar to R6600, except has no bayonet lug, supplied with .22 LR cal. conversion kit.

| | $1,975 | $1,825 | $1,675 | $1,525 | $1,375 | $1,225 | $1,100 | |

Subtract $300 if w/o conversion kit.

Serial numbers SP360200 and below are pre-ban.

* **Delta H-Bar (R6600DH)** – similar to R6600, except has 3-9x rubber armored scope, removable cheekpiece, adj. scope mount, and black leather sling, test range selected for its accuracy, aluminum transport case. Mfg. 1987-1991.

| | $2,300 | $2,150 | $1,925 | $1,775 | $1,575 | $1,375 | $1,125 | *$1,460* |

Serial numbers SP360200 and below are pre-ban.

AR-15, Pre-Ban, 1989-Sept. 11, 1994 Mfg. w/Blue Label Box

Common features of 1989-1994 AR-15 production include a small front takedown pin, internal sear block, reinforcement around the mag. release button, flash hider, no bayonet lug on 20 in. models, A2 sights, brass deflector, and forward bolt assist. Models R6430 and 6450 do not have A2 sights, brass deflector, or forward bolt assist.

Blue label boxed AR-15s were mfg. between 1989-Sept. 11, 1994. Please refer to box description under Pre-1989 AR-15 mfg.

Pre-ban parts rifles are rifles which are not assembled in their proper factory configuration. Counterfeit pre-ban rifles are rifles using post-ban receivers and assembled into a pre-ban configuration.

Add $100 for NIB condition.

AR-15A3 TACTICAL CARBINE (R-6721) – .223 Rem. cal., GIO, M4 flat-top with 16 in. heavy barrel, 1:9 twist, A2 sights, pre-ban configuration with flash hider, bayonet lug, and 4-position, collapsible stock, removable carry handle, 134 were sold commercially in the U.S., most collectible AR-15. Mfg. 1994 only.

| S/N 134 and lower | $2,975 | $2,500 | $2,275 | $2,050 | $1,900 | $1,775 | $1,600 | |
| S/N 135 and higher | $1,250 | $1,075 | $950 | $850 | $750 | $650 | $550 | |

On the R-6721, serial numbers BD000134 and below are pre-ban.

Please note the serial number cutoff on this model, as Colt shipped out a lot of unstamped post-ban law enforcement only "LEO" rifles before finally stamping them as a restricted rifle.

GOVERNMENT CARBINE (R6520) – .223 Rem cal., GIO, receiver is stamped Government Carbine, two-position collapsible buttstock, 800 meter adj. rear sight, 16 in. barrel bayonet lug, 1:7 twist, shortened forearm, 5 lbs. 13 oz. Mfg. 1988-94.

| | $2,275 | $2,125 | $2,025 | $1,875 | $1,750 | $1,625 | $1,425 | *$880* |

Add $200 for green label box.

On the R6520, serial numbers GC018500 and below are pre-ban.

Please note the serial number cutoff on this model, as Colt shipped out a lot of unstamped post-ban law enforcement only "LEO" rifles before finally stamping them as a restricted rifle.

This model was manufactured in both green and blue label configurations.

COLT CARBINE (R6521) – receiver is stamped Colt Carbine, similar to R6520, except has no bayonet lug, 16 in. barrel, 1:7 twist. Disc. 1988.

| | $2,150 | $2,000 | $1,850 | $1,700 | $1,625 | $1,475 | $1,300 | *$770* |

Serial numbers CC001616 and below are pre-ban.

SPORTER LIGHTWEIGHT (R6530) – .223 Rem. cal., GIO, receiver is stamped Sporter Lightweight, 16 in. barrel, 1:7 twist, similar to R6520, except does not have bayonet lug or collapsible stock.

| | $1,650 | $1,500 | $1,350 | $1,100 | $1,000 | $900 | $800 | *$740* |

Serial numbers SI027246 and below are pre-ban.

9mm CARBINE (R6430) – 9mm Para. cal., similar to R6450 Carbine, except does not have bayonet lug or collapsible stock. Mfg. 1992-1994.

| | $1,950 | $1,800 | $1,650 | $1,500 | $1,375 | $1,275 | $1,175 | |

Serial numbers NL004800 are pre-ban.

9mm CARBINE (R6450) – 9mm Para. cal., GIO, carbine model with 16 in. barrel, 1:10 twist, bayonet lug, w/o forward bolt assist or brass deflector, two-position collapsible stock, 20 shot mag., 6 lbs. 5 oz.

| | $2,250 | $2,100 | $1,950 | $1,800 | $1,725 | $1,575 | $1,400 | *$696* |

On the R6450, serial numbers TA010100 are pre-ban.

Please note the serial number cutoff on this model, as Colt shipped out a lot of unstamped post-ban law enforcement only "LEO" rifles before finally stamping them as a restricted rifle.

This model was manufactured with either a green or blue label.

MSR	100%	98%	95%	90%	80%	70%	60%	Last MSR

7.62x39mm CARBINE (R6830) – 7.62x39mm cal., GIO, 16 in. barrel w/o bayonet lug, 1:12 twist, fixed buttstock. Mfg. 1992-1994.

| | $1,850 | $1,700 | $1,550 | $1,400 | $1,275 | $1,175 | $1,075 | |

Serial numbers LH011326 are pre-ban.

TARGET COMPETITION H-BAR RIFLE (R6700) – .223 Rem. cal., GIO, flat-top upper receiver for scope mounting, 20 in. H-Bar barrel (1:9 in. twist), quick detachable carry handle with a 600-meter rear sighting system, dovetailed upper receiver grooved to accept Weaver style scope rings, 8 1/2 lbs.

| | $1,850 | $1,700 | $1,550 | $1,400 | $1,200 | $1,025 | $875 | |

Serial numbers CH019500 and below are pre-ban.

COMPETITION H-BAR CUSTOM SHOP (R6701) – .223 Rem. cal., similar to the R6700, but with detachable scope mount, custom shop enhancements added to trigger and barrel, 2,000 mfg. from Colt Custom Shop.

| | $1,950 | $1,800 | $1,650 | $1,500 | $1,350 | $1,200 | $1,050 | |

MATCH H-BAR (R6601) – GIO, heavy 20 in. H-Bar barrel with 1:7 twist, fixed buttstock. 8 lbs.

| | $1,750 | $1,600 | $1,450 | $1,300 | $1,150 | $1,025 | $950 | |

* **Delta H-Bar (R6601DH)** – similar to R6601, except has 3-9x rubber armored variable scope, removable cheekpiece, adj. scope mount, black leather sling, test range selected for its accuracy, aluminum transport case. Mfg. 1987-91.

| | $2,450 | $2,300 | $2,150 | $2,000 | $1,850 | $1,700 | $1,550 | *$1,460* |

Serial numbers MH086020 and below are pre-ban.

SPORTER TARGET (R6551) – similar to R6601, except had 20 in. barrel with reduced diameter underneath handguard, 7 1/2 lbs.

| | $1,750 | $1,600 | $1,450 | $1,300 | $1,150 | $1,050 | $950 | |

On the R6551, serial numbers ST038100 and below are pre-ban.

AR-15, Post-Ban, Mfg. Sept. 12, 1994-Present

During 2007, Colt released the M-5 Military Carbine and the LE 10-20, with 11 1/2, 14 1/2, or 16 in. barrel. These guns were only available for military and law enforcement.

State compliant variations are not listed in this text. Values are typically similar to the models from which they were derived.

Add $368 for Colt Scout C-More Sight (disc.).
Add $444 for Colt Tactical C-More Sight (disc.).

COMPETITION PRO – .223 Rem. Wylde cal., GIO, 18 in. match grade stainless steel fluted barrel, fully adj. gas block, triple chamber or Sure-Fire muzzle brake, forged upper and lower receiver, flat-top with Picatinny rail, 30 shot mag., matte black finish, Geissele two-stage match trigger, Magpul adj. stock, grip, and forend, approx. 7 lbs. Mfg. 2013.

| | $1,825 | $1,525 | $1,295 | $1,175 | $950 | $775 | $600 | *$2,029* |

PRO CRB-16 – .300 AAC Blackout cal., GIO, patented low profile adj. gas block, forged and precision fitted upper and lower receivers, matte black finish, 16 in. match grade air gauged stainless steel barrel with Colt competition triple port muzzle brake, 10 or 30 shot aluminum mag., Geissele two-stage match trigger, Magpul enlarged triggerguard, Magpul STR six position adj. stock with locking adjustments, Magpul MOE grip with extended backstrap, Hogue 12 in. multi-piece slotted float tube handguard, Competition charging handle with extended tactical latch, matched bolt and bolt carrier with H-buffer, 13 slot Picatinny rail on flat-top upper receiver, 6.7 lbs. New 2013.

| MSR $1,599 | $1,375 | $1,200 | $1,025 | $935 | $750 | $625 | $475 | |

PRO CRG-20 – 6.5mm Grendel cal., GIO, patented low profile adj. gas block, forged and precision fitted upper and lower receivers, matte black finish, 20 in. match grade air gauged chromemoly steel custom barrel with black nitrided finish, 10 or 25 shot aluminum mag., Colt competition match target trigger, nickel Teflon coated, 15 in. vented modular float tube handguard, 10 in. top mounted Picatinny handguard rail with 23 slots and 2-3 accessory rails, oversized trigger guard, Magpul CTR six position adj.buttstock with locking adjustments, Magpul MOE pistol grip with extended backstrap, competition charging handle with extended tactical latch, matched bolt and bold carrier with H-buffer, 13 slot Picatinny rail on flat-top upper receiver. New 2013.

| MSR $1,649 | $1,400 | $1,225 | $1,050 | $950 | $775 | $625 | $495 | |

PRO CRL-16 – .308 Win. cal., GIO, low profile adj. gas block, CNC machined and precision fitted upper and lower receivers, matte black finish, 16 in. tapered midweight match grade air gauged polished stainless steel custom barrel with triple port muzzle brake, 10 or 20 shot Magpul mag., integral enlarged trigger guard, Geissele two-stage SSA-E match trigger, Magpul CTR six position adj. stock with locking adjustments, Magpul MOE pistol grip with extended backstrap, 12 1/2 in. float tube handguard, top mounted Picatinny handguard rail, two 3 in. accessory rails, competition charging handle with extended tactical latch, matched bolt and bolt carrier, 18 slot Picatinny rail on flat-top upper receiver. New 2013.

| MSR $2,339 | $1,995 | $1,750 | $1,495 | $1,350 | $1,095 | $900 | $700 | |

MSR	100%	98%	95%	90%	80%	70%	60%	Last MSR

PRO CRL-20 – .308 Win. cal., similar to Pro CRL-16, except has 20 in. tapered heavy barrel with six flutes. New 2013.

| MSR $2,979 | $2,550 | $2,225 | $1,925 | $1,735 | $1,400 | $1,150 | $895 | |

PRO CRP-16 – .223 Rem. cal., GIO, low profile adj. gas block, forged and precision fitted upper and lower receivers, matte black finish, 16 in. two-diameter heavy weight match grade air gauged polished stainless steel barrel, triple port muzzle brake, 10 or 30 shot Magpul mag., Geissele two-stage match trigger, Magpul enlarged trigger guard, Magpul CTR six position adj. stock with locking adjustments, Magpul MOE grip with extended backstrap, competition 12 in. vented modular float tube handguard, 5 1/2 in. top mounted Picatinny handguard rail with 11 slots, two 3 in. accessory rails, competition charging handle with extended tactical latch matched bolt and bolt carrier with H-buffer, 13 slot Picatinny rail on flat-top upper receiver. New 2013.

| MSR $1,899 | $1,625 | $1,425 | $1,225 | $1,100 | $895 | $725 | $575 | |

PRO CRP-18 – .223 Rem. cal., similar to CRP-16, except has 18 in. custom fluted mid-weight barrel, 15 in. vented modular float tube handguard, and full length Picatinny top handguard rail with one 2 in. accessory rail. New 2013.

| MSR $2,019 | $1,725 | $1,510 | $1,295 | $1,175 | $950 | $775 | $600 | |

PRO CRP-20 – .223 Rem. cal., similar to Pro CRP-18, except has 20 in. two-diameter heavy barrel and 10 in. top mounted Picatinny handguard rail with 23 slots, and two 3 in. accessory rails. New 2013.

| MSR $1,899 | $1,625 | $1,425 | $1,225 | $1,100 | $895 | $725 | $575 | |

EXPERT CRE-18 – .223 Rem. cal., GIO, low profile gas block, forged and precision fitted upper and lower receivers, matte black finish, 18 in. midweight match grade air gauged polish stainless steel barrel, 10 or 30 shot Magpul mag., competition nickel Teflon coated match target trigger, enlarged Magpul trigger guard, Magpul MOE four position adj. stock, 15 in. vented modular float tube handguard, 5 1/2 in. top mounted Picatinny handguard rail with 11 slots, two 3 in. accessory rails with five slots each, Hogue rubber finger groove grip, competition charging handle with extended tactical latch, matched bolt and bolt carrier with H-buffer, 13 slot Picatinny rail on flat-top upper receiver. New 2013.

| MSR $1,599 | $1,375 | $1,200 | $1,050 | $935 | $750 | $625 | $495 | |

SPORTING RIFLE CSR-1516/CSR-1518 – .223 Rem. or 5.56 NATO cal., GIO, solid steel machined low profile gas block, forged alloy upper and lower receivers, matte black finish, 16 (CSR-1516) or 18 (CSR-18) in. midweight match grade chromemoly black manganese phosphate threaded steel barrel with standard flash suppressor, 10 or 30 shot mag., nickel Teflon coated match target trigger, adj. six position carbine (CSR-16) or rifle stock with wide cheekpiece (CSR-18), rubber over-molded finger groove grip with integral beavertail, 12 in. float tube handguard, standard charging handle, bolt, and bolt carrier, top mounted seven slot accessory rail. New 2013.

| MSR $990 | $850 | $750 | $650 | $575 | $475 | $385 | $300 | |

Add $59 for CSR-18.

MARKSMAN CRX-16/CRX-16E – .223 Rem. cal., GIO, low profile gas block, forged and precision fitted upper and lower receivers, matte black finish, 16 in. midweight match grade manganese phosphated chromemoly steel barrel, twin port muzzle brake, 10 or 30 shot Magpul mag., competition match target nickel Teflon coated trigger, enlarged Magpul trigger guard, carbine style four position adj. buttstock or Magpul MOE fixed rifle stock (CRX-16E), checkered A2 style finger groove grip, 12 in. vented modular float tube handguard, 5 1/2 in. top mounted Picatinny handguard rail with 11 slots, two 3 in. accessory rails with five slots each, matched bolt and bolt carrier with H-buffer, 13 slot Picatinny rail on flat-top upper receiver. New 2013.

| MSR $1,399 | $1,195 | $1,050 | $895 | $815 | $650 | $550 | $425 | |

COLT ACCURIZED RIFLE (CR6720/CR6724) – .223 Rem. cal., GIO, 20 (CR6720) or 24 (CR6724, disc. 2012, reintroduced 2014) in. stainless match barrel, matte finish, accurized AR-15, 8 (disc. 1998) or 9 (new 1999) shot mag., 9.41 lbs. New 1997.

| MSR $1,374 | $1,095 | $950 | $825 | $750 | $600 | $500 | $400 | |

MATCH TARGET COMPETITION H-BAR RIFLE (MT6700/MT6700C) – .223 Rem. cal., GIO, features flat-top upper receiver for scope mounting, 20 in. barrel (1:9 in. twist), quick detachable carry handle which incorporates a 600-meter rear sighting system, counterbored muzzle, dovetailed upper receiver is grooved to accept Weaver style scope rings, supplied with two 5 (disc.), 8 (disc.), or 9 (new 1999) shot mags., cleaning kit, and sling, matte black finish, 8 1/2 lbs. Mfg. 1992-2013.

| | $975 | $850 | $725 | $675 | $535 | $450 | $395 | $1,230 |

Add $57 for compensator (MT6700C, mfg. 1999-disc).

MATCH TARGET COMPETITION H-BAR II (MT6731) – .223 Rem. cal., GIO, flat-top, 16.1 in. barrel (1:9 in.), 9 shot mag., matte finish, 7.1 lbs. Mfg. 1995-2012.

| | $950 | $825 | $700 | $650 | $525 | $425 | $395 | $1,173 |

MATCH TARGET LIGHTWEIGHT (MT6430, MT6530, or MT6830) – .223 Rem. (MT6530, 1:7 in. twist), 7.62x39mm (MT6830, disc. 1996, 1:12 in. twist), or 9mm Para. (MT6430, disc. 1996, 1:10 in. twist) cal., GIO, features 16 in. barrel (non-threaded per C/B 1994), initially shorter stock and handguard, rear sight adjustable for windage and elevation, includes two detachable 5, 8, or 9 (new 1999) shot mags., approx. 7 lbs. Mfg. 1991-2002.

| | $895 | $795 | $675 | $625 | $525 | $425 | $395 | $1,111 |

Add $200 for .22 LR conversion kit (disc. 1994).

MSR	100%	98%	95%	90%	80%	70%	60%	Last MSR

MATCH TARGET M4 CARBINE (MT6400/MT6400R) – .223 Rem. cal., GIO, similar to current U.S. armed forces M4 model, except semi-auto, 9 or 10 shot mag., 16.1 in. barrel, 1:7 in. twist, matte black finish, fixed tube buttstock, A3 detachable carrying handle, 7.3 lbs. Mfg. 2002-2013.

| | $950 | $850 | $750 | $650 | $450 | $425 | $395 | *$1,211* |

Add $341 for quad accessory rail (MT6400R).

MATCH TARGET 6400001 – 5.56 NATO cal., GIO, 16.1 in. M4 barrel with flash suppressor, flat-top receiver, fixed tube stock, 10 shot mag., Magpul Gen. II rear back up sight, two-piece ribbed handguard with post front sight, black finish, 7 lbs. Mfg. 2013 only.

| | $1,300 | $1,100 | $975 | $825 | $725 | $575 | $500 | *$1,461* |

MATCH TARGET 6400R001 – 5.56 NATO cal., 16.1 in. M4 barrel with flash suppressor, 10 shot mag., flat-top receiver with Picatinny rail integrated with quad rail handguard, Magpul Gen. II rear sight and flip-up adj. post front sight, black finish, 7.2 lbs. Mfg. 2013 only.

| | $1,595 | $1,375 | $1,250 | $1,000 | $825 | $650 | $550 | *$1,825* |

MATCH TARGET H-BAR RIFLE (MT6601/MT6601C) – .223 Rem. cal., GI, heavy 20 in. H-Bar barrel, 1:7 in. twist, A2 sights, 8 lbs. Mfg. 1986-2010.

| | $1,125 | $975 | $875 | $775 | $675 | $600 | $550 | *$1,218* |

Add $200 for .22 LR conversion kit (mfg. 1990-94).

Add $1 for compensator (MT6601C, new 1999).

TACTICAL ELITE MODEL (TE6700) – .223 Rem. cal., GIO, 20 in. heavy barrel, 1:8 in. twist, Hogue finger groove pistol grip, Choate buttstock, fine tuned for accuracy, scope and mount included, approx. 1,000 rifles made by the Custom Shop circa 1996-97.

| | $1,650 | $1,450 | $1,250 | $1,075 | $900 | $725 | $575 | |

TARGET GOVT. MODEL RIFLE (MT6551) – .223 Rem. cal., GIO, semi-auto version of the M-16 rifle with forward bolt assist, 20 in. barrel (1:7 in.), straight line black nylon stock, aperture rear and post front sight, 5, 8, or 9 (new 1999) shot mags., 7 1/2 lbs. Disc. 2002.

| | $925 | $810 | $700 | $650 | $550 | $450 | $400 | *$1,144* |

Add $200 for .22 LR conversion kit (mfg. 1990-94).

SPORTER CARBINE (SP6920) – .223 Rem. cal., GIO, has M-4 features including flat-top receiver with A3 removeable carry handle, 16.1 in. barrel with flash hider, 4-position collapsible buttstock, ribbed oval handguard, matte black finish, 5.95 lbs. Mfg. 2011 only.

| | $995 | $875 | $775 | $675 | $600 | $500 | $400 | *$1,155* |

Add 15% for the legal LE6920 variation that were sold to civilians.

The last 100 carbines of the Model LE6920 marked "Law Enforcement Carbine" and "Restricted" were sold as commercial guns to FFL dealers. Each of these has a factory letter stating as such.

COLT SPORTER (SP6940) – .223 Rem. cal., GIO, flat-top receiver with full-length quad Picatinny rails, 16.1 in. fully floated barrel, flip up adj. sights, 4-position collapsible stock, 1-piece monolithic upper receiver, 20 shot mag., matte black metal finish, 6.1 lbs. Mfg. 2011 only.

| | $1,275 | $1,000 | $900 | $800 | $700 | $625 | $550 | *$1,500* |

Add 15% for the legal LE6940 variation that were sold to civilians.

The last 100 carbines of the Model LE6940 marked "Law Enforcement Carbine" and "Restricted" were sold as commercial guns to FFL dealers. Each of these has a factory letter stating as such.

SP901 RIFLE – .308 Win. cal., GIO, 16 in. full floated heavy chrome lined barrel, direct gas system, locking bolt, matte black finish, one piece monolithic upper receiver with rail, upper receiver can be swapped out for .223, ambidextrous operating controls, flip up post sights, bayonet lug and flash hider. Mfg. mid-2011.

While advertised in 2011, this model never went into production (see LE901-16S).

COLT CARBINE AR6450 – 9mm Para. cal., GIO, 16.1 in. barrel with flash suppressor, A3 detachable carrying handle, 32 shot mag., grooved aluminum handguard, A2 post front sight, adj. Rogers Super Stoc, matte finish, 6.35 lbs. Mfg. 2012 only.

| | $1,050 | $925 | $850 | $725 | $600 | $550 | $425 | *$1,176* |

* **Colt Carbine AR6951** – 9mm Para. cal., similar to AR6450, except has flat-top receiver and folding rear sight. New 2012.

| MSR $1,248 | $1,075 | $950 | $850 | $725 | $600 | $550 | $425 | |

COLT CARBINE AR6520TRI – 5.56 NATO cal., GIO, 16.1 in. barrel, matte black finish, 30 shot mag., adj. sights. Mfg. 2013 only.

| | $1,050 | $925 | $850 | $725 | $600 | $550 | $425 | *$1,223* |

MSR	100%	98%	95%	90%	80%	70%	60%	Last MSR

COLT CARBINE AR6720/AR6721 – 5.56 NATO cal., GIO, choice of 16.1 in. heavy (AR6721) or light (AR6720) barrel with flash hider and A2 front sight, ribbed aluminum forearm, A3 detachable carrying handle, 20 shot mag., matte black finish, adj. stock, 6.2 or 7.3 lbs. New 2012.

| MSR $1,136 | $950 | $825 | $725 | $650 | $550 | $450 | $400 | |

COLT CARBINE CR6724001 – 5.56 NATO cal., GIO, 24 in. stainless barrel without sights, one-piece flat-top upper receiver with integrated 2/3 length quad Picatinny rail, fixed non-adj. stock, 10 shot mag., black finish, 8.8 lbs. New 2013.

| MSR $1,653 | $1,425 | $1,250 | $1,075 | $975 | $825 | $725 | $575 | |

COLT CARBINE AR6720LECAR – 5.56 NATO cal., GIO, 16.1 in. barrel, Magpul Gen. II rear sight with adj. post front sight, 30 shot mag., matte black finish, 6 lbs. Mfg. 2013 only.

| | $1,250 | $1,075 | $925 | $825 | $675 | $550 | $425 | *$1,468* |

AR15 A4 – 5.56 NATO cal., GIO, 20 in. barrel with flash suppressor, 30 shot mag., flat-top receiver with removable carry handle, A2 style buttstock and front sight, ribbed handguard, Black finish, 7.7 lbs. New 2013.

| MSR $1,270 | $1,075 | $950 | $850 | $725 | $600 | $550 | $425 | |

AR15 A4MP-FDE – 5.56 NATO cal., GIO, 20 in. barrel with flash suppressor, Flat Dark Earth (FDE) furniture, 30 shot mag., 2/3 quad rail with cover, A2 front sight with Magpul Gen. II rear sight, fixed stock, matte black barrel, matte black or FDE (new 2014) receiver finish, 7 1/2 lbs. New 2013.

| MSR $1,304 | $1,095 | $975 | $850 | $725 | $600 | $550 | $425 | |

Add $35 for FDE receiver finish.

AR-15 SCOPE (3X/4X) AND MOUNT – initially offered with 3x magnification scope, then switched to 4x. Disc.

| | $395 | $300 | $240 | $185 | $160 | $130 | $115 | *$344* |

LE901-16S (SP901) – .308 Win. cal., GIO, 16.1 in. heavy full floated barrel with bayonet lug and flash hider, flat-top with Picatinny rail, 1-piece upper receiver with BUIS, ambidextrous controls, flip-up adj. front sight post, flip-up adj. rear sight, 20 shot mag., fixed stock, matte black finish, 9.4 lbs. New 2012.

| MSR $2,544 | $2,275 | $1,995 | $1,700 | $1,550 | $1,250 | $1,025 | $795 | |

LE6900 – 5.56 NATO cal., GIO, 16.1 in. barrel, no sights, 30 shot mag., matte black finish, 6 lbs. Mfg. 2012-mid 2013.

| | $800 | $725 | $625 | $550 | $475 | $425 | $395 | *$899* |

LE6920 – 5.56 NATO cal., GIO, 16.1 in. barrel with bayonet lug and flash hider, adj. front sight post, ribbed handguard, Magpul Gen2 back-up rear sight, flat-top receiver with Picatinny rail, collapsible stock, 30 shot mag., matte black finish, 6.9 lbs. New 2012.

| MSR $1,155 | $995 | $875 | $750 | $675 | $550 | $450 | $400 | |

LE6920AE – 5.56 NATO cal., 16.1 in. barrel, ambidextrous mag. release, bolt catch and fire selector, 30 shot PMag., MBUS rear Gen. 2 sights, collapsible stock, matte black finish, 6.38 lbs. New 2014.

| MSR $1,374 | $1,225 | $1,075 | $925 | $825 | $675 | $550 | $425 | |

LE6920 SOCOM – 5.56 NATO cal., GIO, 16.1 in. barrel with bayonet lug and flash hider, flat-top receiver with BUIS, Knights Armament rail system, 30 shot mag., adj. front sight post, flip-up adj. rear sight, non-adj. tube stock, matte black finish, 7.2 lbs. New 2012.

| MSR $1,602 | $1,395 | $1,220 | $1,050 | $950 | $775 | $625 | $495 | |

LE6920MP-R – 5.56 NATO cal., 16.1 in. barrel, 30 shot PMag., MBUS rear Gen. 2 sight, Troy rail, Magpul MOE furniture, Black furniture, 7.11 lbs. New 2014.

| MSR $1,268 | $1,125 | $985 | $850 | $775 | $625 | $500 | $400 | |

LE6920MP – 5.56 NATO cal., GIO, 16.1 in. barrel with bayonet lug and flash hider, 30 shot mag., adj. front sight post, Magpul Gen2 back up rear sight, collapsible stock, flat-top receiver with Picatinny rail, Magpul MOE furniture in Black (LE6920MP-B), Flat Dark Earth (LE6920MP-FDE), A-TACS Foliage/Green (LE6920MPFG, new 2013), Olive Drab (LE6920MP-OD), USA One Nation Hydro-dipped (LE6920MP-USA, new 2014), or ATAC camo hydro-dipped (LE6920MPATAC, new 2014), 6.9 lbs. New 2012.

| MSR $1,229 | $1,095 | $950 | $825 | $750 | $600 | $500 | $400 | |

Add $87 for USA One Nation Hydro-Dipped Magpul furniture (LE6920-USA, new 2014).

Add $166 for ATACS Foliage/Green finish (LE6920MPFG).

Add $247 for ATAC camo Hydro-Dipped Magpul furniture (LE6920MPATAC, new 2014).

* LE6920MPG – 5.56 NATO cal., similar to LE6920MP, except features Olive Drab Green upper and lower receivers, OD Green Magpul furniture (LE6920MPG-OD) or Black Magpul furniture (LE6920MPG-B, new 2014), vertical grip. New 2012.

| MSR $1,361 | $1,195 | $1,050 | $895 | $825 | $650 | $550 | $425 | |

MSR	100%	98%	95%	90%	80%	70%	60%	Last MSR

* LE6920MPFDE – 5.56 NATO cal., similar to LE6920MP, except features Flat Dark Earth Magpul MOE furniture with vertical grip, Flat Dark Earth finish. New 2012.

| MSR $1,361 | $1,195 | $1,050 | $895 | $825 | $650 | $550 | $425 | |

* LE6920MPFDE-R – 5.56 NATO cal., similar to LE6920MP, except features Flat Dark Earth coated upper and lower receivers, FDE Troy Rail, FDE Magpul furniture. New 2014.

| MSR $1,572 | $1,350 | $1,175 | $1,025 | $925 | $750 | $625 | $475 | |

LE6940 – 5.56 NATO cal., GIO, 16.1 in. full floated barrel with bayonet lug and flash hider, 1-piece upper receiver, 30 shot mag., flip-up adj. front sight post, Magpul Gen2 back-up rear sight, collapsible stock, matte black finish, 6.9 lbs. New 2012.

| MSR $1,546 | $1,295 | $1,150 | $975 | $875 | $725 | $585 | $450 | |

LE6940P – 5.56 NATO cal., GPO, 16.1 in. full floated barrel with bayonet lug and flash hider, 1-piece upper receiver, 30 shot mag., flip-up adj. front sight post, Magpul Gen2 back-up rear sight, collapsible stock, matte black finish, 6.9 lbs. New 2012.

| MSR $2,105 | $1,750 | $1,525 | $1,325 | $1,195 | $975 | $795 | $625 | |

* LE6940MPFG – 5.56 NATO cal., similar to LE6940P, except features ATACS Forest Green Camo. Mfg. 2012-2013.

| | $1,195 | $1,050 | $895 | $825 | $650 | $550 | $425 | *$1,395* |

LE6940AE-3G – 5.56 NATO cal., 16.1 in. barrel, Colt articulating piston system, 30 shot PMag., MBUS rear Gen. 2 sight, Black furniture, 7.2 lbs. New 2014.

| MSR $1,945 | $1,650 | $1,450 | $1,250 | $1,125 | $925 | $750 | $575 | |

LT6720-R – 5.56 NATO cal., 16.1 in. barrel, 30 shot PMag., MBUS front and rear Gen. 2 sights, Troy rail, Black furniture, 6.48 lbs. New 2014.

| MSR $1,321 | $1,125 | $985 | $850 | $775 | $625 | $500 | $400 | |

RIFLES: SEMI-AUTO, RIMFIRE, AR-15 & VARIATIONS

The following models are manufactured by Carl Walther, located in Ulm, Germany, under license from New Colt Holding Corp., and imported/distributed by Umarex USA, located in Fort Smith, AR.

M4 CARBINE – .22 LR cal., GIO, 16.2 in. shrouded barrel, flat-top receiver, 10 or 30 shot mag., detachable carry handle, single left-side safety lever, four position retractable stock, ribbed aluminum handguard, black finish, approx. 6 lbs. Mfg. by Umarex under license from Colt. New 2009.

| MSR $500 | $425 | $375 | $325 | $300 | $275 | $250 | $200 | |

* M4 Ops – .22 LR cal., GIO, 16.2 in. barrel, 10 or 30 shot mag., aluminum upper and lower receiver, black finish, quad tactical rail interface system with elongated Picatinny rail on top of barrel and frame, inline barrel/stock design, cartridge case deflector, muzzle compensator, detachable rear sight, four position collapsible stock, ejection port cover, approx. 6 1/2 lbs. Mfg. by Umarex under license from Colt. New 2009.

| MSR $579 | $495 | $425 | $360 | $330 | $300 | $275 | $225 | |

M16 – .22 LR cal., GIO, 21.2 in. barrel, 10 or 30 shot mag., flat-top receiver with detachable carry handle, fixed stock, elongated ribbed aluminum handguard, removable rear sight, ejection port cover, single left-side safety lever, black finish, approx. 6 1/4 lbs. Mfg. 2009-2010.

| | $575 | $525 | $475 | $425 | $395 | $375 | $350 | *$599* |

* M16 SPR (Special Purpose Rifle) – .22 LR cal., GIO, 21.2 in. barrel, 30 shot mag., black finish, fixed stock, aluminum upper and lower receiver, quad tactical rail interface system with Picatinny rail, flip up front and rear sights, inline barrel/stock design, cartridge case deflector, muzzle compensator. Mfg. 2009-2010.

| | $625 | $575 | $525 | $475 | $450 | $415 | $395 | *$670* |

COMMANDO ARMS

Previous manufacturer located in Knoxville, TN.

Commando Arms became the new name for Volunteer Enterprises in the late 1970s.

CARBINES: SEMI-AUTO

MARK 45 – .45 ACP cal., carbine styled after the Thompson sub-machine gun, 16 1/2 in. barrel.

| | $495 | $425 | $350 | $315 | $280 | $225 | $195 | |

COMMANDO ARMS (NEW MFG.)

Current trademark of shotguns manufactured in Konya, Turkey. Currently imported under private label by Webley & Scott USA.

In addition to shotguns, parent company Komando Av Sa. Tic. Ltd. Sti. also manufactures air rifles.

MSR	100%	98%	95%	90%	80%	70%	60%	Last MSR

SHOTGUNS

Current SxS models include the Estate, Prestige, and the Classic. Current O/U models include the Ultra, Hunter, Elite, Gold, Royal, Osso, and the Classic. Current semi-auto models include the Gold and Classic Series. Current single barrel models include the Star Series. Slide action defense guns include the Pump Series. None of these models are currently imported into the U.S. Please contact the company directly for more information, including U.S. availability and pricing on non-Webley & Scott labeled models (see Trademark Index).

COMPETITIVE EDGE GUNWORKS LLC

Current rifle manufacturer located in Bogard, OR.

RIFLES: BOLT ACTION

Competitive Edge Gunworks LLC builds custom order bolt action rifles based on its patented action. Tactical, Hunting, Varmint, and Competition configurations are available. Please contact the company directly for more information, including available options, delivery time and a price quotation (see Trademark Index).

CONTROLLED CHAOS ARMS

Current custom AR-15 manufacturer located in Baxter, IA.

Controlled Chaos Arms builds and manufactures AR rifles and carbines, and offers other firearm industry products such as suppressors, gunsmithing services, provides finishes and weapon maintenance, as well as gun and rifle training. Please contact the company directly for more information on all their products and services including current models, options, pricing, and availability (see Trademark Index).

RIFLES: SEMI-AUTO

AR-15 CARBINE PACKAGE – 5.56 NATO cal., GIO, 16 in. M4 profile barrel with A2 birdcage flash hider, tactical charging handle assembly, removable rear sight, Gen. 2 six-position stock, standard trigger, Ergo pistol grip, M4 polished feed ramp, includes soft case, takedown tool, and two Extreme Duty 30 shot mags.

MSR $1,300	$1,150	$1,000	$875	$775	$650	$525	$400	

CORE RIFLE SYSTEMS

Current trademark of carbines and rifles manufactured by Good Time Outdoors, Inc. (GTO), located in Ocala, FL.

RIFLES: SEMI-AUTO

GTO Guns manufactures a complete line of AR-15 style carbines and rifles, in addition to uppers in various cals., lower receivers, and related accessories.

CORE15 M4 PISTON RIFLE – 5.56 NATO cal., AR-15 style, utilizes Core15/Adams Arms GPO, 16 in. M4 chrome-lined barrel with A2 flash hider, M1913 Picatinny optics rails, Magpul 20 shot PMag., Tapco 6-position adj. stock, black furniture, M4 style thermoset molded polymer handguards with dual heat shields, A2 pistol grip, flat-top receiver, matte black finish or custom colors also available, marked GTO near gas block, 6.2 lbs. New 2011.

MSR $1,250	$1,095	$950	$850	$695	$575	$495	$375	

CORE15 M4 RIFLE – 5.56 NATO cal., utilizes standard GIO, A-2 elevated front sight, with one Picatinny rail, otherwise similar to Core15 M4 Piston Rifle, 5.9 lbs. New 2011.

MSR $900	$800	$675	$625	$550	$475	$400	$350	

CORE 15 M4 SCOUT RIFLE – 5.56 NATO cal., GIO, 16 in. M4 profile barrel with A-2 flash hider, mil-spec forged upper and lower receiver, stainless steel gas tube, chrome lined stainless steel bolt carrier, 30 shot mag., six-position retractable stock, M4 style thermoset molded polymer hand guards, A-2 pistol grip, Hardcore billet charging handle, Type III Class II hard coat anodized finish, 6 lbs. New 2014.

MSR $800	$725	$625	$550	$495	$425	$375	$325	

CORE15 MOE .300 BLACKOUT RIFLE – .300 AAC Blackout cal., GIO, 16 in. stainless steel barrel with SureFire 3 prong flash hider, forged T6 M4 flat-top upper with internal dry lube and Laser-T markings, V.2 charging handle, forged lower receiver with hard coat anodized finish, M4 feed ramps, and beveled magwell, Magpul MOE 6-position stock and pistol grip, Magpul MOE handguard, Magpul 30 shot PMag., black furniture, 5.8 lbs. New 2013.

MSR $1,240	$1,075	$925	$835	$675	$550	$475	$375	

CORE15 MOE M4 RIFLE – 5.56 NATO cal., 16 in. M4 profile barrel with A2 flash hider, choice of GIO or GOP, 30 shot Magpul mag., forged upper and lower receivers, M4 feed ramps, Magpul MOE handguard, MBUS rear sight, Magpul MOE 6-position stock and pistol grip, oversized trigger guard, black furniture, low profile or Picatinny gas block, 5.9-6.2 lbs. New 2012.

MSR $1,100	$975	$825	$750	$600	$500	$450	$350	

Add $439 for Core15 MOE M4 Piston rifle with gas piston assembly.

MSR	100%	98%	95%	90%	80%	70%	60%	Last MSR

CORE15 MOE MID-LENGTH RIFLE – 5.56 NATO cal., GIO, 18 in. heavy stainless steel barrel polygonal rifling and A2 flash hider, Magpul MOE 6-position and pistol grip, Magpul 30 shot PMag., oversized trigger guard, forged upper receiver with flat-top Picatinny rail, forged lower with M4 feed ramps and beveled magwell, enclosed vent forearm, black furniture, 6.2 lbs. New 2012.

| MSR $1,420 | $1,250 | $1,075 | $975 | $795 | $650 | $495 | $400 | |

* *Core15 MOE Mid-Length Piston Rifle* – 5.56 NATO cal., similar to Core15 MOE Mid-Length rifle, except has GPO, Magpul MOE handguard, MOE Black or Desert Tan (mfg. 2012 only) hardware, 6.9 lbs. New 2012.

| MSR $1,730 | $1,525 | $1,295 | $1,175 | $950 | $775 | $600 | $500 | |

CORE15 TAC M4 RIFLE – 5.56 NATO cal., GIO or GPO, similar to Core15 MOE M4 rifle, except has TAC free floating quad rail, approx. 6 lbs. New 2012.

| MSR $1,240 | $1,075 | $925 | $835 | $675 | $550 | $475 | $375 | |

Add $440 for Core15 TAC M4 Piston rifle with gas piston assembly.

CORE15 TAC M4 UL RIFLE – 5.56 NATO cal., GIO, 16 in. chromemoly M4 profile barrel with A2 flash hider, stainless steel gas tube, A frame front sight base (forged), optional low profile or Picatinny gas block, Magpul MBUS rear sight, 6-position retractable stock with A2 pistol grip, Magpul 30 shot PMag., forged upper receiver with flat-top Picatinny rail and M4 feed ramps, forged lower with beveled magwell, black furniture, 5.2 lbs. New 2013.

| MSR $1,130 | $1,000 | $850 | $775 | $650 | $550 | $450 | $375 | |

CORE15 TAC M4 V.2 RIFLE – 5.56 NATO cal., 16 in. M4 profile barrel with A2 flash hider, choice of GIO or GPO, flat-top model with full length Picatinny rail on top of receiver and quad rail, Magpul ACS six position stock and pistol grip, 30 shot Magpul mag., approx. 6 lbs. Mfg. 2012-2013.

| | $1,150 | $975 | $885 | $725 | $585 | $475 | $400 | *$1,299* |

CORE15 TAC II .300 BLACKOUT RIFLE – .300 AAC Blackout cal., carbine length GIO, 16 in. stainless steel barrel, forged T6 M4 flat-top upper with internal dry lube and Laser-T markings, V.2 charging handle, Gen 2 free float mid-length quad rail, forged lower receiver with anodized finish, M4 feed ramps, and beveled magwell, Magpul ACS 6-position stock, Magpul MOE pistol grip, Magpul 30 shot PMag., low profile gas block, black furniture. New 2013.

| MSR $1,350 | $1,175 | $1,025 | $925 | $750 | $615 | $475 | $400 | |

CORE15 TAC II M4 RIFLE – 5.56 NATO cal., GIO, 16 in. M4 profile barrel with A2 flash hider, forged lower receiver with M4 feed ramps and beveled magwell, forged upper receiver with full length flat-top Picatinny rail, Gen 2 mid-length 2-piece quad rail, Magpul ACS six position stock and pistol grip, 30 shot Magpul mag., V.2 charging handle, oversized trigger, 5.9 lbs. New 2012.

| MSR $1,300 | $1,150 | $1,000 | $900 | $750 | $600 | $475 | $400 | |

CORE15 TAC III RIFLE – 5.56 NATO cal., GIO, 16 in. chromemoly barrel with A2 flash hider, low profile gas block, forged lower receiver with beveled magwell, forged upper with M4 feed ramps, flat-top Picatinny rail, and Gen 2 SS Series free float forearm, stainless steel gas tube, V.2 charging handle, Magpul MOE 6-position stock and pistol grip, Magpul 30 shot PMag., oversized trigger guard, black furniture, 5.9 lbs. New 2013.

| MSR $1,350 | $1,175 | $1,025 | $925 | $750 | $615 | $475 | $400 | |

CORE15 TAC MID-LENGTH RIFLE – 5.56 NATO cal., GIO, 18 in. heavy stainless steel match grade barrel with polygonal rifling and A2 flash hider, forged upper and lower receivers, flat-top receiver with Gen 2 mid-length two piece quad rail system, V.2 charging handle, Magpul UBR buttstock, Magpul MIAD grip, Magpul 30 shot PMag., black finish, 8 lbs. New 2012.

| MSR $1,630 | $1,425 | $1,225 | $1,100 | $895 | $725 | $575 | $475 | |

* *Core15 TAC Mid-Length Piston Rifle* – 5.56 NATO cal., similar to Core15 TAC Mid-Length rifle, except has mid-length GPO, adjustable gas settings, Picatinny flat-top gas block, 8.5 lbs. New 2012.

| MSR $1,850 | $1,625 | $1,395 | $1,250 | $1,025 | $835 | $650 | $525 | |

CORE30 MOE RIFLE – .308 Win. cal., GIO, 16 in. CMV mid-length barrel with SureFire SOCOM 3 Prong flash hider, low profile gas block, Magpul MOE 6-position stock and grip, Magpul 20 shot PMag., Magpul MOE mid-length forearm, aluminum alloy lower and upper with Picatinny rail and Laser engraved T-markings, integral oversized trigger guard, billet charging handle V3, hard coat anodized finish. New 2013.

| MSR $1,900 | $1,675 | $1,425 | $1,300 | $1,050 | $850 | $675 | $550 | |

CORE30 MOE LR RIFLE – .308 Win. cal., GIO, 16 in. CMV mid-length barrel with SureFire SOCOM muzzle brake, low profile gas block, aluminum alloy upper receiver with Picatinny rail, Geissele SSA-E two-stage match trigger, integral oversized trigger guard, MOE mid-length forearm, Magpul MOE rifle stock and grip, billet charging handle V3, anodized finish, Magpul 20 LR PMag. New 2013.

| MSR $2,250 | $1,975 | $1,700 | $1,525 | $1,250 | $1,025 | $800 | $600 | |

MSR	100%	98%	95%	90%	80%	70%	60%	Last MSR

CORE30 TAC RIFLE – .308 Win. cal., GIO, 16 in. CMV mid-length barrel with SureFire SOCOM muzzle brake, low profile gas block, Magpul 20 shot LR PMag., Magpul ACS 6-position stock, Magpul MOE grip, Samson STAR 13.2 in. quad rail, billet charging handle V3, integral oversized trigger guard, hard coat anodized finish, aluminum alloy lower and upper receiver with Picatinny rail and laser engraved T-markings, black furniture. New 2013.

	MSR $2,400	$2,100	$1,800	$1,625	$1,325	$1,075	$850	$725

CORE30 TAC LR RIFLE – .308 Win. cal., GIO, 18 in. stainless steel match grade mid-length barrel with SureFire SOCOM muzzle brake, low profile gas block, Magpul 20 LR PMag., aluminum alloy upper receiver with Picatinny rail, Geissele SSA-E two-stage match trigger, integral oversized trigger guard, Magpul UBR stock, Magpul MIAD grip, APEX Gator grip 15 in. free float modular forearm, billet charging handle V3, anodized finish. New 2013.

	MSR $2,800	$2,450	$2,100	$1,900	$1,550	$1,275	$975	$795

CORONADO ARMS

Current bolt action rifle manufacturer located in Dixon, CA.

CARBINES/RIFLES: SEMI-AUTO

CA-15 CARBINE – 5.56 NATO or 6.8 SPC cal., AR-15 style, GIO, Lothar Walther button rifled barrel, 10 shot mag., Geissele trigger, extended upper and lower receivers, flared and broached magwell, Magpul MOE grip, Magpul STR stock, Black hard anodized finish, 7 1/4 lbs.

	MSR $ 2,275	$2,025	$1,775	$1,525	$1,375	$1,125	$925	$725

CA-15 RIFLE – 5.56 NATO or 6.8 SPC cal., AR-15 style, GIO, Lothar Walther button rifled and fluted bull barrel, 10 shot mag., mid-length gas system, Geissele two-stage trigger, extended upper and lower receivers, flared and broached magwell, Black hard anodized finish, Magpul MOE grip, Magpul PRS stock. New 2014.

	MSR $2,695	$2,425	$2,125	$1,825	$1,650	$1,350	$1,100	$850

CROSS CANYON ARMS

Current bolt action rifle manufacturer located in West Haven, UT.

RIFLES: BOLT ACTION

Cross Canyon Arms manufactures high quality custom bolt action hunting and tactical style rifles chambered for its proprietary Tejas cartridge, as well as short and long actions calibers. There are six base models: the Grand Canyon ($5,213 MSR for short action, $5,288 MSR for long action), Africa Game (dangerous game cals., $5,213 MSR for short action, $5,288 MSR for long action), Grand Teton ($5,213 MSR for short action, $5,288 for long action), Death Valley ($5,213 MSR for short action, $5,288 MSR for long action), Big Cottonwood ($2,750 MSR), and the King's Canyon ($2,395 MSR). A multitude of options and finishes are available. Additionally, a 1,000 Yard Package ($8,995 MSR) and a 1,200 Yard Package ($9,250 MSR) are available. Please contact the company for more information, including options, delivery time, and pricing (see Trademark Index).

CROSSFIRE LLC

Previous manufacturer located in La Grange, GA 1998-2001.

COMBINATION GUNS

CROSSFIRE MK-I – 12 ga. (3 in. chamber) over .223 Rem. cal., unique slide action O/U design allows stacked shotgun/rifle configuration, 18 3/4 in. shotgun barrel with invector chokes over 16 1/4 in. rifle barrel, detachable 4 (shotgun) and 5 (rifle) shot mags., open sights, Picatinny rail, synthetic stock and forearm, choice of black (MK-I) or RealTree 100% camo (MK-1RT) finish, single trigger with ambidextrous fire control lever, 8.6 lbs. Limited mfg. mid-1998-2001.

		$1,295	$1,150	$995	$895	$795	$695	$595	*$1,895*

Add $100 for camo finish.

CRUSADER WEAPONRY

Current manufacturer located in Murray, UT.

PISTOLS: SEMI-AUTO

G20 WRAITH – 10mm cal., SA, SFO, Generation 3 Glock frame, tungsten guide rod, factory weight recoil spring, ghost ring tactical 5 lb. connector (hand fit), extended slide stop, PSI Tac-Rac plug/tool, Trijicon night sights, Slipstream Permanent Pistol Treatment.

	MSR $769	$675	$600	$500	$475	$375	$300	$250

* **G21 Phantom** – .45 ACP cal., otherwise similar to G20 Wraith.

	MSR $769	$675	$600	$500	$475	$375	$300	$250

* **G23 Reaper** – .40 S&W cal., otherwise similar to G20 Wraith.

	MSR $725	$650	$575	$500	$450	$375	$300	$225

MSR	100%	98%	95%	90%	80%	70%	60%	Last MSR

* **G26 Specter** – 9mm Para. cal., otherwise similar to G20 Wraith.

MSR $725 $650 $575 $500 $450 $375 $300 $225

RIFLES: SEMI-AUTO

BROADSWORD – 7.62 NATO cal., AR-10 patterned rifle, 16, 18, 20, or 24 in. polygonal rifled barrel with BattleComp compensator, billet receiver, Apex free floating handguard, accepts Magpul PMags., treated with Slipstream weapon lubricant, includes Plano tactical hard case.

MSR $2,900 $2,600 $2,275 $1,950 $1,775 $1,425 $1,175 $925

GUARDIAN – 5.56 NATO or 6.8 SPC cal., mid-length gas system, 16 in. polygonal rifled barrel with Vortex flash hider, free float handguard, Magpul CTR buttstock, Magpul MIAD grip, Magpul MBUS back-up sights, ambi single point sling attachment, quad rail forend with end cap, Slipstream basic rifle treatment, includes Bulldog hard sided rifle case.

MSR $2,000 $1,800 $1,575 $1,350 $1,225 $1,000 $825 $625

LONGBOW – 7.62 NATO cal., 24 in. polygonal rifled barrel with BattleComp muzzle brake, Magpul PRS stock, DPMS Panther target grip, JP adj. trigger, Apex handguard, Slipstream basic rifle treatment (cerakote finishes and airbrushed camo are optional), rifle gas system with low profile gas block.

MSR $2,700 $2,425 $2,125 $1,825 $1,650 $1,325 $1,100 $850

PALADIN – 5.56 NATO cal., 24 in. match grade polygonal rifled heavy barrel with target crown, rifle length gas system, low profile gas block, APEX free float tube forearm, target grip, JP trigger, Magpul PRS stock, Slipstream treatment, includes hard case.

MSR $2,100 $1,875 $1,650 $1,400 $1,275 $1,025 $850 $650

TEMPLAR – 5.56 NATO cal., AR-15 style, mid-length gas system, 18 in. polygonal rifled barrel with BattleComp compensator, Magpul UBR buttstock, Magpul MIAD grip, Magpul MBUS sights, Apex handguard with top rail, Slipstream basic rifle treatment, Plano tactical hard rifle case.

MSR $2,200 $1,975 $1,725 $1,475 $1,350 $1,075 $900 $700

SHOTGUNS: SLIDE ACTION

WRAITH – 12 ga., adj. rifle sights, extended 6 shot mag., stainless steel magazine follower, Mesa Tactical SureShell shotshell carrier, oversized safety button, Speedfeed stock set, action job, trigger job, Slipstream treatment, Dark Grey cerakote finish (other colors and camo available upon request).

MSR $999 $900 $800 $675 $625 $500 $400 $325

CZECHPOINT INC.

Current distributor located in Knoxville, TN.

Czechpoint Inc. distributes tactical style semi-auto rifles, including a line of AK-47 design carbines/rifles with milled receivers in various configurations, Skorpion pistols (see model listing under Skorpion heading), and revolvers manufactured in the Czech Republic by D-Technik, Alfa Proj., and others. Please contact the company directly regarding current model availability and pricing (see Trademark Index).

NOTES

D SECTION

D&L SPORTS, INC.

Current manufacturer located in Chino Valley, AZ.

Gunsmith Dave Lauck manufactures a complete line of 1911 style custom pistols, AR-15 style semi-auto carbines, and precision bolt action rifles. A wide variety of options and accessories are available. Additionally, D&L offers custom gunsmithing services. Please contact the company directly for more information, including pricing, options, and delivery time (see Trademark Index).

D.A.R. GmbH

Dynamics Arms Research (DAR) manufactures AR-15 style rifles and carbines and is located in Lichentanne, Germany. No current U.S. importation. Please contact the company directly for more information and availability on its models (see Trademark Index).

DPMS FIREARMS (LLC)

Current manufacturer established in 1986 and located in St. Cloud, MN. Previously located in Becker, MN. Previous company name was DPMS, Inc. (Defense Procurement Manufacturing Services, Inc.) DPMS Firearms assembles high quality AR-15 style rifles (including a conversion for .22 cal.), in addition to selling related parts and components. Distributor, dealer, and consumer direct sales.

In December 2007, Cerberus Capital Management acquired the assets of DPMS. The new company name became DPMS Firearms, LLC, and currently is DPMS Firearms.

MSR	100%	98%	95%	90%	80%	70%	60%	Last MSR

PISTOLS: SEMI-AUTO

PANTHER .22 LR PISTOL – .22 LR cal., GIO, blowback action, 8 1/2 in. heavy chromemoly steel barrel, 10 shot mag., black aircraft aluminum flat-top upper receiver, black forged aircraft aluminum lower receiver, phosphate and hard chrome finished bolt and carrier, aluminum trigger guard, ribbed aluminum tubular handguard, no sights, 4 1/4 lbs. Limited mfg. 2006-2007.

	100%	98%	95%	90%	80%	70%	60%	Last MSR
	$775	$700	$625	$550	$475	$425	$375	$850

PISTOLS: SLIDE ACTION

PANTHER PUMP PISTOL – .223 Rem. cal., GIO, 10 1/2 in. threaded heavy barrel, aluminum handguard incorporates slide action mechanism, pistol grip only (no stock), carrying handle with sights, 5 lbs. Disc. 2007.

	100%	98%	95%	90%	80%	70%	60%	Last MSR
	$1,475	$1,200	$1,025	$925	$825	$700	$575	$1,600

RIFLES: SEMI-AUTO

Each new DPMS rifle/carbine comes equipped with two mags. (high cap where legal), a nylon web sling, and a cleaning kit. Post-crime bill manufactured DPMS rifles may have pre-ban features, including collapsible stocks, high capacity mags, and a flash hider/compensator. Models with these features are not available in certain states.

The Panther AR-15 Series was introduced in 1993 in various configurations, including semi-auto and slide action, and feature a tactical design in various barrel lengths and configurations, with a 10 or 30 shot mag.

300 AAC BLACKOUT – .300 AAC Blackout cal., 16 in. heavy chrome lined barrel, equipped with Blackout suppressor adapter, or an inert slipover mock suppressor, AP4 stock, choice of carbine or mid-length handguard, 7-7 1/2 lbs. New 2012.

MSR $1,199		$1,075	$995	$850	$725	$625	$525	$425

COMPACT HUNTER – .308 Win. cal., 16 in. Teflon coated stainless steel barrel, B5 System SOPMOD stock, two-stage match trigger, carbon fiber free float handguard, Hogue rubber pistol grip, 7 3/4 lbs. New 2012.

MSR $1,499		$1,275	$995	$850	$725	$600	$525	$450

LITE HUNTER (PANTHER LITE 308/338) – .243 Win., .260 Rem., .308 Win. or .338 Federal cal., 18 (disc. 2012) or 20 (new 2012) in. free float barrel, no sights, carbon fiber free float hand guard, bipod stud, A3 style flat-top, Picatinny rail, A2 stock (new 2012), Hogue rubber grips, various accessories and options available. New 2009.

MSR $1,499		$1,275	$995	$850	$725	$600	$525	$450

LONG RANGE LITE – .308 Win. cal., 24 in. stainless steel barrel, A2 fixed stock, two-stage match trigger, carbon fiber free float handguard, Hogue rubber pistol grip, 10 1/4 lbs. New 2012.

MSR $1,499		$1,275	$995	$850	$725	$600	$525	$450

MOE WARRIOR – 5.56 NATO cal., 16 in. heavy barrel, Magpul MOE stock, handguard, and pistol grip, back-up sights, sling adapter, enhanced trigger guard, suppressor adapter, Black or Dark Earth Magpul MOE furniture, 7.3 lbs. New 2012.

MSR $1,159		$975	$850	$725	$625	$525	$475	$425

MSR	100%	98%	95%	90%	80%	70%	60%	Last MSR

TAC2 – 5.56 NATO cal., 16 in. barrel with Panther flash hider, Magpul ACS stock, MOE pistol grip, new M111 modular handguard system, utilizes a full rifle length gas system, A2 front and Magpul rear sights, 8 1/2 lbs. New 2012.

| MSR $1,299 | $1,100 | $900 | $775 | $675 | $575 | $500 | $450 | |

TAC20 – .308 Win. cal., 20 in. heavy chromemoly barrel, A2 fixed stock, detachable carry handle, Panther flash hider, 11 1/2 lbs. New 2012.

| MSR $1,299 | $1,100 | $900 | $775 | $675 | $575 | $500 | $450 | |

TPR – 5.56 NATO cal., 20 in. heavy stainless steel barrel with AAC flash hider, M111 modular handguard, Magpul MOE pistol grip and B5 Systems Sopmod stock, two stage trigger, 7 3/4 lbs. New 2012.

| MSR $1,349 | $1,150 | $1,000 | $875 | $750 | $650 | $600 | $550 | |

PANTHER A2/A3 CLASSIC – 5.56 NATO cal., 16 (disc.) or 20 in. heavy barrel, ribbed barrel shroud, A3 stock with detachable carrying handle with sights, or A2 fixed stock 9 lbs.

| MSR $869 | $750 | $650 | $575 | $475 | $425 | $375 | $335 | |

Add $10 for A3 stock.

Add $76 for left-hand variation (Southpaw Panther, disc.)

* **Panther Classic Bulldog** – 20 in. stainless fluted bull barrel, flat-top, adj. buttstock, vented free float handguard, 11 lbs. Disc. 1999.

| | $1,025 | $850 | $725 | $625 | $550 | $475 | $425 | *$1,219* |

PANTHER CARBINE – 5.56 NATO cal., 16 in. heavy barrel with A2 birdcage flash hider, A3 flat-top upper, Pardus 6-position collapsible stock, GlacierGuard handguard, A2 pistol grip, 7.1 lbs.

| MSR $829 | $725 | $625 | $525 | $450 | $400 | $350 | $325 | |

PANTHER 7.62x39mm CARBINE/RIFLE – 7.62x39mm Russian cal., 16 or 20 in. heavy barrel, black Zytel buttstock with trap door assembly, A2 flash hider, A2 pistol grip, 7-9 lbs. Mfg. 2000-2011.

| | $725 | $650 | $575 | $475 | $425 | $375 | $335 | *$850* |

Add $10 for 20 in. barrel.

PANTHER DCM – .223 Rem. cal., 20 in. stainless steel heavy barrel, National Match sights, two-stage trigger, black Zytel composition buttstock, 9 lbs. Mfg. 1998-2003, reintroduced 2006-2012.

| | $965 | $800 | $675 | $595 | $52 | $460 | $415 | *$1,129* |

PANTHER CLASSIC SIXTEEN – 5.56 NATO cal., 16 in. lightweight chromemoly (new 2012) or heavy (disc. 2011) barrel with A2 Birdcage flash hider, adj. sights, black Zytel composition buttstock (disc.) or A2 fixed pistol grip stock, 7.1 lbs. New 1998.

| MSR $859 | $735 | $650 | $575 | $475 | $425 | $375 | $335 | |

Add $55 for Panther Free Float Sixteen with free floating barrel and vent. handguard (disc. 2008).

A1 LITE 20 (PANTHER LITE A1/A3) – 5.56 NATO cal., 16 (disc.) or 20 (new 2007) in. post-ban chromemoly barrel with A2 Birdcage flash hider (new 2007), 1:9 in. twist, non-collapsible fiberite CAR (disc.) or A2 fixed pistol grip stock, choice of forged A1 upper with forward bolt assist or A3 (disc.) carry handle, black Teflon finish, 6-7.3 lbs. New 2002.

| MSR $829 | $700 | $625 | $550 | $450 | $400 | $360 | $325 | |

PANTHER LO-PRO CLASSIC – 5.56 NATO cal., 16 in. bull barrel, A2 fixed stock, features flat-top lo-pro upper receiver with push pin, 7 3/4 lbs. Mfg. 2002-2012.

| | $650 | $600 | $525 | $450 | $400 | $360 | $325 | *$769* |

PANTHER TUBER – 5.56 NATO cal., features 16 in. post-ban heavy free float barrel with full length 2 in. dia. aluminum free float handguard, adj. A2 rear sights. Mfg. 2002-2008.

| | $675 | $600 | $500 | $475 | $375 | $300 | $250 | *$754* |

PANTHER A2 TACTICAL – 5.56 NATO cal., features 16 in. heavy manganese phosphated barrel, standard A2 handguard, 9 3/4 lbs. Mfg. 2004-2013.

| | $735 | $650 | $575 | $475 | $425 | $375 | $335 | *$859* |

PANTHER AP4 CARBINE – 5.56 NATO cal., features 16 in. M4 contour barrel with A2 flash hider, with or w/o attached Miculek compensator, fixed fiberglass reinforced polymer M4 stock, 7 1/4 lbs. Mfg. 2004-2012.

| | $825 | $750 | $625 | $475 | $425 | $375 | $335 | *$959* |

Add $54 for Miculek compensator.

* **Panther AP4 Carbine (Disc.)** – 6.8x43mm SPC or 5.56x45mm cal., 16 in. barrel, collapsible stock, includes carrying handle, 6 1/2 lbs. Disc.

| | $775 | $695 | $600 | $525 | $450 | $400 | $360 | *$904* |

MSR	100%	98%	95%	90%	80%	70%	60%	Last MSR

PANTHER AP4 A2 CARBINE – 5.56 NATO cal., 16 in. chromemoly steel heavy barrel with A2 flash hider, standard A2 front sight assembly, A2 fixed carry handle and adj. rear sight, forged aircraft aluminum upper and lower receiver, hard coat anodized teflon coated black AP4 six position telescoping fiber reinforced polymer stock, GlacierGuard handguard, 7.1 lbs. New 2006.

| MSR $959 | $815 | $725 | $650 | $550 | $475 | $425 | $375 | |

PANTHER A2 CARBINE "THE AGENCY" – 5.56 NATO cal., 16 in. chromemoly steel barrel with A2 flash hider, A3 flat-top forged receiver, two-stage trigger, tactical charging handle, package includes Surefire quad-rail and flashlight, EoTech and "Mangonel" rear sights, Ergo Suregrip forearm and collapsible stock, supplied with two 30 shot mags., 7 lbs. Mfg. 2007-2012.

| | $1,725 | $1,575 | $1,400 | $1,250 | $1,025 | $900 | $775 | *$2,069* |

LR-6.5 (PANTHER 6.5) – 6.5 Creedmoor cal., 24 in. stainless steel free float bull barrel, single rail gas block, no sights, ribbed aluminum free float tube handguard, bipod stud, A3 style flat-top, black Teflon coated, standard A2 black Zytel mil spec stock, A2 pistol grip, 11.3 lbs. New 2009.

| MSR $1,239 | $1,050 | $875 | $750 | $650 | $575 | $500 | $450 | |

PANTHER 6.8mm CARBINE/RIFLE – 6.8x43mm Rem. SPC cal., 16 (new 2007) or 20 in. chromemoly manganese phosphated steel barrel with A2 flash hider, standard A2 front sight assembly, A3 flat-top upper receiver with detachable carry handle and adj. rear sight, aluminum aircraft alloy lower receiver, black standard A2 Zytel mil spec stock with trap door assembly, A2 handguard, includes two 25 shot mags., approx. 9 lbs. Mfg. 2006-2011.

| | $875 | $795 | $700 | $600 | $500 | $425 | $375 | *$1,019* |

Add $10 for 20 in. barrel.

PANTHER 6.8 SPCII HUNTER – 6.8x43mm Rem. SPC cal., 18 in. steel barrel with Miculek compensator, aluminum A3 flat-top with forward assist, black Zytel skeletonized A2 stock, mid-length carbine fiber free-floating forearm tube, 7.65 lbs. Mfg. 2011-2012.

| | $1,050 | $950 | $825 | $725 | $625 | $550 | $495 | *$1,269* |

PANTHER RECON MID-LENGTH CARBINE – 5.56 NATO or 7.62 NATO (new 2012) cal., 16 in. stainless steel heavy barrel with AAC blackout flash hider, flat-top aluminum upper receiver with Magpul BUIS front and rear sights, mid-length quad rail free floating forearm tube, Magpul MOE stock and pistol grip, 7.7 lbs. New 2011.

| MSR $1,129 | $950 | $795 | $675 | $595 | $525 | $460 | $415 | |

Add $430 for .308 Recon (new 2012).

PANTHER LBR CARBINE – 5.56 NATO cal., 16 in. lightweight stainless barrel with A2 flash hider, muzzle brake, flat-top receiver with integral Picatinny rail, Magpul MOE stock with A2 pistol grip, vent free floating handguard with front upper Picatinny rail, 7 1/4 lbs. New 2011.

| MSR $979 | $825 | $725 | $625 | $495 | $450 | $395 | $350 | |

This model is also available in a DIVAS Edition with 16 in. chromemoly barrel and Leopard print especially for women (new 2012).

PRAIRIE PANTHER – 20 in. heavy fluted free float barrel, flat-top, vented handguard, 8 3/4 lbs. Disc. 1999.

| | $795 | $725 | $625 | $550 | $475 | $425 | $375 | *$959* |

PRAIRIE PANTHER (CURRENT MFG.) – .223 Rem. or 6.8 SPC (black finish only) cal., 20 in. stainless steel fluted heavy barrel, target crown, carbon fiber free float tube, no sights, hard anodized finish, choice of black with carbon fiber handguard (new 2011), King's Desert Shadow (Desert), King's Snow Shadow (new 2011) or Mossy Oak Brush (Brush) camo coverage, A3 Picatinny rail flat-top, tactical charging handle assembly, Magpul winter trigger guard, skeletonized black Zytel mil spec stock with trap door assembly, A2 pistol grip stock, two-stage trigger, approx. 7.1 lbs. New 2010.

| MSR $1,239 | $1,050 | $925 | $825 | $725 | $625 | $525 | $425 | |

Add $30 for 6.8 SPC cal. (black finish only).
Add $50 for camo finishes.

ARCTIC PANTHER – .223 Rem. cal., 20 in. barrel, similar to Prairie Panther, except has white powder coat finish on receiver and aluminum handguard, railed gas block, 9 lbs. New 1997.

| MSR $1,129 | $960 | $825 | $700 | $600 | $525 | $460 | $415 | |

PANTHER BULL – .223 Rem. cal., features 16 (Sweet 16), 20, or 24 in. stainless free float bull barrel, flat-top, aluminum forearm, A2 fixed stock, aluminum pistol grip, A2 handguard, railed gas block/optics ready, 7 3/4 - 9 1/2 lbs.

| MSR $939 | $795 | $700 | $600 | $525 | $450 | $400 | $360 | |

Add $40 for 20 in. barrel (Panther Bull 20).
Add $60 for 24 in. barrel (Panther Bull 24).

* ***Panther Bull Classic*** – .223 Rem. cal., features 20 in. long, 1 in. bull barrel, adj. sights, 10 lbs. Mfg. 1998-2008.

| | $775 | $700 | $600 | $525 | $450 | $400 | $360 | *$910* |

Add $200 for SST lower.

MSR	100%	98%	95%	90%	80%	70%	60%	Last MSR

* Panther Bull Twenty-Four Special – .223 Rem. cal., features 24 in. stainless fluted barrel, adj. A2 buttstock with sniper pistol grip, 10 1/4 lbs. New 1998.

| MSR $1,229 | $1,050 | $875 | $750 | $625 | $525 | $460 | $415 | |

* Panther Super Bull – .223 Rem. cal., 16, 20, or 24 in. extra heavy free float bull barrel, flat-top receiver, handguard; approx. 11 lbs. Mfg. 1997-98, 24 in. model reintroduced during late 2004, disc. 2006.

| | $1,025 | $835 | $725 | $600 | $525 | $460 | $415 | $1,199 |

* Panther Super Bull 24 – features 24 in. extra heavy stainless steel bull barrel (1 1/8 in. diameter barrel), flat-top, hi-rider upper receiver, skeletonized A2 buttstock, 11 3/4 lbs. Mfg. 1999-2004.

| | $1,025 | $835 | $725 | $600 | $525 | $460 | $415 | $1,199 |

PANTHER PARDUS – .223 Rem. cal., 16 in. stainless steel free float bull barrel, integrated compensator, titanium nitride plated steel bolt and carrier, three rail extruded upper receiver, aluminum alloy upper and lower receiver, Teflon coated tan or black six position telescoping fiber reinforced polymer stock, curved and serrated buttplate, four-rail aluminum handguard, no sights, includes two 30 shot mags., 8.1 lbs. Mfg. 2006-2008.

| | $1,350 | $1,150 | $950 | $800 | $675 | $575 | $525 | $1,600 |

PANTHER MK-12 5.56 NATO – 5.56 NATO cal., 18 in. stainless heavy free float barrel with flash hider, features one-piece four rail tube and six long rail covers, A3 flat-top receiver, 5-position Sopmod collapsible stock with tactical pistol grip, two-stage trigger, two 30 round mags., Midwest Industry flip-up sights, 8 3/4 lbs. New 2007.

| MSR $1,649 | $1,395 | $1,125 | $950 | $800 | $700 | $600 | $500 | |

PANTHER MK-12 7.62 NATO – 7.62 NATO cal., 18 in. stainless steel heavy barrel, flash hider, Midwest Industries flip up rear sight, gas block with flip up front sight, A3 Picatinny rail flat-top, aluminum lower receiver, integral trigger guard, Magpul CTR adj. stock, Hogue rubber grip with finger grooves, two stage match trigger, hard anodized black finish, four rail free float tube, six rail covers, approx. 9.6 lbs. New 2010.

| MSR $1,799 | $1,525 | $1,225 | $975 | $850 | $725 | $625 | $525 | |

PANTHER SDM-R – .223 Rem. cal., 20 in. heavy stainless free float barrel with A2 flash hider, features four rail aluminum tube, pistol grip stock, National Match front sight, Harris bipod with rail adapter, two 30 shot mags., 8.85 lbs. Mfg. 2007-2008.

| | $1,175 | $1,050 | $925 | $825 | $725 | $650 | $575 | $1,404 |

PANTHER 20TH ANNIVERSARY – .223 Rem. cal., 20 in. stainless steel fluted bull barrel, phosphated steel bolt and carrier, hi-rider forged high polished chrome upper and lower receiver with commemorative engraving, chrome plated charging handle, semi-auto trigger group, aluminum trigger guard and mag. release button, A2 black Zytel mil spec stock with trap door assembly and engraved DPMS logo, no sights, vented aluminum handguard, includes two 30 shot mags., approx. 9 1/2 lbs. Limited mfg. of 100 rifles in 2006.

| | $1,795 | $1,575 | $1,350 | $1,225 | $985 | $825 | $625 | $1,995 |

PANTHER RACE GUN – .223 Rem. cal., 24 in. stainless steel barrel with Hot Rod hand guard, IronStone steel and aluminum stock with rubber buttplate and brass weights, 16 lbs. Mfg. 2001-2008.

| | $1,450 | $1,250 | $1,050 | $950 | $850 | $725 | $600 | $1,724 |

PANTHER SINGLE SHOT – 5.56 NATO cal., 20 in. barrel, A2 black Zytel stock and handguard, single shot only w/o magazine, 9 lbs. Disc. 2008.

| | $695 | $600 | $550 | $495 | $445 | $395 | $350 | $819 |

AP4 .22 CAL. CARBINE – .22 LR cal., GIO, 16 in. barrel, GlacierGuard M4 handguard, A2 pistol grip and flash hider, AP4 stock with detachable carry handle, 6 1/2 lbs.

| MSR $935 | $775 | $700 | $600 | $525 | $450 | $395 | $325 | |

.22 CAL. BULL CARBINE – .22 LR cal., GIO, 16 in. bull barrel, aluminum handguard, A2 pistol grip and flash hider, fixed A2 stock, no sights, 7.3 lbs.

| MSR $935 | $775 | $700 | $600 | $525 | $450 | $395 | $325 | |

PANTHER .22 RIFLE – .22 LR cal., AR-15 style receiver, GIO, 16 in. bull barrel, black Teflon metal finish, Picatinny rail, black Zytel A2 buttstock, 7.8 lbs. Mfg. 2003-2008.

| | $675 | $595 | $525 | $475 | $425 | $375 | $335 | $804 |

PANTHER DCM .22 LR RIFLE – .22 LR cal., GIO, 20 in. fluted stainless steel H-Bar barrel with 1:16 in. twist, A2 upper receiver with National Match sights, black teflon finish, A2 stock and handguards, also available with optional DCM handguard system. Mfg. 2004-2008.

| | $850 | $750 | $650 | $550 | $475 | $425 | $375 | $994 |

MSR	100%	98%	95%	90%	80%	70%	60%	Last MSR

PANTHER AP4 .22 LR RIFLE – .22 LR cal., GIO, features 16 in. M4 contoured barrel with 1:16 in. twist, M4 handguards and pinned carstock, A3 flat-top upper receiver, detachable carry handle with A2 sights and black teflon finish, 6 1/2 lbs. Mfg. 2004-2008.

	100%	98%	95%	90%	80%	70%	60%	Last MSR
	$750	$675	$600	$500	$450	$400	$350	*$894*

This model was also available in a pre-ban configuration for law enforcement.

PANTHER LR-.308 – .308 Win. cal., 24 in. free float bull barrel with 1:10 in. twist, ribbed aluminum forearm tube, aircraft alloy upper/lower, A2 fixed pistol grip stock, black Teflon finish, 11 1/4 lbs. New mid-2003.

MSR $1,199	$995	$875	$750	$650	$575	$500	$450	

* **Panther LR-.308B** – .308 Win. cal., similar features as the Long Range Rifle, except has 18 in. chromemoly bull barrel and carbine length aluminum handguard. Mfg. late 2003-2012.

	$995	$875	$750	$650	$575	$500	$450	*$1,189*

* **Panther LR-.308T** – 7.62 NATO cal., similar features as the .308B, except has 16 in. H-Bar barrel. Mfg. 2004-2012.

	$995	$875	$750	$650	$575	$500	$450	*$1,189*

* **Panther LR-.308 AP4** – 7.62 NATO cal., similar to Panther .308 Long Range, except has AP4 six position telescoping fiber reinforced polymer stock. Disc. 2012.

	$1,095	$950	$825	$725	$650	$600	$550	*$1,299*

* **Panther LR-.308 Classic** – 7.62 NATO cal., similar to Panther LR-308, except has 20 in. barrel, A3 style flat-top receiver and removeable carry handle. New mid-2008.

MSR $1,199	$995	$875	$750	$650	$575	$500	$450	

PANTHER LR-308C – .308 Win. cal., 20 in. heavy steel free float barrel, features A3 flat-top receiver with detachable carrying handle, standard A2 front sight assembly, four rail standard length tube, two 19 shot mags., 11.1 lbs. Mfg. 2007-2008.

	$1,050	$925	$825	$725	$650	$600	$550	*$1,254*

PANTHER LRT-SASS – 7.62 NATO cal., 18 in. stainless steel contoured barrel with Panther flash hider, A3 style flat-top upper receiver solid alumnium lower receiver, AR-15 trigger group, ambi-selector, JP adj. trigger, black waterproof Vltor Clubfoot carbine 5 position (disc.) or Magpul stock, vented handguard and Panther tactical pistol grip, Magpul sights, approx. 11 1/2 lbs. New 2006.

MSR $2,179	$1,850	$1,625	$1,350	$1,125	$950	$825	$700	

PANTHER MINI-SASS – 5.56 NATO cal., 18 in. stainless steel fluted barrel with Panther flash hider, forged A3 flat-top upper receiver, aircraft aluminum alloy lower receiver, aluminum trigger guard, Magpul PRS stock, tactical pistol grip, Magpul sights, includes Harris bipod, 10 1/4 lbs. New 2008.

MSR $1,649	$1,395	$1,200	$950	$800	$700	$600	$550	

PANTHER LR-30S – .300 RSUM cal., 20 in. stainless steel free float fluted bull barrel, aluminum upper and lower receiver, hard coat anodized teflon coated black skeletonized synthetic stock, integral trigger guard, ribbed aluminum tube handguard, includes two 4 shot mags., nylon web sling and cleaning kit. Mfg. 2004-2008.

	$1,050	$925	$825	$725	$650	$575	$500	*$1,255*

PANTHER LR-204 – .204 Ruger cal., 24 in. fluted stainless steel bull barrel, no sights, A3 flat-top forged upper and lower receiver, semi-auto trigger group, standard A2 black Zytel mil spec stock with trap door assembly, includes two 30 shot mags., 9 3/4 lbs. New 2006.

MSR $1,059	$895	$800	$700	$600	$500	$450	$395	

PANTHER LR-243 – .243 Win. cal., 20 in. chromemoly steel heavy (disc. 2012) or lightweight (Lite Hunter) free float barrel, no sights, raised Picatinny rail, aluminum upper and lower receiver, standard AR-15 trigger group, skeletonized black Zytel mil spec stock with trap door assembly, ribbed aluminum free float handguard, includes two 19 shot mags., 10 3/4 lbs. Mfg. 2006-2013.

	$1,275	$995	$850	$725	$600	$525	$450	*$1,499*

PANTHER LR-260 SERIES – .260 Rem. cal., 18 (mfg. 2007-2012, LR-260L), 20 (LR-260H, Lite Hunter) or 24 (LR-260) in. stainless steel fluted bull barrel, no sights, raised Picatinny rail, thick walled aluminum upper receiver, solid lower receiver, standard AR-15 trigger group, integral trigger guard, A2 black Zytel stock with trap door assembly, includes two 19 shot mags., 11.3 lbs. New 2006.

MSR $1,239	$1,050	$950	$825	$725	$650	$600	$550	

Add $260 for 18 in. barrrel (LR-260L) with skeletonized stock, Miculek compensator and JRD trigger (disc. 2012).

PANTHER ORACLE – 5.56 NATO or 7.62 NATO cal., 16 in. chromemoly heavy barrel, A2 flash hider, gas block with single rail, no sights, GlacierGuards oval carbine length handguard, A3 Picatinny flat-top, hard anodized black finish, integral trigger guard, Pardus six position telescoping stock with cheekpiece, A2 pistol grip, curved and serrated buttplate, multiple sling slots, approx. 8.3 lbs. New 2010.

MSR	100%	98%	95%	90%	80%	70%	60%	Last MSR

* Panther Oracle 5.56 NATO cal.

MSR $739 — $625, $550, $495, $450, $400, $350, $295

Add $30 for stainless steel barrel.

Add $80 for quad rail handguard.

Add $110 for ATACS Oracle Carbine (includes ATACS camo coverage), new 2011.

* Panther Oracle 7.62 NATO cal.

MSR $1,099 — $950, $850, $750, $675, $600, $525, $450

Add $90 for ATACS Oracle Carbine (includes ATACS camo coverage), new 2011.

PANTHER SPORTICAL – 5.56 NATO or 7.62 NATO cal., 16 in. chromemoly heavy or lite contour barrel, single rail gas block, A2 flash hider, various rails and accessories. New mid-2008.

MSR $729 — $650, $575, $500, $450, $400, $350, $295

Add $300 for 7.62 NATO cal.

PANTHER REPR – 7.62 NATO cal., 18 in. chromemoly (disc.) or 20 in. fluted stainless steel free float barrel, Gem Tech flash hider/suppressor, micro gas block, A3 style flat-top upper receiver, milled aluminum lower receiver, hard coat anodized coyote brown finish, removable hinged trigger guard, Picatinny rail, four rail tube handguard, Magpul Precision Rifle Stock, Hogue rubber grip with finger grooves, 9 1/2 lbs. New 2009.

MSR $2,589 — $2,195, $1,925, $1,725, $1,400, $1,200, $975, $850

PANTHER RAPTR CARBINE – 5.56 NATO cal., 16 in. chromemoly steel contoured barrel, 30 shot mag., flash hider, A2 front sight, Mangonel flip up rear sight, Ergo Z-Rail two piece four rail handguard, Crimson Trace vertical grip with integrated light and laser combination, A3 Picatinny rail flat-top, hard coat anodized black finish, dust cover, aluminum trigger guard, AP4 six position telescoping polymer stock, Ergo Ambi-Sure grip, 8.2 lbs. Mfg. 2010-2011.

$1,395, $1,150, $950, $825, $725, $600, $500 — *$1,649*

PANTHER CSAT TACTICAL – 5.56 NATO cal., 16 in. chromemoly steel contoured barrel, 30 shot mag., A2 front sight assembly with A2 front sight post, detachable rear sight, four rail free float tube, A3 Picatinny rail flat-top, aluminum lower receiver, Magpul CTR adj. stock, Magpul MIAD pistol grip, 7.8 lbs. Mfg. 2010-2012.

$1,495, $1,250, $1,025, $850, $725, $625, $550 — *$1,799*

PANTHER CSAT PERIMETER – 5.56 NATO cal., similar to Tactical, except has 16 in. heavy barrel, approx. 8 lbs. Mfg. 2010-2011.

$1,495, $1,250, $1,025, $850, $725, $625, $550 — *$1,799*

PANTHER 3G1 – 5.56 NATO or 7.62 NATO (new 2012) cal., 18 in. stainless standard or heavy barrel, 30 shot mag., Miculek compensator, no sights, VTAC modular handguard, bipod stud, A3 Picatinny rail flat-top, black anodized finish, aluminum trigger guard, JP adj. trigger group, Magpul CTR adj. stock, Hogue rubber pistol grip, 7 3/4 lbs. New 2010.

MSR $1,299 — $1,095, $900, $775, $650, $575, $500, $450

Add $400 for 7.62 NATO cal. (new 2012).

PANTHER 3G2 – 5.56 NATO cal., similar to 3G1, except has 16 in. barrel, Magpul STR buttstock, M111 modular handguard, Ergo rubber pistol grip, and Magpul Gen. 2 BUS sights, 7 lbs., 2 oz. New 2013.

MSR $1,239 — $1,050, $900, $775, $650, $575, $500, $450

RIFLES: SLIDE ACTION

PANTHER PUMP RIFLE – .223 Rem. cal., GIO, 20 in. threaded heavy barrel with flash hider, aluminum handguard incorporates slide action mechanism, carrying handle with sights, bayonet lug, designed by Les Branson, 8 1/2 lbs. Disc. 2009.

$1,395, $1,175, $995, $875, $725, $575, $495 — *$1,700*

DSA INC.

Current manufacturer, importer, and distributor of semi-auto rifles and related components located in Barrington, IL. Previously located in Round Lake and Grayslake, IL.

DSA Inc. is a manufacturer of FAL design and SA58 style rifles for both civilian and law enforcement purposes (L.E. certificates must be filled out for L.E. purchases). Until recently, DSA, Inc. also imported a sporterized Sig 550 rifle.

PISTOLS: SEMI-AUTO

SA58TAC – 7.62x51 cal., 8 in. barrel, based on SA58 FAL design, 20 shot mag., Type 1 or 2 receiver, Trident flash hider, black glass filled nylon furniture, Para extended scope mount, lightweight alloy lower receiver, SAW pistol grip, folding cocking handle, includes sling and hard case. New 2013.

MSR $1,695 — $1,475, $1,275, $1,150, $950, $775, $625, $550

MSR	100%	98%	95%	90%	80%	70%	60%	Last MSR

RIFLES: BOLT ACTION

DS-MP1 – .308 Win. cal., 22 in. match grade barrel, Rem. 700 action with Badger Ordnance precision ground heavy recoil lug, trued bolt face and lugs, hand lapped stainless steel barrel with recessed target crown, black McMillan A5 pillar bedded stock, Picatinny rail, includes test target guaranteeing 1/2 MOA at 100 yards, black or camo Duracoat finish, 11 1/2 lbs. Mfg. 2004-2009.

	$2,500	$2,150	$1,800	$1,550	$1,250	$1,000	$850	$2,800

RIFLES: SEMI-AUTO

The SA-58 rifles listed are available in either a standard DuraCoat solid (OD Green or GrayWolf), or optional camo pattern finishes - add $250 for camo. Patterns include: Underbrush, Woodland Prestige, Desert MirageFlage, Urban MirageFlage, Wilderness MirageFlage, OD MirageFlage, Black Forest MirageFlage, Winter Twig, Tiger Stripe, Advanced Tiger Stripe, Vietnam Tiger Stripe, Marsh, AmStripe, Urban Camo, Belgian Camo, ACU, Afghan Camo, Multicolor or Mossy Oak Breakup (disc.). DSA Inc. makes three types of forged steel receivers, and they are distinguished by the machining cuts on Types I and II, and no cuts on Type III.

Add $300-$350 for camo, depending on pattern.

SA58 STANDARD RIFLE/CARBINE – .308 Win. cal., FAL design using high precision CNC machinery, 16 (carbine), 18 (carbine), 19 (disc. 2012), 21 (standard or bull), or 24 in. (bull only, disc. 2009) steel or stainless steel cyrogenically treated barrel, black synthetic stock, pistol grip (standard 2001) attached to frame, 10 or 20 shot mag., 8.7-11 lbs.

MSR $1,700	$1,495	$1,250	$1,050	$875	$775	$675	$575	

Add $250 for stainless steel barrel.
Add $150 for bull barrel.

* **SA58 Standard Rifle Predator** – .243 Win., .260 Rem., or .308 Win. cal., Type 1 or Type 3 receiver, 16 or 19 in. barrel with target crown, green fiberglass furniture, Picatinny rail, 5 or 10 shot mag., approx. 9 lbs. Mfg. 2003-2012.

	$1,525	$1,275	$1,050	$875	$775	$675	$575	$1,750

* **SA58 Standard Rifle Gray Wolf** – .300 WSM (disc. 2005) or .308 Win. cal., Type 1 or Type 3 receiver, 21 in. bull barrel with target crown, gray aluminum handguard, synthetic stock and adj. pistol grip, Picatinny rail, 5 or 10 shot mag., approx. 13 lbs. Mfg. 2003-2010.

	$1,950	$1,750	$1,450	$1,250	$1,050	$875	$775	$2,295

* **SA58 Tactical Carbine** – similar to SA58 Standard Rifle, except has 16 1/4 in. barrel, 8 1/4 lbs. Mfg. 1999-2012.

	$1,495	$1,250	$1,050	$875	$775	$675	$575	$1,700

Add $275 for Para folding stock.
Add $200 for SA58 Lightweight Carbine with aluminum receiver components (disc. 2004).
Add $250 for SA58 Stainless Steel Carbine (included scope mount through 2000).
Subtract 5% if w/o fluted barrel (became standard 2009).

* **SA58 Carbine** – .308 Win. cal., 16 1/4 or 18 in. threaded barrel, Type I or II receiver, standard synthetic or X-Series buttstock, pistol grip, threaded flash hider, lightweight alloy lower. New 2011.

MSR $1,700	$1,495	$1,250	$1,050	$875	$775	$675	$575	

* **SA58 Standard Para. Rifle/Carbine** – .308 Win. cal., 16 (carbine, fluted or non-fluted), 18 (carbine), or 21 in. threaded barrel, Type I or II receiver, standard synthetic, X-Series buttstock (disc. 2012), or Para. folding stock, pistol grip, threaded flash hider, lightweight alloy lower. New 2011.

MSR $1,975	$1,775	$1,575	$1,350	$1,150	$950	$750	$625	

* **SA58 Medium Contour** – .223 Rem. or .308 Win. cal., 21 in. medium contour barrel, Type I or II receiver, standard synthetic or X-Series buttstock, pistol grip, threaded flash hider, lightweight alloy lower. New 2011.

MSR $1,700	$1,495	$1,250	$1,050	$875	$775	$675	$575	

Add $150 for .223 Rem. cal.

* **SA58 Standard Rifle Collectors Series** – .308 Win. cal., configurations included the Congo ($1,970 - last MSR), Para Congo ($2,220 - last MSR), and the G1 ($2,000 - last MSR). Mfg. 2003-2010.

Add $230 for Dura-coat finish.

* **SA58 Standard Rifle T48 Replica** – .308 Win. cal., 10 or 20 shot fixed mag., stripper clip top cover, cryogenically treated barrel, wood furniture, replica Browning flash hider. Imported 2002-2008.

	$1,500	$1,275	$1,050	$850	$725	$625	$525	$1,795

* **SA58 SPR (Special Purpose Rifle)** – .308 Win. cal., Type I forged receiver, 19 in. fully fluted premium barrel, match grade speed trigger, rail interfaced handguard, extended extreme duty scope mount, SPR side folding adj. stock, SAW pistol grip, Versa-Pod bipod and BUIS included, detachable 10 or 20 shot mag., includes adj. sling, hard case, 13.8 lbs. New 2009.

MSR $4,795	$4,375	$3,950	$3,500	$3,100	$2,750	$2,450	$2,150	

MSR	100%	98%	95%	90%	80%	70%	60%	*Last MSR*

* SA58 Spartan – .308 Win. cal., Type 1 non-carry handle cut receiver with Spartan Series logo, aluminum lower receiver, 16 or 18 in. standard weight barrel with Steyr short flash hider or YHM Phantom flashider, DSA custom shop speed trigger, tactical para. rear sight, post front sight, standard synthetic buttstock, military grade handguard, black finish or black with OD Green furniture, three detachable 20 shot mags., adj. sling and case. New 2009.

| MSR $2,595 | $2,295 | $1,995 | $1,750 | $1,550 | $1,325 | $1,125 | $925 | |

Add $200 for Spartan TAC model with 16 in. medium contour fluted barrel, side folding stock, and A2 flash hider.

STG58 AUSTRIAN FAL – .308 Win. cal., features choice of DSA Type I or Type II upper receiver, carry handle, steel lower receiver, rifle has long flash hider, carbine has Steyr short flash hider, steel handguard with bipod cut, metric FAL buttstock and pistol grip, adj. front and rear sight, 10 or 20 shot detachable mag., 10 - 10.4 lbs. Imported 2006-2008, reimported 2011-2012.

| | $995 | $895 | $800 | $700 | $600 | $500 | $400 | *$1,150* |

Add $50 for carbine.
Add $290 for rifle with folding stock (disc. 2008).
Add $340 for carbine with folding stock (disc. 2008).

IMBEL 58 – .308 Win. cal., Imbel FAL standard rifle with 21 in. original Imbel barrel, DSA Type 1 carry handle cut receiver, original flash hider, U.S. humpback stock and handguard. Mfg. 2011-2012.

| | $875 | $775 | $650 | $525 | $450 | $375 | $325 | *$995* |

DS-S1 – .223 Win. cal., GIO, 16, 20, or 24 in. match chamber stainless steel free float bull barrel, A2 buttstock, aluminum handguard, Picatinny gas block sight base, forged lower receiver, NM two-stage trigger, forged flat-top upper receiver, optional fluted barrel, variety of Duracoat solid or camo finishes available, 8-10 lbs. Mfg. 2004-2005.

| | $825 | $750 | $625 | $525 | $425 | $375 | $325 | *$950* |

DS-CV1 CARBINE – 5.56 NATO cal., GIO, 16 in. chromemoly D4 barrel with press on mock flash hider, fixed Shorty buttstock, D4 handguard and heatshield, forged front sight base, forged lower receiver, forged flat-top upper receiver, variety of Duracoat solid or camo finishes available, 6 1/4 lbs. Mfg. 2004-2005.

| | $775 | $700 | $625 | $550 | $500 | $450 | $400 | *$850* |

DS-LE4 CARBINE – 5.56 NATO cal., GIO, 14 1/2 or 16 in. chromemoly D4 barrel with threaded A2 flash hider, collapsible CAR buttstock, D4 handguard with heatshield, forged lower receiver, forged front sight base with bayonet lug, forged flat-top upper receiver, Duracoat solid or camo finish, 6.15 or 6 1/4 lbs. Mfg. 2004-2012.

Please contact the factory directly for pricing on this model.

The 14 1/2 in. model was for military/law enforcement only.

DS-AR SERIES – .223 Rem cal., GIO, available in a variety of configurations including carbine and rifle, standard or bull barrels, various options, stock colors and features. Mfg. 2006-2008.

| | $875 | $775 | $675 | $575 | $495 | $450 | $395 | *$1,000* |

Add $243 for SOPMOD Carbine. Add $30 for 1R Carbine. Add $150 for 1V Carbine. Add $130 for S1 Bull rifle. Add $500 for DCM rifle. Add $30 for XM Carbine.
Add $1,395 - $1,515 for monolithic rail platform. Add $675 for Z4 GTC Carbine with corrosion resistant operating system.

ZM-4 SERIES – .223 Rem. cal., GIO, 16 or 20 in. barrel, forged upper and lower receiver, various configurations, black finish, detachable magazine, hard case. New 2004.

* ZM-4 Standard – .223 Rem. cal., GIO, 20 in. chromemoly heavy barrel with A2 flash hider, mil-spec forged lower receiver and flat-top upper, front sight base with lug, standard handguard with heat shield, fixed A2 buttstock, 9 lbs.

| MSR $788 | $695 | $595 | $500 | $450 | $395 | $350 | $295 | |

Add $24 for A2 carry handle (mfg. 2011-2012)
Add $62 for chrome lined barrel.

* ZM-4 Mid-Length – similar to Standard, except has 16 in. barrel and M4 six position collapsible stock, 6.65 lbs.

| MSR $834 | $750 | $625 | $550 | $475 | $425 | $395 | $350 | |

Add $13 for fluted barrel. Add $55 for A2 carry handle (disc.). Add $102 for Magpul MOE pistol grip and ACE FX fixed skeleton stock (new 2013).

* ZM-4 Standard Carbine – similar to ZM-4 Mid-Length, except has 16 in. non-fluted barrel, also available in OD Green, A2 carry handle.

| MSR $831 | $750 | $625 | $550 | $475 | $425 | $395 | $350 | |

Add $219 for flat-top receiver.

* ZM-4 Standard MRP – .223 Rem. cal., GIO, 16 or 18 in. chrome lined (16 in.) or stainless steel free float barrel, mil-spec forged lower receiver, LMT MRP forged upper receiver with 20 1/2 in. full length quad rail, LMT enhanced bolt, dual extractor springs, collapsible CAR stock, detachable 30 shot mag., A2 flash hider. Disc. 2010.

| | $2,275 | $1,995 | $1,750 | $1,550 | $1,325 | $1,125 | $950 | *$2,695* |

Add $100 for stainless steel barrel.

MSR	100%	98%	95%	90%	80%	70%	60%	Last MSR

* **ZM-4 Gas Piston CQB** – .223 Rem. cal., GPO, 16 in. chrome lined free floating barrel, Mil-spec forged lower receiver, CQB forged upper receiver, one piece bolt carrier, quick change barrel system, collapsible CAR stock, detachable 30 shot mag., A2 flash hider. Disc. 2010.

| | $2,425 | $2,150 | $1,625 | $1,475 | $1,300 | $1,125 | $950 | $2,870 |

* **ZM-4 Spartan** – .223 Rem. cal., GIO, 16 in. fluted chromemoly barrel, Yankee Hill Machine Phantom flash hider, mil-spec forged lower and flat-top upper receiver, forged front sight base with lug, M4 collapsible stock, Magpul trigger guard, Robar NP3 bolt, carrier, and charging handle, Hogue pistol grip, LEO model with Chip McCormick match trigger, SOPMOD collapsible stock, and two-piece rail system became standard 2013, 6.65 lbs.

| MSR $1,455 | $1,225 | $1,075 | $925 | $825 | $700 | $575 | $450 | |

* **ZM-4 .300 Blackout** – .300 Blackout cal., GIO, 16 in. blue or stainless steel barrel, matte black finish, A3 flat-top alloy receiver, forged front sight base with bayonet lug, M4 handguard with heat shield, Trident flash hider, Hogue pistol grip, six position collapsible stock. New 2013.

| MSR $853 | $750 | $625 | $550 | $475 | $425 | $395 | $350 | |

Add $20 for stainless.

* **ZM-4 Enhanced Carbine** – 5.56 NATO cal., GIO, 16 in. enhanced MK16 fluted M4 barrel, matte black finish, alloy flat-top receiver, forged front sight base with bayonet lug, ambidextrous selector switch, YHM muzzle brake, Magpul MOE pistol grip, enhanced Delta ring, Magpul MOE handguard, six position MOE stock. New 2013.

| MSR $929 | $825 | $700 | $600 | $525 | $450 | $395 | $350 | |

RPD TRADITIONAL RIFLE – 7.62x39 cal., 20 1/2 in. barrel, billet machined receiver, belt-fed, wood stock, includes two 100 shot belt and drum sets, carry bag, sling, hard case, approx. 17 lbs. New 2013.

| MSR $2,100 | $1,775 | $1,575 | $1,325 | $1,100 | $950 | $800 | $675 | |

RPD CARBINE – 7.62x39 cal., 17 1/2 in. fluted barrel, billet machined receiver, belt-fed, quad rail handguard, SAW style pistol grip, fully adj. AR15 style stock, lightweight alloy lower trigger frame, includes two 100 shot belt and drum sets, carry bag, sling, hard case, approx. 14 lbs. New 2013.

| MSR $2,850 | $2,395 | $2,100 | $1,800 | $1,575 | $1,300 | $1,050 | $900 | |

DAEWOO

Previous commercial firearms manufacturer located in Korea. Previous limited importation by Century International Arms, located in Delray Beach, FL. Previous importation included Kimber of America, Inc. until 1997, Daewoo Precision Industries, Ltd., until mid-1996, located in Southampton, PA, and previously distributed by Nationwide Sports Distributors 1993-96. Previously imported by KBI, Inc. and Firstshot, Inc., both located in Harrisburg, PA, and B-West located in Tucson, AZ.

Daewoo made a variety of firearms available for commercial use, and most of these were never imported into the U.S.

PISTOLS: SEMI-AUTO

DH380 – .380 ACP cal., DA/SA, styled after the Walther PPK. Imported 1995-96.

| | $330 | $285 | $260 | $235 | $210 | $185 | $165 | $375 |

DH40 – .40 S&W cal., otherwise similar to DP51, 32 oz. Imported 1995-disc.

| | $325 | $270 | $245 | $225 | $200 | $185 | $170 | |

DP51 STANDARD/COMPACT – 9mm Para. cal., "fast action" allows lowering hammer w/o depressing trigger, 3 1/2 (DP51 C or S, disc.) or 4.1 (DP51) in. barrel, 10 (C/B 1994), 12* (.40 S&W), or 13* (9mm Para.) shot mag., 3-dot sights, tri-action mechanism (SA, DA, or fast action), ambidextrous manual safety, alloy receiver, polished or sand-blasted black finish, 28 or 32 oz., includes lockable carrying case with accessories. Recently imported in various configurations circa 1991-2009.

| | $315 | $265 | $240 | $220 | $200 | $185 | $170 | |

Add 10% for DP51 Compact (disc.).

DP52 – .22 LR cal., DA/SA, similar to DH380, 3.8 in. barrel, alloy receiver, 10 shot mag., blue finish, 23 oz. Imported 1994-96.

| | $320 | $275 | $225 | $200 | $180 | $165 | $150 | $380 |

RIFLES: SEMI-AUTO

MAX II (K2) – .223 Rem. cal., 18 in. barrel, gas operated rotating bolt, folding fiberglass stock, interchangeable mags. with the Colt M16, 7 lbs. Importation disc. 1986.

| | $950 | $875 | $800 | $725 | $625 | $550 | $475 | $609 |

MAX I (K1A1) – similar to Max II (K2), except has retractable stock. Importation disc. 1986.

| | $1,050 | $925 | $850 | $750 | $650 | $575 | $500 | $592 |

MSR	100%	98%	95%	90%	80%	70%	60%	Last MSR

DR200 – .223 Rem. cal., sporterized stock, 10 shot mag. Imported 1995-96.

	100%	98%	95%	90%	80%	70%	60%	Last MSR
	$650	$550	$475	$425	$395	$375	$350	*$535*

DR300 – 7.62x39mm cal., with or w/o thumbhole stock. Importation disc.

	100%	98%	95%	90%	80%	70%	60%
	$650	$550	$475	$425	$395	$375	$350

DAKOTA ARMS, INC.

Current manufacturer and previous importer established in 1986, located in Sturgis, SD. Dealer and direct sales through manufacturer only. This company is not affiliated with Dakota Single Action Revolvers.

On June 5, 2009, Remington Arms Company purchased Dakota Arms, Inc.

Dakota Arms Inc. also owned the rights to Miller Arms and Nesika actions. Please refer to these individual sections for more information.

Dakota Arms models listed below are also available with many custom options - please contact the factory directly for availability and pricing. Left-hand actions are available on all bolt action rifles at no extra charge. Actions (barreled or unbarreled) may also be purchased separately. Please contact the manufacturer directly for individual quotations.

RIFLES: BOLT ACTION

DAKOTA LONGBOW T-76 TACTICAL – .300 Dakota Mag., .300 Win. Mag. (new 2006), .330 Dakota Mag., .308 Win. (new 2006), .338 Lapua Mag., or .338 Dakota Mag. cal., 28 in. stainless barrel, long range tactical design, black synthetic stock with adj. comb, includes Picatinny optical rail, Model 70 style trigger, matte finish metal, controlled round feeding, and deployment kit, 13.7 lbs. Mfg. 1997-2009.

	100%	98%	95%	90%	80%	70%	60%	Last MSR
	$4,300	$3,760	$3,225	$2,925	$2,365	$1,935	$1,505	*$4,795*

DAKOTA SCIMITAR TACTICAL – .308 Win. or .338 Lapua cal., 24 or 27 in. match grade chromemoly barrel, 2nd generation Longbow with solid top receiver, long and short action, one-piece bolt handle, oversized claw extraction system, true controlled round feed, three postition safety, non-glare matte black finish, synthetic stock, optical rail. Mfg. 2008-2009.

	100%	98%	95%	90%	80%	70%	60%	Last MSR
	$5,850	$5,120	$4,385	$3,980	$3,215	$2,630	$2,045	*$6,295*

DAN WESSON

Current trademark manufactured by Dan Wesson Firearms beginning 2005, and located in Norwich, NY. Distributed beginning 2005 by CZ-USA, located in Kansas City, KS. Previously manufactured by New York International Corp. (NYI) located in Norwich, NY 1997-2005. Distributor and dealer sales.

PISTOLS: SEMI-AUTO

Until 2005, Dan Wesson manufactured a complete line of .45 ACP 1911 style semi-auto pistols. Previously manufactured models include: Seven (last MSR was $999), Seven Stainless (last MSR was $1,099), Guardian (last MSR was $799), the Guardian Deuce (last MSR was $799), the Dave Pruit Signature Series (last MSR was $899), and the Hi-Cap (last MSR was $689).

ELITE SERIES HAVOC – .38 Super or 9mm Para. cal., 4 1/4 in. barrel with compensator, SA, all steel construction, designed for Open IPSC/USPSA Division, C-More sights, 21 shot mag., black finish, 38 oz. New 2011.

MSR $4,299	$3,700	$3,225	$2,800	$2,400	$2,000	$1,650	$1,400

ELITE SERIES MAYHEM – .40 S&W cal., SA, Limited IPSC/USPSA, 6 in. bull barrel with tactical rail, 18 shot mag., adj. fiber optic sights, black finish, 38 3/4 oz. New 2011.

MSR $3,899	$3,400	$2,950	$2,550	$2,100	$1,800	$1,500	$1,325

ELITE SERIES TITAN – 10mm cal., 4 3/4 in. bull barrel, SA, 18 shot mag., all steel construction, lower frame tactical rail, black finish, tritium sights, 26 oz. New 2011.

MSR $3,829	$3,350	$2,925	$2,550	$2,100	$1,800	$1,500	$1,325

GUARDIAN – 9mm Para., .38 Super (new 2014), or .45 ACP (new 2011) cal., 8 or 9 shot mag., 4 1/4 in. barrel, SA, black light alloy commander frame, bobtail mainspring housing, tritium sight, checkered cocobolo grips, 28.8 oz. New 2010.

MSR $1,558	$1,350	$1,150	$950	$825	$725	$625	$525

Add $61 for .45 ACP cal. (new 2011).

RZ-45 HERITAGE – .45 ACP cal. only, 8 shot mag., 5 in. barrel, stainless steel frame, SA, fixed night sights, manual thumb safety, rubber grips, 38 1/2 oz. New 2009.

MSR $1,298	$1,075	$900	$800	$700	$600	$500	$400

SPECIALIST – .45 ACP cal., SA, 5 in. barrel, features serrated rib and tritium night sights, G10 VZ Operator II grips, two 8 shot mags., frame has lower Picatinny rail, matte stainless or black duty finish. New 2012.

MSR $1,558	$1,350	$1,150	$950	$825	$725	$625	$525

Add $312 for black duty finish.

MSR	100%	98%	95%	90%	80%	70%	60%	Last MSR

VALOR – .45 ACP cal., 8 shot mag., 5 in. barrel, SA, choice of black ceramic coated finish or matte stainless steel (new 2010), slimline VZ or G10 grips, adj. (disc.) or Heinie Ledge Straight 8 (new 2010) tritium night sights, 38 oz. New 2008.

| MSR $1,701 | $1,525 | $1,225 | $975 | $850 | $725 | $625 | $550 | |

Add $311 for black finish.

* ***Valor Bobtail Commander*** – similar to Valor, except has 4 1/4 in. barrel, and bobtail commander style features, 35.2 oz. New 2010.

| MSR $1,766 | $1,525 | $1,225 | $975 | $850 | $725 | $625 | $550 | |

Add $311 for black finish.

REVOLVERS: DOUBLE ACTION

Dan Wesson has also manufactured a variety of revolver packages that were available by special order only.

MODEL 715 SMALL FRAME SERIES – .357 Mag. cal., 6 shot, stainless steel, 2 1/2, 4, 6, 8, or 10 in. heavy barrel with VR and full ejector shroud, rubber wraparound finger groove grips, interchangeable barrels. Mfg. 2002-2004.

| | $625 | $550 | $475 | $425 | $375 | $325 | $275 | $709 |

Add $50 for 4 in., $90 for 6 in., $150 for 8 in., or $190 for 10 in. barrel.

This model was also available as a pistol pack with 4 barrels and case. MSR was $1,699.

DANE ARMORY LLC

Previous AR-15 style rifle manufacturer located in Mesa, AZ until 2013.

RIFLES: SEMI-AUTO

All rifles included a case and manual.

DCM SERVICE AR-15 – .223 Rem. cal., National Match barrel and chromed bolt carrier, free float forend tube, F-marked front sight base, fixed synthetic stock, matte black finish, A4 configuration with carry handle, pistol grip. Disc. 2013.

| | $1,575 | $1,375 | $1,175 | $1,075 | $865 | $710 | $550 | $1,850 |

HIGH POWER MATCH AR – .223 Rem. or .308 Win. cal., heavy barrel, Dane Armory exclusive free float handguard, Sinclair or Centra sight options, wide variety of stocks, handguard, and accessories. Disc. 2013.

Base price on this model was $1,950.

PISTOL CALIBER AR – .223 Rem. or .308 Win. cal., heavy barrel, Dane Armory exclusive free float handguard, Sinclair or Centra sight options, wide variety of stocks, handguard, and accessories. Disc. 2013.

Base price on this model was $2,150.

DANIEL DEFENSE

Current AR-15 style rifle and related components manufacturer located in Savannah, GA.

CARBINES: SEMI-AUTO

In addition to the models listed below, Daniel Defense can build a custom rifle based on customer specifications. Please contact the company directly for this service (see Trademark Index). Daniel Defense also offers a complete line of tactical accessories and parts.

DDM4 CARBINE SERIES – 5.56 NATO cal., GIO, 16 in. chrome lined barrel, A2 birdcage flash hider, 10, 20, or 30 shot mag., mil-spec enhanced mag. well, A4 feed ramp, A1.5 BUIS sight, pinned "F" marked front sight base, Omega X rails, Magpul 5 position collapsible buttstock, A2 vertical grip, includes plastic case.

* ***DDM4V1*** – 5.56 NATO cal., GIO, 16 in. chrome lined barrel with flash suppressor, standard or lightweight (new 2012) barrel, original Daniel Defense rifle, 6 lbs.

| MSR $1,799 | $1,595 | $1,375 | $1,125 | $925 | $825 | $725 | $625 | |

* ***DDM4V2*** – 5.56 NATO cal., GIO, 16 in. chrome lined barrel, similar to DDM4V1, except lightweight configuration with Omega X 7.0 rail system, also available with lightweight carbine barrel (DDM4V2LW). Mfg. 2011-2013.

| | $1,575 | $1,375 | $1,125 | $925 | $800 | $700 | $600 | $1,759 |

* ***DDM4V3*** – 5.56 NATO or 6.8 SPC (new 2012) cal., GIO, 16 in. chrome lined barrel, similar to DDM4V2, except has mid-length gas system, 9 in. free float Omega quad rail, also available with lightweight carbine barrel (DDM4V3LW).

| MSR $1,799 | $1,595 | $1,375 | $1,125 | $925 | $825 | $725 | $625 | |

* ***DDM4V4*** – 5.56 NATO cal., 16 in. hammer forged carbine barrel, pinned low profile gas block, Omega X 9.0 rail system, available in lightweight profile (disc. 2011), no sights, fixed sights, or flip up sights. Disc. 2013.

| | $1,475 | $1,275 | $1,050 | $900 | $775 | $650 | $550 | $1,639 |

Add $120 for fixed sights.
Add $299 for flip up sights (disc. 2011).

MSR	100%	98%	95%	90%	80%	70%	60%	Last MSR

* **DDM4V5** – 5.56 NATO or .300 Blackout (new mid-2012) cal., GIO, 16 in. hammer forged carbine barrel, 30 shot mag., pinned low profile gas block, Omega X 12.0 rail system, available in lightweight profile, no sights, fixed sights, or flip up sights, approx. 6 lbs.

| MSR $1,689 | $1,525 | $1,500 | $1,125 | $925 | $825 | $725 | $575 | |

Add $120 for fixed sights.
Subtract $80 for 5.56 NATO cal.
Add $299 for flip up sights (disc. 2011).

* **DDM4V7** – 5.56 NATO or 6.8 SPC cal., GIO, 16 (5.56 NATO) or 18 (6.8 SPC) in. standard or lightweight barrel with flash hider, with or w/o sights, flat-top receiver, full length top Picatinny rail, forearm features three modular Picatinny rails that are moveable, 30 shot mag. New 2012.

| MSR $1,559 | $1,395 | $1,275 | $1,050 | $875 | $750 | $650 | $550 | |

Add $110 for fixed sights.

DDM4 ISR 300 – .300 AAC Blackout cal., GIO, 10.3 in. barrel or 16.2 in. barrel with permanently attached pinned and welded, integral stainless steel suppressor, 30 shot mag., modular 12 in. float rail, flared mag well, Mil spec upper receiver with M4 feed ramps, Magpul MOE stock, A2 grip, Black finish, 7 lbs., 10 oz. New 2013.

| MSR $3,199 | $2,850 | $2,300 | $1,950 | $1,700 | $1,450 | $1,225 | $1,050 | |

All NFA rules apply to this firearm.

DD CARBINE SERIES – 5.56 NATO or 6.8mm SPC cal., GIO, 16 in. chrome lined barrel, similar to DDM4 Series, except mil-spec buttstock. New 2010.

* **DDXV/XV EZ** – GIO, 16 in. cold hammer forged barrel, "F" marked fixed front sight base, flared mag well on lower receiver, Magpul enhanced trigger guard, M16 bolt carrier group, rear receiver QD sling swivel attachment, with (XV EZ) or w/o (XV, disc. 2011) EZ CAR 7.0 rail system and A1 fixed rear sight. Disc. 2013.

| | $1,275 | $1,100 | $950 | $825 | $700 | $600 | $500 | $1,419 |

Add $68 for EZ CAR 7.0 rail system.
Add $129 for XVM model with mid-length barrel.

* **DDV6.8** – 6.8mm SPC cal., GIO, 16 in. cold hammer forged mid-length barrel, Omega X 9.0 VFG and A1.5 fixed rear sight. Disc. 2011.

| | $1,375 | $1,100 | $975 | $850 | $725 | $625 | $525 | $1,537 |

DAUDSONS ARMOURY

Current manufacturer located in Peshawar, Pakistan. No current U.S. importation.

Daudsons Armoury's origins stretch back over two centuries dealing in the sporting arms and defense firearms trade. The company provides firearms for the armed forces of Pakistan as well as the Defense Ministry.

Daudsons Armoury manufactures the DSA line of 12 ga. shotguns. There are four basic models: DSA Shooter, DSA Commando, DSA Sure Shot, and the DSA Security. All are manufactured from high grade alloy steel, with black synthetic stocks and forearms, and all parts are completely interchangeable. Daudsons also manufactures double barrel rifles and a semi-auto .22 cal. rifle. For more information on these guns, including pricing and U.S. availability, please contact the company directly (see Trademark Index).

DEL-TON INCORPORATED

Current rifle manufacturer located in Elizabethtown, NC. Dealer sales. Previously distributed until 2011 by American Tactical Imports, located in Rochester, NY.

CARBINES/RIFLES: SEMI-AUTO

Del-Ton manufactures a wide variety of AR-15 style carbines/rifles. Many options, accessories, and parts are also available. Please contact the company for more information, including current availability and options (see Trademark Index). All rifles includes a hard case, two mags., and buttstock cleaning kit.

A2 CARBINE – .223 Rem. cal., GIO, 16 in. heavy chromemoly barrel, fixed A2 stock, CAR handguard with single heat shield, A2 flash hider, black furniture, carry handle, includes sling. Disc. 2012.

| | $695 | $625 | $550 | $500 | $450 | $395 | $350 | $750 |

A2 DT-4 CARBINE – .223 Rem. cal., GIO, 16 in. chromemoly barrel, six position M4 stock, 30 shot mag., CAR handguard with single heat shield, A2 flash hider, black furniture, includes sling. Disc. 2012.

| | $695 | $625 | $550 | $500 | $450 | $395 | $350 | $750 |

ALPHA 220H – 5.56 NATO cal., GIO, 20 in. chromemoly heavy profile barrel with threaded muzzle and A2 flash hider, forged aluminum T6 upper and lower receiver, 30 shot mag., A2 configuration with rear sight, rifle length handguard with single heat shield, standard A2 Black Zytel buttstock with trap door assembly, A2 grip, Black furniture, 8.2 lbs.

| MSR $793 | $700 | $625 | $550 | $500 | $450 | $395 | $350 | |

MSR	100%	98%	95%	90%	80%	70%	60%	Last MSR

ALPHA 320H – 5.56 NATO cal., similar to Alpha 220H, except features M4 feed ramps, no sights, and A3 flat-top receiver, 8 lbs.

MSR $788	$695	$625	$550	$500	$450	$395	$350	

ALPHA 320G (STANDARD GOVERNMENT PROFILE RIFLE) – 5.56 NATO cal., GIO, 20 in. chromemoly standard or heavy profile barrel with threaded muzzle and A2 flash hider, Government profile, M4 feed ramps, A2 reinforced Zytel buttstock, A2 grip, 30 shot mag., standard length handguard with single heat shield, black furniture, forged aluminum upper and lower receivers, A3 flat-top or A2 upper with carry handle, includes sling.

MSR $788	$695	$625	$550	$500	$450	$395	$350	

ALPHA 320P – 5.56 NATO cal., GIO, post ban rifle, 20 in. heavy chromemoly barrel with crowned muzzle, M4 feed ramps, 10 shot mag., fixed A2 reinforced Zytel buttstock with trap door assembly, A2 grip, Black furniture, rifle length handguard with single heat shield, flat-top A3 or A2 upper with carry handle, includes sling, 7.8 lbs. Disc. 2013.

	$695	$625	$550	$500	$450	$395	$350	$780

DTI-4 CARBINE – .223 Rem. cal., GIO, 16 in. chromemoly M4 profile barrel, six position M4 stock, 30 shot mag., CAR handguard with single heat shield, A2 flash hider, black furniture, A3 flat-top or A2 upper with carry handle, includes sling. Disc. 2012.

	$695	$625	$550	$500	$450	$395	$350	$750

DTI-15 CARBINE – .223 Rem. cal., GIO, 16.1 in. barrel, 30 shot mag., hard anodized black oxide finish, adj. six position collapsible stock with M249-style pistol grip, fixed front sights, approx. 7 3/4 lbs. Mfg. mid-2011-2012.

	$750	$650	$575	$525	$465	$400	$350	$859

DTI EVOLUTION – 5.56 NATO cal., GIO, lightweight profile 16 in. chrome-lined barrel with threaded muzzle and A2 flash hider, low profile gas block, M4 feed ramps, Samson Evolution free float forend with accessory rails, Samson quick flip dual aperture rear sight, Samson folding front sight, forged aluminum upper and lower receiver, A3 flat-top with white T marks, hard coat anodized, two-stage trigger, Magpul CTR stock, buffer tube, and Magpul MOE + grip, Black or Dark Earth furniture, 6 1/2 lbs. New 2013.

MSR $1,299	$1,125	$975	$850	$725	$625	$525	$425	

DTI EXTREME DUTY – 5.56 NATO cal., GIO, 16 in. hammer forged chrome lined barrel with threaded muzzle/A2 flash hider, Black finish, T6 aluminum upper and lower receiver, M4 carbine handguard with double heat shield, M4 5-position reinforced fiber buttstock with Mil-Spec buffer tube, A2 grip, Samson quick flip dual aperture rear sight, 6.4 lbs. New 2012.

MSR $1,100	$950	$825	$700	$600	$525	$475	$375	

DTI TRX MID-LENGTH RIFLE/CARBINE – 5.56 NATO cal., GIO, 16 in. barrel, A2 flash hider, threaded muzzle, Troy TRX battlerail handguard, 30 shot mag., and BattleAx CQB adj. stock, Black or Tan finish, 7.2 lbs. Mfg. 2012 only.

	$1,075	$950	$825	$700	$600	$500	$425	$1,250

DT SPORT CARBINE – 5.56 NATO cal., GIO, lightweight profile 16 in. barrel with threaded muzzle/A2 flash hider, forged aluminum A3 flat-top upper receiver with forward assist, forged alum. lower with A2 grip, M4 6 position buttstock with commercial buffer tube, oval ribbed handguard with A2 front sight and single heat shield, 10 or 30 shot mag., manganese phosphated under front sight base, 5.8 lbs. New 2011.

MSR $707	$650	$575	$525	$475	$425	$395	$335	

* **DT Sport OR** – 5.56 NATO cal., similar to DT Sport Carbine, except is Optics Ready, so does not include the A2 front sight tower, manganese phosphated under low pro gas block, 5.6 lbs. New 2013.

MSR $707	$650	$575	$525	$475	$425	$395	$335	

ECHO 216 (A2 LIGHTWEIGHT) – 5.56 NATO cal., GIO, 16 in. chromemoly M4 barrel with threaded muzzle and A2 flash hider, forged T6 aluminum upper and lower receiver, carry handle, 30 shot mag., carbine length handguard with single heat shield, A2 configuration with rear sight, M4 5-position stock with buffer tube, A2 grip, Black furniture, 6.6 lbs. New 2012.

MSR $793	$700	$625	$550	$500	$450	$395	$350	

* **Echo 216F** – 5.56 NATO cal., similar to Echo 216, except features A2 reinforced Zytel buttstock with trap door assembly, 6.8 lbs. Mfg. 2012-2013.

	$695	$625	$550	$500	$450	$395	$350	$788

* **Echo 216H** – 5.56 NATO cal., similar to Echo 216, except features 16 in. chromemoly heavy barrel, A2 reinforced Zytel buttstock and A2 grip, trap door assembly, 7 lbs.

MSR $793	$700	$625	$550	$500	$450	$395	$350	

MSR	100%	98%	95%	90%	80%	70%	60%	Last MSR

ECHO 314/15 – 5.56 NATO cal., GIO, 14 1/2 in. M4 profile barrel with pinned YHM Phantom flash hider making it 16 in. total length, M4 feed ramps, forged aluminum T6 upper and lower receiver, A3 flat-top upper with white T marks, M4 6-position reinforced fiber buttstock with buffer tube, A2 grip, carbine length handguard with single heat shield, 30 shot mag., Black furniture, 6 lbs. New 2012.

| MSR $814 | $725 | $625 | $550 | $500 | $450 | $395 | $350 | |

ECHO 316 – 5.56 NATO cal., forged aluminum upper and lower receiver, hard coat anodized mil-spec matte black finish, 16 in. barrel with threaded muzzle and Manganese phosphated finished, A2 flash hider, aluminum triggerguard, M4 front sight base, M4 five position reinforced fiber buttstock with mil-spec buffer tube, carbine length aluminum delta ring single heat shield handguards, A2 grip, A3 flat-top. New 2014.

| MSR $788 | $695 | $625 | $550 | $500 | $450 | $395 | $350 | |

ECHO 316L LIGHTWEIGHT CARBINE – 5.56 NATO cal., GIO, 16 in. chromemoly barrel with A2 flash hider and threaded muzzle, forged T6 aluminum upper and lower receiver, carbine length handguard with single heat shield, M4 six position reinforced carbon fiber buttstock, 5.8 lbs. Mfg. 2012 only.

| | $695 | $625 | $550 | $500 | $450 | $395 | $350 | *$750* |

ECHO 316H – 5.56 NATO cal., GIO, 16 in. chromemoly heavy barrel with threaded muzzle and A2 flash hider, M4 feed ramps, carbine length handguard with single heat shield, front sight base, T6 aluminum upper and lower, A3 flat-top with white T marks, M4 5-position reinforced carbon buttstock with buffer tube, A2 grip, black furniture, 6.6 lbs. New 2012.

| MSR $788 | $695 | $625 | $550 | $500 | $450 | $395 | $350 | |

* ***Echo 316H OR*** – 5.56 NATO cal., similar to Echo 316H, except has single rail gas block and is optics ready, 6.4 lbs. New 2013.

| MSR $859 | $775 | $675 | $575 | $525 | $475 | $425 | $375 | |

ECHO 316 MOE – 5.56 NATO cal., GIO, 16 in. chromemoly heavy profile barrel, threaded muzzle, A2 flash hider, A3 flat-top, Magpul MOE polymer stock with buffer tube and Magpul MOE grip, 30 shot PMag, forged T6 aluminum upper and lower receiver, Magpul MOE carbine length handguard with heat resistant construction, OD Green, Black or Tan finish, 6.8 lbs. New 2012.

| MSR $858 | $775 | $675 | $575 | $525 | $475 | $425 | $375 | |

ECHO 316P – 5.56 NATO cal., GIO, M4 Post Ban rifle, 16 in. chromemoly barrel with pinned YHM muzzle brake, 10 shot mag., M4 feed ramps, forged aluminum T6 upper and lower receivers, A3 flat-top upper, pinned M4 reinforced carbon fiber buttstock with commercial buffer tube, black furniture, carbine length handguard with single heat shield, 6.9 lbs.

| MSR $816 | $725 | $625 | $550 | $500 | $450 | $395 | $350 | |

ECHO 316PF (POST-BAN CARBINE) – 5.56 NATO cal., GIO, A3 Post Ban rifle, 16 in. heavy profile chromemoly barrel with target crowned muzzle, no flash hider, 10 shot mag., M4 feed ramps, fixed A2 reinforced Zytel buttstock with trap door assembly, A2 grip, black furniture, carbine length handguard with single heat shield, forged aluminum T6 upper and lower receivers, A3 upper, 6.9 lbs. Disc. 2013.

| | $695 | $625 | $550 | $500 | $450 | $395 | $350 | *$780* |

M4 CARBINE – .223 Rem. cal., GIO, 16 in. chromemoly barrel, 30 shot mag., black furniture, six position M4 stock, CAR handguard with single heat shield, A2 flash hider, includes sling. Disc. 2012.

| | $695 | $625 | $550 | $500 | $450 | $395 | $350 | *$750* |

Add $9 for Tapco Model with Tapco buttstock, SAW grip, polymer mags., and short vertical grip (new 2012).

SIERRA 216H (A2 MID-LENGTH CARBINE) – 5.56 NATO cal., GIO, 16 in. chromemoly barrel with threaded muzzle and A2 flash hider, heavy profile, forged aluminum T6 upper and lower receiver, carry handle, 30 shot mag., A2 configuration with rear sight, A2 reinforced Zytel buttstock with trap door assembly, A2 grip, mid-length handguard with single heat shield, Black furniture, 7.4 lbs.

| MSR $793 | $700 | $625 | $550 | $500 | $450 | $395 | $350 | |

SIERRA 316H (MID-LENGTH CARBINE) – 5.56 NATO cal., GIO, 16 in. mid-length chromemoly barrel with A2 flash hider, heavy profile, 30 shot mag., black furniture, six postition M4 stock, A2 grip, forged aluminum T6 upper and lower receiver, A3 flat-top, mid-length handguard with single heat shield, M4 feed ramps, 7 lbs.

| MSR $788 | $695 | $625 | $550 | $500 | $450 | $395 | $350 | |

SIERRA 316 MOE – 5.56 NATO cal., GIO, 16 in. chromemoly barrel, threaded muzzle, A2 flash hider, A3 flat-top, Magpul MOE polymer stock and Magpul MOE grip and trigger guard, 30 shot PMag, forged T6 aluminum upper and lower receiver, Magpul MOE mid-length handguard with heat resistant polymer construction, OD Green, Black or Dark Earth finish, 7.1 lbs. New 2012.

| MSR $858 | $775 | $675 | $575 | $525 | $475 | $425 | $375 | |

SIERRA 316P – 5.56 NATO cal., GIO, A3 mid-length post ban rifle, 16 in. chromemoly barrel with pinned YHM muzzle

MSR	100%	98%	95%	90%	80%	70%	60%	*Last MSR*

brake, 10 shot mag., M4 feed ramps, pinned M4 reinforced carbon fiber buttstock with commercial buffer tube, black furniture, mid-length handguard with single heat shield, A3 flat-top, forged aluminum T6 upper and lower receivers, 6.9 lbs. Disc. 2013.

	100%	98%	95%	90%	80%	70%	60%	Last MSR
	$800	$700	$600	$550	$450	$375	$300	*$806*

DEMRO

Previous manufacturer located in Manchester, CT.

RIFLES: SEMI-AUTO

T.A.C. MODEL 1 RIFLE – .45 ACP or 9mm Luger cal., blow back operation, 16 7/8 in. barrel, open bolt firing system, lock-in receiver must be set to fire, also available in carbine model.

	100%	98%	95%	90%	80%	70%
	$650	$595	$525	$475	$425	$395	$360

XF-7 WASP CARBINE – .45 ACP or 9mm Luger cal., blow back operation, 16 7/8 in. barrel.

	100%	98%	95%	90%	80%	70%
	$650	$595	$525	$475	$425	$395	$360

Add $45 for case.

DERYA HUNTING ARMS

Current manufacturer established in 2000, and located in Konya, Turkey. Distributed by Societe Fayoumi, located in Beirut, Lebanon.

Derya Hunting Arms currently manufactures semi-auto, slide action, and single shot shotguns in various configurations, in addition to air rifles and tactical accessories. Currently, there is no U.S. importation of this trademark. Please contact the distributor directly for more information, values, and availability (see Trademark Index).

DESERT ORDNANCE

Current rifle manufacturer located in McCarren, NV. Current distributor for U.S. Ordnance.

RIFLES: BOLT ACTION

Desert Ordnance offers several bolt action models, including the Desert Dog Custom, Coyote, and the Prong Horn, in various calibers, colors, and stock options. Please contact the company directly for more information, including pricing and availbility (see Trademark Index).

RIFLES: SEMI-AUTO

Desert Ordnance offers a complete line of AR-15 style tactical and hunting rifles, mostly in 5.56 NATO cal. Many options and configurations are available, as well as a wide variety of parts and accessories. Please contact the company directly for more information, including pricing and availability (see Trademark Index).

DESERT TECH (DESERT TACTICAL ARMS)

Current rifle manufacturer located in West Valley City, UT beginning 2014. Previously named Desert Tactical Arms located in Salt Lake City, UT from 2007-2013.

Desert Tech currently manufacutures accessories, ammunition, silencers, and conversion kits. Please contact the company directly for more information on these products (see Trademark Index).

RIFLES: BOLT ACTION

SRS-A1 (STEALTH RECON SCOUT) – .260 Rem. (new 2014), .300 Win. Mag., .308 Win., .338 Lapua Mag. (new 2014), 6.5 Creedmoor (new 2014), 6.5x47 Lapua (new 2014), or 7mm WSM (new 2014) cal., GIO, 6 shot mag., bullpup design with 22 or 26 in. free floating threaded chromemoly match grade barrel, fully adj. match trigger, quad rail, monolithic upper aluminum receiver, Black, OD Green, or FDE finish, adj. buttstock and cheekpiece, 5 or 6 shot detachable box mag., 11 lbs., 8 oz. New 2013.

	100%	98%	95%	90%	80%	70%	60%
MSR $3,086	$2,625	$2,295	$1,975	$1,785	$1,450	$1,175	$925

Add $200 for OD Green or FDE finish.
Add $350 for monopod.
Add $1,460-$1,827 for conversion kit, depending on caliber.

Please contact the company directly for more information on the wide variety of options and accessories available for this model.

RIFLES: SEMI-AUTO

HTI SNIPER – .50 BMG, .375 Cheytac, .408 Cheytac (new 2014), or .416 Barrett (new 2014) cal., GIO, 29 in. match grade, free floating, fluted barrel, 5 shot, ergonomic stock, designed to be lighter and more portable, compact bullpup design, Black, OD Green, or FDE finish, 19.4 lbs. New 2012.

	100%	98%	95%	90%	80%	70%	60%
MSR $4,630	$4,300	$3,850	$3,300	$2,800	$2,300	$1,925	$1,775

Add $200 for OD Green or FDE finish.

MSR	100%	98%	95%	90%	80%	70%	60%	Last MSR

MDR RIFLE – .223 Rem., .308 Win., or 7.62x39mm cal., bullpup design, 16 in. barrel, fully ambidextrous, lightweight, ergonomic, Black finish, 7 1/2 lbs. New 2014.

| MSR $1,500 | | $1,350 | $1,175 | $1,025 | $925 | $750 | $615 | $475 | |

SRS-A1 COVERT (STEALTH RECON SCOUT) – .243 Win. (disc. 2013), .300 Win. Mag., .308 Win. or .338 Lapua cal., GIO, 16 or 18 in. match grade free floating barrel, 5 or 6 shot mag., bullpup designed to be eleven inches shorter than conventional M16A2 rifles, tactical stock with adj. LOP, pistol grip, black or olive drab hard coat anodizing, Black, Coyote Brown (disc. 2013), Flat Dark Earth, or Olive Drab finish, full length rail, ambidextrous mag release, 9.4-15.1 lbs.

| MSR $3,086 | | $2,775 | $2,425 | $2,100 | $1,800 | $1,550 | $1,300 | $1,050 | |

Add $203 for OD Green or Flat Dark Earth finish.

Add $350 for Monopod.

Above values are for rifle or covert chassis and do not include a conversion kit. Add $1,491-$1,859, depending on caliber.

DESERT TOYS

Previous rifle manufacturer located in Mesa, AZ.

Desert Toys manufactured a single shot bolt action .50 BMG rifle called the Rebel. The standard Rebel was available with an 18 or 26 in. barrel in black finish. A variety of accessories and options were also available. Base price for this model was $2,950.

DETONICS DEFENSE TECHNOLOGIES, LLC

Current semi-auto pistol manufacturer established in 2007 and located in Millstadt, IL.

During 2013, Detonics changed its name to Detonics Defense Technologies, LLC.

PISTOLS: SEMI-AUTO

COMBAT MASTER HT – .40 S&W cal., 3 1/2 in. barrel, SAO, 7 shot mag., two-tone cerakote finish, stainless steel frame, low profile sights, aluminum/dymondwood grips, 30 oz. New 2010.

| MSR $1,849 | | $1,650 | $1,450 | $1,250 | $950 | $750 | $550 | $450 | |

NEMESIS HT – .40 S&W cal., similar to Combat Master HT, except has 5 in. barrel, 9 shot, 38 oz. New 2011.

| MSR $2,249 | | $1,950 | $1,750 | $1,550 | $1,250 | $995 | $750 | $550 | |

DTX – 9mm Para. or .40 S&W cal., DAO, 4 1/4 in. barrel, two-tone cerakote finish, aluminum/polymer frame, 14 (.40 S&W) or 16 (9mm Para.) shot, low profile sights, aluminum/polymer grips, 25 1/2 oz. New mid-2011.

| MSR $1,099 | | $995 | $850 | $725 | $625 | $500 | $400 | $300 | |

MTX – .45 ACP cal., DAO, 4 1/4 in. match barrel, Black finish, 10 shot mag., aluminum frame with steel receiver, fixed combat sights, 27 oz. New 2014.

| MSR $1,500 | | $1,350 | $1,125 | $925 | $800 | $675 | $575 | $500 | |

DETONICS FIREARMS INDUSTRIES

Previous manufacturer located in Bellevue, WA 1976-1988. Detonics was sold in early 1988 to the New Detonics Manufacturing Corporation, a wholly owned subsidiary of "1045 Investors Group Limited."

Please refer to the New Detonics Manufacturing Corporation listing available on www.bluebookofgunvalues.com for complete model listings of both companies.

DETONICS USA

Previous manufacturer located in Pendergrass, GA circa 2004-mid-2007.

PISTOLS: SEMI-AUTO

SCOREMASTER – .45 ACP cal., stainless steel construction, 5 in. barrel, SAO, 7 shot, MMC adj. rear sight, logo engraved checkered rosewood grips, available in Tactical (adj. sights and rail) or Target (Bo-Mar adj. sights, ext. slide stop, mag. release, and ambidextrous safety) configuration, 43 oz.

| | | $1,475 | $1,250 | $1,050 | $925 | $800 | $775 | $625 | $1,650 |

MILITARY TACTICAL – .45 ACP cal., SAO, black bonded finish, adj. sights, includes rail, forward serrations, checkered front strap, and lanyard ring.

| | | $1,750 | $1,525 | $1,350 | $1,125 | $950 | $800 | $675 | $1,975 |

DEZ TACTICAL ARMS, INC.

Current AR-15 style rifle manufacturer established in 2012 and located in south central WI.

MSR	100%	98%	95%	90%	80%	70%	60%	Last MSR

CARBINES/RIFLES: SEMI-AUTO

COVERT OPS CARBINE – .223 Rem. cal., GIO, 16 in. HBar chromemoly Vanadium steel button rifled barrel, 30 shot Magpul PMag with transparent round count window, forged upper receiver with M4 grooved feed ramps, charging handle with extended tactical latch, forged aluminum lower receiver, Mil-Spec bolt carrier group, carbine length gas tube, YHM smooth profile mid-length free floating forearm with end cap, stainless steel military grade trigger, YHM Phantom muzzle brake, FAB Defense six-position adj. stock with adj. cheekpiece, Ambi ERGO grip (v2) or UTG combat sniper grip with FAB Defense magwell grip, 7.1 lbs.

| MSR $1,550 | $1,325 | $1,160 | $995 | $900 | $725 | $595 | $475 | |

DTA-4 ENHANCED CARBINE – .223 Rem. or .300 Blackout cal., GIO, 16 in. chromemoly Vanadium steel button rifled barrel, 30 shot Magpul PMag, forged upper receiver with M4 grooved feed ramps, A2 front sight base with carbine length gas tube, Magpul MOE handguard, carbine length forearm, forged aluminum lower receiver, A2 flash hider, stainless steel military grade trigger, Magpul MOE six position adj. stock, Israeli grip, approx. 6 lbs., 13 oz.

| MSR $1,349 | $1,150 | $1,000 | $875 | $775 | $635 | $525 | $400 | |

Add $50 for .300 Blackout cal.

DTA-4 CARBINE – .223 Rem. cal., GIO, 16 in. chromemoly Vanadium steel button rifled barrel, 30 shot aluminum mag., forged upper receiver with M4 grooved feed ramps and charging handle, A2 front sight base with carbine length gas tube, military handguard, M4 military style carbine length forearm, forged aluminum lower receiver, A2 flash hider, stainless steel military grade trigger, tactical six position collapsible adj. stock, military style grip, approx. 6 1/2 lbs.

| MSR $974 | $825 | $725 | $625 | $560 | $450 | $375 | $295 | |

FLAWLESS RIFLE – .223 Rem. cal., GIO, 20 or 24 in. chromemoly HBar Vanadium steel button rifled diamond fluted barrel, 30 shot Magpul PMag with transparent round count window, forged upper receiver with M4 grooved feed ramps and charging handle with extended tactical latch, forged aluminum lower receiver, Mil-Spec bolt carrier group, quad rail with rifle length gas tube, YHM diamond profle free floating rifle length forearm with end cap, stainless steel military grade trigger, .50 cal. style flash enhancer, FAB Defense six-position adj. stock with adj. cheekpiece, ERGO SureGrip, 9 lbs.

| MSR $1,600 | $1,360 | $1,195 | $1,025 | $925 | $750 | $610 | $475 | |

Add $10 for 24 in. barrel.

TRU-FLIGHT CARBINE – .223 Rem. cal., GIO, 16 in. chromemoly Vanadium steel button rifled barrel, 30 shot Magpul PMag with transparent round count window, forged upper receiver with M4 grooved feed ramps and extended charging handle, forged aluminum lower receiver, Mil-Spec bolt carrier group, single rail Picatinny gas block with carbine length gas tube, YHM carbine length free floating forearm, stainless steel military grade trigger, three port compensator, FAB Defense six-position adj. stock with adj. cheekpiece, Israeli grip with FAB Defense magwell grip, 6.8 lbs.

| MSR $1,370 | $1,175 | $1,025 | $875 | $800 | $650 | $525 | $410 | |

TWISTED ELITE CARBINE – .223 Rem. cal., GIO, 16 in. chromemoly HBar Vanadium steel button rifled twist fluted barrel, 30 shot Magpul PMag with transparent round count window, forged upper receiver with M4 grooved feed ramps and extended charging handle, forged aluminum lower receiver, Mil-Spec bolt carrier group, low profile gas block with carbine length gas tube, YHM carbine length free floating "Tod Jarrett Competition" forearm, stainless steel military grade trigger, YHM Phantom muzzle brake, FAB Defense six-position adj. stock with adj. cheekpiece, ERGO SureGrip with FAB Defense magwell grip, 7.2 lbs.

| MSR $1,570 | $1,325 | $1,150 | $995 | $900 | $725 | $595 | $475 | |

DIAMONDBACK FIREARMS

Current pistol and AR-15 style rifle manufacturer located in Cocoa, FL. Distributor and dealer sales.

During late 2012, Taurus Holdings purchased an exclusive global distribution agreement with Diamondback Firearms, LLC. Taurus will assume all sales and marketing efforts of the Diamondback branded products from its Miami office.

PISTOLS: SEMI-AUTO

DB15 – 5.56 NATO or .300 Blackout cal., GIO, 7 1/2 or 10 1/2 in. chromemoly barrel, forged aluminum lower and A3 flat-top forged aluminum upper receiver, SST, no sights, Diamondback aluminum modified four rail handguard, A2 style pistol grip, Black, Flat Dark Earth, or OD Green finish. New 2014.

| MSR $899 | $800 | $700 | $600 | $550 | $450 | $350 | $275 | |

Add $15 for Flat Dark Earth or OD Green finish.

CARBINES: SEMI-AUTO

DB15 5.56 NATO – 5.56 NATO cal., GIO, 16 in. standard handguard or M4 contour free floating barrel with A2 flash hider, A3 flat-top upper receiver, 4-position M4 stock, Black or Flat Dark Earth finish, available with no sights, A2 front sights, or MagPul sights, 6.65 lbs. New 2013.

| MSR $899 | $800 | $700 | $600 | $550 | $450 | $350 | $295 | |

Add $142 for Flat Dark Earth finish.

MSR	100%	98%	95%	90%	80%	70%	60%	Last MSR

Add $120 for M4 countour free-floating barrel with no sights.

Add $153 for MagPul sights.

* **DB15 Camo** – 5.56 NATO cal., similar to DB15, except has Digital Green Camo or Digital Tan Camo finish. New 2013.

MSR $1,221	$1,100	$975	$825	$750	$600	$500	$395

Add $33 for MagPul sights.

* **DB15 Nickel** – 5.56 NATO cal., GIO, 30 shot mag., 16 in. M4 contour free floating barrel with A2 flash hider, A3 flat-top upper receiver, aluminum four rail handguard, nickel boron coating, 6-position MagPul CTR stock, Magpul MIAD grip, no sights, 6.65 lbs. New 2013.

MSR $1,199	$1,075	$950	$800	$725	$600	$485	$375

Add $28 for MagPul sights.

DB15 .300 BLACKOUT – .300 AAC Blackout cal., similar to DB15 5.56 NATO.

MSR $1,010	$900	$800	$675	$625	$550	$495	$435

Add $130 for free floating quad rail, no sights.

Add $160 for Flat Dark Earth finish.

Add $231 for free floating quad rail with MagPul sights.

Add $234 for Magpul CTR stock, Miad grip, and nickel boron coating or $333 if Magpul sights are added.

Add $254 for digital green camo or $358 for ATACS camo coverage.

DLASK ARMS CORP.

Current manufacturer and distributor located in British Columbia, Canada. Direct sales.

PISTOLS: SEMI-AUTO

Dlask Arms Corp. manufactures custom M-1911 style custom guns for all levels of competition. Previous models included the TC Tactical Carry at $1,250 last MSR, Gold Team at $2,000 last MSR, Silver Team L/S at $1,700 last MSR, and the Master Class at $3,500 last MSR. Dlask also imported a DAC 394 during 1997-1998, it's a 9mm Para. copy of the Sig 225, limited importation. Current values range from $225-$400, depending on condition. In addition, Dlask also manufactures a wide variety of custom parts for the M-1911. For more information, please contact the company directly (see Trademark Index).

DLASK 1911 – .45 ACP cal., available in all calibers, Suregrip safety by Ed Brown, slide fit to frame, Novak fixed sight, full length guide rod, black checkered grips.

MSR $1,250	$1,125	$975	$850	$775	$625	$500	$400

DLASK 1911 PRO – .45 ACP cal., avail. in all calibers, adj. rear sight and dovetail front sight, Suregrip safety by Ed Brown, slide is fit to frame, checkered brown grips, includes full length guide rod. New 2008.

MSR $1,560	$1,400	$1,225	$1,050	$950	$775	$625	$500

DLASK 1911 PRO PLUS – .45 ACP cal., other cals. available, hand fit, will accept all standard parts, adj. rear sight and dovetail front, ambidextrous safety, Suregrip safety by Ed Brown, includes full length guide rod. New 2008.

MSR $2,500	$2,250	$1,975	$1,695	$1,525	$1,250	$1,015	$800

DLASK 1911 SLICK – .45 ACP cal., tactical 1911 style, heavy flanged, tapered cone match grade barrel, Tactical Novak sights, extreme dehorn. New mid-2011.

MSR $1,400	$1,250	$1,095	$950	$850	$700	$575	$450

RIFLES: SEMI-AUTO

BASIC DAR 22 – .22 LR cal., GIO, 16 1/2 in. barrel, Dlask DAR 22 receiver with integral Picatinny rail, Hogue overmolded stock (customer's choice of color), anodized black finish. New 2012.

MSR $600	$550	$475	$425	$375	$350	$325	$295

DAR-701 TARGET – AR-15 style, GIO, 22, 24, or 26 in. stainless steel or blue barrel, aluminum alloy construction, two front sling swivels on the tube.

MSR $2,200	$1,975	$1,725	$1,475	$1,350	$1,075	$900	$700

DOLPHIN GUN COMPANY

Current rifle manufacturer located in Lincolnshire, United Kingdom.

Dolphin Gun Company was founded circa 2006 by competitive shooters Mik Maksimovic and Pete Hobson. The company builds competition "F Class" and tactical style rifles, utilizing Accuracy International or tactical style stocks. Many calibers and options are available. Base price is £2460 for the repeater, £2500 for repeater with F/TR stock, and £2360 for the single shot, including VAT. Please contact the company directly for more information, including pricing, delivery time, and availability (see Trademark Index).

MSR	100%	98%	95%	90%	80%	70%	60%	*Last MSR*

DOMINION ARMS

Previous trademark of slide action shotguns manufactured by Rauch Tactical, located in Blaine, WA.

Rauch manufactured 12 ga. tactical style slide action shotguns until circa 2010.

DOUBLE STAR CORP.

Current manufacturer located in Winchester, KY. Distributed by JT Distributing. Dealer sales only.

Double Star Corp. currently also manufactures AR-15 accessories and uppers. Please contact the company directly for more information (see Trademark Index).

PISTOLS: SEMI-AUTO

1911 COMBAT PISTOL – .45 ACP cal., SA, forged steel frame, stainless steel slide, optional 1913 Picatinny rail, Novak white dot front and LoMount rear sights, memory groove beavertail grip safety, 8 shot mag., 25 LPI checkering, black nitride or nickel finish, 39 oz. New 2010.

	100%	98%	95%	90%	80%	70%	60%
MSR $2,000	$1,800	$1,575	$1,350	$1,225	$995	$825	$625

Add $150 for nickel finish.

DSC .300 BLACKOUT AR PISTOL – .300 Blackout cal., 7 1/2 or 9 in. rifled barrel, pistol length free float aluminum handguard, pistol tube, 4 3/4 lbs. New 2014.

	100%	98%	95%	90%	80%	70%	60%
MSR $1,150	$1,025	$895	$775	$695	$575	$450	$350

DSC 7.5 AR PISTOL – 5.56 NATO or 9mm Para. cal., AR-15 style, GIO, Picatinny rail gas block, 7 1/2 in. chromemoly steel barrel, free float aluminum tube handguard, flat-top or standard A2 upper receiver, CAR length pistol receiver extension, standard A2 grip, 4.7 lbs.

	100%	98%	95%	90%	80%	70%	60%
MSR $1,010	$925	$825	$725	$650	$575	$500	$450

Add $220 for 9mm Para. cal.

DSC 10.5 AR PISTOL – 5.56 NATO or 9mm Para. cal., AR-15 style, GIO, Picatinny rail gas block, 10 1/2 in. chromemoly steel barrel, single heat shield CAR handguard, flat-top or standard A2 upper receiver, CAR length pistol receiver extension, standard A2 pistol grip, 5 1/2 lbs.

	100%	98%	95%	90%	80%	70%	60%
MSR $1,070	$950	$825	$700	$575	$500	$425	$375

Add $220 for 9mm Para. cal.

DSC 11.5 AR PISTOL – 5.56 NATO or 9mm Para. cal., AR-15 style, GIO, Picatinny rail gas block, 11 1/2 in. chromemoly steel barrel, single heat shield CAR handguard, flat-top or standard A2 upper receiver, CAR length pistol receiver extension, standard A2 pistol grip, 5.7 lbs.

	100%	98%	95%	90%	80%	70%	60%
MSR $1,070	$950	$825	$700	$575	$500	$425	$375

Add $220 for 9mm Para. cal.

DSC STAR-15 PISTOL – .223 Rem. cal., AR-15 style, GIO, 7 1/2, 10 1/5, or 11 1/2 in. chromemoly match barrel, A2 flash hider, front sight assembly or rail gas block. Disc. 2010.

	100%	98%	95%	90%	80%	70%	60%	*Last MSR*
	$875	$750	$675	$600	$525	$450	$395	*$950*

RIFLES/CARBINES: SEMI-AUTO

Double Star Corp. makes a complete line of AR-15 style carbines/rifles, as well as a line of SBRs (Short Barreled Rifles) for military/law enforcement.

DSC .204 RUGER – .204 Ruger cal., GIO, 20 or 24 in. stainless steel fluted or non-fluted bull barrel, Picatinny rail gas block, mil-spec flat-top, free float aluminum tube handguard, A2 pistol grip and buttstock. Mfg. 2013 only.

	100%	98%	95%	90%	80%	70%	60%	*Last MSR*
	$995	$900	$800	$700	$600	$500	$425	*$1,125*

DSC .300 BLACKOUT – .300 Blackout cal., GIO, 16 in. HBAR barrel, black nitride coating, Picatinny rail gas block, CAR handguard, mil-spec flat-top with M4 feed ramp, A2 pistol grip, six position commercial spec DS-4 stock, 6.7 lbs. New 2013.

	100%	98%	95%	90%	80%	70%	60%
MSR $1,030	$925	$825	$725	$650	$575	$500	$450

DSC 3 GUN RIFLE – 5.56 NATO cal., AR-15 style, GIO, 30 shot, 18 in. fluted stainless barrel with Carlson Comp muzzle brake, Samson 15 in. Evolution handguard, Ace ARFX buttstock, Timney trigger, Hogue or ERGO ambi sure grip, 7 1/2 lbs. New 2012.

	100%	98%	95%	90%	80%	70%	60%
MSR $1,700	$1,525	$1,325	$1,125	$975	$850	$750	$650

DSC COMMANDO – 5.56 NATO cal., GIO, 16 in. chromemoly HBAR lightweight barrel, permanently attached flash hider, Picatinny rail gas block or "F" marked FSB, two-piece CAR length polymer handguard, mil-spec flat-top or A2 upper receiver, A2 pistol grip, six position DS-4 buttstock, front sight base, 6.45 lbs. New 2013.

	100%	98%	95%	90%	80%	70%	60%
MSR $1,030	$925	$825	$725	$650	$575	$500	$450

MSR	100%	98%	95%	90%	80%	70%	60%	Last MSR

DSC CONSTANT CARRY CARBINE – 5.56 NATO cal., GIO, 16 in. lightweight A-1 profile barrel, steel low profile gas block, Samson Evolution 9 in. handguard, mil-spec flat-top with M4 feedramp, A2 pistol grip, Ace Ltd. AR-UL-E buttstock, Magpul MBUS front and rear sights, 5 1/2 lbs. New 2013.

| MSR $1,350 | $1,195 | $1,000 | $900 | $775 | $675 | $550 | $450 | |

DSC CRITTERSLAYER – .223 Rem. cal., AR-15 style, GIO, 24 in. fluted Shaw barrel, full length Picatinny rail on receiver and Badger handguard, two-stage match trigger, palmrest, ergonomic pistol grip with finger grooves, includes Harris LMS swivel bipod, flat-top or high rise upper receiver, 11 1/2 lbs. Disc. 2010.

| | $1,300 | $1,150 | $925 | $850 | $750 | $650 | $550 | *$1,430* |

Add $40 for ported barrel.

* DSC CritterSlayer Jr. – .223 Rem. cal., GIO, similar to CritterSlayer, except has 16 in. barrel and fully adj. A2 style buttstock, DSC flat-top or high rise upper receiver. Disc. 2010.

| | $1,050 | $875 | $775 | $675 | $575 | $475 | $400 | *$1,150* |

Add $65 for detachable carrying handle or $35 for removable front sight.

Add $200 for Enhanced CritterSlayer Jr. with 16 in. Expedition barrel, CAR hand guard, and adj. buttstock.

DSC DEER RIFLE – 6.8 SPC cal., AR-15 style, GIO, 20 in. chromemoly heavy barrel with A2 phantom flash hider, 5 shot mag., Ace ARFX skeleton stock, Next Camo water transfer finish, winter trigger guard, 7 3/4 lbs. New 2012.

| MSR $1,450 | $1,295 | $1,125 | $875 | $800 | $700 | $600 | $500 | |

DSC DS-4 – 5.56 NATO, 6.5 Grendel, 6.8 SPC, or 7.62x39mm cal., AR-15 style, patterned after the Military M-4, GIO, matte black, tactical pink, or OD Green finish, 16 in. chromemoly barrel, double heat shield handguard, A2 or flat-top upper receiver, A2 pistol grip, 6-position buttstock, 6.3 lbs.

| MSR $1,050 | $950 | $775 | $650 | $575 | $495 | $450 | $395 | |

DSC FDE DS-4 MOE – 5.56 NATO cal., AR-15 style, GIO, 16 in. chromemoly barrel, Magpul MOE features include handguard, upper receiver, pistol grip, enhanced trigger guard, rear BUIS, 6 position commercial spec Magpul MOE stock, 30 shot mag., FDE (Flat Dark Earth) finish, 6.3 lbs.

| MSR $1,230 | $1,095 | $975 | $850 | $725 | $600 | $500 | $425 | |

DSC FDE DS-4 – 5.56 NATO cal., GIO, 16 in. chromemoly M4 barrel, Flat Dark Earth teflon coated finish, Picatinny rail gas block or "F" marked FSB, double heat shield two-piece polymer handguard, flat-top upper receiver, A2 pistol grip, six position buttstock, Magpul Rear BUS, FDE or OD Green finish. New mid-2012.

| MSR $1,070 | $950 | $825 | $700 | $625 | $550 | $475 | $395 | |

DSC EXPEDITION CARBINE/RIFLE – 5.56 NATO cal., AR-15 style, GIO, 16 or 20 (disc.) in. lightweight contour barrel with integrated muzzle brake, single heat shield CAR handguard, A2 or flat-top upper receiver, A2 pistol grip, A2 or 6-position commercial spec stock, 6.35lbs.

| MSR $1,030 | $925 | $825 | $675 | $550 | $450 | $395 | $350 | |

Add $65 for detachable carry handle (disc.).

DSC LIGHTWEIGHT TACTICAL – 5.56 NATO cal., GIO, fluted 16 in. chromemoly HBAR barrel, Picatinny rail gas block or "F" marked FSB, single heat shield two-piece CAR length polymer handguard, mil-spec flat-top or A2 upper receiver, D-4 six position buttstock, 6.9 lbs. New mid-2012.

| MSR $1,130 | $995 | $850 | $750 | $650 | $575 | $500 | $450 | |

DSC MARKSMAN RIFLE – 5.56 NATO cal., AR-15 style, GIO, 20 in. Wilson Arms stainless steel barrel, Daniel Defense free float handguard, Picatinny rail gas block, A2 Phantom flash hider, Magpul PRS buttstock, adj. LOP, Magpul MIAD pistol grip, two-stage trigger, front and rear flip sight, approx. 9 lbs.

| MSR $1,800 | $1,595 | $1,350 | $1,100 | $925 | $750 | $625 | $550 | |

Add $185 for bipod.

DSC MIDLENGTH CARBINE – 5.56 NATO cal., 16 in. barrel with A2 flash hider, mid-length polymer handguard, DS-4 stock, 6.7 lbs. New 2014.

| MSR $1,000 | $900 | $800 | $675 | $625 | $500 | $400 | $325 | |

DSC MIDNIGHT DRAGON – 5.56 NATO cal., AR-15 style, GIO, 24 in. stainless steel bull barrel with spiral fluting and black nitride coating, aluminum free float handguard with bipod stud, A3 flat-top upper receiver, ARFX buttstock, ERGO tactical pistol grip, DSC two-stage trigger, Badger TAC latch, DSC enhanced trigger guard, 9 1/4 lbs. New 2012.

| MSR $1,350 | $1,195 | $1,050 | $925 | $800 | $700 | $600 | $475 | |

DSC MSD MIL-SPEC DRAGON – 5.56 NATO cal., 16 in. barrel, "F" marked front sight tower, DS-4 Mil-Spec stock, 6.1 lbs. New 2014.

| MSR $1,200 | $1,075 | $950 | $800 | $725 | $600 | $475 | $400 | |

MSR	100%	98%	95%	90%	80%	70%	60%	Last MSR

DSC PATROL CARBINE – 5.56 NATO cal., AR-15 style, GIO, 16 in. chromemoly lightweight barrel with A2 phantom flash hider, Slimline quad rail handguard with three low profile rail covers, flip up rear sight, six position DS-4 buttstock, Hogue overmolded pistol grip, 6 1/2 lbs.

MSR $1,350	$1,200	$1,050	$900	$825	$675	$550	$450	

DSC STAR-CAR CARBINE – 5.56 NATO, 6.5 Grendel, 6.8 SPC, or 9mm Para. cal., AR-15 style, GIO, 16 in. chromemoly steel heavy barrel with A2 flash hider, fixed post-ban CAR type stock, single heat shield CAR handguard, A2 or flat-top upper receiver, standard A2 pistol grip, 6.7 lbs.

MSR $980	$875	$750	$650	$550	$475	$425	$375	

Add $75 for 6.8 SPC, $125 for 6.5 Grendel, or $220 for 9mm Para. cal.

DSC STAR M4 CARBINE – .223 Rem. cal., AR-15 M4 carbine design, GIO, fixed M4 style post-ban buttstock, 16 in. barrel, M4 handguard, 6.76 lbs. Disc. 2012.

	$825	$725	$650	$565	$500	$465	$430	*$910*

Add $85 for detachable carrying handle.

DSC STAR DISSIPATOR – 5.56 NATO cal., AR-15 style, GIO, 16 in. dissipator chromemoly steel barrel with full length handguard, A2 or 6 position CAR buttstock, A2 or flat-top upper receiver, 6.9 lbs.

MSR $1,030	$925	$825	$700	$625	$525	$425	$350	

DSC STAR-15 LIGHTWEIGHT TACTICAL – .223 Rem. cal., AR-15 style, GIO, 16 in. fluted H-Bar barrel with attached muzzle brake, shorty A2 buttstock, A2 or flat-top upper receiver, 6 1/4 lbs. Disc. 2004, reintroduced 2009-2010.

	$825	$725	$650	$565	$500	$465	$430	*$930*

Add $65 for detachable carrying handle.

DSC STAR-15 RIFLE/CARBINE – 5.56 NATO, 6.5 Grendel, 6.8 SPC, or 7.62x39mm (disc. 2013) cal., AR-15 style, GIO, 16 (disc.) or 20 in. match barrel with A2 flash hider, ribbed forearm, two-piece rifle handguard, standard A2 buttstock and pistol grip, A2 or flat-top upper receiver, 8 lbs.

MSR $980	$875	$750	$650	$550	$475	$425	$375	

Add $65 for flat-top with detachable carrying handle.

Add $75 for 6.8 SPC,or 7.62x39mm (disc. 2013) cal. or $125 for 6.5 Grendel cal.

DSC STAR-15 9MM CARBINE – 9mm Para. cal., AR-15 style, GIO, 16 in. barrel, ribbed forearm, A2 or flat-top upper receiver, 7 1/2 lbs. Mfg. 2004, reintroduced 2009-2010.

	$950	$825	$725	$650	$575	$500	$450	*$1,080*

Add $65 for detachable carry handle.

DSC STAR-15 6.8 SPC RIFLE/CARBINE – 6.8 SPC cal., GIO, 16 or 20 in. chromemoly barrel, A2 upper or flat-top, A2 (rifle) or 6-position DS-4 buttstock, 7-8 lbs. Disc. 2010

	$825	$725	$650	$565	$500	$465	$430	*$935*

Add $65 for detachable carry handle.

DSC STAR-15 6.8 SPC SUPER MATCH RIFLE – 6.8 SPC cal., GIO, 20, 22, or 24 in. free float super match stainless steel bull barrel, Picatinny rail gas block, two-piece NM free floating handguard. Disc. 2010.

	$950	$825	$725	$650	$575	$500	$450	*$1,075*

DSC STAR-15 .204 RUGER RIFLE – .204 Ruger cal., GIO, 24 in. chromemoly barrel, A2 buttstock, A2 flash hider. Disc. 2010.

	$925	$850	$750	$650	$575	$500	$450	*$1,050*

DSC STAR-15 6.5 GRENDEL CARBINE/RIFLE – 6.5 Grendel cal., GIO, 16 or 20 in. chromemoly barrel, A2 or six position (Carbine) buttstock. Disc. 2010.

	$875	$775	$675	$600	$525	$450	$395	*$985*

Add $65 for detachable carry handle.

DSC STAR-15 6.5 GRENDEL SUPER MATCH RIFLE – 6.5 Grendel cal., GIO, 20, 22, or 24 in. free floating match bull barrel, A2 buttstock, Picatinny rail gas block, two-piece NM free floating hand guard. Disc. 2010.

	$995	$875	$775	$675	$575	$475	$400	*$1,125*

DSC STAR-15 DCM SERVICE RIFLE – 5.56 NATO cal., AR-15 style, GIO, 20 in. free-float match barrel, National Match front and rear sights, two-stage match trigger, DCM handguard, 8 lbs. Disc.

	$900	$825	$725	$650	$550	$485	$440	*$1,000*

DSC SUPERMATCH RIFLE – 5.56 NATO, 6.5 Grendel, or 6.8 SPC cal., AR-15 style, GIO, 16, 20, 22 (disc. 2013), or 24 in. free-float stainless steel Super Match barrel, flat-top or high rise upper receiver, includes Picatinny rail and one-piece National Match handguard, A2 stock, 7.8 - 9 3/4 lbs.

MSR $1,130	$995	$850	$750	$650	$575	$500	$450	

Add $65 for 6.8 SPC or $115 for 6.5 Grendel cal.

MSR	100%	98%	95%	90%	80%	70%	60%	Last MSR

DSC TARGET CARBINE – .223 Rem. cal., AR-15 style, GIO, features 16 in. dissipator barrel with full length round one-piece National Match handguard, flip-up sights, Picatinny rail, flat-top upper receiver. Disc.

	100%	98%	95%	90%	80%	70%	60%	Last MSR
	$1,050	$875	$775	$695	$625	$550	$485	$1,175

DSC ZOMBIE SLAYER – 5.56 NATO cal., AR-15 style, GIO, 14 1/2 in. DS4 barrel (16 in. with permanently attached A2 phantom flash hider), flat-top upper receiver with detachable GI carry handle, two 30 shot magazines, 6 position D4 stock, double heat shield handguards, USMC multi-purpose bayonet, "Zombie Slayer" lasered lower, 6.1 lbs. New 2012.

MSR	100%	98%	95%	90%	80%	70%	60%
$1,245	$1,100	$975	$875	$775	$675	$575	$475

NOTES

_____

_____

_____

_____

_____

_____

_____

_____

_____

_____

_____

_____

_____

_____

_____

_____

_____

_____

_____

_____

_____

E SECTION

E.D.M. ARMS

Current manufacturer established in 1997 and located in Hurricane, UT since 2008. Previously located in Redlands, CA 1997-2008. Dealer and consumer direct sales.

MSR	100%	98%	95%	90%	80%	70%	60%	Last MSR

RIFLES: BOLT ACTION

WINDRUNNER MODEL 96 (XM107) – .338 Lapua (mfg. 2002-2010) or .50 BMG cal., takedown repeater action, EDM machined receiver, fully adj. stock, match grade 28 in. detachable barrel that removes within seconds, allowing exact head space every time the barrel is reinstalled, includes two 5 (.50 BMG cal.) or 8 (.338 Lapua) shot mags., Picatinny rail, and bipod, 24 (Lightweight Tactical Takedown) or 36 lbs.

| MSR $7,500 | $6,375 | $5,575 | $4,775 | $4,325 | $3,500 | $2,875 | $2,225 | |

Add $1,000 for left hand action.

* **Windrunner Model 96 SS99** – similar to Windrunner, except is single shot, w/o mag., includes bipod and sling, 32 lbs. New 2002.

| MSR $5,250 | $5,250 | $4,600 | $4,150 | $3,450 | $2,850 | $2,250 | $1,850 | |

MODEL 06 MINI-WINDRUNNER – .308 Win. cal., 20 in. barrel, 10 shot mag., Picatinny rail, lightweight, tactical, takedown version of the Windrunner Model 96, 11.2 lbs. Mfg. 2007-2010.

| | $4,250 | $3,750 | $3,300 | $2,900 | $2,550 | $2,175 | $1,800 | *$4,250* |

MODEL XM04 CHEYENNE TACTICAL – .408 CheyTac cal., takedown repeater, tactical bolt action configuration, 5 shot mag., 30 in. fluted barrel with suppressor, desert camo finish, retractable stock, effective range is 2,500+ yards, 27 lbs. New 2002.

| MSR $6,750 | $6,750 | $6,200 | $5,500 | $5,000 | $4,500 | $4,000 | $3,500 | |

Subtract $1,400 for single shot action (disc.).

MODEL 12 – .223 Rem. or 7.62 NATO cal., fluted barrel with muzzle brake, 4 shot detachable mag., Savage AccuTrigger standard, includes twin rail adj. stock with heavy recoil pad, receiver with Picatinny rail, pistol grip, guaranteed one MOA at 100 yards. New 2012.

| MSR $2,975 | $2,975 | $2,600 | $2,250 | $1,875 | $1,600 | $1,400 | $1,200 | |

MODEL 50 – .50 BMG cal., bolt action, single shot, twin rail adj. skeletonized stock, Picatinny rail and bipod. Mfg. 2003.

| | $4,250 | $3,750 | $3,250 | $2,850 | $2,450 | $2,050 | $1,650 | *$4,250* |

MODEL 98 – .338 Lapua cal., takedown repeating bolt action, single rail adj. stock, pistol grip, 22 lbs. New 2003.

| MSR $6,750 | $6,750 | $6,200 | $5,500 | $5,000 | $4,500 | $4,000 | $3,500 | |

510 DTC EUROP – .50 DTC Europ cal. (1 in. shorter than .50 BMG), designed for CA shooters and legal in CA. Mfg. 2007-2008.

| | $7,500 | $6,850 | $6,200 | $5,500 | $5,000 | $4,500 | $4,000 | *$7,500* |

RIFLES: SEMI-AUTO

WINDRUNNER .50 CAL. – .50 BMG cal., 28 in. Lilja match grade chromemoly barrel, integrated Picatinny rail, removable black stock with cheekrest and adj. buttpad. New 2006.

| MSR $9,250 | $8,750 | $7,500 | $6,750 | $6,000 | $5,250 | $4,500 | $3,750 | |

E.M.F. CO., INC.

Current importer and distributor established 1956 and located in Santa Ana, CA. Distributor and dealer sales. E.M.F. stands for Early & Modern Firearms Inc.

For information on Great Western, Dakota Single Action and Hartford revolvers, rifles and carbines imported by E.M.F., please refer to the Great Western, Dakota Single Action Revolvers and Hartford sections. Please refer to the *Blue Book of Modern Black Powder Arms* by John Allen (also online) for more information and prices on E.M.F.'s lineup of modern black powder models.

Black Powder Revolvers - Reproductions & Replicas and *Black Powder Long Arms & Pistols - Reproductions & Replicas* by Dennis Adler are also invaluable sources for most black powder revolver reproductions and replicas, and include hundreds of color images on most popular makes/models, provide manufacturer/trademark histories, and up-to-date information on related items/accessories for black powder shooting - www.bluebookofgunvalues.com

PISTOLS: SEMI-AUTO

All current semi-auto pistols are manufactured in the U.S.

MSR	100%	98%	95%	90%	80%	70%	60%	Last MSR

HARTFORD 1911-A1 – .45 ACP cal., 5 in. barrel, SA, 7 shot mag., patterned after original 1911, parkerized finish, fixed sights, flat or arched mainspring housing, black ergo, brown plastic military, ultra stag, or checkered hardwood grips, includes two mags. Mfg. 2009-2013.

| | $515 | $465 | $400 | $360 | $330 | $300 | $275 | *$585* |

HARTFORD 1911 COMBAT MODEL – .45 ACP cal., 7 shot mag., similar to 1911-A1 model, except has choice of fixed Tritium low profile, or adj. sights with Tritium inserts, parkerized, blue, Duracoat, or nickel finish, black ergo or checkered hardwood grips, includes two mags, lock, and hard case. Mfg. 2009-2013.

| | $595 | $525 | $450 | $395 | $360 | $330 | $300 | *$685* |

HARTFORD 1911 CCC MODEL – .45 ACP cal., 4 1/4 in. barrel, SA, 8 shot mag., choice of fixed low profile, Novak style fixed night, or Bo-Mar adj. sights, parkerized, blue, stainless, Duracoat, or nickel finishes, includes two mags., lock, and hard case. Mfg. 2009-2013.

| | $950 | $825 | $700 | $575 | $475 | $425 | $375 | *$1,075* |

Add $710 for night sights and skip checkered grips.

FMK MODEL 9C1 – 9mm Para. cal., 4 in. barrel, SA, SFO, lightweight polymer frame, 10 or 14 shot mag., blue steel slide with engraved Bill of Rights, five interchangable front sights, eighteen interchangable rear sights, "Mag Out" safety, striker indicator, and loaded chamber indicator, black or desert tan finish, includes two mags., lock, and case, 23 1/2 oz., mfg. by FMK Firearms. New 2009.

| MSR $400 | $360 | $325 | $285 | $260 | $235 | $215 | $200 | |

RIFLES: SEMI-AUTO

J R CARBINE – 9mm Para., .40 S&W, or .45 ACP cal., GIO, blowback operation, utilizes standard M4/AR-15 furniture and trigger components, right or left hand action, Glock magazine, can be converted to other popular pistol mags., flat-top receiver, quad rail forend, black adj. stock, extended pistol grip, tri-flatted barrel design, patented ejection and extraction features, compatible with AR15 accessories, mfg. in U.S.A. by J R Carbines, LLC. Mfg. mid-2010-2013.

| | $675 | $600 | $525 | $475 | $425 | $400 | $350 | *$750* |

Please refer to Just Right Carbines listing for current manufacture.

RIFLES: SEMI-AUTO, REPRODUCTIONS

These models are authentic shooting reproductions previously mfg. in Italy.

AP 74 – .22 LR or .32 ACP cal., GIO, copy of the Colt AR-15, 15 shot mag., 20 in. barrel, 6 3/4 lbs. Importation disc. 1989.

| | $350 | $295 | $250 | $200 | $175 | $155 | $145 | *$295* |

Add $25 for .32 cal.

* **AP74 Sporter Carbine** – .22 LR cal. only, GIO, wood sporter stock. Importation disc. 1989.

| | $375 | $325 | $275 | $225 | $195 | $175 | $160 | *$320* |

* **AP74 Paramilitary Paratrooper Carbine** – .22 LR cal. only, GIO, folding wire, black nylon or wood folding stock. Importation disc. 1987.

| | $395 | $350 | $300 | $260 | $215 | $175 | $165 | *$325* |

Add $10 for wood folding stock.

* **AP74 "Dressed" Military Model** – GIO, with Cyclops scope, Colt bayonet, sling, and bipod. Disc. 1986.

| | $395 | $350 | $300 | $265 | $240 | $220 | $200 | *$450* |

GALIL – .22 LR cal. only, reproduction of the Israeli Galil. Importation disc. 1989.

| | $350 | $295 | $250 | $200 | $175 | $155 | $145 | *$295* |

KALASHNIKOV AK-47 – .22 LR cal. only, reproduction of the Russian AK-47, semi-auto. Importation disc. 1989.

| | $350 | $295 | $250 | $200 | $175 | $155 | $145 | *$295* |

FRENCH M.A.S. – .22 LR cal. only, reproduction of the French bullpup combat rifle, with carrying handle, 29 shot mag. Importation disc. 1989.

| | $375 | $325 | $265 | $240 | $220 | $200 | $185 | *$320* |

M1 CARBINE – .30 cal. only, copy of the U.S. Military M1 Carbine. Disc. 1985.

| | $295 | $250 | $225 | $200 | $175 | $150 | $125 | *$205* |

Add 50% for Paratrooper variation.

EAGLE ARMS, INC.

Previous manufacturer located in Geneseo, IL. Previous division of ArmaLite, Inc. 1995-2002, located in Geneseo, IL. Manufacture of pre-1995 Eagle Arms rifles was in Coal Valley, IL.

MSR	100%	98%	95%	90%	80%	70%	60%	*Last MSR*

During 1995, Eagle Arms, Inc. reintroduced the ArmaLite trademark. The new company was organized under the ArmaLite name. In 2003, Eagle Arms became a separate company, and no longer a division of ArmaLite.

Eagle Arms also made lower receivers only.

RIFLES: SEMI-AUTO, RECENT MFG.

On the following M-15 models manufactured 1995 and earlier, A2 accessories included a collapsible carbine type buttstock (disc. per 1994 C/B) and forward bolt assist mechanism. Accessories are similar, with the addition of National Match sights. The A2 suffix indicates the rifle is supplied with carrying handle, A4 designates a flat-top receiver, some are equipped with a detachable carrying handle.

AR-10 MATCH RIFLE – .308 Win. cal., GIO, very similar to the Armalite AR-10 A4 rifle, 20 or 24 (Match rifle) in. chromemoly barrel, A2 (Service rifle) or A4 style flat-top upper receiver (no sights), black stock with pistol grip and forearm, 10 shot mag., 9.6 lbs. Mfg. 2001-2005.

	$925	$850	$750	$650	$550	$450	$395	*$1,000*

Add $65 for Service rifle with A2 front/rear sights.
Add $480 for 24 in. barrel and aluminum free-floating handguard.

MODEL M15 A2/A4 RIFLE (EA-15 E-1) – .223 Rem. or .308 Win. cal., patterned after the Colt AR-15A2, GIO, 20 in. barrel, A2 sights or A4 flat-top, with (pre 1993) or w/o forward bolt assist, 7 lbs. Mfg. 1990-1993, reintroduced 2002-2005.

	$750	$675	$600	$550	$500	$450	$395	*$795*

Add $40 for .223 cal. flat-top (Model E15A4B).
Add $205 for .308 Win. cal. flat-top.
Add 10% for .308 Win. cal.

* **Model M15 A2/A4 Rifle Carbine (EA9025C/EA9027C)** – GIO, features collapsible (disc. per C/B 1994) or fixed (new 1994) buttstock and 16 in. barrel, 5 lbs. 14 oz. Mfg. 1990-95, reintroduced 2002-2005.

	$750	$675	$600	$550	$500	$450	$395	*$795*

Add $40 for flat-top (Model E15A4CB).
1997 retail for the pre-ban models was $1,100 (EA9396).

Beginning 1993, the A2 accessory kit became standard on this model.

* **Model M15 A2 H-BAR Rifle (EA9040C)** – GIO, features heavy Target barrel, 8 lbs. 14 oz., includes E-2 accessories. Mfg. 1990-95.

	$850	$750	$675	$575	$525	$450	$395	*$895*

1997 retail for this pre-ban model was $1,100 (EA9200).

* **Model M15 A4 Rifle Eagle Spirit (EA9055S)** – GIO, includes 16 in. premium air gauged National Match barrel, fixed stock, full length tubular aluminum handguard, designed for IPSC shooting, includes match grade accessories, 8 lbs. 6 oz. Mfg. 1993-95, reintroduced 2002 only.

	$800	$700	$625	$550	$500	$450	$395	*$850*

The 1995 pre-ban variation of this model retailed at $1,475 (EA9603).

* **Model M15 A2 Rifle Golden Eagle (EA9049S)** – similar to M15 A2 H-BAR, except has National Match accessories and two-stage trigger, 20 in. extra heavy barrel, 12 lbs. 12 oz. Mfg. 1991-1995, reintroduced 2002 only.

	$1,000	$875	$775	$675	$575	$475	$425	*$1,125*

The 1997 pre-ban variation of this model retailed at $1,300 (EA9500).

* **Model M15 A4 Rifle Eagle Eye (EA9901)** – GIO, includes 24 in. free floating 1 in. dia. barrel with tubular aluminum handguard, weighted buttstock, designed for silhouette matches, 14 lbs. Mfg. 1993-95.

	$1,350	$1,175	$995	$850	$725	$625	$525	*$1,495*

* **Model M15 Rifle Action Master (EA9052S)** – GIO, match rifle, flat-top, solid aluminum handguard tube, for free floating 20 in. barrel with compensator, N.M. accessories, fixed stock, 8 lbs. 5 oz. Mfg. 1992-95, reintroduced 2002 only.

	$750	$675	$600	$550	$500	$450	$395	*$850*

The 1995 pre-ban variation of this model retailed at $1,475 (EA5600).

* **Model M15 A4 Rifle Special Purpose (EA9042C)** – GIO, 20 in. barrel, flat-top (A4) or detachable handle receiver. Disc. 1995.

	$895	$825	$725	$625	$525	$450	$395	*$955*

The 1995 pre-ban variation of this model retailed at $1,165 (EA9204).

* **Model M15 A4 Rifle Predator (EA9902)** – GIO, post-ban only, 18 in. barrel, National Match trigger, flat-top (A4) or detachable handle receiver. Mfg. 1995 only.

	$1,225	$1,050	$925	$825	$700	$600	$495	*$1,350*

MSR	100%	98%	95%	90%	80%	70%	60%	Last MSR

EAST RIDGE GUN COMPANY, INC.

Current rifle manufacturer located in Bancroft, WI.

RIFLES: BOLT ACTION, SINGLE SHOT

BIG BERTHA – .50 BMG cal., 36 in. Lothar Walther premium target bull barrel, muzzle brake, all steel bipod, special tactical or custom laminated wood stock, scope rail, approx. 40 lbs.

| MSR $2,750 | $2,475 | $2,165 | $1,850 | $1,685 | $1,365 | $1,115 | $865 | |

COMPETITOR 2000 – .50 BMG cal., 30 or 36 in. Lothar Walther fluted bull barrel, extra large muzzle brake, all steel bipod, adj. aluminum stock with military hard coat finish, scope mount, Jewell trigger, pistol grip with palm swell, accuracy guaranteed to be less than 1 minute of angle with custom ammo.

| MSR $3,400 | $3,075 | $2,695 | $2,300 | $2,095 | $1,695 | $1,385 | $1,075 | |

LIGHT WEIGHT COMPETITOR – .50 BMG cal., 30 in. Lothar Walther fluted bull stainless or chromemoly barrel, reduced weight muzzle brake, adj. skeletonized aluminum stock with black hard coat finish, scope mounting rail, Jewell trigger, sniper type pistol grip with palm swell, optional carrying handle, 28 lbs. Disc. 2010.

| | $3,075 | $2,695 | $2,300 | $2,095 | $1,695 | $1,385 | $1,075 | $3,400 |

Add $200 for stainless steel barrel.

REBEL – .50 BMG cal., 36 in. Lothar Walther bull barrel, muzzle brake, all steel bipod, adj. aluminum tactical stock with removable carrying handle, or custom laminated wood stock, scope rail, AR-15 grip, approx. 38 lbs.

| MSR $2,450 | $2,195 | $2,000 | $1,725 | $1,550 | $1,250 | $1,025 | $800 | |

Add $200 for custom laminated wood stock.

SHORTY – .50 BMG cal., 30 in. Lothar Walther tapered barrel, muzzle brake, all steel bipod, adj. aluminum tactical stock with removable carry handle, or custom laminated wood stock, scope rail, approx. 31 lbs.

| MSR $2,250 | $2,050 | $1,795 | $1,525 | $1,395 | $1,125 | $925 | $715 | |

Add $200 for custom laminated wood stock.

TITAN BENCH – .50 BMG cal., 30 in. Lothar Walther stainless steel fluted barrel, muzzle brake, adj. trigger, bench rest style laminated stock in choice of colors, precision ground tapered or flat steel scope base, 26 lbs. 6 oz.

| MSR $2,550 | $2,295 | $2,015 | $1,725 | $1,560 | $1,260 | $1,035 | $800 | |

ED BROWN CUSTOM, INC.

Current rifle manufacturer established during 2000 and located in Perry, MO. During 2009, the rifle division was transferred to Ed Brown Products, Inc.

Please refer to Ed Brown Products, Inc. for currently manufactured rifles.

RIFLES: BOLT ACTION

702 LIGHT TARGET (TACTICAL) – .223 Rem. or .308 Win. cal., features Ed Brown short repeater action, aluminum trigger guard and floorplate, 21 in. match grade barrel, includes Talley scope mounts, approx. 8 3/4 lbs. Disc. 2005.

| | $2,495 | $2,185 | $1,870 | $1,695 | $1,370 | $1,125 | $875 | $2,495 |

A3 TACTICAL – various cals., top-of-the-line sniper weapon, 26 in. heavyweight match grade hand lapped barrel, Shilen trigger, McMillan fiberglass A-3 tactical stock, 11 1/4 lbs. Disc. 2008.

| | $2,995 | $2,620 | $2,245 | $2,035 | $1,645 | $1,350 | $1,050 | $2,995 |

ED BROWN PRODUCTS, INC.

Current manufacturer established during 1988 located in Perry, MO. Consumer direct sales.

PISTOLS: SEMI-AUTO

All the models in this category except the Classic Custom are available with Gen. III black coating at no extra charge.

The following MSRs represent each model's base price, with many options available at an additional charge.

Add $75 for ambidextrous safety on certain models.

COMMANDER BOBTAIL – various cals., M1911 style, SA, carry configuration, features round butt variation of the Class A Limited frame, incorporating frame and grip modifications, including a special housing w/o checkering, 4 1/4 in. barrel, Hogue exotic wood grips, 34 oz. Disc. 2003.

| | $2,350 | $2,055 | $1,760 | $1,600 | $1,290 | $1,055 | $820 | $2,350 |

EXECUTIVE TARGET – .45 ACP cal., similar to Executive Elite, except modified for target and range shooting, adj. Ed Brown rear sight, 5 in. barrel, single stack mag., matte stainless or matte black Gen. III stainless finish, cocobolo diamond checkered grips, approx. 38 oz. New 2006.

| MSR $2,945 | $2,675 | $2,400 | $2,000 | $1,800 | $1,425 | $1,175 | $925 | |

MSR	100%	98%	95%	90%	80%	70%	60%	Last MSR

Add $75 for California Executive Target Model with matte blue frame/slide finish and black Gen II coating.

EXECUTIVE ELITE – .45 ACP cal., M1911 style, 5 in. barrel, SA, choice of all blue (disc.) stainless blue (disc.), or full stainless slide/barrel, features Hardcore components, flared and lowered ejection port, Commander style hammer, 25 LPI checkering on front and rear grip strap, beveled magwell, fixed 3-dot night sights, checkered cocobolo wood grips, matte stainless or matte black Gen. III stainless finish, 34 oz. New 2004.

MSR $2,695 $2,525 $2,200 $1,875 $1,650 $1,325 $1,075 $850

EXECUTIVE CARRY – .45 ACP cal., similar to Executive Elite, except has 4 1/4 in. barrel and Bobtail grip, 34 oz. New 2004.

MSR $2,945 $2,675 $2,400 $2,000 $1,800 $1,425 $1,175 $925

KOBRA – .45 ACP cal., M1911 style, 7 shot, 5 in. barrel, SA, features "snakeskin" metal treatment on frame, mainspring housing and slide, 3-dot night sights, exotic wood grips, matte stainless or matte black Gen. III stainless finish, 39 oz. New 2002.

MSR $2,495 $2,325 $2,000 $1,725 $1,500 $1,225 $995 $775

KOBRA CARRY – .45 ACP cal., M1911 style, 4 1/4 in. barrel, SA, features Bobtail and "snakeskin" metal treatment on frame, mainspring housing and slide, 3-dot night sights, matte stainless or matte black Gen. III stainless finish, 34 oz. New 2002.

MSR $2,745 $2,575 $2,250 $1,925 $1,700 $1,400 $1,100 $875

* ***Kobra Carry Lightweight*** – .45 ACP, 7075 aluminum single stack commander frame and Bobtail housing, 4 1/4 in. barrel, 10-8 black sight, front night sight, slim cocobolo wood grips, black Gen. III coating, 27 oz. New 2010.

MSR $3,120 $2,925 $2,600 $2,200 $1,850 $1,525 $1,200 $975

SPECIAL FORCES – .45 ACP cal., M1911 style, 7 shot mag, 5 in. barrel, SA, Commander style hammer, special Chainlink treatment on front and rear grip straps, checkered diamond pattern cocobolo grips, 3-dot night sights, Generation III black coating applied to all metal surfaces, 38 oz. New 2006.

MSR $2,495 $2,325 $2,000 $1,725 $1,500 $1,225 $995 $775

Add $100 for stealth gray Gen. III finish and carbon fiber grips (new 2011).

Add $75 for California Special Forces Model with matte blue frame/slide finish and black G3 coating.

SPECIAL FORCES LIGHT RAIL – .45 ACP cal., 5 in. barrel, SA, forged Government style frame with integral light rail, Chainlink treatment on forestrap and mainspring housing, fixed 3-dot night sights, traditional square cut cocking serrations, diamond cut wood grips, approx. 40 oz. Mfg. 2009-2012.

                 $2,275 $1,975 $1,725 $1,550 $1,275 $1,050 $825   *$2,395*

SPECIAL FORCES CARRY/CARRY II – .45 ACP cal., 4 1/2 in. Commander style barrel, SA, single stack bobtail frame, 8 shot, chainlink treatment on forestrap and mainspring housing, stainless or optional Gen. III finish, low profile combat rear sights, fixed dovetail 3-dot night front sights, diamond cut wood grips, approx. 35 oz. New 2009.

MSR $2,745 $2,445 $2,140 $1,835 $1,660 $1,345 $1,100 $855

JIM WILSON SPECIAL LIMITED EDITION – .45 ACP cal., SA, features black frame with Jim Wilson signature on slide, smooth Tru-Ivory grips, 7 shot mag., 38 oz. Limited mfg. 2007.

                 $2,295 $2,010 $1,720 $1,560 $1,260 $1,035 $800   *$2,295*

JEFF COOPER COMMEMORATIVE LIMITED EDITION – .45 ACP cal., 5 in. barrel, SA, Govt. style, forged frame and slide, matte finish, square cut serrations on rear of slide, Jeff Cooper signature on slide, fixed Novak Lo-mount dovetail rear sight, dovetail front sight, 7 shot mag., exhibition grade cocobolo grips with Jeff Cooper pen and sword logo, includes ltd. ed. leather bound copy of *Principles of Self Defense*, 38 oz. Ltd. mfg. 2008.

                 $2,295 $2,010 $1,720 $1,560 $1,260 $1,035 $800   *$2,295*

MASSAD AYOOB SIGNATURE EDITION – .45 ACP cal., 4 1/4 in. barrel, commander bobtail stainless steel frame, SA, 25 LPI checkering on frame and mainspring housing, Massad Ayoob signature on right side of slide, ambidextrous safety, fixed 3-dot sights, black G10 checkered grips, 4 1/2 lb. trigger pull, includes a copy of *Gun Digest Book of Concealed Carry* by Massad Ayoob. Limited mfg. 2009-2010.

                 $2,700 $2,365 $2,025 $1,835 $1,485 $1,215 $945   *$2,700*

CHAMPION MOLON LABE 1911 – .45 ACP cal., 5 in. barrel, designed by certified law enforcement instructor Dave Champion, hand fitted and assembled, "Molon Labe" in Greek letters is laser engraved on the left side of the frame, "Champion" is laser engraved on the right side of the slide, custom G10 grips with engraved Spartan battle helmet, custom Snakeskin metal treatment on front and back grip straps, wide notch rear sight with tritium front night sight, solid aluminum trigger, black Gen. III coating. Limited mfg. 2011 only.

                 $2,595 $2,150 $1,850 $1,625 $1,450 $1,275 $1,050   *$2,595*

MSR	100%	98%	95%	90%	80%	70%	60%	Last MSR

RIFLES: BOLT ACTION

In August of 2010, Ed Brown Products announced that all bolt action rifle production had been put on hold indefinitely. The following last MSRs represent each model's base price, and many options were available at additional cost. Beginning 2006, all M-702 actions were disc. in favor of Ed Brown's new Model 704 controlled feed action with spring-loaded extractor integral with the bolt. All recently manufactured rifles have stainless steel barrels and the entire rifle is coated with Generation III black coating (new 2007).

A5 TACTICAL – .300 Win. Mag. or .308 Win. cal., features adj. McMillan A-5 tactical stock, 5 shot detachable mag., black finish, Shilen trigger, 12 1/2 lbs. Mfg. 2008-2010.

	$4,495	$3,935	$3,370	$3,055	$2,470	$2,025	$1,575	$4,495

M40A2 MARINE SNIPER – .30-06 or .308 Win. cal., 24 in. match grade barrel, special McMillan GP fiberglass tactical stock with recoil pad, Woodlands camo is molded into stock, this model is a duplicate of the original McMillan Marine Sniper rifle used in Vietnam, except for the Ed Brown action, 9 1/4 lbs. Mfg. 2002-2010.

	$3,695	$3,235	$2,770	$2,515	$2,030	$1,665	$1,295	$3,695

EDWARD ARMS COMPANY

Current manufacturer located in Phoenix, AZ.

Edward Arms Company manufactures precision weapons systems from the AR-15 platform to custom 1911 handguns. Please contact the company directly for more information including options, pricing, and delivery time (see Trademark Index).

RIFLES: SEMI-AUTO

Current Edward Arms Company models include: SLR Combat Rifle (MSR $1,750), 15V2L Rifle (MSR $1,750), B.A.R. Rifle (MSR $1,750), and the EA10 Rifle (MSR $3,000). Please contact the company directly for more information including options, availability, and delivery time (see Trademark Index).

ENFIELD AMERICA, INC.

Previous manufacturer located in Atlanta, GA.

PISTOLS: SEMI-AUTO

MP-9 – 9mm Para. cal., design similar to MP-45. Mfg. 1985.

	$550	$475	$425	$350	$295	$260	$240	

Add $150 for carbine kit.

MP-45 – .45 ACP cal., 4 1/2, 6, 8, 10, or 18 1/2 in. shrouded barrel, parkerized finish, 10, 30, 40, or 50 shot mag., 6 lbs. Mfg. 1985 only.

	$550	$475	$425	$350	$295	$260	$240	$350

ENFIELDS

Originally manufactured by the Royal Small Arms Factory at Enfield situated on the northern outskirts of London, in Middlesex, England. Various Enfield rifles, carbines and revolvers were produced and/or converted by other British factories (B.S.A., L.S.A., S.S.A., N.R.F., P. Webley & Son, Webley & Scott Ltd., Albion Motors, W.W. Greener, Westley Richards, Vickers (VSM), ROF Fazakerley, ROF Maltby, BSA Shirley (M47C), as well as Australia at Lithgow (from 1913), in Canada at Long Branch (from 1941), the United States by Stevens-Savage (also from 1941), RFI Ishapore, India (from 1905), Nakhu, Pyuthan and Sundrijal in Nepal (from 1911), and at Wah Cantt in Pakistan (from the late 1950s).

The publisher would like to thank Mr. Bob Maze and Mr. Ian Skennerton for making the following information available.

RIFLES & CARBINES

.303 RIFLE No. 1 Mk III* H.T. SNIPER – factory fitted telescopic sight and heavy barrel, converted at Lithgow, Australia at the end of WWII, special bedding of furniture, some were also fitted with a cheekpiece, British and Lithgow actions.

	$7,000	$6,000	$5,500	$5,000	$4,250	$3,750	$3,250	

Buyer beware - check for authentic serial nos., as there have been some fakes on this model.

.303 No. 3 Mk I* (T) (PATTERN 1914 SNIPER) – converted in England by Periscope Prism Co. (1918) & B.S.A. (1938) from Winchester rifles, the Pattern 1918 telescope on crawfoot mounts was fitted.

	$8,500	$7,500	$6,000	$5,250	$4,750	$4,000	$3,750	

MSR	100%	98%	95%	90%	80%	70%	60%	Last MSR

.303 No. 3 Mk I* (T) A SNIPER – converted in England by Alex Martin in WWII from Winchester MK I* (F) rifles, Great War Aldis and P.P. Co. telescopes (ex-SMLE snipers) were fitted, original SMLE rifle engraved number is usually visible, usually scope is offset (left) of the bore line. 421 mfg. beginning of WWII.

| | $7,500 | $6,750 | $6,000 | $5,250 | $4,750 | $4,000 | $3,500 | |

.303 No. 5 MK. I JUNGLE CARBINE – 20 1/2 in. barrel with flash hider, lightened action body and shortened furniture. From 1944, for service in the Far East.

| | $850 | $750 | $650 | $575 | $475 | $385 | $300 | |

Add 50% for BSA Shirley (M47C) rifle grenade trials rifles with serial numbers beginning with "BB" and a hung trigger.

Add approx. $2,500 for the .22 No. 5 Mk I rifle produced during 1945 in limited quantities for trials.

Subtract 20% for Indian service issues that have a transverse wood screw in the forend which is less desirable.

Beware of recently imported (circa 1990s) No. 4 rifles converted to appear as Jungle Carbines. These models do not have the lightning cuts on the receiver, barrel, and trigger guard.

7.62mm L42A1 SNIPER – Enfield conversion and extensive rebuild of the No. 4 Mk I(T) sniper rifle, fitted with an upgraded No. 32 telescopic sight to L1A1, half-stocked furniture, 7.62mm magazine with integral ejector, with heavy target barrel.

| | $8,500 | $7,750 | $7,250 | $6,750 | $5,750 | $5,250 | $4,500 | |

Add 30% for Iraq war issue with 6x Schmidt & Bender scope (beware of non-originals!)

ENTRÉPRISE ARMS INC.

Current manufacturer located in Irwindale, CA, since 1996. Dealer and consumer sales.

Due to space considerations, individual Enterprise Arms Inc. model listings are not listed in this text, but are provided free of charge through our website. Please visit www.bluebookofgunvalues.com.

ERMA SUHL, GmbH

Previous manufacturer located in Suhl, Germany January 1998 - circa 2004. Erma Suhl purchased the remaining assets of Erma-Werke.

RIFLES: BOLT ACTION

SR100 SNIPER RIFLE – .300 Win. Mag., .308 Win., or .338 Lapua Mag. cal., bolt action, tactical rifle featuring brown laminated wood stock with thumbhole, adj. buttplate/cheekpiece, and vent. forend, forged aluminum receiver, 25 1/2 or 29 1/2 in. barrel, muzzle brake, adj. match trigger, approx. 15 lbs. Limited importation 1997-98 only.

| | $6,500 | $5,750 | $5,000 | $4,350 | $3,750 | $3,000 | $2,350 | *$8,600* |

This model was imported exclusively by Amtec 2000, Inc., located in Gardner, MA.

Most recent importation was in .300 Win. Mag., and included a Steyr scope mount.

ERMA-WERKE

Previous manufacturer located in Dachau, Germany (Erma-Werke production) until bankruptcy occurred in October of 1997. Pistols were previously imported and distributed by Precision Sales International, Inc. located in Westfield, MA, Nygord Precision Products located in Prescott, AZ, and Mandall's Shooting Supplies, Inc. located in Scottsdale, AZ. Previously distributed by Excam located in Hialeah, FL.

Erma-Werke also manufactured private label handguns for American Arms Inc. (refer to their section for listings).

RIFLES

Models listed were available from Mandall Shooting Supplies, unless otherwise noted.

EM-1 .22 CARBINE – .22 LR cal., M1 copy, 10 or 15 shot mag., 18 in. barrel, rear adj. aperture sight, 5.6 lbs. Mfg. 1966-97.

| | $365 | $295 | $250 | $215 | $190 | $175 | $160 | *$400* |

EGM-1 – similar to EM-1 except for unslotted buttstock, 5 shot mag.

| | $260 | $230 | $195 | $175 | $150 | $125 | $100 | *$295* |

ESCORT

Current trademark of shotguns manufactured by Hatsan Arms Co., located in Izmir, Turkey, and imported beginning 2002 by Legacy Sports International, located in Reno, NV. Previously located in Alexandria, VA.

SHOTGUNS: O/U

* *Escort Shorty Home Defense* – 12 ga. only, 3 in. chambers, 18 in. VR barrels with choke tubes, fiber optic front sight, accessory rail on lower barrel, nickel plated receiver, black synthetic stock with adj. comb and vent recoil pad, 7 lbs. New 2011.

| MSR $663 | | $575 | $500 | $450 | $365 | $325 | $285 | $265 |

MSR	100%	98%	95%	90%	80%	70%	60%	Last MSR

SHOTGUNS: SEMI-AUTO

Beginning 2004, all models have a round back receiver with 3/8 in. dovetail milled along top for mounting sights. Beginning in 2009, all Escort semi-auto shotguns use a bottom feed system similar to a Remington 11-87.

ESCORT SERIES - 3 IN. – 12 or 20 (new 2005) ga., 3 in. chamber, gas operated action with 2 position adj. screw (disc. 2003), 20 (disc. 2008), 22 (AS Youth and PS Slug, new 2005), 24 (disc. 2008), 26 (new 2005), or 28 in. VR barrel with 3 multi-chokes, blue finish, vent recoil pad, gold trigger, checkered walnut (Model AS) or polymer (Model PS) black or 100% camo coverage Mossy Oak Break Up (disc. 2004), Mossy Oak Obsession (mfg. 2005-2008), Shadowgrass (disc. 2008), King's Woodland (mfg. 2009-2010), King's Desert (mfg. 2009-2010), King's Snow (mfg. 2009-2010), or Muddy Girl (new 2013) camo stock and forearm, 6.4-7 lbs. Importation began 2002.

MSR $489	$395	$350	$325	$285	$250	$225	$195	

Add $169 for AS Supreme model with gloss finished walnut stock and forearm (disc.). Add $99 for Model PS Slug with rifled slug barrel and cantilever mount (disc. 2011).

Add $182 for AS Select Model with select walnut (mfg. 2007-2008). Add $100 for 100% camo coverage (disc. 2010). Add $74 for HiViz Spark front sight and King's Field metal finish (mfg. 2009). Add $175 for Model PS Slug Combo (mfg. 2006-2008). Add $81 for 24 in. barrel with Model PS TriViz sights and Mossy Oak Break Up camo coverage (disc. 2004).

* ***Escort Series - 3 in. - Aimguard*** – similar to Escort model, except has black chrome finish, black polymer stock, 18 (new 2006) or 20 (disc. 2005) in. barrel, cylinder bore. Imported 2004-2007.

	$340	$295	$275	$250	$230	$215	$195	*$392*

* ***Escort Series 3 In. Home Defense*** – 12 ga., 18 in. barrel with cyl. bore choke, muzzle brake, receiver features upper Picatinny rail, adj. ghost ring rear sight and adj. fiber optic front sight, black MP-SA TacStock2 with cushioned pistol grip, forearm has Picatinny rail on bottom, recoil pad, built-in holder for 2 extra shells, 6.9 lbs. New 2011.

MSR $529	$475	$415	$350	$325	$275	$215	$175	

TURKEY/COYOTE TACTICAL – 12 ga., FAST loading system, 24 in. chromemoly barrel, extended full choke Turkey tube, fiber optic ghost ring sights, 100% Realtree AP camo stock with cushioned pistol grip, built-in shell storage in the stock, upper and lower Picatinny rails, mag. cut off, sling swivel studs included, 7.4 lbs. New 2013.

MSR $659	$595	$525	$450	$400	$325	$275	$215	

SHOTGUNS: SLIDE ACTION

ESCORT SERIES – 12 or 20 (new 2005) ga., 3 in. chamber, matte blue finish, Black synthetic or 100% camo (disc.) stock and forearm, 18 (Aimguard or MarineGuard Model), 22 (Field Slug, mfg. 2005-2011), 24 (Turkey, includes extra turkey choke tube and FH TriViz sight combo with Mossy Oak Break Up [disc. 2004] or Obsession camo coverage, disc. 2008), 26 (new 2005, Field Hunter), or 28 (Field Hunter) in. barrel, alloy receiver with 3/8 in. milled dovetail for sight mounting, trigger guard safety, 4 or 5 shot mag. with cut off button, two stock adj. shims, 6.4-7 lbs. Importation began 2003.

* ***Escort Series Aimguard*** – 12 ga., 3 in. chamber, 18 in. barrel, fixed cyl. bore choke, 5 shot mag., matte black synthetic stock, includes sling swivel studs, large slide release button, 6.4 lbs.

MSR $312	$260	$225	$195	$175	$150	$135	$120	

* ***Escort Series Marine Guard*** – 12 ga., 18 in. barrel with black synthetic stock, nickel receiver, 5 shot mag., fixed cyl. bore choke, 6.4 lbs.

MSR $379	$325	$285	$250	$225	$200	$185	$150	

* ***Escort Series Home Defense (Tactical Entry/Special Ops)*** – 12 ga. only, 3 in. chamber, 18 in. barrel, synthetic stock, cushioned vertical pistol grip, available in a variety of configurations, forearm features upper and lower Picatinny rail, current mfg. features the MP-P/A TacStock2 with pistol grip and built in holder for two extra shells, fiber optic front sight, fully adj. ghost ring rear, 6.85 lbs. New 2009.

MSR $393	$350	$295	$260	$225	$200	$180	$160	

Subtract approx. 15% if w/o TacStock2 (new 2010).

EUROPEAN AMERICAN ARMORY CORP.

Current importer and distributor established in late 1990 and located in Rockledge, FL. Previously located in Sharpes, FL 1990-2006. Distributor and dealer sales.

EAA currently imports the Tanfoglio Witness series of semi-auto pistols, located in Italy, H. Weihrauch revolvers, located in Germany, and select Zastava firearms, located in Serbia. All guns are covered by EAA's lifetime limited warranty. EAA has also imported various trademarks of long guns, including Saiga, and Izhmash. Please refer to those individual sections.

Baikal shotguns, Zastava Z98 and Z5 bolt actions, Sarpa slide action shotguns manufactured by Sarzilmaz, and Sabatti double rifles are currently imported by U.S. Sporting Goods Inc. Please refer to individual listings for more information and current pricing.

PISTOLS: SEMI-AUTO

EAA has issued a safety upgrade notice regarding any Witness style semi-auto pistol bearing a serial number between AE00000 - AE700000.

MSR	100%	98%	95%	90%	80%	70%	60%	Last MSR

Owners are requested to field strip the pistol and send the slide assembly directly to EAA. EAA will replace the firing pin and return it to you. See Trademark Index for contact information.

The following Witness pistols also have a .22 LR conversion kit available for $234.

WITNESS EA 9 SERIES – 9mm Para. cal., action patterned after the CZ-75, DA/SA, 4 1/2 in. unported or ported (polymer, New Frame only, new 2002) barrel, steel or polymer frame/steel slide (new 1997), 10 (C/B 1994), 16*, or 18 (new late 2004) shot mag., choice of Wonder (new 1997), stainless steel (disc. 1996), blue, blue/chrome (disc. 1993), or brushed chrome (disc. 1996) finish, combat sights, black neoprene grips, 33 oz. Importation began late 1990.

| MSR $607 | $495 | $430 | $375 | $320 | $285 | $230 | $185 | |

Add $181 for 9mm Para/.22 LR combo.

Subtract $36 for polymer New Frame.

* ***Model EA 9 (L) Compact*** – similar to EA 9, except has 3 5/8 in. unported or ported (polymer frame only, mfg. 2002-2006) barrel and 10 (C/ B 1994), 12 (new late 2004), or 13* shot mag., 27 oz.

| MSR $607 | $495 | $430 | $375 | $320 | $285 | $230 | $185 | |

Subtract $36 for polymer frame.

Add $10-$20 for ported barrel (polymer frame only, disc. 2006).

WITNESS EA 10 SUPER SERIES – 10mm cal., action patterned after the CZ-75, DA/SA, 4 1/2 in. barrel, polymer or steel frame, 10, 12*, or 15 (new late 2004) shot mag., choice of stainless steel (disc.), blue, chrome (disc.), or Wonder (new 1999) finish, combat sights, black neoprene grips, 33 oz. Imported 1994 only, and again begining 1999.

| MSR $607 | $495 | $430 | $375 | $320 | $285 | $230 | $185 | |

Add $30 for chrome finish (disc.).

Add $65 for stainless steel (disc.).

Subtract $36 for polymer frame.

* ***Model EA 10 Carry Comp*** – similar to EA 10, except has 4 1/2 in. compensated barrel, blue or Wonder (new 2005) finish. Mfg. 1999-2005.

| | $415 | $365 | $310 | $280 | $230 | $185 | $145 | *$489* |

Subtract $20 for blue finish.

* ***Model EA 10 Compact*** – similar to EA 10, except has 3 5/8 in. barrel, 8 or 12 (new late 2004) shot mag., 27 oz.

| MSR $607 | $495 | $430 | $375 | $320 | $285 | $230 | $185 | |

Subtract $36 for polymer frame.

WITNESS EA 38 SUPER SERIES – .38 Super cal., action patterned after the CZ-75, DA/SA, 4 1/2 in. barrel, steel or polymer frame/steel slide (mfg. 1997-2004), 10 (C/B 1994), 18 (new late 2004) or 19* shot mag., choice of Wonder (heat treated grey satin finish, new 1997), stainless steel (disc. 1996), blue (disc.), blue/chrome (disc. 1994), or brushed chrome (disc. 1996) finish, combat sights, black neoprene grips, 33 oz. Importation began 1994.

| MSR $607 | $495 | $430 | $375 | $320 | $285 | $230 | $185 | |

Subtract $31 for polymer frame (disc. 2004).

* ***Model EA 38 Compact*** – similar to EA 38 Super Series, except has 3 5/8 in. unported or ported barrel, choice of matte blue or Wonder finish, 30 oz. Mfg. 1999-2004.

| | $370 | $325 | $275 | $250 | $205 | $165 | $130 | *$449* |

Subtract $20 for polymer frame.

Add $20 for Wonder finish or ported barrel (polymer frame only).

WITNESS EA 40 SERIES – .40 S&W cal., action patterned after the CZ-75, DA/SA, 4 1/2 in. barrel, steel or polymer frame/steel slide (new 1997), 10 (C/B 1994), 12*, or 15 (new late 2004) shot mag., choice of Wonder (new 1997), stainless steel (disc. 1996), blue, blue/chrome (disc.), or brushed chrome (disc. 1996) finish, combat sights, black neoprene grips, 33 oz. Importation began late 1990.

| MSR $607 | $495 | $430 | $375 | $320 | $285 | $230 | $185 | |

Subtract $36 for polymer New Frame.

* ***Model EA 40 (L) Compact*** – similar to EA 40, except has 3 5/8 in. unported or ported barrel, 9 or 12 (new late 2004) shot mag.

| MSR $607 | $495 | $430 | $375 | $320 | $285 | $230 | $185 | *$557* |

Subtract $36 for polymer frame.

Add $10-$20 for ported barrel (polymer frame only, disc. 2005).

WITNESS EA 41 SERIES – .41 Action Express cal., action patterned after the CZ-75, DA/SA, 4 1/2 in. barrel, steel frame, 11 shot mag., blue, blue/chrome, or brushed chrome finish, combat sights, black neoprene grips, 33 oz. Importation disc. 1993.

| | $450 | $395 | $335 | $305 | $245 | $200 | $155 | *$595* |

Add $40 for blue/chrome or brushed chrome finish.

MSR	100%	98%	95%	90%	80%	70%	60%	Last MSR

* Model EA 41 Compact – similar to EA 41, except has 3 1/2 in. barrel and 8 shot mag.

	$495	$435	$370	$335	$270	$225	$175	$625

Add $40 for blue/chrome or brushed chrome finish.

WITNESS EA 45 SERIES – .45 ACP cal., action patterned after the CZ-75, DA/SA, 4 1/2 in. standard or compensated (mfg. 1998-2005) barrel, steel frame, polymer full size frame (new 2004), or polymer frame/steel slide (new 1997), 10 (C/ B 1994) or 11* shot mag., choice of Wonder (new 1997), stainless steel (disc. 1996), blue, blue/chrome (disc. 1993), or brushed chrome (disc. 1996) finish, combat sights, walnut grips, 35 oz. Importation began late 1990.

MSR $607	$495	$430	$375	$320	$285	$230	$185	

Add $145 for .45 ACP/.22 LR combo.
Add $40 for ported barrel (steel only, with Wonder finish, disc. 2004).
Subtract $36 for polymer frame or blue finish.

* Model EA 45 (L) Compact – similar to EA 45, except has 3 5/8 in. unported or ported barrel and 8 shot mag., 26 oz.

MSR $607	$495	$430	$375	$320	$285	$230	$185	

Add $30 for ported barrel (polymer frame only, disc. 2004).
Add $50 for single port barrel compensator or carry configuration with compensator (disc.).
Subtract $36 for polymer frame.

WITNESS P CARRY – 9mm Para., 10mm, .40 S&W, or .45 ACP cal., SA/DA, 3.6 in. barrel, 10 (.45 ACP), 15 (10mm or .40 S&W), or 17 (9mm Para.) shot mag., full size polymer frame, compact slide, Commander style, Wonder finish, integral M-1913 rail, 27 oz. New 2006.

MSR $691	$560	$465	$410	$360	$325	$265	$225	

WITNESS CARRY COMP GUN – .38 Super (disc. 1997), 9mm Para. (disc. 1997), .40 S&W cal. (disc. 1997), 10mm (disc. 1994, reintroduced 1999), or .45 ACP cal., DA/SA, full size frame with compact slide and 1 in. compensator, 10 (C/B 1994), 12* (.40 S&W), or 16* (9mm Para.) shot mag., Wonder (new 1997), blue, Duo-Tone (disc. 1994) finish. Imported 1992-2004.

	$425	$370	$320	$290	$235	$190	$150	$479

Add $10 for Wonder finish.

WITNESS ELITE MATCH – 9mm Para., 10mm, .38 Super, .40 S&W, or .45 ACP cal., 4 3/4 in. barrel, two-tone finish, checkered black polymer grips, SA, extended mag. release, 10 (.45 ACP), 15 (.40 S&W or 10mm), or 17 (9mm Para. or .38 Super) shot mag., approx. 44 oz. New mid-2013.

MSR $778	$625	$525	$450	$385	$340	$315	$275	

SAR K2 – 9mm Para., .40 S&W (disc. 2013), 10mm (disc. 2013) or .45 ACP cal., 4 1/2 in. barrel, blue finish, DA/SA, 14 (.45 ACP), 17 (.40 S&W and 10mm), or 18 (9mm Para.) shot mag., steel frame and slide, ergonomic grip, accessory rail, extended beavertail, elongated trigger guard with serrations, removable dovetail front sight, mfg. by Sarsilmaz for Turkish military, 40 oz. Importation began mid-2011.

MSR $459	$390	$335	$285	$250	$225	$200	$185	

Add $104 for stainless steel.
Add $277 for .45 ACP cal.
Add $354 for Sport Configuration in .45 ACP cal.
Add $521 for stainless steel in .45 ACP cal.

SAR K2P – 9mm Para. cal., 3.8 in. barrel, blue or stainless, lower accessory rail, 16 shot mag., ambidextrous safety, full size grip, compact slide, polymer frame, 24 oz. Mfg. 2013 only.

	$365	$325	$275	$250	$200	$165	$125	$433

Add $98 for stainless.

SAR ST10 – 9mm Para. cal., 4.4 in. barrel, blue or two-tone finish, ergonomic polymer grips, steel frame and slide, adj. rear sights, lower accessory rail, 16 shot mag., removable dovetail front sight, includes carry case, holster, two-pocket mag. pouch, two mags., lock and cleaning tools, 34 oz. New mid-2013.

MSR $754	$650	$575	$495	$450	$400	$365	$335	

Add $69 for stainless steel.

SARGUN – 9mm Para., .40 S&W, or .45 ACP cal., 4 1/2 in. barrel, polymer frame, blue or stainless steel slide, 15 or 17 shot mag., matte black finish, ambidextrous controls, loaded chamber indicator, adj. front and rear sights, integral accessory rail, includes case, holster, and other shooting accessories, 20 oz. New mid-2013.

MSR $613	$540	$475	$425	$360	$325	$295	$250	

Add $26 for 9mm Para. or $64 for .40 S&W cal.
Add $101 for stainless.

MSR	100%	98%	95%	90%	80%	70%	60%	Last MSR

ZASTAVA EZ – 9mm Para., .40 S&W, or .45 ACP (disc. 2010) cal., DA/SA, ambidextrous controls, 10 (.45 ACP), 11 (.40 S&W), or 15 (9mm Para.) shot mag., 4 in. barrel, aluminum frame, accessory rail, spur hammer, blue or chrome finish, 33 oz. Imported 2007-2011.

| | $495 | $435 | $375 | $335 | $285 | $250 | $215 | $573 |

Add $47 for chrome finish (disc. 2010).

   * ***Zastava EZ Compact*** – similar to Zastava EZ Model, except has compact frame, 7 (.45 ACP), 8 (.40 S&W), or 12 shot mag., 3 1/2 in. barrel. Imported 2007-2010.

| | $495 | $435 | $375 | $335 | $285 | $250 | $215 | $573 |

Add $47 for chrome finish (disc. 2010).
Subtract 10% if without ported barrel (disc. 2010).

ZASTAVA EZ CARRY – 9mm Para. or .40 S&W cal., full size frame, 3 1/2 in. ported barrel, DA/SA, 10 or 14 shot mag. Imported 2010-2011.

| | $550 | $495 | $450 | $395 | $350 | $300 | $250 | $619 |

RIFLES

Some EAA rifles were manufactured by Sabatti in Italy (est. 1674), Lu-Mar in Italy, and H. Weihrauch in Germany (see separate listing in the H. Weihrauch section). Imported 1992-96.

ZASTAVA PAP 762 SEMI-AUTO – 7.62x39mm cal., patterned after the AK-47, blond hardwood thumbhole stock and furniture, 10 shot mag., 16 3/4 in. barrel, removable accessory rail, 10 lbs. Imported 2008-2013.

| | $435 | $375 | $335 | $295 | $265 | $240 | $220 | $488 |

TANFOGLIO APPEAL SEMI-AUTO – .22 LR or .22 WMR cal., bull pup design, 16 in. barrel with muzzle brake, features elevated Picatinny rail, adj. front and rear sights, ambidextrous controls, black synthetic thumbhole stock with pistol grip has adj. LOP, 10 shot mag., black finish, 4.8 lbs. Importation began 2012.

| MSR $450 | $385 | $335 | $295 | $260 | $240 | $220 | $195 | |

Add $17 for .22 WMR cal.

M-93 BLACK ARROW BOLT ACTION – .50 BMG cal., Mauser action, 36 in. fluted heavy barrel with muzzle brake, adj. folding bipod, iron sights, detachable 5 shot mag., carry handle, detachable scope mount, wood case, 35 lbs. Mfg. by Zastava, imported 2007-2011.

| | $6,400 | $5,800 | $5,000 | $4,250 | $3,500 | $2,900 | $2,300 | $6,986 |

SHOTGUNS: SLIDE ACTION

MODEL PM2 – 12 ga. only, slide action, unique 7 shot detachable mag., 20 in. barrel, black wood stock and composite forearm, dual action bars, cross-bolt safety on trigger guard, available in matte blue or chrome finish, 6.81 lbs. Imported 1992 only.

| | $550 | $480 | $410 | $375 | $300 | $245 | $190 | $695 |

Add $200 for night sights.
Add $75 for matte chrome finish.

EVOLUTION USA

Current rifle manufacturer located in White Bird, ID since 1984. Distributor and dealer sales.

RIFLES: BOLT ACTION

Evolution USA uses four different types of actions for its rifles. They include the MSR-10 that is a faceted and highly customized Remington M700 receiver, the MSX-10 that uses a Post-64 Win. Model 70 with claw extractor, the Pre-64 Win. Model 70 action, and the Mauser Express 98 action manufactured by CZ USA. Most models can be ordered by selecting one of the previous receivers.

BOLT ACTION SNIPER/VARMINT SERIES – various cals., 3 different configurations included Sniper, Informal Target Varmint, and Field Grade Varmint, featured match barrel, action, and tuned trigger. Disc. 2000.
   Prices for the Sniper rifle started at approx. $3,000 while the Varmint guns started at approx. $2,000.

RIFLES: SEMI-AUTO

GRENADA – .223 Rem. cal., GIO, design based on the AR-15 with flat upper receiver, 17 in. stainless steel match barrel with integral muzzle brake, NM trigger. Disc. 2000.

| | $985 | $825 | $675 | $600 | $525 | $465 | $400 | $1,195 |

DESERT STORM – similar to Grenada, except has 21 in. match barrel. Disc. 2003.

| | $975 | $825 | $665 | $560 | $500 | $450 | $400 | $1,189 |

MSR	100%	98%	95%	90%	80%	70%	60%	Last MSR

IWO JIMA – features GIO, carrying handle incorporating iron sights, 20 in. stainless steel match barrel, A2 HBAR action, tubular handguard. Limited mfg.

	$1,000	$875	$775	$700	$600	$475	$425	

RIFLES : SINGLE SHOT

PHANTOM III SINGLE SHOT – .50 BMG or .700 NE cal., Evolution M-2000 stainless single shot action, 28 in. Lilja match barrel with flutes and muzzle brake, approx. 30 lbs. Mfg. 2000-2011.

	$4,700	$4,300	$3,850	$3,500	$2,950	$2,400	$2,250	*$4,700*

Add $1,700 for Delta Model (50-80 lbs.) or .700 NE cal. (24-30 lbs.), disc.

EXCAM

Previous importer and distributor located in Hialeah, FL, which went out of business late 1990. Excam distributed Dart, Erma, Tanarmi, Targa, and Warrior exclusively in the U.S. These trademarks will appear under Excam. All importation of Excam firearms ceased in 1990.

All Targa and Tanarmi pistols were manufactured in Gardone V.T., Italy. All Erma and Warrior pistols and rifles were manufactured in W. Germany. Senator O/U shotguns were manufactured by A. Zoli located in Brescia, Italy.

Due to space considerations, this section is now available online free of charge at www.bluebookofgunvalues.com.

EXCEL ARMS

Current trademark of pistols and rifles manufactured by Excel Industries, Inc., located in Ontario, CA. Previously located in Chino, CA.

PISTOLS: SEMI-AUTO

ACCELERATOR MP – .17 HMR (MP-17), .17 Mach 2 (new 2007, SP-17), .22 LR (new 2007, SP-22), or .22 WMR (MP-22) cal., 6 1/2 (new 2007) or 8 1/2 in. barrel, SA, polymer frame with stainless steel slide, adj. sights, 9 shot mag., 45 or 54 oz. Mfg. 2005-2009.

	$385	$325	$285	$260	$240	$220	$195	*$433*

Add $63 for red/green dot optic sight or $87 for 4x32mm scope with illuminated crosshairs.
Add $87 for choice of Realtree Hardwoods HD Green or Digital Desert camo coverage (new 2008).

MP-17 – .17 HMR cal., 8 1/2 in. barrel, SA, 9 shot, stainless steel, polymer grip, adj. sights, available with red dot optic or scope and rings, matte black, Digital Desert or Realtree Hardwoods HD camo. Mfg. late 2008-2010.

	$375	$325	$285	$260	$240	$220	$195	*$433*

Add $63 for red dot optic front sight. Add $87 for scope and rings. Add $87 for camo.

MP-22 – .22 WMR cal., 6 1/2 or 8 1/2 in. stainless steel bull barrel, SA, 9 shot, polymer grip, adj. sights, integral weaver base, available with red dot optic or scope and rings, stainless steel, Black cerakote, Digital Desert (disc. 2010) or Realtree Hardwoods HD camo (disc. 2010), 3 3/8 lbs. New late 2008.

MSR $477	$415	$345	$300	$260	$240	$220	$195	

Add $71 for red dot optic front sight. Add $97 for scope and rings. Add $87 for camo (disc. 2010).

MP-5.7 – 5.7x28mm cal., stainless steel construction, 8 1/2 in. bull barrel with integral top Picatinny rail, SA, fully adj. target sights, available with red dot optic or scope and rings, polymer grip, 9 shot mag., blow-back action, last round hole open, stainless steel or black Cerakote finish, 3 3/8 lbs. New 2011.

MSR $615	$550	$475	$425	$375	$300	$250	$200	

Add $70 for red dot optic sights. Add $96 for scope and rings.

X-5.7P – 5.7x28mm cal., 8 1/2 in. barrel, SA, 10 or 25 shot mag., no sights or adj. iron sights (25 shot mag. only), Black finish. New 2011.

MSR $715	$650	$575	$500	$450	$400	$350	$295	

Add $121 for adj. iron sights (25 shot mag. only).

X-22P – .22 LR cal., 4 1/2 in. barrel, SA, black synthetic stock, 10 or 25 shot mag., adj. sights, Picatinny rail. New 2009.

MSR $455	$400	$335	$290	$250	$225	$200	$185	

X-30P – .30 Carbine cal., features aluminum frame with integral Picatinny rail, 8 1/2 in. partially shrouded barrel, delayed blow-back action, tilted black synthetic pistol grip with finger grooves, 10 or 20 shot mag., no sights or adj. iron sights (20 shot mag. only), Black finish, 4 1/2 lbs. New 2011.

MSR $715	$650	$575	$500	$450	$400	$350	$295	

Add $121 for adj. iron sights (20 shot mag. only).

MSR	100%	98%	95%	90%	80%	70%	60%	Last MSR

SP-17 – .17 Mach 2 cal., 6 1/2 or 8 1/2 in. barrel, SA, 10 shot, stainless steel, polymer grip, adj. sights, available with red dot optic or scope and rings, matte black, Digital Desert or Realtree Hardwoods HD camo. Mfg. late 2008-2010.

	100%	98%	95%	90%	80%	70%	60%	Last MSR
	$375	$325	$285	$260	$240	$220	$195	*$433*

Add $63 for red dot optic front sight. Add $87 for scope and rings. Add $87 for camo.

SP-22 – .22 LR cal., 6 1/2 or 8 1/2 in. barrel, SA, 10 shot, stainless steel, polymer grip, adj. sights, available with red dot optic or scope and rings, matte black, Digital Desert or Realtree Hardwoods HD camo. Mfg. late 2008-2010.

	100%	98%	95%	90%	80%	70%	60%	Last MSR
	$375	$325	$285	$260	$240	$220	$195	*$433*

Add $63 for red dot optic front sight. Add $87 for scope and rings. Add $87 for camo.

RIFLES: SEMI-AUTO

CR-9 – 9mm Para. cal., stainless steel construction, 18 in. stainless bull barrel, full length Weaver rail and two side rails, adj. and detachable sights, 10 shot mag., nylon sling and detachable swivels. Mfg. 2008.

	100%	98%	95%	90%	80%	70%	60%	Last MSR
	$550	$480	$415	$375	$305	$250	$195	*$635*

MR/SR SERIES – .17 HMR (MR17), .17 Mach 2 (SR17, new 2007), .22 LR (SR22, new 2007), or .22 WMR (MR22) cal., black composite stock with large thumbhole, fluted 18 in. stainless steel barrel and receiver with shroud, black, silver, or camo finish, fully adj. sights, 9 shot mag., standard package is supplied with red dot optic and hard sided case, 8 lbs. Mfg. 2004-2009.

	100%	98%	95%	90%	80%	70%	60%	Last MSR
	$435	$380	$325	$295	$240	$195	$150	*$488*

Add $195 for choice of Realtree Hardwoods HD Green or Digital Desert camo coverage (new 2008).
Add $35 for red dot optical sight.
Add $147 for iron sights or 3-9x40mm scope.
Add $231 for iron sights and 6x9 in. bipod.

MR-17 – .17 HMR cal., 18 in. bull barrel, 9 shot mag., silver or black shroud, available options include no sights, red dot optic, iron sights, scope and rings, sling, bipod, side rails, and flashlight, black, Digital Desert or Realtree Hardwoods HD Green camo. Mfg. late 2008-2010.

	100%	98%	95%	90%	80%	70%	60%	Last MSR
	$425	$370	$320	$290	$235	$190	$150	*$488*

Add $35 for red dot optic sights. Add $147 for iron sights or 3-9x40mm scope. Add $84 for bipod (iron sights or scope only). Add $257 for side rails and flashlight. Add $195 for camo.

The no sight model is only available with one magazine - all other variations include two.

MR-22 – .22 WMR cal., 18 in. bull barrel, 9 shot mag., silver or black shroud, full length top Picatinny rail, available options include no sights, red dot optic, iron sights, scope and rings, sling, bipod, side rails, and flashlight, blow back action, black, Digital Desert (disc. 2010) or Realtree Hardwoods HD Green camo (disc. 2010) finish, 8 lbs. New late 2008.

MSR $538	100%	98%	95%	90%	80%	70%	60%	
	$450	$385	$335	$300	$250	$195	$150	

Add $39 for red dot optic sights. Add $162 for iron sights or 3-9x40mm scope. Add $255 for bipod (iron sights or scope only). Add $446 for side rails and flashlight. Add $195 for camo (disc. 2010).

The no sight model is only available with one magazine - all other variations include two.

* MR-22 Camo – .22 WMR cal., similar to MR-22, except features Desert Digital or Timbers Edge camo stock and shroud, no sights. New 2014.

MSR $600	100%	98%	95%	90%	80%	70%	60%	
	$510	$450	$385	$350	$275	$225	$185	

MR-5.7 – 5.7x28mm cal., 18 in. fluted bull barrel, 9 shot mag., black or silver shroud, full length upper Picatinny rail, no sights, black synthetic pistol grip stock with thumbhole, last round hole open, 8 lbs. New 2011.

MSR $672	100%	98%	95%	90%	80%	70%	60%	
	$595	$515	$460	$400	$350	$300	$275	

Add $163 for 3.9x40mm scope.

SR-17 – .17 Mach 2 cal., 18 in. bull barrel, 10 shot mag., silver or black shroud, available options include no sights, red dot optic, iron sights, scope and rings, sling, bipod, side rails, and flashlight, black, Digital Desert or Realtree Hardwoods HD Green camo. Mfg. 2008-2010.

	100%	98%	95%	90%	80%	70%	60%	Last MSR
	$425	$370	$320	$290	$235	$190	$150	*$488*

Add $35 for red dot optic sights. Add $147 for iron sights or 3-9x40mm scope. Add $84 for bipod (iron sights or scope only). Add $257 for side rails and flashlight. Add $195 for camo.

The no sight model is only available with one magazine - all other variations include two.

SR-22 – .22 LR cal., 18 in. bull barrel, 10 shot mag., silver or black shroud, available options include no sights, red dot optic, iron sights, scope and rings, sling, bipod, side rails, and flashlight, black, Digital Desert or Realtree Hardwoods HD Green camo. Mfg. late 2008-2010.

	100%	98%	95%	90%	80%	70%	60%	Last MSR
	$425	$370	$320	$290	$235	$190	$150	*$488*

Add $35 for red dot optic sights. Add $147 for iron sights or 3-9x40mm scope. Add $84 for bipod (iron sights or scope only). Add $257

MSR		100%	98%	95%	90%	80%	70%	60%	*Last MSR*

for side rails and flashlight. Add $195 for camo.

The no sight model was only available with one magazine - all other variations included two.

X-22R – .22 LR cal., 18 in. barrel, fixed (new 2011) or collapsible black synthetic stock, blow back action, no sights, 10 or 25 shot mag., drilled and tapped, accepts Ruger 10/22 mags., 4 3/4 lbs. New 2009.

MSR $504		$450	$400	$350	$300	$250	$200	$175	

Add $15 for fixed stock (new 2011).
Add $90 for 3-9x40 scope.

X-30R – .30 Carbine cal., 18 in. partially shrouded barrel, features aluminum receiver with integral Picatinny top rail, blow-back action, fixed or collapsible stock, no sights or adj. iron sights (20 shot mag. only), 10 or 20 shot mag., approx. 6 1/4 lbs. New 2011.

MSR $795		$725	$650	$575	$500	$450	$400	$350	

Add $15 for fixed stock (10 shot mag. only).
Add $121 for adj. iron sights (20 shot mag. only).

X-5.7R – 5.7x28mm cal., otherwise similar to the X-30R, 10 or 25 shot mag. New 2011.

MSR $795		$725	$650	$575	$500	$450	$400	$350	

Add $15 for fixed stock (10 shot mag. only).
Add $121 for adj. Iron Sights (25 shot mag. only).

NOTES

_____
_____
_____
_____
_____
_____
_____
_____
_____
_____
_____
_____
_____
_____
_____
_____
_____

F SECTION

F&D DEFENSE

Current manufacturer located in New Braunfels, TX.

MSR	100%	98%	95%	90%	80%	70%	60%	Last MSR

RIFLES: SEMI-AUTO

FD308 – .308 Win. cal., FAL type action with GPO, 17 (disc. 2013), 18 (new 2014), 21 (disc. 2013), or 22 (new 2014) in. stainless barrel with two chamber muzzle brake, full length Picatinny rail with folding battle tritium sights, side charging system with integrated forward asssist, removeable guide rails, Geissele trigger group, tan Magpul stock and pistol grip, storage compartment in the buttstock, 8.7 lbs. New 2012.

MSR $3,395	$3,050	$2,675	$2,295	$2,075	$1,675	$1,375	$1,075	

Add $100 for 22 in. barrel.

FD338 – .338 Lapua Mag. cal., GPO, 22 or 25 in. stainless steel barrel, 10 or 15 shot double stack mags., non-reciprocating side charging handle, matched lower, upper, rail, bolt, and extension, Geissele trigger group, full length Picatinny rail, Magpul stock and pistol grip. New 2013.

MSR $5,450	$4,900	$4,300	$3,675	$3,325	$2,700	$2,200	$1,800	

FD260 – .260 Rem. cal., similar to FD338, except features 22 in. stainless Bartlein barrel, Magpul 20 shot PMag.

MSR $3,595	$3,225	$2,825	$2,425	$2,200	$1,775	$1,450	$1,200	

FD65C – 6.5mm Creedmoor cal., similar to FD338, except has 22 in. barrel.

MSR $3,595	$3,225	$2,825	$2,425	$2,200	$1,775	$1,450	$1,200	

FEG

Current manufacturer located in Hungary (FEG stands for Fegyver es Gepgyar) since 1891. Previously imported 2007-2010 by SSME Deutsche Waffen, Inc., located in Plant City, FL. A few models were imported by Century International Arms located in Delray Beach, FL (see additional information under the Century International Arms in this text). Previously imported and distributed by K.B.I., Inc. located in Harrisburg, PA, and distributed until 1998 by Interarms located in Alexandria, VA.

RIFLES: SEMI-AUTO

MODEL SA-85M – 7.62x39mm cal., sporter rifle utilizing AKM action, 16.3 in. barrel, 6 shot detachable mag., thumbhole stock, 7 lbs. 10 oz. Imported 1991, banned 1998.

	$550	$480	$410	$375	$300	$245	$190	*$429*

SA-85 S (SA-2000M) – .223 Rem. (disc. 2000) or 7.62x39mm cal., sporter rifle with skeletonized Choate synthetic stock, 16.3 (new 2007) or 17 3/4 (disc. 2000) in. barrel with muzzle brake, 6, 10, or 30 shot detachable mag. Imported 1999-2000, reimported 2007-2011.

	$950	$830	$710	$645	$520	$425	$330	*$1,075*

F.I.E.

Previous importer (F.I.E. is the acronym for Firearms Import & Export) located in Hialeah, FL until 1990.

F.I.E. filed bankruptcy in November of 1990 and all models were discontinued. Some parts or service for these older firearms may be obtained through Numrich Gun Parts Corp. (see Trademark Index), even though all warranties on F.I.E. guns are void.

Due to space considerations, this section is now available through our website: www.bluebookofgunvalues.com.

FMK FIREARMS

Current pistol manufacturer located in Placentia, CA. Dealer direct sales beginning 2014. Previously distributed by American Tactical Imports, located in Rochester, NY until 2013.

PISTOLS: SEMI-AUTO

FMK 9C1/9C1G2 – 9mm Para. cal., 4 in. barrel, blue steel, DAO, SFO, features FAT trigger mechanism for quick and short trigger pull, polymer frame with steel slide, 10 or 14 shot mag., loaded chamber indicator, with or w/o Bill of Rights engraving, matte black, Dark Earth, or Pink finish, Picatinny rail, trigger safety, includes two mags. New 2010.

MSR $400	$350	$300	$265	$240	$220	$200	$180	

FMR

Current rifle manufacturer located in Pantin, France. No current U.S. importation.

MSR	100%	98%	95%	90%	80%	70%	60%	Last MSR

RIFLES: BOLT ACTION

FMR owns the rights to the French trademark Unique, and manufactures a line of bolt action rifles based on the original Unique design. All rifles have an aluminum ERGAL or stainless steel action, interchangeable barrels and fully adjustable stocks. The RS1 Sniper is available as a single shot or a repeater, and has an MSR of €1,930. The RS1 Commando has a heavy barrel and muzzle brake and has an MSR of €1,570. Various options are also available, including an unmodified adjustable stock for the CZ22. Please contact the company directly for more information, including options, pricing, and U.S. availability (see Trademark Index).

FNH USA

Current manufacturer and importer established in 1998, and located in McLean, VA. Dealer and distributor sales.

In the U.S., FN (Fabrique Nationale) is represented by two entities - FNH USA, which is responsible for sales, marketing, and business development, and FNM, which stands for FN Manufacturing, which handles manufacturing. FNH USA has two separate divisions - commercial/law enforcement, and military operations. FN Manufacturing is located in Columbia, SC. Design, research and development are conducted under the authority of FN Herstal S.A. Some of the firearms that FNM currently produces for the U.S. government are M16 rifles, M249 light machine guns, and M240 medium machine guns. FNM also produces the FNP line of handguns for the commercial, military, and law enforcement marketplaces. FNM is one of only three small arms manufacturers designated by the U.S. government as an industry base for small arms production. In November 2004, the FN model was chosen by the U.S. Special Operations Command (USSOCOM) for the new SCAR military rifle.

CARBINES/RIFLES: SEMI-AUTO

PS90 – 5.7x28mm cal., blowback operation, bullpup configuration, 16 in. barrel, 10 or 30 shot box mag. runs horizontally along the top, empty cases are ejected downward, integrated muzzle brake, olive drab or black finish, configurations include PS90 RD with reflex sight module (mfg. 2009), PS90 USG with non-magnifying black reticle optical sight, and the PS90 TR with three M-1913 rails for optional optics, 6.3 lbs. Disc. 2011.

	100%	98%	95%	90%	80%	70%	60%	Last MSR
	$1,925	$1,675	$1,450	$1,295	$1,075	$925	$800	*$2,199*

* ***PS90 Standard*** – 5.7x28mm cal., similar to PS90, except no optical sights, 10 (new 2012) or 30 shot mag., black, OD Green, or olive drab (disc.) finish. New 2010.

	100%	98%	95%	90%	80%	70%	60%	
MSR $1,449	$1,300	$1,100	$925	$800	$700	$600	$500	

Add $391 for red-dot sights.

FS2000 STANDARD/TACTICAL – .223 Rem. cal., bullpup configuration, 17.4 in. barrel, gas operated with rotating bolt, 10 or 30 shot AR-15 style mag., empty cases are ejected through a forward port, includes 1.6x optical sighting package on Standard Model (disc. 2010), Tactical Model features emergency back up folding sights, CQB model features lower accessory rail, ambidextrous polymer stock, top mounted M-1913 rail, olive drab green or black finish, 7.6 lbs. Disc. 2013.

	100%	98%	95%	90%	80%	70%	60%	Last MSR
	$2,425	$2,100	$1,825	$1,675	$1,450	$1,250	$995	*$2,779*

SCAR 16S – .223 Rem. cal., semi-auto only version of U.S. SOCOM's newest service rifle, gas operated short stroke piston system, free floating 16 1/4 in. barrel with hard chrome bore, 10 or 30 shot detachable box mag., folding open sights, fully ambidextrous operating controls, three optical rails, side folding polymer stock, fully adj. comb and LOP, black or Flat Dark Earth finish on receiver and stock, 7 1/4 lbs. New 2009.

	100%	98%	95%	90%	80%	70%	60%	
MSR $2,995	$2,695	$2,375	$2,050	$1,850	$1,575	$1,275	$1,050	

SCAR 17S – .308 Win. cal., 10 or 20 shot mag., otherwise similar to SCAR 16S, 8 lbs. New 2009.

	100%	98%	95%	90%	80%	70%	60%	
MSR $3,349	$2,925	$2,550	$2,175	$1,900	$1,575	$1,275	$1,050	

FNAR STANDARD – .308 Win. cal., 16 (new 2010) or 20 in. light or heavy fluted contoured barrel, 10 or 20 shot detachable box mag., one-piece M-1913 optical rail, three accessory rails attached to forearm, matte black synthetic pistol grip stock with soft cheekpiece, adj. comb, ambidextrous mag. release, 8.8 - 9 lbs. Mfg. 2009-2013.

	100%	98%	95%	90%	80%	70%	60%	Last MSR
	$1,550	$1,325	$1,100	$975	$850	$725	$650	*$1,699*

FNAR COMPETITION – 7.62x51mm cal., gas operated, 20 in. fluted barrel, target crowned, front barrel mounted sight rail for aftermarket sights, 20 shot detachable box mag., alum. alloy receiver with one-piece Mil-Std. 1913 optics rail, hard anodized blue receiver finish with Team FNH USA markings, blue/grey laminated stock assembly with checkered gripping surfaces, adj. for cheekpiece, non-slip recoil pad, crossbolt safety, 8.9 lbs. New 2013.

	100%	98%	95%	90%	80%	70%	60%	
MSR $1,767	$1,500	$1,315	$1,125	$1,025	$825	$675	$525	

FN15 – 5.56x45mm cal., available in 16 (carbine), 18 (competition), or 20 (rifle) in. non-free floating barrel, collapsible stock, flat-top upper receiver with rail, matte black finish. New 2014.

	100%	98%	95%	90%	80%	70%	60%	
MSR $1,149	$975	$850	$725	$675	$535	$440	$340	

PISTOLS: SEMI-AUTO

In addition to the models listed, FNH USA also imported the HP-SA ($800 last MSR), and the HP-SFS until 2006.

All FNP guns come standard with three magazines and a lockable hard case.

MSR	100%	98%	95%	90%	80%	70%	60%	Last MSR

FNP-9 – 9mm Para. cal., 4 in. barrel, 10 or 16 (disc. 2010) shot mag., polymer frame, matte black or matte stainless steel slide, DA/SA, matte black or flat Dark Earth (mfg. 2010 only) finish, ambidextrous frame mounted decocker, underframe rail, interchangeable backstrap inserts, 25.2 oz. Disc. 2011.

	$575	$495	$435	$380	$340	$300	$275	*$649*

Add $125 for night sights (disc. 2009).
Add $50 for USG operation (DA/SA, ambidextrous frame mounted decocker/manual safety), disc. 2010.

FNP-9M – 9mm Para. cal., 3.8 in. barrel, DA/SA, 10 or 15 shot mag., polymer frame, similar to the FNP-9, except is smaller frame, 24.8 oz. Disc. 2008.

	$525	$450	$400	$365	$335	$300	$275	*$593*

Add $118 for night sights.

FNP-357 – .357 SIG cal., similar to FNP-9, black finish only, 14 shot mag., 27.2 oz. Mfg. 2009.

	$565	$475	$425	$375	$335	$300	$275	*$629*

Add $65 for USG operation (features ambidextrous frame mounted decocker/manual safety levers).

FNP-40 – .40 S&W cal., 4 in. barrel, 10 or 14 (disc. 2010) shot mag., DA/SA, black or flat Dark Earth (mfg. 2010 only) polymer frame, optional stainless steel slide, underframe rail, interchangeable backstrap, external hammer, 25.2 or 26.7 oz. Disc. 2011.

	$575	$495	$435	$380	$340	$300	$275	*$649*

Add $125 for night sights (disc. 2009).
Add $50 for USG operation (features ambidextrous frame mounted decocker/manual safety levers), disc. 2010.

FNP-45 – .45 ACP cal., 4 1/2 in. barrel, DA/SA, 10 (disc. 2011), 14, or 15 (new 2011) shot mag., polymer frame, matte black finish with optional stainless steel slide, or flat Dark Earth (new 2010) finish, external extractor, underframe rail, interchangeable backstraps, 33.2 oz. Disc. 2013.

	$725	$625	$575	$525	$450	$400	$350	*$795*

Add $125 for night sights (disc.).
Subtract approx. 5% if without USG operation (features ambidextrous frame mounted decocker/manual safety levers).
Add approx. $186 for pistol package, which include three mags., molded polymer holster, double mag. pouch, and training barrel (mfg. 2009 only).

* **FNP-45 Competition** – .45 ACP cal., DA/SA, matte black finish, 15 shot mag., lower accessory rail, interchangeable arched and flat backstrap inserts with lanyard holes, 33.2 oz. Mfg. 2011-2012.

	$1,075	$925	$825	$725	$625	$550	$475	*$1,239*

* **FNP-45 Tactical** – .45 ACP cal., 5.3 in. threaded barrel, 15 shot mag., DA/SA, polymer frame with MIL-STD 1913 mounting rail and interchangeable backstraps with lanyard eyelets, serrated trigger guard, ambidextrous mag. release, manual safety, and slide stop, fixed combat sights, Black or Flat Dark Earth finish, stainless steel slide, includes fitted soft case. Mfg. 2010-2012.

	$1,200	$1,025	$875	$775	$675	$575	$495	*$1,395*

FNS-9/FNS-40 – 9mm Para. or .40 S&W cal., DAO, SFO, 4 in. barrel, matte black or matte silver slide finish, black or Flat Dark Earth finished polymer frame, 14 (FNS-40) or 17 (FNS-9) shot mag., fixed 3-dot sights, loaded chamber indicator, front and rear cocking serrations, lower accessory rail, interchangeable backstrap inserts, serrated trigger guard, ambidextrous safety, 25.2 - 27 1/2 oz. New 2012.

MSR $699	$625	$525	$450	$395	$350	$300	$275	

Add $50 for night sights or for left hand.

FNS-9 LONGSLIDE (COMPETITION) – 9mm Para. cal., striker fired, DAO, SFO, 5 in. hammer forged stainless steel barrel, stainless steel slide, fixed 3 dot sights, loaded chamber indicator, front and rear cocking serrations, 17 shot mag., Mil-Std 1913 accessory mounting rail, serrated trigger guard, black frame finish, 27.2 oz. New 2013.

MSR $749	$675	$575	$475	$425	$375	$325	$295	

FNX-9/FNX-40 – 9mm Para. or .40 S&W cal., DA/SA, 4 in. barrel, 10 (new 2012), 14 (.40 S&W) or 17 (9mm Para.) shot mag., matte black or matte black with stainless steel slide, front and rear cocking serrations, MIL-STD mounting rail, deep V fixed combat sights, serrated trigger guard, ambidextrous mag. release and manual safety, four interchangeable backstrap inserts, 21.9-24.4 oz. New 2010.

MSR $699	$625	$525	$450	$395	$350	$300	$275	

Add $50 for night sights (disc. 2013).

FNX-45 – .45 ACP cal., DA/SA, 4 1/2 in. barrel, 10, 12 (disc. 2013), or 15 shot mag., matte black or stainless steel slide, low profile fixed 3-dot sights, matte black polymer frame, front and rear cocking serrations, four interchangeable backstrap inserts, lower accessory rail, ambidextrous decocking levers, ring style external hammers, Black or Flat Dark Earth finish, approx. 32 oz. New 2012.

MSR $824	$740	$665	$550	$500	$400	$350	$250	

MSR	100%	98%	95%	90%	80%	70%	60%	Last MSR

* FNX-45 Tactical – .45 ACP cal., similar to FNX-45, except has threaded barrel, 15 shot mag., high profile night sights, includes fitted Cordura nylon soft case, 33.6 oz. New 2012.

| MSR $1,399 | $1,200 | $1,025 | $875 | $775 | $675 | $575 | $495 | |

FIVE-SEVEN – 5.7x28mm cal., 4 3/4 in. barrel, SA, SFO, USG (disc. 2012) or MK2 variation, 10 or 20 shot mag., reversible mag. release, textured grip, black, OD Green (disc. 2011) or Flat Dark Earth (disc. 2012) finish, polymer frame, MIL-STD mounting, choice of fixed 3-dot (standard mfg.), adj. (USG model), C-More fixed (disc.), or C-More fixed night sights (disc.), underframe rail, includes three mags., hard case and cleaning kit, 20.8 oz.

| MSR $1,329 | $1,145 | $985 | $845 | $765 | $625 | $500 | $395 | |

Add 10% for early mfg. that incorporated a larger trigger guard than current mfg.

RIFLES: BOLT ACTION

FNH USA imports a wide range of tactical rifle systems for military and law enforcement only. FNH USA also imported a line of modular system rifles, including the Ultima Ratio Intervention, the Ultima Ratio Commando II, and the .338 Lapua Model. Please contact the company directly for more information, including availability and pricing (see Trademark Index).

BALLISTA – .308 Win. (mfg. 2013 only), .300 Win. Mag. (mfg. 2013 only), or .338 Lapua cal., 26 in. fluted barrel, ambidextrous fully adj. folding stock, 5 or 8 shot detachable box mag., aluminum alloy receiver with top mounted mil-std 1913 rail plus multiple rail segments for other accessories, fully adj. single or two-stage trigger, Flat Dark Earth or Desert Tan finish, 14 1/2 lbs. Mfg. by Unique Alpine AG. New 2013.

| MSR $6,999 | $6,450 | $5,900 | $5,300 | $4,750 | $4,100 | $3,500 | $2,950 | |

PBR (PATROL BOLT RIFLE) – .300 WSM (XP Model) or .308 Win. cal., 22 in. heavy free floating barrel standard, stippled black Hogue overmolded stock, Picatinny rail, four shot fixed or removable box mag., some models may be marked "FN Herstal", later production marked "FNH", approx. 9 1/2 lbs.

| | $1,075 | $925 | $825 | $750 | $625 | $500 | $425 | *$1,075* |

Add $170 for XP Model in .300 WSM cal.

SPR A1/A1a – .308 Win. cal., 20 in. fluted (A1a) or 24 (disc. 2013) in. non-fluted barrel, 4 shot detachable box mag., pre-'64 Model 70 action, external claw extractor, matte black McMillan fiberglass stock with adj. comb and LOP, textured gripping surfaces, 12.4 lbs.

| MSR $2,245 | $2,000 | $1,775 | $1,575 | $1,375 | $1,175 | $975 | $750 | |

SPR A2 – .308 Win. cal., similar to A1, 20 in. fluted or 24 in. non-fluted barrel, 11.6 or 12.2 lbs. Disc. 2009.

| | $2,500 | $2,185 | $1,875 | $1,700 | $1,375 | $1,125 | $875 | *$2,745* |

SPR A3 G (SPECIAL POLICE RIFLE) – .308 Win. cal., 24 in. fluted barrel with hard chromed bore, hinged floorplate, one-piece steel MIL-STD 1913 optical rail, A3 fiberglass tactical stock with adj. comb and LOP, steel sling studs, designed to achieve 1/2 MOA accuracy standard, 14.3 lbs.

| MSR $3,495 | $3,175 | $2,750 | $2,350 | $2,125 | $1,700 | $1,395 | $1,075 | |

SPR A5 XP – .308 Win. or .300 WSM cal., 20 or 24 in. chrome lined heavy contour match grade barrel, 5 shot box mag., one piece 20 MOA optics rail, tactical bolt knob, matte black finish, McMillan A5 stock with cheekpiece, threaded muzzle, 11 lbs., 5 oz. New 2013.

| MSR $2,899 | $2,625 | $2,325 | $1,975 | $1,750 | $1,475 | $1,250 | $950 | |

SPR A5 M – .308 Win. or .300 WSM cal., 20 in. fluted (.308 Win. cal. only) or 24 in. non-fluted barrel, 3 or 4 shot mag., black synthetic tactical stock, 11.6 or 12.2 lbs.

| MSR $2,899 | $2,625 | $2,325 | $1,975 | $1,750 | $1,475 | $1,250 | $950 | |

Add $100 for traditional hinged floorplate in .300 WSM cal. or $200 for hinged floorplate in .308 Win. cal. (both disc. 2013).

Add $200 for TBM (tactical box mag.) with 20 or 24 in. fluted barrel (mfg. 2011-2013).

PSR I – .308 Win. cal., 20 in. fluted or 24 in. non-fluted barrel, 3, 4, or 5 shot internal mag., FN tactical sport trigger system, hinged floorplate, matte black McMillan sporter style fiberglass stock, raised comb, recoil pad, steel sling studs, 7.7 or 8.7 lbs. Disc. 2009.

| | $2,000 | $1,750 | $1,500 | $1,360 | $1,100 | $900 | $700 | *$2,253* |

PSR II/III – .308 Win. or .300 WSM (PSR II) cal., 22 in. fluted or 24 in. non-fluted barrel, 3, 4 (PSR III), or 5 shot internal or detachable box mag., FN tactical sport trigger system, matte olive drab McMillan sporter style fiberglass stock, raised comb, recoil pad, steel sling studs, 8.7 - 9.8 lbs. Disc. 2009.

| | $2,000 | $1,750 | $1,500 | $1,360 | $1,100 | $900 | $700 | *$2,253* |

TSR XP/XP USA (TACTICAL SPORT RIFLES) – .223 Rem. (XP USA), 7.62x39mm (XP USA, disc. 2009), .300 WSM (disc. 2013), or .308 Win. (disc. 2013) cal., Model 70 short (XP) or ultra short (XP USA) action, 20 in. fluted (disc. 2010), 20 or 24 (disc. 2013) in. non-fluted barrel, 3, 4 (detachable box mag., XP Model only), 5, or 6 shot mag., one-

MSR	100%	98%	95%	90%	80%	70%	60%	Last MSR

piece steel MIL-STD 1913 optical rail, full aluminum bedding block molded into FN/Hogue synthetic stock, olive drab overmolded surface, recoil pad, steel sling studs, 8.7 - 10.1 lbs.

MSR $1,199　　　$1,050　$925　$800　$700　$600　$500　$400

Add $100 for .300 WSM cal. with floorplate (disc. 2013).

SHOTGUNS

FNH USA manufactured tactical style shotguns, including the FN Police Shotgun ($500 last MSR) and the FN Tactical Police Shotgun (with or w/o fixed stock, $923 last MSR).

MODEL SLP (SELF LOADING POLICE) – 12 ga., 18 (SLP Standard) or 22 in. standard cantilever Invector choked (Mark I/Tactical) or rifled (Mark I Rifled) in. barrel, 6 or 8 shot mag., adj. rear sight, black synthetic stock with half or full pistol grip, rail mounted adj. ghost ring rear sight, two gas pistons for heavy and light loads, 7.7 - 8.2 lbs.

MSR $1,379　　　$1,075　$995　$875　$750　$650　$525　$410

Add $50 for 22 in. Cantilever barrel (SLP MK1 Tactical) with pistol grip stock, rifle sight.

Add $100 for Tactical Model with pistol grip, 18 in. barrel and adj. rifle sights (6 shot mag.).

Subtract $55 for SLP MK1 Competition Model with 22 in. cantilever barrel.

FN SLP MK1 COMPETITION – 12 ga., 3 in. chamber, gas operated, semi-auto, 22 in. barrel with inv. choke, vent rib, adj. rear and fiber optic front sights, 8 shot extended tube mag., aluminum alloy blue hard anodized receiver, matte black synthetic stock with checkered gripping panels on forearm and grip, non-slip recoil pad, sling swivel studs, 8.2 lbs. New 2013.

MSR $1,449　　　$1,295　$1,125　$925　$835　$675　$550　$425

MODEL SC1 O/U – 12 ga., 2 3/4 in. chambers, 28 (disc. 2013) or 30 in. VR barrel with invector plus choking, silver receiver, blue/gray, black, or green adj. comb laminate stock with recoil pad. New 2011.

MSR $2,449　　　$2,150　$1,850　$1,625　$1,400　$1,175　$935　$725

Subtract $300 for green stock.

P-12 SLIDE ACTION – 12 ga., 2 3/4 or 3 in. chrome lined chamber, 18 in. cantilever barrel, matte black finish, aluminum alloy receiver, checkered synthetic stock, recoil pad, Invector cylinder choke Weaver rail pattern, sling swivels, 7 lbs., 7 oz. New 2013.

MSR $669　　　$595　$525　$450　$395　$360　$330　$295

FABARM, S.p.A.

Current manufacturer established in 1900 and located in Brescia, Italy. Currently imported by Fabarm USA beginning 2012, and located in Cambridge, MD. Previously imported by Tristar, located in Kansas City, MO circa 2007-2009. Select models previously retailed until 2012 by Bill Hanus Birdguns, LLC, located in Newport, OR. Previously imported by SIG Arms during 2005, located in Exeter, NH, and by Heckler & Koch, Inc. 1998-2004. Certain models had limited importation by Ithaca Acquisition Corp. located in King Ferry, NY during 1993-1995. Previously imported and distributed (1988-1990) by St. Lawrence Sales, Inc. located in Lake Orion, MI. Previously imported until 1986 by Beeman Precision Arms, Inc. located in Santa Rosa, CA.

Fabarm currently manufactures approx. 35,000 long guns annually.

Fabarm manufactures a wide variety of shotguns, rifles, and double rifles in assorted configurations, with many options available. Most models, however, are not currently being imported into the U.S. at this time. Please contact the importer directly for more information, including current model availability and pricing (see Trademark Index).

Due to space considerations, this manufacturer is available online free of charge at www.bluebookofgunvalues.com.

FABRIQUE NATIONALE

Current manufacturer located in Herstal, near Liege, Belgium. The current company name is "Group Herstal." However, the company is better known as "Fabrique Nationale" or "Fabrique Nationale d'Armes de Guerre". FN entered into their first contract with John M. Browning in 1897 for the manufacture of their first pistol, the FN 1899 Model. Additional contracts were signed and the relationship further blossomed with the manufacture of the A-5 shotgun. FN was acquired by GIAT of France in 1992. In late 1997, the company was purchased by the Walloon government of Belgium. Additional production facilities are located in Portugal, Japan, and the U.S.

Also see: Browning Arms under Rifles, Shotguns, and Pistols, and FNH USA for current offerings in the U.S.

The author would like to express his sincere thanks to Anthony Vanderlinden for making FN contributions to this edition.

RIFLES: BOLT ACTION

FN SNIPER RIFLE (MODEL 30) – .308 Win. cal., this model was a Mauser actioned Sniper Rifle equipped with 20 in. extra heavy barrel, flash hider, separate removable diopter sights, Hensoldt 4x scope, hardcase, bipod, and sling. 51 complete factory sets were imported into the U.S., with additional surplus rifles that were privately imported.

$4,750　$4,250　$4,000　$3,500　$3,000　$2,750　$2,500

MSR	100%	98%	95%	90%	80%	70%	60%	Last MSR

Subtract 15% if removable diopter sights or bipod is missing.

Subtract 10% if scope is not marked with F.N. logo.

Values assume complete factory outfit with all accessories.

RIFLES: SEMI-AUTO

MODEL 1949 – 7x57mm Mauser, 7.65mm Mauser, 7.92mm Mauser, or .30-06 cal., (.308 Win. cal. for Argentine conversion rifles), gas operated, 10 shot box mag. (20 round detachable mag. for Argentine conversions), 23 in. barrel, military rifle, tangent rear sight.

	100%	98%	95%	90%	80%	70%	60%
Columbia	$1,700	$1,400	$1,150	$1,000	$900	$750	$700
Luxembourg	$1,500	$1,250	$1,000	$900	$800	$650	$600
Venezuela	$1,350	$1,100	$900	$850	$700	$600	$550
Argentina	N/A	$1,250	$1,100	$950	$850	$750	$650
Egyptian	$1,600	$1,350	$1,100	$995	$895	$725	$675

Add $100 for detachable grenade launcher.

Subtract 30% for U.S. rebuilt, non-matching rifles with reproduction stocks.

Original FN-49 sniper rifles are extremely rare and may add $2,500+.

Beware of U.S. assembled "sniper" configurations, and Belgian military "ABL" scopes mounted on other contract rifles and sold as original sniper configurations.

FN-49 contract rifles not listed above are very rare in the U.S. and will demand a premium.

Carefully inspect black paint finish for factory originality, as all FN-49s were factory painted.

RIFLES: SEMI-AUTO, FAL/LAR/CAL/FNC SERIES

After tremendous price increases between 1985-88, Fabrique Nationale decided in 1988 to discontinue this series completely. Not only are these rifles not exported to the U.S. any longer, but all production has ceased in Belgium as well. The only way FN will produce these models again is if they are given a large military contract - in which case a "side order" of commercial guns may be built. 1989 Federal legislation regarding this type of tactical design also helped push up prices to their current level. FAL rifles were also mfg. in Israel by I.M.I.

F.N. FAL – semi-auto, French designation for the F.N. L.A.R. (light automatic rifle), otherwise similar to the L.A.R.

	100%	98%	95%	90%	80%	70%	60%
	$4,175	$3,950	$3,750	$3,475	$3,150	$3,100	$2,750

* F.N. FAL G

	100%	98%	95%	90%	80%	70%	60%
Standard	$4,800	$4,000	$3,500	$2,950	$2,450	$2,150	$2,000
Paratrooper	$5,200	$4,400	$3,900	$3,350	$2,850	$2,550	$2,400
Heavy Barrel	$6,800	$6,250	$4,950	$4,400	$3,750	$3,250	$2,750
Lightweight	$5,200	$4,250	$3,750	$3,100	$2,600	$2,350	$2,100

Values listed assume inclusion of factory bipod.

The Standard G Series was supplied with a wooden stock and wood or nylon forearm. The Heavy Barrel variant had all wood furniture and was supplied with a bipod. The Lightweight Model had an aluminum lower receiver, piston tube and magazine.

G Series FALs were imported between 1959-1962 by Browning Arms Co. This rifle was declared illegal by the GCA of 1968, and was exempted 5 years later. Total numbers exempted are: Standard - 1,822, Heavy Barrel - 21, and Paratrooper - 5.

F.N. L.A.R. COMPETITION (50.00, LIGHT AUTOMATIC RIFLE) – .308 Win. (7.62x51mm) cal., semi-auto, competition rifle with match flash hider, 21 in. barrel, adj. 4 position fire selector on automatic models, wood stock, aperture rear sight adj. from 100-600 meters, 9.4 lbs. Mfg. 1981-83.

	100%	98%	95%	90%	80%	70%	60%
	$4,250	$4,025	$3,850	$3,625	$3,450	$3,175	$2,950

This model was designated by the factory as the 50.00 Model.

Mid-1987 retail on this model was $1,258. The last MSR was $3,179 (this price reflected the last exchange rate and special order status of this model).

* FN L.A.R. Competition Heavy barrel rifle (50.41 & 50.42) – barrel is twice as heavy as standard L.A.R., includes wood or synthetic stock, short wood forearm, and bipod, 12.2 lbs. Importation disc. 1988.

	100%	98%	95%	90%	80%	70%	60%
	$4,495	$4,275	$4,150	$4,000	$3,675	$3,500	$3,250

Add $500 for walnut stock.

Add $350 for match sights.

There were 2 variations of this model. The Model 50.41 had a synthetic buttstock while the Model 50.42 had a wood buttstock with steel buttplate incorporating a top extension used for either shoulder resting or inverted grenade launching.

Mid-1987 retail on this model was $1,497 (Model 50.41) or $1,654 (Model 50.42). The last MSR was $3,776 (this price reflected the last exchange rate and special order status of this model).

MSR	100%	98%	95%	90%	80%	70%	60%	Last MSR

* FN L.A.R. Competition Paratrooper rifle (50.63 & 50.64) – similar to L.A.R. model, except has folding stock, 8.3 lbs. Mfg. 1950-88.

| | $4,275 | $3,700 | $3,300 | $3,000 | $2,550 | $2,300 | $2,150 | |

There were 2 variations of the Paratrooper L.A.R. Model. The Model 50.63 had a stationary aperture rear sight and 18 in. barrel. The Model 50.64 was supplied with a 21 in. barrel and had a rear sight calibrated for either 150 or 200 meters. Both models retailed for the same price.

Mid-1987 retail on this model was $1,310 (both the Model 50.63 and 50.64). The last MSR was $3,239 (this price reflected the last exchange rate and special order status of this model).

CAL – originally imported in 1980, FN's .223 CAL military rifle succeeded the .308 FAL and preceeded the .223 FNC, at first declared illegal but later given amnesty, only 20 imported by Browning.

| | $7,800 | $7,000 | $6,250 | $5,500 | $4,750 | $4,100 | $3,600 | |

FNC MODEL – .223 Rem. (5.56mm) cal., lightweight combat carbine, 16 or 18 1/2 in. barrel, NATO approved, 30 shot mag., 8.4 lbs. Disc. 1987.

| | $2,950 | $2,700 | $2,550 | $2,100 | $1,900 | $1,650 | $1,500 | |

Add $350 for Paratrooper model (16 or 18 1/2 in. barrel).

While rarer, the 16 in. barrel model incorporated a flash hider that did not perform as well as the flash hider used on the standard 18 1/2 in. barrel.

Mid-1987 retail on this model was $749 (Standard Model) and $782 (Paratrooper Model). The last MSR was $2,204 (Standard Model) and $2,322 (Paratrooper Model) - these prices reflected the last exchange rate and special order status of these models.

FAXON FIREARMS

Current rifle manufacturer located in Cincinnati, OH.

RIFLES: SEMI-AUTO

ARAK-21 – 5.56 NATO or .300 Blackout cal., utilizes both AR-15 and AK-47 design elements, gas piston actuated (four position), 16 or 20 in. barrel with A2 flash suppressor, MAG tactical lower, upper receiver with charging block and standard charging handle, aluminum full length upper Picatinny rails and partial lower and side rails, three insulating shims, bolt carrier assembly, lower recoil lug with spring guide rod, dual recoil spring system, 30 shot mag., matte black, blue, silver, green or red finish, includes plastic hard case.

| MSR $1,849 | $1,750 | $1,525 | $1,350 | $1,075 | $950 | $825 | $695 | |

Add $265 for extra BAU (barrel assembly unit).

FEATHER INDUSTRIES, INC.

Previous manufacturer located in Boulder, CO until 1995.

RIFLES: SEMI-AUTO

AT-22 – .22 LR cal., semi-auto blowback action, 17 in. detachable shrouded barrel, collapsible metal stock, adj. rear sight, with sling and swivels, 20 shot mag., 3 1/4 lbs. Mfg. 1986-95.

| | $325 | $275 | $250 | $240 | $230 | $220 | $215 | *$250* |

F2 – similar to AT-22, except is equipped with a fixed polymer buttstock. Mfg. 1992-95.

| | $295 | $240 | $215 | $200 | $185 | $175 | $160 | *$280* |

AT-9 – 9mm Para. cal., semi-auto blowback action, 16 in. barrel, available with 10 (C/B 1994), 25*, 32 (disc.), or 100 (disc. 1989) shot mag., 5 lbs. Mfg. 1988-95.

| | $850 | $775 | $700 | $650 | $600 | $550 | $500 | *$500* |

Add $250 for 100 shot drum mag.

F9 – similar to AT-9, except is equipped with a fixed polymer buttstock. Mfg. 1992-95.

| | $725 | $675 | $600 | $550 | $485 | $450 | $375 | *$535* |

SATURN 30 – 7.62x39mm Kalashnikov cal., semi-auto, gas operated, 19 1/2 in. barrel, composite stock with large thumbhole pistol grip, 5 shot detachable mag., drilled and tapped for scope mounts, adj. rear sight, 8 1/2 lbs. Mfg. in 1990 only.

| | $800 | $700 | $625 | $575 | $525 | $450 | $425 | *$695* |

KG-9 – 9mm Para. cal., semi-auto blowback action, 25 or 50 shot mag., tactical configuration. Mfg. 1989 only.

| | $850 | $775 | $700 | $650 | $600 | $550 | $500 | *$560* |

Add $100 for 50 shot mag.

MSR	100%	98%	95%	90%	80%	70%	60%	Last MSR

SAR-180 – .22 LR cal., semi-auto blowback action, 17 1/2 in. barrel, 165 shot drum mag., fully adj. rear sight, walnut stock with combat style pistol grip and forend, 6 1/4 lbs. Mfg. 1989 only.

	$695	$625	$575	$525	$475	$440	$400	$500

Add $250 for 165 shot drum mag.
Add $200 for retractable stock.
Add $395 for laser sight.

This variation was also manufactured for a limited time by ILARCO (Illinois Arms Company), previously located in Itasca, IL.

KG-22 – .22 LR cal., similar to KG-9, 20 shot mag. Mfg. 1989 only.

	$395	$350	$300	$275	$255	$245	$235	$300

FEATHER USA/AWI LLC

Current manufacturer established 1996 and located in Eaton, CO.

PISTOLS: SEMI-AUTO

TACTICAL PISTOL SERIES – 9mm Para., .357 Sig., .40 S&W, .45 ACP, 10mm, or .460 Rowland cal., blowback action, steel construction, 9.2 in. barrel, SA, front and rear sights, scope rail, super rails, pre-drilled for sling, accepts high cap Glock magazines, Black matte finish, no tools needed for takedown or cleaning, includes Backpack carry case, 4 1/2 lbs.

MSR $619	$550	$475	$425	$375	$300	$250	$200	

Add $150 for high accuracy bull barrel on any caliber.

RIFLES: SEMI-AUTO

BACKPACKER SERIES – 9mm Para., .22 LR, .357 Sig., .40 S&W, .45 ACP, 10mm, or .460 Rowland cal., takedown action, modular design, 17.2 in. barrel, 2-position steel stock, 8 shot mag., pre-drilled for scope rail, super rails, and sling, Black matte finish, includes case that is waterproof and floatable, 2 1/2 lbs. (.22 LR).

MSR $399	$350	$300	$275	$250	$200	$150	$125	

Add $250 for 9mm Para., .357 Sig., .40 S&W, .45 ACP, 10mm, or .460 Rowland cal.

DELUXE SERIES – 9mm Para., .22 LR, .357 Sig., .40 S&W, .45 ACP, 10mm, and .460 Rowland cal., takedown action, modular design, 17.2 in. barrel, front and rear sight, 2-position steel stock, scope rail, super rails and pre-drilled for sling, 10 or 20 shot mag., Black matte finish, includes case (holds rifle and optional 4 mags., barrel, barrel shroud, bipod, front grip, car stock), 2 1/2-5 lbs.

MSR $499	$450	$400	$350	$300	$250	$200	$150	

Add $100 for high accuracy fluted barrel (.22 LR).
Add $250 for 9mm Para., .357 Sig., .40 S&W, .45 ACP, 10mm, or .460 Rowland cal.
Add $350 for high accuracy tapered bull barrel for all calibers except .22 LR.

TACTICAL RIGID STOCK SERIES – 9mm Para., .357 Sig., .40 S&W, .45 ACP, 10mm, or .460 Rowland cal., blowback action, modular design, 17.2 in. barrel, front and rear sights, drilled and tapped for sling and comes standard with scope rail and super rail system, includes full tactical carry case, 6 1/2 lbs.

MSR $849	$750	$650	$575	$525	$425	$350	$275	

Add $150 for high accuracy bull barrel on any caliber.

FEDERAL ENGINEERING CORPORATION

Previous manufacturer located in Chicago, IL.

RIFLES: SEMI-AUTO

XC-220 – .22 LR cal., 16 5/16 in. barrel, 28 shot mag., machined steel action, 7 1/2 lbs. Mfg. 1984-89.

	$495	$450	$400	$350	$320	$295	$275	

XC-450 – .45 ACP cal. only, 16 1/2 in. barrel length, 30 shot mag., fires from closed bolt, machined steel receiver, 8 1/2 lbs. Mfg. 1984-89.

	$950	$825	$750	$675	$600	$550	$500	

XC-900 – 9mm Para. cal., 16 1/2 in. barrel length, 32 shot mag., fires from closed bolt, machined receiver action, 8 lbs. Mfg. 1984-89.

	$950	$825	$750	$675	$600	$550	$500	

FEDERAL ORDNANCE, INC.

Previous manufacturer, importer, and distributor located in South El Monte, CA from 1966-1992. Briklee Trading Co. bought the remaining assets of Federal Ordnance, Inc. in late 1992, and continued to import various firearms until circa 1998.

Federal Ordnance imported and distributed both foreign and domestic military handguns and rifles until 1992. In addition, they also fabricated firearms using mostly newer parts.

MSR	100%	98%	95%	90%	80%	70%	60%	Last MSR

RIFLES/CARBINES

M-14 SEMI-AUTO – .308 Win. cal., legal for private ownership (no selector), 20 shot mag., refinished original M-14 parts, available in either filled fiberglass, G.I. fiberglass, refinished wood, or new walnut stock. Mfg. 1986-91.

| | $1,275 | $1,075 | $995 | $940 | $865 | $800 | $750 | $700 |

Add $50 for filled fiberglass stock.
Add $110 for refinished wood stock.
Add $190 for new walnut stock with handguard.

During the end of production, Chinese parts were used on this model. Values are the same.

TANKER GARAND SEMI-AUTO – .30-06 or .308 Win. cal., original U.S. GI parts, 18 in. barrel, new hardwood stock, parkerized finish. Mfg. began late 1991.

| | $975 | $900 | $850 | $800 | $750 | $700 | $625 | |

CHINESE RPK 86S-7 SEMI-AUTO – 7.62x39mm cal., semi-auto version of the Peoples Republic of China RPK light machine gun, 75 shot drum mag., 23 3/4 in. barrel, with bipod. Imported 1989 only.

| | $1,450 | $1,275 | $1,075 | $1,000 | $825 | $775 | $650 | $500 |

Add $100 for 75 shot drum mag.

FIERCE FIREARMS, LLC

Current custom manufacturer located in Gunnison, UT.

Fierce Firearms manufactures custom bolt action rifles in various calibers to customer specifications with many options to choose from including stainless steel or titanium action, stainless steel or carbon barrels, stock dipping, paint jobs, and various finishes.

RIFLES: BOLT ACTION

TACTICAL EDGE – .300 Win., .308 Win., or .338 Lapua cal., stainless steel match grade barrel with 5 flutes, target crown, 3-position True Lock safety, tactical style receiver with built-in Picatinny rail, speed detachable box mag., Triad bolt, Last Guard coating on barrel and action, carbon fiber stock available in Black & Gray, Camo, or True Timber finish. New 2014.

| MSR $2,475 | $2,225 | $1,950 | $1,700 | $1,475 | $1,250 | $1,050 | $875 | |

Add $110 for Camo or True Timber finish.
Add $180 for muzzle brake.
Add $750 for fully adj. stock.

57 CENTER LLC

Please refer to AR57 LLC listing in the A section.

FIREARMS INTERNATIONAL, INC.

Current manufacturer established in 1998, and located in Houston, TX. Dealer sales.

In September, 2004, a new company called Crusader Group Gun Company, Inc. was formed, and is the corporate parent of Firearms International, Inc., High Standard Manufacturing Co., AMT-Auto Mag, and Arsenal Line Products.

While IAI (Israel Arms International) was originally established to market firearms manufactured by Israel Arms, Ltd. through Firearms International, Inc., IAI defaulted on this agreement without any sales being made.

RIFLES/CARBINES: SEMI-AUTO

M1 CARBINE – .30 Carbine cal., 18 in. barrel, parkerized finish, wood stock, adj. rear sight, 10 shot mag., mfg. in the U.S., and patterned after the WWII design, 5 1/2 lbs. Limited mfg. 2001-2003.

| | $500 | $425 | $375 | $335 | $300 | $275 | $250 | $575 |

P50 RIFLE/CARBINE – .50 BMG cal., designed by Robert Pauza, gas operation, 24 or 29 in. barrel, MOA accuracy at 1,000 yards, includes two 5 shot mags. and hard case, 25 (carbine) or 30 lbs. Limited mfg. 2001-2003.

| | $7,500 | $6,750 | $5,750 | $5,000 | $4,500 | $4,000 | $3,500 | $7,950 |

FIREBIRD PRECISION

Current manufacturer located in Mountainair, NM.

Firebird Precision builds custom made AR-15 rifles and shotguns in a variety of configurations and calibers. Each gun is built to individual customer specifications, and a wide variety of options and features are available. Please contact the company directly for available options, delivery time, and an individualized price quotation (see Trademark Index).

MSR	100%	98%	95%	90%	80%	70%	60%	Last MSR

FIRESTORM

Previous trademark of pistols and revolvers manufactured by Industria Argentina, Fabrinor, S.A.L., and Armscor. Distributed (master distributor) and imported from late 2000-2011 by SGS Imports, International Inc., located in Wanamassa, NJ.

PISTOLS: SEMI-AUTO

Beginning 2004, all Firestorm pistols were available with an integral locking system (ILS).

FIRESTORM SERIES – .22 LR, .32 ACP (disc. 2007), or .380 ACP cal., DA/SA, 3 1/2 or 6 (.22 LR cal. only, Sport Model) in. barrel, matte or duo-tone finish, 7 (.380 ACP) or 10 (.22 LR or .32 ACP) shot mag., 3 dot combat sights, anatomic rubber grips with finger grooves, 23 oz. Imported 2001-2011.

	100%	98%	95%	90%	80%	70%	60%	Last MSR
	$280	$235	$185	$155	$145	$135	$125	$329

Add $6 for duo-tone finish.

MINI-FIRESTORM – 9mm Para., .40 S&W, or .45 ACP (new 2002) cal., DA/SA, 3 1/2 in. barrel, nickel, matte or duo-tone finish, 7 (.45 ACP cal.), 10, or 13 (9mm Para. only) shot mag., 3 dot sights, polymer grips, safeties include manual, firing pin, and decocking, 24 1/2 - 27 oz. Imported 2001-2009.

	100%	98%	95%	90%	80%	70%	60%	Last MSR
	$365	$315	$275	$230	$195	$180	$165	$425

Add $10 for duo-tone finish.
Add $20 for nickel finish.

FIRESTORM 45 GOVERNMENT – .45 ACP cal., SA, 5 1/8 in. barrel, matte or duo-tone finish, 7 shot mag., anatomic rubber grips with finger grooves, 36 oz. Imported 2001-2005.

	100%	98%	95%	90%	80%	70%	60%	Last MSR
	$260	$230	$200	$180	$165	$150	$135	$309

Add $8 for duo-tone finish.

FIRESTORM 45 GOVT. 1911 – .45 ACP cal., SA, patterned after the M1911, choice of matte or deluxe blue finish, 7 shot mag., current mfg. has skeletonized hammer, forward slide serrations, Novak style sights, diamond checkered walnut grips, and flared ejection port, 36 oz. Imported 2006-2007, reintroduced 2009.

	100%	98%	95%	90%	80%	70%	60%	Last MSR
	$395	$360	$330	$295	$275	$250	$200	$460

Add $39 for deluxe blue finish.

FORT SOE SIA

Current trademark manufactured by the Science Industrial Association Fort of the Ministry of Internal Affairs of Ukraine, located in Vinnitsa, Ukraine. No current U.S. importation.

The Ministry manufactures a line of good quality semi-auto pistols and semi-auto rifles in various tactical configurations with a wide variety of options. Currently, these guns are not imported into the U.S. Please contact the company directly for more information, including pricing and availability (see Trademark Index).

FORT WORTH FIREARMS

Previous manufacturer located in Fort Worth, TX 1995-2000.

SHOTGUNS: SLIDE ACTION

GL 18 – 12 ga. only, security configuration with 18 in. barrel with perforated shroud, thumb operated laser/xenon light built into end of 7 shot mag. tube, ammo storage. Mfg. 1995-96.

	100%	98%	95%	90%	80%	70%	60%	Last MSR
	$295	$265	$240	$210	$190	$170	$160	$347

FOX CARBINE

Previous rifle trademark manufactured by FoxCo Products Inc., located in Manchester, CT, and by Tri-C Corporation, located in Meridan, CT circa 1974-1976.

CARBINES: SEMI-AUTO

FOX CARBINE – 9mm Para. (mfg. by FoxCo Products) or .45 ACP (mfg. by Tri-C Corp.) cal., patterned after the Tommy Gun, 16 in. barrel with muzzle brake, grip safety, open bolt with fixed firing pin, removable wood rear stock and grooved forearm, uses M-3 30 shot mags., three safeties including a three-digit combination lock on left side of frame, loaded chamber indicator, adj. rear sight, matte metal finish, approx. 8 lbs.

	100%	98%	95%	90%	80%	70%	60%	
	$995	$875	$750	$625	$550	$500	$450	

In 1977, the rights to manufacture the FoxCo carbine were sold to Demro Products Inc., which continued to manufacture this configuration until the mid-1980s.

MSR	100%	98%	95%	90%	80%	70%	60%	Last MSR

FRANCHI, LUIGI

Current manufacturer established during 1868, and located in Brescia, Italy. This trademark has been imported for approximately the past 50 years. Currently imported exclusively by Benelli USA, located in Accokeek, MD, since 1998. Previously imported and distributed by American Arms, Inc. located in North Kansas City, MO. Some models were previously imported by FIE firearms located in Hialeah, FL.

Also see Sauer/Franchi heading in the S section.

SHOTGUNS: SEMI-AUTO & SLIDE ACTION

MODEL 612 DEFENSE – 12 ga. only, 18 1/2 in. barrel with cyl. bore, matte finish metal with black synthetic stock and forearm, 6 1/2 lbs. Imported 2000-2002.

| | $525 | $450 | $375 | $325 | $285 | $265 | $245 | $635 |

This model was previously designated the Variopress 612 Defense.

SAS-12 – 12 ga. only, 3 in. chamber, slide action only, synthetic stock with built-in pistol grip, 8 shot tube mag., 21 1/2 in. barrel, 6.8 lbs. Imported 1988-90 only.

| | $600 | $525 | $450 | $395 | $350 | $295 | $250 | $473 |

This model was imported exclusively by FIE Firearms located in Hialeah, FL.

SPAS-12 – 12 ga., 2 3/4 in. chamber, tactical shotgun, slide action or semi-auto operation, 5 (new 1991) or 8 (disc.) shot tube mag., alloy receiver, synthetic stock with built-in pistol grip (limited quantities were also mfg. with a folding stock or metal fixed stock), one-button switch to change operating mode, 21 1/2 in. barrel, 8 3/4 lbs. Importation disc. 1994.

| | $1,500 | $1,300 | $1,175 | $1,000 | $900 | $800 | $700 | $769 |

This model was imported exclusively by FIE Firearms located in Hialeah, FL until 1990.

SPAS-15 – 12 ga. only, 2 3/4 in. chamber, tactical shotgun, slide action or semi-auto operation, 6 shot detachable box mag., 21 1/2 in. barrel, lateral folding skeleton stock, carrying handle, one button switch to change operating mode, 10 lbs. Limited importation 1989 only.

Even though the retail was in the $700 range, demand and rarity have pushed prices up dramatically, with NIB examples in the $5,000 - $7,500 range.

This model had very limited importation (less than 200) as the BATFE disallowed further importation almost immediately.

LAW-12 – 12 ga. only, 2 3/4 in. chamber, gas operated semi-auto, synthetic stock with built-in pistol grip, 5 (new 1991) or 8 (disc.) shot tube mag., 21 1/2 in. barrel, 6 3/4 lbs. Imported 1988-94.

| | $570 | $485 | $400 | $360 | $320 | $300 | $280 | $719 |

FRANKLIN ARMORY

Current manufacturer of semi-auto pistols and rifles/carbines located in Morgan Hill, CA.

Franklin Armory specializes in producing legal firearms for restrictive jurisdictions such as California (O7/FFL and Class II SOT manufacturer), as well as for the non-restrictive states.

PISTOLS: SEMI-AUTO

SALUS PISTOL – 5.56 NATO or 7.62x39mm cal., GIO, 7 1/2 in. barrel with threaded barrel, crowned muzzle, and Triad flash hider, knurled free float handguard tube, aluminum upper receiver with full Picatinny rail and forward assist, alum. lower receiver with flared mag. well, padded receiver extension/buffer tube, Ergo Ambi Sure grip, 30 shot mag., black finish, includes tactical soft side case.

| MSR $1,495 | | $1,350 | $1,175 | $1,025 | $925 | $750 | $625 | $475 |

Add $155 for 7.62x39mm cal.

SE-SSP 7 1/2 IN. PISTOL – 5.56 NATO or 7.62x39mm cal., GIO, 7 1/2 in. barrel with A2 flash hider, single rail Picatinny gas block, optional forged front sight gas block with integral bayonet lug and front sling swivel, knurled free float handguard tube, A4 forged aluminum upper receiver with full Picatinny rail and forward assist, forged alum. lower receiver with ambi sling mount, padded receiver extension/buffer tube, A2 pistol grip, 30 shot mag., black finish, includes tactical soft side case.

| MSR $1,040 | | $935 | $825 | $700 | $625 | $525 | $425 | $325 |

Add $15 for forged front sight gas block.
Add $135 for 7.62x39mm cal.

SE-SSP 11 1/2 IN. PISTOL – 5.56 NATO, 6.8 SPC, 7.62x39mm, .300 Blackout, or .450 Bushmaster cal., GIO, 11 1/2 in. threaded barrel, crowned muzzle, and flash hider or compensator (on .450 Bushmaster only), CAR handguards with alum. liners, A4 forged aluminum flat-top upper receiver, otherwise similar to SE-SSP 7 1/2 in. pistol.

| MSR $1,020 | | $925 | $810 | $700 | $625 | $510 | $415 | $325 |

Add $20 for forged front sight gas block.

MSR	100%	98%	95%	90%	80%	70%	60%	Last MSR

Add $50 for .300 Blackout cal.
Add $155 for 7.62x39mm cal.
Add $180 for .450 Bushmaster cal.
Add $215 for 6.8 SPC cal.

XO-S SALUS PISTOL – 5.56 NATO, 6.8 SPC, 7.62x39mm, .300 Blackout, or .450 Bushmaster cal., GIO, 11 1/2 in. threaded barrel, crowned muzzle, Phantom toothed flash hider, 9 (450 Bushmaster), 25 (6.8 SPC), or 30 shot mag., Black, Desert Smoke, or Olive Drab Green finish, otherwise similar to Salus pistol.

	100%	98%	95%	90%	80%	70%	60%	
MSR $1,495	$1,350	$1,175	$1,025	$925	$750	$625	$475	

XO-26 – 5.56 NATO, 6.8 SPC, .300 Blackout, 7.62x39mm, or .450 Bushmaster cal., GIO, 11 1/2 in. barrel with Phantom toothed flash hider or Ross Schuler Compensator (on .450 Bushmaster only), Specter length free float forearm quad rail, low profile gas block, A4 forged alum. flat-top upper receiver with full Picatinny rail, pop-up front and rear sights and forward assist, forged alum. lower receiver with ambi sling mount, custom tuned trigger, padded receiver extension/buffer tube, Magpul MIAD grip, 9 (.450 Bushmaster), 25 (6.8 SPC), or 30 shot mag., black finish, includes tactical soft side case.

	100%	98%	95%	90%	80%	70%	60%	
MSR $1,560	$1,400	$1,225	$1,050	$950	$775	$625	$500	

Add $30 for .300 Blackout cal.
Add $140 for 7.62x39mm cal.
Add $210 for 6.8 SPC or .450 Bushmaster cal.

* **XO-26b** – 5.56 NATO, 6.8 SPC, .300 Blackout, or 7.62x39mm cal., similar to XO-26, except features single rail Picatinny gas block and carbine length gas system, Magpul MOE handguard, 25 (6.8 SPC) or 30 shot mag.

	100%	98%	95%	90%	80%	70%	60%	
MSR $1,130	$1,025	$900	$775	$700	$575	$450	$350	

Add $45 for .300 Blackout cal.
Add $170 for 7.62x39mm cal.
Add $225 for 6.8 SPC cal.

XOW – 5.56 NATO or 7.62x39mm cal., GIO, 7 1/2 in. barrel with PWS CQB flash hider, A4 forged aluminum flat-top upper receiver with carbine length forearm quad rail, rail covers, Magpul RVG forward vertical grip, Magpul MBUS pop-up front and rear sights, forward assist, full Picatinny rail, forged alum. lower receiver with ambi sling mount, padded receiver extension/buffer tube, Magpul MIAD grip, Magpul enganced trigger guard, PWS enhanced padded buffer tube, 30 shot mag., Black, FDE, FOL, or Olive Drab Green furniture, includes tactical soft side case. Disc. 2013.

	100%	98%	95%	90%	80%	70%	60%	
	$1,450	$1,275	$1,095	$985	$800	$650	$515	*$1,595*

Add $140 for 7.62x39mm cal.

RIFLES: SEMI-AUTO

3GR – 5.56 NATO cal., GIO, 18 in. barrel with threaded muzzle crown, EGW compensator, A4 forged aluminum upper receiver with Desert Smoke finish, full Picatinny rail, ambi tac latch, forward assist, forged aluminum lower receiver with black finish, Ergo Ambi Sure grip and Magpul MOE trigger guard, 10 or 20 shot mag., Ace ARFX stock with bottom Picatinny rail, adj. comb and LOP, sling mountable. Disc. 2013.

	100%	98%	95%	90%	80%	70%	60%	
	$1,475	$1,300	$1,100	$1,000	$825	$675	$525	*$1,650*

* **3GR-L** – 5.56 NATO cal., similar to 3GR, except has 18 in. fluted barrel, aluminum upper and lower receivers with Desert Smoke finish, flared mag. well, Magpul PRS stock with bottom Picatinny rail, and push button QD sling mounts.

	100%	98%	95%	90%	80%	70%	60%	
MSR $2,310	$2,075	$1,825	$1,550	$1,425	$1,150	$950	$725	

10-8 CARBINE – 5.56 NATO, 6.8 SPC, or 7.62x39mm cal., GIO, 16 in. contour barrel with Triad flash suppressor, forged front sight, free float forearm quad rail, A4 forged aluminum upper receiver with full Picatinny rail, Magpul MBUS rear sight, forward assist, forged aluminum lower receiver with custom tuned trigger, Ergo Gapper, Ergo Ambi Sure grip, M4 6-position adj. stock with rear sling mount positions, 10, 20, 25 (6.8 SPC only), or 30 shot mag., black furniture.

	100%	98%	95%	90%	80%	70%	60%	
MSR $1,395	$1,250	$1,095	$950	$850	$700	$575	$450	

Add $85 for 6.8 SPC cal.
Add $155 for 7.62x39mm cal.

F17-L – .17 Win. Super Mag., GIO, 20 in. stainless steel bull barrel, target crown, free float fluted and vented handguard, forward assist, alum. upper and lower receivers, anodized Black finish, flared mag. well, integral cold weather trigger guard, 10 shot mag., Magpul MOE rifle stock, Magpul MIAD adj. grip, ambidextrous push button QD sling mounts. New 2014.

	100%	98%	95%	90%	80%	70%	60%	
MSR $1,800	$1,625	$1,425	$1,225	$1,100	$895	$750	$575	

HBAR 16 IN. – 5.56 NATO, 6.8 SPC, or 7.62x39mm cal., GIO, 16 in. HBAR contour barrel, threaded muzzle crown with A2 flash hider, CAR handguards, Picatinny rail gas block with carbine length gas system, or optional forged front sight gas block with integral bayonet lug and front sling swivel, A4 forged aluminum upper receiver with full Picatinny rail and forward assist, forged alum. lower receiver with A2 pistol grip, 10, 20, 25 (6.8 SPC only), or 30 shot mag., M4 6-position collapsible stock with rear sling mounts and alum. receiver extension, black furniture.

	100%	98%	95%	90%	80%	70%	60%	
MSR $1,080	$975	$850	$725	$675	$550	$450	$350	

MSR	100%	98%	95%	90%	80%	70%	60%	Last MSR

Add $20 for forged front sight gas block.

Add $95 for 6.8 SPC cal.

Add $140 for 7.62x39mm cal.

* **HBAR 20 IN.** – 5.56 NATO, 6.8 SPC, 7.62x39mm, or .450 Bushmaster cal., similar to HBAR 16 in., except has 20 in. HBAR contour barrel, threaded muzzle crown with flash hider or compensator (.450 Bushmaster only), A2 handguard, forged front sight gas block with integral bayonet lug and front sling swivel, or optional Picatinny rail gas block with carbine length gas system, A2 stock with storage compartment.

| MSR $1,095 | $985 | $875 | $750 | $675 | $550 | $450 | $350 | |

Add $20 for forged front sight gas block.

Add $90 for 6.8 SPC cal.

Add $130 for 7.62x39mm cal.

Add $165 for .450 Bushmaster cal.

LTW – 5.56 NATO cal., similar to HBAR 16 in., except has lightweight contour barrel and A2 flash hider.

| MSR $1,100 | $995 | $875 | $750 | $675 | $550 | $450 | $350 | |

Add $25 for forged front sight gas block.

M4 – 5.56 NATO or .300 Blackout cal., GIO, 16 in. M4 contour barrel with threaded muzzle crown A2 flash hider, M4 double heat shield handguard with aluminum liners, forged front sight gas block with integral bayonet lug and front sling swivel or optional Picatinny rail gas block, A4 forged aluminum upper receiver with full Picatinny rail and forward assist, forged alum. lower receiver, 10, 20, or 30 shot mag., M4 6-position collapsible stock with aluminum CAR receiver extension, A2 pistol grip, black furniture.

| MSR $1,100 | $995 | $875 | $750 | $675 | $550 | $450 | $350 | |

Add $25 for forged front sight gas block.

Add $45 for .300 Blackout cal.

M4-HTF – 5.56 NATO cal., GIO, 16 in. M4 contour fluted barrel, steel construction, low-pro gas block, EGW compensator, forged aluminum A4 upper receiver with Specter length free float forearm quad rail, pop up front and rear sights, forward assist, forged aluminum lower receiver with Ergo Gapper, Ergo Ambi Sure grip, ACE ARFX stock with rubber buttpad and foam padded receiver extension, 10, 20, or 30 shot mag., black furniture.

| MSR $1,735 | $1,550 | $1,350 | $1,175 | $1,050 | $850 | $700 | $550 | |

M4-L – 5.56 NATO or .300 Blackout cal., GIO, 16 in. M4 contour barrel, threaded muzzle crown with A2 flash hider, forged front sight with carbine length gas system, Magpul MOE carbine length handguard, 10 or 20 shot mag., Magpul ACS stock with integral storage compartment, aluminum upper and lower receivers, Black, Desert Smoke, or Olive Drab Green finish, full Picatinny rail with MBUS rear sight, Magpul MIAD adj. grip.

| MSR $1,770 | $1,575 | $1,375 | $1,175 | $1,075 | $875 | $725 | $550 | |

Add $65 for .300 Blackout cal.

* **M4-OPL** – 5.56 NATO or .300 Blackout cal., GPO, similar to M4-L, except utilizes the Osprey Defense Piston System.

| MSR $2,200 | $1,975 | $1,725 | $1,475 | $1,350 | $1,075 | $895 | $695 | |

Add $70 for .300 Blackout cal.

M4-MOE – 5.56 NATO or .300 Blackout cal., GIO, 16 in. M4 contour barrel with threaded muzzle crown A2 flash hider, Magpul MOE handguard, forged front sight gas block with integral bayonet lug and front sling swivel or optional Picatinny rail gas block, A4 forged aluminum upper receiver with full Picatinny rail and forward assist, forged alum. lower receiver with Magpul MOE grip and trigger guard, 10 or 20 shot mag., Magpul MOE 6-position collapsible stock with rubber buttpad, aluminum carbine length receiver extension, black furniture.

| MSR $1,200 | $1,080 | $950 | $825 | $750 | $595 | $475 | $375 | |

Add $25 for forged front sight gas block.

Add $60 for .300 Blackout cal.

M4-SBR-L – 5.56 NATO cal., GIO, 14 1/2 in. M4 contour barrel with Phantom flash hider, threaded muzzle crown, low profile gas block, aluminum upper receiver with full Picatinny rail, MBUS front and rear sights, and forward assist, alum. lower receiver with flared mag. well, bullet button mag. release, QD sling mounts, 10 or 30 shot mag., Magpul CTR stock, Ergo Ambi Sure grip, black furniture.

| MSR $2,000 | $1,800 | $1,575 | $1,350 | $1,225 | $995 | $825 | $625 | |

TMR-L – 5.56 NATO or 6.8 SPC cal., GIO, 20 in. full heavy contour barrel with recessed muzzle crown, low profile gas block with rifle length gas system, aluminum upper and lower receiver with Black, Desert Smoke, or Olive Drab Green finish, full Picatinny rail, Gen. 1 tac latch, flared mag. well, 10 or 20 shot mag., Magpul PRS stock with bottom Picatinny rail, adj. comb and LOP, Ergo Ambi Sure grip.

| MSR $2,035 | $1,825 | $1,600 | $1,375 | $1,250 | $1,000 | $825 | $650 | |

Add $45 for 6.8 SPC cal.

MSR	100%	98%	95%	90%	80%	70%	60%	Last MSR

V1 – 5.56 NATO cal., GIO, 24 in. full heavy contour stainless steel fluted barrel with recessed muzzle crown, single rail Picatinny rail gas block, free float fluted and vented handguard with bipod stud, A4 forged aluminum upper receiver with full picatinny rail, Gen 1 tac latch, forward assist, forged aluminum lower receiver with Magpul MIAD adj. grip, Magpul MOE trigger guard, 10 shot mag., Magpul PRS stock, adj. comb and LOP, bottom Picatinny rail, black furniture.

| MSR $1,640 | $1,475 | $1,295 | $1,100 | $1,000 | $825 | $675 | $525 | |

* V2 – 5.56 NATO or 6.5 Grendel cal., similar to V1, except does not have fluted barrel.

| MSR $1,560 | $1,400 | $1,225 | $1,050 | $950 | $775 | $625 | $500 | |

Add $90 for 6.5 Grendel cal.

V3 – 5.56 NATO or 6.5 Grendel cal., GIO, 24 in. full heavy contour stainless steel barrel with recessed muzzle crown, single rail Picatinny rail gas block with rifle length gas system, free float fluted and vented handguard, A4 forged aluminum upper receiver with full Picatinny rail, forward assist, forged aluminum lower receiver with A2 grip, 10 shot mag, A2 stock with storage compartment and rear sling mount, black furniture.

| MSR $1,110 | $1,000 | $875 | $750 | $675 | $550 | $450 | $350 | |

Add $80 for 6.5 Grendel cal.

* V4 – 5.56 NATO or 6.8 SPC cal., similar to V3, except has 20 in. full heavy non-stainless contour barrel.

| MSR $1,095 | $985 | $875 | $750 | $675 | $550 | $450 | $350 | |

Add $50 for 6.8 SPC cal.

V1-L – 5.56 NATO cal., GIO, 24 in. full heavy contour stainless steel fluted barrel with recessed muzzle crown, Picatinny rail gas block with rifle length gas system, fluted and vented free float rail with sling/bipod stud, aluminum upper receiver with free float fluted and vented handguard, Gen 1 tac latch, forward assist, alum. lower receiver with flared mag. well, push button QD sling mounts, Magpul MIAD adj. grip, 10 or 20 shot mag., Magpul PRS stock, adj. comb and LOP, bottom Picatinny rail, black furniture.

| MSR $2,090 | $1,875 | $1,650 | $1,400 | $1,275 | $1,025 | $850 | $650 | |

* V2-L – 5.56 NATO or 6.5 Grendel cal., similar to V1-L, except does not have fluted barrel.

| MSR $2,000 | $1,800 | $1,575 | $1,350 | $1,225 | $995 | $825 | $625 | |

Add $115 for 6.5 Grendel cal.

FEATURELESS RIFLE – 5.56 NATO cal., GIO, 16 in. HBAR contour barrel with threaded muzzle crown and Phantom brake, Magpul MOE handguard, A4 forged aluminum upper receiver with full Picatinny rail and forward assist, forged alum. lower receiver with Hammerhead grip, 10 or 20 shot mag., ACE ARUL stock with rubber buttpad, alum. receiver extension, Black, Flat Dark Earth (FDE), FOL, or Olive Drab Green furniture. Disc. 2013.

| | $1,080 | $950 | $825 | $750 | $595 | $475 | $37 | *$1,200* |

FULTON ARMORY

Current rifle manufacturer and parts supplier located in Savage, MD. Dealer sales.

CARBINES/RIFLES: SEMI-AUTO

Fulton Armory makes a comprehensive array of the four US Gas Operated Service Rifles: M1 Garand, M1 Carbine, M14 and AR-15-style, including corresponding commercial versions and upper receiver assemblies and related parts and components. All current models are described below.

Previous Fulton Armory M14-style rifles using Fulton Armory's semi-auto M14 receiver included the M14 Competition Rifle (NRA/CMP Service Rifle Match-Legal), and the M14 JSSW with Sage Stock/Accuracy System.

Additionally, Fulton Armory manufactures U.S. military and enhanced civilian configurations of the M1 Garand and M1 Carbine, using genuine U.S.G.I. receivers. Previous models included the M1 Garand Competition Rifle (John C. Garand Match-Legal) - $1,600 last MSR, and the M1 Garand Peerless Rifle (NRA/CMP Service Rifle Match-Legal) - $2,000 last MSR.

Fulton Armory also produces FAR-15 models. Previous models included the Legacy, a '60s semi-auto M16 replica, Classics, mirroring current military M16A2/A4 and M4 models, Guardian Carbines - disc., $1,000-$1,100 last MSR, Liberator and Phantom Tactical Carbines and Enhanced Battle Rifles, Mirage NRA/DCM National Match Rifles - $l,400-$1,800 last MSR, Accutron NRA Match Rifles - $1,300-$2,200 last MSR, Hornet Lightweight Rifle - $750 MSR, disc. 2003, and the Millennial Lightweight Rifle and Carbine - $750-$850 MSR, disc. 2002.

Other previously manufactured rifles included: the UPR (Universal Precision Rifle) - $1,798 last MSR, the UBR (Universal Battle Rifle) - $1,100 last MSR, Predator Varmint Rifle - $1,100 last MSR, National Match - $1,375 last MSR, M14 - $2,500 last MSR, SOPMOD M14 - $3,370 last MSR, Titan UPR - $3,370 last MSR, and the Titan UPR - $1,100 last MSR.

M1 GARAND SERVICE RIFLE – .30-06 cal., GIO, 24 in. GI contour barrel, USGI receiver, walnut stock and handguard with linseed oil finish, includes 8 shot clip and canvas sling.

| MSR $1,700 | $1,525 | $1,350 | $1,150 | $1,050 | $850 | $675 | $550 | |

MSR	100%	98%	95%	90%	80%	70%	60%	Last MSR

* M1 Garand Enhanced Service Rifle – .30-06 cal., GIO, similar to M1 Garand Service Rifle, except comes standard with several National Match upgrades including remove spacer, Loctite and epoxy front handguard hardware, knurl and Loctite lower band to barrel, and modified trigger.

MSR $1,800 $1,625 $1,425 $1,225 $1,100 $900 $725 $575

M1 PEERLESS SERVICE RIFLE – .30-06 cal., GIO, 24 in. GI contour barrel, milled trigger guard, USGI receiver, rear sight, National Match upgrades, glass bedded action, walnut stock with linseed oil finish, includes 8 shot mag. and canvas sling.

MSR $2,500 $2,250 $1,975 $1,700 $1,525 $1,250 $1,015 $800

M1 SERVICE CARBINE – .30 cal., GIO, 18 in. barrel, barrel band with bayonet lug, Fulton Armory's M1 carbine receiver, walnut stock with Linseed oil finish, includes one 10 shot mag., oiler, and canvas sling.

MSR $1,500 $1,350 $1,175 $1,015 $925 $750 $610 $475

* M1A1 Paratrooper Carbine – .30 cal., GIO, similar to M1 Service Carbine, except features a high quality reproduction of the folding wood "Paratrooper" stock with matching wood handguard.

MSR $1,500 $1,350 $1,175 $1,015 $925 $750 $610 $475

* M3 Scout Carbine – .30 cal., GIO, similar to M1 Service Carbine, except features a Picatinny handguard rail for mounting a wide variety of optics.

MSR $1,600 $1,450 $1,275 $1,100 $985 $800 $650 $525

M1C ENHANCED SNIPER RIFLE – .30-06 cal., GIO, 24 in. GI contour barrel with T-37 pronged flash suppressor, USGI receiver (drilled, tapped, and fitted to the scope mount by Griffin & Howe, Inc.), Griffin & Howe scope mount, National Match upgrades, walnut stock with linseed oil finish, includes 8 shot mag., tan leather sling, tan leather lace-up cheekpiece, and professionally fitted.

MSR $2,600 $2,350 $2,050 $1,775 $1,600 $1,300 $1,075 $825

M1C PEERLESS SNIPER RIFLE – .30-06 cal., GIO, 24 in. GI contour barrel with T-37 pronged flash suppressor, USGI receiver (drilled, tapped, and fitted to the scope mount by Griffin & Howe, Inc.), milled trigger guard, National Match upgrades, glass bedded action, walnut stock and handguard with linseed oil finish, includes 8 shot mag., tan leather lace-up cheekpiece, tan leather M1907 sling.

MSR $3,200 $2,875 $2,525 $2,150 $1,950 $1,575 $1,300 $1,000

M1E SCOUT RIFLE – .30-06 cal., GIO, 24 in. GI contour barrel, walnut stock with linseed oil finish, USGI receiver, Super Scout rear handguard with 3-way Picatinny rail, iron sights, includes 8 shot mag. and canvas sling.

MSR $1,850 $1,650 $1,450 $1,250 $1,125 $925 $750 $575

M14 SERVICE RIFLE – GIO, 16 in. SOCOM GIT contour chromemoly barrel with 3-prong trident flash suppressor, Fulton Armory's semi-auto M14 receiver, front sight base, SEI gas cylinder lock with dovetail, fiberglass reinforced black handguard, GI contour walnut stock with linseed oil finish, includes one 10 shot mag., and canvas sling.

MSR $2,800 $2,525 $2,200 $1,900 $1,725 $1,400 $1,150 $875

M14 ENHANCED SERVICE RIFLE – GPO, 22 in. GI Contour chromemoly barrel with National Match flash suppressor with bayonet lug, Fulton Armory's M14 semi-auto receiver, National Match upgrades include gas cylinder with welded front band, Sadlak NM Op rod spring guide, modified trigger, and modified handguard, fiberglass reinforced brown handguard, GI Contour walnut stock with linseed oil finish, includes one 10 shot mag. and canvas sling.

MSR $2,900 $2,600 $2,275 $1,950 $1,775 $1,425 $1,175 $925

M14 PEERLESS NM SERVICE RIFLE – GPO, 22 in. medium contour stainless steel barrel, National Match flash suppressor with bayonet lug, hand milled trigger guard latch, aperture sights, fiberglass reinforced brown handguard, threaded M14 rear lug receiver glass bedded to heavy contour walnut stock with linseed oil finish or McMillan fiberglass stock, glass bedded action, includes National Match upgrades (including Sadlak tin gas piston, ferrule with modified front end, front sling swivel and front sight, modified trigger and handguard), one 10 shot mag., and canvas sling.

MSR $3,550 $3,200 $2,800 $2,400 $2,175 $1,750 $1,450 $1,125

M21 ENHANCED SNIPER RIFLE – GIO, 22 in. GI contour chromemoly barrel, National Match flash suppressor with bayonet lug, Fulton Armory marked "M21" receiver with scope mount and Picatinny rail, fiberglass reinforced brown handguard, GI contour walnut stock with linseed oil finish, adj. cheekpiece, and front stock swivel with Picatinny rail, includes National Match upgrades, one 10 shot mag. and canvas sling.

MSR $3,200 $2,875 $2,525 $2,150 $1,950 $1,575 $1,300 $1,000

FAR-15 PREDATOR VARMINT RIFLE – .223 Rem./5.56 NATO cal., GIO, 24 in. stainless steel bull barrel with plain muzzle, compression fit gas block, flat-top upper, bolt carrier drilled and tapped for side cocking handle, forged lower receiver with Accu-Wedge, fixed A2 buttstock with A2 butt plate and aluminum door assembly, Ergo Sure grip, single stage trigger, includes one 10 shot mag. and Nylon "Silent" sling.

MSR $1,350 $1,225 $1,075 $925 $850 $675 $550 $425

MSR		100%	98%	95%	90%	80%	70%	60%	*Last MSR*

T26 GARAND TANKER – .30-06 cal., GIO, 18 1/4 in. Tanker contour barrel and shortened "Tanker Variant" front handguard, USGI receiver, walnut stock with linseed oil finish, includes 8 shot mag. and canvas sling, 8 1/2 lbs.

    MSR $1,900 $1,700 $1,490 $1,275 $1,155 $935 $765 $595

  * *T26S Garand Scout* – .30-06 cal., GIO, similar to T26 Garand Tanker, except comes standard with Super Scout rear handguard with 3-way Picatinny rail.

    MSR $2,150 $1,925 $1,675 $1,450 $1,325 $1,050 $875 $675

NOTES

G SECTION

GA PRECISION

Current manufacturer established in 1999, and located in N. Kansas City, MO.

MSR	100%	98%	95%	90%	80%	70%	60%	Last MSR

RIFLES: BOLT ACTION

BASE CUSTOM – customer choice of caliber, Rem. 700 short or long action, GIO, 20-26 in. stainless steel barrel with 5R rifling, McMillan M40A-1 HTG stock with Pachmayr decelerator recoil pad, three sling studs, Rem. X-mark trigger, custom steel trigger guard, matte cerakote finish in OD Green, Mil Spec OD, Black, or Coyote Tan finish.

	100%	98%	95%	90%	80%	70%	60%
MSR $3,200	$2,875	$2,525	$2,150	$1,950	$1,575	$1,300	$1,000

CRUSADER – .308 Win. cal., Templar short action, GIO, 23 in. stainless steel barrel, M16 extractor, left side bolt release, McMillan A5 stock in GAP camo pattern, 5 and 10 shot detachable mag., matte Cerakote OD Green finish, T.A.B. Gear sling in OD Green also included.

	100%	98%	95%	90%	80%	70%	60%
MSR $3,990	$3,600	$3,150	$2,700	$2,450	$1,975	$1,625	$1,250

FBI HRT – .308 Win. cal., Templar short action, GIO, 22 in. stainless steel barrel with Surefire suppressor/muzzle brake, 5 and 10 shot detachable mag., McMillan A3-5 adj. stock in OD Green, adj. cheekpiece, spacer system butt pad, left side bolt release, EFR rail installed, OD Green matte Cerakote finish, T.A.B. Gear sling in OD Green also included.

	100%	98%	95%	90%	80%	70%	60%
MSR $4,600	$4,150	$3,625	$3,125	$2,825	$2,275	$1,875	$1,450

GAP-10 – .260 Rem. or .308 Win. cal., semi-auto, GIO, 16-22 in. stainless steel barrel, 20 shot mag., GAP-10 upper and lower receiver with Sniper/Tac handguard, rifle length or mid-length handguard, A2 stock standard (Magpul PRS optional), SST, ambidextrous bolt release, Badger Ordnance Universal safety, includes one-piece scope mount, matte black hard coat anodized finish. New 2012.

	100%	98%	95%	90%	80%	70%	60%
MSR $2,750	$2,475	$2,175	$1,850	$1,675	$1,350	$1,125	$875

GLADIUS – .308 Win. cal., Rem. 700 action, GIO, 18 in. stainless steel special Gladius contour barrel with Surefire brake/adaptor, Manners T-2A stock in Multicam camo pattern, adj. KMW Loggerhead cheek, 5 and 10 shot detachable mag. system, matte black Cerakote finish, includes T.A.B. Gear sling in OD Green.

	100%	98%	95%	90%	80%	70%	60%
MSR $4,100	$3,675	$3,225	$2,750	$2,500	$2,025	$1,650	$1,275

HOSPITALLER – .308 Win. cal., Surgeon Mod. 591 integral short action, GIO, 24 in. stainless steel fluted barrel, Manners T4 adj. stock, KMW cheekpiece, Pachmayr decelerator pad, 5 shot detachable box mag., matte Cerakote OD Green, Tan, or Black finish.

	100%	98%	95%	90%	80%	70%	60%
MSR $4,500	$4,050	$3,550	$3,050	$2,750	$2,225	$1,825	$1,425

NON-TYPICAL – .243 Win., .260 Rem., .270 WSM, .300 WSM, .308 Win., .325 WSM, 7mm-08, 7mm WSM, all Remington RSAUMs, custom .338 WSM and .358 WSM cal., custom GAP Templar Hunter short action, GIO, 25 in. stainless steel contour barrel, B&C GAP Hunter integral aluminum stock in OD Green with Black/Tan webbing, Pachmayr decelerator pad, Rem. X-Mark Pro trigger, custom steel trigger guard, M16 extractor, 1913 rail, matte Cerakote finish in OD Green, Tan, or Black, leather Montana rifle sling included, 7 lbs. 3 oz.

	100%	98%	95%	90%	80%	70%	60%
MSR $2,995	$2,675	$2,350	$2,000	$1,825	$1,475	$1,200	$950

ROCK – customer choice of caliber, Rem. 700 short or long action, GIO, 22 in. stainless steel fluted barrel, McMillan M40A1 HTG stock with choice of camo, Pachmayer Decelerator pad installed, matte Cerakote finish in OD Green, Coyote Tan, or Black.

	100%	98%	95%	90%	80%	70%	60%
MSR $3,495	$3,125	$2,725	$2,325	$2,110	$1,700	$1,400	$1,075

THUNDER RANCH – .308 Win. cal., Templar short action, GIO, 22 in. stainless steel barrel, Manners MCS-T molded-in Field Grade GAP camo stock, 5 and 10 shot mag., OD Cerakote finish, M16 extractor, left-side bolt release, marked with TR logo and comes with a special certificate from Thunder Ranch, T.A.B. Gear sling in OD Green also included.

	100%	98%	95%	90%	80%	70%	60%
MSR $3,870	$3,475	$3,050	$2,600	$2,375	$1,910	$1,575	$1,225

XTREME HUNTER – 6.5 SAUM 4S cal., Templar short action Hunter, 24 in. fluted #3 contour stainless steel barrel, Vais micro muzzlebrake, detachable box mag., X-Mark Pro trigger, M-16 extractor, oversized tactical bolt knob, Manners super light carbon fiber stock, matte cerakote finish in customer's choice of color, leather Montana gun sling, 7 1/2 lbs. New 2014.

	100%	98%	95%	90%	80%	70%	60%
MSR $4,370	$3,925	$3,435	$2,950	$2,675	$2,160	$1,765	$1,375

USMC M40A1 – 7.62 NATO cal., Rem. 700 short action, 25 in. USMC contour stainless steel barrel, matte black finish, steel trigger guard, McMillan M40A1-HTG stock in Forest Camo, red 1/2 in. Pachmayr recoil pad, custom made trigger guard and floorplate.

	100%	98%	95%	90%	80%	70%	60%
MSR $3,700	$3,325	$2,910	$2,495	$2,250	$1,825	$1,495	$1,175

MSR	100%	98%	95%	90%	80%	70%	60%	Last MSR

USMC M40A3 – 7.62 NATO cal., Rem. 700 short action, 25 in. USMC contour stainless steel barrel, matte black finish, Badger Ordnance M5 trigger guard, McMillan A4 stock with OD Green molded-in color, adj. saddle cheekpiece, spacer system buttpad.

MSR $3,970	$3,575	$3,125	$2,675	$2,425	$1,975	$1,625	$1,250	

USMC M40A5 – 7.62 NATO cal., Rem. 700 short action, 25 in. USMC contour stainless steel barrel, Surefire comp/suppressor, matte black finish, Badger M5 DBM trigger guard, one 5 shot mag., adj. McMillan A4 stock in OD Green, PGW PVS-22 night vision mount mounted in stock, spacer system LOP adjustment.

MSR $4,490	$4,040	$3,535	$3,025	$2,750	$2,225	$1,825	$1,415	

US ARMY M-24 – .308 Win. or .300 Win. Mag. cal., Rem. 700 Long action, 24 in. stainless steel barrel, matte black finish, steel M-24 trigger guard, drilled and tapped, one-piece M24 steel scope base, Black HS Precision M-24 stock, adj. LOP, matte black cerakote finish.

MSR $3,670	$3,300	$2,895	$2,475	$2,250	$1,815	$1,485	$1,150	

G.A.R. ARMS

Current AR-15 manufacturer located in Fairacres, NM.

CARBINES/RIFLES: SEMI-AUTO

GR-15 EVOLUTION – 5.56 NATO cal., GIO, 16 in. Government contour barrel with A2 flash hider, threaded muzzle, Parkerized finish, M4 feed ramps, charging handle, Samson 7 in. free float with add-on rails, forged alum. lower receiver and forged A3 flat-top upper, M4 collapsible buttstock, two 30 shot mags., right hand ejection, includes hard rifle case.

MSR $1,158	$1,025	$900	$775	$700	$575	$475	$400	

GR-15 MTCSS – .223 Wylde cal., GIO, 16 in. LW50 stainless steel barrel, Phantom flash hider, YHM quad rail gas block, Daniel Defense 9 in. modular free float rail, Magpul bolt catch B.A.D. lever (battery assist device), two-stage match trigger, Hogue grip, Magpul PRS black sniper stock, charging handle with tactical latch, A3 flat-top upper, Magpul alum. trigger guard, two 30 shot mags., hard rifle case.

MSR $1,800	$1,625	$1,425	$1,225	$1,100	$900	$750	$600	

GR-15 ORHS (OPTICS READY HUNTER STANDARD) – 5.56 NATO cal., GIO, 16 or 20 in. E.R. Shaw chromemoly heavy weight barrel, M4 feed ramps, charging handle, free float aluminum forend, mil-spec trigger, 5 (20 in.) or 10 (16 in.) shot mag., A3 flat-top upper, high riser block for optics, A2 fixed stock, hard rifle case.

MSR $1,359	$1,225	$1,075	$925	$850	$675	$550	$450	

Add $11 for 20 in. barrel.

GR-15 STAINLESS 16 IN. – .223 Rem. cal., GIO, 16 in. stainless steel bison barrel, carbine length free floating handguard, charging handle, forged alum. A3 flat-top upper receiver, forged alum. lower, right hand ejection, two 20 shot mags., A2 buttstock.

MSR $1,205	$1,075	$950	$800	$725	$600	$500	$400	

* **GR-15 Stainless 20 In.** – .223 Wylde cal., similar to A3 Stainless 16 in., except features 20 in. stainless steel barrel and rifle length handguard.

MSR $1,216	$1,075	$950	$800	$725	$600	$500	$400	

GR-15 STANDARD CARBINE – 5.56 NATO cal., GIO, 16 in. Government contour M4 barrel with A2 flash hider, threaded muzzle, M4 feed ramps, Parkerized finish, charging handle, carbine length handguard with single heat shield, forged aluminum lower and A3 flat-top upper receiver, right hand ejection, 6-position collapsible buttstock, single rail gas block, 30 shot mag., standard sling, includes hard rifle case.

MSR $999	$875	$775	$650	$600	$500	$400	$325	

* **GR-15 Standard Rifle** – 5.56 NATO cal., similar to GR-15 A3 Standard Carbine, except features 20 in. barrel, rifle length handguard, and A2 fixed buttstock.

MSR $1,010	$900	$800	$675	$625	$500	$400	$325	

GR-15 TAC DEFENDER – 5.56 NATO cal., GIO, 16 in. Government contour barrel with A2 flash hider, Troy Industries 7, 10, or 13.8 in. free float quad rails, Parkerized finish with M4 feed ramps, charging handle, forged alum. lower receiver and A3 flat-top upper, ejection port cover and round forward assist, right hand ejection, 6-position collapsible buttstock, carbine length handguard and single heat shield (13.8 in. model only).

MSR $1,132	$1,025	$900	$775	$700	$575	$475	$400	

Add $20 for 10 in. Troy Industries free float quad rail.
Add $31 for 13.8 in. Troy Industries free float quad rail.

MSR	100%	98%	95%	90%	80%	70%	60%	*Last MSR*

GR-15 TACDE7 – 5.56 NATO cal., GIO, elite version of Tac Defender model, 16 in. M4 barrel, Parkerized finish, M4 feed ramps, Troy 7 in. free float quad rail in FDE, Troy rail covers in FDE, single rail gas block, YHM (disc.) or Troy gas block mounted flip-up front sight, YHM (disc.) or Troy flip-up rear sight, Vortex (disc.) or Troy Medieval flash suppressor, Magpul trigger guard in FDE, Troy Battle Axe pistol grip FDE, Troy Battle Axe CQB lightweight stock in FDE, Troy 30 shot Battlemag, Troy rifle sling, charging handle with tactical latch, 2-stage match trigger.

MSR $1,884	$1,675	$1,475	$1,250	$1,150	$925	$750	$575	

* **GR-15 TACDE10** – 5.56 NATO cal., similar to GR-15 TACDE7, except features Troy 10 in. free float quad rail, black finish.

MSR $1,917	$1,725	$1,525	$1,300	$1,175	$950	$775	$600	

GR-15 VTAC DEFENDER – 5.56 NATO cal., GIO, 16 in. Govt. contour barrel with A2 flash hider, Troy Industries 9 in. VTAC free float rails, charging handle, forged alum. A3 flat-top upper receiver, forged lower, right hand ejection, two 30 shot mags., M4 collapsible buttstock, Parkerized finish, includes hard rifle case.

MSR $1,180	$1,050	$925	$800	$725	$575	$475	$400	

GR-15 TACE CARBINE – 5.56 NATO cal., GIO, 16 in. fluted barrel, Parkerized finish, M4 feed ramps, 2-stage match trigger, A3 flat-top upper, Midwest Industries flash hider/impact device, Midwest Industries free float quad rail, gas block with flip-up front sight, flip-up rear sight, Magpul ACS stock, Magpul OD Green 30 shot mag., Magpul enhanced aluminum trigger guard, Hogue OD Green pistol grip.

MSR $1,845	$1,650	$1,450	$1,250	$1,125	$925	$750	$600	

GR-15 TACPB CARBINE – 5.56 NATO cal., GIO, 16 in. barrel, Parkerized finish, M4 feed ramps, mil-spec trigger, Troy Industries free float 7.2 in. Alpha BattleRail, YHM single rail gas block, Troy Industries rear flip-up Tritium Battlesight, Troy Industries front gas block mounted flip-up Battlesight, Magpul MOE fixed stock, standard A2 pistol grip, charging handle with tactical latch, 30 shot mag., hard rifle case.

MSR $1,687	$1,525	$1,350	$1,150	$1,050	$850	$700	$550	

GR-15 TACTC – 5.56 NATO cal., GIO, 16 in. M4 barrel with A2 flash hider, charging handle, Tapco M4 six position commercial stock, Tapco saw cut pistol grip, Tapco vertical foregrip and Tapco Intrafuse handguard with quad rails for mounting lights/lasers, Tapco bipod, two Tapco 30 shot mags., Tapco sling system, hard rifle case.

MSR $1,222	$1,100	$975	$825	$750	$600	$500	$400	

GR-15 TACTICAL – 5.56 NATO cal., GIO, 16 in. Govt. contour M4 barrel with A2 flash hider, Parkerized finish, M4 feed ramps, charging handle, carbine length handguard, single heat shield, drop-in quad rails, A3 flat-top forged alum. upper and lower receiver, right hand ejection, M4 6-position collapsible buttstock, two 30 shot mags., hard rifle case.

MSR $1,197	$1,075	$950	$800	$725	$600	$500	$400	

GR-15 ZTAC ZOMBIE TACTICAL CARBINE – 5.56 NATO cal., GIO, 16 in. M4 Govt. contour barrel with A2 flash hider, Parkerized finish, M4 feed ramps, Ergo Z free float rail, Ergo vertical forward grip, Ergo ambidextrous pistol grip in Zombie Green, Ergo Zombie Green Magwell cover, Ergo Zombie Green rail covers and ladder rail covers, Zombie Hunter dust cover, Zombie Hunter magazine catch, Zombie Hunter charging handle, front and rear flip-up sights, Ergo F93 eight position stock, BullDog Zombie coffin soft rifle case.

MSR $1,722	$1,550	$1,350	$1,175	$1,050	$850	$700	$550	

GWACS ARMORY

Current manufacturer of AR-15 style carbines/rifles, receivers, and accessories, and located in Tulsa, OK.

RIFLES: SEMI-AUTO

CAV-15 – 5.56 NATO cal., gas operated, 16 in. chromemoly Nitride M4 Wilson barrel contour with A2 flash suppressor, flat-top receiver with tactical A4 quad rail, Magpul MOE stock, Magpul MOE handguard, Magpul Gen2 backup rear sight, standard charging handle, Milspec trigger assembly, M16 bolt carrier group, optics ready, Black, Coyote Tan, Flat Dark Earth, OD Green, or Zombie Green, approx. 6 lbs.

MSR $889	$800	$700	$600	$550	$450	$375	$295	

GALIL

Current trademark manufactured by Israel Weapon Industries Ltd. (IWI), formerly Israel Military Industries (IMI). No current consumer importation. Recent Galil semi-auto sporterized rifles and variations with thumbhole stocks were banned in April, 1998. Beginning late 1996, Galil rifles and pistols were available in selective fire mode only (law enforcement, military only) and are currently imported by UZI America, Inc., a subsidiary of O.F. Mossberg & Sons, Inc. Previously imported by Action Arms, Ltd. located in Philadelphia, PA until 1994. Previously imported by Springfield Armory located in Geneseo, IL and Magnum Research, Inc., located in Minneapolis, MN.

Magnum Research importation can be denoted by a serial number prefix "MR", while Action Arms imported rifles have either "AA" or "AAL" prefixes.

MSR	100%	98%	95%	90%	80%	70%	60%	Last MSR

RIFLES: SEMI-AUTO

Models 329, 330 (Hadar II), 331, 332, 339 (sniper system with 6x40 mounted Nimrod scope), 361, 372, 386, and 392 all refer to various configurations of the Galil rifle.

MODEL AR – .223 Rem. cal. or .308 Win. cal., gas operated, rotating bolt, 16.1 in. (.223 Rem. cal. only) or 19 in. (.308 Win. cal. only) barrel, parkerized, folding stock, flip-up Tritium night sights. 8.6 lbs.

| | $3,150 | $2,650 | $2,475 | $2,150 | $1,925 | $1,750 | $1,625 | $950 |

Add $500 for .308 Win. cal.

MODEL ARM – similar to Model AR, except includes folding bipod, vented hardwood handguard, and carrying handle.

| | $3,450 | $3,100 | $2,850 | $2,600 | $2,300 | $2,100 | $1,900 | $1,050 |

Add $500 for .308 Win. cal.

GALIL SPORTER – similar to above, except has one-piece thumbhole stock, 4 (.308 Win.) or 5 (.223 Rem.) shot mag., choice of wood (disc.) or polymer hand guard, 8 1/2 lbs. Imported 1991-93.

| | $1,650 | $1,525 | $1,375 | $1,200 | $1,100 | $1,000 | $950 | $950 |

Add $400 for .308 Win. cal.

HADAR II – .308 cal., gas operated, tactical type configuration, 1 piece walnut thumbhole stock with pistol grip and forearm, 18 1/2 in. barrel, adj. rear sight, recoil pad, 4 shot (standard) or 25 shot mag., 10.3 lbs. Imported 1989 only.

| | $1,575 | $1,375 | $1,275 | $1,050 | $950 | $825 | $750 | $998 |

SNIPER OUTFIT – .308 Win. cal., semi-auto, limited production, sniper model built to exact I.D.F. specifications for improved accuracy, 20 in. heavy barrel, hardwood folding stock (adj. recoil pad and adj. cheekpiece) and forearm, includes Tritium night sights, bipod, detachable 6x40mm Nimrod scope, two 25 shot mags., carrying/storage case, 14.1 lbs. Imported 1989 only.

| | $6,500 | $5,750 | $5,000 | $4,350 | $3,750 | $3,250 | $2,850 | $3,995 |

GAMBA, RENATO

Current trademark established in 1748, and located in Gardone V.T., Italy. Gamba firearms are currently manufactured by Bre-Mec srl beginning 2007, and are not currently being imported into the U.S. Previously imported in limited quantities circa 2005-2010 by Renato Gamba U.S.A., located in Walnut, CA. The U.S. service center is located in Bernardsville, NJ. Gamba of America, a subsidiary of Firing Line, located in Aurora, CO, was the exclusive importer and distributor for Renato Gamba long guns from 1996-2000. Pistols were previously imported and distributed (until 1990) by Armscorp of America, Inc. located in Baltimore, MD. Shotguns were previously (until 1992) imported by Heckler & Koch, Inc. located in Sterling, VA.

Filli Gamba (Gamba Brothers) was founded in 1946. G. Gamba sold his tooling to his brother, Renato, in 1967 when Renato Gamba left his brothers and S.A.B. was formed. Filli Gamba closed in 1989 and the Zanotti firm was also purchased the same year.

Renato Gamba firearms have had limited importation since 1986. In 1989, several smaller European firearms companies were purchased by R. Gamba and are now part of the Renato Gamba Group - they include Gambarmi and Stefano Zanotti. The importation of R. Gamba guns changed in 1990 to reflect their long term interest in exporting firearms to America. Earlier imported models may be rare but have not enjoyed much collectibility to date.

Due to space considerations, this section is now available through our website: www.bluebookofgunvalues.com.

GERMAN SPORT GUNS GmbH

Current firearms and air soft manufacturer and distributor located in Ense-Höingen, Germany. Currently imported by American Tactical Imports, located in Rochester, NY.

In May 2013, the L&O Group (owners of Blaser, Mauser, J.P. Sauer & Sohn, John Rigby, and Sig Sauer) purchased a majority stake in German Sport Guns. The L&O Group is owned by Michael Lüke and Thomas Ortmeier.

CARBINES: SEMI-AUTO

GSG-522 – .22 LR cal., semi-auto design patterned after the H&K MP-5 with forearm cocking handle, 16.3 in. barrel with choice of flash hider or faux elongated suppressor, open sights, 10 or 22 shot detachable mag., rail system, black, camo (disc. 2011), or nickel (disc. 2011) finish, synthetic, lightweight synthetic, or wood fixed stock with pistol grip, optional textured pistol grip, Weaver rail, and gold accents (disc. 2012), 6.2-6.6 lbs. New 2002, importation began 2008.

| MSR $451 | | $385 | $335 | $295 | $275 | $250 | $225 | $200 |

Add $100 for 110 round drum mag. (new 2013).
Subtract $56 for lightweight synthetic stock.
Add $28 for nickel (disc. 2011) or $51 for camo finish (special order only, disc. 2011).
Add $47 for wood (disc. 2011).
Add $115 for gold accents (disc. 2012).

MSR	100%	98%	95%	90%	80%	70%	60%	Last MSR

* GSG-522 Retractable Stock – .22 LR cal., 16 1/4 in. barrel with choice of flash hider or faux elongated suppressor, open sights, 22 shot detachable mag., rail system, black finish, lightweight synthetic retractable stock, optional textured pistol grip and integrated Weaver rail. New 2013.

MSR $467	$425	$375	$325	$300	$250	$200	$150

GSG-522 SD – .22 LR cal., similar to GSG-522, except has textured pistol grip and integrated Weaver rail as standard, ribbed hand guard and barrel shroud, black finish only.

MSR $467	$425	$375	$325	$300	$250	$200	$150

Add $100 for 110 round drum mag. (new 2013). Add $12 for retractable stock (new 2013). Subtract $75 for lightweight stock.

GSG STG-44 – .22 LR cal., 17.2 in. barrel, 10 or 25 shot detachable mag., adj. trigger (new 2013), patterned after the Nazi Sturmgewehr 44, wood furniture, blue finish, optional WWII period style wooden crate made in U.S. New 2012.

MSR $500	$450	$400	$350	$300	$250	$200	$160

Add $25 for wooden crate.

KALASHNIKOV – .22 LR cal., patterned after the AK-47 design action, blowback operated, 10, 15 (disc.), 22 (disc.), or 24 (new 2011) shot mag., 16 1/2 in. barrel with protected front sight, available with black synthetic or hardwood pistol grip (mfg. 2012 only) stock. New 2009.

MSR $416	$375	$325	$275	$250	$200	$175	$125

Add $174 for hardwood stock and gold receiver (mfg. 2012 only).

Add $120-$150 for Strikeforce Elite package with adj. polymer stock, pistol grip, recoil system, removable cheekpiece and three Picatinny rails (new 2012).

* Kalashnikov Rebel – .22 LR cal., 16 1/2 in. barrel, wood furniture, features strapping tape wrapped around front of upper handguard and magazine, and bandana added to buttstock, 10 or 24 shot mag., 7 lbs. New 2013.

MSR $483	$425	$375	$325	$285	$260	$230	$200

Add $120-$150 for Strikeforce Elite package with adj. polymer stock, pistol grip, recoil system, removable cheekpiece and three Picatinny rails.

GSG MP-40 – .22 LR cal., 17.2 in. barrel, blued finish, 10 or 28 shot mag., black Bakelite furniture, all metal construction, iron sights, shipped in WWII period-style wooden crate, approx. 9 lbs. New 2014.

MSR $540	$485	$425	$375	$325	$275	$225	$175

PISTOLS: SEMI-AUTO

GSG-522 P – .22 LR cal., 9 in. barrel with flash suppressor, 10 or 22 shot mag., choice of standard or lightweight (new 2013) configuration, black finish, patterned after the MP-5 pistol, adj. diopter rear sight with optional Picatinny rail, top lever charging, integrated Weaver rail (new 2011), textured pistol grip, integrated sling bracket, 5.89 lbs. New 2009.

MSR $429	$365	$335	$315	$285	$265	$245	$225

Subtract $19 for lightweight configuration (new 2013).

GSG-522 PK – .22 LR cal., 10 or 22 shot mag., 4 5/8 in. barrel flush with top of frame, forward mounted charging lever, blued finish, operating mechanism similar to GSG-522 P, integrated Weaver rail and textured pistol grip (new 2011), 5.2 lbs. New 2009.

MSR $421	$365	$335	$315	$285	$265	$245	$225

GSG-922 – .22 LR cal., 3.4 in. threaded barrel, SA, with or w/o faux suppressor, beavertail grip safety, black finish, lower Picatinny rail, checkered black plastic grips, compatible with 1911 parts. New mid-2012.

MSR $380	$340	$300	$275	$250	$225	$200	$185

Add $30 for faux suppressor.

GSG 1911 SERIES – .22 LR cal., patterned after the M1911, 5 in. barrel, SA, front and rear slide serrations, checkered diamond walnut (GSG 1911) or black plastic (GSG Black) grips, skeletonized trigger and hammer, beavertail grip safety, 10 shot mag. New 2009.

MSR $380	$340	$300	$275	$250	$225	$200	$185

Subtract $10 for GSG Black Model.

Add $180 for .22 LR conversion kit (new 2013).

* GSG 1911 Series Target Model – .22 LR cal., similar to 1911 Series, except has threaded barrel and target style checkered molded grips, Picatinny under rail. New late 2013.

MSR $430	$365	$325	$275	$250	$200	$165	$130

Add $17 for Skorpion Pro Gear pistol case.

GSG 1911 AD OPS – .22 LR cal., similar to GSG 1911, except has black plastic grips, lower Picatinny rail, and threaded barrel with 4 in. faux suppressor.

MSR $400	$350	$315	$285	$260	$235	$210	$190

MSR	100%	98%	95%	90%	80%	70%	60%	Last MSR

GIBBS GUNS, INC.

Previously manufactured by Volunteer Enterprises in Knoxville, TN and previously distributed by Gibbs Guns, Inc. located in Greenback, TN.

CARBINES

MARK 45 CARBINE – .45 ACP cal. only, based on M6 Thompson machine gun, 16 1/2 in. barrel, 5, 15, 30, or 90 shot mag. U.S. mfg. Disc. 1988.

	100%	98%	95%	90%	80%	70%	60%	Last MSR
	$750	$625	$525	$450	$375	$330	$300	$279

Add $200 for 90 shot mag.
Add 10% for nickel plating.

GIBBS RIFLE COMPANY, INC.

Current manufacturer, importer, and distributor located in Martinsburg, WV. Gibbs manufactured rifles with the Gibbs trademark in Martinsburg, WV 1991-1994, in addition to importing Mauser-Werke firearms until 1995. Dealer and distributor sales.

In the past, Gibbs Rifle Company, Inc. imported a variety of older firearms, including British military rifles and handguns (both original and refurbished condition), a good selection of used military contract pistols and rifles, in addition to other shooting products and accessories, including a bipod patterned after the Parker-Hale M-85.

Gibbs Rifle Company, Inc. has imported and manufactured military collectibles, historical remakes, and special sporting rifles. All rifles are carefully inspected, commercially cleaned and boxed to ensure their quality, and all have a limited lifetime warranty. Gibbs Rifle Company, Inc. also offered membership in the Gibbs Military Collectors Club, an organization dedicated to military firearms collectors.

RIFLES: BOLT ACTION

ENFIELD NO. 5 JUNGLE CARBINE – .303 British cal., older No. 4 Enfield barreled action with newly manufactured stock, bayonet lug and flash hider have been added, 20 in. barrel, 7 3/4 lbs. Imported 1999-2004, reintroduced 2010 with camo synthetic stock.

	100%	98%	95%	90%	80%	70%	60%	
	$700	$650	$575	$525	$450	$375	$295	

A bayonet and scabbard were also available for this model.

ENFIELD NO. 7 JUNGLE CARBINE – .308 Win. cal., older 2A action with reconfigured original wood, flash hider and bayonet lug have been added, 20 in. barrel, 8 lbs. Imported 1999-2004.

	100%	98%	95%	90%	80%	70%	60%	Last MSR
	$275	$225	$175	$155	$125	$115	$100	$200

QUEST EXTREME CARBINE – .303 British cal., updated No. 5 Enfield action with 20 in. barrel with compensator and flash hider, electroless nickel metal finish, new buttstock with survival kit packaged in butt trap, 7 3/4 lbs. Imported 2000-2004.

	100%	98%	95%	90%	80%	70%	60%	Last MSR
	$295	$265	$225	$185	$170	$160	$150	$250

QUEST II – .308 Win. cal., modern 2A Enfield barreled action, mfg. from chrome vanadium steel, 20 in. barrel with compensator/flash-hider and adj. rear sight, front sight protector, pre-fitted see-through scope mount accepts all Weaver based optics and accessories, electroless nickel finish, hardwood stock with survival kit included, 12 shot mag., 8 lbs. Imported 2001-2004.

	100%	98%	95%	90%	80%	70%	60%	Last MSR
	$375	$325	$265	$235	$200	$185	$170	$280

QUEST III – .308 Win. cal., similar to Quest II, except has black synthetic stock, w/o survival kit. Imported 2002-2004.

	100%	98%	95%	90%	80%	70%	60%	Last MSR
	$395	$345	$280	$240	$200	$185	$170	$300

MODEL 85 SNIPER RIFLE – .308 Win. cal., bolt action, 24 in. heavy barrel, 10 shot mag., camo green synthetic McMillan stock with stippling, built in adj. bipod and recoil pad, enlarged contoured bolt, adj. sights, 12 lbs. 6 oz.

	100%	98%	95%	90%	80%	70%	60%	Last MSR
	$1,825	$1,450	$1,275	$1,050	$875	$750	$625	$2,050

M1903-A4 SPRINGFIELD SNIPER MODEL – .30-06 cal., replica of original M1903-A3 Springfield, drilled and tapped, Redfield replica rings and mounts, new C stock, barrel marked with modern dates of mfg., includes U.S. issue leather sling and OD Green canvas carrying case. M73G2 scope became standard during 2012. New 2009.

	100%	98%	95%	90%	80%	70%	60%	
MSR $1,250	$1,100	$975	$875	$775	$675	$575	$475	

M1903-A4-82 SPRINGFIELD SNIPER MODEL – .30-06 cal., similar to M1903, except has improved M82 rifle scope and 7/8 in. rings. Mfg. 2010-2012.

	100%	98%	95%	90%	80%	70%	60%	Last MSR
	$1,075	$950	$825	$700	$600	$500	$400	$1,200

M1903-A4-84 SPRINGFIELD SNIPER MODEL – .30-06 cal., similar to M1903A4-82, except has improved M84 rifle scope and 7/8 in. rings. Mfg. 2010-2012.

	100%	98%	95%	90%	80%	70%	60%	Last MSR
	$1,100	$950	$825	$700	$600	$500	$400	$1,250

MSR	100%	98%	95%	90%	80%	70%	60%	Last MSR

GILA RIVER GUN WORKS

Current custom rifle manufacturer located in Pocatello, ID, and previously located in Yuma, AZ.

RIFLES: CUSTOM

Michael Scherz specializes in high-quality, bolt action rifles in .550 Magnum caliber. During late 2011 Gila River Tactical was formed and is a division of Gila River Gun Works. This tactical division offers a wide variety of long range precision tactical rifles. Please contact the company directly for more information, including pricing and availability (see Trademark Index).

GIRSAN MACHINE & LIGHT WEAPON INDUSTRY COMPANY

Current handgun and shotgun manufacturer established in 1994, and located in Giresun, Turkey. No current U.S. importation.

PISTOLS: SEMI-AUTO

Girsan manufactures a complete line of good quality semi-auto pistols in a variety of configurations, calibers, frame sizes, and finishes. Many options are available. Current models include: MC13, MC14, Compact M.C., Regard M.C., Tugra, Zirve, Bora, Bora Light, MC 21, MC23, MC 25, MC27, MC27E, MC T40, MC R40, MC C40, MC 21.40, MC 21.45, MC 23.40, MC 23.45, MC 1911, MC 1911S. Please contact the company directly for more information, including U.S. availability and pricing (see Trademark Index).

SHOTGUNS: SEMI-AUTO

During 2012, the company also expanded its line into the 312 series of semi-auto hunting shotguns. Please contact the company directly for more information including current models, pricing, and U.S. availability (see Trademark Index).

GLOCK

Currently manufactured by Glock GmbH in Austria beginning 1983. Sales in the U.S. began in 1986. Glock also opened a production facility for manufacturing its polymer frames and assembling complete pistols in Smyrna, GA during late 2005. Exclusively imported and distributed by Glock, Inc. USA, located in Smyrna, GA. Distributor and dealer sales.

All Glock pistols have a "safe action" constant operating system (double action mode) which includes trigger safety, firing pin safety, and drop safety. Glock pistols have only 35 parts for reliability and simplicity of operation. With approximately 170 or more variations, over 10 million Glock semi-auto pistols have been manufactured since 1983.

In 1995 the Glock Collector's Association was formed. To date Glock has manufactured commemoratives (see Pistols: Semi-Auto, Commemoratives in this section), specially marked, and engraved models, plus the agency and police marked variations. By joining the Glock Collector's Association, members can find out the history of the most desirable G17-G42 civilian models. Please refer to Firearms/Shooting Organizations for more information on the Glock Collector's Association, including how to join.

PISTOLS: SEMI-AUTO

To date, there have been four generations of Glock pistols. Generation 1, circa 1986-1988 features a pebbled finish frame without horizontal grooves on the front or back strap. Generation 2, circa 1988-1997 can be identified by a checkered grenade finish with horizontal grooves on both the front and rear grip straps. Generation 3, circa 1995-2014 started out with transition finger grooves and no front rail with thumb rests, then transitioned into finger grooves and a rail with thumb rests, checkered finished frame. This was followed by Variant 2 which is identified by an (extreme polymid traction) Rough Texture Frame (RTF-2), finger grooves rail, with recessed thumb rests. During 2010, Glock introduced Generation 4 (RTF-4) Rough Textured Frame, this enables standard frame Glock pistols to adopt the new short frame technology, which can be almost instantly fitted to any hand size, and features the (less polymid traction) Rough Textured Frame with recessed thumb rests, finger grooves, rail, and interchangeable frame back straps. It also includes a reversible enlarged magazine catch, dual recoil spring assembly, and a new trigger system, and in 2014, the first model 4th generation slim frame (less than 1 inch width), sub-compact "Less Aggressive" "Rough Textured Frame" (RTF) with thumb rest, reversible enlarged magazine catch, dual recoil spring assembly and new trigger system. Glock has been transitioning all its pistols to Gen4 since 2010.

Add $18 for adj. rear sight, $22 for Glock steel sights (new 2004), or $47 for Glock night sights (new 2004).

Add $80 for fixed Meprolight sight or $105 for fixed Trijicon sight (disc. 2003-2004, depending on model.)

Add $25 for internal locking system (ILS) on most currently manufactured models listed below (new 2004).

Add $95 for tactical light or $284 for tactical light with laser for most currently manufactured pistols listed below.

MODEL 17/17C SPORT/SERVICE – 9mm Para. cal., striker fired constant double action mode, polymer frame, mag., trigger and other pistol parts, 4.48 in. hexagonal rifled barrel, Gen1 (new 1986), Gen2 (new 1989), Gen3 (new 1998) or Gen4 (new 2010), with (Model 17C, Gen2 checkered grip, new 1997) (Model 17C Gen3 ported non-ported (new 1997-98), steel slide and springs, 5 1/2 lb. trigger pull, 10 (C/B 1994), 17* (reintroduced late 2004), or 19* (reintroduced late 2004) shot mag., adj. (Sport Model) or fixed (Service Model) rear sight, includes a lockable pistol box, cable lock, cleaning rod, and other accessories, extra mag. and a spare rear sight, 24 3/4 oz. Importation began late 1985.

MSR	100%	98%	95%	90%	80%	70%	60%
MSR $599	$475	$425	$395	$365	$335	$295	$250

MSR		100%	98%	95%	90%	80%	70%	60%	Last MSR

Add $22 for Model 17C with fixed rear sight (new 1997).

Add $119 for competition model w/adj. sights (Model 17CC, mfg. 2000-2003).

This model is still available with the RTF-2 finish (extreme polymid traction) Rough Textured Frame (Model 17 RFT-2 mfg. 2009).

During 2011 Glock released its 25th Silver Anniversary Limited Edition of the Model 17 Gen4. It featured a 25 year marking on the top of the slide in addition to special 25th year silver medallion inletted in polymer frame - only 2,500 were produced.

All Gen3-4 models have recessed thumb rests and finger grooved mounting accessories rail, except Gen3 standard, compact, sub-compact Transition models (mfg. 1995-1998) have finger grooves, but no mounting accessories rail.

* **Model 17 Gen4** – 9mm Para. cal., similar to Model 17, except features (less polymid traction) Rough Textured Frame (RTF-4) with recessed thumb rests, finger grooves rail, and interchangeable frame back straps, includes a reversible enlarged magazine catch, dual recoil spring assembly, and a new trigger system, fixed rear, adj. rear Glock steel, or Glock night sights. All Gen4 models shipped with 3 magazines. New 2010.

| MSR $649 | | $500 | $440 | $400 | $375 | $335 | $295 | $250 | |

* **Model 17 Gen4 25th Silver Anniversary Limited Edition** – 9mm Para. cal., Glock steel sights only, features 25th year silver medallion inletted in polymer frame and special inscription in back of slide on top, includes silver case. 2,500 to be mfg. during 2011.

| MSR $850 | | $700 | $600 | $500 | $450 | $375 | $350 | $295 | |

* **Model 17L Sport/Service Competition** – 9mm Para. cal., 6.02 in. barrel, slotted relieved slide, recalibrated trigger pull (4 1/2 lb. pull), adj. rear sight, 26.3 oz. mfg. Gen1 pebbled grip (new 1988), Gen2 checkered grip, has no mounting accessories rail (new 1990), Gen3 has thumb rests, finger grooves, mounting accessories rail (new 1998).

| MSR $750 | | $625 | $550 | $475 | $425 | $350 | $325 | $275 | |

Add $28 for adj. sight.

Early Gen1 production with barrel ports, will command a high premium (new 1988).

This model is a long barreled competition version of the Model 17 "pebbled frame". Gen1 production non ported model (new 1988).

MODEL 19/19C COMPACT SPORT/SERVICE – 9mm Para. cal., 4.01 in. barrel with hexagonal rifling ported (Model 19C, Gen2 checkered grip, new 1997), or unported barrel and checkered grip Gen2 has no accessories rail, (new 1988). 10 (C/B 1994), 15* (reintroduced late 2004), or 17* (reintroduced late 2004) shot mag., fixed (Service Model) or adj. (Sport Model) rear sight, 23 1/2 oz., Gen1 cut-down pebbled grip, has no mounting accessories rail (new 1988), Gen3 early transition model has finger grooves, thumb rests, no mounting accessories rail, (new 1997). Later Gen3 models ported/non-ported barrel have thumb rests, finger grooves, mounting accessories rail, (new 1997-1998).

| MSR $599 | | $475 | $425 | $395 | $365 | $335 | $295 | $250 | |

Add $22 for Model 19C with fixed sight only (new 1997).

Add $119 for competition model w/adj. sights (Model 19CC, mfg. 2000-2003).

This model is still available with RTF-2 finish (extreme polymid traction, Rough Textured Frame, Model 19 RTF-2, mfg. 2009).

This model is similar to Model 17, except has scaled down dimensions.

During 1996, AcuSport Corp. commissioned Glock to make a special production run of matching 9mm Para. cal. sets. Each set consists of a Model 19 and 26 with serialization as follows: Model 19 (ser. prefix AAA0000-AAA0499) and Model 26 (ser. prefix AAB0000-AAB0499).

* **Model 19 Gen4** – 9mm Para. cal., similar to Model 19, except features (less polymid traction) Rough Textured Frame (RTF-4) with recessed thumb rests, finger grooves, rail, and interchangeable frame back straps, includes a reversible enlarged magazine catch, dual recoil spring assembly, and a new trigger system, fixed rear, adj. rear Glock steel, or Glock night sights. New 2010.

| MSR $649 | | $500 | $440 | $400 | $375 | $335 | $295 | $250 | |

MODEL 20/20C SPORT/SERVICE – 10mm Norma cal., similar to Model 17 features except has 4.61 in. barrel ported Model 20C, Gen3 with hexagonal rifling, early transition model has recessed thumb rests, finger grooves, no mounting accessories rail (new 1997), 10 (C/B 1994) or 15* (reintroduced late 2004) shot mag., larger slide and receiver, fixed (Service Model) or adj. (Sport Model) rear sight, Gen3 ported/non-ported barrel have recessed thumb rests, finger grooves, mounting accessories rail, (new 1997-1998), Gen2 non-ported barrel, checkered grip, has no mounting accessories rail, 30 oz. New 1990.

| MSR $637 | | $500 | $440 | $410 | $375 | $350 | $325 | $295 | |

Add $39 for compensated barrel (Model 20C, fixed sight only, new 1997).

Add $145 for competition model w/adj. sights (Model 20CC, mfg. 2000-2003).

* **Model 20SF** – 10mm Norma cal., similar to Model 20, except has Gen3 (short frame), have recessed thumb rests, finger grooves, mounting accessories rail, 4.61 in. barrel with hexagonal rifling, 15 shot mag., all Glock sight options

MSR	100%	98%	95%	90%	80%	70%	60%	Last MSR

available, new trigger position, 30.7 oz. New 2009.

MSR $637 $500 $440 $410 $375 $350 $325 $295

* **Model 20 Gen4** – 10mm Norma cal., similar to Model 20 except features (less polymid traction) Rough Textured Frame (RTF-4) with recessed thumb rests, finger grooves, rail and interchangeable frame back straps, includes a reversible enlarged magazine catch, dual recoil assembly and new trigger system, fixed rear, adj. rear Glock steel or Glock night sights. New 2012.

MSR $687 $535 $460 $385 $330 $300 $265 $230

MODEL 21/21C SPORT/SERVICE

– .45 ACP cal., similar to Model 17, except has 4.61 in. barrel with octagonal rifling ported Model 21C, Gen3 early transition model has recessed thumb rests, finger grooves, no mounting accessories rail (new 1997), 10 (C/B 1994) or 13* (reintroduced late 2004) shot mag., Gen3 ported/non-ported barrel, have recessed thumb rests, finger grooves, mounting accessories rail (new 1997-1998), Gen2 non-ported barrel, checkered grip, has no mounting accessories rail, 29 oz. New 1990.

MSR $637 $500 $440 $410 $375 $350 $325 $295

Add $39 for compensated barrel (Model 21C, fixed rear sight only, new 1997).

Add $145 for competition model w/adj. sights (Model 21CC, mfg. 2000-2003).

* **Model 21 Gen4** – .45 ACP cal., similar to Model 21, except features (less polymid traction) Rough Textured Frame (RTF-4) with recessed thumb rests, finger grooves rail and interchangeable frame back straps, includes a reversible enlarged magazine catch, dual recoil spring assembly, and a new trigger system, fixed rear, adj. rear Glock steel, or Glock night sights. New 2011.

MSR $687 $535 $460 $430 $395 $365 $335 $300

* **Model 21SF/21SF (RTF-2)** – .45 ACP cal., similar to Model 21, except has Gen3 (short frame), new trigger position, recessed thumb rests, finger grooves, mounting accessories rail, 4.61 in. barrel with octagonal rifling, 13 shot mag., 29 oz. (new 2007). Gen3 RTF-2 (extreme polymid traction) Rough Textured Frame (new 2009).

MSR $637 $500 $440 $410 $375 $350 $325 $295

MODEL 22/22C SPORT/SERVICE

– .40 S&W cal., similar to Model 17, except has 4.48 in. barrel with hexagonal barrel ported Model 22C Gen2 checkered grip (new 1997), 10 (C/B 1994), 15* (reintroduced late 2004), or 17 shot mag., all Glock sight variations available, Gen3 has ported/non-ported barrel, have recessed thumb rests, finger grooves mounting accessories rail (new 1997-1998), Gen2 has non-ported barrel, checkered grip has no mounting accessories rail, 25 1/2 oz. New 1990.

MSR $599 $475 $425 $395 $365 $335 $295 $250

Add $22 for Model 22C with compensated barrel (fixed rear sight only, new 1997).

Add $119 for competition model with adj. sights (Model 22CC, mfg. 2000-2004).

This model is still available with RTF-2 finish (extreme polymid traction, Rough Textured Frame, Model 22 RTF-2, mfg. 2009).

* **Model 22 Gen4** – .40 S&W cal., similar to Model 22, except features (less polymid traction) Rough Textured Frame (RTF-4) with recessed thumb rests, finger grooves rail and interchangeable frame back straps, includes a reversible enlarged magazine catch, dual recoil spring assembly, and a new trigger system, fixed rear, adj. rear Glock steel, or Glock night sights. New 2010.

MSR $649 $500 $440 $400 $375 $335 $295 $250

MODEL 23/23C COMPACT SPORT/SERVICE

– .40 S&W cal., compact variation of the Model 22, 4.01 in. barrel with hexagonal rifling ported (Model 23C), Gen2 checkered grip (new 1997), 10 (C/B 1994), 13* (reintroduced 2004), or 15 shot mag., available in all Glock sight variations, Gen3 ported/non-ported barrel have recessed thumb rests, finger grooves, mounting accessories rail (new 1997-1998.), Gen2 non-ported barrel, checkered grip has no mounting accessories rail, 23 1/2 oz. New 1990.

MSR $599 $475 $425 $395 $365 $335 $295 $250

Add $22 for compensated barrel (Model 23C, fixed rear sight only).

Add $145 for competition model w/adj. sights (Model 23CC, mfg. 2000-2003).

This model is still available with RTF-2 finish (extreme polymid traction) Rough Textured Frame (Model 22 RTF-2 mfg. 2009).

During 1996, AcuSport Corp. commissioned Glock to make a special production run of matching .40 S&W cal. sets. Each set consists of a Model 23 and 27 with serialization as follows: Model 23 (ser. prefix AAC0000-AAC1499) and Model 27 (ser. prefix AAD0000-AAD1499).

* **Model 23 Gen4** – .40 S&W cal., similar to Model 23 Compact, except features (less polymid traction) Rough Textured Frame (RTF-4) with recessed thumb rests, finger grooves, rail, and interchangeable frame back straps, includes a reversible enlarged magazine catch, dual recoil spring assembly, and a new trigger system, fixed rear, adj. rear Glock steel, or Glock night sights. New 2010.

MSR $649 $500 $440 $400 $375 $335 $295 $250

MSR		100%	98%	95%	90%	80%	70%	60%	Last MSR

MODEL 24/24C SPORT/SERVICE COMPETITION – .40 S&W cal., Gen3, 6.02 in. barrel with hexagonal rifling, internally compensated, recessed thumb rest, finger grooves, accessory rail (Model 24C, new 1999), adj. rear sight, 10, 15, or 17 shot mag., recalibrated trigger pull (4 1/2 lb. pull), Gen2 checkered grip has no rail, "P" ported/non-ported series, 29 1/2 oz. New 1994.

| MSR $750 | | $625 | $550 | $475 | $425 | $350 | $325 | $275 | |

Add $40 for compensated barrel (Model 24C).

MODEL 25 COMPACT SPORT/SERVICE – .380 ACP cal., similar to Model 19 Compact, except has 4.02 in. barrel, 15 or 17 shot mag., recessed thumb rest, finger grooves, accessory rail, 22.5 oz. New 2008.

This model is available for law enforcement only (USA).

MODEL 26 SUB-COMPACT – 9mm Para. cal., sub-compact variation of the Model 19 Compact, except has shortened grip, 3.42 in. barrel with hexagonal rifling, 10 or 12 shot mag., available with all Glock sight variations, thumb rest, finger grooves, no mounting rail, first Gen3 production run Transition model, 21 3/4 oz. New 1995.

| MSR $599 | | $475 | $425 | $395 | $365 | $335 | $295 | $250 | |

* **Model 26 Gen4** – 9mm Para. cal., similar to Model 26 Sub-Compact, except features (less polymid traction) Rough Textured Frame (RTF-4) with recessed thumb rests, finger grooves, and interchangeable frame back straps, includes a reversible enlarged magazine catch, dual recoil spring assembly, and a new trigger system, fixed rear, adj. rear Glock steel, or Glock night sights. New 2010.

| MSR $649 | | $500 | $440 | $400 | $375 | $335 | $295 | $250 | |

MODEL 27 SUB-COMPACT – .40 S&W cal., sub-compact variation of the Model 23 Compact, except has shortened grip, 3.42 in. barrel with hexagonal rifling, 9 or 10 shot mag., all Glock sight variations available, thumb rest, finger grooves, no mounting rail, 21 3/4 oz. New 1995.

| MSR $599 | | $475 | $425 | $395 | $365 | $335 | $295 | $250 | |

* **Model 27 Gen4** – .40 S&W cal., similar to Model 27 Sub-Compact, except features (less polymid traction) Rough Textured Frame (RTF-4) with recessed thumb rests, finger grooves, and interchangeable frame back straps, includes a reversible enlarged magazine catch, dual recoil spring assembly, and a new trigger system, fixed rear, adj. rear Glock steel, or Glock night sights. New 2010.

| MSR $649 | | $500 | $440 | $400 | $375 | $335 | $295 | $250 | |

MODEL 28 SUB-COMPACT – .380 ACP cal., similar to Model 26/27/33/39 Sub-Compact, except has scaled down dimensions with 3.42 in. barrel, thumb rest, finger grooves, no mounting rail, approx. 20 oz. New 1998.

This model is available for law enforcement only (USA).

MODEL 29 SUB-COMPACT – 10mm Norma cal., sub-compact variation of the Model 20, featuring 3.77 in. barrel with hexagonal rifling, 10 shot mag., all Glock sight variations are available, thumb rest, finger grooves, with or w/o (early mfg.) rail, 27 oz. New 1996.

| MSR $637 | | $500 | $440 | $410 | $375 | $350 | $325 | $295 | |

* **Model 29SF** – 10mm Norma cal., 3.77 in. barrel, Gen3, short frame, all Glock sight options available, new trigger position, thumb rest, finger grooves, mounting accessories rail, otherwise similar to Model 29. New 2009.

| MSR $637 | | $500 | $440 | $410 | $375 | $350 | $325 | $295 | |

* **Model 29 Gen4** – 10mm Norma cal., similar to Model 29 Sub-compact except features (less polymid traction) Rough Textured Frame (RTF-4) with recessed thumb rest, finger grooves, rail and interchangeable frame back straps, reversible enlarged magazine catch, dual recoil spring assembly, and new trigger system, fixed rear, adj. rear Glock steel, or Glock night sights. New 2012.

| MSR $637 | | $500 | $440 | $410 | $375 | $350 | $325 | $295 | |

MODEL 30 SUB-COMPACT – .45 ACP cal., sub-compact variation of the Model 21 featuring 3.77 in barrel with octagonal rifling, mag. extension, 10 shot mag., all Glock sight options available, thumb rest, finger grooves, with or w/o (early mfg.) rail, 26 1/2 oz. New 1996.

| MSR $637 | | $500 | $440 | $410 | $375 | $350 | $325 | $295 | |

* **Model 30SF** – .45 ACP cal., 3.77 in. barrel, Gen3 short frame, all Glock sight options available, new trigger position, thumb rest, finger grooves, mounting accessory rail, otherwise similar to Model 30. New 2008.

| MSR $637 | | $500 | $440 | $410 | $375 | $350 | $325 | $295 | |

* **Model 30S** – .45 ACP cal., 3.78 in. barrel, Gen3 short frame, all Glock sight options available, new trigger position, recessed thumb rest, finger grooves, accessory rail, otherwise similar to Model 30SF. Model 36 slim style slide. New 2012.

| MSR $637 | | $500 | $440 | $410 | $375 | $350 | $325 | $295 | |

MSR	100%	98%	95%	90%	80%	70%	60%	Last MSR

* ***Model 30 Gen4*** – .45 ACP cal, similar to Model 30 Sub-compact except features (less polymid traction) Rough Textured Frame (RTF-4) with recessed thumb rest, finger grooves, rail and interchangeable frame back straps, reversible enlarged magazine catch, dual recoil spring assembly, and new trigger system, fixed rear, adj. rear Glock steel, or Glock night sights. New 2012.

| MSR $637 | $500 | $440 | $410 | $375 | $350 | $325 | $295 | |

MODEL 31/31C SPORT/SERVICE

– .357 SIG cal., similar to Model 22, 4.48 in. barrel with hexagonal rifling, ported/non-ported (Model 31-31C Gen3) thumb rests, finger grooves, mounting accessories rail (new 1998), all Glock sight options available, 10, 15, or 16 shot mag., Model 31 Gen2 non-ported barrel, checkered grip has no mounting accessories rail, 26 oz. New 1997.

| MSR $599 | $475 | $425 | $395 | $365 | $335 | $295 | $250 | |

Add $22 for compensated barrel (Model 31C, fixed rear sight only, new 1998).

Add $119 for competition model w/adj. sights (Model 31CC, mfg. 2000-2004).

* ***Model 31 Gen4*** – .357 SIG cal., similar to Model 31, except features (less polymid traction) Rough Textured Frame (RTF-4) with recessed thumb rests, finger grooves rail, and interchangeable frame back straps, includes a reversible enlarged magazine catch, dual recoil spring assembly, and a new trigger system, fixed rear, adj. rear Glock steel, or Glock night sights. New 2010.

| MSR $649 | $500 | $440 | $400 | $375 | $335 | $295 | $250 | |

MODEL 32/32C COMPACT SPORT/SERVICE

– .357 SIG cal., similar to Model 23, 4.01 in. barrel with hexagonal rifling ported/non-ported (Model 32-32C Gen3), thumb rests, finger grooves, mounting accessories rail (new 1998), Model 32 Gen2 non-ported barrel checkered grip, has no mounting accessories rail, all Glock sight options are available, 10, 13, or 14 shot mag., 24 oz. New 1997.

| MSR $599 | $475 | $425 | $395 | $365 | $335 | $295 | $250 | |

Add $22 for compensated barrel (Model 32C, fixed rear sight only, new 1998).

Add $119 for competition model w/adj. sights (Model 32CC, mfg. 2002-2004).

* ***Model 32 Gen4*** – .357 SIG cal., similar to Model 32 Compact, except features (less polymid traction) Rough Textured Frame (RTF-4) with recessed thumb rests, finger grooves, rail, and interchangeable frame back straps, includes a reversible enlarged magazine catch, dual recoil spring assembly, and a new trigger system, fixed rear, adj. rear Glock steel, or Glock night sights. New 2012.

| MSR $649 | $500 | $440 | $400 | $375 | $335 | $295 | $250 | |

MODEL 33 SUB-COMPACT

– .357 SIG cal., sub-compact variation of the Model 32 Compact, shortened grip, 3.42 in. barrel with hexagonal rifling, 9 or 10 shot mag., thumb rest, finger grooves, no mounting rail, 22 oz. New 1997.

| MSR $599 | $475 | $425 | $395 | $365 | $335 | $295 | $250 | |

* ***Model 33 Gen4*** – .357 SIG cal., similar to Model 33 Sub-compact, except features (less polymid traction) Rough Textured Frame (RTF-4) with recessed thumb rests, finger grooves, and interchangeable back straps, includes a reversible enlarged magazine catch, dual recoil spring assembly, and a new trigger system, fixed rear, adj. rear Glock steel, or Glock night sights. New 2012.

| MSR $614 | $535 | $450 | $375 | $325 | $295 | $260 | $225 | |

MODEL 34 SPORT/SERVICE COMPETITION

– 9mm Para. cal., similar features as the Model 17, except has 5.31 in. barrel, recalibrated trigger pull (4 1/2 pull), relieved slide, with hexagonal rifling, extended slide stop lever and magazine catch, adj. rear sights, target grips have recessed thumb rests, mounting accessories rail, 10, 17, or 19 shot mag., 25.75 oz. New 1998.

| MSR $679 | $525 | $450 | $375 | $325 | $295 | $260 | $225 | |

* ***Model 34 Gen4*** – 9mm Para. cal., similar to Model 34, except features (less polymid traction) Rough Textured Frame (RTF-4) with recessed thumb rests, finger grooves, rail, and interchangeable frame back straps, includes a reversible enlarged magazine catch, dual recoil spring assembly, and a new trigger system, adj. rear sight only. New 2011.

| MSR $729 | $575 | $475 | $400 | $350 | $325 | $295 | $265 | |

MODEL 35 SPORT/SERVICE COMPETITION

– .40 S&W cal., 10, 15, or 16 shot mag., recessed thumb rest, finger grooves, accessory rail, otherwise similar to Model 34, 27.5 oz. New 1998.

| MSR $679 | $525 | $450 | $375 | $325 | $295 | $260 | $225 | |

* ***Model 35 Gen4*** – .40 S&W cal., similar to Model 35, except features (less polymid traction) Rough Textured Frame (RTF-4) with recessed thumb rests, finger grooves, rail, and interchangeable frame back straps, includes a reversible enlarged magazine catch, dual recoil spring assembly, and a new trigger system, adj. rear sight only. New 2010.

| MSR $729 | $575 | $475 | $400 | $350 | $325 | $295 | $265 | |

MODEL 36 SUB-COMPACT

– .45 ACP cal., similar to Model 30 Sub-compact, except has single column 6 shot mag., 3.77 in. barrel with octagonal rifling, recessed thumb rest, finger grooves, no rail, all Glock sight options are available, slimmest Glock .45 ACP cal. for concealment, 22 1/2 oz. New 1999.

| MSR $637 | $500 | $440 | $410 | $375 | $350 | $325 | $295 | |

MSR		100%	98%	95%	90%	80%	70%	60%	Last MSR

MODEL 37 SPORT/SERVICE – .45 G.A.P. (Glock Automatic Pistol) cal., 4.48 in. barrel with octagonal rifling, all Glock sight options are available, similar to Model 17, except has extended slide stop lever, wider and heavier slide, improved locking block and ejector, 10 shot semi-staggered column mag., recessed thumb rest, finger grooves, accessory rail, 28 3/4 oz. New 2003.

| MSR $614 | | $535 | $450 | $375 | $325 | $295 | $260 | $225 | |

* ***Model 37 Gen4*** – .45 G.A.P. (Glock Automatic Pistol) cal. similar to Model 37, except features (less polymid traction) Rough Textured Frame (RTF-4) with recessed thumb rests, finger grooves, rail, and interchangeable frame back straps, includes a reversible enlarged magazine catch, dual recoil spring assembly, and a new trigger system, fixed rear, adj. rear Glock steel, or Glock night sights. New 2010.

| MSR $664 | | $515 | $450 | $375 | $325 | $295 | $260 | $225 | |

MODEL 38 COMPACT SPORT/SERVICE – .45 G.A.P. cal., similar to Model 37, except has 4.01 in. barrel with octagonal rifling, 8 shot semi-staggered column mag., thumb rest, finger grooves, accessory rail, all Glock sight options are available, 26 oz. New 2005.

| MSR $614 | | $535 | $450 | $375 | $325 | $295 | $260 | $225 | |

MODEL 39 SUB-COMPACT – .45 G.A.P. cal., sub-compact variation of the Model 38 Compact, except has shortened grip, 6 shot semi-staggered column mag., 3.42 in. barrel with octagonal rifling, all Glock sight options are available, recessed thumb rest, finger grooves, no rail, 22 oz. New 2005.

| MSR $614 | | $535 | $450 | $375 | $325 | $295 | $260 | $225 | |

MODEL 41 SPORT/SERVICE COMPETITION – .45 ACP cal., Gen4 similar to Model 21, except has 5.31 in. barrel, 5 1/2 lb. trigger pull, (less polymid traction) Rough Textured Frame (RTF-4), recessed thumb rest, finger grooves, rail, interchangeable frame backstrap, reversible enlarged magazine catch, dual recoil spring assembly, new trigger system, octagonal rifling, adj. rear Glock sites, 13 shot mag., 27 oz. New 2014.

| MSR $749 | | $675 | $575 | $495 | $425 | $375 | $325 | $295 | |

MODEL 42 SUB-COMPACT – .380 ACP cal., (Gen4) features "Less Aggressive" Polymid Traction Rough Textured Frame (RTF) single column, fires from standard Glock locked breech, 3 1/4 in. barrel with hexagonal rifling, 6 shot mag., measures less than 1 inch width, slimmest Glock frame for concealment, reversible enlarged magazine catch, dual recoil spring assembly, new trigger system, thumb rest, 5 1/2 lb. trigger pull, adj. rear Glock sights, 13 3/4 oz. New 2014.

| MSR $637 | | $575 | $500 | $425 | $365 | $335 | $295 | $275 | |

This model is manufactured in the U.S.

Blue Book Publications selected this model as one of its Top 10 Industry Awards from all the new firearms at the 2014 SHOT Show.

GONCZ ARMAMENT, INC.

Previous manufacturer located in North Hollywood, CA circa 1984-1990.

While advertised, BATF records indicate very few Goncz pistols or carbines were actually produced. All of these guns were prototypes or individually hand-built and none were ever mass produced through normal fabrication techniques.

In 1990, Claridge Hi-Tec, Inc. purchased Goncz Armament, Inc.

GRENDEL, INC.

Previous manufacturer located in Rockledge, FL, circa 1990-1995.

PISTOLS: SEMI-AUTO

MODEL P-30 – .22 WMR cal., blowback similar action to P-12, 5 in. barrel, hammerless, matte black finish, 10 (C/B 1994) or 30* shot mag., 21 oz. Mfg. 1990-95.

| | | $350 | $300 | $250 | $225 | $200 | $185 | $175 | $225 |

Add $25 for electroless nickel finish (disc. 1991).
Add $35 for scope mount (Weaver base).

* ***Model P-30M*** – similar to Model P-30, except has 5.6 in. barrel with removable muzzle brake. Mfg. 1990-95.

| | | $350 | $300 | $250 | $225 | $200 | $185 | $175 | $235 |

Add $25 for electroless nickel finish (disc. 1991).

MODEL P-30L – similar to Model P-30, except has 8 in. barrel with removable muzzle brake, 22 oz. Mfg. 1991-92.

| | | $395 | $350 | $325 | $285 | $250 | $230 | $220 | $280 |

Add $15 for Model P-30LM that allows for fitting various accessories.

MODEL P-31 – .22 WMR cal., same action as P-30, except has 11 in. barrel, enclosed synthetic barrel shroud and flash hider, 48 oz. Mfg. 1990-95.

| | | $450 | $400 | $365 | $325 | $290 | $265 | $235 | $345 |

MSR	100%	98%	95%	90%	80%	70%	60%	Last MSR

RIFLES & CARBINES

MODEL R-31 – .22 WMR cal., similar design to Model P-31 pistol, except has 16 in. barrel and telescoping stock, 64 oz. Mfg. 1991-1995.

	100%	98%	95%	90%	80%	70%	60%	Last MSR
	$495	$450	$425	$375	$335	$310	$285	*$385*

SRT-20F COMPACT – .243 Win. or .308 Win. cal., bolt action based on the Sako A-2 action, 20 in. match grade finned barrel with muzzle brake, folding synthetic stock, integrated bipod rest, no sights, 9 shot mag., 6.7 lbs. Disc. 1989.

	100%	98%	95%	90%	80%	70%	60%	Last MSR
	$775	$725	$675	$595	$565	$540	$520	*$525*

Grendel previously manufactured the SRT-16F, SRT-20L, and SRT-24 - all were disc. 1988. Values are approx. the same as the SRT-20F.

GUNCRAFTER INDUSTRIES

Current pistol manufacturer located in Huntsville, AR.

PISTOLS: SEMI-AUTO

MODEL NO. 1 – .45 ACP or .50 GI cal., 1911 style, SA, 7 shot mag., 5 in. heavy match grade barrel, parkerized or hard chrome finish, front strap checkering, Heinie Slant Pro tritium sights, Aluma checkered grips, includes two mags. and cordura case, 41.3 oz.

MSR $3,185	$2,925	$2,400	$2,050	$1,775	$1,575	$1,350	$1,075

MODEL NO. 2 – .45 ACP or .50 GI cal., 1911 style, 7 shot mag., 5 in. heavy match grade barrel, full profile slide with dust cover frame, integral light rail, parkerized or hard chrome finish, front strap checkering, Heinie Slant Pro tritium sights, Aluma checkered grips, includes two mags. and cordura case, 45.9 oz.

MSR $3,185	$2,925	$2,400	$2,050	$1,775	$1,575	$1,350	$1,075

MODEL NO. 3 – .50 GI cal., similar to Model No. 1, except has Commander style frame. New 2010.

MSR $3,185	$2,925	$2,400	$2,050	$1,775	$1,575	$1,350	$1,075

PISTOL WITH NO NAME – .45 ACP cal., similar to Model No. 3, available with 4 1/2 (either Commander size, or with Officer size frame, Commander size slide/barrel), or 5 in. barrel. New 2010.

MSR $2,695	$2,400	$2,050	$1,750	$1,550	$1,250	$1,000	$800

Add $100 for Officer size frame with Commander size slide/barrel.

NOTES

H SECTION

H-S PRECISION, INC.

Current custom pistol and rifle manufacturer established in 1990 and located in Rapid City, SD. H-S Precision, Inc. also manufactures synthetic stocks and custom machine barrels as well. Dealer and consumer direct sales.

H-S Precision introduced the aluminum bedding block for rifle stocks in 1981, and has been making advanced composite synthetic stocks and custom ballistic test barrels for more than two decades.

In addition to the following models, H-S Precision, Inc. also built rifles using a customer's action (mostly Remington 700 or Winchester Post-'64 Model 70). 2004 MSRs ranged from $1,520-$1,830.

MSR	100%	98%	95%	90%	80%	70%	60%	Last MSR

RIFLES: BOLT ACTION, PRO-SERIES 2000

All H-S Precision rifles feature Kevlar/graphite laminate stocks, cut rifle barrels, and other high tech innovations including a molded aluminum bedding block system. Beginning in 1999, H-S Precision began utilizing their H-S 2000 action, and model nomenclature was changed to begin with Pro-Series 2000.

Add approx. $175-$300 for left-hand action, depending on the model.

PRO-SERIES 2000 LONG RANGE (HEAVY TACTICAL MARKSMAN, HTR) – various cals., stainless fluted barrel standard, Remington BDL (disc. 1999) or Pro-Series 2000 (new 2000) action. New 1990.

MSR	100%	98%	95%	90%	80%	70%	60%
MSR $3,600	$3,060	$2,675	$2,295	$2,075	$1,675	$1,375	$1,075

Add $100 for extended barrel port (Model HTR EP, disc.).

PRO SERIES 2000 RAPID DEPLOYMENT RIFLE (RDR) – .308 Win. cal., Pro-Series 2000 stainless steel short action only, 20 in. fluted barrel, black synthetic stock with or w/o thumbhole, black teflon metal finish, approx. 7 1/2 lbs. New 2000.

MSR	100%	98%	95%	90%	80%	70%	60%
MSR $3,495	$3,125	$2,800	$1,375	$2,100	$1,700	$1,375	$1,075

Add $400 for RDT model (new 2006).

Add $125 for PST60A Long Range stock (disc.).

PRO-SERIES 2000 SHORT TACTICAL (STR) – .308 Win. cal., matte Teflon finished action and barrel, 20 in. fluted barrel with standard porting, Pro Series Tactical stock. New 2004.

MSR	100%	98%	95%	90%	80%	70%
MSR $3,795	$3,400	$3,050	$2,675	$2,295	$2,075	$1,675	$1,375

PRO-SERIES 2000 TAKEDOWN TACTICAL LONG RANGE (TTD) – various short and long action cals., stainless steel barrel, Remington BDL takedown action, matte blue finish. Mfg. 1990-2005, reintroduced 2008.

MSR	100%	98%	95%	90%	80%	70%	60%
MSR $5,995	$5,450	$4,995	$4,500	$4,100	$3,700	$3,200	$2,750

Add $100 for extended barrel port (Model TTD EP, disc.).

Add $2,995 - $3,595 for extra take-down barrel, depending on cartridge case head size.

TAKEDOWN LONG RANGE (TACTICAL MARKSMAN) – .223 Rem., .243 Win., .30-06, .308 Win., 7mm Rem. Mag., .300 Win. Mag., or .338 Win. Mag. cal., includes "kwik klip" and stainless fluted barrel. Mfg. 1990-97.

100%	98%	95%	90%	80%	70%	60%	Last MSR
$2,495	$2,050	$1,675	$1,350	$995	$850	$750	*$2,895*

A complete rifle package consisting of 2 calibers (.308 Win. and .300 Win. Mag.), scope and fitted case was available for $5,200 retail.

HAGELBERG ARMS DESIGN

Current manufacturer located in Denmark. No current US importation.

RIFLES: BOLT ACTION, SINGLE SHOT

FH-50 – .50 BMG cal., bolt action, single shot rifle, loaded from the buttstock (buttstock is bolt), 23.6 (Variant K) or 35.8 (Variant L) in. barrel, pistol grip, approx. 27 lbs.

Please contact the company directly for pricing and U.S. availability on this model.

HAKIM

Previous trademark of rifle adopted by the Egyptian army during the early 1950s.

RIFLES: SEMI-AUTO

HAKIM – 7.92x57mm or 8x57mm cal., gas operated, 25.1 in. barrel with muzzle brake, cocking the bolt is done by sliding the top cover forward, then pulling it back, manual safety is located in rear of receiver, 10 shot detachable box mag., can also be reloaded using stripper clips, adj. rear sight, hardwood stock, 9.7 lbs. Approx. 70,000 mfg. circa 1950s-1960s, with Swedish machinery.

100%	98%	95%	90%	80%	70%	60%
$495	$450	$400	$360	$320	$285	$245

MSR	100%	98%	95%	90%	80%	70%	60%	Last MSR

HALO ARMS, LLC

Previous rifle manufacturer located in Phoenixville, PA from 2003-2013.

Halo Arms also manufactured custom alloy stocks. Due to space considerations, information regarding their rifles is available online free of charge at www.bluebookofgunvalues.com.

HARRINGTON & RICHARDSON, INC.

Previous manufacturer located in Gardner, MA - formerly from Worcester, MA. Successors to Wesson & Harrington, manufactured from 1871 until January 24, 1986. H & R 1871, LLC was formed during 1991 (an entirely different company). H & R 1871, LLC is not responsible for the warranties or safety of older pre-1986 H & R firearms.

A manufacturer of utilitarian firearms for over 115 years, H & R ceased operation on January 24, 1986. Even though new manufacture (under H & R 1871, LLC) is utilizing the H & R trademark, the discontinuance of older models in either NIB or mint condition may command slight asking premiums, but probably will not affect values on those handguns only recently discontinued. Most H & R firearms are still purchased for their shooting value rather than collecting potential. In recent years, Pre-1950s examples have become increasingly more collectible.

Further recent research indicates that many H&R frames were manufactured and stamped with serial numbers in the mid-1930s, but not assembled as complete guns until the WWII era. Therefore, H&R serial numbers alone will not always indicate the variation number.

Please refer to H & R listing in the Serialization section online at www.bluebookofgunvalues.com for alphabetical suffix information on how to determine year of manufacture for most H & R firearms between 1940-1982.

The author would like to thank the late Mr. Jim Hauff and the late Mr. W.E. "Bill" Goforth for providing pricing and information on many of the H&R models.

RIFLES

MODEL 60 REISING SEMI-AUTO – .45 ACP cal., delayed blow back action, 18 1/4 in. barrel, parkerized finish, 10 or 20 shot detachable box mag., front post and adj. rear sight, pistol grip walnut stock, sling swivels, semi-auto version of the Model 50. Mfg. 1944-1946.

$2,800	$2,400	$1,925	$1,575	$1,275	$1,050	$900	

MODEL M-4 SURVIVAL – .22 Hornet cal., 5 shot mag., 14 or 16 in. barrel, wire collapsible stock, mfg. for U.S. military during the 1950s.

$2,000	$1,650	$1,425	$1,125	$965	$855	$750	

Add $400 for barrels less than 16 in. (sales restricted).

This model was packaged in survival kits for U.S. pilots, and is usually encountered with a replacement barrel of 16 inches or more.

MODEL M-1 GARAND – .30-06 cal., semi-auto, 8 shot internal mag., some may be arsenal refinished, mfg. for the U.S. military during the 1950s.

$1,550	$1,325	$1,150	$895	$750	$625	$495	

Subtract 60% if w/o correct parts.

MODEL T-48 FAL/T223 (H&R MFG. FAL) – .308 Win. cal., 20 shot mag., selective fire, approx. 200 mfg. for U.S. military during the 1960s.

Recent values are approx. $10,000 for 98% condition.

Since sales of this rifle are restricted, it is not often encountered in the used marketplace.

M-14 RIFLE/GUERILLA GUN – .308 Win. cal., selective fire, 20 shot mag., Guerilla gun mfg. in prototype only, mfg. for the U.S. military during the 1960s.

Recent values are approx. $20,000 for 98% condition.

Since sales of this rifle are restricted, it is not often encountered in the used marketplace.

M-16 AUTOMATIC BATTLE RIFLE – 5.56 NATO cal., selective fire, 20 or 30 shot mag., mfg. for the U.S. military during the 1960s-1970s.

Recent values are approx. $15,000 for 98% condition.

Since sales of this rifle are restricted, it is not often encountered in the used marketplace.

T-223 (H&R MFG. H&K 93) – .223 Rem. or .308 Win. cal., selective fire, 20 shot mag., approx. 200 mfg. for the U.S. military during the 1960s.

Recent values are approx. $15,000 for 98% condition.

Since sales of this rifle are restricted, it is not often encountered in the used marketplace.

MSR	100%	98%	95%	90%	80%	70%	60%	Last MSR

HARRIS GUNWORKS

Previous firearms manufacturer located in Phoenix, AZ 1995-March 31, 2000. Previously named Harris-McMillan Gunworks and G. McMillan and Co., Inc.

RIFLES: BOLT ACTION

M-40 SNIPER RIFLE – .308 Win. cal., Remington action with McMillan match grade heavy contour barrel, fiberglass stock with recoil pad, 4 shot mag., 9 lbs. Mfg. 1990-2000.

| | $1,825 | $1,450 | $1,125 | $925 | $800 | $700 | $600 | $2,000 |

M-86 SNIPER RIFLE – .300 Phoenix (disc. 1996), .30-06 (new 1989), .300 Win. Mag., or .308 Win. cal., fiberglass stock, variety of optical sights. Mfg. 1988-2000.

| | $2,450 | $2,000 | $1,675 | $1,325 | $1,000 | $895 | $800 | $2,700 |

Add $300 for .300 Phoenix cal. with Harris action (disc. 1996).

Add $200 for takedown feature (mfg. 1993-96).

M-87 LONG RANGE SNIPER RIFLE – .50 BMG cal., stainless steel bolt action, 29 in. barrel with muzzle brake, single shot, camo synthetic stock, accurate to 1500 meters, 21 lbs. Mfg. 1988-2000.

| | $3,450 | $2,800 | $2,375 | $2,000 | $1,850 | $1,700 | $1,575 | $3,885 |

* **M-87R Long Range Sniper Rifle** – similiar specs. as Model 87, except has 5 shot fixed box mag. Mfg. 1990-2000.

| | $3,725 | $2,950 | $2,550 | $2,200 | $2,000 | $1,850 | $1,700 | $4,000 |

M-88 U.S. NAVY – .50 BMG cal., reintroduced U.S. Navy Seal Team shell holder single shot action with thumbhole stock (one-piece or breakdown two-piece), 24 lbs. Mfg. 1997-2000.

| | $3,250 | $2,600 | $2,200 | $1,625 | $1,250 | $1,125 | $900 | $3,600 |

Add $300 for two-piece breakdown stock.

M-89 SNIPER RIFLE – .308 Win. cal., 28 in. barrel with suppressor (also available without), fiberglass stock adj. for length, and recoil pad, 15 1/4 lbs. Mfg. 1990-2000.

| | $2,875 | $2,525 | $2,250 | $1,875 | $1,650 | $1,325 | $1,100 | $3,200 |

Add $425 for muzzle suppressor (disc. 1996).

M-92 BULL PUP – .50 BMG cal., bullpup configuration with shorter barrel. Mfg. 1993-2000.

| | $4,300 | $3,250 | $2,750 | $2,300 | $2,050 | $1,850 | $1,700 | $4,770 |

M-93 – .50 BMG cal., similar to M-87, except has folding stock and detachable 5 or 10 shot box mag. Mfg. 1993-2000.

| | $3,800 | $3,250 | $2,750 | $2,300 | $2,000 | $1,850 | $1,700 | $4,150 |

Add $300 for two-piece folding stock or dovetail combo. quick disassembly fixture.

M-95 TITANIUM/GRAPHITE – .50 BMG cal., features titanium alloy M-87 receiver with graphite barrel and steel liner, single shot or repeater, approx. 18 lbs. Mfg. 1997-2000.

| | $4,650 | $4,175 | $3,475 | $2,875 | $2,300 | $2,050 | $1,850 | $5,085 |

Add $165 for fixed mag.

Add $315 for detachable mag.

M-96 SEMI-AUTO – .50 BMG cal., gas-operated with 5 shot detachable mag., carry handle scope mount, steel receiver, 30 lbs. Mfg. 1997-2000.

| | $6,200 | $5,625 | $5,075 | $4,650 | $4,175 | $3,475 | $2,875 | $6,800 |

HATCHER GUN COMPANY

Current custom pistol, rifle, and shotgun manufacturer located in Elsie, NE and established in 1983.

Hatcher Gun Company manufactures custom pistols, rifles, and shotguns for both the civilian and law enforcement marketplaces. Rifles include a series of AR-15 models in various barrel lengths and configurations, pistols include a bolt action model based on the Remington XP-100, and shotguns include a modified Saiga semi-auto with a short barrel (LE only). Please contact the company directly for more information, availability, and pricing (see Trademark Index).

HEAD DOWN PRODUCTS, LLC

Current AR-15 style semi-auto rifle manufacturer located in Dallas, GA. Previously distributed until 2013 by American Tactical Imports, located in Rochester, NY.

CARBINES/RIFLES: SEMI-AUTO

All Head Down rifles are available in a short barreled configuration for military/law enforcement, include a hard case and limited lifetime warranty.

HDX TAC7 – 5.56 NATO cal., GIO, 16 in. profile melonite coated barrel, 7 in. free floating rail system handguard, matte black hard coat anodized finish, six position collapsible stock with standard pistol grip, two 30 shot mags., A2 flash hider,

MSR	100%	98%	95%	90%	80%	70%	60%	Last MSR

forged upper and lower receiver, flared magazine well, vertical bipod grip, two rail covers. Disc. 2013.

| | $995 | $875 | $750 | $675 | $550 | $450 | $350 | *$1,099* |

TRITON M4 BILLET RIFLE (HDX M4) – 5.56 NATO cal., GIO, 16 in. profile melonite coated barrel, matte black hard coat anodized finish, mil-spec handguard, six position collapsible stock with standard pistol grip, two 30 shot mags., A2 flash hider, forged upper and lower receiver, flared magazine well.

| MSR $849 | $750 | $650 | $575 | $510 | $415 | $350 | $275 | |

TRITON 10 BILLET RIFLE (HDX TAC10) – 5.56 NATO cal., GIO, 16 in. profile melonite coated steel barrel, 10 in. free floating rail system handguard, matte black hard coat anodized finish, six position collapsible stock with standard pistol grip, two 30 shot mags., A2 flash hider, forged upper and lower receiver, flared magazine well, vertical bipod grip, two rail covers, mil-spec bolt carrier group.

| MSR $999 | $895 | $795 | $675 | $610 | $495 | $400 | $325 | |

TRITON 12 BILLET RIFLE (HDX TAC12) – 5.56 NATO cal., GIO, 16 in. profile melonite coated steel barrel, 12 in. free floating rail system handguard, matte black hard coat anodized finish, six position collapsible stock with standard pistol grip, two 30 shot mags., A2 flash hider, forged upper and lower receiver, flared magazine well, vertical bipod grip, two rail covers, mil-spec bolt carrier group.

| MSR $1,099 | $995 | $850 | $750 | $675 | $550 | $450 | $350 | |

MK12 – 5.56 NATO cal., GIO, similar to PV9, except has 15 in. Provectus quad rail and 18 in. match grade barrel with muzzle brake. New 2013.

| MSR $2,299 | $2,000 | $1,800 | $1,600 | $1,400 | $1,200 | $1,000 | $850 | |

PV9 – .300 AAC Blackout or 5.56 NATO cal., GIO, flat-top Picatinny receiver with integrated 9, 13, or 15 in. Provectus quad rail, billet upper/lower receiver, 16 in. barrel with flash suppressor, HDF 6-position buttstock, pistol grip, 30 shot mag. New 2013.

| MSR $1,760 | $1,595 | $1,375 | $1,175 | $995 | $875 | $750 | $625 | |

Add $85 for 13 in., or $350 for 15 in. Provectus quad rail.
Add $100 for .300 AAC Blackout cal.

PV13 – 5.56 NATO or .300 AAC Blackout cal., GIO, 16 in. profile melonite coated barrel, matte black hard coat anodized finish, 13 in. Provectus rail system handguard, HDF adj. stock with Ergo rubber ambi pistol grip, 30 shot mag., A2 flash hider, nickel boron carrier group, precision milled upper and lower receiver, integral trigger guard, flared magazine well.

| MSR $1,845 | $1,650 | $1,450 | $1,250 | $1,125 | $915 | $750 | $575 | |

Add $125 for .300 AAC Blackout cal.

PV15 – 5.56 NATO or .300 AAC Blackout cal., GIO, 16 in. profile melonite coated barrel, matte black hard coat anodized finish, 15 in. Provectus rail system handguard, HDF adj. stock with Ergo rubber ambi pistol grip, 30 shot mag., A2 flash hider, Geissle two-stage trigger, nickel boron carrier group, precision milled upper and lower receiver, integral trigger guard, flared magazine well.

| MSR $2,110 | $1,900 | $1,675 | $1,425 | $1,295 | $1,050 | $850 | $675 | |

Add $115 for .300 AAC Blackout cal.

HECKLER & KOCH

Current manufacturer established in 1949, and located in Oberndorf/Neckar, Germany. Currently imported and distributed beginning mid-2008 by H & K USA, located in Columbus, GA. Previously imported by Merkel USA, located in Trussville, AL, by Heckler & Koch, Inc. located in Sterling, VA (previously located in Chantilly, VA). During 2004, H & K built a new plant in Columbus, GA, primarily to manufacture guns for American military and law enforcement.

In early 1991, H & K was absorbed by Royal Ordnance, a division of British Aerospace (BAE Systems) located in England. During December 2002, BAE Systems sold Heckler & Koch to a group of European investors. Heckler & Koch, Inc. and HKJS GmbH are wholly owned subsidiaries of Suhler Jag und Sportwaffen Holding GmbH and the sole licensees of Heckler & Koch commercial firearms technology.

PISTOLS: SEMI-AUTO, RECENT MFG.

USP and USP Compact (with bobbed hammer) Models are divided into 10 variants. They include: USP Variant 1 (DA/SA with control safety decocking lever on left), USP Variant 2 (DA/SA with control safety decocking lever on right), USP Variant 3 (DA/SA with control safety decocking lever on left), USP Variant 4 (DA/SA with control safety decocking lever on right), USP Variant 5 (DAO with control safety decocking lever on left), USP Variant 6 (DAO with control safety decocking lever on right), USP Variant 7 (DAO with no control lever), USP Variant 9 (DA/SA with safety control lever on left), and USP Variant 10 (DA/SA with safety control lever on right). Please contact your H&K dealer for pricing on these variants.

LEM refers to Law Enforcement Modification (enhanced DAO and conventional SA/DA with serrated decocking button on rear of frame).

All currently manufactured H&K pistols feature a patented lock-out safety device which blocks the hammer strut and slide.

MSR	100%	98%	95%	90%	80%	70%	60%	Last MSR

Add $65 for variant change or night sights prior to shipping on currently manufactured USP and USP Compact models.
Add $387 for laser sighting device BA-6 (mfg. 2002-2005).

P9S – .45 ACP or 9mm Para. cal., DA/SA combat model, 4 in. barrel, roller locked delayed blowback action, blue (early mfg.) or phosphate finish, sculptured plastic grips, fixed sights. Although production ceased in 1984, limited quantities were available until 1989.

	$950	$875	$775	$650	$525	$450	$375	$1,299

Add 20% for .45 ACP.
Add 50% for pistols marked "P9".

P9S TARGET – .45 ACP or 9mm Para. cal., 4 in. barrel, DA/SA, phosphate finish, adj. sights and trigger. Although production ceased in 1984, limited quantities were available until 1989.

	$1,500	$1,275	$1,050	$925	$800	$700	$600	$1,382

Add 20% for .45 ACP cal.

P9S COMPETITION KIT SPORT MODEL – 9mm Para. or .45 ACP (rare) cal., similar to P9S Target, except extra 5 1/2 in. barrel and weight, competition walnut grip, 2 slides, with factory case. Disc. 1984.

		100%	98%	95%	90%	80%	70%	60%	Last MSR
Sport 1		$3,000	$2,650	$2,300	$2,050	$1,800	$1,600	$1,400	
Sport 2		$4,000	$3,500	$3,000	$2,500	$2,000	$1,600	$1,400	
Sport 3		$5,000	$4,500	$4,000	$3,500	$3,000	$2,500	$2,000	$2,250

P7 PSP – 9mm Para. cal., SFO, older variation of the P7 M8, without extended trigger guard, ambidextrous mag. release (European style), or heat shield. Standard production ceased 1986. A reissue of this model was mfg. in 1990, with approx. 150 produced. Limited quantities remained through 1999.

	$1,200	$1,075	$900	$800	$700	$600	$500	
European Model	$2,000	$1,800	$1,500	$1,300	$1,000	$800	$700	$1,111

The PSP is serial numbered 001-239. The PSP/P7 is serial numbered 240-251, and the P7 serialization starts at 252.

P7 M8 – 9mm Para. cal., unique squeeze cocking single action, SFO, extended square combat type trigger guard with heat shield, 4.13 in. fixed barrel with polygonal rifling, 8 shot mag., ambidextrous mag. release, fixed 3-dot sighting system, stippled black plastic grips, black phosphate or nickel (mfg. 1992-2000) finish, includes 2 mags., 28 oz. Disc. 2005.

	$2,250	42,000	$1,750	$1,500	$1,175	$800	$650	$1,515

Add 30% for nickel/hard chrome finish.
Add $100 for Tritium sights (various colors, new 1993).
Add $1,200 for .22 LR conversion kit (barrel, slide, and two mags., disc. 1999).

P7 M13 – similar to P7 M8, only with staggered 13 shot mag., SFO, 30 oz. Disc. 1994.

	$3,200	$2,825	$2,500	$2,250	$1,875	$1,475	$1,250	$1,330

Add 20% for nickel/hard chrome finish.
Add $85 for Tritium sights (various colors, new 1993).
Add $150 for factory wood grips.

P7 M10 – .40 S&W cal., similar specifications as P7 M13, except has 10 shot mag., SFO, 39 oz. Mfg. 1991-1994.

	$3,200	$2,825	$2,500	$2,250	$1,875	$1,475	$1,250	$1,315

Add 20% for nickel/hard chrome finish.
Add $85 for Tritium sights (various colors, new 1993).

HK45 – .45 ACP cal., DA/SA and variants (10), 10 shot mag., 4.53 in. O-ring barrel with polygonal rifling, features black polymer frame with finger groove grips, integrated Picatinny rail, low profile 3-dot sights, interchangable grip panels, twin slide serrations, internal mechanical recoil reduction system reduces recoil 30%, 27.7 oz. New 2008.

MSR $1,193	$1,025	$900	$800	$675	$550	$500	$450	

Add $67 for LEM trigger, DAO.

* **HK45 Tactical** – .45 ACP cal., choice of DA/SA with safety decocking lever on left or LEM trigger, or DAO with no safety/decocking lever, with threaded barrel, choice of black, tan, or green frame, supplied with night sights and one additional grip. New 2013.

MSR $1,392	$1,225	$1,050	$925	$800	$675	$550	$475	

Add $69 for LEM trigger, DAO.

* **HK45 Compact** – similar to HK45, except has 3.9 in. barrel, 8 or 10 shot mag., small grip frame, and bobbed hammer, 28.5 oz. New 2008.

MSR $1,193	$1,025	$900	$800	$675	$550	$500	$450	

Add $67 for LEM trigger, DAO.

MSR	100%	98%	95%	90%	80%	70%	60%	Last MSR

* HK45 Compact Tactical – .45 ACP cal., similar to HK45 Compact, except has 4.57 in. threaded barrel, and 10 shot mag. with extended floorplate, safety/decocking lever on left side, and spur hammer, 29 oz. New 2011.

| MSR $1,392 | $1,225 | $1,050 | $925 | $800 | $675 | $550 | $475 | |

Add $69 for decocking lever on left side.

P30 – 9mm Para. or .40 S&W (new 2011) cal., 3.86 in. barrel with polygonal rifling, 10 (CA only), 13 (.40 S&W cal.) or 15 (9mm Para. cal. only) shot mag., 3-dot sights, lower Picatinny rail, self decocking DA spur hammer, multiple trigger variants including DA/SA, or standard (disc. 2012) or lightened LEM DAO (new 2012) trigger, firing pin block safety, loaded chamber indicator, ergonomic grips with interchangeable side panels and backstraps, double slide serrations, internal recoil reduction system, approx. 23 oz. Importation began mid-2007.

| MSR $1,054 | $925 | $775 | $650 | $550 | $450 | $400 | $375 | |

* P30L – similar to P30, except has 4.5 in. barrel and 1/2 in. longer slide, 27.5 oz. New 2009.

| MSR $1,108 | $950 | $800 | $675 | $575 | $475 | $425 | $400 | |

P2000 – 9mm Para., .357 SIG (mfg. 2005-2012), or .40 S&W cal., DA/SA or LEM (Law Enforcement Modification) DAO (w/o control lever), compact design, patterned after USP Compact Model, features pre-cocked hammer system with very short trigger reset distance, lockout safety device, 3-dot sights, 3.66 in. barrel with polygonal rifling, 10 or 12 shot mag. with finger extension, or optional 13 shot mag. (new late 2004), with or w/o decocker, interchangeable rear grip panels, black finish, approx. 25 oz.

| MSR $992 | $850 | $750 | $650 | $525 | $450 | $400 | $375 | |

Subtract approx. $50 for .357 SIG cal. (mfg. 2005-2012).

* P2000 SK SubCompact – similar to P2000, choice of LEM (Law Enforcement Modification) or regular DA/SA trigger system, 3.26 in. barrel, 9 (.357 SIG (disc. 2012) or .40 S&W cal.) or 10 (9mm Para.) shot mag., approx. 24 oz. Importation began 2005.

| MSR $1,037 | $950 | $800 | $675 | $550 | $495 | $450 | $375 | |

Subtract approx. $50 for .357 SIG cal. (mfg. 2005-2012).

USP CUSTOM COMBAT – 9mm Para. or .40 S&W cal., DA/SA, Variant 1, Novak combat sight system, includes jet funnel kit and two 16 (.40 S&W cal.) or 18 (9mm Para. cal.) shot mags. Mfg. 2009.

| | $1,150 | $975 | $875 | $775 | $675 | $550 | $450 | *$1,295* |

USP COMBAT COMPETITION – 9mm Para. or .40 S&W cal., 4 1/4 in. barrel, includes jet funnel kit with two 16 (.40 S&W) or 18 (9mm Para) mags., Novak combat sight system, DA/SA or LEM trigger (became standard mid-2008), lower accessory rail on frame, 26 1/2 oz. Imported 2007-2010.

| | $1,250 | $1,025 | $925 | $825 | $700 | $600 | $500 | *$1,450* |

Subtract approx. $100 if w/o LEM trigger.

USP COMPETITION – similar to USP Combat Competition, except features LEM match trigger system. Imported 2007-2008.

| | $1,125 | $975 | $850 | $750 | $625 | $500 | $450 | *$1,279* |

USP 9 – 9mm Para. cal., available in 9 variants of DA/SA/DAO, 4 1/4 in. barrel with polygonal rifling, Browning-type action with H & K recoil reduction system, polymer frame, all metal surfaces specially treated, can be carried cocked and locked, stippled synthetic grips, bobbed hammer, 3-dot sighting system, multiple safeties, 10 (C/B 1994), 15 (new late 2004), or 16* shot polymer mag., 26.5 oz. New 1993.

| MSR $952 | $825 | $725 | $600 | $500 | $450 | $400 | $350 | |

Add $67 for LEM trigger, DAO.

Add $107 for Tritium sights (various colors, mfg. 1993-2010).

* USP 9 SD – similar to USP 9, except has target sights and 4.7 in. threaded barrel, approx. 27 oz. Imported 2004-2006, reintroduced 2011.

| MSR $1,313 | $1,150 | $975 | $875 | $725 | $600 | $500 | $450 | |

* USP 9 Stainless – similar to USP 9, except has satin finished stainless steel slide. Mfg. 1996-2001.

| | $700 | $565 | $475 | $415 | $360 | $300 | $255 | *$817* |

USP 9 COMPACT – 9mm Para. cal., compact variation of the USP 9 featuring 3.58 in. barrel, 10 or 13 (new late 2004) shot mag., LEM trigger became available 2003, 25.5 oz. New 1997.

| MSR $992 | $850 | $750 | $650 | $525 | $450 | $400 | $375 | |

Add $68 for LEM trigger, DAO.

* USP 9 Compact Stainless – similar to USP 9 Compact, except has satin finished stainless steel slide. Mfg. 1997-2004.

| | $735 | $595 | $500 | $430 | $375 | $315 | $270 | *$849* |

MSR	100%	98%	95%	90%	80%	70%	60%	Last MSR

* USP 9 Compact LEM – 9mm Para. cal., DAO, blue finish only, LEM trigger mechanism decreases trigger pull to 7 1/2 - 8 1/2 lbs., 24 1/2 oz. Imported 2003-2004.

	$695	$575	$495	$450	$400	$350	$315	$799

USP 9x19 TACTICAL – 9mm Para. cal. enhanced variation of the USP 9, 4.92 in. threaded barrel with rubber o-ring, 10 or 15 shot mag., adj. target type sights and trigger, approx. 28 1/2 oz. Mfg. 2007-2010.

	$975	$850	$750	$625	$525	$450	$400	$1,112

USP 357 – .357 SIG cal., available in 4.25 (Standard, disc. 2004) or 3.58 (Compact) in. barrel, 10 or 12 (optional beginning 2004) shot mag., black finish, approx. 24.5 oz. Imported 2001-2005.

	$695	$560	$500	$450	$395	$350	$300	$799

Subtract $30 for Standard Model (disc. 2004).

USP 40 – .40 S&W cal., similar to USP 9, 9 variants of DA/SA/DAO, 10 (C/B1994), 13* (reintroduced late 2004), or 16 (optional, new 2005, needs jet funnel modification) shot mag., LEM trigger (new 2013), 27.75 oz. New 1993.

MSR $952	$825	$725	$600	$500	$450	$400	$350	

Add $67 for LEM trigger (new 2013).

Add $107 for Tritium sights (various colors, mfg. 1993-disc.).

A desert tan finish became available during 2005 at no extra charge (includes matching nylon carrying case). Limited mfg. 2005-2006.

* USP 40 Stainless – similar to USP 40, except has satin finished stainless steel slide. Mfg. 1996-2003.

	$700	$565	$470	$415	$360	$300	$255	$817

USP 40 COMPACT – .40 S&W cal., compact variation of the USP 40 featuring 3.58 in. barrel, 10 or 12 (new late 2004) shot mag., LEM trigger became available 2002, 27 oz. New 1997.

MSR $992	$850	$750	$650	$525	$450	$400	$375	

Add $68 for LEM trigger, DAO.

A desert tan finish became available during 2005-2006 at no extra charge (includes matching nylon carrying case). Grey was also available in limited quantities during 2005 only.

* USP 40 Compact Stainless – similar to USP 40 Compact, except has satin finished stainless steel slide. Mfg. 1997-2004.

	$735	$595	$500	$430	$375	$315	$270	$849

* USP 40 Compact LEM – .40 S&W cal., DAO, blue finish only, LEM trigger mechanism decreases trigger pull to 7 1/2 - 8 1/2 oz., 24 1/2 oz. Imported 2002-2005.

	$695	$575	$495	$450	$400	$350	$315	

USP 40 TACTICAL – .40 S&W cal., enhanced variation of the USP 40, 4.92 in. threaded barrel with rubber o-ring, 10 (standard) or 13 shot mag., adj. target type sights and match trigger, 30 1/2 oz. New 2005.

MSR $1,333	$1,150	$995	$850	$750	$625	$550	$495	

USP 45 – .45 ACP cal., similar to USP 9, 9 variants of DA/SA/DAO, 10 (C/B 1994), 12 (new late 2004) or 13* shot mag., 27 3/4 oz. New 1995.

MSR $988	$850	$750	$650	$525	$450	$400	$375	

Add $68 for LEM trigger, DAO (new 2011).

Add $107 for Tritium sights (various colors, mfg. 1993-2010).

A desert tan or green finish became available during 2005-2006 at no extra charge (includes matching nylon carrying case). Grey was also available in limited quantities during 2005 only.

* USP 45 Stainless – similar to USP 45, except has satin finished stainless steel slide. Mfg. 1996-2003.

	$760	$600	$500	$430	$375	$315	$270	$888

* USP 45 Match Pistol – .45 ACP cal., features 6.02 in. barrel with polygonal rifling, micrometer adj. high relief and raised rear sight, raised target front sight, 10 shot mag., barrel weight, fluted, and ambidextrous safety, choice of matte black or stainless steel slide, supplied with additional o-rings and setup tools, 38 oz. Mfg. 1997-98.

	$2,150	$1,850	$1,575	$1,300	$1,050	$900	$800	$1,369

Add $72 for stainless steel slide model.

USP 45 COMPACT – .45 ACP cal., compact variation of the USP 45, featuring 3.8 in. barrel, 8 shot mag., 28 oz. New 1998.

MSR $1,040	$895	$775	$650	$550	$475	$425	$375	

Add $68 for LEM trigger, DAO (new 2011).

MSR	100%	98%	95%	90%	80%	70%	60%	Last MSR

* **USP 45 Compact Stainless** – similar to USP 45 Compact, except has satin finished stainless steel slide. Mfg. 1998-2004.

| | $775 | $615 | $510 | $440 | $385 | $325 | $275 | $894 |

* **USP 45 Compact 50th Anniversary** – commemorates the 50th year of H & K (1950-2000), 1 of 1,000 special edition featuring high polish blue slide with 50th Anniversary logo engraved in gold and silver, supplied with presentation wood case and commemorative coin. Limited mfg. 2000 only.

| | $1,150 | $895 | $795 | N/A | N/A | N/A | N/A | $999 |

USP 45 TACTICAL PISTOL – .45 ACP cal., enhanced variation of the USP 45, 5.09 in. threaded barrel with rubber o-ring, 10 or 12 (new late 2004) shot mag., adj. 3-dot target type sights and match trigger, limited availability, 36 oz. New 1998.

| MSR $1,352 | $1,175 | $1,000 | $875 | $775 | $650 | $550 | $495 | |

A desert tan finish became available during 2005-2006 at no extra charge (includes matching nylon carrying case).

* **USP 45 Tactical Pistol Compact** – .45 ACP cal., compact variation of the USP 45 Tactical, 3.78 in. barrel, 8 shot mag., 28 oz. Imported 2006-2012.

| | $1,100 | $950 | $850 | $750 | $650 | $550 | $450 | $1,242 |

USP EXPERT – 9mm Para. (mfg. 2003-2005, reintroduced 2013), .40 S&W (mfg. 2002-2009), or .45 ACP (disc. 2009) cal., features new slide design with 5.2 in. barrel, 10 (standard), 12 (.45 ACP, disc. 2009), 13 (.40 S&W, disc. 2009), 15 (9mm Para.) or 18 (new 2013) shot mag., match grade SA or DA trigger pull, recoil reduction system, reinforced polymer frame, adj. rear sight, approx. 30 oz. Imported 1999-2009, reintroduced 2013.

| MSR $1,372 | $1,225 | $1,075 | $925 | $825 | $725 | $625 | $525 | |

Add $123 for jet funnel frame and two 18 shot mags. (new 2013).

USP ELITE – 9mm Para. (disc. 2005) or .45 ACP cal., long slide variation of the USP Expert, 6.2 in. barrel, match trigger parts, target sights, ambidextrous control levers, blue finish, includes two 10 shot mags. or 12 (.45 ACP) or 15 (9mm Para.) shot mag. Imported 2003-2009.

| | $1,375 | $1,150 | $1,000 | $900 | $800 | $700 | $600 | $1,406 |

MARK 23 SPECIAL OPERATIONS PISTOL – .45 ACP cal., 5.87 in. threaded barrel with O-ring and polygonal rifling, DA/SA, polymer frame with ribbed integral grips, 3-dot sights, 10 or 12 (optional beginning late 2004) shot mag., squared off trigger guard, lower frame is grooved for mounting accessories, mechanical recoil reduction system, 39 oz. Limited availability. New 1996.

| MSR $2,253 | $2,000 | $1,750 | $1,500 | $1,250 | $1,000 | $875 | $775 | |

The "MK23" is the official military design that is not available to civilians.

A desert tan finish became available during 2005-2006 at no extra charge (includes matching nylon carrying case).

SP 89 – 9mm Para. cal., roller locked delayed blowback, 4 1/2 in. barrel, 15 shot mag., adj. aperture rear sight (accepts HK claw-lock scope mounts), 4.4 lbs. Mfg. 1990-1993.

| | $4,950 | $4,500 | $4,150 | $4,000 | $3,750 | $3,625 | $3,500 | $1,325 |

VP 70Z – 9mm Para. cal., 18 shot, DAO, SFO, 4 1/2 in. barrel, parkerized finish, plastic receiver/grip assembly. Disc. 1984.

| | $750 | $675 | $600 | $550 | $500 | $450 | $400 | |

Add 125% if frame cut for shoulder stock (Model VP 70M, NFA Class III).

The majority of pistols that were cut for shoulder stock are the Model VP 70M, and are subject to NFA Class III regulation. A complete M stock with sear is also considered NFA.

HK-416 – .22 LR cal., 10 or 20 shot mag., pistol variation of the Model 416 rifle, blowback action, 9 in. barrel, SA, steel receiver, fixed front sight, external safety, quad Picatinny rail with open sights, including diopter adj. rear sight, black finish, approx. 5 lbs, mfg. by Carl Walther in Ulm, Germany, and imported by Umarex USA. New mid-2009.

| MSR $499 | $450 | $395 | $360 | $330 | $300 | $265 | $235 | |

RIFLES: BOLT ACTION

BASR – .22 LR, .22-250 Rem., 6mm PPC, .300 Win. Mag., .30-06, or .308 Win. cal., Kevlar stock, stainless steel barrel, limited production. Special order only. Mfg. 1986 only.

| | $5,750 | $5,000 | $4,500 | $4,000 | $3,650 | $3,300 | $2,600 | $2,199 |

Less than 135 of this variation were manufactured and they are extremely rare. Contractual disputes with the U.S. supplier stopped H & K from receiving any BASR models.

RIFLES: SEMI-AUTO

Most of the models listed, being of a tactical design, were disc. in 1989 due to Federal legislation. Sporterized variations mfg. after 1994 with thumbhole stocks were banned in April, 1998.

MSR	100%	98%	95%	90%	80%	70%	60%	Last MSR

In 1991, the HK-91, HK-93, and HK-94 were discontinued. Last published retail prices (1991) were $999 for fixed stock models and $1,199 for retractable stock models.

In the early '70s, S.A.C.O. importers located in Virginia sold the Models 41 and 43 which were the predecessors to the Model 91 and 93, respectively. Values for these earlier variations will be higher than values listed.

G3 SEMI-AUTO – .308 Win. cal., patterned after the H&K G3 select-fire military rifle, two variations were imported by Golden State Arms circa 1962.

| | $8,500 | $7,500 | $6,500 | $5,500 | $4,750 | $4,000 | $3,250 | |

SR-9 – .308 Win. cal., semi-auto sporting rifle, 19.7 in. barrel, Kevlar reinforced fiberglass thumbhole stock and forearm, 5 shot mag., diopter adj. rear sight, accepts H & K claw-lock scope mounts. Mfg. 1990-93.

| | $2,075 | $1,725 | $1,400 | $1,225 | $1,075 | $950 | $850 | $1,199 |

While advertised again during 1998, this model was finally banned in April, 1998.

SR-9T – .308 Win. cal., precision target rifle with adj. MSG 90 buttstock and PSG-1 trigger group, 5 shot mag. Mfg. 1992-93.

| | $2,795 | $2,375 | $2,050 | $1,775 | $1,375 | $1,295 | $1,050 | $1,725 |

While advertised again during 1998, this model was finally banned in April, 1998.

SR-9TC – .308 Win. cal., similar to SR-9T except has PSG-1 adj. buttstock. Mfg. 1993 only.

| | $3,350 | $2,925 | $2,600 | $2,275 | $1,925 | $1,475 | $1,250 | $1,995 |

While advertised again during 1998, this model was finally banned in April, 1998.

PSG-1 – .308 Win. cal. only, high precision marksman's rifle, 5 shot mag., adj. buttstock, includes accessories (Hensholdt illuminated 6x42mm scope) and case, 17.8 lbs. Importation disc. 1998.

| | $13,950 | $12,500 | $10,950 | $9,500 | $8,500 | $7,500 | $7,000 | $10,811 |

MODEL 41 A-2 – .308 Win. cal., predecessor to the Model 91 A-2, originally imported by Golden State Arms.

| | $4,500 | $4,000 | $3,750 | $3,500 | $3,350 | $3,200 | $3,000 | |

MODEL 43 A-2 – predecesor to the Model 93 A-2. Disc.

| | $4,500 | $4,000 | $3,750 | $3,500 | $3,350 | $3,200 | $3,000 | |

MODEL 91 A-2 – .308 Win. cal., roller locked delayed blowback action, attenuated recoil, black cycolac stock, 17.7 in. barrel, 20 shot mag., 9.7 lbs. Importation disc. 1989.

* **Model 91 A-2 Fixed stock model**

| | $2,350 | $2,000 | $1,800 | $1,600 | $1,400 | $1,250 | $1,000 | $999 |

Add $200 for desert camo finish.
Add $275 for NATO black finish.

* **Model 91 A-2 SBF (Semi-Beltfed)** – supplied with bipod and M60 link (200 shot with starter tab) and MG42 modified belt (49 shot with fixed starter tab), limited mfg. Disc.

| | $10,500 | $9,500 | $8,500 | N/A | N/A | N/A | N/A | |

* **Model 91 A-3** – with retractable metal stock.

| | $3,100 | $2,900 | $2,700 | $2,500 | $2,150 | $2,000 | $1,895 | $1,114 |

Add $775 for .22 LR conversion kit.

* **Model 91 A-2 Package** – includes A.R.M.S. mount, B-Square rings, Leupold 3-9x compact scope with matte finish. Importation disc. 1988.

| | $3,150 | $2,750 | $2,400 | $2,150 | $1,900 | $1,700 | $1,475 | $1,285 |

Add 30% for retractable stock.

MODEL 93 A-2 – .223 Rem. cal., smaller version of the H & K 91, 25 shot mag., 16.14 in. barrel, 8 lbs.

* **Model 93 A-2 Fixed stock model**

| | $2,500 | $2,250 | $2,000 | $1,750 | $1,500 | $1,250 | $1,000 | $946 |

Add 10% for desert camo finish.
Add 15% for NATO black finish.

* **Model 93 A-3** – with retractable metal stock.

| | $3,400 | $3,250 | $3,000 | $2,800 | $2,650 | $2,500 | $2,250 | $1,114 |

* **Model 93 A-2 Package** – includes A.R.M.S. mount, B-Square rings, Leupold 3-9x compact scope with matte finish. Importation disc. 1988.

| | $3,500 | $3,100 | $2,850 | $2,550 | $2,400 | $2,100 | $1,895 | $1,285 |

Add 10% for retractable stock.

MSR	100%	98%	95%	90%	80%	70%	60%	Last MSR

MODEL 94 CARBINE A-2 – 9mm Para. cal., semi-auto carbine, 16.54 in. barrel, aperture rear sight, 15 shot mag. New 1983.

* **Model 94 Carbine A-2 Fixed stock model**

	$3,950	$3,750	$3,500	$3,400	$3,000	$2,600	$2,500	$946

* **Model 94 Carbine A-3** – retractable metal stock.

	$4,150	$3,900	$3,700	$3,550	$3,200	$2,800	$2,700	$1,114

* **Model 94 Carbine A-2 Package** – includes A.R.M.S. mount, B-Square rings, Leupold 3-9x compact scope with matte finish. Importation disc. 1988.

	$4,300	$3,875	$3,650	$3,300	$3,000	$2,800	$2,500	$1,285

Add 10% for retractable stock.

* **Model 94 Carbine A-2 SGI** – 9mm Para. cal., target rifle, aluminum alloy bipod, Leupold 6X scope, 15 or 30 shot mag. Imported 1986 only.

	$3,950	$3,750	$3,500	$3,000	$2,750	$2,500	$2,150	$1,340

MODEL HK 416 – .22 LR cal., GIO, 10 or 20 shot mag., blowback action with last shot bolt hold open, 16.1 in. barrel with muzzle brake, H&K style diopter sight, black ergonomic pistol grip with storage compartment, manual safety, steel flat-top receiver with quad Picatinny rail, H&K style 5 position buttstock with storage compartment and recoil pad, black finish, 6.8 lbs, mfg. by Carl Walther in Ulm, Germany. Mfg. mid-2010-2011.

	$500	$450	$400	$375	$350	$325	$295	$569

MODEL 416 D145RS – .22 LR cal., GIO, blowback action, 16.1 in. barrel, fixed front sight, adj. rear sight, external safety, 10 or 20 shot mag., metal receiver, black finish, upper and lower rail interface system, pistol grip with compartment, adj. buttstock, functional dust cover, 6.8 lbs., mfg. by Carl Walther in Ulm, Germany, and imported by Umarex USA. New late 2009.

MSR $599	$550	$495	$450	$395	$350	$300	$275	

MODELS SL6 & SL7 CARBINE – .223 Rem. or .308 Win. cal., 17.71 in. barrel, roller locked delayed blowback action, reduced recoil, vent. wood hand guard, 3 or 4 shot mag., 8.36 lbs., matte black metal finish, HK-SL6 is .223 Rem. cal., HK-SL7 is .308 Win. cal. Importation disc. in 1986.

	$1,650	$1,450	$1,250	$1,050	$925	$800	$650	

Add $250-$300 for factory H & K scope mount system.
Add $200 for .308 Win. cal.

These models were the last sporter variations H & K imported into the U.S. - no U.S. importation since 1986.

MODEL SL8-1 – .223 Rem. cal., short stroke piston actuated gas operating system, advanced grey carbon fiber polymer construction based on the German Army G36 rifle, thumbhole stock with adj. cheekpiece and buttstock, 10 shot mag., modular and removable Picatinny rail, removable sights, 20.8 in. cold hammer forged heavy barrel, adj. sights, 8.6 lbs. Imported 2000-2003, reimported 2007-2010.

	$1,950	$1,650	$1,500	$1,350	$1,200	$1,000	$900	$2,449

Add $338 for carrying handle with 1.5X-3x optical sights (disc. 2009).
Add $624 for carrying handle with 1.5X-3x optical sights and red dot reflex sight (disc. 2009).

MODEL SL8-6 – .223 Rem. cal., similar to SL8-1, except has elevated Picatinny rail that doubles as carrying handle. Mfg. 2010-2011.

	$1,950	$1,650	$1,500	$1,350	$1,200	$1,000	$900	$2,388

MODEL USC .45 ACP CARBINE – .45 ACP cal., similar design/construction as the Model SL8-1, except is blowback action, and has 16 in. barrel and grey skeletonized buttstock, 10 shot mag., 6 lbs. Imported 2000-2003, reimported beginning 2007-2011.

	$1,500	$1,275	$1,050	$925	$825	$725	$625	$1,788

MR556A1 CARBINE – 5.56 NATO cal., GPO, 10 or 30 shot steel mag., 16 1/2 in. heavy barrel with muzzle brake, free floating rail system hand guard with four Mil Std 1913 Picatinny rails, Picatinny rail machined into top of upper receiver, two-stage trigger, diopter sights, black anodized finish, adj. buttstock with storage compartment, pistol grip with optional configurations. Mfg. in the U.S. using American and German made components. New 2009.

MSR $3,295	$2,995	$2,600	$2,300	$2,000	$1,700	$1,500	$1,250	

MR762A1 CARBINE – 7.62x51mm cal., GPO, 16 1/2 in. barrel, free floating rail system, flip up front and diopter rear sights, black anodized finish, 10 or 20 shot polymer mag., upper and lower accessory rails, adj. buttstock with storage compartment, pistol grip with optional configurations, 9.84 lbs. Limited mfg. in the U.S. New late 2009.

MSR $3,995	$3,600	$3,150	$2,700	$2,350	$1,950	$1,725	$1,400	

Add $2,000 for LRP Package that includes a Leupold 3-9VX-R Patrol 3-9x40mm scope, G28 adj. cheekpiece buttstock, LaRue Tactical BRM-6 bipod, ERGO pistol grip, cleaning kit, sling, two mags. and Pelican case.

MSR	100%	98%	95%	90%	80%	70%	60%	Last MSR

MODEL MP5 A5 – .22 LR cal., blowback action, 10 or 25 shot mag., 16.1 in. barrel with compensator, black finish, metal receiver, Navy pistol grip, H&K adj. front and rear sights, 3 lug, standard forearm, retractable stock, external safety, 5.9 lbs., mfg. by Carl Walther in Ulm, Germany, imported by Umarex USA. New late 2009.

MSR $499	$450	$395	$360	$330	$300	$275	$250	

MODEL MP5 SD – .22 LR cal., blowback action, 10 or 25 shot mag., 16.1 in. barrel with compensator, black finish, metal receiver, adj. rear sights, interchangeable front post sight, 3 lug imitation, SD type ribbed forearm, Navy pistol grip, retractable stock, external safety, 5.9 lbs. Mfg. by Carl Walther in Ulm, Germany, imported by Umarex USA. New late 2009.

MSR $599	$525	$475	$425	$395	$360	$330	$300	

SHOTGUNS: SEMI-AUTO

Benelli shotguns previously imported by H&K can be found under Benelli.

MODEL 512 – 12 ga. only, mfg. by Franchi for German military contract, rifle sights, matte finished metal, walnut stock, fixed choke pattern diverter giving rectangular shot pattern. Importation disc. 1991.

	$1,500	$1,300	$1,100	$925	$800	$700	$600	

Last Mfg.'s Wholesale was $1,895

HEINIE SPECIALTY PRODUCTS

Previous pistol manufacturer established in 1973, and located in Quincy, IL. Heinie currently manufactures sights only.

Heinie manufactured both scratch built personal defense and tactical/carry 1911 packages in a wide variety of chamberings.

HENRY REPEATING ARMS COMPANY

Current rifle manufacturer established during 1997, and located in Bayonne, NJ beginning 2008. Previously located in Brooklyn, NY. Distributor and dealer sales.

RIFLES: SEMI-AUTO

U.S. SURVIVAL AR-7 – .22 LR cal., patterned after the Armalite AR-7 with improvements, takedown design enables receiver, 2 mags., and barrel to stow in ABS plastic stock, 100% Mossy Oak Break-Up camo (new 2000) or weather resistant silver (disc.) or black (new 1999) stock/metal finish, two 8 shot mags., adj. rear and blade front sights, 16 1/2 in. long when disassembled and stowed in stock, includes plastic carrying case, 3 1/2 lbs. New 1997.

MSR $290	$250	$215	$190	$175	$165	$155	$145	

Add $60 for 100% camo finish (new 2000).

HERA ARMS

Current firearms manufacturer located in Triefenstein, Germany. No current U.S. importation.

Hera Arms manufactures a complete line of AR-15 style semi-auto rifles in .223 Rem cal., as well as several styles of conversions for SIG, Glock, Walther, CZ, and H&K pistols. Hera Arms also manufactures a variety of tactical accessories geared towards military, law enforcement, and sport shooters. Please contact the company directly for more information, including options, US availability, and pricing (see Trademark Index).

HESSE ARMS

Previous manufacturer located in Inver Grove Heights, MN.

Hesse Arms manufactured very limited quantities of semi-auto pistols, bolt action rifles, and semi-auto rifles. Due to space considerations, this information is available free of charge on www.bluebookofgunvalues.com.

HI-POINT FIREARMS

Current trademark marketed by MKS Supply, Inc. located in Dayton, Ohio. Hi-Point firearms have been manufactured by Beemiller Inc. located in Mansfield, OH since 1988. Dealer and distributor sales.

Prior to 1993, trademarks sold by MKS Supply, Inc. (including Beemiller, Haskell Manufacturing, Inc., Iberia Firearms, Inc., and Stallard Arms, Inc.) had their own separate manufacturers' markings. Beginning in 1993, Hi-Point Firearms eliminated these individualized markings and chose instead to have currently manufactured guns labeled "Hi-Point Firearms". All injection molding for Hi-Point Firearms is done in Mansfield, OH.

CARBINES: SEMI-AUTO

MODEL 995TS – 9mm Para. cal., 16 1/2 in. barrel, one-piece camo (disc.) or black polymer stock features pistol grip (target stock became standard 2013), 10 shot mag., aperture rear sight, parkerized or chrome (disc. 2007) finish. New 1996.

MSR $297	$235	$185	$140	$120	$100	$85	$75	

Add $110 for laser sight.
Add $38 for 4x scope or for red dot scope.
Add $23 for forward grip or $52 for forward grip and light.

MSR	100%	98%	95%	90%	80%	70%	60%	*Last MSR*

Add $143 for 4x RGB scope.

Add $30 for forward grip.

Add $153 for forward grip, light, and laser sight (new 2011).

Add $49 for Pro Pack Kit with target stock (new 2011).

Add $15 for camo stock (mfg. 2002-disc.).

Add $85 for detachable compensator, laser, and mount (mfg. 1999-2010).

Add $10 for chrome finish (disc. 2007).

This model is manufactured by Beemiller, located in Mansfield, OH.

MODEL 4095TS – .40 S&W cal., 17 1/2 in. barrel, one-piece camo (disc.) or black polymer stock features pistol grip (target stock became standard 2013), 10 shot mag., aperture rear sight, parkerized or chrome (disc. 2007) finish. Mfg. 2003-2008, reintroduced 2011.

MSR $315	$250	$190	$150	$125	$110	$90	$80	

Add $84 for laser sight.

Add $136 for forward grip, light, and laser sight (new 2011).

Add $32 for Pro Pack Kit with target stock (new 2011).

Add $13 for 4x scope or red dot scope.

Add $111 for 4x RGB scope (new 2013).

Add $6 for forward grip or $35 for forward grip and light.

Add $85 for detachable compensator, laser, and mount (mfg. 1999-2010).

MODEL 4595TS – .45 ACP cal., 17 1/2 in. barrel, black polymer stock (target stock became standard 2013), 9 shot mag., aperture rear sight, black finish. New 2011.

MSR $330	$260	$195	$160	$130	$115	$90	$80	

Add $109 for laser sight.

Add $152 for forward grip, light, and laser sight (new 2011).

Add $49 for Pro Pack Kit with target stock (new 2011).

Add $32 for 4x scope or $30 for red dot scope.

Add $106 for 4x RGB scope (new 2013).

Add $22 for forward grip or $51 for forward grip and light.

HIGH STANDARD

Previous manufacturer located in New Haven, Hamden, and East Hartford, CT. High Standard Mfg. Co. was founded in 1926. They entered the firearms business when they purchased Hartford Arms and Equipment Co. in 1932. The original plant was located in New Haven, CT. During WWII High Standard operated plants in New Haven and Hamden. After the war, the operations were consolidated in Hamden. In the late 1940's and early 1950's the pistol plant was located in East Haven but the guns continued to be marked New Haven. In 1968, the company was sold to the Leisure Group, Inc. A final move was made to East Hartford, CT in 1977 where they remained until the doors were closed in late 1984. In early 1978, the Leisure Group sold the company to the management and the company became High Standard, Inc.

Many collectors have realized the rarity and quality factors this trademark has earned. 13 different variations (Models C, A, D, E, H-D, H-E, H-A, H-B First Model, G-380, , GD, GE, and Olympic, commonly called the GO) had a total production of less than 28,000 pistols. For these reasons, top condition High Standard pistols are getting more difficult to find each year.

As a final note on High Standard pistols, they are listed under the following category names: Letter Series, Letter Series w/Hammer, Lever Letter Series, Lever Name Series, 100 Series, 101 Series, 102 Series, 103 Series, 104 Series, 105 Series, 106 Series - Military Models, 107 Series, Conversion Kits, and SH Series.

Note: catalog numbers were not always consistent with design series, and in 1966-1967 changed with accessories offered, but not design series.

The approx. ser. number cut-off for New Haven, CT marked guns is 442,XXX.

The approx. ser. number range for Hamden, CT marked guns is 431,XXX-2,500,811, G 1,001-G 13,757 (Shipped) or G15,650 (Packed) or ML 1,001-ML 23,065. One exception is a 9211 Victor serial number 3,000,000 shipped 1 March, 1974.

The first gun shipped 16 June, 1977 from E. Hartford was a Victor 9217 serial number EH0001.

The approx. ser. number ranges for E. Hartford, CT manufacture is ML 25,000-ML 86,641 and SH 10,001-SH 34,034. One exception is a single gun numbered ML90,000.

All "V" marked guns were shipped during June 1984 or later independent of serial number.

Original factory boxes have become very desirable. Prices can range from $50-$100 for a good condition Model 106 or 107 factory box to over $150 for an older box of a desirable model.

SHOTGUNS: DEFENSE & LAW ENFORCEMENT

SEMI AUTOMATIC MODEL – 12 ga., 20 in. cylinder bore barrel, 4 shot mag., recoil pad walnut stock and forearm.

	$325	$300	$275	$250	$225	$200	$150	

MSR	100%	98%	95%	90%	80%	70%	60%	*Last MSR*

C-1200, 12 ga., 20 in. barrel, cylinder bore, Riot 20-5, catalog #8294, mfg. 1969. C-1200, 12 ga., 20 in. barrel, cylinder bore, rifle sights, Riot 20-5, catalog #8295, mfg. 1969.

MODELS 10A/10B SEMI-AUTO
– 12 ga., combat model, 18 in. barrel, semi-auto, unique bullpup design incorporates raked pistol grip in front of receiver and metal shoulder pad attached directly to rear of receiver, black cycolac plastic shroud and pistol grip, very compact size (28 in. overall). Disc.

* *Model 10-A Semi-Auto* – 4 shot mag., fixed carrying handle and integral flashlight. Between 1,700 and 1,800 were produced beginning 1967.

	100%	98%	95%	90%	80%	70%	60%	
	$875	$795	$725	$650	$575	$500	$425	

12 ga., 18 in. barrel, cylinder bore, catalog #8290, mfg. 1967-69.

* *Model 10-B Semi-Auto* – 12 ga., folding carrying handle, provisions made for attaching a Kel-lite flashlight to receiver top, extended blade front sight, 4 shot mag., carrying case.

	100%	98%	95%	90%	80%	70%	60%	
	$850	$775	$715	$650	$575	$515	$450	

Add 15% for flashlight.

Cat. No. 50284 optional carrying case and attachable flashlight; Cat. No. 50285 sold optionally. 12 ga., 18.13 in. barrel, cylinder bore, catalog #8291, mfg. 1970-77.

SLIDE ACTION RIOT SHOTGUN
– 12 ga. only on the Flite King Action, 18 or 20 in. barrel, police riot gun, available with or w/o rifle sights, plain pistol grip oiled walnut stock & forearm, changed to walnut stained and lacquered birch in the mid-1970s.

	100%	98%	95%	90%	80%	70%	60%	
	$325	$275	$250	$200	$175	$125	$115	

Catalog #8111/#8113 magazine capacity 6. # 8104/#8129 magazine capacity 5. A 1963 flyer mentions the #8105 Flite King Brush 20 in. and the #8107 Flite King Deluxe 20 in. as riot guns. The data on the #8105 and #8107 is listed under the Flite King Brush. K-101, K-120, K-1200, 12 ga., 20 in. barrel, cylinder bore, Riot 20-6, catalog #8104, mfg. 1963-1977. K-120, K-1200, 12 ga., 18 1/8 in. barrel, cylinder bore, Riot 18-7, catalog #8111, mfg. 1964-1978. K-120, K-1200,12 ga., 18 in. barrel, cylinder bore, rifle sights, Riot 18-7, catalog #8113, mfg. 1965-1978. K-120, 12 ga., 18 1/8 in. barrel, cylinder bore, rifle sights, Riot 18-6, catalog #8118, mfg. 1968. 12 ga., 20 in. barrel, cylinder bore, rifle sights, catalog #8129, mfg. 1976-77. K-102, 12 ga., 20 in. barrel, cylinder bore, catalog #8112, 1964-65. 12 ga., 18 in. barrel, cylinder bore, rifle sights, catalog #8128, mfg. 1976-77.

HIGH STANDARD MANUFACTURING CO.

High Standard is a current trademark of firearms manufactured by Firearms International Inc., established in 1993 and located in Houston, TX.

This company was formed during 1993, utilizing many of the same employees and original material vendors which the original High Standard company used during their period of manufacture (1926-1984). During 2004, Crusader Group Gun Company, Inc. was formed, and this new company includes the assets of High Standard Manufacturing Co, Firearms International Inc., AMT-Auto Mag, Interarms, and Arsenal Line Products.

RIFLES/CARBINES: SEMI-AUTO

HSA-15 – 5.56 NATO or 6x45mm (new 2012) cal., AR-15 style, A2 configuration, 16 (carbine), or 20 (rifle) in. barrel with muzzle brake, fixed (rifle) or collapsible (carbine) stock, 30 shot mag., with or w/o adj. sights.

	100%	98%	95%	90%	80%	70%	60%	
MSR $925	$850	$750	$650	$575	$525	$475	$425	

Add $40 for adj. sights.
Subtract $72 for 6x45mm cal. (new 2012).

HSA-15 CRUSADER – 5.56 NATO cal., 16 in. M4 barrel with A2 flash hider, alum. forged upper and lower receivers, 30 shot mag., quad rail in choice of carbine, mid, or rifle length, low profile gas block or Picatinny gas block, M4 style 6-position adj. stock, ambidextrous safety, Ergo pistol grip, ambidextrous single point sling adaptor, Black or Tan finish. New 2014.

	100%	98%	95%	90%	80%	70%	60%	
MSR $1,200	$1,075	$950	$800	$725	$600	$485	$375	

HSA-15 ENFORCER – 5.56 NATO or .300 Blackout cal., 16 in. M4 style barrel with A2 flash hider, 30 shot mag., alum. forged upper and lower receivers with hard coat anodized finish, quad rail in choice of carbine, mid, or rifle length, low profile gas block or Picatinny rail, M4 6-position adj. stock, Ergo pistol grip, front and rear flip-up rail mounted sights, ambidextrous single point sling adaptor, Black or Tan finish. New 2014.

	100%	98%	95%	90%	80%	70%	60%	
MSR $1,100	$975	$850	$725	$675	$550	$450	$350	

Add $50 for .300 Blackout cal.

HSA-15 NATIONAL MATCH – 5.56 NATO cal., AR-15 style, available with either 20 in. (National Match) or 24 in. (Long Range Rifle) fluted barrel, includes Knight's military two-stage trigger. Mfg. 2006-2012.

	100%	98%	95%	90%	80%	70%	60%	
	$1,125	$950	$850	$750	$650	$550	$495	*$1,238*

Add $12 for Long Range Rifle.

MSR	100%	98%	95%	90%	80%	70%	60%	Last MSR

M-4 CARBINE – 5.56 NATO or 9mm Para. cal., 16 in. barrel, fixed A2 (.223 Rem. cal. only, new 2010) or six position adj. stock, fixed or adj. sights. New 2009.

MSR $880	$825	$725	$625	$550	$475	$400	$350	

Add $30 for 9mm Para. cal. (adj. stock only).

Add $35 for adj. sight (disc.).

Add $65 for quad rail with Picatinny gas block.

Add $450 for chrome lined barrel, free floating quad rails, flip up sights, flash hider and two-stage match trigger (.223 Rem. cal. only, disc. 2009).

M-4 ENFORCER CARBINE – 5.56 NATO cal., 16 in. barrel with A2 flash hider, Socom style six position collapsible stock, flip up battle sights, full length flat-top receiver, YHM quad rail with smooth sides, ergo grip, 30 shot mag. New 2012.

MSR $2,275	$1,950	$1,700	$1,475	$1,250	$1,050	$875	$725	

HOGAN MANUFACTURING LLC

Current AR-15 style carbine/rifle manufacturer located in Glendale, AZ.

RIFLES: SEMI-AUTO

H-223 STANDARD CARBINE – .223 Rem. cal., AR-15 style, GPO, 16 in. button rifled barrel with 5 prong muzzle brake, aluminum alloy free floating monolithic Tactical or Hunter handguards, aluminum forged A3 flat-top upper receiver, lower receiver, Hogan "Gold Standard" trigger system, VLTOR 6-position retractable buttstock with Mil-Spec tube, rubber butt pad, Ergo pistol grip, Black or OD Green anodized, Dark Earth or OD Green Cerakote, or NP3 finish, includes hard case with foam liner, one Magpul PMag., Ergo LowPro rail covers.

MSR $2,399	$2,150	$1,875	$1,625	$1,450	$1,175	$975	$750	

Add $200 for Dark Earth or OD Green Cerakote finish.

* **H-223 Designated Marksman** – .223 Rem. cal., GPO, similar to H-223 Standard carbine, except features 18 in. barrel, 7 lbs. 3 oz. (with Hunter X-Rail) or 8 lbs. 3 oz. (with Tactical X-rail).

MSR $2,399	$2,150	$1,875	$1,625	$1,450	$1,175	$975	$750	

Add $200 for Dark Earth or OD Green Cerakote finish.

* **H-223 Sniper Elite** – .223 Rem. cal., GPO, similar to H-223 Standard Carbine, except features 20 in. barrel, 8 lbs. 5 oz.

MSR $2,574	$2,325	$2,050	$1,750	$1,575	$1,275	$1,050	$825	

Add $200 for Dark Earth or OD Green Cerakote finish.

H-223 HERO MODEL – .223 Rem. cal., AR-15 style, GPO, 16 in. barrel with A2 flash hider, Magpul MOE mid-length plastic handguard, forged alum. A3 flat-top upper, alum. alloy lower receiver, M4 retractable buttstock with Mil-spec tube, A2 pistol grip, Black anodized finish.

MSR $1,699	$1,525	$1,350	$1,150	$1,025	$850	$675	$550	

H-308 STANDARD CARBINE – .308 Win. cal., AR-15 style, GPO, 16 in. button rifled barrel with 5 prong muzzle brake, aluminum alloy free floating monolithic Tactical or Hunter handguards, aluminum forged A3 flat-top upper receiver, lower receiver, Hogan "Gold Standard" trigger system, VLTOR 6-position retractable buttstock with Mil-Spec tube, rubber butt pad, Ergo pistol grip, Black or OD Green anodized, Dark Earth or OD Green Cerakote, or NP3 finish, includes hard case with foam liner, one Magpul PMag., Ergo LowPro rail covers.

MSR $2,899	$2,600	$2,275	$1,950	$1,775	$1,425	$1,175	$925	

Add $200 for Dark Earth or OD Green Cerakote finish.

* **H-308 Designated Marksman** – .308 Win.cal., GPO, similar to H-308 Standard carbine, except features 18 in. barrel.

MSR $2,899	$2,600	$2,275	$1,950	$1,775	$1,425	$1,175	$925	

Add $200 for Dark Earth or OD Green Cerakote finish.

* **H-308 Sniper Elite** – .308 Rem. cal., GPO, similar to H-308 Standard Carbine, except features 20 in. barrel.

MSR $3,049	$2,750	$2,400	$2,075	$1,875	$1,525	$1,250	$975	

Add $200 for Dark Earth or OD Green Cerakote finish.

HOLLOWAY ARMS CO.

Previous manufacturer located in Fort Worth, TX.

Holloway made very few rifles or carbines before operations ceased and existing specimens are scarce.

RIFLES: SEMI-AUTO

HAC MODEL 7 RIFLE – .308 Win. cal., gas operated, 20 in. barrel, adj. front and rear sights, 20 shot mag., side

MSR	100%	98%	95%	90%	80%	70%	60%	Last MSR

folding stock, right or left-hand action. Mfg. 1984-1985 only.

	$3,750	$3,350	$3,100	$2,800	$2,650	$2,350	$2,000	$675

* **HAC Model 7C Rifle Carbine** – 16 in. carbine, same general specifications as Model 7. Disc. 1985.

	$3,750	$3,350	$3,100	$2,800	$2,650	$2,350	$2,000	$675

Also available from the manufacturer were the Models 7S and 7M (Sniper and Match models).

HOLMES FIREARMS

Previous manufacturer located in Wheeler, AR. Previously distributed by D.B. Distributing, Fayetteville, AR.

PISTOLS: SEMI-AUTO

These pistols were mfg. in very limited numbers, most were in prototype configuration and exhibit changes from gun to gun. These models were open bolt and subject to 1988 federal legislation regulations.

MP-83 – 9mm Para. or .45 ACP cal., 6 in. barrel, walnut stock and forearm, blue finish, 3 1/2 lbs.

	$700	$600	$500	$450	$400	$375	$350	$450

Add 10% for deluxe package.
Add 40% for conversion kit (mfg. 1985 only).

MP-22 – .22 LR cal., 2 1/2 lbs., steel and aluminum construction, 6 in. barrel, similar appearance to MP-83. Mfg. 1985 only.

	$395	$360	$320	$285	$250	$230	$210	$400

SHOTGUNS

COMBAT 12 – 12 ga., riot configuration, cylinder bore barrel. Disc. 1983.

	$795	$720	$650	$595	$550	$500	$450	$750

HOULDING PRECISION FIREARMS

Current AR-15 style manufacturer located in Madera, CA.

RIFLES: SEMI-AUTO

HPF-15 MOE – 5.56 NATO cal., GIO, 16 in. M4 barrel with HPF Irish Curse muzzle brake, BTE SST, Magpul MBUS sights, MOE handguard, Magpul MOE 6-position stock, Magpul MOE grip, Cerakote finish, 8.4 lbs.

MSR $1,799	$1,625	$1,425	$1,225	$1,100	$900	$725	$575	

HPF-15 MOE-C – 5.56 NATO cal., GIO, 16 in. M4 profile barrel with Troy Medieval muzzle brake, modular 2-piece handguard, pistol grip, flip up sights, integrated oversized trigger guard and flared magwell, receiver height gas block, all Magpul MOE furniture including MOE carbine length handguard, grip, stock, and Magpul MBUS sights, Cerakote ceramic finish, 7 lbs.

MSR $1,799	$1,625	$1,425	$1,225	$1,100	$900	$725	$575	

HPF-15 MOE-M – 5.56 NATO cal., GIO, 16 in. mid-length barrel with Troy muzzle brake, integrated oversized trigger guard and flared magwell, BTE receiver height gas block, all Magpul MOE furniture including MOE mid-length handguard, grip, 6-position stock, and Magpul MBUS sights, Cerakote ceramic finish, 7 lbs.

MSR $1,799	$1,625	$1,425	$1,225	$1,100	$900	$725	$575	

HPF-15 MOE-R – 5.56 NATO cal., GIO, 18 in. rifle length barrel with Troy muzzle brake, integrated oversized trigger guard and flared magwell, BTE receiver height gas block, all Magpul MOE furniture including MOE rifle-length handguard, grip, 6-position stock, and Magpul MBUS sights, Cerakote ceramic finish, 7 lbs.

MSR $1,799	$1,625	$1,425	$1,225	$1,100	$900	$725	$575	

HPF-15 UBR – 5.56 NATO cal., GIO, 16 or 18 in. mid-length match grade barrel with custom muzzle brake, diamond head gas block, interchangeable Picatinny rail segments, 2-stage Geissele trigger, aluminum upper and lower receivers, polished M4 feed ramps, Troy or JP Enterprise modular handguard, integrated oversized trigger guard and flared magwell, Magpul ACS stock, Ergo grip or Magpul Plus grip, or Vltor collapsible buttstock, Magpul MBUS sights or optic ready, cerakote finish, 6.14 lbs.

MSR $2,350	$2,125	$1,850	$1,595	$1,450	$1,175	$950	$750	

HPF-3 TGR – 5.56 NATO cal., GIO, 16 or 18 in. barrel by Daniel Defense, JP Enterprise tactical compensator or Talon brake, Geissele Super 3-gun SST, HPF upper and lower receiver, large latch BCM Gunfighter charging handle, Magpul plus grip ACS stock. Mfg. 2013 only.

	$2,150	$1,875	$1,625	$1,450	$1,175	$975	$750	$2,403

MSR	100%	98%	95%	90%	80%	70%	60%	Last MSR

HPF-15 TGR – 5.56 NATO cal., GIO, 16 or 18 in. mid-length barrel with custom muzzle brake, Vltor low pro gas block, large or medium latch BCM Gunfighter, polished M4 feed ramps, 15 in. Troy modular handguard, Magpul BUIS sights or optic ready, billet aluminum upper and lower receiver, integrated oversized trigger guard and flared magwell, Geissele SSA 2-stage or duty trigger, Magpul ACS stock, Ergo grip or Magpul Plus grip, or Vltor collapsible stock, 6.14 lbs.

MSR $2,499	$2,250	$1,975	$1,700	$1,525	$1,250	$1,025	$800	

HOUSTON ARMORY

Current rifle manufacturer located in Stafford, TX.

RIFLES

Houston Armory manufactures a line of AR-15 style semi-auto rifles, including the .440 Hash (MSR $3,485), .50 Beowulf ($3,485 MSR), H300IC ($3,085 MSR), H16IC ($3,085 MSR), H308IC ($4,085 MSR), and HASPR16 ($2,890 MSR). Houston Armory also offers a bolt action rifle (MSRs $1,900-$2,900), as well as a complete line of suppressors. Please contact the company directly for more information, including availability and options (see Trademark Index).

HOWA

Current manufacturer established in 1967, and located in Tokyo, Japan. Howa sporting rifles are currently imported beginning Oct., 1999 by Legacy Sports International, LLC, located in Reno, NV. Previously located in Alexandria, VA. Previously imported until 1999 by Interarms/Howa, located in Alexandria, VA, Weatherby (Vanguard Series only), Smith & Wesson (pre-1985), and Mossberg (1986-1987).

RIFLES: BOLT ACTION

Howa also manufactures barreled actions in various configurations. MSRs range from $476-$596. During mid-2011, detachable magazines became available for all Model 1500s.

MODEL 1500 PCS – .308 Win. cal., police counter sniper rifle featuring 24 in. barrel, choice of blue metal or stainless steel, black synthetic or checkered walnut stock, no sights, approx. 9.3 lbs. Imported 1999-2000.

	$385	$335	$290	$260	$210	$175	$135	$465

Add $20 for wood stock.
Add $60 for stainless steel.

HULDRA ARMS

Current trademark of AR-15 style semi-auto rifles manufactured by Adams Arms and sold exclusively by Fleet Farm.

RIFLES: SEMI-AUTO

All rifles include magazine and soft sided tactical case.

MARK IV CARBINE – 5.45x39mm or 5.56 NATO cal., AR-15 style, GPO, 16 in. M4 contour barrel with A2 flash hider, SST, 6-position tactical buttstock with A2 pistol grip, M4 handguards, forged aluminum upper and lower receivers, 6.2 lbs.

MSR $1,050	$895	$785	$675	$610	$495	$400	$315

Add $65 for 5.45x39mm cal.

MARK IV TACTICAL ELITE – 5.56 NATO cal., AR-15 style, GPO, 16 in. Government contour barrel with A2 flash hider, SST, Vltor IMod Mil-Spec stock with non-slip removable butt pad, Ergo ambi pistol grip, free floating extended quad rail forearm with Picatinny rail, forged aluminum upper and lower receivers, includes magazine and soft sided tactical case, 7.2 lbs.

MSR $1,550	$1,350	$1,175	$1,015	$925	$750	$610	$475

MARK IV TACTICAL EVO – 5.56 NATO cal., 14 1/2 in. government contour barrel with permanently affixed elongated flash hider, M4 feed ramps, mid-length gas system, SST, Samson Evolution Series aluminum forearm, mil-spec hardcoat anodized finish, 6.8 lbs.

MSR $1,400	$1,195	$1,050	$895	$815	$650	$540	$425

X-PRE 1 – 5.56 NATO cal., GPO, 16 in. medium contour fluted stainless steel barrel with Adams Arms compensator, SST, Vitor IMod Mil-Spec stock with non-slip removable butt pad, Ergo ambi grip, monolithic fluted forearm, forged aluminum upper and lower receivers, 7.2 lbs. Disc. 2013.

	$1,800	$1,575	$1,350	$1,225	$990	$810	$625	$2,000

I SECTION

IAI INC. - AMERICAN LEGEND

Previous manufacturer, importer, and distributor located in Houston, TX. Firearms were manufactured by Israel Arms International, Inc., located in Houston, TX. IAI designates Israel Arms International, and should not be confused with Irwindale Arms, Inc. (also IAI).

The models listed were part of an American Legend Series that are patterned after famous American and Belgian military carbines/rifles and semi-auto pistols.

MSR	100%	98%	95%	90%	80%	70%	60%	Last MSR

CARBINES/RIFLES: SEMI-AUTO

MODEL 888 M1 CARBINE – .22 LR or .30 Carbine cal., 18 in. barrel, mfg. from new original M1 parts and stock by IAI (barrel bolt and receiver) and unused GI parts, 10 shot mag., choice of birch or walnut stock, parkerized finish, metal or wood handguard, 5 1/2 lbs. Mfg. by IAI in Houston, TX 1998-2004.

	100%	98%	95%	90%	80%	70%	60%	Last MSR
	$675	$595	$565	$435	$395	$315	$295	$556

Add $11 for .22 LR cal.
Add $31 for walnut/metal forearm or $47 for walnut/wood forearm.

MODEL 333 M1 GARAND – .30-06 cal., patterned after the WWII M1 Garand, 24 in. barrel, internal magazine, 8 shot en-bloc clip, parkerized finish, 9 1/2 lbs. Mfg. 2003-2004.

	100%	98%	95%	90%	80%	70%	60%	Last MSR
	$950	$875	$775	$625	$525	$400	$350	$972

PISTOLS: SEMI-AUTO

MODEL 2000 – .45 ACP cal., patterned after the Colt Govt. 1911, 5 or 4 1/4 (Commander configuration, Model 2000-C) in. barrel, SA, parkerized finish, plastic or rubber finger groove grips, 36-38 oz. Mfg. in South Africa 2002-2004.

	100%	98%	95%	90%	80%	70%	60%	Last MSR
	$415	$365	$325	$295	$275	$250	$225	$465

I.O., INC.

Current manufacturer/importer established in 2008, and located in Palm Bay, FL. Previously located in Monroe, NC until mid-2013.

PISTOLS: SEMI-AUTO

HELLCAT .380 II – .380 ACP cal., 2 3/4 in. steel alloy barrel with 6 grooves, DAO, SFO, 6 shot stainless steel mag., fixed sights, available in three finishes, includes custom pocket pouch, 9.4 oz. Disc. 2013.

	100%	98%	95%	90%	80%	70%	60%	Last MSR
	$200	$175	$150	$135	$110	$90	$75	$250

HELLPUP – 7.62x39mm cal., AK-47 design, parkerized finish, 9 1/4 in. barrel, Krinkov style flash hider, 30 shot metal mag., adj. front and rear sights, black polymer furniture, tactical pistol grip, mil-spec receiver, 5 lbs. Mfg. by Radom, importation disc. 2013.

	100%	98%	95%	90%	80%	70%	60%	Last MSR
	$775	$675	$575	$525	$425	$350	$275	$864

POLISH PPS-43C – 9x19mm (new 2014) or 7.62x25mm TT cal., SA, stamped steel barrel and receiver, L-shaped flip up rear sight, fixed blade front sight, muzzle brake, stock has no function and is permanently fixed in its folded position, safety located at front of trigger guard, includes 2 (9x19mm cal.) or 4 curved box magazines (each holds 35 rounds) and cleaning kit. Mfg. at Radom Plant in Poland.

MSR $500	100%	98%	95%	90%	80%	70%	60%	
	$425	$375	$325	$295	$235	$190	$150	

POLISH AK PISTOL – 7.62x39mm cal., AK-47 style similar to Hellpup, 11 1/2 in. barrel, 30 shot curved mag. (includes two), black polymer furniture, Krink flash hider, wood pistol grip. Mfg. by Radom. Importation began 2014.

MSR $700	100%	98%	95%	90%	80%	70%	60%	
	$595	$525	$450	$400	$325	$275	$210	

VENOM .45 1911 – .45 ACP cal., manganese phosphate finish, 8 shot mag., bobbed hammer, skeletonized trigger, diamond checkered grips, serrated front and back grip strap, Picatinny under rail, includes plastic case. New 2014.

MSR $550	100%	98%	95%	90%	80%	70%	60%	
	$475	$415	$350	$325	$260	$215	$165	

RIFLES: SEMI-AUTO

I.O. Inc. imports AK-47 style semi-auto rifles manufactured in Poland and Bulgaria. Previous models included the AK47-C with fixed, folding, collapsible or polymer stock (Galil-type forearm), synthetic or wood stock (last MSR was $500-$670, disc. 2010), an AK-22 rifle (last MSR was $500, disc. 2010), STG-22 rifle (last MSR was $500, disc. 2010), and a CASAR AK series of rifles (last MSR was $648, disc. 2011).

HELLHOUND TACTICAL – 7.62x39mm cal., AK-47 design, aluminum quad rail tactical handguard, 30 shot mag., CNC machined scope mount rail, parkerized finish, fixed polymer or wire folding stock. New 2011.

MSR $800	100%	98%	95%	90%	80%	70%	60%	
	$675	$595	$500	$460	$375	$300	$235	

MSR	100%	98%	95%	90%	80%	70%	60%	Last MSR

POLISH BERYL "ARCHER" – 7.62x39mm cal., AK-47 design, 16 1/4 in. hammer forged barrel with flash hider, 30 shot mag., mil spec receiver, tactical pistol grip, black polymer furniture, collapsible stock, features a bolt hold open integrated into the safety lever on right side of receiver, and FB (Fabryka Broni) trademark on left side of receiver, adj. front and rear sights, tactical swivel sling, 7 lbs. Mfg. in Radom, Poland.

| MSR $1,250 | $1,075 | $940 | $800 | $725 | $595 | $485 | $375 | |

Add $200 for Picatinny rail.

SPORTER – 7.62x39mm cal., AK-47 design, 16 1/4 in. barrel, 30 shot, mil spec receiver, Picatinny rail forearm, black polymer fixed or Tantal folding stock, tactical pistol grip, tactical sling swivel, CNC machined scope mount rail, adj. front and rear sights, available in Parkerized, Dark Earth, or Pink finish/furniture, 7 lbs. New 2011.

| MSR $790 | $675 | $595 | $500 | $460 | $375 | $300 | $235 | |

Add $10 for Tantal folding stock.

* **Laminate Sporter** – 7.62x39mm cal., similar to Sporter model, except features laminate wood stock, parkerized finish only. Importation began 2011.

| MSR $750 | $675 | $600 | $500 | $450 | $375 | $300 | $250 | |

* **Polish Sporter** – 7.62x39mm cal., similar to Sporter Laminate model, except does not have scope mount rail. Importation began 2014.

| MSR $720 | $615 | $540 | $460 | $425 | $340 | $275 | $215 | |

SPORTER ECON – 7.62x39mm cal., AK-47 design, 16 1/4 in. barrel, mil-spec receiver, 30 shot mag., Picatinny rail forearm, Black polymer stock, tactical pistol grip, tactical sling swivel, adj. front and rear sights, Parkerized finish, 7 lbs. Disc. 2013.

| | $600 | $525 | $450 | $410 | $325 | $275 | $225 | $677 |

STG2000-C – 7.62x39mm cal., AK-47 design, 16 1/4 in. barrel, 30 shot mag., mil spec receiver, Picatinny rail, tactical pistol grip, tactical sling swivel, CNC machined scope mount rail, front sight/gas block, Black polymer stock, Parkerized, Dark Earth, or Pink furniture.

| MSR $800 | $675 | $595 | $500 | $460 | $375 | $300 | $235 | |

AR-15A1 – .223 Rem. cal., I.O. made lower receiver machined solid aircraft aluminum billets, 16.1 in. barrel, two 30 shot mags., fixed black polymer stock and forend, pistol grip, carry handle, original Colt Vietnam style upper receiver and bolt assembly. New 2014.

| MSR $900 | $765 | $675 | $575 | $525 | $425 | $345 | $275 | |

CAR-15 – .223 Rem. cal., I.O. made lower receiver machined out of solid aircraft aluminum billets, matte black finish, 16.1 in. barrel with flash hider, two 30 shot mags., adj. six position stock, pistol grip, carry handle, original Colt Vietnam style upper receiver and bolt assembly. New 2014.

| MSR $790 | $675 | $595 | $500 | $460 | $375 | $300 | $235 | |

VEPR IV – please refer to Vepr. section for this model.

BSR-74 – 5.45x39mm cal., AK-47 style, 16.1 in. chrome lined barrel with bayonet lug, removable compensator, 30 shot detachable mag., matte black finish, wood or polymer furniture, wood stock with sling swivel or wire folding stock, pistol grip. Mfg. in Bulgaria, assembled in the US. Importation began 2014.

| MSR $730 | $625 | $550 | $475 | $425 | $350 | $275 | $225 | |

Add $100 for wire folding stock.

SHOTGUNS: SEMI-AUTO

Please refer to Vepr. section.

ISSC HANDELSGESELLSCHAFT

Current manufacturer of semi-auto firearms located in Ried, Austria. Currently imported by Legacy Sports International located in Reno, NV beginning late 2011. Previously imported by Austrian Sporting Arms, located in Ware, MA until 2011.

PISTOLS: SEMI-AUTO

M22 – .22 LR cal., patterned after the Glock semi-auto, 4, 4 3/4 (new 2012), or 5 1/2 (new 2012) in. threaded (new 2012), standard, or target (new 2012) barrel, SA, 10 shot mag., white dot front and adj. rear sights, lower accessory rail, loaded chamber indicator, safety decocker, magazine disconnect, black polymer frame with contoured grip, adj. rear sight, black, two-tone desert tan, OD Green, pink, Harvest Moon camo (new 2013), Outshine camo (new 2013), or Muddy Girl camo (new 2013) finish, with or w/o brushed chrome (new 2012) slide, 21 oz. New 2009.

| MSR $429 | $365 | $325 | $285 | $265 | $245 | $225 | $200 | |

Add $72 for Harvest Moon camo, Outshine camo, or Muddy Girl camo (new 2013) stock.

Add $110 for 4 3/4 in. threaded barrel.

Add $38 for 5 1/2 in. target barrel.

MSR	100%	98%	95%	90%	80%	70%	60%	*Last MSR*

RIFLES: SEMI-AUTO

MK22 – .22 LR cal., 10 or 22 shot mag., 16.6 in. L. Walther match barrel with muzzle brake, multiple charge bar locations on right and left side of receiver, ambidextrous safety and mag. release, Back or Desert Tan (new 2012) finish, variable and folding adj. open sight, Picatinny quad rail, fixed, folding or collapsible stock with adj. cheekpiece, features Ucas system (Universal cocking adaptation system), 6 1/2 lbs. New 2011.

MSR $665	$575	$500	$450	$400	$365	$335	$300	

Add $37 for Desert Tan finish.

INGRAM

Previously manufactured until late 1982 by Military Armament Corp. (MAC) located in Atlanta, GA.

PISTOLS: SEMI-AUTO

MAC 10 – .45 ACP or 9mm Para. cal., open bolt, semi-auto version of the sub-machine gun, 10 (.45 ACP cal.), 16 (9mm Para. cal.), 30 (.45 ACP cal.), or 32 (9mm Para. cal.) shot mag., compact all metal welded construction, rear aperture and front blade sight. Disc. 1982.

	$950	$875	$800	$700	$650	$575	$525	

Add approx. $160 for accessories (barrel extension, case, and extra mag.).

MAC 10A1 – similar to MAC 10 except fires from a closed bolt.

	$395	$375	$350	$280	$265	$225	$210	

MAC 11 – similar to MAC 10 except in .380 ACP cal.

	$750	$695	$650	$575	$550	$535	$485	

INTEGRITY ARMS & SURVIVAL

Current custom AR-15 manufacturer located in Watkinsville, GA.

RIFLES: SEMI-AUTO

Integrity Arms & Survival manufactures custom AR-15 rifles in 5.56 NATO, 6.8 SPC, .223 Wylde, or .300 AAC Blackout caliber per customer specifications. Current models include: Battle Rifle (MSR $1,270), Premium Lightweight Wylde Chambered Carbine (MSR $1,050), Muddy Girl Carbine (MSR $900), Burnt Bronze Battle Rifle (MSR $1,200), Foliage Green Premium Carbine (MSR $1,300), and Tungsten Grey Carbine (MSR $1,350). Please contact the company directly for more information on options, pricing, and availability (see Trademark Index).

INTERARMS ARSENAL

Current trademark of firearms imported and distributed by High Standard Manufacturing Company, located in Houston, TX.

RIFLES: SEMI-AUTO

POLISH MODEL WZ.88 TANTAL – 5.45x39mm cal., choice of side folding stock with wood forend furniture or fixed stock, chrome lined barrel, mfg. in U.S.

MSR $619	$525	$465	$415	$365	$335	$300	$275	

Add $10 for side folding stock.

POLISH UNDERFOLDER – 7.62x39mm cal., underfolding stock.

MSR $975	$825	$675	$575	$475	$400	$350	$300	

HUNGARIAN ADM 65 STYLE AKM – 7.62x39mm cal., side folding stock.

MSR $837	$750	$650	$525	$475	$425	$375	$350	

Add $28 for wood stock.
Add $38 for Tactical model.

HUNGARIAN UNDERFOLDER – 7.62x39mm cal., underfolding stock.

MSR $875	$750	$625	$550	$475	$400	$350	$300	

AKM SERIES – 7.62x38mm cal., black polymer stock, Russian, Egyptian or Polish configurations.

MSR $619	$525	$465	$415	$365	$335	$300	$275	

Add $40 for Polish import with under folding stock (AKMS Model).

AK-74 – 5.45x39mm cal., Bulgarian style mfg., choice of wood or polymer furniture.

MSR $679	$575	$500	$450	$400	$350	$300	$275	

AK-47 – 7.62x39mm cal., AK-47 design with milled receiver, choice of Yugoslavian Zastava or other Eastern Bloc mfg.

MSR $1,195	$1,050	$925	$800	$675	$550	$475	$400	

MSR	100%	98%	95%	90%	80%	70%	60%	*Last MSR*

AR-15 A2 RIFLE – 5.56 NATO cal., AR-15 style, GIO, choice of flat-top (no sights), or A2 configuration, 20 in. barrel with flash hider, choice of black synthetic fixed or collapsible stock, 30 shot mag.

MSR $925	$825	$750	$675	$600	$525	$450	$400

Add $40 for A2 adj. sights.

M4 CARBINE – 5.56 NATO cal., GIO, 16 in. barrel with muzzle brake, choice of flat-top or A2 configuration, M4 6-position collapsible stock.

MSR $880	$775	$675	$600	$525	$450	$400	$375

Add $35 for A2 configuration.

INTERCONTINENTAL ARMS INC.
Previous importer located in Los Angeles, CA circa 1970s.

Intercontinental Arms Inc. imported a variety of SA revolvers, an AR-15 type semi-auto rifle, a derringer, a rolling block single shot rifle, and a line of black powder pistol reproductions and replicas. While these firearms were good, utilitarian shooters, they have limited desirability in today's marketplace. The single action revolvers manufactured by Hämmerli are typically priced in the $200-$395 range, the derringer is priced in the $115-$175 range, the AR-15 copy is priced in the $425-$675 range, and the single shot rolling block rifle is priced in the $150-$200 range, depending on original condition.

INTERDYNAMIC OF AMERICA, INC.
Previous distributor located in Miami, FL 1981-84.

PISTOLS: SEMI-AUTO

KG-9 – 9mm Para. cal., 3 in. barrel, SA, open bolt, tactical design pistol. Disc. approx. 1982.

	$850	$800	$700	$675	$650	$600	$575

KG-99 – 9mm Para. cal., 3 in. barrel, SA, tactical design pistol, closed bolt, 36 shot mag., 5 in. vent. shroud barrel, blue only, a stainless steel version of the KG-9. Mfg. by Interdynamic 1984 only.

	$425	$375	$325	$275	$250	$225	$195

* **KG-99M Mini Pistol**

	$495	$450	$400	$325	$275	$250	$225

INTERSTATE ARMS CORP.
Current importer located in Billerica, MA.

Interstate Arms Corp. has imported a variety of Chinese made cowboy action shotguns and reproductions, as well as pistols from Turkey.

SHOTGUNS: SLIDE ACTION

MODEL 97T WWI TRENCH GUN – 12 ga. only, authentic reproduction of the original Winchester WWI Trench Gun, complete with shrouded barrel, proper markings, finish, and wood. Imported mid-2002-2006, reintroduced 2010. Mfg. by Sun City Machinery Ltd.

MSR $465	$395	$350	$295	$275	$215	$180	$160

MODEL 372 – 12 ga., 3 in. chamber, 18 1/2 in. barrel with heat shield and ghost ring sights, bottom ejection port, cylinder choke, black synthetic stock and forearm. Limited importation 2007-2009.

	$200	$175	$150	$135	$110	$90	$70	*$250*

HAWK 982 – 12 ga. only, 3 in. chamber, defense configuration with 18 1/2 in. cylinder bore barrel with fixed choke, black synthetic stock and forearm, matte black metal finish, current mfg. uses ghost ring sights. Importation began 2001.

MSR $292	$250	$225	$195	$180	$17	$160	$150

INTRAC ARMS INTERNATIONAL INC.
Previous importer located in Knoxville, TN. Intrac imported trademarks manufactured by Arsenal Bulgaria, and by IM Metal Production facility in Croatia late 2000-2004. Previously imported by HS America, located in Knoxville, TN.

RIFLES: SEMI-AUTO

ROMAK 1 & 2 – 7.62x39mm (Romak 1) or 5.45x39mm (Romak 2) cal., AK-47 copy with 16 1/2 in. barrel and scope mount on left side of receiver, wood thumbhole stock, includes 5 and 10 shot mags., and accessories. Imported 2002-2004.

	$595	$550	$525	$475	$450	$400	$350	*$329*

MSR	100%	98%	95%	90%	80%	70%	60%	*Last MSR*

SLR-101 – similar to Romak, except has 17 1/4 in. cold hammer forged barrel and black polymer stock and forearm, includes 2 mags. and accessories. Imported 2002-2004.

	$650	$575	$500	$450	$425	$350	$325	*$359*

ROMAK 3 – 7.62x54R cal., based on current issue PSL/FPK sniper configuration, 5 or 10 shot mag., last shot bolt hold open, 26 1/2 in. barrel with muzzle brake, mil-spec scope with range finder, bullet drop compensator and illuminated recticle. Imported 2002-2004.

	$900	$825	$750	$650	$575	$525	$475	*$899*

INTRATEC
Previous manufacturer circa 1985-2000 located in Miami, FL.

PISTOLS: SEMI-AUTO

TEC-DC9 – 9mm Para. cal., 5 in. shrouded barrel, SA, matte black finish, 10 (C/B 1994) or 32* shot mag. Mfg. 1985-1994.

	$475	$425	$375	$300	$275	$225	$200	*$269*

 * **TEC-9DCK** – similar to TEC-9, except has new durable Tec-Kote finish with better protection than hard chrome. Mfg. 1991-94.

	$495	$465	$425	$375	$325	$295	$260	*$297*

 * **TEC-DC9S** – matte stainless version of the TEC-9. Disc. 1994.

	$550	$500	$450	$400	$350	$300	$250	*$362*

Add $203 for TEC-9 with accessory package (deluxe case, 3-32 shot mags., tactical design grip, and recoil compensator).

TEC-DC9M – mini version of the Model TEC-9, including 3 in. barrel and 20 shot mag. Disc. 1994.

	$495	$465	$425	$375	$325	$295	$260	*$245*

 * **TEC-DC9MK** – similar to TEC-9M, except has Tec-Kote rust resistant finish. Mfg. 1991-94.

	$525	$450	$400	$350	$300	$250	$200	*$277*

 * **TEC-DC9MS** – matte stainless version of the TEC-9M. Disc. 1994.

	$575	$500	$450	$400	$350	$300	$275	*$339*

TEC-22 "SCORPION" – .22 LR cal., 4 in. barrel, SA, ambidextrous safety, military matte finish, or electroless nickel, 30 shot mag., adj. sights, 30 oz. Mfg. 1988-1994.

	$375	$325	$275	$225	$200	$175	$160	*$202*

Add $20 for TEC-Kote finish.

 * **TEC-22N** – similar to TEC-22, except has nickel finish. Mfg. 1990 only.

	$395	$345	$300	$275	$250	$230	$220	*$226*

Add $16 for threaded barrel (Model TEC-22TN).

TEC-22T – threaded barrel variation of the TEC-22 "Scorpion." Mfg. 1991-94.

	$395	$350	$300	$250	$225	$195	$175	*$161*

Add $23 for Tec-Kote finish.

AB-10 – 9mm Para. cal., design similar to Luger, 2 3/4 in. non-threaded barrel, SA, choice of 32* (limited supply) or 10 shot mag., black synthetic frame, firing pin safety block, black or stainless steel finish, 45 oz. Mfg. 1997-2000.

	$325	$275	$235	$200	$180	$160	$150	*$225*

Add $20 for stainless steel (new 2000).
Add $100 for 32 shot mag.

INTRATEC U.S.A., INC.
Previous manufacturer located in Miami, FL.

CARBINES

TEC-9C – 9mm Para. cal., carbine variation with 16 1/2 in. barrel, 36 shot mag.
   Only 1 gun mfg. 1987 - extreme rarity precludes pricing.

PISTOLS: SEMI-AUTO

TEC-9 – 9mm Para. cal., 5 in. shrouded barrel, SA, 32 shot mag. Disc.

	$550	$495	$450	$395	$350	$295	$250	

MSR	100%	98%	95%	90%	80%	70%	60%	*Last MSR*

IRON BRIGADE ARMORY

Current rifle manufacturer located in Jacksonville, NC established 1979. Consumer direct sales through FFL.

RIFLES: BOLT ACTION

Iron Brigade Armory makes four bolt action rifles currently, including the XM-3, Chandler Sniper Rifle, Super/Standard Grade, and the Tactical Precision. Please contact the company directly for more information, availability, and current prices (see Trademark Index).

IRON RIDGE ARMS CO.

Current manufacturer located in Longmount, CO.

Iron Ridge Arms Co. manufactures the IRA-X Rifle platform available in three different configurations. Please contact the company directly for more information including customizing, options, pricing, and availability (see Trademark Index).

ISRAEL ARMS INTERNATIONAL, INC.

Previous importer (please refer to IAI listing) and manufacturer located in Houston, TX, 1997-2004.

ISRAEL ARMS LTD.

Previous manufacturer located in Kfar Saba, Israel. Imported and distributed exclusively by Israel Arms International, Inc. located in Houston, TX 1997-2001.

RIFLES: SEMI-AUTO

MODEL 333 M1 GARAND – .30-06 cal., 24 in. barrel, parts remanufactured to meet GI and mil specs, parkerized finish, 8 shot en-bloc clip, 9 1/2 lbs. Mfg. 2000-2001.

	$895	$850	$800	$700	$600	$500	$400	*$852*

MODEL 444 FAL – .308 Win. cal., patterned after the FN FAL model. Mfg. by Imbel, located in Brazil, 2000-2001.

	$925	$850	$795	$725	$675	$595	$550	*$897*

ISRAEL MILITARY INDUSTRIES (IMI)

Previous manufacturer established 1933-circa 2009, and located in Israel.

IMI manufactured guns (both new and disc. models) include Galil, Jericho, Magnum Research, Timberwolf, Uzi, and others, and can be located in their respective sections.

ITHACA GUN COMPANY (NEW MFG.)

Current manufacturer established in 2006 and located in Upper Sandusky, OH.

During December of 2007, Ithaca Gun Company bought out the remaining assets and equipment of Ithaca Gun Company LLC and moved production to Upper Sandusky, OH. Please contact the company directly for more information, including price and options on available models (see Trademark Index).

SHOTGUNS: SLIDE ACTION

Ithaca currently offers shotguns in 12, 16, 20 and 28 ga. (2 3/4 or 3 in. chambers).

M37 SERIES – 12, 16, 20 (2 3/4 and 3 in. chamber), or 28 ga. (2 3/4 in. chamber), 26, 28, or 30 in. barrel, 5 or 8 shot, wood, synthetic, or laminated stock, vent. rib or field barrel, brass bead front sight, fixed scope mount (DeerSlayer only), or Marble Arms rear sight (Featherweight Upland), bottom ejection action, Pachmayr recoil pad, high luster, matte blue or Perma-Guard finish, 5.8-8.2 lbs. New 2007.

Current/recent models with MSRs are as follows: Featherlight Series - $895-$1,150 MSR, Featherlight Combo - $1,180 MSR, 28 ga. Featherlight Deluxe - $1,150 MSR, Featherlight Waterfowl - $885-$925 MSR, Featherlight Youth Model - $7895 MSR, Featherlight Trap - disc. 2013, $899 last MSR, Ultralight - disc. 2012, last $859-$959 MSR, Deerslayer - $1,029-$1,199 MSR, Turkeyslayer - $925 MSR, Hogslayer - $870-$925 MSR, new 2012, Tactical - $799-$925 MSR, and the Home Defense Model - $799-$885 MSR.

ITHACA GUN COMPANY LLC (OLDER MFG.)

Previous manufacturer located in Ithaca, NY from 1883-1986, King Ferry, NY circa 1989-2005, and Auburn, NY right before it closed in June, 2005.

Ithaca Gun Company, LLC had resumed production on the Model 37 slide action shotgun and variations during 1989, and then relocated to King Ferry, NY shortly thereafter. In the past, Ithaca also absorbed companies including Syracuse Arms Co., Lefever Arms Co., Union Fire Arms Co., Wilkes-Barre Gun Co., as well as others.

SHOTGUNS: SLIDE ACTION

In 1987, Ithaca Acquisition Corp. reintroduced the Model 37 as the Model 87. Recently manufactured Model 87s are listed in addition to both new and older Model 37s (produced pre-1986). During late 1996, Ithaca Gun Co., LLC resumed manufacture of the Model 37, while discontinuing the Model 87.

MSR	100%	98%	95%	90%	80%	70%	60%	Last MSR

Over 2 million Model 37s have been produced.

Model 37s with ser. nos. above 855,000 will accept both 2 3/4 and 3 in. chambered barrels interchangeably. Earlier guns have incompatible threading for the magnum barrels.

MODEL 37 DS POLICE SPECIAL – 12 ga. only, 18 1/2 in. barrel with rifle sights, Parkerized finish on metal, oil finished stock, typically subcontracted by police departments or law enforcement agencies, with or without unit code markings.

| | $325 | $275 | $235 | $200 | $185 | $170 | $160 | |

MODEL 37 PROTECTION SERIES – 12 ga. only, 18 1/2 or 20 in. smoothbore barrel w/o chokes, 5 or 8 shot tube mag., approx. 6 3/4 lbs. Limited mfg. 2005.

| | $425 | $375 | $325 | $275 | $250 | $225 | $195 | *$482* |

Add $27 for 20 in. barrel.

MODEL 87 MILITARY & POLICE – 12 (3 in.) or 20 (new 1989) ga., short barrel Model 37 w/normal stock or pistol grip only, 18 1/2, 20, or 24 3/4 (scarce) in. barrel, choice of front bead or rifle sights, front blade was usually a flourescent orange plastic, 5, 8, or 10 shot. Originally disc. 1983, reintroduced 1989-95.

| | $265 | $230 | $200 | $180 | $170 | $160 | $150 | *$323* |

Add $104 for nickel finish (mfg. 1991-92 only).

IVER JOHNSON ARMS, INC. (NEW MFG.)

Current manufacturer established during 2004 and located in Rockledge, FL. Dealer and distributor sales.

The new Iver Johnson Arms, Inc. company was formed during 2004, and currently manfactures a line of 1911A1 pistols in .45 ACP cal. Current models include: The 1911 Officer (MSR $636-$851), Commander (MSR $617-$698), Thrasher (disc. 2013, last MSR was $608-$817), Model 1911A1 (MSR $608-$743), the Eagle (MSR $713-$794), the Eagle LR (new 2011, MSR $959), the Falcon (MSR $617), and the Hawk (MSR $698-$749). Additionally, Iver Johnson Arms, Inc. imports a line of PAS 12 slide-action shotguns manufactured by Armed in Turkey (MSRs range from $270-$456), and during 2013, introduced a 1911A1 Carbine/Rifle with Mech-Tech Systems upper and Iver Johnson lower (MSR $775).

Iver Johnson Arms, Inc. previously manufactured the Raven Series in both .22 LR and .45 ACP cals. until 2009, and the last MSR was $532. Also discontinued during 2009 was the Frontier Four Derringer and the Model PM 30G M1 Carbine. The Trojan was discontinued in 2012 (last MSR was $574).

Please contact the company directly for more information, including availability and pricing (see Trademark Index).

IVER JOHNSON ARMS & CYCLE WORKS

Previously located in Worchester, MA, 1883-1890, Fitchburg, MA, 1890-1975, Middlesex, NJ 1975-1983 (name changed to Iver Johnson Arms Inc.) and Jacksonville, AR 1984-1993. Formerly Johnson Bye & Co. 1871-1883. Renamed Iver Johnson's Arms & Cycle Works mid-year 1894-1975 (incorporated as Iver Johnson's Arms & Cycle Works Inc. in 1915). Renamed Iver Johnson's Arms & Cycle Works in 1891 with manufacturing moving to Fitchburg, MA. In 1975 the name changed to Iver Johnson's Arms, Inc., and two years later, company facilities were moved to Middlesex, NJ. In 1982, production was moved to Jacksonville, AR under the trade name Iver Johnson Arms, Inc. In 1983, Universal Firearms, Inc. was acquired by Iver Johnson Arms, Inc.

The author and publisher would like to thank the late Mr. Bill Goforth for providing much of the information on Iver Johnson Arms & Cycle Works.

PISTOLS: SEMI-AUTO

I.J. SUPER ENFORCER (M1 CARBINE) – .30 Carbine cal., gas operated pistol version of the M1 Carbine, 5, 10, or 15 shot mag., walnut stock, fires from closed bolt, 9 1/2 in. barrel, 4 lbs. Mfg. 1978-1993.

| | $850 | $745 | $640 | $580 | $470 | $385 | $300 | |

UNIVERSAL ENFORCER (M1 CARBINE) – .30 Carbine cal., gas operated, blue finish, single action, pistol version of the M1 carbine, 5, 10, or 15 shot mag., 9 1/2 in. barrel, hard wood stock, fires from close bolt, trigger block safety, 4 lbs. Mfg. 1986.

| | $850 | $745 | $640 | $580 | $470 | $385 | $300 | |

RIFLES

Iver Johnson's first rifle was manufactured in 1928 and remained the only rifle manufactured entirely within the Iver Johnson factory in Fitchburg. The later .22 cal. rifles were all imported from either Canada or Germany, except the Lil Champ Model, which was manufactured in Jacksonville, AR. The M1 Carbine models were manufactured in either Middlesex, NJ or Jacksonville, AR.

MSR	100%	98%	95%	90%	80%	70%	60%	Last MSR

I.J. SEMI-AUTO CARBINE – .22 LR cal., 15 shot mag., recoil operated, blue finish, copy of the M1 carbine, 18 1/2 in. barrel, military type front sight protected by wings, rear aperture adj. sight, walnut finished hardwood stock and handguard, sling swivels, imported from Germany, 5 3/4 lbs. Mfg. 1985-1990.

| | $425 | $365 | $315 | $275 | $235 | $195 | $175 | |

I.J. MAGNUM SEMI-AUTO CARBINE – .22 WMR cal., gas operated, otherwise similar to Semi-Auto Carbine, imported from Germany. Mfg. 1985-1990.

| | $525 | $465 | $395 | $340 | $295 | $250 | $220 | |

I.J. PLAINSFIELD SEMI-AUTO CARBINE – .30 Carbine, 9mm Para. (new 1986), or 5.7mm (disc. 1986) cal., gas operated, copy of WWII U.S. Military Carbine, 5, 10, 15, or 30 shot detachable mag., stainless steel or blue finish, 18 in. barrel, American walnut or hardwood stock, model names and numbers changed several times, M2 full auto model available during the 1980s, 6 1/2 lbs. Mfg. 1978-1993.

| | $450 | $395 | $335 | $285 | $245 | $210 | $180 | |

Add 10% for walnut stock.
Add 20% for stainless steel.
Add 35% for 5.7mm cal. (Spitfire Model) or 9mm Para. cal.

I.J. PARATROOPER SEMI-AUTO CARBINE – .30 Carbine cal., gas operated, copy of WWII U.S. Military Carbine, 5, 10, 15, or 30 shot detachable mag., stainless steel or blue finish, 18 in. barrel, American walnut or hardwood stock, with collapsible stock extension, model names and numbers changed several times, M2 full auto model available with 12 in. barrel, 4 1/2 lbs. Mfg. 1978-1989.

| | $595 | $550 | $500 | $460 | $430 | $395 | $360 | |

Add 10% for walnut stock.
Add 20% for stainless steel.

I.J. SURVIVAL CARBINE SEMI-AUTO – .30 Carbine or 5.7mm cal., gas operated, copy of WWII military carbine, 5, 10, 15, or 30 shot detachable mag., stainless steel or blue finish, Zytel black plastic pistol grip stock, 6 1/2 lbs.

| | $450 | $395 | $335 | $285 | $245 | $210 | $180 | |

Add 20% for stainless steel.
Add 35% for 5.7mm cal. (Spitfire Model).

* ***I.J. Survival Carbine Semi-Auto w/Folding Stock*** – .30 Carbine or 5.7mm cal., similar to Survival Carbine, except has folding stock. Mfg. 1983-1989.

| | $585 | $500 | $425 | $375 | $325 | $275 | $235 | |

Add 20% for stainless steel.
Add 35% for 5.7mm cal. (Spitfire Model).

I.J. UNIVERSAL CARBINE SEMI-AUTO – .30 Carbine or .256 Win. Mag. cal., gas operated, GI military type carbine, 5 or 10 shot detachable mag., 18 in. barrel, stainless steel or blue finish, walnut stained hardwood, sling swivel, drilled and tapped, known as Model 1003 (.30 Carbine) or Model 1256 (.256 Win. Mag., 5 shot only). Mfg. 1986.

| | $450 | $395 | $335 | $285 | $245 | $210 | $180 | |

Iver Johnson marked models are rare.

I.J. UNIVERSAL PARATROOPER SEMI-AUTO CARBINE – 30 Carbine cal., similar to Universal Carbine model, except has Schmeisser-type hardwood folding stock, 5 or 10 shot detachable mag., drilled and tapped. Mfg. 1986.

| | $550 | $475 | $415 | $360 | $315 | $265 | $230 | |

Iver Johnson marked models are rare.

MODEL 5100 BOLT ACTION SNIPER – .338 Win., .416 Win., or .50 BMG cal., single shot, free floating 29 in. barrel, no sights, drilled and tapped, marketed with Leupold Ultra M1 20X scope, adj. composite stock, adj. trigger, two different model numbers, ltd. mfg., 36 lbs. Mfg. 1985-1993.

| | $4,550 | $3,775 | $3,375 | $3,000 | $2,600 | $2,300 | $2,000 | |

J SECTION

J.B. CUSTOM INC.

Current manufacturer and restorer located in Huntertown, IN. Previously located in Fort Wayne, IN. Consumer direct sales.

J.B. Custom also offers service parts and restoration services for Winchester commemorative lever action rifles and carbines. Due to space considerations, information regarding this manufacturer is available online free of charge at www.bluebookofgunvalues.com.

J.L.D. ENTERPRISES, INC.

Previous rifle manufacturer located in Farmington, CT. In 2006, the company name was changed to PTR 91, Inc.

Please refer to PTR 91, Inc. listing for current information.

JMC FABRICATION & MACHINE, INC.

Previous manufacturer located in Rockledge, FL 1997-99.

MSR	100%	98%	95%	90%	80%	70%	60%	Last MSR

RIFLES: BOLT ACTION

MODEL 2000 M/P – .50 BMG cal., rapid takedown, 30 in. barrel, matte black finish, cast aluminum stock with Pachmayr pad, fully adj. bipod, 10 shot staggered mag., two-stage trigger, includes 24X U.S. Optics scope, prices assume all options included, 29 1/2 lbs. Limited mfg. 1998-99.

	100%	98%	95%	90%	80%	70%	60%	Last MSR
	$7,950	$7,400	$6,800	$6,150	$5,500	$4,900	$4,200	$8,500

Subtract $2,800 if w/o options.

JP ENTERPRISES, INC.

Current manufacturer and customizer established in 1978, and located in Hugo, MN beginning 2010, previously located in White Bear Lake, MN 2000-2009, Vadnais Heights, MN 1998-2000, and in Shoreview, MN 1995-98. Distributor, dealer, and consumer sales.

JP Enterprises is a distributor for Infinity pistols, and also customizes Remington shotgun Models 11-87, 1100, and 870, the Remington bolt action Model 700 series, Glock pistols, and the Armalite AR-10 series.

JP Enterprises also manufactures a complete line of high quality parts and accessories for AR-15 style rifles, including upper and lower assemblies, sights and optics, machined receivers, barrels/barrel kits, fire control kits, handguards, etc. and gunsmithing services. Please contact the company directly for more information and pricing regarding these parts, accesssories, and services (see Trademark Index).

PISTOLS: SEMI-AUTO

Level I & Level II custom pistols were manufactured 1995-97 using Springfield Armory slides and frames. Only a few were made, and retail prices were $599 (Level I) and $950 (Level II).

RIFLES: BOLT ACTION

MOR-07 – .260 Rem., 7mm WSM (new 2009), or .308 Win. cal., 24 in. stainless steel cryo-treated bull barrel, benchrest quality bolt action, Picatinny rail, JP Tactical Chassis system, Timney trigger, benchrest or tactical style forend, Precision grip system, matte black hard coat anodizing, 10 shot detachable, includes hard case. Disc. 2010.

	100%	98%	95%	90%	80%	70%	60%	Last MSR
	$4,250	$3,850	$3,350	$2,925	$2,500	$2,000	$1,600	$4,499

MR-10 – .260 Rem. (new 2012), 7mm WSM (new 2012), .308 Win., .300 WSM, or 6.5 Creedmoor cal., 3 lug short through bolt action with upper Picatinny rail, spiral cut bolt, 24 in. JP Supermatch fluted stainless steel barrel with large profile JP compensator, folding Magpul stock with tactical grip including palmrest, benchrest style forend or JP modular handguard system. New 2011.

	100%	98%	95%	90%	80%	70%	60%	
MSR $3,999	$3,850	$3,500	$3,150	$2,700	$2,300	$1,900	$1,650	

RIFLES: SEMI-AUTO

The rifles in this section utilize a modified AR-15 style operating system.

BARRACUDA 10/22 – .22 LR cal., features customized Ruger 10/22 action with reworked fire control system, choice of stainless bull or carbon fiber superlight barrel, 3 lb. trigger pull, color laminated "Barracuda" skeletonized stock. Mfg. 1997-2003.

	100%	98%	95%	90%	80%	70%	60%	Last MSR
	$1,075	$950	$775	$650	$575	$475	$400	$1,195

A-2 MATCH – .223 Rem. cal., GIO, JP-15 lower receiver with JP fire control system, 20 in. JP Supermatch cryo-treated stainless barrel, standard A-2 stock and pistol grip, DCM type free float forend, MIL SPEC A-2 upper assembly with Smith National Match rear sight. Mfg. 1995-2003.

	100%	98%	95%	90%	80%	70%	60%	Last MSR
	$1,525	$1,300	$1,100	$925	$825	$700	$600	$1,695

MSR	100%	98%	95%	90%	80%	70%	60%	Last MSR

JP-15 & VARIATIONS (GRADE I A-3 FLAT TOP)

– .204 Ruger (new 2012), .223 Rem., or 6.5 Grendel (new 2012) cal., GIO, features Eagle Arms (disc. 1999), DPMS (disc. 1999) or JP15 lower assembly with JP fire control system, Mil Spec A-3 type upper receiver with 18 or 24 in. JP Supermatch cryo-treated stainless barrel, 10 shot mag., synthetic modified thumbhole (disc. 2011), synthetic A2 or ACE ARFX buttstock (new 2012), or laminated wood thumbhole (disc. 2002) stock, JP vent. two-piece free float forend, recoil eliminator, black teflon hard coat anodized finish, JP Compensator muzzle treatment, Hogue pistol grip. New 1995.

| MSR $1,999 | $1,850 | $1,600 | $1,300 | $1,225 | $995 | $850 | $650 | |

Add $80 for Tactical Ready Rifle (new 2013).
Add $400 for NRA Hi-Power version with 24 in. bull barrel and sight package (disc. 2002).
Add $200 for laminated wood thumbhole stock (disc. 2002).
Subtract $275 for Optic Ready Rifle (new 2013).
Subtract $34 for Kyle Lamb signature rifle (JP-15/VTAC).
Subtract $300 for Duty Defense rifle (JP-15D).
Subtract $500 for LE/Military rifle (JP-15LE).

* **JP-15 Grade I IPSC Limited Class** – similar to Grade I, except has quick detachable match grade iron sights, Versa-pod bipod. Mfg. 1999-2004.

| | $1,650 | $1,400 | $1,150 | $995 | $775 | $625 | $550 | $1,795 |

* **JP-15 Grade I Tactical/SOF** – similar to Grade I, all matte black non-glare finish, 18, 20, or 24 in. Supermatch barrel. Mfg. 1999-2003.

| | $1,425 | $1,225 | $1,050 | $925 | $800 | $700 | $600 | $1,595 |

Add $798 for Trijicon ACOG sight with A-3 adapter.

GRADE II

– .223 Rem. cal., GIO, features MIL SPEC JP lower receiver with upper assembly finished in a special two-tone color anodizing process, JP fire control, 18-24 in. cryo treated stainless barrel, composite skeletonized stock, Harris bipod, choice of multi-color or black receiver and forend, includes hard case. Mfg. 1998-2002.

| | $1,750 | $1,500 | $1,275 | $1,025 | $825 | $700 | $600 | $1,895 |

Add $200 for laminated wood thumbhole stock.

GRADE III (THE EDGE)

– .223 Rem. cal., GIO, RND machined match upper/lower receiver system, 2-piece free floating forend, standard or laminated thumbhole wood stock, 18 to 24 in. barrel (cryo treated beginning 1998) with recoil eliminator, includes Harris bipod, top-of-the-line model, includes hard case. Mfg. 1996-2002.

| | $2,550 | $2,125 | $1,750 | $1,450 | $1,150 | $875 | $750 | $2,795 |

Add $250 for laminated thumbhole stock.

AR-10T

– .243 Win. or .308 Win. cal., GIO, features Armalite receiver system with JP fire control, flat-top receiver, vent. free floating tubular handguard, 24 in. cryo treated stainless barrel, black finish. Mfg. 1998-2004.

| | $2,175 | $1,825 | $1,600 | $1,450 | $1,150 | $875 | $750 | $2,399 |

Add $150 for anodized upper assembly in custom color. Add $350 for laminated wood thumbhole stock.

* **AR-10LW** – GIO, lightweight variation of the Model AR-10T, includes 16-20 in. cryo treated stainless barrel, composite fiber tubular handguard, black finish only, 7-8 lbs. Mfg. 1998-2004.

| | $2,175 | $1,825 | $1,600 | $1,450 | $1,150 | $875 | $750 | $2,399 |

Add $200 for detachable sights.

CTR-02 COMPETITION TACTICAL RIFLE

– .204 Ruger (new 2012), .223 Rem., or 6.5 Grendel (new 2012) cal., GIO, state-of-the-art advanced AR design with many improvements, integral ACOG interface, beveled mag well, black synthetic A2 or ACE ARFX buttstock, 10 shot mag., JP recoil eliminator and fire control system, 1/4 MOA possible, JP Supermatch polished stainless steel barrel, rifle or mid-length JP modular hand guard system, Hogue pistol grip, JP low mass or full mass operating system, black teflon over hard coat anodized finish. New 2002.

| MSR $2,599 | $2,350 | $2,050 | $1,775 | $1,600 | $1,295 | $1,075 | $825 | |

Add $599 for presentation grade finish (disc. 2011).

LRP-07

– .260 Rem., .308 Win., 6.5 Creedmoor (new 2012), or .338 Federal (new 2012) cal., GIO, 18 (LRP-07H, Hunter's package) or 22 in. stainless steel cryo-treated barrel, left side charging system (new 2009), tactical compensator, matte black hard coat anodizing, aluminum components, 10 or 19 shot mag., A2 or ACE ARFX black synthetic stock, JP modular hand guard, JP low mass operating system, Hogue pistol grip, upper accessory rail.

| MSR $3,299 | $2,975 | $2,600 | $2,250 | $2,025 | $1,650 | $1,350 | $1,050 | |

Add $100 for Hunter's package.
Add $295 for Bench Rest variation with 22 in. barrel.

* **SASS LRP-07** – .308 Win. cal., similar to LRP-07, except has SASS (Semi-Auto Sniper System) package that includes 20 in. Supermatch barrel, Magpul PRS buttstock, Magpul MIAD grip, scope mount, three 20 shot mags., and soft backpack case. New 2013.

| MSR $4,600 | $4,250 | $3,650 | $3,125 | $2,825 | $2,295 | $1,875 | $1,450 | |

MSR	100%	98%	95%	90%	80%	70%	60%	Last MSR

Add $500 for suppressor.
Add $1,375 for Leupold Mark 4 scope.
Add $1,599 for Bushnell Elite Tactical scope.
Add $2,500 for U.S. Optics SN-3-T-PAL scope.

PSC-11 – .204 Ruger (new 2012), .223 Rem., or 6.5 Grendel (new 2012) cal., GIO, practical side charging rifle with left side charge system, upper has same features as SCR-11 model, but lower unit is cross compatible with any standard AR-15 platform, black teflon hardcoat anodized finish, A2 or ACE ARFX buttstock with Hogue pistol grip, small frame with upper accessory rail. New 2011.

MSR $2,599	$2,350	$2,050	$1,775	$1,600	$1,295	$1,075	$825

PSC-12 – .260 Win., .308 Win., 6.5 Creedmoor, or 6.5 Grendel cal., GIO, similar to PSC-11, except has larger frame, dual charging upper assembly compatible with DPMS lower receivers. New 2012.

MSR $3,499	$3,150	$2,750	$2,375	$2,150	$1,750	$1,425	$1,100

SCR-11 – .204 Ruger, .223 Rem., or 6.5 Grendel cal., competition side-charging rifle with left side charge system, features JP Supermatch polished stainless barrel with JP compensator, flat-top receiver with Picatinny rail, vent. modular handguard, choice of A2 or ACE ARFX buttstock, Hogue pistol grip, matte black anodizing on aluminum components. New 2011.

MSR $2,799	$2,525	$2,225	$1,895	$1,725	$1,395	$1,150	$895

NC-22 – .22 LR cal., precision machined Nordic Component upper receiver, 18 in. lightweight stainless steel barrel with JP Compensator, extra long JP modular hand guard system, matte black anodized hard coat finish. New 2013.

MSR $1,499	$1,350	$1,175	$1,025	$925	$750	$610	$475

JAMES RIVER ARMORY

Current restoration company specializing in the restoration of military firearms from WWI and WWII and located in Baltimore, MD.

James River Armory currently restores selected U.S. Military WWI and WWII rifles, and puts on new Criterion barrels and in some cases, new stocks. When completed, all rifles are test fired for safety. Please contact the company directly for current model availability and pricing on its restored military firearms (see Trademark Index).

JARD, INC.

Current rifle manufacturer located in Sheldon, IA.

RIFLES: SEMI-AUTO

MODEL J16 – .223/5.56 NATO cal., GIO, 16. in. barrel, 20 shot mag., folding/telescoping stock, free floating barrel and handguard, Picatinny rail upper, JARD sight compensation system, optional quad rail or muzzle brake, Black finish.

MSR $1,015	$900	$800	$675	$610	$500	$400	$315

Add $100 for quad rail kit.
Add $75 for muzzle brake.

MODEL J17 – .17 HMR or .22 WMR cal., blowback operation, adj. stock, pistol grip, Picatinny rail receiver, detachable magazine, side charging handle, ergonomic safety and magazine release operation, Black finish.
Please contact the company directly for more information on options, pricing, and delivery time (see Trademark Index).

MODEL J18 – .243 WSSM, .25 WSSM, or 7mm WSSM cal., GIO, 22 in. barrel, enlarged bolt design, side charging handle, flat-top Picatinny rail, free floating barrel and handguard, QD sling stud standard, 3 shot mag.

MSR $1,151	$1,025	$900	$775	$700	$575	$475	$375

MODEL J19 – .223/5.56 NATO cal., GIO, standard AR lower, left non-reciprocating charging handle, right fold adj. length stock with adj. cheek pad, Picatinny rail upper, free float barrel and forearm, JARD sight compensation system, brass deflector.
Please contact the company directly for more information on options, pricing, and delivery time (see Trademark Index).

MODEL J22 – .22 LR cal., blowback operation, 16.2 in. barrel, 26 shot mag., side charging handle, upper Picatinny rail, free floating barrel and handguard, pistol grip, quad rail/muzzle brake is optional, Black finish.

MSR $735	$650	$575	$500	$450	$375	$300	$225

Add $99 for quad rail/muzzle brake.

MODEL J50 – .50 BMG cal., GIO, rotating bolt, 30 in. fixed barrel, free floating handguard, detachable 5 shot mag., adj. trigger, Black finish, 24 lbs.

MSR $8,450	$7,600	$6,650	$5,700	$5,175	$4,175	$3,425	$2,675

MSR	100%	98%	95%	90%	80%	70%	60%	Last MSR

MODEL J1022 – .22 LR cal., blowback operation, accepts Ruger 10/22 magazines/barrels/stocks, Sporter or heavy barrel (multiple barrel configurations available), Picatinny rail standard, Jard Sporter trigger standard, Hogue or wood laminate thumbhole stock.

MSR $549	$500	$450	$375	$350	$275	$225	$175	

Add $15 for sporter barrel with Hogue stock.
Add $75 for heavy barrel with wood laminate thumbhole stock.

JARRETT RIFLES, INC.

Current manufacturer established in 1979, and located in Jackson, SC. Direct custom order sales only.

RIFLES: BOLT ACTION

Jarrett Rifles, Inc. is justifiably famous for its well-known Beanfield rifles (refers to shooting over a beanfield at long range targets). A Jarrett innovation is the Tri-Lock receiver, which has 3 locking lugs, and a semi-integral recoil lug. Jarrett blueprints every action for proper dimensioning and rigid tolerances, and this explains why their rifles have set rigid accuracy standards.

A wide variety of options are available for Jarrett custom rifles (holders of 16 world records in rifle accuracy). Jarrett also manufactures its own precision ammunition for discriminating shooters/hunters. The manufacturer should be contacted directly for pricing and availability regarding these special order options, and custom gunsmithing services (see Trademark Index).

Current pricing does not include 11% excise tax or scope.

BENCHREST/YOUTH/TACTICAL – various cals., various configurations depending on application. Mfg. 1999-disc.

	$4,625	$4,150	$3,650	$3,150	$2,750	$2,150	$1,750	*$4,625*

ORIGINAL BEANFIELD RIFLE – built on customer supplied action, choice of caliber, stock style, color, barrel length and finish, with or w/o muzzle brake, supplied with 20 rounds of ammo and test target. New 2005.

MSR $5,380	$4,995	$4,500	$3,925	$3,400	$3,000	$2,600	$2,200	

.50 CAL. – .50 BMG cal., McMillan custom receiver, choice of repeater or single shot, 30 or 34 in. barrel with muzzle brake, 28-45 lbs. Mfg. 1999-2003.

	$8,050	$6,500	$5,300	$4,350	$3,650	$3,000	$2,500	*$8,050*

Add $300 for repeater action.

JERICHO

Previous trademark of Israel Military Industries (I.M.I.). Previously imported by K.B.I., Inc. located in Harrisburg, PA.

PISTOLS: SEMI-AUTO

JERICHO 941 – 9mm Para. cal. or .41 Action Express (by conversion only) cal., DA/SA, 4.72 in. barrel with polygonal rifling, all steel fabrication, 3 dot Tritium sights, 11 or 16 (9mm Para.) shot mag., ambidextrous safety, polymer grips, decocking lever, 38 1/2 oz. Imported 1990-1992.

	$625	$550	$475	$425	$375	$325	$295	*$649*

Add $299 for .41 AE conversion kit.

Industrial hard chrome or nickel finishes were also available for all Jericho pistols.

* ***Jericho 941 Pistol Package*** – includes 9mm Para. and .41 AE conversion kit, cased with accessories. Mfg. 1990-91 only.

	$850	$775	$700	$625	$575	$495	$450	*$775*

JOHNSON AUTOMATICS, INC.

Previous manufacturer located in Providence, RI. Johnson Automatics, Inc. moved many times during its history, often with slight name changes. M.M. Johnson, Jr. died in 1965, and the company continued production at 104 Audubon Street in New Haven, CT as Johnson Arms, Inc. mostly specializing in sporter semi-auto rifles with Monte Carlo stocks in .270 Win. or .30-06 cal.

RIFLES: SEMI-AUTO

MODEL 1941 – .30-06 or 7x57mm cal., 22 in. removable air cooled barrel, recoil operated, perforated metal handguard, aperture sight, military stock. Most were made for Dutch military, some used by U.S. Marine Paratroopers, during WWII all .30-06 and 7x57mm were ordered by South American governments.

	$7,350	$6,750	$6,000	$5,250	$4,500	$3,950	$3,250	

MilTech offers a restored version of this model. Inspect this model carefully for originality before considering a possible purchase. Values are somewhat lower for restored guns.

MSR	100%	98%	95%	90%	80%	70%	60%	Last MSR

JUST RIGHT CARBINES

Current trademark of carbines established in 2011, and manufactured in Canandaigua, NY. Dealer and distributor sales. Previously distributed by LDB Supply LLC located in Dayton, OH, by American Tactical Imports (ATI), located in Rochester, NY, and by E.M.F., located in Santa Ana, CA.

CARBINES: SEMI-AUTO

JUST RIGHT CARBINE – 9mm Para., .40 S&W, or .45 ACP (new mid-2011) cal., blowback action, 16 1/4 in. barrel, features ambidextrous bolt handle and ejection, flat-top receiver with Picatinny rail and half length barrel quad rail, uses Glock or M1911 (.45 ACP only) magazines, collapsible 6-position stock, matte black, Desert Camo (new 2013), or Muddy Girl (new 2013) finish, approx. 6 1/2 lbs. New 2011.

MSR $774	$695	$610	$525	$475	$400	$350	$300

Add $25 for .40 S&W cal.

Add $50 for .45 ACP cal.

Add $75 for Desert Camo or Muddy Girl camo coverage.

Add $95 for Reaper Z Green and 33 shot mag. (new 2013).

Add $100 for tactical package (includes red dot scope, forward folding grip, Tuff1 grip cover and two magazines.

NOTES

K SECTION

K.B.I., INC.

Previous importer and distributor located in Harrisburg, PA until Jan. 29, 2010. Distributor sales.

K.B.I., Inc. imported Charles Daly semi-auto pistols, Bul Transmark semi-auto pistols, SA revolvers, AR-15 style rifles, and shotguns in many configurations, including O/U, SxS, semi-auto, lever action, and slide action. K.B.I. also imported Armscor (Arms Corp. of the Philippines), FEG pistols, and Liberty revolvers and SxS coach shotguns. These models may be found within their respective alphabetical sections. K.B.I. previously imported the Jericho pistol manufactured by I.M.I. from Israel. Older imported Jericho pistols may be found under its own heading in this text, and more recently imported pistols are listed under the Charles Daly listing.

MSR	100%	98%	95%	90%	80%	70%	60%	Last MSR

RIFLES: BOLT ACTION

KASSNAR GRADE I – available in 9 cals., GIO, thumb safety that locks trigger, with or w/o deluxe sights, 22 in. barrel, 3 or 4 shot mag., includes swivel posts and oil finished standard grade European walnut with recoil pad, 7 1/2 lbs. Imported 1989-93.

	100%	98%	95%	90%	80%	70%	60%	Last MSR
	$445	$385	$325	$275	$225	$195	$175	*$499*

NYLON 66 – .22 LR cal., GIO, patterned after the Remington Nylon 66. Imported until 1990 from C.B.C. in Brazil, South America.

	100%	98%	95%	90%	80%	70%	60%	Last MSR
	$125	$110	$95	$85	$75	$70	$65	*$134*

MODEL 122 – .22 LR cal., GIO, bolt action design with mag. Imported from South America until 1990.

	100%	98%	95%	90%	80%	70%	60%	Last MSR
	$125	$110	$95	$85	$75	$70	$65	*$136*

MODEL 522 – .22 LR cal., GIO, bolt action design with tube mag. Imported from South America until 1990.

	100%	98%	95%	90%	80%	70%	60%	Last MSR
	$130	$115	$100	$85	$75	$70	$65	*$142*

BANTAM SINGLE SHOT – .22 LR cal., GIO, outh dimensions. Imported 1989-90 only.

	100%	98%	95%	90%	80%	70%	60%	Last MSR
	$110	$90	$85	$75	$70	$65	$60	*$120*

KDF, INC.

Previous rifle manufacturer until circa 2007 and current custom riflesmith specializing in restocking and installing muzzle brakes, in addition to supplying specialized rifle parts. Located in Seguin, TX. KDF utilized Mauser K-15 actions imported from Oberndorf, Germany for many rifle models. Previously, KDF rifles were manufactured by Voere (until 1987) in Vöhrenbach, W. Germany.

Older KDF rifles were private labeled by Voere and marked KDF. Since Voere was absorbed by Mauser-Werke in 1987, model designations changed. Mauser-Werke does not private label (i.e. newer guns are marked Mauser-Werke), and these rifles can be found under the Mauser-Werke heading in this text.

Due to space considerations, information regarding this manufacturer is available online free of charge at www.bluebookofgunvalues.com.

KSN INDUSTRIES LTD.

Previous distributor (1952-1996) located in Houston, TX. Previously imported until 1996 exclusively by J.O. Arms, Inc. located in Houston, TX. Currently manufactured Israel Arms, Ltd. pistols may be found under their individual listing.

PISTOLS: SEMI-AUTO

The pistols listed were mfg. by Israel Arms, Ltd.

KAREEN MK II – 9mm Para. or .40 S&W (new late 1994) cal., SA, 4.64 in. barrel, two-tone finish, rubberized grips, regular or Meprolite sights, 10 (C/B 1994), 13*, or 15* shot mag., 33 oz. Imported 1993-1996.

	100%	98%	95%	90%	80%	70%	60%	Last MSR
	$360	$305	$255	$225	$200	$185	$170	*$411*

Add approx. $160 for two-tone finish with Meprolite sights.

* Kareen Mk II Compact – compact variation with 3.85 in. barrel. Imported 1993-96.

	100%	98%	95%	90%	80%	70%	60%	Last MSR
	$415	$360	$315	$255	$225	$200	$185	*$497*

K-VAR CORP.

Current importer located in Las Vegas, NV. MSR Distribution is the distributor for K-Var Corp.

K-VAR Corp. currently distributes Saiga rifles and shotguns, in addition to importing select Zastava bolt action rifles and pistols, Vepr rifles mfg. by Molot, Arsenal Inc. SLR series, AK-47 design rifles and an RPK milled rifle. Additionally, K-Var Crop. manufactures a Model SA M-7 SFK AK-47 design rifle in the U.S. See separate listings for Saiga rifles/shotguns, Zastava bolt action rifles, Vepr rifles, Arsenal, and the RPK model. Please contact the company directly for availability and pricing (see Trademark Index).

MSR	100%	98%	95%	90%	80%	70%	60%	Last MSR

KAHR ARMS

Current manufacturer established in 1993, with headquarters located in Blauvelt, NY, and manufacturing in Worchester, MA. Distributor and dealer sales.

PISTOLS: SEMI-AUTO

All Kahr pistols are supplied with two mags (except CW Series), hard polymer case, trigger lock, and lifetime warranty. Except for the CW Series, all pistols feature Lothar Walther polygonal rifled match grade barrels.

CW9 – 9mm Para. cal., black polymer frame, matte stainless steel slide, 7 shot mag., DAO, 3.6 in. barrel, textured polymer grips, adj. rear sight, pinned in polymer front sight, white dot combat sights, 15.8 oz. New 2005.

| MSR $485 | $425 | $375 | $325 | $295 | $275 | $250 | $225 | |

CW40 – .40 S&W cal., black polymer frame, matte stainless steel slide, 6 shot mag., DAO, 3.6 in. barrel, textured polymer grips, adj. rear sight, pinned in polymer front sight, white dot combat sights, 16.8 oz. New 2008.

| MSR $485 | $425 | $375 | $325 | $295 | $275 | $250 | $225 | |

CW45 – .45 ACP cal., otherwise similar to CW40, 19.7 oz. New 2008.

| MSR $485 | $425 | $375 | $325 | $295 | $275 | $250 | $225 | |

K9 COMPACT – 9mm Para. cal., trigger cocking, DAO with passive striker block, locked breech with Browning type recoil lug, steel construction, 3 1/2 in. barrel with polygonal rifling, 7 shot mag., wraparound black polymer grips, matte black, black titanium (Black-T, mfg. 1997-98), or electroless nickel (mfg. 1996-99) finish, 25 oz. Mfg. 1993-2003.

| | $560 | $485 | $435 | $385 | $340 | $315 | $285 | $648 |

Add $74 for electroless nickel finish (disc.).
Add $126 for black titanium finish (Black-T, disc.).
Add $103 for tritium night sights (new 1996).

* **K9 Compact Stainless** – similar to K9 Compact, except is matte finished stainless steel, NYCPD specs became standard 2006 (trigger LOP is 1/2 in. compared to 3/8 in.). New 1998.

| MSR $855 | $750 | $665 | $550 | $450 | $385 | $335 | $280 | |

Add $130 for tritium night sights.
Add $36 for matte black finish (new 2004).

P9 POLYMER COMPACT – 9mm Para. cal., similar to K9 Compact, except has 3.6 in. barrel, lightweight polymer frame, 7 shot mag., matte stainless slide, 17.9 oz. New 1999.

| MSR $739 | $630 | $525 | $450 | $375 | $325 | $285 | $250 | |

Add $118 for tritium night sights (new 2000).
Add $47 for matte black stainless slide (new 2004).
Add $137 for external safety and loaded chamber indicator with new enhanced trigger (new 2012).

MK9 MICRO SERIES – 9mm Para. cal., micro compact variation of the K9 Compact featuring 3 in. barrel, double action only with passive striker block, overall size is 4 in. H x 5 1/2 in. L, duo-tone finish with stainless frame and black titanium slide, includes two 6 shot flush floor plate mags. Mfg. 1998-99.

| | $650 | $575 | $515 | $465 | $425 | $395 | $375 | $749 |

Add $85 for tritium night sights.

* **MK9 Micro Series Elite 2000 Stainless** – similar to MK9 Elite 98 Stainless, except features black stainless frame and slide, black Roguard finish. Mfg. 2001-2002.

| | $575 | $485 | $425 | $360 | $315 | $260 | $225 | $694 |

PM9 MICRO POLYMER COMPACT – 9mm Para. cal., 3 in. barrel with polygonal rifling, black polymer frame, trigger cocking DAO, blackened stainless steel slide, 6 or 7 (with mag. grip extension, disc.) shot mag., 16 oz. New 2003.

| MSR $786 | $665 | $550 | $460 | $400 | $350 | $300 | $275 | |

Add $122 for tritium night sights.
Add $51 for matte black stainless slide (new 2004).
Add $42 for external safety, loaded chamber indicator (new 2010), and enhanced trigger (new 2012).
Add $168 for stainless slide with Crimson Trace trigger guard laser (new 2010).
Add $263 for custom engraved slide (Custom Shop only), new 2012.

TP9 – 9mm Para. cal., similar to T9, except has black polymer frame and standard sights, 20 oz. New 2004.

| MSR $697 | $600 | $500 | $425 | $360 | $315 | $260 | $225 | |

Add $141 for Novak night sights.

K40 COMPACT – .40 S&W cal., similar to K9, except has 6 shot mag., matte black or electroless nickel finish (disc. 1999), 26 oz. Mfg. 1997-2003.

| | $560 | $485 | $435 | $385 | $340 | $315 | $285 | $648 |

MSR	100%	98%	95%	90%	80%	70%	60%	Last MSR

Add $103 for tritium night sights (new 1997).
Add $74 for electroless nickel finish (disc. 1999).
Add $126 for black titanium finish (Black-T, disc. 1998).

* **K40 Compact Stainless** – similar to K40 Compact, except is stainless steel. New 1997.

MSR $855	$695	$575	$475	$375	$325	$260	$225	

Add $130 for tritium night sights.
Add $36 for matte black stainless steel (new 2004).

P40 COMPACT POLYMER – .40 S&W cal., similar to P9 Compact Polymer, 6 shot mag., 18.9 oz. New 2001.

MSR $739	$630	$525	$450	$375	$325	$285	$250	

Add $118 for tritium night sights.
Add $47 for matte black stainless slide (new 2004).
Add $137 for external safety and loaded chamber indicator.

MK40 MICRO – .40 S&W cal., micro compact variation of the Compact K40, featuring 3 in. barrel, matte stainless frame and slide, supplied with one 5 shot and one 6 shot (with grip extension) mag., 25 oz. New 1999.

MSR $855	$750	$665	$550	$450	$385	$335	$280	

Add $103 for tritium night sights.

PM40 COMPACT POLYMER – .40 S&W cal., black polymer frame, 3 in. barrel, supplied with one 5 shot and one 6 shot (with grip extension) mag., matte finished stainless slide, 17 oz. New 2004.

MSR $786	$665	$550	$460	$400	$350	$300	$275	

Add $122 for tritium night sights.
Add $51 for matte black stainless slide (new 2005).
Add $168 for stainless slide and Crimson Trace trigger guard laser (new 2010).
Add $42 for external safety and loaded chamber indicator with enhanced trigger (new 2012).

TP40 – .40 S&W cal., similar to T40, except has polymer frame. New 2006.

MSR $697	$600	$500	$425	$370	$325	$285	$250	

Add $141 for Novak night sights (TP40 Tactical).

P45 POLYMER – .45 ACP cal., DAO, black polymer frame with matte or black stainless steel slide, 3.54 in. barrel, 6 shot mag., ribbed grip straps, low profile white dot combat sights, 18 1/2 oz. New 2005.

MSR $805	$685	$560	$460	$410	$340	$290	$250	

Add $116 for Novak night sights.
Add $50 for black stainless slide (new 2006).

PM45 POLYMER – similar to TP45 Polymer, except has 3.24 in. barrel and 5 shot mag., approx. 19 oz. New 2007.

MSR $855	$750	$665	$550	$450	$385	$335	$280	

Add $119 for Novak night sights.
Add $48 for black stainless steel slide (new late 2008).
Add $89 for Crimson Trace trigger guard laser (new 2011).

TP45 POLYMER – .45 ACP cal., DAO, 4.04 in. barrel, 7 shot mag., matte stainless slide only, otherwise similar to P45, approx. 23 oz. New 2007.

MSR $697	$595	$495	$430	$365	$325	$285	$250	

Add $142 for Novak sights.

KEL-TEC CNC INDUSTRIES, INC.

Current manufacturer established in 1991, and located in Cocoa, FL. Dealer sales.

CARBINES/RIFLES: SEMI-AUTO

RFB CARBINE – .308 Win. cal., GPO, bullpup configuration with pistol grip and rear detachable mag., 18 (Carbine), or 32 (Target, disc. 2012) in. barrel with A2 style flash hider, Picatinny rail, front ejection from tube located above barrel, 10 or 20 shot mag., accepts FAL type mags., tilting breech block design, ambidextrous controls, black synthetic lower, adj. trigger, choice of Black, OD Green, or Tan finish, 8.1-11.3 lbs. New 2009.

MSR $1,927	$1,795	$1,550	$1,375	$1,150	$900	$800	$700	

Add $158 for OD Green or Tan finish.

* **RFB Hunter** – .308 Win. cal., similar to RFB Carbine, except features 24 in. heavy profile threaded barrel, includes hard case, thread protector, and one 20 shot mag., 9.7 lbs. New 2009.

MSR $2,204	$1,975	$1,250	$1,475	$1,350	$1,085	$900	$700	

Add $75 for OD Green or Tan finish.

MSR	100%	98%	95%	90%	80%	70%	60%	Last MSR

SUB-9/SUB-40 CARBINE – 9mm Para. or .40 S&W cal., unique pivoting 16.1 in. barrel rotates upwards and back, allowing overall size reduction and portability (16 in. x 7 in.), interchangable grip assembly will accept most popular double column high capacity handgun mags., including Glock, S&W, Beretta, SIG, or Kel-Tec, tube stock with polymer buttplate, matte black finish, 4.6 lbs. Mfg. 1997-2000.

	100%	98%	95%	90%	80%	70%	60%	Last MSR
	$365	$335	$300	$265	$235	$200	$180	*$700*

Add $25 for .40 S&W cal.

SUB-2000 CARBINE – 9mm Para. or .40 S&W (new 2004) cal., similar to Sub-9/Sub-40, but features a completely new design, 16.1 in. barrel, aperture rear and adj. front sights, internal keyed deployment lock, push bolt safety, choice of blued, parkerized, or hard chrome finish with Black, OD Green, or Tan grips, 4 lbs. New 2001.

MSR $425	$375	$340	$300	$265	$235	$200	$180	

Add $32 for parkerized finish.
Add $42 for hard chrome finish.
Add $9 for OD Green or Tan grips with parkerized finish. Add $12 for OD Green or Tan grips with blued or hard chrome finish.

This model accepts magazines from the Glock 17, 19, 22, or 23, Beretta 92 or 96, S&W Model 59, or Sig 226.

SU-16 SERIES CARBINE/RIFLE – 5.56 NATO cal., unique downward folding stock, forearm folds down to become a bipod, 16 (new 2005) or 18 1/2 in. barrel, Picatinny receiver rail, M16 breech locking and feeding system, choice of Black, OD Green (new 2012), or Tan (new 2012) synthetic stock (stores extra mags.) and forearm, approx. 4.7 lbs. New 2003.

* ***SU-16A*** – 5.56 NATO cal., features 18 1/2 in. barrel, 10 shot AR-15 compatible mag., right hand reciprocating bolt handle and mag. catch, buttstock can store two 10 shot mags., Black, OD Green, or Tan finish, 5 lbs.

MSR $682	$635	$550	$500	$450	$400	$365	$335	

Add $140 for OD Green or Tan finish.

* ***SU-16B*** – 5.56 NATO cal., similar to SU-16, except has lightened 16 in. barrel, 4 1/2 lbs.

MSR $736	$660	$580	$525	$465	$415	$365	$335	

Add $139 for OD Green or Tan finish.

* ***SU-16C*** – .300 AAC Blackout (new 2013) or 5.56 NATO cal., similar to SU-16A, except front sight is integrated into the gas block, and also has a true folding stock, parkerized finish with black polymer components, 4.7 lbs.

MSR $788	$725	$650	$600	$550	$500	$450	$400	

Add $141 for OD Green or Tan finish.

* ***SU-16E*** – .223 Rem. or .300 AAC Blackout cal., 16 in. barrel, flat-top Picatinny receiver, collapsible buttstock, pistol grip, small quad rail, accepts AR-15 compatible magazines, Black, OD Green, or Tan finish, 4.7 lbs. New 2012.

MSR $901	$825	$750	$675	$600	$550	$500	$450	

Add $138 for OD Green or Tan finish.

* ***SU-16F*** – 5.56 NATO cal., similar to SU-16A, except features Canadian Black or choice of OD Green or Tan finish. New 2012.

MSR $682	$635	$550	$500	$450	$400	$365	$335	

Add $140 for OD Green or Tan finish.

SU-22 RIFLE SERIES – similar to SU-16, except is .22 LR cal., parkerized finish, Picatinny rail on top of receiver and bottom of aluminum quad forearm, open sights, 27 shot mag., 4 lbs. New 2008.

MSR $460	$410	$360	$320	$285	$266	$245	$225	

Add $10 for under folding stock with 15 shot mag. (SU-22C).
Add $41 for pistol grip style AR stock (SU-22E).
Add $126 for OD Green or Tan finish.

RMR-30 CARBINE – .22 WMR cal., 16.1 in. threaded barrel, rifle version of the PMR-30 featuring a skeletonized collapsible stock, upper and lower Picatinny rails, flat-top design, ambidextrous operating handles, aluminum construction, 30 shot mag., 3.8 lbs. New 2011.

MSR $588	$525	$465	$425	$385	$350	$325	$295	

PISTOLS: SEMI-AUTO

PLR-16 – 5.56 NATO cal., gas operation, 9.2 in. threaded barrel, upper frame has integrated Picatinny rail, 10 shot detachable mag., black composite frame, 3.2 lbs. New 2006.

MSR $682	$600	$550	$500	$460	$420	$380	$340	

Add $119 for OD Green or Tan finish.

PLR-22 – .22 LR cal., similar to PLR-16, except has 26 shot mag., 2.8 lbs. New 2008.

MSR $400	$340	$300	$275	$250	$225	$200	$185	

Add $193 for OD Green or Tan finish.

MSR	100%	98%	95%	90%	80%	70%	60%	*Last MSR*

PF-9 – 9mm Para. cal., similar operating system as P-11, 3.1 in. barrel, single stack 7 shot mag., includes lower accessory rail, black finish, 12.7 oz. Limited mfg. 2006, reintroduced 2008.

MSR $340	$275	$220	$185	$165	$150	$135	$125	

Add $45 for parkerized finish.
Add $60 for hard chrome finish.

PMR-30 – .22 WMR cal., 4.3 in. barrel, 30 shot mag., blowback action, manual safety, fiber optic sights, steel slide and barrel, black finished aluminum frame, lower Picatinny rail, 19 1/2 oz. New 2010.

MSR $436	$375	$325	$295	$275	$250	$225	$200	

Add $27 for OD Green or Tan finish.

SHOTGUNS: SLIDE ACTION

KSG – 12 ga., 2 3/4 in. chamber, unique bullpup configuration, utilizing an 18 1/2 in. cyl. bore barrel, twin mag. tubes under the barrel allow 14 shot capacity, downward ejection, steel and polymer construction, upper and lower Picatinny rails w/o sights, pistol grip, 26.1 in. overall length, 6.9 lbs. New 2011.

MSR $1,212	$1,095	$975	$875	$774	$675	$575	$475	

Add $50 for OD Green or Tan finish.

KEPPELER - TECHNISCHE ENTWICKLUNGEN GmbH

Current rifle manufacturer located in Fichtenberg, Germany. No current U.S. importation.

Keppeler manufactures a wide variety of top quality rifles, in many target configurations (including UIT-CISM, Prone, Free, and Sniper Bullpup). Both metric and domestic calibers are available as well as a variety of special order options. Keppeler also manufactures precision caliber conversion tubes for the shotgun barrel(s) on combination guns and drillings. Please contact the factory directly for more information and current pricing (see Trademark Index).

KIMBER

Current trademark manufactured by Kimber Mfg., Inc., established during 1997, with company headquarters and manufacturing located in Elmsford, NY. Previously located in Yonkers, NY until 2011. Previous rifle manufacture was by Kimber of America, Inc., located in Clackamas, OR circa 1993-1997. Dealer sales.

PISTOLS: SEMI-AUTO

Kimber pistols, including the very early models marked "Clackamas, Oregon", have all been manufactured in the Yonkers, NY plant. Prior to the 1998 production year, the "Classic" model pistols were alternately roll-scrolled "Classic", "Classic Custom" or "Custom Classic". During 1997-98, the "Classic" moniker was dropped from Kimber pistol nomenclature as a specific model.

All Kimber 1911 pistols are shipped with lockable high impact synthetic case with cable lock and one magazine, beginning 1999.

Beginning in 2001, the "Series II" pistol, incorporating the Kimber Firing Pin Safety System, was again phased into some centerfire models. All pistols incorporating the firing pin block have the Roman Numeral "II" following the name of the pistol presented on the slide directly under the ejection port. This conversion was completed by February 2002, and about 50% of subsequent Kimber 1911 pistol production has been Series II. There was no "Series I" pistol per se, but pre-series II models are often referred to in that manner.

During 2003, external extractors were phased many .45 ACP models. Due to consumer demand, production was phased back to traditional (internal) extractors during 2006.

All three changes (disuse of the term "Classic" for pistols, Series II safety system, and external extractor) were "phased in" throughout normal production cycles. Therefore, no distinctive cut-off dates or serial numbering series were established to identify specific product runs or identify when these features were incorporated.

Almost all Kimber pistols (exceptions are Royal II, Classic Carry Pro, rimfires and some pistols sold in California) have stainless steel match grade barrels beginning 2013.

Add $339 for .22 LR cal. or $344-$379 for .17 Mach 2 cal. (mfg. 2005-2006) conversion kit for all mil-spec 1911 pistols (includes complete upper assembly, lightweight aluminum slide, premium bull barrel, and 10 shot mag.). Available in satin black and satin silver. Kimber began manufacture of these kits in early 2003. Prior to that, they were manufactured by a vendor.

CUSTOM II – .45 ACP cal., patterned after the Colt Government Model 1911, 5 in. barrel, SA, various finishes, 7 shot mag., steel frame, match grade barrel, bushing and trigger group, dovetail mounted sights, frame machined from solid steel, high ride beavertail grip safety, choice of rubber, laminated wood (disc.), walnut or rosewood (disc.) grips, 38 oz. New 1995.

MSR $871	$725	$625	$525	$475	$375	$325	$265	

Add $34 for walnut or rosewood (disc.) grips.
Add $117 for night sights.
Add $185 for Royal II finish (polished blue and checkered rosewood grips, disc. 2010, and replaced by new Custom Shop version with same name.)

This series' nomenclature added the Roman numeral "II" during 2001.

MSR	100%	98%	95%	90%	80%	70%	60%	Last MSR

* ***Custom Target II*** – .45 ACP cal., similar to Custom II, except features Kimber adj. rear sight. New 1998.

| MSR $974 | $850 | $750 | $625 | $550 | $450 | $360 | $280 | |

CUSTOM STAINLESS II – .38 Super (advertised in 1999, mfg. late 2005-2008), 9mm Para. (advertised in 1999, new 2008), .40 S&W (mfg. 1999-2007), or .45 ACP cal., similar to Custom II, except has stainless steel slide and frame.

| MSR $998 | $850 | $750 | $650 | $550 | $440 | $360 | $280 | |

Add $18 for 9mm Para. or $11 for .40 S&W (disc. 2007) cal.
Add $130 for night sights (.45 ACP cal. only).
Add $143 for high polish stainless in .38 Super cal. only (mfg. late 2005-2008).
Subtract $27 for Stainless Limited Edition marked "Stainless LE" (disc. 1998).

* ***Custom Stainless Target II*** – similar to Custom Stainless II, except is available in .38 Super (new 2002), 9mm Para., 10mm (new 2003), or .45 ACP cal., features Kimber adj. rear sight. New 1998.

| MSR $1,108 | $975 | $850 | $725 | $625 | $500 | $425 | $350 | |

Add $100 for .40 S&W cal. (disc. 2002).
Add $84 for .38 Super, 10mm or 9mm Para. cal.
Add $130 for high polish stainless in .38 Super cal. only (mfg. late 2005-2008).

ROYAL II – .45 ACP cal., 5 in. barrel, similar to Custom II, except features charcoal blue slide and frame, solid bone grips, 38 oz. New 2010.

| MSR $2,020 | $1,850 | $1,575 | $1,325 | $1,100 | $950 | $825 | $700 | |

GOLD MATCH II – .45 ACP cal., features Kimber adj. sight, 5 in. stainless steel match barrel and bushing, SA, premium aluminum match grade trigger, ambidextrous thumb safety became standard in 1998, 8 shot mag., fancy checkered rosewood grips in double diamond pattern, high polish blue, hand fitted barrel by Kimber Custom Shop, 38 oz.

| MSR $1,393 | $1,250 | $1,125 | $950 | $850 | $700 | $575 | $450 | |

This series' nomenclature added the Roman numeral "II" during 2001.

* ***Gold Match Stainless II*** – .38 Super (advertised in 1999, never mfg.), 9mm Para. (advertised in 1999, new 2008), .40 S&W (mfg. 1999-2007), or .45 ACP cal., similar to Gold Match, except is stainless steel, 38 oz.

| MSR $1,574 | $1,375 | $1,175 | $1,025 | $900 | $750 | $625 | $550 | |

Add $75 for 9mm Para. or $100 for .40 S&W (disc. 2007) cal.

TEAM MATCH II – 9mm Para. (new 2009), .45 ACP, or .38 Super (limited mfg. 2003-2004, reintroduced 2006-2010) cal., same pistol developed for USA Shooting Team (2004 Olympics Rapid Fire Pistol Team) competition, satin finish stainless steel frame and slide, 5 in. match grade barrel, SA, 30 LPI front strap checkering, match grade trigger, Tactical Extractor system (disc.) or internal extractor, extended magazine well, 8 shot mag., laminated red/white/blue grips, 38 oz. Total production just over 10,000 units. Later mfg. had a gold logo on slide, red/blue grips and black DLC coating on slide. Mfg. 2003-2012.

| | $1,315 | $1,150 | $975 | $775 | $725 | $575 | $450 | *$1,563* |

Add $13 for 9mm Para. cal.
Add $48 for .38 Super cal. (disc. 2010).

A $100 donation is made to the U.S.A. Shooting Team for every Team Match II sold.

GOLD COMBAT II – .45 ACP cal. only, 5 in. barrel (bushingless bull became standard 2008), SA, full size carry pistol based on the Gold Match, steel frame and slide, stainless steel match grade barrel and bushing, matte black KimPro II finish, serrated flat-top and scalloped French shoulders also became standard 2008, Tritium night sights, checkered walnut (disc. 2008) or 24 LPI herringbone pattern Micarta grips, ambidextrous thumb safety, extended and beveled mag. well, full length guide rod, 38 oz, mfg. by Custom Shop. Mfg. 1994-2008, reintroduced 2011.

| MSR $2,307 | $2,075 | $1,800 | $1,575 | $1,350 | $1,100 | $900 | $750 | |

This series' nomenclature added the Roman numeral "II" during 2001.

* ***Gold Combat Stainless II*** – similar to Gold Combat, except is all stainless steel. Mfg. 1994-2008, reintroduced 2011.

| MSR $2,251 | $2,000 | $1,775 | $1,550 | $1,375 | $1,100 | $900 | $700 | |

* ***Gold Combat RL II*** – similar to Gold Combat, except has Picatinny rail machined into the lower forward frame to accept optics and other tactical accessories. Mfg. 1994-2008, reintroduced 2011.

| MSR $2,405 | $2,100 | $1,800 | $1,575 | $1,375 | $1,125 | $925 | $800 | |

SUPER MATCH II – .45 ACP cal. only, 5 in. barrel, SA, top-of-the-line model, two-tone stainless steel construction, KimPro finish on slide, match grade trigger, Custom Shop markings, accuracy guarantee, 38 oz. New 1999.

| MSR $2,313 | $2,075 | $1,800 | $1,575 | $1,350 | $1,100 | $900 | $750 | |

This series' nomenclature added the Roman numeral "II" during 2001.

MSR	100%	98%	95%	90%	80%	70%	60%	Last MSR

LTP II – .45 ACP cal., designed for Limited Ten competition, Tactical Extractor, steel frame and slide, KimPro finish, 20 LPI front strap checkering, 30 LPI checkering under trigger guard, tungsten guide rod, flat-top serrated slide, beveled mag. well, ambidextrous thumb safety, adj. rear sight. Mfg. by Custom Shop 2002-2006.

	100%	98%	95%	90%	80%	70%	60%	Last MSR
	$1,850	$1,620	$1,385	$1,260	$1,015	$830	$645	$2,106

RIMFIRE TARGET – .17 Mach 2 (mfg. 2004-2005) or .22 LR cal., 5 in. barrel, SA, 10 shot mag., aluminum frame in silver or black anodized finish (disc. 2006), black oxide steel or satin stainless slide (.17 Mach 2 cal. only), black synthetic grips, Kimber adj. rear sight, 28 oz. New 2003.

MSR $871	$775	$675	$575	$500	$400	$325	$275	

Add $75 for .17 Mach 2 cal. (disc. 2005).

RIMFIRE SUPER – .22 LR cal., similar to Rimfire Target, except has flat-top slide with aggressive fluting on upper sides, premium aluminum trigger, ambidextrous safety, rosewood grips with logo inserts, guaranteed to fire a sub-1.5 in. 5 shot group at 25 yards, test target included, 23 oz., mfg. by Kimber Custom Shop. New 2004.

MSR $1,220	$1,075	$925	$800	$700	$600	$500	$425	

POLYMER – .45 ACP cal., SA, features widened black polymer frame offering larger mag. capacity, choice of fixed (Polymer) or adj. Kimber target (Polymer Target, disc. 1999) rear sight, matte black slide, 10 shot mag., 34 oz. Mfg. 1997-2001.

	$675	$595	$500	$450	$375	$300	$225	$795

Add $88 for Polymer Target.

All Polymer models were disc. in 2002 in favor of the new "Ten" Series with improved Kimber made frame. Magazines are interchangeable.

* **Polymer Stainless** – .38 Super (advertised in 1999, never mfg.), 9mm Para. (advertised in 1999, never mfg.), .40 S&W (mfg. 1999 only), or .45 ACP cal., similar to Polymer, except has satin finish stainless steel slide. Mfg. 1998-2001.

	$745	$650	$550	$500	$410	$335	$250	$856

Add $88 for Polymer Stainless Target (disc. 1999).

* **Polymer Gold Match** – .45 ACP cal. only, similar to Gold Match, except has polymer frame, supplied with 10 shot double stack mag., 34 oz. Mfg. 1999-2001.

	$925	$810	$695	$630	$510	$415	$325	$1,041

»**Polymer Gold Match Stainless** – similar to Gold Match, except has polymer frame and stainless steel slide, 34 oz. Mfg. 1999-2001.

	$1,025	$895	$770	$695	$565	$460	$360	$1,177

* **Polymer Pro Carry** – .45 ACP cal. only, 4 in. bushingless bull barrel, steel slide, 32 oz. Mfg. 1999-2001.

	$725	$635	$545	$495	$400	$325	$255	$814

»**Polymer Pro Carry Stainless** – similar to Polymer Pro Carry, except has stainless steel slide. Mfg. 1999-2001.

	$755	$660	$565	$515	$415	$340	$265	$874

* **Polymer Ultra Ten II** – .45 ACP cal., black polymer frame with aluminum frame insert, stainless slide, 3 in. barrel, 10 shot staggered mag., low profile sights, lighter version of the Polymer Series frame, Kimber Firing Pin Safety, 24 oz. **While advertised during 2001 with an MSR of $896, this model never went into production.**

COMPACT II – .45 ACP cal., features 4 in. barrel, SA, .4 in. shorter aluminum or steel frame, 7 shot mag., Commander style hammer, single recoil spring, low profile combat sights, checkered black synthetic grips, 28 (aluminum) or 34 (steel) oz. Mfg. 1998-2001.

	$635	$555	$475	$430	$350	$285	$220	$764

* **Compact Stainless II** – .40 S&W (mfg. 1999-2001) or .45 ACP cal., features stainless steel slide, 4 in. bull barrel, 4 in. shorter aluminum (disc., reintroduced 2009) or stainless (mfg. 2002-2008) frame, 7 shot mag., Commander style hammer, single recoil spring, low profile combat sights, black synthetic grips, 34 oz. New 1998.

MSR $1,052	$925	$825	$725	$625	$525	$450	$350	

Add $32 for .40 S&W cal. (disc. 2001).

This model's nomenclature added the Roman numeral "II" during 2001.

COMBAT CARRY – .40 S&W or .45 ACP cal., 4 in. barrel, SA, carry model featuring aluminum frame and trigger, stainless steel slide, tritium night sights, and ambidextrous thumb safety, 28 oz. Limited mfg. 1999 only.

	$940	$825	$700	$650	$515	$425	$325	$1,044

Add $30 for .40 S&W cal.

PRO CARRY II – 9mm Para. (new mid-2005), .40 S&W (disc. 2001) or .45 ACP cal., 4 in. barrel, SA, features full length grip similar to Custom Model, aluminum frame, steel slide, 7 or 8 shot mag., 28 oz. New 1999.

MSR $919	$825	$725	$625	$525	$450	$350	$295	

MSR	100%	98%	95%	90%	80%	70%	60%	*Last MSR*

Add $50 for 9mm Para. cal.
Add $35 for .40 S&W cal. (disc.).
Add $120 for night sights (.45 ACP cal. only).

This series' nomenclature added the Roman numeral "II" during 2001.

* ***Stainless Pro Carry II*** – similar to Pro Carry, except has stainless steel slide, not available in 9mm Para. cal. New 1999.

MSR $1,016	$900	$800	$700	$600	$500	$400	$300

Add $38 for .40 S&W (disc. 2007) cal.
Add $112 for night sights (.45 ACP cal. only).
Add $295 for Crimson Trace grips (.45 ACP cal. only, disc. 2009).

* ***Pro Carry HD II*** – .38 Super (new 2002) or .45 ACP cal., similar to Pro Carry Stainless, except has heavier stainless steel frame, 35 oz. New 2001.

MSR $1,046	$925	$825	$700	$600	$500	$425	$350

Add $48 for .38 Super cal.

ULTRA CARRY II – .40 S&W (disc. 2001) or .45 ACP cal., 3 in. barrel, SA, aluminum frame, 7 shot mag., 25 oz. New 1999.

MSR $919	$795	$675	$575	$525	$450	$375	$325

Add $120 for night sights.
Add $39 for .40 S&W cal. (disc. 2001).
Add $375 for Crimson Trace grips (disc. 2009).

This series' nomenclature added the Roman numeral "II" during 2001.

* ***Stainless Ultra Carry II*** – 9mm Para. (new 2008), .40 S&W (disc. 2007), and .45 ACP cal., similar to Ultra Carry, except has stainless steel slide. New 1999.

MSR $1,016	$895	$775	$650	$575	$475	$400	$350

Add $50 for 9mm Para. (new 2008) or $45 for .40 S&W cal. (disc. 2007).
Add $109 for night sights (.45 ACP cal. only, disc. 2009).

CLASSIC CARRY PRO – .45 ACP cal., features 4 in. bushingless match grade bull barrel, round heel frame, charcoal blue metal finish, uncheckered bone grips, night sights, front strap checkering, 35 oz. New 2012.

MSR $2,056	$1,825	$1,575	$1,350	$1,150	$950	$825	$700

SUPER CARRY SERIES – .45 ACP cal., 3 (Ultra), 4 (Pro), or 5 (Custom) in. barrel, SA, stainless steel slide, aluminum frame, KimPro II finish, night sights, rounded edges, checkered double diamond wood or Micarta (Ultra+, new 2011) grips, recessed slide stop pin with surrounding bevel, rear slide serrations. New 2010.

MSR $1,596	$1,350	$1,150	$975	$875	$775	$650	$525

* ***Super Carry HD Series*** – .45 ACP cal., 3 (Ultra), 4 (Pro), or 5 (Custom) in. barrel, similar to Super Carry, except has matte black finish and checkered blue/black Micarta grips, 32 oz. New 2011.

MSR $1,699	$1,525	$1,300	$1,100	$950	$825	$700	$575

MASTER CARRY SERIES – .45 ACP cal., 3 (Ultra), 4 (Pro), or 5 (Custom) in. stainless steel barrel, SA, aluminum frame on Carry Pro and Carry Ultra models, stainless steel frame on Carry Custom, black KimPro II finish on slide and satin finish frame, skeletonized trigger, includes Crimson Trace master series laser grips with red beam, round heel frame, tactical wedge night sights, 25-30 oz. New 2013.

MSR $1,568	$1,325	$1,175	$1,025	$900	$775	$650	$550

SOLO CARRY – 9mm Para. cal., micro-compact aluminum frame, DA, SFO, 2.7 in. barrel, 6 or 8 (extended mag.) shot, matte black (Solo Carry) or satin silver (Solo Carry Stainless) KimPro II finish, stainless steel slide and barrel, amidextrous thumb safety, removable grips, amidextrous mag. release, steel sights, 17 oz. New 2011.

MSR $815	$725	$625	$525	$450	$395	$340	$315

* ***Solo CDP (LG)*** – 9mm Para. cal., SFO, matte black aluminum frame with satin stainless steel slide, 6 or 8 shot mag., features fixed 3 dot Tritium night sights and rosewood Crimson Trace laser grips, 17 oz. New late 2011.

MSR $1,223	$1,050	$875	$750	$675	$550	$450	$350

* ***Solo Carry DC*** – 9mm Para. cal., SA, SFO, features black DLC finished slide and barrel, night sights, Carry Melt treatment, 6 shot mag., 17 oz. New 2012.

MSR $904	$825	$750	$675	$600	$550	$500	$450

Add $300 for Crimson Trace laser grips.

MICRO CDP – .380 ACP cal., 2 3/4 in. barrel, SA, 6 shot mag., stainless steel slide and barrel, aluminum frame, 30 LPI front strap checkering, steel dovetail mounted 3-dot night sights, ambidextrous thumb safety, high cut under the trigger guard, double diamond checkered rosewood grips, matte black finish, checkered mainspring housing, 13.4 oz. Built in Kimber Custom Shop. New late 2012.

MSR $951	$800	$700	$600	$550	$450	$360	$280

Add $259 for Crimson Trace laser grips (LG Model).

MSR	100%	98%	95%	90%	80%	70%	60%	Last MSR

MICRO CARRY – .380 ACP cal., SA, stainless steel slide, 2 3/4 in. stainless steel barrel, aluminum frame, all satin or black frame finish, 6 shot mag., steel sights, 15.4 oz. New 2013.

| MSR $651 | $575 | $500 | $450 | $415 | $385 | $350 | $295 | |

Add $18 for all satin finish.

ECLIPSE II SERIES – 10mm (Eclipse Custom II, new 2004) or .45 ACP cal., SA, stainless steel slide and frame, black matte finish with brush polished flat surfaces for elegant two-tone finish, Tritium night sights, target models have adj. bar/dot sights, silver/grey laminated double diamond grips, black small parts, 30 LPI front strap checkering, include Eclipse Ultra II (3 in. barrel, short grip), Eclipse Pro II and Eclipse Pro-Target II (4 in. barrel, standard grip, disc. 2012), Eclipse Custom II, and Eclipse Target II (full size). New 2002.

| MSR $1,289 | $1,150 | $1,000 | $875 | $775 | $625 | $500 | $395 | |

Add $62 for Eclipse Custom II in 10mm cal.

Add $104 for Eclipse Target II or Eclipse Pro-Target II (disc. 2012).

The initial Custom Shop version of these pistols was mfg. during late 2001, featuring an ambidextrous thumb safety, and "Custom Shop" markings on left side of slide, 7,931 were mfg.

CUSTOM TLE II – 10mm (new 2012) or .45 ACP cal., 5 in. barrel, SA, tactical law enforcement pistol (TLE) with exactly the same features as the Kimber pistols carried by LAPD SWAT, black oxide coated frame and slide, same features as Custom II, except has 30 LPI front strap checkering and night sights, approx. 38 oz. New 2003.

* **Custom TLE II** – 9mm Para. (new 2014, TFS Model only), 10mm (new 2013), .45 ACP cal., features 5 in. barrel, black finish, low-profile 3 dot sights, double diamond black synthetic grips, 38 oz.

| MSR $1,080 | $950 | $825 | $700 | $625 | $525 | $425 | $350 | |

Add $73 for TFS Model with threaded barrel (new 2014).

Add $61 for 9mm Para. (new 2014) or 10mm cal. (new 2013).

Add $274 for Crimson Trace laser grips (disc. 2010).

* **Custom TLE/RL II** – 9mm Para. (new 2014), 10mm (new 2013) or .45 ACP cal., similar to Custom TLE II, except has Picatinny rail machined into the frame to accept optics and other tactical accessories. New 2003.

| MSR $1,178 | $1,050 | $925 | $825 | $725 | $600 | $500 | $425 | |

Add $73 for TFS Model with threaded barrel (new 2014).

Add $61 for 9mm Para. (new 2014) or 10mm cal. (new 2013).

* **Stainless TLE II** – .45 ACP cal., similar to TLE II, except has stainless steel slide and frame. New 2004.

| MSR $1,211 | $1,050 | $925 | $800 | $725 | $600 | $500 | $425 | |

* **Stainless TLE/RL II** – .45 ACP cal., similar to Custom TLE/RL II, except is stainless. New 2004.

| MSR $1,323 | $1,150 | $975 | $825 | $750 | $650 | $550 | $450 | |

* **Pro TLE/RL II** – .45 ACP cal., similar to Custom TLE/RL II, except has 4 in. bushingless bull barrel. New 2004.

| MSR $1,248 | $1,075 | $950 | $825 | $725 | $625 | $525 | $425 | |

* **Pro TLE II (LG)** – .45 ACP cal., similar to Custom TLE/RL II, except has 4 in. bushingless bull barrel and Crimson Trace laser grips (disc. 2008 only). Mfg. 2006-2008, reintroduced 2010.

| MSR $1,150 | $995 | $850 | $725 | $650 | $575 | $500 | $425 | |

Subtract $240 if w/o Crimson Trace laser grips (mfg. 2008 only).

* **Stainless Pro TLE II** – .45 ACP cal., similar to Pro TLE II, except is stainless steel, and Crimson Trace laser grips optional.

| MSR $1,253 | $1,075 | $950 | $825 | $725 | $625 | $525 | $425 | |

Add $265 for Crimson Trace laser grips.

* **Stainless Pro TLE/RL II** – .45 ACP cal., similar to Stainless TLE/RL II, except has 4 in. bushingless bull barrel. New 2004.

| MSR $1,379 | $1,225 | $1,050 | $900 | $800 | $700 | $600 | $475 | |

ULTRA TLE II – .45 ACP cal., 3 in. bull barrel, SA, 7 shot mag., dovetail mounted night sights, matte black finish, aluminum frame. New 2010.

| MSR $1,150 | $950 | $825 | $700 | $600 | $500 | $425 | $350 | |

Add $243 for Crimson Trace laser grips.

* **Stainless Ultra TLE II** – .45 ACP cal., similar to Ultra TLE II, except is stainless steel. New 2010.

| MSR $1,253 | $1,075 | $950 | $825 | $725 | $625 | $525 | $425 | |

Add $265 for Crimson Trace laser grips.

TACTICAL II SERIES – 9mm Para. (Tactical Pro II, new 2004) or .45 ACP cal., SA, lightweight tactical pistol, gray anodized (disc. 2008) or gray KimPro II finished frame with black steel slide, fixed tritium 3-dot night sights, extended magazine well, 30 LPI front strap checkering, black/gray laminated logo grips, 7 shot mag. with bumper pad, available

MSR	100%	98%	95%	90%	80%	70%	60%	Last MSR

in Tactical Ultra II (3 in. barrel, short grip, 25 oz.), Tactical Pro II (4 in. barrel, standard grip, 28 oz.), Tactical Custom II (5 in. barrel, standard grip, 31 oz.). Tactical Custom HD II (.45 ACP only, new 2009), or Tactical Entry II (.45 ACP only, includes integral rail and night sights). New 2003.

| MSR $1,317 | $1,125 | $975 | $850 | $725 | $600 | $525 | $450 | |

Add $34 for Tactical Pro II in 9mm Para. cal.

Add $70 for Tactical Custom HD II.

Add $163 for Tactical Entry II.

A Custom Shop version of the Pro Tactical II was manufactured in 2002, but w/o checkering and night sights.

STAINLESS TEN II – .45 ACP cal., SA, high capacity polymer frame, stainless steel slide with satin finish, impressed front grip strap checkering and serrations under trigger guard, textured finish, polymer grip safety and mainspring housing, 10 or 13 (new 2005) round double stack mag., includes Ultra Ten II (3 in. barrel, short grip, disc. 2003), Pro Carry Ten II (4 in. barrel, standard grip), Stainless Ten II (full size), and Gold Match Ten II (stainless steel barrel, polished stainless steel slide flats, hand fitted barrel/bushing to slide, adj. sight), 14 (pre-ban) round mags. also available, accepts magazines from older Kimber mfg. polymer pistols. Mfg. 2002-2007.

| | $715 | $625 | $535 | $485 | $395 | $320 | $250 | *$812* |

Add $9 for Pro-Carry Ten II, $35 for Ultra Ten II (disc. 2003), or $294 for Gold Match Ten II.

* **BP Ten II** – similar to Stainless Ten II, except has black oxide carbon steel slide, and aluminum frame for lighter weight. Mfg. 2003-2007.

| | $570 | $500 | $425 | $385 | $315 | $255 | $200 | *$652* |

* **Pro BP Ten II** – similar to Pro Carry Ten II, except has black oxide carbon steel slide, and aluminum frame for lighter weight. Mfg. 2003-2007.

| | $570 | $500 | $425 | $385 | $315 | $255 | $200 | *$666* |

CDP II (CUSTOM DEFENSE PACKAGE) SERIES – 9mm Para. (new 2008), .40 S&W (disc. 2007), or .45 ACP cal., Custom Shop pistol featuring tritium night sights, stainless steel slide with black anodized aluminum frame, 3 in. (Ultra CDP II, 25 oz.), Ultra+ (3-inch barrel with full length grip, new 2011), 4 in. (Pro CDP II and Compact CDP II, 28 oz.), or 5 in. (Custom CDP II, 31 oz.) barrel, SA, carry bevel treatment, ambidextrous thumb safety, double diamond pattern checkered rosewood grips, 30 LPI checkered front strap and under trigger guard (new 2003), two-tone finish. New 2000.

| MSR $1,331 | $1,150 | $1,000 | $875 | $775 | $625 | $525 | $400 | |

Add $28 for 9mm Para cal. (new 2008).

Add $300 for Crimson Trace laser grips (new 2010).

Add $40 for .40 S&W cal., available in either Ultra CDP II or Pro CDP II configuration (disc. 2007).

The Pro CDP II has a full length grip frame.

This series' nomenclature added the Roman numeral "II" during 2001.

ULTRA TEN CDP II – .45 ACP cal., tritium night sights, stainless steel slide with black polymer frame, 3 in. barrel, SA, carry bevel treatment, standard manual safety, 10 shot mag., 24 oz. Mfg. 2003 only.

| | $825 | $720 | $620 | $560 | $455 | $370 | $290 | *$926* |

RAPTOR II – .45 ACP cal., SA, full size carbon steel or stainless steel (new 2008) frame with "scales" on front strap, continuing on slide in lieu of standard serrations, flats on frame and slide polished, black oxide finish, back cut flat-top, 5 in. stainless barrel with engraved "Raptor II" and "Custom Shop", black anodized trigger, ambidextrous safety, scaled Zebra wood grip panels with Kimber logo, fixed slant night sights, 38 oz. New mid-2004.

| MSR $1,434 | $1,250 | $1,075 | $925 | $800 | $700 | $600 | $475 | |

Add $134 for stainless steel frame (new 2008).

PRO RAPTOR II – .45 ACP cal., SA, full size stainless steel frame with "scales" on front strap, continuing on carbon steel slide in lieu of standard serrations, flats on frame and slide polished, black oxide finish, back cut flat-top, 4 in. stainless barrel with engraved "Pro Raptor II" and "Custom Shop", black anodized trigger, ambidextrous safety, scaled Zebra wood grip panels with Kimber logo, fixed slant night sights, 38 oz. New mid-2004.

| MSR $1,295 | $1,100 | $975 | $850 | $725 | $600 | $500 | $450 | |

Add $120 for Stainless Pro Rapter II (new 2009).

ULTRA RAPTOR II – .45 ACP cal., all-matte black finish, 3 in. ramped bushingless barrel, SA, lightweight aluminum frame, scale serrations on flat-top slide and frontstrap, feathered logo wood grips, flats on frame and slide polished, night sights, mfg. by Custom Shop. New 2006.

| MSR $1,295 | $1,100 | $975 | $850 | $725 | $600 | $525 | $450 | |

Add $120 for Stainless Ultra Raptor II.

GRAND RAPTOR II – .45 ACP cal., SA, full-size stainless steel frame, blued slide, flats on frame and slide polished, two-tone finish, scale rosewood grips with Kimber logo, extended ambidextrous thumb safety, bumped beavertail grip safety, night sights, mfg. by Custom Shop. New 2006.

| MSR $1,657 | $1,425 | $1,250 | $1,050 | $925 | $800 | $675 | $525 | |

MSR	100%	98%	95%	90%	80%	70%	60%	Last MSR

WARRIOR – .45 ACP cal., SA, production began following adoption of this pistol by the Marine Expeditionary Unit (MEU) Special Operations Capable (SOC), Detachment 1 (Det. 1), civilian version with 5 in. barrel, Series I (no firing pin block), carbon steel slide and frame, integral Picatinny light rail, internal extractor, lanyard loop, bumped grip safety, G-10 material grip (coyote brown), wedge night sights, ambidextrous safety, GI length (standard) guide rod finished in black KimPro II, 38 oz. New mid-2004.

MSR $1,512	$1,325	$1,150	$975	$850	$725	$600	$550	

* ***Warrior SOC*** – .45 ACP cal., tan/green KimPro II finish, features lower front rail with removable Desert Tan Crimson Trace Rail Master laser sight, ambidextrous thumb safety, lanyard ring, textured G10 grips, 40 oz. New 2013.

MSR $1,665	$1,495	$1,300	$1,100	$1,025	$900	$775	$650	

DESERT WARRIOR – .45 ACP cal., similar to Warrior, except has Dark Earth KimPro II metal finish and light tan G-10 grips. New mid-2005.

MSR $1,512	$1,325	$1,125	$950	$825	$700	$600	$500	

COVERT II SERIES – .45 ACP cal., 3 (Ultra Covert II), 4 (Pro Covert II), or 5 (Custom Covert II) in. bushingless barrel in 3 and 4 in. models, SA, Custom Covert II has Kimber logo and digital camo pattern, carry bevel treatment, 30 LPI front strap checkering, night sights, Desert Tan finish, matte black oxide slide, approx. 25-30 oz. New 2007.

MSR $1,657	$1,495	$1,300	$1,100	$1,025	$900	$775	$650	

SIS SERIES – .45 ACP cal., SA, stainless steel slide, frame, and serrated mainspring housing, 7 or 8 shot mag., 3 (Ultra), 4 (Pro), or 5 (Custom or Custom RL) in. barrel, SIS night sights, cocking shoulder for one-hand cocking, lightweight hammer, solid trigger, slide serrations, gray KimPro II finish, beavertail grip safety, stippled black laminate logo grips, ambidextrous thumb safety, choice of rounded frame and mainspring housing (SIS Ultra), Picatinny rail (SIS Pro & Custom RL), standard length guide rod (Custom & Custom RL), 31-39 oz. Mfg. 2008-2009.

	$1,250	$1,095	$935	$850	$685	$560	$435	$1,427

Add $95 for SIS Custom RL model with standard length guide rod and Picatinny rail.

AEGIS II SERIES – 9mm Para. cal., 3 (Ultra), 4 (Pro), or 5 (Custom) in. barrel, SA, 8 or 9 shot mag., aluminum frame w/satin silver premium KimPro II finish, matte black slide, thin rosewood grips, 30 LPI front strap checkering, high relief cut under trigger guard, Tactical Wedge night sights, bumped and grooved grip safety, hammer, thumb safety and mag. release button are bobbed, carry melt treatment on both frame and slide, 25 oz. New 2006.

MSR $1,331	$1,125	$975	$850	$725	$625	$525	$450	

ULTRA RCP II – .45 ACP cal., SA, (Refined Carry Pistol), black anodized frame, carry melt treatment, matte black slide with premium KimPro II finish, no sights, bobbed mag. release, hammer, beavertail grip safety and thumb safety, round mainspring housing and rear of frame, thin black micarta grip panels, older mfg. had distinctive "hook" on hammer, new mfg. has straight hammer, 25 oz. Mfg. 2003-2005 by Custom Shop, reintroduced 2007.

MSR $1,351	$1,150	$975	$850	$725	$625	$525	$450	

CRIMSON CARRY II – .45 ACP cal., SA, satin silver aluminum frame, 3 (Ultra), 4 (Pro), or 5 (Custom) in. barrel, matte black slide with black sights, shortened slide stop pin, beveled frame, rosewood Crimson Trace laser grips. New mid-2008.

MSR $1,206	$1,050	$900	$800	$700	$600	$500	$400	

Add $87 for Crimson Trace laser grips with green beam (new 2013).

Pistols: Kimber Non-Cataloged Models

Over the years, Kimber has manufactured a number of models that did not appear in their catalog. To help identify non-cataloged models, pistols are listed in two categories: Custom Shop/Special Edition Pistols and Limited Edition Pistols.

Pistols: Kimber Custom Shop/Special Editions, Single Action

Beginning in 1998, the Kimber Custom Shop began producing special edition pistols. Special edition models have been issued in either fixed numbers, or time limited. Where available, time limited models show the actual number produced. All models are .45 ACP caliber unless otherwise specified.

ROYAL CARRY – compact aluminum frame, 4 in. bushingless barrel, highly polished blue, night sights, ambidextrous safety, hand checkered rosewood grips, 28 oz. 600 mfg. 1998.

Last MSR was $903.

GOLD GUARDIAN – highly polished stainless steel slide and frame, hand fitted 5 in. match barrel and bushing, tritium night sights, ambidextrous safety, extended magazine well, skeletonized match trigger, hand checkered rosewood grips, 38 oz. 300 mfg. 1998.

Last MSR was $1,350.

ELITE CARRY – black anodized compact aluminum frame, stainless slide, 4 in. barrel, meltdown treatment on slide and frame, tritium night sights, 20 LPI checkered front strap, ambidextrous safety, aluminum match trigger, hand checkered rosewood grips, 28 oz. 1,200 mfg. 1998.

Last MSR was $1,019.

MSR	100%	98%	95%	90%	80%	70%	60%	Last MSR

STAINLESS COVERT – meltdown stainless slide and frame finished in silver KimPro, 4 in. barrel, 30 LPI front strap checkering, 3-dot tritium night sights, hand checkered rosewood grips, 34 oz. 1,000 mfg. 1999.

Last MSR was $1,135.

PRO ELITE – aluminum frame with silver KimPro finish, stainless slide with black KimPro finish, full meltdown treatment on slide and frame, 4 in. barrel, 30 LPI front strap checkering, 3-dot tritium night sights, hand checkered rosewood grips, 28 oz. 2,500 mfg. 1999.

Last MSR was $1,140.

ULTRA ELITE – aluminum frame with black KimPro finish, satin stainless slide, full meltdown treatment on slide and frame, 3 in. barrel, 30 LPI front strap checkering, 3-dot tritium night sights, hand checkered rosewood grips, 25 oz. 2,750 mfg. 1999.

Last MSR was $1,085.

HERITAGE EDITION – black oxide steel frame and slide, 30 LPI front strap checkering, ambidextrous safety, premium aluminum trigger, NSSF Heritage medallion and special markings on slide, ser. no. begins with KHE, 38 oz. 1,041 mfg. 2000.

Last MSR was $1,065.

STAINLESS GOLD MATCH SE II – .38 Super or .45 ACP cal., stainless steel frame and slide, 5 in. barrel, serrated flat-top slide, 30 LPI front strap checkering, hand checkered rosewood grips, ambidextrous safety, polished flats, ser. no. begins with KSO, 38 oz. 260 (.38 Super) and 294 (.45 ACP) mfg. 2001.

Last MSR was $1,487.

Add $88 for .38 Super cal.

ULTRA SHADOW II – black steel slide and anodized aluminum frame, 3 in. barrel, fixed tritium night sights, 30 LPI front strap checkering, grey laminate grips, silver grip and thumb safeties and mainspring housing, ser. no. begins with KUSLE, 25 oz.

Last MSR was $949.

PRO SHADOW II – black steel slide and anodized aluminum frame, 4 in. barrel, fixed tritium night sights, 30 LPI front strap checkering, grey laminate grips, silver grip and thumb safeties and mainspring housing, ser. no. begins with KPSLE, 28 oz.

Last MSR was $949.

ULTRA CDP ELITE II – .45 ACP cal., first Kimber .45 pistols with ramped match grade barrels, black anodized aluminum frame, black oxide carbon steel slide, 3 in. barrel, carry melt treatment for rounded and blended edges, Meprolight 3-dot tritium night sights, 30 LPI checkering on front strap and under trigger guard, ambidextrous thumb safety and charcoal/ruby laminated logo grips, 25 oz. Mfg. 2002-Jan., 2003.

Last MSR was $1,216.

ULTRA CDP ELITE STS II – .45 ACP cal., first Kimber .45 pistols with ramped match grade barrels, silver anodized aluminum frame, satin stainless steel slide, 3 in. barrel, carry melt treatment for rounded and blended edges, Meprolight 3-dot tritium night sights, 30 LPI checkering on front strap and under trigger guard, ambidextrous thumb safety and charcoal/ruby laminated logo grips, 25 oz. Mfg. 2002-Jan. 2003.

Last MSR was $1,155.

ULTRA SP II – special anodized frame colors (black/blue, black/red, and black/silver) with black oxide slide, 7 shot mag., 3 in. bushingless barrel, 3-dot sights, carry melt, ball milled micarta grips, standard fixed sights, 25 oz. Mfg. 2003-2005.

MSR	100%	98%	95%	90%	80%	70%	60%	Last MSR
	$1,025	$900	$800	$725	$625	$575	$495	*$1,175*

25th ANNIVERSARY CUSTOM LIMITED EDITION – .45 ACP cal., black oxide frame and slide, 5 in. barrel, premium aluminum trigger, fancy walnut anniversary logo grips, "1979-2004" engraving on slide, Series I safeties and traditional extractor, ser. no. range is KAPC0001-KAPC1911. Limited production of 1,911 during 2004-2005.

MSR	100%	98%	95%	90%	80%	70%	60%	Last MSR
	$825	$725	$650	$575	$500	$425	$350	*$923*

* ***25th Anniversary Custom Limited Edition Gold Match*** – blued frame and slide, deep polish on flats, 5 in. stainless barrel, premium aluminum trigger, ambidextrous safety, adj. sights, fancy walnut anniversary logo grips, "1979-2004" engraving in slide, Series I safeties and traditional extractor, ser. no. range KAPG0001-KAPG0500, 38 oz. Limited production of 500 during 2004-2005.

MSR	100%	98%	95%	90%	80%	70%	60%	Last MSR
	$1,175	$995	$875	$775	$700	$625	$550	*$1,357*

* ***25th Anniversary Custom Limited Edition Pistol Set*** – includes one Custom (ser. no. range KMSC0001-KMSC250) and one Gold Match (ser. no. range KMSG0001 - KMSG250), matched ser. nos., wood presentation case. Limited production of 250 during 2004-2005.

MSR	100%	98%	95%	90%	80%	70%	60%	Last MSR
	$2,250	$2,000	$1,775	$1,525	$1,300	$1,100	$900	*$2,620*

CENTENNIAL EDITION – .45 ACP cal., steel frame with finish by Turnbull Restoration, ivory grips, adj. target sights, light scroll engraving, aluminum trigger, includes presentation case, Limited mfg. of 250 during 2010.

MSR	100%	98%	95%	90%	80%	70%	60%	Last MSR
	$3,995	$3,650	$3,275	N/A	N/A	N/A	N/A	*$4,352*

MSR	100%	98%	95%	90%	80%	70%	60%	Last MSR

SAPPHIRE ULTRA II – 9mm Para. cal., 3 in. barrel, G10 grips, polished stainless steel slide and small parts feature a bright blue PVD finish with fine engraved border accents, rounded heel, ambidextrous thumb safety, Tactical Wedge nightsights. New 2012.

| MSR $1,652 | $1,425 | $1,200 | $1,000 | $875 | $750 | $650 | $550 | |

Pistols: Kimber Limited Editions, Single Action

Kimber has produced limited runs of pistols for dealer groups, NRA, sporting goods stores, law enforcement agencies, special requests, etc. Limited run pistols can be as small as 25 mfg.

PRO CARRY SLE – all stainless steel slide and frame, 4 in. barrel, identicial to Stainless Pro Carry Model, except has stainless frame, mfg. for Kimber Master Dealers, cataloged in 2001, later production known as Pro Carry HD II, 1,329 mfg. during 2000.

Last MSR was $815.

PRO COMBAT – black oxide stainless steel frame and slide, 4 in. barrel, ambidextrous safety, tritium 3-dot night sights, match grade aluminum trigger, 30 LPI front strap checkering, hand checkered rosewood grips, 35 oz. Marketed by RGuns. 52 mfg. 2000.

Last MSR was $860.

TARGET ELITE II – two-tone stainless frame and slide, black oxide coating on frame, slide natural stainless, adj. rear sight, rosewood double diamond grips, sold through stores affiliated with Sports Inc. buying group, 38 oz. 220 mfg. 2001.

Last MSR was $950.

CUSTOM DEFENDER II – two-tone stainless frame and slide, black oxide coating on frame, slide natural stainless, fixed low profile rear sight, double diamond rosewood grips, sold only through stores affiliated with National Buying Service, 38 oz. 290 mfg. 2001.

Last MSR was $839.

CUSTOM ECLIPSE II – stainless slide and frame, 5 in. barrel, black oxide finish brush polished on the flats, 30 LPI front strap checkering, adj. night sights, laminated grey grips, ser. no. begins with KEL, 38 oz. 4,522 mfg. 2001.

Last MSR was $1,121.

PRO ECLIPSE II – stainless steel frame and slide, 4 in. barrel, black oxide finish brush polished on the flats, 30 LPI front strap checkering, fixed 3-dot night sights, laminated grey grips, ambidextrous safety, ser. no. begins with KRE, 35 oz. 2,207 mfg. 2001.

Last MSR was $1,065.

ULTRA ECLIPSE II – stainless steel frame and slide, 3 in. barrel, black oxide finish brush polished on the flats, 30 LPI front strap checkering, fixed 3-dot night sights, laminated grey grips, ambidextrous safety, 34 oz. 1,202 mfg. 2001.

Last MSR was $1,054.

STRYKER TEN II – Ultra Ten II with black polymer frame and frame insert and small parts, natural stainless slide, 25 oz. 200 mfg. 2002.

Last MSR was $850.

LAPD SWAT – black oxide coated stainless frame and slide, 5 in. barrel, low profile Meprolight 3-dot night sights, 30 LPI front strap checkering, black rubber double diamond grips, 38 oz. 300 mfg. 2002.

Following extensive testing to select a duty pistol, LAPD SWAT chose a Kimber Stainless Custom II and had it enhanced to their specifications. This model was made strictly for law enforcement and not sold to the public. A civilian version called the Tactical law Enforcement (TLE) Series went into production in 2003. Pistols marked "LAPD SWAT" were not sold to the public.

NRA EPOCH II – stainless slide and frame, 5 in. barrel, black oxide finish brush polished on flats, 30 LPI front strap checkering, standard safety, fixed tritium night sights, laminated grey grips, ser. no. begins with KNRAE, Friends of NRA pistol available only at NRA banquets, 38 oz. 58 mfg. 2002.

This model had no established MSR.

THE BOSS II – limited edition to commemorate Blythe Sports 50th anniversary, stainless steel slide and frame, carry melt treatment, fixed white dot sights, premium aluminum 2 hole trigger, 5 in. barrel, engraved "The BOSS II" on ejection port side, and "SPECIAL EDITION", black and sliver laminate grips with Blythe 50th anniversary logo in center on white insert, ser. no. KBSS000-KBSS024, 25 mfg.

This model had no established MSR.

ECLIPSE CLE II – 5 in. barrel, Eclipse Custom II finish on slide with black over stainless frame (no front strap checkering), charcoal/ruby Kimber logo grips, sold only through stores affiliated with National Buying Service, 38 oz. 271 mfg. 2003.

Last MSR was $917.

* **Eclipse PLE II** – similar to Eclipse CLE II, except has 4 in. bushingless barrel, sold only through stores affiliated with Sports Inc. buying group, 35 oz. 232 mfg. 2003.

Last MSR was $877.

MSR	100%	98%	95%	90%	80%	70%	60%	Last MSR

* Eclipse ULE II – Eclipse Ultra II finish on slide with black over stainless frame (no front strap checkering), 3 in. bushingless barrel, charcoal/ruby Kimber logo grips, sold only through stores affiliated with National Buying Service, 34 oz. 227 mfg. 2003.

Last MSR was $890.

TEAM MATCH II 38 SUPER – .38 Super cal., identical to original Team Match II, with .38 Super ramped barrel, match grade chamber, bushing and trigger group, special Team Match features, including 30 LPI checkered front strap, adj. sight, extended magazine well, premium aluminum trigger and red, white, and blue USA Shooting Team logo grips, 38 oz. Mfg. 2003-2004.

	100%	98%	95%	90%	80%	70%	60%	Last MSR
	$1,150	$995	$875	$775	$675	$575	$475	$1,352

MCSOCOM ICQB (2004) – .45 ACP cal., at the request of the Marine Corps Special Operations Command (MCSOCOM) Detachment 1 (Det. 1), Kimber produced Interim Close Quarters Battle (ICQB) 1911 patterned pistols in accordance with very high specific requirements: steel frame and slide finished in matte black, internal extractor, GI length guide rod and plug, light rail, bumped grip safety and ambidextrous manual safety, lanyard loop, Simonich G-10 "Gunner" grips, and Novak Lo-Mount night sights.

There was no MSR on this model, as it was not available for sale to the general public.

The civilian version of this pistol is called the Warrior.

TARGET MATCH – .45 ACP cal., oversized 5 in. stainless steel barrel, matte black frame and slide with brush polished flats, high relief cut under trigger guard, wide cocking serrations, solid match trigger, engraved bullseye inlaid burl walnut logo grips, 30 LPI checkering on front strap and under trigger guard, special ser. no. starting with "KTM", 38 oz. 1,000 mfg. 2006-2009.

	100%	98%	95%	90%	80%	70%	60%	Last MSR
	$1,215	$1,025	$875	$775	$700	$600	$500	$1,427

CLASSIC TARGET II – .45 ACP cal., two-tone stainless steel frame, matte black oxide slide, no cocking serrations, adj. sights, premium match grade trigger, smooth/stippled logo grips, match grade chamber, barrel, and barrel bushing, 38 oz. Sold exclusively through Gander Mountain. Mfg. 2006-2008.

	100%	98%	95%	90%	80%	70%	60%	Last MSR
	$825	$675	$555	$460	$395	$350	$300	$999

FRANKLIN CUSTOM II – similar to Custom II, silver finished slide stop, bushing, mag. release, grip safety and mainspring housing, red, white and blue laminate grips with Franklin's Gun Shop logo, commemorates 44th anniversary of Franklin's Gun Shop, ser. no. KFGS01 - KFGS50, 50 mfg. 2006.

This model had no established MSR.

RIFLES: BOLT ACTION

Centerfire Models

The models listed feature a Mauser style action with controlled round feeding and extraction.

MODEL 84M LPT (LIGHT POLICE TACTICAL) – .223 Rem. or .308 Win. cal., 24 in. matte blue heavy sporter contour fluted barrel, 5 shot mag., black laminate stock with panel stippling, Picatinny rail, oversize bolt handle, sling swivels, recoil pad, full length Mauser claw extractor, 3-position Model 70 style safety, adj. trigger, 8 lbs., 7 oz. New 2008.

	100%	98%	95%	90%	80%	70%	60%	Last MSR
MSR $1,495	$1,295	$1,075	$925	$825	$725	$625	$500	

MODEL 8400 TACTICAL SERIES – .300 Win. Mag. or .308 Win. cal., matte blue (Tactical) or KimPro II Dark Earth (Advanced Tactical) finish, grey (Tactical) or Desert Camo (Advanced Tactical) McMillan synthetic stock, 24 in. fluted bull barrel, 5 shot mag., 9 lbs., 4 oz. Mfg. 2007-2013.

	100%	98%	95%	90%	80%	70%	60%	Last MSR
	$1,675	$1,450	$1,250	$1,125	$900	$750	$575	$1,971

Add $680 for Advanced Tactical with desert tan or black Pelican case.

MODEL 8400 ADVANCED TACTICAL II – .308 Win. or .300 Win. Mag. cal., match grade stainless steel threaded barrel with SureFire muzzle brake, full-length Mauser claw extractor, controlled round feeding, Manners MCS-TF4 folding stock with adj. comb, oversized bolt knob and extended bolt handle, upper and lower Picatinny rails, 5 or 10 shot detachable box mag., Desert Tan finish. New 2014.

	100%	98%	95%	90%	80%	70%	60%	Last MSR
MSR $4,351	$3,695	$3,235	$2,775	$2,515	$2,025	$1,675	$1,295	

* Model 8400 Advanced Tactical SOC – .308 Win. or .300 Win. Mag. cal., similar to Model 8400 Advanced Tactical II, except has adj. aluminum folding stock and two forend rails. New 2014.

	100%	98%	95%	90%	80%	70%	60%	Last MSR
MSR $4,419	$3,750	$3,275	$2,825	$2,550	$2,075	$1,695	$1,325	

MODEL 8400 PATROL/POLICE TACTICAL – .300 Win. Mag. or .308 Win. (new 2010) cal., features 20 (Patrol), 24, or 26 in. match grade barrel, chamber, and trigger, trued bolt face, custom McMillan glass bedded stock, fixed Picatinny rail, enlarged bolt handle and knob, 8 3/4 lbs. Mfg. 2009-2013.

	100%	98%	95%	90%	80%	70%	60%	Last MSR
	$1,325	$1,160	$995	$900	$725	$595	$475	$1,495

MSR	100%	98%	95%	90%	80%	70%	60%	Last MSR

MODEL 8400 PATROL TACTICAL – .308 Win. or .300 Win. Mag. cal., match grade stainless steel fluted barrel, full-length Mauser claw extractor, controlled round feeding, Manners MCS-T6 reinforced carbon fiber black synthetic stock with squared forend and grooved forearm, vertical pistol grip, ambidextrous palm swell, oversized bolt knob and extended bolt handle, top rail, 5 or 10 shot detachable box mag. New 2014.

| MSR $2,447 | $2,075 | $1,825 | $1,550 | $1,400 | $1,150 | $935 | $725 | |

KIMEL INDUSTRIES, INC.

Previously manufactured until late 1994 by A.A. Arms located in Monroe, NC. Previously distributed by Kimel Industries, Inc. located in Matthews, NC.

CARBINES: SEMI-AUTO

AR-9 CARBINE – 9mm Para. cal., carbine variation of the AP-9 with 16 1/2 in. barrel, 20 shot mag., and steel rod folding stock. Mfg. 1991-94.

| | $625 | $550 | $475 | $425 | $365 | $315 | $275 | $384 |

PISTOLS: SEMI-AUTO

AP-9 PISTOL – 9mm Para. cal., SA, blowback operation, bolt knob on left side of receiver, 5 in. barrel with vent. shroud, front mounted 10 (C/B 1994) or 20* shot detachable mag., black matte finish, adj. front sight, 3 lbs. 7 oz. Mfg. 1989-1994.

| | $475 | $425 | $375 | $325 | $300 | $275 | $250 | $279 |

* **AP-9 Pistol Mini** – compact variation of the AP-9 Model with 3 in. barrel, blue or nickel finish. Mfg. 1991-94.

| | $550 | $500 | $425 | $375 | $325 | $300 | $275 | $273 |

* **AP-9 Pistol Target** – target variation of the AP-9 with 12 in. match barrel with shroud, blue finish only. Mfg. 1991-94.

| | $600 | $550 | $475 | $425 | $375 | $350 | $325 | $294 |

* **P-95 Pistol** – similar to AP-9, except without barrel shroud and is supplied with 5 shot mag., parts are interchangeable with AP-9. Mfg. 1990-91 only.

| | $395 | $350 | $300 | $250 | $200 | $175 | $150 | $250 |

KING'S ARSENAL

Current manufacturer established in 2011 and located in Abilene, TX.

RIFLES: SEMI-AUTO

Add $110 for Samson Quad Rail.
Add $99 for custom barrel fluting.
Add $75 for bull barrel.
Add $75 for 6.8 SPC or 6.5 Grendel cal.
Add $49 for nickel boron bolt carrier group coating.

CROWN 15 BASE MODEL – 5.56 NATO, 6.8 SPC, or 6.5 Grendel cal., GIO, 16, 18, or 20 in. barrel, lightweight or midweight, King's Arsenal upper and lower, M4 collapsible stock with A2 grip, A2 flash hider, 15 in. Samson Evo handguard or 12.4 in. Quad Rail.

| MSR $1,785 | $1,525 | $1,335 | $1,150 | $1,035 | $840 | $685 | $535 | |

Add $109 for Magpul CTR stock.

CROWN 15 KUSTOM MODEL – 5.56 NATO, 6.8 SPC, 6.5 Grendel, or .300 Blackout cal., GIO, 16, 18, or 20 in. Noveske stainless steel barrel, lightweight or midweight, King's Arsenal upper and lower, Geissele SSA trigger, Magpul CTR stock, King's Arsenal grip, A2 flash hider, 15 in. Samson Evo handguard or 12.4 in. Quad Rail.

| MSR $2,285 | $1,995 | $1,750 | $1,475 | $1,325 | $1,075 | $880 | $685 | |

Add $75 for Noveske Switchblock.
Add $75 for .300 Blackout cal.
Add $165 for Geissele SD3G trigger.

KINTREK, INC.

Previous rifle manufacturer located in Owensboro, KY.

RIFLES: SEMI-AUTO

BULLPUP MODEL – .22 LR cal., bullpup configuration, hinged dust cover, clear Ram-Line type coil spring mag., black synthetic thumbhole stock, A-2 type front/rear sight. Disc.

| | $350 | $300 | $250 | $225 | $200 | $175 | $150 | |

MSR	100%	98%	95%	90%	80%	70%	60%	Last MSR

KNIGHT'S ARMAMENT COMPANY

Current manufacturer established in 1983, and located in Titusville, FL. Previously located in Vero Beach, FL. Dealer and consumer direct sales.

RIFLES: SEMI-AUTO

Some of the models listed were also available in pre-ban configurations. SR-25 Enhanced Match model has 10 or 20 shot mag. Some of the following models, while discontinued for civilian use, may still be available for military/law enforcement.

STONER SR-15 M-5 RIFLE – .223 Rem. cal., GIO, 20 in. standard weight barrel, flip-up low profile rear sight, two-stage target trigger, 7.6 lbs. Mfg. 1997-2008.

	100%	98%	95%	90%	80%	70%	60%	Last MSR
	$1,775	$1,550	$1,300	$1,100	$900	$825	$725	$1,837

* Stoner SR-15 M-4 Carbine – .223 Rem. cal., similar to SR-15 rifle, except has 16 in. barrel, choice of fixed synthetic or non-collapsible buttstock. Mfg. 1997-2005.

	100%	98%	95%	90%	80%	70%	60%	Last MSR
	$1,495	$1,250	$1,050	$925	$825	$725	$625	$1,575

Add $100 for non-collapsible buttstock (SR-15 M-4 K-Carbine, disc. 2001).

* Stoner SR-15 URX E3 Carbine – .223 Rem. cal., GIO, features 16 in. free floating barrel with URX forearm, E3 type rounded lug improved bolt. New 2004.

MSR $2,207	100%	98%	95%	90%	80%	70%	60%	Last MSR
	$2,200	$1,925	$1,650	$1,500	$1,225	$1,000	$775	

STONER SR-15 MATCH RIFLE – .223 Rem. cal., GIO, features flat-top upper receiver with 20 in. match grade stainless steel free floating barrel with RAS forend, two-stage match trigger, 7.9 lbs. Mfg. 1997-2008.

	100%	98%	95%	90%	80%	70%	60%	Last MSR
	$1,850	$1,625	$1,375	$1,150	$950	$850	$750	$1,972

STONER SR-25 SPORTER – .308 Win. cal., GIO, 20 in. lightweight barrel, AR-15 configuration with carrying handle, 5, 10, or 20 (disc. per C/B 1994) shot detachable mag., less than 2 MOA guaranteed, non-glare finish, 8.8 lbs. Mfg. 1993-97.

	100%	98%	95%	90%	80%	70%	60%	Last MSR
	$2,650	$2,250	$1,900	$1,600	$1,300	$1,000	$850	$2,995

* Stoner RAS Sporter Carbine (SR-25 Carbine) – .223 Rem. cal., GIO, 16 in. free floating barrel, grooved non-slip handguard, removable carrying handle, 7 3/4 lbs. Mfg. 1995-2005.

	100%	98%	95%	90%	80%	70%	60%	Last MSR
	$3,100	$2,650	$2,200	$1,800	$1,500	$1,250	$1,000	$3,495

Subtract 15% if w/o RAS.

In 2003, the Rail Adapter System (RAS) became standard on this model.

SR-25 STANDARD MATCH – .308 Win. cal., GIO, free-floating 24 in. match barrel, fiberglass stock, includes commercial gun case and 10 shot mag. Disc. 2008.

	100%	98%	95%	90%	80%	70%	60%	Last MSR
	$3,600	$3,300	$2,950	$2,600	$2,300	$2,000	$1,600	$3,918

SR-25 RAS MATCH – .308 Win. cal., similar to SR-25 Standard, except has 24 in. free floating match barrel and flat-top receiver, less than 1 MOA guaranteed, RAS became standard 2004, 10 3/4 lbs. Mfg. 1993-2008.

	100%	98%	95%	90%	80%	70%	60%	Last MSR
	$3,350	$2,800	$2,300	$1,800	$1,500	$1,250	$1,000	$3,789

Subtract approx. 15% if w/o Rail Adapter System (RAS).

Over 3,000 SR-25s were mfg.

* SR-25 RAS Match Lightweight – .308 Win. cal., GIO, features 20 in. medium contour free floating barrel, 9 1/2 lbs. Mfg. 1995-2004.

	100%	98%	95%	90%	80%	70%	60%	Last MSR
	$2,950	$2,550	$2,175	$1,700	$1,400	$1,200	$995	$3,244

Add approx. 15% for Rail Adapter System.

SR-25 ENHANCED MATCH RIFLE/CARBINE – .308 Win. cal., GIO, 16 or 20 in. barrel, 10 or 20 shot mag., URX rail system, two-stage trigger, ambidextrous mag. release, integrated adj. folding front sight, micro adj. folding rear sight, EM gas block, combat trigger guard, chrome plated multi-lug bolt and bolt carrier, fixed or nine position adj. stock, black anodized finish, flash hider (carbine only), approx. 8 1/2 lbs. Disc. 2013.

	100%	98%	95%	90%	80%	70%	60%	Last MSR
	$4,750	$4,375	$3,750	$3,400	$2,750	$2,250	$1,750	$4,994

Add $625 for 16 in. carbine.

SR-25 MK11 MOD O CIVILIAN DELUXE SYSTEM PACKAGE – .308 Win. cal., GIO, consumer variation of the Navy Model Mark Eleven, Mod O, w/o sound suppressor, includes Leupold 3.5-10X scope, 20 in. military grade match barrel, backup sights, cell-foam case and other accessories. Mfg. 2003-2008.

	100%	98%	95%	90%	80%	70%	60%	Last MSR
	$7,950	$7,250	$6,350	$5,850	$5,100	$4,500	$4,000	$8,534

SR-25 MK11 MATCH RIFLE – .308 Win. cal., GIO, includes MK11 Mod O features and 20 in. heavy barrel. Mfg. 2004-2008.

	100%	98%	95%	90%	80%	70%	60%	Last MSR
	$5,675	$5,200	$4,775	$4,400	$3,750	$3,150	$2,700	$6,325

MSR	100%	98%	95%	90%	80%	70%	60%	*Last MSR*

SR-25 MK11 CARBINE – .308 Win. cal., GIO, includes MK11 Mod O features and 16 in. match grade stainless steel barrel with muzzle brake, URX 4x4 rail forend, 4-position buttstock. Mfg. 2005-2013.

| | $6,350 | $5,800 | $5,200 | $4,700 | $3,950 | $3,400 | $2,850 | *$6,636* |

SR-25 BR CARBINE – .308 Win. cal., similar to SR-25 MK11 Carbine, except has chrome lined steel barrel. Mfg. 2005-2008.

| | $5,675 | $5,200 | $4,775 | $4,400 | $3,750 | $3,150 | $2,700 | *$6,307* |

SR-M110 SASS – 7.62x51mm cal., GIO, 20 in. military match grade barrel, full RAS treatment on barrel, civilian variation of the Army's semi-auto sniper rifle system, includes Leupold long-range tactical scope, 600 meter back up iron sights, system case and other accessories. Mfg. 2006-2009.

| | $13,000 | $11,000 | $9,500 | $8,000 | $7,000 | $6,000 | $5,000 | *$14,436* |

"DAVID TUBB" COMPETITION MATCH RIFLE – .260 Rem. or .308 Win. cal., GIO, incorporates refinements by David Tubb, top-of-the-line competition match rifle, including adj. and rotating buttstock pad. Mfg. 1998 only.

| | $5,200 | $4,000 | $3,600 | $3,150 | $2,700 | $2,300 | $1,995 | *$5,995* |

STONER SR-50 – .50 BMG cal., GIO, features high strength materials and lightweight design, fully locked breech and two lug rotary breech bolt, horizontal 5 shot box mag., tubular receiver supports a removable barrel, approx. 31 lbs. Limited mfg. 2000, non-commercial sales only.

Last MSR was $6,995

Extreme rarity factor precludes accurate pricing on this model.

KORRIPHILA

Previous trademark manufactured until 2004 by Intertex, located in Eislingen, Germany. Previously imported 1999-2004 by Korriphila, Inc., located in Pineville, NC., and by Osborne's located in Cheboygan, MI until 1988.

PISTOLS: SEMI-AUTO

Less than 30 Korriphila pistols were made annually.

HSP 701 – 7.65 Luger, .38 Super, 9mm Para., 9mm Police, 9mm Steyr, .45 ACP, or 10mm Norma cal., DA/SA, Budischowsky delayed roller block locking system assists in recoil reduction, 40% stainless steel parts, 4 or 5 in. barrel, blue or satin finish, walnut grips, 7 or 9 shot mag., based on earlier HSP 70, approx. 2.6 lbs, very limited production.

| | $6,500 | $5,500 | $3,750 | $2,950 | $2,150 | $1,850 | $1,675 | |

KORSTOG

Current trademark of AR-15 style rifles manufactured by Adams Arms, and retailed exclusively by Fleet Farm.

Korstog is an ancient Norwegian word meaning "crusade."

CARBINES/RIFLES: SEMI-AUTO

All rifles include a soft sided tactical case.

BRANN – 5.56 NATO cal., carbine length direct impingement gas system, high quality aluminum forged upper and lower receivers, aluminum precision machined receiver extension/buffer tube, hard coat anodized finish, 16 in. melonite coated chromemoly valadium steel barrel with M4 contour, single stage trigger, F-marked front sight base and A2 front sight post, six-position tactical butt stock with carbine USGI forearm, A2 grip, upper receiver adaptable for rear sight or optics, A4 flat-top receiver with M4 feed ramps. New 2013.

| MSR $1,000 | $850 | $750 | $640 | $575 | $475 | $425 | $350 | |

JAGER – 5.56 NATO cal., rifle length direct impingement gas system, low profile gas block, high quality aluminum upper and lower receivers, hard coat anodized finish, 20 in. heavy precision fluted stainless steel barrel with Adams Arms Jet compensator, JP-EZ single stage trigger, no sights, Magpul PRS precision adjustable stock with 15 in. Sampson Evolution Series T6 aluminum mil-spec forearm, ERGO Ambi grip, A4 flat-top receiver with M4 feed ramps, steel bolt carrier group, heat-treated gas key, 9.1 lbs. New 2013.

| MSR $2,050 | $1,750 | $1,550 | $1,325 | $1,195 | $975 | $825 | $725 | |

VAR – 5.56 NATO cal., mid-length direct impingement gas system, low profile gas block, high quality aluminum forged upper and lower receivers, machined aluminum mil-spec receiver extension/buffer tube, hard coat anodized finish, 16 in. melonite coated chromemoly valadium steel barrel with permanently attached flash hider, JP-EZ single stage trigger, no sights, six-position Vltor IMod collapsible stock with Sampson Evolution Series T6 aluminum forearm, ERGO Ambi grip, A4 flat-top receiver with M4 feed ramps, steel bolt carrier group, heat-treated gas key. New 2013.

| MSR $1,550 | $1,325 | $1,175 | $995 | $900 | $725 | $595 | $475 | |

MSR	100%	98%	95%	90%	80%	70%	60%	Last MSR

VOLI – 5.56 NATO cal., mid-length direct impingement gas system, high quality aluminum upper and lower receivers, hard coat anodized finish, 16 in. melonite coated chromemoly valadium steel barrel, single stage trigger, F-marked front sight base and A2 Magpul front sight post, Magpul MBUS Gen 2 rear sight, six position Magpul MOE adjustable collapsible stock, pistol grip, A4 flat-top receiver with M4 feet ramps, steel bolt carrier group, heat treated gas key. New 2013.

MSR $1,250	$1,075	$940	$800	$750	$595	$485	$395	

KRICO

Current trademark manufactured by Kriegeskorte Handels GmbH, located in Pyrbaum, Germany. No current U.S. importer. Previously imported exclusively mid-2005-2010 by Northeast Arms LLC, located in Fort Fairfield, ME. Previously distributed by Precision Sales, Int'l, located in Westfield, MA 1999-2002. Previously manufactured in Vohburg-Irsching, Germany 1996-1999, and in Fürth-Stadeln, Germany by Sportwaffenfabrik Kriegeskorte GmbH pre-1996.

During 2000, Krico was purchased by Marocchi. Krico has been imported/distributed by over ten U.S. companies/individuals. Krico manufactures high quality rifles, and to date, has mostly sold their guns in Europe. Many of the discontinued models listed may still be current within the European marketplace. Please contact the company directly for more information, including U.S. availability and pricing (see Trademark Index). The Krico name is an abridgement of the family name Kriegeskorte.

Due to space considerations, information regarding this manufacturer is available online free of charge at www.bluebookofgunvalues.com.

KRISS SYSTEMS SA

Current manufacturer of civilian and law enforcement firearms established in 2008 with factories located in Nyon, Switzerland and Virginia Beach, VA. Dealer sales.

Kriss Systems SA is a division of the Gamma Applied Visions Group SA, a Swiss-based global technology development firm. The company's previous name was Transformational Defense Industries, Inc. In late 2010, the company acquired Swiss pistol maker Sphinx Sytems Ltd.

Kriss Systems SA also manufactures a semi-auto pistol variation of its SBR (short barrel rifle) with a standard 5 1/2 in. barrel and other lengths available.

Please contact Kriss USA directly for more information, including configurations, availability, and pricing (see Trademark Index).

PISTOLS: SEMI-AUTO

KRISS VECTOR SDP – .45 ACP cal., pistol variation of the Kriss Vector carbine, 5 1/2 or 6 1/2 in. threaded or unthreaded (optional) barrel, full length Picatinny receiver rail, accepts Glock 21 mags., 5.4 lbs. New 2011.

MSR $1,895	$1,750	$1,550	$1,375	$1,200	$1,100	$1,000	$900	

RIFLES: SEMI-AUTO

Kriss also manufactures a .45 ACP Vector submachine gun for military and law enforcement only.

KRISS VECTOR CRB – .45 ACP cal., delayed blowback utilizing patented Super V System redirects recoil downward and away from the shooter, 16 in. steel barrel w/o sights, Ultramid Nylon 6/6 polymer receiver with A2 steel plates, 13 shot Glock type mag., Picatinny rail, flip up front and rear sights, two-stage trigger, folding vertical forearm grip, rail type folding stock, 5.8 lbs. New 2011.

MSR $1,895	$1,750	$1,550	$1,375	$1,200	$1,100	$1,000	$900	

Add $100 for Kriss Vector SBR model with 5 1/2 or 6 1/2 in. barrel (NFA weapon).

Add $884 for TacPac option (includes tactical sling, bipod grip pod system, Surefire tactical light, and L-3 Eotech holographic sight system), new 2012.

L SECTION

L.A.R. MANUFACTURING, INC.

Previous rifle manufacturer established in 1968 and located in West Jordan, UT until 2012. L.A.R. was acquired by the Freedom Group in late 2012 and closed its doors during 2013.

In addition to its .50 cal. bolt action rifles, L.A.R. also made upper receiver assemblies, and associated parts/accessories for AR-15 style carbines/rifles.

MSR	100%	98%	95%	90%	80%	70%	60%	Last MSR

RIFLES: BOLT ACTION

GRIZZLY BIG BOAR COMPETITOR RIFLE – .50 BMG cal., single shot, bolt action design in bullpup configuration, alloy steel receiver and bolt, 36 in. heavy barrel with compensator, thumb safety, match or field grade, includes bipod, scope mount, leather cheek pad and hard carry case, 30.4 lbs. Mfg. 1994-2011.

	$2,150	$1,725	$1,575	$1,375	$1,175	$1,050	$950	$2,350

Add $100 for parkerizing.
Add $250 for nickel trigger housing finish.
Add $350 for full nickel frame (disc. 2010).
Add $250 for stainless steel Lothar Walther barrel (disc. 2010).
Add $522 for redesigned (2002) tripod and pintle mount.
Last MSR was $4,841 for the Big Bore Hunter Rifle Package in 2011. This included: Nightforce scope and rings, cleaning kit, tripod with pintle mount, drag bag, and hard carry case.

GRIZZLY T-50 – .50 BMG cal., single shot, 32-36 in. barrel with muzzle brake, extended barrel shroud with top and bottom Picatinny rails, black parkerized finish, cheek saddle on frame, carry handle in front of trigger guard, extended bolt handle, 30 1/2 - 32 lbs. Mfg. 2009-2012.

	$3,000	$2,800	$2,600	$2,400	$2,200	$2,000	$1,800	$3,200

MSR on the A T-50 Tactical Package was $5,618. This package included: Nightforce scope and rings, cleaning kit, heavy duty bipod, carry handle, Accu-Shot monopod, drag bag, and hard carry case.

RIFLES: SEMI-AUTO

GRIZZLY 15 – .223 Rem. cal., GIO, patterned after the AR-15, available in either A2 or A3 configuration, limited mfg. 2004-2005.

	$825	$725	$650	$575	$525	$475	$425	$795

Add $85 for detachable carry handle.

GRIZZLY A2 SPEC CARBINE – 5.56 NATO cal., AR-15 style, GIO, 16 in. M4 chromemoly threaded barrel with A2 Bird cage flash suppressor, 5 position collapsible carbine stock, Grizzly A2 aluminum upper receiver, mil spec forged aluminum LAR Grizzly lower receiver, mil spec or LAR split carbine quad rail handguard, A2 front sight, standard trigger group, A2 mil spec pistol grip. Mfg. 2011-2012.

	$895	$775	$675	$575	$525	$475	$425	$999

GRIZZLY A3 SPEC CARBINE – 5.56 NATO cal., GIO, similar to Grizzly A2 Spec Carbine, except has Grizzly A3 aluminum flat-top upper receiver. Mfg. 2011-2012.

	$880	$765	$675	$575	$525	$475	$425	$979

OPS-4 GRIZZLY H-TACTICAL – 5.56 NATO cal., AR-15 style, GPO, 16 in. M4 chromemoly threaded barrel with A2 birdcage flash suppressor, 5 position collapsible carbine stock, LAR side charged forged aluminum flat-top upper receiver, mil spec forged aluminum LAR Grizzly lower receiver, mil spec or LAR split carbine quad rail handguard, hard anodized aluminum charging handle. Mfg. 2011-2012.

	$975	$850	$725	$625	$550	$500	$450	$1,111

OPS-4 GRIZZLY HUNTER – .223 Rem./5.56 NATO (.223 Wylde chamber) cal., AR-15 style, GIO, 18, 20, or 24 in. bull chromemoly (20 or 24 in.) or stainless steel (18 or 20 in.) barrel, standard A2 black stock, standard trigger or 2 stage match trigger group, OPS-4 side charged forged aluminum flat-top upper receiver, mil spec forged aluminum LAR Grizzly lower receiver, LAR free float tube rifle length handguard, LAR aluminum gas block, hard anodized aluminum charging handle. Mfg. 2011-2012.

	$885	$765	$675	$575	$525	$475	$425	$989

OPS-4 GRIZZLY OPERATOR – 5.56 NATO cal., AR-15 style, GIO, 16 in. chromemoly heavy threaded barrel with 5 port muzzle brake and compensator, Magpul CTR collapsible stock, Hogue rubber grip with finger grooves or Magpul MIAD pistol grip, standard trigger group, OPS-4 side charged forged aluminum flat-top upper receiver, mil spec forged aluminum LAR Grizzly lower receiver, LAR mid length quad rail handguard, LAR aluminum gas block with rail, hard anodized aluminum charging handle. Mfg. 2011-2012.

	$975	$825	$725	$625	$550	$500	$450	$1,099

MSR	100%	98%	95%	90%	80%	70%	60%	Last MSR

OPS-4 GRIZZLY PRECISION OPERATOR – .223 Rem./5.56 NATO (.223 Wylde chamber) cal., AR-15 style, GIO, 18 or 20 in. bull stainless steel barrel, Magpul PRS stock, Magpul pistol grip and trigger guard or Magpul MIAD, standard trigger or 2 stage match trigger group, LAR rifle length free floating quad rail handguard, LAR aluminum low profile gas block, otherwise similar to OPS-4 Grizzly Operator. Mfg. 2011-2012.

	$1,125	$950	$825	$725	$625	$550	$475	$1,299

OPS-4 GRIZZLY SPEC CARBINE – 5.56 NATO cal., AR-15 style, GIO, 16 in. M4 chromemoly threaded barrel with A2 Bird cage flash suppressor, standard trigger group, 5 position collapsible carbine stock, OPS-4 side charged forged aluminum flat-top upper receiver, mil spec forged aluminum LAR Grizzly lower receiver, A2 front sight, mil-spec or LAR split carbine quad rail handguard, hard anodized aluminum charging handle. Mfg. 2011-2012.

	$865	$750	$675	$575	$525	$475	$425	$959

OPS-4 GRIZZLY SPEC RIFLE – 5.56 NATO cal., AR-15 style, GIO, 20 in. chromemoly heavy threaded barrel with A2 birdcage flash suppressor, standard trigger or 2 stage match trigger group, standard A2 black stock, otherwise similar to OPS-4 Grizzly Spec Carbine. Mfg. 2011-2012.

	$895	$775	$675	$575	$525	$475	$425	$999

OPS-4 GRIZZLY STANDARD CARBINE – 5.56 NATO cal., AR-15 style, GIO, 16 in. M4 chromemoly threaded barrel with A2 birdcage flash suppressor, standard trigger group, 5 position collapsible carbine stock, LAR side charged forged aluminum flat-top upper receiver, mil spec forged aluminum LAR Grizzly lower receiver, LAR aluminum gas block with rail, full chrome bolt carrier and gas key, hard anodized aluminum charging handle. Mfg. 2011-2012.

	$895	$775	$675	$575	$525	$475	$425	$999

OPS-4 GRIZZLY STANDARD RIFLE – 5.56 NATO cal., AR-15 style, GIO, 20 in. chromemoly heavy threaded barrel with A2 birdcage flash suppressor, standard trigger or 2 stage match trigger group, standard A2 black stock, otherwise similar to OPS-4 Grizzly Standard Carbine. Mfg. 2011-2012.

	$975	$850	$725	$625	$550	$500	$450	$1,099

OPS-22 TERMINATOR – .22 LR cal., GIO, 16 in. carbon steel barrel, free float tube, 30 shot mag., collapsible buttstock. Mfg. 2011-2012.

	$575	$500	$425	$375	$325	$295	$275	$649

L E S INCORPORATED

Previous manufacturer located in Morton Grove, IL.

PISTOLS: SEMI-AUTO

P-18 ROGAK – 7.65mm Para. (limited mfg.) or 9mm Para. cal., DA/SA gas delayed blowback, 18 shot, 5 1/2 in. barrel, stainless steel, black plastic grips with partial thumb rest. Disc.

	$450	$395	$350	$325	$295	$275	$250	
High Polish Finish	$525	$450	$395	$375	$325	$295	$275	

Add 25% for 7.65mm Para. cal.

This pistol was patterned after the Steyr Model GB. Approx. 2,300 P-18s were mfg. before being disc.

LRB ARMS

Current manufacturer located in Floral Park, NY. Currently distributed by LRB of Long Island, NY.

RIFLES: SEMI-AUTO

M14SA BASE – .308 Win./7.62 NATO cal., GIO, 22 in. barrel with NM modified flash suppressor, 10 shot mag., hammer forged receiver, forged LRB bolt, reconditioned brown fiberglass or New Boyds walnut stock, sling.

MSR $2,541	$2,275	$2,000	$1,700	$1,550	$1,250	$1,025	$800	

Add $133 for Boyds walnut stock.

M14SA CLASSIC – .308 Win./7.62 NATO cal., GIO, authentic Vietnam era "As Issue" rifle, Criterion 22 in. chrome-lined barrel with USGI flash suppressor, 10 shot mag., M14SA receiver, LRB bolt, USGI reconditioned brown fiberglass or USGI reconditioned walnut stock, sling.

MSR $2,641	$2,375	$2,075	$1,775	$1,625	$1,300	$1,075	$825	

Add $83 for walnut stock.

M14SA TANKER – .308 Win./7.62 NATO cal., GIO, Criterion 18 1/2 in. chrome-lined barrel with LRB muzzle brake, 10 shot mag., M14SA receiver, LRB bolt, USGI reconditioned brown fiberglass or New Boyds walnut stock, sling.

MSR $2,663	$2,400	$2,100	$1,800	$1,625	$1,325	$1,075	$850	

Add $83 for walnut stock.

MSR	100%	98%	95%	90%	80%	70%	60%	Last MSR

M14SA MEDIUM MATCH – .308 Win./7.62 NATO cal., GIO, choice of 22 in. stainless steel or chromemoly barrel with NM modified flash suppressor, NM front and rear sight, NM spring guide, Boyds walnut stock, 10 shot mag., sling.

MSR $3,005	$2,700	$2,375	$2,025	$1,825	$1,475	$1,225	$950	

M25 MEDIUM MATCH – .308 Win./7.62 NATO cal., choice of 22 in. stainless steel or chromemoly barrel with NM modified flash suppressor, M25 receiver, LRB bolt, NM front and rear sight, NM spring guide, unitized gas cylinder, Boyds walnut stock, 10 shot mag., sling.

MSR $3,090	$2,775	$2,425	$2,075	$1,875	$1,525	$1,250	$975	

M25 TANKER – .308 Win./7.62 NATO cal., GIO, Criterion 18 1/2 in. chrome-lined barrel with LRB muzzle brake, 10 shot mag., M25 receiver, USGI reconditioned brown fiberglass or New Boyds walnut stock, sling.

MSR $2,748	$2,475	$2,175	$1,850	$1,675	$1,375	$1,125	$875	

Add $134 for walnut stock.

10TH ANNIVERSARY SPECIAL – .308 Win./7.62 NATO cal., GIO, choice of 22 in. stainless steel or chromemoly barrel with USGI flash suppressor, NM front sight, NM OP rod spring guide, Boyds M1A style walnut stock, laser engraved number on left side of receiver, buttstock displays a 10th Anniversary coin mounted on right side. Limited mfg. of 200 beginning 2012. Disc. 2013.

	$2,325	$2,025	$1,750	$1,575	$1,275	$1,050	$825	*$2,592*

LWRC INTERNATIONAL, INC.

Current manufacturer of pistols, rifles, and related AR-15 accessories established during 2006, and located in Cambridge, MD. Dealer and distributor sales.

PISTOLS: SEMI-AUTO

PSD (PERSONAL SECURITY DETAIL) PISTOL – 5.56 NATO cal., GPO, 8 in. ultra compact hammer forged steel barrel, A2 flash hider, 30 shot Magpul P-Mag, MIAD pistol grip, shortened recoil system, Troy front sight, folding BUIS rear sight, NiCorr surface treatment, Black, FDE, Patriot Brown, or OD Green finish, 5 1/2 lbs.

MSR $2,097	$1,875	$1,650	$1,400	$1,275	$1,025	$850	$650	

Add $150 for FDE, OD Green, or Patriot Brown finish.

RIFLES: SEMI-AUTO

LWRC manufactures a complete line of short-stroke, gas-piston operated AR-15 style, M-16, and M-4 semi-auto rifles. These models have a wide variety of sights, accessories, and related hardware available. Please contact the company directly for more information on the available options (see Trademark Index).

M6-A2 – 5.56 NATO or 6.8mm SPC cal., GPO, 16.1 in. cold hammer forged match grade barrel, six position Vltor EMod or Magpul MOE stock, Magpul MIAD pistol grip, 30 shot mag., A2 flash hider, folding BUIS front and rear sights, mid-length free float rail system, Black, FDE, OD Green, or Patriot Brown finish, 7.3 lbs.

MSR $2,217	$1,995	$1,725	$1,550	$1,375	$1,125	$975	$775	

Add $150 for FDE, OD Green, or Patriot Brown finish.

This model is also available with a 10 1/2 or 14.7 in. barrel for law enforcement/military. A M6A2 DEA variation is also available with 14.7 in. barrel.

M6-A3 – 5.56 NATO or 6.8mm SPC cal., GIO, 16.1 or 18 in. barrel, Vltor EMod adj. stock, Magpul MIAD pistol grip, integrated flip down sight, ARM-R free float rail system, front sight is folding and incorporated in gas block, 30 shot mag., A2 flash hider, Olive Drab or Black finish, 7.3 lbs.

	$2,075	$1,775	$1,575	$1,400	$1,125	$975	$800	*$2,317*

M6-A4 – 5.56 NATO or 6.8mm SPC cal., GPO, 16 1/2 in. hammer forged steel barrel, short stroke piston system, Vltor EMod adj. stock, Magpul MIAD pistol grip, folding rear BUIS sight, folding front sight incorporated in gas block, 30 shot mag., black finish, front handle, quad rail, 7.4 lbs.

While advertised during 2011, this model has yet to be manufactured.

M6-G – 5.56 NATO or 6.8mm SPC cal., 16.1 in. hammer forged steel barrel, short stroke piston system, Magpul MOE pistol grip stock, folding BUIS front and rear sights, 30 shot mag., enhanced fire control group, black finish, approx. 7 lbs.

While advertised during 2011, this model has yet to be manufactured.

M6-IC – 5.56 NATO cal., GPO, 16 in. fluted (first 500) or non-fluted barrel with A2 Birdcage flash hider, Monoforge upper receiver, 9 in. M6 modular rail, FDE (initial run of 500 only) or Black finish, available in standard, A5 (law enforcement only), SPR, PSD, and MK configurations, Magpul MOE pistol grip stock, 7.3 lbs. New 2013.

MSR $2,349	$2,100	$1,800	$1,525	$1,300	$1,100	$900	$750	

Add $100 for fluted barrel.

MSR	100%	98%	95%	90%	80%	70%	60%	Last MSR

M6-IC-SPR – 5.56 NATO cal., GPO, 16.1 in. helical fluted barrel with A2 Birdcage flash hider, 30 shot PMag., ambidextrous charging handle, 12 in. IC modular rail, Magpul MIAD pistol grip stock, LWRCI folding BUIS front and rear sights, Black, OD Green, FDE, or Patriot Brown finish, 7.1 lbs. New 2014.

MSR $2,349	$2,100	$1,800	$1,525	$1,300	$1,100	$900	$750	

Add $150 for FDE, OD Green, or Patriot Brown finish.

M6-SL – 5.56 NATO or 6.8mm SPC cal., GPO, 16.1 in. light contour cold hammer forged barrel, six position Magpul CTR stock, MOE mid length handguard and pistol grip, 30 shot mag., A2 flash hider, EXO (nickel boron) plated advanced combat bolt, one piece coated carrier, and enhanced fire control group, Daniel Defense fixed rear sight, fixed A2 front sight, Black, FDE, Patriot Brown, or OD Green finish, 7.2 lbs.

MSR $1,675	$1,500	$1,300	$1,100	$900	$775	$650	$575	

Add $100 for FDE, Patriot Brown, or OD Green finish.

This model is also available with a 10 1/2, 12.7, and 14.7 in. barrel for law enforcement/military. A M6A1-S Patrolman's Carbine is also available with 14.7 in. barrel and M4 collapsible stock.

M6-SPR (SPECIAL PURPOSE RIFLE) – 5.56 NATO or 6.8mm SPC cal., GPO, 16.1 in. cold hammer forged fluted barrel, Magpul ACS stock, Magpul MIAD pistol grip, 30 shot mag., A2 flash hider, folding BUIS front and rear sights, Black, OD Green, FDE or Patriot Brown finish, SPR-MOD rail, Bravo Company Mod4 Gunfighter charging handle, nickel coated bolt carrier and fire control group, Skirmish sights, 7.3 lbs.

MSR $2,479	$2,225	$1,850	$1,625	$1,425	$1,150	$995	$800	

This model is also available with a 14.7 in. barrel for law enforcement/military.

R.E.P.R. (RAPID ENGAGEMENT PRECISION RIFLE) – 7.62mm NATO cal., GPO, variations include 16 (medium light, fluted or non-fluted), 18 (DMR, medium), and 20 (Sniper, heavy) in. cold hammer forged barrel, Birdcage flash hider, Geissele two-stage trigger, six position Vltor Emod, Magpul UBR, or Magpul PRS stock, 5, 10, or 20 shot mag., Magpul MIAD pistol grip, folding BUIS sights, sculpted ARM-R top rail, adj. four position gas block, ambidextrous bolt release, left side mounted charging handle, matte black, FDE, Patriot Brown, or OD Green finish, 9 1/2 - 11 1/4 lbs.

MSR $3,600	$3,240	$2,900	$2,550	$2,175	$1,650	$1,425	$1,200	

Add $150 for 16 in. fluted barrel.
Add $150 for FDE, Patriot Brown, or OD Green finish.
Add $200 for 20 in. heavy barrel.

SIX8-A2 – 6.8 SPC II cal., GPO, 16.1 in. barrel with LWRCI flash hider, 30 shot PMag., nickel boron coated bolt carrier group, enhanced fire control group, claw extractor, Black, FDE, Patriot Brown, or OD Green finish, Magpul MOE pistol grip stock, 9 in. Picatinny quad rail, mil-spec trigger, flip-up sights, two-position safety, fully ambidextrous, 7.3 lbs. New 2013.

MSR $2,499	$2,250	$1,850	$1,595	$1,425	$1,175	$950	$800	

Add $150 for FDE, Patriot Brown, or OD Green finish.

This model is also available with 8 1/2 or 14.7 in. barrels for military/law enforcement.

* **SIX8-SPR** – 6.8 SPC II cal., similar to SIX8-A2, except features Magpul MIAD pistol grip stock, LWRCI folding BUIS front and rear sights, 12 in. user configurable rail system, Patriot Brown Cerakote finish, 7 1/4 lbs. New 2013.

MSR $2,249	$2,000	$1,775	$1,525	$1,375	$1,125	$925	$725	

Add $150 for FDE, Patriot Brown, or OD Green finish.

LABANU INCORPORATED

Labanu, Inc. SKSs were manufactured by Norinco in China, and imported exclusively until 1998 by Labanu, Inc., located in Ronkonkoma, NY.

RIFLES: SEMI-AUTO

MAK 90 SKS SPORTER RIFLE – 7.62x39mm cal., sporterized variation of the SKS with thumbhole stock, 16 1/2 in. barrel, includes accessories, 5 lbs. Importation began 1995, banned 1998.

	$625	$550	$475	$425	$375	$325	$295	*$189*

LAKESIDE MACHINE LLC

Previous manufacturer located in Horseshoe Bend, AR until late 2013. Previously located in Pound, WI.

RIFLES: SEMI-AUTO

Lakeside manufactured half-scale, semi-auto, belt fed replicas of many of America's famous machine guns, including the 1919 A4 ($3,995 last MSR), 1919 M37 ($3,895 last MSR, only 2 mfg.), 1917 A1 ($4,495 last MSR), M2 HB ($4,995 last MSR), M2 WC ($5,495 last MSR), and a dual mount M2 HB (was POR). Calibers included: .22 LR, .17 Mach 2 (optional), and .22 WMR. Additionally, Lakeside also manufactured a semi-auto, closed bolt, belt fed .22 LR cal. Model Vindicator BF1 with 16 1/4 in. shrouded barrel ($2,695 last MSR).

MSR	100%	98%	95%	90%	80%	70%	60%	Last MSR

LANCER SYSTEMS

Current AR-15 style rifle and accessories manufacturer located in Allentown, PA.

RIFLES: SEMI-AUTO

L15 COMPETITION – 5.56 NATO cal., GIO, 18 in. stainless steel barrel, Wheaton Arms compensator, extra long free floating handguard, EFX-A2 fixed stock, Ergo grip, CMC trigger, 7.7 lbs. New 2013.

MSR $2,225	$1,975	$1,750	$1,475	$1,225	$1,000	$850	$750

* L15 Super Competition – 5.56 NATO cal., GIO, upgraded version of the L15 Competition featuring 17 in. stainless steel Krieger barrel, Wheaton Arms SS compensator, Lancer extra long handguard, EFX-A2 fixed stock, Ergo grip, CMC trigger, 7.8 lbs. New 2013.

MSR $2,525	$2,300	$1,925	$1,600	$1,275	$1,075	$875	$775

L15 SHARP SHOOTER – 5.56 NATO cal., GIO, 20 in. heavy profile Krieger barrel, Lancer extra long free-float handguard, tactical Magwell lower receiver, EFX-A2 fixed stock, Ergo grip, CMC trigger, 8.9 lbs. New 2013.

MSR $2,180	$1,925	$1,675	$1,400	$1,1150	$975	$775	$700

L15 SPORTER – 5.56 NATO cal., GIO, 16 in. lightweight CHF chrome lined barrel with A2 flash hider, Lancer handguard with 2 in. sight rail, tactical Magwell lower receiver, F93 Pro stock, Ergo grip, Milspec trigger, 7.2 lbs. New 2013.

MSR $1,750	$1,575	$1,375	$1,125	$900	$775	$675	$575

LARUE TACTICAL

Current manufacturer located in Leander, TX.

RIFLES: SEMI-AUTO

Continued high demand for Larue's AR-15 models have resulted in 100%-60% values being higher than normal.

OBR (OPTIMIZED BATTLE RIFLE) – 5.56 NATO (new 2011) or .308 Win. cal., AR-15 style, GIO, 16.1, 18, or 20 in. stainless steel barrel, adj. gas block, 20 shot box mag., flared magwell, A2 fixed stock, black anodized finish, Mil-Std 1913 one piece upper rail, Troy front and optional BUIS rear sight, A2 flash hider, detachable side rails, approx. 10 lbs. **A variety of accessories are available on this model for additional cost.**

* 5.56 NATO Cal.

MSR $2,245	$2,950	$2,600	$2,250	$2,000	$1,800	$1,600	$1,400

* .308 Win. Cal.

MSR $3,370	$3,995	$3,500	$3,000	$2,600	$2,200	$1,850	$1,500

PREDATOBR – 5.56 NATO or 7.62 NATO cal., GIO, 16.1 or 18 in. threaded barrel, 30 shot, Picatinny rail, 6-position Retract Action Trigger (R.A.T.) stock. New 2014.

MSR $2,245	N/A	N/A	N/A	N/A	N/A	N/A	N/A

Add $1,125 for 7.62 NATO cal.

Due to continued demand for this trademark, values for this new model are currently unpredictable.

TACTICAL PREDATAR – 5.56 NATO or .308 Win. (new 2013) cal., GIO, 16.1 or 18 in. contoured stainless steel barrel, skeletonized handguard, A2 flash hider, quad rail forend, black phosphate finish, six position Magpul stock, 30 shot mag., charging lever, forward assist, Geissele two-stage trigger, approx. 6 1/2 lbs. New mid-2011.

* 5.56 NATO Cal.

MSR $1,682	$2,250	$2,000	$1,800	$1,600	$1,400	$1,200	$1,000

* .308 Win. Cal.

MSR $2,807	$3,650	$3,300	$2,950	$2,600	$2,300	$2,000	$1,750

COSTA SIGNATURE EDITION – 5.56 NATO cal., GIO, 16.1 in. barrel, SureFire muzzle brake, FDE KG GunKote finish, "COSTA LUDUS" logo engraved on left side of receiver, black parts and rail covers, first 500 units are match numbered on the upper and lower. New 2013.

MSR $2,895	$4,995	$4,500	$4,000	$3,500	$3,000	$2,500	$2,000

LASERAIM ARMS, INC.

Previous distributor located in Little Rock, AR. Previously manufactured until 1999 in Thermopolis, WY. Laseraim Arms, Inc. was a division of Emerging Technologies, Inc.

PISTOLS: SEMI-AUTO

SERIES I – .40 S&W, .400 Cor-Bon (new 1998), .45 ACP, or 10mm cal., SA, 3 3/8 (Compact Model), 5, or 6 in. barrel with compensator, ambidextrous safety, all stainless steel metal parts are Teflon coated, beveled mag. well, integral

MSR	100%	98%	95%	90%	80%	70%	60%	Last MSR

accessory mounts, 7 (.45 ACP) or 8 (10mm or .40 S&W) shot mag., 46 or 52 oz. Mfg. 1993-99.

| | $325 | $295 | $265 | $215 | $185 | $150 | $125 | *$349* |

Add $120 for wireless laser combo (new 1997).

* ***Series I Compact*** – .40 S&W or .45 ACP cal., features 3 3/8 in. non-ported slide and fixed sights. Mfg. 1993-99.

| | $325 | $295 | $265 | $215 | $185 | $150 | $125 | *$349* |

Series I Illusion and Dream Team variations were made during 1993-94. Retail prices respectively were $650 and $695.

SERIES II – .40 S&W (disc. 1994), .45 ACP, or 10mm cal., SA, similar technical specs. as the Series I, except has non-reflective stainless steel finish, fixed or adj. sights, and 3 3/8 (Compact Model, .45 ACP only), 5, or 7 (.45 ACP only) in. non-compensated barrel, 37 or 43 oz. Mfg. 1993-1996.

| | $485 | $385 | $300 | $240 | $210 | $180 | $155 | *$550* |

Series II Illusion and Dream Team variations were made during 1993-94. Retail prices respectively were $500 and $545.

SERIES III – .45 ACP cal., 5 in. ported barrel, SA, serrated slide, Hogue grips. Mfg. 1994-disc.

| | $595 | $465 | $415 | $375 | $345 | $310 | $275 | *$675* |

SERIES IV – .45 ACP cal., 3 3/8 (Compact Model) or 5 in. ported barrel, SA, serrated slide, diamond checkered wood grips. Mfg. 1994-disc.

| | $550 | $450 | $400 | $360 | $330 | $300 | $265 | *$625* |

LAUER CUSTOM WEAPONRY

Current manufacturer of AR-15 style carbines/rifles located in Chippewa Falls, WI.

RIFLES: SEMI-AUTO

Please contact the manufacturer directly for current pricing and availability on these models (see Trademark Index).

LCW15 BATTLE RIFLE – 5.56 NATO cal., AR-15 style, GIO (available with LCW's MaxGas proprietry high performance gas system), 16 in. barrel, A3 flat-top or A2 carry handle on upper receiver, shorty carbine handguard, A2 buttstock, one 30 shot GI mag., Black or Afghan camo finish.

LCW15 TARGET RIFLE – 5.56 NATO cal., GIO (MaxGas proprietary gas system), 24 in. stainless steel bull barrel, matching serial number on upper and lower receiver, A3 flat-top upper receiver, match target trigger, free float aluminum handguard, A2 buttstock, one 20 shot mag., includes hard case and ear plugs.

LCW15 URBAN RESPONDER – 5.56 NATO cal., AR-15 style, GIO, CQB precision carbine, M4 barrel with A2 flash hider, TriPower illuminated sight, M6 tactical laser illuminator with remote switch, lightweight 4-rail tactical free float handguard, forward grip, compact skeleton stock, tactical grip with storage compartment, DPMS quick response rear flip-up sight, A.R.M.S. 17 mount, LCW 3-point tactical sling, 30 shot mag., Urban MirageFlage finish, 7 1/2 lbs.

VINDICATOR – .22 LR cal., GIO, belt-fed model.

LAW ENFORCEMENT ORDNANCE CORPORATION

Previous manufacturer located in Ridgway, PA until 1990.

SHOTGUNS: SEMI-AUTO

STRIKER-12 – 12 ga., 12 shot rotary mag., 18 1/4 in. alloy shrouded barrel with PG extension, folding or fixed tactical design stock, 9.2 lbs., limited mfg. 1986-1990.

| | $1,000 | $875 | $750 | $675 | $600 | $550 | $500 | *$725* |

Add $200 for folding stock.
Add $100 for Marine variation ("Metal Life" finish).

Earlier variations were imported and available to law enforcement agencies only. In 1987, manufacture was started in PA and these firearms could be sold to individuals (18 in. barrel only). This design was originally developed in South Rhodesia.

LAZZERONI ARMS COMPANY

Current manufacturer located in Tucson, AZ since 1995. Direct/dealer sales.

RIFLES: BOLT ACTION

Lazzeroni ammunition is precision loaded in Lazzeroni's Tucson facility under rigid tolerances. All ammunition is sealed for absolute weatherproofing. Lazzeroni proprietary calibers are already established as being extremely effective at long distances.

MODEL L2012/L2005 GLOBAL HUNTER SERIES – available in various Lazzeroni proprietary cals., various configurations including Short Magnum Lite, Long Magnum Lite, Long Magnum Thumbhole, Long Magnum Special Long Range (disc. 2010), Short Magnum Dangerous Game (disc. 2010) and Long Magnum Dangerous Game, features stainless steel receiver, match grade fluted or unfluted barrel with muzzle brake, Jewell competition trigger, diamond

MSR	100%	98%	95%	90%	80%	70%	60%	Last MSR

fluted or helical cut bolt shaft, titanium firing pin, Limbsavr recoil pad, slim line graphite composite stock, approx. 6.1-8.7 lbs. Mfg. 2005-disc.

	$4,650	$4,250	$3,600	$3,100	$2,650	$2,150	$1,675	$5,000

Add $1,000 for heavy barrel Long Magnum (disc. 2010).
Add $3,000 for Dangerous Game (Model L2012-LD) or Long Magnum Tactical Model (Model L2012-TAC, mfg. 2011-2013).

LEGACY SPORTS INTERNATIONAL

Current importer located in Reno, NV. Previously located in Alexandria, VA.

Legacy Sports International imports a wide variety of firearms trademarks in various configurations, including pistols, rifles, and shotguns. Trademarks include: Citadel, Escort, Howa, ISSC, Pointer, Puma, and Verona (disc.). Please refer to these individual listings.

LEGION FIREARMS LLC

Current firearms and accessories manufacturer located in Temple, TX.

CARBINES: SEMI-AUTO

LF-10D CARBINE – .308 Win. or 7.62x51 NATO cal., GIO, 16 in. stainless steel barrel, three land polygonal rifling, M4 feed ramps, hex milled fluting, SureFire muzzle brake micro MOA adj. gas block, aluminum aircraft grade nickel boron coated upper and lower receiver, 12 in. Legion quad-channel concept handguard, ceramic wear resistant coating, Raptor .308 charging handle, ambidextrous bolt release, Phase 5 tactical REVO sling attachment system, BAD lever 90 degree ambi safety selector, Magpul MOE pistol grip, B5 Systems enhanced SOPMOD stock, H3 heavy buffer, steel bolt carrier, single stage trigger, available in Alpha Grey, Burnt Bronze, Flat Dark Earth, OD Green, Sniper Grey, or Black finish. New 2011.

MSR $3,390	$3,100	$2,875	$2,515	$2,150	$1,950	$1,575	$1,295

LF-15D CARBINE – 5.56 NATO cal., GIO, 16 in. stainless steel barrel, three land polygonal rifling, M4 feed ramps, hex milled fluting, aluminum aircraft grade nickel boron coated upper and lower receiver, Wilson Combat handguard, ceramic wear resistant coating, drilled and tapped, ambidextrous bolt release, available in Alpha Grey, Burnt Bronze, Flat Dark Earth, OD Green, Sniper Grey, or Black finish, Noveske QD endplate, single stage trigger, adj. tactical stock, H2 heavy buffer, lightweight billet modular design. New 2011.

MSR $2,390	$2,175	$1,995	$1,775	$1,525	$1,375	$1,115	$910

PISTOLS: SEMI-AUTO

LF-P – 9mm Para., .40 S&W, or .45 ACP cal., 5 in. stainless steel threaded or non-threaded barrel, SA, 1911 style chromemoly frame and slide, 13 (.45 ACP), 18 (.40 S&W), or 20 (9mm Para.) shot mag., omni-directional serrations, EGW melt barrel bushing, Legion hex hammer, Ameri Glow rear sights, STI machined front sights, Springco cryotreated recoil and main spring, custom trigger assembly, available in Flat Dark Earth, Naked Nickel Boron, Burnt Bronze, OD Green, or Black finish, includes three magazines.

MSR $2,595	$2,350	$2,200	$1,925	$1,650	$1,495	$1,210	$995

LEITNER-WISE DEFENSE, INC.

Current AR-15 style parts/accessories manufacturer located in Alexandria, VA. The company discontinued its semi-auto line of rifles circa 2010.

RIFLES: SEMI-AUTO

M.U.L.E. MOD. 1 (MODULAR URBAN LIGHT ENGAGEMENT CARBINE) – 5.56 NATO cal., GPO, 16 in. steel barrel standard, other lengths optional, op-rod operating system, single stage trigger, Magpul ACS buttstock, MOE pistol grip, black finish, upper and lower rails, 30 shot mag., flared magwell, E sights, includes one mag., manual, and cleaning kit, 7.9 lbs. Disc. circa 2010.

	$1,550	$1,375	$1,175	$1,000	$850	$700	$575	$1,680

Add $100 for precision trigger.

M.U.L.E. MOD. 2 (MODULAR URBAN LIGHT ENGAGEMENT CARBINE) – .308 Win. cal., GPO, 16 or 20 in. steel barrel, similar to Mod. 1, except has heavier barrel, 8 1/2 lbs. Disc. circa 2010.

	$1,895	$1,700	$1,500	$1,300	$1,100	$900	$700	$2,100

Add $100 for 20 in. barrel.

LEITNER-WISE RIFLE CO. INC.

Previous manufacturer located in Springfield, VA circa 2006. Previously located in Alexandria, VA 1999-2005.

MSR	100%	98%	95%	90%	80%	70%	60%	Last MSR

RIFLES: SEMI-AUTO

LW 15.22 – .22 LR or .22 WMR cal., GIO, patterned after the AR-15, 16 1/2 or 20 in. barrel, forged upper and lower receivers, choice of carry handle or flat-top upper receiver, forward bolt assist, last shot hold open, 10 or 25 shot mag. Mfg. 2000-2005.

| | $775 | $675 | $600 | $550 | $500 | $450 | $425 | *$850* |

Add $50 for A2 carrying handle.

LW 15.499 – .499 (12.5x40mm) cal., receiver and action patterned after the AR-15, mil spec standards, 16 1/2 in. steel or stainless steel barrel, flat-top receiver, 5 (disc.), 10, or 14 (new 2006) shot mag., approx. 6 1/2 lbs. Mfg. 2000-2005.

| | $1,350 | $1,150 | $995 | $875 | $750 | $675 | $600 | |

Add $92 for stainless steel barrel.

LW 6.8/5.56 S.R.T. – 5.56x45mm NATO or 6.8x43mm SPC cal., 16.1 in. barrel, hard chrome lined bore, gas operated, locking bolt, Troy front and rear sights, forged T7075 aluminum flat-top upper receiver, six position collapsible stock, Picatinny rail, removable carry handle, A2 flash hider, LW forged lower receiver, 28 or 30 shot mag., 5.38 lbs. Ltd. mfg. 2006.

| | $2,050 | $1,800 | $1,600 | $1,400 | $1,200 | $1,000 | $850 | |

Add $100 for 6.8x43mm SPC cal.

LES BAER CUSTOM, INC.

Current manufacturer and customizer established in 1993, and located in LeClaire, IA since 2008. Previously located in Hillsdale, IL until 2008. Dealer sales only.

PISTOLS: SEMI-AUTO, 1911 SERIES, SINGLE ACTION

The following current models are available with the following features unless otherwise noted: lowered and flared ejection port, tuned and polished extractor, Baer extended ejector, and beveled mag. well.

Add $70 for Tactical Package (rounds the edges of the pistol).

ULTIMATE MASTER COMBAT SERIES – .38 Super, .400 Cor-Bon, or .45 ACP cal., steel frame and slide with blued finish, compensated, 5 or 6 in. barrel, two 8 shot mags., checkered Cocobolo grips, low mount LBC adj. sight with hidden rear leaf, dovetailed front sight, double serrated slide, deluxe Commander hammer and sear, full length recoil rod, extended ambi safety, speed trigger.

* **Compensated Model** – .38 Super or .45 ACP cal., compensated barrel.

| MSR $2,880 | $2,500 | $2,250 | $2,000 | $1,750 | $1,575 | $1,350 | $995 | |

Add $260 for .38 Super cal.

* **5 Inch Model** – .38 Super, .400 Cor-Bon, or .45 ACP cal., 5 in. barrel.

| MSR $2,790 | $2,425 | $2,150 | $1,900 | $1,650 | $1,525 | $1,275 | $925 | |

Add $50 for .400 Cor-Bon cal. Add $100 for .38 Super cal.

* **6 Inch Model** – .38 Super, .400 Cor-Bon, or .45 ACP cal., 6 in. barrel.

| MSR $2,790 | $2,425 | $2,150 | $1,900 | $1,650 | $1,525 | $1,275 | $925 | |

Add $70 for .400 Cor-Bon cal. Add $180 for .38 Super cal.

NATIONAL MATCH HARDBALL PISTOL – .45 ACP cal., NM steel frame, slide, and 5 in. barrel with stainless bushing, 7 shot mag., blued finish, checkered front strap, checkered Cocobolo grips, low mount LBC adj. sight with hidden rear leaf, dovetailed front sight, rear serrated slide, match trigger.

| MSR $1,960 | $1,725 | $1,550 | $1,325 | $1,100 | $975 | $825 | $675 | |

BULLSEYE WADCUTTER PISTOL – .45 ACP cal., NM frame, slide, and barrel with stainless bushing, 7 shot mag., blued finish, checkered Cocobolo grips, double serrated slide, high checkered front strap, Baer deluxe hammer and sear, beavertail grip safety with pad, Baer speed trigger, optical scope mount.

| MSR $2,140 | $1,900 | $1,675 | $1,450 | $1,225 | $1,025 | $850 | $700 | |

Add $50 for 6 in. slide with Lo-Mount LBC adj. sights and Baer optical mount.

PPC DISTINGUISHED MATCH PISTOL – 9mm Para. or .45 ACP cal., NM steel frame, slide, and barrel with stainless bushing, 8 shot mag., 5 in. barrel, blued finish, checkered Cocobolo grips, PPC sight, Baer dovetail front sight, double serrated slide, Baer deluxe Commander hammer and sear, beavertail grip safety with pad, Baer speed trigger, extended ambi safety.

| MSR $2,240 | $2,000 | $1,775 | $1,525 | $1,275 | $1,050 | $875 | $725 | |

Add $390 for 9mm Para. cal. with supported chamber.

MSR	100%	98%	95%	90%	80%	70%	60%	Last MSR

PPC OPEN CLASS – 9mm Para. or .45 ACP cal., similar to PPC Distinguished Match, except features 6 in. barrel.

MSR $2,350	$2,100	$1,850	$1,600	$1,325	$1,100	$900	$750	

Add $390 for 9mm Para. cal. with supported chamber.

PREMIER II 5 INCH MODEL – .38 Super, .400 Cor-Bon, or .45 ACP cal., NM steel frame, slide, and barrel with stainless bushing, 5 in. barrel, low mount LBC adj. sight with hidden rear leaf, dovetail front sight, two 8 shot mags., blued finish or stainless steel, checkered Cocobolo grips, beavertail grip safety with pad, speed trigger, extended ambi safety.

MSR $1,905	$1,675	$1,425	$1,225	$1,050	$925	$775	$650	

Add $45 for stainless steel.
Add $185 for .400 COR-BON cal. Add $365 for .38 Super cal. Add $505 for .45 ACP/.400 COR-BON dual cylinder combo.

PREMIER II 6 INCH MODEL – .38 Super or .45 ACP cal., similar to Premier II 5 Inch Model, except features 6 in. barrel, blued finish only.

MSR $2,090	$1,825	$1,600	$1,375	$1,175	$995	$825	$675	

Add $100 for .400 COR-BON cal. Add $420 for .38 Super cal.

PREMIER II SUPER-TAC – .38 Super, .400 Cor-Bon, .45 ACP, or .45 ACP/.400 Cor-Bon combo cal., NM steel frame, slide, and barrel with stainless bushing, double serrated slide, low mount LBC adj. rear sight and Baer dovetail front sight, both fitted with tritium night sights, two 8 shot mags., Dupont S coating, checkered Cocobolo grips, deburred for tactical carry, beavertail grip safety with pad, Baer speed trigger, extended ambi safety.

MSR $2,370	$2,125	$1,850	$1,600	$1,325	$1,100	$900	$750	

Add $25 for .400 Cor-Bon cal.
Add $200 for .38 Super cal.
Add $520 for .45 ACP/.400 Cor-Bon dual cylinder combo.

BOSS – .45 ACP cal., similar to the Premier II series, except features blued slide, extended combat safety, rear cocking serrations on the slide, fiber optic front sight, chromed complete lower, special tactical package.

MSR $2,260	$2,025	$1,775	$1,525	$1,275	$1,050	$875	$725	

PROWLER III – .45 ACP cal., NM steel frame, slide, and 5 in. barrel with tapered cone stub weight, Bear reverse plug, slide fitted to frame, double serrated slide, low mount BoMar sight with hidden leaf rear, dovetail front sight, checkered slide stop, Baer speed trigger, deluxe Commander hammer, beavertail grip safety with pad, extended ambi safety, blued finish, two 8 shot mags., checkered Cocobolo grips.

MSR $2,710	$2,400	$2,125	$1,800	$1,575	$1,300	$1,100	$925	

CUSTOM CARRY – .38 Super (4 1/4 in. only), or .45 ACP cal., NM steel frame, slide, and barrel with stainless bushing, 4 1/4 (Comanche length) or 5 in. throated barrel, blued or stainless steel finish, deluxe fixed combat sight, dovetail front sight, improved ramp style night sights, double serrated slide, checkered slide stop, Baer speed trigger, extended ambi safety, two 8 shot mags., checkered Cocobolo grips.

MSR $1,920	$1,700	$1,525	$1,300	$1,075	$950	$800	$650	

Add $120 for stainless steel finish.
Add $300 for .38 Super cal. with 4 1/4 in. barrel and stainless steel finish.

SUPER COMANCHE – .38 Super cal., steel construction only, 4 1/4 in. throated barrel, NM slide with rear serrations only, stainless steel bushing, deluxe fixed combat rear sight with night sight, dovetail front sight ramp style with night sight, blue finish or optional chrome or DuPont S finish, checkered slide stop, speed trigger, extended ambi safety, checkered Cocobolo grips, high checkered front strap, two 9 shot mags. with base pads. New 2013.

MSR $2,220	$1,995	$1,775	$1,525	$1,275	$1,050	$875	$725	

ULTIMATE RECON PISTOL – .45 ACP cal., full size Caspian frame with integral Picatinny rail system for frame mounted light, comes standard with a Streamlight TLR-1, NM slide and 5 in. barrel with stainless bushing, deluxe fixed combat rear sight with night sights, dovetail front sight, double serrated slide, bead blast blue finish or optional bead blast chrome finish, deluxe hammer and sear, checkered slide stop, speed trigger, tactical style extended combat safety, checkered Cocobolo grips, high checkered front strap, two 8 shot mags.

MSR $2,370	$2,125	$1,850	$1,600	$1,325	$1,100	$900	$750	

Add $240 for bead blast chrome finish.

ULTIMATE TACTICAL CARRY – .45 ACP cal., steel NM frame and slide with front and rear serrations, slide fitted to frame, 5 in. barrel with stainless match bushing, LBC deluxe fixed combat rear sight with tritium inserts, dovetail front sight with tritium insert, blued finish, deluxe hammer and sear, checkered slide stop, combat extended safety, aluminum match trigger, deluxe special slim line grips, three stainless steel 8 shot mags.

MSR $1,930	$1,695	$1,450	$1,225	$1,050	$925	$775	$650	

MSR	100%	98%	95%	90%	80%	70%	60%	Last MSR

THUNDER RANCH SPECIAL – .45 ACP cal., similar to Ultimate Tactical Carry, except has beavertail grip safety with pad, high checkered front strap, deluxe special slim line grips with Thunder Ranch logo, three stainless steel 7 shot mags., special Thunder Ranch logo engraved on slide, special serial numbers with "TR" prefix.

MSR $1,980	$1,695	$1,495	$1,225	$1,050	$925	$775	$650	

SHOOTING USA CUSTOM PISTOL – .45 ACP cal., similar to Premier II 5 in. model, except also features tactical extended safety, a special serial number prefix with "S USA" and the number, the famous Shooting USA logo engraved on the right side of the slide, blued finish, two 8 shot stainless steel mags., and a special DVD produced by Shooting USA.

MSR $1,905	$1,675	$1,425	$1,225	$1,050	$925	$775	$650	

CUSTOM CENTENNIAL MODEL 1911 PISTOL – .45 ACP cal., made to commemorate the 100th anniversary year of "Old Ironsides", similar to Premier II 5 in. model, except features rear serrated slide with the model name engraved on the slide, ivory grips, deluxe charcoal blue finish, extended tactical safety, three 8 shot mags., special presentation box.

MSR $4,050	$3,600	$3,200	$2,750	$2,250	$1,875	$1,500	$1,350	

1911 S.R.P. (SWIFT RESPONSE PISTOL) – .45 ACP cal., NM steel frame and slide with front and rear serrations, 4 1/4 (Comanche Model) or 5 in. barrel with stainless match bushing, deluxe fixed combat sight, dovetail front sight, checkered slide stop, speed trigger, deluxe Commander hammer, beavertail grip safety with pad, tactical style ambi safety, Tritium night sights installed front and rear, Deburred for tactical carry, Dupont S coating on complete pistol, three 8 shot mags., checkered Cocobolo grips, special wooden presentation box with glass lid.

MSR $2,490	$2,150	$1,800	$1,575	$1,300	$1,050	$875	$775	

MONOLITH – .38 Super or .45 ACP cal., NM steel Monolith frame, Monolith flat bottom double serrated slide, 5 in. barrel with stainless match bushing, low mount LBC adj. sight with hidden rear leaf, Baer dovetail front sight, checkered slide stop, speed trigger, deluxe Commander hammer, beavertail grip safety with pad, extended ambi safety, two 8 shot mags., checkered Cocobolo grips, blued finish, extra long dust cover.

MSR $1,990	$1,695	$1,495	$1,225	$1,050	$925	$775	$650	

Add $400 for supported chamber .38 Super.

* Monolith Heavyweight – .38 Super or .45 ACP cal., similar to Monolith, except has a heavier frame.

MSR $2,060	$1,750	$1,525	$1,250	$1,075	$950	$800	$675	

Add $335 for supported chamber .38 Super.

MONOLITH COMANCHE – .45 ACP cal., NM steel Monolith frame, Monolith flat bottom double serrated slide, 4 1/4 in. barrel with stainless match bushing, Tritium night sights front and rear and deluxe fixed rear sight, checkered slide stop, speed trigger, deluxe Commander hammer, beavertail grip safety with pad, extended ambi safety, two 8 shot mags., checkered Cocobolo grips, blued finish, extra long dust cover.

MSR $1,995	$1,725	$1,450	$1,225	$1,050	$925	$775	$650	

* Monolith Comanche Heavyweight – .45 ACP cal., similar to Monolith Comanche, except dust cover is slightly thicker to add weight and is flat on the bottom.

MSR $2,060	$1,750	$1,525	$1,250	$1,075	$950	$800	$675	

.38 SUPER STINGER – .38 Super cal., NM Stinger frame, NM Commanche length slide with rear serrations only, 4 1/4 in. barrel with supported chamber and stainless steel bushing, deluxe fixed combat rear sight with night sight, dovetail ramp type with night sight, checkered slide stop, speed trigger, deluxe Commander hammer, beavertail grip safety with pad, tactical ambi safety, three 8 shot mags. with pads, checkered Cocobolo grips, blue finish or optional chrome or Dupont S finish. New 2013.

MSR $2,495	$2,250	$1,975	$1,700	$1,475	$1,225	$1,050	$850	

STINGER MODEL – .45 ACP cal., NM Stinger frame, NM Commanche length slide with rear serrations, slide fitted to frame, 4 1/4 in. barrel with stainless bushing, low mount combat fixed rear sight, dovetail front sight, checkered slide stop, speed trigger, deluxe Commander hammer, beavertail grip safety with pad, extended ambi safety, two 7 shot mags., checkered Cocobolo grips, blued finish.

MSR $1,930	$1,695	$1,450	$1,225	$1,050	$925	$775	$650	

* Stinger Model Stainless – .45 ACP cal., similar to Stinger Model, except features stainless steel frame and slide.

MSR $1,990	$1,695	$1,495	$1,225	$1,050	$825	$725	$650	

CONCEPT I/CONCEPT II – .45 ACP cal., NM steel frame and slide, 5 in. barrel with stainless bushing, slide fitted to frame, double serrated slide, LBC adj. deluxe low mount rear sight with hidden leaf, dovetail front sight, or deluxe fixed combat sight (Concept II), checkered slide stop, fitted speed trigger with action job, deluxe Commander hammer, beavertail grip safety with pad, extended ambi safety, two 8 shot mags., checkered Cocobolo grips, blued finish.

MSR $1,770	$1,595	$1,350	$1,150	$975	$825	$700	$575	

MSR	100%	98%	95%	90%	80%	70%	60%	Last MSR

* **Concept III/Concept IV** – .45 ACP cal., similar to Concept I/Concept II, except has stainless steel frame and blued steel slide, and checkered front strap.

| MSR $1,910 | | $1,675 | $1,450 | $1,225 | $1,050 | $925 | $775 | $650 | |

* **Concept V** – .45 ACP cal., similar to Concept I, except both frame and slide are stainless steel, available with 5 or 6 in. barrel, LBC adj. rear sight, checkered front strap.

| MSR $1,940 | | $1,700 | $1,450 | $1,225 | $1,050 | $925 | $775 | $650 | |

Add $85 for 6 in. barrel.

* **Concept VI** – .45 ACP cal., similar to Concept V, except has 5 in. barrel, Baer deluxe fixed combat rear sight.

| MSR $1,910 | | $1,675 | $1,450 | $1,225 | $1,050 | $925 | $775 | $650 | |

* **Concept VII** – .45 ACP cal., similar to Concept I, except has Commanche size 4 1/4 in. barrel, all blued steel, Baer deluxe fixed combat rear sight, and checkered front strap.

| MSR $1,920 | | $1,675 | $1,450 | $1,225 | $1,050 | $925 | $775 | $650 | |

* **Concept VIII** – .45 ACP cal., similar to Concept I, except has Commanche size 4 1/4 in. barrel, all stainless steel, Baer deluxe fixed combat rear sight, and checkered front strap.

| MSR $1,955 | | $1,695 | $1,450 | $1,225 | $1,050 | $925 | $725 | $650 | |

HEMI 572 – .45 ACP cal., inspired by Chrysler's fast and fearsome 1970 Hemi Cuda, double serrated slide, fiber optic front sight with green insert, Hex head grip screws, special tactical package with ambi safety, VZ black recon grips, complete hard chrome finish on all major components, Dupont S coating on slide stop, mag. catch and mag. catch lock, two 8 shot mags. New 2013.

| MSR $2,395 | | $2,050 | $1,725 | $1,500 | $1,225 | $1,000 | $825 | $725 | |

LIMITED EDITION LES BAER PRESENTATION GRADE 1911 – .45 ACP cal., similar to Premier II, except also features detailed hand chiseled engraving, special charcoal blueing on all polished surfaces, rich nitre blue is used on pins, thumb safety, slide stop, grip screws, mag catch lock and hammer, real ivory grips, "LBC" engraving on top of the slide is inlaid with gold, optional to add name of the recipient engraved on the slide with the legend "To (name) by Les Baer", includes special presentation box.

| MSR $6,590 | | $5,950 | $5,500 | $4,750 | $4,000 | $3,250 | $2,500 | $2,100 | |

Add $100 for name engraving on slide.

CUSTOM 25TH ANNIVERSARY SPECIAL COLLECTORS MODEL – .45 ACP cal., similar to Premier II, except also includes hand engraving on both sides of the slide and frame, Les Baer's actual signature and the legend "25th Anniversary" have been engraved, then inlaid with white gold on the top of the slide, rich charcoal blue finish, real ivory grips, also includes a special presentation box.

| MSR $6,995 | | $6,250 | $5,750 | $4,850 | $4,100 | $3,300 | $2,550 | $2,200 | |

RIFLES: BOLT ACTION

CUSTOM TACTICAL VARMINT CLASSIC – .243 Win., .260 Rem., .300 Win. Mag. (new 2011) or .308 Win. cal., 24 in. match grade barrel, Still Tac 30 action and thick lug, Timney match trigger, front and back of action are glass bedded and lug is bedded into Bell & Carlson precision varmint stock, fitted Wyatts precision floorplate with box mag., Picatinny one piece rail, Dupont S coated finish. Mfg. 2010-2011.

| | | $3,250 | $2,850 | $2,450 | $2,000 | $1,650 | $1,375 | $1,125 | *$3,410* |

Add $150 for .300 Win. Mag. cal. with Harris bipod and muzzle brake.

CUSTOM TACTICAL/TACTICAL RECON – .243 Win., .260 Rem., .308 Win., .338 Lapua, 6.5x284 Norma, or .300 Win. Mag. cal., 24, 26, or 27 in. match grade barrel with or w/o muzzle brake, Still Tac 30 action and thick lug, Timney match trigger, front and back of action are glass bedded and lug is bedded into Bell & Carlson adj. stock, fitted Wyatts precision floorplate with box mag., Picatinny one piece rail, Dupont S coated finish, Harris bipod. Limited mfg. 2011 only.

| | | $3,300 | $2,950 | $2,500 | $2,075 | $1,695 | $1,375 | $1,125 | *$3,560* |

Add $200 for .300 Win. Mag. with enforcer muzzle brake or $330 for .338 Lapua with enforcer muzzle brake.

RIFLES: SEMI-AUTO

CUSTOM ULTIMATE AR MODEL – .204 Ruger (new 2004), .223 Rem., or 6.5 Grendel (mfg. 2007-2009) cal., 18-24 in. stainless steel barrel, Picatinny flat-top rail, individual rifles are custom built with no expense spared, everything made in-house ensuring top quality and tolerances, all models are guaranteed to shoot 1/2-3/4 MOA groups, various configurations include Varmint Model (disc.), Super Varmint Model, NRA Match Rifle, Super Match Model (new 2002), M4 Flattop Model, Custom Special Tactical (new 2011), and IPSC Action Model. New 2001.

| MSR $2,240 | | $2,100 | $1,900 | $1,700 | $1,500 | $1,300 | $1,100 | $900 | |

Add $950-$1,305 for Super Varmint scope packages (includes Leupold Vari-X III 4.5-14x40mm scope). Add $140 for Super Match model. Add $90 for M4 flat-top model. Add $320 for IPSC action model. Add $349 for Thunder Ranch rifle (disc. 2010). Add $849 for CMP competition rifle. Add $240 for NRA match rifle w/o sights. Add $245 for Super Varmint model (.204 Ruger cal.) Add $210 for 6.5 Grendel cal. with M4 style barrel. Add $110 for Custom Special Tactical rifle (new 2011).

MSR	100%	98%	95%	90%	80%	70%	60%	Last MSR

.264 LBC-AR – .264 LBC-AR cal., 18-24 in. stainless steel barrel, available in Ultimate Super Varmint, Ultimate Super Match, and Ultimate M4 Flat-top configurations, fixed stock, black finish, 14 shot mag., features similar to Ultimate Model in .223 cal. New 2010.

	100%	98%	95%	90%	80%	70%	60%	Last MSR
MSR $2,240	$2,100	$1,900	$1,700	$1,500	$1,300	$1,100	$900	

Add $50 for Super Varmint model.
Add $150 for Super Match model.

6x45 ULTIMATE AR – 6x45mm cal., 18-24 in. stainless steel barrel, available in Super Varmint, Super Match, and M4 Flat-top configurations, black finish, fixed stock, similar to Ultimate AR in .223 configuration. New 2010.

	100%	98%	95%	90%	80%	70%	60%	Last MSR
MSR $2,240	$2,100	$1,900	$1,700	$1,500	$1,300	$1,100	$900	

Add $50 for Super Varmint model.
Add $150 for Super Match model.

POLICE SPECIAL – .223 Rem., .264 LBC-AR (disc.), or 6x45mm (disc.) cal., 16 in. precision button rifled steel barrel, 14 or 30 shot mag., removable carry handle with rear sight, Picatinny flat-top upper rail, National Match chromed carrier, flip up front sight, six position ATI collapsible stock with adj. cheekpiece and grip, Picatinny four-way handguard, A2 flash hider, Timney match trigger group, lockable sling swivel mounted on stud on four-way handguard, includes two mags. New 2010.

	100%	98%	95%	90%	80%	70%	60%	Last MSR
MSR $1,790	$1,625	$1,425	$1,150	$1,000	$875	$750	$625	

.308 LBC ULTIMATE MATCH/SNIPER – .308 Win. cal., 18 or 20 in. stainless steel barrel with precision cut rifling, matte black finish, 20 shot mag., machined upper and lower, no forward assist, Picatinny flat-top rail, steel gas block, free float handguard with lock ring, two-stage trigger group, Dupont S coating on barrel, Harris bipod, fixed or adj. Magpul stock, with or w/o enforcer muzzle brake, available in Match or Sniper configuration. New 2011.

	100%	98%	95%	90%	80%	70%	60%	Last MSR
MSR $3,190	$2,850	$2,725	$2,600	$2,275	$1,750	$1,500	$1,250	

Add $30 for Match model with PRS Magpul stock or $300 for Sniper model with adj. stock and enforcer muzzle brake.

.308 ULTIMATE MONOLITH SWAT MODEL – .308 Win. cal., 18 or 24 in. stainless steel barrel with precision cut rifling, matte black finish, 20 shot mag., similar to .308 Ultimate Match/Sniper, except has integrated Mil-Std 1913 Picatinny rail system, Magpul PRS adj. stock, Versa pod and adapter, integral trigger guard is bowed on bottom so shooter can wear gloves. New 2011.

	100%	98%	95%	90%	80%	70%	60%	Last MSR
MSR $3,940	$3,750	$3,475	$3,000	$2,725	$2,450	$2,250	$1,750	

Add $250 for Enforcer muzzlebrake.

LEWIS MACHINE & TOOL COMPANY (LMT)

Current tactical rifle and accessories manufacturer established in 1980, and located in Milan, IL.

CARBINES/RIFLES: SEMI-AUTO

LMT manufactures AR-15 style rifles and carbines.

CQB SERIES – 5.56 NATO cal., GPO, 16 in. chrome lined barrel, 30 shot mag., standard trigger, SOPMOD stock, monolithic rail platform, tactical charging handle assembly, includes sling, manual, tactical adj. front and rear sights, torque wrench/driver, and three rail panels, 6.8 lbs.

	100%	98%	95%	90%	80%	70%	60%	Last MSR
MSR $2,100	$1,875	$1,550	$1,350	$1,225	$975	$800	$625	

* **CQB16 6.8** – 6.8 SPC cal., GPO, similar to CQB16 Standard, except has 25 shot mag. New 2010.

	100%	98%	95%	90%	80%	70%	60%	Last MSR
MSR $2,198	$1,975	$1,725	$1,475	$1,350	$1,085	$895	$695	

* **CQBPS16** – 5.56 NATO cal., GPO, 16 in. barrel, tactical charging handle assembly, Defender lower with SOPMOD buttstock, 30 shot mag., standard trigger group, includes sling, tactical front and rear sights, torque wrench/driver, and three rail panels. New 2010.

	100%	98%	95%	90%	80%	70%	60%	Last MSR
MSR $2,351	$2,100	$1,750	$1,500	$1,375	$1,100	$900	$700	

* **CompCQB16** – 5.56 NATO cal., GPO, similar to CQB16 Standard Model, except has 10 shot mag.

	100%	98%	95%	90%	80%	70%	60%	Last MSR
MSR $2,100	$1,875	$1,550	$1,350	$1,225	$975	$800	$625	

COMP16 – 5.56 NATO cal., GIO, 16 in. chrome lined barrel, standard flat-top upper receiver, 10 shot mag., tactical charging handle assembly, Defender lower with fixed SOPMOD buttstock, standard trigger group, includes sling, tactical adj. rear sight.

	100%	98%	95%	90%	80%	70%	60%	Last MSR
MSR $1,685	$1,500	$1,250	$1,075	$975	$825	$675	$550	

CMP556 – 5.56 NATO cal., 16 in. chrome lined target style barrel, standard flat-top upper receiver, tactical charging handle, Defender lower with fixed SOPMOD buttstock and standard trigger group, 10 shot mag., heavy duty push button swivel, adj. rear sight.

	100%	98%	95%	90%	80%	70%	60%	Last MSR
MSR $2,100	$1,875	$1,550	$1,350	$1,225	$975	$800	$625	

MSR	100%	98%	95%	90%	80%	70%	60%	Last MSR

CQB16300 – .300 Whisper cal., 16 in. chrome lined barrel, tactical charging handle, Defender lower with SOPMOD buttstock and standard trigger group, adj. rear sight, tactical front sight, 30 shot mag., includes torque wrench, 3 rail panels, and sling.

| MSR $2,100 | $1,875 | $1,550 | $1,350 | $1,225 | $975 | $800 | $625 | |

CQBPU16 – 5.56 NATO cal., GPO, 16 in. chrome lined barrel, charging handle, H2 buffer, includes torque wrench and 3 rail panels.

| MSR $1,558 | $1,395 | $1,225 | $1,050 | $950 | $775 | $625 | $500 | |

STD16 – 5.56 NATO cal., GIO, 16 in. chrome lined barrel, standard trigger and bolt, choice of SOPMOD or Gen. 2 collapsible stock, 5.9 - 6.2 lbs.

| MSR $1,594 | $1,425 | $1,225 | $1,075 | $950 | $775 | $650 | $500 | |

SPM16 – 5.56 NATO cal., GIO, similar to STD16, except has Generation 2 buttstock. New 2010.

| MSR $1,371 | $1,225 | $1,075 | $900 | $800 | $675 | $550 | $495 | |

LM8MWS – .308 Win. cal., GPO, 16 in. steel or stainless steel barrel, 20 shot mag., monolithic rail platform, Defender lower with SOPMOD stock, two stage trigger, includes sling, manual, tactical front and rear sights, torque wrench/driver, and three rail panels. New 2010.

| MSR $3,149 | $2,825 | $2,475 | $2,125 | $1,850 | $1,525 | $1,250 | $975 | |

Add $563 for matte black stainless steel barrel.
Add $340 for Pigman Signature Model (new 2012).

LM8MRP – 5.56 NATO cal., GPO, otherwise similar to LM8MWS. New 2012.

| MSR $2,254 | $2,025 | $1,750 | $1,450 | $1,300 | $1,050 | $875 | $675 | |

Add $134 for 16 in. stainless steel barrel.

LM308MWSE/MWSF – .308 Win. cal., GIO, 16 in. barrel, two stage trigger group, SOPMOD buttstock, tactical sights, 20 shot mag., includes 3 rail panels. New 2012.

| MSR $3,003 | $2,700 | $2,350 | $2,000 | $1,750 | $1,450 | $1,175 | $895 | |

Add $563 for matte black stainless steel barrel.

LM308 COMP16 – .308 Win. cal., GIO, standard 16 in. crowned target barrel, 10 shot mag., includes 3 rail panels. New 2012.

| MSR $3,003 | $2,700 | $2,350 | $2,000 | $1,750 | $1,450 | $1,175 | $895 | |

LM308MWSK – .308 Win. cal., GIO, 20 in. stainless steel barrel with matte black finish, SOPMOD buttstock, two stage trigger, 20 shot mag., includes three rail panels. New 2012.

| MSR $3,566 | $3,200 | $2,800 | $2,400 | $2,175 | $1,750 | $1,450 | $1,125 | |

LM8308SS SHARPSHOOTER WEAPON SYSTEM – .308 Win. cal., GIO, 16 in. stainless steel matte black barrel, tactical charging handle, SOPMOD buttstock, flip up sights, includes eight 20 shot magazines, cleaning kit, Harris bipod and pelican case, Flat Dark Earth furniture. New 2012.

| MSR $5,198 | $4,675 | $4,200 | $3,600 | $3,250 | 2,800 | $2,400 | $2,000 | |

LIBERTY ARMS INTERNATIONAL LLC

Current importer and manufacturer currently located in Victoria, TX. Previously located in Albion, NY until 2010.

RIFLES: SEMI-AUTO

Liberty Arms assembles an AK-47 design carbine manufactured from U.S. milled or stamped receivers, U.S. chrome lined barrels, and Bulgarian manufactured part kits. MSRs are $900 for the milled receiver, and $750 for the stamped receiver. Additionally, the company imports a variety of European firearms and ammunition. Please contact the company directly for current surplus offerings, availability, and pricing (see Trademark Index).

LIBERTY ARMS WORKS, INC.

Previous manufacturer located in West Chester, PA circa 1991-1996.

PISTOLS: SEMI-AUTO

L.A.W. ENFORCER – .22 LR, 9mm Para., 10mm, .40 S&W (new 1994), or .45 ACP cal., patterned after the Ingram MAC 10, SA, 6 1/4 in. threaded barrel, closed bolt operation, manual safety, 10 (C/B 1994) or 30* shot mag., 5 lbs. 1 oz. Mfg. 1991-96.

| | $575 | $500 | $450 | $415 | $385 | $335 | $295 | *$545* |

LJUNGMAN

Previously manufactured by Carl Gustaf, located in Eskilstuna, Sweden.

MSR	100%	98%	95%	90%	80%	70%	60%	*Last MSR*

RIFLES: SEMI-AUTO

AG 42 – 6.5x55mm Swedish cal., 10 shot mag., wood stock, tangent rear and hooded front, bayonet lug, designed in 1941.

	$850	$700	$600	$495	$450	$400	$365	

This was the first mass produced, direct gas operated rifle. This weapon was also used by the Egyptian armed forces and was known as the Hakim, and chambered in 8x57mm Mauser.

LOKI WEAPON SYSTEMS, INC.

Previous manufacturer and distributor circa 2009-2012 and located in Coalgate, OK.

Loki Weapon Systems manufactured AR-15 style tactical rifles and 1911 style pistols. Loki was also the U.S. distributor until 2012 for A.M.S.D., located in Geneva, Switzerland.

CARBINES/RIFLES: SEMI-AUTO

Other calibers were available by request. Loki offered a limited lifetime warranty on all rifles and carbines.

FENRIR – 5.56 NATO, .300 Whisper, .458 SOCOM, 6.5 Grendel, 6.8 SPC, or 6.8 Grendel cal., 16 in. barrel, 40 shot mag., mid length gas operating system, M4 ramps and extension, machined upper and lower, Fail Zero coated bolt carrier group, 12 in. eight sided forend with full length Picatinny rail, YHM Phantom flash hider, Ergo F93 eight position stock, hard case, approx. 8 lbs. Mfg. 2009-2011.

	$1,450	$1,295	$1,125	$900	$800	$700	$600	*$1,575*

Subtract $125 for ambidextrous safety selector and 15 in. eight sided forend.

HUNTING RIFLE – .223 Rem./5.56 NATO (.223 Wylde chamber) cal., 20 in. varmint barrel, eight sided forend with three Picatinny rails, single stage trigger, 10 shot mag., fixed stock with ERGO grip, includes hard case. Mfg. mid-2010-2011.

	$1,475	$1,295	$1,125	$900	$800	$700	$600	*$1,625*

PRECISION SNIPER TACTICAL RIFLE – .223 Rem./5.56 NATO (.223 Wylde chamber) cal., M4 upper and lower, 18 in. fluted stainless steel barrel, three port compensator, eight sided forend with full length Picatinny rail, ambidextrous safety, two-stage trigger, 30 shot mag., F93 ERGO stock and grip, includes hard case. Disc. 2011.

	$1,625	$1,475	$1,295	$1,125	$900	$800	$700	*$1,795*

LWSF 3G COMPETITION – 5.56 NATO cal., 18 in. double fluted stainless steel barrel, 15 in. vented carbon fiber forend, Vltor A2 fixed stock, adj. gas block, lightened buffer system and carrier, standard mil-spec charging handle, hardcoat anodized teflon coated black finish, two-stage trigger, integrated CQB Magwell grip with XL magwell and ERGO pistol grip, Nordic Corvette compensator, approx. 6 1/2 lbs. Mfg. 2012.

	$1,675	$1,450	$1,225	$1,050	$900	$750	$675	*$1,850*

LWSF DMR (DESIGNATED MARKSMAN) – .223 Rem./5.56 NATO (.223 Wylde chamber) cal., 20 in. fluted stainless steel SDMR contoured barrel with Rolling Thunder compensator, standard mil-spec charging handle, A2 stock with Magpul MOE grip, hardcoat anodized Teflon coated black finish, multiple picatinny rails, LOKI 14.5 handguard, pinned Lo Pro gas block, M4 feed ramps, 7.8 lbs. Mfg. 2012.

	$1,495	$1,300	$1,100	$900	$700	$600	$550	*$1,645*

LWSF MAGPUL MOE – .264 LBC, .300 BLK, or 5.56 NATO cal., 16.1 in. chromemoly vanadium alloy barrel, A2 birdcage flash hider, Magpul MOE stock with pistol grip, mid-length forend and low profile gas block or YHM flip sight tower gas block, integrated Picatinny rail, oversized trigger guard, hardcoat anodized teflon coated finish, forward assist and dust cover, polished M4 feed ramps, fail zero full-auto bolt carrier, nickel-boron coated charging handle and fire control group, approx. 6 1/2 lbs. Mfg. 2012 only.

	$1,195	$1,000	$850	$725	$600	$500	$450	*$1,349*

LWSF PATROL – .264 LBC, .300 BLK, or 5.56 NATO cal., 16 (.300 BLK cal.), 18 (.264 LBC) or 18 in. double fluted stainless steel barrel, mid-length gas block, phantom flash hider, Vltor EMOD retractable stock with Magpul MOE grip, full length Picatinny rail, free floating forend, integrated winter trigger guard, creep-adj. polished trigger, M4 feed ramps, forward assist and dust cover, black hard coat anodized finish, also available with optional tactical comp or Battlecomp, 7 1/2 lbs. Mfg. 2012.

	$1,275	$1,075	$975	$775	$625	$525	$475	*$1,479*

LWSF STD – .300 BLK, 6.5 Grendel, or 5.56 NATO cal., 16.1 in. chromemoly vanadium alloy barrel, A2 birdcage flash hider, Magpul MOE stock, low profile gas block with rail, black hard coat anodized finish, mid-length free floating forend, standard M4 pistol grip, oversized trigger guard, integrated CQB Magwell grip with XL magwell, fail zero full-auto rated bolt carrier, polished M4 feed ramps, forward assist and dust cover, optional YHM flip sight tower gas block, Vltor EMOD or Ergo F93 stock, 6.7 lbs. Mfg. 2012 only.

	$1,195	$1,000	$850	$725	$600	$500	$450	*$1,349*

MSR	100%	98%	95%	90%	80%	70%	60%	*Last MSR*

LWSF TACTICAL – .300 BLK or 5.56 NATO cal., 16 in. nitride treated M4 barrel, 14 1/2 in. modular forend, A2 birdcage flash hider, Vltor EMOD six-position retractable stock with Magpul MOE grip, black hard coat anodized teflon coated finish, Nib-X coated full-auto rated bolt carrier, integrated winter trigger guard, CQB Magwell grip with XL magwell, creep-adj. polished trigger, optional 9 in. top rail and three 3 in. rails or Troy TRX Extreme handguard, standard mil-spec charging handle, forward assist and M4 feed ramps. Mfg. 2012 only.

	$1,300	$1,100	$1,000	$800	$650	$550	$500	*$1,525*

LWS M4 MOE – 5.56 NATO cal., 16 in. nitride treated barrel, M4 extension, A2 birdcage flash hider, six-position Magpul MOE stock with pistol grip and trigger guard, standard A2 sight post low profile gas block with integrated rail or YHM gas block with integrated flip up front sight, mil-spec BCG nickel boron bolt carrier, mid-length handguard, black hardcoat anodized teflon coated finish, forward assist and dust cover, creep-adj. hand stoned trigger, standard mil-spec charging handle. Mfg. 2012 only.

	$895	$825	$750	$650	$550	$450	$350	*$999*

LWS M4 PATROL – .300 BLK or 5.56 NATO cal., 16 in. nitride treated barrel, M4 extension, A2 birdcage flash hider, choice of six-position Magpul MOE stock with pistol grip and trigger guard, EMOD or F93 collapsible stock and ERGO pistol grip, mil-spec BCG nickel boron bolt carrier, Loki 12 in. rifle length handguard, black hardcoat anodized teflon coated finish, forward assist and dust cover, creep-adj. hand stoned trigger, standard mil-spec charging handle, optional 12 in. top Picatinny rail and three 3 in. side and bottom rails. Mfg. 2012 only.

	$1,050	$925	$825	$700	$600	$500	$400	*$1,199*

LWS M4 STD – .300 BLK or 5.56 NATO cal., 16 in. nitride treated barrel, M4 extension, six-position Magpul MOE stock with M4 pistol grip and trigger guard, black, flat Dark Earth, or OD Green hardcoat anodized teflon coated finish, M4 flat-top upper, 30 shot PMAG, creep-adj. hand stoned single stage trigger, standard mil-spec charging handle, low profile gas block with integrated rail, mid-length handguard, includes case. Mfg. 2012 only.

	$925	$850	$775	$675	$575	$475	$375	*$1,049*

LWS M4 TACTICAL – .300 BLK or 5.56 NATO cal., 16 in. nitride treated M4 barrel, 14 1/2 in. free floating forend, A2 birdcage flash hider, choice of six-position Magpul MOE, EMOD, or F93 stock with ERGO pistol grip, black hard coat anodized teflon coated finish, standard mil-spec charging handle, forward assist and dust cover, mid-length gas system, optional 9 in. Picatinny rail, three 3 in. side and bottom rails, hand stoned trigger, XL modular handguard. Mfg. 2012 only.

	$1,075	$925	$825	$700	$600	$500	$400	*$1,225*

PISTOLS: SEMI-AUTO

Loki manufactured custom built 1911 style pistols in .45 ACP cal. Base price began at $1,800 and went up according to options and accessories.

LONE STAR ARMAMENT, INC.

Previous pistol manufacturer circa 1970-2004, and located in Stephenville, TX. During 2003, Lone Star Armament was absorbed by STI, located in Georgetown, TX.

PISTOLS: SEMI-AUTO

Lone Star Armament manufactured a lineup of M1911 style pistols. Models included: Ranger Match ($1,595 last MSR), Lawman Match ($1,595 last MSR), Lawman Series ($1,475 last MSR), Ranger Series ($1,475 last MSR), and the Guardian Series ($895 last MSR).

LONE STAR TACTICAL SUPPLY

Current firearms manufacturer and dealer located in Tomball, TX.

In addition to manufacturing semi-auto pistols, rifles, and shotguns, Lone Star is also a dealer for Saiga rifles, and offers many shooting accessories.

PISTOLS: SEMI-AUTO

COMPETITION 9 – 9mm Para. cal., GIO, SA, TimberWolf frame, choice of 2 quick change grips, rounded trigger guard, extended beaver tail, round mag. catch, improved checkering, extended slide lock and slide stop, two Glock 17 shot mags., forged stainless steel slides, front and rear cocking serrations, bull nose, beveled rails, lowered ejection port, adj. rear sights.

MSR $750		$675	$600	$500	$475	$375	$300	$250	

COMPETITION 40 – .40 S&W cal., SA, similar to Competition 9, except features two Glock 17 shot mags.

MSR $750		$675	$600	$500	$475	$375	$300	$250	

DUTY 9 – 9mm Para. cal., GIO, SA, TimberWolf frame, choice of 2 quick change grips, rounded trigger guard, extended beaver tail, round mag. catch, improved checkering, extended slide lock and slide stop, two Glock 17 shot mags., forged stainless steel slides, front and rear cocking serrations, bull nose, beveled rails, lowered ejection port, standard sights.

MSR $750		$675	$600	$500	$475	$375	$300	$250	

MSR	100%	98%	95%	90%	80%	70%	60%	Last MSR

DUTY 40 – .40 S&W cal., SA, similar to Duty 9, except features two Glock 15 shot mags.

	100%	98%	95%	90%	80%	70%	60%	
MSR $750	$675	$600	$500	$475	$375	$300	$250	

Add $120 for diamond speed sights with tritium inserts.

RIFLES: SEMI-AUTO

BORDER PATROL – .223 Rem./5.56 NATO (.223 Wylde chamber) cal., AR-15 style, 16 in. chromemoly barrel with A2 flash hider, extended M4 feed ramps, "F" marked A2 front sight base, forged charging handle, laser engraved "T" markings, dry film lube inside upper receiver, ST-T2 Tungsten buffer, Lone Star Tactical logo, bullet pictogram selector markings, 6-position stock, 6-position buffer tube, castle nut, staked latch plate, standard pistol grip, Black finish. Mfg. for Lone Star Tactical by Spike's Tactical.

	100%	98%	95%	90%	80%	70%	60%	
MSR $1,025	$925	$810	$700	$625	$525	$425	$325	

SHOTGUNS

870 TACTICAL – 12 ga., 18 1/2 in. tactical barrel with XS front blade sight, XS ghost ring sight rail, 870 Picatinny rail forward handguard, 2 shot magazine extension, receiver drilled and tapped for scope mounts, sidesaddle ammunition carrier, Blackhawk recoil reducing stock with powerpack, custom textured pistol grip and forward handguard, Black finish.

	100%	98%	95%	90%	80%	70%	60%	
MSR $850	$775	$675	$575	$525	$425	$350	$275	

SAIGA 12 – 12 ga., Kalashnikov style, Blackhawk SpecOps recoil reducing stock, Lone Star stock adapter with single point sling capability, custom trigger, TAC-47 custom 3-position gas plug, Tromix Shark Break door breacher muzzle brake, SGM forward handguard, SGM tactical 10 shot mag., custom textured pistol grip and forward handguard.

	100%	98%	95%	90%	80%	70%	60%	
MSR $1,500	$1,350	$1,175	$1,025	$925	$750	$625	$475	

LOSOK CUSTOM ARMS

Current semi-auto rifle manufacturer located in Delaware, OH.

RIFLES: SEMI-AUTO

VALKYR – various cals. between .30-06-.458 Win. Mag., various barrel configurations 18 in. to 28 in. sporter through heavy, choice of M1 Garand or M14 operating system, milled receiver, modified M1918 Browning BAR magazine, McMillan stock, Picatinny top rail, 16 1/2 lbs. New 2012.

Please contact the company directly for more information on this model including availability, pricing, and options (see Trademark Index).

LUSA USA

Current manufacturer located in Hooksett, NH. Dealer and distributor sales.

CARBINES: SEMI-AUTO

Lusa USA manufactures a 9mm Para. cal. carbine with a 16 in. barrel in three configurations - the 94 LE (MSR $1,295), 94 SP89 Pistol (MSR $999), 94 SA (A2 Standard, MSR $999), the 94 PDW (side folding stock, MSR $1,099), and the 94 AWB (fixed stock, MSR $999-$1,099). Please contact the company directly for more information, including options and availability (see Trademark Index).

M SECTION

M+M, INC.
Current importer and distributor located in Eastlake, CO.

MSR	100%	98%	95%	90%	80%	70%	60%	Last MSR

RIFLES: SEMI-AUTO

M10-762 RIFLE – 7.62x39mm cal., AK-47 design, 16 1/4 in. barrel, 30 shot mag., RPK graduated rear sight. Imported from Romania with six U.S. made parts and assembled in America.

No MSR	$625	$550	$495	$450	$400	$375	$350	

PISTOLS: SEMI-AUTO

SAN P553 – 5.56 NATO cal., upper receiver has Picatinny rail with integrated synthetic handguard, pistol grip, muzzle brake, 30 shot mag. Mfg. in Switzerland. Importation began 2013.

MSR $3,200	$2,725	$2,395	$2,050	$1,850	$1,500	$1,225	$950	

MG ARMS INCORPORATED
Current manufacturer established in 1980, and located in Spring, TX. MG Arms Incorporated was previously named Match Grade Arms & Ammunition. Consumer direct sales.

PISTOLS: SEMI-AUTO

WRAITHE – .45 ACP cal., M1911 design, 4 1/2 in. match grade barrel, SA, choice of fixed or night sights, 3 1/2 lb. trigger, custom grip panels, choice of Olive Drab, Black, Desert Tan, or titanium finish. New 2013.

MSR $2,750	$2,400	$2,125	$1,800	$1,400	$1,150	$925	$850	

RIFLES: SEMI-AUTO

K-YOTE VARMINT SYSTEM – various cals. from .17 Rem. - .458 Lott, AR-15 style, GIO, target trigger, stainless match grade free floating barrel, standard or camo finish four rail aluminum handguard, adj. stock, A3 flat-top upper receiver, machined lower receiver, scope rail. New 2009.

MSR $3,695	$3,450	$3,100	$2,850	$2,550	$2,300	$2,250	$1,995	

CK-4 – .223 Rem. or .300 Fireball cal., AR-15 style, GIO, MGA 3-piece lower receiver, A3 flat-top receiver, 5 position collapsible stock, 16 in. barrel with flash hider, free floating quad rail handguard, choice of PTFE resin finish, basic, or camo coverage. New 2011.

MSR $1,995	$1,695	$1,475	$1,275	$1,150	$925	$775	$595	

TARANIS – 5.56 NATO cal., AR-15 style, GIO, 16 in. lightweight match grade tapered barrel with titanium flash hider, upper receiver with flat-top Picatinny rail, carbon fiber handguard, CTR 6-position collapsible stock, 20 or 30 shot mag., PTFE resin, basic, or zebra camo finish. New 2013.

MSR $2,195	$1,975	$1,750	$1,425	$1,150	$995	$850	$675	

MGI
Current rifle manufacturer located in Old Town, ME. Previously located in Bangor, ME until late 2010.

RIFLES: SEMI-AUTO

MARCK-15 (HYDRA) – .22 LR, .223 Rem., .300 AAC Blackout, .450 Thumper, .458 Socom, 5.56 NATO, 6.5 Grendel, 6.8 SPC, and .50 Beowulf cal., AR-15 style, GIO, complete weapon system, with or w/o a low profile gas block, 16 in. barrel, modular lower receiver with a 5.56mm mag. well, QCB-D upper receiver, change barrels in seconds with no tools required, and utiliize the correct magazine for the caliber you desire. A wide variety of configurations are available.

MSR $1,299	$1,175	$1,025	$875	$800	$650	$525	$425	

* ***Marck-15 Piston*** – similar to Marck-15 Base System, except features GPO.

MSR $1,599	$1,425	$1,245	$1,075	$975	$775	$650	$500	

* ***Marck-15-9mm SMG/LE*** – 9mm Para. cal., GIO, similar to Marck-15 Base System, except utilizes SMG mags. and comes standard with 16 in. blow back barrel and blow back bolt. New 2012.

MSR $1,299	$1,175	$1,025	$875	$800	$650	$525	$425	

This model is also available utilizing Glock magazines in 9mm Para. (Marck-15-9mm LE), or .45 ACP (Marck-15-45LE) cal. New 2012.

* ***Marck-15-AK47-003*** – 7.62x39mm cal., similar to Marck-15 Base System, except offered in AK configuration utilizing standard AK-47 magazines and includes enhanced reliability firing pin and bolt and low profile gas block.

MSR $1,299	$1,175	$1,025	$875	$800	$650	$525	$425	

MSR	100%	98%	95%	90%	80%	70%	60%	Last MSR

* Marck 15-308 Configuration (.308 Hydra) – .308 Win. cal., similar to Marck-15 Base System, except offered in .308 configuration, takes a modified M14 magazine, includes a rate recoil reducing buffer and 18 in. barrel.

MSR $1,750	$1,575	$1,375	$1,175	$1,075	$875	$725	$550	

M-K SPECIALTIES INC.

Previous rifle manufacturer circa 2000-2002 located in Grafton, WV.

RIFLES: SEMI-AUTO

M-14 A1 – .308 Win. cal., forged M-14 steel receiver using CNC machinery to original government specifications, available as Rack Grade, Premier Match, or Tanker Model, variety of National Match upgrades were available at extra cost, base price is for Rack Grade. Mfg. 2000-2002.

	$1,475	$1,275	$995	$875	$750	$625	$500	$1,595

National Match upgrades ranged from $345-$955.

MK ARMS INC.

Previous manufacturer located in Irvine, CA circa 1992.

CARBINES: SEMI-AUTO

MK 760 – 9mm Para. cal., steel frame, 16 in. shrouded barrel, fires from closed bolt, 14, 24, or 36 shot mag., parkerized finish, folding metal stock, fixed sights. Mfg. 1983-approx. 1992.

	$725	$650	$575	$525	$475	$415	$375	$575

MKE

Current manufacturer located in Ankara, Turkey. No current U.S. importation. Previously imported beginning 2011 by American Tactical Imports, located in Rochester, NY. Previously distributed by Mandall Shooting Supplies, Inc., located in Scottsdale, AZ.

MKE manufactures a wide variety of military and law enforcement models, in addition to a line of consumer semi-auto hunting rifles and a semi-auto pistol. Please contact the importer directly for more information, including pricing and availability (see Trademark Index).

PISTOLS: SEMI-AUTO

AT-94P – 9mm Para. cal., MP5 style, 16.4 in. barrel, matte black finish, roll locked delayed blowback system, 30 shot mag. Imported 2011-2012.

	$1,395	$1,200	$1,000	$850	$700	$600	$525	$1,596

AT-94K – 9mm Para. cal., MP5 style, roll locked delayed blowback system, 4 1/2 in. barrel, matte black finish, 30 shot mag., open sights. Imported 2011-2012.

	$1,395	$1,200	$1,000	$850	$700	$600	$525	$1,596

RIFLES/CARBINES: SEMI-AUTO

AT-94R2 CARBINE – 9mm Para. cal., 16.4 in. barrel, patterned after H&K Model 94, roll delayed blowback action, A2 style MP5 stock, steel receiver, matte black finish, 10 shot detachable box mag. Imported 2011-2012.

	$1,350	$1,125	$900	$800	$700	$600	$500	$1,550

AT-43 RIFLE – .223 Rem. cal., 17 in. barrel, patterned after H&K Model 93, roll delayed blowback action, A2 style fixed stock, steel receiver, matte black finish, 30 shot detachable box mag. Imported 2011-2012.

	$1,300	$1,075	$875	$775	$675	$575	$475	$1,495

MKS SUPPLY, INC.

Marketing company representing various companies including Chiappa Firearms Ltd. and Hi-Point Firearms. MKS firearms are manufactured by Chiappa Firearms Ltd. located in Dayton, OH.

SHOTGUNS

MKS Supply, Inc. currently offers the following shotguns: Aimpro Tactical 590 A1 with choice of 18 1/2 or 20 in. barrel with Hogue standard stock, and TacStar side saddle - MSRs are $897 and $945, Aimpro Tactical 590 A1 Breacher - MSR $868, and the Aimpro Tactical 590 A1 Elite with holographic sight and other accessories - MSR $1,495. Please contact the company directly for more information and availability (see Trademark Index).

MMC ARMORY

Current AR-15 manufacturer established in 2008 and located in Mark, IL.

MSR	100%	98%	95%	90%	80%	70%	60%	*Last MSR*

PISTOLS: SEMI-AUTO

MA15 CQP (CLOSE QUARTER PISTOL) – 5.56 NATO cal., 7 or 11 in. barrel with Blast Shield, 30 shot mag., flared magazine well, enhanced SST, hard coat anodized receivers with M4 feed ramps, flared magazine well, Troy Bravo handguard with full Picatinny quad rail system, A2 style grip, flat trigger guard, Black furniture.

	100%	98%	95%	90%	80%	70%	60%	
MSR $1,950	$1,750	$1,525	$1,325	$1,200	$975	$795	$700	

RIFLES: SEMI-AUTO

MA15 3GCR (3 GUN COMPETITION READY) – 5.56 NATO cal., GIO, 17 in. barrel with compensator, 15 in. Troy Alpha handguard, enhanced SST, nickel coated bolt carrier group, low profile gas block, ambidextrous charging handle, 30 shot mag., flat trigger guard, Rodgers Superstoc and 6-position polished buffer tube, polymer A2 style grip, Black furniture, 6.2 lbs. New 2014.

	100%	98%	95%	90%	80%	70%	60%	
MSR $1,709	$1,525	$1,325	$1,150	$1,050	$850	$695	$550	

MA15 PATROL ELITE – 5.56 NATO cal., GIO, 16 in. chromemoly M4 profile nitride hardened barrel, nickel boron coated carrier group, polished buffer tube, single stage trigger, Matte Black or Muddy Girl (new 2014) finish, two-piece mid-length handguard with double heat shield, six position collapsible polymer stock, A2 style pistol grip, Picatinny gas block, 30 shot mag., A2 dimension compensator, flat mil-spec trigger guard, 6.1 lbs.

	100%	98%	95%	90%	80%	70%	60%	
MSR $1,339	$1,125	$995	$850	$775	$625	$500	$395	

Add $214 for Muddy Girl furniture (new 2014).

MA15 PREDATOR XV – 5.56 NATO cal., GIO, 17.1 in. threaded barrel with M4 extension and thread protector, 30 shot mag., enhanced SST, hard coat anodized receivers with M4 feed ramps and flared magazine well, 13 in. Troy Alpha rail, low profile gas block, ambidextrous charging handle, Troy 13 in. Bravo handguard, Rodgers Superstoc and 6-position polished buffer tube, A2 style pistol grip, Black furniture, 6.2 lbs. New 2014.

	100%	98%	95%	90%	80%	70%	60%	
MSR $1,599	$1,350	$1,175	$1,000	$915	$735	$600	$475	

MA15 RECON – 5.56 NATO cal., GIO, 16 in. chromemoly M4 profile nitride hardened cerakoted barrel, available with flash hider or compensator, nickel boron coated carrier group, polished buffer tube, enhanced single stage trigger, matte black finish, 13 in. Troy Bravo quad rail handguard, six position Rodgers Superstoc collapsible polymer stock, A2 style grip, 30 shot mag., A2 dimension compensator, winter trigger guard, low profile gas block, ambidextrous charging handle, 6.8 lbs.

	100%	98%	95%	90%	80%	70%	60%	
MSR $1,599	$1,350	$1,175	$1,000	$915	$735	$600	$475	

Add $60 for compensator.

MA15 TACTICAL – 5.56 NATO cal., GIO, 16 in. chromemoly nitride hardened barrel with M4 extension, available with flash hider or compensator, nickel boron coated carrier group, polished buffer tube, SST, Matte Black finish, 13 in. Troy Alpha modular handguard with movable Picatinny rail, six position Rodgers Superstoc collapsible polymer stock, A2 style grip, 30 shot mag., A2 dimension compensator, flat trigger guard, low profile gas block, ambidextrous charging handle, 6.1 lbs.

	100%	98%	95%	90%	80%	70%	60%	
MSR $1,579	$1,335	$1,175	$1,000	$915	$735	$600	$475	

Add $60 for compensator.

MAADI-GRIFFIN CO.

Previous rifle manufacturer located in Mesa, AZ until 2003. Consumer direct sales.

RIFLES: SEMI-AUTO

MODEL MG-6 – .50 BMG cal., gas operated, bullpup configuration, one piece cast lower receiver, 5, 10, or 15 shot side mounted mag., 26-30 in. barrel, includes bipod, hard carrying case, and 3 mags. 23 lbs. Mfg. 2000-2003.

	100%	98%	95%	90%	80%	70%	60%	
	$5,500	$4,750	$3,850	$3,250	$2,600	$2,200	$1,800	*$5,950*

Add $450 for MK-IV tripod.

RIFLES: SINGLE SHOT

MODEL 89 – .50 BMG cal., one piece cast lower receiver, 36 in. barrel, felt recoil is less than 12 ga., tig-welded interlocking assembly, no screws, tripod optional, 22 lbs. Mfg. 1990-2003.

	100%	98%	95%	90%	80%	70%	60%	
	$3,100	$2,750	$2,400	$2,050	$1,775	$1,500	$1,250	*$3,150*

Add $600 for stainless steel.

MODEL 92 CARBINE – .50 BMG cal., 20 in. barrel, 5 lbs. trigger pull, 18 1/2 lbs. Mfg. 1990-2003.

	100%	98%	95%	90%	80%	70%	60%	
	$2,950	$2,550	$2,225	$1,875	$1,650	$1,400	$1,200	*$2,990*

Add $650 for stainless steel.

MODEL 99 – .50 BMG cal., similar to Model 89, except has 44 in. barrel, 28 lbs. Mfg. 1999-2003.

	100%	98%	95%	90%	80%	70%	60%	
	$3,150	$2,725	$2,450	$2,050	$1,775	$1,500	$1,250	*$3,350*

Add $650 for stainless steel.

MSR	100%	98%	95%	90%	80%	70%	60%	Last MSR

MAGNUM RESEARCH, INC.

Current trademark of pistols and rifles with company headquarters located in Blauvelt, NY beginning 2010, with manufacturing facilities located in Pillager, MN, and by I.W.I. (Baby and Desert Eagle Series), located in Israel. During June of 2010, Kahr Arms purchased the assets of Magnum Research, Inc. Desert Eagle Series was manufactured 1998-2008 by IMI, located in Israel. Previously manufactured by Saco Defense located in Saco, ME during 1995-1998, and by TAAS/IMI (Israeli Military Industries) 1986-1995. .22 Rimfire semi-auto pistols (Mountain Eagle) were previously manufactured by Ram-Line. Single shot pistols (Lone Eagle) were manufactured by Magnum Research sub-contractors. Distributed by Magnum Research, Inc., in Minneapolis, MN. Dealer and distributor sales.

PISTOLS: SEMI-AUTO, RIMFIRE

THE MOUNTAIN EAGLE – .22 LR cal., SA, 6 (new 1995) or 6 1/2 (disc. 1994) in. polymer and steel barrel, features alloy receiver and polymer technology, matte black finish, adj. rear sight, 15 or 20 shot mag. 21 oz. Mfg. 1992-96.

	100%	98%	95%	90%	80%	70%	60%	Last MSR
	$185	$155	$135	$115	$100	$85	$75	*$239*

* ***The Mountain Eagle Compact Edition*** – similar to Mountain Eagle, except has 4 1/2 in. barrel with shortened grips, adj. rear sight, 10 or 15 shot mag., plastic case, 19.3 oz. Mfg. 1996 only.

	100%	98%	95%	90%	80%	70%	Last MSR
	$165	$135	$120	$105	$95	$80	$70	*$199*

* ***The Mountain Eagle Target Edition*** – .22 LR cal., Target variation of the Mountain Eagle, featuring 8 in. accurized barrel, 2-stage target trigger, jeweled bolt, adj. sights with interchangeable blades, 23 oz. Mfg. 1994-96.

	100%	98%	95%	90%	80%	70%	Last MSR
	$235	$185	$150	$135	$120	$105	$95	*$279*

PICUDA MLP-1722 – .17 Mach 2 or .22 LR cal., 10 in. graphite barrel, no sights, features MLR-22 frame, choice of laminated nutmeg, forest camo, or pepper colored Barracuda stock, integral scope base, target trigger, 10 shot mag., approx. 3 lbs. Mfg. 2007-2009.

	100%	98%	95%	90%	80%	70%	Last MSR
	$595	$525	$450	$400	$350	$300	$250	*$699*

PISTOLS: SEMI-AUTO, CENTERFIRE

IMI SP-21 – 9mm Para., .40 S&W, or .45 ACP cal., DA/SA, traditional Browning operating system, SFO, polymer frame with ergonomic design, 3.9 in. barrel with polygonal rifling, 10 shot mag., finger groove grips, 3 dot adj. sights, reversible mag. release, multiple safeties, matte black finish, decocking feature, approx. 29 oz. Limited importation from IMI late 2002-2005.

	100%	98%	95%	90%	80%	70%	Last MSR
	$550	$395	$335	$300	$280	$260	$240	*$499*

The IMI SP-21 uses the same magazines as the Baby Eagle pistols. This model is referred to the Barak SP-21 in Israel.

PISTOLS: SEMI-AUTO, CENTERFIRE - EAGLE SERIES

Magnum Research also offers a Collector's Edition Presentation Series. Special models include a Gold Edition (serial numbered 1-100), a Silver Edition (serial numbered 101-500), and a Bronze Edition (serial numbered 501-1,000). Each pistol from this series is supplied with a walnut presentation case, 2 sided medallion, and certificate of authenticity. Prices are available upon request by contacting Magnum Research directly.

Alloy frames on the Desert Eagle Series of pistols were discontinued in 1992. However, if sufficient demand warrants, these models will once again be available to consumers at the same price as the steel frames.

Beginning late 1995, the Desert Eagle frame assembly for the .357 Mag., .44 Mag., and .50 AE cals. is based on the .50 caliber frame. Externally, all three pistols are now identical in size. This new platform, called the Desert Eagle Pistol Mark XIX Component System, enables .44 Mag. and .50 AE conversions to consist of simply a barrel and a magazine - conversions to or from the .357 Mag. also include a bolt.

The slide assembly on the Mark I and Mark VII is physically smaller than the one on a Mark XIX. Also, the barrel dovetail on top is 3/8 in. on a Mark I or Mark VII, while on a Mark XIX, it is 7/8 in., and includes cross slots for scopes.

Individual Desert Eagle Mark XIX 6 in. barrels are $389-$564, depending on finish, and 10 in. barrels are $459-$634, depending on finish. Add $129 for Trijicon night sights (new 2006). Add $49-$89 for Hogue Pau Ferro wooden grips (new 2007) or $49 for Hogue soft rubber grips with finger grooves (disc. 2008).

MR9/MR40 EAGLE – 9mm Para. or .40 S&W cal., SA, SFO, fully adj. rear sight, 4 (9mm Para. cal., disc. 2013), 4.15 (.40 S&W cal., disc. 2013), or 4 1/2 in. barrel, interchangeable palm swells, 10, 11(.40 S&W cal.), or 15 (9mm Para. cal.) shot mag., lower Picatinny rail, internal safeties, square trigger guard, cooperative manufacturing effort with Carl Walther supplying the black polymer frame with integral steel rails, while the stainless steel slide and barrel are manufactured and assembled in Pillager, MN, approx. 25 oz. New 2011.

	100%	98%	95%	90%	80%	70%	60%	
MSR $559	$475	$425	$375	$325	$295	$275	$250	

* ***The Baby Eagle II Semi-Compact*** – 9mm Para., .40 S&W, or .45 ACP cal., similar to Baby Eagle II Full Size, except has 3.7 (disc.), or 3.93 (new 2011) in. barrel, DA/SA, ergonomic rear sight and lower Picatinny rail. Importation began 2008 by I.W.I.

	100%	98%	95%	90%	80%	70%	60%	
MSR $656	$560	$475	$425	$375	$325	$275	$225	

Add $235 for brushed or polished chrome (disc. 2009).
Subtract $27 for polymer frame.

MSR	100%	98%	95%	90%	80%	70%	60%	Last MSR

MARK I DESERT EAGLE .357 MAG – .357 Mag. cal., SA, similar to Mark VII, except has standard trigger and safety lever is teardrop shaped, and slide catch release has single serration. Disc.

| | $925 | $825 | $725 | $625 | $525 | $450 | $400 | |

MARK XIX .357 MAG. DESERT EAGLE – features .50 cal. frame and slide, SA, standard Black, Brushed Chrome, Matte Chrome, Polished Chrome, Bright Nickel, Satin Nickel, 24K Gold, Titanium Gold, or Titanium Gold w/Tiger Stripes finish, 6 or 10 (disc. 2011) in. barrel, full Picatinny top rail with fixed sights became standard late 2009 (U.S. mfg.), 4 lbs., 6 oz. Mfg. by Saco 1995-98, by IMI 1998-2009, and domestically beginning 2010.

| MSR $1,563 | $1,350 | $1,125 | $875 | $775 | $650 | $550 | $475 | |

Add $275 for Brushed Chrome, Matte Chrome, Polished Chrome, Bright Nickel or Satin Nickel finish.

Add $507 for 24K Gold or Titanium Gold finish.

Add $618 for Titanium Gold w/Tiger Stripe finish.

Add $87 for 10 in. barrel (disc. 2011).

MARK VII .357 MAG. DESERT EAGLE – .357 Mag. cal., SA, gas operated, 6 (standard barrel length), 10, or 14 in. barrel length with 3/8 in. dovetail rib, steel (58.3 oz.) or alloy (47.8 oz.) frame, adj. trigger, safety lever is hook shaped, slide catch/release lever has three steps, adaptable to .44 Mag. with optional kit, 9 shot mag. (8 for .44 Mag.). Mfg. 1983-95, limited quantities were made available again during 1998 and 2001.

| | $1,100 | $1,000 | $875 | $750 | $650 | $550 | $475 | *$929* |

Add approx. $150 for 10 or 14 in. barrel (disc. 1995).

Add $495 for .357 Mag. to .41 Mag./.44 Mag. conversion kit (6 in. barrel). Disc. 1995.

Add approx. $685 for .357 Mag. to .44 Mag. conversion kit (10 or 14 in. barrel). Disc. 1995.

* **Mark VII .357 Mag. Desert Eagle Stainless Steel** – similar to .357 Mag. Desert Eagle, except has stainless steel frame, 58.3 oz. Mfg. 1987-95.

| | $1,100 | $1,000 | $875 | $750 | $650 | $550 | $475 | *$839* |

Add approx. $150 for 10 or 14 in. barrel.

MARK VII .41 MAG. DESERT EAGLE – .41 Mag. cal., SA, similar to .357 Desert Eagle, 6 in. barrel only, 8 shot mag., steel (62.8 oz.) or alloy (52.3 oz.) frame. Mfg. 1988-1995, limited quantities available during 2001.

| | $1,050 | $975 | $850 | $725 | $625 | $525 | $475 | *$899* |

Add $395 for .41 Mag. to .44 Mag. conversion kit (6 in. barrel only).

* **Mark VII .41 Mag. Desert Eagle Stainless Steel** – similar to .41 Mag. Desert Eagle, except has stainless steel frame, 58.3 oz. Mfg. 1988-95.

| | $1,100 | $1,000 | $875 | $750 | $650 | $550 | $475 | *$949* |

MARK I DESERT EAGLE .44 MAG – .44 Mag. cal., SA, similar to Mark VII, except has standard trigger and safety lever is teardrop shaped, and slide catch release has single serration. Disc.

| | $1,200 | $1,075 | $925 | $775 | $675 | $575 | $495 | |

MARK XIX .44 MAG. DESERT EAGLE – features .50 cal. frame and slide, SA, standard Black, brushed chrome, polished chrome, matte chrome, satin nickel, bright nickel, 24K Gold, Titanium Gold, or Titanium Gold w/Tiger Stripes finish, 6 or 10 in. barrel, full Picatinny top rail with fixed sights became standard late 2009 (U.S. mfg.), 4 lbs., 6 oz. Mfg. by Saco 1995-98, by IMI 1998-2009, domestically by CCI beginning 2009, and by I.W.I. beginning 2012.

| MSR $1,534 | $1,350 | $1,125 | $875 | $775 | $650 | $550 | $475 | |

Add $116 for 10 in. barrel.

Add $29 for U.S. mfg.

Add $238 for 6 in. barrel with muzzle brake, black finish (new 2013), or $615 for muzzle brake with brushed or polished chrome (new 2013).

Add $341 for Brushed chrome, matte chrome, polished chrome, satin nickel, or bright nickel finish.

Add $577 for 24K Gold or Titanium Gold finish. Add $689 for Titanium Gold w/Tiger Stripes finish.

Add $199 for black muzzle brake (limited mfg. 2010 only).

MARK VII .44 MAG. DESERT EAGLE – .44 Mag. cal., SA, similar to .357 Desert Eagle, 8 shot mag., steel (62.8 oz.) or alloy (52.3 oz.) frame. Originally mfg. 1986-1995, re-released 1998-2000.

| | $1,100 | $1,000 | $875 | $750 | $650 | $550 | $475 | *$1,049* |

Add $100 for 10 (current) or 14 (disc. 1995) in. barrel.

Add $475 for .44 Mag. to .357 Mag. conversion kit (6 in. barrel). Disc. 1995.

Add $675 for .44 Mag. to .357 Mag. conversion kit (10 or 14 in. barrel). Disc. 1995.

Add $395 for .44 Mag. to .41 Mag. conversion kit (6 in. barrel). Disc. 1995.

* **Mark VII .44 Mag. Desert Eagle Stainless Steel** – similar to .44 Mag. Desert Eagle, except has stainless steel frame, 58.3 oz. Mfg. 1987-95.

| | $1,175 | $1,050 | $900 | $775 | $675 | $575 | $475 | *$949* |

Add approx. $210 for 10 or 14 in. barrel.

MSR	100%	98%	95%	90%	80%	70%	60%	Last MSR

MARK VII .50 MAG. DESERT EAGLE – .50 AE cal., SA, 6 in. barrel with 7/8 in. rib with cross slots for Weaver style rings, steel only, black standard finish, frame slightly taller than the Mark VII .357 Mag./.44 Mag., 7 shot mag., 72.4 oz. Mfg. 1991-1995 by IMI, limited quantities were made available again during 1998 only.

	$1,175	$950	$825	$700	$575	$500	$450	*$1,099*

This cartridge utilized the same rim dimensions as the .44 Mag. and was available with a 300 grain bullet. The .50 Action Express cal. has 20%-25% more stopping power than the .44 Mag., with a minimal increase in felt recoil.

MARK XIX CUSTOM 440 – .440 Cor-Bon cal., SA, similar to Mark XIX .44 Mag. Desert Eagle, 6 or 10 in. barrel, standard black finish, rechambered by MRI Custom Shop, limited mfg. 1999-2001.

	$1,175	$995	$850	$725	$575	$500	$450	*$1,389*

Add $40 for 10 in. barrel.

MARK XIX .50 MAG. DESERT EAGLE – .50 AE cal., SA, larger frame, standard black finish, 6 or 10 in. barrel, full Picatinny top rail with fixed sights became standard late 2009 (U.S. mfg.), 4 lbs., 6 oz. Mfg. by Saco 1995-1998, by IMI (1998-2008 disc.), I.W.I. (new 2009), and CCI in the U.S. beginning 2010.

MSR $1,563	$1,350	$1,125	$875	$775	$650	$550	$475	

Add $120 for 10 in. barrel.
Add $31 for domestic mfg.
Add $240 for muzzle brake (black finish, 6 in. barrel only).
Add $349 for brushed chrome, matte chrome, polished chrome, bright nickel or satin nickel finish.
Add $590 for 24K Gold or Titanium Gold finish. Add $701 for Titanium Gold w/Tiger Stripes finish.
Add $199 for black muzzle brake (mfg. 2010 only), or $623 for muzzle brake with brushed chrome (new 2011) or polished chrome (new 2013) finish.

MARK XIX 3 CAL. COMPONENT SYSTEM – includes Mark XIX .44 Mag. Desert Eagle and 5 barrels including .357 Mag. (6 and 10 in.), .44 Mag., and .50 AE (6 and 10 in.) cals., .357 bolt assembly and ICC aluminum carrying case. Also available in custom finishes at extra charge. Mfg. 1998-2011.

	$3,900	$3,450	$2,800	$2,400	$2,000	$1,750	$1,500	*$4,402*

* **Mark XIX 3 Cal. Component System (6 or 10 in. Barrel)** – includes component Mark XIX system in 6 or 10 in. barrel only. Mfg. 1998-2011.

	$2,550	$2,225	$1,775	$1,500	$1,250	$1,000	$850	*$2,910*

Add $262 for 10 in. barrel (disc. 2011).

RIFLES: BOLT-ACTION

MOUNTAIN EAGLE TACTICAL RIFLE – .223 Rem. (new 2002), .22-250 Rem. (new 2002), .308 Win., .300 Win. Mag., or .300 WSM (new 2002) cal., accurized Rem. M-700 action, 26 in. Magnum Lite barrel, H-S Precision tactical stock, adj. stock and trigger, 9 lbs., 4 oz. Mfg. 2001-2011.

	$2,150	$1,825	$1,475	$1,150	$850	$700	$575	*$2,475*

Add $96 for any cal. other than .300 WSM (disc. 2011).

MAJESTIC ARMS, LTD.

Previous firearms manufacturer established during 2000, and located on Staten Island, NY. The company now produces firearms components, conversion kits, and accessories.

CARBINES: SEMI-AUTO

MA 2000 – .22 LR cal., Henry Repeating Arms Co. AR-7 takedown action, fiberoptic sights, American walnut forearm, pistol grip, and buttplate, fixed tubular stock with butt bag, 16 1/4 in. Lothar Walther barrel with crown, black teflon or silver bead blast finish, 4 lbs. Mfg. 2000-2008.

	$350	$295	$250	$225	$195	$175	$150	*$389*

MA 4 – .17 HMR, .17 Mach 2 (new 2005), .22 LR (new 2005), or .22 WMR cal., takedown action, traditional or wire frame stock, interchangeable barrel/bolt assembly.

While intially advertised during 2004 with an MSR of $399, this model did not go into production past the prototype stage.

SHOTGUNS: SLIDE ACTION

BASE-TAC – 12 or 20 ga., 3 in. chamber, based on M870 Remington action, approx. 18 in. barrel with ghost ring sights, black synthetic (12 ga.) or hardwood stock and forearm, extended 6 shot tube mag., 6-7 lbs. Mfg. 2004-2010.

	$675	$575	$500	$450	$400	$350	$300	*$759*

Add $30 for 20 ga.

MSR	100%	98%	95%	90%	80%	70%	60%	*Last MSR*

MARLIN FIREARMS COMPANY

Current trademark with headquarters located in Madison, NC beginning 2010. Currently manufactured by Remington in Ilion, NY beginning early 2011. Previous manufacturer located in North Haven, CT (1969-2010), and in New Haven, CT (1870-1969). The Marlin company manufactured firearms between 1870-2010. Distributor sales only.

On Nov. 10th, 2000, Marlin Firearms Company purchased H&R 1871, Inc. This includes the brand names Harrington & Richardson, New England Firearms, and Wesson & Harrington (please refer to individual sections in this text).

During 2005, Marlin Firearms Company once again started manufacturing a L.C. Smith line of both SxS and O/U shotguns.

Remington Arms. Company, Inc. and The Freedom Group acquired Marlin Firearms Company, H&R 1871, LLC., New England Firearms (NEF), and L.C. Smith brand in January of 2008. The Freedom Group, Inc. announced the closure of its Marlin manufacturing facility, located in North Haven, Connecticut. During 2011, production was moved to Ilion, NY. Marlin Firearms Company had been a family-owned and operated business from 1921-2007.

SHOTGUNS: BOLT ACTION

* ***Model 512DL Slugmaster*** – similar to Model 512 Slugmaster, except has black Rynite stock, Fire Sights (with red fiberoptic inserts) became standard 1998. Disc. 1998.

	100%	98%	95%	90%	80%	70%	60%	Last MSR
	$310	$230	$200	$180	$160	$145	$130	*$372*

* ***Model 512P Slugmaster*** – 12 ga., 3 in. chamber, features 21 in. ported fully rifled barrel with front and rear Fire Sights (high visibility red and green fiberoptic inserts), 2 shot detachable box mag., black fiberglass synthetic stock with molded-in checkering, receiver is drilled and tapped, 8 lbs. Mfg. 1999-2001.

	100%	98%	95%	90%	80%	70%	60%	Last MSR
	$315	$235	$200	$180	$165	$155	$145	*$388*

MASTERPIECE ARMS

Current pistol and rifle manufacturer located in Gomer, GA. Previously located in Carrollton, GA until 2013, also previously located in Braselton, GA. Dealer sales only.

CARBINES: SEMI-AUTO

MPA manufactures a line of semi-auto carbines patterned after the MAC Series with 30 or 35 shot mags. (interchangable with its pistols).

MPA460 CARBINE – .460 Rowland cal., 16 in. threaded barrel, 30 shot mag., side cocking, muzzle brake, black finish, with or w/o .45 ACP upper. Mfg. 2010 only.

	100%	98%	95%	90%	80%	70%	60%	Last MSR
	$725	$650	$575	$500	$425	$375	$325	*$800*

Add $54 for scope mount, hand guard, and Mark III tactical scope.

MPAR556/MPAR300 – 5.56 NATO or .300 Blackout (new 2014) cal., 16.26 in. barrel with combat muzzle brake, short stroke piston, ATACS Hyrographic (new 2014), phosphate or hardcoat anodized finish, two-piece free floating aluminum handguard with front cover and Picatinny rails, MBA buttsock, side folding design, locked bolt action, side charging handle, forward assist, angled foregrip, full length top rail, dust cover on side charger, full length scope mount, accepts M16 magazines, 7.8 lbs. New 2013.

MSR $950	100%	98%	95%	90%	80%	70%	60%
	$850	$750	$650	$575	$500	$450	$395

Add $108 for ATACS Hyrographic finish (new 2014), 5.56 NATO cal. only.

MPAR68 – 6.8 SPC cal., 16 in. threaded barrel with combat muzzle brake, locked bolt, short stroke piston, 25 shot mag., MPA aluminum handguard, side charger, full length scope mount, MPA buttstock, side folding design, Black or MultiCam Hydrographic finish. New 2014.

MSR $1,028	100%	98%	95%	90%	80%	70%	60%
	$925	$810	$695	$625	$525	$450	$395

Add $75 for MultiCam Hydrographic finish.

MPA MINI TACTICAL CARBINE – 9mm Para. cal., side cocker, 16 in. threaded barrel with birdcage muzzle brake, 30 shot mag., mag. loader, adj. front and rear sights, tactical pistol grip, aluminum quad rail, multi-reticle hollow sight, MPA low profile aluminum or side folding (new 2014) stock. New 2011.

MSR $816	100%	98%	95%	90%	80%	70%	60%
	$725	$625	$525	$450	$425	$400	$375

Add $53 for side folding stock.

Models MPA9300SST and MPA9300SST-SF

MPA TACTICAL CARBINE – 9mm Para. or .45 ACP cal., side charger, 16 in. threaded barrel, scope mount, 30 (.45 ACP cal.) or 35 (9mm Para. cal.) shot mag., Intrafuse handguard and vertical grip, Defender stock, multi-reticle hollow sight. Mfg. 2011-2012.

	100%	98%	95%	90%	80%	70%	60%	Last MSR
	$850	$750	$650	$575	$500	$425	$375	*$956*

Add $16 for .45 ACP cal.

SIDE COCKING MODEL – 9mm Para (MPA20SST), .45 ACP (MPA1SST), or 5.7x28mm (MPA5700SST) cal., side cocker, 16 in. threaded barrel, muzzle brake, 20 (5.7x28mm only) or 30 shot mag., scope mount, mag. loader, MPA

MSR	100%	98%	95%	90%	80%	70%	60%	Last MSR

low profile aluminum or side folding (new 2014)stock, MPA aluminum handguard, adj. front and rear sights, quick mag. release, tactical pistol grip (9mm Para. only).

MSR $816	$725	$625	$525	$450	$425	$400	$375	

Add $53 for side folding stock.

TOP COCKING MODEL – 9mm Para. (MPA20T-A) or .45 ACP (MPA1T-A) cal., top cocking, 16 in. threaded barrel, black skeletonized stock, 30 shot mag. Disc. 2010.

	$480	$425	$360	$325	$265	$215	$170	$530

Add $30 for .45 ACP cal.

PISTOLS: SEMI-AUTO

MPA manufactures a line of tactical style pistols patterned after the original MAC Series from Ingram.

MPA10T – .45 ACP cal., top cocking, 6 or 10 (disc.) in. threaded barrel, 30 shot mag., short Picatinny rail mounted to lower receiver for attachment of flashlight, barrel extension, magazine loader, quick magazine release, adj. front and rear sights.

MSR $499	$375	$325	$275	$225	$200	$175	$150	

Add $80 for 10 in. barrel and AR-15 hand guard (disc.).

* *MPA10SST* – .45 ACP cal., similar to MPA10T, except is side cocking, available with optional muzzle brake.

MSR $574	$495	$425	$375	$325	$275	$225	$195	

MPA30T – 9mm Para. cal., top cocking, 6 in. threaded barrel, 30 shot mag., barrel extension, mag. loader, adj. front and rear sights, quick mag. release, flashlight lower Picatinny rail, hammer with disconnect.

MSR $499	$375	$325	$275	$225	$200	$175	$150	

* *MPA30SST* – 9mm Para. cal., similar to MPA30T, except is side cocking.

MSR $574	$495	$425	$375	$325	$275	$225	$195	

MPA57SST – 5.7x28mm cal., side cocker, 5 in. threaded barrel, 20 shot mag., scope mount, muzzle brake, adj. front and rear sights, quick mag. release, flashlight lower Picatinny rail, hammer with disconnect, Black, ATACS, or Grim Reaper finish.

MSR $605	$535	$475	$400	$365	$295	$240	$185	

Add $60 for ATACS (MPA57SSA-ATACS) or Grim Reaper (MPA57SST-GR) finish.

MPA570SST – 5.7x28mm cal., side cocker, 8 in. threaded barrel, muzzle brake, 20 shot mag., scope mount, short aluminum handguard, angled foregrip, adj. front and rear sights, quick mag. release, flashlight lower Picatinny rail, hammer with disconnect, Black finish.

MSR $756	$675	$595	$500	$460	$375	$300	$235	

MPA930 MINI PISTOL – 9mm Para. cal., 3 1/2 in. threaded barrel, SA, 35 shot mag., optional scope mount, black finish. Disc. 2013.

	$375	$325	$275	$225	$200	$175	$150	$489

Add $81 for side cocker with scope mount.

MPA930T MINI PISTOL – 9mm Para. cal., top cocking, 4 1/2 in. threaded barrel, 30 shot mag., mag. loader, barrel extension, adj. front and rear sights, quick mag. release, hammer with disconnect, Black, Camo (Model MPA930T-AC), or Grim Reaper (MPA930T-GR) finish.

MSR $499	$375	$325	$275	$225	$200	$175	$150	

Add $45 for camo (MPA930T-AC) or Grim Reaper (MPA930T-GR) finish.

* *MPA930SST Mini Pistol* – 9mm Para. cal., similar to MPA930T, except is side cocking and features tactical pistol grip, flashlight lower Picatinny rail.

MSR $574	$495	$425	$375	$325	$275	$225	$195	

MPA22T MINI PISTOL – .22 LR cal., 5 in. threaded barrel, SA, 30 shot mag., top cocker or side cocker with scope mount, black finish. Mfg. 2010-2012.

	$385	$350	$315	$275	$250	$225	$195	$440

Add $85 for side cocker with scope mount.

MPA460 PISTOL – .460 Rowland cal., 6 or 10 in. threaded barrel, SA, 30 shot mag., side cocker, scope mount, muzzle brake, black finish. Mfg. 2009-2010.

	$495	$450	$395	$365	$335	$300	$275	$580

Add $90 for .45 ASP upper.
Add $96 for 10 in. barrel.

MSR	100%	98%	95%	90%	80%	70%	60%	Last MSR

MPA TACTICAL PISTOL – 9mm Para. or .45 ACP cal., side cocker, 6 in. threaded barrel, SA, 30 (.45 ACP) or 35 (9mm) shot mag., multi-reticle hollow sight, includes Picatinny rail, flash light and pressure switch, adj. front and rear sights, quick magazine release, safety barrel extension, tactical pistol grip. New 2011.

| MSR $657 | $575 | $525 | $450 | $400 | $350 | $300 | $275 | |

Model MPA10SST-X and MPA30SST-X

MPA MINI TACTICAL PISTOL – .22 LR (disc. 2012) or 9mm Para. cal., side cocker, 3 1/2 (9mm Para. cal.) or 5 (.22 LR cal., disc. 2012) in. threaded barrel, SA, 30 (.22 LR cal.) or 35 (9mm Para. cal.) shot mag., multi-reticle red-dot sight, adj. front and rear sights, tactical pistol grip, includes flash light, ring rail, and safety extension. New 2011.

| MSR $657 | $575 | $525 | $450 | $400 | $350 | $300 | $275 | |

Model MPA930SST-X

MPA SUB-COMPACT – .32 ACP or .380 ACP cal., DAO, 2 1/4 in. barrel, sub-compact design, 6 shot mag., solid steel construction, black or two-tone finish, black synthetic grips, 11.8 oz. Mfg. 2011-2012.

| | $275 | $250 | $225 | $195 | $175 | $150 | $135 | *$323* |

Add $23 for two-tone finish.

RIFLES: BOLT ACTION

MPA308BA – .308 cal., 22 in. match grade fluted hand lapped stainless threaded barrel with muzzle brake, Jewel trigger, aluminum V-bedded chassis, Rem. 700 type action, stainless one-piece fluted bolt, ground recoil lugs, AICS detachable magazine, Magpul PRS sniper stock, Ergo pistol grip with palm shelf. New 2014.

| MSR $3,475 | $3,125 | $2,750 | $2,350 | $2,125 | $1,725 | $1,400 | $1,095 | |

Add $300 for side folding chassis (MPA308BA-SF).

MAUNZ MATCH RIFLES LLC (MAUNZ, KARL)

Current manufacturer located in Grand Rapids, OH. Previously located in Toledo and Maumee, OH circa 1960s-1987.

RIFLES: SEMI-AUTO

Maunz Rifles were manufactured in Toledo and Maumee Ohio from 1960's until 1987 by Karl Maunz for high-end military, law enforcement and competition. Models included the Model 87 Maunz Match Rifle, Model 77 Service Match Rifle, Model 67 Match Grade for practice, Model 67 Sniper Rifle, Model 57 and the Model 47 rifle. All models made on or prior to 2011 are custom order only.

MODEL 57 M1A – various cals. including .30-06, .308 Win., .276 Maunz or .45 Maunz (rare), other custom calibers were available, utilizes M1 Garand receiver with M14 parts, National Match barrel, custom-built glass bedded stock.

| | $1,800 | $1,600 | $1,350 | $1,125 | $900 | $775 | $625 | |

MODEL 66 MATCH SERVICE RIFLE – .308 Win. cal., 22 in. barrel, M1A configuration with M1 and M14 G.I. parts, fiberglass stock, NM sights, M1 trigger assembly, 10 lbs., approx. 200 mfg.

| | $2,500 | $2,250 | $2,000 | $1,800 | $1,500 | $1,250 | $1,050 | |

MODEL 67 MATCH GRADE PRACTICE RIFLE – 7.62 NATO/.308 Win. (.308x224, .308x244, .308x264), 6.30 Maunz, .338 Maunz (ltd. mfg.), or .45 Maunz (ltd. mfg.) cal., other custom calibers were available, M1A configuration with combination of M1 Garand and M14 parts, not allowed for service rifle competition.

| | $2,000 | $1,775 | $1,525 | $1,250 | $1,000 | $875 | $700 | |

MODEL 67 ASSAULT SNIPER RIFLE – 7.62 NATO/.308 Win. (.308x224, .308x244, .308x264), or 6.30 Maunz cal., 22 in. barrel standard, medium and heavy barrels were also available, M14 sights standard, 5, 10, 20, or 30 shot mag.

| | $2,000 | $1,775 | $1,525 | $1,250 | $1,000 | $875 | $700 | |

MODEL 77 SERVICE MATCH RIFLE – 7.62 NATO/.308 Win. cal., custom calibers were also available, 22 in. barrel standard, medium and heavy barrels were also available, 5, 10, or 20 shot mag., NM/2A sights, special removable front globe sight, charcoal grey parkerized finish, heavyweight Kevlar or graphite/fiberglass stock with black gel coat, red/white/blue stocks also available.

| | $2,850 | $2,500 | $2,250 | $1,975 | $1,700 | $1,350 | $1,075 | |

MODEL 87 – various cals., 26 in. medium weight barrel, synthetic stock, G.I. parts with TRW bolts, satin black finish, open sights, ser. nos. 00001-03030, 11 lbs. Mfg. 1985-89.

| | $2,300 | $2,100 | $1,800 | $1,500 | $1,250 | $1,050 | $925 | |

MODEL 87 MATCH RIFLE – 7.62 NATO/.308 Win. (.308x224, .308x244, .308x264), 6.30 Maunz, .338 Maunz (ltd. mfg.), or .45 Maunz (ltd. mfg.) cal., other custom calibers were available, charcoal grey parkerized finish, heavyweight Kevlar or graphite/fiberglass stock with black gel coat, red/white/blue stocks also available.

| | $2,500 | $2,250 | $1,925 | $1,675 | $1,350 | $1,125 | $975 | |

MSR	100%	98%	95%	90%	80%	70%	60%	Last MSR

MODEL 007 – .30 Custom, 6.30 Maunz, or .45 Maunz cal., accuracy metal full lined bedded with long action to accept the M1 Garand bolt, modified M14 type gas system, stainless steel or metal receiver, scope mount, classic wood, heavyweight Kevlar, or graphite/fiberglass stock covered in black gel coat, accepts many different type of magazines, custom weight barrels available.

| MSR $1,650 | $1,495 | $1,300 | $1,100 | $950 | $825 | $700 | $600 | |

MODEL 007 NRA MATCH RIFLE – chambered in 6.30 Maunz caliber with die sets for 6mm, 6.5mm, 7mm, 7.62x51mm, and .30-06 cal., 50 mfg. - one for each state, custom fit to the shooter and using his chosen serial number.

| | $1,650 | $1,450 | $1,250 | $1,050 | $925 | $800 | $700 | |

MODEL 97 MATCH/VARMINT RIFLE – chambered for custom calibers, modeled after the US M16/AR-15, GIO, custom weight barrels, fiberglass stock, custom color stock or classic wood stock.

| MSR $1,250 | $1,100 | $975 | $850 | $725 | $600 | $500 | $400 | |

MODEL 97 SERVICE RIFLE – 5.56 NATO or .223 Rem. cal., modeled after the US M16/AR-15, GIO, black gel coated GI fiberglass stock. Disc. 2013.

| | $1,075 | $950 | $800 | $725 | $595 | $485 | $375 | *$1,200* |

MODEL M14SA – service Standard grade rifle modeled after the M14.
Previous MSR on this model was $1,400.

MODEL M16SA – Service Standard grade rifle modeled after the M16.
Previous MSR on this model was $650.

MAUSER JAGDWAFFEN GmbH

Current trademark established during 1871, and currently owned by SIG Arms AG beginning late 2000. Mauser Model 98 Magnum bolt action rifles are currently manufactured by Mauser Jagdwaffen GmbH, located in Isny, Germany. Currently imported beginning 2009 by Mauser USA, located in San Antonio, TX.

In late 2000, SIG Arms AG, the firearms portion of SIG, was purchased by two Germans named Michael Lüke and Thomas Ortmeier, who have a background in textiles. Today the Lüke & Ortmeier group (L&O Group) includes independently operational companies such as Blaser Jadgwaffen GmbH, Mauser Jagdwaffen GmbH, J.P. Sauer & Sohn GmbH, SIG-Sauer Inc., SIG-Sauer GmbH and SAN Swiss Arms AG.

From late March, 2006-2009, Models 98 and 03 were distributed exclusively by Briley Manufacturing, located in Houston, TX. The former transition name was Mauser Jagd-und Sportwaffen GmbH. On January 1, 1999, Mauser transferred all production and distribution rights of both hunting and sporting weapons to SIG-Blaser. Mauser-Werke Oberndorf Waffensysteme GmbH continues to manufacture military defense contracts (including making small bore barrel liners for tanks), in addition to other industrial machinery.

Previously imported exclusively by Brolin Arms, located in Pomona, CA during 1997-98 only. During 1998, the company name was changed from Mauser-Werke Oberndorf Waffensysteme GmbH. During 1994, the name was changed from Mauser-Werke to Mauser-Werke Oberndorf Waffensysteme GmbH. Previously imported by GSI located in Trussville, AL, until 1997, Gibb's Rifle Co., Inc. until 1995, Precision Imports, Inc. located in San Antonio, TX until 1993, and KDF located in Seguin, TX (1987-89).

PISTOLS: SEMI-AUTO, RECENT IMPORTATION

M-2 – .357 SIG (disc. 2001), .40 S&W, or .45 ACP cal., short recoil operation, SFO, rotating 3.54 in. barrel lockup, manual safety, 8 (.45 ACP) or 10 shot, DAO, hammerless, aluminum alloy frame with nickel chromium steel slide, black finish, includes case and trigger lock, approx. 29 or 32 1/2 oz. Mfg. by SIG in Europe, limited importation 2000-04.

| | $450 | $400 | $350 | $300 | $275 | $250 | $225 | |

RIFLES: BOLT ACTION, RECENT PRODUCTION

Values on currently manufactured models include single rifle case, scope mount, and matching sling.

Add $620-$815 for left-hand action, depending on model. Add $1,287 per interchangeable standard cal. barrel. Add $675 per bolt assembly, and/or $211 per bolt head. Add $996 for barrel fluting (standard cals. only). Beginning late 2006, Mauser began grading wood between grades 2-11. Grade 2 is standard wood, and the following additional charges apply to the additional wood upgrades (2011 MSRs): Grade 3 - $300, N/A domestically, Grade 4 - $480, Grade 5 - $969, Grade 6 - $1,939, Grade 7 - $2,905, Grade 8 - $4,063, Grade 9 - $5,227, Grade 10 - $6,772, Grade 11 - from $8,708.

MODEL SR 93 – .300 Win. Mag. cal., precision rifle employing skeletonized cast magnesium/aluminum stock, combination right-hand/left-hand bolt, adj. ergonomics, 27 in. fluted barrel with muzzle brake, integrated bipod, 4 or 5 shot mag., approx. 13 lbs. without accessories. Disc. 1996.

| | $20,000 | $17,250 | $14,750 | $11,950 | $8,700 | $6,500 | $5,000 | *$21,995* |

MSR	100%	98%	95%	90%	80%	70%	60%	Last MSR

* **Model 2000 Classic Sniper** – .300 Win. Mag. or .308 Win. cal., features heavy fluted barrel, special set trigger system, bipod rail, and other special shooting performance features, satin blue metal finish, custom built with individual certificate. Limited importation 1998 only.

| | $1,900 | $1,550 | $1,350 | $1,100 | $900 | $775 | $650 | *$2,200* |

LIGHTNING SNIPER MODEL – .300 Win. Mag. or .308 Win. cal., slide-bolt action, features free floating heavy fluted barrel w/o sights, special wood or synthetic stock with built-in bipod rail, detachable mag., satin blue metal finish. Limited importation 1998 only.

| | $895 | $775 | $675 | $600 | $525 | $475 | $425 | *$1,000* |

* **Lightning Sniper Model Stainless** – similar to Lightning Sniper Model, except is satin stainless steel. Limited importation 1998 only.

| | $895 | $775 | $675 | $600 | $525 | $475 | $425 | *$1,000* |

MAVERICK ARMS, INC.

Currently manufactured by Maverick Arms, Inc. located in Eagle Pass, TX. Administrative offices are at O.F. Mossberg & Sons, located in North Haven, CT. Distributor sales only.

SHOTGUNS

Beginning 1992, all Maverick slide action shotguns incorporate twin slide rails in the operating mechanism.

* **Model 88 Field Slide Action Security** – 12 ga., 18 1/2 (6 shot) or 20 (8 shot) in. barrel with cyl. bore fixed choke, regular or pistol grip (disc. 1997) synthetic stock, 6 or 8 shot, plain synthetic forearm, 7 lbs. New 1993.

| MSR $298 | $235 | $200 | $175 | $150 | $125 | $100 | $85 | |

Add $7 for 8 shot model with 20 in. barrel (disc. 2009).
Add $98 for Bullpup configuration (6 or 9 shot) (disc. 1994).
Add $47-$65 for combo package (disc.).

* **Model 88 Field Slide Action Combat** – 12 ga. only, combat design featuring pistol grip stock and forearm, black synthetic stock is extension of receiver, 18 1/2 in. cyl. bore barrel with vented shroud with built-in carrying handle, open sights. Mfg. 1990-92.

| | $375 | $330 | $280 | $255 | $205 | $170 | $130 | *$282* |

MODEL HS-12 TACTICAL O/U – 12 ga., 2 3/4 or 3 in. chambers, 18 1/2 in. barrels cylinder bore or Imp. Mod chokes, matte black finish, synthetic stock, rear slot sight with fiber optic front sight, no under barrel mounted Picatinny rail beginning 2012. New 2011.

| MSR $547 | $465 | $400 | $340 | $300 | $250 | $200 | $160 | |

Add $16 for choke tubes.
Add $18 for Thunder Ranch model with left and right side Picatinny rails and neoprene stock shell holder (new 2013).

MODEL HS-12 THUNDER RANCH – 12 ga., 3 in. chamber, 2 shot, 18 1/2 in. barrel, matte black finish, side mounted Picatinny rails, tang mounted safety and barrel selector, checkered black synthetic pistol grip stock and forearm with nylon shell holder, fiber optic front sight, engraved Thunder Ranch logo, 6 1/4 lbs. New 2013.

| MSR $565 | $475 | $425 | $365 | $335 | $300 | $275 | $250 | |

MAWHINNEY, CHUCK

Current trademark of sniper rifles manufactured by Rifle Craft, Ltd. located in the United Kingdom. Imported by Chuck Mawhinney, located in Baker City, OR.

RIFLES: BOLT ACTION

M40 SNIPER – .308 Win. cal., based on the M700 Remington action, 24 in. matte black pillar bedded free floating barrel, walnut stock, engraved aluminum floorplate with Chuck Mawhinney's signature (former sniper for the Marines), includes 3-9x40mm Leupold scope. Serial numbered 1-103. New 2012.

| MSR $5,000 | $5,000 | $4,400 | $3,750 | $3,150 | $2,500 | $2,000 | $1,650 | |

McCANN INDUSTRIES

Previous rifle and current accessories manufacturer located in Spanaway, WA.

McCann Industries manufactured new Garand semi-auto rifles with design improvements that utilize a .338 or .458 Mag cal. cartridge (not Win. Mag.), in addition to a .300 Win. Mag. bolt action pistol. For more information, including pricing and availability, contact the company directly (see Trademark Index).

McDUFFEE ARMS

Current AR-15 rifle manufacturer established in 2010 and located in Westminster, CO.

McDuffee Arms is a family owned and operated business specializing in AR-15 rifles and receivers. They offer a lifetime warranty on all their products.

MSR	100%	98%	95%	90%	80%	70%	60%	Last MSR

RIFLES: SEMI-AUTO

BANSHEE AR-15 CARBINE – 5.56 NATO, .300 Blackout, or 7.62x39mm cal., 16 in. M4 contour chromemoly barrel, railed gas block, free float quad rail handguards, A3 flat-top upper receiver, six-position adj. stock, power extractor spring, 6.6 lbs.

| MSR $975 | $875 | $775 | $650 | $600 | $475 | $400 | $300 | |

* **Banshee AR-15 Carbine SS** – 5.56 NATO, .300 Blackout, 6.8 SPC, or 7.62x39mm cal., similar to Banshee AR-15 Carbine, except features 16 in. M4 contour stainless steel barrel and steel flash suppressor, 6.6 lbs.

| MSR $1,000 | $900 | $795 | $675 | $625 | $500 | $400 | $325 | |

BANSHEE AR-15 RIFLE – .223 Wylde cal., 20 in. stainless steel barrel and custom flash suppressor, railed gas block, free float quad rail handguard, A3 flat-top upper receiver, six position adj. stock, power extractor spring.

| MSR $1,190 | $1,050 | $925 | $800 | $725 | $575 | $475 | $375 | |

McMILLAN BROS. RIFLE CO.

Previous division of McMillan Group International, located in Phoenix, AZ. Dealer and consumer direct sales. During 1998, the company name changed from McBros Rifles to McMillan Bros. Rifle Co. The company name changed again during 2007 to McMillian Firearms Manufacturing. Please refer to McMillian Firearms Manufacturing LLC listing.

RIFLES: BOLT ACTION

MCR TACTICAL – .308 Win. or .300 Win. Mag. cal. Mfg. 1993-2007.

| | $2,950 | $2,400 | $1,900 | $1,500 | $1,250 | $1,050 | $925 | $3,300 |

This model was formerly designated the MCR Sniper Model.

* **MCRT Tactical** – .300 Win. Mag. or .338 Lapua (new 1998), similar to MCR Tactical. Mfg. 1993-2007.

| | $3,050 | $2,550 | $2,100 | $1,825 | $1,550 | $1,375 | $1,100 | $3,500 |

Add $500 for .338 Lapua Mag (muzzle brake is standard).

This model was formerly designated the MCRT Sniper Model.

BIG MAC/BOOMER – .50 BMG cal., available as either single shot sporter, repeater sporter, light benchrest, or heavy benchrest variation. Mfg. 1993-2007.

| | $4,450 | $3,850 | $3,250 | $2,700 | $2,225 | $1,825 | $1,525 | $4,900 |

Add $300 for repeating action.
Add $500 for Tactical 50 variation.
Add $100 for Tactical single shot.
Add $100 for heavy benchrest variation.

McMILLAN FIREARMS MANUFACTURING, LLC

Current manufacturer located in Phoenix, AZ beginning 2007.

McMillan Group International is a group of McMillan family companies: McMillan Fiberglass Stocks, McMillan Firearms Manufacturing, and McMillan Machine Company.

RIFLES: BOLT ACTION, TACTICAL SERIES

TAC-300 – .300 Win. Mag. cal., 26 in. medium heavy free floating contoured threaded barrel with cap and polygon rifling, detachable 5 shot box mag. or hinged floorplate, drilled and tapped, McMillan G30 long action, A-5 fiberglass buttstock, black, olive, gray, dark earth, or tan finish, adj. cheekpiece, two sling swivels, 11 lbs.

| MSR $6,750 | $5,725 | $5,000 | $4,295 | $3,895 | $3,150 | $2,575 | $2,000 | |

TAC-308 – .308 Win. cal., 20 or 24 in. match grade stainless steel medium heavy contoured threaded barrel with cap, detachable 5 shot box mag. or hinged floorplate, drilled and tapped, McMillan G30 short action, A-3 fiberglass buttstock, black, olive, gray, dark earth, or tan finish, adj. cheekpiece, two sling swivels.

| MSR $6,495 | $5,525 | $4,825 | $4,150 | $3,750 | $3,050 | $2,475 | $1,925 | |

TAC-338 – .338 Lapua cal., 26 1/2 in. match grade stainless steel medium heavy contoured threaded barrel with muzzle brake, detachable 5 shot box mag. or hinged floorplate, drilled and tapped, McMillan G30 short action, A-5 fiberglass buttstock, black, olive, gray, dark earth, or tan finish, adj. cheekpiece, 6 flushmount cups with sling loops.

| MSR $6,895 | $5,850 | $5,125 | $4,395 | $3,975 | $3,225 | $2,625 | $2,050 | |

TAC-416 R/SS – .416 Barrett cal., single shot action, 29 in. match grade Navy contour or 30 in. light contour fluted threaded barrel with muzzle brake, drilled and tapped, McMillan synthetic stock with butthook and adj. saddle style cheekpiece, six flushmount cups with sling loops, bipod, decelerator pad, spacer system, adj. trigger, black, olive, gray, tan, or dark earth finish. New 2013.

| MSR $9,990 | $8,495 | $7,425 | $6,375 | $5,775 | $4,675 | $3,825 | $2,975 | |

MSR	100%	98%	95%	90%	80%	70%	60%	Last MSR

TAC-50 A1 – .50 BMG cal., 29 in. match grade Navy contour fluted threaded barrel with muzzle brake, drilled and tapped, detachable box mag., McMillan synthetic stock with butthook and adj. saddle style cheekpiece, four flushmount cups with sling loops, bipod, black, olive, gray, tan, or dark earth finish, adj. trigger.

| MSR $9,990 | $8,495 | $7,425 | $6,375 | $5,775 | $4,675 | $3,825 | $2,975 | |

TAC-50 A1-R2 – .50 BMG cal., similar to Tac-50 A1, except has McMillan Tac-50 A1-R2 stock and R2 recoil mitigation system. New 2013.

| MSR $11,990 | $10,195 | $8,925 | $7,650 | $6,925 | $5,600 | $4,595 | $3,575 | |

ALIAS STAR – 6.5x47 Lapua, 6.5 Creedmoor, or .308 Win. cal., 18 to 24 in. stainless steel match grade barrel, threaded muzzle with thread cap, detachable 10 or 20 shot mag., tactical pistol grip, matte black finish, tube or quad rail forend, Anschutz trigger, includes case, 11.6 lbs. New 2013.

| MSR $8,300 | $7,350 | $6,825 | $6,000 | $5,150 | $4,675 | $3,775 | $3,000 | |

ALIAS TARGET – .260 Rem., 6.5x47 Lapua, 6.5 Creedmoor, .308 Win., .308 Palma, or 6XC cal., 24 to 30 in. barrel, includes two detachable 10 shot mags. and one single shot loading block, competition pistol grip, matte black finish, competition buttstock and forend, Anschutz trigger, 12 lbs. New 2013.

| MSR $8,300 | $7,350 | $6,825 | $6,000 | $5,150 | $4,675 | $3,775 | $3,000 | |

CS5 STANDARD – .308 Win cal., matte black finish, 18 1/2 in. stainless steel match grade barrel with threaded muzzle and thread cap., 10 or 20 shot detachable box magazine, Anschutz trigger, adj. butt stock, pistol grip, tactile safety button, upper Picatinny rail, optional suppressor and bipod, includes full-size gun case. New 2012.

Please contact the company directly for pricing on this model (see Trademark Index).

Thid model is also available in a "Stubby" variation with 12 1/2 in. barrel for military/law enforcement.

RIFLES: SEMI-AUTO

M1A – .308 Win. cal., 18 or 20 in. barrel, 10 shot mag., McMillan MFS-14 modular tactical system, SOCOM five position adj. buttstock, pistol grip with finger groove, M3A fiberglass stock with saddle type cheekpiece, Picatinny style side and bottom rails, four flushmount cups with sling swivels, two-stage military trigger, many other options available.

| | $2,995 | $2,750 | $2,450 | $2,125 | $1,800 | $1,525 | $1,300 | *$3,399* |

Add $200 for compact model with 18 in. barrel.

M3A – .308 Win. cal., features McMillan M3A fiberglass stock with adj. cheekpiece, standard or full length upper handguard tactical rail. Mfg. 2011-2012.

Retail pricing was not obtainable for this model.

McMILLAN, G. & CO., INC.

Previous trademark established circa 1988, located in Phoenix, AZ.

G. McMillan & Co., Inc. had various barrel markings from 1988-1995 including G. McMillan, Harris - McMillan, and Harris Gunworks.

RIFLES: BOLT ACTION

The models listed were also available with custom wood stocks at varying prices. McMillan also manufactured a custom rifle from a supplied action. Features included new barreling, a fiberglass stock, matte black finish, and range testing to guarantee 3/4 M.O.A. Prices started at $1,400.

Add $150 for stainless steel receiver on most models.

M-40 SNIPER RIFLE – .308 Win. cal., Remington action with McMillan match grade heavy contour barrel, fiberglass stock with recoil pad, 4 shot mag., 9 lbs. Mfg. 1990-95.

| | $1,775 | $1,475 | $1,150 | $925 | $825 | $725 | $625 | *$1,800* |

M-86 SNIPER RIFLE – .300 Phoenix, .30-06 (new 1989), .300 Win. Mag. or .308 Win. cal., fiberglass stock, variety of optical sights. Mfg. 1988-95.

| | $1,825 | $1,500 | $1,150 | $975 | $85 | $775 | $675 | *$1,900* |

Add $550 for .300 Phoenix cal.

Add $200 for takedown feature (new 1993).

* M-86 Sniper Rifle System – includes Model 86 Sniper Rifle, bipod, Ultra scope, rings, and bases. Cased. Mfg. 1988-92.

| | $2,460 | $2,050 | $1,825 | $1,600 | $1,350 | $1,100 | $950 | *$2,665* |

M-87 LONG RANGE SNIPER RIFLE – .50 BMG cal., stainless steel bolt action, 29 in. barrel with muzzle brake, single shot, camo synthetic stock, accurate to 1500 meters, 21 lbs. Mfg. 1988-95.

| | $3,650 | $2,950 | $2,500 | $2,150 | $1,900 | $1,700 | $1,575 | *$3,735* |

* M-87 Long Range Sniper Rifle System – includes Model 87 Sniper Rifle, bipod, 20X Ultra scope, rings, and bases. Cased. Mfg. 1988-92.

| | $4,200 | $3,400 | $2,875 | $2,550 | $2,250 | $2,100 | $1,800 | *$4,200* |

MSR	100%	98%	95%	90%	80%	70%	60%	Last MSR

* M-87R Long Range Sniper Rifle – same specs. as Model 87, except has 5 shot fixed box mag. Mfg. 1990-95.

| | $3,995 | $3,300 | $2,700 | $2,300 | $2,000 | $1,850 | $1,700 | $4,000 |

Add $300 for Combo option.

M-89 SNIPER RIFLE – .308 Win. cal., 28 in. barrel with suppressor (also available without), fiberglass stock adj. for length and recoil pad, 15 1/4 lbs. Mfg. 1990-95.

| | $2,200 | $1,825 | $1,575 | $1,250 | $1,050 | $875 | $750 | $2,300 |

Add $425 for muzzle suppressor.

M-92 BULLPUP – .50 BMG cal., bullpup configuration with shorter barrel. Mfg. 1993-95.

| | $3,750 | $2,950 | $2,550 | $2,200 | $2,000 | $1,850 | $1,700 | $4,000 |

M-93SN – .50 BMG cal., similar to M-87, except has folding stock and detachable 5 or 10 shot box mag. Mfg. 1993-95.

| | $3,950 | $3,250 | $2,750 | $2,300 | $2,000 | $1,850 | $1,700 | $4,300 |

.300 PHOENIX LONG RANGE RIFLE – .300 Phoenix cal., special fiberglass stock featuring adj. cheekpieces to accommodate night vision optics, adj. buttplate, 29 in. barrel, conventional box mag., 12 1/2 lbs. Mfg. 1992 only.

| | $2,700 | $2,195 | $1,850 | $1,450 | $1,100 | $925 | $825 | $3,000 |

.300 Phoenix was a cartridge developed to function at ranges in excess of 800 yards. It produced muzzle velocities of 3100 ft. per second with a 250 grain bullet.

MCREES PRECISION

Previous firearms and current accessories manufacturer located in Lesterville, MO. McRees Precision is a division of McRees Multi Services. Consumer sales through FFL dealers.

RIFLES: BOLT ACTION

McRees Precision manufactured a bolt action rifle in various calibers with a 22 in. barrel. All rifles were guaranteed at least 1/2 MOA at 100 yards.

METROARMS CORPORATION

Current manufacturer of American Classic trademarked 1911 style semi-auto pistols imported and distributed by Eagle Imports, located in Wanamassa, NJ.

MetroArms Corporation was established in late 2011 under the expertise of former competitive shooter Hector Rodriquez.

PISTOLS: SEMI-AUTO: AMERICAN CLASSIC SERIES

AMERICAN CLASSIC COMMANDER MODEL – 9mm Para. (new 2013) or .45 ACP cal., SA, 4 1/4 in. barrel, 8 (.45 ACP) or 9 (9mm) shot mag., blue, hard chrome, or duo-tone (new 2012) finish, steel frame and slide, Novak rear sight, dovetail front sight, flared and lowered ejection port, extended slide stop, beavertail grip safety, combat hammer, combat trigger, rear slide serrations, diamond cut checkered mahogany grips, approx. 36 oz. New 2010.

| MSR $624 | $520 | $450 | $375 | $325 | $295 | $275 | $250 |

Add $95 for hard chrome finish.
Add $75 for duo-tone finish (new 2012).

AMERICAN CLASSIC AMIGO MODEL – .45 ACP cal., Officer's Model configuration with 3 1/2 in. barrel, otherwise similar to Commander Model, 7 shot mag., deep blue, hard chrome, or duo-tone (new 2012) finish, approx. 32 1/2 oz. New 2011.

| MSR $714 | $610 | $515 | $425 | $365 | $325 | $285 | $250 |

Add $90 for hard chrome finish.
Add $60 for duo-tone finish (new 2012).

AMERICAN CLASSIC TROPHY MODEL – .45 ACP cal., 5 in. barrel, 8 shot mag., hard chrome finish, steel frame and slide, SA, dovetail fiber optic front sight, adj. Novak rear sight, flared and lowered ejection port, ambidextrous thumb safety, reverse plug recoil system with full length guide rod, beveled mag well, combat hammer and trigger, front and rear slide serrations, diamond cut checkered mahogany grips, checkered main spring housing, approx. 38 oz. New 2010.

| MSR $819 | $715 | $6235 | $575 | $495 | $450 | $425 | $375 |

PISTOLS: SEMI-AUTO, MAC SERIES

MAC 1911 BOBCUT – .45 ACP cal., SA, 4 1/4 in. barrel, steel frame, blue, hard chrome, or black chrome (new 2014) finish, 8 shot mag., hammer forged steel slide, fully adj. Novak style rear sight, dovetail fiber optic front sight, custom hard wood grips with MAC logo, approx. 35 oz. New 2013.

| MSR $902 | $765 | $675 | $575 | $525 | $425 | $350 | $275 |

Add $76 for hard chrome finish.
Add $143 for black chrome finish (new 2014).

MSR	100%	98%	95%	90%	80%	70%	60%	Last MSR

MAC 1911 CLASSIC – .45 ACP cal., blue or hard chrome finish, 8 shot mag., 5 in. ramped match bull barrel, SA, steel frame, hammer forged steel slide, fully adj. Bomar style rear sight, dovetail fiber optic front sight, flared and lowered ejection port, standard slide stop, enhanced beavertail grip safety, skeletal hammer, combat trigger, wide front and rear slide serrations, ambidextrous thumb safety, custom hard wood grips with MAC logo, wide magwell, approx. 41 oz. New 2013.

| MSR $1,045 | $895 | $795 | $650 | $595 | $475 | $395 | $300 | |

Add $75 for hard chrome finish.

MAC 1911 BULLSEYE – .45 ACP cal., blue, hard chrome, or black chrome (new 2014) finish, 8 shot mag., similar to Mac 1911 Classic model, except has 6 in. ramped match bull barrel, approx. 47 oz. New 2013.

| MSR $1,204 | $1,025 | $895 | $775 | $695 | $575 | $450 | $350 | |

Add $15 for black chrome finish (new 2014).
Add $90 for hard chrome finish.

MAC 3011 SSD – .45 ACP or .40 S&W (new 2014) cal., SA, steel frame, 5 in. ramped match grade bull barrel, blue or hard chrome finish, 14 (.45 ACP) or 15 (.40 S&W) shot mag., hammer forged steel slide, fully adj. Bomar style rear sight, dovetail fiber optic front sight, flared and lowered ejection port, standard slide stop, enhanced beavertail grip safety, skeletal hammer, combat trigger, wide front and rear slide serrations, ambidextrous thumb safety, aluminum grips with MAC logo, wide magwell, approx. 46 oz. New 2013.

| MSR $1,136 | $975 | $865 | $735 | $650 | $525 | $425 | $325 | |

Add $76 for hard chrome finish.

PISTOLS: SEMI-AUTO, SPS SERIES

SPS Series pistols are manufactured by S.P.S. in Spain, then assembled in the U.S.

SPS PANTERA – .45 ACP or .40 S&W (new 2014) cal., black chrome finish, 12 (.45 ACP) or 16 (.40 S&W, new 2014) shot mag., 5 in. ramped match bull barrel, SA, steel frame, hammer forged steel slide, fully adj. Bomar style rear sight, dovetail fiber optic front sight, flared and lowered ejection port, standard slide stop, enhanced beavertail grip safety, skeletal hammer, lightweight polymer trigger, wide front and rear slide serrations, ambidextrous thumb safety, glass filled nylon polymer grips with S.P.S. logo, wide magwell, approx. 37 oz. New 2013.

| MSR $1,895 | $1,600 | $1,400 | $1,200 | $1,095 | $875 | $725 | $550 | |

SPS VISTA – 9mm Para. (Vista Short) or .38 Super (Vista Long) cal., black chrome finish, 21 shot mag., 5 1/2 in. ramped match threaded barrel, SA, steel frame, hammer forged steel slide, scope mount, flared and lowered ejection port, standard slide stop, enhanced beavertail grip safety, skeletal hammer, lightweight polymer trigger, wide front and rear slide serrations, ambidextrous thumb safety, glass filled nylon polymer grips with S.P.S. logo, wide magwell, approx. 42-43 oz. New 2013.

| MSR $2,450 | $2,175 | $1,900 | $1,625 | $1,475 | $1,195 | $975 | $750 | |

MICOR DEFENSE, INC.

Current manufacturer established in 1999 and located in Decatur, AL.

Micor manufactures a line of defense products available to the general public, as well as custom weapons and products for the defense and other related industries. Micor consists of two companies - Micor Industries, Inc. and Micor Defense, Inc.

RIFLES: SEMI-AUTO

Micor manufactures the Leader 416 semi-auto bullpup rifle, Leader T2 semi-auto rifle, and the Leader 338 Bullpup rifle. Additionally, Micor offers the Leader 50, a lightweight .50 BMG cal. rifle (MSR $9,995). All models were designed by Charles St. George, original designer of the Bushmaster M17 bullpup rifle. Please contact the company directly for pricing, availability, and options (see Trademark Index).

MICROTECH SMALL ARMS RESEARCH, INC. (MSAR)

Current rifle manufacturer located in Bradford, PA.

CARBINES/RIFLES: SEMI-AUTO

MSAR manufactures American-made semi-auto bullpup carbines and rifles, patterned after the Steyr AUG.

STG-556 – .223 Rem. cal., 16 or 20 in. chrome lined barrel, gas operated rotating bolt, short piston drive, 10, 20, 30, or 42 shot mag., black, tan, or OD Green finish, with or w/o 9 inch Picatinny rail, right or left hand ejection, synthetic stock, 7.2 lbs.

| MSR $1,839 | $1,675 | $1,400 | $1,200 | $995 | $800 | $700 | $625 | |

Add $156 for 1.5x Optic.

* **STG-556 Gebirgsjager Limited Edition** – similar to STG-556, engraved Edelweiss flower insignia, except includes all OD Green finish, 1.5x CQB optical sight, 6 in. Picatinny side rail, three 30 shot mags., OD Green Currahee knife with nylon sheath, Giles sling with Uncle Mike's sling swivels, custom Pelican 1700 green case, and certificate of authenticity.

| | $3,495 | $3,100 | $2,750 | $2,525 | $2,300 | $2,100 | $1,875 | |

MSR	100%	98%	95%	90%	80%	70%	60%	Last MSR

STG-680 – 6.8mm Rem. cal., 16 or 20 in. chrome lined barrel, 10, 20, 30, or 42 shot mag., black, tan, or OD Green synthetic stock, with or w/o 9 inch Picatinny rail, right or left hand action, 7.2 lbs.

| | $1,725 | $1,575 | $1,395 | $1,275 | $1,150 | $995 | $825 | |

Add $156 for 1.5x Optic.

STG-E4 – 5.56 NATO or .300 AAC Blackout cal., semi-auto rifle, bull pup design, gas operated rotating bolt short piston drive, 16 1/2 or 18 1/2 in. chromemoly barrel with dedicated sound flash suppressor, 9 in. Picatinny rail, re-engineered bolt carrier, black composite stock with quick detach shell deflector, improved trigger modual, 2-position safety, 30 shot mag., 7.2 lbs. New 2013.

| MSR $2,200 | $1,975 | $1,675 | $1,450 | $1,200 | $1,000 | $800 | $700 | |

MILLER PRECISION ARMS

Current AR-15 manufacturer located in Columbia Falls, MT.

RIFLES: SEMI-AUTO

MPA300 GUARDIAN – .300 Win. Mag. cal., 20 in. stainless steel ultra match SPR barrel, Precision Reflex forearm, Magpul PRS stock, Dark Earth Cerakote finish.

| MSR $5,399 | $4,850 | $4,250 | $3,650 | $3,300 | $2,675 | $2,195 | $1,700 | |

MPAR 10 – .308 Win. cal., 16-24 in. stainless steel SPR contour barrel, free float aluminum forearm, LMT Sopmod stock, bead blasted stainless steel finish.

| MSR $2,199 | $1,975 | $1,725 | $1,475 | $1,350 | $1,075 | $900 | $700 | |

MPAR 15 – 5.56 NATO cal., 16 in. M4 button rifled chromemoly barrel, Troy Industries forearm, Magpul MOE stock, Black anodized finish.

| MSR $1,599 | $1,425 | $1,250 | $1,075 | $975 | $775 | $650 | $500 | |

MPA 556 – .223 Wylde cal., 18 in. stainless steel ultra match SPR barrel, Hammerhead muzzle brake, precision machined billet upper and lower receiver, forward assist, Picatinny flat-top rail, extractor, Geissele two-stage trigger, Precision Reflex free float carbon fiber handguard, integral trigger, LMT Sopmod stock, Armour Black Cerakote finish.

| MSR $3,600 | $3,250 | $2,850 | $2,450 | $2,225 | $1,800 | $1,475 | $1,150 | |

MPA 762 – .308 Win. cal., 18 in. stainless steel ultra match SPR contour barrel, Precision Reflex Delta forearm, LMT Sopmod stock, anodized finish.

| MSR $3,750 | $3,375 | $2,950 | $2,525 | $2,300 | $1,850 | $1,525 | $1,175 | |

MILTAC INDUSTRIES, LLC

Current AR-15 manufacturer located in Boise, ID.

RIFLES: SEMI-AUTO

ALPHA SERIES – 5.56 NATO cal., GIO, 16 in. M4 chrome lined barrel with Smith Enterprises Vortex flash hider, two Magpul 30 shot PMags., 13 in. modular free float Alpha rail, Geissele Super two-stage trigger, flared mag. well, oversized trigger guard, 3D engraving on lower receiver, Troy Industries M4 flip-up iron battle sights, Hard coat anodized and Cerakote finish in Black, Flat Dark Earth, or Two-Tone, Magpul 6-position collapsible or extended stock, Magpul MIAD grip, includes Crossfire tactical carry case, 6 lbs. 12 oz.

| MSR $2,899 | $2,600 | $2,275 | $1,950 | $1,775 | $1,425 | $1,175 | $925 | |

BRAVO SERIES – .300 Blackout cal., GIO, 16 in. stainless barrel with SP ATC muzzle brake, two Magpul 30 shot PMags., 13 in. modular free float Alpha rail, Geissele Super two-stage trigger, flared mag. well, oversized trigger guard, 3D engraving on lower receiver, Troy Industries M4 flip-up iron battle sights, Hard coat anodized and Cerakote finish in Black, Flat Dark Earth, or Two-Tone, Magpul 6-position collapsible or extended stock, Magpul MIAD grip, includes Crossfire tactical carry case, 7 lbs. 4 oz.

| MSR $2,899 | $2,600 | $2,275 | $1,950 | $1,775 | $1,425 | $1,175 | $925 | |

ECHO SERIES – 5.56 NATO cal., GIO, 16 in. M4 chrome lined barrel with Smith Enterprises Vortex flash hider, 13 in. modular free float Alpha rail, flared mag. well, oversized trigger guard, 3D engraving on lower receiver, no sights, Hard coat anodized and Cerakote finish in Black, Flat Dark Earth, or Two-Tone, Magpul MOE carbine mil-spec stock, Magpul MOE grip, 6 lbs. 4 oz.

| MSR $2,349 | $2,100 | $1,850 | $1,575 | $1,425 | $1,150 | $950 | $775 | |

MITCHELL ARMS, INC.

Previous manufacturer, importer, and distributor located in Fountain Valley, CA.

Due to space considerations, information regarding this manufacturer is available online free of charge at www.bluebookofgunvalues.com.

MSR	100%	98%	95%	90%	80%	70%	60%	Last MSR

MITCHELL'S MAUSERS

Current importer located in Fountain Valley, CA.

Please refer to the Escalade and Sabre sections for previously imported semi-auto and slide action shotguns.

PISTOLS: SEMI-AUTO

Mitchell's Mausers previously imported older Luger pistols in many variations. Last MSRs circa 2010 on the following models were: P08 WWI 4 in. $4,995, P08 WWII 4 in. $4,495, Navy Model 6 in. $6,495, Artillery Model 8 in. $7,995, P08 Treaty of Versailles $5,995, and $9,995 for Carbine w/stock. All were restored and were cased with accessories. Additionally, the company also imported a restored WWII P.38, cased with accessories - last MSR was $1,295.

FALCON SERIES – 9mm Para., .40 S&W, or .45 ACP cal., DA/SA operation, Browning locking system operation, 3.9 (semi-compact) or 4 1/4 (compact) in. barrel, low profile sights, aluminum frame with steel frame and barrel, 12, 16, or 20 shot mag., loaded chamber indicator, approx. 32 oz. Mfg. in Serbia. Importation began late 2011.

MSR $795	$725	$650	$575	$495	$425	$350	$295	

RIFLES: BOLT ACTION

Beginning 1999, Mitchell's Mausers imported a sizeable quantity of WWII Mauser 98Ks manufactured in Yugoslavia during/after WWII. These guns are basically in new condition, having been only test fired over the past 50 years. They are supplied with bayonet and scabbard, military leather sling, original field cleaning kit, and leather ammo pouch. Caliber is 8mm Mauser (7.9x57mm), and all parts numbers match on these rifles.

MODEL M48 – 8mm Mauser cal., original Mauser 98K rifle manufactured with German technology in Serbia, various grades, matching serial numbers on all parts. Importation began 2006.

MSR $349	$325	$295	$275	$250	$240	$230	$220	

The above price is for the Service grade rifle without accessories. Add $100 for Collector Grade, $150 for Custom Select Grade, $200 for BO (Stealth), $200 for Premium Grade, $250 for Premium Select Grade, and $300 for Premium Grade BO (Stealth).
A special Museum Grade with bayonet, scabbard, belt hanger, and other accessories was also available for $1,000.

TANKER MAUSER M63 (MODEL M48) – .243 Win., .270 Win., .30-06, 8mm Mauser, or .308 Win. cal., similar to Model 48, except the barrel length is 17.4 in., 5 shot internal mag., 1400m adj. rear sight, hardwood stock with semi-gloss finish, 7.4 lbs. Imported 2006-approx. 2010.

	$450	$395	$375	$345	$295	$265	$235	*$495*

NEW K98 – 8mm Mauser cal., original WWII Mauser mfg., all matching parts, various configurations available, including Souvenir, Collector, and Premium Grades.

MSR $789	$725	$625	$525	$450	$395	$350	$295	

BLACK ARROW – .50 BMG cal., Mauser action, 5 shot detachable box mag., fluted and compensated barrel, includes bipod and quick detachable scope mount, shock absorbing buttstock. Imported 2003-2006.

	$5,750	$4,950	$4,275	$3,600	$3,000	$2,400	$2,150	*$6,500*

SOVIET MOSIN-NAGANT – various cals., original gun dated 1942 to commemorate the battle of Stalingrad. Limited importation 2009.
U.S. pricing was not available on this model.

RIFLES: SEMI-AUTO

BLACK LIGHTNING – .17 Mach 2 (disc.), .17 HMR (disc.), .22 LR (disc.), or .22 WMR cal., black polymer oversized thumbhole stock with full length aluminum shroud and Picatinny rail, 18 in. stainless steel fluted heavy barrel, stainless steel action, 9 shot mag., detachable carry handle, detachable front sight, sling swivels. New 2006.

MSR $650	$550	$475	$425	$375	$335	$300	$275	

PPSH 41/22/PPS50/22 – .22 LR cal., patterned after the Russian PPSh-41, 16.1 in. barrel, features stained hardwood stock, full length perforated barrel heat shield, fixed sights, 10, 30, or 50 shot detachable drum magazine, 4.4 lbs. Importation began 2012.

MSR $495	$450	$400	$350	$300	$275	$250	$225	

Add $150 for 50 shot detachable drum mag.

MOHAWK ARMORY

Current AR-15 style manufacturer located in Midway, TN.

Mohawk Armory offers a line of AR-15 style semi-auto rifles and pistols. The company is also a Class III dealer and offers many products for law enforcement/military. Please contact the company directly for more information, including pricing and available options (see Trademark Index).

MSR		100%	98%	95%	90%	80%	70%	60%	*Last MSR*

MOLOT

Current manufacturer established during 1941, and located in Vyatskie Polyany, Kirov region, Russia.

Currently manufactured trademarks include: Vepr. rifles and shotguns, a SKS semi-auto rifle line, several models of bolt action rifles, including target models, in addition to Becas slide action and semi-auto shotguns. Please refer to these sections for more information.

MOSSBERG, O.F. & SONS, INC.

Current manufacturer located in North Haven, CT, 1962-present and New Haven, CT, 1919-1962.

Oscar Mossberg developed an early reputation as a designer and inventor for the Iver Johnson, Marlin-Rockwell, Stevens, and Shattuck Arms companies. In 1915, he began producing a 4-shot, .22 LR cal. palm pistol known as the "Novelty," with revolving firing pin. After producing approx. 600 of these pistols, he sold the patent to C.S. Shattuck, which continued to manufacture guns under the name "Unique." The first 600 had no markings except serial numbers, and were destined for export to South America. Very few of these original "Novelty" pistols survived in this country, and they are extremely rare specimens.

Mossberg acquired Advanced Ordnance Corp. during 1996, a high quality manufacturer utilizing state-of-the-art CNC machinery.

RIFLES: BOLT ACTION, CURRENT PRODUCTION

* *ATR Night Train Special (Model 100)* – .308 Win. cal., 22 in. fluted barrel, short action, 4 shot mag., matte blue, Multi Cam camo (new 2013), or digital green camo finish, synthetic stock, Picatinny rail, top load magazine, adj. LBA trigger, available with 4-16x50mm scope w/sun shade, flip open lens protector and bipod, or Barska 6-24x60mm illuminated reticle scope and Harris bipod. New 2010.

MSR $615		$515	$450	$385	$325	$295	$275	$250

Add $276 for Barska scope and Harris bipod (Night Train 2 or IV).
Add $43 for 4-16x50mm scope, bipod, and digital green camo (Night Train III).

MVP FLEX – 5.56mm or 7.62 NATO cal., 18 1/2 or 20 in. threaded or non-threaded sporter or medium bull barrel, matte blue finish, spiral fluted bolt, optional A2 flash suppressor, 10 shot mag., LBA trigger, Picatinny top rail, FLEX TLS-compatible six position adj. stock in black or tan (new 2014), 6 1/2-7 lbs. New 2013.

MSR $966		$815	$695	$600	$550	$425	$350	$275

Add $21 for threaded barrel with A2 flash suppressor.
Subtract $266 for Tan stock (new 2014).

MVP PATROL – 5.56mm, 7.62 NATO, or .300 ACC Blackout cal., 16 1/4 in. medium bull threaded or non-threaded barrel, spiral fluted bolt, LBA adj. trigger, matte blue finish, textured stock in black or Tan (new 2014) with checkered grip and forend, 10 shot mag., no sights or rifle sights, Picatinny rail, 6 3/4 - 7 1/2 lbs. New 2013.

MSR $709		$595	$515	$430	$395	$315	$285	$260

Add $17 for threaded barrel and A2 flash suppressor.

RIFLES: LEVER ACTION

MODEL 464 SPX – .22 LR (disc. 2013) or .30-30 Win. cal., 16 1/4 or 18 1/2 (disc. 2013) in. barrel, 7 (.30-30 Win. cal.) or 14 (disc. 2013) shot mag., matte black finish, six position adj. tactical stock with elevated comb, tri-rail forearm with ladder rail covers, rifle sights, 6 (.22 LR cal.) or 7 (.30-30 Win. cal.) lbs. New 2012.

MSR $543		$450	$385	$325	$285	$240	$190	$150

Add $9 for flash suppressor.
Subtract approx. $40 for .22 LR cal. (disc. 2013).

MODEL 464 ZMB – .30-30 Win. cal., 6 (disc. 2013) or 7 (new 2014) shot mag., compact 16 1/4 in. barrel with removable A2 flash suppressor, matte blue finish, six position adj. tactical stock, tri-rail forend with rail covers, 3-dot adj. fiber optic or rifle sights, drilled and tapped, sling swivel studs, ZMB receiver engraving, 7 lbs. New 2012.

MSR $581		$480	$410	$350	$300	$250	$210	$175

RIFLES: SEMI-AUTO

MODEL 715T TACTICAL CARRY (TACTICAL 22) – .22 LR cal., AR-15 style, GIO, 18 in. barrel, matte black finish, 10 or 25 shot mag., synthetic fixed or six-position adj. stock, front post sight, adj. rifle sights, Picatinny quad-rail forend, handle mounted top rail, mag. loading assist tool, integrated A2 style carry handle, 5 1/4 lbs. New 2011.

MSR $308		$255	$215	$175	$150	$125	$100	$95

MSR	100%	98%	95%	90%	80%	70%	60%	Last MSR

MODEL 715T FLAT-TOP – .22 LR cal., GIO, 16 1/4 in. barrel with A2 style muzzle brake, blue barrel finish, 10 or 25 shot mag., flat-top with full length top rail, removeable/adj. sights or 30mm red dot sights, fixed or adj. synthetic stock, Black, Mossy Oak Brush, or Muddy Girl (new 2014) camo finish, 5 1/2 - 5 3/4 lbs. New 2012.

MSR $366	$300	$255	$230	$200	$175	$150	$125	

Add $9 for removable A2 style Picatinny mounted front and rear sights.
Add $64 for Muddy Girl camo finish (new 2014).
Add $69 for Mossy Oak Brush camo finish.

MMR HUNTER – 5.56 NATO cal., GIO, 20 in. carbon steel barrel with black phosphate metal finish, 5 shot mag., SST, anodized aluminum receiver, Picatinny top rail, A2 black synthetic stock, SE-1 pistol grip with battery compartment, checkered aluminum tubular forend, Mossy Oak Treestand or Mossy Oak Brush camo finish, no sights, 7 1/2 lbs. New mid-2011.

MSR $1,028	$895	$775	$675	$625	$550	$475	$400	

Add $99 for camo finish.

MMR TACTICAL – 5.56 NATO cal., GIO, 16 1/4 in. carbon steel barrel with black phosphate metal finish, 10 or 30 shot mag., anodized aluminum receiver, black synthetic fixed or six-position collapsible stock, A2 style muzzle brake, no sights or removable Picatinny rail, Stark SE-1 deluxe pistol grip, quad rail forend, approx. 7 - 7 1/2 lbs. New mid-2011.

MSR $987	$875	$775	$650	$550	$450	$395	$350	

Add $41 for Picatinny rail.

SHOTGUNS: SEMI-AUTO & SLIDE ACTION, RECENT PRODUCTION

In 1985, Mossberg purchased the parts inventory and manufacturing rights for the shotguns that Smith & Wesson discontinued in 1984. These 1000 and 3000 Series models (manufactured in Japan) are identical to those models which S&W discontinued. Parts and warranties are not interchangeable.

Beginning 1989, all Mossbergs sold in the U.S. and Canada have been provided with a Cablelock which goes through the ejection port, making the gun's action inoperable.

To celebrate its 75th anniversary, Mossberg released a new Crown Grade variation within most models during 1994, including the slide action 500 and 835 Series. These can be differentiated from previous manufacture by cut checkering, redesigned walnut or American hardwood stocks and forearms, screw-in choke tubes, and 4 different camo patterns. The Crown Grade was discontinued in 2000.

On April 30, 2013, Mossberg announced the manufacture of its 10 millionth Mossberg 500 model.

At the SHOT Show during 2014, Mossberg unveiled its new Duck Commander Series. Please refer to individual listings.

MODEL 500 CAMPER – 12, 20 ga., or .410 bore only, 18 1/2 in. barrel, synthetic pistol grip (no stock), camo carrying case optional, blued finish. Mfg. 1986-90 only.

	$250	$220	$185	$170	$135	$110	$85	*$276*

Add $25 for .410 bore. Add $30 for camo case.

MODEL 500 BULLPUP – 12 ga., 18 1/2 (6 shot) or 20 (9 shot) in. barrel, bullpup configuration, 6 or 9 shot mag., includes shrouded barrel, carrying handle, ejection port in stock, employs high impact materials. Mfg. 1986-90.

	$650	$525	$450	$415	$325	$275	$215	*$425*

Add $15 for 8 shot mag. (disc.).

MODEL 500 HOME SECURITY – 20 (1996 only) ga. or .410 bore, 3 in. chamber, 18 1/2 in. barrel with spreader choke, Model 500 slide-action, 5 shot mag., blue metal finish, synthetic field stock with pistol grip forearm, 6 1/4 lbs. New 1990.

MSR $459	$395	$345	$295	$275	$215	$180	$140	

* **Model 500 Home Security Laser .410** – includes laser sighting device in right front of forearm. Mfg. 1990-93.

	$400	$350	$300	$270	$220	$180	$140	*$451*

MODEL 500 PERSUADER – 12 or 20 (new 1995) ga., 6 or 8 shot, 18 1/2 in. plain barrel, cyl. bore or Accu-chokes (new 1995), optional rifle (12 ga./20 in. cyl. bore barrel only) or ghost ring (new 1999) sights, blue, matte (new 2006, 12 ga. only), or parkerized (12 ga. with ghost ring sights only) finish, Speedfeed stock was disc. 1990, optional bayonet lug, plain pistol grip wood (disc. 2004) or synthetic stock, approx. 6 3/4 lbs.

MSR $447	$380	$335	$285	$260	$210	$175	$135	

Add $18 for tri-rail Picatinny forend (new 2011).
Add $14 for pistol grip.
Add $159 for ghost ring sights (new 2013).
Add $146 for tactical light forend (blue finish only, new 2013).
Add $46 for 20 ga. with 18 1/2 in. stand off barrel (new 2009).
Add $38 for 20 ga. Bantam Model w/ghost ring sights (new 2013).
Add $127 for parkerized finish and ghost ring sights (disc. 2004).
Add $40 for combo with pistol grip (disc.).
Add $23 for rifle sights (disc., 12 ga. only).

MSR	100%	98%	95%	90%	80%	70%	60%	Last MSR

* **Model 500 Persuader Night Special Edition** – 12 ga. only, includes synthetic stock and factory installed Mepro-Light night sight bead sight, only 300 mfg. for Lew Horton Distributing in 1990 only.

	$350	$260	$225	$200	$160	$135	$115	*$296*

MODEL 500 TACTICAL – 12 ga. only, 3 in. chamber, 18 1/2 in. cylinder bore barrel, 6 or 8 shot, adj. tactical synthetic stock, choice of matte blue or Marinecoate finish, optional tri-rail forend with removable side rails and integral bottom rail (new 2011), approx. 6 3/4 lbs. New 2006.

MSR $578	$500	$395	$335	$300	$245	$200	$155	

Add $148 for Marinecote finish.
Add $15 for tri-rail forend (new 2011) or $53 for tri-rail and ghost ring sights.

MODEL 500 CHAINSAW – 12 ga., 3 in. chamber, 18 1/2 in. stand-off barrel with cyl. bore choke, 5 shot mag., pistol grip synthetic stock, matte black finish, easily removable unique "chainsaw" forend grip provides muzzle control and stability, drilled and tapped, tri-rail forend, white dot sights, 6 lbs. New 2011.

MSR $525	$450	$395	$340	$300	$250	$200	$160	

MODEL 500 CHAINSAW ZMB – 12 ga., 3 in. chamber, 18 1/2 in. stand-off barrel with cyl. bore choke, 6 shot mag., pistol grip synthetic stock, matte black finish, easily removable unique "chainsaw" forend grip provides muzzle control and stability, drilled and tapped, tri-rail forend, white dot sights, includes light and laser combo, ZMB engraved logo on receiver, 6 lbs. New 2012.

MSR $614	$500	$425	$335	$280	$230	$185	$145	

MODEL 500 SPX SPECIAL PURPOSE – 12 ga. only, 18 1/2 in. ported barrel with M16 style front sight, LPA ghost ring rear sight, Picatinny rail, adj. tactical black synthetic stock with pistol grip, 6 3/4 lbs. New 2009.

MSR $704	$600	$525	$450	$410	$325	$275	$210	

MODEL 500 SPECIAL PURPOSE ROAD BLOCKER – 12 ga. only, features pistol grip (no stock), 18 1/2 in. barrel with heat shield and large muzzle brake, 6 lbs. New 2009.

MSR $544	$460	$400	$350	$315	$250	$200	$160	

MODEL 500 SPECIAL PURPOSE – 12 ga. only, 18 in. cylinder bored barrel, choice of blue or parkerized finish, synthetic stock with or without Speedfeed. Disc. 1996.

	$350	$295	$250	$225	$200	$175	$160	*$378*

Add $21 for Speedfeed stock.
Add $76 for ghost ring sight (parkerized finish only).

MODEL 500 SPECIAL PURPOSE (CURRENT MFG.) – 12 ga., 2 3/4 or 3 in. chamber, 18 1/2 in. cylinder bore barrel, 6 shot, matte blue finish, synthetic stock, plain bead sight, recoil reduction system. New 2013.

MSR $493	$425	$375	$325	$295	$235	$195	$150	

MODEL 500 THUNDER RANCH – 12 ga., 3 in. chamber, 18 1/2 in. cylinder bore barrel, 5 shot mag., matte black synthetic stock with 12 3/4 in. LOP, white dot sights, tri-rail Picatinny forend, non-glare matte blue metal finish, sling swivel studs, Thunder Ranch logo engraved on receiver, includes black padded sling. New mid-2011.

MSR $509	$435	$375	$325	$295	$235	$195	$150	

MODEL 500 CRUISER – 12, 20, or .410 (new 1993) ga., 14 (12 ga. only, Law Enforcement Model, disc. 1995), 18 1/2, 20, or 21 (20 ga. only - mfg. 1995-2002) in. cylinder bored barrel, shroud is available in 12 ga. only, 6 or 8 (12 ga. only) shot mag., pistol grip forearm only, 5 3/4 - 7 lbs. New 1989.

MSR $447	$380	$335	$285	$260	$210	$175	$135	

Add $17 for heat shield around barrel (12 ga. only).
Add $44 for tactical Cruiser with matte blue metal finish, bead sight, and pistol grip stock.
Add $96 for 14 in. barrel (disc.).
Add approx. $34 for camper case (1993-1996).
Add $14 for 8 shot (20 in. barrel, 12 ga. only).
Add $90 for Rolling Thunder model with heat shield and large barrel stabilizer (new 2009).

* **Model 500 Cruiser Mil-Spec** – 12 ga. only, 20 in. cylinder bored barrel with bead sights, built to Mil-Specs., parkerized finish. Mfg. 1997 only.

	$395	$345	$295	$270	$215	$180	$140	*$478*

* **Model 500 Crusier Blackwater Series** – 12 ga., 3 in. chamber, 18 1/2 in. cylinder bore barrel, synthetic pistol grip, matte black finish, white dot front sight, ported stand off door breacher at muzzle, 6 shot, half-round ribbed forearm with nylon web strap, Blackwater logo on right side of receiver, approx. 6 lbs. New 2011.

MSR $478	$400	$350	$300	$275	$225	$180	$140	

MSR	100%	98%	95%	90%	80%	70%	60%	Last MSR

MODEL 500 GHOST RING SIGHT – 12 ga. only, 3 in. chamber, 18 1/2 or 20 in. cyl. bore or Accu-choke (20 in. only - new 1995) barrel, 6 or 9 shot tube mag., blue or parkerized finish, synthetic field stock, includes ghost ring sighting device. Mfg. 1990-97.

	100%	98%	95%	90%	80%	70%	60%	Last MSR
	$270	$235	$200	$185	$150	$120	$95	*$332*

Add $53 for parkerized finish.
Add $49 for 9 shot mag. (20 in. barrel only).
Add $123 for Accu-choke barrel (parkerized finish only).
Add $134 for Speedfeed stock (new 1994 - 9 shot, 20 in. barrel only).

MODEL 500 MARINER – 12 ga. only, 3 in. chamber, 18 1/2 or 20 in. cyl. bore barrel, 6 or 9 (disc. 2008) shot, Marinecote finish on all metal parts (more rust-resistant than stainless steel), pistol grip black synthetic stock and forearm, fixed or ghost ring (mfg. 1995-99) sights, approx. 6 3/4 lbs.

MSR	100%	98%	95%	90%	80%	70%	60%	
MSR $611	$525	$460	$395	$350	$295	$235	$185	

Add $51 for 9 shot model with 20 in. barrel (disc. 2008).
Add $68 for ghost ring rear sight (disc. 1999).
Add $23 for Speedfeed stock (mini-combo only - disc.).

MODEL 500 J.I.C. (JUST IN CASE) – 12 ga., 3 in. chamber, 18 in. cyl. bore barrel, 6 or 8 (new 2013) shot, comes with pistol grip, impact resistant tube and strap, available in four configurations: 5.11 Pack (w/takedown 500 and tools), Crusier (survival kit in a can, blue metal, OD Green tube), Mariner (multi-tool and knife, Orange tube, Marinecote finish), Sandstorm (Desert camo tube and finish), or Black (8 shot only, new 2013), 5 1/2 lbs. New 2007.

MSR	100%	98%	95%	90%	80%	70%	60%	
MSR $435	$375	$330	$280	$250	$200	$170	$130	

Add $44 for Cruiser or Black, $105 for Sandstorm or $142 for Marinecote.

MODEL 500 FLEX TACTICAL – 12 or 20 (new 2014) ga., 18 1/2 or 20 in. cylinder bore barrel, matte blue, OD Green, or tan finish, white dot, XS ghost ring, or plain bead sight, Picatinny rail, black pistol grip, standard or six position adj. synthetic stock, TLS tooless locking system. New mid-2012.

MSR	100%	98%	95%	90%	80%	70%	60%	
MSR $643	$575	$500	$450	$400	$375	$350	$325	

Add $202 for XS ghost ring sight.
Add $234 for six position adj. stock.

MODEL 500/590 INTIMIDATOR LASER – 12 ga. only, 3 in. chamber, 18 1/2 (Model 500) or 20 (Model 590) in. cyl. bore barrel, 6 (Model 500) or 9 (Model 590) shot tube mag., blue or parkerized finish, synthetic field stock, includes laser sighting device. Mfg. 1990-93.

* ***Model 500 Intimidator***

	100%	98%	95%	90%	80%	70%	60%	Last MSR
	$500	$385	$340	$300	$265	$230	$195	*$505*

Add $22 for parkerized finish.

* ***Model 590 Intimidator***

	100%	98%	95%	90%	80%	70%	60%	Last MSR
	$550	$495	$440	$375	$340	$295	$260	*$556*

Add $45 for parkerized finish.

MODEL 590 SPECIAL PURPOSE SLIDE ACTION – 12 ga., 3 in. chamber, similar to Model 500, except has 9 shot mag., 20 in. cyl. bore barrel with or w/o 3/4 shroud, and bayonet lug, blue or parkerized finish, regular black synthetic stock, with or w/o Speedfeed, 7 1/4 lbs. New 1987.

MSR	100%	98%	95%	90%	80%	70%	60%	
MSR $537	$450	$395	$340	$300	$250	$200	$160	

Add $103 for tri-rail Picatinny forend and Speedfeed stock (new 2011).
Add $140 for tactical light forend in blue finish with heat shield.
Add $38 for parkerized finish.
Add $75 for heavy barrel with ghost ring sights, metal trigger guard and safety (disc. 2011).
Add $80 for ghost ring sights (parkerized finish only).
Add $33 for Speedfeed (blue, disc. 1999) or $90 for Speedfeed (parkerized) stock.

* ***Model 590 Special Purpose Slide Action Mariner*** – 12 ga., similar to Model 500 Mariner except is 9 shot and has 20 in. barrel, 7 lbs. Mfg. 1989-1993, reintroduced 2009.

MSR	100%	98%	95%	90%	80%	70%	60%	
MSR $671	$575	$500	$425	$395	$315	$260	$200	

Add 5% for Speedfeed stock (disc. 1990).
Subtract 10% if w/o pistol grip adapter (disc.)

* ***Model 590 Special Purpose Slide Action Bullpup*** – similar to Model 500 Bullpup except is 9 shot and has 20 in. barrel. Mfg. 1989-90 only.

	100%	98%	95%	90%	80%	70%	60%	Last MSR
	$650	$525	$450	$410	$325	$275	$210	*$497*

MSR	100%	98%	95%	90%	80%	70%	60%	Last MSR

* Model 590 Special Purpose Slide Action Double Action – 12 ga. only, 3 in. chamber, world's first double action shotgun (long trigger pull), 18 1/2 or 20 in. barrel, 6 or 9 shot, bead or ghost ring sights, black synthetic stock and forearm, top tang safety, parkerized metal finish, 7-7 1/4 lbs. Mfg. 2000-2003.

	100%	98%	95%	90%	80%	70%	60%	Last MSR
	$450	$395	$335	$305	$245	$200	$155	*$510*

Add $31 for 9 shot capacity.
Add $48 for ghost ring sights.
Add $124 for Speedfeed stock (20 in. barrel with ghost ring sights only).

* Model 590 Special Purpose Slide Action Line Launcher – special purpose Marine and rescue shotgun with blaze orange synthetic stock, line dispensing canister, floating and distance heads, nylon and spectra line refills, includes case and two boxes of launching loads.

	100%	98%	95%	90%	80%	70%	60%	Last MSR
	$850	$745	$635	$580	$465	$380	$295	*$927*

MODEL 590 FLEX TACTICAL
– 12 ga., 20 in. cylinder bore barrel, matte blue finish, bead sight, six position adj. black synthetic stock with rail. New mid-2012.

MSR $842	$715	$625	$535	$485	$395	$325	$250	

MODEL 590A1 SLIDE ACTION
– 12 ga., 3 in. chamber, 6 or 9 shot mag., 18 1/2 or 20 (new 2010) in. fluted or non-fluted cylinder bore heavy barrel, parkerized finish, metal trigger guard and top safety, black synthetic stock, optional Speedfeed or six position aluminum tube adj. stock, choice of 3-dot, bead, or ghost ring sights, approx. 7 1/2 lbs. New 2009.

MSR $581	$495	$435	$375	$335	$275	$225	$175	

Add $40 for fluted barrel and LDA adj. trigger (new 2011).
Add $39 for ghost ring sights.
Add $53 for Speedfeed stock.
Add $35 for choice of 3-dot or ghost rings sights with Speedfeed stock.
Add $89 for Bantam Model with shortened LOP and ghost ring sights (6 shot only, limited mfg.).
Add $69 for 9 shot.

* Model 590A1 Adj. Stock Slide Action – 12 ga. only, similar to Model 590A1, except has six position adj. aluminum stock with pistol grip, 9 shot model has 20 in. barrel, 3 dot (6 shot) or ghost ring (9 shot) sights, 7 1/2 lbs. New 2009.

MSR $789	$675	$595	$500	$460	$375	$300	$235	

Add $50 for 6 shot model with 3 dot sights.
Add $56 for tri-rail Picatinny forend (new 2011).

* Model 590A1 Special Purpose Slide Action (Disc.) – 12 ga., marked 590A1 on receiver, parkerized, ghost ring rear sight, synthetic stock and forend, ramp front sight. Disc. 1997.

	100%	98%	95%	90%	80%	70%	60%	Last MSR
	$550	$480	$410	$375	$300	$245	$190	

* Model 590A1 Special Purpose Slide Action Blackwater Series – 12 ga., 3 in. chamber, 20 in. heavy wall cylinder bore barrel, 9 shot extended mag., military trigger guard, bayonet lug, parkerized metal finish, matte black furniture, Blackwater logo on right side of receiver, top Picatinny rail, integral adj. ghost ring rear sight, white post front sight, half-round ribbed forearm with three Picatinny rails, Speedfeed buttstock with two spare shell holders on each side, rubber buttpad, 7 1/4 lbs. New 2011.

MSR $732	$625	$550	$475	$425	$345	$280	$220	

* Model 590A1 Mariner Slide Action – 12 ga. only, 18 1/2 in. cyl. bore barrel with bead sights, Marinecote finish, black synthetic stock and forearm, 6 shot only, 6 3/4 lbs. New 2009.

MSR $727	$615	$540	$460	$425	$340	$275	$215	

* Model 590A1 SPX Slide Action – 12 ga. only, 20 in. cyl. bore barrel with ghost ring sights, parkerized finish, black synthetic stock and forearm, 9 shot, includes M9 bayonet and scabbard, receiver Picatinny rail, fiber optic front sight, 7 1/4 lbs. New 2009.

MSR $867	$735	$645	$550	$500	$400	$330	$250	

MODEL 590A1 TACTICAL
– 12 ga., 18 1/5 or 20 in. cylinder bore barrel, 6 or 9 shot extended tube mag., adj. pistol grip stock, matte black finish, ghost ring sights, Picatinny top rail. New 2013.

MSR $845	$715	$625	$535	$485	$395	$325	$250	

MODEL 590A1 SLIDE ACTION CLASS III RESTRICTED
– 12 ga. only, law enforcement/military use only with 14 in. barrel, 6 shot, seven different configurations, plus X12 model designed to use Taser International products. Retail pricing is not available on this model.

* Model 930 Semi-Auto Tactical – 12 ga., 18 1/2 in. cylinder bore barrel, blue finish, 5 shot, synthetic stock.

MSR $660	$550	$480	$415	$375	$300	$250	$195	

Add $23 for heat shield.

MSR	100%	98%	95%	90%	80%	70%	60%	Last MSR

* **Model 930 Semi-Auto Special Purpose Home Security** – 12 ga., 3 in. chamber, 18 1/2 in. cylinder bore barrel, bead sights, blue finish, black synthetic stock, 7 1/2 lbs. New 2007.

MSR $612	$525	$450	$385	$350	$285	$230	$180	

Add $46 for tactical barrel in matte blue finish or $68 for tactical barrel with heat shield (new 2011).
Add $67 for Field/Security combo (new 2010).

* **Model 930 Semi-Auto Special Purpose Roadblocker** – 12 ga., similar to Home Security Model, except has 18 1/2 in. barrel with large muzzle brake, 5 shot, 7 3/4 lbs. Mfg. 2009-2011.

	$575	$495	$415	$375	$300	$245	$190	*$670*

* **Model 930 Semi-Auto Special Purpose SPX** – 12 ga., 3 in. chamber, features 8 shot mag., Picatinny rail, LPA ghost ring rear sight, and winged fiber optic front sight, with or w/o pistol grip stock, 7 3/4 lbs. New 2008.

MSR $787	$675	$595	$500	$460	$370	$300	$235	

Add $96 for pistol grip stock.
Add $151 for pistol grip stock with coyote tan finish.

* **Model 930 Semi-Auto Special Purpose SPX Blackwater Series** – 12 ga., 3 in. chamber, 8 shot, XS sight system, 18 1/2 in. cylinder bore barrel, receiver mounted sliding safety, matte black finish with Blackwater logo on right side of receiver, black composite pistol grip stock, Picatinny rail with integral adj. ghost ring sight, oversized cocking handle and bolt release, 7 3/4 lbs. New 2011.

MSR $865	$700	$615	$525	$475	$385	$315	$245	

* **Model 930 Semi-Auto JM Pro Series** – 12 ga., 3 in. chamber, 22 or 24 in. barrel, 9 or 10 shot, matte black or Kryptek Typhon camo (new 2014, 24 in. bbl. only) synthetic stock, fiber optic front sight, engraved receiver, beveled loading gate, shorter forend, extended magazine tube, adj. overtravel, built to Jerry Miculek's specifications. New 2012.

MSR $752	$635	$550	$475	$425	$345	$280	$225	

Add $28 for Kryptek Typhon camo finish (new 2014).

* **Model 3000 Slide Action Law Enforcement** – 12 or 20 ga. only, 18 1/2 or 20 in. cylinder bore only, rifle or bead sights. Mfg. 1986-87 only.

	$325	$285	$245	$220	$180	$145	$115	*$362*

Add $25 for rifle sights.
Add $33 for black speedfeed stock.

* **Model 9200 Crown Semi-Auto Jungle Gun** – 12 ga. only, 18 1/2 in. plain barrel with cyl. bore, parkerized metal, synthetic stock. Mfg. 1998-2001.

	$610	$535	$455	$415	$335	$275	$215	*$704*

NOTES

N SECTION

NAVY ARMS COMPANY

Current importer established during 1958, and located in Martinsburg, WV beginning 2005. During 2012, Navy Arms temporarily suspended the importation of firearms. Previously located in Union City, NJ, 2001-2005, in Ridgefield, NJ. Navy Arms imports are fabricated by various manufacturers including the Italian companies Davide Pedersoli & Co., Pietta & Co., and A. Uberti & C. Navy Arms also owns Old Western Scrounger ammo, which markets obsolete and hard-to-find ammo. Distributor and dealer sales.

Navy Arms has also sold a wide variety of original military firearms classified as curios and replics. Handguns included the Mauser Broomhandle, Japanese Nambu, Colt 1911 Government Model, Tokarev, Browning Hi-Power, S&W Model 1917, and others. Rifles included Mauser contract models, Japanese Type 38s, Enfields, FNs, Nagants, M1 Carbines, M1 Garands, Chinese SKSs, Egyptian Rashids, French MAS Model 1936s, among others. Most of these firearms are priced in the $75-$500 price range depending on desirability of model and condition.

In 2014, Navy Arms made an agreement with Browning Arms Company, licensees of the Winchester brand name for firearms, to have Winchester-branded 1873 replica rifles made for Navy Arms with features and upgrades unique to Navy Arms guns. These improvements include a factory installed short-stroke kit, squared off shotgun style buttstock, deluxe grade American walnut stocks fully checkered with an oil finish and full octagonal barrels. Navy Arms receives these guns from Winchester without finish on the metal and they are sent to Turnbull Manufacturing Co. to have the receiver and all furniture color case hardened and the barrels blued. These guns will be produced annually on a limited basis and are only available from Navy Arms. For information and up-to-date pricing regarding recent Navy Arms black powder models, please refer to the *Blue Book of Modern Black Powder Arms* by John Allen (also online).

Black Powder Revolvers - Reproductions & Replicas and *Black Powder Long Arms & Pistols - Reproductions & Replicas* by Dennis Adler are also invaluable sources for most black powder revolver reproductions and replicas, and include hundreds of color images on most popular makes/models, provide manufacturer/trademark histories, and up-to-date information on related items/accessories for black powder shooting - www.bluebookofgunvalues.com.

MSR	100%	98%	95%	90%	80%	70%	60%	Last MSR

RIFLES: MODERN PRODUCTION

In addition to the models listed, Navy Arms in late 1990 purchased the manufacturing rights of the English firm Parker-Hale. In 1991, Navy Arms built a manufacturing facility, Gibbs Rifle Co., located in Martinsburg, WV and produced these rifles domestically 1991-1994 (see Gibbs Rifle Co. listing for more info on models the company currently imports).

RPKS-74 – .223 Rem. or 7.62x39mm (new 1989) cal., semi-auto version of the Chinese RPK Squad Automatic Weapon, Kalashnikov action, 19 in. barrel, integral folding bipod, 9 1/2 lbs. Imported 1988-89 only.

	100%	98%	95%	90%	80%	70%	60%	Last MSR
	$525	$445	$350	$250	$195	$175	$150	$649

MODEL 1 CARBINE/RIFLE – .45-70 Govt. cal., action is sporterized No. 1 MKIII Enfield, choice of 18 (carbine) or 22 (rifle) in. barrel with iron sights, black Zytel Monte Carlo (rifle) or straight grip walnut (carbine) stock, 7 (carbine) or 8 1/2 (rifle) lbs. Limited importation 1999 only.

	100%	98%	95%	90%	80%	70%	60%	Last MSR
	$325	$255	$200	$175	$160	$145	$130	$375

MODEL 4 CARBINE/RIFLE – .45-70 Govt. cal., action is sporterized No. 4 MKI Enfield, choice of 18 (carbine) or 22 (rifle) in. barrel, blue metal, choice of checkered walnut Monte Carlo (rifle) or uncheckered straight grip (carbine, disc. 1999) stock, 7 or 8 lbs. Mfg. 1999-2001.

	100%	98%	95%	90%	80%	70%	60%	Last MSR
	$325	$255	$200	$175	$160	$145	$130	$375

NEMESIS ARMS

Current rifle manufacturer located in Calimesa, CA.

RIFLES: BOLT ACTION

VANQUISH (WINDRUNNER) – .243 Win., .260 Rem., 6.5 Creedmoor (new 2011), .300 Win. (new 2013), .308 Win., or .338 Federal cal., take down action, 16 or 20 in. chromemoly steel heavy fluted barrel, steel alloy upper, steel lower, adj. stock, 10 shot detachable mag., Weaver rail, Versapod bipod, 12 lbs.

MSR $4,450		$3,850	$3,500	$3,150	$2,725	$2,400	$2,125	$1,775

During 2010, this model's nomenclature changed from Windrunner to the Vanquish.

NEMO (NEW EVOLUTION MILITARY ORDNANCE)

Current centerfire rifle manufacturer located in Kalispell, MT. Dealer sales.

RIFLES: SEMI-AUTO

NEMO manufactures many variations of rifles built on the AR-15 style platform. It currently sells weapon systems to the military, law enforcement, special operations, and the civilian marketplace. NEMO also makes tactical bolt action rifles per individual specifications.

MSR	100%	98%	95%	90%	80%	70%	60%	Last MSR

OMEN/OMEN MATCH 2.0 – .300 Win. Mag. cal., GIO, 22 in. match grade (disc. 2013) or fluted stainless steel (new 2014) barrel with NEMO PC Tornado flash hider (disc. 2013) or NEMO A-10 muzzle brake (new 2014), nickel boron barrel extension and feed ramp, two NEMO 14 shot mags., Geissele two-stage trigger, two detachable handguard accessory rails with built-in QD mounts, NEMO integrated free floated customizable handguard with hard black anodized finish, low profile (disc. 2013) or adj. (new 2014) gas block, NEMO steel side charging handle, Mako adj. SSR-25 sniper stock and Hogue overmolded pistol grip with Black finish, Tru-Spec Drag Bag, Billet upper and lower receivers with SF Tiger Stripe finish, 10 1/2 lbs. New 2012.

MSR $5,699		$4,850	$4,250	$3,640	$3,300	$2,675	$2,185	$1,700

The Omen model was upgraded in 2014 and renamed the Omen Match 2.0.

OMEN PRATKA – .300 Win. Mag. cal., GIO, 20 in. ultra-lightweight fluted stainless steel barrel with NEMO A-10 muzzle brake, two NEMO 14 shot polymer mags., nickel boron barrel extension and feed ramp, steel side charging handle, Geissele two-stage trigger, NEMO integrated free floated customizable handguard with Black anodized finish, two detachable handguard accessory rails with built-in QD mounts, Mission First Tactical Battlelink ultra lightweight minimalist stock with sling mounts and Hogue overmolded pistol grip with Black finish, includes carry case, 9 1/2 lbs. New 2014.

MSR $3,995		$3,400	$2,975	$2,550	$2,325	$1,875	$1,550	$1,300

OMEN RECON – .300 Win. Mag. cal., 18 in. fluted stainless steel barrel, adj. gas block, nickel boron barrel extension, feed ramp, bolt release, and bolt carrier with recoil reduction system, Geissele two-stage trigger, two 14 shot polymer mags., billet aluminum receivers with Custom Tiger Stripe finish, NEMO integrated free float customizable handguard with Black finish, two detachable handguard accessory rails with built-in QD mounts, steel side charging handle, Magpul STR collapsible carbine stock and Hogue overmolded pistol grip with Black finish, includes custom drag bag, 10 lbs. New 2014.

MSR $5,699		$4,850	$4,250	$3,640	$3,300	$2,675	$2,185	$1,700

OMEN WATCHMAN – .300 Win. Mag. cal., adj. gas block, 24 in. stainless cut-rifling barrel with A-10 muzzle brake, Picatinny rail on top of aluminum handguard and aluminum receiver, Geissele SSA-E match trigger, nickel boron bolt release, feed ramp, barrel extension, and bolt carrier with recoil reduction system, two 14 shot polymer mags., two detachable accessory rails, solid billet receiver with Tiger Stripe finish, Magpul PRS Black stock with Hogue grip, includes custom drag bag, 12.6 lbs. New 2014.

MSR $7,375		$6,275	$5,500	$4,700	$4,275	$3,450	$2,825	$2,400

TANGO2 – 5.56 NATO/.223 Rem. cal., GIO, NEMO barrel with PC Tornado flash hider, Billet upper and lower receivers with SF Tiger Stripe finish, free float customizable handguard with removable rail system in Black, low profile gas block, charging handle with tactical latch, Troy micro sights, adj. buttstock with battery storage in black finish, Hogue overmolded pistol grip, ambi safety, one PMag., Timney trigger, foam lined case.

MSR $2,975		$2,525	$2,225	$1,900	$1,725	$1,400	$1,150	$975

* **TANGO6** – similar to Tango2, except available in .300 AAC Blackout cal.

MSR $2,975		$2,525	$2,225	$1,900	$1,725	$1,400	$1,150	$975

TANGO8 – .308 Win. cal., 16 in. stainless steel barrel with NEMO flash hider and black nitride finish, low profile gas block, Geissele SSA-E two-stage trigger, NEMO integrated free floated customizable handguard, two detachable handguard accessory rails with built-in QD mounts, Troy micro sights, charging handle with tactical latch, billet aluminum receiver with Custom Tiger Stripe finish, NEMO adj. buttstock assembly with battery storage, Hogue overmolded pistol grip, Black finish, includes one Magpul PMag. and foam lined case.

MSR $4,200		$3,575	$3,125	$2,675	$2,425	$1,975	$1,625	$1,250

» **Tango 8 SASS** – .308 Win. cal., same as Tango 8, except features 20 in. SASS Profile stainless steel barrel, NEMO rifle-length integrated free floated customizable handguard, Magpul PRS buttstock, black finish, 10.8 lbs.

MSR $4,675		$3,975	$3,475	$3,000	$2,700	$2,185	$1,800	$1,475

Ti ONE TITANIUM RIFLE – .308 Win. cal., AR-15 style, GIO, 16 in. stainless steel H-Bar profile barrel, titanium matched receiver set, customizable tube handguard, Troy Tritium micro set back up iron sights, titanium Picatinny handguard rails, low profile gas block, charging handle with tactical latch, 6-pos. buttstock, Hogue grip with battery management system, titanium DRK compensator, Timney trigger, titanium buffer tube, Black nitride finish, 8.65 lbs. Serial No. 1.

Current MSR on this rifle is $95,000.

NESIKA

Current trademark of actions and rifles (new 2014) manufactured by Nesika Bay Precision, Inc., located in Sturgis, SD. Actions are currently distributed by Dakota Arms. Nesika also manufactured rifles circa 2004-2005. Previously located in Poulsbo, WA until 2003. Dealer and consumer sales.

On June 5, 2009, Remington Arms Company purchased Dakota Arms, Inc., including the rights to Nesika.

MSR	100%	98%	95%	90%	80%	70%	60%	Last MSR

RIFLES: BOLT ACTION

In 2014, Nesika once again began offering its proprietary actions. Current models include the Tactical Model (MSR $1,400-$1,700), Classic Model (MSR $1,275-$1,475), Hunter Model (MSR $1,050-$1,450), and Round Model (MSR $1,000-$1,350).

Nesika also sold its proprietary rifle actions until 2009 in Classic ($1,275 - $1,475 MSR), Round ($1,000 - $1,350 MSR), Hunter ($1,050 - $1,450 MSR), and Tactical ($1,400 - $1,700 MSR) configurations and in a variety of cals. A Model NXP bolt action single shot pistol model was also available. Last MSR was $1,100 circa 2008.

URBAN TACTICAL – various tactical cals., heavy duty receiver with Picatinny rail and fluted 24 or 28 in. barrel, detachable box mag., black synthetic stock with adj. recoil pad. Mfg. 2004-2005.

	100%	98%	95%	90%	80%	70%	60%	Last MSR
	$4,500	$4,000	$3,500	$3,000	$2,500	$2,000	$1,650	*$5,040*

Add $160 for heavy .308 Win. cal. or $520 for Lapua or Lazzeroni Warbird or Patriot cals.

NEW DETONICS MANUFACTURING CORPORATION

Previous manufacturer located in Phoenix, AZ 1989-1992. Formerly named Detonics Firearms Industries (previous manufacturer located in Bellevue, WA 1976-1988). Detonics was sold in early 1988 to the New Detonics Manufacturing Corporation, a wholly owned subsidiary of "1045 Investors Group Limited."

Due to space considerations, information regarding this manufacturer is available online free of charge at www.bluebookofgunvalues.com.

NEW ENGLAND FIREARMS

Current trademark established during 1987, located and previously manufactured in Gardner, MA until Nov. 1, 2007. Beginning Nov. 1, 2007, the NEF trademark applies to imported guns only. Distributor sales.

During late Jan. of 2008, Remington acquired the Marlin Firearms Company, which had purchased the H&R, New England Firearms (NEF), and L.C. Smith brands during 2000. On May 31st, 2007, Remington Arms Co. was acquired by Cerberus Capital.

During 2000, Marlin Firearms Co. purchased the assets of H&R 1871, Inc., and the name was changed to H&R 1871, LLC. Brand names include Harrington & Richardson, New England Firearms, and Wesson & Harrington.

All NEF firearms utilize a transfer bar safety system and have a $10 service plan which guarantees lifetime warranty.

New England Firearms should not be confused with New England Arms Corp.

RIFLES: SINGLE SHOT

Beginning Nov. 1, 2007, H&R 1871 decided that all products built in the USA will carry the H&R brand name, and all imported products will be sold under the NEF brand name. The Handi-Rifle, Super Light Handi-Rifle, Sportster, and Survivor are now under the H&R brand name.

SURVIVOR – .223 Rem., .308 Win. (new 1999), .357 Mag. (disc. 1998) or .410/45 LC (new 2007) cal., similar in design to the Survivor Series shotgun, removable forearm with ammo storage, thumbhole stock with storage compartment, no iron sights, 20 (.410/45 LC cal. only) or 22 in. barrel, blue or nickel finish, .357 Mag. cal. has open sights, .223 Rem. and .308 Win. cal. have heavy barrels and scope mount rail, 6 lbs. Mfg. 1996-2008.

	100%	98%	95%	90%	80%	70%	60%	Last MSR
	$230	$180	$145	$110	$80	$70	$60	*$281*

Add approx. $15 for nickel finish (disc. 1998, reintroduced 2007 for .410/45 LC cal. only).
Subtract $76 for .410/45 LC cal. (new 2007).

SHOTGUNS: SINGLE SHOT

Beginning Nov. 1, 2007, H&R 1871 decided that all products built in the U.S.A. will carry the H&R brand name, and all imported products will be sold under the NEF brand name. The Pardner Series and Tracker Slug are now under the H&R brand name.

SURVIVOR SERIES – 12 (disc. 2003), 20 ga. (disc. 2003), or .410/.45 LC (new 1995) bore, 3 in. chamber, 20 (.410/.45 LC) or 22 in. barrel with Mod. choke, blue or electroless nickel finish, synthetic thumbhole designed hollow stock with pistol grip, removable forend holds additional ammo, sling swivels, and black nylon sling, 13 1/4 in. LOP, 6 lbs. Mfg. 1992-93, reintroduced 1995-2006.

	100%	98%	95%	90%	80%	70%	60%	Last MSR
	$175	$150	$120	$100	$85	$75	$65	*$219*

Add $18 for electroless nickel finish.
Subtract 20% for 12 or 20 ga.

SHOTGUNS: SLIDE ACTION

Beginning Nov. 1, 2007, H&R 1871 decided that all products built in the U.S.A. will carry the H&R brand name, and all imported products will be sold under the NEF brand name. The Pardner Series is now under the H&R brand name.

* *Pardner Pump Protector* – .12 ga., black synthetic stock, 18 1/2 in. barrel, bead front sight, matte finished metal, swivel studs, vent. recoil pad, 5 shot tube mag., crossbolt safety. Mfg. 2006-2007.

	100%	98%	95%	90%	80%	70%	60%	Last MSR
	$155	$135	$115	$100	$85	$75	$65	*$186*

MSR	100%	98%	95%	90%	80%	70%	60%	Last MSR

* ***Pardner Pump Slug*** – 12 or 20 ga., take-down action, 21 (20 ga.) or 22 (12 ga.) in. rifled barrel, matte metal finish, black synthetic (12 ga.) or walnut (20 ga.) pistol grip stock with fluted comb, swivel studs, vent. recoil pad, ramp front sight, adj. rear sight, drilled and tapped, 5 shot mag., crossbolt safety, approx. 6 1/2 lbs. Mfg. 2006-2008.

	100%	98%	95%	90%	80%	70%	60%	Last MSR
	$250	$215	$190	$160	$140	$115	$100	$298

Add $33 for full cantilever scope mount (new 2009).

Add $44 for walnut stock and forearm.

NEWTOWN FIREARMS

Current manufacturer located in Hangtown, CA.

CARBINES: SEMI-AUTO

NF-15/GEN 2 TACTICAL – 5.56 NATO cal., AR-15 style, choice of GIO or GPO, 16 in. match grade Vanadium steel fluted barrel with flash hider, quad Picatinny rail, black furniture, collapsible stock, sub MOA accuracy guaranteed, 10 or 20 shot mag., 8 lbs. Disc. 2013.

	100%	98%	95%	90%	80%	70%	60%	Last MSR
	$2,775	$2,300	$1,950	$1,575	$1,250	$1,000	$875	$2,950

NF-15 GEN 3 MATCH – .223 Wylde cal., GPO, 16 in. McGowen H-Bar match stainless steel barrel with black nitride coating, Gen-3 mil-spec T6 heavy mass billet upper and lower receiver set, Timney match trigger, modular free float quad rail, Adams Arms 4-pos. carbine length piston system with Adams Arms piston carrier, Battle Arms ambi safety, billet tactical charging handle, Magpul ACS mil-spec stock, Ergo Suregrip pistol grip. New 2014.

MSR $2,800	100%	98%	95%	90%	80%	70%	60%	
	$2,375	$2,075	$1,775	$1,625	$1,300	$1,075	$925	

GEN-4 NF-15 – .223 Wylde cal., 16 in. McGowen H-Bar match stainless steel barrel with black nitride coating and Barnes Precision A2 enhanced flash hider, billet tactical latch charging handle, Battle Arms ambidextrous safety selector, Gen-4 mil-spec T6 forged or Gen-4 mil-spec T6 billet lower receiver, forged upper receiver, modular free float quad rail, handguard with low heat-sync barrel nut, Barnes Precision gas block or Troy low pro gas block, 6-pos. carbine buffer tube, Magpul CTR stock, Ergo Sure pistol grip. New 2014.

MSR $1,499	100%	98%	95%	90%	80%	70%	60%	
	$1,275	$1,125	$950	$875	$700	$575	$475	

Add $200 for Gen. 4 mil-spec T6 billet lower receiver.

GEN-4 NF-15 PISTON – .223 Wylde cal., S.M.A.A.R.T. Infinitely adj. gas piston system, 16 in. McGowen H-Bar match stainless steel barrel with black nitride coating and Barnes Precision A2 enhanced flash hider, Gen-4 mil-spec T6 forged or Gen-4 mil-spec billet lower receiver, forged upper receiver, ACT combat trigger, modular free float quad rail, handguard with low heat-sync barrel nut, 6-pos. carbine buffer tube, billet tactical latch charging handle, Battle Arms ambidextrous safety selector, Magpul CTR stock, Ergo Sure pistol grip. New 2014.

MSR $2,099	100%	98%	95%	90%	80%	70%	60%	
	$1,785	$1,575	$1,350	$1,225	$975	$800	$675	

Add $300 for Gen-4 mil-spec T6 billet lower receiver.

NEXT GENERATION ARMS

Previous rifle manufacturer located in Hayden, ID until circa 2012.

RIFLES: SEMI-AUTO

Next Generation Arms manufactured AR-15 style rifles with an emphasis on being lighter, shorter, more reliable and easier to clean. There were many configurations possible, but most used a Noveske 14 1/2 in. barrel and a Geissele trigger. These are combined with advanced design and manufacturing as well as ceramic coatings.

NIGHTHAWK CUSTOM

Current manufacturer located in Berryville, AR, since 2004. Consumer custom order sales.

PISTOLS: SEMI-AUTO, SINGLE ACTION

Nighthawk Custom offers a complete line of high quality 1911 style semi-auto pistols. Please contact the company directly for more information on custom pistols, a wide variety of options, gunsmithing services and availability (see Trademark Index).

Add $200 for Crimson Trace laser grips on any applicable model (not bobtail). Add $150 for Ed Brown bobtail. Add $65 for ambidextrous safety. Add $50 for crowned barrel. Add $50 for beveled and recessed slide stop. Add $350 for Complete Hard Chrome Finish. Add $350 for Complete Diamond Black Finish.

10-8 – .45 ACP cal., 5 in. barrel, SA, green or black linen micarta grips, black Perma Kote finish, 8 shot, Hilton Yam/10-8 performance designed U-notched rear and serrated front sights with tritium inserts, low profile Dawson Light Speed Rail, front/rear cocking serrations, long solid trigger with hidden fixed over travel stop, strong side only safety, 42 oz. Mfg. 2009-2010.

	100%	98%	95%	90%	80%	70%	60%	Last MSR
	$2,350	$2,025	$1,650	$1,325	$1,175	$900	$775	$2,595

MSR	100%	98%	95%	90%	80%	70%	60%	Last MSR

AAC (ADVANCED ARMAMENT CORPORATION) – 9mm Para. or .45 ACP cal., 5 in. threaded barrel, SA, stainless steel thread protector, done in collaboration with Advanced Armament Corporation, lightening cuts on the top and sides of the slide, mainspring housing and front strap that match the Advanced Armament M4-2000 suppressor, tall Heinie Slant Pro Straight Eight front sights designed for use with suppressor, black Perma Kote finish in black, ultra thin Nighthawk Custom Alumagrips, solid, black aluminum trigger, 39 oz. New 2010.

MSR $3,295 $2,950 $2,625 $2,325 $1,825 $1,450 $1,225 $1,000

Add $100 for AAC Recon Model with integrated lower rail.

BOB MARVEL CUSTOM 1911 – .45 ACP cal., 4 1/4 in. barrel, proprietary bull barrel system, hand stippling on top of slide, bull nose front taper, fully adjustable sights, one-piece mainspring housing and magwell, high cut front strap, lightweight aluminum medium solid match trigger, Nighthawk Custom/Marvel EVERLAST recoil system, Black Melonite finish, 2 lbs. 6 oz. New 2012.

MSR $3,995 $3,525 $3,050 $2,600 $2,000 $1,650 $1,425 $1,250

CHRIS COSTA RECON – 9mm Para. (2012 only) or .45 ACP cal., 5 in. crowned barrel and beveled flush with the bushing, 8 (.45 ACP) or 10 (9mm Para.) shot mag., fully machined slide and one piece mainspring housing, top serrations, red fiber optic or tritium dot front sights, EVERLAST recoil system, magwell with rounded butt, Jardine Tactical Hook rear sights, extreme high cut checkered front strap, integrated recon light rail, multi-faceted slide top, lightweight aluminum medium solid match trigger, 10-8 Performance Hyena Brown grips, Black Melonite finish, COSTA logo engraved in silver, 2 lbs. 6 oz. New 2012.

MSR $3,695 $3,250 $2,800 $2,425 $1,875 $1,525 $1,300 $1,075

  * **Chris Costa Compact** – .45 ACP cal. only, similar to Chris Costa Recon, except has smaller, officer-style frame, 4 1/4 in. barrel, black 10-8 Performance 5 LPI grips, 2 lbs. 4 oz. New 2012.

MSR $3,695 $3,250 $2,800 $2,425 $1,875 $1,525 $1,300 $1,075

DOMINATOR – .45 ACP cal., 5 in. crowned match grade barrel, stainless steel frame with black Perma Kote slide, Nighthawk Custom fully adjustable rear sights, 8 shot, hand serrated rear og slide with serrated top slide, front and rear slide serrations, 25 LPI checkering on front strap, cocobolo double diamond grips with laser engraved Nighthawk Custom logo, 40 oz.

MSR $3,250 $2,875 $2,525 $2,100 $1,700 $1,350 $1,000 $875

Add $100 for Recon Model with integrated lower rail.

Add $350 for the FLX high capacity double stack frame (disc. 2011).

ENFORCER – .45 ACP cal., SA only, 5 in. barrel, Novak low mount tritium or Heinie Slant Pro night sights, extended tactical mag. catch, aggressive no slip G10 Golf Ball grips or Mil-Tac G-10 spiral logo grips in either Black/Gray or Black/Green (new 2012), unique frame with integrated plunger tube and mag well, hand serrations on rear of slide with serrated top slide, front and rear slide cocking serrations, lanyard loop mainspring housing, complete de-horn and ready for carry, Perma Kote finish in Black, Green, Sniper Gray, Coyote Tan, or Titanium Blue, 39 oz.

MSR $3,395 $3,050 $2,700 $2,375 $1,850 $1,450 $1,225 $1,000

Add $100 for Recon Model with integrated lower rail.

FALCON – 9mm Para., 10mm, or .45 ACP cal., 5 in. match grade stainless steel or carbon steel crowned barrel with chamfered bushing, one-piece fully machined mainspring/magwell combination, rear cocking serrations, golf ball dimple-pattern G10 grips in Coyote Tan, Black, or OD Green finish with or without the Nighthawk logo, Heinie ledge rear sight, 39 oz. New 2011.

MSR $3,295 $2,950 $2,575 $2,225 $2,000 $1,625 $1,325 $1,025

  * **Falcon Commander** – .45 ACP cal., similar to Falcon, except in Commander size. New 2013.

MSR $3,295 $2,950 $2,575 $2,225 $2,000 $1,625 $1,325 $1,025

GRP (GLOBAL RESPONSE PISTOL) – 9mm Para. (new 2012), 10mm (new 2012), or .45 ACP cal., SA only, 5 in. match grade barrel, 8 shot mag., match grade trigger, front and rear cocking serrations, Heinie or Novak Extreme Duty adj. night sights, Gator Back (disc.) or Golf Ball grips, Perma Kote ceramic based finish in Black, Sniper Gray, Green, Coyote Tan, or Titanium Blue, tactical single side or Ambi safety, 2 lb. 7 oz.

MSR $2,896 $2,650 $2,225 $1,900 $1,550 $1,200 $975 $825

Add $100 for GRP II with 4 1/4 in. barrel (disc. 2011).

Add $200 Crimson Trace laser grips.

Add $350 for the FLX high capacity double stack frame (disc. 2011).

  * **GRP Recon** – 9mm Para., 10mm, or .45 ACP cal., similar to GRP, except includes frame with integrated lower rail for Surefire X300 weapon light, 2 lb. 9 oz.

MSR $3,100 $2,775 $2,425 $2,075 $1,875 $1,525 $1,250 $975

Add $200 Crimson Trace laser grips.

MSR	100%	98%	95%	90%	80%	70%	60%	Last MSR

HEINE LADY HAWK – 9mm Para. or .45 ACP cal., 4 1/4 in. crowned match grade barrel, ultra thin aluminum grips, Heinie Slant Pro Straight Eight sights, modified ultra thin chain link front strap and mainspring housing for reduced grip circumference, titanium blue Perma Kote finish with hard chromed controls, 36 oz.

   MSR $3,450 $3,050 $2,650 $2,375 $1,850 $1,450 $1,225 $1,000

   Add $100 for Recon Model with integrated lower rail.
   Add $200 for anodized aluminum lightweight frame.
   Add $200 for complete stainless steel model.

HEINIE LONG SLIDE – 10mm or .45 ACP cal., 6 in. match grade barrel, black Perma Kote ceramic based finish, cocobolo wood grips with Heinie logo, Nighthawk Custom fully adjustable rear or fixed sights, 25 LPI checkering on front strap, contoured for carry, 44 oz.

   MSR $3,595 $3,175 $2,750 $2,425 $1,925 $1,550 $1,300 $1,000

   Add $100 for Recon Model with integrated lower rail.
   Add $150 for extended magazine well.
   Add $350 for unique Nighthawk Custom camouflage finish; available in Digital, Woodland or Desert Camo (disc. 2011).

HEINIE PDP – .45 ACP cal., 4 1/4 (Commander size) or 5 (Government size) in. Heinie match grade barrel, cocobolo wood grips with Heinie logo, fixed sights, scalloped front strap and mainspring housing, extended combat safety, contoured for carry magwell, Heinie match hammer, sear, and disconnector, serrated rear of slide & slide top, Heinie aluminum trigger, tactical mag release, 38 oz.

   MSR $3,395 $3,000 $2,600 $2,150 $1,700 $1,350 $1,000 $875

HEINIE SIGNATURE SERIES – 9mm Para. cal., available in Competition, Government Recon, and Officer Compact configurations, features silver Heinie Signature Series engraved logo on right of slide, features same thin frame as Lady Hawk model.

   * **Heinie Signature Series Compact** – 9mm Para. cal., similar to the RECON and the Competition model, except has smaller officer-style frame designed for concealed carry, 4 1/2 in. barrel, and G10 grips. New 2012.

   MSR $3,450 $3,050 $2,650 $2,350 $1,850 $1,500 $1,275 $1,000

   * **Heinie Signature Series Competition** – 5 in. barrel, hand signed thin grip panels, fully machined one piece mainspring housing and magwell combination that has been thinned and scalloped, red fiber optic front sights, black Heinie Slant Pro rear sights, hand serrated rear of slide, slide top serrations, crowned and recessed match grade barrel, tool steel hammer and hammer strut, lightweight aluminum match grade trigger, recessed slide stop, chamfered frame, 40 oz. New 2012.

   MSR $3,450 $3,050 $2,650 $2,350 $1,850 $1,500 $1,275 $1,000

   * **Heinie Signature Series RECON** – 9mm Para. cal., 5 in. match grade barrel, similar features as the Competition, except has integrated recon light rail X300 tactical light, and Heine Slant Pro Night Sights. New 2012.

   MSR $3,550 $3,150 $2,700 $2,375 $1,850 $1,525 $1,300 $1,075

HEINIE TACTICAL CARRY – .45 ACP cal., 5 in. Heinie match grade barrel, black Perma Kote ceramic based finish, double diamond cocobolo or aluminum grips with Heinie logo, Heinie Straight Eight Slant Pro night sights, Heinie trigger, complete carry dehorned, Heinie signature magwell, flat slide top with 40 LPI serrations, done in collaboration with renowned gunsmith Richard Heinie, 40 oz. Disc. 2013.

                 $3,600 $3,250 $2,850 $2,450 $2,000 $1,600 $1,200   *$3,895*

PREDATOR – 9mm Para., 10mm, or .45 ACP cal., SA only, 5 in. stainless steel barrel, black Perma Kote ceramic based finish with black slide, double diamond cocobolo, walnut, or black cristobal checkered grips, Heinie Slant Pro Straight Eight or Novak Lo-Mount night sights, hand checkering on rear of slide with serrated top slide, front and rear slide serrations, 25 LPI checkering on front strap, unique one piece precision fit barrel designed to reduce muzzle flip and felt recoil, one inch at 25 yards guaranteed accuracy, top-of-the-line model, available in Black, Sniper Gray, Coyote Tan, Titanium Blue, Hard Chrome, or Stainless steel, 32-34 oz.

   MSR $3,450 $3,050 $2,650 $2,350 $1,850 $1,500 $1,275 $1,000

   Add $100 for Recon Model with integrated lower rail.
   Add $350 for the FLX high capacity double stack frame. (9mm & 10mm Government size only, disc. 2011)

   * **Predator II** – 9mm Para., 10mm, or .45 ACP cal., similar to Predator, except has 4 1/4 in. barrel, checkered rear of slide, top serrations, 2 lbs. 4 oz.

   MSR $3,450 $3,050 $2,650 $2,350 $1,850 $1,500 $1,275 $1,000

   * **Predator III** – 9mm Para., 10mm, or .45 ACP cal., similar to Predator, except features Officer frame and 4 1/4 in. barrel, 2 lbs. 6 oz.

   MSR $3,450 $3,050 $2,650 $2,350 $1,850 $1,500 $1,275 $1,000

MSR	100%	98%	95%	90%	80%	70%	60%	Last MSR

T3 – 9mm Para, .40 S&W (disc. 2011) or .45 ACP cal., 4 1/4 in. match grade stainless steel fully crowned barrel, Officer size frame, extended mag. well, flush forged slide stop with chamfered frame, tactical mag. release, unique Nighthawk T3 magwell, horizontally serrated no-snag mainspring housing and rear of slide, skeletonized aluminum match trigger, Heinie straight 8 slant pro sights, Perma Kote finish, in Black, Gun Metal Grey, Green, Coyote Tan, Titanium Blue, or hard chrome, 38 oz.

MSR $3,250	$2,900	$2,400	$1,975	$1,650	$1,300	$1,050	$850	

Add $200 for anodized aluminum lightweight frame.

Add $495 for T3 Comp model (.45 ACP cal. only), with Schuemann AET hybrid comp. ported barrel (new 2010).

* **T3 Stainless** – 9mm Para, .40 S&W (disc. 2011) or .45 ACP cal., similar to T3, except stainless steel.

MSR $3,400	$3,000	$2,625	$2,325	$1,850	$1,450	$1,225	$1,000	

* **T3 Thin** – similar to the T3, except is smaller design for concealed carry. New 2012.

MSR $3,400	$3,000	$2,625	$2,325	$1,850	$1,450	$1,225	$1,000	

T4 – 9mm Para. cal., 3.8 in. crowned barrel, steel or aluminum frame, thin grips. New 2013.

MSR $3,350	$2,975	$2,625	$2,325	$1,850	$1,450	$1,225	$1,000	

TALON – 9mm Para., .40 S&W (disc. 2011), 10mm, or .45 ACP cal., 5 in. match grade, lightweight aluminum match trigger, hand checkering on rear of slide with serrated top slide, front and rear slide serrations, 25 LPI checkering on front strap, Novak night sights, cocobolo, walnut, or black cristobal grips, tactical mag. release, Perma Kote ceramic based finish in Black, Sniper Gray, Coyote Tan, Titanium Blue, Hard Chrome, or Diamond Black option available, 36-41 oz.

MSR $3,095	$2,750	$2,400	$1,975	$1,600	$1,300	$1,000	$875	

Add $100 for Recon Model with integrated lower rail.

Add $200 for anodized aluminum lightweight frame.

Add $350 for the FLX high capacity double stack frame (disc. 2011).

* **Talon II** – 9mm Para., .40 S&W (disc. 2011), 10mm, or .45 ACP cal., similar to Talon, except features Commander size frame, 4 1/4 in. barrel, 2 lbs. 4 oz.

MSR $3,095	$2,750	$2,400	$1,975	$1,600	$1,300	$1,000	$875	

»**Talon II Bobtail** – 9mm Para., .40 S&W (disc. 2011), 10mm, or .45 ACP cal., similar to Talon II, except features Ed Brown Bobtail.

MSR $3,245	$2,875	$2,525	$2,100	$1,700	$1,350	$1,000	$875	

* **Talon IV** – similar to Talon, except compact model with 3.6 in. barrel, gray frame and black slide, rear slide serrations, and black grips. Disc. 2010.

	$2,225	$1,950	$1,600	$1,300	$1,050	$875	$750	$2,425

RIFLES: BOLT ACTION

HUNTING RIFLE – various cals., bolt action, available in Hunting, Varmint, and Bench Rest configurations, Broughton barrel, synthetic stock. Disc. 2011.

	$3,500	$3,100	$2,650	$2,250	$1,800	$1,375	$1,125	$3,895

TACTICAL RIFLE – .308 Win., 7mm Rem. Mag., .300 Rem. Mag., or .338 Lapua cal., with or w/o Surgeon action, with or w/o bolt on Picatinny rail with choice of 0 or 20 MOA integral elevation, Jewell trigger, Perma Kote finish in choice of Desert Sand, OD Green, Sniper Gray, Desert camo, Woodland camo, or Urban camo finish, tactical synthetic stock with adj. comb. Mfg. 2009-2011.

	$3,800	$3,350	$2,900	$2,500	$2,000	$1,500	$1,225	$4,250

Add $550 for short Surgeon action.

Add $595 for 100% coverage Custom woodland or digital camouflage finish.

Add $625 for Magnum Surgeon action.

Add $650 for long Surgeon action.

Add $875 for XL action in .338 Lapua cal.

SHOTGUNS

TACTICAL SLIDE ACTION – 12 ga., reworked 3 in. chambered action for faster, smoother cycling, Hogue Over Molded style stock with 12 or 14 in. LOP, Big Dome large safety, 2-shot extension, fully adjustable and protected ghost ring rear sight with red fiber optic front, 4 or 6 round shell carrier. Rust-Proof ceramic finish in a variety of colors including camo, (Hillbilly223 camo finish became standard in 2014).

MSR $1,350	$1,150	$995	$825	$700	$500	$450	$375	

Add $35 for Tritium front sight upgrade.

Add $75 for Picatinny rail on top of receiver.

Add $85 for magazine clamp with rail & swing swivel.

Add $125 for breaching tool.

Add $125 for Surefire Tactical light with ring mount.

Add $165 for 5-position stock.

MSR	100%	98%	95%	90%	80%	70%	60%	Last MSR

TACTICAL SEMI-AUTO – 12 ga., 2 3/4 in. chamber, 18 in. barrel, pistol grip synthetic stock, Surefire fore end weapon light, hand tuned action, Rust-Proof ceramic finish in a variety of colors including camouflage patterns. tactical charging handle on the bolt, fully adjustable and protected ghost ring rear sight, red fiber optic front sight, 2-shot extension, 4 or 6 round shell carrier. Disc. 2011.

	100%	98%	95%	90%	80%	70%	60%	Last MSR
	$1,800	$1,550	$1,250	$1,125	$800	$675	$550	*$2,060*

Add $35 for Tritium front sight blade.

Add $75 for Picatinny rail on top of receiver.

Add $299 for Surefire forend tactical weapon light.

NOREEN FIREARMS LLC

Current manufacturer located in Belgrade, MT.

RIFLES

Noreen manufactures a complete line of long range precision rifles in .338 Lapua to .50 BMG cal. A wide variety of options, configurations, and accessories are available. Please contact the company directly for more information (see Trademark Index).

BAD NEWS ULTRA LONG RANGE SEMI-AUTO (ULR) – .300 Win. Mag. or .338 Lapua cal., GPO, matte black finish, aluminum receiver, mil-spec or adj. trigger, 5 or 10 shot detachable box mag., 26 in. barrel, custom muzzle brake, one piece bolt carrier, Picatinny quad rail on handguard, Magpul PRA adj. stock.

MSR $5,995		$5,450	$4,475	$3,825	$3,475	$2,800	$2,295	$1,775

ULTRA LONG RANGE BOLT ACTION (ULR) – .338 Lapua, .408 Cheytac, .416 Barrett, or .50 BMG cal., single shot, 34 in. button rifled chromemoly barrel, tactical black or desert camo finish, shell holder bolt, Timney adj. trigger, Picatinny top rail, muzzle brake, folding rotating bipod, collapsible shoulder stock.

MSR $2,599		$2,200	$1,925	$1,650	$1,495	$1,210	$995	$775

Add $300 for .338 Lapua, .408 Cheytac, or .416 Barrett cal.

Add $900 for XLR Extreme stock.

BN36 SEMI-AUTO – .25-06 Rem., .270 Win., or .30-06 cal., GIO, 22 in. barrel, side charging, matte black finish, fixed A2 stock with pistol grip, 5, 10, or 20 shot box mag., mil-spec or optional match trigger, muzzle brake. New 2013.

MSR $1,999		$1,700	$1,495	$1,275	$1,150	$935	$765	$595

NORINCO

Current division of China North Industries Corp. established in 1981, and located in Beijing, China. Norinco currently manufactures small arms and large military weapons for commercial, law enforcement, and military applications. No current U.S. importation. Distributed throughout Europe by Norconia GmbH, located in Rottendorf, Germany. Previously imported and distributed exclusively by Interstate Arms Corp., located in Billerica, MA. Previous importers have included: Norinco Sports U.S.A., located in Diamond Bar, CA, Century International Arms, Inc. located in St. Albans, VT; China Sports, Inc. located in Ontario, CA; Interarms located in Alexandria, VA; KBI, Inc. located in Harrisburg, PA; and others.

Norinco pistols, rifles, and shotguns are manufactured in the People's Republic of China by China North Industries Corp. (Norinco has over 100 factories). Currently, due to government legislation, Norinco cannot legally sell weapons in the U.S.

Due to space considerations, information regarding this manufacturer is available online free of charge at www.bluebookofgunvalues.com.

NORTHERN COMPETITION

Current rifle manufacturer located in Racine, WI. Consumer direct sales through FFL.

RIFLES: SEMI-AUTO

Northern Competition manufactures a line of AR-15 style rifles in various calibers and configurations. Current/recent models are described within this section. Previous models included the Predator and Ranch models.

CHEETAH – .22-250, .243 Win., or .308 Win. cal., AR-15 style, GIO, 24 or 26 in. chromemoly barrel, quad rail Picatinny handguard, Magpul PRS stock, NM 2-stage trigger, one 19 shot Magpul mag., Black finish, 12 1/2 lbs. Disc. 2013.

	100%	98%	95%	90%	80%	70%	60%	Last MSR
	$1,800	$1,575	$1,350	$1,225	$995	$810	$625	*$2,019*

COUGAR – .22-250, .243 Win., or .308 Win. cal., AR-15 style, GIO, 24 or 26 in. chromemoly barrel, single stage trigger, A2 style buttstock, pistol grip, Black finish, 12 lbs. Disc. 2013.

	100%	98%	95%	90%	80%	70%	60%	Last MSR
	$1,550	$1,350	$1,175	$1,050	$850	$700	$550	*$1,719*

MSR	100%	98%	95%	90%	80%	70%	60%	*Last MSR*

COMPLETE SERVICE RIFLE (NCSR15) – .22-250, .243 Win., or .308 Win. cal., AR-15 style Classic A2 design, pre or post-ban configuration, GIO, 20 in. heavy barrel, A2 style buttstock, two-stage trigger, charging handle, NM float tube assembly, NM front sight housing, NM double pinned minute sights, Black finish.

MSR $1,495	$1,350	$1,175	$1,025	$925	$750	$625	$475	

Add $200 for Geissele trigger.

NOSLER, INC.

Current rifle, ammunition, and bullet manufacturer located in Bend, OR.

John Nosler founded Nosler, Inc. in 1948, and is responsible for the development of numerous bullet designs optimized for accuracy or dangerous game hunting.

RIFLES: BOLT ACTION

* ***Model 48 Professional*** – various cals., features black Bell & Carlson composite stock, matte black Cerakote finish, no sights, 6 1/2 -7 1/2 lbs. Mfg. 2012-2013.

	$2,295	$2,000	$1,725	$1,550	$1,250	$1,025	$800	*$2,695*

Add $100 for detachable magazine.
Add $200 for factory installed muzzle brake.

RIFLES: SEMI-AUTO

VARMAGEDDON – 5.56 NATO cal., AR-15 style, GIO, 18 in. stainless steel barrel, forged Vltor upper receiver with Picatinny rail and integrated 13 1/2 in. NSR handguard with KeyMod system, extended feed ramp, Magpul PRS stock, MOE grip, Geissele SD-E trigger. New 2013.

MSR $2,695	$2,400	$2,075	$1,775	$1,575	$1,350	$1,100	$925	

Add $900 for package with Leupold Varmageddon scope and CDS turret.

NOVESKE RIFLEWORKS LLC

Current manufacturer located in Grants Pass, OR. Dealer and distributor sales.

CARBINES/RIFLES: SEMI-AUTO

.300 BLK CARBINE LO-PRO/NSR – .300 AAC Blackout cal., GIO, 16 in. stainless steel barrel, low-profile gas block pinned to barrel, forged Gen. II lower, forged Vltor MUR upper with anti-rotation interfaced with handguard, Gun Fighter charging handle, 11 in. free float handguard with 1913 rails or 13 1/2 in. NSR free floating handguard with 1913 top rail, Blackout 51T flash suppressor, Mil-Spec receiver extension, black finish, extended feed ramp, H2 buffer, Vltor iMod carbine stock, flip up front and rear sights, approx. 6 lbs. Disc. 2013.

	$1,995	$1,750	$1,495	$1,350	$1,095	$900	$700	*$2,335*

Add $160 for Lo-Pro Model.

BASIC LIGHT RECCE CARBINE – 5.56 NATO cal., GIO, 16 in. cold hammer forged chrome lined barrel, forged lower, flat-top upper, Gun Fighter charging handle, mid-length A2 handguards, Blackout flash suppressor, Mil-Spec receiver extension, black phosphate finish, approx. 6 lbs.

MSR $1,730	$1,475	$1,300	$1,100	$1,000	$825	$675	$575	

GEN III RIFLE – 5.56 NATO or .300 Blackout cal., 16 or 18 in. barrel, 30 shot mag., carbine or mid-length gas system, Gen. III upper receiver with extended feed ramps and anti-rotation interface with handguard, Raptor ambidextrous charging handle, Gen. III lower receiver with 6-pos. receiver extension, ALG Defense ACT trigger, Noveske 13 1/2 in. quad rail with 1913 rails, NSR 13 1/2 in. free floating handguard with top Picatinny rail, Noveske Signature back up iron sights by Troy Ind., Magpul STR carbine stock, MIAD pistol grip, Black Cerakote finish. New mid-2014.

MSR $2,575	$2,195	$1,925	$1,650	$1,500	$1,200	$1,000	$850	

Add $20 for 18 in. barrel.

GEN III SWITCHBLOCK RIFLE – 5.56 NATO cal., 16 in. barrel, mid-length gas system, Gen. III upper receiver with extended feed ramps, Raptor ambidextrous charging handle, Gen. III lower receiver with 6-pos. receiver extension, staked Noveske QD end plate, ALG Defense ACT trigger, 11 1/2 in. Noveske split rail w/1913 rails, Noveske Signature back up iron sights by Troy Ind., 30 shot mag., Magpul STR Carbine stock, MIAD pistol grip, Black Cerakote finish. New mid-2014.

MSR $2,930	$2,495	$2,185	$1,875	$1,700	$1,375	$1,125	$975	

INFANTRY RIFLE – 5.56 NATO or .300 Blackout cal., 16 in. barrel, 30 shot mag., low pro gas block, carbine or mid-length gas system, Gen. I flat-top upper receiver with extended feed ramps, MOD 4 Gun Fighter charging handle, Gen. I forged lower receiver with 6-pos. receiver extension, ALG Defense ACT trigger, Noveske Signature back-up iron sights by Troy Ind., Noveske 11 in. quad rail w/1913 rails, Magpul CTR stock, Magpul MOE grip.

MSR $2,365	$2,025	$1,775	$1,525	$1,375	$1,125	$925	$775	

MSR	100%	98%	95%	90%	80%	70%	60%	*Last MSR*

LIGHT RECCE CARBINE – 5.56 NATO or .300 AAC Blackout cal., GIO, 16 in. cold hammer forged chrome lined barrel, low-profile gas block or Switchblock pinned to barrel, forged Gen. II lower, forged Vltor upper with anti-rotation interfaced with handguard, Gun Fighter charging handle, NSR 13 1/2 in. free float handguard with 1913 top rail or 11 1/2 in. free float handguard with 1913 rails (Switchblock only), Blackout 51T flash suppressor, ALG combat trigger, Mil-Spec receiver extension, black phosphate finish, approx. 6 lbs. Disc. 2013.

| | $1,895 | $1,650 | $1,425 | $1,295 | $1,050 | $850 | $675 | *$2,215* |

Add $320 for Switchblock.
Subtract $35 for 5.56 NATO cal.

LIGHT RECCE LO-PRO CARBINE – 5.56 NATO cal., GIO, 16 in. cold hammer forged chrome lined barrel, low-profile gas block pinned to barrel, forged Gen. II lower, forged Vltor MUR upper with anti-rotation interfaced with handguard, Gun Fighter charging handle, 11 in. free float handguard with 1913 top rail, Blackout flash suppressor, Mil-Spec receiver extension, black phosphate finish, extended feed ramp, approx. 6 lbs. Disc. 2013.

| | $1,995 | $1,750 | $1,495 | $1,350 | $1,095 | $900 | $700 | *$2,340* |

RECON CARBINE – 5.56 NATO cal., GIO, 16 in. stainless steel barrel, low-profile gas block, forged Gen. II lower, forged Vltor upper receiver featuring an anti-rotation interface with handguard, Gun Fighter charging handle, 11 in. free float handguard with 1913 rails or NSR 13 1/2 in. free float handguard with 1913 top rail, Blackout flash suppressor, ALG combat trigger, Mil-Spec receiver extension, black finish, Vltor iMod carbine stock, H buffer, flip up front and rear sights, extended feed ramps, optional Switchblock pinned to barrel, approx. 6 lbs. Disc. 2013.

| | $2,125 | $1,875 | $1,595 | $1,450 | $1,175 | $950 | $750 | *$2,485* |

Add $195 for Switchblock.
Subtract $160 for NSR handguard.

ROGUE HUNTER – 5.56 NATO cal., GIO, 16 or 18 in. lightweight stainless steel barrel, low-profile gas block pinned to barrel, forged lower, M4 upper, Gun Fighter charging handle, 13 1/2 in. free float handguard with 1913 top rail, A2 flash suppressor, ALG combat trigger, Mil-Spec receiver extension, black finish, Vltor iMod carbine stock, H buffer, Tango Down pistol grip, 30 shot mag., extended feed ramp, approx. 6 lbs., 4 oz.

| MSR $1,825 | $1,550 | $1,350 | $1,175 | $1,050 | $850 | $700 | $600 | |

Add $20 for 18 in. barrel.

SHOOTING TEAM RIFLE – 5.56 NATO cal., 18 in. stainless steel barrel, 30 shot mag., Gen. III upper receiver with extended feed ramps and anti-rotation interface with handguard, Gen. III lower receiver, Geissele DMR trigger, STS ambidextrous selector, Raptor ambidextrous charging handle, 16.7 in. free floating handguard with Picatinny top rail, Magpul PRS stock, MIAD pistol grip, Cerakote (Tungsten) finish. New mid-2014.

| MSR $3,010 | $2,575 | $2,250 | $1,925 | $1,750 | $1,425 | $1,175 | $1,000 | |

SPR – 5.56 NATO cal., GIO, 18 in. stainless steel barrel, low-profile gas block pinned to barrel, forged Gen II lower, forged Vltor MUR upper featuring an anti-rotation interface with handguard, Gun Fighter charging handle, NSR 13 1/2 in. free float handguard with 1913 top rail, Blackout flash suppressor, ALG combat trigger, Mil-Spec receiver extension, black finish, Vltor iMod carbine stock, H buffer, flip up front and rear sights, extended feed ramp, approx. 6 lbs. Disc. 2013.

| | $1,995 | $1,750 | $1,495 | $1,350 | $1,095 | $900 | $700 | *$2,350* |

NOWLIN MFG., INC.

Previous custom handgun manufacturer. Nowlin Guns continues to manufacture a wide variety of pistol components. The company was established in 1982, and is currently located in Claremore, OK.

PISTOLS: SEMI-AUTO

Nowlin discontinued all its pistols in late 2010. The following is a listing of its products with last MSRs. Nowlin Mfg., Inc. manufactured a complete line of high quality M1911 A1 styled competition and defense pistols, available in 9mm Para., 9x23mm, .38 Super, .40 S&W, or .45 ACP cal. Various frame types are available, including a variety of Nowlin choices. Recent models (available in blue or nickel finish) included the NRA Bianchi Cup (approx. 1997 retail was $2,750 - disc.), 007 Compact ($1,395 - disc.), Compact X2 ($1,436 - disc.), Match Classic ($1,695 - disc. 2010), Crusader ($1,999 - disc. 2010), Avenger w/STI frame ($2,279 - disc. 2010), Challenger ($2,049 - disc. 2010), World Cup PPC ($2,219 - disc. 2010), STI High Cap. Frame ($1,595 - disc. 1999), Mickey Fowler Signature Series ($2,187 - disc. 2010), Compact Carry ($1,695 - disc. 1999), Compact 4 1/4 in. ($1,750, .45 ACP, disc. 2002), Gladiator ($1,447 in .45 ACP cal., disc. 2002), Match Master ($2,795 - disc. 2010), Bianchi Cup Master Grade ($5,019, .38 Super cal., disc. 2010) and the Custom Shop Excaliber Series ($3,029 - disc. 2010).

O SECTION

OBERLAND ARMS

Current manufacturer located in Huglfing, Germany. Previously located in Habach, Germany. No current U.S. importation.

Oberland Arms manufactures a wide variety of high quality rifles, including an OA-15 series based on the AR-15 style. Oberland Arms also used to manufacture pistols. Many rifle options and configurations are available. Please contact the company directly for more information, including pricing, options, and U.S. availability (see Trademark Index).

OHIO ORDNANCE WORKS, INC.

Current rifle and related components manufacturer established in 1981, and located in Chardon, OH.

Ohio Ordnance Works also manufactures machine guns, components, and accessories.

MSR	100%	98%	95%	90%	80%	70%	60%	Last MSR

RIFLES: SEMI-AUTO

MODEL BAR 1918A3 – .30-06 cal., patterned after the original Browning BAR (M1918A2) used during WWI, all steel construction utilizing original parts except for lower receiver, 24 in. barrel, original folding type rear sight, includes two 20 shot mags., matte metal and wood finish, Bakelite or American walnut stock and forearm, carrying handle, web sling, bipod, flash hider, bolt open hold device, 20 lbs.

MSR $4,300	$3,650	$3,195	$2,750	$2,475	$2,000	$1,650	$1,275	

MODEL BAR A1918 SLR – .30-06 cal., similar to Model BAR 1918A3, except does not have A3 carry handle, mfg. by Ohio Ordnance Works, Inc. 2005-2007.

	$3,100	$2,800	$2,450	$2,100	$1,800	$1,575	$1,300	*$3,350*

Add $200 for walnut stock.

MODEL 1928 BROWNING – .30-06, 7.65mm, .308 Win., or 8mm (disc.) cal., semi-auto action patterned after the 1928 Browning watercooled machine gun, blue (disc.) or parkerized finish, includes tripod, water hose, ammo can, 3 belts, and belt loader. Limited production late 2001-2007.

	$3,750	$3,400	$3,000	$2,650	$2,300	$2,100	$1,900	*$4,000*

Add $200 for .308 Win. or 8mm (disc.) cal.
Add approx. $2,000 for blue finish (limited mfg.).

MODEL M-240 SLR – 7.62 NATO cal., belt fed, gas operated, air cooled, fires from closed bolt, sling, cleaning kit, ruptured case extractor, gas regulator cleaning tool, disassembly tools, 2500 M-13 links, custom fit hard case, 24.2 lbs. New 2007.

Please contact the company directly for pricing and availability on this model.

MODEL VZ2000/VZ2000 SBR – 7.62x39mm cal., Czech VZ 58 copy, new milled receiver, original barrels, heat cured paint finish (matches original Czech finish), choice of bakelite furniture with folding stock or pistol grip with quad Picatinny rail and vertical grip (VZ2000 Tactical), includes four 30 shot mags., pouch, sling, cleaning kit, original bayonet, 6 lbs.

MSR $1,026	$875	$765	$650	$595	$475	$395	$300	

MODEL 1917A1 WATERCOOLED – .30-06 or .308 Win. cal., semi-auto copy of the military 1917A1 machine gun, various packages are available. Mfg. 2011-2012.

	$6,500	$5,750	$5,000	$4,650	$4,250	$3,850	$3,450	*$5,000*

Add $1,005 for deluxe package including 1917A1 tripod.
Add $1,500 for "The Works" package including 1917A1 tripod, water hose and can, wooden box, and linker.

MODEL 1919A4 SEMI-AUTO BELTFED – .308 Win. cal., copy of military 1919A4 machine gun, various packages available. Mfg. 2011-2012.

	$3,250	$2,650	$2,200	$1,800	$1,650	$1,500	$1,375	*$2,000*

Add $550 for Deluxe Package including M2 tripod and pintle.
Add $945 for "The Whole Enchilada" package including M2 tripod with pintle, trunnion shield, 1919A4 linker, and .30-06 barrel.

OLYMPIC ARMS, INC.

Current manufacturer established during 1976, and located in Olympia, WA. Sales through Olympic dealers only.

Olympic Arms, Inc. was founded by Robert C. Schuetz, and began as Schuetzen Gun Works (SGW) in 1956, manufacturing barrels in Colorado Springs, Colorado. Prior to that Mr. Schuetz had been partnered in business with well known gunsmith P.O. Ackley. In 1975 the company moved to Olympia, Washington, and while its business in rifle barrels and barrel blanks thrived, it also began manufacturing complete custom bolt action rirfles. In 1982, Schuetzen Gun Works began to manufacture AR-15/M16 rifles and components under the trade name of Olympic Arms, Inc., while custom bolt action rifles

MSR	100%	98%	95%	90%	80%	70%	60%	Last MSR

continued to be produced under the SGW brand. In late 1987, Olympic Arms, Inc. acquired Safari Arms of Phoenix, AZ. As of Jan. 2004, the Safari Arms product name was discontinued, and all 1911 style products are now being manufactured in the Olympic Arms facility in Olympia, WA. Schuetzen Pistol Works is the in-house custom shop of Olympic Arms. Olympic Arms is one of the few AR-15 manufacturers to make every major component part in-house.

PISTOLS: SEMI-AUTO

Please refer to the Safari Arms section for previously manufactured pistols made under the Safari Arms trademark.

BIG DEUCE – .45 ACP cal., 6 in. longslide version of the MatchMaster, SA, matte black slide with satin stainless steel frame, smooth walnut (disc.) or cocobolo grips with double diamond checkering, double slide serrations, 44 oz. Mfg. 1995-2004, reintroduced 2006.

MSR $1,164	$1,025	$900	$725	$600	$500	$400	$350	

COHORT – .45 ACP cal., features Enforcer slide and MatchMaster frame, 4 in. stainless steel barrel, SA, beavertail grip safety, extended thumb safety and slide release, commander style hammer, smooth walnut grips with laser etched Black Widow logo (disc.) or checkered walnut grips, finger grooved front grip strap, fully adj. rear sight, 37 oz. New 1995.

MSR $974	$850	$750	$650	$550	$450	$400	$350	

ENFORCER – .45 ACP cal., 3.8 (disc.) or 4 in. bushingless stainless bull barrel, SA, 6 shot mag., shortened grip, available with max hard finish aluminum frame, parkerized, electroless nickel, or lightweight (disc.) anodized finishes, Triplex counterwound self-contained spring recoil system, flat or arched mainspring housing, adj. sights, ambidextrous safety, neoprene or checkered walnut grips, finger grooved front grip strap, 27 (lightweight model) or 35 oz.

MSR $1,034	$925	$825	$675	$575	$475	$400	$350	

This model was originally called the Black Widow. After Safari Arms became Schuetzen Pistol Works, this model was changed extensively to include stainless construction, beavertail grip safety, and combat style hammer.

MATCHMASTER – .45 ACP cal., similar to the Enforcer, except has 5 or 6 in. barrel and 7 shot mag. rounded (R/S) or squared off trigger guard, finger grooved front grip strap, single or double (6 in. barrel) slide serrations, approx. 40 oz.

MSR $1,034	$850	$725	$600	$500	$425	$395	$375	

Add $70 for 6 in. barrel.

BLAK-TAC MATCHMASTER – .45 ACP cal., 5 in. National Match barrel, SA, 7 shot mag., widened and lowered ejection port, Blak-Tac treated frame and slide, low profile combat sights, adj. trigger, approx. 40 oz. Mfg. 2003-2008.

	$875	$775	$675	$575	$500	$450	$400	*$995*

K22 – .22 LR cal., GIO, SA, 1/2 in. button rifled stainless steel barrel, forged flat-top with Picatinny rails, gas block, free floating aluminum tube handguard with knurling, non-chromed bore, A2 flash suppressor, 4.3 lbs. New 2011.

MSR $896	$775	$675	$575	$475	$425	$395	$375	

K23P – 5.56 NATO cal., GIO, SA, 6 1/2 in. chromemoly steel barrel, A2 upper w/aluminum handguard, A2 flash suppressor, recoil buffer in back of frame, 5.12 lbs. New 2007.

MSR $975	$895	$825	$725	$625	$525	$450	$400	

Add $95 for A3 upper receiver (disc. 2011) or $144 for A3 upper w/Picatinny rail and Firsh handguard (disc. 2011).

OA-93 PISTOL – .223 Rem. (older mfg.), 5.56 NATO (current mfg.), or 7.62x39mm (very limited mfg., disc.) cal., GIO without buffer tube stock, or charging handle, 6 (most common, disc.), 6 1/2 (new 2005), 9 (disc.), or 14 (disc.) in. free-floated match stainless steel threaded barrel with flash suppressor, upper receiver utilizes integral scope mount base, 30 shot mag., 4 lbs. 3 oz., approx. 500 mfg. 1993-94 before Crime Bill discontinued production, reintroduced late 2004.

MSR $1,268	$1,150	$1,050	$900	$825	$750	$700	$650	

Last MSR in 1994 was $2,700.

Add 100% for 7.62x39mm cal.

OA-96 AR PISTOL – .223 Rem. cal., GIO, 6 in. barrel only, similar to OA-93 Pistol, except has pinned (fixed) 30 shot mag. and rear takedown button for rapid reloading, 5 lbs. Mfg. 1996-2000.

	$860	$775	$650	$575	$495	$450	$395	*$860*

OA-98 PISTOL – .223 Rem. cal., GIO, skeletonized, lightweight version of the OA-93/OA-96, 6 1/2 in. non-threaded barrel, 10 shot fixed (disc.) or detachable (new 2006) mag., denoted by perforated appearance, 3 lbs. Mfg. 1998-2003, reintroduced 2005-2007.

	$995	$875	$800	$750	$700	$650	$600	*$1,080*

RIFLES: BOLT ACTION

In 1993, Olympic Arms purchased the rights, jigs, fixtures, and machining templates for the Bauska Big Bore Magnum Mauser action. Please contact Olympic Arms (see Trademark Index) for more information regarding Bauska actions both with or without fluted barrels.

MSR	100%	98%	95%	90%	80%	70%	60%	Last MSR

ULTRA CSR TACTICAL RIFLE – .308 Win. cal., Sako action, 26 in. broach cut heavy barrel, Bell & Carlson black or synthetic stock with aluminum bedding, Harris bipod, carrying case. Mfg. 1996-2000.

	$1,450	$1,250	$1,100	$1,000	$800	$700	$600	$1,140

COUNTER SNIPER RIFLE – .308 Win. cal., bolt action utilizing M-14 mags., 26 in. heavy barrel, camo-fiberglass stock, 10 1/2 lbs. Disc. 1987.

	$1,300	$1,100	$975	$895	$750	$650	$600	$1,225

SURVIVOR I CONVERSION UNIT – .223 Rem. or .45 ACP cal., converts M1911 variations into carbine, bolt action, collapsible stock, 16 1/4 in. barrel, 5 lbs.

	$275	$225	$195	$150	$125	$110	$95	

This kit was also available for S&W and Browning Hi-Power models.

RIFLES: SEMI-AUTO

Olympic Arms is currently shipping high capacity mags. with its rifles/carbines to those states where legal.

The PCR (Politically Correct Rifle) variations listed refer to those guns manufactured after the Crime Bill was implemented in September 1994 through 2004. PCR rifles have smooth barrels (no flash suppressor), a 10 shot mag., and fixed stocks. Named models refer to the original, pre-ban model nomenclature.

Olympic Arms has also made some models exclusively for distributors. They include the K30R-16-SST (Sports South, LLC), K16-SST (Sports South, LLC), and the PP FT M4 SS (Lew Horton). Please contact these distributors for more information, availability, and pricing.

Add $30 for Coyote Brown, Desert Tan, or Pink furniture on models with carbine length handguards, pistol grip, and collapsible buttstock (new 2010).

Add $142 for A3 forged flat-top upper receiver with Picatinny rails and detachable carry handle.

COMPETITOR RIFLE – .22 LR cal., GIO, Ruger 10/22 action with 20 in. barrel featuring button cut rifling, Bell & Carlson thumbhole fiberglass stock, black finish and matte stainless fluted barrel, includes bipod, 6.9 lbs. Mfg. 1996-99.

	$575	$500	$450	$400	$360	$330	$300	$575

ULTRAMATCH/PCR-1 – .223 Rem. cal., GIo, AR-15 action with modifications, 20 or 24 in. match stainless steel barrel, Picatinny flat-top upper receiver, Williams set trigger optional, scope mounts, 10 lbs. 3 oz. New 1985.

* **Ultramatch PCR-1** – disc. 2004.

	$950	$850	$750	$675	$625	$575	$525	$1,074

* **Ultramatch PCR-1P** – .223 Rem. cal., GIO, premium grade ultramatch rifle with many shooting enhancements, including Maxhard treated upper and lower receiver, 20 or 24 in. broach cut Ultramatch bull barrel, 1x10 in. or 1x8 in. rate of twist. Mfg. 2001-2004.

	$1,175	$1,050	$925	$825	$725	$625	$550	$1,299

* **Ultramatch UM-1** – .223 Rem. cal., GIO, 20 in. stainless Ultramatch barrel with non-chromed bore, gas block, free floating aluminum tube with knurling, approx. 8 1/2 lbs. Disc. 1994, reintroduced late 2004-2012.

	$1,250	$1,075	$950	$825	$750	$675	$600	

Last MSR in 1994 was $1,515, last MSR in 2012 was $1,329

* **Ultramatch UM-1P** – .223 Rem. cal., similar to UM-1 Ultramatch, except has 20 (disc. 2006) or 24 in. Ultramatch bull stainless barrel, premium grade ultramatch rifle with many shooting enhancements, 9 1/2 lbs. New 2005.

MSR $1,624	$1,495	$1,325	$1,100	$975	$825	$775	$700	

INTERCONTINENTAL – .223 Rem. cal., GIO, features synthetic wood-grained thumbhole buttstock and aluminum handguard, 20 in. Ultramatch barrel (free floating). Mfg. 1992-1993.

	$1,650	$1,350	$1,050	$875	$750	$600	$550	$1,371

INTERNATIONAL MATCH – .223 Rem. cal., similar to Ultramatch, except has custom aperture sights. Mfg. 1991-93.

	$1,475	$1,150	$950	$800	$675	$575	$525	$1,240

SERVICE MATCH/PCR SERVICE MATCH – .223 Rem. cal., AR-15 action with modifications, GIO, 20 in. SS Ultramatch barrel, carrying handle, standard trigger, choice of A1 or A2 flash suppressor (Service Match only), 8 3/4 lbs.

* **Service Match SM-1** – GIO, 9.7 lbs., disc. 1994, reintroduced late 2004-2012.

	$1,095	$995	$875	$775	$700	$625	$550	

Last MSR in 1994 was $1,200, last MSR in 2012 was $1,273

* **Service Match SM-1P Premium Grade** – .223 Rem. cal., GIO, Maxhard upper and lower receiver, 20 in. broach cut Ultramatch super heavy threaded barrel (1 turn in 8 in. is standard), flash suppressor, 2-stage CMP trigger, Blak-Tak Armour bolt carrier assembly, Bob Jones NM interchangeable rear sight system, AC4 pneumatic recoil buffer, Turner Saddlery competition sling, GI style pistol grip. Mfg. 2005-2012.

	$1,575	$1,350	$1,200	$1,025	$900	$800	$725	$1,728

MSR	100%	98%	95%	90%	80%	70%	60%	Last MSR

* Service Match PCR – disc. late 2004.

	100%	98%	95%	90%	80%	70%	60%	Last MSR
	$825	$750	$675	$625	$550	$500	$450	$1,062

* Service Match PCR-SMP Premium Grade – .223 Rem. cal., Maxhard upper and lower receiver, 20 in. broach cut Ultramatch super heavy barrel (1 turn in 8 in. is standard), 2-stage CMP trigger, Blak-Tak Armour bolt carrier assembly, Bob Jones NM interchangeable rear sight system, AC4 pneumatic recoil buffer, Turner Saddlery competition sling, GI style pistol grip. Mfg. 2004 only.

	100%	98%	95%	90%	80%	70%	60%	Last MSR
	$1,100	$950	$800	$700	$600	$550	$475	$1,613

MULTIMATCH ML-1/PCR-2 – .223 Rem. cal., tactical short range rifle, 16 in. Ultramatch barrel with A2 upper receiver, aluminum collapsible (Multimatch ML-1) or fixed (PCR-2) stock, carrying handle, A2 flash suppressor (Multimatch ML-1 only). New 1991.

* Multimatch ML-1 – 7.35 lbs. Disc. 2012.

	100%	98%	95%	90%	80%	70%	60%	
	$1,050	$950	$850	$750	$675	$600	$525	

Last MSR in 1994 was $1,200, last MSR in 2012 was $1,188

* Multimatch PCR-2 – disc. late 2004.

	100%	98%	95%	90%	80%	70%	60%	Last MSR
	$750	$675	$600	$525	$450	$425	$400	$958

MULTIMATCH ML-2/PCR-3 – .223 Rem. cal., GIO, features Picatinny flat-top upper receiver with stainless steel 16 in. Ultramatch bull (new 2005) barrel, carrying handle (disc.), approx. 7 1/2 lbs. New 1991.

* Multimatch ML-2 – .223 Rem. cal., 16 in. stainless steel bull barrel, crowned muzzle, forged flat-top with Picatinny rails, tubular aluminum handguard, A2 stock, 7 1/2 lbs. Disc. 1994, reintroduced late 2004.

MSR $1,253

	100%	98%	95%	90%	80%	70%	60%	
	$1,095	$975	$850	$750	$675	$600	$525	

Last MSR in 1994 was $1,200

* Multimatch PCR-3 – disc. late 2004.

	100%	98%	95%	90%	80%	70%	60%	Last MSR
	$850	$750	$650	$550	$500	$450	$350	$958

AR-15 MATCH/PCR-4 – .223 Rem. cal., GIO, patterned after the AR-15 with 20 in. barrel and solid synthetic stock, 8 lbs. 5 oz. Mfg. 1975-2004.

* PCR-4

	100%	98%	95%	90%	80%	70%	60%	Last MSR
	$850	$750	$650	$575	$525	$475	$425	$803

* AR-15 Match

	100%	98%	95%	90%	80%	70%	60%	Last MSR
	$1,095	$995	$875	$775	$650	$575	$495	$1,075

CAR-15/PCR-5 – GIO, modified AR-15 with choice of 11 1/2 (disc. 1993) or 16 in. barrel, stow-away pistol grip and collapsible stock (CAR-15 only), 7 lbs. Mfg. 1975-1998, PCR-5 reintroduced 2000-2004.

* PCR-5 – .223 Rem., 9mm Para. (new 1996), .40 S&W (new 1996), or .45 ACP (new 1996) cal., GIO. Disc. 1998, reintroduced 2000-2004.

	100%	98%	95%	90%	80%	70%	60%	Last MSR
	$950	$850	$800	$725	$650	$600	$550	$755

Add $45 for 9mm Para., .40 S&W, or .45 ACP cal.

* CAR-15 – .223 Rem., 9mm Para., .40 S&W, .45 ACP, or 7.62x39mm cal.

	100%	98%	95%	90%	80%	70%	60%	Last MSR
	$1,050	$950	$850	$775	$650	$575	$495	$1,030

Add $170 for pistol cals.

PCR-6 – 7.62x39mm cal., 16 in. barrel, post-ban only, GIO, A-2 stowaway stock, carrying handle, 7 lbs. Mfg. 1995-2002.

	100%	98%	95%	90%	80%	70%	60%	Last MSR
	$895	$795	$725	$650	$500	$475	$425	$870

PCR-7 ELIMINATOR – .223 Rem. cal., similar to PCR-4, except has 16 in. barrel, 7 lbs. 10 oz. Mfg. 1999-2004.

	100%	98%	95%	90%	80%	70%	60%	Last MSR
	$850	$750	$675	$625	$585	$540	$510	$844

PCR-8 – .223 Rem. cal., same configuration as the PCR-1, except has standard 20 in. stainless steel heavy bull barrel with button rifling. Mfg. 2001-2004.

	100%	98%	95%	90%	80%	70%	60%	Last MSR
	$825	$725	$675	$640	$600	$550	$525	$834

* PCR-8 Mag. – .223 WSSM or .243 WSSM cal., otherwise similar to PCR-8. Mfg. 2004.

	100%	98%	95%	90%	80%	70%	60%	Last MSR
	$925	$825	$750	$675	$600	$550	$500	$1,074

This model was also scheduled to be available in .308 Olympic Mag. and 7mm Olympic Mag. cals.

PCR-9/10/40/45 – 9mm Para., 10mm, .40 S&W, or .45 ACP cal., similar to PCR-5 Carbine except for pistol cal., GIO, A2 upper standard, 16 in. barrel, A2 buttstock, mil spec lower receiver. Mfg. 2001-2004.

	100%	98%	95%	90%	80%	70%	60%	Last MSR
	$875	$775	$675	$600	$550	$495	$450	$835

MSR	100%	98%	95%	90%	80%	70%	60%	Last MSR

PCR-16 – .223 Rem. cal., GIO, 16 in. match grade bull barrel, two-piece aluminum free-floating handguard, Picatinny receiver rail, 7 1/2 lbs. Mfg. 2003-2004.

	$825	$750	$650	$600	$565	$535	$500	*$714*

PCR-30 – .30 Carbine cal., GIO, forged aluminum receiver with matte black anodizing, parkerized steel parts, A-2 adj. rear sight, accepts standard GI M1 .30 Carbine mags., 16 in. barrel with 1 turn in 12 in. twist, 7.15 lbs. Mfg. 2004.

	$875	$825	$750	$700	$650	$600	$575	*$899*

PLINKER – .223 Rem. cal., similar to PCR-5, except has 16 in. button rifled barrel standard, A1 sights, cast upper/lower receiver, 100% standard mil spec parts, 7 lbs. Mfg. 2001-2004.

	$650	$595	$550	$500	$495	$450	$425	*$598*

PLINKER PLUS – 5.56 NATO cal., similar to Plinker, except has 16 (disc. 2009, reintroduced 2011) in. button rifled threaded chromemoly steel barrel with A2 flash suppressor, standard A1 upper, cast upper/lower receiver, 100% standard Mil-spec parts, A2 stock with trapdoor, 7-8.4 lbs. New 2005.

MSR $727	$625	$550	$450	$395	$350	$300	$275	

* **Plinker Plus Flat Top** – 5.56 NATO cal., similar to Plinker Plus, except has flat-top with Picatinny rails, M4 six point collapsible stock. New 2012.

MSR $727	$625	$550	$450	$395	$350	$300	$275	

* **Plinker Plus 20** – 5.56 NATO cal., similar to Plinker Plus, except has 20 in. button rifled threaded chromemoly steel barrel with A2 flash suppressor, choice of A2 configuration or flat-top upper receiver with Picatinny rails, cast upper/lower receiver, 100% standard Mil-spec parts, A2 stock, 7-8.4 lbs. New 2012.

MSR $908	$900	$825	$725	$650	$600	$575	$550	

CAR-97 – .223 Rem., 9mm Para., 10mm, .40 S&W, or .45 ACP cal., similar to PCR-5, except has 16 in. button rifled barrel, A2 sights, fixed CAR stock, post-ban muzzle brake, approx. 7 lbs. Mfg. 1997-2004.

	$795	$750	$675	$600	$550	$500	$450	*$780*

Add approx. $65 for 9mm Para., .40 S&W, or .45 ACP cal.

* **CAR-97 M4** – .223 Rem. cal., M4 configuration with contoured barrel, GIO, fixed carbine tube stock, factory installed muzzle brake, oversized shortened handguard. Mfg. 2003-2004.

	$800	$750	$675	$600	$550	$500	$450	*$839*

Add $95 for detachable carrying handle (new 2004).

FAR-15 – .223 Rem. cal., GIO, featherweight model with A1 contour lightweight button rifled 16 in. barrel, fixed collapsible stock, 9.92 lbs. Mfg. 2001-2004.

	$775	$700	$650	$600	$550	$500	$450	*$822*

GI-16 – 5.56 NATO cal., GIO, forged aluminum receiver with black matte finish, A1 type upper receiver, parkerized steel parts, A1 adj. rear sights, 16 in. button rifled match grade barrel, M4 collapsible stock, 6.6 lbs. Mfg. 2004, reintroduced 2006-2012.

	$800	$750	$700	$625	$575	$525	$475	*$857*

GI-20 – .223 Rem. cal., similar to GI-16, except has 20 in. heavy barrel and A-2 lower receiver, 8.4 lbs. Mfg. 2004.

	$725	$650	$595	$550	$495	$450	$425	*$749*

OA-93 CARBINE – .223 Rem. cal., GIO, 16 in. threaded barrel, design based on OA-93 pistol, aluminum side folding stock, flat-top receiver, round aluminum handguard, Vortex flash suppressor, 7 1/2 lbs. Mfg. 1995 - civilian sales disc. 1998, reintroduced 2004-2007.

	$1,250	$1,050	$925	$825	$750	$675	$625	

Last MSR in 1998 was $1,550.

Last MSR in 2007 was $1,074

* **OA-93PT Carbine** – .223 Rem. cal., GIO, aluminum forged receiver, black matte hard anodized finish, no sights, integral flat-top upper receiver rail system, match grade 16 in. chromemoly steel barrel with removable muzzle brake, push button removable stock, vertical pistol grip, 7.6 lbs. Mfg. 2004 only, reintroduced 2006-2007.

	$985	$875	$825	$750	$675	$600	$550	*$1,074*

LTF/LT-MIL4 LIGHTWEIGHT TACTICAL RIFLE – 5.56 NATO cal., GIO, available in LTF (fluted), LT-M4 (new 2011), or LT-MIL4 (disc. 2009) configuration, black matte anodized receiver, Firsh type forearms with Picatinny rails, parkerized steel parts, adj. flip-up sight system, 16 in. non-chromed fluted, M4 stainless steel (new 2011), or MIL4 threaded barrel with flash suppressor, tube style Ace FX buttstock, 6.4 lbs. New 2005.

MSR $1,240	$1,125	$975	$850	$775	$700	$650	$600	

Subtract $97 for M4 style stainless steel barrel (new 2011).

Subtract approx. 10% if w/o fluted barrel.

MSR	100%	98%	95%	90%	80%	70%	60%	Last MSR

LTF PREDATOR – .204 Ruger (new 2012), 5.56 NATO, or 6.8 SPC (new 2012) cal., similar to LTF, except has ERGO grip and available in black or 100% camo coverage. New 2011.

| MSR $1,240 | $1,125 | $975 | $850 | $775 | $700 | $650 | $600 | |

K3B CARBINE – 5.56 NATO cal., GIO, 16 in. match grade chromemoly steel threaded barrel with flash suppressor, adj. A2 rear sight, A2 (disc.) or M4 collapsible (new 2012) buttstock, adj. front post sight, A3 flat-top receiver became standard 2011, 6 3/4 lbs.

| MSR $1,006 | $925 | $825 | $700 | $600 | $550 | $500 | $450 | |

* **K3B-FAR Carbine** – 5.56 NATO cal., similar to K3B Carbine, except has smaller stainless barrel diameter and is lightweight, 6 lbs. New 2005.

| MSR $1,071 | $975 | $850 | $725 | $625 | $550 | $500 | $450 | |

* **K3B-M4 Carbine** – 5.56 NATO cal., similar to K3B Carbine, except has M4 handguard, collapsible stock, and 16 in. M4 stainless barrel, 6.3 lbs. New 2005.

| MSR $1,104 | $1,000 | $875 | $750 | $650 | $575 | $525 | $475 | |

* **K3B-M4-A3-TC Carbine** – 5.56 NATO cal., similar to K3B-M4, except is tactical carbine version with Firsh handguard, flat-top upper receiver with Picatinny rail, and detachable carry handle, 6.7 lbs. New 2005.

| MSR $1,247 | $1,150 | $1,025 | $925 | $825 | $775 | $700 | $650 | |

K4B/K4B68 – 5.56 NATO or 6.8 SPC (new 2010) cal., GIO, 20 in. match grade chromemoly steel button rifled threaded barrel with flash suppressor, adj. A2 rear sight, A2 buttstock, adj. front post sight, A2 upper receiver and handguard, 8 1/2 lbs.

| MSR $1,033 | $950 | $825 | $725 | $625 | $550 | $500 | $450 | |

Add $65 for 6.8 SPC cal.

K4B-A4 – .223 Rem. cal., GIO, features 20 in. barrel with A2 flash suppressor, elevation adj. post front sight, bayonet lug, Firsh rifle length handguard with Picatinny rails, flat-top receiver, 9 lbs. Mfg. 2006-2008.

| | $850 | $760 | $675 | $600 | $550 | $500 | $450 | *$941* |

K7 ELIMINATOR – 5.56 NATO cal., GIO, 16 in. stainless steel threaded barrel with flash suppressor, adj. A2 rear sight, A2 buttstock, adj. front post sight, 6.8 lbs. New 2005.

| MSR $1,039 | $950 | $825 | $725 | $625 | $550 | $500 | $450 | |

K8 – .204 Ruger (new 2012), 6.8 SPC (new 2012) or 5.56 NATO cal., GIO, 20 in stainless steel button rifled bull barrel, A2 buttstock, Picatinny flat-top upper receiver, gas block, free floating aluminum knurled tube, satin bead blast finish on barrel, 8 1/2 lbs. New 2005.

| MSR $909 | $895 | $800 | $700 | $625 | $550 | $500 | $450 | |

Add $58 for .204 Ruger cal.
Add $125 for 6.8 SPC cal.

This model is marked "Target Match" on mag. well.

* **K8-MAG** – similar to K8, except available in .223 WSSM, .243 WSSM, .25 WSSM, or .300 OSSM (new 2006) cals., and has 24 in. barrel, 5 shot mag., 9.4 lbs. New 2005.

| MSR $1,364 | $1,250 | $1,125 | $995 | $900 | $800 | $700 | $600 | |

K9/K10/K40/K45 – 9mm Para. (K9), 10mm Norma (K10), .40 S&W (K40), or .45 ACP (K45) cal., blow back action, GIO, adj. A2 rear sight, 10 shot converted Uzi (10mm, .40 S&W or .45 ACP cal.) or 32 (9mm Para.) shot converted Sten detachable mag., 16 in. threaded stainless steel barrel with flash suppressor, M4 collapsible buttstock, bayonet lug, 6.7 lbs. New 2005.

| MSR $1,006 | $925 | $825 | $700 | $600 | $550 | $500 | $450 | |

* **K9GL/K40GL** – 9mm Para. or .40 S&W cal., otherwise similar to K9 Series, lower receiver designed to accept Glock magazines, 16 in. barrel with flash suppressor, collapsible stock, does not include magazine. New 2005.

| MSR $1,157 | $1,050 | $975 | $850 | $750 | $650 | $575 | $500 | |

K16 – 5.56 NATO, 6.8 SPC (new 2012), 7.62x39mm (new 2012), or .300 AAC Blackout (new 2012) cal., GIO, 16 in. free floating button rifled barrel, A2 buttstock, flat-top upper receiver with Picatinny rails, 7 1/2 lbs. New 2005.

| MSR $829 | $775 | $725 | $650 | $600 | $550 | $500 | $450 | |

Add $62 for 7.62x39mm, 6.8 SPC, or .300 AAC Blackout cal.

K22 M4 – .22 LR cal., GIO, 16 in. stainless steel barrel, M4 six-point collapsible stock, forged A2 upper, adj. rear sight, adj. post front sight with bayonet lug, A1 flash suppressor, fiberite carbine length handguard with heat shield, 6.6 lbs. Mfg. 2011-2012.

| | $950 | $850 | $725 | $625 | $575 | $525 | $475 | *$1,039* |

MSR	100%	98%	95%	90%	80%	70%	60%	Last MSR

K22 RIMFIRE TARGET MATCH – .22 LR cal., GIO, 16 in. stainless steel bull barrel, A2 fixed trapdoor stock, flat-top with Picatinny rails, no sights, free floating aluminum handguard tube with knurling, muzzle crown, 8.6 lbs. New 2011.

| MSR $831 | $775 | $725 | $650 | $600 | $550 | $500 | $450 | |

K22 SURVIVAL LIGHT – .22 LR cal., GIO, 16 in. stainless steel featherweight barrel, side folding stock, flat-top with Picatinny rails, gas block, free floating slotted aluminum handguard, A1 flash suppressor, 6 lbs. Mfg. 2011-2012.

| | $825 | $795 | $715 | $625 | $575 | $525 | $475 | $883 |

K30 – .30 Carbine cal., similar to K16, except has A2 upper receiver, collapsible stock, and threaded barrel with flash suppressor, 6.6 lbs. Mfg. 2005-2006.

| | $825 | $700 | $625 | $550 | $500 | $450 | $400 | $905 |

Add $95 for A3 upper receiver.

K30R – 7.62x39mm cal., GIO, 16 in. stainless steel barrel, M4 six-point collapsible stock, A2 flash suppressor, pistol grip, matte black anodized receiver, parkerized steel parts, A2 upper with adj. rear sight, 6 3/4 lbs. New 2007.

| MSR $974 | $895 | $795 | $695 | $595 | $550 | $500 | $450 | |

K68 – 6.8 SPC cal., GIO, 16 or 20 (optional) in. stainless steel barrel, M4 six-position collapsible stock, A2 upper with adj. rear sight, matte black anodized receiver, parkerized steel parts, pistol grip, A2 flash suppressor, 6.62 lbs. New 2007.

| MSR $1,104 | $995 | $875 | $750 | $625 | $575 | $525 | $475 | |

K74 – 5.45x39mm cal., GIO, 16 in. button rifled stainless steel barrel with A2 flash suppressor, A2 upper with adj. front sight, M4 type six-position collapsible stock, 6 3/4 lbs. New 2009.

| MSR $1,058 | $975 | $875 | $775 | $675 | $600 | $550 | $495 | |

UMAR (ULTIMATE MAGNUM AR) – .22-250 Rem., .223 WSSM, .243 WSSM, .25 WSSM, or .300 WSSM cal., GIO, 24 in. heavy match grade stainless steel bull barrel, black matte anodized aluminum forged receiver, parkerized steel parts, flat-top/gas block with Picatinny rails, sling swivel mount, A2 stock w/trapdoor, Ergo tactical deluxe pistol grip, Predator Firsch free floating handguard, 9.4 lbs. New 2012.

| MSR $1,589 | $1,395 | $1,225 | $1,075 | $925 | $825 | $725 | $625 | |

The upper receiver of this model will not work on standard AR-15 lowers.

GAMESTALKER/GSG2 – .204 Ruger (mfg. 2011 only), 6.8 SPC (GSG2, new 2011), 5.56 NATO (GSG2, new 2011), 7.62x39mm (GSG2, new 2011), .243 WSSM, .25 WSSM, or .300 OSSM cal., GIO, 22 in. stainless steel barrel, flat-top upper receiver with Picatinny rail, free floating aluminum handguard, ACE skeleton stock with ERGO Sure Grip, 100% camo coverage, approx. 7 1/2 lbs. New 2010.

| MSR $1,364 | $1,250 | $1,125 | $995 | $900 | $800 | $700 | $600 | |

Subtract $130 for GSG2 Model (new 2011).

OMEGA WEAPONS SYSTEMS INC.

Previous shotgun manufacturer established circa 1998, and located in Tucson, AZ. Previously distributed by Defense Technology, Inc., located in Lake Forest, CA.

SHOTGUNS: SEMI-AUTO

OMEGA SPS-12 – 12 ga. only, 2 3/4 in. chamber, features gas operation and 5 shot detachable mag., 20 in. barrel, protected ghost ring rear and front sight, synthetic stock (with or w/o pistol grip) and forearm, 9 lbs. Mfg. 1998-2005.

| | $195 | $180 | $165 | $150 | $135 | $125 | $115 | $225 |

OMNI

Previous manufacturer located in Riverside, CA 1992-1998. During 1998, Omni changed its name to E.D.M. Arms. Previously distributed by First Defense International located in CA.

RIFLES: BOLT ACTION

LONG ACTION SINGLE SHOT – .50 BMG cal., competition single shot, chromemoly black finished receiver, 32-34 in. steel or stainless steel barrel with round muzzle brake, benchrest fiberglass stock, designed for FCSA competition shooting, 32 lbs. Mfg. 1996-98.

| | $3,600 | $3,200 | $2,800 | $2,500 | $2,150 | $1,800 | $1,500 | $3,500 |

Add $400 for painted stock (disc. 1996).

SHELL HOLDER SINGLE SHOT – similar to Long Action Single Shot, except has fiberglass field stock with bipod, 28 lbs. Mfg. 1997-98.

| | $2,975 | $2,750 | $2,525 | $2,150 | $1,800 | $1,500 | $1,250 | $2,750 |

MSR	100%	98%	95%	90%	80%	70%	60%	Last MSR

MODEL WINDRUNNER – .50 BMG cal., long action, single shot or 3 shot mag., 1-piece I-beam, chromemoly black finished receiver, 36 in. barrel with round muzzle brake, fiberglass tactical stock, 35 lbs. Mfg. 1997-1998.

| | $6,950 | $6,425 | $5,875 | $5,325 | $4,750 | $4,175 | $3,500 | $7,500 |

    Add $750 for 3 shot repeater.

MODEL WARLOCK – .50 BMG or 20mm cal., single, 3 (20mm), or 5 (.50 BMG) shot fixed mag., fiberglass field stock, massive design chromemoly black finished receiver, muzzle brake, 50 lbs. Mfg. 1997-1998.

| | $10,750 | $8,950 | $7,750 | $6,750 | $5,500 | $4,750 | $3,950 | $12,000 |

E.D.M. ARMS MODEL 97 – available in most cals. up to .308 Win., single shot or repeater (cals. .17 Rem. through .223 Rem. only), wire-cut one-piece receiver, black tactical stock with pillar-bedded chromemoly barrel, black finished receiver, unique trigger with safety, 9 lbs. Mfg. 1997-98.

| | $2,525 | $2,150 | $1,800 | $1,500 | $1,250 | $1,100 | $925 | $2,750 |

E.D.M. ARMS WINDRUNNER WR50 – .50 BMG cal., sniper rifle, 5 shot mag., removable tactical adj. stock, takedown action with removable barrel, wire-cut one-piece receiver, titanium muzzle brake, blackened chromemoly barrel, approx. 29 lbs. Mfg. 1998 only.

| | $11,750 | $10,250 | $9,500 | $8,250 | $7,000 | $5,750 | $4,500 | $12,900 |

ORSIS

Current tactical rifle manufacturer located in Moscow, Russia.

RIFLES: BOLT ACTION

T-5000 – .308 Win. or .338 Lapua cal., fluted barrel with muzzle brake, interchangeable bolt handles, twin upper Picatinny rails, adj. buttstock and cheekpiece, various metal finishes, 14 1/2 lbs.

    Please contact the company directly for U.S. availability and pricing.

P/Q SECTIONS

P.A.W.S., INC.

Previous manufacturer located in Salem, OR. Distributor and dealer sales. Previously distributed by Sile Distributors, Inc. located in New York, NY.

MSR	100%	98%	95%	90%	80%	70%	60%	Last MSR

CARBINES: SEMI-AUTO

ZX6/ZX8 CARBINE – 9mm Para. or .45 ACP cal., semi-auto, 16 in. barrel, 10 or 32* shot mag., folding metal stock, matte black finish, aperture rear sight, partial barrel shroud, 7 1/2 lbs. Mfg. 1989-2004.

| | $715 | $635 | $550 | $475 | $375 | $300 | $250 | |

The ZX6 is chambered for 9mm Para., while the ZX8 is chambered for .45 ACP.

PGW DEFENCE TECHNOLOGIES, INC.

Current manufacturer established in 1992, and located in Winnipeg, Manitoba, Canada. Previous company name was Prairie Gun Works until 2003. Currently imported by Leroy's Big Valley Gun Works, located in Glasgow, MT.

RIFLES: BOLT ACTION

PGW manufactures approx. 50-60 guns annually. They also sell their actions separately for $400-$2,300, depending on caliber and configuration.

LRT-3 (PGW/GIBBS) – .50 BMG cal., single shot action, Big Mac stock. Mfg. 1999-2009.

| | $4,150 | $3,700 | $3,400 | $3,100 | $2,800 | $2,500 | $2,250 | |

PTR INDUSTRIES, INC.

Current rifle manufacturer located in Aynor, SC beginning in 2014. Previously located in Bristol, CT and Farmington, CT. Represented by Vincent A. Pestilli & Associates, located in Brownfield, ME. Previous company names were PTR 91, Inc. and J.L.D. Enterprises.

PISTOLS: SEMI-AUTO

PTR-91 PDW – .308 Win. cal., 8 1/2 in. barrel with flash hider, tactical handguard, black aluminum butt cap, H&K type polymer trigger group, includes one 20 shot mag., approx. 7 1/2 lbs. New 2012.

| MSR $1,150 | | $1,025 | $895 | $775 | $695 | $575 | $500 | $450 | |

PTR-32 PDW – 7.62x39mm cal., otherwise similar to PTR-91 PDW, except has one banana shaped 30 shot mag. Limited mfg. 2012 only.

| | $1,050 | $950 | $800 | $700 | $600 | $500 | $450 | *$1,199* |

This model was also available with a Picatinny rail (Model PTW-32 PDW-R), limited mfg. 2012 only.

RIFLES: SEMI-AUTO

The following rifles utilize an H&K style roller bloacked delayed blowback action. PTR-91 also manufactures the SBR (Short Barrel Rifle) for military/law enforcement.

PTR-91F – .308 Win. cal., CNC machined scope mounts, H&K style hooded front blade and four position diopter rear sight, 18 in. barrel with 1:12 twist, black furniture, pre-ban H&K flash hider, or welded muzzle brake (PTR-91C), H&K Navy type polymer trigger group, 20 shot mag., one piece forged cocking handle, parkerized finish, matte black coated.

| MSR $1,245 | | $1,150 | $1,025 | $900 | $800 | $700 | $600 | $550 | |

Add $200 for tactical handguard, side folding stock, and pre-ban flash hider (PTR-91R, disc. 2008).
Add $200 for tactical handguard, side folding stock, and muzzle brake (PTR-91 RC, disc. 2008).

* **PTR-91T** – .308 Win. cal., similar to Model PTR-91, except has green furniture and original H&K flash hider. Limited mfg. 2005.

| | $895 | $800 | $700 | $600 | $500 | $450 | $400 | *$995* |

PTR-91 AI – .308 Win. cal., match grade rifle with polymer trigger group, match grade barrel, H&K style hooded front blade and four position diopter rear sight, 20 shot mag., steel bipod, steel handguard with bipod recesses, pre-ban H&K flash hider, with (PTR-91 AI C) or w/o (PTR-91 AI F) muzzle brake with match grade barrel. Mfg. 2005-2008.

| | $1,150 | $925 | $825 | $725 | $600 | $500 | $425 | *$1,295* |

PTR-91 G.I. – .308 Win. cal., 18 in. H&K type profile barrel and polymer trigger group, 20 shot mag., OD Green furniture, matte parkerized finish. New 2012.

| MSR $1,049 | | $950 | $850 | $725 | $625 | $500 | $450 | $425 | |

MSR	100%	98%	95%	90%	80%	70%	60%	Last MSR

* *PTR-91 G.I. K* – .308 Win. cal., similar to PTR-91 G.I., except has 16 in barrel. New 2014.

| MSR $1,049 | $950 | $850 | $750 | $675 | $550 | $450 | $350 | |

PTR-91 CLASSIC – .308 Win. cal., 18 in. H&K type profile barrel with flash hider, 20 shot mag., black (Classic Black) or wood (Classic Wood) furniture with slimline handguard, black powdercoated finish, H&K navy type polymer trigger group. Limited mfg. 2012 only.

| | $875 | $750 | $625 | $550 | $500 | $450 | $395 | *$969* |

Add $30 for Classic Wood.

PTR-91 KC – .308 Win. cal., "Kurz" law enforcement carbine with 16 in. barrel, H&K style hooded front blade and four position diopter rear sight, 10 (compliant) or 20 (disc.) shot mag., tropical green (disc.) or black furniture, wide handguard with bipod recesses, pre-ban H&K flash hider or welded muzzle compensator (PTR-91KC). New 2005.

| MSR $1,245 | $1,150 | $1,025 | $900 | $800 | $700 | $600 | $550 | |

Add $100 for PTR-91 KFO with side folding stock and pre-ban flash hider (disc. 2006).

PTR-91 KFM4 – .308 Win. cal., "Kurz" paratrooper carbine, 16 in. barrel, H&K style hooded front blade and four position diopter rear sight, 20 shot mag., tropical green (disc.) or black furniture, wide handguard with bipod recesses and three complete rails, H&K Navy type polymer trigger group, M4 type 6 position telescoping stock and flash hider. New 2005.

| MSR $1,450 | $1,295 | $1,095 | $975 | $850 | $725 | $600 | $500 | |

Add $100 for welded scope mount (Model PTR-91 KFM4R, new 2011).

PTR-91 KF – .308 Win. cal., 16 in. barrel, 20 shot mag., black furniture with tactical handguard, pre-ban H&K flash hider, standard fixed stock, H&K Navy polymer trigger group.

| MSR $1,245 | $1,150 | $1,025 | $900 | $800 | $700 | $600 | $550 | |

PTR-91 KPF GERMAN PARATROOPER – .308 Win. cal., 16 in. barrel, 20 shot mag., black furniture, three rails, pre-ban H&K flash hider, H&K Navy polymer trigger group, original German telescoping stock.

| MSR $1,915 | $1,775 | $1,575 | $1,375 | $1,150 | $925 | $800 | $675 | |

Add $100 for welded scope mount (Model PTR-91 KPFR, new 2011).

PTR-MSG 91 SNIPER – .308 Win. cal., 18 in. fluted target barrel, black furniture, tactical aluminum handguard, welded Picatinny accessory rail, Harris bipod, adj. Magpul stock with cheekpiece, pre-ban H&K flash hider, with (Model PTR-MSG 91 C) or w/o (PTR-MSG 91) welded muzzle compensator.

| MSR $2,125 | $1,975 | $1,775 | $1,575 | $1,375 | $1,150 | $900 | $750 | |

PTR-MSG 91 SS SUPER SNIPER – .308 Win. cal., 20 in. fluted free floating match barrel, 10 shot mag., black furniture with tactical super sniper handguard, welded Picatinny accessory rail, Harris bipod, no sights, adj. Magpul stock.

| MSR $2,825 | $2,575 | $2,275 | $1,975 | $1,750 | $1,500 | $1,225 | $975 | |

PTR-91 SC SQUAD CARBINE – .308 Win. cal., 16 in. fluted barrel, H&K style hooded front blade and four position diopter rear sight, black furniture, tactical aluminum handguard with three rails, welded Picatinny accessory rail, 20 shot mag., standard stock, pre-ban H&K flash hider, with or w/o welded compensator (compliant model).

| MSR $1,550 | $1,425 | $1,250 | $1,050 | $925 | $800 | $675 | $550 | |

PTR-32 KF – 7.62x39mm cal., 16 in. barrel, H&K style hooded front blade and four position diopter rear sight, 30 shot mag., black furniture, tactical aluminum handguard, pre-ban H&K flash hider, H&K Navy type polymer trigger group, standard stock. Disc. 2013.

| | $1,050 | $925 | $825 | $725 | $600 | $500 | $450 | *$1,175* |

Add $50 for welded scope mount (Model PTR-32KFR, new 2011).

PTR-32 KC – 7.62x39mm cal., 16 in. barrel, H&K style hooded front blade and four position diopter rear sight, 10 shot mag., black furniture, tactical aluminum handguard, H&K Navy type polymer trigger group, welded muzzle compensator. Disc. 2013.

| | $1,050 | $925 | $825 | $725 | $600 | $500 | $450 | *$1,175* |

Add $50 for welded scope mount (Model PTR-32 KCR, new 2011).

PTR-32 KFM4 – 7.62x39mm cal., 16 in. barrel, H&K style hooded front blade and four position diopter rear sight, 30 shot mag., black furniture, tactical aluminum handguard with three rails, pre-ban H&K flash hider, H&K Navy type polymer trigger group, M4 six position telescoping stock. Disc. 2013.

| | $1,325 | $1,100 | $975 | $850 | $725 | $600 | $500 | *$1,485* |

Add $100 for welded scope mount (model PTR-32 KFM4R, new 2011).

PTR-32 KCM4 – 7.62x39mm cal., 16 in. barrel, H&K style hooded front blade and four position diopter rear sight, 10 shot mag., black furniture, tactical aluminum handguard with three rails, H&K Navy type polymer trigger group, M4 style fixed stock, welded compensator. Disc. 2013.

| | $1,325 | $1,100 | $975 | $850 | $725 | $600 | $500 | *$1,485* |

Add $100 for welded scope mount (Model PTR-32 KCM4R, new 2011).

MSR	100%	98%	95%	90%	80%	70%	60%	Last MSR

PTR-32 KPF – 7.62x39mm cal., 16 in. barrel, 30 shot mag., black furniture, three rails, original German telescoping stock. Mfg. 2011-2013.

	100%	98%	95%	90%	80%	70%	60%	Last MSR
	$1,825	$1,600	$1,400	$1,150	$925	$800	$675	*$1,980*

Add $100 for welded scope mount (Model PTR-32 KPF4).

PTR-91 MSR – .308 Win. cal., 18 in. crown tapered target barrel, 5 shot mag., H&K Navy type polymer trigger group, sling swivel, earth tone furniture with free floating handguard, 8 in. welded scope mount, black synthetic stock with adj. cheekpiece. New 2012.

MSR $1,200	$1,075	$950	$825	$700	$675	$550	$425	

PALMETTO STATE ARMORY

Current AR-15 style rifle and related parts manufacturer with corporate offices located in Columbia, SC.

RIFLES: SEMI-AUTO

Palmetto State Armory currently manufactures the SPX and Freedom Series rifles. Please contact the company directly for more information, including availability and pricing (see Trademark Index).

PALMETTO STATE DEFENSE, LLC

Current manufacturer located in Greer, SC.

RIFLES: SEMI-AUTO

Palmetto State Defense manufactures custom AR-15 style rifles in several calibers and configurations. Current models include: MOE 16 in. Carbine, M4 Carbine, Limited Edition Blue, A2.5 20 in. Rifle, .300 BLK, Straightjacket, and gas piston operated Suppressor Ready Carbine. Please contact the company directly for more information including options, pricing, and availability (see Trademark Index).

PARA USA, LLC

Current manufacturer established in 1985, and located in Pineville, NC. Previous company names were Para-Ordnance Mfg. Inc. and Para USA Inc. Para-Ordnance Mfg. Inc was located in Scarborough, Ontario, Canada until June 2009. Previously located in Ft. Lauderdale, FL. Dealer and distributor sales.

Para-Ordnance Mfg. was founded by Ted Szabo and Thanos Polyzos. Szabo was born in Hungary and his family fled the country when the Russians invaded during the Hungarian Revolution of 1956. Polyzos was born in Greece and later emigrated to Canada.

On Jan. 30, 2012, Freedom Group, Inc. purchased the assets of Para USA, Inc. Manufacturing is scheduled to remain in Pineville, NC.

PISTOLS: SEMI-AUTO

From 1985-2009, pistols were marked "Made in Canada" with a Canadian maple leaf on the slide.

In 1999, Para-Ordnance introduced their LDA trigger system, originally standing for Lightning Double Action. During 2002, all alloy frame pistols were discontinued, and the abbreviation LDA became Light Double Action. Beginning 2003, all Para-Ordnance models were shipped with two magazines. Beginning Jan. 1, 2004, all Para-Ordnance models were replaced for the general market (except California) with the introduction of the new Power Extractor (PXT) models. The Griptor system, featuring front grip strap grasping grooves, became available during 2005, and the accessory mounting rail option became available during 2006.

Previous Para-Ordnance model nomenclature typically listed the alphabetical letter of the series, followed by a one or two digit number indicating magazine capacity, followed by the number(s) of the caliber. Hence, a Model P14.45 is a P Series model with a 14 shot mag. in .45 ACP cal., and a 7.45LDA indicates a .45 ACP cal. in Light Double Action with a 7 shot mag.

Current Para nomenclature typically features the configuration type on the left side of the slide. The model designation is located on the right side of the slide and underneath it on the frame the product code (new 2006)/order number (changed to product code during 2006), which is alpha-numeric, may also appear. For current product codes for the various Para models, please visit www.para-usa.com.

Para offers the following finishes on its pistols: Regal (black slide, black frame w/stainless fire controls), Midnight Blue (blue slide, blue frame w/blue fire controls), Coyote Brown, Covert Black (black slide, black frame, and black fire controls), Black Watch (black slide, green frame, green (double stack) or black (single stack) fire controls), Spec Ops (green slide, green frame w/black fire controls), or Sterling (all stainless, black slide w/polished sides), in addition to stainless steel construction.

6.45 LDA/LLDA – Models 6.45 LDA (changed to Para-Companion, marked Para-Companion on left side of slide and C7.45LDA on right side of slide) and 6.45 LLDA were advertised in the 2001 Para-Ordnance catalog (became the Para-Carry, marked Para-Carry on left side of slide and 6.45 LLDA on right side of frame), the 6.45 LLDA was never mfg., prototype only. Mfg. 2001-2003.

C SERIES MODELS – .45 ACP cal., DAO, 3 (Carry), 3 1/2 (Companion or Companion Carry), 4 1/2 (CCW or Tac-Four), or 5 in. barrel, stainless steel only, single or double (Tac-Four only) stack mag., 6 (Carry), 7, or 10 (Tac-Four only) shot mag., approx. 30-34 oz. Mfg. 2003.

	100%	98%	95%	90%	80%	70%	60%	Last MSR
	$775	$680	$580	$525	$425	$350	$270	*$939*

Add $70 for Companion Carry Model.

MSR	100%	98%	95%	90%	80%	70%	60%	*Last MSR*

D SERIES MODELS – 9mm Para., .40 S&W, or .45 ACP cal., DAO, 3 1/2 or 5 in. barrel, 7 or 10 shot single stack mag., steel receiver, matte black finish or stainless steel. Mfg. 2003.

	$715	$625	$535	$485	$395	$320	$250	*$859*

Add $80 for stainless steel.

P SERIES MODELS – 9mm Para., .40 S&W, or .45 ACP cal., SA, 3 1/2, 4 1/4, or 5 in. barrel, 10 shot mag., matte black (5 in. barrel only) or stainless steel finish.

* **P Series Model P12** – .40 S&W (disc. 2002) or .45 ACP cal., compact variation of the P14 featuring 10 (C/B 1994) or 11* shot mag. and 3 1/2 in. barrel, 33 oz. with steel frame (disc. 2002) or 24 oz. with alloy frame (disc. 2002) or stainless steel (standard beginning 2003, duo-tone stainless was disc. 2000). Mfg. 1990-2003.

	$750	$655	$560	$510	$410	$335	$260	*$899*

Subtract 10% for steel frame (disc. 2002).

* **P Series Model P13** – .40 S&W (disc. 2000) or .45 ACP cal., similar to P14, except has 10 (C/B 1994) or 12* shot mag., 4 1/4 in. barrel, 35 oz. with steel frame (disc. 2002) or 25 oz. with alloy frame (disc. 2002), stainless steel became standard 2003 (duo-tone stainless was disc. 2000). Mfg. 1993-2003.

	$750	$655	$560	$510	$410	$335	$260	*$899*

* **P Series Model P14** – .40 S&W (mfg. 1996-2000) or .45 ACP cal., patterned after the Colt Model 1911A1 except has choice of alloy (matte black, disc. 2002), steel (matte black), or stainless steel (stainless or duo-tone finish) frame that has been widened slightly for extra shot capacity (13* shot), 10 shot (C/B 1994) mag., single action, 3-dot sight system, rounded combat hammer, 5 in. ramped barrel, 38 oz. with steel frame or 28 oz. with alloy frame (disc. 2002), duo-tone stainless steel was disc. 2000. Mfg. 1990-2003.

	$685	$600	$515	$465	$375	$310	$240	*$829*

Add $70 for stainless steel.

* **P Series Model P16** – .40 S&W cal., otherwise similar to P14, steel or stainless steel (new 1997) frame only. New 1995-2002.

	$640	$560	$480	$435	$350	$290	$225	*$750*

Add $49 for stainless steel.
Add $35 for duo-tone stainless steel (disc. 2000).

* **P Series Model P18** – 9mm Para. cal., 5 in. ramped barrel, stainless steel, solid barrel bushing, flared ejection port, quadruple safety, adj. rear sight, 40 oz. Mfg. 1998-2003.

	$800	$700	$600	$545	$440	$360	$280	*$960*

PXT 1911 SINGLE STACK SERIES – .38 Super or .45 ACP cal., SA, features new power extractor design with larger claw (PXT), left slide is marked "Para 1911", right side marked with individual model names, various configurations, barrel lengths, and finishes, single stack mag., spurred or spurless (light rail models only) hammer. New 2004.

* **Slim Hawg** – .45 ACP cal. only, 3 in. barrel, 6 shot mag., 3-dot sights, choice of stainless steel (disc. 2009) or Covert Black (new 2006) finish, 24 or 30 (stainless) oz. Disc. 2012.

	$850	$750	$650	$595	$475	$395	$325	*$949*

Add $140 for stainless steel (disc. 2009).

* **Super Hawg Single Stack** – .45 ACP cal., similar to S14.45 Ltd., except has 6 in. barrel and stainless finish, 8 shot mag. Mfg. 2008-2010.

	$1,250	$1,095	$935	$850	$685	$560	$435	*$1,369*

* **GI Expert** – .45 ACP cal., 5 in. barrel, 8 shot mag., 3 dot sights, steel frame, black finish. Mfg. 2009-2012.

	$575	$495	$425	$375	$300	$245	$200	*$649*

» **GI Expert Stainless** – .45 ACP cal., 5 in. barrel, 8 shot mag., similar to GI Expert, except is weather resistant stainless steel. Mfg. 2010-2012.

	$615	$550	$475	$400	$350	$300	$250	*$699*

» **GI Expert ESP** – .45 ACP cal., 5 in. barrel, 8 shot mag., similar to GI Expert, except has beavertail grip safety with speed bump, lightweight match trigger with adj. overtravel, fiber optic front sight. Mfg. 2010.

	$625	$525	$450	$400	$350	$300	$250	*$699*

» **GI Expert LTC** – .45 ACP cal., 4 1/4 in. barrel, 8 shot mag., similar to GI Expert, except has compact frame, beavertail grip safety, competition trigger, fiber optic front sight, double diamond checkered wood grips, alloy receiver, black slide, black frame. Mfg. 2011-2012.

	$700	$625	$525	$425	$375	$325	$295	*$799*

* **1911 OPS** – .45 ACP cal. only, 3 1/2 in. barrel, 7 shot mag., 3-dot sights, stainless steel construction, 32 oz. Disc. 2008.

	$975	$855	$730	$665	$535	$440	$340	*$1,099*

MSR	100%	98%	95%	90%	80%	70%	60%	Last MSR

* 1911 LTC – 9mm Para. (mfg. 2008-2010) or .45 ACP cal., 4 1/4 in. barrel, 8 or 9 (9mm Para) shot mag., 3-dot sights, steel (disc.), alloy or stainless steel (disc. 2009) construction, Covert black (9mm Para.) or Regal finish, 28 (alloy) or 35 oz. Disc. 2012.

| | $775 | $675 | $550 | $425 | $375 | $325 | $295 | $899 |

Add $20 for steel (disc.), or $150 for stainless steel (disc. 2009).

* 1911 SSP Series – .38 Super (disc. 2008) or .45 ACP cal., 5 in. barrel, SA, 8 or 9 (.38 Super cal. only) shot mag., fiber optic (new 2011) 3-dot or Novak adj. (Tactical Duty Model only, disc.) sights, carbon or stainless steel (mfg. 2006-2008) construction, Black Covert (new 2008) or Regal (disc.) finish, steel frame (new 2011), stainless (disc. 2008), or bright stainless (.38 Super cal. only), premium cocobolo (new 2011), checkered wood (disc.) or pearl (.38 Super cal.) grips, 39 oz. Disc. 2008, reintroduced 2011-2012.

| | $775 | $675 | $550 | $425 | $375 | $325 | $295 | $899 |

Add $230 for stainless steel.
Add $250 for .38 Super cal., or $280 for .38 Super with pearl grips.
Add $250 for Tactical Duty SSP with Novak adj. sights (disc. 2008).

* 1911 SSP Gun Rights – .45 ACP cal., 14 shot, 5 in. barrel, stainless steel construction, 40 oz. Mfg. mid-2009-2011.

| | $1,025 | $895 | $775 | $695 | $565 | $475 | $375 | $1,149 |

Para USA made a donation to the NRA-ILA fund for every pistol sold.

* 1911 Black Ops/Black Ops Ltd. – .45 ACP cal., 5 in. barrel, 8 shot mag., fiber optic front and adj. rear sight (Black Ops Ltd.) or night sights (Black Ops), stainless steel with black finish, gold Para. emblem on checkered wood grips, adj. trigger. New 2012.

| MSR $1,257 | $1,110 | $975 | $835 | $750 | $610 | $500 | $395 | |

* Black Ops 10.45 – .45 ACP cal., 5 in. barrel, 10 shot mag., stainless steel slide and frame, G10 grips, IonBond finish, night sights. New 2013.

| MSR $1,299 | $1,100 | $965 | $825 | $750 | $600 | $495 | $385 | |

* Black Ops 14.45 – .45 ACP cal., 5 in. barrel, 14 shot mag., stainless steel slide and frame, G10 grips, IonBond finish, night sights. New mid-2012.

| MSR $1,299 | $1,100 | $965 | $825 | $750 | $600 | $495 | $385 | |

* Black Ops Combat – .45 ACP cal., 5 1/2 in. barrel, 14 shot mag., stainless steel slide and frame, G10 grips, IonBond finish, high profile night sights. New 2013.

| MSR $1,325 | $1,125 | $985 | $850 | $765 | $625 | $500 | $395 | |

* Black Ops Recon – 9mm Para (new 2014) or .45 ACP cal., 4 1/4 in. barrel, 14 shot mag., stainless steel slide and frame, G10 grips, IonBond finish, night sights. New 2013.

| MSR $1,299 | $1,100 | $965 | $825 | $750 | $600 | $495 | $385 | |

* 1911 Nite-Tac – .45 ACP cal. only, 5 in. barrel, 8 shot mag., 3-dot sights, stainless steel construction, Covert Black finish or stainless, features light rail on frame, flush spurless hammer, 40 oz. Disc. 2008.

| | $1,025 | $875 | $750 | $650 | $550 | $450 | $375 | $1,149 |

* Todd Jarrett USPSA Limited Edition – .45 ACP cal., 5 in. barrel, 8 shot mag., features Novak adj. sights, steel construction, Covert Black/Sterling finish, 39 oz.

| | $1,550 | $1,355 | $1,160 | $1,055 | $850 | $695 | $540 | $1,729 |

PXT HIGH CAPACITY SERIES – 9mm Para., 40 S&W, or .45 ACP cal., SA, 10 shot or high capacity mag., various barrel lengths, construction, and finishes.

* Hawg 9 – 9mm Para. cal., compact frame, 12 shot mag., 3 in. ramped barrel with guide rod, dovetailed low mount 3-dot fixed sights, alloy receiver, steel slide, spurred competition hammer, match grade trigger, black polymer grips, Regal black finish, three safeties, 24 oz. Mfg. 2005-2010.

| | $875 | $765 | $655 | $595 | $480 | $395 | $305 | $959 |

* Lite Hawg 9 – similar to Hawg 9, except is steel and has light rail, flush spurless hammer, Covert Black finish. Disc. 2008.

| | $990 | $865 | $740 | $675 | $545 | $445 | $345 | $1,099 |

* Lite Hawg .45 – .45 ACP cal., similar to Lite Hawg 9, except has 10 shot mag., flush spurless hammer, Covert Black finish. Disc. 2008.

| | $990 | $865 | $740 | $675 | $545 | $445 | $345 | $1,099 |

* Warthog – .45 ACP cal., lightweight, compact design, 3 in. ramped barrel, alloy or stainless steel frame, 10 shot mag., tritium night (disc.) or 3-dot (upgraded fiber optic became standard during 2011) sights, spur competition hammer, match grade trigger, extended slide lock, beavertail grip and firing pin safeties, black polymer grips, matte black (new 2011), Covert Black (Para-Kote, disc.), or Regal (disc.) finish, 24 or 31 oz. New 2004.

| MSR $884 | $750 | $650 | $565 | $510 | $415 | $340 | $265 | |

Add $35 for stainless steel.

MSR	100%	98%	95%	90%	80%	70%	60%	Last MSR

* ***Nite Hawg*** – .45 ACP cal., 3 in. barrel, 10 shot mag., tritium night sights, compact alloy frame, Covert Black finish, black plastic grips, 24 oz.

| | $995 | $870 | $745 | $675 | $545 | $450 | $350 | *$1,099* |

* ***Big Hawg*** – .45 ACP cal., 5 in. barrel, 14 shot mag., 3-dot sights, alloy frame, Regal finish with chrome accents, black plastic grips, 28 oz.

| | $875 | $765 | $655 | $595 | $480 | $395 | $305 | *$959* |

* ***Super Hawg High Capacity*** – .45 ACP cal., similar to S14.45 Ltd., except has 6 in. barrel and stainless finish. Mfg. 2008-2010.

| | $1,250 | $1,095 | $935 | $850 | $685 | $560 | $435 | *$1,369* |

* ***P14.45*** – .45 ACP cal., 5 in. barrel, 14 shot mag., 3-dot (fiber optic became standard 2011) sights, Covert Black finish steel (new 2008) or stainless steel (disc.) construction, black synthetic grips, brushed stainless steel, 40 oz.

| | $795 | $725 | $625 | $575 | $475 | $375 | $295 | *$879* |

Add $230 for stainless steel (disc.2009).

* ***P14.45 Stainless*** – .45 ACP cal., 5 in. barrel, 14 shot mag., similar to P14.45, except is all stainless steel, 40 oz. Mfg. 2012.

| | $750 | $650 | $525 | $425 | $375 | $325 | $295 | *$899* |

Add $30 for light rail.

* ***P14.45 Gun Rights*** – .38 Super or .45 ACP cal., 8 or 9 shot, 5 in. barrel, steel or stainless steel construction, Covert Black or bright stainless, 39 oz. Mfg. mid-2009-2011.

| | $1,025 | $895 | $775 | $695 | $565 | $475 | $375 | *$1,159* |

Para USA made a donation to the NRA-ILA fund for every pistol sold.

* ***P18.9*** – 9mm Para. cal., 5 in. barrel, 18 shot mag., adj. sights, stainless steel construction, black synthetic grips, brushed stainless steel, 40 oz.

| | $1,025 | $895 | $770 | $695 | $565 | $460 | $360 | *$1,139* |

* ***S14.45 Limited (PXT High Capacity Limited)*** – .45 ACP cal., single action, 10 (disc.) or 14 shot mag., adj. sights, 3 1/2 (stainless steel, disc. 2005), 4 1/4 (stainless steel, disc. 2005), or 5 (steel, disc. 2005, or stainless steel) in. barrel, Covert (disc. 2005) or Sterling finish, black synthetic grips, 40 oz.

| | $1,150 | $995 | $850 | $775 | $625 | $500 | $395 | *$1,289* |

Add $110 for Long Slide Limited Model (mfg. 2011).
Add $75 for 3 1/2 or 4 1/4 in. barrel or stainless steel (disc. 2006).

* ***S16.40 Limited (PXT High Capacity Limited)*** – .40 S&W cal., single action, 10 (disc.) or 16 shot mag., adj. sights, 3 1/2 (stainless steel, disc. 2005), 4 1/4 (stainless steel, disc. 2005), or 5 (steel, disc. 2005, or stainless steel) in. barrel, Covert (disc. 2005) or Sterling finish, black synthetic grips, 40 oz.

| | $1,150 | $995 | $850 | $775 | $625 | $500 | $395 | *$1,289* |

Add $75 for 3 1/2 or 4 1/4 in. barrel or stainless steel (disc. 2006).

* ***S12-45 Limited*** – .45 ACP cal., 3 1/2 in. ramped barrel, 10 or 12 shot mag., stainless steel frame with black slide, Novak adj. rear sight, spur competition hammer, checkered cocobolo grips with gold medallions, 34 oz. Mfg. 2005-2006.

| | $995 | $870 | $745 | $675 | $545 | $450 | $350 | *$1,105* |

* ***18.9 Limited*** – 9mm Para. cal., 5 in. barrel, stainless steel frame, black Sterling finish, stainless slide, 10 or 18 shot mag., fiber optic front sights, adj. rear sights, includes two mags. Mfg. 2011-2012.

| | $1,150 | $995 | $850 | $775 | $625 | $500 | $395 | *$1,289* |

* ***Todd Jarrett USPSA .40 Limited Edition*** – .40 S&W cal., SA, 16 shot mag., 5 in. barrel, Novak adj. sights, steel construction, Covert Black/Sterling finish, flared magwell, black synthetic grips, 40 oz. Disc. 2008.

| | $1,495 | $1,310 | $1,120 | $1,015 | $820 | $675 | $525 | *$1,729* |

14.45 TACTICAL – .45 ACP cal., 4 1/4 (disc.) or 5 in. match grade barrel, SA, 8 shot mag., stainless steel frame, black finish, checkered front grip strap, Ed Brown National Match bushing and slide stop, Tactical II hammer, power extractor, flat checkered mainspring housing, alloy base pads, fiber optic sights. Mfg. 2011-2012.

| | $1,375 | $1,200 | $1,025 | $925 | $750 | $625 | $475 | *$1,599* |

16.40 TT – .40 S&W cal., SA, 16 shot mag., 5 in. barrel, stainless steel frame, duo-tone finish, adj. sights, 42 oz. Mfg. 2012.

| | $1,695 | $1,450 | $1,250 | $1,050 | $875 | $750 | $650 | *$1,899* |

PXT LDA SINGLE STACK (CARRY OPTION SERIES) – 9mm Para. (new mid-2006), .45 GAP (new mid-2006) or .45 ACP cal., DAO, single stack mag., various barrel lengths and finishes, features Griptor grips (grooved front grip strap), spurless flush hammer and rounded grip safety.

MSR	100%	98%	95%	90%	80%	70%	60%	Last MSR

* Carry Gap – .45 GAP cal., 3 in. barrel, 6 shot mag., 3-dot sights, steel frame, Covert Black finish, 30 oz. Disc. 2008.

| | $975 | $855 | $730 | $665 | $535 | $440 | $340 | *$1,079* |

* CCO Gap – similar to Carry Gap, except has 7 shot mag. and 3 1/2 in. barrel, 31 oz. Mfg. 2006-2008.

| | $975 | $855 | $730 | $665 | $535 | $440 | $340 | *$1,079* |

* Covert Black Carry – .45 ACP cal., 6 shot mag., 3 in. barrel, Novak adj. sights, stainless steel construction, Covert Black finish, 30 oz.

| | $1,025 | $895 | $770 | $695 | $565 | $460 | $360 | *$1,149* |

* Carry – similar to Covert Black Carry, except has 3-dot sights and is brushed stainless steel.

| | $1,025 | $895 | $770 | $695 | $565 | $460 | $360 | *$1,149* |

* Carry 9 – 9mm Para. cal., 8 shot mag., 3 in. barrel, 3-dot sights, alloy frame, Covert Black finish, 24 oz. Mfg. mid-2006-2011.

| | $900 | $785 | $675 | $610 | $495 | $405 | $315 | *$999* |

* Stealth – .45 ACP cal., 3 in. barrel, alloy frame, black anodized finish, night sights, 24 oz. Mfg. 2012-2013.

| | $1,175 | $1,025 | $875 | $800 | $650 | $525 | $450 | *$1,339* |

* PDA – 9mm Para cal., 3 in. barrel with fiber optic front and two-dot rear sights, alloy frame with Sterling/Covert Black finish. Mfg. 2008-2011.

| | $1,125 | $975 | $825 | $750 | $605 | $495 | $385 | *$1,249* |

* PDA .45 – .45 ACP cal., 3 in. barrel with three dot sights, 6 shot mag., alloy frame with stainless/Covert Black finish. Mfg. 2008-2011.

| | $1,150 | $995 | $850 | $775 | $625 | $500 | $395 | *$1,299* |

* CCO – .45 ACP cal., 7 shot mag., 3 1/2 in. barrel, 3-dot sights, stainless steel construction, brushed stainless finish, 32 oz. Disc. 2008.

| | $1,000 | $875 | $750 | $680 | $550 | $450 | $350 | *$1,129* |

* CCW – similar to CCO model, except has 4 1/4 in. barrel, 34 oz. Disc. 2008.

| | $1,000 | $875 | $750 | $680 | $550 | $450 | $350 | *$1,129* |

* Companion – .45 ACP cal., 3 1/2 in. barrel, 7 shot mag., stainless steel frame, LDA trigger system, black finish, fiber optic front sight, 2-dot rear sight. Mfg. 2011-2012.

| | $895 | $775 | $650 | $595 | $475 | $395 | $300 | *$999* |

* Companion II – .45 ACP cal., 4 1/4 in. barrel, 8 shot mag., stainless steel frame, black finish, fiber optic sight, single stack, DA trigger system, gold trigger, checkered wood grips with gold Para logo, includes two mags. Mfg. 2011.

| | $750 | $650 | $525 | $425 | $375 | $325 | $295 | *$899* |

PXT LDA SINGLE STACK – .45 ACP cal., DAO, non-carry option models, spurless flush hammer, various configurations and barrel lengths.

* CCO Companion Black Watch – .45 ACP cal., 7 shot mag., 3 1/2 in. barrel, 3-dot sights, stainless steel construction, Black Watch finish, 32 oz.

| | $975 | $855 | $730 | $665 | $535 | $440 | $340 | *$1,099* |

* Tac-S – .45 ACP cal., 8 shot mag., 4 1/4 in. barrel, 3-dot sights, steel frame, Spec Ops finish, 35 oz.

| | $865 | $755 | $650 | $590 | $475 | $390 | $305 | *$999* |

* Covert Black Nite-Tac SS – .45 ACP cal., 8 shot mag., 5 in. barrel, 3-dot sights, stainless steel construction, Covert Black finish, includes light rail, checkered wood grips, 40 oz. Mfg. 2006-2007.

| | $1,000 | $875 | $750 | $650 | $550 | $450 | $375 | *$1,125* |

* Nite-Tac SS – .45 ACP cal., 8 shot mag., 5 in. barrel, 3-dot sights, stainless steel construction, brushed stainless finish, includes light rail, checkered wood grips, 40 oz. Mfg. 2006-2007.

| | $1,000 | $875 | $750 | $650 | $550 | $450 | $375 | *$1,125* |

PXT LDA HIGH CAPACITY (CARRY OPTION SERIES) – 9mm Para., .40 S&W, or .45 ACP cal., DAO, spurless flush hammer, rounded grip safety, various options, barrel lengths and magazine capacity.

* Carry 12 – .45 ACP cal., 12 shot mag., 3 1/2 in. barrel, low mount 3-dot tritium night sights, stainless steel construction, black synthetic grips, brushed stainless finish, 34 oz.

| | $1,050 | $920 | $785 | $715 | $575 | $470 | $365 | *$1,199* |

* Tac-Four – .45 ACP cal., 13 shot mag., 4 1/4 in. barrel, 3-dot sights, stainless steel construction, black synthetic grips, brushed stainless finish, 36 oz.

| | $960 | $840 | $735 | $625 | $525 | $425 | $350 | *$1,099* |

MSR	100%	98%	95%	90%	80%	70%	60%	Last MSR

* **Tac-Forty** – .40 S&W cal., 15 shot mag., 4 1/4 in. barrel, 3-dot sights, stainless steel construction, black synthetic grips, brushed stainless finish, 36 oz. Mfg. 2007.

	$925	$825	$725	$625	$525	$425	$350	$1,049

* **Tac-Five** – 9mm Para cal., 18 shot mag., 5 in. barrel, Novak adj. sights, stainless steel construction, black synthetic grips, Covert Black finish, 37 1/2 oz. Mfg. 2007.

	$1,050	$920	$785	$715	$575	$470	$365	$1,185

This model was also available in a limited edition "Canadian Forces" model with a maple leaf on the slide.

PXT LDA HIGH CAPACITY SERIES – .45 ACP cal., DAO, 14 shot mag., 5 in. barrel, 3-dot sights, steel or stainless steel construction, spurless flush hammer, Covert Black finish or stainless steel.

* **Covert Black Hi-Cap .45** – steel frame, Covert Black finish. Disc. 2008.

	$950	$830	$710	$645	$520	$425	$330	$1,099

* **Hi-Cap .45** – stainless steel construction, brushed stainless finish. Disc. 2008.

	$955	$840	$730	$625	$525	$425	$350	$1,099

* **Covert Black Nite-Tac .45** – steel frame, Covert Black finish, includes light rail. Mfg. 2006-2008.

	$955	$840	$730	$625	$525	$425	$350	$1,099

* **Coyote Brown Nite-Tac .45** – .45 ACP cal., similar to Covert Black Nite-Tac, except has adj. fiber optic sights and Coyote Brown finish.

	$1,175	$1,030	$880	$800	$645	$530	$410	$1,349

* **Nite-Tac .45** – stainless steel construction, brushed stainless finish, includes light rail. Mfg. 2006-2008.

	$1,025	$900	$775	$650	$550	$450	$350	$1,199

* **Colonel** – .45 ACP cal., 4 1/4 in. ramped barrel, low mount white 3-dot fixed sights, steel frame, 10 or 14 shot mag., spur competition hammer, LDA trigger, black polymer grips with medallions, green spec. ops. finish, 37 oz. Mfg. 2005-2006.

	$795	$695	$595	$540	$435	$360	$280	$899

PXT LDA HIGH CAPACITY LIMITED – 9mm Para., .40 S&W, or .45 ACP cal., DAO, 10, 14, 16, or 18 shot mag., steel or stainless steel, 5 in. barrel. Disc. 2006.

	$935	$800	$700	$600	$500	$400	$350	$1,035

Add $75 for stainless steel.

PXT LTC HIGH CAPACITY – .45 ACP cal., 4 1/4 in. barrel, DAO, 10 or 14 shot mag., 3-dot fixed sights, stainless steel frame, match grade trigger, black polymer grips with medallions, green spec. ops. finish, three safeties, 37 oz. Mfg. 2005-2006.

	$750	$655	$560	$510	$410	$335	$260	$855

S SERIES MODELS – .40 S&W or .45 ACP cal., SA, 3 1/2, 4 1/4, or 5 in. barrel, 10 shot mag., matte black (5 in. barrel only) or stainless steel finish.

* **S Series Model S10 Limited** – similar to P10, except has competition shooting features, including beavertail grip safety, competition hammer, tuned trigger, match grade barrel, front slide serrations, choice of steel or alloy frame with matte black finish or stainless steel, 40 oz. Mfg. 1999-2002.

	$765	$670	$575	$520	$420	$345	$270	$865

Add $10 for steel receiver.
Add $24 for stainless steel.

* **S Series Model S12 Limited** – .40 S&W (disc. 2002) or .45 ACP cal., similar to P12, except has competition shooting features, including beavertail grip safety, competition hammer, tuned trigger, match grade barrel, front slide serrations, choice of steel or alloy (disc. 2002) frame, matte black (disc. 2002) or stainless steel finish, 40 oz. Mfg. 1999-2003.

	$895	$785	$670	$610	$490	$405	$315	$1,049

Subtract 10% for steel frame (disc. 2002).

* **S Series Model S13 Limited** – .40 S&W (disc. 2002) or .45 ACP cal., similar to P13, except has competition shooting features, including beavertail grip safety, competition hammer, tuned trigger, match grade barrel, front slide serrations, choice of steel or alloy (disc. 2002) frame, matte black (disc. 2002) or stainless steel finish, 40 oz. Mfg. 1999-2003.

	$895	$785	$670	$610	$490	$405	$315	$1,049

* **S Series Model S14 Limited** – .40 S&W (disc. 2002) or .45 ACP cal., similar to P14, except has competition shooting features, including beavertail grip safety, competition hammer, tuned trigger, match grade barrel, front slide serrations, matte black or stainless steel, 40 oz. Mfg. 1998-2003.

	$850	$745	$635	$580	$465	$380	$295	$989

Add $60 for stainless steel.

MSR	100%	98%	95%	90%	80%	70%	60%	Last MSR

* **S Series Model S16 Limited** – .40 S&W cal., similar to P16, except has 5 in. barrel and competition shooting features, including beavertail grip safety, competition hammer, tuned trigger, match grade barrel, front slide serrations, matte black steel or stainless steel, 40 oz. Mfg. 1998-2003.

	$850	$745	$635	$580	$465	$380	$295	$989

Add $60 for stainless steel.

T SERIES MODELS – 9mm Para., .40 S&W (stainless steel only), or .45 ACP cal., DAO, 5 in. barrel, 7 (.45 ACP cal. only, single stack mag.) or 10 shot mag., steel or stainless steel, matte black finish or stainless steel. Mfg. 2003.

	$825	$720	$620	$560	$455	$370	$290	$1,009

Add $80 for stainless steel.

RIFLES: SEMI-AUTO

TTR SERIES – .223 Rem. cal., tactical design, GIO, 16 1/2 in. chrome lined barrel, DIGS (delayed impingement gas system) operation, 30 shot mag., flip up front sight and adj. flip up rear sight, flat-top receiver with full length Picatinny rail, black finish, single stage trigger, available in Short Rail with fixed stock (TTR-XASF, mfg. 2009), or 5 position folding stock with Short Rail (TTR-XAS), Long Rail (TTR-XA), and Nylatron (TTR-XN, mfg. 2009) forearm configurations. Mfg. 2009-late 2011.

	$2,050	$1,800	$1,575	$1,350	$1,150	$975	$825	$2,397

Add $100 for Nylatron forearm (mfg. 2009).

PARDINI, ARMI S.r.l.

Current manufacturer located in Lido di Camaiore, Italy. Currently imported by Pardini USA, LLC beginning 2012 located in Tampa, FL. Previously imported until 2012 by Larry's Guns, located in Gray, ME. Previously imported until 2004 by Nygord Precision Products located in Prescott, AZ, and distributed until 1996 by Mo's Competitor Supplies & Range, Inc. located in Brookfield, CT, and until 1990 by Fiocchi of America, Inc., located in Ozark, MO.

For more information and current pricing on both new and used Pardini airguns, please refer to the *Blue Book of Airguns* by Dr. Robert Beeman & John Allen (also online).

PISTOLS: SEMI-AUTO

PC45 – .40 S&W, .45 ACP, or 9x21mm cal., single action mechanism designed for stock competition category, adj. trigger pull. Limited importation by Nygord 2000-2004.

	$1,295	$1,050	$840	$715	$575	$500	$440	

Add $75 for 6 in. barrel and slide.

* **PC45S** – .40 S&W, .45 ACP, or 9x21mm cal., similar to PC, except has compensator and scope mount with optical sight.

	$1,500	$1,250	$1,100	$950	$850	$725	$600	

* **PCS-Open** – similar to PCS, except w/o scope and frame mount, top-of-the-line semi-auto.

	$1,650	$1,400	$1,250	$1,100	$950	$850	$725	

GT9/PC40/GT45 DEFENSE/SPORT – 9mm Para., 9x21mm (disc. 2011), .40 S&W, or .45 ACP cal., 5 or 6 in. barrel, SA, diamond wood grips, matte silver, 13 or 17 (9x21mm) shot mag., black, silver, bronze, or two-tone finish. Importation began late 2004.

MSR $2,299	$1,950	$1,700	$1,465	$1,325	$1,075	$880	$685	

Add $150 for 6 in. barrel.
Add $100 for silver or bronze (disc. 2013) finish.
Add $50 for .45 ACP cal.
Add $95 for 6 in. barrel and slide (disc.).
Add $700 for titanium finish in 9mm Para. cal. with 6 in. barrel only.
Add $999 for 9mm Para. or .40 S&W cal. conversion kit for GT45 Model (disc. 2013).
Add $230 for GT45S Model with compensator in silver finish (disc. 2011).

* **GT9/GT40 Defense Sport Inox** – 9mm Para. or .40 S&W (IPSC) cal., features 5 or 6 in. stainless steel barrel, black or Ergal finish.

MSR $2,899	$2,465	$2,150	$1,850	$1,675	$1,350	$1,100	$875	

Add $100 for Ergal finish.
Add $800 for 5 in. barrel and 9mm Para. cal. or $1,100 for 9mm Para. cal. with 6 in. barrel (all disc. 2013).

PARKER-HALE LIMITED

Previous gun manufacturer located in Birmingham, England. Rifles were manufactured in England until 1991 when Navy Arms purchased the manufacturing rights and built a plant in West Virginia for fabrication. This new company was called Gibbs Rifle Company, Inc. and they manufactured models very similar to older Parker-Hale rifles during 1992-94. Shotguns were manufactured in Spain and imported by Precision Sports, a division of Cortland Line Company, Inc. located in Cortland, NY until 1993.

Parker was the previous trade name of the A.G. Parker Company, located in Birmingham, England, which was formed from a gun making business founded in 1890 by Alfred Gray Parker. The company became the Parker-Hale company in 1936. The company was purchased by John Rothery Wholesale circa 2000.

Parker-Hale Ltd. continues to make a wide variety of high quality firearms cleaning accessories for both rifles and shotguns, including their famous bipod.

Due to space considerations, information regarding this manufacturer is available online free of charge at www.bluebookofgunvalues.com.

PATRIOT ORDNANCE FACTORY (POF)

Current rifle manufacturer located in Glendale, AZ.

CARBINES/RIFLES: SEMI-AUTO

Patriot Ordnance Factory manufactures AR-15 style rifles and carbines, as well as upper and lower receivers and various parts. The semi-auto carbines and rifles use a unique gas piston operating system that requires no lubrication. A wide variety of options are available for each model. Please contact the company directly for more information, including option pricing (see Trademark Index).

P308 MID-LENGTH RIFLE – .308 Win. cal., GPO, 16 1/2 or 20 in. heavy contour fluted barrel, 3-position gas regulation for normal, suppressed and single action modes, FMP-A3 muzzle device, corrosion resistant operating system, chrome plated mil spec bolt, optional fixed hooded front sight, optional Troy or Diamondhead flip up sights, hunter/sniper or tactical aircraft aluminum alloy modular railed receiver, nickel, black, Olive Drab (new 2013), and CeraKote Burnt Bronze (new 2013) hard coat anodized Teflon finish, oversized trigger guard, Magpul MOE pistol grip, Magpul CTR six position collapsible stock, Ergo ladder rail covers, sling, bipod mount, Magpul PMAG 20 shot mag., approx. 9 lbs.

| MSR $3,220 | $2,675 | $2,150 | $1,825 | $1,600 | $1,350 | $1,175 | $1,000 |

Add $100 for Olive Drab (new 2013) or Cerakote Burnt Bronze (new 2013) finish.
Add $25 for NP3 nickel/alloy plating.

This model is also available with a 12 1/2 or a 14 1/2 in. barrel for military/law enforcement.

GEN 4 MODEL 308 CARBINE/RIFLE – .308 Win. cal., regulated piston system, black anodize, NP3 nickel alloy plating, or Cerakote Olive Drab finish, 16 or 20 in. deep fluted barrel, 30 shot PMAG, 11 in. modular rail. New 2014.

| MSR $3,245 | $2,690 | $2,150 | $1,825 | $1,600 | $1,350 | $1,175 | $1,000 |

Add $25 for NP3 nickel alloy plating or $100 for Cerakote Olive Drab finish.

This model is also available with a 14 or 14 1/2 in. barrel for military/law enforcement.

P308 HUNTING RIFLE – .243 Win or .308 Win. cal., GPO, 20 in. heavy contour fluted barrel, 3-position gas regulation for normal, suppressed and single action modes, FMP-A3 muzzle device, corrosion resistant operating system, chrome plated mil spec bolt, optional fixed hooded front sight, optional Troy or Diamondhead flip up sights, hunter/sniper aircraft aluminum alloy Olive Drab Cerakote modular railed receiver, Olive Drab Cerakote finish, oversized trigger guard, Magpul MOE pistol grip, fixed polymer buttstock, Ergo ladder rail covers, sling, bipod mount, 5 shot stainless steel mag., approx. 9 lbs. Disc. 2013.

| | $2,675 | $2,150 | $1,825 | $1,600 | $1,350 | $1,175 | $1,000 | *$3,220* |

P415 MID-LENGTH RIFLE – 5.56 NATO cal., GPO, 16 1/2 or 18 in. heavy contour fluted barrel, 3-position gas regulation for normal, suppressed and single action modes, FMP-A3 muzzle device, corrosion resistant operating system, chrome plated mil spec bolt, optional fixed hooded front sight, optional Troy or Diamondhead flip up sights, hunter/sniper or tactical aircraft aluminum alloy modular railed receiver, nickel and black hard coat anodized Teflon finish, oversized trigger guard, Magpul MOE pistol grip, Magpul CTR six position collapsible stock, Ergo ladder rail covers, sling, bipod mount, Magpul PMAG 30 shot mag., approx. 8 lbs. New 2012.

| MSR $2,320 | $2,100 | $1,800 | $1,750 | $1,500 | $1,050 | $875 | $725 |

Add $30 for NP3 nickel/alloy plating (new 2014).

This model is also available with a 14 1/2 in. barrel for military/law enforcement.

GEN 4 MODEL 415 CARBINE/RIFLE – .223 Rem. cal., regulated piston system, black anodize, NP3 nickel alloy plating, or Cerakote Olive Drab finish, 16 or 18 in. deep fluted barrel, 30 shot PMAG, 11 in. modular rail. New 2014.

| MSR $2,375 | $2,124 | $1,800 | $1,750 | $1,500 | $1,050 | $875 | $725 |

Add $50 for NP3 nickel alloy plating or $100 for Cerakote Olive Drab finish.

This model is also available with a 14 1/2 in. barrel for military/law enforcement.

P415 HUNTING RIFLE – 5.56 NATO cal., GPO, 18 in. heavy contour fluted barrel, 3-position gas regulation for normal, suppressed and single action modes, FMP-A3 muzzle device, corrosion resistant operating system, chrome plated mil spec bolt, optional fixed hooded front sight, optional Troy or Diamondhead flip up sights, hunter/sniper aircraft aluminum alloy modular railed receiver, Olive Drab Cerakote finish, oversized trigger guard, Magpul MOE pistol

MSR	100%	98%	95%	90%	80%	70%	60%	Last MSR

grip, fixed polymer buttstock, Ergo ladder rail covers, sling, bipod mount, 5 shot stainless steel mag., approx. 8 lbs. Disc. 2013.

	$1,825	$1,650	$1,425	$1,295	$1,050	$875	$675	$2,320

P415 SPECIAL PURPOSE RIFLE – .223 Rem. cal., GPO, 18 in. heavy contour chrome lined fluted barrel, A3 muzzle device, corrosion resistant operating system, nickel plated A3 flat-top upper receiver and charging handle, M4 feed ramp, nickel and black hard coat anodized Teflon finish, fixed removable hooded front sight, optional Troy flip up sight, single stage trigger, Magpul PRS or six position adj. buttstock, tactical rail handguard, approx. 9 lbs. Disc. 2011.

	$1,825	$1,650	$1,425	$1,295	$1,050	$875	$675	$1,999

P415 RECON CARBINE – .223 Rem. cal., GPO, 16 in. heavy contour chrome lined fluted barrel, A3 muzzle device, corrosion resistant operating system, nickel plated A3 flat-top upper receiver and charging handle, M4 feed ramp, nickel and black hard coat anodized Teflon finish, fixed removable hooded front sight, optional Troy flip up sight, single stage trigger, oversized trigger guard, Magpul PRS or six position adj. buttstock, tactical rail handguard, approx. 8 lbs. Disc. 2011.

	$1,825	$1,650	$1,425	$1,295	$1,050	$875	$675	$1,999

P415 CARBINE – .223 Rem. cal., GPO, 16 in. heavy contour chrome lined fluted barrel, A3 muzzle device, corrosion resistant operating system, nickel plated A3 flat-top upper receiver and charging handle, M4 feed ramp, nickel and black hard coat anodized Teflon finish, fixed removable hooded front sight, optional Troy flip up sight, single stage trigger, oversized trigger guard, Magpul CTR retractable six position buttstock, M4 plastic handguard or Predator P-9 tactical rail system, sling/bipod mount, approx. 7-7.4 lbs. Disc. 2011.

	$1,825	$1,650	$1,425	$1,295	$1,050	$875	$675	$1,999

Add $300 for Predator P-9 tactical rail system.

PISTOLS: SEMI-AUTO

P308 PISTOL – .308 Win. cal., GPO, 12 1/2 in. heavy contour fluted barrel, 3-position gas regulation for normal, suppressed and single action modes, FMP-A3 muzzle device, corrosion resistant operating system, chrome plated mil spec bolt, optional fixed hooded front sight, optional Troy or Diamondhead flip up sights, hunter/sniper or tactical aircraft aluminum alloy modular railed receiver, nickel and black hard coat anodized Teflon finish, oversized trigger guard, Magpul MOE pistol grip, PWS enhanced pistol buffer tube, Ergo ladder rail covers, sling, bipod mount, Magpul PMAG 20 shot mag., approx. 7 1/2 lbs.

MSR $3,220	$2,850	$2,250	$1,900	$1,650	$1,350	$1,175	$1,000	

P415 PISTOL – 5.56 NATO cal., GPO, 7 1/4 or 10 1/2 in. heavy contour fluted barrel, 3-position gas regulation for normal, suppressed and single action modes, FMP-A3 muzzle device, chrome plated mil spec bolt, optional fixed hooded front sight, optional Troy or Diamondhead flip up sights, hunter/sniper or tactical aircraft aluminum alloy modular railed receiver, nickel and black hard coat anodized Teflon finish, oversized trigger guard, Magpul MOE pistol grip, PWS enhanced pistol buffer tube, Ergo ladder rail covers, sling, bipod mount, Magpul PMAG 30 shot mag., approx. 6 1/2 lbs. Disc. 2013.

	$2,075	$1,800	$1,525	$1,375	$1,100	$900	$725	$2,320

GEN 4 AR PISTOL – .223 Rem. (Model 415) or .308 Win. (Model 308) cal., black anodize finish or NP3 nickel alloy plating, 7 1/4 or 12 1/2 (.308 Win. cal. only) in. deep fluted barrel, 6 or 11 (.308 Win. cal. only) in. modular rail. New 2014.

MSR $2,345	$2,100	$1,825	$1,525	$1,375	$1,100	$900	$750	

Add $25 for NP3 nickel alloy plating.
Add $100 for Model 308.

PAUZA SPECIALTIES

Previously manufactured by Pauza Specialties circa 1991-96, and located in Baytown, TX. Previously distributed by U.S. General Technologies, Inc. located in South San Francisco, CA.

Pauza previously manufactured the P50 semi-auto rifle for Firearms International, Inc. - please refer to that section for current information.

RIFLES: SEMI-AUTO

P50 SEMI-AUTO – .50 BMG cal., semi-auto, 24 (carbine) or 29 (rifle) in. match grade barrel, 5 shot detachable mag., one-piece receiver, 3-stage gas system, takedown action, all exterior parts Teflon coated, with aluminum bipod, 25 or 30 lbs. Mfg. 1992-96.

	$5,950	$5,250	$4,600	$4,100	$3,650	$3,200	$2,800	$6,495

PEACE RIVER CLASSICS

Previous manufacturer located in Bartow, FL until 2001. Peace River Classics was a division of Tim's Guns.

MSR	100%	98%	95%	90%	80%	70%	60%	*Last MSR*

RIFLES: SEMI-AUTO

PEACE RIVER CLASSICS SEMI-AUTO – .223 Rem. or .308 Win. (new 1998, possible prototypes only) cal., available in 3 configurations including the Shadowood, the Glenwood, and the Royale, GIO, hand-built utilizing Armalite action, patterned after the AR-15, match grade parts throughout, special serialization, laminate thumbhole stock. Very limited mfg. 1997-2001.

Last MSR on the .223 Rem. cal. in 2001 was $2,695, or $2,995 for .308 Win. cal.

Due to this model's rarity factor, accurate values are hard to ascertain.

PETERS STAHL GmbH

Previous pistol manufacturer located in Paderborn, Germany until 2010. Previously imported until 2009 by Euro-Imports, located in Yoakum, TX. Previously distributed by Swiss Trading GmbH, located in Bozeman, MT. Previously imported 1998-1999 by Peters Stahl, U.S.A. located in Delta, UT, and by Franzen International Inc. located in Oakland, NJ until 1998.

PISTOLS: SEMI-AUTO

Peters Stahl manufactured high quality semi-auto pistols based on the Model 1911 design, but had limited U.S. importation. Models include the Multicaliber, 92-Sport, O7-Sport, HC-Champion and variations, 1911-Tactical/Classic, PLS, and a .22 LR. Peters-Stahl also manufactures multicaliber conversion kits of the highest quality. Recent models previously imported (until 2000) included the Model Millennium (MSR was $2,195), Match 22 LR (MSR was $1,995), Trophy Master (MSR was $1,995), Omega Match (MSR was $1,995), High Capacity Trophy Master (MSR was $1,695), O7 Multicaliber (MSR was $1,995), and the 92 Multicaliber (MSR was $2,610-$2,720). In the past, Peters Stahl has manufactured guns for Federal Ordnance, Omega, Schuetzen Pistol Works, and Springfield Armory.

PISTOL DYNAMICS

Current semi-auto pistol manufacturer located in Palm Bay, FL.

PISTOLS: SEMI-AUTO

Pistol Dynamics manufactures high quality 1911-style semi-auto pistols. Series include the Signature (base price $3,800 MSR), Combat Special Evolution (base price $3,600 MSR), Combat Special Classic (base price $4,600 MSR), Scout (base price $2,900 MSR), and the X-O (base price $2,400 MSR). Options and delivery times vary from each model. Please contact the company directly for availability and pricing (see Trademark Index).

POLY TECHNOLOGIES, INC.

Previously distributed by PTK International, Inc. located in Atlanta, GA. Previously imported by Keng's Firearms Specialty, Inc., located in Riverdale, GA. Manufactured in China by Poly Technologies, Inc.

Poly Technologies commercial firearms are made to Chinese military specifications and have excellent quality control. These models were banned from domestic importation due to 1989 Federal legislation.

RIFLES: SEMI-AUTO

Add 10% for NIB.

AKS-762 – 7.62x39mm or .223 Rem. cal., 16 1/4 in. barrel, semi-auto version of the Chinese AKM (Type 56) rifle, 8.4 lbs., wood stock. Imported 1988-1989.

	$1,495	$1,325	$1,100	$975	$875	$795	$750	*$400*

Add $100 for side-fold plastic stock.

This model was also available with a downward folding stock at no extra charge.

SKS – 7.62x39mm cal., 20 9/20 in. barrel, full wood stock, machined steel parts to Chinese military specifications, 7.9 lbs. Imported 1988-89.

	$550	$475	$400	$350	$300	$275	$250	*$200*

AK-47/S (LEGEND) – 7.62x39mm cal., 16 3/8 in. barrel, semi-auto configuration of the original AK-47, fixed, side-folding, or under-folding stock, with or w/o spike bayonet, 8.2 lbs. Imported 1988-89.

	$2,000	$1,800	$1,600	$1,350	$1,200	$1,000	$925	*$550*

Add 10% for folding stock.

The "S" suffix in this variation designates third model specifications.

* ***AK-47/S National Match Legend*** – utilizes match parts in fabrication.

	$1,950	$1,750	$1,550	$1,275	$1,050	$975	$900	

RPK – 7.62x39mm cal. Disc.

	$1,475	$1,300	$1,150	$1,025	$925	$850	$775	

MSR	100%	98%	95%	90%	80%	70%	60%	Last MSR

M-14/S – .308 Win. cal., 22 in. barrel, forged receiver, patterned after the famous M-14, 9.2 lbs. Imported 1988-89.

	100%	98%	95%	90%	80%	70%	60%	Last MSR
	$1,100	$950	$850	$775	$725	$650	$575	*$700*

PRECISION FIREARMS LLC

Current firearms manufacturer located in Martinsburg, VA beginning in late 2013. Previously located in Hagerstown, MD. Dealer and consumer sales through FFL.

Precision Firearms manufactures high quality AR-15 style rifles and upper assemblies. Calibers currently include .17 Rem., .204 Ruger, .223 Rem., 5.56 NATO, 6.5 Grendel, .264 LBC, 6.8 SPC II, and .308 Win. Please contact the manufacturer directly for more information, availability, and pricing (see Trademark Index).

PRECISION REFLEX, INC.

Current AR-15 manufacturer located in New Bremen, OH.

Precision Reflex, Inc. manufactures AR-15 style rifles and shooting accessories for commercial, law enforcement, and military use. For more information on the many products they have available, please contact the company directly (see Trademark Index).

RIFLES: SEMI-AUTO

3 GUN SHOOTER RIFLE – 5.56 NATO or 6.8 SPC cal., 18 in. stainless steel barrel with threaded muzzle, M4 feed ramps, low profile steel gas block, forged upper and lower receivers, 15 in. black forearm, AR trigger, 6-position carbine stock with recoil pad, A2 pistol grip, flip-up rear sights, Gas Buster charging handle with military latch, 7 1/2 lbs. New 2014.

	100%	98%	95%	90%	80%	70%	60%	
MSR $1,320	$1,175	$1,025	$875	$800	$650	$525	$425	

DELUXE RIFLE – 5.56 NATO or 6.8 SPC cal., 16 in. Douglas stainless steel or 17 in. Bergara chromemoly barrel, threaded muzzle, M4 feed ramps, flip-up front and rear sights, AR trigger, intermediate round forearm with natural finish, intermediate length top rail, 6-position carbine stock with recoil pad, A2 pistol grip, Gas Buster charging handle w/military latch, Black finish, 7.9 lbs. New 2014.

	100%	98%	95%	90%	80%	70%	60%	
MSR $1,325	$1,175	$1,025	$875	$800	$650	$525	$425	

Add $215 for Douglas stainless steel barrel.

ENTRY LEVEL RIFLE – 5.56 NATO cal., 17 in. Bergara chromemoly barrel, threaded muzzle, M4 feed ramps, forged upper and lower receivers, rifle length round forearm in Natural, Black, or Flat Dark Earth, AR trigger, 6-position carbine stock with recoil pad, A2 pistol grip, Gas Buster charging handle w/military latch, approx 8 lbs. New 2014.

	100%	98%	95%	90%	80%	70%	60%	
MSR $1,190	$1,050	$925	$800	$725	$575	$475	$375	

Add $30 for forearm with Black or Flat Dark Earth finish.

* **Entry Level Rifle Stainless** – 5.56 NATO or 6.8 SPC cal., similar to Entry Level rifle, except features 16 in. stainless steel barrel, rifle length round forearm in Natural, Black, or Flat Dark Earth finish. New 2014.

	100%	98%	95%	90%	80%	70%	60%	
MSR $1,322	$1,175	$1,025	$875	$800	$650	$525	$425	

Add $11 for forearm with Black or Flat Dark Earth finish.

ENTRY LEVEL DELTA RIFLE – 5.56 NATO cal., 17 in. Bergara chromemoly barrel, threaded muzzle, M4 feed ramps, forged upper and lower receivers, rifle length Delta forearm in Black or Flat Dark Earth finish, AR trigger, 6-position carbine stock with recoil pad, A2 pistol grip, Gas Buster charging handle w/military latch, approx 8 lbs. New 2014.

	100%	98%	95%	90%	80%	70%	60%	
MSR $1,205	$1,075	$950	$800	$725	$575	$475	$375	

* **Entry Level Delta Rifle Stainless** – 5.56 NATO or 6.8 SPC cal., similar to Entry Level Delta rifle, except features 16 in. stainless steel barrel, rifle length Delta forearm in Black or Flat Dark Earth finish, approx 8 lbs. New 2014.

	100%	98%	95%	90%	80%	70%	60%	
MSR $1,339	$1,200	$1,050	$900	$800	$650	$525	$425	

MARK 12 MOD O SPR RIFLE – 5.56 NATO or 6.8 SPC cal., 18 in. stainless steel barrel, threaded muzzle, forged upper and lower receivers, flip-up front and rear sights, AR trigger, Black rifle length forearm, full length SPR top rail, 6-position carbine stock with recoil pad, A2 pistol grip, Gas Buster charging handle w/military latch, 8.68 lbs. New 2014.

	100%	98%	95%	90%	80%	70%	60%	
MSR $1,790	$1,625	$1,425	$1,225	$1,100	$900	$725	$575	

* **Mark 12 Mod Delta Rifle** – 5.56 NATO or 6.8 SPC cal., similar to Mark 12 Mod O SPR rifle, except features a full length SPR Delta top rail, 7.9 lbs. New 2014.

	100%	98%	95%	90%	80%	70%	60%	
MSR $1,790	$1,625	$1,425	$1,225	$1,100	$900	$725	$575	

MARK 12 MOD O SPR VARIANT RIFLE – 5.56 NATO or 6.8 SPC cal., 16 in. stainless steel or 17 in. Bergara chromemoly barrel, threaded muzzle, M4 feed ramps, forged upper and lower receivers, AR trigger, 6-position carbine stock with recoil pad, A2 pistol grip, Black finish, intermediate length top rail, flip-up front and rear sights, 7.9 lbs. New 2014.

	100%	98%	95%	90%	80%	70%	60%	
MSR $1,494	$1,350	$1,175	$1,025	$925	$750	$625	$500	

Add $134 for stainless steel barrel in 5.56 NATO or $181 if in 6.8 SPC cal.

MSR	100%	98%	95%	90%	80%	70%	60%	*Last MSR*

TACTICAL OPERATOR RIFLE – 5.56 NATO or 6.8 SPC cal., 16 in. Douglas stainless steel barrel or 17 in. Bergara (5.56 NATO only) chromemoly barrel, threaded muzzle, M4 feed ramps, forged upper and lower receivers, AR trigger, rifle length round forearm with Flat Dark Earth finish, flip-up front and rear sights, 6-position carbine stock with recoil pad, A2 pistol grip, top rail, Gas Buster charging handle w/military latch, 7.9 lbs. New 2014.

MSR $1,504	$1,350	$1,175	$1,025	$925	$750	$625	$500

Add $134 for Douglas stainless steel barrel in 5.56 NATO or $171 if with 6.8 SPC cal.

PREDATOR CUSTOM SHOP

Current custom manufacturer located in Knoxville, TN.

RIFLES: BOLT ACTION

Predator Custom Shop manufactures custom bolt action rifles built to customer specifications. Base rifles start at $2,050. Please contact the company directly for more information including options, pricing, availability, and delivery time (see Trademark Index).

RIFLES: SEMI-AUTO

Predator Custom Shop manufactures custom AR-15 rifles built to customer specifications. Current models include the 5.56 Carnivore, and the 5.56 DMR. Please contact the company directly for more information including options, pricing, availability, and delivery time (see Trademark Index).

PREDATOR TACTICAL LLC

Current manufacturer located in Tempe, AZ.

Predator Tactical LLC was founded by champion competition shooter Matt Burkett.

PISTOLS: SEMI-AUTO

For the following models personalization is available on any part of the build and finishing. You can have your name on the magazines, side of the gun, etc. Each pistol also includes one hour of private training in Arizona by the Predator Team, one complete refinishing, and a range bag.

1911 SHRIKE – 9mm Para., 10mm, .38 Super, or .45 ACP cal., Caspian Arms frame, Briley custom match barrel with spherical bushing, 8 shot mag., stainless steel, high polished silver sides with engraved lettering and logos, checkering on front strap, Extreme Engineering hammer, sear, and disconnector.
    Current MSR on this model is $3,575.

1911 TOTAL CUSTOM – .45 ACP cal., carbon frame and slide, 5 in. barrel with bushing, tactical guide rod, Rosewood, walnut, or VZ OP2 black grips, blued finish.
    Current MSR on this model is $3,250-$5,850, depending on customer specifications.

BANSHEE OPEN GUN – 9mm Para., .38 Super, .38 Super Comp., .40 S&W, or .45 ACP cal., STI tactical or standard frame, Shuemann Hybrid 3 port barrel, PT exclusive compensator, C-More scope, PT sideways mount or Allchin scope mount, Extreme Engineering hammer, sear, and disconnector, Aftec extractor, Dawson magwell, ambi safety, Ed Brown beavertail, blued, hard chrome, or PVD coated finish.
    Current MSR on this model is $4,450-$5,575, depending on customer specifications.

IRON SHRIKE – .45 ACP cal., heat treated carbon steel Caspian Arms frame, checkering on front strap, tactical guide rod, G10 grips, adj. rear sight, front night sight, front and rear serrations, high grip beavertail safety, blued finish.
    Current MSR on this model is $3,450.

NIGHT SHRIKE – .45 ACP cal., 4 in. ultra match barrel, stainless steel slide on top of aluminum short rail frame, high polished silver sides with engraved lettering and logos, stainless steel, checkering on front strap, tactical rail, tactical guide rod, adj. or fixed rear sights, front night sight, front and rear serrations, high grip beavertail, 8 shot mag.
    Current MSR on this model is 3,950.

SCARAB – 9mm Para., 10mm, .38 Super, .38 Super Comp., .40 S&W, or .45 ACP cal., STI frame, Briley or Schuemann match barrel, Extreme Engineering hammer, sear, and disconnector, front and rear serrations, Ed Brown beavertail grip safety.
    Current MSR on this model is $3,625-$5,175, depending on customer specifications.

3 GUN NATION CUSTOM SCARAB – 9x19mm, .38 Super, .38 Super Comp., .40 S&W, or .45 ACP cal., STI frame, bull barrel, stainless billet machined slide, stainless small parts, Extreme Engineering fire control group, Burkett grip, two-tone finish.
    Current MSR on this model is $3,495-$4,130, depending on customer specifications.

WRAITH OPEN GUN – 9mm Para., .38 Super, or .38 Super Comp. cal., STI frame, PT exclusive compensator, C-More scope, PT tactical side or PT Allchin scope mount, Extreme Engineering hammer, sear, and disconnector, Aftec extractor, ambi safety, Ed Brown beavertail, blued, hard chrome, or black nitride finish.
    Current MSR on this model is $4,750-$5,875, depending on customer specifications.

MSR	100%	98%	95%	90%	80%	70%	60%	Last MSR

RIFLES: SEMI-AUTO

Predator Tactical offers customized rifles - base price for the PT-10 Model is $2,750. Please contact the company for more information, including pricing and availability (see Trademark Index).

PRIMARY WEAPONS SYSTEMS

Current manufacturer located in Boise, ID.

Primary Weapons Systems manufactures a series of AR-15 style semi-auto pistols, rifles, and bolt action rifles, as well as SBR models for law enforcement and military.

PISTOLS: SEMI-AUTO

MK107 SERIES – .223 Rem./5.56 NATO (.223 Wylde chamber), 7.62x39mm (disc. 2012) cal., AR-15 style, GPO, 30 shot mag., 7 1/2 in. Isonite QPQ treated, 1:8 twist button rifled barrel. Mil-Spec upper and lower receiver, ALG Defense QMS trigger, enhanced bolt carrier group, PWS KeyMod rail system, BCM Gunfighter charging handle, Magpul MOE furniture and sights.

MSR $1,950	$1,700	$1,500	$1,275	$1,150	$950	$775	$600	

MK109 SERIES – .300 BLK cal., GPO, 9 3/4 in. stainless steel, 30 shot polymer mag., Isonite QPD treated, button rifled barrel, mil-spec upper and lower receiver, quad rail, available in matte black or Flat Dark Earth finish, enhanced charging handle and bolt carrier group, Micro-slicked Internals, Magpul XT rail panels, Magpul MOE grip, MBUS sights, approx. 5 1/5 lbs. Disc. 2012.

	$1,525	$1,300	$1,100	$925	$750	$675	$575	*$1,700*

Add $200 for Flat Dark Earth finish.

MK110 SERIES – .223 Rem. cal. (.223 Wylde chamber), similar to MK107 Series, except has 10 1/2 in. barrel. New 2014.

MSR $1,950	$1,700	$1,500	$1,275	$1,150	$950	$775	$600	

RIFLES: BOLT ACTION

MK3 SERIES – .308 Win. (new 2014) or .300 Win. Mag., 20 (.308 Win. cal. only) or 21 3/4 in. stainless steel barrel, 5 shot mag., Isonite QPQ treated barrel and receiver, Jewell trigger, PRC muzzle device, KRG Whisky-3 folding chassis, AI mag. compatibility, 11 1/2 lbs. New 2012.

MSR $7,000	$6,250	$5,475	$4,700	$4,250	$3,450	$2,825	$2,200	

T3 RIMFIRE SERIES – .22 LR cal., 21 1/2 in. barrel, choice of stock, Summit 10/22 action, 30 shot mag., approx. 4 lbs.

MSR $800	$675	$595	$500	$450	$375	$300	$235	

RIFLES: SEMI-AUTO

MK1 SERIES – .223 Rem./5.56 NATO (.223 Wylde chamber), or .300 BLK cal., GPO, 16 or 18 (new 2014) in. stainless steel, Isonite QPD treated, button rifled barrel, 30 shot polymer mag., mil-spec upper and lower receiver, quad rail, available in matte black, flat dark earth, or Kryptek camo (new 2014) finish, enhanced bolt carrier group, Micro-slicked Internals, Magpul XT rail panels, Magpul MOE grip, MBUS sights, Triad 30 flash suppressor, ALG Defense QMS trigger, PWS KeyMod rail system, BCM GUNFIGHTER charging handle, approx. 7 lbs.

MSR $1,950	$1,695	$1,485	$1,275	$1,150	$925	$775	$600	

Add $50 for Kryptek camo finish.
Add $250 for Ranger proof logo.

This series is also available with 7, 9 1/2, 10 1/2 or 14 1/2 in. barrels for military/law enforcement.

MK2 SERIES – .308 Win. cal., SR-25 platform, GPO, 16.1 or 20 in. Isonite QPD treated button rifled barrel, 30 shot polymer mag., mil-spec upper and lower receiver, quad rail, available in matte black or Flat Dark Earth finish, enhanced bolt carrier group, Micro-slicked Internals, Magpul XT rail panels, Magpul MOE grip, MBUS sights, ALG Defense QMS trigger, PWS KeyMod rail system, BCM Gunfighter charging handle, 8 lbs. 12 oz.

MSR $2,900	$2,575	$2,250	$1,925	$1,750	$1,425	$1,160	$900	

This series is also available with 12 1/2 or 14 1/2 barrels for military/law enforcement.

WOODLAND SPORTING RIFLE – .223 Rem./5.56 NATO (.223 Wylde chamber), or .300 BLK cal., GIO, 16.1 or 18 in. free floating stainless steel, Isonite QPQ treated, button rifled barrel, enhanced charging handle, PWS Mil Spec upper and lower receiver, enhanced DI carrier, black olive (disc.) or walnut stock, 30 shot polymer mag. approx. 7 1/2 - 8 lbs. New 2012.

MSR $1,500	$1,325	$1,160	$1,000	$900	$725	$600	$500	

MSR	100%	98%	95%	90%	80%	70%	60%	*Last MSR*

WRAITH 3GUN COMPETITION RIFLE – .223 Rem./5.56 NATO (.223 Wylde chamber) cal., GIO, 18 in. free floating stainless steel, Isonite QPQ treated, button rifled barrel, enhanced charging handle, PWS mil-spec upper and lower receiver, enhanced DI carrier, black, olive or walnut stock, 30 shot polymer mag., Daniel Defense free float handguard, JP Tactical EZ trigger, 7 lbs., 14 oz. Mfg. 2012.

	$1,800	$1,575	$1,275	$1,025	$900	$775	$675	*$2,000*

PROARMS ARMORY s.r.o

Current manufacturer located in Czech Republic. No U.S. importation.

RIFLES: SEMI-AUTO

PAR MK3 – 5.56 NATO cal., GPO, 5, 10, 20, or 30 shot mag., 16 3/4 or 18 in. Lothar Walther barrel, four-position adj. gas block, aluminum alloy frame and upper receiver, ergonomic beaver tail pistol grip, free float handguard with four fixed rails, telescopic 6-position fixed stock, folding MBUS sights.

Retail pricing is not available for this model.

PROFESSIONAL ORDNANCE, INC.

Previous manufacturer located in Lake Havasu City, AZ 1998-2003. Previously manufactured in Ontario, CA circa 1996-1997. Distributor sales only.

During 2003, Bushmaster bought Professional Ordnance and the Carbon 15 trademark. Please refer to the Bushmaster section for currently manufactured Carbon 15 rifles and pistols (still manufactured in Lake Havasu City).

PISTOLS: SEMI-AUTO

CARBON-15 TYPE 20 – .223 Rem. cal., GIO, Stoner type operating system with recoil reducing buffer assembly, carbon fiber upper and lower receiver, hard chromed bolt carrier, 7 1/4 in. unfluted stainless steel barrel with ghost ring sights, 30 shot mag. (supplies were limited), also accepts AR-15 type mags., 40 oz. Mfg. 1999-2000.

	$950	$800	$725	$650	$575	$525	$475	*$1,500*

CARBON-15 TYPE 21 – .223 Rem cal., GIO, ultra lightweight carbon fiber upper and lower receivers, 7 1/4 in. "Profile" stainless steel barrel, quick detachable muzzle compensator, ghost ring sights, 10 shot mag., also accepts AR-15 type mags., Stoner type operating system, tool steel bolt, extractor and carrier, 40 oz. Mfg. 2001-2003.

	$850	$750	$675	$600	$550	$500	$450	*$899*

CARBON-15 TYPE 97 – .223 Rem. cal., similar to Carbon 15 Type 20, except has fluted barrel and quick detachable compensator, 46 oz. Mfg. 1996-2003.

	$925	$800	$725	$625	$575	$525	$475	*$964*

RIFLES: SEMI-AUTO

CARBON-15 TYPE 20 – .223 Rem. cal., GIO, same operating system as the Carbon-15 pistol, 16 in. unfluted stainless steel barrel, carbon fiber buttstock and forearm, includes mil spec optics mounting base, 3.9 lbs. Mfg. 1998-2000.

	$975	$850	$795	$725	$650	$550	$475	*$1,550*

CARBON-15 TYPE 21 – .223 Rem. cal., GIO, ultra light weight carbon fiber upper and lower receivers, 16 in. "Profile" stainless steel barrel, quick detachable muzzle compensator, Stoner type operating system, tool steel bolt, extractor and carrier, optics mounting base, quick detachable stock, 10 shot mag., also accepts AR-15 type mags., 3.9 lbs. Mfg. 2001-2003.

	$975	$850	$795	$725	$650	$550	$475	*$988*

CARBON-15 TYPE 97/97S – .223 Rem. cal., GIO, ultra lighweight carbon fiber upper and lower receivers, Stoner type operating system, hard chromed tool steel bolt, extractor and carrier, 16 in. fluted stainless steel barrel, quick detachable muzzle compensator, optics mounting base, quick detachable stock, 30 shot mag., also accepts AR-15 type mags., 3.9 lbs. Mfg. 2001-2003.

	$1,075	$900	$825	$750	$675	$600	$550	*$1,120*

Add $165 for Model 97S (includes Picatinny rail and "Scout" extension, double walled heat shield forearm, ambidextrous safety, and multi-point silent carry).

PROOF RESEARCH

Current rifle manufacturer located in Columbia Falls, MT. Consumer sales through FFL dealers.

RIFLES: BOLT ACTION

TERMINUS (MONTE CARLO) – .204 Ruger-.338 Win. cal., H6 hunting action, 16-28 in. Proof carbon fiber wrapped barrel, Monte Carlo lightweight ergonomic stock with raised cheepiece, Jewell or Timney trigger, optics are optional, Cerakote finish is standard, Matte Black, Timber, and other custom finishes also available.

MSR $5,690		$5,125	$4,485	$3,850	$3,485	$2,825	$2,300	$1,795

MSR	100%	98%	95%	90%	80%	70%	60%	Last MSR

SUMMIT – .204 Ruger-.338 Win. Mag. cal., lightweight mountain carry rifle, Proof H6 bolt action, 16-28 in. Proof Research carbon fiber wrapped barrel, Jewell and Timney trigger, Proof summit stock, Cerakote finish is standard, Matte Black, Black Granite, and other custom finishes available.

| MSR $5,540 | $4,950 | $4,325 | $3,715 | $3,365 | $2,725 | $2,225 | $1,750 | |

   * ***Summit YL*** – .204 Ruger-.338 Win. Mag. cal., similar to Summit model, except developed for the female or youth shooter, features 16-26 in. barrel, Summit CFB lightweight stock with slim profile, and Leupold 4.5-14x40 CDX optics.

| MSR $5,700 | $5,125 | $4,485 | $3,850 | $3,485 | $2,825 | $2,300 | $1,800 | |

TAC II – .243 Rem.-.338 Win. cals., AR-15 style, GIO, lightweight, long range rifle, Proof T6 action, 16-28 in. Proof Research carbon fiber wrapped Sendero barrel, Proof Tactical II stock with cheekpiece, vertical grip, and lower profile forearm, Jewell or Timney trigger, optics are optional and customer defined, Cerakote finish is standard, Flat Dark Earth, OD Green, camo, and other finishes available, 8.81 lbs.

| MSR $6,750 | $6,100 | $5,340 | $4,575 | $4,150 | $3,350 | $2,750 | $2,150 | |

Pricing is for base rifle only w/o options.

RIFLES: SEMI-AUTO

MONOLITHIC AR10 – .243 Rem.-.338 RCM cals., GIO, 20 in. carbon fiber wrapped barrel, carbine, mid-rifle, or rifle length available, Mega Machine Monolithic upper receiver, Mega Machine lower receiver, Magpul PRS stock is standard, Geiselle trigger, Premier 3-15x50LT optics, LaRue Tactical LT 104 mount, anodized Type III Black, Cerakote, and custom option finishes available.

| MSR $3,417 | $3,075 | $2,700 | $2,300 | $2,100 | $1,700 | $1,400 | $1,075 | |

MONOLITHIC AR15 – .204 Ruger-6.8 SPC cal., GIO, 16 in. carbon fiber wrapped barrel, available in carbine, mid-length, and rifle length, Mega Machine Monolithic upper and matched lower receiver, Magpul ACS stock standard, Geiselle trigger, optics are optional and customer defined, LaRue Tactical LT 104 mount, anodized Type II Black, OD Green, and other Cerakote custom finishes available.

| MSR $3,113 | $2,800 | $2,450 | $2,100 | $1,900 | $1,550 | $1,275 | $975 | |

SOCOM I – 243 Rem.-.338 Win. cals., AR-15 style, GIO, "tactical hunter" rifle, Proof T6 action, 16-28 in. Proof Research carbon fiber wrapped barrel, Proof Socom I composite stock with adj. cheekpiece and straight grip, Jewell or Timney trigger, optics are optional and customer defined, Cerakote finish is standard, Flat Dark Earth, OD Green, camo, and other finishes available.

| MSR $6,850 | $6,150 | $5,375 | $4,625 | $4,175 | $3,375 | $2,775 | $2,150 | |

TUBE GUN SYSTEM – .204 Ruger-.338 Win. cals., Proof C6 action, GIO, 16-28 in. Proof Research carbon fiber wrapped bull barrel, Eliseo tube chasis RTS stock, optics are optional and customer defined, Cerakote finish is standard, matte black and other custom colors are available.

| MSR $4,695 | $4,250 | $3,725 | $3,200 | $2,900 | $2,350 | $1,925 | $1,500 | |

PUMA

Current trademark of firearms imported by Legacy Sports International LLC, located in Reno, NV. Previously located in Alexandria, VA.

RIFLES: SEMI-AUTO

PPS/22 – .22 LR cal., 16 in. shrouded barrel with open sights, choice of uncheckered wood or black, green, or sand colored synthetic or Wildcat tactical adj. stock, 10 (clip), 30 (clip or drum) or 50 shot drum mag., Wildcat stock includes optional Picatinny rail, pistol grip, and vertical forend grip, mfg. by Pietta. Mfg. 2009-2010.

| | $475 | $425 | $375 | $325 | $295 | $275 | $250 | *$519* |

   Add $40 for 50 shot drum mag or wood stock.

   Add $50 for black, green, or sand colored, or Wildcat synthetic stock.

QUALITY ARMS

Current rifle manufacturer located in Rigby, ID.

RIFLES: BOLT ACTION

THE TAC 21 – .308 Win., 6.5x47 Lapua, or .338 Lapua cal., GIO, built on Rem. receiver, full length accessories mounting rail, Magpul PRS stock, Magpul pistol grip, heavy duty bipod, 5 or 10 shot AICS mag., American Defense 35mm quick detach scope mount and 6-25x56 LRS-1 Millett Tactical rifle scope, includes Condor drag bag.

| MSR $1,895 | $1,700 | $1,500 | $1,275 | $1,150 | $950 | $775 | $600 | |

MSR	100%	98%	95%	90%	80%	70%	60%	Last MSR

RIFLES: SEMI-AUTO

6.5 GRENDEL – 6.5 Grendel cal., GIO, this rifle will be custom built, but basics specs are as follows: 18, 20, or 24 in. match grade free floated stainless barrel, tactical free float rail, front and rear Magpul or ARMS flip-up sights, SST, Magpul ACS 6-position collapsible stock, nickel plated 4 1/2 lb. single stage trigger, hammer, bolt, and carrier, 10 and 26 shot mag., includes black soft tactical case.

MSR $1,795	$1,625	$1,425	$1,225	$1,100	$900	$725	$575

THE BATTLESTORM – 5.56 NATO cal., GIO, 16 in. free floated M4 profile barrel, free float lightweight Spectre length quad rail handguard with ladder rail covers and end cap, low profile gas block, front and rear RTS sights, Primary Arms 1-4x24 optical red dot scope, ergonomic pistol grip, Battle Blades knife and scabbard, winter trigger guard, nickel plated single stage trigger, hammer, bolt and carrier, Battlelink 6-position collapsible stock with storage, 30 shot Magpul mag., includes cleaning kit and black soft tactical case.

MSR $1,595	$1,450	$1,275	$1,100	$975	$800	$650	$525

THE DEVASTATOR – 5.56 NATO cal., GIO, 16 in. M4 profile barrel, free float carbine length quad rail handguard with ladder rail covers and end cap, YHM flip-up front sight gas block, rear flip-up sights, single stage trigger, 6-position collapsible stock, 30 shot Mapgul mag., forged upper and lower receivers, includes cleaning kit and black soft tactical case.

MSR $975	$875	$775	$650	$600	$475	$400	$300

THE DOMINATOR – 5.56 NATO cal., GIO, 18 in. free floated medium profile stainless barrel, low profile gas block, tactical free float rail or YHM custom rail, forged lower receiver, standard M3/M4 forged upper receiver, ergonomic grip, Magpul ACS 6-position collapsible stock, front and rear Magpul or ARMS polymer sights, Primary Arms M3 style red dot scope with cantilever mount, single point sling egg plate, single stage nickel plated trigger, hammer, and bolt carrier, 30 shot Magpul mag., includes black soft tactical case.

MSR $1,395	$1,250	$1,095	$950	$850	$700	$575	$450

THE LIBERATOR – 5.56 NATO cal., GIO, 16 in. free floated M4 profile barrel, free float lightweight Spectre length quad rail handguard with ladder rail covers and end cap, low profile gas block, front and rear Magpul or ARMS flip-up polymer sights, forged mil spec upper and lower receivers, Primary Arms red dot with cantilever mount, ergonomic pistol grip, upgraded 6-position collapsible stock, 30 shot Magpul mag., nickel plated single stage trigger, hammer, bolt, and carrier, includes black soft tactical case.

MSR $1,295	$1,150	$1,000	$875	$775	$650	$525	$400

THE LRAR DOMINATOR – 5.56 NATO cal., GIO, 18 in. match grade free floated stainless barrel, tactical free float rail, front and rear Magpul or ARMS flip-up sight, Primary Arms M3 red dot with cantilever mount, Magpul ACS 6-position collapsible stock, nickel plated single stage trigger, hammer, bolt, and carrier, 30 shot Magpul mag., ambidextrous upper receiver with fully automatic upward opening ejection port doors, includes black soft tactical case.

MSR $1,495	$1,350	$1,175	$1,025	$925	$750	$625	$475

THE M4 CARBINE – 5.56 NATO cal., GIO, 16 in. M4 barrel, forged lower receiver, A3/A4 forged flat-top upper, rear flip-up sight, forged front sight, A2 grip, M4 6-position collapsible stock, SST, 30 shot Magpul mag.

MSR $750	$675	$600	$500	$450	$375	$300	$225

QUALITY PARTS CO./BUSHMASTER

Quality Parts Co. was a division of Bushmaster Firearms, Inc. located in Windham, ME that manufactured AR-15 type rifles and various components and accessories for Bushmaster. Please refer to the Bushmaster listing in the B section for current model listings and values.

R SECTION

R GUNS

Current manufacturer, importer, and dealer located in Carpentersville, IL.

R Guns offers a line of AR-15 style rifles and carbines in various configurations, upper and lower receivers, accessories, and related components. Please contact the company directly for more information on its various models, availability, and pricing (see Trademark Index).

RAAC

Current importer located in Scottsburg, IN.

MSR	100%	98%	95%	90%	80%	70%	60%	Last MSR

RIFLES AND SHOTGUNS

Russian American Armory Company is an import company for Molot, located in Russia. Current product/model lines include Vepr. rifles, in addition to a line of bolt action rifles, including the LOS/BAR Series, CM-2 Target rifle, Korshun, and Sobol hunting model. Please check individual heading listings for current information, including U.S. availability and pricing. Please contact the company directly for current offerings (see Trademark Index).

MKA 1919 – 12 ga., 3 in. chamber, AR-15 style, self-adjusting GIO, 18 1/2 in. barrel with three choke tubes, 5 shot box mag., A2 configuration with carry handle and front sight, Picatinny rail, bolt hold open after last round, choice of matte black or 100% camo coverage. Mfg. by Ücyildyz Arms Ind. Co. Ltd. located in Turkey.

MSR $700	$650	$575	$525	$475	$435	$400	$375

Add $100 for 100% camo coverage.
Add $500 for flat-top receiver and adj. stock.

R.I.P. TACTICAL

Current AR-15 manufacturer located in Utah.

RIFLES: SEMI-AUTO

R.I.P. Tactical builds custom AR-15 rifles to individual customer specifications. Current models include: RIP-BM (base model), RIP-NT (nickel teflon coated), RIP-DC (camo), RIP-BA (black anodized), RIP-OD (ceramic coated dark green), and the RIP-SBR (short barreled rifle). Base MSR starts at $1,495. Several options are available for each model. Please contact the company directly for options, delivery time, and an individualized price quotation (see Trademark Index).

RND MANUFACTURING

Current manufacturer established in 1978, and located in Longmont, CO. Previously distributed by Mesa Sportsmen's Association, L.L.C. located in Delta, CO. Dealer or consumer direct sales.

PISTOLS: SEMI-AUTO

RND PISTOL – 5.56 NATO cal., AR-15 style, GIO, round shrouded handguard, 7 1/2 in. barrel with muzzle brake, pistol grip, full length vent. Picatinny rail, titanium firing pin, 9 1/2 lbs. New 2010.

MSR $2,000	$1,800	$1,600	$1,350	$1,100	$900	$750	$650

RIFLES: SEMI-AUTO

RND EDGE SERIES – .223 Rem. (RND 400), .300 WSM (RND 1000, new 2003), .300 Ultra (RND 2100, new 2003), .308 Win. (RND 800, new 2010), .338 Lapua Mag. (RND 2000, new 1999), .375 Super Mag. (RND 2600), .408 Cheytac (RND 2500) or 7.62x39mm (disc.) cal., patterned after the AR-15 style, CNC machined, GIO, 18, 20, 24, or 26 in. barrel, choice of synthetic (Grade I), built to individual custom order, handmade laminated thumbhole (Grade II, disc. 1998), or custom laminated thumbhole stock with fluted barrel (Grade III, disc. 1998), vented aluminum shroud, many options and accessories available, approx. 11 1/2-16 lbs., custom order only, values represent base model. New 1996.

Add $355 for Grade II (disc. 1998) or $605 for Grade III (disc.).

* **RND 400** – .223 Rem. cal., GIO, AR-15 style, 18-26 in. barrel, CNC machined upper and lower receivers, integral picatinny rail, titanium firing pin, free floating handguard, synthetic A2 style stock, hard black anodized with grey or black finish, 9.5 lbs.

MSR $2,295	$2,000	$1,750	$1,300	$1,050	$850	$750	$650

* **RND 800** – .308 Win./7.62 NATO cal., GPO, AR-15 style, 20-26 in. super match free floating barrel, CNC machined matched upper and lower receivers, left side non-reciprocating charging handle, hard black anodized with black or gray gun coat, integral Picatinny rail, titanium firing pin, modular handguard, adj. stock, 11 lbs. New 2010.

MSR $3,795	$3,400	$2,975	$2,550	$2,310	$1,875	$1,525	$1,200

MSR	100%	98%	95%	90%	80%	70%	60%	Last MSR

* **RND 1000** – .300 Win. Mag. cal., GPO, 20-26 in. Super match free floating barrel, CNC machined matched upper and lower receivers, left sided non-reciprocating charging handle, integral Picatinny rail, RND integrated buffer system, modular handguard, fully adj. stock, single feed double stack mag., hard black anodized with black or gray gun coat finish, 11 lbs. New 2003.

| MSR $2,295 | $2,000 | $1,750 | $1,300 | $1,050 | $850 | $750 | $650 | |

* **RND 2000** – .338 Lapua Mag. cal., GPO, AR-15 style, 20-26 in. Super match free floating barrel, CNC machined matched upper and lower receivers, left sided non-reciprocating charging handle, integral Picatinny rail, single feed double stack mag., RND integrated buffer system, modular handguard, fully adj. stock, hard black anodized with black or gray gun coat finish, 14 lbs. New 1999.

| MSR $4,795 | $4,325 | $3,785 | $3,250 | $2,950 | $2,375 | $1,950 | $1,525 | |

» **RND 2100** – .300 Rem. Ultra Mag. cal., otherwise similar to RND 2000. New 2003.

| MSR $4,795 | $4,325 | $3,785 | $3,250 | $2,950 | $2,375 | $1,950 | $1,525 | |

» **RND 2500** – .408 CheyTac cal., GPO, similar to RND 2000, except features 26 in. Super match free floating barrel, 18 lbs. New 2004.

| MSR $10,500 | $9,450 | $8,275 | $7,100 | $6,425 | $5,200 | $4,250 | $3,325 | |

» **RND 2600** – .375 Cheytac cal., GPO, 20-26 in. Super match free floating barrel, CNC machined matched upper and lower receivers, left sided non-reciprocating charging handle, integral Picatinny rail, single feed double stack mag., RND integrated buffer system, modular handguard, fully adj. stock, hard black anodized with black or gray gun coat finish, 18 lbs.

| MSR $10,500 | $9,450 | $8,275 | $7,100 | $6,425 | $5,200 | $4,250 | $3,325 | |

* **RND 3000** – .50 BMG cal., GPO, 26 in. Super match barrel with muzzle brake, full length integrated Picatinny rail, fully adj. stock, double stack mag., includes optics and scope, black or various camo colors, includes bipod, 28 lbs.

| MSR $11,500 | $10,350 | $9,250 | $8,250 | $7,500 | $6,750 | $6,000 | $5,250 | |

» **RND 3100** – .416 Rem. Mag. cal., otherwise similar to RND 3000. Mfg. 2012 only.

| | $10,350 | $9,250 | $8,250 | $7,500 | $6,750 | $6,000 | $5,250 | $11,500 |

RPB INDUSTRIES

Previous company located in Avondale, GA. RPB Industries' guns were made by Masterpiece Arms.

CARBINES: SEMI-AUTO

RPB CARBINE – .45 ACP cal., closed bolt blowback action, 16 1/4 in. barrel, fixed skeletonized stock and forearm pistol grip, accepts M-3 military submachine gun mags., black finish, 9 1/2 lbs. Mfg. 2000-2004.

| | $450 | $375 | $325 | $285 | $260 | $235 | $210 | |

Add $75 for Deluxe Model with EZ cocker and installed scope mount.

RADOM

Current trademark manufactured by Fabryka Broni, Lucznik - Radom Sp. z o.o., located in Radom, Poland. Currently imported on a limited basis by I.O., Inc., located in Monroe, NC. Previously manufactured 1925-1945 by the Polish Arsenal located in Radom, Poland & Steyr, Austria. Post WWII also manufactured by Z.M. Lucznik (Radom Factory) in Radom, Poland. Recent importation was by Dalvar of U.S.A., located in Seligman, AZ. Previously located in Richardson, TX and Henderson, NV.

RIFLES: SEMI-AUTO

Fabryka Broni Lucznik currently manufactures a variety of semi-auto rifles and carbines designed after the Model 96 Beryl rifle. Please contact the importer directly for U.S. availability and pricing (see Trademark Index).

RAMO DEFENSE SYSTEMS

Previous rifle manufacturer 1999-2003 and located in Nashville, TN.

RIFLES: BOLT ACTION

TACTICAL .308 – .308 Win. cal., Rem. M-700 long action, match grade stainless steel barrel, skeletonized black synthetic stock with cheekpad, matte black metal finish, 4 shot mag., 16 lbs. Mfg. 1999-2003.

| | $2,495 | $2,100 | $1,850 | $1,600 | $1,400 | $1,200 | $995 | $2,495 |

M91/M91A2 – .308 Win. or .300 Win. Mag. cal., Rem. M-700 long action, black Kevlar and fiberglass stock, matte black metal finish, 4 shot mag., 14 lbs. Mfg. 1999-2003.

| | $2,695 | $2,250 | $1,950 | $1,675 | $1,475 | $1,250 | $995 | $2,695 |

Add $200 for .300 Win. Mag. cal.

MSR	100%	98%	95%	90%	80%	70%	60%	Last MSR

M600 SINGLE SHOT – .50 BMG cal., single shot, twin tube skeletonized stock with pistol grip and cheekpiece, 32 in. barrel with fins at breech and muzzle brake, 23 lbs. Mfg. 1999-2003.

	$4,195	$3,700	$3,200	$2,750	$2,250	$1,950	$1,675	$4,195

M650 REPEATER – .50 BMG cal., repeater action with 6 shot detachable rotary mag., stock and barrel (30 in.) similar to M600, approx. 30 lbs. Mfg. 1999-2003.

	$6,395	$5,750	$5,150	$4,500	$3,750	$3,000	$2,250	$6,395

RANGEMASTER PRECISION ARMS (RPA INTERNATIONAL LTD.)

Current rifle manufacturer located in Kent, England. No current U.S. importation.

Company name changed in mid-2013 from RPA International Ltd. to Rangemaster Precision Arms.

RIFLES

Rangemaster Precision Arms manufactures high quality bolt action rifles, including a tactical long range sniper model, the Rangemaster RM 7.62 Stubby (£4,175 MSR), Rangemaster RM 7.62 (£4,175 MSR), Rangemaster 338 (£4,430 MSR), and the Rangemaster 50 (£5,306 MSR). The Rangemaster Series includes a folding stock, stainless steel barrel and muzzle brake, Picatinny rails and tactical bipod. The Interceptor is available in a single shot (£2,533 MSR) and a Repeater (£2,813 MSR) version. The Hunter rifle comes with or w/o a thumbhole stock (£2,723 base MSR), Highland Stalker (£2,758 MSR), Woodland Stalker (£2,723 MSR). The Target Rifle Series includes the Elite Single Shot (£2,550 MSR), and the Ranger (£2,398 MSR). The G2 Series is a high performance tactical rifle in 7.62x51mm caliber with a 26 in. (G2 7.62) or 16 in. (G2 7.62 STBY) steel fluted barrel, muzzle brake and integral Picatinny rail. Both models are £4,740 MSR. In late 2013, RPA introduced the Ultra tactical rifle (POR). All pricing does not include VAT. Additionally, the company makes custom rifles and actions. Please contact the company directly for complete pricing, U.S. availability and options (see Trademark Index).

RASHEED (RASHID)

Previous Egyptian military rifle mfg. circa mid-1960s.

RIFLES: SEMI-AUTO

RASHEED – 7.62x39mm cal., gas operated mechanism with tilting bolt, 20 1/2 in. barrel with folding bayonet, bolt cocking is by separate bolt handle installed on right side of receiver, detachable 10 shot mag., open type sights, hardwood stock with vent. forend, approx. 8,000 mfg. circa mid-1960s.

	$795	$700	$600	$500	$400	$300	$250	

RED ROCK ARMS

Current manufacturer established April 2003 and located in Mesa, AZ. During late 2006, the company name was changed from Bobcat Weapons, Inc. to Red Rock Arms.

PISTOLS: SEMI-AUTO

BWA5 FSA – 9mm Para. cal., H&K tactical design, roller locked delayed blowback action, 8.9 in. stainless steel barrel, black Duracoat finished stock, pistol grip, and forearm, 10, 30, or 40 shot mag., approx. 5.3 lbs. Mfg. 2007-2008.

	$1,525	$1,350	$1,125	$900	$775	$650	$550	$1,700

RIFLES: SEMI-AUTO

ATR-1 CARBINE – .223 Rem. cal., H&K tactical design, 16 1/4 in. barrel, adj. front and rear sight, black furniture, 30 shot AR-15 style mag., available with or w/o flash suppressor, 8 lbs. New 2007.

MSR $1,400	$1,250	$1,075	$925	$825	$750	$650	$575	

BW5 FSA – 9mm Para. cal., H&K tactical design, stamped steel lower receiver, roller locked delayed blowback action, 16 1/2 in. stainless steel barrel (3-lug barrel and 9 in. fake suppressor), black Duracoat finished stock, pistol grip, and forearm, 10, 30, or 40 shot mag., approx. 6.7 lbs. Mfg. 2006-2008.

	$1,525	$1,350	$1,125	$900	$775	$650	$550	$1,700

RED X ARMS

Current semi-auto rifle manufacturer located in central MN.

CARBINES: SEMI-AUTO

X-TREME 16 TACTICAL SS – 5.56 NATO cal., GIO, 16 in. button rifled stainless steel heavy H-Bar contour barrel, A2 birdcage muzzle brake, A3 aluminum flat-top upper and lower receiver, forward assist, dust cover, black hardcoat anodized finish, six position adj. M4 stock with sling hook, chrome lined bolt carrier and staked gas key, chrome plated firing pin, aluminum charging handle, 30 shot Magpul mag., two-piece quad rail aluminum handguard, carbine length gas tube, optional sights and bipod.

MSR $725	$650	$575	$525	$475	$450	$425	$395	

MSR	100%	98%	95%	90%	80%	70%	60%	Last MSR

GARY REEDER CUSTOM GUNS

Current custom manufacturer located in Flagstaff, AZ. Consumer direct sales.

HANDGUNS

For over 30 years, Gary Reeder has specialized in customizing revolvers from various manufacturers, and is now building several series of custom revolvers on his own frames, in addition to customizing customer supplied handguns. Gary's son Kase also manufactures several series of Model 1911 style pistols built to customers specifications in .45 ACP and 10mm. Reeder currently produces well over 60 different series of custom hunting handguns, cowboy guns, custom 1911s, and large caliber hunting rifles. For more information on his extensive range of custom guns, please contact the factory directly (see Trademark Index).

REGENT

Current trademark of semi-auto pistols manufactured by Trabzon Gun Industry Corp., located in Turkey, and imported by Umarex USA, Inc.

PISTOLS: SEMI-AUTO

R350CR – .45 ACP cal., 4 in. barrel, 7 shot mag., lower Picatinny rail, bobbed hammer and skeletonized trigger, checkered front grip strap, double diamond checkered Hogue synthetic grips, 35 oz. New 2012.

MSR $499	$425	$375	$350	$325	$300	$275	$250	

REMINGTON ARMS COMPANY, INC.

Current manufacturer and trademark established in 1816, with factories currently located in Ilion, NY, Lonoke, AR, and Mayfield, KY.

Founded by Eliphalet Remington II and originally located in Litchfield, Herkimer County, NY circa 1816-1828. Remington established a factory in Ilion, NY next to the Erie Canal in 1828, and together with his sons Philo, Samuel, and Eliphalet III pioneered many improvements in firearms manufacture. Corporate offices were moved to Madison, NC in 1996. DuPont owned a controlling interest in Remington from 1933-1993, when the company was sold to Clayton, Dubilier & Rice, a New York City based finance company. The Mayfield, KY plant opened in 1997. On May 31st, 2007, a controlling interest in the company was sold to Cerberus Capital. Currently, Remington employs 2,500 workers in the U.S., including 1,000 in its Ilion, NY plant alone. Recently, Remington has acquired Harrington & Richardson Firearms (H & R), and Marlin Firearms. The company has moved manufacturing to their Remington plant in Ilion, New York. Remington management has every intention of keeping all three product identities separate.

During 2013, Remington made significant improvements, including the expansion of its ammunition facility, growth of its firearms manufacturing capacity, secured some competitive military and law enforcement contracts, and introduced a series of new products including the Ultimate Defense Handgun Ammunition and Model 783 bolt action rifle.

In February of 2014, Remington announced a major expansion with new manufacturing to occur at the old Chrylser building in Huntsville, AL. The company has indicated that more than 2,000 new jobs will be created in the next 10 years.

For recent information on long guns imported by Spartan Gun Works, a Remington subsidiary, please refer to the Spartan Gun Works listing in the S section.

PISTOLS: SEMI-AUTO, POST-WWII PRODUCTION

MODEL 1911 R1 ENHANCED – 9mm Para. (new 2014) or .45 ACP cal., SA, steel construction with blued finish, 5 in. barrel, front and rear slide serrations, skeletonized trigger, bobbed hammer, checkered black laminate grips, 8 shot mag., low profile rear sight and fiber optic front sight, 40 oz. New 2013.

MSR $940	$825	$725	$625	$550	$500	$450	$400	

Add $200 for Crimson Trace laser sight (.45 ACP cal. only), new 2014.

* ***Model 1911 R1 Enhanced Stainless*** – .45 ACP cal., 5 in. barrel, all stainless steel construction, features front and rear slide serrations, skeletonized trigger, bobbed hammer, checkered black laminate grips, 8 shot mag., low profile rear sight and fiber optic front sight, 40 oz. New 2013.

MSR $1,140	$975	$850	$725	$625	$550	$500	$450	

* ***Model 1911 R1 Enhanced Threaded Barrel*** – .45 ACP cal., features 5 3/4 in. threaded stainless steel barrel, all steel construction with blue finish, 8 shot mag., twin slide serrations, checkered black laminate grips, skeletonized trigger, bobbed hammer, 40 oz. New 2013.

MSR $1,140	$975	$850	$725	$625	$550	$500	$450	

MODEL 1911 R1 CARRY – .45 ACP cal., 5 in. stainless steel match grade barrel and bushing, SA, steel construction with satin black oxide finish, beavertail grip safety, skeletonized aluminum trigger, bobbed hammer, ambidextrous safety, Novak low profile sights with Tritium front sight, partially checkered Cocobolo grips, supplied with one 7 shot and one 8 shot mag., 38 1/2 oz. New 2013.

MSR $1,299	$1,100	$995	$875	$775	$675	$575	$475	

MSR	100%	98%	95%	90%	80%	70%	60%	Last MSR

RIFLES: SEMI-AUTO - CENTERFIRE

The models have been listed in numerical sequence for quick reference.

Remington also manufactures models R4, R5, R10, R11, and ACR for military and law enforcement only. These models are not covered in this text.

* **Model 7400 SP (Special Purpose)** – .270 Win. or .30-06 cal., similar to Model 7400, except has non-reflective matte finish on both wood and metalwork. Mfg. 1993-94.

	100%	98%	95%	90%	80%	70%	60%	Last MSR
	$435	$370	$300	$255	$230	$210	$185	$524

* **Model 7400 Weathermaster** – .270 Win. or .30-06 cal., features matte nickel plated receiver, barrel, and magazine, black synthetic stock and forearm, 22 in. barrel with open sights, 7 1/2 lbs. Mfg. 2003-2004.

	$495	$400	$315	$255	$230	$210	$185	$624

* **Model 7400 Synthetic** – same cals. as Model 7400, features black fiberglass reinforced synthetic stock and forend, matte black metal finish, 22 in. barrel only. Mfg. 1998-2006.

	$465	$385	$330	$285	$265	$240	$220	$589

»**Model 7400 Synthetic Carbine** – .30-06 cal., similar to Model 7400 Synthetic, except has 18 1/2 in. barrel. 7 1/4 lbs. Mfg. 1998-2006.

	$465	$385	$330	$285	$265	$240	$220	$589

MODEL R-15 HUNTER – .30 Rem. AR cal., GIO, 22 in. fluted barrel, receiver length Picatinny rail, ergonomic pistol grip, 4 shot detachable mag., 100% Realtree AP HD camo coverage, approx. 7 3/4 lbs. New 2009.

MSR $1,327	$1,150	$1,000	$900	$775	$700	$625	$550	

MODEL R-15 VTR (VARMINT TARGET RIFLE) PREDATOR – .204 Ruger (disc. 2009) or .223 Rem. cal., GIO, 18 (carbine, .204 Ruger disc. 2009) or 22 in. free floating chromemoly fluted barrel, fixed or telestock (Carbine CS) with pistol grip, 5 shot fixed (new 2012, .223 Rem. cal. only) or detachable mag. (compatible with AR-15 style mags.), R-15 marked on magwell, single stage trigger, flat-top receiver with Picatinny rail, no sights, round vent. forearm, 100% Advantage Max-1 HD camo coverage except for barrel, includes lockable hard case, mfg. by Bushmaster in Windham, ME 2008-2011, and in Ilion, NY beginning 2011, 6 3/4 - 7 3/4 lbs. Mfg. 2008-2013.

	$1,150	$1,000	$900	$775	$700	$625	$550	$1,327

* **Model R-15 VTR Stainless** – .223 Rem. cal., similar to Predator, except has 24 in. stainless triangular barrel, OD Green (disc.) or Advantage Max-1 HD camo, fixed stock, pistol grip, and tubed forearm, 7 3/4 lbs. New 2009.

MSR $1,529	$1,530	$1,350	$1,150	$1,050	$850	$700	$550	

* **Model R-15 VTR Thumbhole** – .223 Rem. cal., similar to VTR Stainless, except has 24 in. fluted barrel, OD Green camo thumbhole stock. Mfg. 2009-2010.

	$1,275	$1,125	$1,000	$900	$800	$700	$625	$1,470

* **Model R-15 VTR Byron South Signature Edition** – .223 Rem. cal., GIO, 18 in. barrel, Advantage Max-1 HD camo pistol grip stock. Mfg. mid-2008-2011.

	$1,625	$1,400	$1,225	$1,050	$900	$800	$700	$1,845

* **Model R-15 VTR Predator Carbine** – .223 Rem. cal., GIO, 18 (disc. 2013) or 22 in. free floating button rifled fluted barrel with recessed hunting crown, 5 shot mag., single stage trigger, receiver length Picatinny rail, ergonomic pistol grip, fixed or collapsible (CS, disc. 2013) synthetic stock, Advantage Max-1 HD camo coverage on stock, receiver, and forearm furniture, 6 3/4-7 3/4 lbs.

MSR $1,327	$1,150	$1,000	$900	$775	$700	$625	$550	

MODEL R-25 – .243 Win., 7mm-08 Rem., or .308 Win. cal., GIO, 20 in. free floating fluted chromemoly barrel, single-stage trigger, ergonomic pistol grip fixed stock with 100% Mossy Oak Treestand camo coverage, front and rear sling swivels, 4 shot fixed (.308 Win. cal. only, new 2012) or detachable mag., R-25 marked on magwell, includes hard case, 7 3/4 lbs. New 2009.

MSR $1,697	$1,495	$1,225	$1,075	$950	$850	$750	$650	

RIFLES: SLIDE ACTION, CENTERFIRE

* **Model 7600P Patrol Rifle** – .308 Win. cal., 16 1/2 in. barrel, synthetic stock, parkerized finish, Wilson Combat ghost ring sights, designed for police/law enforcement only.

Remington does not publish consumer retail pricing for this police/law enforcement model. Secondary prices for this model will be slightly higher than for current pricing on the Model 7600 Synthetic.

* **Model 7600 Synthetic** – same cals. as Model 7600, features black fiberglass reinforced synthetic stock and forend, matte black metal finish, 22 in. barrel only, SuperCell recoil pad became standard 2011, 7 1/2 lbs. New 1998.

MSR $772	$610	$475	$385	$315	$265	$240	$225	

During 2007, Grice offered 500 Model 7600 QWAC (Quick Woods Action Carbine) in .308 Win. cal. with 18 1/2 in. barrels, Realtree AP camo synthetic stocks and fiber optic front and rear sights.

MSR	100%	98%	95%	90%	80%	70%	60%	Last MSR

»Model 7600 Synthetic Carbine – .30-06 cal., similar to Model 7600 Synthetic, except has 18 1/2 in. barrel, SuperCell recoil pad became standard in 2011, 7 1/4 lbs. New 1998.

| MSR $772 | $610 | $475 | $385 | $315 | $265 | $240 | $225 | |

MODEL 7615 – .223 Rem., 10 shot AR-15 compatible detachable box mag., accepts AR-15 and M16 style magazines, 16 1/2 (tactical model with pistol grip and non-collapsible tube stock and Knoxx Special Ops NRS recoil suppressor), 18 1/2 (ranch rifle, walnut stock and forearm), or 22 (camo hunter, 100% Mossy Oak Brush camo coverage) in. barrel w/o sights, synthetic or walnut (ranch carbine) stock and forearm, drilled and tapped, approx. 7 lbs. Mfg. 2007-2008, mfg. in Ilion, NY.

| | $790 | $685 | $575 | $500 | $450 | $400 | $350 | *$955* |

Add $54 for Camo Hunter with 100% camo coverage.

MODEL 7615P PATROL RIFLE – .223 Rem. cal., 16 1/2 in. barrel, 10 shot or extended mag., synthetic stock, parkerized finish, accepts AR-15 and M16 style magazines, Wilson Combat ghost ring sights, designed for police/law enforcement, 7 lbs.

Remington does not publish consumer retail pricing for this police/law enforcement model. Secondary prices for this model will be slightly higher than for current pricing on the Model 7600 Carbine.

MODEL 7615 SPS – .223 Rem. cal., 16 1/2 in. blue barrel, Picatinny rail, action, slide release and safety based on the Model 870, 10 shot mag, accepts AR-15 and M16 style mags., black pistol grip synthetic stock. Mfg. 2008.

| | $695 | $625 | $550 | $500 | $450 | $400 | $350 | *$805* |

This model was available through Remington Premier dealers only.

RIFLES: RIMFIRE, SEMI-AUTO

Please note: Model 597 rifles in .17 HMR caliber have been recalled by Remington - please visit Remington's website for more information: www.remington.com, or call 1-800-243-9700, #3.

* Model 597 AAC-SD – .22 LR cal., black synthetic stock, 16 1/2 in. threaded barrel with thread protector, includes scope rail, 10 shot mag., no sights, 5 1/2 lbs. New 2011.

| MSR $257 | $200 | $160 | $130 | $110 | $100 | $85 | $75 | |

MODEL 597 VTR (VARMINT TARGET RIFLE) – .22 LR or .22 WMR cal., 16 in. heavy barrel, 10 or 30 shot mag., Picatinny top rail, fixed A2 or Pardus collapsible stock with pistol grip, with (collapsible stock only) or w/o free-floating Quad rail, choice of matte black or A-TACS digital camo finish, nickel Teflon plating, 5 1/2 lbs. Mfg. 2010-2011.

| | $415 | $375 | $330 | $300 | $275 | $250 | $225 | *$465* |

Add $26 for .22 WMR cal. (fixed A-2 stock only).
Add $153 for A-TACS overmolded stock or free-floating Quad Rail system.

* Model 597 Heavy Barrel – .22 LR cal., features 16 1/2 in. heavy barrel w/o sights, scope rail installed, OD Green or A-TACS digital camo (disc. 2013) synthetic stock, 5 3/4 lbs. New 2012.

| MSR $254 | $200 | $160 | $130 | $110 | $100 | $85 | $75 | |

Add $100 for A-TACS Digital camo stock (last MSR was $349, disc. 2013).

RIFLES: BOLT ACTION, MODEL 700 & VARIATIONS

Remington also currently manufactures Models M24, M24A2, M24A3, R700, XM2010, and MSR for military and law enforcement only. These models are not covered in this text.

MODEL 700P & VARIATIONS – various cals., long or short action, various barrel lengths, designed for police/law enforcement and military, current configurations include: 700P, 700P TWS (Tactical Weapons System, includes scope, bipod and case), 700P LTR (Light Tactical Rifle), 700P LTR TWS (Light Tactical Rifle/Tactical Weapons System, includes scope, bipod, and case), 700P USR (Urban Sniper Rifle), Model M24/M24A2/M24A3 Sniper Weapon System (combination of Model 700 and Model 40-XB design, with scope, case, and bipod), and from the Remington Custom Shop Model 40-XS Tactical Rifle System, Model 40-XB Tactical, and the Model 40-XS 338 Tactical.

Remington does not publish consumer retail pricing for these police/law enforcement models. Secondary prices for base models w/o scopes and other options will be slightly higher than for current pricing on the Model 700BDL Custom Deluxe. Prices for rifles with scopes and other features will be determined by how much the individual options and accessories add to the base value.

MODEL 700 SPS (SPECIAL PURPOSE SYNTHETIC) – various cals., 20 (Youth Model), 24 or 26 in. barrel, standard or Youth synthetic stock with SuperCell (became standard 2010, except on Youth Model) or R3 (disc. 2009) recoil pad, X-Mark Pro adj. trigger standard, except on Youth model, approx. 7 3/8 lbs. New 2005, mfg. in Ilion, NY.

| MSR $731 | $575 | $475 | $415 | $350 | $310 | $270 | $230 | |

Subtract $7 for .260 Rem. cal. (new 2014).

This model is available in a Youth variation in cals. .243 Win., .270 Win. (disc.), 7mm-08 Rem., .30-06 (disc.) or .308 Win. (disc.) at no extra charge.

MSR	100%	98%	95%	90%	80%	70%	60%	*Last MSR*

This model is also available in left-hand action at no extra charge - calibers are .270 Win., .30-06, .300 Win. Mag., or 7mm Rem. Mag. (new 2009).

MODEL 700 SPS TACTICAL – .223 Rem. or .308 Win. cal., 20 in. heavy contour barrel, black oxide finish, black synthetic overmolded Hogue stock, X-Mark Pro adj. trigger, matte black finish, 7 1/2 lbs. Mfg. 2008, reintroduced 2010.

MSR $788	$625	$515	$450	$385	$335	$295	$250	

This model was available through Remington Premier dealers only in 2008.

* ***Model 700 SPS Tactical AAC-SD*** – .300 Blackout (new 2013) or .308 Win. cal., features 16 1/2 (new 2013) or 20 in. heavy barrel with threaded muzzle, Hogue overmold Ghillie Green Pillar bedded stock, X-Mark Pro adj. trigger. New 2011.

MSR $842	$675	$575	$475	$400	$365	$335	$300

* ***MODEL 700 SPS Tactical Blackhawk*** – .223 Rem. or .308 Win. cal., 20 in. triangular contoured barrel, Bell & Carlson Metalist adj. stock, pistol grip cap, steel floorplate and trigger guard, X-Mark Pro trigger, synthetic stock, tactical bolt handle, 8 1/2 lbs. Mfg. 2012 only.

	$695	$625	$560	$520	$485	$435	$395	*$850*

* ***Model 700 SPS Tactical Laser Engraved*** – .223 Rem. or .308 Win. cal., 16 1/2 in. barrel with threaded muzzle, laser engraved "Tactical" on barrel, carbon receiver and barrel with matte finish, Hogue Ghillie Green synthetic stock, X-Mark Pro externally adj. trigger, 7 1/2 lbs. New 2013.

MSR $842	$675	$575	$475	$400	$365	$335	$300

MODEL 700 TACTICAL – 6.8mm SPC cal., 20 in. parkerized barrel, synthetic stock, approx. 9 lbs. Limited availability 2005-2006.

	$800	$650	$550	$450	$400	$300	$275	*$990*

MODEL 700 TACTICAL TARGET – .308 Win. cal., 26 in. triangular contour barrel with 5-R tactical rifling, 4 shot mag., steel trigger guard and floorplate, X-Mark Pro adj. trigger, Bell & Carlson Medalist adj. stock, tactical bolt handle, OD Green finish, 11 3/4 lbs. New 2009.

MSR $2,138	$1,860	$1,600	$1,375	$1,150	$950	$825	$700

MODEL 700 XCR TACTICAL – .223 Rem., .308 Win. or .300 Win. Mag. cal., 3-5 shot mag., features 26 in. fluted stainless steel receiver/barrel with black TriNyte PVD coating, tactical Bell & Carlson OD Green with Black web stock with full length aluminum bedding, X-Mark Pro adj. trigger, 9 1/8 lbs. New 2007.

MSR $1,525	$1,260	$1,050	$925	$825	$725	$625	$500

* ***Model 700 XCR Tactical .338 Lapua*** – .338 Lapua cal., similar to Model 700 XCR Tactical, except has 5 round detachable mag. box, steel trigger guard, and AAC muzzle brake. New 2011.

MSR $2,493	$2,085	$1,825	$1,575	$1,325	$1,100	$925	$775

* ***Model 700 XCR Tactical Compact*** – .223 Rem. or .308 Win. cal., similar to Model 700 XCR, except has 20 in. fluted varmint contour barrel, compact dimensions, 7 1/2 lbs. New 2008.

MSR $1,525	$1,260	$1,050	$925	$825	$725	$625	$500

RIFLES: BOLT ACTION, MODEL 40X & VARIATIONS

MODEL 40-XB TACTICAL – .308 Win. cal., repeater action with adj. 40-X trigger, aluminum bedding block, 27 1/4 in. button rifled fluted stainless barrel, Teflon coated metal, matte black H-S Precision synthetic tactical stock with vertical pistol grip, 10 1/4 lbs. New 2004.

MSR $2,992	$2,550	$2,200	$1,800	$1,450	$1,200	$925	$800

MODEL 40-XB TDR/TIR (TARGET DEPLOYMENT/INTERDICTION RIFLE) – .308 Win. cal., super match stainless steel hand lapped barrel, BCS 1000 (TDR) or H-S PST25 tactical/vertical pistol grip stock (TIR), custom tuned match trigger, one-piece heavy duty steel trigger guard, heavy stainless recoil lug, integral mounting system with #8 screws, Picatinny rail, double pinned bolt handle, muzzle brake, MOA accuracy guaranteed to 600 yards, includes hard carrying case, mfg. by Custom Shop.

These models are POR.

MODEL 40-XS TACTICAL – .308 Win. or .338 Lapua cal., stainless steel action and barrel, adj. trigger, non-reflective black polymer coating, titanium bedded McMillan A5 adj. stock, AR type extractor, detachable mag., muzzle brake (.338 Lapua cal.), steel trigger guard and floorplate, mfg. by Custom Shop.

MSR $4,400	$3,675	$3,050	$2,500	$2,000	$1,650	$1,350	$1,175

Add $550 for .338 Lapua cal.

Add $2,731 for Model 40-XS Tactical Weapons System with Harris bipod, Picatinny rail, Leupold Mark IV 3.5-10x40mm long range M1 scope, Turner AWS tactical sling, and military grade hard case.

MSR	100%	98%	95%	90%	80%	70%	60%	*Last MSR*

MODEL 40-X TACTICAL MOD – .308 Win. cal., 20 in. barrel, barreled action colors include flat dark earth (FDE), OD Green, or black. Limited mfg. 2011 only.

	$4,300	$3,600	$3,000	$2,300	$1,875	$1,500	$1,325	*$4,850*

MODEL 40-X TDR – .308 Win. cal., repeater action, 20 in. barrel, features various stock/receiver colors, including black, OD Green, tan and flat dark earth. Limited mfg. 2011 only.

	$2,775	$2,300	$1,875	$1,500	$1,200	$995	$825	*$3,170*

MODEL 40-X TIR – .308 Win. cal., repeater action, 20 in. barrel, stock/slash receiver colors include black/black, black/OD Green, or black/tan. Limited mfg. 2011 only.

	$3,600	$3,100	$2,400	$1,925	$1,500	$1,250	$1,000	*$4,087*

MODEL XM3 TACTICAL – .308 Win. cal., choice of steel or titanium action, match grade 18 1/2 in. stainless threaded barrel, Model 40-X action, custom bedded McMillan stock with adjustable LOP, Harris bipod, steel trigger guard, Nightfore NXS 3.5-15x50mm mil dot scope, guaranteed MOA accuracy to 1,000 yards, Hardigg Storm case with all tools and maintenance equipment, mfg. by Custom Shop. Mfg. 2009-2011.

	$9,250	$8,000	$7,000	$6,000	$5,000	$4,000	$3,500	*$10,281*

Add $2,128 for steel action.

SHOTGUNS: SEMI-AUTO, DISC.

MODEL 48A RIOT GUN – 12 ga. only, 20 in. plain barrel.

	$275	$220	$195	$165	$150	$140	$110	

Shotguns: Semi-Auto, Model 1100 & Variations

3 in. shells (12 or 20 ga.) may be shot in Magnum receivers only, regardless of what the barrel markings may indicate (the ejection port is larger in these Magnum models with "M" suffix serialization).

Model 1100 serial numbers on the receiver started with the number 1001. All but the early guns also have a prefix letter. All Model 1100 Remington shotguns were serial numbered in blocks of numbers. Each serial number has a suffix and the following indicates the meaning: V = 12 ga. standard, M = 12 ga. Mag., W = 16 ga., X = 20 ga., N = 20 ga. Mag., K = 20 ga. lightweight, U = 20 ga. lightweight Mag., J = 28 ga., H = .410 bore.

Add $877 for custom shop Etchen stock and forearm installed on new Model 1100s (mfg. 2000-circa 2010).

MODEL 1100 TACTICAL – 12 ga. only, 3 in. chamber, choice of Speedfeed IV pistol grip or black synthetic stock and forearm, 6 (Speedfeed IV) or 8 (22 in. barrel only) shot mag., 18 (Speedfeed IV with fixed IC choke) or 22 (synthetic with Rem Chokes and HiViz sights) in. VR barrel, OD Green metal finish, R3 recoil pad, approx. 7 1/2 lbs. Disc. 2006.

	$640	$575	$515	$450	$400	$350	$295	*$759*

Add $40 for 22 in. barrel.

MODEL 1100 TAC-2/TAC-4 – 12 ga., 2 3/4 in. chamber, 18 (bead sight) or 22 in. VR barrel, Hi-Viz sights, bead blasted black oxide metal finish, black synthetic stock with (Tac-2 with SFIV stock) or w/o (Tac-4) pistol grip, fixed (18 in.) or Rem Chokes, 6 or 8 shot mag., sling swivels, R3 recoil pad, 7 1/2 - 7 3/4 lbs. New 2007.

MSR $943	$795	$675	$575	$500	$450	$400	$350	

Add $72 for Tac-4 with 4 shot mag. and 22 in. VR barrel.

Shotguns: Semi-Auto, Model 11-87 & Variations

Model 11-87 barrels will not fit the Model 1100 or Model 11-87 Super Magnum models.

Remington MSRs on extra barrels (3 in. chamber standard) for the following currently manufactured models range from $282-$336 per barrel, depending on configuration.

Many options are available from the Custom Shop, and are POR.

MODEL 11-87 P (POLICE) – 12 ga. only, 18 in. barrel, improved cylinder choke, synthetic stock, parkerized finish, choice of bead or rifle sights, 7 shot extended mag., designed for police/law enforcement.

Remington does not publish consumer retail pricing for this police/law enforcement model. Secondary prices for this model will be slightly higher than for current pricing on the Model 11-87 SPS.

MODEL 11-87 SPS (SPECIAL PURPOSE SYNTHETIC) – see individual sub-models listed below.

* ***Model 11-87 SPS 3 in. Magnum*** – similar to Model 11-87 SP 3 in. Mag., except is supplied with black synthetic stock and forearm. Disc. 2004.

	$610	$475	$400	$360	$315	$275	$250	*$791*

* ***Model 11-87 SPS-BG Camo (Special Purpose Synthetic Big Game)*** – 12 ga. only, 21 in. plain barrel with rifle sights and Rem Choke. Mfg. 1994 only.

	$555	$425	$350	$290	$250	$225	$200	*$692*

MSR	100%	98%	95%	90%	80%	70%	60%	Last MSR

* **Model 11-87 SP/SPS (Special Purpose Deer Gun)** – 12 ga. only, 3 in. chamber, 21 in. IC or Rem Choke (Model SP, mfg. 1989-2003) or fully rifled (new 1993, became standard 2004) barrel with rifle sights, parkerized metal with matte finished wood or black synthetic (Model SPS, new 1993) stock and forearm, vent. recoil pad, includes camouflaged nylon sling, 7 1/4 lbs. Mfg. 1987-2005.

	$695	$525	$450	$395	$350	$300	$250	$908

Subtract 10% for fixed choke barrel or if w/o cantilever (became standard 2005) scope mount.

Rem Chokes were standard on this model between 1989-1992.

SHOTGUNS: SLIDE ACTION, DISC.

MODEL 17R – 20 ga. only, security configuration, 20 in. cylinder bore barrel, 4 shot mag. Mfg. circa 1920s.

	$325	$265	$235	$200	$150	$120	$100	

MODEL 29R – 12 ga. only, security configuration, 20 in. cylinder bore barrel, 5 shot mag. Mfg. circa 1920s.

	$375	$325	$265	$235	$200	$150	$120	

MODEL 31R "RIOT" GRADE – features shortened barrel.

	$425	$365	$325	$295	$270	$230	$190	

SHOTGUNS: SLIDE ACTION, MODEL 870 & RECENT VARIATIONS

3 in. shells (12 or 20 ga.) may be shot in Magnum receivers only regardless of what the barrel markings may indicate (the ejection port is larger in these Magnum models with M suffix serialization).

Remington has manufactured many limited production runs for various distributors and wholesalers over the years. These shotguns are usually built to a specific configuration (gauge, stock, barrel length, finish, etc.), and are usually available until supplies run out. While these models are not included in this section, pricing in most cases will be similar to the base models from which they were derived.

In April 2009, Remington made its 10 millionth Model 870 slide action shotgun, making it the most manufactured shotgun in firearms history.

Remington also manufactures the Models R870 and MCS for military and law enforcement only. These models are not covered in this text.

Many custom shop options are available, all are POR.

Add 25%-35% for 16 ga. on older mfg., if original condition is 95%+.

Remington MSRs on extra barrels (3 in. chamber is standard, except for Skeet barrel) for the following currently manufactured models range from $124-$327 per barrel, depending on configuration.

MODEL 870 EXPRESS SYNTHETIC TACTICAL (HD, HOME DEFENSE) – 12 or 20 (new 2007, 7 shot mag. only) ga., 18 1/2 in. with fixed cyl. choked barrel with bead front sight, black synthetic stock and forend, black oxide metal finish, 7 1/2 lbs. New 1991.

MSR $420	$335	$270	$220	$190	$170	$155	$135	

Add $23 for 12 ga. 6 shot tube mag. or $39 for 20 ga. 7 shot tube mag.

Add $181 for ghost ring sights with Rem chokes.

* **Model 870 Express Tactical Knoxx 20 Ga.** – 20 ga., features black Knoxx Spec-Ops stock with 7 shot mag., 18 1/2 in. barrel with fixed cyl. choke, black synthetic stock, matte black finish, drilled and tapped, 6 lbs. New 2009.

MSR $555	$450	$375	$320	$280	$240	$210	$180	

* **Model 870 Express Tactical Camo** – 12 ga., 6 shot mag. with 2 shot mag. extension, 18 1/2 in. barrel with Rem choke, XS Ghost Ring Sight Rail and XSR Ghost Ring sights, synthetic stock with A-TACS camo coverage, 7 1/2 lbs. New 2010.

MSR $720	$585	$485	$435	$380	$325	$275	$225	

* **Model 870 Express Specialty** – 12 or 20 ga., 18 in. cylinder bore or Rem Choke barrel, folding or Knoxx Spec-Ops pistol grip stock, 2 or 7 shot mag extension. Mfg. 2008.

	$365	$315	$270	$235	$200	$180	$160	$452

Add $27 for 2 shot mag. extension with Knoxx Spec-Ops stock.

Add $53 for synthetic folding stock with 7 shot mag extension.

This model was available through Remington Premier dealers only.

MODEL 870 SPECIAL PURPOSE MARINE MAGNUM – 12 ga. only, 3 in. chamber, 18 in. plain barrel bored cyl., electroless nickel plated metal finish, 6 or 7 (disc.) shot mag., R3 recoil pad became standard during 2004, sling swivels and Cordura sling, 7 1/2 lbs.

MSR $841	$665	$560	$460	$400	$350	$300	$250	

Add $117 for XCS Marine Model with black TriNyte metal coating (mfg. 2007-2008).

MSR	100%	98%	95%	90%	80%	70%	60%	Last MSR

MODEL 870 POLICE – 12 ga. only, 18 or 20 in. plain barrel, choice of blue or parkerized finish, bead or rifle (disc. 1995, 20 in. barrel only) sights, Police cylinder (disc.) or IC choke. Mfg. 1994-2006 (last year of civilian sales).

	$385	$315	$250	$200	$175	$160	$145	$492

Add $13 for parkerized finish.

Add $44 for rifle sights (disc. 1995).

Remington also offers a Model 870P, 870P MAX, 870MCS, and 870P Synthetic for police/law enforcement, featuring extended capacity magazines, improved cylinder chokes, collapsible stocks, with some models having shorter than 18 in. barrels. While Remington does not publish consumer retail pricing for these police/law enforcement models, secondary prices for these guns will be slightly higher than for current pricing on the Model 870 Police.

MODEL 870 TACTICAL – 12 ga. only, 3 in. chamber, 18 or 20 in. fixed IC choke barrel, 6 or 7 (20 in. barrel only) shot mag., OD Green metal finish, black synthetic tactical or Knoxx Spec-Ops adj. recoil absorbing stock with pistol grip, open sights, approx. 7 1/2 lbs. Mfg. 2006.

	$515	$465	$425	$385	$350	$320	$290	$599

Add $26 for Spec-Ops adj. stock.

MODEL 870 TAC-2/TAC-3 – 12 ga., 3 in. chamber, 18 or 20 (disc) in. cyl. bore barrel, black oxide metal finish, black synthetic stock and forearm, pistol grip with choice of Knoxx Spec-Ops folding stock (Tac-2 FS), Knoxx Spec-Ops tube stock or regular synthetic (disc. 2008) stock, 6 (Tac-2 w/18 in. barrel) or 8 (Tac-3 w/20 in. barrel, disc. 2008) shot mag., bead sights, R3 recoil pad on fixed stock, approx. 7 lbs. New 2007.

MSR $750	$615	$535	$470	$415	$380	$340	$300	

MODEL 870 TACTICAL DESERT RECON – 12 ga., 18 or 20 in. barrel, Digital Tiger TSP Desert Camo stock and forend, special ported tactical extended Rem Choke tube, Speedfeed stock with 2 or 3 shot carrier. Mfg. 2008-2009.

	$575	$500	$450	$400	$365	$335	$295	$692

Add $67 for 20 in. barrel.

MODEL 870 RIOT – 12 ga. only, 18 or 20 in. barrel, choice of blue or parkerized metal finish. Disc. 1991.

	$295	$265	$225	$200	$170	$150	$130	$355

Add $40 for police rifle sights (20 in. barrel only).

MODEL 887 NITRO MAG TACTICAL – 12 ga., 3 in. chamber, 18 1/2 in. barrel with Rem Choke and Hi-Viz front sight, black synthetic stock and forearm, 4 shot mag. and 2 shot extension with mag. tube hanger bracket, Picatinny rail, SuperCell recoil pad, ArmorLokt coated metal finish, 6 7/8 lbs. New 2010.

MSR $534	$425	$380	$335	$295	$260	$230	$195	

REPUBLIC ARMS, INC.

Previous manufacturer 1997-2001, and located in Chino, CA.

PISTOLS: SEMI-AUTO

THE PATRIOT – .45 ACP cal., DAO, ultra compact with 3 in. barrel, 6 shot mag., ultra compact black polymer frame and stainless steel slide (either brushed or with black Melonite coating, new 2000), locked breech action, checkered grips, 20 oz. Mfg. 1997-2001.

	$265	$230	$210	$185	$175	$165	$155	$299

REPUBLIC ARMS OF SOUTH AFRICA

Previous manufacturer located in Jeppestown, Union of South Africa. Previously imported until 2002 by TSF Ltd., located in Fairfax, VA.

PISTOLS: SEMI-AUTO

RAP 401 – 9mm Para. cal., 8 shot mag., otherwise similar to Rap-440. Importation 1999-circa 2002.

	$495	$425	$375	$350	$325	$300	$275	

RAP-440 – .40 S&W cal., compact DA/SA, 3 1/2 in. barrel with high contrast 3-dot sights, last shot hold open, hammer drop safety/decocking lever, firing pin block safety, 7 shot mag., all steel construction, 31 1/2 oz., includes case, spare magazine, and lock. Imported 1998-circa 2002.

	$545	$475	$425	$395	$375	$330	$300	

Add $50 for Trilux tritium night sights.

SHOTGUNS: SLIDE ACTION

MUSLER MODEL – 12 ga., lightweight shotgun, polymer reinforced stock and forearm, action opening release lever, action locks open after the last round. Imported 1998-circa 2002.

	$549	$475	$425	$395	$375	$330	$300	

MSR	100%	98%	95%	90%	80%	70%	60%	Last MSR

RHINO ARMS

Current rifle manufacturer located in St. Louis, MO. Previously located in Washington, MO.

RIFLES: SEMI-AUTO

Rhino Arms manufactures a complete line of AR-15 style carbines/rifles.

Add $45 for Magpul ACS stock, $155 for Magpul PRS stock, or $165 for Magpul UBR stock.

RA-4B SERIES – .223 Rem. cal., GIO, 16 or 20 (RA-4BV only) in. chromemoly heavy barrel, aluminum lower receiver, flat-top upper, A2 flash hider, choice of A2 buttstock (RA-4B or RA-4BV) or M4 buttstock (RA-4BG or RA-4BT), 10 or 30 shot mag., anti-walk receiver retaining pins. Disc. 2010.

	100%	98%	95%	90%	80%	70%	60%	Last MSR
	$895	$825	$750	$675	$595	$550	$495	*$978*

Add $44 for RA-4BG model with rail gas block and M4 buttstock.
Add $248 for RA-BT model with four rail handguard and M4 buttstock.
Add $119 for RA-4BV model with 20 in. barrel, free float tube and A2 buttstock.

RA-4P SERIES – .223 Rem. cal., GIO, 16 or 20 (RA-4PV) in. chromemoly steel barrel, flat-top upper, aluminum lower, A2 or Rhino flash hider, 10 or 30 shot mag., ERGO grip, Magpul CTR or PRS buttstock, anti-walk receiver retaining pins. Disc. 2010.

	100%	98%	95%	90%	80%	70%	60%	Last MSR
	$1,150	$1,000	$875	$750	$625	$550	$500	*$1,243*

Add $35 for RA-4PG model with four rail gas block, CAR handguard, and CTR buttstock.
Add $185 for RA-4PT model with four rail gas block, four rail handguard, and CTR buttstock.
Add $247 for RA-PV model with four rail gas block, free float tube, and PRS buttstock.

DOUBLE V SERIES II 5.56/.300 BLACKOUT – 5.56 NATO or .300 Blackout cal., GIO, 16 (5.56 NATO cal. only) or 18 (.300 Blackout cal. only) in. chromemoly fluted bull with muzzle brake or non-fluted barrel, machined aluminum receiver, gas block with integrated Picatinny rail, free floating carbon fiber handguard, Ergo grip, 10 or 30 shot Rhino Skin coated mag., Magpul CTR stock standard, nickel boron coated precision bolt carrier group, 7.8 (5.56 NATO) or 8.1 lbs.

	100%	98%	95%	90%	80%	70%	60%	Last MSR
MSR $2,405	$2,100	$1,850	$1,575	$1,425	$1,150	$950	$750	

Add $270 for .300 Blackout cal.
Add $45 for Magpul ACS stock, $155 for Magpul PRS stock, or $165 for Magpul UBR stock.

DOUBLE V SERIES II 308 (RA-5D) – .308 Win. cal., GIO, 18 in. chromemoly heavy fluted bull with muzzle brake or non-fluted barrel, aluminum upper and lower receiver, rail gas block, 10 or 20 shot mag., Rhino flash hider, free float tube, Magpul UBR or CTR stock, ERGO grip, anti-walk receiver retaining pins, 8.8 lbs.

	100%	98%	95%	90%	80%	70%	60%	Last MSR
MSR $3,015	$2,700	$2,365	$2,025	$1,835	$1,485	$1,215	$950	

Add $45 for Magpul ACS stock, $155 for Magpul PRS stock, or $165 for Magpul UBR stock.

RIB MOUNTAIN ARMS, INC.

Previous rifle manufacturer circa 1992-2000, and located in Beresford and Sturgis, SD.

RIFLES: BOLT ACTION

MODEL 92 – .50 BMG cal., match grade barrel with muzzle brake, long action, walnut thumbhole stock, Timney trigger, approx. 28 lbs. Mfg. 1997-2000.

	100%	98%	95%	90%	80%	70%	60%	Last MSR
	$3,175	$2,725	$2,275	$2,000	$1,750	$1,575	$1,300	*$3,475*

MODEL 93 – similar to Model 92, except has short action with removable shell holder bolt, approx. 25 lbs. Mfg. 1997-2000.

	100%	98%	95%	90%	80%	70%	60%	Last MSR
	$3,175	$2,725	$2,275	$2,000	$1,750	$1,575	$1,300	*$3,475*

RIFLES, INC.

Current custom rifle manufacturer located in Pleasanton, TX. Previously located in Cedar City, UT. Dealer or direct consumer sales.

Riflemaker and custom gunsmith Lex Webernick has been manufacturing lightweight sporting rifles for more than 20 years.

RIFLES: BOLT ACTION

On the following models, the customer must provide a Remington or Winchester action.

Add $175 for muzzlebrake (stainless quiet Slimbrake II) on Classic and Master Series.

CANYON – various cals., designed for long range shooting, synthetic stock with adj. cheekpiece available in 6 colors, stainless steel action/barrel with muzzle brake, 10 lbs. New 2011.

	100%	98%	95%	90%	80%	70%	60%	Last MSR
MSR $3,500	$3,150	$2,650	$2,100	$1,775	$1,500	$1,215	$1,000	

MSR		100%	98%	95%	90%	80%	70%	60%	*Last MSR*

THE ROBAR COMPANIES, INC.

Current customizer established during 1986, and located in Phoenix, AZ.

Robar is a leader in custom metal finishing, including combination finishes. These include the Roguard black finish, NP3 surface treatment, and additional finishes including bluing, electroless nickel, Polymax camoflauge, and Polymax finish. Please contact Robar directly (see Trademark Index) for more information, including current prices on their lineup of firearms, custom metal and wood finishes, and customizing services, including shotguns.

ROBERT HISSERICH COMPANY

Previous gunsmith and previous custom rifle manufacturer located in Mesa, AZ. Previous company name was Stockworks.

RIFLES: BOLT ACTION

ROBERT HISSERICH BOLT GUN – various cals., features Weatherby Vanguard action, Pac-Nor stainless steel barrel, Pachmayr decelerator pad, hinged floor plate, black synthetic stock. Mfg. 2003 - disc.

			$1,795	$1,500	$1,250	$1,050	$875	$750	$625

LIGHTWEIGHT RIFLES SLR – various cals., Rem. long or short action, Kevlar/fiberglass MPI stock, match grade Pac-Nor barrel, straight flutes in bolt body, Timney trigger, straight line muzzle brake, pillar bedded action, free floating barrel, "window" cuts in action for lightening, black oxide finish on carbon or stainless steel, English or Claro walnut deluxe checkered stock, custom order only. Approx. 4 3/4-5 lbs.

			$2,600	$2,300	$2,000	$1,800	$1,600	$1,400	$1,200

Add $200 for stainless steel.

SHARPSHOOTER – various cals., Win. Model 70 action with controlled feeding, precision long range hunting rifle with Schnieder stainless steel fluted barrel, laminated stock with ebony forend tip, titanium firing pin, pillar glass bedded with free floating barrel, includes Leupold 6.5-20x40mm scope, custom order only.

			$5,950	$5,100	$4,500	$3,900	$3,400	$2,850	$2,150

ROBINSON ARMAMENT CO.

Current rifle manufacturer located in Salt Lake City, UT. Previously distributed by ZDF Import/Export, Inc., located in Salt Lake City, UT. Dealer and consumer direct sales.

PISTOLS: SEMI-AUTO

XCR-L MICRO PISTOL – 5.56 NATO, 6.8 SPC, or 7.62x39mm cal., GPO, 7 or 7 1/2 in. chrome lined barrel, upper, side, and lower rails, two stage trigger, accepts M-16 magazines, left side charging handle, various sight options, approx. 5 lbs. New 2010.

MSR $1,795			$1,625	$1,425	$1,225	$1,100	$895	$750	$575

XCR-M – .243 Win., .260 Rem., or 7.62 NATO cal., GPO, 9 1/2 in. barrel, 15 in. full top rail, 5 1/2 in. side and bottom rail, various options available, matte black, flat dark earth, or olive drab finish, 6.2 lbs. New 2012.

MSR $2,300			$2,075	$1,825	$1,550	$1,400	$1,150	$935	$725

RIFLES: SEMI-AUTO

M96 EXPEDITIONARY RIFLE/CARBINE – .223 Rem. cal., GPO, tactical modular design, unique action allows accessory kit (new 2000) to convert loading from bottom to top of receiver, 16.2 (Recon Model, new 2001), 17 1/4 (carbine, new 2000) or 20 1/4 in. barrel with muzzle brake, stainless steel receiver and barrel, matte black finish metal, black synthetic stock and forearm, adj. sights, gas operated with adjustment knob, last shot hold open, rotating bolt assembly, 8 1/2 lbs. Mfg. 1999-2006.

			$1,495	$1,300	$1,100	$925	$850	$775	$700

Add $750 for rifle/carbine with top feed.

XCR-L MODEL – .223 Rem., 6.8 SPC, 7.62x39mm, 5.45x39mm or .308 Win. (mfg. 2008-2013) cal., GPO, tactical design, 16 or 18.6 in. full floating barrel, handguard with 8 in. side and bottom Picatinny rails, open sights, quick change barrel system, bolt hold open, side folding stock standard until 2008, stock configuration optional beginning 2009, two-stage trigger, uses M16 mags., 7 1/2 lbs. New 2006.

MSR $1,778			$1,600	$1,400	$1,200	$1,095	$895	$725	$575

Add $560 for conversion kit (includes barrel, bolt, and 25 shot mag.).
Add $150-$250 for stock option, depending on configuration.
Add $50 for 18.6 in. barrel.
Add $185 for sights.
Add $32 for rail covers.
Add $200 for flat dark earth or olive drab or $300 for white or tiger stripe.

The model nomenclature was changed from XCR to XCR-L (lightweight) during 2008.

MSR	100%	98%	95%	90%	80%	70%	60%	Last MSR

XCR-M – .260 Rem. (disc. 2013) or .308 Win. cal., GPO, 16, 18.6 or 20 in. light or heavy stainless steel barrel, 20 in. full top rail, 9 1/2 in. side and bottom rail, matte black, flat dark earth, olive drab, white, or tiger stripe finish, approx. 8 lbs. New 2012.

MSR $2,178	$1,975	$1,750	$1,475	$1,350	$1,085	$895	$695	

Add $200 for flat dark earth, olive drab, white or tiger stripe finish.
Add $32 for rail covers.
Add $185 for sights.

ROCK ISLAND ARMORY (CURRENT MFG.)

Current trademark manufactured by Arms Corp. of the Philippines. Currently imported by Armscor Precision International, located in Pahrump, NV.

PISTOLS: SEMI-AUTO

M1911-A1 FSP – 9mm Para. (new 2011), .38 Super or .45 ACP cal., patterned after the Colt Govt. Model, SA, 7 shot mag. (2 provided), 5 in. barrel, parkerized (disc. 2001), nickel, blue (new 2002), two-tone (new 2002), or stainless steel (new 2002), skeletonized combat hammer and trigger, front and rear slide serrations, hard rubber grips, 38 oz. Imported 1996-97, reintroduced 2001.

No MSR	$395	$360	$320	$295	$280	$260	$240	

Add $10 for MSP Model or for .38 Super cal.
Add $18 for Duracoat finish.
Add $34 for two-tone finish.
Add $100 for stainless steel (disc. 2011)
Add $60 for a high capacity configuration (Model 1911-A2 HC, 13 shot mag., disc. 2009).
Add $60 for Model 1911-A1 FS RIA Tactical (.45 ACP cal. only) or $84 for FS RIA Tactical with Duracoat (new 2012).
Add $205 for Model 1911-A2 FS RIA Match Model (.45 ACP cal. only).
Add $55 for nickel finish (Model 1911-A1 FSNP).
Add $100 for night sights (new 2012).

M1911-A1 FS TACTICAL – .45 ACP cal., SA, features skeletonized trigger, bobbed hammer, and lower Picatinny rail, diamond checkered walnut or VZ (new 2013) grips, parkerized finish, 8 shot mag., standard or Meprolite night sights. New 2011.

No MSR	$525	$450	$400	$365	$335	$300	$275	

Add $100 for Meprolite night sights.

M1911-A1 MAP/MAPP SERIES – 9mm Para. cal., DA/SA, MAP 1 Series is standard configuration, while MAPP 1 Series is tactical with lower Picatinny rail, 3 1/2 (MAPP 1), or 4 (MAP 1) in. barrel, fixed front and adj. rear sight, double slide serrations, ambidextrous safety, 16 shot mag., synthetic grip frame with steel slide. New 2010.

No MSR	$450	$400	$350	$300	$275	$250	$225	

TCM SERIES – .22 TCM or 9mm Para. cal., available in MicroMag, Target, Midsize Standard, VZ Midsize, or VZ Fullsize configurations, SA, dovetail ramp tactical or target adj. sights, parkerized finish, black checkered synthetic grips, 17 shot mag., combat hammer, skeletonized trigger, includes extra 9mm barrel. New 2013.

No MSR	$750	$650	$550	$500	$410	$335	$260	

ROCK RIVER ARMS, INC.

Current handgun and rifle manufacturer established in 1996 and located in Colona, IL beginning 2004. Previously located in Cleveland, IL until 2003. Dealer and consumer direct sales.

CARBINES/RIFLES: SEMI-AUTO

Rock River Arms makes a variety of AR-15 style rifles/carbines in .223 Rem. cal. Previous models include the CAR UTE (disc. 2004, last MSR was $850), Tactical Carbine A2, M4 Entry (disc. 2003, last MSR was $875), and NM A2-DCM Legal (disc. 2005, last MSR was $1,265).

Beginning 2006, Rock River Arms released a series of rifles in 9mm Para. cal. Also during 2006, the company released a series of rifles in .308 Win. cal.

A wide variety of options are available for each rifle. Base model assumes black furniture.

LAR-15 STANDARD A2 – .223 Rem. cal., GIO, forged A2 upper receiver, 20 in. Wilson chromemoly barrel, A2 flash hider, two-stage match trigger, A2 pistol grip, handguard, and buttstock, 8.6 lbs. Disc. 2012.

	$900	$775	$650	$595	$475	$395	$300	*$980*

LAR-15 STANDARD A4 – similar to Standard A2 model, except has forged A4 upper receiver, 8.2 lbs.

MSR $1,010	$875	$765	$650	$595	$480	$395	$300	

Add $125 for Hogue free float tube, $185 for quad rail free float with three rail covers, or $190 for advanced half quad with three rail covers.
Add $145 for left hand (LAR-15LH, Lef-T, new 2013).

MSR	100%	98%	95%	90%	80%	70%	60%	*Last MSR*

LAR-15 NATIONAL MATCH A2 – .223 Rem. cal., GIO, forged A2 upper receiver, 20 in. Wilson heavy match stainless barrel, 20 shot mag., two-stage match trigger, A2 flash hider, A2 pistol grip and buttstock, free floating handguard, 9.7 lbs.

| | MSR $1,335 | $1,150 | $1,000 | $875 | $775 | $635 | $525 | $400 |

LAR-15 NATIONAL MATCH A4 – .223 Rem. cal., GIO, similar to National Match A2 model, except has forged A4 upper receiver with NM carry handle, 9.7 lbs.

| | MSR $1,415 | $1,200 | $1,050 | $900 | $815 | $660 | $540 | $425 |

LAR-15 CAR A2 – .223 Rem. cal., GIO, forged A2 upper receiver, 16 in. Wilson chromemoly barrel, A2 flash hider, two-stage match trigger, CAR length handguard, A2 pistol grip, fixed or tactical CAR stock, 7 1/2 lbs. Disc. 2012.

| | | $875 | $750 | $635 | $580 | $465 | $380 | $295 | *$960* |

Add $15 for six-position tactical stock.
Add $175 for tactical carry handle.
Add $145 for quad rail and tactical CAR stock.

LAR-15 CAR A4 – .223 Rem. cal., similar to CAR A2, except has forged A4 upper receiver, 7.1 lbs.

| | MSR $1,035 | $895 | $785 | $670 | $610 | $495 | $400 | $315 |

Add $145 for left hand (LAR-15LH Lef-T, new 2013).
Add $15 for six-position tactical stock.
Add $145 for quad rail and tactical stock.
Add $175 for tactical carry handle.

LAR-15 DELTA CAR – .223 Rem. cal., GIO, forged upper and lower, 16 in. chromemoly H-Bar barrel, A2 flash hider, low profile gas block, two-stage trigger, winter trigger guard, Delta CAR stock, ERGO Suregrip, Delta quad rail CAR two-piece drop-in handguard, 7 lbs. New 2013.

| | MSR $1,085 | $925 | $815 | $695 | $625 | $510 | $415 | $325 |

LAR-15 DELTA CAR MID-LENGTH – .223 Rem. cal., similar to Delta CAR, except has mid-length handguard, 7.3 lbs. New 2013.

| | MSR $1,100 | $950 | $825 | $700 | $625 | $525 | $450 | $400 |

LAR-15 MID-LENGTH A2 – .223 Rem. cal., forged A2 upper receiver, 16 in. Wilson chromemoly barrel, two-stage match trigger, mid-length handguard, A2 pistol grips and buttstock, 7 1/2 lbs. Disc. 2012.

| | | $875 | $750 | $625 | $575 | $465 | $375 | $295 | *$960* |

Add $15 for six-position tactical stock.

LAR-15 MID-LENGTH A4 – .223 Rem. cal., similar to Mid-Length A2 model, except has forged A4 upper receiver, 7.1 lbs.

| | MSR $1,035 | $895 | $785 | $670 | $610 | $495 | $400 | $315 |

Add $15 for six-position tactical stock.
Add $170 for quad rail and tactical stock.
Add $175 for tactical carry handle.

LAR-15 R3 COMPETITION – 5.56 NATO cal., GIO, 18 in. barrel with factory tuned muzzle brake, low profile gas block, RRA adj. Operator A2 or CAR stock, 30 shot mag., two-stage trigger, RRA TRO-XL handguard, matte black finish, top rail, 7 lbs., 10 oz. New 2013.

| | MSR $1,310 | $1,125 | $985 | $850 | $765 | $625 | $500 | $395 |

LAR-15 TACTICAL CAR A4 – .223 Rem. cal., GIO, forged A4 upper receiver, detachable tactical carry handle, 16 in. Wilson chromemoly barrel, A2 flash hider, two-stage match trigger, Hogue rubber pistol grip, R-4 handguard, six-position tactical CAR stock, 7 1/2 lbs.

| | MSR $1,065 | $925 | $810 | $695 | $630 | $510 | $415 | $325 |

Add $115 for left hand (LAR-15LH, Lef-T, new 2013).
Add $40 for chrome lined barrel.
Add $45 for A2 carry handle or $80 for tactical carry handle.

LAR-15 ELITE CAR A4 – .223 Rem. cal., similar to Tactical CAR A4, except has mid-length handguard, 7.7 lbs.

| | MSR $1,065 | $925 | $810 | $695 | $630 | $510 | $415 | $325 |

Add $40 for chrome lined barrel.
Add $45 for A2 carry handle or $80 for tactical carry handle.

LAR-15 ELITE COMP – .223 Rem. cal., GIO, 16 in. barrel with tactical muzzle brake, MagPul CTR stock, features free floating half-round, half-quad handguard, Pads flip up rear sight, pistol grip, 8.4 lbs. New 2008.

| | MSR $1,515 | $1,295 | $1,135 | $975 | $880 | $710 | $585 | $450 |

MSR	100%	98%	95%	90%	80%	70%	60%	Last MSR

LAR-15 TACTICAL CAR UTE2 – .223 Rem. cal., GIO, forged Universal Tactical Entry 2 upper receiver, 16 in. Wilson chromemoly barrel, A2 flash hider, two-stage match trigger, Hogue rubber pistol grip, R-4 handguard, six-position tactical CAR stock, 7 1/2 lbs. Disc. 2012.

	100%	98%	95%	90%	80%	70%	60%	Last MSR
	$965	$825	$700	$625	$510	$415	$325	*$1,060*

LAR-15 ELITE CAR UTE2 – .223 Rem. cal., similar to Tactical CAR UTE2, except has mid-length handguard, 7.7 lbs. Disc. 2012.

	100%	98%	95%	90%	80%	70%	60%	Last MSR
	$965	$825	$700	$625	$510	$415	$325	*$1,060*

LAR-15 ENTRY TACTICAL – .223 Rem. cal., GIO, forged A4 upper receiver, 16 in. Wilson chromemoly R-4 heavy barrel, detachable tactical carry handle, A2 flash hider, two-stage match trigger, Hogue rubber pistol grip, R-4 handguard with double heat shields, six-position tactical CAR stock, 7 1/2 lbs.

MSR	100%	98%	95%	90%	80%	70%	60%	Last MSR
MSR $1,065	$925	$810	$695	$630	$510	$415	$325	

Add $40 for chrome lined barrel.
Add $45 for A2 carry handle or $80 for tactical carry handle.

LAR-15 PRO-SERIES GOVERNMENT – .223 Rem. cal., GIO, forged A4 upper receiver, 16 in. chrome lined Wilson chromemoly barrel, A2 flash hider, two-stage match trigger, flip-up rear sight, Hogue rubber pistol grip, six-position tactical CAR stock, Surefire M73 quad rail handguard, Surefire M951 WeaponLight light system, EOTech 552 Holosight red-dot optical sight, side mount sling swivel, 8.2 lbs. Disc. 2012.

	100%	98%	95%	90%	80%	70%	60%	Last MSR
	$2,150	$1,850	$1,575	$1,425	$1,150	$950	$725	*$2,375*

LAR-15 PRO-SERIES ELITE – .223 Rem. cal., GIO, forged A4 upper receiver, chrome lined 16 in. Wilson chromemoly barrel, RRA tactical muzzle brake, flip front sight and gas block assembly, two-stage match trigger, winter trigger guard, Badger tactical charging handle latch, A.R.M.S. #40L low profile flip-up rear sight, ERGO sure-grip pistol grip, six-position tactical CAR stock, MWI front sling adapter, MWI CAR stock end plate adapter loop rear sling mount, Daniel Defense 12.0 FSPM quad rail handguard, SureFire M910A-WH vertical foregrip weaponlight, Aimpoint Comp M2 red dot optical sight and QRP mount with spacer, 9 1/2 lbs. Disc. 2012.

	100%	98%	95%	90%	80%	70%	60%	Last MSR
	$2,500	$2,175	$1,975	$1,595	$1,300	$1,025	$975	*$2,750*

LAR-15 VARMINT EOP (ELEVATED OPTICAL PLATFORM) – .223 Rem. cal., GIO, forged EOP upper receiver, 16, 18, 20, or 24 in. Wilson air gauged stainless steel bull barrel, Weaver style light varmint gas block with sight rail, two-stage match trigger, Winter trigger guard, knurled and fluted free floating aluminum tube handguard, Hogue rubber pistol grip, A2 buttstock, approx. 8.2 - 10 lbs.

MSR	100%	98%	95%	90%	80%	70%	60%	Last MSR
MSR $1,250	$1,075	$950	$800	$725	$595	$485	$375	

Add $15 for 18, $30 for 20, or $40 for 24 in. barrel.

LAR-15 VARMINT A4 – .223 Rem. or .308 Win. (mfg. 2010-2011) cal., similar to Varmint EOP, except has forged A4 upper receiver., 7.9 - 11.6 lbs.

MSR	100%	98%	95%	90%	80%	70%	60%	Last MSR
MSR $1,215	$1,050	$925	$795	$715	$580	$475	$375	

Add $145 for left hand (LAR-15LH, Lef-T, new 2013).
Add $15 for 18, $30 for 20, or $40 for 24 in. barrel.
Add $395 for .308 Win. cal. (mfg. 2010-2011).

LAR-15 PREDATOR PURSUIT RIFLE – .223 Rem. cal., similar to Varmint A4, except has 16 (Predator Mid-Length, new 2011) or 20 in. Wilson heavy match stainless steel barrel, 8.1 lbs.

MSR	100%	98%	95%	90%	80%	70%	60%	Last MSR
MSR $1,190	$1,025	$895	$775	$695	$565	$460	$360	

Add $145 for left hand (LAR-15LH, Lef-T, new 2013).

FRED EICHLER SERIES PREDATOR RIFLE – .223 Rem. cal., GIO, 16 in. mid-length stainless steel cryogenically treated barrel, low profile hidden gas block, chrome RRA National Match two-stage trigger with parkerized finish on trigger shoe, RRA winter trigger guard, RRA free-floating handguard with full length Picatinny top rail and 2 1/2 in. rails at 3, 6, and 9 o'clock positions, over molded pistol grip, RRA six position or Operator stock, 20 shot mag., forged A4 upper flat-top, custom muzzle break, two-tone black/tan finish, includes hard case. New 2012.

MSR	100%	98%	95%	90%	80%	70%	60%	Last MSR
MSR $1,510	$1,295	$1,135	$975	$880	$710	$585	$450	

LAR-15 COYOTE CARBINE/RIFLE – .223 Rem. cal., GIO, forged A4 upper receiver, 16 or 20 in. Wilson chromemoly HBar barrel, Smith Vortex flash hider, Weaver style light varmint gas block with sight rail (disc. 2013) or low profile gas block (new 2014), two-stage match trigger, winter trigger guard, Hogue rubber pistol grip, Hogue overmolded free float tube handguard (disc. 2013) or RRA deluxe extended free float rail (new 2014), ACE ARFX skeleton (disc. 2013) or RRA Operator A2 (new 2014) or Operator CAR (new 2014) stock, 8.4 lbs.

MSR	100%	98%	95%	90%	80%	70%	60%	Last MSR
MSR $1,260	$1,075	$925	$775	$695	$575	$450	$350	

Add $45 for 20 in. barrel.
Add $145 for left hand (LAR-15LH, Lef-T, new 2013).

MSR	100%	98%	95%	90%	80%	70%	60%	Last MSR

LAR-15 OPERATOR SERIES – .223 Rem. cal., GIO, 16 in. chromemoly barrel, tactical muzzle brake, forged LAR-15 lower, forged A4 upper receiver, upper Picatinny rail, Operator CAR stock, matte black finish, two-stage trigger, winter trigger guard, ERGO SureGrip, configurations include the Entry (R-4 handguard and barrel profile), the Tactical (R-4 handguard), and the Elite (half-quad free float handguard with mid-length gas system), designed for left-handed shooters, 7.2-8 lbs. New 2011.

| MSR $1,360 | $1,175 | $1,050 | $875 | $800 | $650 | $525 | $410 | |

Beginning 2013, this model became available in left hand only (LAR-15LH, Lef-T).

LAR-15 ATH (ADVANCED TACTICAL HUNTER) CARBINE – .223 Rem. cal., GIO, forged A4 upper and LAR-15 lower receiver, 18 in. heavy match cryo treated stainless steel barrel, muzzle brake, matte black finish, low profile gas block, two-stage trigger, winter trigger guard, ERGO Sure Grip pistol grip, half-quad free float handguard with three rail covers, Operator CAR stock, 7.7 lbs. New 2011.

| MSR $1,370 | $1,175 | $1,050 | $875 | $800 | $650 | $525 | $410 | |

LAR-15 9.11 COMMEMORATIVE – .5.56 NATO or .223 Rem. cal., GIO, 16 in. lightweight chromemoly barrel, forged A4 upper receiver, low profile gas block, chromed bolt carrier group, RRA tactical muzzle brake, two-stage chrome trigger group, winter trigger guard, star safety, overmolded pistol grip, Hogue free float tube handguard, non-collapsible or six position tactical CAR stock, flat black finish with American flag, and "9*11 Tenth Year Commemoration" engraved on receiver. Limited mfg. mid-2011.

| | $995 | $850 | $725 | N/A | N/A | N/A | N/A | *$1,011* |

Add $25 for non-collapsible stock, pinned/welded tactical muzzle brake, and 10 shot mag.

LAR-15 HUNTER – .223 Rem. cal., GIO, 16 in. chromemoly barrel, forged A4 upper receiver, tactical muzzle brake, low profile gas block, two-stage trigger, winter trigger guard, half-quad free float mid-length handguard with three rail covers, Operator CAR stock, Hogue rubber pistol grip, WYL-Ehide or PRK-Ehide anodized camo finish, 7.6 lbs. New 2012.

| MSR $1,550 | $1,350 | $1,200 | $1,000 | $925 | $750 | $625 | $480 | |

LAR-15 X-1 RIFLE – .223 Wylde chambered for 5.56 NATO and .223 cal., 18 in. fluted stainless steel barrel, RRA Beast or Hunter muzzle brake, forged upper and lower receivers, low profile gas block, two-stage trigger, Winter trigger guard, RRA TRO-XL extended length free float rail, Operator A2 or Operator CAR stock, Hogue rubber pistol grip, Black or Tan finish, 7.7 lbs. New 2014.

| MSR $1,450 | $1,225 | $1,025 | $900 | $825 | $675 | $625 | $475 | |

Add $50 for RRA Hunter muzzle brake and tan finish.

LAR-PDS CARBINE (PISTON DRIVEN SYSTEM) – .223 Rem. cal., GPO, 16 in. chromemoly barrel, A2 flash hider, black finish, full length upper and partial lower Picatinny rails, Hogue rubber pistol grip, ribbed forend, two stage trigger, injection molded ribbed or tri-rail handguard, folding ambidextrous non-reciprocating charging handles, two-position regulator, side folding six-position tactical stock with receiver extension storage compartment, approx. 7.4 lbs. New 2011.

| MSR $1,595 | $1,375 | $1,200 | $1,050 | $935 | $750 | $625 | $480 | |

Add $155 for tri-rail handguard.

LAR-6.8 A2/A4 – 6.8mm SPC cal., GIO, forged A2 (disc. 2012) or A4 upper receiver, 16 in. Wilson chromemoly barrel, A2 flash hider, two-stage match trigger, A2 pistol grip and buttstock, choice of CAR length or mid-length handguard, 7 1/2 lbs.

| MSR $1,055 | $900 | $795 | $675 | $610 | $495 | $400 | $315 | |

Add approx. $150 for quad rail.
Add $50 for Operator stock.

LAR-6.8 COYOTE – 6.8mm SPC cal., GIO, forged A4 upper receiver, 16 in. Wilson chromemoly HBar barrel, Smith Vortex flash hider, Weaver style light varmint gas block with sight rail, two-stage match trigger, winter trigger guard, Hogue rubber pistol grip, Hogue overmolded free float tube handguard, A2 stock, 7 lbs.

| MSR $1,270 | $1,095 | $960 | $825 | $750 | $600 | $495 | $385 | |

LAR-6.8 X-1 RIFLE – 6.8 SPC II cal., 18 in. fluted stainless steel HBAR barrel, RRA Beast or Hunter muzzle brake, low profile gas block, forged lower and A4 upper receiver, two-stage trigger, Winter trigger guard, RRA TRO-XL extended length free float rail, RRA Operator A2 or Operator CAR stock, Hogue rubber pistol grip, Black or Tan finish, 7.9 lbs. New 2014.

| MSR $1,200 | $1,025 | $925 | $795 | $715 | $575 | $475 | $375 | |

Add $50 for RRA Hunter muzzle brake and tan finish.

LAR-458 CAR A4 – .458 SOCOM cal., GIO, forged A4 upper receiver, 16 in. Wilson chromemoly bull barrel, A2 flash hider, Weaver style varmint gas block with sight rail, two-stage match trigger, knurled and fluted free floating aluminum tube handguard, A2 buttstock and pistol grip, 7.6 lbs.

| MSR $1,220 | $1,050 | $925 | $795 | $715 | $575 | $475 | $375 | |

Add $280 for Operator model with half quad free float with full length top rail and CAR stock (new 2010).

MSR	100%	98%	95%	90%	80%	70%	60%	*Last MSR*

LAR-458 MID-LENGTH A4 – .458 SOCOM cal., GIO, forged A4 upper receiver, 16 in. chromemoly bull barrel, A2 flash hider, gas block with sight rail, two-stage match trigger, knurled and fluted free floating aluminum tube handguard, A2 buttstock and pistol grip, 7.8 lbs. New 2010.

MSR $1,220	$1,050	$925	$795	$715	$575	$475	$375	

Add $290 for Operator model with half quad free float with full length top rail, Vortex flash hider and CAR stock (new 2010).

LAR-458 X-1 RIFLE – .458 Socom cal., 18 in. fluted stainless steel bull barrel, RRA Beast or Hunter muzzle brake, low profile gas block, forged RRA LAR-458 lower and A4 upper receiver, two-stage trigger, Winter trigger guard, RRA TRO-XL extended length free float rail, RRA Operator A2 or Operator CAR stock, Hogue rubber pistol grip, Black or Tan finish, 8.7 lbs. New 2014.

MSR $1,220	$1,050	$925	$795	$715	$575	$475	$375	

Add $50 for RRA Hunter muzzle brake and tan finish.

LAR-8 MID LENGTH A2/A4 – .308 Win. cal., GIO, 16 in. barrel with A2 flash hider, CAR buttstock, gas block sight base, Hogue rubber grip, two stage trigger, forged A2 (disc. 2012) or A4 upper receiver, mid-length handguard, approx. 8 lbs. New 2010.

MSR $1,335	$1,150	$1,000	$865	$780	$635	$525	$400	

LAR-8 ELITE OPERATOR – .308 Win. cal., GIO, 16 in. barrel, similar to Mid-length A4, except has advanced half quad rail, flip front sight, gas block sight base, Operator stock and Smith Vortex flash hider. New 2010.

MSR $1,740	$1,495	$1,310	$1,125	$1,015	$825	$675	$525	

LAR-8 STANDARD A2/A4 – .308 Win. cal., GIO, forged lower and A2 (disc. 2012) or A4 upper receiver, 20 in. chromemoly barrel, A2 flash hider, gas block sight base, two stage trigger, A2 buttstock, A2 handguard, Hogue rubber pistol grip, approx. 9 lbs. New 2010.

MSR $1,370	$1,175	$1,025	$880	$800	$650	$525	$410	

LAR-8 STANDARD OPERATOR – .308 Win. cal., GIO, 16 in. barrel, similar to LAR-8 Standard A4, except has advanced half quad rail, flip front sight, gas block sight base, Operator stock and Smith Vortex flash hider. New 2010.

MSR $1,790	$1,550	$1,315	$1,100	$900	$700	$600	$550	

LAR-8 PREDATOR HP – .308 Win. cal., GIO, forged lower and upper receiver, 20 in. bead blasted lightweight stainless steel barrel, gas block sight base, two stage trigger, A2 buttstock, free float tube handguard, Hogue rubber pistol grip, approx. 8.6 lbs. New 2010.

MSR $1,605	$1,375	$1,200	$1,025	$935	$750	$625	$480	

Add $50 for Operator A2 stock.

LAR-8 VARMINT A4 – .308 Win. cal., GIO, forged LAR-8 lower, forged A4 upper receiver with forward assist and port door, 20 or 26 in. cryo treated stainless steel bull barrel, varmint gas block with sight rail, two-stage trigger, winter trigger guard, Hogue rubber pistol grip, A2 buttstock, aluminum free float tube handguard, 10.4-11.6 lbs. New 2011.

MSR $1,570	$1,400	$1,200	$1,000	$925	$750	$625	$475	

Add $5 for 26 in. barrel.
Add $110 for quad rail.

LAR-8 X-1 RIFLE – 7.62 NATO cal., 18 in. fluted stainless steel HBAR barrel, RRA Beast or Hunter muzzle brake, RRA custom low profile gas block, forged lower and A4 upper with forward assist and port door, two-stage trigger, Winter trigger guard, RRA TRO-STD rifle length free float rail, RRA Operator A2 or Operator CAR stock, Hogue rubber pistol grip, Black or Tan finish, 9 1/2 lbs. New 2014.

MSR $1,800	$1,550	$1,325	$1,100	$900	$700	$600	$550	

Add $50 for RRA Hunter muzzle brake and tan finish.

LAR-9 CAR A2/A4 – 9mm Para. cal., forged A2 (disc. 2012) or A4 upper receiver, 16 in. Wilson chromemoly barrel, A1 flash hider, standard single stage trigger, CAR length handguard, A2 pistol grip, six-position tactical CAR stock, approx. 7 lbs.

MSR $1,180	$1,000	$875	$750	$675	$550	$450	$350	

Add $50 for Operator stock.

LAR-9 MID-LENGTH A4 – 9mm Para. cal., forged A4 upper receiver, forged lower with integral magwell, 16 in. Wilson chromemoly barrel with gas block sight base, A2 flash hider, standard single stage trigger, mid-length handguard, Hogue pistol grip, six-position tactical CAR stock, approx. 7 lbs.

MSR $1,180	$1,000	$875	$750	$675	$550	$450	$350	

Add $50 for Operator stock.

LAR-10 VARMINT A4 – .308 Win. cal., forged A4 upper reciever with forward assist and port door, 26 in. Wilson stainless steel bull barrel, Weaver type sight base gas block, two-stage match trigger, knurled and fluted free floating aluminum tube handguard, Hogue pistol grip, A2 buttstock, 11.6 lbs. Disc. 2010.

	$1,225	$1,070	$925	$825	$675	$550	$425	*$1,350*

MSR	100%	98%	95%	90%	80%	70%	60%	*Last MSR*

LAR-10 MID-LENGTH A2/A4 – .308 Win. cal., GIO, forged A2 or A4 upper receiver with forward assist and ejection port door, 16 in. Wilson chromemoly barrel, A2 flash hider, A2 front sight or A4 gas block with sight base, two-stage match trigger, mid-length handguard, Hogue rubber pistol grip, six-position tactical CAR stock, approx. 8 lbs. Disc. 2009.

	$1,000	$875	$750	$675	$550	$450	$350	*$1,100*

Add $50 for A2 sights.

LAR-10 STANDARD A2/A4 – .308 Win. cal., forged A2 or A4 upper receiver, with forward assist and ejection port door, 20 in. Wilson chromemoly barrel, A2 flash hider, A2 front sight or A4 gas block sight base, two-stage match trigger, A2 handguard, Hogue rubber pistol grip, A2 buttstock, 9.3 lbs. Disc. 2009.

	$1,000	$875	$750	$675	$550	$450	$350	*$1,100*

Add $45 for A2 sights.

LAR-40 MID-LENGTH A2/A4 – .40 S&W cal., forged A2 (disc. 2011) or A4 (new 2013) upper, 16 in. chromemoly barrel, A2 flash hider, two-stage match trigger, mid-length handguard, Hogue rubber pistol grip, six-position tactical CAR stock, approx. 7 lbs. Mfg. 2010-2011, reintroduced 2013.

MSR $1,260	$1,075	$940	$800	$725	$595	$485	$375	

LAR-40 CAR A2/A4 – .40 S&W cal., GIO, forged A2 (disc. 2011) or A4 upper receiver, 16 in. chromemoly barrel, A2 flash hider, single stage trigger, R-4 handguard, six-position tactical CAR stock with Hogue pistol grip, approx. 7 lbs. Disc. 2011, reintroduced 2013.

MSR $1,260	$1,075	$940	$800	$725	$595	$485	$375	

Add $145 for quad rail.
Add $50 for Operator stock.

LAR-47 CAR A4 – 7.62x39mm cal., GIO, forged lower and A4 upper, 16 in. chrome lined HBar barrel, gas block front sight base, A2 flash hider, two-stage trigger, winter trigger guard, CAR handguard, six position CAR stock, A2 pistol grip, ambidextrous mag. release, 6.4 lbs. New 2013.

MSR $1,270	$1,095	$960	$825	$750	$600	$495	$385	

LAR-47 DELTA CARBINE – 7.62x39mm cal., GIO, forged lower and A4 upper, 16 in. chrome lined HBar barrel, gas block front sight base, A2 flash hider, two-stage trigger, winter trigger guard, two-piece quad rail handguard, six position Delta CAR stock, ERGO Suregrip, ambidextrous mag. release, 7 3/4 lbs. New 2013.

MSR $1,545	$1,325	$1,160	$995	$900	$730	$595	$465	

TASC RIFLE – .223 Rem. cal., GIO, forged A2 upper receiver with lockable windage and elevation adj. rear sight, 16 in. Wilson chromemoly barrel, A2 flash hider, two-stage match trigger, Hogue rubber pistol grip, A2 buttstock or six-position CAR tactical buttstock, choice of R-4 or mid-length handguard, approx. 7 1/2 lbs. Disc. 2009.

	$875	$765	$655	$595	$475	$395	$300	*$950*

Add $15 for six-position collapsible stock.

PRO-SERIES TASC – .223 Rem. cal., GIO, forged A2 upper receiver, chrome lined 16 in. Wilson chromemoly barrel, Smith Vortex flash hider, two-stage match trigger, oversize winter trigger guard, A2 rear sight with lockable windage and elevation, Hogue rubber pistol grip, six-position tactical CAR stock, Surefire M85 mid-length quad rail, graphite fore grip, EOTech 511 Holosight, Midwest Industries A2 adj. cantilever sight mount, 8.7 lbs. Disc. 2009.

	$1,850	$1,600	$1,400	$1,200	$1,000	$800	$675	*$2,000*

PISTOLS: SEMI-AUTO

Rock River Arms made a variety of high quality M-1911 based semi-autos through 2011. They specialized in manufacturing their own National Match frames and slides. Previous models included: the Standard Match (disc. 2003, last MSR was $1,150), Ultimate Match Achiever (disc. 2003, last MSR was $2,255), Matchmaster Steel (disc. 2001, last MSR was $2,355), Elite Commando (disc. 2005, last MSR was $1,725), Hi-Cap Basic Limited (disc. 2003, last MSR was $1,895), and the Doug Koenig Signature Series (disc. 2003, last MSR was $5,000, .38 Super cal.). Rock River Arms still offers parts, and reintroduced a 1911 model in 2013.

BASIC LIMITED MATCH – 9mm Para., .38 Super, .40 S&W, or .45 ACP cal., blue, hard chrome, black "T", or black/green "T" duotone finish, 4 1/4, 5, or 6 in. barrel, SA, National Match frame and slide with low mount Bo-Mar hidden leaf rear sight, match Commander hammer and match sear, tuned and polished extractor and extended ejector, lowered and flared ejection port, beavertail grip safety, aluminum speed trigger, two piece recoil guide rod and polished feed ramp, RRA dovetail front sight, serrated slide stop and ambidextrous safety, deluxe checkered grips. Disc. 2010.

	$1,675	$1,465	$1,255	$1,140	$920	$755	$585	*$1,840*

LIMITED MATCH – 9mm Para., .38 Super, .40 S&W, or .45 ACP cal., SA, blue, hard chrome, black "T" or black/green duotone finish, National match frame with beveled mag well and choice of 20, 25, or 30 LPI checkered front and rear strap, 4 1/4, 5, or 6 in. barrel with double slide serrations and RRA borders, low mount Bo-Mar hidden leaf rear sight,

MSR	100%	98%	95%	90%	80%	70%	60%	Last MSR

RRA dovetail front sight, 40 LPI checkering under trigger guard, Match Commander hammer and match sear, aluminum speed trigger, beavertail grip safety with raised pad, extended mag. release button, deluxe checkered grips, two-piece recoil guide rod. Disc. 2010.

	$1,975	$1,700	$1,500	$1,300	$1,100	$900	$750	$2,185

NATIONAL MATCH HARDBALL – 9mm Para., .38 Super, .40 S&W, or .45 ACP cal., blue, hard chrome, black "T" or black/green "T" duotone finish, forged National Match frame with 4 1/4, 5, or 6 in. barrel, SA, beveled mag well, choice of rear or double slide serrations, aluminum speed trigger, milled in Bo-Mar rear sight with hidden rear leaf, lowered and flared ejection port, tuned and polished extractor and extended ejector, checkered rosewood grips. Disc. 2011.

	$1,400	$1,225	$1,050	$950	$770	$630	$490	$1,550

BULLSEYE WADCUTTER – 9mm Para., .38 Super, .40 S&W, or .45 ACP cal., blue, hard chrome, black "T" or black/green "T" duotone finish, 7 shot mag., 4 1/4, 5, or 6 in. barrel, SA, National Match frame with choice of RRR Slide mount, Bo-Mar rib, Caspian frame mount sights, or Weigand 3rd Gen. frame mount, double slide serrations, beavertail grip safety with raised pad, lowered and flared ejection port, Commander hammer and match sear, aluminum speed trigger, checkered rosewood grips. Disc. 2011.

	$1,550	$1,355	$1,160	$1,055	$850	$695	$540	$1,715

Add $35 for Caspian frame mount or Bo-Mar rib.

TACTICAL PISTOL – 9mm Para., .38 Super, .40 S&W, .45 ACP cal., blue, hard chrome, black "T" or black/green "T" duotone finish, 5 in. barrel with double slide serrations, SA, RRA bar stock frame with integral light rail, lowered and flared ejection port, RRA dovetail front sight with tritium inserts, Heinie rear sight with tritium inserts, optional Novak rear sight, aluminum speed trigger, tuned and polished extractor, extended ejector, beavertail grip safety, tactical mag. catch and safety, standard recoil system, completely dehorned for carry, checkered rosewood grips, optional ambidextrous safety, optional Smith & Alexander magwell. Disc. 2011.

	$1,850	$1,620	$1,385	$1,260	$1,015	$830	$645	$2,040

BASIC CARRY – .45 ACP cal., 5 in. National Match barrel with double slide serrations, SA, parkerized finish, checkered rosewood grips, RRA forged National Match frame, lowered and flared ejection port, RRA dovetail front sight, Heinie rear sight, Match Commander hammer and match sear, aluminum speed trigger, beavertail grip safety, standard mag. catch, safety, and standard recoil system. Disc. 2010.

	$1,450	$1,270	$1,085	$985	$795	$650	$505	$1,600

RRA PRO CARRY – 9mm Para., .38 Super, .40 S&W, or .45 ACP cal., 4 1/4, 5, or 6 in. barrel with slide serrations, SA, RRA National Match frame with choice of 20, 25, or 30 LPI checkered front strap, lowered and flared ejection port, RRA dovetail front sight with tritium inserts, Match Commander hammer, aluminum speed trigger, tuned and polished extractor, extended ejector, deluxe rosewood grips, choice of Heinie or Novak rear sight with tritium inserts, beavertail grip safety. Disc. 2010.

	$1,675	$1,465	$1,255	$1,140	$920	$755	$585	$1,920

RRA SERVICE AUTO – 9mm Para. cal., similar to RRA Pro Carry, except with 5 in. barrel and double slide serrations. Mfg. 2009-2010.

	$1,575	$1,380	$1,180	$1,070	$865	$710	$550	$1,790

LIMITED POLICE COMPETITION – 9mm Para. cal., 5 in. National Match barrel, SA, blue, hard chrome, black "T", or black/green "T" duotone finish, RRA forged National Match frame with beveled mag well with choice of 20, 25, or 30 LPI checkered front strap, double slide serrations, 3-position rear sight, choice of wide or narrow blade, RRA dovetail front sight, tall, thinned, and relieved for PPC, Smith & Alexander flared mag well, lowered and flared ejection port, Match Commander hammer and match sear, tuned and polished extractor and extended ejector, beavertail grip safety and flat checkered mainspring housing, deluxe checkered grips, ambidextrous safety, tuned and polished feed ramp, two-piece recoil spring guide rod. Disc. 2010.

	$2,095	$1,825	$1,600	$1,375	$1,250	$1,000	$775	$2,375

UNLIMITED POLICE COMPETITION – 9mm Para. cal., forged 6 in. National Match barrel, SA, RRA forged National Match frame with beveled mag well, choice of 20, 25, or 30 LPI checkered front strap, double slide serrations, similar configuration as Limited Police Competition. Disc. 2010.

	$2,095	$1,825	$1,600	$1,375	$1,250	$1,000	$775	$2,375

LAR-15 – .223 Rem. cal., GPO, 7 or 10 1/2 in. chromemoly barrel, A2 or A4 configuration, A2 flash hider, single stage trigger, Hogue rubber pistol grip, R-4 handguard (10 1/2 in. barrel only) or aluminum free float tube, pistol length handguard (7 in. barrel only), matte black finish, approx. 5 lbs.

MSR $1,015	$875	$765	$650	$595	$480	$395	$300	

Add $45 for 7 in. barrel or for gas block sight base.
Add $50 for A2 configuration.
Add $75 for quad rail free float three rail covers.

MSR	100%	98%	95%	90%	80%	70%	60%	Last MSR

LAR-9 – similar to LAR-15, except is 9mm Para. cal., A2 flash hider, 4.8 - 5.2 lbs.

| MSR $1,160 | $995 | $875 | $750 | $675 | $550 | $450 | $350 | |

Add $50 for 7 in. barrel, $65 for aluminum free floating forearm with A2 front sight, $45 for aluminum free floating handguard with gas block sight base, or $145 for quad rail with three rail covers.

LAR-40 – .40 S&W cal., GPO, 7 or 10 1/2 in. barrel, forged lower receiver with integral magwell, A2 or A4 upper, single stage trigger, Hogue rubber pistol grip, approx. 5 lbs. Mfg. 2010-2011.

| | $1,050 | $900 | $800 | $700 | $600 | $500 | $400 | $1,120 |

Add $45 for 7 in. barrel and free float tube handguard.

Add $10-$15 for gas block sight base.

PDS PISTOL (PISTON DRIVEN SYSTEM) – .223 Rem. cal., GPO, 8 (disc. 2012) or 9 (new 2013) in. chromemoly barrel, features A2 flash hider, full length upper and partial lower Picatinny rails, Hogue rubber pistol grip, ribbed forend, single (disc. 2012) or two-stage (new 2013) stage trigger, injection molded ribbed handguard, folding ambidextrous non-reciprocating charging handles, two-position regulator, approx. 5 lbs. New 2010.

| MSR $1,245 | $1,075 | $940 | $800 | $725 | $595 | $485 | $375 | |

Add $150 for aluminum tri-rail handguard.

1911 POLY – .45 ACP cal., 1911 style polymer frame, 5 in. chromemoly barrel, SA, steel slide, 7 shot mag., overmolded pistol grips, beavertail grip safety, Commander hammer, parkerized finish, aluminum speed trigger, dovetail front and rear sight, includes two mags., polymer holster, mag loader, lock and fitted case, 36 oz. Advertised 2013.

Pricing has yet to be established on this model.

ROCKY MOUNTAIN ARMS, INC.

Current firearms manufacturer located in Longmont, CO since 1991.

Rocky Mountain Arms is a quality specialty manufacturer of rifles and pistols. All firearms are finished in a Dupont Teflon-S industrial coating called "Bear Coat".

PISTOLS: SEMI-AUTO

BAP (BOLT ACTION PISTOL) – .308 Win., 7.62x39mm, or 10mm Rocky Mountain Thunderer (10x51mm) cal., features 14 in. heavy fluted Douglas Match barrel, Kevlar/graphite pistol grip stock, supplied with Harris bipod and black nylon case. Mfg. 1993 only.

| | $1,425 | $1,275 | $1,100 | $950 | $825 | $700 | $575 | $1,595 |

22K PISTOLS – .22 LR cal., AR style pistols featuring GIO, 7 in. barrel, choice of matte black or NATO Green Teflon-S finish, will use Colt conversion kit, choice of carrying handle or flat-top upper receiver, 10 or 30 shot mag., includes black nylon case. Mfg. 1993 only.

| | $475 | $425 | $375 | $350 | $325 | $295 | $275 | $525 |

Add $50 for flat-top receiver with Weaver style bases.

PATRIOT PISTOL – .223 Rem. cal., AR-15 style, GIO, featuring 7 in. match barrel with integral Max Dynamic muzzle brake, 21 in. overall, available with either carrying handle upper receiver and fixed sights or flat-top receiver with Weaver style bases, fluted upper receiver became an option in 1994, accepts standard AR-15 mags, 5 lbs. Mfg. 1993-94 (per C/B), reintroduced 2005.

| MSR $3,000 | $2,850 | $2,500 | $2,250 | $2,000 | $1,750 | $1,500 | $1,250 | |

KOMRADE – 7.62x39mm cal., includes carrying handle upper receiver with fixed sights, floating 7 in. barrel, Teflon red or black finish, 5 lbs., 5 shot mag. Mfg. 1994-95.

| | $1,825 | $1,650 | $1,425 | $1,200 | $975 | $850 | $775 | $1,995 |

RIFLES: BOLT ACTION

PROFESSIONAL SERIES – .223 Rem., .30-06, .308 Win., or .300 Win. Mag. cal., bolt action rifle utilizing modified Mauser action, fluted 26 in. Douglas premium heavy match barrel with integral muzzle brake, custom Kevlar-Graphite stock with off-set thumbhole, test target. Mfg. 1991-95.

| | $2,050 | $1,650 | $1,275 | $995 | $850 | $725 | $600 | $2,200 |

Add $100 for .300 Win. Mag. cal.

Add $300 for left-hand action.

PRAIRIE STALKER – .223 Rem., .22-250 Rem., .30-06, .308 Win., or .300 Win. Mag. cal., choice of Remington, Savage, or Winchester barreled action, includes Choate ultimate sniper stock, lapped bolt and match crown, "Bear Coat" all-weather finish, includes factory test target. Limited mfg. 1998 only.

| | $1,595 | $1,350 | $1,150 | $950 | $875 | $775 | $675 | $1,795 |

MSR	100%	98%	95%	90%	80%	70%	60%	Last MSR

* Prairie Stalker Ultimate – similar to Prairie Stalker, except custom barrel and caliber specifications are customer's choice. Limited mfg. 1998 only.

	100%	98%	95%	90%	80%	70%	60%	Last MSR
	$2,200	$1,875	$1,625	$1,400	$1,200	$1,000	$895	$2,495

PRO-VARMINT – .22-250 Rem., or .223 Rem. cal., RMA action, 22 in. heavy match barrel with recessed crown, "Bear Coat" metal finish, Choate stock with aluminum bedding. Mfg. 1999-2002.

	$995	$875	$800	$725	$650	$575	$450	$1,095

POLICE MARKSMAN – .308 Win. or .300 Win. Mag. cal., similar to Professional Series, except has 40X-C stock featuring adj. cheekpiece and buttplate, target rail, Buehler micro-dial scope mounting system. Mfg. 1991-95.

	$2,325	$1,995	$1,650	$1,325	$1,100	$900	$700	$2,500

Add $100 for .300 Win. Mag. cal.
Add $400 for left-hand action.
Add $400 for illuminated dot scope (4-12x56mm).

* Police Marksman II – .308 Win. cal., RMA action, 22 in. heavy match barrel with recessed crown, "Bear Coat" metal finish, Choate stock with aluminum bedding. Mfg. 1999-2002.

	$995	$875	$800	$725	$650	$575	$450	$1,095

PRO-GUIDE – .280 Rem., .35 Whelen, .308 Win., 7x57mm Mauser, or 7mm-08 Rem. cal., Scout Rifle design with 17 in. Shilen barrel, "Bear Coat" finish, approx. 7 lbs. Mfg. 1999-2002.

	$2,025	$1,800	$1,600	$1,425	$1,200	$1,000	$825	$2,295

NINJA SCOUT RIFLE – .22 WMR cal., takedown rifle based on Marlin action, black stock, 16 1/2 in. match grade crowned barrel, forward mounted Weaver style scope base, adj. rear sight, 7 shot mag. Mfg. 1991-95.

	$640	$575	$525	$460	$430	$390	$360	$695

Add $200 for illuminated dot scope (1.5-4X) w/extended eye relief.

SCOUT SEMI-AUTO – .22 WMR cal., patterned after Marlin action. Mfg. 1993-95.

	$650	$575	$495	$395	$350	$295	$260	$725

Add $200 for illuminated dot scope (1.5-4X) w/extended eye relief.

RIFLES: SEMI-AUTO

M-SHORTEEN – .308 Win. cal., compact highly modified M1-A featuring 17" match crowned barrel, custom front sight, mod. gas system, hand honed action and trigger, custom muzzle brake. Mfg. 1991-94.

	$1,650	$1,425	$1,175	$995	$850	$725	$600	$1,895

Add $200 for Woodland/Desert camo.

VARMINTER – .223 Rem. cal. only, AR-15 style, GIO, 20 in. fluted heavy match barrel, flat-top receiver with Weaver style bases, round metal National Match handguard, free float barrel, choice of NATO green or matte black Teflon-S finish, supplied with case and factory test target (sub-MOA accuracy). Mfg. 1993-94.

	$2,195	$1,800	$1,600	$1,400	$1,200	$1,000	$875	$2,495

PATRIOT MATCH RIFLE – .223 Rem. cal., AR-15 style, GIO, 20 in. Bull Match barrel, regular or milled upper and lower receivers, two-piece machined aluminum hand guard, choice of DuPont Teflon finish in black or NATO green, 1/2 MOA accuracy, hard case. Mfg. 1995-97, reintroduced 2005.

MSR $2,500	$2,350	$2,050	$1,700	$1,425	$1,200	$1,000	$895	

SHOTGUNS: SLIDE ACTION

870 COMPETITOR – 12 ga., 3 in. chamber, security configuration with synthetic stock, hand-honed action, ghost ring adj. sights, "Bear Coat" finish, high visibility follower. Mfg. 1996-97.

	$695	$625	$550	$500	$450	$400	$360	$795

ROHRBAUGH FIREARMS CORP.

Current manufacturer located in Bayport, NY, previously located in Deer Park, NY.

PISTOLS: SEMI-AUTO

R-9 – 9mm Para. or .380 ACP (new 2007) cal., DAO, 2.9 in. barrel, free bored to reduce felt recoil, frame is 7075-T651 aluminum, stainless steel or black Stealth slide, 6 shot mag., parts cut from solid billets, all internal parts are stainless, short recoil locked breech with cam operated tilting barrel locking system, recessed hammer, carbon fiber (disc.) or G10 grips, no sights, 12.8 (carbon fiber grips) or 13 1/2 (G10 grips) oz. New 2003.

MSR $1,150	$1,000	$875	$750	$680	$550	$450	$350	

Add $45 for black Stealth slide.

MSR	100%	98%	95%	90%	80%	70%	60%	Last MSR

* **R9S Model** – similar to Model R-9, except has fixed open sights, 9mm Para. cal. variations include Tribute (silver gun with black/blue CF grips, new 2012), Coyote (Coyote Tan metal finish, new 2012), and Covert (black with sights, new 2012). New 2004.

MSR $1,150	$1,000	$875	$750	$680	$550	$450	$350	

Add $45 for black Stealth slide.

Add $200 R9S Tribute (new 2012). Add $600 for R9S Coyote or Covert (new 2012).

Add $45 for Elite Custom Model (Model R9SE, disc.).

ROHRBAUGH ROBAR R9 SERIES – similar to original R9, except frame, barrel, slide and trigger are treated with Robar Industries NP3 coating (corrosion resistant and self lubricating), polished stainless steel, limited lifetime warranty. Mfg. 2010 only.

	$1,500	$1,315	$1,125	$1,020	$825	$675	$525	$1,795

RUSSIAN AMERICAN ARMORY COMPANY

See RAAC listing.

RUSSIAN SERVICE PISTOLS AND RIFLES

Previously manufactured at various Russian military arsenals (including Tula).

RIFLES

Original Soviet Mosin-Nagant bolt action rifles/carbines include: M1891 rifle, M1891 Dragoon, M1891/30 Rifle, M1891/30 Sniper Model, M1910 Carbine, M1938 Carbine, and the M1944 Carbine. Values for these older original military configurations will approximate values listed for the original mfg. Mosin-Nagant.

TOKAREV M1938 & M1940 (SVT) SEMI-AUTO – 7.62x54R cal., SVT M40 is the more common variation, while the SVT M38 sniper is very rare, 10 shot mag., first Russian military semi-auto, large quantities manufactured beginning 1938, but original surviving specimens in excellent condition are now very scarce.

SVT M38	$4,500	$4,000	$3,500	$3,000	$2,500	$2,000	$1,500	
SVT M40	$1,800	$1,500	$1,200	$1,000	$800	$700	$600	

RPD SEMI-AUTO – 7.62x39mm cal., converted from belt fed to semi-auto only, fired from closed bolt, milled receiver, includes 50 shot mag., recent importation.

	$3,795	$3,495	$2,950	$2,600	$2,300	$2,000	$1,750	

S SECTION

S.W.A.T. FIREARMS

Current manufacturer of AR-15 style rifles located in Campbell, TX since 1999.

S.W.A.T. Firearms manufactures upper and lower receivers, standard billet and tactical rifles, and will customize each firearm to customer specifications.

MSR	100%	98%	95%	90%	80%	70%	60%	Last MSR

RIFLES: SEMI-AUTO

BASE MODERN SPORTING RIFLE – 5.56 NATO or 7.62 cal., 16-20 in. heavy chromemoly barrel, free float round handguard, 7 lbs.

MSR $1,125	$1,000	$875	$750	$675	$550	$450	$350	

DESERT STORM – 5.56 NATO cal., 16 in. lightweight chromemoly barrel with FH-1 flash hider, rifle length free float quad rail, Magpul MOE stock, Magpul AFG forward grip, Cerakote Magpul FDE finish, 6.97 lbs.

MSR $1,609	$1,450	$1,275	$1,095	$975	$800	$650	$525	

DRAGON SLAYER – 5.56 NATO cal., 16 in. barrel with MB-2 muzzle brake, mid-length quad rail, Crimson Cerakote finish, 6.2 lbs.

MSR $1,485	$1,325	$1,175	$1,000	$900	$725	$600	$475	

M4 – 5.56 NATO cal., 16 in. M4 contour barrel with FH-1 flash hider, Ergo grip, carbine length free float quad rail, 7 lbs.
Please contact the company directly for pricing and options on this model.

PRISON PINK CONVICTION – 5.56 NATO cal., 16 in. lightweight chromemoly barrel, 2-piece quad rail, Prison Pink Cerakote finish, 6.6 lbs.

MSR $1,458	$1,300	$1,150	$975	$875	$725	$600	$475	

TASTANIUM DEVIL – 5.56 NATO cal., 16 in. heavy barrel with MB-3 muzzle brake, carbine length free float quad rail, Titanium Cerakote finish, 6 1/2 lbs. New 2014.

MSR $1,410	$1,250	$1,100	$950	$850	$700	$575	$450	

TOP GUN – 5.56 NATO cal., 16 in. heavy barrel with MB-1 muzzle brake, 2-stage trigger, YHM quad rail, extended charging handle, Ergo pistol grip, Magpul CTR stock, ambi-sling mount, 7.7 lbs.

MSR $1,669	$1,500	$1,325	$1,125	$1,025	$825	$675	$550	

S.W.D., INC.

Previous manufacturer located in Atlanta, GA.

Similar models have previously been manufactured by R.P.B. Industries, Inc. (1979-82), and met with BATF disapproval because of convertibility into fully automatic operation. "Cobray" is a trademark for the M11/9 semiautomatic pistol.

CARBINES

SEMI-AUTO CARBINE – 9mm Para. cal., same mechanism as M11, 16 1/4 in. shrouded barrel, telescoping stock.

	$550	$495	$450	$400	$325	$275	$235	

PISTOLS: SEMI-AUTO

COBRAY M-11/NINE mm – 9mm Para. cal., fires from closed bolt, SA, 3rd generation design, stamped steel frame, 32 shot mag., parkerized finish, similar in appearance to Ingram Mac 10.

	$475	$395	$350	$300	$295	$275	$250	

This model was also available in a fully-auto variation, Class III transferable only.

REVOLVERS

LADIES HOME COMPANION – .45-70 Govt. cal., double action design utilizing spring wound 12 shot rotary mag., 12 in. barrel, steel barrel and frame, 9 lbs. 6 oz. Mfg. 1990-94.

	$650	$525	$400	$360	$335	$310	$290	

SHOTGUNS: SINGLE SHOT

TERMINATOR – 12 or 20 ga., tactical design shotgun with 18 in. cylinder bore barrel, parkerized finish, ejector. Mfg. 1986-88 only.

	$150	$125	$95	$80	$70	$60	$55	*$110*

SI DEFENSE, INC.

Current AR-15 style carbine/rifle manufacturer located in Kalispell, MT.

MSR	100%	98%	95%	90%	80%	70%	60%	*Last MSR*

CARBINES/RIFLES: SEMI-AUTO

SI-C .223 STANDARD CARBINE – .223 Rem./5.56x45mm cal., internal gas block system, 16 in. parkerized barrel with SI DRK muzzle brake, A2 style fixed front sight, flip-up rear sight, billet upper and lower receivers, custom carbine length handguard, available in Black, Flat Dark Earth, or OD Green finish.

| N/A | $950 | $850 | $725 | $650 | $525 | $425 | $335 | |

SI-C M4 CARBINE – 5.56 NATO cal., nickel boron coated bolt carrier group, 16 in. M4 contour, nitride coated barrel with muzzle brake, 30 shot Magpul mag., Magpul MBUS flip rear sight, YHM flip- up front sight, 6-position adj. stock, Magpul MOE handguard, standard black or flat dark earth finish, 7 lbs. New 2014.

| N/A | $1,025 | $895 | $775 | $695 | $575 | $475 | $375 | |

SI-C ATC – 5.56 NATO cal., 16 in. M4 contour, nitride coated barrel with muzzle brake, 30 shot Magpul mag., 6-position adj. stock, 15 in. floating handguard, Hogue grip, fixed front and adj. rear sight, standard black or flat dark earth finish, 6 1/2 lbs. New 2014.

| N/A | $1,600 | $1,400 | $1,200 | $1,095 | $895 | $725 | $575 | |

SI-D .308 BATTLE RIFLE – .308 Win./7.62 NATO cal., 16 1/2 in. parkerized barrel with SI DRK muzzle brake, A2 style fixed front sight, carbine length gas system, billet upper and lower receivers, SI Defense carbine handguard, 6-position adj. buttstock, black finish.

| N/A | $1,575 | $1,375 | $1,175 | $1,075 | $875 | $725 | $550 | |

SI-D .308 CARBINE (HUNTING/SPORTSMAN) – .308 Win. cal., 16 in. M4 contour barrel with SI Defense DRK compensator, Weaver extra tall scope rings and Nikon 3x9 power scope with BDC reticle, free floating carbine length tube handguard, SI Defense adj. quad rail gas block, adj. 6-position Choate stock, 20 shot Magpul mag., flat dark earth finish, 9.1 lbs.

| N/A | $2,100 | $1,850 | $1,575 | $1,425 | $1,150 | $950 | $735 | |

MID-LENGTH CUSTOM – .223 Rem./5.56x45mm cal., internal gas block system, 18 in. stainless steel fluted barrel with SI DRK muzzle brake, flip-up front and rear sights, billet upper and lower receivers, black mid-length handguard, Ace stock, Black finish. Disc. 2013.

Retail pricing was not available on this model.

TREAD – 5.56x45mm cal., 18 in. parkerized barrel with SI Defense DRK muzzle brake, flip-up front and rear sights, billet upper and lower receivers, custom handguard, Ace buttstock, "Don't Tread On Me" engraving, custom Timney skeletonized trigger group, extended charging handle latch, red and white colored lettering. Disc. 2013.

Retail pricing was not available on this model.

SKS

SKS designates a semi-auto rifle design originally developed by the Russian military, and manufactured in Russia by both Tula Arsenal (1949-1956) and by Izhevsk Arsenal from 1953-1954. Currently manufactured in Russia, China, and many other countries. Previously manufactured in Russia, China (largest quantity), N. Korea, East Germany, Romania, Albania, Yugoslavia, and North Vietnam.

SKS DEVELOPMENT & HISTORY

SKS (Samozaryadnyi Karabin Simonova) - developed by Sergei Gavrilovich Simonov in the late 1940s to use the 7.62 cartridge of 1943 (7.62x39mm). The SKS is actually based on an earlier design developed by Simonov in 1936 as a prototype self-loading military rifle. The SKS was adopted by the Soviet military in 1949, two years after the AK-47, and was originally intended as a complement to the AK-47s select-fire capability. It served in this role until the mid-to-late 1950s, when it was withdrawn from active issue and sent to reserve units and Soviet Youth "Pioneer" programs. It was also released for use in military assistance programs to Soviet Bloc countries and other "friendly" governments. Much of the original SKS manufacturing equipment was shipped to Communist China prior to 1960. Since then, most of the SKS carbines produced, including those used by the Viet Cong in Vietnam, have come from China.

Like the AK-47, the Simonov carbine is a robust military rifle. It, too, was designed to be used by troops with very little formal education or training. It will operate reliably in the harshest climatic conditions, from the Russian arctic to the steamy jungles of Southeast Asia. Its chrome-lined bore is impervious to the corrosive effects of fulminate of mercury primers and the action is easily disassembled for cleaning and maintenance.

The SKS and a modified sporter called the OP-SKS (OP stands for Okhotnichnyi Patron) are the standard hunting rifles for a majority of Russian hunters. It is routinely used to take everything from the Russian saiga antelope up to and including moose, boar, and brown bear. The main difference between the regular SKS and the OP variant is in the chamber dimensions and the rate of rifling. The OP starts as a regular SKS, then has the barrel removed and replaced with one designed to specifically handle a slightly longer and heavier bullet.

Prior to the "assault weapons" ban, hundreds of thousands of SKS carbines were imported into the U.S. The SKS was rapidly becoming one of the favorites of American hunters and shooters. Its low cost and durability made it a popular "truck gun" for those shooters who spend a lot of time in the woods, whether they are ranchers, farmers, or plinkers. While the Russian made SKS is a bonafide curio and relic firearm and legal for importation, the Clinton administration suspended all import permits for firearms having a rifled bore and

MSR	100%	98%	95%	90%	80%	70%	60%	Last MSR

ammunition from the former Soviet Union in early 1994. In order to get the ban lifted, the Russian government signed a trade agreement, wherein they agreed to deny export licenses to any American company seeking SKS rifles and a variety of other firearms and ammunition deemed politically incorrect by Clinton & Gore. The BATF then used this agreement as a reason to deny import licenses for any SKS from any country.

Most of the SKS carbines imported into the U.S. came from the Peoples Republic of China. They were a mix of refurbished military issue, straight military surplus, and even some new manufacture. Quality was rather poor. Compared to the SKS Chinese carbines, only a few Russian made SKSs ever made it into the U.S. All are from military stockpiles and were refurbished at the Tula Arms Works, probably the oldest continuously operating armory in the world. Recently, more SKS carbines have been imported from the former Yugoslavia by Century International Arms. These carbines carry the former Soviet Bloc designation of "Type 58" and feature milled receivers. Quality is generally good, and values are comparable to other Russian/European SKS imports. Values for unmodified Russian and Eastern European made SKS carbines (those with the original magazines and stock) are higher than the Chinese copies.

The most collectible SKS is East German mfg., and SKS rifles mfg. in N. Korea and N. Vietnam are also quite rare in the U.S.

Over 600 million SKS carbines have been manufactured in China alone, by over 45 different manufacturers, in addition to the millions manufactured in other former Soviet Bloc countries. The Simonov carbine was the best selling semi-auto rifle in America (and other countries) during 1993-94, and remains a popular choice for plinking, hunting, and protection in the new millennium.

RIFLES: SEMI-AUTO

SKS – 7.62x39mm Russian cal., Soviet designed, original Soviet mfg. as well as copies mfg. in China, Russia, Yugoslavia, and many other countries, gas operated weapon, 10 shot fixed mag., wood stock (thumbhole design on newer mfg.), with or w/o (newer mfg.) permanently attached folding bayonet, tangent rear and hooded front sight, no current importation from China, Russia, or the former Yugoslavia.

Please refer to individual importers for other SKS listings, including Norinco, Poly-Technologies, and Mitchell Arms.

* **SKS Mfg. in Russia, Yugoslavia, Romania**

	100%	98%	95%	90%	80%	70%	60%
	$395	$365	$325	$295	$275	$235	$195

* **SKS Chinese Recent Mfg. w/Thumbhole Stock**

	100%	98%	95%	90%	80%	70%	60%
	$295	$275	$250	$225	$200	$185	$165

SRM ARMS

Current shotgun manufacturer located in Meridan, ID. Exclusively distributed by GSA Direct LLC located in Boise, ID. Dealer sales.

SHOTGUNS: SEMI-AUTO

SRM Arms also manufactures a 10 (Model 1208) or 13 (Model 1212) in. barrel shotgun for military/law enforcement.

MODEL 1216 – 12 ga., 3 in. chamber, 18 1/2 in. barrel with fixed choke, bullpup with pistol grip configuration, semi-auto roller-locked delayed blowback system, matte black finish, features a rotating detachable 16 shot mag with four separate tubes, ambidextrous receiver with tip up action, full length top Picatinny rail and three handguard rails, ghost rear and post front sights, 34 1/2 in. OAL, 7 1/4 lbs. New late 2011.

MSR $2,399	100%	98%	95%	90%	80%	70%	60%
	$2,175	$1,875	$1,575	$1,300	$1,150	$925	$800

The concept of the SRM shotgun began in the early 2000's when special forces personnel described their dream shotgun to the SRM developers. The first model was previewed in 2008, with final versions arriving late 2011.

SSK INDUSTRIES

Current customizer and Class II manufacturer located in Wintersville, OH.

SSK Industries manufactures complete guns, and furnishes a wide variety of gunsmithing services.

SSK Industries manufactures complete rifles and suppressors for police, military, and civilian use (where legal in accord with BATFE regulations). Their custom shop works on virtually anything 20mm or smaller.

SSK Industries used Thompson Center flatside frames and applied an industrial hard chrome finish prior to the introduction of stainless steel receivers. Most SSK handguns and rifles are extensively customized in exotic calibers, finishes, and various engraving options. Receivers and barrels could be purchased separately - values below are for complete assembled pistols.

SSK has also manufactured various limited editions including the Handgun Hunters International (HHI) Models 1, 2, and 3. Issue prices on these guns were $1,100 (Model 3), $1,200 (Model 2), and $1,300 (Model 1). Only 50 were mfg. total in 1987. SSK also customized a Ruger Super Redhawk (.44 Mag. or .45 LC cal.). This variation came with either a scoped 7 1/2 in. octagon barrel (Beauty Model) or a 6 in. bull barrel with muzzle brake (Beast Model). Prices started at $1,430 - add $245 extra for .45 LC cal.

PISTOLS: SINGLE SHOT

Values listed are for basic models with no options or special features.

MSR	100%	98%	95%	90%	80%	70%	60%	Last MSR

SSK-CONTENDER – over 150 cals. available from .17 Bee to .50-70, various custom barrels available, basically, this is a custom order only gun.

| | $1,500 | $1,375 | $1,250 | $1,125 | $1,000 | $900 | $825 | |

Individual barrels were available starting at $268.
An arrestor muzzle brake was available on special order.

This model included barrel, frame, stocks, and sights as standard equipment.

SSK-XP100 – various cals. between .17 and .50, includes TSOB mount and rings.

| | $1,700 | $1,500 | $1,300 | $1,150 | $1,025 | $925 | $850 | *$1,700* |

The .50 cal. XP100 (12.9 X 50.8 JDJ) came with SSK muzzle brake, scope, dies, and new reinforced fiberglass stock.

SSK ENCORE – over 400 calibers available with plain, fluted, and heavy barrels.
Please contact the company directly for pricing on this model.

RIFLES

Values listed are for basic models with no options or special features. In addition, SSK custom manufactures a bolt action rifle available in almost any caliber and configuration - prices started at approx. $2,000 and can go as high as $6,000, depending on the customer's individual special orders. SSK also has developed a 6.5mm, 7mm, or .30 cal. upper unit conversion for AR-15s and M-16s utilizing heavy sub-sonic "whisper" ammunition. SSK also manufactures a line of .50 cal. rifles, and a complete AR-15 starts at $1,500.

SSK TCR 87 – .14 through .500 cals., Nitro Express cals. are also available, features Thompson Center TRC 87 receiver, and SSK custom barrels, muzzle brakes, and exotic finishes were available at extra cost.

| | $1,700 | $1,500 | $1,300 | $1,150 | $1,025 | $925 | $850 | |

SSK RUGER NO. 1 – many cals. including .577 NE (optional), custom order rifle based on a Ruger No. 1 frame.

| | $2,000 | $1,800 | $1,600 | $1,400 | $1,250 | $1,100 | $1,000 | |

SSK BOLT ACTION – various cals., ground up custom order rifle.

| | $2,500 | $2,250 | $1,800 | $1,600 | $1,400 | $1,250 | $1,100 | |

STI INTERNATIONAL

Current manufacturer established during 1993, and located in Georgetown, TX. Distributor and dealer sales.

In addition to manufacturing the pistols listed, STI International also makes frame kits in steel, stainless steel, aluminum, or titanium - prices range between $206-$691.

PISTOLS: SEMI-AUTO, SINGLE ACTION

The beginning numerals on all STI pistols designate the barrel length, and most of the following models are listed in numerical sequence.

2.5 NEMESIS – 7mm Penna/7x23mm cal., 2 1/2 in. barrel. Mfg. 2010-2011.

| | $840 | $725 | $625 | $525 | $450 | $400 | $350 | *$870* |

3.0 DUTY ONE – 9mm Para., .40 S&W, or .45 ACP cal., 3 in. ramped bull barrel, forged steel frame with integral tactical rail, grid front strap, undercut trigger guard, front and rear slide serrations, with or w/o tritium sights (new 2014), 8 shot mag., G10 grip panels, high ride beavertail grip safety, matte blue, blue/anodized (new 2014), or hard chrome (new 2014) finish, 36.3 oz. New 2013.

| MSR $1,384 | $1,175 | $1,025 | $875 | $800 | $650 | $525 | $400 | |

Add $79 for tritium sights.
Add $363 for hard chrome finish.

3.0 ELEKTRA – 9mm Para., .40 S&W (disc. 2012), or .45 ACP cal., forged aluminum frame, 3 in. bull barrel, stainless steel slide, rear cocking serrations, beavertail grip safety, 6 or 8 shot mag., fixed tritium 2 dot sights, black anodized, silver/blue, silver/purple, silver/red, or silver/pink finish. New 2010.

| MSR $1,472 | $1,250 | $1,095 | $950 | $850 | $695 | $565 | $440 | |

3.0 ESCORT – 9mm Para., .40 S&W (new 2013) or .45 ACP cal., 3 in. bull barrel, checkered cocobolo grips, round top slide with rear cocking serrations, adj. 3-dot sights, 6 or 8 shot mag., blue slide with Duracoated frame, stippled front strap, 22.8 oz. New 2009.

| MSR $1,233 | $1,050 | $925 | $795 | $715 | $575 | $475 | $375 | |

3.0 LAWMAN – .38 Super (new 2014), 9mm Para. or .45 ACP cal., 3.24 in. STI ramped bushing barrel, polished blue finish, forged steel frame with 30 LPI front strap checkering, undercut trigger guard, G10 grip panels, front and rear slide cocking serrations, long curved aluminum trigger, high-ride beavertail safety, recoil master guide rod, ramped front sight, tactical adj. rear sight, optional tritium sights, 6 or 8 shot mag., single sided thumb safety, blue, black, green, or brown/tan finish, 24.8 oz. New 2012.

| MSR $1,514 | $1,285 | $1,125 | $965 | $875 | $700 | $575 | $450 | |

Add $79 for tritium sights.

MSR	100%	98%	95%	90%	80%	70%	60%	Last MSR

3.0 OFF DUTY – 9mm Para. or .45 ACP cal., compact frame, blued or hard chrome matte finish, 3 in. barrel with blue slide, checkered cocobolo grips, stippled front strap, competition front sight, tactical rear sight, 31.3 oz. Mfg. 2009-2013.

| | $1,075 | $950 | $800 | $725 | $595 | $485 | $375 | *$1,265* |

3.0 ROGUE – 9mm Para. cal., 3 in. bull barrel, forged aluminum compact frame, STI stippled front strap, undercut trigger guard, blued slide with Duracoated frame, integral sights, 21 oz. Mfg. 2009.

| | $925 | $825 | $725 | $650 | $575 | $500 | $425 | *$1,024* |

3.0 SHADOW – 9mm Para., .40 S&W, or .45 ACP cal., 3 in. bull barrel, matte black KG coated finish, forged aluminum frame, undercut trigger guard, stippled front strap, ultra thin G-10 grips with STI logo, rear cocking serrations, curved trigger, beavertail grip safety, fixed tritium 2 dot sights, 6 or 8 shot mag., 23.4 oz. New 2010.

| MSR $1,472 | $1,250 | $1,095 | $950 | $850 | $695 | $565 | $440 | |

3.0 SPARTAN III – 9mm Para. or .45 ACP cal., 1911 Commander steel frame, parkerized finish, bald front strap, hand checkered double diamond mahogany grips, rear slide serrations, STI long curved trigger, 3.24 in. chrome non-ramped bull bushing barrel, STI high ride beavertail grip safety, competition front sights, fixed rear sights, 6 or 8 shot mag., 32.7 oz. New 2012.

| MSR $754 | $650 | $575 | $495 | $440 | $360 | $295 | $225 | |

3.0 TACTICAL SS – .38 Super (new 2014), 9mm Para., .40 S&W, or .45 ACP cal., 3.8 in. ramped bull or threaded (new 2014) barrel, matte blue or hard chrome (new 2014) finish, forged steel frame with integral tactical rail, 30 LPI front strap checkering, undercut trigger guard, G10 grip panels, long curved trigger, high ride beavertail grip safety, ambidextrous thumb safeties, ramped front sight, fixed ledge style rear sight, 6 or 8 shot mag., 34.4 oz. New 2013.

| MSR $1,940 | $1,650 | $1,450 | $1,240 | $1,125 | $910 | $750 | $575 | |

Add $168 for threaded barrel.
Add $79 for tritium sights.
Add $340 for hard chrome finish.

3.0 TACTICAL – .38 Super, 9mm Para., .40 S&W, or .45 ACP cal., matte blue or hard chrome finish, 3 in. bull or threaded barrel, modular steel frame with integral tactical rail, flat-top slide with rear cocking serrations, black glass filled nylon polymer grips, long curved trigger, high ride beavertail grip safety, fixed rear sight, ramped front sight, 10, 12, 14, or 17 shot mag., 34 oz. New 2014.

| MSR $2,144 | $1,825 | $1,595 | $1,375 | $1,240 | $1,000 | $825 | $640 | |

Add $102 for tritium sights, or $167 for threaded barrel with tritium sights.
Add $340 for hard chrome finish.

> * **3.0 Tactical Lite** – .38 Super, 9mm Para, .40 S&W, or .45 ACP cal., 3 in. bull or threaded barrel, 10, 12, 14, or 17 shot mag., wih or w/o tritium sights, blue finish. New 2014.
>
> | MSR $2,144 | $1,825 | $1,595 | $1,375 | $1,240 | $1,000 | $825 | $640 | |
>
> Add $62 for tritium sights or $167 for threaded barrel and tritium sights.

3.0 TOTAL ECLIPSE – 9mm Para., .40 S&W, or .45 ACP cal., 3 in. barrel, skeletonized trigger, aluminum frame, polymer grips, beavertail safety, fixed 2-dot tritium sights, blue finish, 23.1 oz. Mfg. 2011-2013.

| | $1,575 | $1,375 | $1,175 | $1,075 | $865 | $710 | $550 | *$1,870* |

3.25 GP5 – 9mm Para. cal., 3 1/4 in. barrel, DAO, blue finish, chromemoly steel frame with integral tactical rail, textured polymer grips, double slide serrations, ambidextrous safety, internal extractor, adj. sights, 24.2 oz. Mfg. by Grand Power, Ltd. 2010-2011.

| | $595 | $550 | $500 | $450 | $400 | $375 | $350 | *$663* |

3.4 BLS9/BLS40 – 9mm Para. or .40 S&W cal., blue finish, Govt. length grips, Heinie low mount sights, single stack mag., 30 oz. Mfg. 1999-2005.

| | $765 | $650 | $565 | $460 | $400 | $360 | $330 | *$889* |

3.4 LS9/LS40 – 9mm Para. or .40 S&W (disc. 2008) cal., blue finish, Commander length grips, single stack mag., Heinie low mount rear sight, slide integral front sight, 28 oz. Mfg. 1999-2013.

| | $925 | $750 | $625 | $525 | $450 | $400 | $350 | *$1,002* |

3.4 ESCORT – 9mm Para. or .45 ACP cal., 1911 forged aluminum Commander style frame, 3.4 in. ramped bull barrel, slide with rear cocking serrations, Duracoat finish with blue slide, undercut trigger guard, stippled front strap, rosewood grips, STI hi-ride beavertail grip safety, fixed Novak style 3-dot sights, 22.8 oz. Mfg. 2007-2008.

| | $925 | $825 | $725 | $650 | $575 | $500 | $425 | *$1,024* |

3.9 FALCON – .38 Super, .40 S&W, or .45 ACP cal., STI standard frame, 3.9 in. barrel, size is comparable to Officers Model, adj. rear sight. Limited mfg. 1993-98.

| | $1,875 | $1,375 | $1,175 | $925 | $850 | $775 | $675 | *$2,136* |

MSR	100%	98%	95%	90%	80%	70%	60%	Last MSR

3.9 GUARDIAN – 9mm Para. (new 2009), .40 S&W (new 2014), or .45 ACP cal., 1911 Commander style blue frame, 3.9 in. ramped bull barrel, stainless slide with polished sides, stippled front strap, undercut trigger guard, rosewood grips, fixed 3-dot sights, 6 or 8 shot mag., stainless/blue or hard chrome finish, 32.4 oz. New 2007.

	100%	98%	95%	90%	80%	70%	60%	Last MSR
MSR $1,181	$1,000	$875	$750	$675	$550	$450	$350	

Add $340 for hard chrome finish.

3.9 STINGER – 9mm Para. or .38 Super cal., black frame, designed for IPSC and USPSA competition, 38 oz. Mfg. 2005-2008.

	100%	98%	95%	90%	80%	70%	60%	Last MSR
	$2,500	$2,225	$1,975	$1,750	$1,575	$1,375	$1,150	$2,773

3.9 TACTICAL – 9mm Para., .40 S&W, or .45 ACP cal., matte blue finish, 3.9 in. bull barrel, modular steel frame with integral tactical rail, flat-top slide with rear cocking serrations, black glass filled nylon polymer grips, long curved trigger, high ride beavertail grip safety, fixed rear sight, ramped front sight, 34 oz. Mfg. 2012-2013.

	100%	98%	95%	90%	80%	70%	60%	Last MSR
	$1,775	$1,500	$1,250	$1,000	$875	$800	$675	$2,109

4.0 DUTY ONE – 9mm Para., .40 S&W, or .45 ACP cal., 4.4 in. ramped bull (disc. 2013) or bushing (new 2014) barrel, forged steel frame with integral tactical rail, grid front strap, undercut trigger guard, front and rear slide serrations, G10 grip panels, matte blue, blue/anodized or hard chrome finish, high ride beavertail grip safety, 8 or 9 shot mag., 36.3 oz. New 2013.

	100%	98%	95%	90%	80%	70%	60%	Last MSR
MSR $1,384	$1,175	$1,025	$875	$800	$650	$525	$400	

Add $79 for tritium sights.
Add $340 for hard chrome finish.

3.9 V.I.P. – 9mm Para. (new 2009), .40 S&W (new 2009), or .45 ACP cal. only, aluminum frame, STI modular polymer frame, stainless steel slide, 3.9 in. bull barrel with STI Recoilmaster muzzle brake, 10, 13, or 16 shot double stack mag., STI fixed sights, blue or hard chrome finish or stainless steel, 25 oz. Mfg. 2001-2006, reintroduced 2009.

	100%	98%	95%	90%	80%	70%	60%	Last MSR
MSR $1,775	$1,500	$1,325	$1,125	$1,025	$825	$675	$525	

Add $340 for hard chrome finish.

4.0 LAWMAN – 9mm Para. or .45 ACP cal., 4.26 in. STI ramped bushing barrel, polished blue finish, forged steel frame with 30 LPI front strap checkering, undercut trigger guard, G10 grip panels, front and rear slide cocking serrations, long curved aluminum trigger, high-ride beavertail safety, recoil master guide rod, ramped front sight, tactical adj. rear sight, single sided thumb safety, 8 or 9 shot mag., blue, black/green, or brown/tan finish, 37.3 oz. New 2012.

	100%	98%	95%	90%	80%	70%	60%	Last MSR
MSR $1,514	$1,285	$1,125	$965	$875	$700	$575	$450	

Add $79 for tritium sights.

4.0 SPARTAN IV – 9mm Para. or .45 ACP cal., 1911 Commander steel frame, parkerized finish, bald front strap, hand checkered double diamond mahogany grips, rear slide serrations, STI long curved trigger, 4.26 in. chrome non-ramped bull bushing barrel, STI high ride beavertail grip safety, competition front sights, fixed rear sights, 8 or 9 shot mag., 34.3 oz. New 2012.

	100%	98%	95%	90%	80%	70%	60%	Last MSR
MSR $754	$650	$575	$495	$440	$360	$295	$225	

4.0 TACTICAL SS – 9mm Para., .40 S&W, or .45 ACP cal., 4.3 in. ramped bull or threaded (new 2014) barrel, matte blue or hard chrome (new 2014) finish, forged steel frame with integral tactical rail, 30 LPI front strap checkering, undercut trigger guard, G10 grip panels, long curved trigger, high ride beavertail grip safety. ambidextrous thumb safeties, ramped front sight, fixed ledge style rear sight, 6, 8, or 9 shot mag., 38.2 oz. New 2013.

	100%	98%	95%	90%	80%	70%	60%	Last MSR
MSR $1,940	$1,650	$1,450	$1,240	$1,125	$910	$750	$575	

Add $79 for tritium sights or threaded barrel.
Add $340 for hard chrome finish.

4.0 TACTICAL – 9mm Para., .40 S&W, or .45 ACP cal., matte blue or hard chrome finish, 3 in. bull or threaded barrel, modular steel frame with integral tactical rail, flat-top slide with rear cocking serrations, black glass filled nylon polymer grips, long curved trigger, high ride beavertail grip safety, fixed rear sight, ramped front sight, 10, 12, 14, or 17 shot mag., 34 oz. New 2014.

	100%	98%	95%	90%	80%	70%	60%	Last MSR
MSR $2,144	$1,825	$1,595	$1,375	$1,240	$1,000	$825	$640	

Add $102 for tritium sights, or $167 for threaded barrel with tritium sights.
Add $340 for hard chrome finish.

   * **4.0 Tactical Lite** – 9mm Para., .40 S&W, or .45 ACP cal., 4 in. bull or threaded barrel, 10, 12, 14, or 17 shot mag., with or w/o tritium sights, blue finish. New 2014.

	100%	98%	95%	90%	80%	70%	60%	Last MSR
MSR $2,144	$1,825	$1,595	$1,375	$1,240	$1,000	$825	$640	

Add $62 for tritium sights or $167 for threaded barrel and tritium sights.

4.15 TACTICAL – 9mm Para., .40 S&W, or .45 ACP cal., blue steel, fixed sights, short trigger, ambidextrous safety, 34 1/2 oz. Mfg. 2004-2013.

	100%	98%	95%	90%	80%	70%	60%	Last MSR
	$1,725	$1,500	$1,295	$1,175	$950	$775	$600	$2,045

MSR	100%	98%	95%	90%	80%	70%	60%	Last MSR

4.15 RANGER II (3.9 RANGER) – 9mm Para. (new 2009), .40 S&W (new 2009), or .45 ACP cal. only, Officer's Model with 3.9 (Ranger, disc. 2004) or 4.15 (Ranger II, new 2005) in. bull barrel and 1/2 in. shortened grip frame, 6 shot mag., blue or hard chrome (new 2014) steel frame with stainless steel slide, single stack mag., low mount STI/Heinie sights, 8 or 9 shot mag., 29 oz. New 2001.

| MSR $1,181 | $1,000 | $875 | $750 | $675 | $550 | $450 | $350 | |

Add $340 for hard chrome finish.

Add $192 for Ranger III configuration (mfg. 2010-2013).

4.15 DUTY CT – 9mm Para., .40 S&W or .45 ACP cal., 5 in. bull barrel, matte blue finish, integral tactical rail, flat-top slide with rear cocking serrations, ramped front sight, fixed rear sight, 36.6 oz. Mfg. 2006-2008.

| | $1,100 | $950 | $825 | $700 | $600 | $525 | $450 | *$1,286* |

4.15 STEELMASTER – 9mm Para. cal., 4.15 in. Trubore barrel, blue or hard chrome (new 2014) finish with polished classic slide, sabertooth cocking serrations, C-More red dot scope with blast shield and thumbrest, black glass filled nylon polymer grips with aluminum magwell, 10 or 20 shot mag., 38.9 oz. New 2009.

| MSR $3,048 | $2,595 | $2,275 | $1,950 | $1,765 | $1,425 | $1,175 | $910 | |

Add $395 for hard chrome finish.

4.15 MATCHMASTER – .38 Super or 9mm Para. (new 2014) cal., 4.15 in. Trubor barrel, blue or hard chrome (new 2014) finish with polished classic slide, sabertooth front and rear cocking serrations, black glass filled nylon polymer grips with aluminum magwell, drilled and tapped, 10 or 20 shot mag., C-More red dot scope with blast shield and thumb rest, 38.9 oz. New 2009.

| MSR $3,193 | $2,715 | $2,375 | $2,035 | $1,850 | $1,495 | $1,225 | $950 | |

Add $395 for hard chrome finish.

4.25 GP6 – 9mm Para. cal., 4 1/4 in. barrel, DA/SA, blue finish, chromemoly steel frame with integral tactical rail, textured polymer grips, double slide serrations, ambidextrous safety, internal extractor, adj. sights, 26.1 oz. Mfg. by Grand Power, Ltd. Mfg. 2009-2012.

| | $595 | $550 | $500 | $450 | $400 | $375 | $350 | *$663* |

Add $34 for GP6-C model with fiber optic front sight and adj. rear sight (mfg. 2010-2011).

4.25 EL COMMANDANTE – 9mm Para. cal., blue matte finish, Government steel frame, 4.25 in. non-ramped bushing barrel, beavertail grip safety, steel trigger, single sided thumb safety, one-piece original GI style guide rod, GI steel sights, smooth wood grips, rear slide cocking serrations, 34 1/2 oz. Mfg. 2011 only.

| | $895 | $725 | $625 | $525 | $450 | $400 | $350 | *$942* |

4.3 HAWK – various cals., 4.3 in. barrel, STI standard frame (choice of steel or aluminum), 27 or 31 oz. Mfg. 1993-1999.

| | $1,725 | $1,275 | $1,075 | $875 | $800 | $700 | $600 | *$1,975* |

4.3 NIGHT HAWK – .45 ACP cal., 4.3 in. barrel, STI wide extended frame, blue finish, 33 oz. Limited mfg. 1997-99.

| | $1,875 | $1,375 | $1,175 | $925 | $850 | $775 | $675 | *$2,136* |

5.0 G.I. – .45 ACP cal., 5 in. non-ramped bushing barrel, matte blue finish, steel frame and trigger, beavertail grip safety, matte blue slide with rear cocking serrations, smooth wood grips, GI steel sights, 8 shot mag., 35.3 oz. New 2010.

| MSR $874 | $750 | $650 | $565 | $510 | $415 | $340 | $265 | |

5.0 FB7 – 7mm or 9mm Para. cal., 5 in. barrel. Mfg. 2010-2011.

| | $1,750 | $1,500 | $1,250 | $1,000 | $875 | $800 | $675 | *$1,940* |

5.0 EAGLE – 9mm Para., .357 SIG, .38 Super, .40 S&W, or .45 ACP cal., 5.1 in. barrel, STI standard full size wide body govt. model frame (choice of steel or aluminum), 10, 12, 14, or 17 shot double stack mag., adj. rear sight, polished blue or hard chrome (new 2014) finish, high ride beavertail grip safety, black glass filled nylon polymer grips, 31 or 35 oz.

| MSR $2,123 | $1,800 | $1,575 | $1,350 | $1,225 | $995 | $810 | $625 | |

Add $340 for hard chrome finish.

Add $266 for .38 Super with .45 ACP conversion kit (disc. 2011).

5.0 EDGE – .38 Super (new 2014), 9mm Para., 10mm Norma (disc. 2008), .40 S&W, or .45 ACP cal., 5 in. bull barrel, designed for limited/standard IPSC competition, STI extended wide body frame, 10, 12, 14, or 17 shot double stack mag., blue or hard chrome finish, 39 oz. New 1998.

| MSR $2,180 | $1,850 | $1,625 | $1,395 | $1,260 | $1,025 | $835 | $650 | |

Add $340 for hard chrome finish.

MSR	100%	98%	95%	90%	80%	70%	60%	Last MSR

5.0 DUTY ONE – 9mm Para., .40 S&W, or .45 ACP cal., 5.1 in. ramped bull barrel, forged steel frame with integral tactical rail (new 2013), grid front strap, undercut trigger guard, front and rear slide serrations, checkered wood (disc. 2012) or G10 grip panels (new 2013), matte blue, blue/anodized (new 2014), or hard chrome (new 2014) finish, high ride beavertail grip safety, 8 or 9 shot mag., 37.2 oz. New 2005.

MSR $1,384	$1,175	$1,025	$875	$800	$650	$525	$400	

Add $363 for hard chrome finish.

Add $79 for tritium sights.

5.0 LAWMAN (LSA) – 9mm Para. (new 2013) or .45 ACP cal., 1911 Govt. style, 5 in. barrel, hammer forged carbon steel frame, designed for duty, self-defense, IPSC, USPSA, and IDPA competition, with or w/o tritium sights, 8 or 9 shot mag., blue, black/green, or brown/tan finish, 36 oz. New 2005.

MSR $1,514	$1,285	$1,125	$965	$875	$700	$575	$450	

5.0 SENTRY – 9mm Para., .40 S&W, or .45 ACP cal., 5 in. ramped barrel with bushing, classic polished flat-top slide with front and rear cocking serrations, checkered cocobolo grips, blue or hard chrome finish, competition front and adj. rear sights, 6 or 9 shot mag., 35.3 oz. New 2009.

MSR $1,753	$1,495	$1,300	$1,125	$1,000	$825	$675	$525	

Add $315 for hard chrome finish.

5.0 APEIRO – .38 Super (new 2014), 9mm Para., .40 S&W, or .45 ACP cal., 5 in. Schuemann Island style bull barrel, long wide steel frame, stainless steel slide, blue finish, black glass filled nylon polymer grips, stainless flared and blended magwell, Dawson fiber optic front and adj. rear sights, 10, 12, 14, or 17 shot mag., 38 oz. New 2010.

MSR $2,934	$2,495	$2,185	$1,875	$1,695	$1,375	$1,125	$875	

5.0 SPARROW – .22 LR cal. only, unlocked blowback action, STI standard extended frame, 5.1 in. ramped bull barrel, fixed sights, blue finish, 30 oz. Limited mfg. 1998-1999 only.

	$1,025	$900	$800	$700	$600	$500	$400	*$1,090*

5.0 EXECUTIVE – .40 S&W cal. only, STI long/wide frame, 5 in. bull barrel, 10 or 14 shot double stack mag., stainless construction, grey nylon polymer grips and square trigger guard, hard chrome finish with black inlays, fiberoptic front and STI adj. rear sights, approved for IPSC standard and USPSA limited edition, 38 oz. New 2001.

MSR $2,638	$2,250	$1,975	$1,695	$1,525	$1,240	$1,015	$795	

* **5.0 Executive IPSC 30th Commemorative** – 9mm Para., .40 S&W, or .45 ACP cal., ramped bull barrel, two-tone hard chrome finish, special engraved slide with "IPSC 30th Anniversary" on side, 39 oz. Mfg. 2005-2006.

	$2,500	$2,225	$1,975	N/A	N/A	N/A	N/A	*$2,775*

* **5.0 Executive Special Edition** – 9mm Para., .40 S&W, or .45 ACP cal., ramped bull barrel, 24Kt. gold on all steel surfaces, checkered black grips, "Special Edition" engraved on slide, 39 oz. Mfg. 2005-2006.

	$2,625	$2,325	$2,000	N/A	N/A	N/A	N/A	*$2,930*

5.0 STI 20TH ANNIVERSARY – 9mm Para., .40 S&W, or .45 ACP cal., 5 in. bull barrel, steel frame, PVD and TIN (titanium nitride) finish, black glass filled nylon polymer filled grips, TIN coated magwell, beavertail grip safety, Dawson fiber optic front and STI adj. rear sight, 38 oz. Limited edition of 200 during 2010.

	$3,300	$2,950	$2,600	N/A	N/A	N/A	N/A	*$3,623*

5.0 100TH ANNIVERSARY SPECIAL EDITION – .45 ACP cal., consists of 2 pistols - one is traditional GI style 1911, and the other gun is built on STI's patented high capacity modular frame, boxed with 2011 STI "challenge" coin, 500 sets mfg. 2011-2012.

	$3,875	$3,400	$2,900	$2,400	$2,100	$1,950	$1,700	*$4,154*

5.0 TROJAN – 9mm Para., .40 S&W, .38 Super, or .45 ACP, 5 in. barrel with bushing, standard Govt. length grips, single stack mag., stainless steel available 2006, blue, blue/anodized, or hard chrome finish, 8 or 9 shot mag., 36 oz. New 1999.

MSR $1,222	$1,035	$900	$775	$700	$575	$465	$360	

Add $340 for hard chrome finish.

Add $288 for .38 Super with .45 ACP conversion kit (disc. 2011).

Add $412 for stainless steel (disc. 2011).

5.0 TRUBOR (COMPETITOR) – 9mm Para. or .38 Super cal. only, standard frame, classic slide with front and rear serrations, square hammer, compensator, double stack mag., match sear, STI "Alchin" style blast deflector mount, TruBor compensator became standard 2005, C-More rail scope, wide ambidextrous and grip safeties, 41.3 oz. Mfg. 1999-2011.

	$2,475	$2,050	$1,750	$1,450	$1,200	$995	$875	*$2,864*

MSR	100%	98%	95%	90%	80%	70%	60%	Last MSR

5.0 TRUBOR GM – 9mm Para. or .38 Super cal., 5 in. TruBor bull barrel, hard chrome finish with blue color inlays, classic flat-top slide, sabertooth cocking serrations, blue glass filled nylon polymer grips with stainless steel magwell, drilled and tapped, C-More gray scope, 44.6 oz. Mfg. 2009-2011.

| | $3,350 | $3,000 | $2,700 | $2,250 | $1,800 | $1,400 | $1,175 | *$3,655* |

5.0 SPARTAN V – 9mm Para. (new 2013), or .45 ACP cal., 1911 Govt. steel frame, parkerized finish, bald front strap, hand checkered double diamond wood grips, front and rear slide serrations, STI long curved trigger, 5 in. chrome ramped bushing barrel, STI high ride beavertail grip safety, fiber optic front sights, adj. rear sights, 9 shot mag., 35.3 oz. New 2007.

| MSR $754 | $650 | $575 | $495 | $440 | $360 | $295 | $225 | |

5.0 USPSA SINGLE STACK – 9mm Para., .38 Super (new 2013), .40 S&W, or .45 ACP cal., 5 in. stainless steel barrel with bushing, tri-top two-tone slide with sabertooth cocking serrations, blue frame, 30 LPI front strap checkering, checkered steel D&T mainspring housing and magwell, competition front and adj. rear sight, 8 or 9 shot mag., 38.3 oz. New 2009.

| MSR $1,976 | $1,675 | $1,475 | $1,250 | $1,140 | $925 | $750 | $585 | |

5.0 USPSA DOUBLE STACK – 9mm Para., .40 S&W, or .45 ACP cal., 5 in. stainless steel barrel, tri-top two-tone slide with sabertooth cocking serrations, blue frame, 30 LPI front strap checkering, checkered steel D&T mainspring housing and magwell, competition front and adj. rear sight, 38.3 oz. Mfg. 2009-2012.

| | $2,425 | $2,000 | $1,750 | $1,450 | $1,200 | $1,000 | $900 | *$2,818* |

5.0 IPSC DOUBLE STACK – 9mm Para., .40 S&W, or .45 ACP cal., 5 in. bull barrel, blue frame, two-tone hard chrome slide with sabertooth cocking serrations, Dawson fiber optic front and adj. rear sights, black glass filled nylon polymer grips with stainless steel magwell, 38 oz. Mfg. 2009-2012.

| | $2,425 | $2,000 | $1,750 | $1,450 | $1,200 | $1,000 | $900 | *$2,818* |

5.0 RANGEMASTER – .38 Super (new 2014), 9mm Para. or .45 ACP cal., black frame, 5 in. ramped bull barrel, STI Recoilmaster guide rod, blue or hard chrome finish, 8 or 9 shot mag., 38 oz. New 2005.

| MSR $1,618 | $1,375 | $1,200 | $1,025 | $935 | $750 | $625 | $475 | |

Add $340 for hard chrome finish.

5.0 RANGEMASTER II – similar to Rangemaster, except does not have extended frame dust cover. Mfg. 2006.

| | $1,175 | $965 | $850 | $725 | $625 | $525 | $475 | *$1,344* |

5.0 TACTICAL – 9mm Para., .40 S&W, or .45 ACP cal., 5 in. bull or threaded barrel, short trigger, ambidextrous safety, 10, 12, 14, or 17 shot mag., blue steel or hard chrome finish, fixed sights, 39 oz. New 2004.

| MSR $2,144 | $1,825 | $1,595 | $1,375 | $1,240 | $1,000 | $825 | $640 | |

Add $340 for hard chrome finish.
Add $102 for tritium sights or $167 for tritium sights and threaded barrel.

  * **5.0 Tactical Lite** – similar to 5.0 Tactical, except stainless slide, alloy frame, fixed sights, 34 1/2 oz. Mfg. 2004-2005.

| | $1,800 | $1,525 | $1,300 | $1,050 | $900 | $825 | $700 | *$2,002* |

5.0 TACTICAL SS – 9mm Para., .40 S&W, or .45 ACP cal., 5 in. ramped bull or threaded barrel, matte blue or hard chrome finish, forged steel frame with integral tactical rail, 30 LPI front strap checkering, undercut trigger guard, G10 grip panels, long curved trigger, high ride beavertail grip safety, ambidextrous thumb safeties, ramped front sight, fixed ledge style rear sight, 6, 8, or 9 shot mag., 41.1 oz. New 2013.

| MSR $1,940 | $1,650 | $1,450 | $1,240 | $1,125 | $910 | $750 | $575 | |

Add $79 for tritium sights or $168 for threaded barrel and tritium sights.
Add $340 for hard chrome finish.

5.0 TRUSIGHT – 9mm Para., .40 S&W, or .45 ACP (disc. 2008) cal., 5 in. ramped bull barrel with expansion chamber, black glass filled nylon polymer grip with aluminum magwell, Dawson fiber optic front sight, adj. rear sight, blue finish with polished slide, 39 oz. Mfg. 2006-2009.

| | $1,795 | $1,525 | $1,275 | $1,050 | $900 | $825 | $700 | *$1,985* |

5.0 LEGEND – .38 Super, 9mm Para., .40 S&W, or .45 ACP cal., 5 in. bull barrel, STI modular steel long wide frame, Tri-top forged slide with sabertooth cocking serrations and hard chrome with black inlay and polished sides, blue frame, black glass filled nylon polymer grips with hard chrome magwell, Dawson fiber optic front sights, adj. rear sight, 10, 12, 14, or 17 shot mag., 38 oz. New 2007.

| MSR $2,886 | $2,450 | $2,150 | $1,840 | $1,665 | $1,350 | $1,100 | $860 | |

MSR	100%	98%	95%	90%	80%	70%	60%	Last MSR

LEGACY MODEL – 45 ACP cal., 5 in. ramped STI bushing barrel, PVD finish, polished flat-top black slide, rear cocking serrations, front strap checkering, custom cocobolo grips, ambidextrous thumb safety, ramped front sight, 36 oz. Mfg. 2006-2008.

	$1,750	$1,500	$1,250	$1,000	$900	$825	$700	*$1,929*

5.0 NITRO 10 – 10mm cal., 1911 style Government frame, 5 in. ramped bull barrel, 8 shot mag., one piece steel guide rod, long curved trigger, undercut trigger guard, competition front sight, fixed "Ledge" style rear sight, "Nitro" cocobolo grip panels, blue matte finish, high ride beavertail grip safety, single-sided thumb safety, classic slide with front and rear cocking serrations, 38.9 oz. New 2014.

MSR $1,514	$1,285	$1,125	$965	$875	$700	$575	$450	

5.0 MARAUDER – 9mm Para. cal., 5 in. barrel with bushing, 10 or 17 shot mag., black nitride finish. New 2014.

MSR $2,621	$2,225	$1,950	$1,675	$1,515	$1,225	$1,000	$775	

5.0 GM – 9mm Para or .38 Super cal., race gun, modular steel frame, 5 in. one piece, rifle grade, stainless steel Trubor compensated barrel, drilled and tapped mag release, long curved trigger, C-More scope, stainless steel mag well, 2011 glass filled black polymer modular grips, high ride beavertail grip safety, ambidextrous thumb safety, hard chrome finish with blue color inlay, classic flat-top with slide lightening, sabertooth cocking serrations, recoil master guide rod, 17 or 20 shot mag., 44.6 oz. New 2014.

MSR $3,682	$3,125	$2,735	$2,350	$2,125	$1,725	$1,400	$1,095	

5.0 SENTINEL – 9mm Para., .40 S&W, or .45 ACP cal., 1911 Govt. forged frame, 5 in. barrel, flat-top slide with rear cocking serrations, matte blue finish, front strap 30 LPI checkering, checkered steel D&T mainspring housing and flared magwell, STI competition front sights, adj. rear sight, thick rosewood grips, 38.3 oz. Mfg. 2007-2008.

	$1,395	$1,200	$1,025	$875	$750	$625	$550	*$1,598*

5.0 SENTINEL PREMIER – .45 ACP cal., 1911 Govt. forged frame, 5 in. barrel with bushing, polished slide with rear cocking serrations, hard chrome finish, front strap 30 LPI checkering, checkered steel D&T mainspring housing and flared magwell, tritium sights, 6 shot mag., 36.7 oz. New 2009.

MSR $2,410	$2,050	$1,795	$1,540	$1,395	$1,125	$925	$725	

5.0/5.5 TRUBOR – 9mm Para. or .38 Super cal., modular steel frame, 5 or 5.5 (disc. 2013) in. Trubor barrel, polished blue or hard chrome finish, black glass filled nylon polymer grips with aluminum magwell, lightened slide with front and rear cocking serrations, two inch integral compensator, C-More railway red dot sight with blast deflector mount, ambidextrous thumb safety, 10 or 20 shot mag., 41 oz. New 2012.

MSR $3,064	$2,600	$2,275	$1,950	$1,775	$1,425	$1,175	$910	

Add $347 for hard chrome finish.

5.1 LIMITED – while advertised during 1998 with an MSR of $1,699, this model never went into production.

5.5 EAGLE – various cals., features STI standard frame, 5 1/2 in. compensated barrel, 44 oz. Limited mfg. 1994-98.

	$2,100	$1,750	$1,475	$1,200	$995	$895	$775	*$2,399*

5.5 GRANDMASTER – .38 Super cal. standard, custom order gun with any variety of options available, double stack mag., 42 oz. Mfg. 2001-2008.

	$3,075	$2,650	$2,275	$1,900	$1,650	$1,425	$1,200	*$3,371*

5.5 STI GM – 9mm Para. or .38 Super cal., modular steel frame, 5.5 Trubor bull barrel with two inch integral compensator, hard chrome finish with blue, red, or black inlay, C-More red dot sight, blue glass filled polymer grips with stainless flared magwell and drilled and tapped mag. release, lightened slide with sabertooth cocking serrations, high ride beavertail grip safety, ambidextrous thumb safety, 10 or 20 shot mag., 44.6 oz. New 2012.

MSR $3,682	$3,125	$2,735	$2,350	$2,125	$1,725	$1,400	$1,095	

6.0 EAGLE – .38 Super, 9mm Para., .40 S&W, or .45 ACP cal., features STI super extended heavy frame, 6 in. barrel with bushing, blue or hard chrome finish, wide body with 10, 12, 14, or 17 shot double stack mag., 42 oz. New 1998.

MSR $2,243	$1,900	$1,665	$1,425	$1,295	$1,050	$850	$665	

Add $340 for hard chrome finish.
Add $267 for .38 Super with .45 ACP conversion kit (disc. 2008).

6.0 TROJAN – 9mm Para. or .45 ACP cal., similar to Trojan 5.0, except has 6 in. barrel and single stack mag., 36 oz. New 2000.

MSR $1,555	$1,325	$1,160	$995	$900	$725	$595	$465	

Add $143 for .38 Super with .45 ACP conversion kit (disc. 2008).

6.0 HUNTER – 10mm cal. only, 6 in. barrel, STI super extended heavy frame with single stack mag., blue finish, 51 oz. Only 2 mfg. 1998, disc. 2000.

	$2,250	$1,875	$1,650	$1,425	$1,200	$995	$895	*$2,485*

Add $350 for Leupold 2X scope with terminator mount.

MSR	100%	98%	95%	90%	80%	70%	60%	*Last MSR*

6.0 PERFECT 10 – 10mm Norma cal., 6 in. bull barrel, blue or hard chrome finish with polished classic flat-top slide, front and rear cocking serrations, ramped front and Heinie fixed rear sights, 6 inch integral tactical rail, 10 or 14 shot mag., black glass filled nylon polymer grips with aluminum flared magwell, 37 1/2 oz. New 2009.

	100%	98%	95%	90%	80%	70%	60%	
MSR $2,621	$2,225	$1,950	$1,675	$1,515	$1,225	$1,000	$775	

Add $340 for hard chrome finish.

6.0 TARGETMASTER – 9mm Para. or .45 ACP cal., black frame, 6 in. ramped bull barrel, two piece steel guide rod, 8 or 9 shot mag., 40 oz. New 2005.

	100%	98%	95%	90%	80%	70%	60%	
MSR $1,815	$1,550	$1,350	$1,165	$1,0550	$850	$700	$550	

Add $315 for hard chrome finish in 9mm Para. cal, or $340 for hard chrome finish in .45 ACP cal.

6.0 .450 XCALIBER – .450 cal., single stack mag., V-10 barrel and slide porting, stainless grip and thumb safeties, adj. rear sight. Limited mfg. 2000-2002.

	100%	98%	95%	90%	80%	70%	60%	
	$1,000	$850	$750	$650	$525	$450	$395	*$1,122*

6.0 .450+ XCALIBER – .450+ cal., otherwise similar to Xcaliber 6.0 .450, except has 6 in. frame with patented polymer grip and double stack mag. Limited mfg. 2000-2002.

	100%	98%	95%	90%	80%	70%	60%	
	$1,775	$1,575	$1,350	$1,175	$995	$875	$775	*$1,998*

RIFLES/CARBINES: SEMI-AUTO

STI SPORTING/TACTICAL CARBINE – .223 Rem. or 5.56 NATO cal., GIO, 16 in. stainless steel barrel, JP trigger group, STI Valkyrie handguard and gas block, Nordic tactical compensator, black Teflon coating, fixed A2 or collapsible buttstock, optional rails, approx. 7 lbs. New 2010.

	100%	98%	95%	90%	80%	70%	60%	
MSR $1,455	$1,225	$1,075	$925	$835	$675	$550	$425	

SWS 2000

Previous rifle manufacturer located in Krefeld, Germany until 2010. Previously imported until 2009 by Euro-Imports, located in Yoakum, TX.

RIFLES

SWS 2000 manufactured a variety of sporting and tactical style rifles in a variety of configurations.

Prices ranged from €2,600-€3,759 for sporting and hunting models, and €6,162-€7,910 for tactical rifles.

SABRE

Previous trademark of shotguns previously imported by Mitchell's Mausers, located in Fountain Valley, CA.

SHOTGUNS: SEMI-AUTO

SABRE – 12 ga. only, gas operated, 18 1/2 (w/o VR), 22, or 28 in. VR barrel with choke tubes, choice of black fiberglass or checkered walnut stock and forearm, configurations include Hunting, Turkey, Deer Hunter, and Police, mfg. in Turkey. Importation disc. 2007.

	100%	98%	95%	90%	80%	70%	60%	
	$435	$375	$325	$275	$235	$210	$190	*$495*

Add $50 for Police model.

SABRE DEFENCE INDUSTRIES LLC.

Previous manufacturer from 2002-2010, with production headquarters located in Nashville, TN, and sales offices located in Middlesex, U.K. This company was previously known as Ramo Mfg., Inc., which was founded in 1977. Sabre Defence was also the U.S. distributor for Sphinx pistols until 2009.

Due to space considerations, information regarding this manufacturer is available online free of charge at www.bluebookofgunvalues.com.

SACO DEFENSE INC.

Previous firearms manufacturer located in Saco, ME. Saco Defense was purchased by General Dynamics in July of 2000, and continues to produce guns for military defense contracts. This company was previously owned by Colt's Manufacturing Company, Inc. during late 1998-2000.

In the past, Saco Defense utilized their high-tech manufacturing facility to produce guns for Magnum Research, Weatherby (contract ended Sept., 2001), and others.

SADLAK INDUSTRIES LLC

Current rifle and components manufacturer located in Coventry, CT.

MSR	100%	98%	95%	90%	80%	70%	60%	Last MSR

RIFLES: SEMI-AUTO

Sadlak Industries manufactures M14 and M1A style semi-auto rifles, as well as numerous parts and components, including scope mounts and service tools. Please contact the company directly for more information, including pricing and current availability (see Trademark Index).

SAFARI ARMS

Previous trademark manufactured in Olympia, WA. M-S Safari Arms, located in Phoenix, AZ, was started in 1978 as a division of M-S Safari Outfitters. In 1987, Safari Arms was absorbed by Olympic Arms. Safari Arms manufactured 1911 style pistols since the acquisition of M-S Safari Arms in 1987. In Jan. 2004, the Safari Arms name was discontinued and all 1911 style pistols are now being manufactured by Olympic Arms. Please refer to the Olympic Arms section for currently manufactured models.

Safari Arms previously made the Phoenix, Special Forces, Camp Perry, and Royal Order of Jesters commemoratives in various configurations and quantities. Prices average in the $1,500 range except for the Royal Order of Jesters ($2,000).

SCHUETZEN PISTOL WORKS

Schuetzen Pistol Works is the current custom shop of Olympic Arms. Some of the pistols made by Safari Arms had the "Schuetzen Pistol Works" name on them (c. 1994-96). Until Jan. 2004, all pistols were are marked with the Safari Arms slide marking. All pistols, however, have been marked "Safari Arms" on the frame. The pistols formerly in this section have been moved to the PISTOLS: SEMI-AUTO category.

PISTOLS: SEMI-AUTO, SINGLE ACTION

Safari Arms manufactured mostly single action, semi-auto pistols derived from the Browning M1911 design with modifications. Please refer to Olympic Arms listing for currently manufactured pistols.

GI SAFARI – .45 ACP cal., patterned after the Colt Model 1911, Safari frame, beavertail grip safety and commander hammer, parkerized matte black finish, 39.9 oz. Mfg. 1991-2000.

	$500	$455	$395	$350	$295	$275	$250	$550

CARRYCOMP – similar to MatchMaster, except utilizes W. Schuemann designed hybrid compensator system, 5 in. barrel, available in stainless steel or steel, 38 oz. Mfg. 1993-99.

	$1,030	$875	$750	$600	$500	$425	$375	$1,160

* **CarryComp Enforcer** – similar to Enforcer, except utilizes W. Schuemann designed hybrid compensator system, available in stainless steel or steel, 36 oz. Mfg. 1993-96.

	$1,175	$1,025	$875	$750	$600	$500	$425	$1,300

CARRIER – .45 ACP cal. only, reproduction of the original Detonics ScoreMaster, except has upgraded sights, custom made by Richard Niemer from the Custom Shop. New 1999-2001.

	$750	$625	$575	$500	$450	$400	$350	$750

RENEGADE – .45 ACP cal., left-hand action (port on left side), 4 1/2 (4-star, disc. 1996) or 5 (new 1994) in. barrel, 6 shot mag., adj. sights, stainless steel construction, 36-39 oz. Mfg. 1993-98.

	$955	$800	$700	$600	$525	$450	$395	$1,085

Add $50 for 4-star (4 1/2 in. barrel, disc.).

RELIABLE – similar to Renegade, except has right-hand action. Mfg. 1993-98.

	$730	$620	$525	$450	$425	$400	$375	$825

Add $60 for 4-star (4 1/2 in. barrel, disc.).

GRIFFON PISTOL – .45 ACP cal., 5 in. stainless steel barrel, 10 shot mag., standard govt. size with beavertail grip safety, full-length recoil spring guide, commander style hammer, smooth walnut grips, 40 1/2 oz. Disc. 1998.

	$855	$725	$650	$575	$500	$450	$395	$920

SAFETY HARBOR FIREARMS, INC.

Current manufacturer located in Safety Harbor, FL.

Safety Harbor Firearms also manufactures a line of KEG (Kompact Entry Gun) slide action shotguns (12 and 20 ga.), in short barrel lengths that are classified as NFA weapons. Please contact the manufacturer directly for more information, availability and pricing for these models (see Trademark Index).

RIFLES: BOLT ACTION

SHF R50 – .50 BMG cal., 18, 22, or 29 in. barrel, side mounted 3 (disc. 2009) or 5 shot mag., black reinforced fixed tube stock with vent. recoil pad, partially shrouded barrel with muzzle brake, Picatinny rails, 16 1/2-20 lbs.

MSR $2,450	$2,325	$2,100	$1,825	$1,675	$1,350	$1,100	$850	

MSR	100%	98%	95%	90%	80%	70%	60%	Last MSR

SHF S50 – .50 BMG cal., single shot, 18, 22, or 29 in. barrel, similar stock and handguard as the SHF R50. New mid-2009.

| MSR $1,950 | $1,800 | $1,650 | $1,475 | $1,325 | $1,075 | $875 | $775 | |

SHF R/S ZOMBIE – .50 BMG cal., choice of repeater or single shot action. New 2014.

| MSR $2,199 | $1,995 | $1,750 | $1,500 | $1,350 | $1,095 | $900 | $800 | |

Add $500 for Mag. fed repeater action.

SAIGA

Current trademark manufactured by Izhmash, located in Izhevsk, Russia. Currently distributed exclusively beginning 2012 by RWC Group LLC, located in Tullytown, PA. Currently imported beginning late 2011 by US Sporting Goods, Inc., located in Rockledge, FL, RAAC (Russian American Armory Company), located in Scottsburg, IN, Arsenal INc., located in Las Vegas, NV, and K-VAR Corp., located in Las Vegas, NV. Previously imported by European American Armory Corp., located in Sharpes, FL.

CARBINES/RIFLES: SEMI-AUTO

SAIGA RIFLE – .223 Rem. (Model IZ-114), 5.45x39mm (Model IZ-240), or .308 Win. (Model IZ-139) cal., Kalashnikov type action, black synthetic or hardwood (new 2003, only available in .308 Win. cal.) stock and forearm, 16, 20, or 21 (.308 Win. cal. only) in. barrel length, matte black metal, 7-8 1/2 lbs. Imported 2002-2004, reintroduced 2006.

| MSR $560 | $475 | $415 | $350 | $325 | $260 | $215 | $175 | |

Add $20 for 20 in. barrel or 16 in. barrel with adj. cheekpiece.
Add $200 for .308 Win. cal.
Add $80 for 5.45x39mm cal. with AK-style forend and handguard.

* ***Saiga Rifle 7.62x39mm Cal.*** – 7.62x39mm (Model IZ-132) cal., 16.3 or 20 (disc. 2013) in. barrel, 10 shot mag., otherwise similar to Saiga Rifle. Imported 2002-2004, reintroduced 2006.

| MSR $535 | $450 | $395 | $350 | $300 | $250 | $200 | $160 | |

Add $45 for 20 in. barrel or for 16 in. barrel with adj. cheekpiece.
Add $105 for 16 in. barrel with AK-47 style forend and handguard.

SAIGA 100 – .223 Rem., .30-06, .308 Win., or 7.62x39mm cal., hunting configuration with black synthetic stock, 3 or 10 shot mag., 22 in. barrel with open sights, 7.7 lbs. Imported 2006-disc.

| | $650 | $595 | $550 | $495 | $450 | $400 | $350 | |

Add 15% for .308 Win. cal.

SAIGA CARBINE CONVERSION – 7.62x39mm cal., AK-style carbine, polymer furniture. New 2012.

| MSR $900 | $775 | $675 | $575 | $525 | $425 | $350 | $275 | |

Add $20 for Tuning B Model (CBS collapsible stock, RS47SET polymer forward handguard, four rails and G47 pistol grip).
Add $525 for Tuning C Model (ARSNL fully adj. stock, XRS47 aluminum 5 rails handguard, UPG47 pistol grip w/interchangeable finger grooves and backstraps).

SGL21/26 SERIES – 7.62x39mm cal., Russian made, stamped receiver, original Russian chrome lined hammer forged barrel, front sight block with bayonet lug, gas block with accessory lug, US made double stage trigger group, 5 shot mag., 4000 meter rear sight leaf, scope rail, original Warsaw, NATO or black polymer side folding buttstock with trapdoor for cleaning kit, Black, OD Green, Plum, Desert Sand (new 2012) finish. Mfg. by Izhmash, imported by Arsenal, Inc. New 2011.

| MSR $959 | $825 | $725 | $625 | $575 | $450 | $375 | $295 | |

Add $10 for NATO buttstock.
Add $10 for 40 shot mag.
Add $105 for forend rails (new 2012).
Add $422 for black polymer side folding buttstock.

SGL31 – 5.45x39mm cal., Russian made, stamped receiver, 10 shot mag., original Russian chrome lined hammer forged barrel, front sight block with bayonet lug, gas block with accessory lug, US made double stage trigger group, 1000 meter rear sight leaf, scope rail, original Warsaw or black polymer side folding buttstock with trapdoor for cleaning kit, Black, OD Green, Plum or Desert Sand (new 2012) finish. Mfg. by Izhmash, imported by Arsenal Inc. New 2011.

| MSR $1,199 | $1,025 | $895 | $775 | $695 | $565 | $475 | $375 | |

Add $10 for 30 shot mag.
Add $50 for Plum, Green, or Desert Sand (new 2012) finish.
Add $105 for forend rails (new 2012).
Add $150 for black polymer side folding buttstock.

MSR	100%	98%	95%	90%	80%	70%	60%	Last MSR

SHOTGUNS: SEMI-AUTO

SAIGA-12 – 12 or 20 ga., 3 in. chamber, 5 shot detachable box mag., Kalashnikov type action, black synthetic stock and forearm, 19-22 in. barrel length, matte black metal, with or w/o side rail, optional adj. leaf sight or notch rear sight, 6.7-10 lbs. Imported 2002-2004, reintroduced 2006.

| MSR $780 | $675 | $595 | $500 | $450 | $375 | $300 | $235 | |

Add $25 for adj. leaf sight or $13 for notch rear sights.
Add $94 for 20 ga.
Add $40 for RPK handguard (disc.).
Add 10% for choke tubes (12 ga. only, disc.).

* **Saiga .410 Bore** – .410 bore, 19 or 21 in barrel, 4 or 10 (disc.) shot detachable box mag., NATO or Warsaw Pact buttstock, with or w/o side scope rail, otherwise similar to Saiga Shotgun, approx. 6.6 lbs. Imported 2002-2004, reintroduced 2006.

| MSR $646 | $500 | $475 | $415 | $375 | $300 | $250 | $195 | |

* **Saiga Skeletonized Stock** – 12 ga. only, 19 in. barrel, plastic or laminated skeletonized stock, Picatinny rail, with or w/o magwell, 4 or 5 shot mag., AK sights. New 2012.

| MSR $994 | $850 | $750 | $650 | $575 | $475 | $375 | $300 | |

Add $81 for laminated stock.

* **Saiga Hunting Model** – 12 ga. only, 19 in. barrel, wooden or plastic Monte Carlo or hunting style stock, with or w/o mag well, Picatinny rail, optional leaf or AK sights, 4 or 5 shot mag. New 2012.

| MSR $885 | $750 | $650 | $575 | $500 | $415 | $350 | $275 | |

Add $45 for wooden stock.
Add $144 for optional leaf sight.
Add $80 for hunting stock.

SAKO, LTD.

Current rifle manufacturer established circa 1921 and located in Riihimäki, Finland. Current models are presently being imported by Beretta USA, located in Accokeek, MD. Previously imported by Stoeger Industries, Inc. located in Wayne, NJ, Garcia, and Rymac.

During 2000, Sako, Ltd. was purchased by Beretta Holding of Italy. All currently produced Sakos are imported by Beretta USA Corp. located in Accokeek, MD.

Beginning 2000, most Sako rifles (except the Action I in .223 Rem. cal.) are shipped with a Key Concept locking device. This patented system uses a separate key to activate an almost invisible lock which totally blocks the firing pin and prevents bolt movement.

RIFLES: BOLT ACTION, RECENT PRODUCTION

Beginning late 2001, Sako established a custom shop, which allows the consumer to select from a wide variety of finishes, options, and special orders, including individual stock dimensions. Please contact Beretta USA for more information regarding the Sako custom shop.

All Sako left-handed models are available in medium or long action only.

Some older model TRG rifles (Models TRG-S, TRG-22, and TRG-42) have experienced firing pin breakage. Ser. no. ranges on these U.S. distributed rifles are 202238 - 275255 and 973815 - 998594. Please contact Beretta USA directly (str@berettausa.com or 800-803-8869) for a replacement firing pin assembly if you have a rifle within these serial number ranges.

MODEL TRG-21 – .308 Win. cal., bolt action, 25 3/4 in. stainless steel barrel, new design features modular synthetic stock construction with adj. cheekpiece and buttplate, cold hammer forged receiver, and resistance free bolt, 10 shot detachable mag., 10 1/2 lbs. Imported 1993-99.

| | $2,300 | $2,000 | $1,800 | $1,600 | $1,400 | $1,200 | $975 | *$2,699* |

MODEL TRG-22 – .308 Win. cal., bolt action, 20 or 26 in. stainless steel barrel, updated TRG-21 design featuring adj. modular synthetic stock in Green, Desert Tan (disc.), or all black construction with adj. cheekpiece and buttplate, competition trigger, Picatinny rail became standard circa 2011, choice of blue (disc. 2002) or phosphate (new 2002) metal finish, cold hammer forged receiver, and resistance free bolt, 10 shot detachable mag., approx. 10 1/4 lbs. Importation began 2000.

| MSR $3,495 | $2,975 | $2,465 | $1,975 | $1,750 | $1,500 | $1,250 | $1,000 | |

Add $2,580 for folding stock in green finish.
Subtract approx. 10% if without Picatinny rail.

MODEL TRG-41 – .338 Lapua Mag. cal., similar to Model TRG-21, except has long action and 27 1/8 in. barrel, 7 3/4 lbs. Imported 1994-99.

| | $2,700 | $2,425 | $2,150 | $1,850 | $1,625 | $1,400 | $1,200 | *$3,099* |

MSR	100%	98%	95%	90%	80%	70%	60%	Last MSR

MODEL TRG-42 – .300 Win. Mag. (disc. 2012) or .338 Lapua Mag. cal., updated TRG-41 design featuring long action and 27 1/8 in. barrel, Picatinny rail became standard during 2011, choice of black composite/blue finish, desert tan (disc. 2013), or green composite/phosphate (new 2002) finish, 5 shot mag., 11 1/4 lbs. Importation began 2000.

| MSR $4,445 | $4,025 | $3,525 | $3,150 | $2,775 | $2,325 | $1,925 | $1,750 | |

Add $2,650 for folding stock with Picatinny rail (green finish only).

Subtract approx. $775 if without Picatinny rail (desert tan stock only).

MODEL TRG-S – available in medium action (disc. 1993) in .243 Win. or 7mm-08 cal., or long action in .25-06 Rem. (Mfg. 1994-98), .270 Win. (disc. 2000), 6.5x55mm Swedish (disc. 1998), .30-06 (disc.), .308 Win. (disc. 1995), .270 Wby. Mag. (disc. 1998), 7mm Wby. Mag. (Mfg. 1998), 7mm Rem. Mag. (disc.), .300 Win. Mag. (disc.), .300 Wby. Mag. (mfg. 1994-99), .30-378 Wby. Mag. (new 1998, 26 in. barrel only), .338 Win. Mag. (disc. 1999), .338 Lapua Mag. (new 1994), .340 Wby. Mag. (disc. 1998), 7mm STW (26 in. barrel only, disc. 1999), .375 H&H (disc. 1998), or .416 Rem. Mag. (disc. 1998) cal., black synthetic stock, Sporter variation derived from the Model TRG-21, 22 (disc.), 24 (Mag. cals. only, disc.), or 26 in. barrel, 3 or 5 shot detachable mag., fully adj. trigger, 60 degree bolt lift, matte finish, 8 1/8 lbs. Imported 1993-2004.

| | $775 | $650 | $525 | $475 | $440 | $415 | $380 | $896 |

SAMCO GLOBAL ARMS, INC.

Current importer and distributor located in Miami, FL. Dealer sales.

Samco Global Arms purchased the Charles Daly trademark in late 2012, and is currently importing a variety of Charles Daly shotgun configurations (see Charles Daly in the C section). Samco also imports Akkar shotguns from Turkey, as well as a variety of foreign and domestic surplus military rifles, including various contract Mausers, Loewe, Steyr, Czech, Lee Enfield, Mosin-Nagant, etc. Samco also imports European surplus pistols. Most of these guns offer excellent values to both shooters and collectors. Please contact the company directly for current availability and pricing, as its inventory changes weekly (see Trademark Index).

SAN SWISS ARMS AG

Current company established during late 2000, with headquarters located in Neuhausen, Switzerland.

In late 2000, SIG Arms AG, the firearms portion of SIG, was purchased by two Germans named Michael Lüke and Thomas Ortmeier, who have a background in textiles. Today the Lüke & Ortmeier group (L&O Group) includes independently operational companies such as Blaser Jadgwaffen GmbH, Mauser Jagdwaffen GmbH, John Rigby, J.P. Sauer & Sohn GmbH, SIG-Sauer Inc., SIG-Sauer GmbH and SAN Swiss Arms AG. Please refer to individual listings.

RIFLES

In 2010, San Swiss Arms purchased the rights to the A.M.S.D. Model OM 50 Nemesis. Model nomenclature has been changed to the San 511. Please contact the company directly for more information on this model including options, pricing, and U.S. availability (see Trademark Index).

SARCO, INC.

Current importer and wholesaler located in Stirling, NJ.

Sarco Inc. imports a wide variety of foreign and domestic surplus military style rifles and shotguns that offer excellent values for the shooter. Please contact the company directly, as inventory changes constantly (see Trademark Index).

SARSILMAZ (SAR ARMS)

Current manufacturer established during 1880, and located in Istanbul, Turkey. Currently imported under private label by by European American Armory, located in Rockledge, FL. Recently imported by Armalite, Inc., located in Geneseo, IL (refer to listings in Armalite section). Select slide action shotguns are imported by US Sporting Goods Inc. located in Rockledge, FL. Previously distributed 2000-2003 by PMC, located in Boulder City, NV. Previously imported and distributed until 2000 by Armsport, Inc. located in Miami, FL.

PISTOLS: SEMI-AUTO

Sarsilmaz manufactures a wide variety of semi-auto pistols in many configurations. Current models include the K10, K12, Kilinc 2000, B6, V8, CM9, P6, and the P8 Series. These models/series are not currently imported into the U.S. Please refer to the Armalite and European American Armory sections for recent importation.

Please contact Sarsilmaz directly for more information, including pricing on its line of non-imported semi-auto pistols (see Trademark Index).

REVOLVERS

Sarsilmaz manufacturers a line of double action revolvers in .38 Special and .357 Magnum caliber. Currently, these models are not imported into the U.S.

MSR	100%	98%	95%	90%	80%	70%	60%	Last MSR

RIFLES: SEMI-AUTO

Beginning in 2014, Sarsilmaz introduced the SAR 223 semi-auto rifle, based on the AR-15 design. All rifles are gas piston operated, have adjustable telescoping tactical style stocks, matte black finish, and come with a 30 shot aluminum, steel, or polymer magazine. Currently, this line of rifles is not imported into the U.S.

SHOTGUNS

Sarsilmaz manufactures a variety of shotguns in O/U, semi-auto, and slide action configurations. Some of these models have been imported in the past in limited quantities. Sarsilmaz is manufacturing select models for Bernardelli. Recent importation was by US Sporting Goods Inc. (see listings here).

SAR SEMI-AUTO SHOTGUN/SARSA – 12, 20, or 28 ga., 3 in. chamber (12 and 20 ga.), inertia/recoil operation, dual action bars, 22, 26, or 28 in. VR barrel with Benelli style choke tubes, aluminum receiver, steel bolt, polymer stock and forearm, choice of matte black or 100% camo finish, recoil pad, various configurations, 5.5-6.1 lbs. Importation began 2011.

MSR $545	$465	$400	$350	$325	$250	$210	$190

Add $70 for 100% camo coverage (not available in 28 ga.).

SARSASP SEMI-AUTO – 12 ga., 3 in. chamber, 18 1/2 in. barrel, 5 shot mag, black polymer stock with pistol grip, top Picatinny rail, raised fiber optic front sight, adj. ghost ring rear sight, breach-style choke tube, 5 3/4 lbs. New mid-2013.

MSR $659	$560	$495	$425	$380	$310	$250	$195

SAR SLIDE ACTION – 12, 20, or 28 (disc. late 2011) ga., 2 3/4, 3 or 3 1/2 in. (12 ga. only) chamber, dual action bars, 22, 26, or 28 in. VR barrel with Benelli style choke tube, aluminum receiver, polymer stock and forearm, choice of matte black or 100% camo coverage, various configurations, 5.7-6.2 lbs. Importation began 2011.

MSR $381	$325	$285	$250	$230	$210	$190	$175

Add $67 for 100% camo coverage.
Add $81 for combo package with extra barrel (3 1/2 in. chamber only).

SAR SLIDE ACTION SPECIAL PURPOSE – 12 ga., 3 in. chamber, tactical configuration with black polymer pistol grip stock and extended grooved forearm, dual action bars, 18 1/2 in. fixed or screw in choke barrel with muzzle brake, aluminum receiver, optional Picatinny rail with ghost ring sight, 5 3/4 lbs. Importation began 2011.

MSR $368	$315	$275	$250	$230	$210	$190	$175

Add $23 for Picatinny rail.
Subtract $67 for bead sights.

SARPASP SLIDE ACTION – 12 ga., 3 in. chamber, 18 1/2 in. barrel, 5 shot mag, black polymer stock with pistol grip, top Picatinny rail, raised fiber optic front sight, adj. ghost ring rear sight, breach-style choke tube, 5 3/4 lbs. New mid-2013.

MSR $485	$415	$375	$310	$280	$230	$185	$150

SAUER, J.P., & SOHN

Current manufacturer located in Eckernförde, Germany since 1751 (originally Prussia). Currently imported by Sauer USA, located in San Antonio, TX. Previously manufactured in Suhl pre-WWII. Previously imported and warehoused 1995-2007 by SIG Arms, located in Exeter, NH. Rifles were previously imported until 1995 by the Paul Company Inc. located in Wellsville, KS and until 1994 by G.U., Inc. located in Omaha, NE.

In 1972, J.P. Sauer & Sohn entered into a cooperative agreement with SIG. During 2000, SAN Swiss Arms AG purchased SIG Arms AG, including the J.P. Sauer & Sohn trademark. The L&O Group, an international industrial holding company, currently has controlling interest of J.P. Sauer and Sohns. Production remains in Eckernförde, Germany.

RIFLES: BOLT ACTION

Add $1,081-$2,156 per interchangeable barrel depending on rifle configuration on the following models where applicable.
Add $631-$677 per spare bolt, depending on rifle configuration.
Add $683 for left-hand.
Add $1,763 for Model 202 conversion kit or $1,917-$2,776 for Model 202 takedown conversion kit, depending on caliber.

SSE 3000 PRECISION RIFLE – .308 Win. cal., very accurate, law enforcement counter Sniper Rifle, built to customer specifications.

	$4,845	$3,655	$3,200	$2,850	$2,500	$2,275	$2,000	

SSG 2000 – available in .223 Rem., 7.5mm Swiss, .300 Wby. Mag., or .308 Win. (standard) cal., bolt action, 4 shot mag., no sights, deluxe sniper rifle featuring thumbhole style walnut stock with stippling and thumbwheel adj. cheekpiece, 13 lbs. Importation disc. 1986.

	$2,480	$2,260	$1,950	$1,700	$1,500	$1,300	$1,100	$2,850

This model was available in .223 Rem., .300 Wby. Mag., or 7.5mm cal. by special order only.

MSR	100%	98%	95%	90%	80%	70%	60%	*Last MSR*

SSG 3000 – .223 Rem., 22 1/2 in. barrel, Parker-Hale bipod, 2-stage match trigger, includes 2 1/2-10x52mm Zeiss scope, 200 mfg. for Swiss police.

	$12,000	$10,000	$8,500	$7,000	$6,750	$5,500	$4,250	

SSG 3000 (CURRENT MFG.) – See listing under Sig-Sauer.

SAVAGE ARMS, INC.

Current manufacturer located in Westfield, MA since 1959, with sales offices located in Suffield, CT. Previously manufactured in Utica, NY - later manufacture was in Chicopee Falls, MA. Dealer and distributor sales.

This company originally started in Utica, NY in 1894. The Model 1895 was initially manufactured by Marlin between 1895-1899. After WWI, the name was again changed to the Savage Arms Corporation. Savage moved to Chicopee Falls, MA circa 1946 (to its Stevens Arms Co. plants). In the mid-1960s the company became The Savage Arms Division of American Hardware Corp., which later became The Emhart Corporation. This division was sold in September 1981, and became Savage Industries, Inc. located in Westfield, MA (since the move in 1960). On November 1, 1989, Savage Arms Inc. acquired the majority of assets of Savage Industries, Inc. On June 24, 2013, ATK acquired Caliber Company, the parent company of Savage Sports Corporation.

Savage Arms, Inc. will offer service and parts on their current line of firearms only (those manufactured after Nov. 1, 1995). These models include the 24, 99, and 110 plus the imported Model 312. Warranty and repair claims for products not acquired by Savage Arms, Inc. will remain the responsibility of Savage Industries, Inc. For information regarding the repair and/or parts of Savage Industries, Inc. firearms, please refer to the Trademark Index in the back of this text. Parts for pre-1989 Savage Industries, Inc. firearms may be obtained by contacting the Numrich Gun Parts Corporation located in West Hurley, NY (listed in Trademark Index). Savage Arms, Inc. has older records/info. on pistols, the Model 24, older mfg. Model 99s, and Model 110 only. A factory letter authenticating the configuration of a particular specimen may be obtained by contacting Mr. John Callahan (see Trademark Index for listings and address). The charge for this service is $30.00 per gun, and $25.00 per gun for Models 1895, 1899, and 99 rifles. Please allow 8 weeks for an adequate response.

For more Savage model information, please refer to the Serialization section in the back of this text.

Please refer to the *Blue Book of Modern Black Powder Arms* by John Allen (also online) for more information and prices on Savage's lineup of modern black powder models. For more information and current pricing on both new and used Savage airguns, please refer to the *Blue Book of Airguns* by Dr. Robert Beeman & John Allen (also online).

Black Powder Long Arms and Pistols - Reproductions & Replicas by Dennis Adler is also an invaluable source for most black powder reproductions and replicas, and includes hundreds of color images on most popular makes/models, provides manufacturer/trademark histories, and up-to-date information on related items/accessories for black powder shooting - www.bluebookofgunvalues.com

RIFLES: CENTERFIRE, CURRENT/RECENT PRODUCTION

The 110 Series was first produced in 1958. Beginning in 1992, Savage Arms, Inc. began supplying this model with a master trigger lock, earmuffs, shooting glasses (disc. 1992), and test target.

Beginning 1994, all Savage rifles employ a laser etched bolt featuring the Savage logo. During 1996, Savage began using pillar bedded stocks for many of their rifles.

Recent Savage nomenclature usually involves alphabetical suffixes which mean the following: B - laminated wood stock, BT - laminated thumbhole stock, C - detachable box mag., EV - Evolution stock, F - composite/synthetic stock, G - hardwood stock, H - hinged floorplate, K - AccuStock or standard muzzle brake, AK - adj. muzzle brake with fluted barrel, L - left-hand, LE - Law Enforcement, NS - no sights, P - police (tactical) rifle, SB - smooth bore, SE - safari express, SR - suppressor ready, SS - stainless steel, SS-S - stainless steel single shot, T - Target (aperture rear sight), TR - tactical style rimfire, TRR - tactical style rimfire w/rail, U - high luster blue, blue metal finish and/or stock finish, V - Long Range (Varmint w/heavy barrel), XP - package gun (scope, sling, and rings/base), Y - Youth/Ladies Model. A 2 digit model number (10) designates new short action. A 3 digit model number (110) indicates long action.

Hence, the Model 111FCNS designates a 111 Series firearm with synthetic stock, detachable magazine, and no sights. Likewise, a Model 11FYCXP3 indicates a Model 11 Series with synthetic stock, youth dimensions, detachable magazine, is a packaged gun which includes scope. The Model 116FHSAK indicates a long action rifle with hinged floorplate, synthetic stock, stainless steel action/barrel with adj. muzzlebrake.

During 2003, Savage released its new patented AccuTrigger, which allows the consumer to adjust the trigger pull from the outside of the rifle from 1 1/2 lbs. - 6 lbs. using a proprietary tool. The AccuTrigger also has almost no trigger creep and is infinitely adjustable. Initially, it was released in all Varmint, LE, and heavy barrel long range rifles, and during 2004, the AccuTrigger became standard on nearly all Savage centerfire rifles, except the Model 11 and 11FCXP3 and 10/110G Package guns. During 2007, Savage began offering target actions with AccuTrigger, right bolt, and choice of left or right port ejection with .223 Rem. bolt head - MSR is $560-$595.

During 2008, Savage Arms introduced a new personal anti-recoil device (P.A.D.), which is installed in many Savage bolt action centerfire rifles. The P.A.D. reduces recoil by 45% from OEM solid and vented pads.

In 2009, Savage Arms introduced its Accustock, which incorporates a rigid aluminum rail and 3D bedding cradle that is firmly imbedded in the stock throughout the length of the rifles forend. Many Savage Centerfire rifles now incorporate the Accustock bedding system.

Also during 2009/2010, Savage introduced varmint short actions, along with both long and short sporter actions. Sporter actions had

MSR	100%	98%	95%	90%	80%	70%	60%	Last MSR

an MSR of $481, while the varmint short actions' MSR was $505. A dual port receiver, allowing left loading and right ejection was also released in 2009 - MSR was $595.

During 2010, Target actions became available in stainless steel only (in either single or dual port configuration) - MSR on the single port is $613, and $651 for the dual port.

During 2012, Savage introduced its new AXIS Series.

Whenever possible, the models within this category have been listed in numerical sequence.

Subtract approx. 10% on models listed below w/o AccuTrigger (became standard on all centerfire rifles in 2004).

MODEL 10BA/BAS-K – .308 Win. cal., 24 in. barrel with muzzle brake, short action, 10 shot detachable box mag., all aluminum Accustock, AccuTrigger, Magpul PRS-G3 buttstock, Picatinny rail, no sights, matte blued finish, oversize bolt handle, 13.4 lbs. New 2009.

| MSR $2,375 | $2,000 | $1,750 | $1,500 | $1,360 | $1,100 | $900 | $700 | |

* Model 10BAT/S-K – .308 Win. cal., 24 in. barrel with muzzle brake, short action, 10 shot detachable box mag., similar to Model 10BAS-K, except has tactical stock with adj. buttpad. Mfg. 2009-2010.

| | $1,750 | $1,450 | $1,125 | $925 | $800 | $700 | $600 | *$2,071* |

MODEL 10 LAW ENFORCEMENT SERIES – .223 Rem., .260 Rem. (mfg. 1999-2001), .308 Win., or 7mm-08 (mfg. 1999-2001) cal., short action, tactical/law enforcement model, checkered black synthetic stock, features 20 (new 2006) or 24 in. heavy barrel w/o sights, AccuTrigger became standard 2003, 8 lbs. Mfg. 1998-2007.

| | $505 | $395 | $320 | $275 | $230 | $190 | $165 | *$621* |

* Model 10FP/10FLP – .223 Rem. or .308 Win. cal., short action, 20 or 24 in. heavy free floating and button rifled barrel, 4 shot box mag., black McMillan synthetic sporter style stock, drilled and tapped, swivel stud, oversized bolt handle, 6 1/4 lbs. Mfg. 1998-2010.

| | $625 | $500 | $425 | $365 | $335 | $295 | $275 | *$775* |

This model was also available in left-hand action (Model 10FLP, 24 in. barrel only, disc. 2009).

* Model 10FP Duty – similar to Model 10FP, except has open iron sights. Mfg. 2002 only.

| | $435 | $355 | $290 | $250 | $215 | $180 | $165 | *$525* |

* Model 10FP 20 In. (LE1/LE1A) – .223 Rem. (LE1A only, disc. 2007) or .308 Win. cal., similar to Model 10FP, except has 20 in. heavy barrel with no sights, choice of standard (LE1, disc. 2005) or Choate (LE1A) stock (folding only, new 2006). Mfg. 2002-2010.

| | $865 | $695 | $565 | $475 | $425 | $350 | $300 | *$1,034* |

Subtract 20% for standard stock (LE1).

* Model 10FP 26 In. (LE2/LE2A) – .223 Rem. (LE2A only) or .308 Win. cal., similar to Model 10FP-LE1/LE1A, except has 26 in. heavy barrel and choice of standard (LE2, disc. 2005) or Choate stock (LE2A). Mfg. 2002-2006.

| | $625 | $500 | $400 | $360 | $330 | $300 | $275 | *$754* |

Subtract 20% for standard stock.

* Model 10FP McMillan (LE2B) – .308 Win. cal., short action, features McMillan tactical fiberglass stock with stippled grip areas, 4 shot mag., 26 in. heavy barrel. Mfg. 2003-2006.

| | $860 | $725 | $625 | $525 | $425 | $325 | $265 | *$1,033* |

* Model 10FP H-S Precision – .308 Win. cal., 24 in. barrel, features H-S Precision stock. Mfg. 2006 only.

| | $720 | $585 | $475 | $425 | $350 | $300 | $275 | *$864* |

* Model 10FPCPXP/10FPXP (LE/LEA) – .308 Win. cal. only, short action, features skeletonized synthetic stock, 24 (new 2006) or 26 (disc. 2005) in. barrel w/o sights, H-S Precision stock became standard 2006, LEA has Choate stock, LE has standard stock (disc. 2005), includes Burris (disc.) or Leupold (new 2004) 3.5-10x50mm scope with flip covers and sling, 4 shot internal (FPXP, disc. 2006) or detachable (FPCPXP, new 2007) mag., Harris bipod, aluminum case, 10 1/2 lbs. Mfg. 2002-2009.

| | $2,275 | $1,850 | $1,550 | $1,300 | $1,100 | $900 | $750 | *$2,715* |

Subtract 20% for LE standard stock or 10% for Choate stock (Model 10FPXP-LEA package).

* Model 10FCP H-S Precision – .308 Win. cal., 24 in. barrel, features H-S Precision stock, 4 shot detachable box mag., matte blued finish, oversized bolt handle, no sights, 9.6 lbs. New 2007.

| MSR $1,277 | $1,100 | $925 | $750 | $650 | $550 | $475 | $400 | |

»Model 10FCPXP H-S Precision Package – .308 Win. cal., 24 in. barrel, includes top Picatinny rail, 3-9x40mm scope, and bipod, 9.6 lbs. Mfg. 2010-2011.

| | $2,550 | $2,250 | $1,900 | $1,625 | $1,275 | $1,000 | $875 | *$2,908* |

* Model 10FCP Choate – .308 Win. cal., 24 in. barrel, features Choate stock, detachable box mag. Mfg. 2007 only.

| | $700 | $575 | $475 | $425 | $350 | $300 | $275 | *$833* |

MSR	100%	98%	95%	90%	80%	70%	60%	Last MSR

* **Model 10FCP McMillan** – .308 Win. cal., 24 in. barrel, features McMillan stock, 4 shot detachable box mag., no sights, matte blued finish, oversized bolt handle, 10 lbs. New 2007.

| MSR $1,545 | $1,325 | $1,025 | $895 | $750 | $650 | $550 | $475 | |

* **Model 10 FCP-K/ Model 10 FLCP-K** – .223 Rem. or .308 Win. cal., short action, 24 in. heavy blue barrel with muzzle brake, 4 shot detachable box mag., drilled and tapped, black synthetic AccuStock with aluminum spine and 3-D bedding cradle, swivel stud for bipod, oversized bolt handle, 8.9 lbs. Mfg. 2009-2013.

| | $850 | $725 | $595 | $475 | $425 | $350 | $300 | $975 |

This model was also available in left-hand action at no extra charge (Model 10 FLCP-K).

MODEL 10 PRECISION CARBINE

– .223 Rem., .308 Win., or .300 AAC Blackout (mfg. 2012 only) cal., 20 in. matte blue free floating button rifled threaded (new 2012) or un-threaded (disc. 2011) barrel, 4 shot detachable box mag., swivel stud, oversized bolt handle, green camo Accustock with aluminum spine and 3-D bedding cradle, 7 lbs. New 2009.

| MSR $952 | $810 | $675 | $550 | $425 | $375 | $350 | $300 | |

MODEL 12 LONG RANGE PRECISION

– .243 Win., .260 Rem., or 6.5 Creedmoor cal., short action, 26 in. barrel, Target AccuTrigger, H-S Precision fiberglass stock, 4 shot detachable box mag., no sights, oversized bolt handle, 11 lbs. New 2011.

| MSR $1,215 | $1,025 | $895 | $750 | $650 | $550 | $475 | $400 | |

MODEL 12 LONG RANGE PRECISION VARMINTER REPEATER

– .204 Ruger, .22-250 Rem., .223 Rem., or 6mm Norma BR cal., 26 in. barrel, short action, detachable box mag., target AccuTrigger. Mfg. 2008-2010.

| | $1,085 | $925 | $825 | $725 | $625 | $525 | $450 | $1,319 |

MODEL 110-FP LAW ENFORCEMENT (TACTICAL POLICE)

– .223 Rem. (disc. 1998), .25-06 Rem. (new 1995), .300 Win. Mag. (new 1995), .30-06 (mfg. 1996-2006), .308 Win. (disc. 1998), or 7mm Rem. Mag. (mfg. 1995-2007) cal., long action, 24 in. heavy barrel pillar bedded tactical rifle, all metal parts are non-reflective, 4 shot internal mag., black Dupont Rynite stock, right or left-hand (mfg. 1996-2001) action, drilled and tapped for scope mounts, AccuTrigger became standard 2003, 8 1/2 lbs. Mfg. 1990-2001, reintroduced 2003-2008.

| | $575 | $465 | $360 | $310 | $265 | $240 | $210 | $678 |

Was also available in left-hand action at no additional charge (mfg. 1996-2001, Model 110-FLP).

* **Model 110FCP** – .25-06 Rem. or .300 Win. Mag. cal., 24 in. heavy barrel with Savage muzzle brake, 4 shot detachable box mag., black synthetic AccuStock with aluminum spine and 3-D bedding cradle, drilled and tapped, swivel stud for bipod, oversized bolt handle, 9 lbs. Mfg. 2009.

| | $725 | $600 | $500 | $425 | $375 | $350 | $300 | $866 |

MODEL 110BA/BAS

– .300 Win. Mag. or .338 Lapua cal., right or left (new 2013) hand action, 26 in. fluted carbon steel barrel with muzzle brake, 5 or 6 shot detachable box mag., drilled and tapped, open sights, includes Picatinny top rail, matte black aluminum tactical AccuStock with handguard, AccuTrigger, 15 3/4 lbs. New 2010.

| MSR $2,561 | $2,175 | $1,900 | $1,625 | $1,450 | $1,150 | $925 | $775 | |

MODEL 110FCP HS PRECISION

– .300 Win. Mag. or .338 Lapua cal., short or long action, 24 in. carbon steel barrel, matte black metal finish, 4 shot detachable box mag., black fiberglass stock, drilled and tapped, AccuTrigger, 9 lbs. New 2012.

| MSR $1,277 | $1,100 | $925 | $750 | $650 | $550 | $475 | $400 | |

Add $400 for .338 Lapua cal.

MODEL 111 HOG HUNTER

– .338 Win. Mag. cal., long action, 4 shot internal box mag., 20 in. threaded barrel with iron sights, matte black metal finish, AccuTrigger, OD Green synthetic stock, 8 lbs. New 2012.

| MSR $560 | $475 | $425 | $365 | $335 | $295 | $265 | $235 | |

MODEL 111 LONG RANGE HUNTER

– .25-06 Rem., 6.5x284 Norma, 7mm Rem. Mag., .300 Win. Mag., or .338 Lapua (new 2012) cal., 3 or 5 (.338 Lapua cal. only) shot mag., 26 in. fluted carbon steel barrel with adj. muzzle brake, drilled and tapped, AccuTrigger, Karsten adj. and detachable cheekpiece, matte black synthetic AccuStock and forearm, no sights, hinged floorplate, 8.65 lbs. New 2010.

| MSR $1,104 | $950 | $775 | $625 | $525 | $425 | $365 | $325 | |

Add $236 for .338 Lapua cal. (new 2012).

SCATTERGUN TECHNOLOGIES INC. (S.G.T.)

Current manufacturer located in Berryville, AR since 1999. Previously located in Nashville, TN 1991-1999. Distributor, dealer, and consumer sales.

During 1999, Wilson Combat purchased Scattergun Technologies. S.G.T. manufactures practical defense, tactical, and hunting shotguns in 12 ga. only, utilizing Remington Models 870 and 11-87 (disc.) actions in various configurations as listed. All shotguns feature 3 in. chamber capacity and parkerized finish.

MSR	100%	98%	95%	90%	80%	70%	60%	Last MSR

SHOTGUNS: SEMI-AUTO

Add $15 for short stock on models listed.
Add $125 for Armor-Tuff finish on models listed.

K-9 MODEL – 12 ga., 18 in. barrel, adj. ghost ring sight, 7 shot mag., side saddle, synthetic buttstock and forearm. Disc. 2003.

	100%	98%	95%	90%	80%	70%	60%	Last MSR
	$1,100	$875	$775	$665	$560	$465	$410	$1,325

SWAT MODEL – 12 ga., similar to K-9 Model, except has 14 in. barrel and forearm with 11,000 CP flashlight. Disc. 2003.

	100%	98%	95%	90%	80%	70%	60%	Last MSR
	$1,400	$1,150	$895	$785	$655	$550	$465	$1,750

This model was available for military and law enforcement only.

URBAN SNIPER MODEL – 12 ga., 18 in. rifled barrel, scout optics, 7 shot mag., side saddle, synthetic buttstock, forearm and bipod. Disc. 1999.

	100%	98%	95%	90%	80%	70%	60%	Last MSR
	$1,225	$1,075	$950	$835	$685	$585	$485	$1,390

SHOTGUNS: SLIDE ACTION

On the following models, Armor-Tuff finish became standard during 2003.

Add $15 for short stock on models listed.
Subtract approx. $100 if w/o Armor Tuff finish.

STANDARD MODEL – 12 or 20 (disc. 2011) ga., 18 1/2 in. barrel, adj. ghost ring sight, 7 shot mag., side saddle, synthetic buttstock and forearm with 11,000 CP flashlight.

MSR	100%	98%	95%	90%	80%	70%	60%	Last MSR
MSR $1,540	$1,395	$1,150	$975	$875	$650	$550	$450	

Add $15 for short stock.

PROFESSIONAL MODEL – 12 ga., similar to Standard Model, except has 14 in. barrel and 6 shot mag.

This model is NFA and available for military and law enforcement only.

EXPERT MODEL – 12 ga., 18 in. barrel with mod. choke, nickel/Teflon finished receiver, adj. ghost ring sight, forearm incorporates 11,000 CP flashlight. Mfg. 1997-2000.

	100%	98%	95%	90%	80%	70%	60%	Last MSR
	$1,200	$995	$775	$665	$560	$465	$410	$1,350

ENTRY MODEL – 12 ga., 12 1/2 in. barrel with mod. choke, adj. ghost ring sights, 5 shot mag., side saddle, synthetic buttstock with 5,000 CP flashlight and nylon loop strap. Disc.

	100%	98%	95%	90%	80%	70%	60%	Last MSR
	$995	$800	$600	$495	$430	$365	$315	$1,125

This model was available for military and law enforcement only.

COMPACT MODEL – 12 1/2 in. barrel with mod. choke, adj. ghost ring sight, 5 shot mag., synthetic buttstock and forearm. Mfg. 1994-99.

	100%	98%	95%	90%	80%	70%	60%	Last MSR
	$575	$510	$420	$360	$315	$260	$225	$635

This model was available for military and law enforcement only.

PRACTICAL TURKEY MODEL – 20 in. barrel with extra full choke, adj. ghost ring sight, 5 shot mag. for 3 in. shells, synthetic buttstock and forearm. Mfg. 1995-99.

	100%	98%	95%	90%	80%	70%	60%	Last MSR
	$545	$500	$465	$405	$350	$290	$250	$595

LOUIS AWERBUCK SIGNATURE MODEL – 18 in. barrel with fixed choke, adj. ghost ring sight, 5 shot mag., side saddle, wood buttstock with recoil reducer and forearm. Mfg. 1994-99.

	100%	98%	95%	90%	80%	70%	60%	Last MSR
	$625	$490	$385	$325	$275	$230	$200	$705

F.B.I. MODEL – similar to Standard Model, except has 5 shot mag. Disc. 1999.

	100%	98%	95%	90%	80%	70%	60%	Last MSR
	$715	$625	$490	$420	$370	$305	$265	$770

MILITARY MODEL – 18 in. barrel with vent. handguard and M-9 bayonet lug, adj. ghost ring rear sight, 7 shot mag., synthetic stock and grooved corncob forearm. Mfg. 1997-98.

	100%	98%	95%	90%	80%	70%	60%	Last MSR
	$625	$490	$385	$325	$275	$230	$200	$690

PATROL MODEL – 18 in. barrel, adj. ghost ring sight, 5 shot mag., synthetic buttstock and forearm. Disc. 1999.

	100%	98%	95%	90%	80%	70%	60%	Last MSR
	$545	$500	$465	$405	$350	$290	$250	$595

BORDER PATROL (MODEL 20) – 12 or 20 (disc. 2011) ga., 18 1/2 or 20 (disc. 2011) in. barrel, similar to Patrol Model, except has 7 shot mag., black synthetic stock and forearm.

MSR	100%	98%	95%	90%	80%	70%	60%	Last MSR
MSR $1,135	$995	$875	$775	$675	$575	$475	$395	

Add $15 for short stock.
Add $35 for 20 ga. (disc. 2011).

MSR	100%	98%	95%	90%	80%	70%	60%	Last MSR

BORDER PATROL (MODEL 21) – similar to Border Patrol Model 20, except has 14 in. barrel and 6 shot mag. This model is NFA and available for military and law enforcement only.

CONCEALMENT 00, 01, 02, 03, & BREACHING MODELS – 12 ga., short 12 1/2 in. barrel, various configurations, mfg. for military and law enforcement only. Disc. 1998.

| | $490 | $395 | $280 | $230 | $200 | $170 | $145 | |

Last MSRs range from $500-$625.

SCHMEISSER GmbH

Current manufacturer located in Krefeld, Germany. Distributed by American Tactical Imports, located in Rochester, NY.

RIFLES: SEMI-AUTO

Schmeisser GmbH currently manufactures AR-15 style rifles in several calibers and configurations. Current models include AR15 M4, AR15 M5, AR15 A4 (16 and 20 in.), AR15 Ultramatch, AR15 Ultramatch STS, AR15 M4-Solid, and AR15 M5-Solid. Please contact the company directly for more information including options, pricing, and availability (see Trademark Index).

SCHUETZEN PISTOL WORKS

Schuetzen Pistol Works is the in-house custom shop of Olympic Arms. Schuetzen Pistol Works has been customizing Safari Arms and Olympic Arms 1911 style pistols since 1997. For currently manufactured pistols, please refer to the Olympic Arms listing. For discontinued models, please refer to the Safari Arms listing.

SCHWABEN ARMS GMBH

Current manufacturer located in Rottweil, Germany. No current U.S. importation.

Schwaben Arms GmbH manufactures 600-800 guns annually. Production includes an extensive lineup of quality tactical rifles and carbines, primarily patterned after H&K models and other historically significant military rifles/carbines, including a .308 Win. cal. semi-auto MP5. Both commercial and military/law enforcement models are available. Please contact the factory directly for U.S. availability and pricing (see Trademark Index).

SCORPION TACTICAL

Current custom AR-15 manufacturer located in Leander, TX.

RIFLES: SEMI-AUTO

ATS-15 L1 – 5.56 NATO cal., GIO, 16 in. heavy barrel with A2 flash hider, 30 shot mag., fixed front and flip-up adj. rear sights, forged aluminum upper and lower receivers, standard AR charging handle, SST, standard plastic mid-length handguard with heat shield, 6-pos. sliding stock, plastic pistol grip, Black finish.

| MSR $999 | $900 | $800 | $675 | $625 | $500 | $400 | $325 | |

ATS-15 L2 – 5.56 NATO cal., GIO, 16 in. heavy barrel with A2 flash hider, 30 shot PMag., fixed front and Magpul MBUS rear sights, forged aluminum upper and lower receivers, standard AR charging handle, SST, mid-length drop-in quad rail, 6-pos. sliding stock, Ergo grip, Black finish.

| MSR $1,229 | $1,150 | $1,000 | $875 | $775 | $650 | $525 | $400 | |

ATS-15 L3 – 5.56 NATO cal., GIO, 16 in. M4 profile barrel with A2 flash hider, 30 shot PMag., Troy micro flip up Battlesight sights, forged aluminum upper and lower receivers, standard AR charging handle, SST, Magpul enhanced aluminum trigger guard, carbine-length free floating quad rail, Magpul 6-pos. CTR stock, Ergo grip, Black finish, 6.9 lbs.

| MSR $1,449 | $1,300 | $1,150 | $975 | $875 | $725 | $585 | $475 | |

ATS-15 L5 – 5.56 NATO cal., GIO, 16 in. M4 profile barrel with A2 flash hider, 30 shot PMag., Magpul Gen2 MBUS front and rear back up sights, forged aluminum upper and lower receivers, standard AR charging handle, SST, Magpul enhanced aluminum trigger guard, 13.8 in. Troy Alpha rail, Magpul ACS/Adaptable Carbine Storage stock, Ergo grip, FDE finish, 6.9 lbs.

| MSR $2,200 | $1,975 | $1,725 | $1,475 | $1,350 | $1,085 | $900 | $725 | |

SEEKINS PRECISION

Current manufacturer located in Lewiston, ID.

Seekins Precision currently manufactures complete AR-15 style rifles as well as AR-15 parts and accessories. Please contact the company directly for more information on current models and available products (see Trademark Index).

MSR	100%	98%	95%	90%	80%	70%	60%	Last MSR

RIFLES: SEMI-AUTO

CBR – .223 Rem./5.56 NATO (.223 Wylde chamber), or .300 AAC Blackout cal., GIO, 16 in. stainless steel barrel with flash hider, Melonite coated gas tube, bolt carrier and adj. gas block, Magpul MOE stock, ERGO pistol grip, ALG-ACT trigger, BCM Mod 3 charging handle, B.A.D. ambi selector, SP Gen2 billet lower, upper, and 12 in. BAR rail, H buffer, M4 feed ramp.

| MSR $1,875 | $1,675 | $1,475 | $1,250 | $1,150 | $925 | $750 | $575 | |

SP3G – .223 Rem./5.56 NATO (.223 Wylde chamber) cal., GIO, 18 in. 3G contoured super match barrel, 15 in. SP3R rail system, Melonite coated gas tube, bolt carrier, and adj. gas block, Magpul UBR stock, ERGO deluxe tactical pistol grip, Geissele Super 3-Gun trigger, BCM Mod 3 charging handle, SP billet lower Gen 2, Billet iMRT-3 upper, H buffer, M4 feed ramp, and SP Advanced Tactical Compensator.

| MSR $2,800 | $2,525 | $2,225 | $1,900 | $1,725 | $1,400 | $1,150 | $900 | |

SENNI ARMS CO.

Current manufacturer located in Queensland, Australia. No current U.S. importation.

Senni Arms manufactures a complete line of 1911-style semi-auto pistols, including the Stinger, 2010, Black Snake, Lawson, Silhouette, Razorback, and the Trooper. Senni Arms also manufactures the Siege semi-auto tactical shotgun and the Elysium M4 semi-auto tactical carbine. Please contact the company directly for more information, including pricing and domestic availability (see Trademark Index).

SERBU FIREARMS, INC.

Current manufacturer located in Tampa, FL.

Serbu Firearms also manufactures a Super-Shorty short barreled slide action shotgun based on the Remington 870 or Mossberg 500. These shotguns are classified NFA only.

RIFLES: BOLT ACTION

BFG-50 RIFLE/CARBINE – .50 BMG cal., single shot bolt action, 22 (carbine), 29 1/2 (rifle), or 36 (alloy or stainless, new 2011) in. match grade barrel with muzzle brake, AR-15 style trigger and safety, Picatinny rail, parkerized finish, 17-22 lbs. New 1999.

| MSR $2,395 | $2,395 | $2,150 | $1,875 | $1,625 | $1,450 | $1,185 | $975 | |

Add $75 for "Have a Nice Day" engraving on Shark muzzle brake.
Add $175 for bi-pod.
Add $400 for 36 in. barrel (alloy or stainless), new 2011.

BFG-50A – .50 BMG cal., gas operated, 26 in. barrel with 8 port Shark Brake muzzle brake, 10 shot mag., 3-lug bolt, sliding plate extrator, dual plunger ejectors, removable barrel extension and handguard, 23 lbs. New 2008.

| MSR $7,200 | $6,650 | $5,750 | $5,000 | $4,100 | $3,700 | $3,400 | $3,100 | |

SERO LTD.

Current rifle manufacturer located in Budapest, Hungary. No U.S. importation.

RIFLES: SEMI-AUTO

GEPARD GM6 LYNX – 14.5x114mm Soviet or .50 BMG cal., bullpup configuration, 28 3/4 in. barrel with muzzle brake, 100% desert camo coverage, 5 shot mag. is located in back of the pistol grip, full Picatinny rail, 25.3 lbs. New 2012.

Please contact the company directly for U.S. availability and pricing.

SHARPS MILSPEC

Previous trademark and division of Sharps Rifle Company, located in Chamberlain, SD 2011 only.

RIFLES: SEMI-AUTO

SHARPS 2010 CARBINE – 5.56 NATO cal., AR-15 style, GPO, 16 in. 5 groove rifling barrel with muzzle brake, redesigned charging handle, aluminum free floating handguard with quad Picatinny rails, Magpul ACS buttstock and MIAD pistol grip, supplied with two 30 shot mags. Limited mfg. 2011 only.

| | $2,425 | $2,100 | $1,800 | $1,500 | $1,250 | $1,000 | $850 | *$2,695* |

SHOOTERS ARMS MANUFACTURING INCORPORATED

Current manufacturer established in 1992, and located in Cebu, the Philippines. Currently imported by Century International Arms, located in Delray Beach, FL. Previously imported by Pacific Arms Corp. in Modesto, CA.

Shooter Arms Manufacturing Inc. makes semi-auto pistols, including the Elite, Commodore, Military, GI, Desert Storm, Seahawk, 1911A1, Eagle, Hawk, and the Trojan. Previous models have included the React, React-2, Military Enhanced, GI

MSR	100%	98%	95%	90%	80%	70%	60%	Last MSR

Enhanced, Elite Sport, Chief, Scout, Falcon, Raven, Omega, and Alpha. Shooters Arms Manufacuring Inc. also manufactures a revolver, the Protector, and a 12 ga. shotgun called the SAS 12. Please contact the importer directly for more information, including pricing and U.S. availability (see Trademark Index).

SIDEWINDER

Previous trademark manufactured by D-Max, Inc. located in Bagley, MN circa 1993-96. Dealer or consumer sales.

REVOLVERS

SIDEWINDER – .45 LC or 2 1/2/3 in. .410 bore shotshells/slugs, 6 shot, stainless steel construction, 6 1/2 or 7 1/2 in. bull barrel (muzzle end bored for removable choke), Pachmayr grips, transfer bar safety, adj. rear sight, unique design permits one cylinder to shoot above listed loads, cased with choke tube, 3.8 lbs. Mfg. 1993-1996.

	$695	$575	$475	$415	$360	$300	$255	$775

SIG ARMS AG

Current Swiss company (SIG) established during 1860 in Neuhausen, Switzerland. P 210 pistols are currently imported and distributed by Sig Sauer (formerly SIG Arms, Inc.), established in 1985, located in Exeter, NH. Previously located in Herndon, VA and Tysons Corner, VA.

In late 2000, SIG Arms AG, the firearms portion of SIG, was purchased by two Germans named Michael Lüke and Thomas Ortmeier, who have a background in textiles. Today the Lüke & Ortmeier group includes independently operational companies such as Blaser Jadgwaffen GmbH, Mauser Jagdwaffen GmbH, J.P. Sauer & Sohn GmbH, SIG-Sauer Inc., SIG-Sauer GmbH and SAN Swiss Arms AG. Please refer to individual listings.

PISTOLS: SEMI-AUTO

SIG Custom Shop variations of the P 210 were also available in three configurations - United We Stand ($8,990 last MSR) and two variations of the 50 Year Jubilee ($4,995 or $5,999 last MSR).

Add $1,473 for .22 LR conversion kit on the following models (not available on the P 210-8).

P 210 & VARIATIONS – 9mm Para. or 7.65mm Para. (disc.) cal., single action, 4 3/4 in. barrel, 8 shot mag., standard weapon of the Swiss Army, 2 lbs.

Originally mfg. in 1947, this pistol was first designated the SP 47/8 and became the standard military pistol of the Swiss Army in 1949. Later designated the P 210, this handgun has been mfg. continuously for over 55 years.

* **P 210 Danish Army M49** – Danish Army version of the Model P 210, approx. 25,000 mfg.

	$3,000	$2,500	$2,000	$1,750	$1,500	$1,250	$1,000	

* **P 210-1** – polished finish, walnut grips, special hammer, fixed sights. Importation disc. 1986.

	$2,500	$2,000	$1,500	$1,250	$1,000	$900	$750	$1,861

* **P 210-2** – matte finish, field or combat (recent mfg.) sights, plastic (disc.) or wood grips. Limited importation 1987-2002.

	$1,800	$1,500	$1,200	$900	$750	$625	$550	$1,680

Add 25% for high polish Swiss Army pistols with "A" prefix.
Add 50% for West German Police Contract models with unique loaded chamber indicator on slide. Approx. 5,000 mfg. in "D" prefix serial range.

* **P 210-5** – matte finish, heavy frame, micrometer target sights, 150mm or 180mm (disc.) extended barrel, hard rubber (disc.) or wood (current mfg.) grips, bottom (EU) or push-button side mounted (U.S.) mag. release, very limited mfg. Limited importation 1997-2007.

	$2,250	$2,150	$1,675	$1,350	$1,125	$1,000	$895	

Add 15% for side mounted mag. release.
Add 50% for early mfg. guns.

* **P 210-6** – matte blue finish, fixed (recent importation) or micrometer sights, 120mm barrel, checkered walnut grips, bottom (EU) or push-button side mounted (U.S.) mag. release.

	$1,850	$1,700	$1,500	$1,300	$1,125	$1,000	$895	

* **P 210-7** – .22 LR or 9mm Para. cal., regular or target long barrel, limited importation. Disc.

	$3,500	$3,000	$2,700	$2,350	$2,000	$1,750	$1,500	

* **P 210-8** – features heavy frame, target sights, and wood grips. Special order only. Limited importation 2001-2003.

	$3,750	$3,250	$2,650	$2,300	$1,950	$1,600	$1,275	$4,289

* **P 210 Legend** – please refer to listing in the Sig Sauer section, new mfg.

MSR	100%	98%	95%	90%	80%	70%	60%	Last MSR

RIFLES: BOLT ACTION

SHR 970 – .25-06 Rem., .270 Win., .280 Rem., .30-06, .308 Win., .300 Win. Mag., or 7mm Rem. Mag. cal., steel receiver, standard model featuring easy take-down (requires single tool) and quick change 22 or 24 (Mag. cals. only) in. barrel, detachable 3 or 4 shot mag., 65 degree short throw bolt, 3 position safety, standard medium gloss walnut stock with checkering, ultra-fast lock time, nitrided bore, no sights, includes hard carry case, approx. 7.3 lbs. Mfg. 1998-2002.

	100%	98%	95%	90%	80%	70%	60%	Last MSR
	$475	$395	$350	$325	$295	$275	$250	*$550*

Add $395 for extra barrel.

  * **SHR 970 Synthetic** – similar to SHR 970, except has checkered black synthetic stock with stippled grip. Mfg. 1999-2002.

	100%	98%	95%	90%	80%	70%	60%	Last MSR
	$445	$375	$325	$295	$275	$250	$230	*$499*

STR 970 LONG RANGE – .308 Win. or .300 Win. Mag. cal., inlcudes stippled black McMillan composite stock with precision bedding blocks, 24 in. fluted heavy barrel with integral muzzle brake and non-reflective Ilaflon metal coating, cased, 11.6 lbs. Mfg. 2000-2002.

	100%	98%	95%	90%	80%	70%	60%	Last MSR
	$875	$795	$675	$575	$525	$475	$425	*$899*

RIFLES: SEMI-AUTO

MODEL 1908 MONDRAGON – 7.5mm cal. and others, serial number is stamped externally in four locations, unique operating mechanism, first semi-auto military contract rifle, approx. 500 rifles Mexican contract.

	100%	98%	95%	90%	80%	70%	60%
	$25,000	$22,000	$19,000	$16,000	$13,000	$10,000	$7,000

PE-57 – 7.5 Swiss cal. only, semi-auto version of the Swiss military rifle, 24 in. barrel, includes 24 shot mag., leather sling, bipod and maintenance kit. Importation disc. 1988.

	100%	98%	95%	90%	80%	70%	60%	Last MSR
	$8,000	$7,000	$6,000	$5,000	$4,000	$3,000	$2,500	*$1,745*

The PE-57 was previously distributed in limited quantities by Osborne's located in Cheboygan, MI.

SIG-AMT RIFLE – .308 Win. cal., semi-auto version of SG510-4 auto rifle, roller delayed blowback action, 5, 10, or 20 shot mag., 18 3/4 in. barrel, wood stock, folding bipod. Mfg. 1960-1988.

	100%	98%	95%	90%	80%	70%	60%	Last MSR
	$5,500	$4,500	$3,750	$3,250	$2,750	$2,250	$1,750	*$1,795*

SG 550/551 – .223 Rem. cal. with heavier bullet, Swiss Army's semi-auto version of a tactical design rifle (SIG 90), 20.8 (SG 550) or 16 in. (SG 551 Carbine) barrel, some synthetics used to save weight, 20 shot mag., diopter night sights, built-in folding bipod, 7.7 or 9 lbs.

	100%	98%	95%	90%	80%	70%	60%	Last MSR
SG 550 (Rifle)	$8,500	$7,750	$7,000	$6,250	$5,500	$4,950	$4,500	
SG 551 (Carbine)	$9,500	$9,000	$8,500	$8,000	$7,250	$6,500	$5,600	*$1,950*

This model had very limited domestic importation before 1989 Federal legislation banned its configuration.

SIG 556 – Please refer to the Sig Sauer section.

SIG SAUER

Current firearms trademark manufactured by SIG Arms AG (Schweizerische Industrie-Gesellschaft) located in Neuhausen, Switzerland. Most models are currently manufactured in the U.S., and some models continue to be imported from Switzerland. Sig Sauer, Inc. was established in 2007, and is located in Exeter, NH. Previously imported and distributed from 1985-2006 by Sigarms, Inc. located in Exeter, NH. Previously located in Herndon, VA and Tysons Corner, VA.

In late 2000, SIG Arms AG, the firearms portion of SIG, was purchased by two Germans named Michael Lüke and Thomas Ortmeier (L&O Group), who have a background in textiles. Headquarters for L&O are in Emsdetten, Switzerland. Today the Lüke & Ortmeier group includes independently operational companies such as Blaser Jadgwaffen GmbH, Mauser Jagdwaffen GmbH, John Rigby, J.P. Sauer & Sohn GmbH, SIG-Sauer Inc., SIG-Sauer GmbH and SAN Swiss Arms AG. Please refer to individual listings.

On Oct. 1, 2007, SIG Arms changed its corporate name to Sig Sauer.

PISTOLS: SEMI-AUTO

Beginning 2001, SIG started manufacturing variations which are compliant by state. They include CA (10 shot mag. max only), MA (requires a loaded chamber indicator), and NY (must include empty shell casing) are priced slightly higher than the standard models available for the rest of the states.

The Sigarms Custom Shop, located in Exeter, NH, has recently been established, and offers a wide variety of custom shop services, including action enhancement, full servicing, DA/SA conversions, trigger and hammer modifications, barrel replacement, and many refinishing options. Please contact Sigarms Custom Shop directly for more information and current pricing on these services.

During 2005, the Sigarms Custom Shop produced 12 limited editions, including the P229 Rail (January), P245 w/nickel accents and Meprolight night sights (February), P220 .45 ACP Rail (March), P239 Satin Nickel w/Hogue rubber grips (April), GSR 1911 Reverse

MSR	100%	98%	95%	90%	80%	70%	60%	*Last MSR*

Two-Tone (May), P229 Satin Nickel Reverse Two-Tone (June), P232 Rainbow Titanium (July), P226 Rail (August), P220 Sport Stock (September), P239 w/extra .357 SIG cal. barrel (October), P228 Two-Tone (November), and the P226 package w/Oakley glasses (December).

Early SIG Sauer pistols can be marked either with the Herndon or Tysons Corner, VA barrel address, and can also be marked "W. Germany" or "Germany". Earlier mfg. had three proofmarks on the bottom front of the slide, with a fourth on the frame in front of the serial number. Early guns with these barrel markings will command a slight premium over prices listed below, if condition is 98%+. Current mfg. has Exeter, NH barrel address.

Add $302-$379 for caliber X-Change kit on current models.

MODEL MPX-P – 9mm Para. cal., AR-15 style pistol, GPO, 8 in. barrel, aluminum handguard, reflex sights, 30 shot mag. New 2014.

MSR $1,999	$1,825	$1,625	$1,475	$1,275	$1,050	$900	$750	

Add $329 for pistol stabilizing brace (PSB), new 2014.

MOSQUITO – .22 LR cal., compact design similar to P226, 3.98 in. barrel, polymer frame, 10 shot mag., DA/SA, decocker, ambidextrous manual safety, Picatinny rail on bottom of frame, internal locking device, adj. rear sight, molded composite grips, black, nickel (mfg. 2007-2008), blue (disc. 2012), two-tone, desert digital camo (mfg. 2009-2012), pink (new 2009), reverse two-tone (new 2007), carbon fiber (mfg. 2012 only), flat dark earth (FDE) frame (new 2012), multi-cam (mfg. 2012 only), OD frame (new 2012), or deep purple (new 2012) frame finish, 24.6 oz. New 2005.

MSR $408	$350	$300	$260	$230	$210	$190	$170	

Add $18 for hot pink frame, flat dark earth frame (new 2012), OD frame finish, or deep purple frame finish.
Add $34 for threaded barrel.
Add $15 for nickel (disc. 2008) finish. Add $79 for carbon fiber or multi-cam (mfg. 2012 only).
Add $112 for desert digital camo frame with threaded barrel, disc. 2012.
Add $142 for camo finish, threaded barrel, and tactical trainer package (disc. 2009).
Add $75 for long slide with barrel weight (black finish only, new 2007, Sporter model). Disc. 2012.

MODEL P 210 LEGEND – 9mm Para. cal., SA only, 4 3/4 in. barrel with fixed 2-dot or adj. target sights, black nitron finish, side release 8 shot mag., checkered wood grips, improved and extended beavertail, grooved grip straps, nickel plated safety, hammer, trigger, and slide release. Importation began 2011.

MSR $2,428	$2,175	$1,925	$1,700	$1,475	$1,250	$1,050	$875	

Add $214 for adj. target sights.

For pre-2011 manufacture, please refer to listings in the Sig Arms AG section.

MODEL P 210 SUPER TARGET – 9mm Para. cal., SAO, 4.7 in. barrel, Nitron stainless steel slide and frame, 8 shot, redesigned 1911-style safety lever and extended slide catch lever, adj. target sights, enhanced controls, beavertail, stippled ergonomic wood grips with integral magwell, Black nitron finish. New 2014.

MSR $3,993	$3,500	$3,150	$2,750	$2,500	$2,250	$2,000	$1,750	

MODEL P220 – .22 LR (disc.), .38 Super (disc.), 7.65mm (disc.), 9mm Para. (disc 1991), or .45 ACP cal., 7 (.45 ACP, disc.) or 8 shot mag., full size, DA/SA, SAO, or DAO (.45 ACP cal. only), 4.4 in. barrel, decocking lever, choice of matte blue (disc. 2006), black nitron (new 2007), stainless steel (mfg. 2001-2007), K-Kote (disc. 1999), electroless nickel (disc. 1991), two-tone with nickel finished slide (disc. 2011), or Ilaflon (mfg. 2000 only) finish, lightweight alloy frame, black plastic grips, optional DAK trigger system (DAO with 6 1/2 lb. trigger pull) available during 2005 only, tactical rail became standard 2004 at no extra charge (blue or stainless only), contrast (disc. 2013) or Siglite night sights (became standard 2014), approx. 30.4 or 41.8 (stainless steel) oz. New 1976.

MSR $1,108	$885	$730	$625	$525	$450	$400	$350	

Subtract $75 if without Siglite night sights (became standard 2014)
Add $149 for black stainless with Hogue rubber grips and Siglite night sights (mfg. 2012-2013).
Add $40 for DAK trigger system (limited mfg. 2005).
Add $103 for two-tone (nickel slide) finish (disc. 2011).
Add $100 for P220 SAO Model (single action only, disc. 2009).
Add $306 for Crimson Trace laser grips w/night sights (disc. 2009).
Add $95 for stainless steel frame & slide (mfg. 2001-2007).
Add $40 for Ilaflon finish (disc. 2000).
Add $45 for factory K-Kote finish (disc. 1999).
Add $70 for electroless nickel finish (disc. 1991).
Add $285 for .22 LR conversion kit (current mfg.) or $680 for older mfg. .22 LR conversion kit.
Subtract 10% for "European" Model (bottom mag. release - includes 9mm Para. and .38 Super cals.).

Values are for .45 ACP cal. and assume American side mag. release (standard 1986).

This model was also available as a Custom Shop Limited Edition during July, 2004 (MSR was $800 and November, 2004 (MSR was $861).

MSR	100%	98%	95%	90%	80%	70%	60%	Last MSR

* Model P220 Combat – .45 ACP cal., features flat Dark Earth finish, alloy frame, Nitron stainless slide, corrosion resistant parts, 8 shot mag., M1913 Picatinny rail, Siglite night sights, with (Combat TB) or w/o (Combat disc. 2012) threaded barrel. Mfg. 2007-2012, re-introduced 2014.

| MSR $1,316 | $1,100 | $950 | $825 | $725 | $625 | $525 | $425 | |

Subtract $100 if w/out threaded barrel (became standard 2014).

* Model P220 Elite/Dark Elite – .45 ACP cal., similar to P220, except has short reset trigger, DA/SA or SAO, two-tone (limited mfg.), or black Nitron finish, 8 shot mag., ergonomic beavertail, Picatinny rail, front cocking serrations, custom shop wood or black aluminum (Dark Elite) grips. New 2007.

| MSR $1,253 | $1,095 | $950 | $825 | $725 | $625 | $525 | $425 | |

Add $61 for Elite Dark with threaded barrel (disc. 2012).

* Model P220 Elite Stainless – .45 ACP cal., similar to P220 Elite, except is stainless steel, features custom shop wood or checkered aluminum (Platinum Elite, disc. 2011) grips. New 2007.

| MSR $1,396 | $1,250 | $1,050 | $925 | $800 | $700 | $600 | $500 | |

Add $72 for platinum Elite with aluminum grips (stainless only), disc. 2011.

* Model P220 Equinox – .45 ACP cal., similar to P220, except has two-tone accented slide with nitron finish, Truglo TFO front sight, Siglite rear sight, black wood grips w/custom shop logo. New 2007.

| MSR $1,253 | $1,095 | $950 | $850 | $725 | $625 | $525 | $425 | |

* Model P220 Extreme – .45 ACP cal., black nitron finish with stainless reverse two-tone, 4 in. barrel, forward slide serrations, Siglite night sights, and Hogue G-10 grips, approx. 30 oz. New 2012.

| MSR $1,239 | $1,075 | $950 | $850 | $725 | $625 | $525 | $425 | |

* Model P220 Match – .45 ACP cal., similar to P220, except has 5 in. cold hammer forged barrel, DA/SA or SAO, ambidextrous safety, two-tone or stainless (Match Elite) finish, adj. sights, black polymer or custom shop wood (Super Match) grips, Elite Match became standard during 2010. Mfg. 2007-2012.

| | $1,175 | $975 | $850 | $725 | $625 | $550 | $450 | $1,368 |

Add $7 for Super Match model.

Subtract approx. $200 for Match (disc. 2009, last MSR was $1,170).

* Model P220 NRALE – .45 ACP cal., features NRA Law Enforcement logo and the words "NRA Law Enforcement" engraved in 24Kt. gold, cocobolo grips with NRA medallions, gold trigger and appointments. Limited production of 1,000, including P226 NRALE 2002-2003.

| | $850 | $650 | $495 | N/A | N/A | N/A | N/A | $911 |

* Model P220 Scorpion Elite – .45 ACP cal., features flat dark earth (FDE) metal finish, beavertail, stainless reverse two-tone, Siglite night sights and Hogue Extreme G-10 grips. New 2012.

| MSR $1,312 | $1,175 | $995 | $875 | $750 | $650 | $550 | $450 | |

Add $71 for threaded barrel (disc. 2012).

* Model P220 Sport – .45 ACP cal., features 4.8 in. heavy compensated barrel, stainless steel frame and slide, 10 shot mag., target sights, improved trigger pull, single or double action, 46.1 oz. Imported 1999-2000, reintroduced 2003-2005.

| | $1,375 | $975 | $800 | $695 | $585 | $485 | $415 | $1,600 |

* Model P220R – .22 LR cal., 4.4 in. barrel, 10 shot mag., DA/SA, matte black anodized finish, adj. sights, otherwise similar to standard P220. Mfg. 2009-2012.

| | $565 | $500 | $450 | $395 | $350 | $300 | $275 | $642 |

* Model P220 TacPac – .45 ACP cal., features black nitron finish, Siglite sights, one-piece enhanced E2 grip, STL 900L, includes holster. New 2013.

| MSR $1,238 | $1,075 | $925 | $825 | $725 | $625 | $525 | $425 | |

MODEL P220 .22 LR – .22 LR cal., full size, 4.4 in. barrel, DA/SA trigger, black anodized alloy slide, 10 shot mag., adj. sights, black anodized finish. New 2014.

| MSR $642 | $550 | $495 | $450 | $400 | $365 | $335 | $295 | |

MODEL P220 CARRY – .45 ACP cal., compact model w/full size frame, 3.9 in. barrel, 8 shot single stack mag., DA/SA, DAK, or SAO, black Nitron finish, Siglite night sights, Picatinny rail, black polymer wood grips, contrast (disc. 2013) or Siglite night sights (became standard 2014). New 2007.

| MSR $1,108 | $925 | $825 | $725 | $625 | $525 | $425 | $350 | |

Subtract $100 if without Siglite night sights (became standard 2014).

Add $100 for SAO trigger (disc. 2008).

* Model P220 Carry Elite – .45 ACP cal., similar to P220 Elite, except is compact model, stainless or black Nitron (mfg. 2009-2012) finish, Siglite night sights, wood grips. New 2007.

| MSR $1,396 | $1,250 | $1,050 | $925 | $800 | $700 | $600 | $500 | |

Subtract $140 for black nitron finish (disc. 2012).

MSR	100%	98%	95%	90%	80%	70%	60%	Last MSR

* **Model P220 Carry Stainless Elite** – similar to P220 Carry, except has SRT, stainless reverse two-tone, Siglite night sights, beavertail, Hogue rubber (mfg. 2012-2013) or wood grips (new 2013). New 2012.

| MSR $1,396 | $1,250 | $1,050 | $925 | $800 | $700 | $600 | $500 | |

* **Model P220 Carry Equinox** – similar to P220 Carry, except has two-tone accented slide with nitron finish, Truglo TFO front sight, Siglite rear sight, black wood grips w/custom shop logo. New 2007.

| MSR $1,243 | $1,075 | $950 | $850 | $725 | $625 | $525 | $425 | |

* **Model P220 Carry SAS** – similar to P22 Carry, except has SRT, two-tone finish with black frame and stainless steel slide, custom shop brown wood grips (disc.) or one-piece polymer grips, contrast (disc. 2013) or Siglite night sights (became standard 2014), Gen. 2 features became standard 2008. New 2010.

| MSR $1,149 | $995 | $850 | $750 | $650 | $550 | $450 | $400 | |

MODEL P220 COMPACT
– .45 ACP cal., compact beavertail frame, 3.9 in. barrel, 6 shot mag., DA/SA or SAO, black Nitron or two-tone (disc. 2010) finish, contrast or Siglite night sights, lower Picatinny rail, black polymer grips. Mfg. 2007-2013.

| | $940 | $815 | $700 | $600 | $500 | $400 | $350 | *$1,166* |

Add $75 for two-tone finish (disc. 2010).
Add $58 for Siglite night sights only (disc. 2011).

* **Model P220 Compact SAS** – similar to P220 Compact, except DA/SA or SAO (disc.), no beavertail, SRT, w/o lower Picatinny rail, contrast (disc.) or Siglite night sights (became standard 2014), black polymer or custom shop wood (disc.) grips, Gen. 2 features became standard 2012. New 2007.

| MSR $1,166 | $995 | $875 | $750 | $650 | $550 | $450 | $400 | |

MODEL P224
– 9mm Para., 357 Sig., or .40 S&W cal., 3 1/2 in. barrel, DA/SA or DAK trigger (disc. 2013), alloy frame with stainless steel slide, 10 or 12 (9mm Para. only) shot mag., satin nickel slide and controls (P224 Nickel), Siglite night sights, wood (disc.) or one-piece enhanced E2 (new 2013) grips, 25.4 oz. New 2012.

| MSR $1,108 | $885 | $730 | $625 | $525 | $450 | $400 | $350 | |

* **Model P224 SAS Gen. 2** – similar to P224, except has black nitron finish, dehorned metal parts, stainless reverse two-tone, Siglite night sights, and one-piece enhanced E2 grip. New 2012.

| MSR $1,149 | $995 | $850 | $750 | $650 | $550 | $450 | $400 | |

* **Model P224 Extreme** – 9mm Para. or .40 S&W cal., similar to Model P224 SAS Gen. 2, except has Hogue Extreme G-10 grips. New 2012.

| MSR $1,170 | $1,025 | $875 | $750 | $650 | $550 | $450 | $400 | |

* **Model P224 Equinox** – .40 S&W cal. only, two-tone polished nitron finish, Truglo front sight with Siglite rear night sight, black wood grips. New 2012.

| MSR $1,243 | $1,075 | $925 | $775 | $675 | $575 | $475 | $400 | |

MODEL P225
– 9mm Para. cal., regular double action or double action only, similar to P220, shorter dimensions, 3.85 in. barrel, 8 shot, thumb actuated button release mag., fully adj. sights, 28.8 oz. Disc. 1998.

| | $595 | $525 | $450 | $425 | $395 | $350 | $310 | *$725* |

Add $45 for factory K-Kote finish.
Add $105 for Siglite night sights.
Add $45 for nickel finished slide (new 1992).
Add $70 for electroless nickel finish (disc. 1991).

This model was also available as a Custom Shop Limited Edition during March, 2004. MSR was $803.

MODEL P226
– .357 SIG (new 1995), 9mm Para. (disc. 1997, reintroduced 1999), or .40 S&W (new 1998) cal., full size, choice of double action or double action only (new 1992) operation, 10 (C/B 1994), 12 (new mid-2005, .357 SIG or .40 S&W cal.) or 15* (9mm Para. cal. only) shot mag., 4.4 in. barrel, alloy frame, currently available in blackened stainless steel (Nitron finish became standard 2000), two-tone (disc. 2011), reverse two-tone (.40 S&W cal. only - mfg. 2012 only), or nickel (disc. 2002) finish (stainless slide only), tactical rail became standard 2004, choice of traditional DA or DAK (disc.) trigger system (DAO with 6 1/2 lb. trigger pull, not available in all stainless) available beginning 2005, E2 grips became standard 2011, high contrast sights (disc. 2013) or Siglite night sights (became standard 2014), automatic firing pin block safety, 31.7 or 34 oz. New 1983.

| MSR $1,108 | $885 | $730 | $625 | $525 | $450 | $400 | $350 | |

Subtract $100 if without Siglite night sights (became standard 2014).
Add $302 for .22 LR cal. conversion kit.
Add $149 for reverse two-tone finish - all stainless with Siglite night sights and Hogue rubber grips (mfg. 2012 only).
Add $306 for Crimson Trace laser grips w/Siglite night sights (mfg. 2007).
Add $95 for stainless steel frame and slide (mfg. 2004-2005).
Add $103 for two-tone finish (nickel finished stainless steel slide) w/night sights, (disc. 2011).

MSR	100%	98%	95%	90%	80%	70%	60%	Last MSR

Add $45 for K-Kote (Polymer) finish (mfg. 1992-97, 9mm Para. only).

Add $70 for electroless nickel finish (disc. 1991).

This model is also available in double action only (all finishes) at no extra charge.

This model was also available as a Custom Shop Limited Edition during Feb., 2004 (MSR was $1,085). A limited edition P226 America with blue titanium and gold finishes was also available from SIG's Custom Shop (MSR was $7,995).

This model is also available as the P226R Tactical, sold exclusively by Ellett Bros distributors - no pricing information is available.

* **Model P226 Combat** – 9mm Para. cal., DA/SA, 4.4 in. barrel, 10 or 15 shot mag., Siglite night sights, flat dark earth frame and grips, black Nitron slide, Picatinny rail, 34 oz. Mfg. 2008-2012.

	100%	98%	95%	90%	80%	70%	60%	Last MSR
	$1,050	$925	$825	$725	$625	$525	$425	*$1,218*

Add $71 for TB model with threaded barrel.

* **Model P226 Elite** – 9mm (new 2011), .357 SIG (mfg. 2011-2012), .40 S&W (mfg. 2011-2013), or .45 ACP (disc. 2011) cal., similar to P226, except has short reset trigger, SAO, two-tone (disc.), or black Nitron finish, 15 shot mag., Siglite night sights, black polymer grips. New 2007.

MSR $1,243	$1,050	$925	$825	$725	$625	$525	$425	

Add $72 for platinum Elite with aluminum grips (disc. 2011).

Add $71 for TB Model with threaded barrel (9mm Para. only), disc. 2012.

* **Model P226 Elite Dark** – 9mm (new 2011), .357 SIG (mfg. 2011-2012), .40 S&W (new 2011), or .45 ACP (disc. 2011) cal., similar to P226, except has Black Nitron finish 12 or 15 shot mag., aluminum checkered grips. New 2007.

MSR $1,243	$1,050	$925	$825	$725	$625	$525	$425	

* **Model P226 Elite Stainless** – 9mm (new 2011), .357 Sig (disc. 2012), .40 S&W (new 2011), or .45 ACP (disc. 2011) cal., otherwise similar to P226, except has stainless steel, custom shop wood grips (disc.) or checkered Rosewood grips, Siglite night sights. New 2007.

MSR $1,396	$1,250	$1,050	$925	$800	$700	$600	$500	

* **Model P226 Enhanced Elite** – 9mm Para., .357 SIG, or .40 S&W cal., includes lower Picatinny rail in front of trigger guard, black nitron finish, beavertail, stainless reverse two-tone, E2 polymer grips and night sights. Mfg. 2011-2012.

	$1,025	$900	$800	$700	$600	$500	$400	*$1,175*

* **Model P226 Equinox** – .40 S&W cal., 4.4 in. barrel, two-tone Nitron stainless steel slide, lightweight black anodized alloy frame, nickel accents, 10 or 12 shot mag., Truglo tritium front sight, rear Siglite night sight, Picatinny rail, grey laminated wood grips, 34 oz., mfg. by the Custom Shop. Mfg. 2006-2012.

	$1,050	$925	$825	$725	$625	$525	$425	*$1,218*

* **Model P226 Extreme** – 9mm Para. or .40 S&W cal., similar to Model P226 Enhanced Elite, except has Hogue Extreme Series G10 grips. New 2011.

MSR $1,239	$1,075	$950	$800	$700	$600	$550	$450	

* **Model P226 E2** – 9mm Para. cal., 15 shot mag., black Nitron finish, ergonomic slim profile one piece grips, Siglite night sights, short reset trigger, integral accessory rail, includes three mags. New 2010 only.

	$1,000	$895	$775	$675	$575	$525	$450	*$1,149*

* **Model P226 Jubilee** – 9mm Para. cal., limited edition commemorating SIG's 125th anniversary, features gold-plated small parts, carved select walnut grips, special slide markings, cased. Mfg. 1985 only.

	$1,495	$1,175	$950	$835	$685	$585	$485	*$2,000*

* **Model P226 MK25 Navy Version** – 9mm Para. cal., 4.4 in. barrel, black Nitron or Flat Dark Earth (FDE, new 2014) finish with phosphated small components, features anchor engraving, three 15 shot mags., Picatinny rail, UID label on right side of slide, Siglite night sight, otherwise similar to Model P226. New 2012.

MSR $1,166	$1,025	$850	$750	$600	$500	$450	$400	

Add $70 for Flat Dark Earth finish (new 2014).

* **Model P226 NRALE** – .40 S&W cal., features NRA Law Enforcement logo and the words "NRA Law Enforcement" engraved in 24Kt. gold, cocobolo grips with NRA medallions, gold trigger and appointments. Limited production of 1,000, including P220 NRALE, 2002-2003.

	$850	$650	$495	N/A	N/A	N/A	N/A	*$911*

* **Model P226R** – .22 LR cal., Nitron finish, adj. sights, DA/SA or SAO, 10 shot mag., with or w/o beavertail grips and stainless reverse two-tone. Mfg. 2009-2012.

	$585	$515	$465	$400	$350	$300	$275	*$656*

Add $33 for beavertail and stainless reverse two-tone.

MSR	100%	98%	95%	90%	80%	70%	60%	Last MSR

* **Model P226 Scorpion Elite** – 9mm Para. cal. only, features flat dark earth (FDE) finish, beavertail, stainless reverse two-tone, Siglite night sights, and Hogue Extreme G-10 grips. Mfg. 2012 only.

	$1,150	$975	$850	$750	$650	$550	$450	$1,285

Add $71 for threaded barrel.

* **Model P226 Special Editions** – 9mm Para. or .40 S&W (Cops Commemorative only, disc. 2008) cal., engraved, variations include Navy (black Nitron finish, phosphate components and anchor engraving), Cops Commemorative (Siglite night sights and wood grips, disc. 2008). Series disc. 2011.

	$895	$775	$675	$575	$475	$400	$350	$1,020

* **Model P226 Sport** – 9mm Para. cal., features 5.6 in. match or heavy compensated barrel, stainless steel frame and slide, 10 shot mag., target sights, improved trigger pull, single or double action, rubber grips, 48.8 oz. Mfg. 2003-2005.

	$1,375	$975	$800	$695	$585	$485	$415	$1,600

* **Model P226 ST** – 9mm Para., .40 S&W, or .357 Mag. cal., 4.4 in. barrel, white stainless slide and frame, blue barrel, Picatinny rail, 10 shot mag., 38.8 oz.

While advertised during 2006, this model never went into production - prototypes only.

* **Model P226 Super Cap Tactical** – .40 S&W cal., similar to P226 Tactical, black Nitron finish, TruGlo front sight, Siglite rear sight, includes four 15 shot mags. Mfg. 2009-2010.

	$1,025	$925	$825	$725	$625	$525	$425	$1,156

* **Model P226 TACOPS** – 9mm Para., .357 SIG (mfg. 2012 only), or .40 S&W cal., features Truglo tradium fiber optic front sight and Siglite rear night sight, beavertail, stainless reverse two-tone, Magwell grips, black nitron finish, 20 shot mag., 34 oz. New 2011.

MSR $1,316	$1,175	$995	$850	$750	$650	$550	$450	

Add $13 for 9mm Para. cal.

* **Model P226 TacPac** – 9mm Para. or .40 S&W cal., features black nitron finish, Siglite sights, one-piece enhanced E2 grip, STL 900L, includes holster. New 2013.

MSR $1,238	$1,075	$950	$825	$725	$625	$525	$425	

* **Model P226 Tactical/Blackwater Tactical** – similar to P226, black Nitron finish, Picatinny rail, threaded barrel, post and dot contrast Siglite night sights, available in standard (disc. 2009) and Blackwater configuration (black Nitron finish, Siglite night sights, and wood grips). Mfg. 2007-2010.

	$1,150	$975	$850	$750	$650	$550	$450	$1,300

Subtract approx. $50 for standard tactical - (disc. 2009, last MSR was $1,245).

* **Model P226 USPSA** – 9mm Para. cal., short reset trigger, 4.4 in. barrel, 15 shot mag., Dawson fiber optic front sight, Warren rear sight, polymer grips, aluminum frame with stainless steel slide, black Nitron finish, USPSA engraving, includes three mags. Mfg. 2009-2010.

	$1,095	$950	$825	$725	$625	$525	$400	$1,246

MODEL P226 .22 LR – .22 LR cal., 4.4 in. barrel, DA/SA trigger, black anodized alloy slide, 10 shot mag., adj. sights, one-piece enhanced E2 grip, black anodized finish. New 2014.

MSR $636	$550	$495	$450	$400	$365	$335	$295	

Add $43 for beavertail and SRT.

MODEL P226 X-FIVE – 9mm Para. or .40 S&W cal., SA, adj. trigger, 5 in. stainless steel barrel and slide, ambidextrous thumb safety, all stainless construction with magwell, low profile adj. sights, 14 (.40 S&W) or 19 (9mm Para.) shot mag., available in blue, two-tone, stainless or black Nitron finish, checkered walnut grips, includes 25 meter test target, checkered front grip strap, 47.2 oz. Mfg. mid-2005-2012.

	$2,400	$2,050	$1,700	$1,400	$1,225	$1,000	$850	$2,747

* **Model P226 X-Five Competition** – 9mm Para. or .40 S&W cal., similar to X-Five, except has black polymer grips. Mfg. 2007-2012.

	$1,725	$1,475	$1,250	$1,050	$875	$700	$650	$1,976

* **Model P226 X-Five All Around** – 9mm Para. or .40 S&W cal., adj. sights, ergonomic beavertail grip, DA/SA, stainless slide and frame, black polymer grips. Mfg. 2007-2012.

	$1,425	$1,200	$975	$850	$750	$650	$550	$1,696

* **Model P226 X-Five Tactical** – 9mm Para. cal., black Nitron finish, contrast sights, lightweight alloy frame, Picatinny rail, single action trigger, ergonomic beavertail grips. Mfg. 2007-2012.

	$1,425	$1,200	$975	$850	$750	$650	$550	$1,696

MODEL P226 X SERIES – 9mm Para. or .40 S&W cal., individual models are marked on left side of slide between slide serrations. New series introduced 2014.

MSR	100%	98%	95%	90%	80%	70%	60%	Last MSR

* **Model P226 X All Around** – 9mm Para. or .40 S&W cal., DA/SA, natural stainless steel slide and frame extended for 5 in. barrel, adj. rear sight, front cocking serrations, integral Picatinny accessory rail, standard magazine and mag. catch, Black laminated grips. New 2014.

| MSR $2,245 | $1,950 | $1,775 | $1,575 | $1,375 | $1,175 | $975 | $725 | |

* **Model P226 X Classic** – 9mm Para. or .40 S&W cal., SAO, 5 in. barrel, natural stainless steel slide and frame, user adj. SAO trigger, fully adj. target sights, M1913 Picatinny accessory rail, custom walnut grips. New 2014.

| MSR $2,679 | $2,395 | $2,100 | $1,850 | $1,600 | $1,350 | $1,100 | $925 | |

* **Model P226 X Entry** – 9mm Para. or .40 S&W cal., SAO, 5 in. barrel, natural stainless steel slide and frame, fixed rear sight, M1913 Picatinny accessory rail, standard magazine catch, Black polymer grips. New 2014.

| MSR $1,763 | $1,550 | $1,375 | $1,200 | $1,050 | $875 | $725 | $600 | |

* **Model P226 X Match** – 9mm Para. or .40 S&W cal., SAO, natural stainless steel slide and frame extended for a 5 in. barrel, front cocking serrations, skeletonized hammer, fully adj. target sights, M1913 Picatinny accessory rail, extended magazine catch, Black laminate grips. New 2014.

| MSR $1,728 | $1,500 | $1,300 | $1,100 | $900 | $750 | $650 | $575 | |

Add $1,192 for .40 S&W cal.

Add $1,078 for shorter barrel (XFive Match Short model).

* **Model P226 X Open** – 9mm Para. cal., SAO, natural stainless steel slide and frame, 5 in. barrel with compensator, user adj. SAO straight match trigger, Sport takedown lever, M1913 Picatinny accessory rail, Black G10 grips, bridge mount, ambidextrous slide racker, extended magazine catch. New 2014.

| MSR $4,852 | $4,450 | $4,000 | $3,550 | $3,100 | $2,700 | $2,300 | $1,850 | |

* **Model P226 X Super Match** – 9mm Para. or .40 S&W cal., 5 or 6 (XSix Super Match) in. barrel, sport takedown lever, natural stainless steel slide and frame, fully adj. target sights, M1913 Picatinny accessory rail, extended magazine catch, Black G10 grips, straight trigger. New 2014.

| MSR $3,042 | $2,700 | $2,400 | $2,250 | $1,800 | $1,550 | $1,350 | $1,150 | |

Add $241 for 6 in. barrel (XSix Super Match model).

* **Model P226 X Tactical** – 9mm Para. or .40 S&W cal., SAO, Nitron slide, black alloy frame, black polymer grips. New 2014.

| MSR $1,678 | $1,495 | $1,300 | $1,125 | $900 | $775 | $650 | $550 | |

MODEL P227 – .45 ACP cal., DA/SA, 4.4 in. stainless steel barrel, 10 shot mag., black nitron finish, contrast sights (mfg. 2013 only) or Siglite night sights (became standard 2014), lower Picatinny rail, 32 oz. New 2013.

| MSR $1,108 | $975 | $800 | $700 | $600 | $500 | $400 | $350 | |

Subtract $100 if without Siglite night sights (became standard 2014).

* **Model P227 Carry** – .45 ACP cal., DA/SA, 3.9 in. stainless steel barrel, 10 shot mag., black nitron finish, Siglite night sights, lower Picatinny rail, 30 1/2 oz. New 2013.

| MSR $1,108 | $975 | $800 | $700 | $600 | $500 | $400 | $350 | |

* **Model P227 Carry SAS** – .45 ACP cal., Gen. 2, 3.9 in. stainless steel barrel, black nitron finish, dehorning, SRT, contrast or Siglite night sights, Sig anti-snag treatment on slide and frame with no rail, one piece ergonomic grips, 30 1/2 oz. New 2013.

| MSR $1,149 | $995 | $850 | $750 | $625 | $525 | $425 | $375 | |

* **Model P227 Equinox** – .45 ACP cal., DA/SA, two-tone polished nitron finish, TruGlo fiber optic front sight, Siglite night sights, wood grips, 10 shot mag. New 2014.

| MSR $1,250 | $1,050 | $950 | $825 | $725 | $625 | $525 | $425 | |

* **Model P227R** – .45 ACP cal., DA/SA, threaded barrel, 45 Nitron, Siglite sights, SRT, 10 or 14 shot mag., black nitron finish. New 2014.

| MSR $1,228 | $1,050 | $950 | $825 | $725 | $625 | $525 | $425 | |

* **Model P227R TacPac** – .45 ACP cal., DA/SA, 45 Nitron, Siglite sights, STL-900L, 10 shot mag., includes holster. New 2014.

| MSR $1,238 | $1,050 | $950 | $825 | $725 | $625 | $525 | $425 | |

MODEL P228 (OLD MFG.) – 9mm Para., choice of double action or double action only (new 1992) operation, compact design, 3.86 in. (compact) barrel, 10 (C/B 1994) or 13* (reintroduced 2004) shot mag., automatic firing pin block safety, high contrast sights, alloy frame, choice of blue, Nitron (new 2004), nickel (mfg. 1991-97), or stainless steel (new 2004) slide, or K-Kote (disc. 1997) finish, 29.3 oz. Mfg. 1990-97, reintroduced 2004-2006.

| | $700 | $600 | $500 | $450 | $400 | $350 | $310 | $840 |

Add $50 for Siglite night sights.

Add $376 for .22 LR cal. conversion kit.

Add $45 for K-Kote (Polymer) finish (disc. 1997).

MSR	100%	98%	95%	90%	80%	70%	60%	*Last MSR*

Add $45 for nickel finished slide (1991-97).

Add $70 for electroless nickel finish (disc. 1991).

This model was also available in double action only (all finishes) at no extra charge.

This model was also available as a Custom Shop Limited Edition during April, 2004 (MSR was $800).

MODEL P228 (NEW MFG.) – 9mm Para. cal., SA/DA, Siglite night sights, includes two 15 shot mags., choice of black nitron, Flat Dark Earth (new 2014) or stainless reverse two-tone (SRT) finish. New 2013.

MSR $1,149	$1,000	$875	$750	$625	$525	$475	$$25	

Add $71 for Flat Dark Earth finish (new 2014) or threaded barrel (new 2014).

MODEL P229 – .357 SIG (new 1995), 9mm Para. (mfg. 1994-96, reintroduced 1999), or .40 S&W cal., compact size, 3.9 in. barrel, similar to Model P228, except has blackened Nitron or satin nickel (disc.) finished stainless steel slide with aluminum alloy frame, 10 (C/B 1994), 12* (.357 SIG or .40 S&W cal. only), or 13 (9mm Para. cal. only, new 2005) shot mag., choice of traditional DA or DAK (disc. 2013) trigger system (DAO with 6 1/2 lb. trigger pull) available beginning 2005, E2 (enhanced ergonomics) grips became standard 2011, tactical rail became standard in 2004 (Nitron finish only), contrast sights (disc. 2013), Siglite sights became standard 2014, includes lockable carrying case, 31.1 or 32.4 oz. New 1991.

MSR $1,085	$975	$800	$700	$600	$500	$400	$350	

Add $23 for 9mm Para. or .40 S&W cal.

Subtract $100 if without Siglite night sights (became standard 2014).

Add $306 for Crimson Trace laser grips w/Siglite night sights (mfg. 2007-2008).

Add $180 for black Nitron finish with TruGlo TFO front and Siglite rear sights with four hi-cap mags. (Super Cap Tactical model, not available in .357 SIG cal.), disc. 2010.

Add $103 for two-tone finish (nickel finished stainless steel slide) with night sights (disc. 2011).

Add $302 for .22 LR cal. conversion kit.

This model was also available in double action only at no extra charge.

This model was also available as a Custom Shop Limited Edition during June, 2004 (MSR was $873), during August, 2004 (MSR was $916) and during Dec. 2004 (MSR was $844).

* Model P229 Elite – 9mm Para. cal., similar to P229, except has short reset trigger, DA/SA or SAO, two-tone (disc.), dark (Elite Dark, new 2009) or black Nitron (disc. 2011) finish, 8 shot mag., ergonomic beavertail, Picatinny rail, front cocking serrations, custom shop wood or aluminum grips. Mfg. 2007-2012.

	$1,050	$925	$825	$725	$625	$525	$425	*$1,218*

Add $71 for TB model with threaded barrel.

Add $72 for platinum Elite with aluminum grips (disc. 2011).

* Model P229 Elite Stainless – 9mm Para. or .40 S&W cal., SA/DA, stainless steel slide with SRT finish, 10, 12 (.40 S&W only), or 15 (9mm Para.) shot mag., ergonomic beavertail, Picatinny rail, front cocking serrations, Siglite night sights, custom shop wood grips only. New 2007.

MSR $1,396	$1,250	$1,050	$875	$775	$675	$575	$450	

* Model P229 Elite Dark – 9mm Para., .357 Sig (disc. 2012), or .40 S&W cal., DA/SA, 3.9 in. barrel, SRT (short reset trigger), Black Nitron finish, 12 or 15 shot mag., ergonomic beavertail, Picatinny rail, front cocking serrations, front strap checkering, Siglite night sights, custom aluminum grips. New 2009.

MSR $1,243	$1,050	$925	$825	$725	$625	$525	$425	

Add $71 for TB model with threaded barrel (disc. 2013).

* Model P229 Enhanced Elite – 9mm Para.(disc. 2012), .40 S&W (disc. 2012), or .357 SIG cal., includes lower Picatinny rail in front of trigger guard, black nitron finish, beavertail, stainless reverse two-tone, E2 polymer grips and Siglite night sights. Mfg. 2011-2013.

	$1,000	$900	$800	$700	$600	$500	$400	*$1,175*

* Model P229 Scorpion Elite – 9mm Para. or .40 S&W cal., features flat dark earth (FDE) finish, beavertail, stainless reverse two-tone, Siglite night sights, and Hogue Extreme G-10 grips. New 2012.

MSR $1,312	$1,175	$995	$850	$750	$650	$550	$450	

Add $71 for threaded barrel (9mm Para. only), disc. 2012.

* Model P229 Equinox – .40 S&W cal., 4.4 in. barrel, two-tone Nitron stainless steel slide, lightweight black anodized alloy frame, nickel accents, 10 or 12 shot mag., Truglo tritium front sight, rear Siglite night sight, Picatinny rail, grey laminated wood grips, 34 oz., mfg. by the Custom Shop. Mfg. 2007-2012.

	$1,050	$925	$825	$725	$625	$525	$425	*$1,218*

* Model P229 Extreme – 9mm Para. cal., features black nitron finish, stainless reverse two-tone, front slide serrations, Siglite night sights, and Hogue Extreme Series G10 grips. Mfg. 2012 only.

	$1,050	$925	$800	$700	$600	$550	$450	*$1,213*

MSR	100%	98%	95%	90%	80%	70%	60%	Last MSR

* **Model P229 Sport** – .357 SIG or .40 S&W (new 2003) cal., features 4.8 in. match or heavy (disc. 2000) compensated barrel, stainless steel frame and slide, target sights, improved trigger pull, single or double action, 43.6 oz. Mfg. 1998-2000, reintroduced 2003-2005.

| | $1,375 | $975 | $800 | $695 | $585 | $485 | $415 | *$1,600* |

* **Model P229 SAS** – 9mm Para., .357 SIG, or .40 S&W cal., 3.86 in. barrel, 12 shot mag., DAK trigger, smooth dehorned stainless steel slide, two-tone (disc.), or black Nitron (new 2009) finish, Siglite night sights, contrast rear sight, light-weight black hard anodized frame, rounded trigger guard, checkered wood grips, designed for snag-free profile for concealed carry, Generation II features became standard 2009, 32 oz. Mfg. by Custom Shop. Mfg. 2005-2012.

| | $995 | $875 | $750 | $625 | $525 | $475 | $425 | *$1,125* |

Add $30 for two-tone finish (disc. 2010).

* **Model P229 E2** – 9mm Para. cal., 15 shot mag., black Nitron finish, ergonomic slim profile one piece grips, Siglite night sights, short reset trigger, integral accessory rail, includes three mags. Mfg. 2010 only.

| | $1,000 | $895 | $775 | $675 | $575 | $525 | $450 | *$1,149* |

* **Model P229 TacPac** – 9mm Para. or .40 S&W cal., features black nitron finish, Siglite sights, one-piece enhanced E2 grip, STL 900L, includes holster. New 2013.

| MSR $1,238 | $1,075 | $950 | $825 | $725 | $625 | $525 | $425 | |

* **Model P229 HF (Heritage Fund)** – .40 S&W cal., 10 shot, 3.9 in. barrel, slide marked "10th Anniversary P229", frame marked "1992-2002", gold engraving and accents, brushed stainless steel, gold trigger, cocobolo Hogue grips with NSSF Heritage Fund medallion, includes wood display case. Limited mfg. late 2001-2004.

| | $1,195 | $750 | $600 | N/A | N/A | N/A | N/A | *$1,299* |

* **Model P229R .22 LR** – .22 LR cal., 4.4 in. barrel, 10 shot mag., DA/SA, matte black anodized finish, adj. sights, E2 polymer grip, otherwise similar to standard P229. Mfg. 2009-2012.

| | $585 | $515 | $465 | $400 | $350 | $300 | $275 | *$656* |

MODEL P230 – .22 LR (disc.).32 ACP, .380 ACP, or 9mm Ultra (disc.) cal., 7, 8, or 10 shot, 3.6 in. barrel, regular double action or double action only, blue, composite grips, 17.6 oz. Mfg. 1976-1996.

| | $425 | $375 | $300 | $270 | $240 | $215 | $190 | *$510* |

Add $35 for stainless slide (.380 ACP only).

* **Model P230 SL Stainless** – similar to Model P230, except stainless steel construction, 22.4 oz. Disc. 1996.

| | $480 | $400 | $375 | $315 | $270 | $230 | $200 | *$595* |

MODEL P232 – .380 ACP cal., choice of double action or double action only, 3.6 in. barrel, 7 shot mag., aluminum alloy frame, compact personal size, blue (disc.), black nitron or two-tone stainless (disc. 2012) slide, automatic firing pin block safety, composite (disc.) or Hogue rubber grips, Siglite night sights (became standard 2010), 17.6 oz. New 1997.

| MSR $809 | $725 | $650 | $550 | $475 | $425 | $350 | $295 | |

Add $29 for two-tone finish (mfg. 2007-2012).
Subtract $71 if w/o Siglite night sights (became standard 2010).

* **Model P232 Stainless** – .380 ACP cal., similar to Model P232, except stainless steel construction, natural finish, 22.4 oz. New 1997.

| MSR $889 | $795 | $650 | $525 | $450 | $375 | $325 | $295 | |

Subtract approx. $75 if w/o Siglite night sights and Hogue grips (standard beginning 2007).

MODEL P238 – 9mm Para. (mfg. 2012 only), or .380 ACP cal., lightweight aluminum frame, 2.7 in. barrel, stainless steel slide, SAO trigger, thumb safety, black Nitron or two-tone finish, fixed or Siglite night sights, fluted grips (new 2012), 15.2 oz. Mfg. 2009-2013.

| | $550 | $475 | $450 | $375 | $340 | $300 | $275 | *$679* |

Add $14 for two-tone finish.
Subtract $40 if w/o Siglite night sights (standard beginning 2010).

This model with specific features was disc. in 2013, and replacement model is the P238 Two-Tone Tribal (features black tribal engraving pattern on slide).

* **Model P238 Blackwood** – .380 ACP cal., similar to Model P238, except has two-tone finish and blackwood grips. New 2010.

| MSR $738 | $650 | $575 | $475 | $425 | $385 | $325 | $275 | |

Add $28 for Ambi safety (mfg. 2012 only).

* **Model P238 Desert** – .380 ACP cal., similar to Model P238, except has Desert tan finish, Siglite night sights, Hogue one-piece FDE rubber grip, Ambi safety (mfg. 2012 only), and X-Grip 7 shot mag. New 2012.

| MSR $752 | $650 | $575 | $475 | $425 | $375 | $325 | $275 | |

Add $28 Ambi safety (mfg. 2012 only).

MSR	100%	98%	95%	90%	80%	70%	60%	Last MSR

* **Model P238 Diamond Plate** – .380 ACP cal., similar to Model P238, except has two-tone finish or black nitron (mfg. 2012 only), "Diamond Plate" engraving, and black G10 grips. Mfg. 2011-2013.

	$650	$575	$475	$425	$375	$325	$275	*$752*

Add $28 for Ambi safety (mfg. 2012 only).

* **Model P238 Equinox** – .380 ACP cal., similar to Model P238, except has two-tone nitron finish, TruGlo TFO front sight, Siglite rear sight, black wood grips, approx. 16 oz. New 2010.

MSR $752	$650	$575	$475	$425	$385	$325	$275	

Add $28 for Ambi safety (mfg. 2012 only).

* **Model P238 Extreme** – .380 ACP cal., similar to Model P238, except has black nitron finish, Siglite night sights, Hogue Extreme G10 grips, X-Grip 7 shot mag. New 2012.

MSR $752	$650	$575	$475	$425	$385	$325	$275	

* **Model P238 Lady** – .380 ACP cal., similar to Model P238, except built on red Cerakote alloy frame with "rose and scroll" 24K gold engraving, and rosewood grips. Mfg. 2011-2013.

	$650	$575	$475	$425	$375	$325	$275	*$752*

* **Model P238 Polished** – .380 ACP cal., SA, 2.7 in. barrel, 6 shot, features polished frame and engraved stainless steel slide, choice of Hogue pink (Model P238 ESP-nitron) or white pearlite (Model P238 Pearl) grips, Siglite night sights. New 2014.

MSR $766	$665	$615	$525	$475	$425	$375	$325	

Add $13 for pink pearlite grips (Model P238 ESP-Nitron).

* **Model P238 Rainbow** – .380 ACP cal., similar to Model P238, except has Rainbow titanium slide and accents, and rosewood grips. New 2010.

MSR $752	$650	$575	$475	$425	$385	$325	$275	

* **Model P238 Rosewood** – similar to Model P238, except has rosewood grips, black nitron finish only. New 2010.

MSR $723	$650	$575	$475	$425	$385	$325	$275	

Add $29 for Ambi safety (mfg. 2012 only).

* **Model P238 Scorpion** – .380 ACP cal., similar to Model P238, except has flat dark earth (FDE) finish, Siglite night sights, Ambi safety, and Hogue G-10 grips. New 2012.

MSR $795	$695	$600	$525	$475	$400	$350	$295	

* **Model P238 Stainless** – .380 ACP cal., similar to P238, except has stainless steel frame and slide, Siglite night sights, G10 or rosewood (disc. 2012) grips, approx. 20 oz. Mfg. 2010-2013.

	$695	$600	$525	$475	$400	$350	$295	*$786*

* **Model P238 SAS** – .380 ACP cal., features two-tone finish with Siglite night sights, Custom Shop (disc.) or Brown Goncalo checkered wood grips and logo engraved on slide, dehorned frame and slide. New 2011.

MSR $766	$665	$615	$525	$475	$425	$375	$325	

Add $29 for Ambi safety (mfg. 2012 only).

* **Model P238 Tactical Laser** – similar to Model P238, except has two-tone finish, black checkered aluminum grips, Ambi safety (new 2012), Ambi laser module. Mfg. 2010-2012.

	$725	$625	$525	$475	$425	$375	$325	*$829*

* **Model P238 Two-Tone Tribal** – .380 ACP cal., SA, 2.7 in. barrel, 6 shot, two-tone or two-tone with nickel slide, Siglite night sights, choice of aluminum or custom wood grips, standard or Rainbow titanium trible engraving. New 2014.

MSR $752	$650	$575	$475	$425	$385	$325	$275	

Add $14 for Rainbow titanium tribal engraving and two-tone nickel slide.

MODEL P239 – .357 SIG, 9mm Para., or .40 S&W (new 1998) cal., compact personal size, DA or DAO, black Nitron or two-tone (disc. 2009) stainless steel slide and aluminum alloy frame, firing pin block safety, 3.6 in. barrel, 7 or 8 (9mm Para. only) shot mag., contrast sights (disc. 2013) or Siglite night sights (became standard 2014), approx. 29 oz. New 1996.

MSR $1,108	$885	$730	$625	$525	$450	$400	$350	

Add $111 for .357 SIG cal.

Subtract $100 if without Siglite night sights (became standard 2014).

Add $305 for Crimson Trace laser grips and night sights (mfg. 2007).

Add $135 for two-tone stainless slide with night sights (disc. 2009).

This model was also available as a Custom Shop Limited Edition during May, 2004 (MSR was $673).

MSR		100%	98%	95%	90%	80%	70%	60%		Last MSR

* **Model P239 Rainbow** – .40 S&W cal., otherwise similar to Model P239, Rainbow titanium finish, Siglite night sights. Mfg. 2012 only.

		100%	98%	95%	90%	80%	70%	60%		Last MSR
		$925	$825	$725	$625	$525	$450	$350		*$1,000*

* **Model P239 SAS** – 9mm Para. (new 2008), .357 SIG (disc. 2012), or .40 S&W cal., 3.6 in. barrel, 7 or 8 shot mag., DAK trigger, smooth dehorned stainless steel slide, Siglite night sights, contrast rear sight, light-weight black hard anodized frame, black Nitron or two-tone (disc. 2013) finish, rounded trigger guard, checkered/carved wood grips, designed for snag-free profile for concealed carry, Generation II features became standard 2009, 29 1/2 oz. Mfg. by Custom Shop beginning June, 2005.

MSR $1,149		$1,000	$875	$750	$625	$525	$475	$$25		

Add $14 for two-tone finish (disc. 2013).

* **Model P239 Scorpion Elite** – 9mm Para., .357 Sig., or .40 S&W cal., DA/SA, SRT, 7 or 8 shot mag., Siglite sights, Flat Dark Earth finish, Hogue Extreme G10 grips. New 2014.

MSR $1,219		$950	$825	$700	$600	$500	$450	$400		

* **Model P239 Tactical** – 9mm Para. cal., otherwise similar to Model P239, except has threaded barrel, front cocking serrations, stainless reverse two-tone, Siglite night sights. Mfg. 2010-2012.

		$925	$825	$700	$600	$500	$400	$350		*$1,058*

MODEL P245 – .45 ACP cal., compact model featuring 3.9 in. barrel, traditional double action, includes 6 and 8 shot mag., blue, two-tone (disc. 2005), Ilaflon (mfg. 2000 only), or K-Kote (disc. 1999) finish, approx. 30 oz. Mfg. 1999-2006.

		$695	$585	$495	$440	$400	$350	$310		*$840*

Add $75 for Siglite night sights.
Add $56 for two-tone or K-Kote finish (disc.).
Add $50 for Ilaflon finish (mfg. 2000 only).

MODEL P250 – 9mm Para., .357 SIG (disc. 2010), .40 S&W, or .45 ACP cal., DAO, choice of 4.7 (full size), 3.9 (Compact), or 3.1 (Subcompact) in. barrel, steel frame with black polymer grip shell (three different sizes), features modular synthetic frame with removable fire control assembly, 10 (.45 ACP), 17 (.357 SIG or .40 S&W) or 20 (9mm Para.) shot mag., ambidextrous slide release lever, black Nitron or two-tone (disc. 2010) finish, contrast or Siglite night sights, integrated Picatinny rail, converts into various calibers by changing slides, grip modules, and magazine, 27.6 oz. Mfg. mid-2008-2013.

		$475	$415	$365	$325	$285	$260	$230		*$570*

Add $72 for Siglite night sights.
Add $15 for two-tone finish (not available in .45 ACP cal.), disc. 2010.
Add $243 for 2 SUM package, includes sub-compact caliber exchange kit (not available in .357 SIG or .45 ACP cal.).

* **Model P250 Compact** – 9mm Para., .357 SIG (disc.), .40 S&W or .45 ACP cal., similar to P250 Full Size, except has 3.9 in. barrel, 9 (.45 ACP), 13 (.357 SIG or .40 S&W) or 15 (9mm Para.) shot mag., contrast (disc. 2013) or Siglite night sights (became standard 2014), 24.6 oz. New mid-2008.

MSR $642		$550	$475	$400	$350	$300	$275	$250		

Subtract $75 if without Siglite night sights (became standard 2014).
Add $94 for Ambidextrous manual safety (9mm Para. cal. only), mfg. 2012 only.
Add $141 for threaded barrel and Siglite night sights (9mm Para. cal. only), mfg. 2012 only.
Add $15 for two-tone finish (disc. 2010).
Add $215 for desert digital camo finish (9mm Para. cal. only), includes Siglite night sights, medium grips, and DAO (mfg. 2009-2010).

* **Model P250 Compact Diamond** – similar to P250 Compact, except has black nitron or two-tone finish with "Diamond Plate" engraving, Siglite night sights. Mfg. 2012 only.

		$495	$425	$375	$325	$275	$250	$225		*$582*

Add $15 for two-tone finish (disc. 2010).
Add $215 for desert digital camo finish (9mm Para. cal. only), includes Siglite night sights, medium grips, and DAO (mfg. 2009-2010).

* **Model P250 Subcompact** – similar to P250 Compact, except is also available in .380 ACP cal. (new 2012), and has 3.1 in. barrel, 6 (.45 ACP), 10 (.357 SIG - disc. 2010 or .40 S&W) or 12 (9mm Para.) shot mag., contrast (disc. 2013) or Siglite night sights, 22.6 oz. New mid-2008.

MSR $642		$550	$475	$400	$350	$300	$275	$250		

Subtract $75 if without Siglite night sights (became standard 2014).
Add $15 for two-tone finish (9mm Para. or .40 S&W cal.), disc. 2010.
Add $375 for desert digital camo finish (9mm Para. cal. only), includes Siglite night sights, medium grips, and DAO (mfg. 2009-2010).

* **Model P250 TacPac** – 9mm Para. or .40 S&W cal., compact frame, Siglite sights, Black Nitron finish, Picatinny rail, includes STL-900 holster. New 2014.

MSR $769		$675	$600	$525	$450	$395	$350	$295		

MSR	100%	98%	95%	90%	80%	70%	60%	Last MSR

MODEL P290RS (P290) – 9mm Para. cal., DAO, sub-compact design utilizing light polymer frame, 2.9 in. barrel, 6 or 8 (new 2012) shot mag., Re-strike firing pin (became standard in 2012), black polymer (standard) or enhanced black and green G10 (new 2014) grips, Siglite night sights, options include integrated laser module and personalized grip inserts, black nitron, ORB nitron (new 2014) or two-tone finish, 20 oz. New 2011.

MSR $570	$495	$450	$395	$360	$330	$295	$260	

Add $43 for enhanced black and green G10 grips (Black nitron or ORB nitron finish only). New 2014.

Add $72 for two-tone finish with integrated laser module (new 2014).

Add $24 for Diamond Plate engraving (mfg. 2012 only).

In 2014, the model nomenclature changed to P290RS.

MODEL P320 NITRON – 9mm Para. or .40 S&W cal., SFO, DAO, 4.7 in. barrel, 14 (.40 S&W) or 17 (9mm Para.) shot mag., nitron finish, Sig-lite night sights, interchangeable grip panels, lower Picatinny rail, front and rear slide serrations, 29.4 oz. New 2014.

MSR $713	$625	$550	$515	$475	$450	$425	$395	

* **Model P320 Carry Nitron** – 9mm Para., .357 Sig., or .40 S&W cal., 3.9 in. barrel, 13 or 15 (9mm Para.) shot mag., otherwise similar to P320 Nitron, 26 oz. New 2014.

MSR $713	$625	$550	$515	$475	$450	$425	$395	

MODEL PM400 – 5.56 NATO cal., pistol equivalent of the M400 carbine/rifle, features 11 1/2 in. barrel with quad rails. New 2014.

MSR $1,294	$1,125	$995	$875	$750	$625	$500	$450	

Add $86-$120 for pistol stablizing brace (PSB), new 2014.

MODEL P516 – 5.56 NATO cal., short stroke pushrod gas operating system with adj. gas valve, 7 or 10 (new 2012) in. barrel with muzzle brake, Magpul MOE grip, flip up adj. iron sights, 30 shot mag., aluminum quad rail, black finish. Mfg. 2011-2012, re-introduced 2014.

MSR $1,666	$1,475	$1,275	$1,075	$925	$775	$650	$550	

Add $173 for pistol stabilizing brace (PSB). New 2014.

MODEL P522 – .22 LR cal., blowback action, 10.6 in. barrel, aluminum flat-top upper receiver, choice of polymer or quad rail (P522 SWAT) forend, flash suppressor, 10 or 25 shot polymer mag., ambidextrous safety selector, sling attachments, approx. 6 1/2 lbs. Mfg. 2010 only, re-introduced 2014.

MSR $467	$415	$375	$335	$300	$275	$250	$225	

Add $120 for pistol stabilizing brace (PSB), new 2014.

Add $71 for P522 SWAT model with quad rail forend (mfg. 2010 only).

Last MSR for P522 SWAT model (disc. 2010) was $643.

MODEL P556 – 5.56 NATO cal., GPO similar to SIG 556 carbine, 10 in. cold hammer forged barrel with A2 type flash suppressor, Picatinny top rail, pistol grip only, ribbed and vented black polymer forearm, black Nitron finish, mini red dot front sight, aluminum alloy two-stage trigger, ambidextrous safety, 30 shot mag (accepts standard AR-15 style mags.), 6.3 lbs. Mfg. 2009-2010.

	$1,825	$1,650	$1,450	$1,300	$1,200	$1,100	$1,000	$1,876

Add $147 for P556 SWAT model with quad rail forend.

* **Model P556 Lightweight** – similar to Model P556, except has lightweight polymer lower unit and forend. Mfg. 2010-2013.

	$1,075	$950	$825	$725	$625	$525	$425	$1,207

Add $133 for quad rail forend (SWAT Model).

MODEL P556xi – 5.56 NATO (AR-15 style) or 7.62x39mm (AK-47 design) cal., 10 in. barrel, polymer handguard, flip up sights, 30 shot mag. New 2014.

MSR $1,466	$1,350	$1,175	$1,025	$900	$800	$700	$600	

Add $133 for 7.62x39mm cal. with AK-47 design.

Add $120 for pistol stabilizing brace (PSB), new 2014.

MODEL P938 – 9mm Para. cal., SAO, 3 in. barrel, lightweight aluminum frame, stainless steel slide, thumb safety, black nitron or two-tone finish, 6 shot, Siglite night sights, Ambi safety, rosewood, blackwood, or Hogue rubber grips, 16 oz. New 2012.

* **Model P938 Aluminum** – 9mm Para. cal., 3 in. barrel, 6 shot mag., black nitron finish, Siglite night sights, Ambi safety, black aluminum grips. New 2013.

MSR $836	$725	$575	$475	$425	$395	$350	$295	

* **Model P938 Black Rubber** – 9mm Para. cal., 3 in. barrel, 6 shot mag., black nitron finish, Siglite night sights, Ambi safety, black rubber grips. New 2013.

MSR $836	$725	$575	$475	$425	$395	$350	$295	

MSR	100%	98%	95%	90%	80%	70%	60%	Last MSR

* ***Model P938 Blackwood*** – 9mm Para. cal., 3 in. barrel, 6 shot mag., black nitron finish, Siglite night sights, Ambi safety, Hogue blackwood grips, two-tone black nitron frame/stainless slide finish. New 2012.

MSR $819	$700	$575	$475	$425	$395	$350	$295	

* ***Model P938 Equinox*** – 9mm Para. cal., 3 in. barrel, features two-tone polished nitron finish, TruGlo front and Siglite rear sights, Ambi safety, Hogue black diamondwood grips. New 2012.

MSR $833	$725	$575	$475	$425	$395	$350	$295	

* ***Model P938 Extreme*** – 9mm Para. cal., features black nitron finish, Siglite night sights, Hogue Extreme G10 grips, Ambi safety, X-Grip 7 shot mag., otherwise similar to Model P938. New 2012.

MSR $833	$725	$575	$475	$425	$395	$350	$295	

* ***Model P938 Nightmare*** – 9mm Para. cal., 3 in. barrel, 7 shot mag., black nitron finish, Siglite night sights, Ambi safety, Hogue Black G10 grips. New 2013.

MSR $836	$725	$575	$475	$425	$395	$350	$295	

* ***Model P938 Rosewood*** – 9mm Para. cal., 3 in. barrel, 6 shot mag., black nitron finish, Siglite night sights, Ambi safety, rosewood grips. New 2012.

MSR $805	$685	$550	$475	$425	$375	$325	$275	

* ***Model P938 SAS*** – 9mm Para. cal., features two-tone finish, dehorning, Siglite night sights, Brown Goncalo checkered wood grips, Ambi safety. Mfg. 2012-2013.

	$735	$575	$475	$425	$385	$325	$275	*$848*

* ***Model P938 Scorpion*** – 9mm Para. cal., SA, 6 shot mag., Siglite night sights, Ambi safety, Hogue G10 grips, Flat Dark Earth finish. New 2014.

MSR $893	$775	$625	$525	$450	$425	$375	$325	

MODEL 1911 FULL SIZE (GSR REVOLUTION) – .40 S&W (new 2014) or .45 ACP cal., SA, 5 in. match grade barrel, choice of white (disc.), standard blue (disc.), two-tone, reverse two-tone (mfg. 2007-2010), XO Black (new 2007) or black Nitron finish, includes two 8 shot mags., with or w/o (disc. 2012) under frame Picatinny rail, firing pin safety, front and rear strap checkering, Novak (disc.) or low profile sights, checkered wood (all stainless), rosewood, aluminum, or synthetic (blued stainless) grips, approx. 41 oz. Mfg. in Exeter, NH. New 2004.

MSR $1,142	$995	$875	$750	$650	$550	$450	$375	

Subtract $43 if without M-1913 Picatinny rail (disc. 2012).

Add $100 for platinum Elite with two-tone finish, adj. combat night sights and aluminum grips (mfg. 2008-2011).

Add $120 for Blackwater model (mfg. 2009-2010).

Subtract $40 for reverse two-tone finish (disc. 2010).

The abbreviation GSR on this model stands for Granite Series Revolution.

* ***Model 1911 Desert*** – .45 ACP cal., features desert tan finish, contrast sights, Ergo XT OD Green grips, otherwise similar to the 1911. Mfg. 2012 only.

	$950	$825	$725	$625	$525	$450	$375	*$1,070*

* ***Model 1911 Extreme*** – .45 ACP cal., black nitron finish, Hogue Extreme G-10 grips, ambi safety, low profile night sights, magwell housing, flat trigger, otherwise similar to the 1911. Mfg. 2012 only.

	$1,075	$950	$825	$725	$625	$525	$425	*$1,213*

* ***Model 1911 Fastback*** – .45 ACP, Fastback rounded frame, black nitron finish, low profile night sights, two 8 shot mags., and rosewood grips, otherwise similar to the 1911. Mfg. 2012 only.

	$1,025	$875	$750	$625	$525	$450	$375	*$1,170*

* ***Model 1911 Max*** – .40 S&W (new 2014) or .45 ACP cal., Custom Competition, features reverse two-tone finish, fiber optic front and adj. rear sights, ICE Magwell, Wilson Mag., G-10 grips, and Max logo, otherwise similar to the 1911. New 2012.

MSR $1,712	$1,550	$1,250	$1,100	$925	$800	$700	$600	

Add $1 for .40 S&W cal. (new 2014).

* ***Model 1911 Spartan (Molon Labe)*** – .45 ACP cal., SA, 5 in. barrel, features custom oil rubbed bronze nitron finish with 24 Kt. gold inlay Molon Labe engraving on slide (Ancient Greek meaning "Come and Take Them"), Hogue grips with Spartan helmet, and low profile sights, otherwise similar to the 1911. New late 2012.

MSR $1,356	$1,100	$975	$850	$750	$650	$550	$450	

* ***Model 1911 POW-MIA*** – .45 ACP cal., features custom engraved nitron finish, and custom Hogue POW-MIA grips, otherwise similar to the 1911. Mfg. 2012 only.

	$1,100	$975	$850	$750	$650	$550	$450	*$1,356*

Add $143 for custom engraved stainless, engraved KaBar knife, and Pelican case.

MSR	100%	98%	95%	90%	80%	70%	60%	Last MSR

* **Model 1911 Nightmare** – .45 ACP cal., black nitron finish, stainless controls and black G-10 grips. New 2012.

| MSR $1,242 | $1,075 | $975 | $850 | $750 | $650 | $550 | $425 | |

* **Model 1911 Railed Tacpac** – .45 ACP cal., features 1911 XO with lower Picatinny rail, includes holster with attached mag. pouch and two magazines, laser module. New 2013.

| MSR $1,142 | $995 | $875 | $750 | $650 | $550 | $450 | $375 | |

* **Model 1911 Scorpion** – .45 ACP cal., features flat dark earth (FDE) finish, low profile night sights, ambi safety, magwell housing, and Hogue Extreme Series G10 grips, otherwise similar to 1911. New 2011.

| MSR $1,213 | $1,075 | $950 | $825 | $725 | $625 | $525 | $425 | |

Add $72 for threaded barrel (mfg. 2012 only).

* **Model 1911 Spartan** – .45 ACP cal., SAO, 8 shot, stainless steel slide and frame with custom ORB finish, "MOLON LAABE" engraved on slide and grips, stainless steel magwell, custom Spartan grips with bronze inlay, skeletonized trigger, Siglite sights. New 2014.

| MSR $1,356 | $1,150 | $1,050 | $900 | $800 | $700 | $600 | $500 | |

* **Model 1911 Stainless** – .45 ACP cal., features stainless finish and blackwood grips, otherwise similar to the 1911. Disc. 2013.

| | $995 | $875 | $750 | $650 | $550 | $450 | $425 | $1,156 |

Subtract $43 if without M-1913 Picatinny rail (disc. 2012).

* **Model 1911 STX** – .45 ACP cal., features two-tone finish, flat-top, adj. combat night sights and wood grips, ambi safety, magwell, otherwise similar to the 1911.

| MSR $1,213 | $1,075 | $950 | $825 | $725 | $625 | $525 | $425 | |

* **Model 1911 TTT** – .45 ACP cal., features two-tone finish, black controls, adj. combat night sights and wood grips, otherwise similar to the 1911. Disc. 2012.

| | $1,025 | $875 | $750 | $650 | $550 | $450 | $375 | $1,170 |

* **Model 1911 Tacops** – .45 ACP cal., features black nitron finish, integral accessory rail, ambi thumb safety, magwell, Ergo XT grips, 4 magazines, otherwise similar to 1911. New 2011.

| MSR $1,213 | $1,075 | $950 | $825 | $725 | $625 | $525 | $425 | |

Add $72 for threaded barrel.

* **Model 1911 Tacpac** – .45 ACP cal., features 1911 XO, holster with attached mag. pouch, Mag loader, and 3 magazines, otherwise similar to the 1911. Mfg. 2012-2013.

| | $950 | $825 | $725 | $625 | $525 | $450 | $375 | $1,070 |

Add $72 for the Railed Tacpac Model, includes M-1913 rail, laser module, and 2 magazines.

* **Model 1911 Target** – .45 ACP cal., features black nitron or stainless finish, adj. target sights, and rosewood or blackwood grips. Mfg. 2011-2012.

| | $975 | $850 | $725 | $625 | $525 | 4450 | $400 | $1,113 |

Add $29 for stainless finish with blackwood grips.

* **Model 1911 XO** – .45 ACP cal., features black nitron or stainless (disc. 2012) finish, low profile contrast sights, and Ergo XT grips, otherwise similar to the 1911.

| MSR $1,050 | $925 | $795 | $675 | $575 | $475 | $425 | $350 | |

Add $28 for stainless finish (disc. 2012).

MODEL 1911 TRADITIONAL FULL SIZE – .45 ACP cal., SA, 5 in. barrel, rounded top slide, front cocking serrations, stainless frame with matte black nitron slide and small parts, 3 hole speed trigger, Hogue custom black wood grips, low profile Siglite night sights, two 8 shot mags., reverse two-tone finish, approx. 41 oz. Mfg. 2011-2012.

| | $995 | $850 | $725 | $625 | $525 | $450 | $400 | $1,142 |

* **Model 1911 Traditional Compact** – .45 ACP cal., SA, compact slide with 3.9 in. barrel, rounded top slide, stainless frame, 3 hole speed trigger, Hogue custom black wood grips, low profile Siglite night sights, two 7 shot mags., stainless finish, approx. 35 oz. Mfg. 2011-2012.

| | $995 | $850 | $725 | $625 | $525 | $450 | $400 | $1,142 |

* **Model 1911 Traditional Tacops** – .45 ACP cal., alloy frame, features black nitron finish, M1913 rail, ambi thumb safety, magwell, Ergo XT grips, and 4 magazines, flared magwell, lower Picatinny rail, otherwise similar to 1911 Traditional. New 2012.

| MSR $1,213 | $1,075 | $950 | $825 | $725 | $625 | $525 | $425 | |

MODEL 1911 MATCH ELITE – 9mm Para., .40 S&W, or .45 ACP cal., round top, 5 in. barrel, SA, double slide serrations on frame, adj. target sights, 3 hole trigger, Hogue custom wood grips, choice of stainless or two-tone (.45 ACP cal. only) finish. Mfg. 2011-2012.

| | $925 | $875 | $750 | $650 | $550 | $450 | $400 | $1,170 |

MSR	100%	98%	95%	90%	80%	70%	60%	Last MSR

MODEL 1911 TRADITIONAL STAINLESS STEEL – 9mm Para., .38 Super, .40 S&W, or .45 ACP cal., stainless steel. New 2014.

* ***Model 1911 Traditional Stainless Match Elite*** – 9mm Para., .38 Super, or .40 S&W cal., SAO, stainless frame, adj. sights. New 2014.

| MSR $1,170 | $1,025 | $875 | $775 | $675 | $575 | $450 | $425 | |

* ***Model 1911 Traditional Stainless Nightmare*** – .45 ACP cal., SAO, Fastback frame, Siglite sights, nitron finish. New 2014.

| MSR $1,242 | $1,075 | $975 | $850 | $750 | $650 | $550 | $425 | |

* ***Model 1911 Traditional Stainless Scorpion*** – .45 ACP cal., SAO, stainless steel frame, Siglite sights, Flat Dark Earth finish. New 2014.

| MSR $1,213 | $1,075 | $950 | $825 | $725 | $625 | $525 | $425 | |

MODEL 1911 CARRY (REVOLUTION) – similar to Model 1911 GSR, except is carry configuration with short stainless slide, 4 in. barrel, SA, stainless steel frame or black Nitron finish, Novak (disc. 2010) or low profile night sights, 8 shot mag., rosewood grips became standard with black nitron finish during 2011, black wood grips became standard on stainless finish during 2011. Mfg. 2007-2012.

| | $975 | 4850 | $725 | $625 | $525 | $450 | $375 | *$1,128* |

Add $14 for stainless finish with blackwood grips.

* ***Model 1911 Carry Fastback*** – .45 ACP, Fastback rounded frame, black nitron finish, low profile night sights, two 8 shot mags., and rosewood grips, otherwise similar to the 1911 Carry. Mfg. 2012 only.

| | $1,025 | $875 | $750 | $650 | $550 | $450 | $375 | *$1,170* |

* ***Model 1911 Carry Nightmare*** – .45 ACP cal., black nitron finish, stainless controls and black G-10 grips. New 2012.

| MSR $1,242 | $1,075 | $975 | $850 | $750 | $650 | $550 | $425 | |

* ***Model 1911 Carry Scorpion*** – .45 ACP cal., features Flat Dark Earth finish, low profile night sights, ambi safety, magwell housing, and Hogue Extreme Series G-10 grips, otherwise similar to 1911 Carry. New 2012.

| MSR $1,213 | $1,075 | $950 | $825 | $725 | $625 | $525 | $425 | |

Add $72 for threaded barrel (mfg. 2012 only).

* ***Model 1911 Carry Spartan*** – .45 ACP cal., SAO, ORB, Siglite sights, nitron finish. New 2014.

| MSR $1,356 | $1,150 | $1,050 | $900 | $800 | $700 | $600 | $500 | |

* ***Model 1911 Carry Tacops*** – .45 ACP cal., features black nitron finish, M-1913 rail, ambi thumb safety, magwell, Ergo XT grips, and 4 magazines, otherwise similar to 1911 Carry. Mfg. 2012 only.

| | $1,075 | $950 | $825 | $725 | $625 | $525 | $425 | *$1,213* |

Add $72 for threaded barrel.

MODEL 1911 COMPACT (REVOLUTION) – .45 ACP cal., SA, short slide and compact frame, 6 shot, stainless or black Nitron finish, 4 in. barrel, night sights. Mfg. 2007-2009.

| | $975 | $850 | $725 | $625 | $525 | $450 | $400 | *$1,170* |

* ***Model 1911 Compact C3*** – .45 ACP cal., black hard coat anodized alloy frame, stainless slide, two-tone finish, 4 in. barrel, SA, 7 shot, low profile contrast sights, slim profile custom wood grips, otherwise similar to 1911 Compact. New 2011.

| MSR $1,042 | $925 | $825 | $725 | $625 | $525 | $450 | $400 | |

Add $214 for Magwell and black CTC laser grips (mfg. 2012 only) or add $243 for Magwell and wood grain CTC laser grips (mfg. 2012 only).

* ***Model 1911 Compact RCS*** – .45 ACP cal., dehorning and anti-snag treatment, black Nitron or two-tone finish, 7 shot, low profile night sights, custom wood grips, otherwise similar to 1911 Compact. Disc. 2012.

| | $975 | $850 | $725 | $625 | $525 | $450 | $400 | *$1,170* |

Add $15 for two-tone finish.

MODEL 1911 ULTRA COMPACT – .45 ACP cal., 3.3 in. barrel, SA, 3 hole trigger, aluminum frame, slip profile custom wood rosewood or blackwood grips, low profile night sights, two 7 shot mags., nitron or two-tone finish, 28 oz. New 2011.

| MSR $1,142 | $1,000 | $875 | $750 | $650 | $550 | $450 | $400 | |

Add $14 for two-tone finish.

MODEL 1911-22 – .22 LR cal., SA, black frame and slide finish, 5 in. barrel, low profile 3-dot contrast sights, 3 hole trigger, bobbed hammer, beavertail, Hogue custom rosewood grips, one 10 shot mag., black, camo (new 2013), Flat Dark Earth (new 2012), or OD Green (new 2012) finish, 34 oz. New 2011.

| MSR $460 | $395 | $350 | $315 | $275 | $260 | $240 | $200 | |

Add $58 for Flat Dark Earth, OD Green (new 2012), or camo (new 2013) finish.

MSR	100%	98%	95%	90%	80%	70%	60%	Last MSR

MODEL SIG PRO SP2009 – 9mm Para. cal., otherwise identical to SP2340, 28 oz. Mfg. 1999-2005.

	$510	$450	$355	$290	$260	$220	$195	*$640*

Add $60 for Siglite night sights.
Add $31 for two-tone finish.

MODEL SIG PRO SP2022 – 9mm Para., .357 SIG, or .40 S&W cal., 10, 12 or 15 (9mm Para. cal. only) shot mag., 3.85 in. barrel, DA/SA, polymer frame, Picatinny rail, Nitron, blue, or two-tone (disc. 2005) stainless steel slide, black Nitron finish, convertible to DAO, optional interchangeable grips, 26.8 (9mm Para.) or 30 oz. Mfg. 2004-2007.

	$495	$440	$355	$290	$260	$220	$195	*$613*

Subtract 10% if w/o Siglite night sights (became standard 2007).

MODEL SIG PRO SP2340 – .357 SIG, or .40 S&W cal., features polymer frame and one-piece Nitron finished stainless steel or two-tone (new 2001) finished slide, 3.86 in. barrel, DA/SA, includes two interchangeable grips, 10 shot mag., approx. 30.2 oz. Mfg. 1999-2005.

	$510	$450	$355	$290	$260	$220	$195	*$640*

Add $60 for Siglite night sights.
Add $31 for two-tone finish.

MODEL SP2022 – 9mm Para. or .40 S&W cal., DA/SA, 3.9 in. barrel, polymer frame with integrated lower Picatinny rail, choice of black nitron or natural stainless slide, modular fire control unit, interchangeable grip assemblies, 10 (disc.) 12, or 15 (9mm Para. cal. only) shot mag., contrast (disc. 2013, except for FDE finish) or Siglite night sights (became standard 2014), black nitron or FDE (new 2014) finish, 29 oz. New 2011.

MSR $642	$550	$475	$400	$350	$300	$275	$250	

Subtract approx. $75 if without Siglite night sights (became standard 2014).
Add $57 for FDE (flat dark earth) finish with contrast sights (new 2014).
Add $161 for threaded barrel (mfg. 2012 only).

* **Model SP2022 Diamond** – similar to Model SP2022, except has two-tone or black nitron finish with "Diamond Plate" engraving, and Siglite night sights. Mfg. 2012 only.

	$550	$475	$400	$350	$300	$250	$225	*$626*

* **Model SP2022 TacPac** – 9mm Para. or .40 S&W cal., 15 shot mag., features black nitron finish, Siglite sights, one-piece enhanced E2 grip, STL 900L, includes holster. New 2013.

MSR $769	$675	$575	$495	$450	$400	$365	$335	

RIFLES: BOLT ACTION

TACTICAL 2 – .223 Rem. (mfg. 2010-2012), .308 Win., .300 Win. Mag. (disc. 2013), or .338 Lapua cal., left or right hand straight pull action, 24.7 (.308 Win. cal. only), 25.6 (.300 Win. cal. only, disc. 2013), or 27 (.338 Lapua cal. only) in. fluted barrel with muzzle brake, aluminum receiver, black hard coat anodized finish, adj. single stage trigger, 4 or 5 shot polymer box mag., ambidextrous Blaser adj. composite pistol grip stock with adj. buttplate and cheekpiece, Picatinny rail, optional Harris bipod, 12 - 12 1/2 lbs. New 2007.

MSR $4,171	$3,700	$3,300	$2,900	$2,400	$1,900	$1,750	$1,500	

Add $303 for .338 Lapua cal.
Add $299-$565 per individual bolt head depending on caliber.
Add $1,689 per interchangeable barrel.

SIG 50 – .50 BMG cal., 29 in. fluted barrel with muzzle brake, 5 shot detachable mag., helical bolt, Desert Tan finish, detachable butt stock, McMillan tactical stock, includes bipod, 23.4 lbs. Mfg. 2011-2012, re-introduced 2014.

MSR $9,825	$9,100	$7,750	$6,350	$5,100	$4,850	$3,900	$3,200	

SSG 3000 PRECISION TACTICAL RIFLE – .308 Win. cal., modular design, ambidextrous McMillan tactical stock with adj. comb, 23.4 in. barrel with muzzle brake, folding aluminum chassis (new 2012), 5 shot detachable mag., supplied in 3 different levels, Level I does not have bipod or scope, cased, 12 lbs. Mfg. 2000-2012.

	$2,400	$2,100	$1,700	$1,500	$1,250	$1,000	$875	*$2,799*

Add $933 for folding aluminum chassis (new 2012).
Add $1,500 for Level II (includes Leupold Vari-X III 3.5-10x40mm duplex reticle scope and Harris bipod, disc.).
Add $2,300 for Level III (includes Leupold Mark 4 M1 10x40mm Mil-Dot reticle scope and Harris bipod, disc.).
Add $1,500 for .22 LR cal. conversion kit (disc.).

* **SSG 3000 Patrol** – .308 Win. cal., 18 or 23 1/2 in. barrel with (new 2014) or w/o threading, black or FDE (new 2014) finish, Patrol stock with integral aluminum bedding. New 2012.

MSR $1,499	$1,325	$1,100	$950	$825	$700	$575	$495	

RIFLES: SEMI-AUTO

State compliant rifles on some of the currently manufactured models listed within this section include CA, HA, MA, MD, NJ, and NY. Compliance features will vary from state to state, and typically, these compliant state MSR's are slightly higher than the standard models available from the rest of the states.

MSR	100%	98%	95%	90%	80%	70%	60%	Last MSR

SIG M400 – 5.56 NATO cal., GIO, 16 in. barrel, A2 grip, M4 buttstock, 600 meter adj. and removable rear sight, 30 shot mag., includes hard case. New 2012.

| MSR $1,119 | $1,100 | $975 | $875 | $750 | $650 | $550 | $450 | |

Add $93 for aluminum quad rails.

Add $40 for lightweight steady ready platform (mfg. 2012 only).

* SIG M400 Carbon Fiber – 5.56 NATO cal., GIO, 16 in. barrel, carbon fiber forend or choice of SIG or carbon fiber rifle stock, 30 shot Lancer mag. New 2014.

| MSR $1,999 | $1,950 | $1,750 | $1,575 | $1,400 | $1,200 | $995 | $800 | |

Add $133 for carbon fiber forend and carbon fiber rifle stock.

* SIG M400 Classic – 5.56 NATO cal., GIO, M4 style handguard and buttstock, SIG grips, rear flip-up sight, 30 shot mag. New 2014.

| MSR $1,200 | $1,200 | $1,075 | $925 | $850 | $700 | $575 | $450 | |

* SIG M400 Enhanced Carbine – 5.56 NATO cal., GIO, features 16 in. barrel, MOE handguards, MOE grip, MOE stock, and flip up rear sights, available in black, OD Green, or Flat Dark Earth finish, otherwise similar to SIG M400. New 2012.

| MSR $1,234 | $1,200 | $1,075 | $925 | $850 | $700 | $575 | $450 | |

Add $66 for Flat Dark Earth finish.

* SIG M400 Enhanced Patrol – 5.56 NATO cal., GIO, 16 in. barrel, flip up sights, Flat Dark Earth or Muddy Girl finish. New 2014.

| MSR $1,367 | $1,350 | $1,100 | $1,000 | $875 | $800 | $675 | $525 | |

Add $27 for Muddy Girl finish.

* SIG M400 Hunting – 5.56 NATO cal., GIO, features 20 in. barrel, 1:8 twist, MOE handguard, MOE grip, optic ready, black or Mix Pine2 finish, otherwise similar to SIG M400. Mfg. 2012 only.

| | $975 | $875 | $775 | $675 | $600 | $550 | $495 | *$1,099* |

Add $90 for Mix Pine2 finish.

* SIG M400 Magpul – 5.56 NATO cal., GIO, 20 in. barrel, black finish, Magpul rifle stock, MOE grip and forend. New 2014.

| MSR $1,287 | $1,275 | $1,075 | $925 | $825 | $725 | $525 | $450 | |

* SIG M400 Predator – 5.56 NATO cal., GIO, 18 in. heavy match grade threaded and capped stainless steel barrel, 5 shot mag., Geissele two-stage match trigger, Hogue synthetic rubber grip stock with free float forend, flat-top upper, extended charging handle, 7.6 lbs. New 2013.

| MSR $1,384 | $1,375 | $1,100 | $1,000 | $875 | $800 | $675 | $525 | |

* SIG M400 SWAT – 5.56 NATO cal., GIO, features 16 in. barrel, and quad rail, SIG grip, M4 style buttstock, rear flip sight, 20 shot mag. Mfg. 2012 only, re-introduced 2014.

| MSR $1,294 | $1,275 | $1,075 | $925 | $825 | $725 | $525 | $450 | |

* SIG M400 Varmint – 5.56 NATO cal., GIO, 22 in. heavy stainless steel barrel, 5 shot mag., match trigger. New 2014.

| MSR $1,395 | $1,195 | $1,050 | $895 | $815 | $650 | $540 | $425 | |

* SIG M400 Varminter – 5.56 NATO cal., direct impingement system, 22 in. heavy match grade stainless steel threaded and capped barrel, 5 shot mag., Geissele two-stage match trigger, Hogue rubber grip synthetic stock with free float forend, flat-top upper, extended charging handle, 8.1 lbs. New 2013.

| MSR $1,395 | $1,195 | $1,050 | $895 | $815 | $650 | $540 | $425 | |

SIG 516 – 5.56 NATO cal., features short stroke pushrod GPO, 3 or 4 position system gas valve, various configurations. New 2011.

* SIG 516 Basic Patrol – 5.56 NATO cal., GPO, features polymer handguard and 2 Picatinny rails - one on top of receiver and the other in front of handguard, 16 in. free floating barrel with muzzle brake, Magpul stock and pistol grip, 30 shot mag. Mfg. 2011 only.

| | $1,095 | $950 | $800 | $700 | $600 | $500 | $425 | *$1,252* |

* SIG 516 Patrol – 5.56 NATO or 7.62x39mm (mfg. 2012 only) cal., GPO, features Magpul MOE adj. stock and MOE grip, rear charging handle, free floating quad Picatinny rail, 3 position gas valve, 16 in. free floating barrel with muzzle brake, 30 shot mag., ladder rail covers (new 2012), PMag (new 2012), Black, Flat Dark Earth (new 2012) or OD Green (new 2012) finish. New 2011.

| MSR $1,719 | $1,700 | $1,500 | $1,250 | $1,000 | $875 | $725 | $600 | |

Add $67 for Flat Dark Earth finish (new 2012).

The SIG Model 516 is also available in CQB configuration with 10 in. barrel and PDW (Personal Defense Weapon) configuration with 7 1/2 in. barrel for military/law enforcement only.

MSR	100%	98%	95%	90%	80%	70%	60%	Last MSR

* **SIG 516 Carbon Fiber** – 5.56 NATO cal., GPO, 16 in. barrel, flip-up sights, carbon fiber forend and choice of carbon fiber SIG or Rifle stock, 30 shot Lancer mag. New 2014.

| MSR $2,371 | $2,350 | $2,050 | $1,800 | $1,600 | $1,400 | $1,200 | $995 | |

Add $133 for carbon fiber rifle stock and forend.

* **SIG 516 Sport Configuration Model (SCM)** – GPO, features fixed stock, A2 pistol grip, 10 shot mag. Mfg. 2011-2012.

| | $1,375 | $1,150 | $1,000 | $875 | $750 | $625 | $525 | $1,599 |

* **SIG 516 Precision Marksman** – GPO, features 18 in. free floating match barrel w/o muzzle brake, free floating quad Picatinny rail, 2 stage trigger, Magpul PRS stock, MIAD grip, 30 shot mag. Mfg. 2011-2013.

| | $2,400 | $2,100 | $1,800 | $1,625 | $1,325 | $1,075 | $850 | $2,399 |

SIG 522 – .22 LR cal., GIO, 16 in. barrel, blowback action, 10 or 25 shot mag., black polymer lower receiver, folding/telescopic or non-folding Swiss style (disc.) stock, polymer (w/rail kit) or aluminum forend, flash suppressor, approx. 6 1/2 lbs. New 2009.

Add $199 for mini red dot sight (disc. 2012).
Add $53 for non-folding stock (disc.).
Add $222 for rotary front sight (disc. 2009).
Add $210 for Harris bipod (disc. 2010).
Add $66 (Variable Power) or $106 (Prismatic Scope) with polymer handguards and telescopic stock (mfg. 2011 only).

* **SIG 522 Classic** – .22 LR cal., GIO, 16 in. barrel, features folding/telescopic stock, polymer handguards, rail kit, 10 or 25 shot mag.

| MSR $600 | $525 | $450 | $415 | $365 | $335 | $300 | $275 | |

* **SIG 522 Classic SWAT** – .22 LR cal., GIO, features folding/telescopic stock, aluminum quad rail, 10 or 25 shot mag. Disc. 2012.

| | $550 | $475 | $425 | $375 | $325 | $275 | $225 | $640 |

* **SIG 522 Commando** – .22 LR cal., GIO, 16 in. barrel, polymer handguard, folding/telescopic stock, tactical training suppressor, rail kit. New 2011.

| MSR $574 | $495 | $450 | $400 | $350 | $300 | $275 | $250 | |

* **SIG 522 Commando SWAT** – .22 LR cal., GIO, quad rail handguard, folding/telescopic stock, tactical training suppressor. Mfg. 2012 only.

| | $625 | $550 | $475 | $400 | $350 | $300 | $275 | $707 |

* **SIG 522 Field** – .22 LR cal., GIO, 20 in. barrel, folding/telescopic stock, polymer handguard, rail kit, 10 shot mag. New 2012.

| MSR $534 | $465 | $415 | $365 | $335 | $300 | $275 | $250 | |

* **SIG 522 Target** – .22 LR cal., GIO, 20 in. barrel, Hogue free floating forend, folding/telescopic stock, variable power scope, 10 shot mag. New 2012.

| MSR $794 | $695 | $600 | $500 | $425 | $375 | $325 | $295 | |

SIG 551A1 – 5.56 NATO cal., GPO, 16 in. barrel, rotary bolt, utilizes original Swiss 550-style 20 or 30 shot translucent mags., black polymer folding skeletonized stock and forearm that surrounds barrel, gray finish, post front sights, adj. rotary diopter drum rear sight, two-stage trigger, top accessory rail, 7 lbs. New 2012.

| MSR $1,599 | $1,450 | $1,300 | $1,100 | $925 | $800 | $675 | $550 | $1,599 |

SIG 556 CLASSIC – 5.56 NATO cal., GPO, rotary bolt, 16 in. barrel with muzzle brake, polymer forearm, alloy trigger housing, choice of SIG quad-rail (SWAT Model) or tri-rail, integrated Picatinny rails, two-stage trigger, collapsible or collapsible/folding tube stock, Magpul CTR Carbine stock type (SWAT) or M4 style stock (556ER or 556 Holo), 30 shot AR-15 type mag., 7.8-8.7 lbs. Mfg. 2007-2013.

| | $1,265 | $1,110 | $950 | $850 | $700 | $575 | $450 | $1,266 |

Add $133 for quad-rail system (Classic SWAT Model).
Add $45 for Holo model with holographic sight (disc. 2009).
Add $150 for collapsible stock with GLR and Stoplite (disc. 2009).
Add $306 for Classic 16 with adj. folding stock and red dot sight (disc. 2009).
Add $456 for Classic 17 with adj. folding stock and rotary sight (disc. 2009).
Add $300 for 16 in. barrel with GLR and Stoplite (disc. 2009).
Subtract $200 if w/o iron sights (became standard 2008).

MSR	100%	98%	95%	90%	80%	70%	60%	Last MSR

* **SIG 556R** – 7.62x39mm cal., GPO, 16 in. barrel, polymer handguards or aluminum quad rail (mfg. 2012 only) forend, folding/telescopic (mfg. 2011 only), or Swiss style (new 2012) stock, mini red dot sight, 5 (Hunting Model, mfg. 2012 only) or 30 shot AK type mag. Mfg. 2011-2013.

| | $1,330 | $1,175 | $1,000 | $900 | $750 | $600 | $475 | $1,332 |

Add $34 for Hunting Model (mfg. 2012 only).
Add $133 for aluminum quad rail (mfg. 2012 only).

* **SIG 556 DMR** – 5.56 NATO cal., GPO, similar to Model 556, except has 18 in. heavy barrel w/o sights, adj. Magpul PRS stock, vented synthetic forearm, Picatinny rail on bottom of forearm and top of receiver, includes tactical bipod, 12 lbs. Mfg. 2008-2013.

| | $1,730 | $1,525 | $1,300 | $1,175 | $950 | $775 | $600 | $1,732 |

* **SIG 556 Patrol** – 5.56 NATO cal., GPO, similar to SIG 556, 16 in. barrel, 30 shot mag., steel upper receiver, choice of polymer (Patrol) or alloy quad rail (Patrol SWAT) forend, black anodized finish, A2 flash suppressor, folding collapsible Swiss style stock, rotary diopter sight, 7 1/2 lbs. Mfg. 2010-2013.

| | $1,265 | $1,110 | $950 | $850 | $700 | $575 | $450 | $1,266 |

Add $133 for SWAT model with quad rail forend.

* **SIG 556 xi Patrol Swat** – 5.56mm NATO cal., GPO, 16 in. barrel, steel receiver with M1913 rail, flip-up front and rear sights, M1913 quad rail forend, removable barrel, ambi safety, ambi mag. release, Swiss style stock. Mfg. 2012 only.

| | $1,295 | $1,125 | $1,000 | $875 | $750 | $625 | $475 | $1,424 |

SIG 556xi – 5.56 NATO (AR-15 style), 7.62x39mm (AK-47 design), or .300 Blackout (AR-15 style) cal., GPO, 16 in. barrel, flip-up sights, 30 shot mag., polymer handguard. New 2014.

| MSR $1,466 | $1,450 | $1,250 | $1,050 | $900 | $800 | $700 | $600 | |

Add $133 for 7.62x39mm or .300 Blackout cal.

SIG 556/P226 MATCHED PAIR – 5.56 NATO/9mm Para. cals., GPO, includes matched set of Desert Digital Special Editions of SIG 556 ER folding stock and P226 pistol. Both rifle and pistol have unique matching serial numers, includes pelican hard carry case in flat dark earth, certificate of authenticity. Limited production run of 1,500 sets. Mfg. 2012.

Retail pricing was not established on this set.

SIG 716 PATROL – 7.62 NATO cal., GPO, 16 in. barrel, 20 shot mag., MagPul ACS stock and MIAD grip, quad rail, Black, Flat Dark Earth, or OD Green finish. New 2011.

| MSR $2,186 | $2,175 | $1,850 | $1,575 | $1,300 | $1,100 | $925 | $800 | |

Add $36 for Flat Dark Earth finish (new 2012).

SIG 716 PRECISION MARKSMAN – 7.62 NATO cal., 18 in. barrel, short stroke GPO, four position gas valve, threaded muzzle, upper and lower rails, two-stage Geissele match trigger, MIAD grip, Magpul UBR stock, matte black finish, 20 shot PMag., bipod, folding back up iron sights, 11 lbs. Mfg. 2013 only.

| | $2,250 | $1,975 | $1,695 | $1,525 | $1,240 | $1,015 | $795 | $2,666 |

SIG SCM – 5.56 NATO cal., GIO, 16 in. barrel, 10 shot mag., steel upper receiver, polymer forend with lower accessory rail, Holo sight, aluminum lower, target crowned muzzle, A2 fixed stock, Picatinny top rail, approx. 8 lbs. Mfg. 2010-2011.

| | $1,075 | $950 | $825 | $725 | $625 | $525 | $425 | $1,191 |

SIG SCM 22 – .22 LR cal., 18 in. barrel, choice of polymer handguard, or aluminum quad rail, blow-back operating system, adj. iron sights, fixed stock, 10 shot mag. Mfg. 2011 only.

| | $525 | $450 | $395 | $350 | $300 | $275 | $250 | $587 |

Add $103 for aluminum quad rail.

SIG MPX – 9mm NATO cal., converts to .357 SIG or .40 S&W cal., closed, fully locked short stroke pushrod gas system, matte black finish, 16 in. barrel with permanently attached muzzle brake, free float barrel system, 30 shot mag., ambidextrous magazine release, MPX Reflex sight, telescoping or folding stock, pistol grip, extended carbon fiber rail adaptable handguard, ambidextrous safety selector, monolithic upper receiver with integral M1913 rail at 12 o'clock, AR-style controls, rear charging handle. New mid-2013.

| MSR $2,199 | $2,175 | $1,850 | $1,600 | $1,250 | $1,050 | $875 | $725 | |

SIONICS WEAPON SYSTEMS

Current rifle manufacturer located in Tucson, AZ.

CARBINES/RIFLES: SEMI-AUTO, AR-15 STYLE

PATROL RIFLE I – 5.56 NATO cal., GIO, 16 in. medium weight chrome lined barrel, M4 upper receiver, F-marked front sight base, Magpul MBUS rear sight, A2 flash suppressor, nickel plated bolt carrier and key, heavy extractor

MSR	100%	98%	95%	90%	80%	70%	60%	Last MSR

spring, forged aluminum lower receiver, single stage LE trigger, 30 shot Magpul mag., "H" buffer, six position Magpul MOE stock, grip, and handguard, includes soft case.

MSR $1,319 $1,125 $985 $850 $765 $625 $500 $395

PATROL RIFLE II – 5.56 NATO cal., GIO, 16 in. medium weight chrome lined barrel, M4 upper receiver, F-marked front sight base, Magpul MBUS rear sight, A2 flash suppressor, nickel plated bolt carrier and key, heavy extractor spring, forged aluminum lower receiver, single stage LE trigger, 30 shot Magpul mag., "H" buffer, six position Magpul STR stock, Magpul MOE grip, free floating 9 inch quad rail handguard, includes soft case.

MSR $1,609 $1,375 $1,200 $1,025 $935 $750 $625 $480

PATROL RIFLE II PRO – 5.56 NATO cal., similar to Patrol Rifle II, except has 12 in. free float quad rail handguard and low profile gas block.

MSR $1,669 $1,425 $1,250 $1,075 $975 $785 $640 $500

PATROL RIFLE III/III XL – 5.56 NATO cal., GIO, 16 in. medium weight chrome lined barrel, M4 upper receiver, Magpul MBUS front and rear sight, A2 flash suppressor, nickel plated bolt carrier and key, heavy extractor spring, forged aluminum lower receiver, single stage LE trigger, 30 shot Magpul mag., "H" buffer, six position Magpul STR stock, Magpul MOE grip, free floating 12.37 inch "slick side" rail EVO handguard, low profile gas block, includes soft case.

MSR $1,559 $1,325 $1,175 $995 $900 $730 $595 $465

    Add $10 for XL Model with 15 in. "slick side" rail.

PERIMETER MARKSMAN RIFLE – 5.56 NATO cal., GIO, 18 1/2 in. stainless steel chrome lined barrel, M4 upper receiver, Magpul MBUS front and rear sight, Sionics muzzle brake, nickel plated bolt carrier and key, heavy extractor spring, forged aluminum lower receiver, single stage LE trigger, 30 shot Magpul mag., standard rifle buffer, ACE skeleton stock, Magpul MOE grip, free floating 15 inch rail EVO handguard, low profile gas block, includes soft case.

MSR $1,709 $1,450 $1,275 $1,095 $985 $800 $650 $510

SIRKIS INDUSTRIES, LTD.

Previous manufacturer located in Ramat-Gan, Israel. Previously imported and distributed by Armscorp of America, Inc. located in Baltimore, MD.

RIFLES

MODEL 36 SNIPER RIFLE – .308 Win. cal. only, gas operated action, carbon fiber stock, 22 in. barrel, flash suppressor, free range sights. Disc. 1985.

     $670 $580 $520 $475 $430 $390 $350   *$760*

SISK RIFLES LLC

Current rifle manufacturer located in Dayton, TX.

RIFLES: BOLT ACTION

Charlie Sisk builds high quality bolt action rifles per individual customer specifications. The STAR (Sisk Tactical Adaptive Rifle) has a base price of $6,495. Hunting models start at $5,600. A wide variety of options and accessories are available. Please contact the company directly for more information, including availability, delivery time, pricing and options (see Trademark Index).

SKORPION

Current semi-auto or select-fire pistol model manufactured in the Czech Republic. Currently imported by Czechpoint, Inc. located in Knoxville, TN beginning 2010. Previously imported by CZ USA 2009-2010.

PISTOLS: SEMI-AUTO

SA VZ. 61 SKORPION – .32 ACP cal., semi-auto copy of VZ 61 Skorpion submachine gun, blue or nickel finish, SA, forward charging knob, steel frame, 4.52 in. barrel, 20 shot mag., hardwood grips, flip up rear sight, lanyard rings, wood or polymer grips, 41 oz.

MSR $595 $500 $440 $375 $340 $275 $225 $175

SMITH & WESSON

Current manufacturer located in Springfield, MA, 1857 to date. Partnership with Horace Smith & Daniel B. Wesson 1856-1874. Family owned by Wesson 1874-1965. S&W became a subsidiary of Bangor-Punta from 1965-1983. Between 1983-1987, Smith & Wesson was owned by the Lear Siegler Co. On May 22, 1987, Smith & Wesson was sold to R.L. Tomkins, an English holding company. During 2001, Tomkins sold Smith & Wesson to Saf-T-Hammer, an Arizona-based safety and security company. Smith & Wesson was the primary distributor for most Walther firearms and accessories in the United States from 2002-2012. During 2012, Carl Walther GmbH Sportwaffen and Umarex

MSR	100%	98%	95%	90%	80%	70%	60%	Last MSR

announced the formation of Walther Arms, Inc. to import, sell, and market all Walther products in the U.S. beginning Jan. 1, 2013.

The author wishes to express his thanks to Mr. Sal Raimondi, Jim Supica, Rick Nahas, and Roy Jinks, the S&W Historian, for their updates and valuable contributions.

Factory special orders, such as ivory or pearl grips, special finishes, engraving, and other production rarities will add premiums to the values listed. After 1893, all ivory and pearl grips had the metal S&W logo medallions inserted on top.

FACTORY LETTER OF AUTHENTICITY - S&W charges $50 for a formal letter of authenticity. A form is available for downloading on their website: www.smith-wesson.com for this service. Turnaround time is usually 8-12 weeks.

For more information and current pricing on both new and used Smith & Wesson airguns, please refer to the *Blue Book of Airguns* by Dr. Robert Beeman & John Allen (also online).

REVOLVERS: NUMBERED MODEL/RECENT MFG. (MODERN HAND EJECTORS)

Smith & Wesson handguns manufactured after 1957 are stamped with a model number on the frame under the cylinder yoke. The number is visible when the cylinder is open. All revolvers manufactured by S&W from 1946-1956 were produced without model numbers.

To locate a particular revolver in the following section, simply swing the cylinder out to the loading position and read the model number inside the yoke. The designation Mod. and a two- or three-digit number followed by a dash and another number designates which engineering change was underway when the gun was manufactured. Hence, a Mod. 15-7 is a Model 15 in its 7th engineering change (and should be indicated as such when ordering parts). Usually, earlier variations are the most desirable to collectors unless a particular improvement is rare. The same rule applies to semi-auto pistols, and the model designation is usually marked on the outside of the gun.

Beginning 1994, S&W started providing synthetic grips and a drilled/tapped receiver for scope mounting on certain models.

S&W revolvers are generally categorized by frame size. Frame sizes are as follows: J-frame (small), K-frame (medium), L-frame (medium), N-frame (large), and X-frame (extra large). All currently manufactured S&W revolvers chambered for .38 S&W Spl. cal. will also accept +P rated ammunition.

Current S&W abbreviations for revolver feature codes used on its price sheets and literature are as follows: Grips: CTG - Crimson Trace laser grips, RG - rubber grips, WG - wood grips. Sights: ADJ - adjustable, ADJV - adjustable V-notch, BB - black blade, DWD - dovetail white dot, INTCH - interchangeable front, FIX - fixed, FO - fiber optic, GB - gold bead front, INTEG - integral front, PAT - Patridge front, NS - night sight, RR - red ramp front, SN - square notch, WB - white bead, and WO - white outline. Frame Material: AL - alloy, SS - stainless, CS - carbon steel. Frame Sizes: SM - Small/Compact, MD - Medium, LG - Large, XL - Extra Large. Older finish abbreviations include: ZB - Blue/Black, ZC - Clear Cote, ZG - Grey, ZM - Matte, ZS - Satin. Cylinder: CA - alloy, CC - carbon, CS - stainless, CT - titanium. Barrel: BF - full lug, BO - one piece, BP - PowerPort, BT - traditional, B2 - two piece. Action: DAO - double action only, SA/DA - single action/double action. Older finish abbreviations include: ZB - Blue/Black, ZC - Clear Cote, ZG - Grey, ZM - Matte, ZS - Satin. Cylinder: CA - alloy, CC - carbon, CS - stainless, CT - titanium.

Pre-2010 S&W abbreviations for revolver feature codes used on its price sheets and literature are as follows: Grips: GC - Crimson Trace laser grips, GR - rubber grips, GW - wood grips, GF - finger groove grips. Sights: SA - adj., SB - black blade front, SC - interchangeable front, SF - fixed, SG - gold bead front, SH - Hi-Viz, SI - integral front, SP - Patridge front, SN - front night, SR - red ramp front, SW - white outline adj. rear. Frame Material: FA - alloy, FS - stainless, FC - carbon.

During 2009, S&W started manufacture of the Classic Firearms series of revolvers. These guns incorporate many features of S&W's older and most famous/collectible revolvers, but have also been enhanced with modern engineering changes. This series is referred to as Classic or Classics in the model nomenclature, as opposed to Classic which indicates standard production S&W models and nomenclature.

Add 10%-15% for those models listed that are pinned and recessed (pre-1981 mfg.), if in 90% or better condition.

Earlier mfg. on the following models with lower engineering change numbered suffixes are more desirable than later mfg. (i.e., a Model 10-1 is more desirable than a Model 10-14).

Factory error stamped revolvers generally bring a small premium (5%-10%, if in 95%+ original condition) over a non-error gun, if the right collector is found.

BODYGUARD 38 – .38 Spl. + P cal., 5 shot, DAO, 1.9 in barrel, small J-frame, internal hammer, aluminum alloy upper frame, steel reinforced polymer lower frame, stainless steel cylinder, ambidextrous cylinder release, fixed sights with laser module next to cylinder latch behind the recoil shield, and activated with thumb, round butt with integrated black polymer grips, matte black finish, 14.3 oz. New late 2010.

MSR $509	$425	$385	$350	$315	$280	$260	$240	

GOVERNOR – .45 LC/.410 shotshell or .45 ACP/.410 shotshell, 2 1/2 in. shotshell, new Z-frame, 2 3/4 in. barrel, 6 shot, SA/DA, tritium night front sight, fixed rear sight, Scandium alloy frame with stainless steel cylinder, matte black finish, black synthetic finger groove or Crimson Trace Laser grips, 29.6 oz. New 2011.

MSR $869	$695	$595	$475	$400	$350	$300	$275	

Add $310 for Crimson Trace laser grips.

MSR	100%	98%	95%	90%	80%	70%	60%	Last MSR

MODEL 310 NIGHTGUARD – 10mm or .40 S&W cal., 2 1/2 in. barrel, matte black finish, Scandium alloy N-frame with stainless steel cylinder, 6 shot, SA/DA, XS 24/7 standard dot tritium night front sight, fixed rear sight, Pachmayr grips, 28 oz. Mfg. 2009-2010.

	$895	$685	$530	$425	$350	$300	$275	$1,185

MODEL 315 NIGHTGUARD – .38 Spl. + P cal., 2 1/2 in. barrel, K-frame, blue/black finish, 6 shot, rubber grips, front night sight, fixed rear sight, alloy frame with stainless cylinder. Mfg. 2009 only. Scarce.

	$1,150	$1,000	$865	$775	$635	$525	$400	$995

MODEL 325 PD-AIRLITE Sc – .45 ACP cal., 2 1/2 (disc. 2006) or 4 in. barrel, otherwise similar to Model 329 PD, approx. 21 1/2 - 25 oz. Mfg. 2004-2007.

	$800	$625	$485	$400	$335	$300	$275	$1,067

MODEL 325 NIGHTGUARD – .45 ACP cal., two-piece 2 1/2 in. barrel, alloy frame with stainless steel cylinder, black alloy finish, 6 shot, N-frame, SA/DA, rubber grips, fixed rear sight with front night sight, 28 oz. Mfg. 2008-2012.

	$825	$650	$525	$425	$350	$300	$275	$1,049

MODEL 327 PD-AIRLITE Sc – .357 Mag. cal., 8 shot, N-frame, 4 in. two-piece barrel, wood grips, Scandium frame with titanium cylinder, matte black finish, 26 1/2 oz. Mfg. 2008-2009.

	$950	$725	$550	$450	$350	$315	$285	$1,264

MODEL 327 NIGHTGUARD – .357 Mag. cal., two-piece 2 1/2 in. barrel, alloy frame with stainless steel cylinder, black alloy finish, 8 shot, N-frame, SA/DA, rubber grips, fixed rear sight with front night sight, 27.6 oz. Mfg. 2008-2012.

	$825	$650	$525	$425	$350	$300	$275	$1,049

MODEL 329 PD-AIRLITE Sc – .44 Mag. cal., 4 in. barrel, N-frame, 6 shot, Scandium frame and titanium cylinder with matte black metal finish, wood Ahrends grips with finger grooves, and Hogue rubber monogrip, Hi-Viz front sight, approx. 26 oz. New 2003.

MSR $1,159	$915	$715	$550	$450	$375	$325	$300	

MODEL 329 NIGHTGUARD – .44 Mag. cal., two-piece 2 1/2 in. barrel, alloy frame with stainless steel cylinder, black alloy finish, 6 shot, N-frame, SA/DA, rubber grips, fixed rear sight with front night sight, 29.3 oz. Mfg. 2008-2012.

	$825	$650	$525	$425	$350	$300	$275	$1,049

MODEL 337 AIRLITE Ti CHIEFS SPECIAL – .38 S&W Spl.+P cal., J-frame, 5 shot, 1 7/8 in. barrel, similar design as the Model 331, 11.9 oz. Mfg. 1999-2003.

	$675	$595	$500	$460	$370	$300	$235	$716

Add $24 for Dymondwood Boot grips (mfg. 1999 only).

MODEL 340 AIRLITE Sc CENTENNIAL – .357 Mag. cal., J-frame, 5 shot, 1 7/8 in. barrel only, Scandium alloy frame, barrel shroud, and yoke, titanium cylinder, two-tone matte stainless/grey finish, hammerless, Hogue Bantam grips, 12 oz. Mfg. 2001-2008.

	$775	$575	$475	$400	$340	$295	$250	$1,019

MODEL 340 PD AIRLITE Sc (CENTENNIAL) – similar to Model 340 Airlite Sc, except has black/grey finish, Hi-Viz sight became standard 2009, also available with no internal lock (new 2011), "PD" marked, 12 oz. New 2000.

MSR $1,019	$795	$625	$500	$400	$340	$295	$250	

MODEL 340 M & P (CENTENNIAL) – .357 Mag. cal., 5 shot, J-frame, DAO, concealed hammer, 1 7/8 in. barrel, includes XS sights (24/7 tritium night and integral U-notch), Scandium alloy frame with stainless steel cylinder, also available with no internal lock (new 2011), matte black finish, synthetic or Crimson Trace laser grips, "M&P" marked, 13.3 oz. New 2007.

MSR $869	$695	$595	$475	$400	$350	$300	$275	

Add $260 for Crimson Trace laser grips.

MODEL 342 AIRLITE Ti CENTENNIAL – .38 S&W Spl.+P cal., similar to Model 337, except is hammerless and double action only, matte stainless/grey finish, Uncle Mike's Boot grips, 12 oz. Mfg. 1999-2003.

	$575	$445	$390	$345	$310	$280	$250	$734

Add $24 for Dymondwood Boot grips (mfg. 1999 only).

MODEL 342 PD AIRLITE Ti CENTENNIAL – .38 S&W Spl.+P cal., J-frame, 5 shot, double action only, aluminum alloy frame with titanium cylinder and stainless steel 1 7/8 in. barrel, hammerless, black/grey finish, "PD" marked, Hogue Bantam grips, 10.8 oz. Mfg. 2000-2003.

	$595	$460	$390	$340	$310	$280	$250	$758

MSR	100%	98%	95%	90%	80%	70%	60%	Last MSR

MODEL 351 PD AIRLITE Sc (CHIEFS SPECIAL) – .22 MRF (.22 WMR) cal., J-frame, 1 7/8 in. two-piece barrel, 7 shot, black finish, aluminum alloy frame and cylinder, wood grips, 10.6 oz. New 2004.

| MSR $759 | $575 | $495 | $400 | $350 | $300 | $275 | $225 | |

MODEL 357 PD – .41 Rem. Mag. cal., 6 shot, 4 in. two piece barrel, N frame, Scandium alloy frame with titanium cylinder, matte black finish, Ahrends wood grips with finger grooves, Hi-Viz front sight, adj. V-notch rear sight, 27 1/2 oz. Mfg. mid-2005-2007.

| | $815 | $575 | $475 | $400 | $340 | $300 | $275 | *$1,067* |

MODEL 357 NIGHTGUARD – .41 Mag. cal., 2 1/2 in. barrel, N-frame, matte black metal finish, 6 shot, black synthetic grips, alloy frame with stainless steel cylinder, fixed rear sight, front night sight, 29.7 oz. Mfg. 2010 only.

| | $895 | $685 | $530 | $425 | $350 | $300 | $275 | *$1,185* |

MODEL 360 AIRLITE Sc CHIEFS SPECIAL – .357 Mag. cal., J-frame, 5 shot, 1 7/8 in. two piece barrel, Scandium alloy frame with titanium cylinder, matte stainless/grey finish, Hogue Bantam grips, fixed sights, 12 oz. Mfg. 2001-2007.

| | $775 | $575 | $475 | $400 | $340 | $295 | $250 | *$1,019* |

MODEL 360 PD AIRLITE Sc (CHIEFS SPECIAL) – .357 Mag. or .38 Spl. + P cal., J-frame, similar to Model 360 Airlite Sc Chiefs Special, except has matte stainless/grey finish, "PD" marked, Hi-Viz sight became standard 2009, 12 oz. New 2002.

| MSR $1,019 | $850 | $675 | $525 | $400 | $340 | $295 | $250 | |

MODEL 360 M & P (CHIEFS SPECIAL) – .357 Mag. cal., 5 shot, J-frame, SA/DA, 1 7/8 in. barrel, includes XS sights (24/7 tritium night and integral U-notch), Scandium alloy frame with stainless steel cylinder, matte black finish, synthetic grips, M&P marked, 13.3 oz. Mfg. 2007-2012.

| | $725 | $600 | $475 | $350 | $300 | $250 | $225 | *$869* |

MODEL 386 AIRLITE Sc MOUNTAIN LITE – .357 Mag. cal., L-frame, 7 shot, 2 1/2 (new 2007) or 3 1/8 (disc. 2006) in. two piece stainless steel barrel with adj. rear and Hi-Viz front sight, Scandium alloy frame with titanium cylinder, two-tone matte stainless/grey finish, Hogue Bantam grips, 18 1/2 oz. Mfg. 2001-2007.

| | $650 | $510 | $420 | $365 | $325 | $295 | $265 | *$869* |

MODEL 386 PD AIRLITE Sc – .357 Mag. cal., L-frame, 7 shot, 2 1/2 in. stainless barrel with adj. black rear sight, Scandium alloy frame with titanium cylinder, black/grey finish, Hogue Bantam grips, 17 1/2 oz. Mfg. 2001-2005.

| | $665 | $500 | $415 | $355 | $315 | $285 | $250 | *$872* |

Add $22 for Hi-Viz front sight (disc. 2005).

MODEL 386 Sc/S – .357 Mag. cal., L-frame, 7 shot, 2 1/2 in. barrel, synthetic finger groove grips, matte black finish, Scandium alloy frame with stainless steel cylinder, red ramp front sight, adj. rear sight, 21.2 oz. Mfg. mid-2007-2008.

| | $775 | $600 | $475 | $385 | $335 | $295 | $265 | *$948* |

MODEL 386 NIGHTGUARD – .357 Mag. cal., two-piece 2 1/2 in. barrel, alloy frame with stainless cylinder, black alloy finish, 7 shot, L-frame, SA/DA, rubber grips, fixed rear sight with front night sight, 24 1/2 oz. Mfg. 2008-2012.

| | $750 | $595 | $500 | $450 | $400 | $350 | $325 | *$979* |

MODEL 396 AIRLITE Ti MOUNTAIN LITE – .44 S&W Spl. cal., L-frame, 5 shot, 3 1/8 in. two piece barrel, adj. rear and Hi-Viz front sight, aluminum alloy frame with titanium cylinder, matte stainless/grey finish, Hogue Bantam grips, 18 oz. Mfg. 2001-2004.

| | $625 | $475 | $400 | $355 | $315 | $285 | $250 | *$812* |

There has been one engineering change to this model.

MODEL 396 NIGHTGUARD – .44 Spl. cal., two-piece 2 1/2 in. barrel, alloy frame with stainless steel cylinder, black alloy finish, 5 shot, L-frame, SA/DA, rubber grips, fixed rear sight with front night sight, 24.2 oz. Mfg. 2008-2009.

| | $825 | $650 | $550 | $475 | $425 | $375 | $335 | *$1,074* |

MODEL 632 PRO SERIES – .327 Federal Mag. cal., 2 1/8 (new 2010) or 3 (disc.) in. black PowerPort barrel, blue/black finish, 6 shot, stainless small frame and cylinder, rubber grips, SA/DA, adj. sight, night sights (new 2010), approx. 23 oz. Mfg. 2009-2012.

| | $600 | $575 | $550 | $450 | $375 | $350 | $300 | *$809* |

Add $90 for 3 in. PowerPort barrel and blue/black metal finish with SA/DA action (marked MOD 632-1).

MSR	100%	98%	95%	90%	80%	70%	60%	Last MSR

MODEL 637 AIRWEIGHT (CHIEFS SPECIAL)

– .38 S&W Spl.+P cal., J-frame, 5 shot, matte finish, alloy frame with 1 7/8 (current mfg.), 2 1/8 (PowerPort only, disc.), or 2 1/2 full lug (mfg. 2010 only) in. satin stainless steel barrel and cylinder, current production uses Uncle Mike's Boot, Crimson Trace Laser (new 2005), or pink (new 2012) grips, 15 oz., 560 mfg. during 1991, reintroduced 1996.

MSR $469	$355	$315	$275	$225	$190	$170	$150	

Add $20 for pink grips (new 2012).
Add $16 for Carry Combo configuration (mfg. 2004-2008).
Add $230 for Crimson Trace laser grips (new 2005).
Add $50 for 2 1/2 in. full lug barrel (mfg. 2010 only).
Add $142 for 2 1/8 in. barrel with PowerPort (Pro Series, mfg. 2009-2010).

MODEL 638 AIRWEIGHT (BODYGUARD)

– .38 S&W Spl.+P cal., J-frame, 5 shot, alloy frame, 1 7/8 or 2 1/2 full lug (mfg. 2010 only) in. stainless steel barrel and cylinder, shrouded hammer, round butt, Uncle Mike's Boot, Crimson Trace Laser, or pink (new 2012) grips, 15 oz. 1,200 mfg. during 1990 only, reintroduced 1998.

MSR $469	$355	$315	$275	$225	$190	$170	$150	

Add $20 for pink grips (new 2012).
Add $24 for 2 1/2 in. full lug barrel (disc. 2010).
Add $230 for Crimson Trace laser grips (new 2010).

MODEL 681 DISTINGUISHED SERVICE MAGNUM

– .357 Mag. cal., stainless steel, 4 in. barrel, fixed sights, L-Frame. Mfg. 1980-1992.

	$425	$350	$275	$225	$175	$140	$125	*$412*

1991 mfg. includes square butt. There were 5 engineering changes to this model.

MODEL 686 DISTINGUISHED COMBAT MAGNUM

– .357 Mag./.38 Spl.+ P cal., L-Frame, 6 shot, similar to Model 586, except has 2 1/2 (new 1990), 4, 6 (with (disc.) or w/o PowerPort), or 8 3/8 (disc. 2002) in. barrel, fixed (disc.) or adj. sights, blue, stainless, Midnight Black (ltd. ed. 1989 only, 2,876 mfg. in 6 in. barrel, and 1,559 mfg. in 4 in. barrel) finish, current production uses Hogue rubber grips, 35-51 oz. New 1980.

MSR $829	$600	$475	$350	$300	$250	$225	$200	

* ***Model 686 Distinguished Combat Magnum Plus*** – .357 Mag./.38 Spl.+ P cal., L-frame, 7 shot, 2 1/2, 3 (new 2007), 4, or 6 in. barrel, synthetic or Hogue rubber grips, stainless steel, round (2 1/2 in. barrel only) or square butt, white outline rear sight on 4 or 6 in. barrel, 34 1/2 - 43 oz. New 1996.

MSR $849	$615	$485	$350	$300	$250	$225	$200	

MODEL 686/686SSR PRO SERIES

– .357 Mag./.38 Spl. + P cal., 6 shot, L-frame, 4 (Model 686SSR) or 5 (Model 686 with full moon clips, new 2010) in. barrel, SA/DA, interchangeable front sight, adj. rear sight, satin stainless (Model 686SSR) or bead (Model 686) finish, checkered wood grips, stainless steel frame and cylinder, forged hammer and trigger, custom barrel with recessed Precision crown, Bossed mainspring, and tuned action, 38.3 oz. New 2007.

MSR $999	$750	$615	$515	$400	$350	$325	$275	

Subtract $10 for full moon clips (Model 686, new 2010).

PISTOLS: SEMI-AUTO, CENTERFIRE

Listed in order of model number (except .32 and .35 Automatic Pistols). Alphabetical models will appear at the end of this section.

To understand S&W 3rd generation model nomenclature, the following rules apply. The first two digits (of the four digit model number) specify caliber. Numbers 39, 59, and 69 refer to 9mm Para. cal. The third digit refers to the model type. 0 means standard model, 1 is for compact, 2 is for standard model with decocking lever, 3 is for compact variation with decocking lever, 4 is for standard with double action only, 5 designates a compact model in double action only, 6 indicates a non-standard barrel length, 7 is a non-standard barrel length with decocking lever, and 8 refers to non-standard barrel length in double action only. The fourth digit refers to the material(s) used in the fabrication of the pistol. 3 refers to an aluminum alloy frame with stainless steel slide, 4 designates an aluminum alloy frame with carbon steel slide, 5 is for carbon steel frame and slide, 6 is a stainless steel frame and slide, and 7 refers to a stainless steel frame and carbon steel slide. Hence, a Model 4053 refers to a pistol in .40 S&W cal. configured in compact version with double action only and fabricated with an aluminum alloy frame and stainless steel slide. This model nomenclature does not apply to 2 or 3 digit model numbers (i.e., Rimfire Models and the Model 52).

Current S&W abbreviations for pistol feature codes used on its price sheets and literature are as follows: Grips: CTG - Crimson Trace laser grips, PG - plastic grips, RG - rubber grips, WG - wood grips. Sights: ADJ - adjustable, ADJFO - adj. fiber optic, FIXEDB - fixed black, LMC - low mount carry, BB - black blade, BP - black post, FO - fiber optic, GB - gold bead - INTCH - interchangeable, NS - night sights, PAT - Patridge, RR - red ramp, WB - white bead, WD - white dot. Frames: AL - alloy, SS - stainless steel, CS - carbon steel, MCR - maximum corrosion resistant, (SM - stainless melonite), POLY - polymer. Safeties: AMBI - ambidextrous, MS - magazine safety, NMS - no magazine safety, IL - internal lock, TS - thumb safety, TLCI - tacticle loaded chamber indicator. Action: DA - double action only, SA - single action only, SA/DA - single action/double action, SF - striker fire.

Pre-2010 S&W abbreviations are as follows: Grips: GC - Crimson Trace laser grips, GR - rubber grips, GW - wood grips, GF - finger groove grips, GP - plastic grips. Sights: SA - adj., SB - black blade front, SC - interchangeable front, SD - dot front, SF - fixed, SG - gold

MSR	100%	98%	95%	90%	80%	70%	60%	Last MSR

bead front, SH - Hi-Viz, SL - Lo Mount Carry, SP - Patridge front, SR - red ramp front, SV - black post, S1 - front night. Frame Material: FA - alloy, FS - stainless, FC - carbon, FM - stainless Melonite, FP - polymer. Frame Sizes: SM - Small/Compact, MD - Medium, LG - Large, XL - Extra Large. Finishes: ZB - Blue/Black, ZC - Clear Cote, ZG - Grey, ZL - Melonite, ZM - Matte, ZS - Satin Stainless, ZT - Two-Tone, ZW - Camo. Barrel: BC - carbon, BL - light, BO - one piece, BS - stainless, BT - traditional, BX - heavy, B2 - two piece. Action: AD - double action only, AF - striker fire, AS - single action only, AT - traditional double action. Slide: DS - stainless steel, DC- carbon, DM - stainless Melonite.

When applicable, early variations of some of the older semi-auto models listed in this category will be more desirable than later mfg.

BODYGUARD 380 – .380 ACP cal., 2 3/4 in. barrel, sub-compact, black polymer frame with integral laser and finger groove grips, stainless steel slide with black melonite finish, 6 shot mag., DAO (hammer fired), SFO, adj. sight, 11.85 oz. New mid-2010.

MSR $419	$365	$325	$285	$265	$245	$225	$200	

MODEL 59 – 9mm Para. cal., similar to Model 39, except has 14 shot mag., black nylon grips, DA/SA, total production approx. 231,841. Mfg. 1972-1981.

	$550	$400	$350	$275	$250	$225	$215	

Add $50 for nickel finish.
Add $150 for smooth front (ungrooved) grip frame.
Add 200% for smooth front and rear grip straps (20 mfg.).

MODEL 410 – .40 S&W cal., Value Series, DA/SA, steel slide with alloy frame, blue finish, 4 in. barrel, 10 or 11 shot mag., single side safety, 3-dot sights, straight backstrap with synthetic grips, 28 1/2 oz. Mfg. 1996-2007.

	$525	$375	$275	$225	$195	$175	$165	$687

Add $25 for Hi-Viz front sight (mfg. 2002-2003).

* ***Model 410S*** – .40 S&W cal., Value Series, similar to Model 410, except has stainless steel slide with alloy frame, 28 1/2 oz. Mfg. 2005-2006.

	$545	$375	$275	$245	$205	$175	$165	$711

Add $100 for Crimson Trace laser grips.

MODEL 411 – .40 S&W cal., Value Series, 4 in. barrel, DA/SA, 11 shot mag., fixed sights, blue finish, aluminum alloy frame, manual safety. Mfg. 1992-1996.

	$475	$400	$350	$325	$295	$280	$265	$525

MODEL 439 – 9mm Para. cal., DA/SA, 4 in. barrel, blue or nickel finish, alloy frame, 8 shot mag., checkered walnut grips, 30 oz. Mfg. 1981-1988.

	$500	$415	$350	$325	$260	$215	$165	$472

Add $50 for nickel finish (disc. 1986).
Add $26 for adj. sights.

Production began on February 26, 1981 with serial number A669101. The first few thousand were supplied with a short wide extractor before reverting back to the Model 39-2 style extractor. The gun was discontinued in the fall of 1988 and replaced by the third-generation Model 3904.

MODEL 457 COMPACT – .45 ACP cal., Value Series, DA/SA, alloy frame and steel slide, 3 3/4 in. barrel, single side safety, 3-dot sights, 7 shot mag., straight backstrap, blue finish only, black synthetic grips, 29 oz. Mfg. 1996-2006.

	$525	$365	$270	$225	$195	$175	$165	$681

MODEL 459 – 9mm Para. cal., 14 shot version of Model 439, checkered nylon stocks, limited mfg. with squared-off trigger guard with serrations. Mfg. 1981-1988.

	$450	$400	$350	$300	$275	$255	$240	$501

Add $25 for adj. sights.
Add $50 for nickel finish (disc. 1986).
Add 30% for Model 4590 (Transitional 5903).

Production started in 1981, at approximately serial number A668439, and was discontinued in 1988. It is estimated that the first 10,000 guns were produced with the short wide extractor.

MODEL 469 "MINI" – 9mm Para. cal., DA/SA, alloy frame, 12 shot finger extension mag., short frame, bobbed hammer, 3 1/2 in. barrel, sandblast blue or satin nickel finish, ambidextrous safety standard (1986), molded Delrin black grips, 26 oz. Mfg. 1983-1988.

	$475	$435	$325	$275	$240	$225	$210	$478

The first eleven guns were completed in 1982 (serial numbers starting at A796437) and were used for test and evaluation samples. Full production began in August of 1983 with serial number A840000. 25 of the first 100 guns were nickel finish, class "A" engraved and shipped with a presentation case, marked "First 100". However while they were marked "First 100" they were not necessarily the first hundred serial numbers.

MSR	100%	98%	95%	90%	80%	70%	60%	Last MSR

MODEL 559 – The Model 559 is the carbon steel version of the 14 round, double stack magazine second-generation pistol, DA/SA. The gun was introduced in 1980 with shipments starting in 1981, at approximately serial number A672725. The majority of the guns were produced with the short wide extractor. Only 200 to 250 were supplied with the Model 39-2 type extractor. After production of 10,609 units, 8,973 in blue finish and 1,636 in nickel, the gun was discontinued October 1982.

| | $600 | $525 | $450 | $375 | $275 | $250 | $225 | |

Add $50 for nickel finish.
Add $30 for fixed rear sight.

MODEL 639 STAINLESS – 9mm Para. cal., DA/SA, similar to Model 439, only stainless steel, 8 shot mag., ambidextrous safety became standard 1986, 36 oz. Mfg. 1982-1988.

| | $475 | $400 | $350 | $300 | $250 | $200 | $165 | $523 |

Add $27 for adj. sights.

The pistol was introduced on May 24, 1982, with serial number A769806. The gun was first available with the short wide extractor but that was changed to the Model 39-2 type on September 15, 1982 after approximately 600 had been produced.

MODEL 645 STAINLESS – .45 ACP cal. only, 5 in. barrel, SA, 8 shot mag., squared-off trigger guard, black molded nylon grips, ambidextrous safety, fixed sights, 37 1/2 oz. Mfg. 1985-1988.

| | $550 | $475 | $400 | $350 | $300 | $250 | $200 | $622 |

Add approx. 25% for the approx. 479 Model 6450 "Interim" pistols were mfg. in 1988 only.
Add $27 for adj. sight.

The first 28 prototype pistols were produced in October 1984 and were serial numbered from A883222 to A883249. Production started in November 1985 with shipments starting in December of 1985 at serial number TAK0001.

MODEL 659 STAINLESS – 9mm Para. cal., DA/SA, similar to Model 459, only stainless steel, 14 shot mag., ambidextrous safety became standard 1986, 39 1/2 oz. Disc. 1988.

| | $475 | $400 | $350 | $300 | $250 | $215 | $180 | $553 |

Add approx. 30% for the approx. 150 Model 6590 "Interim" or "transitional" pistols were mfg. in 1988 only.
Add $27 for adj. sights.

The gun was introduced in 1982 beginning with serial number A782700 and was discontinued in 1988. It was replaced by the Model 5906. A limited number of this model were supplied with the short wide extractor and are considered scarce.

MODEL 669 STAINLESS – 9mm Para. cal., smaller version of Model 659 with 12 shot finger extension mag., 3 1/2 in. barrel, fixed sights, molded Delrin grips, ambidextrous safety standard, 26 oz. Mfg. 1986-88 only.

| | $475 | $375 | $300 | $250 | $195 | $165 | $140 | $522 |

Add approx. 30% for the approx. 150 Model 6690 "Interim" or "transitional" pistols were mfg. in 1988 only.

The Model 669 was introduced in 1985 beginning with serial number TAE 0001. The gun had a stainless steel slide and barrel with aluminum alloy frame. The first 100 guns were set aside for special orders; 25 of these were class "A" engraved by an outside contractor and marked "1 of 25." It took ten years for all of these engraved guns to be sold. In 1988 the Model 669 was discontinued and replaced by the Model 6906. Total production of the Model 669 was 54,074 pistols.

MODEL 908 COMPACT – 9mm Para. cal., Value Series, compact variation of the Model 909/910, DA/SA, 3 1/2 in. barrel, 3-dot sights, 8 shot mag., straight backstrap, 24 oz. Mfg. 1996-2007.

| | $495 | $355 | $275 | $230 | $195 | $175 | $165 | $648 |

* **Model 908S Compact** – Value Series, similar to Model 908, except has stainless steel slide with alloy frame, 24 oz. Mfg. 2003-2007.

| | $495 | $355 | $275 | $230 | $195 | $175 | $165 | $648 |

Add $24 for carry combo variation (includes Kydex carry holster, new 2004).

MODEL 910 FULL SIZE – Value Series, similar to Model 909, except has 10 or 15 shot mag., 28 oz. Mfg. 1994-2007.

| | $450 | $375 | $300 | $250 | $210 | $190 | $175 | $616 |

Add $22 for Hi-Viz front sight (disc. 2003).

MODEL 915 – 9mm Para. cal., Value Series, 4 in. barrel, fixed sights, 10 (C/B 1994) or 15* shot mag., manual safety, aluminum alloy frame, blue finish. Mfg. 1993-1994.

| | $425 | $350 | $275 | $225 | $200 | $190 | $175 | $467 |

MODEL 1006 STAINLESS – 10mm cal., stainless steel construction, 5 in. barrel, DA/SA, exposed hammer, 9 shot mag., fixed or adj. sights, ambidextrous safety, 26,979 units produced 1990-1993.

| | $750 | $650 | $425 | $350 | $300 | $245 | $215 | $769 |

Add $27 for adj. rear sight.
Product Codes: 104800, 105004, 108234, 108237.

MSR	100%	98%	95%	90%	80%	70%	60%	Last MSR

MODEL 1026 STAINLESS – 10mm cal., 5 in. barrel, DA/SA, features frame mounted decocking lever, 9 shot mag., straight backstrap, 3,135 units produced 1990-1991 only.

	100%	98%	95%	90%	80%	70%	60%	Last MSR
	$850	$675	$550	$425	$325	$245	$215	$755

Product Codes: 105006, 105021, 108239.

MODEL 1046 STAINLESS – 10mm cal., 5 in. barrel, DAO, fixed sights, 9 shot mag., straight backstrap, 151 units produced 1991 only.

	100%	98%	95%	90%	80%	70%	60%	Last MSR
	$1,500	$1,200	$875	$550	$400	$300	$250	$747

Product Codes: 104602, 108233.

MODEL 1066 STAINLESS – 10mm cal., 4 1/4 in. barrel, DA/SA, 9 shot mag., straight backstrap, ambidextrous safety, traditional double action, fixed sights, 5,067 units produced 1990-1992.

	100%	98%	95%	90%	80%	70%	60%	Last MSR
	$750	$625	$500	$400	$325	$250	$225	$730

Add $75 for Tritium night sights - disc. 1991 (Model 1066-NS).

Product Codes: 105500, 108270.

Only 1,000 Model 1066-NSs were manufactured.

MODEL 1076 STAINLESS – similar to Model 1026 Stainless, except has 4 1/4 in. barrel, 13,805 units produced 1990-93.

	100%	98%	95%	90%	80%	70%	60%	Last MSR
	$700	$625	$550	$450	$350	$300	$245	$778

Product Codes: 10506, 105021, 108239.

MODEL 1086 STAINLESS – similar to Model 1066 Stainless, except is double action only, 1,660 units produced 1990-1992.

	100%	98%	95%	90%	80%	70%	60%	Last MSR
	$900	$700	$525	$400	$325	$250	$210	$730

Product Codes: 106004, 108251.

MODEL SW1911 – .45 ACP cal., patterned after the Colt M1911, large frame, SA, 5 in. barrel, 8 shot single stack mag., alloy (disc. 2006), steel or stainless steel frame, steel slide, matte, blue/black (new 2005) or Clear Coat finish, patented S&W firing pin safety release activated by the grip safety, pinned-in external extractor, Wolff springs throughout, Texas Armament match trigger, Hogue rubber (standard) or wood (new 2004) grips, McCormick hammer and thumb safety, Briley barrel bushing, two Wilson magazines, full-length heavy guide rod, high profile Wilson beavertail safety, adj. rear black blade, or Novak Lo-Mount Carry sights, 39 oz. Mfg. 2003-2011.

	100%	98%	95%	90%	80%	70%	60%	Last MSR
	$875	$675	$525	$425	$375	$335	$300	$1,039

Add $60 for rear adj. sight.

Add $270 or Doug Koenig Model w/two-tone finish and adj. rear sight.

* Model SW1911 Stainless – features stainless steel frame and slide, checkered wood or black synthetic grips, 39.4 oz.

MSR $1,079	100%	98%	95%	90%	80%	70%	60%
	$925	$725	$550	$425	$395	$350	$325

Add $120 for wood grips and adj. rear sight.
Add $93 for matte finish with black blade front sight (disc. 2006).
Add $72 for tactical lower frame rail w/wood grips (mfg. 2006-2010).
Add $301 for Crimson Trace laser grips (mfg. 2005-2010).

* Model SW1911 w/no firing pin block – similar to SW1911, except does not have firing pin block, Melonite finish. Mfg. 2009-2011.

	100%	98%	95%	90%	80%	70%	60%	Last MSR
	$925	$750	$525	$450	$400	$375	$350	$1,099

MODEL SW1911 PD (Sc) – similar to Model SW1911, except has 4 1/4 or 5 (new 2007) in. barrel with small Scandium alloy frame, 8 shot, black finish, and wood grips. Mfg. 2004-2011.

	100%	98%	95%	90%	80%	70%	60%	Last MSR
	$950	$725	$550	$475	$425	$375	$325	$1,109

Add $240 for Crimson Trace laser grips.
Add $120 for Gunsite model with gold bead front sight.
Add $30 for tactical lower rail.

MODEL SW1911 E SERIES – .45 ACP cal., 4 1/4 (disc. 2012) or 5 (new 2011) in. barrel, SA, features front and rear scalloped slide serrations, 7 or 8 shot, white dot sights, alloy or stainless steel (new 2011) frame, blue/black (alloy frame), GI Bead (stainless) or Melonite (stainless) finish, wood or Crimson Trace Laser grips, approx. 40 oz. New 2009.

MSR $979	100%	98%	95%	90%	80%	70%	60%
	$815	$665	$535	$450	$400	$350	$300

Add $170 for Crimson Trace Laser grips.
Add $220 for 4 1/4 in. barrel with alloy frame (disc. 2012).
Add $420 for tactical rail (5 in. barrel only, stainless steel, new 2011).

MSR	100%	98%	95%	90%	80%	70%	60%	Last MSR

SW1911 PRO SERIES – .45 ACP or 9mm Para. (new 2009) cal., SA, 5 in. barrel, 8 (.45 ACP) or 10 (9mm Para.) shot mag., 3-dot (9mm Para. cal. only), Novak fiber optic front and rear or Black Dovetail rear adj. sights, checkered wood grips, stainless steel frame and slide, satin stainless finish, Pro Series features include 300 LPI front strap checkering, hand polished barrel feed ramp, crisp 4 1/2 lb. trigger pull, full length guide rod, oversized external extractor, ambidextrous frame safety, precision crowned muzzle, 41 oz. New mid-2007.

MSR $1,459 $1,150 $925 $775 $675 $575 $475 $425

Add $120 for 9mm Para. cal. (new 2009).

Add $150 for adj. Black Dovetail rear sight (new late 2011).

* **SW1911 Pro Series Subcompact** – similar to SW1911 Pro Series, except has 3 in. barrel, 7 shot mag., and subcompact frame, 26 1/2 oz. New 2009.

MSR $1,229 $950 $795 $675 $550 $450 $400 $350

MODEL 3904 – 9mm Para. cal., DA/SA, aluminum alloy frame, 4 in. barrel with fixed bushing, 8 shot mag., Delrin one piece wraparound grips, exposed hammer, ambidextrous safety, beveled magazine well, extended squared-off trigger guard, adj. or fixed rear sight, 3-dot sighting system, 28 oz. Mfg. 1989-1991.

$475 $385 $350 $325 $300 $280 $265 $541

Add $25 for adj. rear sight.

MODEL 3906 STAINLESS – stainless steel variation of the Model 3904, 35 1/2 oz. Mfg. 1989-91.

$510 $435 $375 $315 $270 $230 $200 $604

Add $28 for adj. rear sight.

MODEL 3913 COMPACT STAINLESS – stainless steel variation of the Model 3914, 25 oz. Mfg. 1990-99.

$535 $440 $365 $305 $260 $220 $190 $662

* **Model 3913NL Compact Stainless** – similar to Model 3913 Ladysmith, except does not have Ladysmith on the slide. Disc. 1994.

$550 $475 $395 $350 $295 $250 $220 $622

* **Model 3913 LS Compact Stainless (Ladysmith)** – similar to Model 3913 Stainless, except is matte stainless with white Delrin grips and mag. does not have finger extension, includes case, 25 oz. Mfg. 1990-2006.

$710 $525 $400 $335 $290 $245 $215 $901

MODEL 3913TSW TACTICAL – 9mm Para. cal., DA/SA, compact frame, 3 1/2 in. barrel, 8 shot mag., Novak Lo-Mount 2-dot sights, stainless steel slide, aluminum alloy frame, matte stainless finish, straight black backstrap synthetic grips, 24.8 oz. Mfg. 1998-2006.

$690 $520 $400 $335 $290 $245 $215 $876

MODEL 3914 COMPACT – 9mm Para. cal., DA/SA, aluminum alloy frame, 3 1/2 in. barrel, hammerless, 8 shot finger extension mag., fixed sights only, ambidextrous safety, blue finish, straight backstrap grip, 25 oz. Mfg. 1990-1995.

$495 $425 $350 $325 $295 $280 $265 $562

This model was also available with a single side manual safety at no extra charge - disc. 1991 (Model 3914NL).

* **Model 3914 Compact LadySmith** – similar to Model 3914, except has Delrin grips, 25 oz. Mfg. 1990-91 only.

$485 $415 $365 $305 $260 $220 $190 $568

* **Model 3914 TSW** – similar to Model 3914, except slide is marked "9 Tactical", blue finish, 8 shot mag. 1,060 mfg. 1990 only.

$800 $650 $475 $395 $345 $280 $235

MODEL 3953 COMPACT STAINLESS – 9mm Para. cal., DAO, aluminum alloy frame with stainless steel slide, compact model with 3 1/2 in. barrel, 8 shot mag. Mfg. 1990-1999.

$535 $440 $365 $305 $260 $220 $190 $662

MODEL 3953TSW – similar to Model 3913TSW, except is DAO, 24.8 oz. Mfg. 1998-2002.

$615 $475 $380 $320 $275 $230 $200 $760

MODEL 3954 – similar to Model 3953, except has blue steel slide. Mfg. 1990-92.

$475 $395 $350 $325 $295 $280 $265 $528

MODEL 4003 STAINLESS – .40 S&W cal., DA/SA, 4 in. barrel, 11 shot mag., white dot fixed sights, ambidextrous safety, aluminum alloy frame with stainless steel slide, one piece Xenoy wraparound grips, straight gripstrap, 28 oz. Mfg. 1991-1993.

$575 $495 $395 $330 $285 $240 $215 $698

MSR	100%	98%	95%	90%	80%	70%	60%	Last MSR

* Model 4003TSW Stainless – similar to Model 4003 Stainless, but has aluminum alloy frame, 10 shot mag., stainless steel slide, S&W tactical features, including equipment rail and Novak Lo-Mount Carry sights, traditional double action only, satin stainless finish, 28 1/2 oz. Mfg. 2000-2004.

| | $700 | $600 | $500 | $450 | $400 | $360 | $330 | $940 |

MODEL 4004 – .40 S&W cal., similar to Model 4003, except has aluminum alloy frame with blue carbon steel slide. Mfg. 1991-92.

| | $540 | $460 | $375 | $325 | $295 | $280 | $265 | $643 |

MODEL 4006 STAINLESS – .40 S&W cal., 3 1/2 (Shorty Forty) or 4 in. barrel, DA/SA, 10 (C/B 1994) or 11* shot mag., satin stainless finish, exposed hammer, Delrin one piece wraparound grips, 3-dot sights, 38 1/2 oz. Mfg. 1990-1999.

| | $655 | $545 | $400 | $335 | $290 | $245 | $215 | $791 |

Add $31 for adj. rear sight.

Add $115 for fixed Tritium night sights (new 1992).

The bobbed hammer option on this model was disc. in 1991.

* Model 4006TSW Stainless – similar to Model 4006 Stainless, except has stainless steel frame and slide, S&W tactical features, including equipment rail, traditional double action only, 37.8 oz. Mfg. 2000-2004.

| | $700 | $600 | $500 | $450 | $400 | $360 | $330 | $963 |

Add $38 if w/o Novak Lo-Mount Carry (NLC) sights.

Add $133 for night sights (disc.).

MODEL 4013 COMPACT STAINLESS – .40 S&W cal., DA/SA, 3 1/2 in. barrel, 8 shot mag., fixed sights, ambidextrous safety, alloy frame. Mfg. 1991-1996.

| | $595 | $485 | $385 | $330 | $295 | $280 | $265 | $722 |

MODEL 4013TSW TACTICAL – .40 S&W cal., DA/SA, 3 1/2 in. barrel, 9 shot mag. with reversible mag. catch, aluminum alloy frame with stainless steel slide, satin stainless finish, black synthetic grips, fixed 3-dot Novak Lo-Mount Carry sights, ambidextrous safety, 26.8 oz. Mfg. 1997-2006.

| | $825 | $630 | $450 | $385 | $335 | $280 | $235 | $1,021 |

MODEL 4014 COMPACT – similar to Model 4013, except is steel with blue finish. Mfg. 1991-93.

| | $550 | $475 | $425 | $375 | $330 | $300 | $275 | $635 |

MODEL 4026 STAINLESS – .40 S&W cal., traditional double action with frame mounted decocking lever, 10 (C/B 1994) or 11* shot mag., fixed sights, curved backstrap, 36 oz. Mfg. 1991-93.

| | $625 | $525 | $400 | $335 | $290 | $245 | $215 | $731 |

MODEL 4040 PD – .40 S&W cal., compact frame using Scandium, 3 1/2 in. barrel, DA/SA, Hogue rubber grips, Novak Lo-Mount Carry 3-dot sights, matte black finish, 25.6 oz. Mfg. 2003-2005.

| | $625 | $525 | $400 | $335 | $290 | $245 | $215 | $840 |

MODEL 4043 STAINLESS – .40 S&W cal., DAO, aluminum alloy frame with stainless steel slide, 4 in. barrel, 10 (C/B 1994) or 11* shot mag., one piece Xenoy wraparound grips, straight backstrap, white-dot fixed sights, 30 oz. Mfg. 1991-1999.

| | $635 | $510 | $390 | $325 | $280 | $240 | $210 | $772 |

* Model 4043TSW Stainless – .40 S&W cal., DAO, similar to Model 4043 Stainless, but has S&W tactical features, including equipment rail, 28 1/2 oz. Mfg. 2000-2002.

| | $650 | $550 | $425 | $350 | $290 | $245 | $215 | $886 |

MODEL 4044 – .40 S&W cal., similar to Model 4043, except has carbon steel slide. Mfg. 1991-92.

| | $540 | $460 | $375 | $325 | $295 | $280 | $265 | $643 |

MODEL 4046 STAINLESS – similar to Model 4006 Stainless, except is DAO, 4 in. barrel only. Mfg. 1991-1999.

| | $655 | $540 | $400 | $335 | $290 | $245 | $215 | $791 |

Add $115 for Tritium night sights (new 1992).

* Model 4046TSW Stainless – DAO, similar to Model 4046 Stainless, but has S&W tactical features, including equipment rail, 37.8 oz. Mfg. 2000-2002.

| | $700 | $625 | $500 | $455 | $400 | $360 | $330 | $907 |

Add $133 for night sights.

MODEL 4053 COMPACT STAINLESS – .40 S&W cal., DAO variation of the Model 4013. Mfg. 1991-1997.

| | $625 | $525 | $400 | $335 | $290 | $245 | $215 | $734 |

MSR	100%	98%	95%	90%	80%	70%	60%	Last MSR

MODEL 4053TSW (TACTICAL) – .40 S&W cal., DAO, 3 1/2 in. barrel, 9 shot mag. with reversible mag. catch, alloy frame with stainless steel slide, satin stainless finish, black synthetic grips, fixed sights, ambidextrous safety, 26.8 oz. Mfg. 1997-2002.

	$730	$580	$425	$360	$315	$260	$225	*$886*

MODEL 4054 – .40 S&W cal., DAO variation of the Model 4014. Mfg. 1991-1992.

	$650	$550	$425	$350	$290	$245	$215	*$629*

MODEL 4056TSW (TACTICAL) – .40 S&W cal., DAO, 3 1/2 in. barrel, 9 shot mag. with reversible mag. catch, stainless steel frame and slide, satin stainless finish, black synthetic grips, fixed sights, ambidextrous safety, 37 1/2 oz. Mfg. 1997 only.

	$675	$575	$450	$350	$290	$245	$215	*$844*

MODEL 4505 – .45 ACP cal., carbon steel variation of the Model 4506, fixed or adj. rear sight. 1,200 mfg. 1991 only.

	$650	$550	$425	$350	$290	$245	$215	*$660*

Add $27 for adj. rear sight.

MODEL 4506 STAINLESS – .45 ACP cal., 5 in. barrel, DA/SA, 8 shot mag., combat trigger guard, exposed hammer, fixed or adj. rear sight, straight backstrap (curved is optional), Delrin one-piece grips, 40 1/2 oz. Mfg. 1990-1999.

	$680	$550	$410	$345	$300	$250	$220	*$822*

Add $33 for adj. rear sight.

Approx. 100 Model 4506s left the factory mismarked Model 645 on the frame. In NIB condition they are worth $700.

MODEL 4513TSW – .45 ACP cal., DAO, compact frame, 3 3/4 in. barrel, 7 shot mag., 3-dot Novak Lo-Mount Carry sights, stainless steel slide, aluminum alloy frame, satin stainless finish, 28.6 oz. Mfg. 1998-2004.

	$725	$625	$475	$395	$340	$285	$240	*$980*

MODEL 4516 COMPACT STAINLESS – .45 ACP cal., bobbed hammer, compact variation of the Model 4506, 3 3/4 in. barrel, DA/SA, 7 shot mag., ambidextrous safety, fixed rear sight only, 34 oz. Mfg. 1990-1997.

	$650	$525	$400	$335	$290	$245	$215	*$787*

Original model is marked 4516 while later mfg. changed slide legend to read 4516-1. Original mfg. is more collectible and slight premiums are being asked.

MODEL 4526 STAINLESS – similar to Model 4506 Stainless, except has frame mounted decocking lever. Mfg. 1990-91 only.

	$675	$550	$425	$350	$290	$245	$215	*$762*

MODEL 4536 STAINLESS – .45 ACP cal., similar to Model 4516 Compact, except has frame mounted decocking lever only. Mfg. 1990-91 only.

	$675	$550	$425	$350	$290	$245	$215	*$762*

MODEL 4546 STAINLESS – .45 ACP cal., similar to Model 4506 Stainless, except is double action only. Mfg. 1990-91 only.

	$675	$550	$425	$350	$290	$245	$215	*$735*

MODEL 4553TSW – .45 ACP cal., similar to Model 4513TSW, except is double action only. Mfg. 1998-2002.

	$755	$595	$450	$385	$335	$280	$235	*$924*

MODEL 4556 STAINLESS – .45 ACP cal., DAO, 3 3/4 in. barrel, 7 shot mag., fixed sights. Mfg. 1991 only.

	$675	$550	$425	$350	$290	$245	$215	*$735*

MODEL 4563TSW – .45 ACP cal., DA/SA, 4 1/4 in. barrel, 8 shot mag., aluminum alloy frame with stainless steel slide, satin stainless finish, includes S&W tactical features, including equipment rail and Novak 3-dot sights, synthetic black straight backstrap grips, 30.6 oz. Mfg. 2000-2004.

	$750	$625	$450	$390	$340	$280	$235	*$977*

MODEL 4566 STAINLESS – .45 ACP cal., DA/SA, ambidextrous safety, 4 1/4 in. barrel, 8 shot mag. Mfg. 1990-1999.

	$650	$550	$410	$345	$300	$250	$220	*$822*

* ***Model 4566TSW Stainless*** – similar to Model 4566, except has ambidextrous safety, 39.1 oz. Disc. 2004.

	$725	$600	$450	$390	$340	$280	$235	*$1,000*

MODEL 4567-NS STAINLESS – similar to Model 4566 Stainless, except has Tritium night sights, stainless steel frame and carbon steel slide. 2,500 mfg. in 1991 only.

	$650	$550	$425	$350	$290	$245	$215	*$735*

MSR	100%	98%	95%	90%	80%	70%	60%	Last MSR

MODEL 4576 STAINLESS – .45 ACP cal., features 4 1/4 in. barrel, DA/SA, frame mounted decocking lever, fixed sights. Mfg. 1990-1992.

| | $635 | $535 | $410 | $345 | $300 | $250 | $220 | *$762* |

MODEL 4583TSW – similar to Model 4563TSW, except is DAO, 30.6 oz. Mfg. 2000-2002.

| | $700 | $575 | $450 | $380 | $330 | $275 | $230 | *$921* |

MODEL 4586 STAINLESS – .45 ACP cal., full size 4 1/4 in. barrel, DAO, 8 shot mag. Mfg. 1990-1999.

| | $695 | $575 | $425 | $345 | $300 | $250 | $220 | *$822* |

* ***Model 4586TSW Stainless*** – similar to Model 4566TSW, except is DAO, 39.1 oz. Mfg. 2000-2002.

| | $700 | $600 | $445 | $380 | $330 | $275 | $230 | *$942* |

MODEL 5903 – 9mm Para. cal., DA/SA, 4 in. barrel, stainless steel slide and alloy frame, exposed hammer, 10 (C/B 1994) or 15* shot mag., adj. (disc. 1993) or fixed rear sight, ambidextrous safety. Mfg. 1990-1997.

| | $650 | $575 | $475 | $395 | $365 | $325 | $300 | *$701* |

Add $30 for adj. rear sight (disc).
Add 20% for Model 5903 SSV, only 1,500 mfg.

* ***Model 5903TSW*** – 9mm Para. cal., DA/SA, aluminum alloy frame with stainless slide, satin stainless finish, includes S&W tactical features, such as equipment rail and Novak Lo-Mount Carry sights, black synthetic grips with curved backstrap, 28.9 oz. Mfg. 2000-2004.

| | $725 | $580 | $430 | $385 | $330 | $275 | $250 | *$892* |

MODEL 5904 – 9mm Para. cal., similar to Model 5903, except has blue steel slide and blue alloy frame, 26 1/2 oz. Mfg. 1989-1998.

| | $535 | $445 | $360 | $330 | $300 | $280 | $265 | *$663* |

Add $30 for adj. rear sight (disc. 1993).

MODEL 5905 – 9mm Para. cal., similar to Model 5904, except has blue carbon steel frame and slide. Approx. 5,000 mfg. 1990-1991 only.

| | $650 | $575 | $500 | $440 | $375 | $335 | $300 | |

MODEL 5906 STAINLESS – 9mm Para. cal., stainless steel variation of the Model 5904, 37 1/2 oz. Mfg. 1989-1999.

| | $615 | $500 | $400 | $335 | $290 | $245 | $215 | *$751* |

Add $37 for adj. rear sight.
Add $115 for Tritium night sights.
Add 100% for Model 5906M (South American military model with melonite finish).

* ***Model 5906TSW Stainless*** – 9mm Para. cal., DA/SA, similar to Model 5906 Stainless, but has S&W tactical features, including equipment rail, 38.3 oz. Mfg. 2000-2004.

| | $650 | $575 | $475 | $350 | $300 | $265 | $235 | *$915* |

Add $44 if w/o Novak Lo Mount Carry sight.
Add $132 for night sights (disc.).

MODEL 5924 – 9mm Para. cal., blue steel version of the 5903, 4 in. barrel, features frame mounted decocking lever, 15 shot mag., 37 1/2 oz. Mfg. 1990-91 only.

| | $625 | $550 | $475 | $375 | $335 | $300 | $280 | *$635* |

MODEL 5926 STAINLESS – 9mm Para. cal., stainless variation of the Model 5924. Disc. 1992.

| | $600 | $525 | $425 | $350 | $295 | $250 | $210 | *$697* |

MODEL 5943 STAINLESS – 9mm Para. cal., DAO, 4 in. barrel, aluminum alloy frame with stainless steel slide, straight backstrap, 15 shot mag. Mfg. 1990-1991 only.

| | $550 | $465 | $390 | $325 | $280 | $235 | $205 | *$655* |

* ***Model 5943-SSV Stainless*** – 9mm Para. cal., similar to Model 5943 Stainless, except has 3 1/2 in. barrel, Tritium night sights. Mfg. 1990-91 only.

| | $625 | $550 | $475 | $395 | $330 | $285 | $240 | *$690* |

* ***Model 5943TSW Stainless*** – 9mm Para. cal., DAO, aluminum alloy frame with stainless steel slide, includes S&W tactical features, equipment rail, and Novak Lo-Mount Carry sights, 28.9 oz. Mfg. 2000-2002.

| | $650 | $575 | $450 | $375 | $325 | $280 | $265 | *$844* |

MODEL 5944 – 9mm Para. cal., similar to Model 5943 Stainless, except has blue finish slide and frame. Mfg. 1990-1991 only.

| | $625 | $550 | $475 | $400 | $350 | $300 | $280 | *$610* |

MSR	100%	98%	95%	90%	80%	70%	60%	Last MSR

MODEL 5946 STAINLESS – 9mm Para. cal., DAO, one piece Xenoy wraparound grips, all stainless steel variation of the Model 5943, 39 1/2 oz. Mfg. 1990-1999.

	$615	$500	$400	$335	$290	$245	$215	*$751*

* ***Model 5946TSW Stainless*** – 9mm Para. cal., DAO, includes S&W tactical features, equipment rail, and Novak Lo-Mount Carry sights, 38.3 oz. Mfg. 2000-2002.

	$725	$600	$450	$375	$315	$260	$225	*$863*

MODEL 6904 COMPACT – 9mm Para. cal., compact variation of the Model 5904, 3 1/2 in. barrel, DA/SA, 10 (C/B 1994) or 12* shot finger extension mag., fixed rear sight, 26 1/2 oz. Mfg. 1989-1997.

	$550	$475	$400	$350	$325	$300	$280	*$625*

MODEL 6906 COMPACT STAINLESS – 9mm Para. cal., stainless steel variation of the Model 6904, 26 1/2 oz. Mfg. 1989-1999.

	$585	$470	$380	$320	$275	$235	$200	*$720*

Add $116 for Tritium night sights (new 1992).

MODEL 6926 STAINLESS – 9mm Para. cal., 3 1/2 in. barrel, DA/SA, features frame mounted decocking lever, aluminum alloy frame with stainless slide, 12 shot mag. Mfg. 1990-1991 only.

	$650	$575	$450	$375	$315	$270	$230	*$663*

MODEL 6944 – 9mm Para. cal., DAO, 3 1/2 in. barrel, 12 shot mag., aluminum alloy frame with blue steel slide. Mfg. 1990-1991 only.

	$600	$525	$450	$375	$325	$300	$280	*$578*

MODEL 6946 STAINLESS – 9mm Para. cal., similar to Model 6944, except has stainless steel slide, semi-bobbed hammer, 26 1/2 oz. Mfg. 1990-1999.

	$675	$575	$475	$375	$315	$270	$230	*$720*

SIGMA MODEL SW9F SERIES – 9mm Para. cal., DAO, SFO, 4 1/2 in. barrel, fixed sights, polymer frame and steel slide, blue finish only, 10 (C/B 1994) or 17* shot mag., 26 oz. Mfg. 1994-1996.

	$475	$400	$350	$325	$295	$280	$265	*$593*

Add $104 for Tritium night sights.

* ***Sigma Model SW9C Series Compact*** – 9mm Para. cal., similar to Sigma Model SW9F, except has 4 in. barrel, 25 oz. Mfg. 1996-1998.

	$450	$355	$325	$295	$280	$265	$240	*$541*

* ***Sigma Model SW9M Series Compact*** – 9mm Para. cal., SFO, features 3 1/4 in. barrel, 7 shot mag., fixed channel rear sight, grips integral with frame, satin black finish, 18 oz. Mfg. 1996-1998.

	$300	$270	$240	$220	$195	$175	$160	*$366*

SIGMA MODEL SW9VE/GVE (SW9E/SW9P/SW9G/SW9V) – 9mm Para. cal., DAO, SFO, features 4 in. standard or ported (SW9P, mfg. 2001-2003) barrel, 10 or 16 (new late 2004) shot mag., 3-dot sighting system, grips integral with grey (disc. 2000), Nato Green (SW9G, disc. 2003) or black polymer frame, black (SW9E, mfg. 1999-2002) or satin stainless steel (SW9VE) slide, 24.7 oz. Mfg. 1997-2012.

	$320	$275	$230	$200	$175	$150	$140	*$379*

Add $8 for Allied Forces model w/Melonite slide (mfg. 2007-2009).
Add $380 for SW9VE/SW40VE Allied Forces model w/emergency kit, including space blankets, emergency food, first aid kit, crank radio/flashlight, multi-tool, and pocket survival pack, cased (mfg. 2007-2009).
Add $48 for SW9P or SW9G with night sights (disc. 2003).
Add $210 for Tritium night sights (disc. 2000).

The Enhanced Sigma Series Model SW9VE was introduced during 1999, after the SW9V was discontinued.

SIGMA MODEL SW40F SERIES – .40 S&W cal., DAO, SFO, 4 1/2 in. barrel, fixed sights, polymer frame, blue finish only, 10 (C/B 1994) or 15* shot mag., 26 oz. Mfg. 1994-1998.

	$450	$355	$325	$295	$280	$265	$240	*$541*

Add $104 for Tritium night sights (disc. 1997).

* ***Sigma Model SW40C Series Compact*** – .40 S&W cal., similar to Sigma Model SW40F, except has 4 in. barrel, 26 oz. Mfg. 1996-1998.

	$450	$355	$325	$295	$280	$265	$240	*$541*

MSR		100%	98%	95%	90%	80%	70%	60%	Last MSR

SIGMA MODEL SW40VE/SW40P/SW40G/SW40GVE (SW40E/SW40V) – .40 S&W cal., SFO, features 4 in. standard or ported (SW40P, mfg. 2001-2005) barrel, 10 or 14 (new mid-2004) shot mag., 3-dot sighting system, grips integral with grey (disc. 2000), Nato green (SW40G) or black polymer frame, black slide with Melonite finish (SW40E, mfg. 1999-2002) or satin stainless steel slide, 24.4 oz. Mfg. 1997-2012.

		$320	$275	$230	$200	$175	$150	$140	$379

Add $8 for Allied Forces model w/Melonite slide, (mfg. 2007-2009).
Add $210 for Tritium night sights (disc.).
Add $145 for Model SW40P or SW40G (includes night sights, disc. 2005).
Add $380 for SW9VE/SW40VE Allied Forces model w/emergency kit, including space blankets, emergency food, first aid kit, crank radio/flashlight, multi-tool, and pocket survival pack, cased (mfg. 2007-2009).

The Enhanced Sigma Series Model SW40VE was introduced during 1999, after the SW40V was discontinued.

MODEL SW99 – 9mm Para., .40 S&W, or .45 ACP (new 2003) cal., traditional DA, SFO, 9 (.45 ACP cal.) or 10 shot mag., similar to the Walther P99, black polymer frame with black stainless slide and barrel, 4, 4 1/8 (.40 S&W cal. only), or 4.25 (.45 ACP cal. only, new 2003) in. barrel, black finish, ambidextrous mag. release, frame equipment groove, interchangeable backstraps, decocking lever, cocking indicator, adj. 3-dot or night sights, 25.4 (9mm Para cal.) or 28 1/2 oz. Mfg. 2000-2004.

		$565	$485	$430	$380	$340	$300	$275	$667

Add $123 for night sights.
Add $41 for .45 ACP cal. (new 2003).

* **Model SW99 Compact** – similar to SW99, except is compact version, not available in .45 ACP cal., 3 1/2 in. barrel, 8 (.40 S&W cal.) or 10 (9mm Para cal.) shot mag. with finger extension, approx. 23 oz. Mfg. 2003-2004.

		$565	$485	$430	$380	$340	$300	$275	$667

SIGMA MODEL SW357 – .357 SIG cal., SFO, 4 in. barrel, 10 shot mag., black finish, stainless steel. Mfg. 1998 only.

		$525	$450	$375	$325	$250	$195	$165	

SIGMA MODEL SW380 – .380 ACP cal., DAO, SFO, 3 in. barrel, fixed sights, polymer frame and steel slide, striker firing system, blue finish only, 6 shot mag., shortened grip, 14 oz. Mfg. 1996-2000.

		$285	$245	$210	$190	$180	$170	$160	$358

MODEL SW990L – 9mm Para., .40 S&W, or .45 ACP cal., DAO, SFO, 9 (.45 ACP cal. only), 10 (all cals. except .45 ACP), 12 (.40 S&W cal.) or 16 (9mm Para.) shot mag., similar to the Walther P99, black polymer frame with black stainless Melonite slide and barrel, 4 (9mm Para. cal. only), 4 1/8 (.40 S&W cal. only), or 4.25 (.45 ACP cal. only) in. barrel, black finish, approx. 25 oz. Mfg. 2005-2006.

		$610	$515	$450	$400	$350	$300	$275	$729

Add $44 for .45 ACP cal.

* **Model SW990L Compact** – similar to SW990L, except is compact version with small polymer frame, not available in .45 ACP cal., 3 1/2 in. barrel, 8 (.40 S&W cal.) or 10 (9mm Para cal.) shot mag. with finger extension, approx. 23 oz. Mfg. 2005-2006.

		$610	$515	$450	$400	$350	$300	$275	$729

MODEL SW SD9 – 9mm Para. cal., DAO, SFO, w/o hammer, 4 in. barrel, 10 or 16 shot mag., stainless steel slide/barrel, black polymer frame with Picatinny rail, front and rear slide serrations, Tritium night front sight, two-dot fixed rear sight, black Melanite finish, 22.7 oz. Mfg. 2010-2011.

		$375	$325	$295	$275	$250	$225	$200	$459

Add $40 for home defense kit that includes NanoVault lockable case and S&W Micro90 compact pistol light (disc. 2011).

MODEL SW SD40 – .40 S&W cal., DAO, striker fire action, w/o hammer, 4 in. barrel, 10 or 14 shot mag., stainless steel slide/barrel, black polymer frame with Picatinny rail, front and rear slide serrations, Tritium night front sight, two-dot fixed rear sight, black Melanite finish, 22.7 oz. Mfg. 2010-2011.

		$375	$325	$295	$275	$250	$225	$200	$459

Add $40 for home defense kit that includes NanoVault lockable case and S&W Micro90 compact pistol light (disc. 2011).

MODEL M&P SERIES – 9mm Para., .40 S&W, .357 SIG (disc. 2010), .380 (new 2014), or .45 ACP (new 2007) cal., DAO, SFO, black Melonite finished stainless steel barrel and slide with twin scalloped slide serrations, black Zytel polymer frame reinforced with stainless steel, matte black or Dark Earth brown (new 2007) finish, 6 (new 2014), 8, 10, 12, 15, or 17 shot mag., ramp front sights, Novak Lo-Mount Carry rear sight, ambidextrous manual safety became an option during 2009, 6 1/2 lbs. trigger pull, 18 degree grip angle, Picatinny rail in front of trigger guard, three interchangeable grip sizes, 24 1/4-29 1/2 oz. Approx. 25 variations in each caliber. New 2006.

Add $50 for ambidextrous manual safety with lanyard loop on non-compact models.

M&P357 – .357 SIG cal., SFO, 4 1/4 in. barrel, 10 or 15 shot mag., similar to M&P9. Disc. 2010.

		$575	$475	$375	$335	$285	$260	$230	$727

MSR	100%	98%	95%	90%	80%	70%	60%	*Last MSR*

* M&P357 Compact – .357 SIG cal., 10 shot mag., 3 1/2 in. barrel, similar to M&P9 Compact, 22 oz. Mfg. 2007-2010.

	$575	$475	$375	$335	$285	$260	$230	*$727*

M&P9 – 9mm Para. cal., SFO, 10 or 17 shot mag., 4 1/4 in. barrel, full size polymer frame, white dot or steel ramp dovetail front sight, steel low profile or Novak Lo-Mount carry rear sight, stainless steel slide and barrel, black Melonite finish, with or w/o thumb safety, black grips with three interchangeable palmswell grip sizes or Crimson Trace Laser grips (new 2008), lower accessory rail, includes two magazines, 24 oz.

MSR $569	$425	$350	$315	$285	$260	$230	$200	

Add $120 for carry and range kit - includes Blade Tech Kydex holster, double magazine pouch, Maglula Uplula speed loader, ear plugs, and extra magazine.
Add $260 for Crimson Trace Laser grips (new 2008).
Add $150 for threaded barrel kit (disc. 2013).

* M&P9 JG – 9mm Para. cal., SFO, 17 shot mag., similar to M&P9, except has fiber optic front sight, Warren tactical rear sight, five interchangeable palmswell grip sizes (three black and two pink), breast cancer awareness ribbon engraved on slide, designed in collaboration with champion Julie Goloski-Golob. Disc. 2012.

	$465	$375	$325	$300	$280	$250	$215	*$619*

* M&P9L – 9mm Para. cal., SFO, 17 shot mag., 5 in. barrel, full size polymer frame, white dot or steel ramp dovetail front sight, steel low profile carry rear sight, stainless steel slide and barrel, black Melonite finish, three interchangeable palmswell grip sizes, includes two magazines, 25 oz. Disc. 2011.

	$575	$475	$395	$350	4325	4295	$250	*$758*

* M&P9 VTAC (Viking Tactics) – 9mm Para. cal., SFO, 17 shot mag., 4 1/4 in. barrel, full size polymer frame, VTAC Warrior front and rear sights, durable PVD coated stainless steel slide, Flat Dark Earth finish, 24 oz.

MSR $799	$640	$535	$425	$375	$325	$295	$250	

* M&P9 Compact – 9mm Para. cal., SFO, 12 shot mag., 3 1/2 in. barrel, steel ramp dovetail mount front sight, Novak Lo-Mount carry rear sight, compact Zytel polymer frame with stainless steel slide and barrel, black Melonite finish, with or w/o thumb safety, with or w/o three interchangeable palmswell or Crimson Trace Laser grips, 22 oz. New 2007.

MSR $569	$425	$350	$315	$285	$260	$230	$200	

Add $260 for Crimson Trace laser grips.
Add $150 if w/o thumb safety and interchangeable grips (disc. 2011).

M&P40 – .40 S&W cal., 10 or 15 shot mag., SA or DAO, SFO, 4 1/4 in. barrel, similar to Model M&P9, with or w/o thumb safety, 24 1/4 oz.

MSR $569	$425	$350	$315	$285	$260	$230	$200	

Add $120 for carry and range kit - includes Blade Tech Kydex holster, double magazine pouch, Maglula Uplula speed loader, ear plugs, and extra magazine.
Add $260 for Crimson Trace laser grips.

* M&P40 VTAC (Viking Tactics) – .40 S&W cal., SFO, 15 shot mag., 4 1/4 in. barrel, full size polymer frame, VTAC Warrior front and rear sights, durable PVD coated stainless steel slide, Flat Dark Earth finish, 24 oz.

MSR $799	$640	$535	$425	$375	$325	$295	$250	

* M&P40 Compact – 9mm Para. cal., SFO, 10 or 12 shot mag., 3 1/2 in. barrel, steel ramp dovetail mount front sight, Novak Lo-Mount carry rear sight, compact Zytel polymer frame with stainless steel slide and barrel, black Melonite finish, with or w/o thumb safety, with or w/o three interchangeable palmswell or Crimson Trace Laser grips, 22 oz. New 2007.

MSR $569	$425	$350	$315	$285	$260	$230	$200	

Add $240 for Crimson Trace laser grips.

M&P45 – .45 ACP cal., SFO, 10 shot mag., 4 (Mid-Size) or 4 1/2 in. barrel, full size black polymer frame, Melanite or Dark Earth Brown finish, otherwise similar to M&P9, 29.6 oz.

MSR $599	$450	$375	$325	$295	$260	$230	$200	

Add $90 for night sights (disc. 2012).
Add $20 for Dark Earth Brown finish or ambidextrous safety.
Add $230 for Crimson Trace laser grips (disc. 2012).

* M&P45 Compact – .45 ACP cal., SFO, 8 shot mag., 4 in. barrel, similar to M&P9 Compact, 27 oz. New 2007.

MSR $599	$450	$375	$325	$295	$260	$230	$200	

Add $20 for ambidextrous safety with either melonite or dark brown finish.

MSR	100%	98%	95%	90%	80%	70%	60%	Last MSR

M&P C.O.R.E. (COMPETITION OPTICS READY EQUIPMENT) – 9mm Para. or .40 S&W cal., SFO, 4 1/4 or 5 in. barrel, 10 or 17 shot mag., polymer frame, stainless steel slide, striker-fire action, ambidextrous controls, black Melonite finish, lower Picatinny rail, fixed two dot rear sight, white dot dovetail front sight, accepts six different popular styles of optics, also available in Pro Series configuration, 24 oz. New 2013.

MSR $729	$625	$550	$475	$425	$350	$275	$225	

MODEL M&P 9 PRO SERIES – 9mm Para. cal., N-frame, striker fire action, 5 in. barrel, black polymer frame, 17 shot, lower Picatinny rail, satin (disc.) or stainless steel, plastic grips, Lo-Mount Carry, night sights, Fiber optic Green Novak reduced glare sights (disc. 2013), or optics ready, 26 oz. New 2012.

MSR $699	$575	$475	$400	$350	$300	$265	$235	

Add $70 for optic ready variation (new 2013).

PISTOLS: SEMI-AUTO, RIMFIRE

MODEL M&P15-22P – .22 LR cal., 6 in. threaded carbon steel barrel with A1 style compensator, 25 shot detachable mag., blowback action similar to M&P 15-22 rifle, quad rail handguard, adj. sights on top Picatinny rail, polymer lower receiver, matte black finish, black pistol grip, 51 oz. Mfg. mid-2010-2011.

	$425	$385	$360	$330	$295	$275	$250	$519

Product Code: 813000.

MODEL M&P 22 – .22 LR cal., SFO, 4.1 in. threaded barrel, single action hammerless, 10 or 12 shot mag., plastic grips, fixed backstrap, aluminum alloy slide, adj. rear sight, black blade front sight, ambidextrous safety, blue/black finish, ambidextrous manual safety and slide stop, reversible mag release, lower Picatinny rail, approx. 24 oz. New 2011.

MSR $419	$350	$315	$285	$260	$240	$220	$195	

Revolvers: Performance Center Variations

MODEL PC-13 – .357 Mag. cal., DA, 6 shot, 3 in. Magna ported barrel, fixed rear w/ramp front sight, Eagle Secret Service boot or Uncle Mike's grips on a K-frame, matte blue finish with beveled cylinder latch, trigger, and charge holes, shrouded extractor rod, trigger has an overtravel stop, 400 mfg., distributed by Lew Horton during 1995.

Last MSR was $760.

Product Codes: 170059 (eagle grips) or 170063 (Uncle Mike's grips).

MODEL 19 PERFORMANCE CENTER K COMP – .38 Spl./.357 Mag. cal., DA, blue matte finish, Target K-frame w/round butt, 6 shot fluted cylinder with counterbores, 3 in. full lug ported barrel, blue matte finish, smooth combat trigger, set back tritium night front sight on post, black blade adjustable rear sight, contoured thumbpiece, rubber combat grips, 36 oz. Mfg. 1994 and 2000.

Last MSR was $800.

Product Codes: 170025 (1994 mfg.) and 170163 (2000 mfg.).

MODEL 27-7 – .357 Mag. cal., 8 shot, 100 with 4 in. barrel with black ramp front sight, 100 with 6 1/2 in. barrel with black Patridge front sight, Magna combat grips, 42-45 oz. Distributed by Bangers.

Last MSR was N/A.

Product Codes: 170166 (4 in.) or 170167 (6 1/2 in.).

MODEL 66 F COMP (1993) – .357 Mag. cal., 3 in. full lug barrel w/compensator, dovetailed tritium front night sight, tuned action, round butt w/rubber grips, counterbored cylinder, contoured cylinder latch, "LHF" serial number prefix, approx. 300 mfg. Distributed by Lew Horton, 1993.

Last MSR was N/A.

Product Code: 170024.

MODEL 66 THE SUPER K – .357 Mag. cal., 3 in. specially contoured barrel with 2 port magna porting, white synthetic grip with S&W medallions, Performance Center Tuned action and overtravel trigger stop. Distributed by Lew Horton, 1997.

Last MSR was N/A.

Product Code: 170090.

MODEL 66 F-COMP – .357 Mag. cal., 3 in. full lug ported barrel with drift adj. dovetailed ramp front sight and micrometer click rear sight, 6 shot cylinder with chamfered charge holes, front sight set behind barrel port, glass bead finish, shipped with walnut combat grips and an additional Hogue Bantam monogrip.

Last MSR was $798.

Product Code: 170024FC.

MODEL 67 F-COMP – .38 Spl. cal., 6 shot, SA/DA, 3 in. full lug Power Port barrel, adj. white outline rear and tritium front sights, stainless steel frame, matte black finish, synthetic finger groove grips, 35 oz. Mfg. mid-2007-2009.

	$1,025	$875	$750	$625	$525	$450	$400	$1,311

Product Code: 170324.

MSR	100%	98%	95%	90%	80%	70%	60%	Last MSR

MODEL 325 THUNDER RANCH – .45 ACP cal., SA/DA, 6 shot, 4 in. barrel, interchangeable front sight, adj. rear sight, Scandium alloy N-frame with stainless steel cylinder, matte black finish, rubber finger groove grips, 31 oz. New 2008.

| MSR $1,329 | $1,080 | $895 | $750 | $625 | $525 | $425 | $350 | |

Product code: 170316.

MODEL 327 Sc – .357 Mag. cal., 8 shot, 2 in. barrel with titanium shroud, black finish with natural grey titanium cylinder, Scandium alloy N-frame, teardrop color case hammer and trigger with overtravel stop, Ahrends cocobolo round butt grips with finger grooves, small lanyard pin, PC logo under thumbpiece, fixed or adj. sights, shipped with black PC marked gun rug made by Allen with internal pouch, 2 full moon clips, special ser. no. range. New 2006.

| MSR $1,309 | $1,075 | $885 | $750 | $625 | $525 | $425 | $350 | |

Add $16 for 5 in. barrel with adj. sights (disc.).

Product Codes: 170245FC (black) or 170251FC (clear, disc.).

MODEL 327 Sc JERRY MICULEK – similar to Model 327 Sc, 5 in. barrel, 8 shot, unfluted titanium cylinder with adj. rear sights, orange Hi-Viz fiber optic front sight, unique new two-piece barrel design, Jerry Miculek signature grip and extra Hogue rubber grips. Mfg. 2005.

Last MSR was $1,149.

MODEL 327 TRR8 – .357 Mag. cal., 8 shot, 5 in. barrel, large frame, interchangeable front sight, adj. V-notch rear sight, Scandium alloy with titanium alloy cylinder, synthetic finger groove grips, black finish, equipment rail, 35.3 oz. New mid-2007.

| MSR $1,329 | $1,085 | $895 | $750 | $625 | $525 | $425 | $350 | |

Product code: 170269.

MODEL 327 M&P R8 – .357 Mag. or .38 Spl. + P cal., 8 shot, SA/DA, 5 in. two-piece barrel, large frame, Scandium alloy frame, stainless steel cylinder, interchangeable dot front sight, adj. V-notch rear sight, accessory rail, 36.3 oz. New mid-2007.

| MSR $1,289 | $1,050 | $875 | $750 | $625 | $525 | $425 | $350 | |

Product code: 170292.

MODEL 329-1 AIRLITE PD – .44 Mag. cal. DA, serrated and ported 3 in. barrel, round butt Scandium alloy N-frame, 6 shot titanium cylinder, painted red ramp front sight, adj. black blade front sight, Ahrends cocobolo finger groove wood grips. Mfg. 2003.

Last MSR was $1,100.

Product Codes: 170233 (clear) or 170232FC (matte black).

All Model 329-1 Airlites were recalled by S&W during July, 2004. DO NOT FIRE THIS GUN!

MODEL 586 L COMP – .357 Mag. cal., 3 in. full lug ported barrel with tritium dot front and micrometer click rear sight, Altamont Rosewood grips, 7 shot cylinder rebated for moon clips, black or blue finish, shipped with locking aluminum case & Master Gun Lock, first blue finish revolver in 7 shot offered by S&W, 37 1/2 oz. Distributed by Camfour, 2000 and 2004.

Last MSR was N/A.

Product Code: 170170 (2000 mfg.) or 170248FC (2004 mfg.).

MODEL 625-5 JERRY MICULEK DESIGN – .45 ACP cal., 5 1/4 in. barrel, Patridge front w/gold bead and adj. black blade rear sight, reduced cylinder freebore, 6 shot fluted cylinder w/chamfered charge holes, deep cut broached rifling, hand honed bore, satin stainless finish, "Jerry Miculek" Hogue Laminate combat grips, lockable aluminum case, 42 oz. Distributed by Camfour, 2001.

Last MSR was $899.

Product Code: 170176.

MODEL 625-6 "V COMP" – .45 ACP cal., 4 in. slabside barrel with a removable compensator or a replacement muzzle to protect the crown, 6 shot non-fluted cylinder has a ball-detent lockup in the yoke, Millett dovetailed red ramp front and micrometer click rear sight, Hogue Combat wood grips, semi-target hammer, smooth combat trigger w/overtravel stop, shipped w/double combo lock aluminum carry case, 43 oz. Distributed by RSR, 1999.

Last MSR was $925.

Product Code: 170136.

MODEL 627-2 STAINLESS – .357 Mag./.38 Spl. cal., DA, stainless steel version of the Model 27, 8 shot cylinder, 5 in. tapered barrel, interchangeable front sights, drilled & tapped for scope mount, chamfered charge holes, flash chrome teardrop hammer, Hogue hardwood combat grips, new thumbpiece, engraved ".357 Magnum 8 Times" on barrel, floating firing pin, RJM serial prefix, 44 oz. Distributed by Lew Horton, 1997-1998.

Last MSR was $1,000.

Product Code: 170089.

MSR	100%	98%	95%	90%	80%	70%	60%	*Last MSR*

MODEL 627-3 "V-COMP JERRY MICULEK SPECIAL" – 8 shot cylinder, 5 in. barrel, removable compensator, removable/interchangeable cap to protect the rifling, smooth combat trigger w/overtravel stop pin, TH, drift adj. red ramp front sight, micrometer click rear sight. "Jerry Miculek" design Hogue wooden grips, locking aluminum case, 47 oz. Distributed by RSR in 2000.

Last MSR was N/A.

Product Code: 170142.

On July 24th 1999, Jerry Miculek set a world record for firing a S&W 8 shot revolver. The results were: 8 Shots on 1 target in 1.00 seconds and 8 Shots on 2 targets in 1.06 seconds. Both records were set using a Model 627 from the Performance Center.

MODEL 627-PC – .357 Mag. cal., 8 shot, 2 5/8 in. barrel, Millett red ramp drift adj. front sight with micrometer click white outline rear sight, Eagle wood boot grips, flash chromed custom teardrop hammer, smooth combat trigger, full length extractor, stainless steel with glass bead finish, shipped with aluminum double lock carrying case, 37.6 oz. Approx. 302 mfg. 1999-2000.

Last MSR was $1,025.

Product Code: 170133.

MODEL 627-4 – .38 Super cal., 8 shot, black non-fluted cylinder, 5 1/2 in. barrel, angled cut removable compensator and cap, red/white/blue Jerry Miculek designed grip, Patridge front sight with adj. black outline rear sight, chrome teardrop hammer and chrome trigger with overtravel stop, stainless steel, glass bead finish, drilled and tapped. Mfg. for Banger's 2002.

Last MSR was N/A.

Product Code: 170205.

MODEL 627-5 (CURRENT MFG.) – .357 Mag. cal., large frame, 2 5/8 (new 2010) or 5 in. tapered and contoured barrel with fluted or unfluted cylinder, 8 shot, floating firing pin, interchangeable front sight with black blade rear sight, wood grips, trigger overtravel stop, internal lock system, new frame design, shipped with black PC marked gun rug, 37.6 or 44 oz.

MSR $1,079	$915	$710	$550	$450	$400	$350	$300

Add $210 for 5 in. barrel.

Product Codes: 170210 and 170133.

MODEL 627 V-COMP – .357 Mag. cal., large frame, 8 shot, 5 in. barrel, SA/DA, adj. front and rear sights, stainless steel/alloy frame with two-tone matte or satin stainless (disc. 2011) finish, synthetic rubber or wood laminate (disc. 2011) finger groove grips, chrome tear drop hammer, 47 oz. New 2008.

MSR $1,559	$1,250	$1,100	$975	$850	$725	$600	$525

Product code: 170296.

MODEL 629-4 COMP & CAP – .44 Mag. cal., 6 1/2 in. barrel, removable muzzle brake with replaceable end cap, rosewood grips. Distributed by Lew Horton, 1998.

Last MSR was N/A.

Product code: 170124.

MODEL 629-5 V-COMP – .44 Mag. cal., large frame, 4 in. slabside barrel with removable compensator, muzzle cap, non-fluted cylinder, ball-detent lockup in the yoke, flash chromed semi-target hammer, smooth combat trigger w/overtravel stop, dovetail red ramp front sight, micrometer click rear sight, Hogue wood combat grips w/S&W Monogram, aluminum carry case, 43 oz. Distributed by RSR in 1999, reintroduced in 2009.

MSR $1,559	$1,250	$1,100	$975	$850	$725	$600	$525

Product code: 170137.

MODEL 629-5 DEFENSIVE REVOLVER – .44 Mag. cal., 2 5/8 in. barrel, ball detent lockup system in the yoke, 6 shot non-fluted cylinder, flash chromed teardrop hammer and smooth combat trigger, Millett dovetailed red ramp front sight, micrometer click rear sight, Hogue wood combat grips, glass bead stainless steel finish, aluminum carry case with the Performance Center logo, 39.6 oz. Distributed by Lew Horton, 1999-2000.

Last MSR was $1,026.

Product code: 170135.

MODEL 632-1 – .327 Mag. Federal cal., 3 in. ported barrel, ramp front sight with adjustable rear sight, black overall finish with Uncle Mike's combat grips, stainless steel frame and cylinder and steel internal parts. Mfg. 2009.

Last MSR was N/A.

Product code: 170329.

This model was the first production handgun in this caliber made by S&W.

MSR	100%	98%	95%	90%	80%	70%	60%	*Last MSR*

MODEL 646 – .40 S&W cal., 4 in. ribbed slabside barrel, SA/DA, 6 shot fluted titanium cylinder, drift adj. Patridge front sight, micrometer adj. rear sight, drilled and tapped for scope mount, smooth combat trigger, round butt, L-target frame, "Performance Center" on the left side and "40 S&W" on the right side of barrel, frosted glass bead stainless finish, Altamont wood combat grips, 2 sets of half moon clips and extraction tool, ser. no. prefix "RDA", 36 oz. Mfg. 2000.

Last MSR was $845.

Product code: 170165.

MODEL 657 DEFENSIVE REVOLVER – .41 Mag. cal., 2 5/8 in. barrel, 6 shot non-fluted cylinder, ball detent lockup, full length extractor, round butt, N-frame, adj. Millett red ramp front sight, micrometer adj. white outline rear sight, flash chromed teardrop hammer, chromed trigger with travel overstop, Hogue combat grips, glass bead stainless steel finish, aluminum carry case, 39.6 oz. Distributed by Lew Horton, 1999.

Last MSR was $1,001.

Product code: 170134.

MODEL 681-4 LEW HORTON SPECIAL – .357 Mag. cal., 3 in. Quadra-port barrel, 7 shot chamfered cylinder, trigger overtravel stop, fixed sight, ser. no. prefix "LHB", 300 mfg. Distributed by Lew Horton, 1996.

Last MSR was $700.

Product code: 170080.

MODEL 681-5 SPECIAL FOR CAMFOUR – .357 Mag. cal., 3 or 4 in. full lug barrel, 7 shot fluted cylinder, adj. black ramp front sight, Quad Porting, glass bead stainless steel finish, laminate checkered wood and Hogue Bantam Monogrip, 7 shot moon clips, chamfered cylinder charge holes, Performance Center case. Distributed by Camfour, 2001.

Last MSR was N/A.

Product codes: 170172 (4 in.) or 170178 (3 in.).

MODEL 686 MAG COMP – .357 Mag. cal., 3 in. barrel, integral compensator, adj. front red ramp sight, white outline rear sight, radiused full lug barrel, radiused hammer, radiused combat trigger w/overtravel stop, Uncle Mike's grips, Performance Center logo, contoured thumbpiece, full-length extractor rod, 350 mfg. Distributed by Lew Horton, 1992.

Last MSR was $1,000.

Product code: 170010.

MODEL 686 CARRY COMP 4 IN. – .357 Mag. cal., 4 in. barrel, integral compensator, dovetailed front sight w/ interchangeable post or red ramp, white outline rear sight, Uncle Mike's grips. Distributed by Lew Horton.

Last MSR was $1,000.

Product code: 170016.

MODEL 686 CARRY COMP 6 IN. – .357 Mag. cal., 6 in. barrel, integral port, replaceable front sight, Hogue grips, semi-target hammer, smooth combat trigger, full underlug contour. Mfg. 1994.

Last MSR was $1,099.

Product code: 170009.

MODEL 686 PLUS – .357 Mag. cal., 6 in. tapered barrel, 7 shot fluted cylinder, machined for full moon clips w/ chamfered charge holes, L-frame drilled and tapped for scope mount, round butt, Altamont wood grips, flash chromed semi-target hammer and smooth combat trigger, gold bead Patridge front sight, micrometer adj. white outline rear sight, satin stainless steel finish, 44 oz. Distributed by Lew Horton, 1998.

Last MSR was $929.

Product code: 170103.

MODEL 686-6 LIGHT RAIL – 5 in. barrel with small rail under the full lug for accessories, 6 shot cylinder, green Hi-Viz front sight, white outline rear sight, synthetic rubber grip, internal lock. Mfg. 2007.

Product code: 170322.

Rifles: Performance Center Variations

M&P RIFLE – 5.56 NATO cal., GIO, 10 shot mag., 20 in. stainless steel barrel, Hogue synthetic stock with pistol grip, free-floating anodized forend, two-stage match trigger, billet aluminum receiver with Picatinny rail, no sights, hard coat black or camo anodized finish, includes rifle case, 8 lbs. 2 oz. New 2008.

MSR $1,549	$1,300	$1,075	$925	$825	$725	$625	$525

Add $40 for camo finish.

Product codes: 178016 (black) or 178015 (camo).

MSR	100%	98%	95%	90%	80%	70%	60%	Last MSR

M&P 15-22 PC TB – .22 LR cal., GIO, 18 in. fluted barrel, 10 shot detachable mag., fixed (compliant) or 6-position VLTOR adj. buttstock, polymer receiver with modular rail forend, adj. A2 post front sight and adj. dual aperture rear sight, black finish, 5.6 lbs. New 2011.

	MSR $789	$665	$580	$500	$450	$425	$400	$395

Product Codes: 170335 or 170337 (compliant).

M&P 15PC LIMITED EDITION – 5.56 NATO cal., GIO, 20 in. barrel, 10 shot mag., Wylde Chamber, skeletonized full length buttstock, integral Picatinny style rail system, black matte finish, anodized streamlined free floating forend, black rubber pistol grip, swivel stud for sling or bipod attachment, PC marked soft carry case, master trigger lock and manual, marked "M&P 15PC" laser engraved on the right side, no forward assist on the upper. Mfg. 2006.

	$1,675	$1,425	$1,150	$925	$825	$725	$625	*$1,999*

Product Code: 170293.

Pistols: Semi-Auto, Performance Center Variations

MODEL 41 OPTIC READY – .22 LR cal., Model 41 action, 5 1/2 in. barrel, SA, features full length Picatinny rail on top of barrel, removable front and rear sights, checkered wood grips with thumbrest, 10 shot mag., blue finish, 41 oz. New 2013.

	MSR $1,619	$1,350	$1,100	$950	$850	$750	$650	$550

Product code: 178031.

MODEL 945 SPECIAL PERFORMANCE CENTER .45 MATCH PISTOL – .45 ACP cal., 5 in. barrel, SA, titanium coated spherical barrel bushing, 8 round mag., Performance Center markings, post front sight, adj. Bo-Mar rear sight, checkered two-piece laminated wood grips, bead blast stainless steel finish, ambidextrous frame mounted thumb safety, grip safety as part of the short beavertail, Master trigger lock, "Performance Center" marked foam-filled aluminum case starting in 1999, ser. nos. LEW0001-LEW1368, 43.5 oz. (1998) 42 oz. (1999 and later mfg.) Mfg. 1998-2000.

* **Model 945 Special Performance Center .45 Match Pistol 170104** – 5 in. barrel, stainless steel, 8 shot, 43.5 oz. Mfg. 1998.

Last MSR was $1,618.

* **Model 945 Special Performance Center .45 Match Pistol 170147** – 5 in. barrel, two-tone or blue finish, lightened trigger, grip safety, Bo-Mar rear sight, post front sight, stainless steel, ambidextrous frame mounted safety, 42 oz. Distributed by RSR. Mfg. 1998-2000.

Last MSR was N/A.

* **Model 945 Special Performance Center .45 Match Pistol 170152** – 4 in. barrel, black finish, 8 shot mag., post front and Novak 2 Dot Lo- Mount Carry rear sight, frame mounted safety, titanium coated spherical bushing, 20 LPI checkering front and back strap, extended magazine catch, checkered two-piece wood grips, stainless steel, grip safety, S/N prefix "PCZ", 36 oz. Distributed by Camfour, 2000.

Last MSR was N/A.

* **Model 945 Special Performance Center .45 Match Pistol 170153** – 4 in. barrel, post front and Novak 2 Dot Lo-Mount carry rear sight, grip safety, checkered two piece wood grips, lightened trigger, bead blast stainless steel finish, frame mounted safety, S/N prefix "PCZ", 36 oz. Distributed by RSR, 2000.

Last MSR was N/A.

* **Model 945 Special Performance Center .45 Match Pistol 170169** – 3 3/4 in. barrel, white dot dovetail front and Novak 2 Dot Lo-Mount Carry rear sight, grip and single side frame mounted safety, 7 round mag., checkered laminate wood grips, lightened trigger, black finish alloy frame, stainless steel slide, S/N Prefix "CMF", 28 oz. Distributed by Camfour, 2000.

Last MSR was N/A.

* **Model 945 Special Performance Center .45 Match Pistol 170177** – 3 1/4 in. barrel, white dot dovetail front and Novak 2 Dot Lo-Mount Carry rear sight, beavertail grip and single-side frame mounted safety, 6 round mag., checkered Hogue laminated wood grips, alloy frame with clear glass bead stainless steel slide, Performance Center carry case, 2 mags., 24.5 oz. Distributed by Camfour, 2001.

Last MSR was N/A.

* **Model 945 Special Performance Center Match Pistol 170180** – .40 S&W cal., 3 3/4 in. barrel, white dot dovetail front and Novak 2 Dot Lo-Mount Carry rear sight, beavertail grip and single-side frame mounted safety, 7 round mag., checkered Hogue laminated wood grips, alloy frame w/glass bead finish stainless steel slide, titanium coated barrel bushing, Performance Center carry case, 2 mags., 25.7 oz. 158 mfg. and distributed by Sports South in 2001.

Last MSR was N/A.

MSR	100%	98%	95%	90%	80%	70%	60%	Last MSR

* *Model 945 Special Performance Center .45 Match Pistol 170184* – 3 1/4 in. glass bead black barrel, white dovetail front and Novak 2 Dot Lo-Mount Carry rear sight, grip and single side frame mounted safety, 6 round mag., checkered Hogue laminated wood grips, alloy frame with stainless steel slide, lightened trigger, S/N prefix "PCZ", 24 oz. Distributed by RSR, 2001.

Last MSR was N/A.

MODEL 945-1 – .45 ACP cal., 8 shot mag., SA, 5 in. barrel, features scalloped slide serrations, black (disc.) or two-tone finish, checkered front and rear gripstrap, checkered wood panel grips, stainless steel, adj. rear sight, target trigger and bobbed hammer, 40 1/2 oz., released during 2003, reintroduced 2005-2010.

	$1,925	$1,650	$1,425	$1,225	$1,000	$900	$800	$2,410

Product codes: 170173 (stainless) and 170300 (two-tone).

MODEL 1911 – .45 ACP cal., large frame, 4 1/4 or 5 in. barrel, SA, choice of satin stainless steel frame and slide (5 in. bbl.), or blue scandium alloy frame/stainless steel slide with round butt (4 1/4 in. bbl.), 8 shot mag., two-tone G10 brown (4 1/4 in. bbl.) or blue (5 in. bbl.) custom wood grips, 6 diagonally cut ported slide cuts, skeletonized trigger, bobbed hammer, adj. rear sight, 29.6 oz (4 1/4) or 40 1/2 (5 in.). New 2013.

MSR $1,589	$1,325	$1,075	$950	$850	$750	$650	$550	

Product codes: 170343 (5 in. bbl.) or 170344 (4 1/4 in. bbl.)

MODEL 1911 (2004-2012) – .38 Super (mfg. 2005-2010) or .45 ACP cal., 5 in. barrel, SA, black finish, 8 or 10 (.38 Super cal.) shot mag., dovetailed black front sight with adj. micro-click black rear sight, checkered laminate wood grips, stainless steel or stainless Melonite (new 2005) frame/barrel, glass bead finish, full length guide rod, ambidextrous frame mounted safety, 30 LPI front strap checkering, hand lapped and polished fitted barrel, frame and slide, unique front and rear serrations, includes two magazines, 41 oz., released during 2004.

	$1,795	$1,575	$1,325	$1,150	$1,000	$875	$750	$2,209

Add $160 Melonite finish.

Product codes: 170243, 170261 and 170257.

* *Model 1911 (2005)* – .45 ACP cal., two additional variations of this model were produced during 2005, stainless steel with glass bead satin finish, 8 shot mag., 5 in. barrel, SA, Doug Koenig speed hammer, lightweight match trigger with over travel stop, black dovetail front sight with black micro adj. rear sight, laminate fully checkered grips, oversized external extractor, full length guide rod and oversized mag. well extension, custom front and rear slide serrations, ambidextrous frame mounted safety, shipped with two 8 shot mags, other variation had high polished flats on the slide and barrel.

Last MSR was N/A.

Product codes: 170258 and 170261.

* *Model 1911 .38 Super cal. (2005)* – .38 Super cal., another variation of the original 2004 model, part of Doug Koenig Professional Series, 5 in. barrel, SA, satin stainless steel finish, 10 shot mag., Doug Koenig speed hammer, competition match trigger with overtravel stop, black dovetail front sight, Doug Koenig logo on smooth black Micarta grips, oversized external extractor, full length guide rod, competition mag. well, 30 LPI front strap checkering. Mfg. 2005.

Last MSR was N/A.

Product code: 170257.

THE SHORTY 9 & SHORTY 9 MKIII – 9mm cal., match grade 3 /12 in. barrel w/hand fitted titanium bushing, DA/SA, alloy frame, blue steel slide, over-size slide rails, ambidextrous safety, Performance Center action tuning job, adj. Novak Lo-Mount sights, wraparound plastic grips, the MKIII included Zippo lighter with Performance Center logo. 611 were mfg. and distributed by Lew Horton with ser. nos. PCV0001 - PCV0611 in 1993.

Last MSR was $1,024.

Product code: 170030.

9 RECON – 9mm cal., 3 1/2 in. match grade barrel, DA/SA, titanium coated spherical barrel bushing, double stack 12 + 1 mag., white dot front and Novak 2 Dot Lo-Mount rear sight, traditional DA trigger, hand lapped oversize rails, ambidextrous spring loaded decocker, 20 LPI checkering on the front strap, Hogue wraparound rubber grips, compact frame, two-tone finish with a clear anodized alloy frame and a carbon steel blue slide, aluminum carry case, 27.2 oz. Distributed by RSR, 1999-2000.

Last MSR was N/A.

Product code: 170140.

The 9mm Recon is similar to the Shorty 40 except the 9 Recon was a RSR exclusive while the Shorty 8 was a Lew Horton exclusive. The Recon does have forward slide serrations, ambidextrous safety, Hogue grips and the slide is marked RECON.

MSR	100%	98%	95%	90%	80%	70%	60%	Last MSR

S&W 4006 SHORTY FORTY – .40 S&W cal., 3 1/2 in. barrel, DA/SA, spherical bushing, bobbed hammer, Novak Lo-Mount carry sights, 9-round single stack magazine, alloy frame, grips and frame may be stamped with Performance Center logo, beveled trigger, adj. front dovetail sight, oversize slide rails, 500 mfg., 27 oz. Distributed by Lew Horton, 1992, 1993, and 1995.

Last MSR was $1,500.

A total of 1,583 guns were produced with serial numbers PCS0001 to PCS1583, The initial order was for 500 guns when first released, however they sold so well that the run was extended of the first generation pistols. There were some minor changes within the first group, to the blued hammer and trigger on the later guns. There are subtle differences between the first and second production runs (e.g.: grip tang extended, horizontal checkering added to the front strap, color variations on some parts) product code 170060. The 3rd generation pistols were the ones with the higher production numbers some of which were marked "MK III". These were release in blue, product Code 170061 and stainless steel, Product code 170076. The fourth variation was Model 4006 Shorty Forty PC Y2000 was made for Camfour Dist. product #170164 in blue finish.

* S&W 4006 Shorty Forty Tactical – .40 S&W cal., full size companion to Shorty Forty, 5 in. barrel. Distributed by Lew Horton & RSR, limited production 1993-1997.

Last MSR was $1,500.

Product code: 170020 (Lew Horton) and 170091 (RSR).

* S&W 4006 Shorty Forty Compensated – .40 S&W cal., compensator mounted on 5 1/4 in. ported Bar-Sto barrel. 500 mfg. and distributed by Lew Horton.

Last MSR was $1,700.

Product code: 104401.

* S&W 4006 Shorty Forty MK III – third variation S/N prefix "PCW". Mfg. 1995.

Last MSR was $949.

Product code: 170011.

* S&W 4006 Shorty Forty MKIII 1997 – ambidextrous safety, low mount adj. sights, hand fitted titanium barrel bushing, precision checkered front strap, hand honed double action S/N prefix "KPC". Distributed by Lew Horton.

Last MSR was $1,025.

Product code: 170061.

* S&W 4006 Shorty Forty .40 S&W Tactical – .40 S&W cal., 5 in. match grade barrel, fixed tritium night front and Novak 2-dot rear sight, stainless steel frame w/carbon steel slide materials, tactical black matte slide w/satin stainless frame finish, 10 round mag., box cut frame and slide rails for 100% contact, balanced slide, ambidextrous decocker, 41.6 oz. Distributed by RSR, 1997.

Last MSR was $1,146.

Product code: 170091.

* S&W 4006 Shorty Forty TSW Stocking Dealer – .40 S&W cal., 4 1/4 in. barrel. Mfg. August, 1994.

Last MSR was N/A.

Product code: 170054.

MODEL 4006 SHORTY FORTY Y2000 – .40 S&W cal., 3 1/2 in. barrel, DA/SA, white dovetail front sight, Novak Lo-Mount Carry 2 Dot rear sight, aluminum frame with stainless slide, 9 round mag., two-tone black finish, Performance Center aluminum case. Distributed by Camfour 2000.

Last MSR was N/A.

Product code: 170164.

PERFORMANCE CENTER 40 RECON – .40 S&W cal., 4 1/4 in. match grade barrel w/compensator, DA/SA, titanium coated spherical barrel bushing, white dot post front and all black Novak Lo-Mount rear sight, 7 round magazine, ambidextrous spring loaded decocker, Hogue wraparound rubber grip, stainless steel material with matte black finish, laser etched with "40 RECON Performance Center" on the left side. Distributed by RSR, 1998.

Last MSR was N/A.

Product code: 170099.

PERFORMANCE CENTER 45 RECON – .45 ACP cal., 4 1/4 in. match grade ported barrel, DA/SA, titanium coated spherical barrel bushing, white dot post front and black Novak Lo-Mount rear sight, ambidextrous spring loaded decocker, Hogue wraparound rubber grip, 7 round magazine, stainless steel construction, stainless or matte black finish, laser etched "45 RECON Performance Center" on the left side, aluminum carry case, S/N prefix "SFF", 27.8 oz. Distributed by RSR, 1998.

Last MSR was $1,022.

Product code: 170098 (matte black), 170141 (stainless finish), or 170128 (includes Recon SWAT knife).

MSR	100%	98%	95%	90%	80%	70%	60%	Last MSR

PERFORMANCE CENTER 45 CQB PISTOLS (CLOSE QUARTERS BATTLE) – .45 ACP cal., 4 in. match grade barrel, SA, two variations offered in 1998, Novak Lo-Mount Dot front and Novak Lo-Mount 2 Dot rear sight, 7 round mag., straight backstrap grip, stainless steel slide, titanium coated spherical barrel bushing, alloy frame with a matte black finish (Model CQB-AL) or stainless steel frame with a matte stainless (Model CQB-SS) finish, ".45 C.Q.B. Performance Center" laser etched on the slide's left side. Distributed by Lew Horton, 1998-1999.

Last MSR was $1,235.

Product code: 170106 (alloy) or 170105 (stainless).

THE SHORTY .45 – .45 ACP cal., match grade barrel, ambidextrous safety, adj. sights, hand fitted titanium barrel bushing, oversize frame and slide rails, precision checkered front strap, hand honed double action. Mfg. 1997.

Last MSR was $1,146.

Product code: 170075. This model was the first of the Performance Center compact .45s. Shipped on June 3, 1996. Total production was 660 units with serial numbers starting at SFF0001-SFF0660.

THE .45 LIMITED – 45 ACP cal., match grade barrel, SA, oversize precision cut frame and slide rails, hand fitted titanium barrel bushing and slide lock, adj. sights, oversize mag. well, tuned action, Zippo lighter with Perf. Center logo. Distributed by Lew Horton, 1997.

Last MSR was $1,470.

MODEL 5906 PC-9 – 9mm cal., 3 1/2 in. barrel with spherical titanium bushing, DA/SA, 15 shot mag., blue slide with satin stainless frame, smooth trigger, bobbed hammer, dovetail front and Novak Lo-Mount fixed rear sight, 27 oz. Distributed by Lew Horton in 1993.

Last MSR was N/A

Product code: 170030.

Rifles: Semi-Auto

The following is a listing of abbreviations with related feature codes of both centerfire and rimfire semi-auto rifles: Stock: S/6 ADJ - 6 position adj., S/BLK - black synthetic, S/CAM - camo synthetic, S/SF - solid fixed, S/W - wood stock. Pistol Grip: PG - plastic grip, RG - rubber grip, WG - wood grip, NA - no grip. Rear Sight: R/ADJ - adjustable, R/FS - folding stock, R/FSADJ - folding adjustable, NA - no rear sight. Front Sight: F/BB - Black Blade, F/BP - Black Post, F/FO - fiber optic, F/FS - folding sight, F/FSADJ - folding adjustable, F/GB - Gold Bead, F/WBF - white bead front sight, NA - no front sight. Forend: CFF - custom free float, MR - modular rail, STD - standard, NA - no forend (one piece stock). Receiver Material: AL - alloy, CA - carbon, SS - Stainless steel, POLY - polymer. Action: BA - bolt action, FA - fixed action, SAT - semi-auto.

M&P10 – .308 Win. cal., GIO, 18 in. barrel, enhanced flash hider, 20 shot mag., matte black finish, ambidextrous controls, six-position CAR stock, chromed gas key, bolt carrier, and firing pin, pistol grip, 7 lbs. 11 oz. New 2013.

MSR $1,619	$1,475	$1,275	$1,050	$935	$750	$625	$525

Product Codes: 811308.

MODEL M&P15 CENTERFIRE SEMI-AUTO SERIES – .223 Rem./5.56 NATO or 5.45x39mm cal., GIO, AR-15 style design with 16 in. or longer chrome lined barrel with muzzle brake, aluminum upper and lower receiver, 10 or 30 shot mag. (most are mil-spec), one piece, fixed position, skeletonized, or six position CAR collapsible stock, hard coat black anodized finish, features detachable carrying handle, A2 post front sight, adj. dual aperture rear sight, and thinned handguard, M&P15T features extended Picatinny rail on receiver and barrel, in addition to RAS on both sides and bottom of barrel, adj. front and rear folding battle sights, supplied with hard carry case, approx. 6 1/2 lbs. New 2006.

The lowest serial number encountered to date is SW00200.

* **Model M&P15** – 5.56 NATO cal., GIO, 16 in. carbon steel barrel, 30 shot mag., alloy receiver, black alloy finish, six-position adj. pistol grip stock, adj. rear sight, black post front sight.

MSR $1,249	$1,250	$1,100	$950	$850	$700	$575	$450

Product Code: 811000.

* **Model M&P15A** – 5.56 NATO cal., GIO, AR-15 style design, 16 in. barrel, 30 shot mag., similar to Model M&P15, except features a receiver Picatinny rail and adj. rear folding battle sight with ribbed handguard, 6 1/2 lbs. Mfg. 2006-2012.

	$1,275	$1,125	$950	$850	$700	$575	$450	$1,289

Product Code: 811002.

* **Model M&P15T** – 5.56 NATO cal., GIO, AR-15 style design, fixed 10 (CA compliant) or detachable 30 shot mag., 16 in. barrel, similar to Model M&P15A, except features folding (disc. 2010) or fixed Black Post front sight (new 2011), fixed (new 2011) or folding adj. rear sight (disc. 2010), modular rail (disc. 2010) or custom free float forend (new 2011), 6.85 lbs.

MSR $1,159	$1,150	$1,000	$875	$775	$650	$525	$425

Product Codes: 811001 (disc. 2010), or 811041 (new 2011).

MSR		100%	98%	95%	90%	80%	70%	60%	Last MSR

* **Model M&P15FT** – 5.56 NATO cal., GIO, AR-15 style design, 16 in. barrel, 10 shot mag. (compliant for CT, MA, MD, NJ, and NY), one-piece pistol grip fixed stock, custom free float forend (new 2012), folding adj. (new 2012) front and rear sights, modular rail (disc. 2011), alloy receiver. Mfg. 2008-2011.

MSR $1,159	$1,150	$1,000	$875	$775	$650	$525	$425

Last MSR for product code 811004 was $1,709 in 2011

Product Code: 811004 (disc. 2011), 811048 (new 2012).

* **Model M&P15OR** – 5.56 NATO cal., GIO, 16 in. carbon steel barrel with flat-top Picatinny rail and gas block, 30 shot mag., optics ready alloy receiver, black alloy finish, six-position adj. stock, no rear sight. New 2008.

MSR $1,069	$1,050	$925	$800	$725	$600	$500	$400

Product Code: 811003.

* **Model M&P15ORC** – 5.56 NATO cal., GIO, AR-15 style design, 16 in. barrel, 10 shot mag. (compliant CT, MA, MD, NJ and NY), black alloy finish, pistol grip stock, alloy receiver, optics ready. New mid-2008.

MSR $1,039	$925	$800	$725	$625	$525	$425	$350

Product Code: 811013.

* **Model M&P15X** – 5.56 NATO cal., GIO, AR-15 style design, 16 in. barrel, 30 shot mag., black alloy finish, six-position adj. pistol grip stock, folding rear and black post front sights, modular rail, alloy receiver. New 2008.

MSR $1,379	$1,375	$1,200	$1,025	$950	$775	$650	$500

Product Code: 811008.

* **Model M&P15I** – .223 Rem. cal., GIO, AR-15 style design, 17 in. barrel, 10 shot mag. (compliant CT, MA, MD, NJ, and NY), black alloy finish, pistol grip stock, adj. rear sight, black post front sight, alloy receiver, 7 lbs. Mfg. mid-2008-2011.

	$1,000	$875	$775	$675	$575	$500	$450	$1,259

Product Code: 811010.

* **Model M&P15R** – 5.45x39mm cal., GIO, AR-15 style design, 16 in. barrel, 30 shot mag., black alloy finish, pistol grip stock, adj. rear and black post front sight, alloy receiver, Picatinny rail, 6 1/2 lbs. Mfg. 2008-2011.

	$1,075	$950	$825	$700	$600	$500	$450	$1,089

Product Code: 811011.

* **Model M&P15VTAC** – 5.56 NATO cal., GIO, AR-15 style design, Viking Tactics Model, 16 in. barrel, 30 shot mag., black alloy finish, pistol grip stock, modular rail, alloy receiver. Mfg. mid-2008-2011.

	$1,950	$1,700	$1,475	$1,225	$925	$775	$625	$1,989

Product Code: 811012.

MODEL M&P15VTAC II – 5.56 NATO cal., gas operated, semi-auto, 30 shot mag., 16 in. barrel, features mid-length system for lower recoil, enhanced flash hider, aluminum upper and lower receivers, 13 in. TRX Extreme handguard and VLTOR IMOD 6-position collapsible stock, melaonite/hard coat black anodized finish, 6.28 lbs. New 2012.

MSR $1,949	$1,950	$1,700	$1,475	$1,225	$925	$775	$625

Product Code: 811025.

* **Model M&P15MOE** – 5.56 NATO cal., GIO, AR-15 style design, 16 in. barrel, 30 shot mag., black alloy finish, six position adj. stock, alloy receiver, post front sight, folding rear sight. Mfg. 2010-2011.

	$1,250	$1,075	$900	$775	$650	$525	$425	$1,249

Product Codes: 811020 and 811021.

MODEL M&P15 MOE MID – 5.56 NATO cal., GIO, 16 in. barrel, features Magpul hardware, 30 shot, alloy receiver, 6-position adj. stock, black post front sight and folding adj. rear sight, black or Flat Dark Earth finish. New 2012.

MSR $1,259	$1,260	$1,075	$900	$775	$650	$525	$425

Product Codes: 811053 and 811054.

* **Model M&P15PS** – 5.56 NATO cal., GIO, AR-15 style design, 16 in. barrel, fixed 10 (CA compliant) or 30 shot mag., black alloy finish, six position adj. stock with standard forend, alloy receiver, solid handguard, Picatinny rail above gas block, no sights, flat-top upper, chrome lined bore, gas key, and bolt carrier, adj. gas plug with three settings. Mfg. 2010-2013.

	$1,350	$1,150	$950	$825	$675	$550	$450	$1,359

Product Code: 811022.

* **Model M&P15PSX** – 5.56 NATO cal., GIO, AR-15 style design, 16 in. barrel, 30 shot mag., black alloy finish, six position adj. stock with standard forend and tactical rail, alloy receiver. Mfg. 2010-2013.

	$1,500	$1,325	$1,125	$1,025	$825	$675	$525	$1,499

Product Code: 811023.

MSR	100%	98%	95%	90%	80%	70%	60%	Last MSR

* **Model M&P15 Sport** – 5.56 NATO cal., GIO, 16 in. melonite treated barrel, fixed (CA compliant) or detachable 10 (compliant CT, MA, MD, NJ, and NY), or 30 shot mag., single stage trigger, hard coat black anodized upper and lower receiver, polymer handguard, chrome lined gas key and bolt carrier, adj. A2 post front sight, adj. dual aperture rear sight, six-position telescoping buttstock, A2 flash suppressor. New 2011.

| MSR $739 | $650 | $575 | $500 | $425 | $375 | $325 | $300 | |

Product Codes: 811036 and 811037 (compliant).

* **Model M&P15 TS** – 5.56 NATO cal., GIO, AR-15 style design, 16 in. barrel with flash hider, 30 shot mag., Magpul folding front and rear sights, Magpul MOE stock and mag., full Troy TRX free floating quad rail, 6 1/2 lbs. New 2011.

| MSR $1,569 | $1,550 | $1,350 | $1,175 | $1,050 | $850 | $700 | $550 | |

Product Code: 811024.

MODEL M&P15 300 WHISPER – .300 Whisper cal., GIO, 16 in. barrel with or without sound suppressor, 10 shot mag., low recoil and muzzle blast, six-position CAR stock, Black (new 2014) or Realtree APG camo on all surfaces except barrel, 6.38 lbs. New 2012.

| MSR $1,119 | $1,100 | $975 | $825 | $750 | $600 | $500 | $400 | |

Product Code: 811300 (camo) or 811302 (black).

MODEL M&P15-22 RIMFIRE SEMI-AUTO – .22 LR cal., semi-auto, GIO, blowback action, AR-15 style design, 16 1/2 in. barrel with or w/o threading, 10 (disc. 2011) or 25 shot mag., matte black, Pink Platinum (new 2014), Black and Tan (new 2014), Purple Platinum (new 2014), Harvest Moon Orange (new 2014), or 100% Realtree APG HD camo finish, A2 post front sight and dual aperture rear sight, fixed or six position CAR adj. stock, quad rail handguard, 5 1/2 lbs. New 2009.

| MSR $499 | $425 | $385 | $350 | $325 | $300 | $280 | $260 | |

Add $20 for threaded barrel.
Add $60 for 100% Realtree APG HD camo finish with threaded barrel (new 2011).
Add $60 for Pink Platinum, Black and Tan, Purple Platinum, or Harvest Moon Orange finish (new 2014).

Product Codes: 811030 (Black), 811046 (Camo), 811051 (Pink Platinum), 811059 (Black and Tan), 10041 (Purple Platinum), or 10043 (Harvest Moon Orange).

* **Model M&P15-22 MOE Rimfire Semi-Auto** – .22 LR cal., GIO, similar to Model M&P15-22, except has 16 in. barrel, folding front and rear sight and skeletonized MagPul MOE stock, flat black or Flat Dark Earth (new 2012) finish, approx. 5 1/2 lbs. New 2011.

| MSR $609 | $525 | $450 | $395 | $365 | $335 | $300 | $275 | |

Product Codes: 811034 and 811035.

* **Model M&P15-22 PC TB**
Please see listing under Performance Center rifles.

SHOTGUNS

In 1984 S&W discontinued importation of all Howa manufactured shotguns. Mossberg continued importation utilizing leftover S&W parts in addition to fabricating their own.

MODEL 3000 POLICE – 12 ga. only, 18 or 20 in. barrel, blue or parkerized finish, many combinations of finishes, stock types, and other combat accessories were available for this model.

| | $325 | $255 | $215 | $185 | $170 | $155 | $140 | |

Add $125 for folding stock.

SOG ARMORY

Current rifle manufacturer located in Houston, TX.

SOG Armory also makes a wide variety of components and accessories for both AR-10 and AR-15/M16 carbines and rifles.

CARBINES/RIFLES: SEMI-AUTO

All AR-15 style rifles come standard with one 10 or 30 shot magazine, manual, sling, and hard case.

SOG CRUSADER – .223 Rem. cal., GIO, 16 in. chrome lined steel barrel, 30 shot mag., Mil Spec hard coat anodized upper and lower, black, tan, or OD green phosphate finish, enhanced mag well and trigger guard, M16 bolt and carrier, flash hider, ERGO pistol grip, M4 six position tactical stock, M4 stock pad, charging handle, SOG/Troy four rail handguard, SOG/Troy rear flip up sight.

| MSR $1,700 | $1,500 | $1,250 | $1,025 | $875 | $750 | $725 | $675 | |

MSR	100%	98%	95%	90%	80%	70%	60%	Last MSR

SOG DEFENDER – .223 Rem. cal., GIO, 16 in. chrome lined steel barrel, 30 shot mag., Mil Spec hard coat anodized upper and lower, black, tan, or OD green phosphate finish, enhanced mag well and trigger guard, M16 bolt and carrier, flash hider, ERGO pistol grip, M4 six position tactical stock, M4 stock pad, charging handle, SOG/Troy four rail handguard, detachable carry handle.

| MSR $1,600 | $1,425 | $1,175 | $1,000 | $850 | $725 | $650 | $550 | |

SOG ENFORCER – .223 Rem. cal., 16 in. chrome lined steel barrel, 30 shot mag., Mil Spec hard coat anodized upper and lower, black phosphate finish, enhanced mag well and trigger guard, M16 bolt and carrier, flash hider, ERGO pistol grip, M4 six position tactical stock, M4 stock pad, charging handle, CAR M4 handguard with double heat shield, SOG/Troy rear slip up sight.

| MSR $1,500 | $1,350 | $1,125 | $975 | $825 | $700 | $600 | $495 | |

SOG GUARDIAN – .223 Rem. cal., GIO, 16 in. chrome lined steel barrel, 30 shot mag., Mil Spec hard coat anodized upper and lower, black phosphate finish, enhanced mag well and trigger guard, M16 bolt and carrier, flash hider, ERGO pistol grip, M4 six position tactical stock, M4 stock pad, charging handle, CAR M4 handguard with double heat shield and detachable carry handle.

| MSR $1,400 | $1,275 | $1,075 | $925 | $800 | $700 | $600 | $495 | |

SOG OPERATOR – .223 Rem. cal., GIO, 16 in. chrome lined steel barrel, 30 shot mag., Mil Spec hard coat anodized upper and lower, black, tan, or OD green phosphate finish, enhanced mag well, M16 bolt and carrier, flash hider, ERGO pistol grip, six position tactical stock, M4 stock pad, charging handle, SOG/Troy four rail handguard, SOG/Troy flip up sight, Magpul Winter trigger guard, Wolf Eye's 260 Lumens tactical light, SOG mount, graphite vertical grip.

| MSR $2,300 | $2,075 | $1,825 | $1,675 | $1,450 | $1,200 | $825 | $750 | |

SOG PREDATOR – .223 Rem. cal., GIO, 20 in. Lothar Walther fully fluted barrel with muzzle brake, SOG Extreme vent. handguard with upper and lower Picatinny rails, SOG sights, low profile gas block, Magpul trigger guard and PRS stock, 8.3 lbs. New 2011.

| MSR $2,000 | $1,800 | $1,550 | $1,275 | $1,050 | $850 | $750 | $675 | |

SOG WARRIOR – .223 Rem. cal., GIO, 16 in. chrome lined steel barrel, 30 shot mag., Mil Spec hard coat anodized upper and lower, black or tan phosphate finish, enhanced mag well and trigger guard, M16 bolt and carrier, flash hider, ERGO pistol grip, VLTOR EMOD stock, M4 stock pad, charging handle, SOG/Troy Extreme free float handguard with rails, SOG/Troy flip front and rear sights.

| MSR $1,800 | $1,600 | $1,375 | $1,150 | $1,000 | $875 | $725 | $600 | |

SOMMER + OCKENFUSS GmbH

Previous manufacturer located in Baiersbronn, Germany until 2002. Previously imported by Lothar Walther Precision Tool, located in Cumming, GA. Previously imported by Intertex Carousels Corporation during 1998-2000, and located in Pineville, NC.

Sommer + Ockenfuss also produced a bolt adapter to convert the Remington 700 bolt action into a straight pull repeater, enabling the addition of a firing pin safety and firing chamber lock.

PISTOLS: SEMI-AUTO

P21 – .224 HV, 9mm Para., or .40 S&W cal., 3.11 (Combat) or 3.55 (Police) in. rotating barrel, DA/SA, release grip safety uncocks the hammer, keyed slide lock blocks firing pin and slide, 10 shot mag., approx. 24 oz. Mfg. 2001.

| | $550 | $495 | $450 | $415 | $375 | $340 | $310 | $608 |

Add approx. $320 for conversion slide assemblies.

RIFLES: SLIDE ACTION

SHORTY – most popular cals., unique slide action rifle in bullpup configuration featuring a straight line design with a grip safety pistol grip which also works the slide assembly, stainless or black coated barrel, compact 6-lug bolt with a locking surface of 0.263 sq. in., with or w/o sideplates inlet into walnut or black synthetic (new 1999) stock. Imported 1998-2002.

* ***Shorty Wilderness Rifle*** – match trigger, polymer stock, and stainless steel barrel.

| | $1,495 | $1,275 | $1,100 | $995 | $925 | $850 | $750 | $1,660 |

Add $310 for .375 H&H or .416 Rem. Mag. cal. (Shorty Safari).
Add $200 for walnut stock (Shorty American Hunter).
Add $210 for sight mounts.
Add $88 for recoil brake.

* ***Shorty Marksman Rifle*** – similar to Wilderness Rifle, except has choice of black coated or fluted heavy match barrel and recoil brake.

| | $1,875 | $1,675 | $1,450 | $1,275 | $1,100 | $995 | $850 | $2,020 |

Add $80 for .308 Win. or .300 Win. Mag. (fluted barrel), $420 for .338 Lapua Mag. with black coated barrel, or $710 for .338 Lapua

MSR	100%	98%	95%	90%	80%	70%	60%	*Last MSR*

Mag. with fluted stainless barrel.
Add $80 for stainless barrel.
Add $210 for sight mount, $168 for bipod, $210 for Spigot stock cap.

There were also deluxe variations, limited editions, and Marksman's packages ($4,100-$4,860 MSR) available in this model.

SOUTHERN GUN COMPANY

Current custom rifle manufacturer located in the U.K.

RIFLES

Southern Gun Company manufactures AR-15 style single shot and manual repeating action rifles in several calibers and configurations built to customer specifications. Southern Gun Company also manufactures the LA-30 semi-auto rifle with features built to customer specifications.

Please contact the company directly for more information including options, pricing, and availability (see Trademark Index).

SPARTAN PRECISION RIFLES

Current rifle manufacturer established in early 2011, and located in Concord, CA.

Custom riflemaker Marc Soulie builds rifles per individual specifications, with a specialty in F-Class and sniper rifles. Please contact him directly for more information, including pricing, configurations, options, availability and delivery time (see Trademark Index).

SPECIALIZED DYNAMICS

Current custom manufacturer located in Chandler, AZ.

RIFLES: SEMI-AUTO

MFR (MULTI-FUNCTION RIFLE) – .17 Rem., .204 Ruger, .223 Rem., 6x45, 20 Practical, .264 LBC, or 6.8 SPC cal., GIO, stainless barrel (choice of length), billet aluminum lower, flat-top upper receiver with aluminum free float vented and fluted handguard, RRA 2-stage match trigger, fixed A1 stock, Ergo deluxe pistol grip.

MSR $1,399	$1,250	$1,100	$950	$850	$700	$575	$450

LW-HUNTER – .17 Rem., .223 Rem., .204 Ruger, 20 Practical, 6x45, .264 LBC, or 6.8 SPC cal., GIO, .75 in. stainless steel barrel (choice of length), billet aluminum lower and flat-top upper receiver, RRA two-stage match trigger, ACE skeleton stock, Ergo deluxe pistol grip, carbon fiber free float tube, lightweight profile.

MSR $1,499	$1,350	$1,175	$1,025	$925	$750	$625	$475

LONG RANGE PREDATOR – .243 Win., .260 Rem., 6.5 Creedmoor, or .308 Win. cal., GIO, stainless steel barrel (choice of length), billet large frame lower and flat-top upper receiver, RRA 2-stage match trigger, winter trigger guard, Magpul PRS stock, Ergo deluxe pistol grip.

MSR $2,149	$1,925	$1,675	$1,450	$1,325	$1,075	$875	$675

SPECIALIZED TACTICAL SYSTEMS

Current manufacturer located in Pleasant View, UT.

RIFLES: SEMI-AUTO

TITAN B – 5.56 NATO cal., GPO, 16 in. STS salt bath nitride stainless barrel, STS SX3 lower receiver, VLTOR upper receiver, Magpul MOE stock, grip, and PMAG, Magpul back up sights, 2-stage match trigger, includes STS tactical case, 7 1/2 lbs.

MSR $2,299	$2,050	$1,800	$1,550	$1,400	$1,125	$925	$725

TITAN B DI.L – 5.56 NATO cal., GIO, 16 in. STS salt bath nitride stainless barrel, STS SX3 lower receiver, mil-spec upper, Magpul MOE stock, grip, and PMAG, Magpul back up sights, Mil-spec trigger, hard anodized with teflon coating, includes STS tactical case, 6 7/8 lbs.

MSR $1,699	$1,525	$1,350	$1,150	$1,050	$850	$675	$550

ZOMBIE SLAYER – 5.56 NATO cal., GIO, 16 in. STS salt bath nitride stainless barrel, STS SX3 lower receiver with custom ZOMBIE logo, custom fire control, VLTOR upper receiver, STS "Zombie Muzzle Thumping Device" (ZMTD), Magpul MOE stock, grip, V-grip, and PMAG, Magpul back up sights, 2-stage match trigger, Tungsten Grey cerakote finish, includes STS tactical case and "The Zombie Survival Guide" book. Only 50 mfg.

MSR $2,500	$2,250	$1,975	$1,700	$1,525	$1,250	$1,025	$825

This Zombie themed rifle was custom built for the 2011 SHOT Show. The original model was auctioned off and proceeds went to various charities.Only a limited number of these are planned for production.

MSR	100%	98%	95%	90%	80%	70%	60%	Last MSR

SPECIAL WEAPONS LLC

Previous tactical rifle manufacturer 1999-2002, and located in Mesa, AZ. Previously located in Tempe, AZ.

Special Weapons LLC closed its doors on Dec. 31, 2002. Another company, Special Weapons, Inc., is handling the warranty repairs on Special Weapons LLC firearms (see Trademark Index).

CARBINES: SEMI-AUTO

OMEGA 760 – 9mm Para. cal., reproduction of the S&W Model 76, 16 1/4 in. partially shrouded barrel, fixed wire stock, 30 shot mag., 7 1/2 lbs. Limited mfg. 2002.

	$495	$450	$425	$395	$375	$350	$325	$575

SW-5 CARBINE – 9mm Para. cal., configuration styled after the HK-94 (parts interchangeable), stainless steel receiver, plastic lower housing, 16 1/4 in. stainless steel barrel, A2 style black synthetic stock with wide forearm, 10 shot mag. (accepts high capacity HK-94/MP-5 mags also), approx. 6 3/4 lbs. Mfg. 2000-2002.

	$1,475	$1,225	$1,025	$875	$800	$750	$695	$1,600

SW-45 CARBINE – .45 ACP cal., otherwise similar to SW-5 Carbine. Mfg. 2000-2002.

	$1,550	$1,275	$1,050	$895	$825	$775	$725	$1,700

RIFLES: SEMI-AUTO

SW-3 – .308 Win. cal., styled after the HK-91 (parts interchangeable), tooled receiver, metal steel lower trigger housing, 17.71 stainless steel barrel, A2 style stock, approx. 10 lbs. Mfg. 2000-2002.

	$1,425	$1,175	$995	$850	$800	$750	$695	$1,550

* **SW-3 SP** – similar to SW-3, except has PSG-1 style trigger assembly, 22 in. custom target barrel and Weaver rail welded to top. Mfg. 2000-2002.

	$2,250	$1,975	$1,700	$1,500	$1,250	$1,050	$895	$2,500

SPHINX SYSTEMS LTD.

Current manufacturer established in 1876, and presently located in Matten b. Interlaken, Switzerland. Currently imported by Kriss Arms USA, beginning 2011 and located in Virginia Beach, VA. In late 2010, Kriss Arms acquired Sphinx Systems Ltd., including the Sphinx trademark. Previously distributed until 2009 by Sabre Defence Industries, LLC, located in Nashville, TN. Previously imported by Rocky Mountain Armoury, located in Silverthorne, CO. Previously manufactured by Sphinx Engineering S.A. located in Porrentruy, Switzerland, and by Sphinx U.S.A., located in Meriden, CT until 1996. Previously imported by Sile Distributors located in New York, NY.

PISTOLS: SEMI-AUTO

Please contact the importer directly for current U.S. availability and pricing on the following current models.

MODEL 2000S STANDARD – 9mm Para. or .40 S&W (new 1993) cal., 4.53 in. barrel, DA/SA or DAO, stainless steel fabrication, 10 (C/B 1994), 15* (9mm Para.), or 11* (.40 S&W) shot mag., checkered walnut grips, fixed sights, 35 oz. Importation disc. 2002.

	$965	$750	$625	$525	$450	$410	$375	

Add $117 for .40 S&W cal.

* **Model 2000PS Standard Police Special** – similar to Model 2000S, except has compact slide and 3.66 in. barrel.

	$850	$625	$525	$450	$410	$380	$350	

Add $40 for .40 S&W cal.
Add $87 for N/Pall finish.

* **Model 2000P Standard Compact** – similar to Model 2000 Standard, except has 3.66 in. barrel and 13 shot mag., 31 oz.

	$850	$625	$525	$450	$410	$380	$350	

Add $40 for .40 S&W cal.
Add $87 for N/Pall finish.

* **Model 2000H Standard Sub-Compact** – similar to Model 2000 Compact, except has 3.34 in. barrel and 10 shot mag., 26 oz. Disc. 1996.

	$850	$625	$525	$450	$410	$380	$350	$940

Add $40 for .40 S&W cal.
Add $87 for N/Pall finish.

MSR	100%	98%	95%	90%	80%	70%	60%	Last MSR

MODEL 2000 MASTER – 9mm Para., 9x21mm, or .40 S&W cal., SAO, two-tone finish only, designed for Master's stock class competition.

	$1,795	$1,350	$1,100	$995	$895	$775	$650	$2,035

MODEL AT-2000 (NEW MODEL) – 9mm Para. or .40 S&W cal., 4.53 in. barrel, DA/SA, 10 shot mag., machined slide with electro deposited finish, decocking mechanism. Limited mfg. 2004-2005.

	$1,825	$1,675	$1,450	$1,225	$1,000	$800	$675	$1,995

MODEL AT-2000CS COMPETITOR – 9mm Para., 9x21mm, or .40 S&W cal., DA/SA, competition model featuring many shooting improvements including 5.3 in. compensated barrel, 10 (C/B 1994), 11* (.40 S&W), or 15* shot mag., Bo-Mar adj. sights, two-tone finish. Imported 1993-1996.

	$1,725	$1,275	$1,050	$950	$850	$750	$675	$1,902

Add $287 for Model AT-2000C (includes Sphinx scope mount).
Add $1,538 for AT-2000K conversion kit (new 1995).
Add $1,490 for Model AT-2000CKS (competition kit to convert AT-2000 to comp. pistol, disc. 1994).

MODEL 2000 COMPETITION – similar to Model 2000 Master, except is SAO and includes more advanced competitive shooting features, Bo-Mar sights, top-of-the-line competition model. Imported 1993-96.

	$2,475	$1,925	$1,725	$1,500	$1,250	$1,050	$895	$2,894

Add $78 for Model AT-2000GM (includes Sphinx scope mount).

MODEL 3000 SERIES – 9mm Para., 9x21mm (disc.), .40 S&W, or .45 ACP cal., DA/SA, available in standard (4.53 in. barrel), tactical (3 3/4 in. barrel), or competition (4.53 in. barrel, adj. sights), configuration, choice of manual safety or decocker, titanium upper/lower frame with stainless slide, stainless steel slide with titanium lower frame or stainless steel frame/slide, front/rear gripstrap stipling or grooved, two-tone finish, approx. 40 oz. Imported 2001-circa 2012.

	$2,525	$2,275	$2,000	$1,800	$1,575	$1,375	$1,150	

Add $350 for titanium frame with stainless steel slide.
Add $800 for stainless steel slide with titanium upper/lower frame (disc.).
Add $75 for tactical model.
Add $350 for competition model.

SPHINX .45 ACP – .45 ACP cal., DA/SA, steel construction, 3 3/4 in. barrel, double slide serrations, blue finish, 10 shot mag., fixed Trijicon night sights, black polymer grips, decocker mechanism, approx. 43 oz. New 2007.

MSR N/A	$2,850	$2,500	$2,150	$1,850	$1,500	$1,250	$1,000	

SDP SERIES – 9mm Para. cal., 3 1/8 (Sub-Compact), 3.7 (Compact), 4 1/2 (Standard) in. barrel, DA/SA, aluminum frame and slide, full length guide rails, 13, 15, or 17 shot mag., match grade trigger, six integrated safeties including loaded chamber indicator, notched Picatinny rail avail. on compact and standard models, twin slide serrations, various sight combinations available per individual model, interchangeable aluminum/rubber grip system, 21-31 3/4 oz. New 2012.

SPIDER FIREARMS

Current rifle manufacturer located in St. Cloud, FL.

RIFLES: SINGLE SHOT

These models can also be custom ordered in .510 DTC, .50 Spider, .50 SFBR, .416 Barrett, .408 CheyTac, .338 Harris, .338 Lapua, and .338 Wby. Mag. cals.

SPORTSMAN FERRET 50 – .50 BMG cal., single shot bolt action, A2 style buttstock and pistol grip, Picatinny rail, choice of 18 to 36 in. barrel (LW-19 chromemoly is standard), matte black finish, perforated handguard with bipod, includes muzzle brake. New 2003.

MSR $3,192	$2,850	$2,575	$2,375	$2,100	$1,800	$1,600	$1,400	

Add $265 for LW-50 stainless steel barrel (SS Sportsman)
Add $530 for LW-50 Supermatch stainless super match barrel (SM Sportsman).

SUPERCOMP FERRET – similar to Ferret 50, features solid steel construction, fixed scope rails, 18 to 36 in. Lothar Walther stainless or chromemoly Supermatch barrels, adj. 1 lb. competition style trigger, two-axis cheekrest, and detachable rear monopod. New 2004.

MSR $3,382	$2,875	$2,600	$2,400	$2,200	$1,875	$1,650	$1,425	

Add $275 for LW-50 stainless steel barrel.
Add $530 for LW-50 stainless steel Supermatch barrel.

MSR	100%	98%	95%	90%	80%	70%	60%	Last MSR

SPIKE'S TACTICAL LLC

Current manufacturer located in Apopka, FL.

CARBINES/RIFLES: SEMI-AUTO

ST-15 M4 LE CARBINE – 5.56 NATO cal., carbine length GIO, 16 in. M4 profile barrel with A2 flash hider, 7 in. B.A.R., ST-T2 Tungsten buffer, ST M4 stock, Magpul MBUS rear sight, includes hard plastic carry case.

MSR $1,125	$1,025	$900	$775	$700	$575	$475	$375	

ST-15 M4 LE CARBINE w/B.A.R. – 5.56 NATO cal., carbine length GIO, 16 in. M4 barrel with A2 flash hider, ST Lo profile gas block, 9, 10, or 12 in. B.A.R., ST T2 Tungsten buffer, ST M4 stock, includes hard plastic case.

MSR $1,149	$1,025	$900	$775	$700	$575	$475	$400	

Add $12 for 10 in. B.A.R. Add $22 for 12 in. B.A.R.

ST-15 M4 LE CARBINE w/S.A.R. – 5.56 NATO cal., carbine length GIO, 16 in. M4 barrel with A2 flash hider, F-marked A2 front sight base or ST Lo Profile gas block, 7 or 9 in. S.A.R., ST-T2 Tungsten buffer, ST M4 stock, Magpul MBUS rear sight, includes hard plastic carry case.

MSR $1,203	$1,075	$950	$800	$725	$600	$475	$400	

Add $15 for 9 in. S.A.R. and ST Lo Profile gas block.

ST-15 MID-LENGTH LE CARBINE – 5.56 NATO cal., GIO, 16 in. Govt. profile barrel with A2 flash hider, F-marked A2 front sight base, mid-length handguards, ST-T2 Tungsten buffer, ST M4 stock, includes Magpul MBUS rear sight, hard plastic case.

MSR $960		$850	$750	$650	$600	$475	$400	$325

ST-15 MID-LENGTH LE CARBINE w/HEATSHIELD – 5.56 NATO cal., GIO, 16 in. M4 barrel with A2 flash hider, F-marked A2 front sight base, M4 double heat shield handguards, ST-T2 Tungsten buffer, ST M4 stock, includes Magpul MBUS rear sight, hard plastic carry case.

MSR $950		$850	$750	$650	$575	$475	$400	$325

ST-15 MID-LENGTH LE w/B.A.R. – 5.56 NATO cal., GIO, 16 in. Govt. profile barrel with A2 flash hider, F-marked A2 front sight base, 9 or 10 in. B.A.R., with or w/o ST Lo Profile gas block, ST-T2 Tungsten buffer, ST M4 stock, includes Magpul rear sight, hard plastic carry case.

MSR $1,159		$1,050	$925	$800	$725	$600	$500	$400

Add $12 for 10 in. B.A.R. and Lo Profile gas block.

ST-15 MID-LENGTH LE w/S.A.R. – 5.56 NATO cal., GIO, 16 in. Govt. profile barrel with A2 flash hider, ST Lo Profile gas block, 13.2 in. S.A.R., ST-T2 Tungsten buffer, ST M4 stock, includes hard plastic carry case.

MSR $1,258		$1,125	$1,000	$850	$775	$625	$500	$400

SPIRIT GUN MANUFACTURING COMPANY LLC

Previous manufacturer located in West Palm Beach, FL until 2011.

PISTOLS: SEMI-AUTO

SGM9P – 5.56 NATO cal., GIO, 7 1/2 in. stainless steel barrel with KX3 compensator, 30 shot mag., black, green, or tan finish, SGM9 lower with integral three position sling mount and swivel, VLTOR custom CASV handguard, flip up front sight, VLTOR MUR upper receiver, National Match phosphate and chromed custom bolt carrier. Limited mfg. Disc. 2011.

	$2,200	$1,950	$1,725	$1,500	$1,300	$1,100	$825	*$2,495*

RIFLES/CARBINES: SEMI-AUTO

Spirit Gun Manufacturing offered a complete line of AR-15 style rifles and carbines in law enforcement/military and civilian configurations. Recent models included (last MSRs reflect 2011 pricing): SGM-15, SGM-16, and SGM 17 ($2,495 MSR), SGM-A39, SGM-40, and SGM-41 ($2,495 MSR), SGM-A19 ($2,695 MSR), SGM-A43 ($2,695 MSR), SGM-A23 ($2,795 MSR), SGM-A47 ($2,795 MSR), SGM-A24 ($2,895 MSR), and the SGM-A48 ($2,895 MSR). A variety of options and accessories were available.

SPORT-SYSTEME DITTRICH

Current manufacturer established in 2003 and located in Kulmbach, Germany. Limited importation in North America by Wolverine Supplies, located in Manitoba, Canada. Previously imported by Marstar Canada, located in Ontario, Canada.

Sport-Systeme Dittrich manufactures high quality semi-auto reproductions of famous military guns, including the MP38 (BD 38), Sturmgewehr 44 (BD 44) and the Gerät Neumünster (BD 3008). Its latest model is a reproduction of the Fallschirmjägergewehr FG42 as the BD42 I. Please contact the importer or the company directly for more information, including pricing and U.S. availability (see Trademark Index).

MSR	100%	98%	95%	90%	80%	70%	60%	Last MSR

SPRINGFIELD ARMORY (MFG. BY SPRINGFIELD INC.)

Current trademark manufactured by Springfield Inc., located in Geneseo, IL. Springfield Inc. has also imported a variety of models. This company was named Springfield Armory, Geneseo, IL until 1992.

Springfield Inc. manufactures commercial pistols and rifles, including reproductions of older military handguns and rifles.

COMBINATION GUNS

M6 SCOUT RIFLE – .22 LR, .22 WMR (disc.), or .22 Hornet cal. over smoothbore .410 bore w/3 in. chamber, O/U Survival Gun, 14 (legal transfer needed) or 18 1/4 in. barrels, parkerized or stainless steel (new 1995), approx. 4 lbs. Disc. 2004.

	100%	98%	95%	90%	80%	70%	60%	Last MSR
.22 LR/.22 Win. Mag. cal.	$425	$375	$325	$275	$250	$225	$195	
.22 Hornet cal.	$775	$725	$650	$550	$475	$400	$325	$215

Add approx. 10% for stainless steel.
Add 10% for lockable Marine flotation plastic carrying case.

Early mfg. does not incorporate a trigger guard while late production had a trigger guard.

M6 SCOUT PISTOL/CARBINE – .22 LR or .22 Hornet cal. over .45 LC/.410 bore, 16 in. barrels, parkerized or stainless steel. Mfg. 2002-2004.

	100%	98%	95%	90%	80%	70%	60%	Last MSR
.22 LR cal.	$425	$375	$325	$275	$250	$225	$195	
.22 Hornet cal.	$775	$725	$650	$550	$475	$400	$325	$223

Add 10% for stainless steel.
Add approx. $200 per interchangeable 10 in. pistol barrel assembly.
Add 15% for detachable stock.

This model was also available with an optional detachable stock ($49-$59 MSR, not legal with a rifled barrel less than 16 in. or smoothbore less than 18 in.).

M6 SCOUT PISTOL – .22 LR or .22 Hornet cal. over .45 LC/.410 bore, 10 in. barrels, parkerized or stainless steel. Mfg. 2002-2004.

	100%	98%	95%	90%	80%	70%	60%	Last MSR
.22 LR cal.	$425	$375	$325	$275	$250	$225	$195	
.22 Hornet cal.	$775	$725	$650	$550	$475	$400	$325	$199

Add approx. 10% for stainless steel.
Add approx. $200 per interchangeable 16 in. carbine barrel.

PISTOLS: SEMI-AUTO

OMEGA PISTOL – .38 Super, 10mm Norma, or .45 ACP cal., SA, ported slide, 5 or 6 in. interchangeable ported or unported barrel with Polygon rifling, special lockup system eliminates normal barrel link and bushing, Pachmayr grips, dual extractors, adj. rear sight. Mfg. 1987-1990.

	100%	98%	95%	90%	80%	70%	60%	Last MSR
	$775	$650	$575	$495	$425	$360	$295	$849

Add $663 for interchangeable conversion units.
Add $336 for interchangeable 5 or 6 in. barrel (including factory installation).

Each conversion unit includes an entire slide assembly, one mag., 5 or 6 in barrel, recoil spring guide mechanism assembly, and factory fitting.

Pistols: Semi-Auto - P9 Series

MODEL P9 – 9mm Para., 9x21mm (new 1991) .40 S&W (new 1991), or .45 ACP cal., patterned after the Czech CZ-75, DA/SA, blue (standard beginning 1993), parkerized (standard until 1992), or duotone finish, various barrel lengths, checkered walnut grips. Mfg. in U.S. starting 1990.

* ***Model P9 Standard*** – 4.72 in. barrel, 15 shot (9mm Para.), 11 shot (.40 S&W), or 10 shot (.45 ACP) mag., parkerized finish standard until 1992 - blue finish beginning 1993, 32.16 oz. Disc. 1993.

	100%	98%	95%	90%	80%	70%	60%	Last MSR
	$430	$375	$335	$295	$275	$240	$215	$518

Add $61 for .45 ACP cal.
Add $182 for duotone finish (disc. 1992).
Subtract $40 for parkerized finish.

In 1992, Springfield added a redesigned stainless steel trigger, patented sear safety which disengages the trigger from the double action mechanism when the safety is on, lengthened the beavertail grip area offering less "pinch," and added a two-piece slide stop design.

* ***Model P9 Stainless*** – similar to P9 Standard, except is constructed from stainless steel, 35.3 oz. Mfg. 1991-93.

	100%	98%	95%	90%	80%	70%	60%	Last MSR
	$475	$425	$350	$285	$250	$215	$185	$589

Add $50 for .45 ACP cal.

MSR	100%	98%	95%	90%	80%	70%	60%	Last MSR

* **Model P9 Compact** – 9mm Para. or .40 S&W cal., 3.66 in. barrel, 13 shot (9mm Para.) or 10 shot (.40 S&W) mag., shorter slide and frame, rounded trigger guard, 30 1/2 oz. Disc. 1992.

	$395	$350	$300	$275	$250	$225	$200	$499

Add $20 for .40 S&W cal.
Add $20-$30 for blue finish depending on cal.
Add $78 for duotone finish.

* **Model P9 Sub-Compact** – 9mm Para. or .40 S&W cal., smaller frame than the P9 Compact, 3.66 in. barrel, 12 shot (9mm Para.) or 9 shot (.40 S&W) finger extension mag., squared-off trigger guard, 30.1 oz. Disc. 1992.

	$395	$350	$300	$275	$250	$225	$200	$499

Add $20 for .40 S&W cal.
Add $20-$30 for blue finish depending on cal.

* **Model P9 Factory Comp** – 9mm Para., .40 S&W, or .45 ACP cal., 5 1/2 in. barrel (with compensator attached), extended sear safety and mag. release, adj. rear sight, slim competition checkered wood grips, choice of all stainless (disc. 1992) or stainless bi-tone (matte black slide), dual port compensated, 15 shot (9mm Para.), 11 shot (.40 S&W), or 10 shot (.45 ACP) mag., 33.9 oz. Mfg. 1992-93.

	$595	$525	$450	$420	$390	$360	$330	$699

Add $36 for .45 ACP cal.
Add $75-$100 for all stainless finish.

* **Model P9 Ultra IPSC (LSP)** – competition model with 5.03 in. barrel (long slide ported), adj. rear sight, choice of parkerized (standard finish until 1992 when disc.), blue (disc. 1992), bi-tone (became standard 1993), or stainless steel (disc. 1992) finish, extended thumb safety, and rubberized competition (9mm Para. and .40 S&W cals. only) or checkered walnut (.45 ACP cal. only) grips, 15 shot (9mm Para.), 11 shot (.40 S&W), or 10 shot (.45 ACP) mag., 34.6 oz. Disc. 1993.

	$555	$475	$415	$350	$300	$275	$250	$694

Add $30 for .45 ACP cal.

* **Model P9 Ultra LSP Stainless** – stainless steel variation of the P9 Ultra LSP. Mfg. 1991-92.

	$675	$525	$425	$360	$315	$260	$225	$769

Add $30 for .40 S&W cal.
Add $90 for .45 ACP cal.

* **Model P9 World Cup** – see listing under 1911-A1 Custom Models heading.

Pistols: Semi-Auto - R-Series

PANTHER MODEL – 9mm Para., .40 S&W, or .45 ACP cal., DA/SA, 3.8 in. barrel, hammer drop or firing pin safety, 15 shot (9mm Para.), 11 shot (.40 S&W), or 9 shot (.45 ACP) mag., Commander hammer, frame mounted slide stop, narrow profile, non-glare blue finish only, walnut grips, squared-off trigger guard, 29 oz. Mfg. 1992 only.

	$600	$500	$400	$350	$300	$275	$250	$609

FIRECAT MODEL – 9mm Para. or .40 S&W cal., SA, 3 1/2 in. barrel, 3-dot low profile sights, all steel mfg., firing pin block and frame mounted ambidextrous safety, 8 shot (9mm Para.) or 7 shot (.40 S&W) mag., checkered combat style trigger guard and front/rear gripstraps, non-glare blue finish, 35 3/4 oz. Mfg. 1992-1993.

	$550	$450	$400	$350	$300	$275	$250	$569

BOBCAT MODEL – while advertised in 1992, this model was never mfg.

LINX MODEL – while advertised in 1992, this model was never mfg.

Pistols: Semi-Auto - Disc. 1911-A1 Models

MODEL 1911-A1 STANDARD MODEL – .38 Super, 9mm Para., 10mm (new 1990), or .45 ACP cal., patterned after the Colt M1911-A1, 5.04 (Standard) or 4.025 (Commander or Compact Model) in. barrel, SA, 7 shot (Compact), 8 shot (.45 ACP), 9 shot (10mm), or 10 shot (9mm Para. and .38 Super) mag., walnut grips, parkerized, blue, or duotone finish. Mfg. 1985-1990.

	$400	$360	$330	$300	$280	$260	$240	$454

Add $35 for blue finish.
Add $80 for duotone finish.

This model was also available with a .45 ACP to 9mm Para. conversion kit for $170 in parkerized finish, or $175 in blue finish.

MSR	100%	98%	95%	90%	80%	70%	60%	Last MSR

* **Model 1911-A1 Standard Defender Model** – .45 ACP cal. only, similar to Standard 1911-A1 Model, except has fixed combat sights, beveled mag. well, extended thumb safety, bobbed hammer, flared ejection port, walnut grips, factory serrated front strap and two stainless steel magazines, parkerized or blue finish. Mfg. 1988-90.

	$485	$435	$375	$340	$300	$280	$260	$567

Add $35 for blue finish.

* **Model 1911-A1 Standard Commander Model** – .45 ACP cal. only, similar to Standard 1911-A1 Model, except has 3.63 in. barrel, shortened slide, Commander hammer, low profile 3-dot sights, walnut grips, parkerized, blue, or duotone finish. Mfg. in 1990 only.

	$450	$415	$350	$325	$285	$260	$245	$514

Add $30 for blue finish.
Add $80 for duotone finish.

* **Model 1911-A1 Standard Combat Commander Model** – .45 ACP cal. only, 4 1/4 in. barrel, bobbed hammer, walnut grips. Mfg. 1988-89.

	$435	$385	$325	$295	$275	$250	$230	

Add $20 for blue finish.

* **Model 1911-A1 Standard Compact Model** – .45 ACP cal. only, compact variation featuring shortened Commander barrel and slide, reduced M1911 straight gripstrap frame, checkered walnut grips, low profile 3-dot sights, extended slide stop, combat hammer, parkerized, blue, or duotone finish. Mfg. 1990 only.

	$450	$415	$350	$325	$285	$260	$245	$514

Add $30 for blue finish.
Add $80 for duotone finish.

* **Model 1911-A1 Standard Custom Carry Gun** – .38 Super (special order only), 9mm Para., 10mm (new 1990), or .45 ACP cal., similar to Defender Model, except has tuned trigger pull, heavy recoil spring, extended thumb safety, and other features. Mfg. 1988-disc.

	$860	$725	$660	$535	$460	$420	$385	$969

Add $130 for .38 Super Ramped, 10mm was POR.

Pistols: Semi-Auto - 1911-A1, Single Action (90s Series)

The initials "PDP" refer to Springfield's Personal Defense Pistol series.

Beginning in 2000, Springfield Armory started offering a Loaded Promotion package on their 1911-A1 pistol line. Many of these features and options are found on the FBI's Hostage Rescue Teams (HRT) pistol contract with Springfield Armory. Standard features of this Loaded Promotion package are hammer forged premium air-gauged barrel, front and rear cocking serrations, Novak patented low profile sights or Bo-Mar type adj. sights, extended thumb safety, tactical beavertail, flat mainspring housing, Cocobolo grips, High Hand grip, lightweight match trigger, full length guide rod, and machine beveled mag. well. This promotion includes all pistols except the Mil-Spec Model 1911 A1.

In 2001, Springfield's Custom Loaded 1911-A1 Series pistols came equipped standard with Springfield's integral locking system, carry bevel, hammer forged premium air-gauged barrel, front and rear cocking serrations, Novak patented low profile sights (some models come equipped with Tritium sights or Bo-Mar type adj. sights), extended thumb safety, tactical beavertail, flat mainspring housing, cocobolo grips, high hand grip, lightweight adj. match trigger, full length guide rod, machine beveled magwell, and a "loaded" coupon ($600 consumer savings). These Custom Loaded features will vary by model. All models with less than a 5 in. and all alloy pistols supplied with ramped, fully supported barrels.

Beginning 2002, every Springfield pistol is equipped with a patented integral locking system (I.L.S., keyed in the rear gripstrap) at no extra charge.

Beginning 2007, most models were shipped with an 11 gear system, including one (GI models only) or two mags., belt holster, magazine pouch, and bore brush supplied in a lockable blue plastic case.

PDP DEFENDER MODEL – .40 S&W (disc. 1992) or .45 ACP cal., standard pistol with slide and barrel shortened to Champion length (4 in.), tapered cone dual port compensator system, fully adj. sights, Videcki speed trigger, rubber grips, Commander style hammer, serrated front strap, parkerized (disc. 1992), duotone/bi-tone, or blue (disc. 1993) finish. Mfg. 1991-1998.

	$850	$745	$635	$580	$465	$380	$295	$992

1911-A1 90s EDITION (CUSTOM LOADED) – .38 Super, 9mm Para., 10mm (disc. 1991), .40 S&W, or .45 ACP cal., patterned after the Colt M1911-A1, except has linkless operating system, 5.04 (Standard) or 4 (Champion or Compact Model) in. barrel, 7 shot (Compact), 8 shot (.40 S&W or .45 ACP Standard), 9 shot (9mm Para., 10mm, or .38 Super), or 10 shot (.38 Super) mag., checkered walnut grips, parkerized (.38 Super beginning 1994 or .45 ACP beginning 1993), blue or duotone (disc. 1992) finish. New 1991.

MSR	100%	98%	95%	90%	80%	70%	60%	Last MSR

* 1911-A1 90s Edition Mil-Spec – .38 Super (disc. 2011) or .45 ACP cal., blue (disc.), 5 in. stainless steel barrel, parkerized, bi-tone (mfg. 2004 only), or OD Green (mfg. 2004 only) finish, 3-dot Hi-Viz fixed combat sights, standard loaded features include belt holster, double mag. pouch and extra set of grips (Mil-Spec Package), 39 oz.

| MSR $785 | $655 | $550 | $475 | $400 | $325 | $285 | $245 | |

Add $17 for blue finish (disc. 2001).

Add $21 for OD Green or bi-tone finish (mfg. 2004 only).

Subtract approx. $70 if without Mil-Spec package (became standard in 2012, includes belt holster, double mag. pouch and extra set of grips, introduced 2009).

Add $631 for .38 Super cal. in High Polish Nickel (Acusport exclusive 2004-2007).

* 1911-A1 90s Edition Mil-Spec Operator – .45 ACP cal. only, similar to Mil-Spec 1911-A1, except has Picatinny light mounting system forged into lower front of frame, parkerized finish only. Disc. 2002.

| | $615 | $540 | $460 | $420 | $340 | $275 | $215 | *$756* |

* 1911-A1 90s Edition Loaded Operator – .45 ACP cal. only, similar to full size service model, except has Picatinny light mounting platform forged into lower front of frame, checkered hardwood (disc. 2003) or plastic grips, OD Green with black bi-tone Armory Kote finish, Novak low mount tritium (disc.) or Trijicon night sights. New 2002.

| MSR $1,398 | $1,180 | $1,025 | $875 | $775 | $635 | $515 | $400 | |

* 1911-A1 90s Edition Lightweight Operator – .45 ACP cal. only, 5 in. stainless steel barrel, blue finish, 7 shot mag., fixed low profile combat rear sight, dovetail front sight, cocobolo grips, 34 oz. New 2006.

| MSR $1,299 | $1,125 | $975 | $825 | $750 | $600 | $495 | $385 | |

* 1911-A1 90s Edition Standard or Lightweight Model – .45 ACP cal. (current mfg.), Standard model has parkerized, blue, or OD Green with Armory Kote (new 2002) finish, Custom Loaded features became standard in 2001, Lightweight Model was mfg. 1995-2012 with either matte (disc. 2002), bi-tone (mfg. 2003-2012) or blue (mfg. 1993-disc.) finish, current mfg. is w/either Novak low mount or Trijicon night sights, 28.6 or 35.6 oz.

| MSR $999 | $875 | $750 | $650 | $575 | $475 | $375 | $295 | |

Add $52 for Lightweight Model (with Trijicon night sights), disc. 2012.

Subtract approx. 10%-25% if w/o Custom Loaded features (new 2001), depending on condition.

* 1911-A1 90s Edition Stainless Standard Model – 9mm Para. (mfg. 1994-2012), .38 Super (disc.), .40 S&W (mfg. 2001-2002), or .45 ACP cal., 7 (.45 ACP cal.), 8 (.40 S&W), or 9 (9mm Para.) shot mag., Custom Loaded features became standard in 2001, wraparound rubber (disc.) or checkered hardwood grips, 11 Gear system holster became standard 2009, Novak Lo-Mount (disc.), Bo-Mar type (mfg. 1996-2001), or combat 3 dot sights, beveled mag. well, 39.2 oz. New 1991.

| MSR $1,039 | $915 | $800 | $675 | $595 | $480 | $395 | $325 | |

Add $62 for 9mm Para. cal. (disc. 2012), or $32 for .40 S&W cal. (disc.).

Add $230 for Tactical Combat Model with combat features and black stainless steel (mfg. 2005-disc.).

Add $50 for Bo-Mar type sights (disc. 2001).

Add $202 for long slide variation in .45 Super cal. with V16 porting and Bo-Mar sights (disc.).

* 1911-A1 90s Edition Stainless Super Tuned Standard – .45 ACP cal. only, super tuned by the Custom Shop, 7 shot mag., 5 in. barrel, Novak fixed Lo-Mount sights, 39.2 oz. Mfg. 1997-99.

| | $875 | $765 | $655 | $595 | $480 | $395 | $305 | *$995* |

* 1911-A1 90s Edition Standard High Capacity – 9mm Para. (disc.) or .45 ACP cal., 5 in. barrel, blue (disc. 2001) or matte parkerized (new 1996) finish with plastic grips, 3-dot fixed combat sights, 10 shot (except for law enforcement) mag. Mfg. 1995-2003.

| | $635 | $555 | $475 | $430 | $350 | $285 | $220 | *$756* |

Add $50 for blue finish (disc.).

* 1911-A1 90s Edition Stainless High Capacity – similar to Standard High Capacity, except is stainless steel. Mfg. 1996-2000.

| | $675 | $590 | $505 | $460 | $370 | $305 | $235 | *$819* |

* 1911-A1 90s Edition XM4 High Capacity Model – 9mm Para. or 45 ACP cal., features widened frame for high capacity mag., blue (mfg. 1993 only) or stainless finish only. Mfg. 1993-94.

| | $595 | $520 | $445 | $405 | $325 | $270 | $210 | *$689* |

1911-A1 TRP (TACTICAL RESPONSE PISTOL) OPERATOR – .45 ACP cal., 5 in. standard or bull barrel, 7 shot mag., fixed combat 3-dot tritium or adj. Trijicon sights, black Armory Kote or stainless steel, checkered front strap, available in Standard, Stainless, and Operator configurations, 4 1/2 - 5 lbs. New mid-2008.

| MSR $1,867 | $1,615 | $1,400 | $1,200 | $1,075 | $875 | $750 | $625 | |

MSR	100%	98%	95%	90%	80%	70%	60%	Last MSR

MODEL 1911-A1 GI – .45 ACP cal., 5 in. barrel, parkerized, OD Green Armory Kote finish or stainless steel, 7 (standard) or 13 (high capacity) shot mag., low profile military sights, diamond checkered walnut grips with U.S. initials, includes 5.11 Gear belt holster, 36 oz. Mfg. 2004-2011.

| | $565 | $485 | $415 | $375 | $300 | $245 | $190 | *$656* |

Add $52 for stainless steel.

Add $61 for high capacity magazine (parkerized finish, new 2005).

1911-A1 TACTICAL RESPONSE (TRP SERIES) – .45 ACP only, 5 in. standard or bull (Operator Model only) barrel, 7 shot mag., matte Armory Kote finish or stainless steel, checkered rosewood grips, Trijicon (new 2006), Novak or Hi-Viz (disc., Operator Model only) 3-dot Tritium (disc. 2001) sights, 36 oz. New 1999.

| MSR $1,777 | $1,525 | $1,325 | $1,125 | $1,025 | $825 | $675 | $525 | |

1911-A1 COMMANDER MODEL – .45 ACP cal. only, similar to Standard 1911-A1 Model, except has 3.63 in. barrel, shortened slide, Commander hammer, low profile 3-dot sights, walnut grips, parkerized, blue, or duotone finish. Mfg. 1991-92.

| | $425 | $370 | $320 | $290 | $235 | $190 | $150 | |

* ***1911-A1 Commander Model Combat*** – .45 ACP cal. only, 4 1/4 in. barrel, bobbed hammer, walnut grips. Mfg. 1991 only.

| | $425 | $370 | $320 | $290 | $235 | $190 | $150 | |

1911-A1 CHAMPION MODEL – .380 ACP (Model MD-1, mfg. 1995 only) or .45 ACP cal., similar to Standard Model, except has 4 in. barrel and shortened slide, blue (disc. 2000) or parkerized (Mil-Spec Champion, new 1994) finish, Commander hammer, checkered walnut grips, 3-dot sights (Novak night sights became standard 2001), 7 shot mag., 33 1/2 oz. Mfg. 1992-2002.

| | $695 | $610 | $520 | $470 | $380 | $315 | $245 | *$856* |

Add $30 for Ultra Compact slide (mfg. 1997-98).

Add $79 for ported Champion V10 with Ultra Compact slide (disc.).

Subtract approx. 10%-25% if w/o Custom Loaded features (new 2001), depending on condition.

Subtract approx. $150 for .380 ACP cal. (Model MD-1, disc.).

* ***1911-A1 Champion Model (Custom Loaded)*** – .45 ACP cal. only, stainless steel or Lightweight bi-tone with OD Green with Black Armory Kote finish (new 2004), Trijicon night sights. Mfg. 1992-2012.

| | $900 | $800 | $675 | $615 | $500 | $400 | $315 | *$1,031* |

Add $42 for stainless steel.

Add $119 for Ultra Compact slide (mfg. 1997-98).

Add $52 for ported Champion V10 with Ultra Compact slide (disc. 2000).

Subtract approx. 10%-25% if w/o Custom Loaded features (new 2001), depending on condition.

* ***1911-A1 Champion Model Lightweight Operator*** – .45 ACP cal., 4 in. stainless steel barrel, blue finish, 7 shot mag., fixed low profile combat rear sight, dovetail front sight, cocobolo grips, 34 oz. Mfg. 2006-2012.

| | $940 | $825 | $700 | $630 | $510 | $415 | $325 | *$1,076* |

* ***1911-A1 Champion Model GI*** – .45 ACP cal., parkerized or blued slide with black anodized frame (Lightweight Model, new 2005), low profile military sights, diamond checkered wood grips with U.S. initials, includes belt holster, 34 oz. Mfg. 2004-2012.

| | $560 | $485 | $410 | $375 | $300 | $245 | $190 | *$656* |

* ***1911-A1 Champion Model TRP*** – .45 ACP cal., 4 in. barrel, otherwise similar to TRP Tactical Response. Mfg. 1999-2001.

| | $1,045 | $915 | $785 | $710 | $575 | $470 | $365 | *$1,249* |

* ***1911-A1 Champion Model Lightweight*** – .45 ACP cal., 4 in. barrel, aluminum frame, matte metal finish, night sights became standard during 2001, current mfg. has lower Picatinny rail. New 1999.

| MSR $1,129 | $995 | $850 | $725 | $625 | $500 | $425 | $350 | |

Subtract approx. 10%-25% if w/o Custom Loaded features (new 2001), depending on condition.

* ***1911-A1 Champion Model Comp PDP*** – .45 ACP cal. only, compensated version of the Champion Model, blue. Mfg. 1993-98.

| | $780 | $680 | $585 | $530 | $430 | $350 | $275 | *$869* |

* ***1911-A1 Champion Model Super Tuned*** – .45 ACP cal., super tuned by the Custom Shop, 7 shot mag., 4 in. barrel, blue or parkerized finish, Novak fixed Lo-Mount sights, 36.3 oz. Mfg. 1997-99.

| | $850 | $745 | $635 | $580 | $465 | $380 | $295 | *$959* |

Add $30 for blue finish.

MSR	100%	98%	95%	90%	80%	70%	60%	Last MSR

* ***1911-A1 Champion Model XM4 High Capacity*** – 9mm Para. or .45 ACP cal., high capacity variation. Mfg. 1994 only.

| | $615 | $540 | $460 | $420 | $340 | $275 | $215 | *$699* |

1911-A1 COMPACT MODEL – .45 ACP cal. only, compact variation featuring shortened 4 in. barrel and slide, reduced M1911-A1 curved gripstrap frame, checkered walnut grips, low profile 3-dot sights, 6 or 7 shot mag., extended slide stop, standard or lightweight alloy (new 1994) frame, combat hammer, parkerized, blue, or duotone (disc. 1992) finish, standard or lightweight (new 1995) configuration, 27 or 32 oz. Mfg. 1991-96.

| | $415 | $365 | $310 | $280 | $230 | $185 | $145 | *$476* |

Add $66 for blue finish.
Add $67 for Compact Lightweight Model (matte finish only).

* ***1911-A1 Compact Model Stainless*** – stainless steel variation of the Compact Model. Mfg. 1991-96.

| | $495 | $435 | $370 | $335 | $270 | $225 | $175 | *$582* |

* ***1911-A1 Compact Model Lightweight*** – .45 ACP cal., forged alloy frame, matte metal finish, 6 shot mag., Novak night sights became standard 2001. Mfg. 1999-2003.

| | $585 | $510 | $440 | $395 | $320 | $265 | $205 | *$733* |

Subtract approx. 10%-25% if w/o Custom Loaded features (new 2001), depending on condition.

» **1911-A1 Compact Model Lightweight Stainless** – similar to Compact Lightweight, except is stainless steel. Disc. 2001.

| | $725 | $635 | $545 | $495 | $400 | $325 | $255 | *$900* |

Subtract approx. 10%-25% if w/o Custom Loaded features (new 2001), depending on condition.

* ***1911-A1 Compact Model Comp Lightweight*** – compensated version of the Compact Model, bi-tone or matte finish, regular or lightweight alloy (new 1994) frame. Mfg. 1993-98.

| | $775 | $680 | $580 | $525 | $425 | $350 | $270 | *$869* |

* ***1911-A1 Compact Model High Capacity*** – blue or stainless steel, 3-dot fixed combat sights, black plastic grips, 10 shot (except for law enforcement) mag. Mfg. 1995-96 only.

| | $550 | $475 | $400 | $365 | $295 | $245 | $190 | *$609* |

Add $39 for stainless steel.

* ***1911-A1 Compact Model High Capacity PDP Comp*** – .45 ACP cal. only, features compensated 3 1/2 in. barrel, 10 shot (except law enforcement) mag., blue finish only. Mfg. 1995-96 only.

| | $830 | $725 | $620 | $565 | $455 | $375 | $290 | *$964* |

1911 A-1 ULTRA COMPACT (CUSTOM LOADED) – .380 ACP (lightweight only, mfg. 1995 only), 9mm Para. (new 1998, lightweight stainless only), or .45 ACP cal., 3 1/2 in. barrel, bi-tone (.45 ACP only, disc.), matte (.380 ACP, MD-1), or parkerized (Mil-Spec Ultra Compact) finish, 6, 7 (.380 ACP cal.) or 8 (9mm Para. cal.) shot mag., Custom Loaded features and night sights became standard in 2001, 24 or 30 oz. Mfg. 1995-2003.

| | $680 | $595 | $510 | $460 | $375 | $305 | $240 | *$837* |

Add $12 for V10 porting.
Add $12 for Novak Tritium sights (not available on 9mm Para cal.).
Add $110 for bi-tone finish (disc.).
Subtract $50 for MD-1 variation (.380 ACP only).
Subtract approx. 10%-25% if w/o Custom Loaded features (new 2001), depending on condition.

* ***1911 A-1 Ultra Compact Mil-Spec*** – .45 ACP cal., parkerized (disc.) or blued (new 2004) finish, similar to full size Mil-Spec Model, 6 shot mag., checkered grips, 3-dot fixed Hi-Viz combat sights. Mfg. 2001-2002, reintroduced 2004 only.

| | $550 | $480 | $410 | $375 | $300 | $245 | $190 | *$641* |

Subtract approx. 10%-25% if w/o Custom Loaded features (new 2001), depending on condition.

* ***1911 A-1 Ultra Compact Stainless Custom Loaded*** – 9mm Para. (disc. 2004) or .45 ACP cal., stainless steel, Novak (disc.) or Fixed Combat Trijicon (current mfg.) night sights became standard 2001. Mfg. 1998-2012.

| | $925 | $800 | $675 | $615 | $490 | $400 | $315 | *$1,073* |

Add $17 for 9mm Para cal. (lightweight, disc. 2004).
Subtract approx. 10%-25% if w/o Custom Loaded features (new 2001), depending on condition.

* ***1911 A-1 Ultra Compact Lightweight*** – .45 ACP cal., aluminum frame, matte metal finish, night sights became standard 2001. Mfg. 1999-2001.

| | $695 | $610 | $520 | $470 | $380 | $315 | $245 | *$867* |

Subtract approx. 10%-25% if w/o Custom Loaded features (new 2001), depending on condition.

* ***1911 A-1 Ultra Compact V10 Lightweight Ported*** – .45 ACP cal., bi-tone finish. Mfg. 1999-2001.

| | $750 | $655 | $560 | $510 | $410 | $335 | $260 | *$737* |

MSR	100%	98%	95%	90%	80%	70%	60%	Last MSR

»**1911 A-1 Ultra Compact V10 Lightweight Stainless** – 9mm Para. or .45 ACP (exclusive) cal., similar to Ultra Compact Lightweight, except is stainless steel, Novak Lo-Mount sights. Mfg. 1999-2002.

| | $725 | $635 | $545 | $495 | $400 | $325 | $255 | $870 |

Add $31 for night sights (.45 ACP cal. only).

Subtract approx. 10%-25% if w/o Custom Loaded features (new 2001), depending on condition.

* **1911 A-1 Ultra Compact High Capacity** – 9mm Para. (disc.) or .45 ACP cal., parkerized (Mil-Spec) or blue (disc.) finish, and stainless steel (disc.) construction, 10 shot mag., 3-dot fixed combat (disc.) or Novak Lo-Mount (new 2002) sights, black plastic grips. Mfg. 1996-2002.

| | $735 | $645 | $550 | $500 | $405 | $330 | $255 | $909 |

Add $98 for stainless steel.

Add $145 for stainless steel with V10 ported barrel (disc.).

Subtract approx. 10%-25% if w/o Custom Loaded features (new 2001), depending on condition.

* **1911 A-1 Ultra Compact V10 Ported** – .45 ACP cal. only, 3 1/2 in. specially compensated barrel/slide, blue (disc.), bi-tone, or parkerized (Mil-Spec Ultra Compact) finish, Novak Lo-Mount or 3-dot combat sights, 30 oz. Mfg. 1995-2002.

| | $690 | $605 | $515 | $470 | $380 | $310 | $240 | $853 |

Subtract approx. 10%-25% if w/o Custom Loaded features (new 2001), depending on condition.

* **1911 A-1 Ultra Compact V10 Super Tuned Ported** – .45 ACP cal. only, super tuned by the Custom Shop, 3 1/2 in. ported barrel, bi-tone finish or stainless steel (exclusive), Novak fixed Lo-Mount sights, 32.9 oz. Mfg. 1997-99.

| | $925 | $810 | $695 | $630 | $510 | $415 | $325 | $1,049 |

Add $70 for stainless steel (exclusive).

1911-A1 MICRO COMPACT – .45 ACP cal. only, 3 in. tapered barrel w/o bushing, matte finish, checkered grips, 6 shot mag., Novak Lo-Mount night sights. Mfg. 2002 only.

| | $625 | $545 | $470 | $425 | $345 | $280 | $220 | $749 |

* **1911 A-1 Micro Compact Lightweight Custom Loaded** – similar to Micro Compact 1911 A-1, except also available in .40 S&W (disc.) cal., bi-tone, OD Green (mfg. 2003 only), or black Armory Kote (mfg. 2003-2004) finish with forged steel slide (grey) and aluminum alloy frame (blue), checkered cocobolo grips, Trijicon night sights, 24 oz. Mfg. 2002-2012.

| | $1,195 | $995 | $875 | $750 | $625 | $525 | $425 | $1,377 |

Add $71 for Operator Model with XML X-treme mini light (disc. 2011).

* **1911 A-1 Micro Compact Lightweight Stainless Custom Loaded** – .45 ACP cal. only, similar to Micro Compact 1911 A-1 Custom Loaded, except is stainless or black stainless steel slide. Mfg. 2003.

| | $825 | $720 | $620 | $560 | $455 | $370 | $290 | $993 |

* **1911 A-1 Micro Compact GI** – .45 ACP cal., parkerized finish, checkered diamond walnut grips with U.S. initials, includes belt holster, 32 oz. Mfg. 2004-2011.

| | $615 | $535 | $465 | $400 | $325 | $270 | $210 | $708 |

1911-A1 EMP (ENHANCED MICRO PISTOL) – 9mm Para. or .40 S&W cal., bi-tone finish, 9 shot mag., 3 in. stainless steel bull barrel, polished stainless slide with blue frame, tritium 3-dot sights, available in Standard or Lightweight configuration, reduced dimensions result in narrower profile, cocobolo or G10 grips, 27 (Lightweight) or 33 oz. New 2007.

| MSR $1,345 | $1,175 | $1,025 | $875 | $785 | $635 | $515 | $400 | |

Add $79 for G10 grips (new 2008).

Pistols: Semi-Auto - 1911-A1 Custom Models

In addition to the models listed, Springfield also custom builds other configurations of Race Guns that are available through Springfield dealers. Prices range from $2,245-$2,990.

Add $100 for all cals. other than .45 ACP.

CUSTOM CARRY GUN – .45 ACP (other cals. available upon request) cal., similar to Defender Model, except has tuned trigger pull, 7 shot mag., heavy recoil spring, extended thumb safety, available in blue or phosphate (disc.) finish. New 1991.

| MSR $2,119 | $1,775 | $1,450 | $1,150 | $950 | $800 | $700 | $600 | |

CUSTOM OPERATOR – .45 ACP cal. New 2001.

| MSR $2,810 | $2,495 | $2,225 | $1,775 | $1,400 | $1,100 | $950 | $850 | |

MSR	100%	98%	95%	90%	80%	70%	60%	Last MSR

PROFESSIONAL MODEL – .45 ACP cal., FBI contract model, black finish, custom fitted National Match barrel and bushing, many other custom shop features, low mount Novak rear sight, checkered cocobolo grips, with or w/o integral light rail on lower frame. New 1999.

MSR $2,647	$2,350	$2,100	$1,700	$1,325	$1,025	$925	$825	

Add $101 for lower Picatinny rail.

1911-A1 CUSTOM COMPACT – .45 ACP cal. only, carry or lady's model with shortened slide and frame, compensated, fixed 3-dot sights, Commander style hammer, Herrett walnut grips, other custom features, blue only.

	$1,615	$1,325	$1,100	$950	$850	$750	$675	*$1,815*

1911-A1 CUSTOM CHAMPION – similar to Custom Compact, except is based on Champion model with full size frame and shortened slide.

	$1,615	$1,325	$1,100	$950	$850	$750	$675	*$1,815*

CUSTOM HIGH CAPACITY LTD – .40 S&W cal. Mfg. 2004-2011.

	$2,200	$1,775	$1,425	$1,125	$975	$875	$775	*$2,650*

OPERATOR LIGHTWEIGHT – .45 ACP cal., 3 in. barrel, bi-tone finish, XML mini-light, includes Novak Trijicon night sights. Limited mfg. 2005.

	$1,050	$925	$800	$700	$600	$500	$400	*$1,247*

OPERATOR TACTICAL RESPONSE – .45 ACP cal., 5 in. barrel, black Armory Kote finish, adj. Trijicon night sights. Limited mfg. 2005.

	$1,395	$1,075	$900	$775	$675	$575	$475	*$1,639*

LOADED OPERATOR – .45 ACP cal., 5 in. barrel, OD Green or black Armory Kote finish and slide, Novak or Trijicon night sights. Limited mfg. 2005.

	$1,025	$900	$800	$700	$600	$500	$400	*$1,218*

Pistols: Semi-Auto - XD Series

All XD pistols are manufactured by HS Produkt (formerly I.M. Metal) in Croatia. All XD pistols were originally shipped with two magazines. Beginning 2005, high capacity magazines are legal for civilian sales in those states that permit high cap. mags. During 2006, all XD pistols are shipped with the XD Gear System, consisting of belt holster, double magazine pouch, magazine loader, two magazines and cable lock.

In 2013, Springfield Armory USA released its XD-S Series in .45 ACP cal. with many compact features.

XD 5 IN. TACTICAL (X-TREME DUTY) – 9mm Para., .357 SIG, .40 S&W, .45 ACP (new 2006), or .45 GAP (mfg. 2005-2007) cal., cold hammer forged 5 in. barrel, 9 (.45 GAP), 10, 12 (.40 S&W or .357 SIG), or 15 (9mm Para.) shot mag., lightweight polymer frame, matte black, bi-tone (.45 ACP only), Dark Earth (mfg. 2007-2012) or OD Green finish, steel slide, single action striker fired with U.S.A. trigger system, firing pin and loaded chamber indicators, dual recoil spring system, integral accessory rails standard on frame, ambidextrous mag. release, grip safety, front and rear slide serrations, external thumb safety became separate model in 2008, approx. 29 (9mm Para. cal.) or 33 oz. New 2002.

MSR $599	$535	$450	$400	$350	$300	$265	$235	

Add $30 for thumb safety (.45 ACP cal. only, black or bi-tone finish only).
Add $30 for .45 ACP cal. (new 2006), or $80 for bi-tone finish (.45 ACP cal. only).
Add $92 for Trijicon sights or approx. $90 for Heinie (disc.) tritium Slant Pro sights.
Subtract $7 for .45 GAP cal. black tactical (disc. 2007).

* **XD Tactical Pro** – limited mfg. 2003 only.

	$875	$775	$675	$575	$475	$400	$350	*$1,099*

XD 4 IN. SERVICE (X-TREME DUTY) – 9mm Para., .357 SIG, .40 S&W, .45 ACP (new 2006), or .45 GAP (mfg. 2005-2007) cal., cold hammer forged 4 in. ported or unported barrel, 9 (.45 GAP), 10 (.45 ACP), 12 (.40 S&W or .357 SIG), or 15 (9mm Para.) shot mag., lightweight polymer frame, matte black (only finish available on .357 SIG cal.), bi-tone (new 2003), Dark Earth (mfg. 2007-2012) or OD Green finish, steel slide, single action striker fired with U.S.A. trigger system, firing pin and loaded chamber indicators, dual recoil spring system, integral accessory rails standard on frame, ambidextrous mag. release, grip safety, front and rear slide serrations, thumb safety became separate model during 2008, approx. 28 (9mm Para.) or 30 oz. New 2002.

MSR $578	$515	$435	$365	$310	$275	$235	$200	

Add $29 for .45 ACP cal.
Add $35 for V10 ported barrel (black or OD Green finish, not available in .45 ACP or .45 GAP cal.).
Add $67 for bi-tone finish.
Add $100 for stainless steel slide (.45 ACP cal. only), disc.
Add $29 for thumb safety in .45 ACP cal.
Add $96 for Trijicon or Heinie tritium Slant Pro night sights (not available on .45 GAP cal.).
Subtract $7 for .45 GAP cal. (disc. 2007).

MSR	100%	98%	95%	90%	80%	70%	60%	*Last MSR*

XD 3 IN. SUB-COMPACT (X-TREME DUTY) – 9mm Para. or .40 S&W (new 2004) cal., cold hammer forged 3 in. barrel, 9 (.40 S&W), 10 (9mm Para.), or 13 (9mm Para.) shot mag., lightweight polymer frame, bi-tone (new 2004), matte black or OD Green finish, steel slide, single action striker fired with U.S.A. trigger system, firing pin and loaded chamber indicators, dual recoil spring system, integral accessory rails standard on frame, ambidextrous mag. release, grip safety, front and rear slide serrations, 26 oz. New 2003.

MSR $549	$490	$425	$365	$310	$275	$235	$200

Add $67 for bi-tone finish.

Add $96 for Trijicon or Heinie tritium Slant Pro night sights.

Add $100 for X-treme mini light (disc. 2011).

This model is not available with a thumb safety.

XD COMPACT SERIES – 9mm Para. (mfg. 2007 only), .40 S&W (mfg. 2007 only), or .45 ACP cal., 4 or 5 in. barrel, shortened grip frame, black, OD Green (disc.2012), bi-tone (new 2008), or Dark Earth (disc. 2011) finish, stainless steel slide, OD Green (disc 2012) or Dark Earth (disc. 2011) only, mfg. 2008-2012), 10 or extended 13 shot mag., 29 or 32 oz. New 2007.

MSR $600	$525	$440	$400	$350	$315	$280	$245

Add $46 for 5 in. barrel.

Add $66 for bi-tone finish or stainless steel slide (4 in. barrel only, disc. 2012).

Add $94 for Trijicon night sights (disc. 2011).

Subtract $30 for 9mm or .40 S&W cal. (4 in. barrel only), w/o night sights (disc. 2007).

XD CUSTOM SERIES – the Springfield custom shop makes three variations of the XD pistol, including the XD Carry, XD Production, and XD Custom Competition. Most calibers and sizes are available.

Current MSRs on this series are as follows - XD Carry is $795, XD Production is $1,200, and XD Custom Competition is $1,460.

XD(M) SERIES – 9mm Para., .40 S&W, or .45 ACP (new mid-2010) cal., 3.8 (available in 9mm Para. or .40 S&W only, new 2010) or 4 1/2 in. match grade barrel, 10 (.45 ACP only, new 2012), 13, 16 or 19 shot mag., polymer frame with lower Picatinny rail, minimal reset trigger, contoured frame is slightly modified from XD model, black, bi-tone, or OD Green Melonite oxide finish, deepened and diagonal slide serrations, black or stainless steel slide, interchangeable back straps, includes 3 interchangeable grip straps, includes XD Gear holster and black plastic carrying case, 28-31 oz. New mid-2008.

MSR $697	$615	$540	$465	$410	$360	$310	$265

Add $12 for .45 ACP cal. (new 2011).

Add approx. $66 for bi-tone finish or for OD Green w/stainless slide (not available in .45 ACP cal.).

Add $118 for night sights (Tritium or Trijicon).

XD(M) COMPACT SERIES – 9mm Para., .40 S&W, or .45 ACP (new 2012) cal., 3.8 in. barrel, 9 (flush, disc. 2012) or 13 shot mag., black or bi-tone polymer frame with lower Picatinny rail, Melonite metal finish, low profile dovetail front and rear 3 dot sights, includes the XD(M) Gear System, 26 oz. New 2011.

MSR $705	$620	$550	$465	$410	$360	$310	$265

Add $27 for .45 ACP cal. (new 2012).

Add $64 for bi-tone finish.

Subtract $112 for flush magazines (disc. 2012).

This model is also available with an extended 16 (.40 S&W cal.) or 19 (9mm Para. cal.) shot mag. in states where legal.

XD(M) COMPETITION SERIES – 9mm Para., .40 S&W, or .45 ACP cal., 5 1/4 in. match grade select fit barrel, Melonite fully supported ramp, 13 (.45 ACP), 16 (.40 S&W), or 19 (9mm Para.) shot mag., black polymer frame, red fiber optic front and fully adj. target rear sight, forged steel slide, black or bi-tone finish, 29-32 oz. New late 2011.

MSR $795	$725	$650	$550	$475	$400	$350	$300

Add $40 for .45 ACP cal.

Add $70 for bi-tone finish.

XD(M) CUSTOM SERIES – the Springfield custom shop makes three variations of the XD(M) pistol, including the XD(M) Carry, XD(M) Production, and XD(M) Custom Competition. Most calibers and sizes are available.

Current MSRs on this series are as follows - XD(M) Carry is $910, XD(M) Production is $1,295, and XD(M) Custom Competition is $1,525.

XD-S – 9mm Para. or .45 ACP cal., hammerless striker ignition system, 3.3 or 4 (9mm Para. only, new 2014) in. steel barrel, 5 or 7 shot mag., polymer frame with textured grip panels, fiber optic front and low profile dovetail rear sights, black or bi-tone melonite finish, loaded chamber indicator, single position Picatinny rail system, short reset trigger, rear grip safety, includes XD-S Gear System (paddle holster, double magazine pouch, 2 mags., and cable lock), 21 1/2 oz. New 2013.

MSR $599	$525	$465	$425	$385	$350	$325	$295

Add $70 for bi-tone finish.

MSR	100%	98%	95%	90%	80%	70%	60%	Last MSR

RIFLES: SEMI-AUTO, TACTICAL DESIGN

Many models listed are CA legal, since they do not have a muzzle brake. MSRs are typically the same as those guns available with a muzzle brake. Pricing on CA legal firearms is not included within the scope of this listing - please contact a Springfield dealer directly for this information.

M1 CARBINE – .30 Carbine cal., features new receiver on older military M1 GI stocks. Disc.

	100%	98%	95%	90%	80%	70%	60%	Last MSR
	$495	$435	$370	$335	$270	$225	$175	

M1 GARAND AND VARIATIONS – .30-06, .270 Win. (disc. 1987), or .308 Win. cal., semi-auto, 24 in. barrel, gas operated, 8 shot mag., adj. sights, 9 1/2 lbs.

* **M1 Garand Rifle** – .30-06 or .308 Win. cal., mfg. with original U.S. government issue parts, with new walnut stock, 8 shot mag., 24 in. barrel, 9 1/2 lbs. Limited mfg. 2002-2007.

	100%	98%	95%	90%	80%	70%	60%	Last MSR
	$1,175	$1,030	$880	$800	$645	$530	$410	$1,439

Add $30 for .308 Win. cal.

* **M1 Garand Standard Model** – supplied standard with camo GI fiberglass stock.

	100%	98%	95%	90%	80%	70%	60%	Last MSR
	$725	$635	$545	$495	$400	$325	$255	$761

Subtract $65 if with GI stock.

* **M1 Garand National Match** – walnut stock, match barrel and sights.

	100%	98%	95%	90%	80%	70%	60%	Last MSR
	$850	$745	$635	$580	$465	$380	$295	$897

Add $240 for Kevlar stock.

* **M1 Garand Ultra Match** – match barrel and sights, glass bedded stock, walnut stock standard.

	100%	98%	95%	90%	80%	70%	60%	Last MSR
	$950	$830	$710	$645	$520	$425	$330	$1,033

Add $240 for Kevlar stock.

* **M1-D Sniper Rifle** – .30-06 or .308 Win. cal., limited quantities, with original M84 scope, prong type flash suppressor, leather cheek pad and slings.

	100%	98%	95%	90%	80%	70%	60%	Last MSR
	$1,100	$960	$825	$750	$605	$495	$385	$1,033

* **M1 Garand Tanker Rifle** – similar to T-26 authorized by Gen. MacArthur at the end of WWII, 18 1/4 in. barrel, .30-06 or .308 Win. cal., GI stock standard.

	100%	98%	95%	90%	80%	70%	60%	Last MSR
	$850	$745	$635	$580	$465	$380	$295	$797

Add $23 for walnut full stock.

* **D-Day M1 Garand Rifle** – .30-06 cal., 24 in. barrel, gas operated, military square post front sights, engraved stock, 8 shot mag., two 8 shot clips, leather sling, cleaning kit, includes wooden crate and limited edition lithograph print, 9 1/2 lbs. 1,944 mfg. 2004-2005.

	100%	98%	95%	90%	80%	70%	60%	Last MSR
	$1,375	$1,205	$1,030	$935	$755	$620	$480	$1,490

BM 59 – .308 Win. cal., mfg. in Italy and machined and assembled in the Springfield Armory factory, 19.32 in. barrel, 20 shot detachable box mag., 9 1/2 lbs.

* **BM 59 Standard Italian Rifle** – with grenade launcher, winter trigger, tri-compensator, and bipod.

	100%	98%	95%	90%	80%	70%	60%	Last MSR
	$1,750	$1,530	$1,310	$1,190	$960	$785	$610	$1,950

* **BM 59 Alpine Rifle** – with Beretta pistol grip type stock.

	100%	98%	95%	90%	80%	70%	60%	Last MSR
	$2,025	$1,770	$1,520	$1,375	$1,115	$910	$710	$2,275

This model was also available in a Paratrooper configuration with folding stock at no extra charge.

* **BM 59 Nigerian Rifle** – similar to BM 59, except has Beretta pistol grip type stock.

	100%	98%	95%	90%	80%	70%	60%	Last MSR
	$2,075	$1,815	$1,555	$1,410	$1,140	$935	$725	$2,340

* **BM 59 E Model Rifle**

	100%	98%	95%	90%	80%	70%	60%	Last MSR
	$1,975	$1,730	$1,480	$1,345	$1,085	$890	$690	$2,210

M1A RIFLES – .243 Win. (disc.), .308 Win., or 7mm-08 Rem. (1991 mfg. only) cal., patterned after the original Springfield M14 - except semi-auto, walnut or fiberglass stock, 22 in. steel or stainless steel barrel, fiberglass handguard, "New Loaded" option (see separate listing) beginning 2001 includes NM air gauged barrel, trigger group, front and rear sights, and flash suppressor or Springfield proprietary muzzle brake, 9 lbs.

* **M1A Standard/Basic Model** – 7.62mm, above specifications, choice of Collector (original GI stock, disc. 2001), birch (disc. 2003), walnut (M1A Standard Model beginning 1993), Mossy Oak camo finished (new 2003), Green composite (new 2011), black fiberglass (M1A Basic Model), camo fiberglass (disc.), GI wood (disc. 1992), and brown (disc.) or black laminated (M1A Standard Model mfg. 1996-2000) stock, regular or National Match (disc.) barrel.

MSR $1,640	100%	98%	95%	90%	80%	70%	60%	Last MSR
	$1,425	$1,250	$1,050	$950	$765	$630	$490	

Add $9 for Green composite stock (new 2011).

MSR	100%	98%	95%	90%	80%	70%	60%	Last MSR

Add $99 for new walnut stock.

Add $44 for Mossy Oak camo finished stock.

Add $59 for birch stock (disc. 2003).

Add $44 for stainless steel barrel (disc.), $74 for bipod and stabilizer (disc.) or $159 for brown laminated stock (disc.), $59 for National Match barrel (disc.), $155 for National Match barrel and sights (disc.), $200 for folding stock (disc. 1994).

Subtract $58 for camo fiberglass stock (disc.).

Standard (entry level model) stock configuration for 1996 was black or camo fiberglass.

* **M1A E-2** – standard stock is birch. Disc.

	100%	98%	95%	90%	80%	70%	60%	Last MSR
	$975	$855	$730	$665	$535	$440	$340	$842

Add $30 for walnut stock.

Add $120 for Shaw stock with Harris bipod.

* **M1A Bush Rifle** – .308 Win. cal., 18 in. shrouded barrel, 8 lbs. 12 oz., collector GI, walnut, Mossy Oak camo finished (new 2003), black fiberglass folding (disc. 1994 per C/B), and black fiberglass (disc.) or laminated black (disc.) stock. Disc. 1999, reintroduced 2003 only.

	100%	98%	95%	90%	80%	70%	60%	Last MSR
	$1,300	$1,135	$975	$885	$715	$585	$455	$1,529

Add $29 for walnut stock (disc.), $15 for black fiberglass stock (disc.), $86 for black laminated stock (disc.), $235 for National Match variation (disc.), and $525 for Super Match variation (disc.)

* **M1A National Match** – .308 Win. cal., 22 in. steel or stainless steel (new 1999) barrel, National Match sights, mainspring guide, flash suppressor, and gas cylinder, special glass bedded oil finished match stock, tuned trigger, walnut stock became standard in 1991, 9 lbs.

MSR $2,318	100%	98%	95%	90%	80%	70%	60%
	$2,000	$1,750	$1,500	$1,350	$1,085	$890	$690

Add $55 for stainless steel barrel.

Add $155 for heavy composition stock (disc.).

Add $250 for either fiberglass or fancy burl wood stock (disc.).

.243 Win. and 7mm-08 Rem. cals. were also available at extra charge until discontinued.

* **M1A Super Match** – .308 Win. cal., similar to National Match, except has air-gauged Douglas or Hart (disc.) heavy barrel, oversized walnut, black fiberglass, or Marine Corp Green Camo fiberglass super match stock, modified operating rod guide, rear lugged receiver beginning 1991, approx. 11 1/2 lbs.

MSR $2,905	100%	98%	95%	90%	80%	70%	60%
	$2,550	$2,200	$1,875	$1,685	$1,360	$1,115	$865

Add $230 for stainless steel Douglas barrel.

Add $738 for McMillan black or Marine Corps camo fiberglass stock.

Add $250 for Krieger or Hart barrel (disc.).

Add $200 for fancy burl walnut (disc.) stock.

.243 Win. and 7mm-08 Rem. cals. were also available at extra charge until discontinued.

M1A LOADED STANDARD – .308 Win. cal., 22 in. National Match steel or stainless steel barrel, features shooting upgrades such as National Match trigger assembly, front and rear sights, and National Match flash suppressor, 10 shot mag., black or green fiberglass, Collector GI walnut (disc. 2000), or new walnut stock, approx. 9 1/2 lbs. New 1999.

MSR $1,794	100%	98%	95%	90%	80%	70%	60%
	$1,650	$1,425	$1,225	$1,075	$875	$725	$575

Add $114 for new walnut stock.

Add $16 for green stock.

Add $211 for stainless steel barrel and walnut stock.

Add $99 for stainless steel barrel.

Add $525 for extended cluster rail with black fiberglass stock and National Match stainless steel barrel (mfg. 2006-2011).

Add $100 for Collector GI walnut (disc. 2000).

M1A "GOLD SERIES" – .308 Win. cal., heavy walnut competition stock, gold medal grade heavy Douglas barrel. Mfg. 1987 only.

	100%	98%	95%	90%	80%	70%	60%	Last MSR
	$1,944	$1,700	$1,460	$1,320	$1,070	$875	$680	$1,944

Add $126 for Kevlar stock, add $390 for special Hart stainless steel barrel, add $516 for Hart stainless steel barrel with Kevlar stock.

M1A SCOUT SQUAD – .308 Win. cal., 18 in. barrel, choice of GI Collector (disc. 1998), new walnut, green (disc. 2011) or black fiberglass, Mossy Oak camo finished, or black laminated (disc. 1998) stock, muzzle stabilizer standard, supplied with Scout mount and handguard, approx. 9 lbs. New 1997.

MSR $1,761	100%	98%	95%	90%	80%	70%	60%
	$1,550	$1,350	$1,150	$1,050	$840	$685	$535

Add $132 for walnut stock.

Add $87 for Mossy Oak camo finish.

Add $14 for green stock (disc. 2011).

MSR	100%	98%	95%	90%	80%	70%	60%	Last MSR

M1A SOCOM 16 – .308 Win. cal., 16 1/4 in. barrel with muzzle brake, black or green fiberglass stock with steel buttplate, black finish, upper handguard has been cut out for sight rail, 10 shot box mag., tritium front sight with ghost ring aperture rear sight, two-stage military trigger, 8.8 lbs. New 2004.

MSR $1,893 $1,725 $1,495 $1,275 $1,150 $925 $750 $585

Add $12 for green composite stock.

M1A/M21 TACTICAL – .308 Win. cal., Garand action, 22 in. barrel, tactical variation of the Super Match mfg. with match grade parts giving superior accuracy, adj. walnut cheekpiece stock, choice of Douglas carbon steel or stainless Krieger barrel, 11.6 lbs. New 1990.

MSR $3,555 $3,150 $2,800 $2,325 $2,075 $1,675 $1,350 $1,075

Add $420 for Krieger stainless barrrel.

M25 "WHITE FEATHER" TACTICAL – .308 Win. cal., Garand action, includes black fiberglass M3A McMillan stock, 22 in. Kreiger heavy carbon barrel standard, Rader trigger, White Feather logo and Carlos Hathcock II signature, 10 shot box mag., includes Harris bipod, 12 3/4 lbs. Mfg. 2001-2009.

   $4,750 $4,155 $3,560 $3,230 $2,610 $2,135 $1,660   *$5,278*

SAR-3 – .308 Win. cal., licensed copy of the pre-import ban HK-91, predecessor to the SAR-8, mfg. in Greece.

   $995 $870 $745 $675 $545 $450 $350

SAR-8 – .308 Win. cal., patterned after the H & K Model 91, roller locking delayed blowback action, fluted chamber, rotary adj. rear aperture sight, 18 in. barrel, recent mfg. incorporated a cast aluminum receiver with integrated Weaver rail, pistol grip, slim forearm, and green furniture (for law enforcement only), supplied with walnut (disc. 1994) or black fiberglass thumbhole sporter stock, 10 (C/B 1994) or 20 (disc. 1994) shot detachable mag., 8.7 lbs. Mfg. in U.S. starting 1990, disc. 1998.

   $1,015 $890 $760 $690 $560 $455 $355   *$1,204*

SAR-8 parts are interchangeable with both SAR-3 and HK-91 parts.

* ***SAR-8 Tactical Counter Sniper Rifle*** – .308 Win. cal., tactical sniper variation of the SAR-8. Mfg. 1996-98.

   $1,325 $1,160 $995 $900 $730 $595 $465   *$1,610*

SAR-48 MODEL – .308 Win. cal., GPO, authentic model of the Belgian semi-auto FAL/LAR rifle, 21 in. barrel, 20 shot mag., walnut or synthetic stock, adj. sights, sling, and mag. loader. Mfg. 1985-89.

   $1,675 $1,465 $1,255 $1,140 $920 $755 $585

Add approx. 20% for Israeli configuration with heavy barrel, bipod, flash hider, and flip-up buttplate.

The SAR-48 was disc. in 1989 and reintroduced as the Model SAR-4800 in 1990.

* ***SAR-48 Bush Rifle*** – similar to SAR-48 model, except has 18 in. barrel.

   $1,750 $1,530 $1,310 $1,190 $960 $785 $610

* ***SAR-48 .22 Cal.*** – .22 LR cal., variation of the Sporter Model. Disc. 1989.

   $725 $635 $545 $495 $400 $325 $255   *$760*

SAR-4800 SPORTER MODEL – .223 Rem. (new 1997) or .308 Win. cal., GPO, authentic model of the Belgian semi-auto FAL/LAR rifle, 18 (.223 Rem. cal. only) or 21 in. barrel, 10 (C/B 1994) or 20 (disc.) shot mag., walnut (disc.) or black fiberglass thumbhole sporter stock, adj. sights, sling, and mag. loader. Mfg. 1990-1998.

   $1,080 $945 $810 $735 $595 $485 $380

All SAR - 4800 parts are interchangeable with both SAR-48 and FN/FAL parts. This model is an updated variation of the pre-WWII FN Model 49.

* ***SAR-4800 Bush Rifle Sporter Model*** – similar to standard model, except has 18 in. barrel.

   $1,085 $950 $815 $735 $595 $490 $380   *$1,216*

STAG ARMS LLC

Current rifle and accessories manufacturer located in New Britain, CT.

RIFLES: SEMI-AUTO

All AR-15 style carbines/rifles are available in post-ban configuration for restricted states, and include one mag., instruction manual, plastic rifle case, and lifetime warranty.

MODEL 1 CARBINE – .223 Rem. cal., GIO, 16 in. chrome lined barrel, A3 forged aluminum upper, standard safety, black anodized finish, six position collapsible stock, removable carry handle, standard GI carbine design, available in right or left (Model 1L) hand, 7.1 lbs.

MSR $949 $850 $750 $650 $595 $500 $400 $325

Add $40 for Model 1L.

MSR	100%	98%	95%	90%	80%	70%	60%	Last MSR

MODEL 2 CARBINE – .223 Rem. cal., GIO, 16 in. chrome lined barrel, A3 forged aluminum upper, standard safety, black anodized finish, six position collapsible stock, flip up rear sight, tactical top rail, available in right or left (Model 2L) hand, 6.4 lbs.

| MSR $940 | $850 | $750 | $650 | $595 | $500 | $400 | $325 | |

Add $24 for Model 2L.

* Model 2T Carbine – .223 Rem. cal., GIO, 16 in. chrome lined barrel, A3 forged aluminum upper, ambidextrous (left hand only) or standard safety, six position collapsible stock, flip up rear sight, tactical rail, pistol grip, available in right or left hand, approx. 6.6 lbs.

| MSR $1,130 | $995 | $895 | $775 | $700 | $575 | $500 | $425 | |

Add $25 for left hand (Model 2T-L).

MODEL 3 CARBINE – .223 Rem. cal., GIO, 16 in. chrome lined barrel, A3 forged aluminum upper, standard safety, black anodized finish, six position collapsible stock, tactical top rail, available in right or left (Model 3L) hand, V-RS modular rail platform became standard 2011, 6.1 lbs.

| MSR $895 | $800 | $700 | $600 | $550 | $475 | $425 | $395 | |

Add $25 for Model 3L.

MODEL 3G RIFLE – 5.56mm cal., GIO, 18 in. stainless steel heavy fluted barrel, matte black finish, Samson Evolution handguard, Geissele Super 3-Gun trigger, 30 shot mag., accessory rail, Magpul ACS buttstock and MOE pistol grip, right or left hand action, 7 1/2 lbs. New 2012.

| MSR $1,459 | $1,350 | $1,225 | $1,025 | $900 | $775 | $650 | $525 | |

Add $20 for left hand.

MODEL 3T RIFLE – 5.56 NATO cal., GIO, 16 in. chrome lined barrel with A2 flash hider, DiamondHead VRS-T free float handguard, polymer DiamondHead front and rear flip-up sights, Mil-Spec 6-pos. collapsible buttstock, A2 plastic grip, 7.4 lbs. New 2014.

| MSR $999 | $875 | $775 | $650 | $600 | $525 | $450 | $400 | |

Add $20 for Model 3T-L (left hand).

MODEL 3T-M RIFLE – 5.56 NATO cal., GIO, 16 in. chrome lined barrel with A2 flash hider, DiamondHead VRS-T free float handguard, aluminum DiamondHead front and rear flip-up sights, Magpul ACS 6-pos. buttstock, Magpul MOE grip, 7 1/2 lbs. New 2014.

| MSR $1,160 | $1,015 | $895 | $775 | $700 | $575 | $500 | $425 | |

Add $20 for left hand (Model 3TL-M).

MODEL 4 RIFLE – .223 Rem. cal., GIO, 20 in. heavy barrel, A3 forged aluminum upper, standard safety, black anodized finish, A2 fixed stock, removable carry handle, available in right or left (Model 4L) hand, 7 1/2 lbs.

| MSR $1,015 | $925 | $825 | $725 | $625 | $550 | $475 | $395 | |

Add $50 for left hand (Model 4L).

MODEL 5 CARBINE – 6.8 SPC cal., GIO, 16 in. chrome lined barrel, A3 forged aluminum upper, standard or ambidextrous (left hand only) safety, black anodized finish, six position collapsible stock, available in right or left (Model 5L) hand, 7.1 lbs.

| MSR $1,045 | $950 | $850 | $725 | $650 | $525 | $450 | $400 | |

Add $50 for left hand (Model 5L).

MODEL 6 RIFLE – .223 Rem. cal., GIO, 24 1/8 in. stainless steel heavy barrel, A3 forged aluminum upper, standard or ambidextrous (left hand only) safety, fixed A2 buttstock, black anodized finish, tactical top rail, no sights, Hogue overmolded pistol grip, approx. 10 lbs.

| MSR $1,055 | $950 | $850 | $725 | $650 | $525 | $450 | $400 | |

Add $40 for left hand (Model 6L).

STAG 7 HUNTER – 6.8 SPC cal., GIO, 20.8 in. stainless steel barrel, A3 forged aluminum upper, standard or ambidextrous (left hand only) safety, fixed A2 buttstock, black anodized finish, no sights, tactical top rail, two-stage match trigger, Hogue pistol grip, available in right or left hand, approx. 10 lbs.

| MSR $1,055 | $950 | $850 | $725 | $650 | $525 | $450 | $400 | |

Add $40 for left hand (Model 7L).

MODEL 8 CARBINE – .223 Rem. cal., GPO, 16 in. chrome lined barrel, A3 forged aluminum upper, ambidextrous (left hand only) or standard safety, six position collapsible stock, flip up rear sight. New 2011.

| MSR $1,145 | $1,010 | $895 | $775 | $700 | $575 | $500 | $425 | |

Add $30 for left hand (Model 8L).

* Model 8T Carbine – .223 Rem. cal., GPO, similar to Model 8, except has Diamondhead VRS-T free floating modular handguard, continuous top rail, matched set of Diamondhead flip up sights. New 2013.

| MSR $1,275 | $1,125 | $975 | $850 | $725 | $600 | $500 | $450 | |

Add $20 for Model 8TL.

MSR		100%	98%	95%	90%	80%	70%	60%	*Last MSR*

STANDARD MANUFACTURING CO. LLC

Current manufacturer located in Newington, CT. Dealer and consumer direct sales were through FFL dealer.

RIFLES: SEMI-AUTO

MODEL M1927 .22 CAL. – .22 LR cal., semi-auto, half scale replica patterned after the Thompson Model 1927, thin barrel, 10 shot (standard) or optional aluminum drum magazine, high gloss blue, deluxe walnut stock, pistol grip, and forearm, 5 1/2 lbs. While advertised during 2012, this model has yet to go into production.

The scheduled MSR on this model was $1,299.

STAR, BONIFACIO ECHEVERRIA S.A.

Previous manufacturer located in Eibar, Spain. Star, Bonifacio Echeverria S.A. closed its doors on July 28th, 1997, due to the intense financial pressure the Spanish arms industry experienced during the late 1990s. Previously imported by Interarms, located in Alexandria, VA.

PISTOLS: SEMI-AUTO

MEGASTAR – 10mm or .45 ACP cal., DA/SA, larger variation of the Firestar featuring 4.6 in. barrel and 12 (.45 ACP) or 14 (10mm) shot mag., 47.6 oz. Imported 1992-1994.

		100%	98%	95%	90%	80%	70%	60%	*Last MSR*
		$450	$395	$340	$305	$250	$205	$160	*$653*

Add $29 for Starvel finish.

ULTRASTAR – 9mm Para. or .40 S&W (new 1996) cal., compact double action design, 3.57 in. barrel, DA/SA, 9 shot mag., blue steel metal, triple dot sights, steel internal mechanism, polymer exterior construction, 26 oz. Mfg. 1994-1997.

		100%	98%	95%	90%	80%	70%	60%	*Last MSR*
		$350	$300	$250	$225	$180	$145	$115	*$296*

STERLING ARMAMENT, LTD.

Previous manufacturer established c. 1900, and located in Dagenham, Essex, England. Previously imported and distributed by Cassi Inc. located in Colorado Springs, CO until 1990.

CARBINES: SEMI-AUTO

AR-180 – please refer to Armalite section for more information and pricing on this model.

STERLING MK 6 – 9mm Para. cal., blowback semi-auto with floating firing pin, shrouded 16.1 in. barrel, side mounted mag., folding stock, 7 1/2 lbs. Disc. 1989.

		100%	98%	95%	90%	80%	70%	60%	*Last MSR*
	N/A	$1,750	$1,500	$1,400	$1,200	$1,000	$795		*$650*

PISTOLS: SEMI-AUTO

PARAPISTOL MK 7 C4 – 9mm Para. cal., 4 in. barrel, tactical design pistol, crinkle finish, same action as MK. 6 Carbine, fires from closed bolt, 10, 15, 20, 30, 34 or 68 shot mag., 5 lbs. Disc. 1989.

		100%	98%	95%	90%	80%	70%	60%	*Last MSR*
	N/A	$1,500	$1,400	$1,200	$1,000	$800	$700		*$600*

Add $50 per 30 or 34 shot mag., $125 for 68 shot mag.

PARAPISTOL MK 7 C8 – 9mm Para. cal., similar to C4, except has 7.8 in. barrel, 5 1/4 lbs. Disc. 1989.

		100%	98%	95%	90%	80%	70%	60%	*Last MSR*
	N/A	$1,500	$1,400	$1,250	$1,050	$900	$750		*$620*

Add $50 per 30 or 34 shot mag., $125 for 68 shot mag.

STERLING ARSENAL

Current custom AR-15 manufacturer located in Sterling, VA.

Sterling Arsenal manufactures their own SAR-XV brand of custom AR-15 rifles. They also customize the AR-10 platform, and convert and enhance Saiga-12 and AK-47 models. Please contact the company directly for more information on all their models, including options, pricing, and availability (see Trademark Index).

STEVENS, J., ARMS COMPANY

Current trademark of long arms produced by Savage Arms, Inc. Beginning in 1999, Savage Arms, Inc. began manufacturing/importing Stevens trademarked guns again, including rifles and shotguns. J. Stevens Arms Company was founded in 1864 at Chicopee Falls, MA as J. Stevens & Co. In 1886 the name was changed to J. Stevens Arms and Tool Co. In 1916, the plant became New England Westinghouse, and tooled up for Mosin-Nagant Rifles. In 1920, the plant was sold to the Savage Arms Corp. and manufactured guns were marked "J. Stevens Arms Co." This designation was dropped in the late 1940s, and only the name "Stevens" has been used up to 1990.

Depending on the remaining Stevens factory data, a factory letter authenticating the configuration of a particular specimen may be obtained by contacting Mr. John Callahan (see Trademark Index for listings and address). The charge for this service is $25.00 per gun - please allow 8 weeks for an adequate response.

MSR	100%	98%	95%	90%	80%	70%	60%	Last MSR

SHOTGUNS

Stevens made a wide variety of inexpensive, utilitarian shotguns that, to date, have attracted mostly shooting interest, but little collector interest. A listing of these models may be found in the back of this text under "Serialization."

MODEL 350 SLIDE ACTION SECURITY – 12 ga., 18 1/4 in. barrel, 5 shot tube mag., bottom ejection, matte black synthetic pistol grip stock, bead (disc. 2012), ghost ring, or rifle (disc. 2012) sights, 7.6 lbs. New mid-2010.

MSR $276	$225	$195	$170	$150	$135	$125	$115	

STEYR ARMS (STEYR MANNLICHER)

Currently manufactured by Steyr-Mannlicher AG & Co. KG in Austria. Founded in Steyr, Austria by Joseph Werndl circa 1864. Currently imported beginning mid-2005 by Steyr Arms, Inc., located in Bessemer, AL. Previously located in Trussville, AL until 2013. Previously located in Cumming, GA. Previously imported 2004-mid-2005 by Steyr USA, located in West Point, MS. Previously imported 2002-2003 by Dynamit Nobel, located in Closter, NJ. Previously imported and distributed until 2002 by Gun South, Inc. (GSI) located in Trussville, AL.

In 2007, the firm of Steyr-Mannlicher was sold to new owners and the factory was relocated to Kleinraming, approx. 12 miles from the original site in Steyr, Austria. The new firm, Steyr Arms, was purchased by Dr. Ernst Reichmayr and his friend and partner, Gerhard Unterganschnigg.

Note: also see Mannlicher Schoenauer in the M section for pre-WWII models.

For more information and current pricing on both new and used Steyr airguns, please refer to the *Blue Book of Airguns* by Dr. Robert Beeman & John Allen (also online).

PISTOLS: SEMI-AUTO

MODEL GB – 9mm Para. cal., DA/SA, 18 shot mag., gas delayed blowback action, non-glare checkered plastic grips, 5 1/4 in. barrel with Polygon rifling, matte finish, steel construction, 2 lbs. 6 oz. Importation disc. 1988.

	100%	98%	95%	90%	80%	70%	60%	Last MSR
Commercial	$675	$600	$525	$450	$400	$350	$300	
Military	$795	$725	$650	$600	$525	$450	$400	$514

In 1987, Steyr mfg. a military variation of the Model GB featuring a phosphate finish - only 937 were imported into the U.S.

MODEL SPP – 9mm Para. cal., SA, delayed blow back system with rotating 5.9 in. barrel, 15 or 30 shot mag., utilizes synthetic materials and advanced ergonomics, adj. sights, grooved receiver for scope mounting, matte black finish, 44 oz. Limited importation 1992-1993.

	100%	98%	95%	90%	80%	70%	60%	Last MSR
	$800	$675	$600	$550	$495	$450	$400	$895

MODEL M SERIES – 9mm Para., .357 SIG, or .40 S&W cal., DAO, SFO, features first integrated limited access key lock safety in a semi-auto pistol, 3 different safety conditions, black synthetic frame, 10 shot mag., matte black finish, loaded chamber indicator, triangle/trapezoid sights, 28 oz. Limited importation 1999-2002.

	100%	98%	95%	90%	80%	70%	60%	Last MSR
	$500	$450	$400	$350	$300	$275	$250	$610

Add $65 for night sights.

M-A1 SERIES – .357 SIG (M357 A-1, disc. 2013), 9mm Para. (M9 A-1), or .40 S&W (M40 A-1) cal., DAO, SFO, updated Model M with Picatinny rail on lower front of frame, redesigned grip frame, trigger safety and lockable safety system, black polymer frame with matte black finished slide, 3 1/2 (not available in .357 SIG cal.) or 4 in. barrel, 10, 12 (.40 S&W or .357 SIG) or 15 (9mm Para.) shot mag., white outlined triangular sights, approx. 27 oz. Imported 2004-2009, reintroduced late 2010.

MSR $560	$495	$450	$395	$350	$300	$275	$250	

Add $23 for triangle sights with Trilux (disc.)
Add $40 for night sights (disc. 2013).

S-A1 SERIES – 9mm Para. (S9 A-1), or .40 S&W (S40 A-1) cal., similar to M-A1 Series, 10 shot mag., smaller compact frame.

MSR $560	$495	$450	$395	$350	$300	$275	$250	

C-A1 SERIES – 9mm Para. (C9 A-1), or .40 S&W (C40 A-1, importation disc. 2011) cal., similar to M-A1 Series, 12 or 17 shot mag., compact frame.

MSR $560	$495	$450	$395	$350	$300	$275	$250	

MODEL S – similar to Model M, except has 3 1/2 in. barrel and shorter grip frame, 10 shot mag., 22 1/2 oz. Limited importation 2000-2002.

	100%	98%	95%	90%	80%	70%	60%	Last MSR
	$475	$435	$385	$350	$325	$300	$280	$610

MSR	100%	98%	95%	90%	80%	70%	60%	Last MSR

RIFLES: BOLT ACTION, RECENT PRODUCTION

The Steyr-Mannlicher models were in production 1968-1996.

Current production guns are now called Steyr-Mannlicher models. For models manufactured 1903-1971, please refer to the Mannlicher Schoenauer Sporting Rifles section in this text. All known calibers are listed for each model. Caliber offerings varied often throughout the 28 year run of the Steyr-Mannlicher, stock designs evolved, and sights and magazine styles changed. The only truly rare caliber is the 6mm Rem., which was always special order. Next in North American rarity is the .25-06. Certain additional European calibers are rare in the USA because they were not imported due to lack of popularity - 5.6x57mm, 6.5x57mm, 6x62mm Freres, 6.5x65mm, and 9.3x62mm.

All four action lengths, SL, L, M, S, were offered in numerous deluxe variations with engraving and stock carving on special order blued metal and highly polished engraved actions. Stock carving is heavy and elegant. The "twisted appearance" of the hammer rifles barrels on all firearms of this group lends a unique and unmistakable look to these rifles.

A major irritant for hardcore Steyr-Mannlicher collectors is the continued misidentification of Luxus models by online sellers. First, a standard USA version Luxus has the word "Luxus" engraved on the left side of the receiver. A Luxus also has a steel box magazine instead of a rotary plastic one and a rotary shotgun style safety, although some apparently early Luxus models exist with the sliding side safety.

Pricing shows the result of continued cost increases at Steyr, which finally caused the end of the production run and redesign to the SBS-96 model to save costs, regain competition, and take advantage of improved safety features.

MANNLICHER/STEYR SCOUT
– .223 Rem. (new 2000), .243 Win. (mfg. 2000 only, reintroduced 2005), .308 Win., 7mm-08 Rem. (new 2000), or .376 Steyr (mfg. 1999-2000, reintroduced 2005) cal., designed by Jeff Cooper, features grey, black synthetic Zytel or camo (.308 Win. cal. only beginning 2005) stock, 19 1/4 in. fluted barrel, Picatinny optic rail, integral bipod, Package includes Steyr or Leupold (disc. 2005) M8 2.5x28 IER scope with factory Steyr mounts, and luggage case. New 1998.

| MSR $2,099 | $1,850 | $1,575 | $1,375 | $1,125 | $900 | $750 | $650 | |

Add $100 for camo (disc. 2013).
Add $600 for Steyr Scout Package with Steyr or Leupold (disc. 2004) scope, mounts and luggage case (disc. 2013).

* **Steyr Scout Jeff Cooper** – .223 Rem., .308 Win. or .376 Steyr (disc. 2000, reintroduced 2005) cal., grey synthetic Zytel stock with Jeff Cooper logo and integral bipod, certificate of authenticity with test target, Package (disc. 2004) included Leupold M8 2.5x28 IER scope with factory Steyr mounts, and luggage case. Mfg. 1999-2009.

| | $2,375 | $2,050 | $1,750 | $1,425 | $1,175 | $1,050 | $900 | $2,699 |

Add approx. 15% for Steyr Scout Package with Leupold scope, mounts and luggage case (disc. 2004).

» **Steyr Scout Jeff Cooper Limited Edition** – 308 Win. cal., 20 in. fluted barrel, 10 shot polymer double stack detachable box mag., flip up iron sights, integral top rail, gray Mannox finish, Scout stock with integrated bipod and UIT rail, "JC" crest of arms, special ser. no., single stage trigger, three position safety, two removable sling swivels, includes Leupold 2.5X28mm Scout Scope, Galco Ching Sling, Boyt hard and soft case, Steyr scope mounts, extra magazine, and copy of Cooper's book *Art of the Rifle*, approx. 8 lbs., limited mfg. of 300. New mid-2010.

| MSR $2,995 | $2,625 | $2,250 | $1,875 | $1,550 | $1,275 | $1,050 | $925 | |

* **Steyr Scout** – .243 Win. cal., similar to Jeff Cooper Package, except does not include scope, mounts, or case. Mfg. 1999-2002.

| | $1,525 | $1,350 | $1,200 | $1,050 | $900 | $750 | $625 | $1,969 |

Add $100 for .376 Steyr cal. (black stock only, disc. 2000).
Add $100 for Jeff Cooper grey stock.

* **Steyr Scout Tactical** – .223 Rem. (new 2000) or .308 Win. cal., similar to Steyr Scout, except has black synthetic stock with removable spacers, oversized bolt handle, and emergency ghost ring sights. Mfg. 1999-2002.

| | $1,600 | $1,400 | $1,250 | $1,050 | $900 | $750 | $625 | $2,069 |

» **Steyr Scout Tactical Stainless** – similar to Steyr Scout Tactical, except has stainless steel barrel. Mfg. 2000-2002.

| | $1,650 | $1,425 | $1,150 | $1,025 | $830 | $710 | $590 | $2,159 |

MANNLICHER PRO VARMINT
– .223 Rem. cal., 23.6 in. heavy fluted barrel, black synthetic or camo vented stock, includes tactical rail. Imported 2009-2013.

| | $1,600 | $1,450 | $1,275 | $1,075 | $900 | $775 | $650 | $1,799 |

Add $200 for camo.

SBS TACTICAL
– .308 Win. cal. only, 20 in. barrel w/o sights, features oversized bolt handle and high capacity 10 shot mag. with adapter, matte blue finish. Mfg. 1999-2002.

| | $840 | $735 | $625 | $550 | $500 | $450 | $395 | $969 |

* **SBS Tactical Heavy Barrel** – .300 Win. Mag. (new 2000) or .308 Win. cal., features 20 (carbine, new 2000, .308 Win. only) or 26 in. heavy barrel w/o sights and oversized bolt handle, matte blue finish or stainless steel (carbine only, new 2000). Mfg. 1999-2002.

| | $865 | $745 | $635 | $550 | $500 | $450 | $395 | $1,019 |

MSR	100%	98%	95%	90%	80%	70%	60%	*Last MSR*

Add $30 for .300 Win. Mag. cal.
Add $40 for stainless steel.

* **SBS Tactical McMillan** – similar to SBS Tactical Heavy Barrel, except has custom McMillan A - 3 stock with adj. cheekpiece and oversized bolt handle, matte blue finish. Mfg. 1999-2002.

| | $1,465 | $1,245 | $1,035 | $850 | $725 | $600 | $550 | |

Last was $1,699
Add $30 for .300 Win. Mag. cal.

* **SBS Tactical CISM** – .308 Win. cal., 20 in. heavy barrel w/o sights, laminated wood stock with black lacquer finish, adj. cheekpiece and buttplate, 10 shot detachable mag., vent. forend. Mfg. 2000-2002.

| | $3,050 | $2,650 | $2,300 | $1,950 | $1,600 | $1,300 | $1,150 | *$3,499* |

Subtract approx. 35% for Swiss contract CISM Match in 7.5x55mm cal. with match diopter sights and 23 1/2 in. barrel. (Only 100 were imported.)

STEYR ELITE (SBS TACTICAL) – .223 Rem. (disc. 2008) or .308 Win. cal., 20 (carbine, disc.), 22.4 (new 2006) or 26 (disc. 2005) in. barrel with full length Picatinny spec. mounting rail, oversize bolt handle, two 5 shot detachable mags. (with spare buttstock storage), adj. black synthetic stock, matte blue finish or stainless steel. New 2000.

| MSR $2,299 | $1,950 | $1,725 | $1,500 | $1,275 | $1,050 | $875 | $775 | |

* **Steyr Elite 08** – .308 Win. cal., 23.6 in. blue or stainless steel barrel, Dural aluminum folding stock, 10 shot high capacity box mag., extra long Picatinny rail. Imported 2009-2013.

| | $5,325 | $4,650 | $4,325 | $3,750 | $3,250 | $2,600 | $1,995 | *$5,999* |

MODEL SSG – .243 Win. (disc., PII Sniper only) or .308 Win cal., for competition or law-enforcement use. Marksman has regular sights, detachable rotary mag., teflon coated bolt with heavy duty locking lugs, synthetic stock has removable spacers, parkerized finish. Match version has heavier target barrel and "match" bolt carrier, can be used as single shot. Extremely accurate.

* **Model SSG 69 Sport (PI Rifle)** – .243 Win. or .308 Win. cal., 26 in. barrel with iron sights, 3 shot mag., black or green ABS Cycolac synthetic stock.

| | $1,775 | $1,500 | $1,225 | $1,000 | $850 | $725 | $650 | *$1,989* |

Add 15% for walnut stock (disc. 1992, retail was $448).

* **Model SSG PII/PIIK Sniper Rifle** – .22-250 Rem. (new 2004), .243 Win. (disc.) or .308 Win. cal., 20 in. heavy (Model PIIK) or 26 in. heavy barrel, no sights, green or black synthetic Cycolac or McMillan black fiberglass stock, modified bolt handle, choice of single or set triggers.

| MSR $1,899 | $1,695 | $1,500 | $1,300 | $1,050 | $875 | $750 | $625 | |

Add 15% for walnut stock (disc. 1992, retail was $448).

* **Model SSG PIII Rifle** – .308 Win. cal., 26 in. heavy barrel with diopter match sight bases, H-S Precision Pro-Series stock in black only. Importation 1991-93.

| | $2,300 | $1,875 | $1,425 | $1,050 | $825 | $700 | $600 | *$3,162* |

* **Model SSG PIV (Urban Rifle)** – .308 Win. cal., carbine variation with 16 1/2 in. heavy barrel and flash hider (disc.), ABS Cycolac synthetic stock in green or black. Imported 1991-2002, reimported beginning 2004.

| MSR $1,899 | $1,695 | $1,500 | $1,300 | $1,050 | $875 | $750 | $625 | |

* **Model SSG Jagd Match** – .222 Rem., .243 Win., or .308 Win. cal., checkered wood laminate stock, 23.6 in. barrel, Mannlicher sights, DT, supplied with test target. Mfg. 1991-1992.

| | $1,550 | $1,050 | $950 | $800 | $675 | $600 | $540 | *$1,550* |

* **Model SSG Match Rifle** – .308 Win. only, 26 in. heavy barrel, brown ABS Cycolac stock, Walther Diopter sights, 8.6 lbs. Mfg. disc. 1992.

| | $2,000 | $1,500 | $1,225 | $925 | $800 | $700 | $600 | *$2,306* |

Add $437 for walnut stock.

* **Model SPG-T** – .308 Win. cal., Target model. Mfg. 1993-98.

| | $3,225 | $2,850 | $2,550 | $2,200 | $1,850 | $1,500 | $1,200 | *$3,695* |

* **Model SPG-CISM** – .308 Win. cal., 20 in. heavy barrel, laminated wood stock with adj. cheekpiece and black lacquer finish. Mfg. 1993-99.

| | $2,995 | $2,600 | $2,300 | $1,950 | $1,700 | $1,450 | $1,200 | *$3,295* |

* **Model SSG Match UIT** – .308 Win. cal. only, 10 shot steel mag., special single set trigger, free floating barrel, Diopter sights, raked bolt handle, 10.8 lbs. Disc. 1998.

| | $3,000 | $2,500 | $2,000 | $1,800 | $1,500 | $1,200 | $1,000 | *$3,995* |

UIT stands for Union Internationale de Tir.

MSR	100%	98%	95%	90%	80%	70%	60%	*Last MSR*

* **Model SSG 04** – .308 Win. or .300 Win. Mag. cal., 20 (disc. 2005) or 23.6 heavy hammer forged barrel with muzzle brake, two-stage trigger, matte finished metal, black synthetic stock, adj. bipod, 8 (.300 Win. Mag.) or 10 (.308 Win.) shot mag., Picatinny rail, adj. buttstock, 10.1 lbs. Importation began 2004.

MSR $2,299	$1,950	$1,725	$1,500	$1,275	$1,050	$875	$775

Add $200 for 16.1 in. barrel.

Add $1,300 for A1 model (new 2009).

* **Model SSG 08** – .308 Win., .300 Win. Mag. (new 2014), or .338 Lapua (new 2014) cal., 23.6 in. barrel, folding stock, adj. Picatinny rails.

MSR $5,899	$5,250	$4,800	$4,300	$3,750	$3,250	$2,600	$1,995

HS-50 – .460 Steyr (disc. 2013) or .50 BMG cal., single shot or repeater (M1) action, 33 in. barrel with muzzle brake, includes Picatinny rail and bipod, approx. 28 lbs. Importation began 2004.

MSR $5,295	$4,850	$4,350	$3,900	$3,500	$3,150	$2,850	$2,500

Add $1,200 for M1 Repeater.

RIFLES: SEMI-AUTO

AUG S.A. – .223 Rem. cal., gas operated, design incorporates use of advanced plastics, short stroke piston, integral Swarovski scope or Picatinny rail (24 in. heavy barrel only), 16, 20, 21, or 24 in. barrel, green composite stock (original bullpup configuration), rotating breech bolt, later mfg. was black or desert tan stock , 10, 30 or 42 shot mag., 7.9 lbs. Importation resumed mid-2006.

MSR $2,099	$1,895	$1,675	$1,425	$1,295	$1,050	$850	$675

Add approx. 10% for 24 in. heavy barrel with Picatinny rail and bipod (disc.).

Add $131 for 42 shot mag.

* **AUG S.A. Commercial** – similar to AUG S.A., grey (3,000 mfg. circa 1997), green, or black finish.

SP receiver (Stanag metal)	$2,950	$2,750	$2,450	$2,150	$1,750	$1,575	$1,400
Grey finish	$3,150	$2,875	$2,600	$2,250	$1,825	$1,625	$1,450
Green finish (last finish)	$3,400	$2,975	$2,700	$2,300	$1,875	$1,675	$1,500
Black finish	$4,125	$3,750	$3,300	$2,950	$2,750	$2,500	$2,250

Last MSR was $1,362 (1989) for Green finish.

STEYR USR (UNIVERSAL SPORTING RIFLE) – .223 Rem. cal., unthreaded barrel, USR thumbhole stock, AUG barrels are not interchangeable with this model. Approx. 3,000 imported circa 1996 before the sporting arms ban began.

	$1,650	$1,450	$1,250	$1,050	$900	$775	$650

MODEL MAADI AKM – 7.62x39mm cal., copy of Soviet AKM design rifle, 30 shot mag., open sights.

	$2,250	$2,000	$1,800	$1,600	$1,450	$1,250	$1,125

STOEGER INDUSTRIES, INC.

Current importer/trademark established in 1924, and currently located in Accokeek, MD. Previously located in Wayne, NJ, until 2000. Stoeger Industries, Inc. was purchased by Beretta Holding of Italy in 2000, and is now a division of Benelli USA. Please refer to the IGA listing for currently imported Stoeger shotgun models.

Stoeger has imported a wide variety of firearms during the past seven decades. Most of these guns were good quality and came from known makers in Europe (some were private labeled). Stoeger carried an extensive firearms inventory of both house brand and famous European trademarks - many of which were finely made with beautiful engraving, stock work, and other popular special order features. As a general rule, values for Stoeger rifles and shotguns may be ascertained by comparing them with a known trademark of equal quality and cal./ga. Certain configurations will be more desirable than others (i.e. a Stoeger .22 caliber Mannlicher with double-set triggers and detachable mag. will be worth considerably more than a single shot target rifle).

Perhaps the best reference works available on these older Stoeger firearms (not to mention the other trademarks of that time) are the older Stoeger catalogs themselves - quite collectible in their own right. You are advised to purchase these older catalogs (some reprints are also available) if more information is needed on not only older Stoeger models, but also the other firearms being sold at that time.

PISTOLS: SEMI-AUTO

Stoeger Lugers can be found in the Luger section.

COUGAR – 9mm Para., .40 S&W, or .45 ACP (new 2010) cal., DA/SA, copy of Beretta, 3.6 in. barrel, matte black finish, 8 (.45 ACP), 11 (.40 S&W), 13 (compact version 9mm, new 2011) or 15 (9mm Para.) shot mag., ambidextrous safety, 3-dot sights, Bruniton black, silver or two-tone matte finish, checkered plastic grips, blowback action with rotating bolt, removable front sight, mfg. in Turkey. Importation began 2007.

MSR $469	$375	$335	$290	$255	$225	$200	$180

MSR	100%	98%	95%	90%	80%	70%	60%	Last MSR

Add $40 for .45 ACP cal. in black finish with accessory rail.

Add $30 for silver or two-tone finish.

SHOTGUNS: SxS

DOUBLE DEFENSE – 12 or 20 ga., 3 in. chambers, hammerless, matte blue finish, 20 in. ported barrels, fixed IC chokes, single trigger, non-reflective matte black hardwood stock, fiber optic front sight, top and bottom Picatinny rails, 6 1/2 lbs. New mid-2009.

MSR $499	$435	$350	$275	$225	$180	$150	$130	

SHOTGUNS: SLIDE ACTION

MODEL P350 – 12 ga. only, 3 1/2 in. chamber, 18 1/2 (Home Security, cyl. fixed choke), 24, 26, or 28 in. barrel, includes 5 screw-in chokes, choice of black synthetic, Timber HD (disc. 2008), Realtree APG HD or Realtree Max-4 HD camo coverage, approx. 6.9 lbs. New 2005.

MSR $349	$285	$240	$200	$170	$150	$125	$110	

Add $30 for pistol grip (18 1/2 in. barrel only).

Add $100 for 100% camo coverage.

Add $63 for 13 oz. recoil reducer (disc. 2010).

Add $130 for Turkey configuration with camo, steady grip and 24 in barrel.

STONER RIFLE

Please refer to the Knight's Manufacturing Company listing in the K section.

STRAYER TRIPP INTERNATIONAL

Please refer to the STI International listing in this section.

STRAYER-VOIGT, INC.

Current manufacturer of Infinity pistols located in Grand Prairie, TX. See the Infinity listing for more information.

STREET SWEEPER

Previously manufactured by Sales of Georgia, Inc. located in Atlanta, GA.

SHOTGUNS

STREET SWEEPER – 12 ga. only, 12 shot rotary mag., tactical configuration with 18 in. barrel, double action, folding stock, 9 3/4 lbs. Restricted sales following the ATF classification as a "destructive device." Mfg. 1989-approx. 1995.

	$1,495	$1,350	$1,100	$995	$895	$795	$695

Unless this model was registered with the ATF before May 1st, 2001, it is subject to seizure with a possible fine/imprisonment.

STURM, RUGER & CO., INC.

Current manufacturer with production facilities located in Newport, NH and Prescott, AZ. Previously manufactured in Southport, CT 1949-1991 (corporate and administrative offices remain at this location). A second factory was opened in Newport, NH in 1963, and still produces single action revolvers, rifles and shotguns.

Sturm, Ruger & Co. was founded in 1949 by Alexander Sturm and William B. Ruger to manufacture .22 cal. semi-auto pistols. The original factory was in a wooden structure located across from the train depot in Southport, CT. By 1959, the company moved into a larger modern factory not too far from the original buildings. The product line quickly expanded to a Target Model, single action revolvers, rifles, DA revolvers and shotguns.

Mr. Alex Sturm passed away in November 1951. On July 6, 2002, the legendary William B. Ruger, Sr. passed away in his home in Prescott, AZ.

Beginning 1996, all handguns are supplied with a case and lock. Beginning late 2000, a spent cartridge case was supplied with all handguns.

From four separate factories, Ruger has manufactured and shipped over 27 million guns. The two Southport, CT facilities are no longer utilized. Guns are manufactured at the two large modern facilities located in Newport, NH and Prescott, AZ. Ruger is America's largest small arms maker, and offers a complete line of firearms for sportsmen, law enforcement, and military. Ruger plans to open a third production facility during 2014 in Mayodan, NC.

Please refer to the *Blue Book of Modern Black Powder Arms* by John Allen (also online) for more information and prices on Sturm Ruger black powder models.

Black Powder Revolvers - Reproductions & Replicas and *Black Powder Long Arms & Pistols - Reproductions & Replicas* by Dennis Adler are also invaluable sources for most black powder reproductions and replicas, and include hundreds of color images on most popular makes/models, provide manufacturer/trademark histories, and up-to-date information on related

MSR	100%	98%	95%	90%	80%	70%	60%	Last MSR

items/accessories for black powder shooting - www.bluebookofgunvalues.com

The publisher would like to thank Bill Hamm, Richard Machniak, John Dougan, and Chad Hiddleson for their contributions in this and previous editions.

PISTOLS: SEMI-AUTO, RIMFIRE

Many distributors and customizers have produced special/limited editions of this popular series of .22 cal. pistols; these editions are not listed in either the *Blue Book of Gun Values* or the *Blue Book of Tactical Firearms Values*. After 1999, all non-22/45 model pistols were fitted with Ruger logo medallions with a red background. Note that Ruger's 22/45 series did not have red eagle logo medallions in either grip panel until the P512MKIIRP was introduced in 2010.

* ***Mark III 22/45 Threaded Barrel*** – .22 LR cal., 10 shot mag., similar to Mark III 22/45, except has 4 1/2 in. threaded bull barrel, SA, fixed sights or Picatinny rail, blue finish, 32 oz. New 2011.

| MSR $449 | $360 | $285 | $225 | $200 | $175 | $140 | $125 | |

PISTOLS: SEMI-AUTO, CENTERFIRE

LCP (LIGHTWEIGHT COMPACT PISTOL) – .380 ACP cal., DAO, bobbed hammer, black glass filled nylon frame with molded checkering, blued steel slide, 2 3/4 in. barrel, 6 or 7 (new 2013) shot mag., .82 in. frame width, fixed sights, black Ruger logos inset in grip panels, includes external locking device, pocket holster, optional Crimson trace laser grips (new 2011), Lasermax Centerfire laser (new 2012), 9.4 oz. New 2008.

| MSR $379 | $315 | $270 | $225 | $180 | $160 | $150 | $140 | |

Add $70 for Lasermax Centerfire laser (new 2012).
Add $180 for Crimson trace laser grips (new 2011).

* ***LCP Stainless*** – .380 ACP cal., similar to LCP, except features stainless steel slide, 7 shot, fixed sights, and brushed stainless finish. New 2014.

| MSR $429 | $350 | $275 | $225 | $200 | $175 | $140 | $125 | |

LC9 – 9mm Para. cal., bobbed hammer, DAO, 3.12 in. barrel, alloy steel slide, blue finish, black glass filled nylon grip frame, 7 or 9 (new 2013) shot mag., 3-dot fixed front and adj. rear sights, slightly larger (less than 1 in. in both height and width) than the LCP, finger grip extension, loaded chamber indicator, includes soft case, optional Lasermax Centerfire laser (new 2012) or Crimson trace laser grips,17.1 oz. New 2011.

| MSR $449 | $360 | $285 | $230 | $200 | $175 | $150 | $130 | |

Add $80 for Lasermax Centerfire laser (new 2012).
Add $180 for Crimson trace "Laserguard" laser (new 2013).

LC380 – .380 ACP cal., alloy steel slide and barrel, blued finish, 3.12 in. barrel, DAO, 7 shot mag., black glass-filled checkered nylon grip frame, adj. 3-dot sights, Crimson Trace Laserguard (new 2014) or LaserMax Centerfire (new 2014), includes loaded chamber indicator and soft case, 17.2 oz. New 2013.

| MSR $449 | $360 | $285 | $230 | $200 | $175 | $150 | $130 | |

Add $80 for Lasermax Centerfire laser (new 2014).
Add $180 for Crimson trace laser grips (new 2014).

P85 – 9mm Para. cal., DA/SA, 4 1/2 in. barrel, aluminum frame with steel slide, 3-dot fixed sights, 15 shot mag., oversized trigger, polymer grips, matte black finish, 2 lbs. Mfg. 1987-1990.

| | $350 | $295 | $265 | $235 | $215 | $200 | $185 | *$410* |

Subtract $30 if without case and extra mag.

Any P85 models without the "MKIIR" stamp on either the left or right side of the safety must be returned to the factory for a free safety modification.

* ***KP85*** – stainless variation of the P85. Mfg. 1990 only.

| | $375 | $315 | $280 | $230 | $200 | $165 | $140 | *$452* |

Subtract $30 if without case and extra mag.

Variants included a decocking or double action only version at no extra charge. Any KP85 models without the "MKIIR" stamp on either the left or right side of the safety must be returned to the factory for a free safety modification.

P85 MARK II – 9mm Para. cal., DA/SA, 4 1/2 in. barrel, aluminum frame with steel slide, 3-dot fixed sights, 15 shot mag., ambidextrous safety beginning in 1991, oversized trigger, polymer grips, matte black finish, 2 lbs. Mfg. 1990-1992.

| | $350 | $295 | $265 | $235 | $215 | $200 | $185 | *$410* |

Subtract $30 if without case and extra mag.

Decocker and DAO models were not available in the Mark II series.

* ***KP85 Mark II*** – stainless variation of the P85. Mfg. 1990-1992.

| | $375 | $315 | $280 | $230 | $200 | $165 | $140 | *$452* |

Subtract $30 if without case and extra mag.

MSR		100%	98%	95%	90%	80%	70%	60%	*Last MSR*

P89 – 9mm Para. cal., DA/SA, improved variation of the P85 Mark II, 10 (C/B 1994) or 15 (new late 2005) shot mag., ambidextrous safety or decocker (Model P89D), blue finish, 32 oz. Mfg. 1992-2007.

		100%	98%	95%	90%	80%	70%	60%	*Last MSR*
		$380	$330	$280	$250	$215	$200	$185	*$475*

Variants were available in a decocking (P89DC) or double action only (P-89DAO, disc. 2004) version at no extra charge.

KP89 STAINLESS – stainless variation of the P89, also available in double action only (disc. 2004). Mfg. 1992-2009.

		100%	98%	95%	90%	80%	70%	60%	*Last MSR*
		$425	$360	$305	$250	$215	$200	$185	*$525*

Add $45 for convertible 7.65mm Luger cal. barrel (Model KP89X, approx. 5,750 mfg. during 1994 only).

P90 – .45 ACP cal., DA/SA, similar to KP90 Stainless, except has blue finish, 8 shot mag., 33 1/2 oz. Disc. 2010.

		100%	98%	95%	90%	80%	70%	60%	*Last MSR*
		$475	$395	$335	$265	$215	$200	$185	*$591*

Add $50 for tritium night sights (disc. 2006).

P90 models were produced in a variety of models for law enforcement or government contracts and will be found with any combination of safety model, decocker or double action only with fingergroove tactical rubber grip and/or tritium night sights.

KP90 STAINLESS – .45 ACP cal., DA/SA 4 1/2 in. barrel, oversized trigger, aluminum frame with stainless steel slide, 8 shot single column mag., KP90 or decocking (KP90D), polymer grips, 3-dot fixed sights, ambidextrous safety began approx ser. no. 660-12800. Mfg. 1991-2010.

		100%	98%	95%	90%	80%	70%	60%	*Last MSR*
		$495	$415	$360	$295	$250	$225	$200	*$636*

Add $50 for tritium night sights (disc. 2006).

KP90 models were produced in a variety of models for law enforcement or government contracts and will be found with any combination of safety model, decocker or double action only with fingergroove tactical rubber grip and/or tritium night sights.

KP91 STAINLESS – .40 S&W cal., similar to Model KP90 Stainless, except is not available with external safety and has 11 shot double column mag. Mfg. 1991-1994.

		100%	98%	95%	90%	80%	70%	60%	*Last MSR*
		$385	$335	$295	$240	$210	$180	$155	*$489*

This model was available in a decocking variation (KP91D) or double action only (KP91DAO). Approx. 39,600 of all models were mfg. before being discontinued in favor of the tapered slide KP944 model.

P93D BLUE – similar to KP93 Stainless, except has blue finish, compact model, ambidextrous decocker, 31 oz. Mfg. 1998-2004.

		100%	98%	95%	90%	80%	70%	60%	*Last MSR*
		$395	$330	$285	$240	$215	$200	$185	*$495*

Add $50 for tritium night sights.

P93 models were produced in a variety of models for law enforcement or government contracts and will be found with any combination of decocker model or double action only with fingergroove tactical rubber grip and/or tritium night sights.

P93 CHICAGO POLICE SPECIAL CONTRACT – produced in the late 1990s for a Chicago Police Department contract, this blued stainless P93 was ordered with a special P89M rollmark on the slide so that those who were concerned about having a "compact" pistol would not be alerted to the fact that it was indeed a P93. Extremely rare in civilian hands.

Extreme rarity precludes accurate pricing on this model, and should be examined for authenticity. NIB specimens have been noted at $550.

KP93 STAINLESS – 9mm Para. cal., compact variation with 3 9/10 in. tilting barrel - link actuated, matte blue or REM (mfg. 1996 only) finish, 3-dot sights, 10 (C/B 1994) or 15* shot mag., available with DA/SA ambidextrous decocker action or DAO, 31 oz. Mfg. 1994-2004.

		100%	98%	95%	90%	80%	70%	60%	*Last MSR*
		$450	$370	$315	$260	$220	$200	$185	*$575*

Add $50 for tritium night sights.

KP93 models were produced in a variety of models for law enforcement or government contracts and will be found with any combination of decocker model or double action only with fingergroove tactical rubber grip and/or tritium night sights.

P94 BLUE – similar to KP94 Stainless, except has blue finish. Mfg. 1998-2004.

		100%	98%	95%	90%	80%	70%	60%	*Last MSR*
		$395	$330	$285	$240	$215	$200	$185	*$495*

Add $50 for tritium night sights.

P94 models have been produced in a variety of models for law enforcement or government contracts and will be found with any combination of safety model, decocker or double action only with fingergroove tactical rubber grip and/or tritium night sights.

MSR	100%	98%	95%	90%	80%	70%	60%	Last MSR

* P94/KP94 w/Integral Tac-Star Laser Sight – 9mm Para. cal., 10 (C/B 1994) or 15* shot mag., integral Tac-Star laser sight, tritium night sights, ambidextrous safety, ambidextrous decocker, or double action only. Mfg. 1994 only.

| | $650 | $575 | $495 | $440 | $360 | $295 | $225 | |

Add $50 for tritium night sights.

These factory laser sighted pistol models were also produced in any combination with fingergroove tactical rubber grip and/or tritium night sights. Some were also produced with Ruger's "REM" finish. Reportedly 1,836 made total of all models.

KP94 STAINLESS – 9mm Para. or .40 S&W cal., available with ambidextrous safety, matte stainless or REM (mfg. 1996 only) finish, DA/SA ambidextrous decocker action or DAO, 10 (C/B 1994), or 15* (9mm Para.) shot mag., 33 oz. Mfg. 1994-2004.

| | $450 | $370 | $315 | $260 | $220 | $200 | $185 | $575 |

Add $50 for tritium night sights.

KP94 models have been produced in a variety of models for law enforcement or government contracts and will be found with any combination of safety model, decocker or double action only with fingergroove tactical rubber grip and/or tritium night sights.

P95PR (P95) – 9mm Para. cal., available in DA/SA ambidextrous decocker (D/DPR suffix), ambidextrous safety, or DAO configuration (DAO suffix, mfg. 1996-2004), polymer frame, 3.9 in. barrel, fixed sights, blue finish, 10 or 15 (new late 2005) shot mag., lower Picatinny rail became standard in 2006, (non-Picatinny rail models discontinued 2005), 27 oz. Mfg. 1996-2013.

| | $320 | $275 | $235 | $195 | $165 | $150 | $135 | $399 |

Add $50 for tritium night sights (disc. 2006).

During 2006, this model's nomenclature changed from P95 to P95PR to reflect the Picatinny style rail.

P95 models have been produced in a variety of models for law enforcement or government contracts and will be found with any combination of safety model, decocker or double action only with fingergroove tactical rubber grip and/or tritium night sights. The P95DAO double action only model was disc. 2004.

KP95PR STAINLESS (KP95) – stainless variation of Model P95 and P95PR. Mfg. 1997-2013.

| | $355 | $310 | $250 | $200 | $175 | $140 | $120 | $439 |

Add $50 for tritium night sights.

During 2006, this model's nomenclature changed from KP95 to KP95PR to reflect the Picatinny style rail. Non-Picatinny rail models were disc. 2005. KP95 models have been produced in a variety of models for law enforcement or government contracts, and will be found in any combination of safety model, decocker, or double action only with fingergroove tactical rubber grisp and/or tritium night sights. The KP95DAO double action only model was disc. 2004.

P97D – .45 ACP cal., DA/SA, ambidextrous decocker, 8 shot mag., blue finish, 30 1/2 oz. Mfg. 2002-2004.

| | $370 | $315 | $275 | $235 | $215 | $200 | $185 | $460 |

Add $50 for tritium night sights.

KP97 STAINLESS – .45 ACP cal., similar to KP95 Stainless, except has 8 shot mag., 27 oz. Mfg. 1999-2004.

| | $395 | $315 | $265 | $235 | $215 | $200 | $185 | $495 |

Add $50 for tritium night sights.

P345PR (P345) – .45 ACP cal., ambidextrous safety or decocker (P345DPR, disc. 2006), DA/SA, black polymer frame with blue steel slide, 4.2 in. barrel, fixed sights, polyurethane grips, slimmer profile frame, 8 shot single column mag., with or w/o (disc. 2006) Picatinny rail, loaded chamber indicator, 29 oz. Mfg. 2005-2012.

| | $485 | $425 | $335 | $275 | $225 | $210 | $195 | $599 |

KP345PR (KP345) – .45 ACP cal., decocker (KP345DPR, disc. 2006), similar to P345, except has stainless steel slide, Picatinny rail became standard 2007 (KP345PR), 29 oz. Mfg. 2005-2012.

| | $515 | $440 | $345 | $280 | $230 | $210 | $195 | $639 |

P944 – .40 S&W cal., similar to P94, ambidextrous safety, blue finish, 34 oz. Mfg. 1999-2010.

| | $445 | $360 | $300 | $245 | $215 | $200 | $185 | $557 |

Add $50 for tritium night sights (disc. 2006).

This model has been produced in many versions for law enforcement or government contracts and will be found with any combination of safety type, decocker, or double action only, fingergroove tactical rubber grip, and/or tritium night sights.

KP944 STAINLESS – similar to P944, except is stainless steel, also available as decocker (KP944D). Mfg. 1999-2010.

| | $500 | $400 | $345 | $275 | $230 | $195 | $170 | $647 |

Add $50 for tritum night sights (disc. 2006).

This model has been produced in many versions for law enforcement or government contracts and will be found with any combination of safety type, decocker, or double action only, fingergroove tactical rubber grip, and/or tritium night sights. The KP944DAO double action only model was disc. 2004.

MSR	100%	98%	95%	90%	80%	70%	60%	*Last MSR*

SR9 – 9mm Para. cal., SFO, semi-double action trigger pull, 4 1/8 in. barrel, 10 or 17 shot mag., reversible backstrap, low profile 3-dot sights, glass filled nylon frame, choice of black stainless, brushed stainless steel, alloy steel/Nitridox Pro Black (SR9B Model), or OD Green (mfg. 2009-2010), Picatinny rail, ambidextrous safety, 26 1/2 oz. New late 2007.

MSR $529	$450	$400	$350	$315	$275	$240	$210

    Note that all SR9 models serial numbered 330-29999 and earlier are subject to a factory recall at no charge. If your pistol has not yet had the new parts installed, please contact Sturm, Ruger & Company at 1-800-784-3701 or email SR9Recall@ruger.com and they will provide you with shipping instructions.

   * SR9C – 9mm Para. cal., similar to the Model SR9, except has compact frame and 3 1/2 in. barrel, brushed stainless or Nitridox Pro Black finish, 10 or 17 shot mag., adj. 3-dot sights, 23.4 oz. New mid-2010.

MSR $529	$450	$400	$350	$315	$275	$240	$210

SR40 – .40 S&W cal., hammerless SFO, 10 or 15 shot mag., 4.14 in. barrel, alloy or stainless steel slide with brushed stainless or Nitridox Pro Black finish, adj. 3-dot sights, black glass filled nylon grips, reversible backstrap, integral mounting rail, ambidextrous thumb safety, loaded chamber indicator, includes two mags., 27 1/4 oz. New 2011.

MSR $529	$450	$400	$350	$315	$275	$240	$210

   * SR40c – .40 S&W cal., similar to SR40, except has compact frame, 3 1/2 in. barrel, brushed stainless or Nitridox Pro Black finish, 9 or 15 shot mag., adj. 3-dot sights, 23.4 oz. New mid-2011.

MSR $529	$450	$400	$350	$315	$275	$240	$210

SR45 – .45 ACP cal., similar to SR40, except has 4 1/2 in. barrel, 10 shot mag. only, choice of brushed stainless slide or alloy steel with black nitride finish, 30.15 oz. New 2013.

MSR $529	$450	$400	$350	$315	$275	$240	$210

SR-1911 – .45 ACP cal., SA, patterned after the Colt M1911 Series 70, 5 in. barrel, supplied with one 7 and one 8 shot stainless steel mags., matte stainless steel frame and slide, diamond checkered cocobolo grips with black Ruger medallion inserts, skeletonized trigger and bobbed hammer, Novak 3-dot adj. sights, approx. 40 oz. New mid-2011.

MSR $829	$715	$565	$465	$385	$325	$275	$250

   * SR-1911CMD – .45 ACP cal., similar to SR-1911, except has 4 1/4 in. barrel, 7 shot mag., 36.4 oz. New 2013.

MSR $829	$715	$565	$465	$385	$325	$275	$250

REVOLVERS: DOUBLE ACTION

   During certain years of manufacture, Ruger's changes in production on certain models (cals., barrel markings, barrel lengths, etc.) have created rare variations that are now considered premium niches. These areas of low manufacture will add premiums to the values listed on standard models.

SPEED SIX (MODELS 207, 208 and 209) – .38 Spl., .357 Mag., or 9mm Para. cal., 2 3/4, or 4 in. barrel, fixed sights, checkered walnut grips, round butt, blue finish, some guns have factory speed hammer (no hammer spur). Mfg. 1973-1988. Model 207 and 208 disc. 1988.

	$450	$375	$300	$225	$175	$150	$140	*$292*

Add $300 for 9mm Para. (Model 209 disc. 1984).

   * Speed Six Models 737 and 738 – stainless steel versions of Models 207 and 208, .357 Mag and .38 Spl. cals., 2 3/4, 3 (Postal Inspector contract) or 4 in. barrel. Disc. 1988.

	$475	$400	$325	$225	$175	$150	$140	*$320*

Add 100% for "U.S." and "N.I.S." marked with 2 3/4 in. barrel.

   * Speed Six Model 739 – stainless steel, 9mm Para. Disc. 1984.

	$700	$575	$500	$400	$275	$195	$175	

SECURITY SIX (MODEL 117) – .357 Mag. cal., 6 shot, 2 3/4, 3 (late production only), 4, 4 (heavy), or 6 in. barrel, adj. sights, checkered walnut grips, square butt. Mfg. 1970-1985.

	$450	$375	$300	$225	$175	$150	$140	*$309*

Add $15 for target grips.
Add 50% for .38 Special cal with 6 in. barrel and 150- prefix serial number
Add 50% for .357 Mag. Cal. With 2 3/4 in barrel, adj. sights and round butt (Model RDA-32RB - extremely rare).

   Note that beginning late in the 150- serial number prefix, the grip frame was changed to have a more outward "highback" shape. Revolvers with the earlier "lowback" grip frame are generally considered more collectible. All revolvers having fixed sights and square butt grip frame with "lowback" shape to the backstrap were also marked "SECURITY-SIX". Only when the new highback gripframe came out were the fixed sight and square butt revolvers marked "SERVICE-SIX".

   500 of this model were mfg. for the California Highway Patrol during 1983 (.38 Spl. cal.) in stainless steel only. They are distinguishable by a C.H.P. marking. Other Security Six Model 117 special editions have been made for various police organizations - premiums might exist in certain regions for these variations.

MSR	100%	98%	95%	90%	80%	70%	60%	Last MSR

* Security Six Model 717 – stainless steel version of Model 117. Disc. 1985.

	$450	$375	$300	$225	$175	$150	$140	$338

Add 30% for this model in .38 Special with 4, 4 (heavy) or 6 in. barrel.

Add 50% for .357 Mag. Cal with 2 3/4 in. barrel, adj. sights and round butt (model GA-32RB - extremely rare).

POLICE SERVICE SIX – .357 Mag., .38 Spl., or 9mm Para. cal., blue finish only, square butt, fixed sights, checkered walnut grips.

* Police Service Six Model 107 – .357 Mag. cal., 2 3/4 or 4 in. barrel, fixed sights. Disc. 1988.

	$4050	$375	$300	$225	$175	$150	$140	$287

Add 40% for this model with low-back grip frame, 6 barrel and 150- prefix serial number.

* Police Service Six Model 108 – .38 Spl. cal., 2 3/4 or 4 in. barrel, fixed sights. Disc. 1988.

	$400	$350	$275	$200	$175	$150	$140	$287

Add 125% for "U.S." marked with or without lanyard loop.

Add 100% for .380 Rim cal. With or without lanyard loop.

* Police Service Six Model 109 – 9mm Para. cal., 2 3/4 or 4 in. barrel, fixed sights. Disc. 1984.

	$700	$550	$500	$400	$275	$195	$175	

POLICE SERVICE SIX STAINLESS STEEL – stainless construction, 4 in. barrel only, fixed sights, checkered walnut grips.

* Police Service Six Stainless Steel Model 707 – .357 Mag. cal., 2 3/4 or 4 in. barrel, square butt. Disc. 1988.

	$475	$400	$325	$225	$175	$150	$140	$310

* Police Service Six Stainless Steel Model 708 – .38 Spl. cal., 2 3/4 or 4 in. barrel, square butt. Disc. 1988.

	$400	$350	$275	$200	$175	$150	$140	$310

GP-100 – .357 Mag. or .38 Spl. (disc.) cal., 4.2, or 6 (.357 Mag. only) in. standard or heavy barrel, 6 shot, strengthened design intended for constant use with all .357 Mag. ammunition, rubber cushioned grip panels with polished Goncalo Alves wood inserts, (disc.) or black Hogue grip, fixed (mfg. 1989-2006) or adj. sights with white outlined rear and interchangeable front, 35-46 oz. depending on barrel configuration. New 1986.

MSR $699	$550	$400	$340	$275	$220	$195	$175	

* GP-100 Stainless Steel – .327 Fed. Mag. (mfg. 2009-disc. 2013), .38 Spl. (disc.), or .357 Mag. cal., similar to GP-100, except 3 (new 1990, fixed sights, .357 Mag. only), 4.2, or 6 in. barrel, 6 or 7 shot (.327 Fed. Mag. only, disc. 2013), satin stainless finish. New 1987.

MSR $729	$575	$425	$330	$265	$210	$170	$140	

Add $30 for adj. sights.

SP-101 STAINLESS STEEL – .22 LR (6 shot - mfg. 1990-2004), .32 H&R (6 shot - mfg. 1991-2012), .327 Federal (6 shot - mfg. 2007-2011), .38 Spl.+P (5 shot), 9mm Para. (5 shot - mfg. 1991-2000), or .357 Mag. (5 shot - new 1991) cal., 2 1/4, 3 1/16, 4 (mfg. 1990-2007), or 4.2 (new 2012) in. barrel, small frame variation of the GP-100 Stainless, fiber optic (new 2012) or Black Ramp front sight, fixed or adj. rear (new 1996) sights, cushioned rubber/ black plastic or engraved hardwood insert (new 2012) grips, satin stainless finish, 25-34 oz. New 1989.

MSR $659	$550	$400	$315	$240	$180	$145	$120	

Add $40 for fiber optic sights (new 2012, 4.2 in. barrel only).

Add $170 for Crimson Trace laser grips (mfg. 2008-2011).

Add $100 for .357 Mag. models with "125 GR. BULLET" rollmarked on barrel lug (disc. 2010).

Add $300 for 9mm Para. caliber (disc. 2000).

Add $150 for .22 LR caliber (disc. 2004).

The .327 Federal caliber configuration will also shoot .32 H&R Mag., .32 S&W, and .32 S&W Long cartridges.

The first few thousand SP-101s in .38 Special had green grip inserts. Also, approximately 3,000 total of the earliest KSP-321 and KSP-331 .357 Mag. models were rollmarked with "125 GR. BULLET" on the barrel under the caliber designation (serial range 570-59359 to 570-67976).

Ruger introduced a .357 Mag./2 1/4 in. (new 1993) or .38 Spl./2 1/4 (new 1994) in. configuration featuring a spurless hammer, double action only.

SP-101 barrel lengths are as follows: .22 cal. is available in 2 1/4 or 4 in. standard or heavy barrel, .32 H&R is available in 3 1/16 or 4 (new 1994) in. heavy barrel, .38 Spl. is available in 2 1/4 or 3 1/16 in. length only, 9mm Para. is available in 2 1/4 (mfg. 1992-2000) or 3 1/16 in. length only, and .357 Mag. is available in 2 1/4 or 3 1/16 in. length only.

* SP101 Stainless Steel .22 LR – .22 LR cal., 4 in. barrel, 8 shot, satin stainless steel, black rubber grips with checkered wood panel inserts, adj. rear sight, fiber optic front sight, 30 oz. New late 2011.

MSR $699	$550	$400	$330	$275	$210	$190	$175	

MSR	100%	98%	95%	90%	80%	70%	60%	Last MSR

REDHAWK – .41 Mag. (mfg. 1984-1991), or .44 Mag. cal., 6 shot fluted cylinder, redesigned large frame, 5 1/2 and 7 1/2 (disc. 2005) in. barrel, blue finish, square butt, smooth hardwood grips, 49-54 oz. Disc. 2009.

| | $615 | $460 | $375 | $285 | $225 | $180 | $165 | *$789* |

Add $40 for scope rings (disc. 2005).

.41 Mag. cals. will bring collector premium.

* ***Redhawk Stainless Steel*** – .357 Mag. (mfg. 1984-1985), .41 Mag. (mfg. 1984-1991), .44 Mag. or .45 LC (mfg. 1998-2005, reintroduced 2008, 4 in. barrel only) cal., stainless steel construction, 4.2 (new 2007), 5 1/2, or 7 1/2 in. barrel, choice of regular or Hogue (4 in. barrel only) grips, 6 shot, adj. sights, 49-54 oz. Disc. 2013.

| | $785 | $600 | $475 | $375 | $300 | $250 | $225 | *$989* |

Add $60 for scope rings (Hunter model, .44 Mag. only in 7 1/2 in. barrel).

Models in .357 Mag., .41 Mag. or .45 LC will bring collector premiums.

The 7 1/2 in. barrel was available with or w/o integral scope mounting system.

SUPER REDHAWK STAINLESS – .44 Mag., .454 Casull, or .480 Ruger (mfg. 2001-2007, reintroduced 2013 only) cal., 6 shot, 7 1/2 or 9 1/2 in. barrel, fluted (.44 Mag. cal. only) or non-fluted cylinder, choice of regular or high gloss (mfg. 1996 only) or Target Gray (.454 Casull and .480 Ruger only, disc. 2009) stainless steel, adj. rear sight, cushioned grip panels (GP-100 style), stainless steel scope rings, 53-58 oz. New late 1987.

| MSR $1,049 | $795 | $700 | $575 | $475 | $400 | $350 | $325 | |

Add $30 for .454 Casull or .480 Ruger (disc. 2013) cal.

Add $75 for early .44 Mag. with "SUPER REDHAWK" rollmarked on both sides of cylinder frame extension, serial range 550-00500 to at least 550-00659.

* ***Super Redhawk Stainless Alaskan*** – .44 Mag. (new 2008), .454 Casull, or .480 Ruger (disc. 2007, reintroduced 2013 only) cal., 5 shot (some .480 Ruger only) or 6 shot, 2 1/2 in. barrel, includes Hogue monogrips and unfluted cylinder, 42 oz. New 2005.

| MSR $1,079 | $875 | $750 | $625 | $450 | $400 | $325 | $265 | |

Add 50% for .480 Ruger with 5-shot cylinder (less than 30 believed to have been shipped commercially).

LCR – .22 LR (new 2012), .22 WMR (new 2013), .38 Spl.+P or .357 Mag. cal., 5 (.38 Spl. or .357 Mag.), 6 (.22 WMR only, new 2013), or 8 (.22 LR only, new 2012) shot, DAO, external hammer (LCRX - new 2014) or hammerless, 1 7/8 in. barrel, monolithic aluminum frame, stainless steel cylinder, polymer fire control housing, matte black or blackened stainless (.357 Mag. only) finish, also available with Hogue Tamer or Crimson Trace finger groove grips, integral rear sight with pinned ramp front sight, 13 1/2-16 1/2 oz. New 2010.

| MSR $529 | $450 | $400 | $365 | $335 | $300 | $275 | $250 | |

Add $70 for .357 Mag. cal.

Add $270 for Crimson Trace laser grips.

Add $50 for LCR-XS model with standard dot tritium front sight (.38 Spl.+P cal. only) and U-notch integral rear sight (mfg. 2011-2013).

RIFLES: BOLT ACTION, CENTERFIRE

During certain years of manufacture, Ruger's changes in production on certain models (cals., barrel markings, barrel lengths, etc.) have created rare variations that are now considered premium niches. These areas of low manufacture will add premiums to the values listed on standard models.

Earlier mfg. had flat-bolt handle or hollow round bolt, and will bring $150+ premium, depending on configuration.

Early (pre-1972) mfg. with flat-bolt handle are desirable in the rarer cals. and will command a 100% premium if in 98%+ original condition.

MODEL 77-GS GUNSITE SCOUT – .308 Win. cal., 16 1/2 in. barrel with flash suppressor, 10 shot box mag., alloy steel receiver, matte black finish, forward mounted Picatinny rail, checkered grey laminate stock, recoil pad, sling swivels, protected front sight and adj. ghost ring rear sight, Gunsite engraved logo grip cap, non-rotating Mauser type controlled round feed extractor, right or left hand (new 2012) action, approx. 7 lbs. New 2011.

| MSR $1,039 | $800 | $700 | $600 | $475 | $400 | $325 | $295 | |

* ***Model 77-GS Gunsite Scout Stainless*** – .308 Win. cal., 16 1/2 (disc. 2012) or 18 in. barrel with flash suppressor, 10 shot box mag., alloy steel receiver, matte black finish, forward mounted Picatinny rail, checkered grey laminate stock, recoil pad, sling swivels, protected front sight and adj. ghost ring rear sight, Gunsite engraved logo grip cap, non-rotating Mauser type controlled round feed extractor, right or left hand (new 2012) action, approx. 7 lbs. New 2011.

| MSR $1,099 | $935 | $825 | $700 | $635 | $515 | $425 | $325 | |

* ***Model HM77-VLEHFS Hawkeye Tactical*** – .223 Rem., .243 Win. (disc. 2010), or .308 Win. cal., 4 or 5 shot mag., matte finished blued action and 20 in. bull barrel with flash suppressor, no sights, adj. two-stage target trigger, black Hogue overmolded stock with Harris bipod, 8 3/4 lbs. Mfg. 2009-2013.

| | $1,050 | $900 | $765 | $650 | $575 | $525 | $475 | *$1,199* |

MSR	100%	98%	95%	90%	80%	70%	60%	Last MSR

RIFLES: SEMI-AUTO, RIMFIRE

During certain years of manufacture, Ruger's changes in production on certain models (cals., barrel markings, barrel lengths, etc.) have created rare variations that are now considered premium niches. These areas of low manufacture will add premiums to the values listed on standard models. The Model 10/22 has been mfg. in a variety of limited production models including a multi-colored or green laminate wood stock variation (1986), a brown laminate stock (1988), a Kittery Trading Post Commemorative (1988), a smoke or tree bark laminate stock (1989), a Chief AJ Model, Wal-Mart (stainless with black laminated hardwood stock - 1990), etc. These limited editions will command premiums over the standard models listed, depending on the desirability of the special edition.

Note: All Ruger Rifles, except Stainless Mini-14, all Mini-30s, and Model 77-22s were made during 1976 in a "Liberty" version. Add $50-$75 when in 100% in the original box condition.

10/22 FS TACTICAL – .22 LR cal., 10 shot rotary mag., alloy steel receiver, 16 1/8 in. barrel with SR-556/Mini 14 style flash suppressor and barrel band, black synthetic stock, Picatinny rail on top of receiver, satin black finish, 4.3 lbs. New late-2010.

| MSR $329 | $255 | $210 | $175 | $140 | $115 | $90 | $75 | |

10/22 TACTICAL w/HEAVY BARREL – .22 LR cal., 10 shot rotary mag., alloy steel receiver, 16 1/8 in. heavy hammer forged barrel w/o sights and spiraled exterior, black Hogue overmolded stock, target trigger, adj. bipod, 6.8 lbs. New late-2010.

| MSR $579 | $450 | $375 | $315 | $275 | $240 | $215 | $175 | |

* **K10/22-T Target Tactical** – similar to 10/22-T Target Model, except available in black matte finish, black Hogue overmolded stock, receiver with Picatinny style rail, 16.1 in. barrel with no sights, includes precision adj. bipod, 6.9 lbs. Mfg. 2010 only.

| | $500 | $425 | $325 | $300 | $200 | $160 | $140 | $555 |

SR-22 – .22 LR cal., 16.1 in. barrel with Mini-14 flash suppressor, 10 shot rotary mag., Hogue monogrip pistol grip, six position telescoping buttstock, integrated Picatinny rail on top of receiver, mid-length vented circular handguard with Picatinny rail, Ruger Rapid Deploy sights, 6 1/2 lbs. New 2013.

| MSR $649 | $550 | $475 | $425 | $375 | $325 | $275 | $250 | |

RIFLES: SEMI-AUTO, CENTERFIRE

Beginning 2013, all Mini-14 models and variations include a drilled and tapped receiver.

MODEL 44 STANDARD CARBINE – .44 Mag. cal., 4 shot mag., 18 1/2 in. barrel, blowback action, folding sight, curved butt. Mfg. 1959-1985.

| | $700 | $600 | $525 | $400 | $300 | $250 | $225 | $332 |

* **Model 44 Standard Carbine Deerstalker** – approx. 3,750 mfg. with "Deerstalker" marked on rifle until Ithaca lawsuit disc. manufacture (1962).

| | $925 | $850 | $725 | $600 | $550 | $475 | $400 | |

* **Model 44 Standard Carbine 25th Year Anniversary** – mfg. 1985 only, limited production, has medallion in stock.

| | $675 | $575 | $450 | N/A | N/A | N/A | N/A | $495 |

RUGER CARBINE – 9mm Para. (PC9) or .40 S&W (PC4) cal., 16 1/4 in. barrel, 10 (PC4) or 15 (PC9) shot detachable mag., black synthetic stock, matte metal finish, with or w/o sights, with fully adj. rear sight or rear receiver sight, crossbolt safety, 6 lbs. Mfg. 1998-2006.

| | $575 | $475 | $375 | $310 | $265 | $240 | $215 | $623 |

Add $24 for adj. rear receiver sight.

Beginning 2005, this model came standard with an adjustable ghost ring aperture rear sight and protected blade front sight.

MINI-14 – .223 Rem. or .222 Rem. (disc.) cal., 5 (standard mag. starting in 1989), 10 (disc.), or 20* shot detachable mag., 18 1/2 in. barrel, gas operated, blue finish, aperture rear sight, military style stock, approx. 6 3/4 lbs. Mfg. 1975-2004.

| | $535 | $445 | $385 | $350 | $325 | $300 | $285 | $655 |

Add 20% for .222 Rem. cal.
Add $300 for folding stock (disc. 1989).
Add 25% for Southport Model with gold bead front sight.
Add 100% for Mini-14 GB (primarily used for law enforcement) with a flash hider and bayonet lug (blue or stainless) if in 95%+ original condition.

* **Mini-14 Stainless** – mini stainless steel version, choice of wood or black synthetic (new 1999) stock. Disc. 2004.

| | $565 | $450 | $395 | $365 | $335 | $315 | $295 | $715 |

Add 20% for .222 Rem. cal.
Add $300 for folding stock (disc. 1990).

MSR	100%	98%	95%	90%	80%	70%	60%	Last MSR

MINI-14 RANCH RIFLE – .223 Rem. cal., 5 (standard mag. starting in 1989), 10 (disc.), or 20 shot detachable mag., blued finish, 18 1/2 in. barrel, choice of black synthetic or hardwood stock, receiver cut for factory rings, similar to Mini-14, supplied with scope rings, folding (disc.) or adj. ghost ring aperture rear sight, protected front sight, and flat style recoil pad (became standard 2005), 7 lbs. New 1982.

| MSR $909 | $910 | $800 | $675 | $625 | $550 | $450 | $400 | |

Add $10 for black synthetic stock.

Add $50 for 20 shot mag. (new 2008).

Add $260 for Mini 14 NRA-ILA Limited Edition with 16 1/8 in. barrel and black Hogue overmolded stock (ltd. mfg. 2008-2009).

Due to 1989 Federal legislation and public sentiment at the time, the Mini-14 Ranch Rifle was shipped with a 5 shot detachable mag., 1989-2008.

* ***Mini-14 Stainless Ranch Rifle*** – 5.56 NATO (current mfg.) or .223 Rem. (older mfg.) or 6.8mm SPC (mfg. 2007-2011) cal., stainless steel construction, choice of wood (disc.) or black synthetic (new 1999) stock, 5 or 20 shot mag., adj. rear sight, 6 3/4 lbs. New 1986.

| MSR $979 | $980 | $850 | $725 | $675 | $575 | $475 | $400 | |

Add $60 for 20 shot mag. (not available in 6.8mm SPC cal.).

Add $300 for folding stock (disc. 1990).

MINI-14 TARGET RIFLE w/THUMBHOLE STOCK – .223 Rem. cal., 22 in. stainless steel heavy barrel with adj. harmonic tuner, no sights, ergonomic black or grey (disc.) laminated thumbhole stock, stainless scope rings, 5 shot mag., 3 position rubber recoil pad with adj. LOP, 9 1/2 lbs. New 2007.

| MSR $1,149 | $1,150 | $1,000 | $875 | $775 | $650 | $525 | $400 | |

Add $16 for 20 shot mag. (mfg. 2009-disc.).

MINI-14 TARGET RIFLE w/BLACK SYNTHETIC STOCK – .223 Rem. cal., 22 in. stainless steel heavy barrel with adj. harmonic tuner, black Hogue overmolded stock, stainless scope rings, 5 shot mag., 8 1/2 lbs. New 2007.

| MSR $1,149 | $1,150 | $1,000 | $875 | $775 | $650 | $525 | $400 | |

Add $16 for 20 shot mag. (mfg. 2009-disc.).

MINI-14 TACTICAL RIFLE FIXED STOCK – 5.56 NATO cal., blued steel or stainless steel action and barrel, compact 16 1/8 in. blue barrel with flash suppressor, 5 or 20 shot mag., fixed black synthetic stock with vents on upper forend, blade front and adj. rear sights, 6 3/4 lbs. New 2009.

| MSR $989 | $990 | $875 | $750 | $675 | $550 | $450 | $395 | |

Add $80 for stainless steel action and barrel.

MINI-14 TACTICAL RIFLE w/COLLAPSIBLE STOCK – 5.56 NATO cal., compact 16 1/8 in. blue barrel with flash suppressor, 5 or 20 shot mag., six position ATI folding/collapsible stock, includes quad Picatinny accessory rails on forend, blade front and adj. rear sights, 7 1/4 lbs. New 2009.

| MSR $989 | $990 | $875 | $750 | $675 | $550 | $450 | $395 | |

MINI-THIRTY – 7.62x39mm Russian cal., 18 1/2 in. barrel, 5 shot detachable mag., hardwood stock, includes scope rings, 7 lbs. 3 oz. Mfg. 1987-2004.

| | $550 | $450 | $405 | $375 | $335 | $300 | $260 | *$695* |

* ***Mini-Thirty Stainless*** – 7.62x39mm cal., 18 1/2 in. barrel, stainless steel variation of the Mini-Thirty, black synthetic stock, adj. ghost ring aperture rear sight and protected front sight became standard 2005, 5 or 20 shot mag., integral sling swivels, 6 3/4 lbs. New 1990.

| MSR $979 | $980 | $850 | $725 | $675 | $575 | $475 | $400 | |

Add $60 for 20 shot mag.

* ***Mini-Thirty Tactical*** – 7.62x39mm cal., similar to Mini-Thirty Stainless, except has 16 1/8 in. barrel with flash suppressor, 20 shot mag., adj. ghost ring aperture rear sight and non-glare post front sight, Ruger scope bases, black synthetic stock, approx. 6 3/4 lbs. New late 2010.

| MSR $989 | $990 | $875 | $750 | $675 | $575 | $475 | $400 | |

SR-556/SR-556 CARBINE – 5.56 NATO or 6.8mm SPC (mfg. mid-2010-2011) cal., GPO, 10, 25 (6.8mm SPC only, disc. 2011), or 30 shot mag., 16.1 in. barrel with muzzle brake, matte black finish, four position chrome plated gas regulator, quad rail handguard, with or without Troy folding sights, fixed (556SC) or six position telescoping M4 style buttstock, Hogue monogrip pistol grip with finger grooves, upper receiver has integrated Picatinny rail, chrome plated bolt, bolt carrier, and extractor, includes rail covers, soft sided carry case and three magazines, 7.4 (Carbine) or 7.9 lbs. New mid-2009.

| MSR $1,995 | $1,795 | $1,575 | $1,075 | $900 | $775 | $650 | $575 | |

SR-762 CARBINE – 7.62 NATO cal., two-stage piston driven, AR-15 style, matte black finish, 16.1 in. heavy contour chrome lined cold hammer forged barrel, includes three 20 shot Magpul PMag magazines, folding backup iron sights, six position adj. M4-style stock, Hogue monogrip, lightweight adj. adaptable handguard, full length top Picatinny rail

MSR	100%	98%	95%	90%	80%	70%	60%	Last MSR

and two side rails, one piece bolt carrier, four position gas regulator, sight adjustment tool, includes soft side carry case, 8.6 lbs. New late 2013.

MSR $2,195	$1,875	$1,650	$1,400	$1,275	$1,050	$850	$725	

SUPERIOR ARMS

Current manufacturer established in 2004 and located in Wapello, IA.

PISTOLS: SEMI-AUTO

Superior Arms manufactured complete AR-style semi-auto pistols, with either an A4 flat-top or A2 carry handle, and 10 1/2 or 11 1/2 in. barrel.

RIFLES: SEMI-AUTO

Please contact the company directly for more information on options, delivery, and availability on the following AR-15 style carbines/rifles (see Trademark Index).

S-15 M4 CARBINE – .223 Rem. cal., GIO, A4 flat-top receiver with integral rail, 16 in. chromemoly barrel, A2 flash hider, M4 handguard, six position telescoping stock, A2 pistol grip, front sling swivel.

MSR $995	$900	$800	$675	$625	$550	$500	$450	

S-15 CARBINE – .223 Rem. cal., GIO, A4 flat-top receiver with integral rail, 16 in. chromemoly barrel, A2 flash hider, M4 handguard, bayonet lug, six position telescoping stock, A2 pistol grip, front sling swivel.

MSR $995	$900	$800	$675	$625	$550	$500	$450	

S-15 MID-LENGTH CARBINE – .223 Rem. cal., GIO, A4 flat-top receiver with integral rail, 16 in. chromemoly barrel, A2 flash hider, mid-length handguard, bayonet lug, six position telescoping stock, A2 pistol grip, front sling swivel.

MSR $1,010	$925	$825	$700	$650	$575	$500	$450	

S-15 H-BAR RIFLE – .223 Rem. cal., GIO, A4 flat-top receiver with integral rail, 20 in. chromemoly barrel, A2 flash hider, A2 buttstock, bayonet lug, A2 pistol grip, front sling swivel.

MSR $1,075	$985	$875	$750	$675	$550	$500	$495	

S-15 VARMINT RIFLE – .223 Rem. cal., GIO, A4 flat-top receiver with integral rail, 20 in. stainless steel bull contour barrel, Picatinny rail gas block, aluminum free floating handguard with sling swivel stud, A2 buttstock, bayonet lug, A2 pistol grip.

MSR $1,095	$995	$875	$750	$675	$550	$500	$495	

SURGEON RIFLES, INC.

Current custom rifle manufacturer located in Prague, OK.

RIFLES: BOLT ACTION

Surgeon Rifles manufactures a variety of bolt action rifles, including tactical and long range configurations. Models include the short action Scalpel ($4,255 MSR), the long action Scalpel ($4,380 MSR), and the Remedy ($5,400 MSR). Many options and accessories are available. Please contact the company directly for more information, including delivery time and availability (see Trademark Index).

SURVIVAL ARMS, INC.

Previous manufacturer established in 1990 located in Orange, CT. Previously located in Cocoa, FL, until 1995.

In 1990, Survival Arms, Inc. took over the manufacture of AR-7 Explorer rifles from Charter Arms located in Stratford, CT.

RIFLES: SEMI-AUTO

AR-7 EXPLORER RIFLE – .22 LR cal., takedown or normal wood stock, takedown barreled action stores in Cycolac synthetic stock, 8 shot mag., adj. sights, 16 in. barrel, black matte finish on AR-7, silvertone on AR-7S, camouflage finish on AR-7C, 2 1/2 lbs. Disc.

	$150	$125	$100	$85	$75	$65	$55	*$150*

Add 20% for takedown action.

AR-20 SPORTER – similar to AR-22, except has shrouded barrel, tubular stock with pistol grip, 10 or 20 shot mag. Mfg. 1996-98.

	$195	$165	$140	$120	$105	$95	$80	*$200*

AR-22/AR-25 – .22 LR cal., 16 in. barrel, black rifle features pistol grip with choice of wood or metal folding* stock, includes 20 (1995 only) or 25 (disc. 1994) shot mag. Disc. 1995.

	$175	$150	$125	$100	$80	$70	$60	*$200*

Subtract $50 for wood stock model.

T SECTION

TNW, INC.

Current firearms manufacturer located in Vernonia, OR. Consumer direct sales.

MSR	100%	98%	95%	90%	80%	70%	60%	Last MSR

PISTOLS: SEMI-AUTO

ASR – .45 ACP, 9mm Para., or .40 S&W cal., no optics, Black, Pink, or Green finish. New 2014.

| MSR $799 | $675 | $600 | $550 | $495 | $450 | $400 | $350 | |

SDI – .223 Rem. cal., billet aluminum receivers, newly designed buffer system with rear sling attachment, Black anodized finish. New 2014.

| MSR $799 | $675 | $600 | $550 | $495 | $450 | $400 | $350 | |

RIFLES: SEMI-AUTO

AERO SURVIVAL RIFLE (ASR) – 9mm Para., .40 S&W, or .45 cal., compact design, breaks down efficiently without use of tools, unique configuration allows for easy barrel removal and caliber changes, available in Black, Pink Attitude, Tiger Green, Tan (new 2014) or Matte Green (new 2014) finish.

| MSR $799 | $675 | $600 | $550 | $495 | $450 | $400 | $350 | |

Add $250 for Black conversion kit or $275 for Pink or Green conversion kit.

MG34 – modified original German MG34s remanufactured using genuine parts, semi-auto only, shoots closed bolt, includes manual, 50 round belt, and ATF approved letter.

| MSR $3,995 | $3,750 | $3,400 | $3,000 | $2,600 | $2,200 | $1,800 | $1,400 | |

MG42 – more research is underway on this model. New 2014.

| MSR $4,299 | $3,975 | $3,550 | $3,100 | $2,650 | $2,250 | $1,850 | $1,450 | |

M3HB – .50 BMG cal., modified original Browning M2/M3, heavy barrel, shoots semi-auto only, cannot be converted to full auto, fires commercial ammunition or blanks, includes IM2 training manual, head spacing gauge, 200 .50 cal. links, left and right-hand feed, ATF approval letter.

| MSR $8,600 | $8,350 | $7,600 | $6,775 | $5,825 | $5,275 | $4,275 | $3,500 | |

Add $1,199 for M3HB mount.

M37 – .30 cal., patterned after a Browning 1919, right or left feed, dual tracks for alternate operation of the belt feeding pawl. Only 125 mfg.

| MSR $4,200 | $3,900 | $3,500 | $3,050 | $2,600 | $2,200 | $1,800 | $1,400 | |

MODEL 1919 – .30 cal., modified original Browning 1919-A4 using genuine G.I. parts, shoots semi-auto only and cannot be converted to full auto, internal and external parts finished with gray military type parkerization, includes 250 links, training manual, BATF approval letter. Disc. 2013.

| | $1,850 | $1,625 | $1,400 | $1,275 | $1,025 | $850 | $650 | *$2,050* |

SGP-QCB – .223 Rem. cal., GPO, quick change barrel firearm, Black anodized finish. New 2013.

| MSR $1,599 | $1,350 | $1,175 | $1,025 | $925 | $750 | $625 | $475 | |

SDI – 5.56 NATO cal., AR-15 style. New 2014.

| MSR $799 | $675 | $600 | $550 | $495 | $450 | $400 | $350 | |

SUOMI M31 – 9mm Para. cal., 16 in. barrel, semi-auto copy of the Finnish KP31, blowback action, 36 shot stick or 71 shot drum mag., parkerized finish, metallic sights, uncheckered plain wood stock, approx. 10 lbs. Importation began 2013.

| MSR $599 | $525 | $450 | $395 | $350 | $295 | $235 | $195 | |

TACTICAL ARMS MANUFACTURER, INC.

Current manufacturer located in Huntersville, NC.

RIFLES: SEMI-AUTO

Tactical Arms Manufacturer, Inc. manufactures AR-15 M4 or M16 style rifles in various calibers and configurations. Base prices start at $1,195. Please contact the company directly for more information including options, pricing, and availability (see Trademark Index).

TACTICAL ARMZ

Current rifle and suppressor manufacturer located in Springfield, MO.

MSR	100%	98%	95%	90%	80%	70%	60%	Last MSR

RIFLES: SEMI-AUTO

TA-15 HAVOC – 5.56 NATO cal., 16 in. chromemoly barrel with YHM Phantom muzzle brake, YHM low profile gas block, SST, modified Battle stock, Ergo rubber pistol grip, 12 1/2 in. Tactical Armz quadrail, Magpul MBUS flip-up sights, billet milled upper and lower receiver, enhanced mag well, nickel boron bolt carrier group, Cerakote Tungsten Ceramic finish, includes PMag. M3 maglevel magazine w/MagGrips, hard flight case, 9 lbs.

MSR $1,999	$1,795	$1,575	$1,350	$1,225	$985	$825	$625	

TA-15 LANCER – 5.56 NATO cal., 16 in. chromemoly barrel with YHM Phantom flash hider, YHM low profile gas block, black nitride bolt carrier group, SST, reinforced CQB buttstock, A2 pistol grip, Magpul MBUS flip-up sights, 12 1/2 in. quad rail handguard,Cerakote Armor Black Ceramic finish, 7.2 lbs.

MSR $1,199	$1,075	$950	$800	$725	$600	$485	$375	

TA-15 RONIN – 5.56 NATO cal., 16 in. chromemoly barrel with YHM Phantom flash hider, billet milled lower and forged and milled upper receiver, nickel boron bolt carrier group, YHM low profile gas block, SST, modified Battle stock with Hogue rubber pistol grip, Magpul MBUS flip-up sights, 12 1/2 in. Tactical Armz slim rail handguard, Cerakote Armor Black finish, includes PMag. M3 magazine w/MagGrips, hard case, 7 lbs.

MSR $1,499	$1,350	$1,175	$1,025	$925	$750	$625	$475	

TACTICAL RIFLES

Current rifle manufacturer located in Zephyrhills, FL. Previously located in Dade City, FL until 2010.

RIFLES: BOLT ACTION

Custom Hydrographic finishes are available on all rifles - price is POR.

Add $500 for Rem. 700 action. Add $895 for Chimera match grade receiver. Add $75 for extended Picatinny rail. Add $345 (short action)-$395 (long action) for TR alloy detachable floorplate or $345 for steel hinged floorplate. Add $225 for Tri-port muzzle brake.

M40 – .260 Rem., 6.5x74 Lapua, or 7.62 NATO/.308 Win. cal., Rem. 700 or TR Chimera custom match grade receiver, 17-26 in. stainless steel match grade barrel with recessed target crown, mil-spec parts, heavyweight steel floorplate (detachable floorplate is optional), Picatinny rail, McMillan A1, A2, A3, A4, or A5 stock, raised comb, Black, Green, Woodland camo, and Desert camo finish, 9 1/2 - 12 1/2 lbs.

MSR $2,895	$2,450	$2,150	$1,850	$1,675	$1,350	$1,100	$860	

Price does not include action.

Other precision calibers are available upon request.

* **M40-223** – .223 Rem. cal., similar to M40, except also features tactical floorplate, and tactical bolt knob. Disc. 2013.

This model was POR.

* **M40-300** – .300 WSM cal., similar to M40, long or short action, except also features dual expansion port brake.

MSR $3,295	$2,800	$2,450	$2,100	$1,900	$1,540	$1,260	$975	

Price does not include action.

* **M40-325** – .325 WSM cal., similar to M40, except features lighter weight barrel with muzzle brake. Disc. 2013.

This model was POR.

* **M40-338** – .338 Lapua cal., similar to M40, except has TR Chimera custom match grade receiver, 20-27 in. stainless steel match grade barrel with recessed target crown, 11-14 lbs.

MSR $3,595	$3,050	$2,675	$2,295	$2,075	$1,675	$1,375	$1,075	

Price does not include action.

TACTICAL CHIMERA HUNTER – .300 WSM or .308 Win. cal., Chimera stainless steel match grade action, 24 in. stainless steel select match grade barrel, recessed match grade crown, muzzle brake standard on .300 WSM, single stage adj. trigger, T7 carbon fiber/fiberglass blend stock, Picatinny rail, extreme environment corrosion resistant solid color matte finish, approx. 9 lbs. Disc. 2013.

This model was POR.

TACTICAL CLASSIC SPORTER – .243 Win., .260 Rem., .270 Win., .300 Win. Mag., .308 Win., .25-06, .30-06, 6.5 Creedmore, 6.5 Lapua, 7mm Rem., or 7mm-08 cal., Chimera match grade stainless action, 18-26 in. stainless match grade barrel, two-piece Picatinny base, solid stainless steel heavyweight hinged floorplate assembly, XXX grade English walnut stock with hand rubbed oil finish, full length alloy bedding block, hand checkered, inlaid sling swivels, single stage adj. trigger.

MSR $5,889	$5,000	$4,375	$3,750	$3,400	$2,750	$2,250	$1,750	

MSR	100%	98%	95%	90%	80%	70%	60%	Last MSR

TACTICAL LONG RANGE – 7.62 NATO/.308 Win. cal., .300 Win. Mag., .325 WSM (disc. 2013), or .338 Lapua cal., Rem. 700 or TR Chimera custom action, 20-26 in. stainless steel match grade barrel with recessed target crown, Picatinny rail, adj. trigger, 3 or 5 shot mag., thumbhole stock, raised cheekpiece, includes ambidextrous sling swivel studs and soft rubber recoil pad, available in Black or Green finish, 12-13 1/2 lbs.

| MSR $2,995 | $2,550 | $2,225 | $1,915 | $1,735 | $1,400 | $1,150 | $895 | |

Price does not include action.

Add $355 for .300 Win. Mag. or $700 for .338 Lapua cal.

TACTICAL PARATROOPER – 7.62 NATO/.308 Win. or .300 Win. Mag. cal., Rem. 700 or TR Chimera custom match grade receiver, 16 1/2 - 26 in. stainless steel match grade barrel with recessed target crown, Picatinny rail, folding thumbhole stock with ambidextrous sling swivel studs and soft rubber recoil pad, match grade trigger, Black or Green finish, 10 1/2 - 12 1/4 lbs.

| MSR $3,550 | $3,000 | $2,625 | $2,250 | $2,040 | $1,650 | $1,350 | $1,050 | |

Price does not include action.

Add $245 for .300 Win. Mag. cal.

RIFLES: SEMI-AUTO

Previous models included the Dow Custom AR 10 (disc. 2004, last MSR was $2,695).

Hydrographics or custom painted finishes are available on all rifles - price is POR.

DOW FAL 15 – .223 Rem. or 6.8 SPC cal., patterned after AR-15, GIO, medium weight match grade stainless steel barrel, matte black receiver finish, flat-top Picatinny upper, match grade trigger, hand rubbed oil finished wood stock. Disc. 2013.

This model was POR.

TACTICAL AR-15 – .223 cal., AR-15 style, GIO, Krieger heavy match grade free floating barrel with birdcage flash hider, 2-stage match trigger, mil-spec handguard, black, green, or sand colored stock.

| MSR $2,395 | $2,025 | $1,775 | $1,525 | $1,375 | $1,115 | $910 | $710 | |

Add $95 for titanium or chrome match bolt carrier.

Add $115 for Vortex style tempered steel flash suppressor.

Add $185 for Picatinny machined forend.

TACTICAL M4C – .223 Rem. cal., AR-15 style, GIO, 16 in. heavy match grade barrel with birdcage flash hider, free float CNC machined forend with GI foresight assembly or smooth gas block, flat-top upper, collapsible stock, extreme environment finish.

| MSR $2,285 | $1,950 | $1,700 | $1,465 | $1,325 | $1,075 | $880 | $685 | |

Add $95 for titanium or chrome match bolt carrier.

Add $115 for Vortex style tempered steel flash suppressor.

Add $50 for Harris bipod adapter stud with push button release swivel.

Add $179 for PRI folding front sight.

Add $139 for ARMS low profile folding Picatinny rail mounted rear sight.

TACTICAL M21 – .30 cal., M14 action, GIO, Krieger heavy match grade barrel, M3 bedded stock, vertical pistol grip with wrap-over thumb shelf and vertically adj. saddle type cheek piece, butt has removable spacer system, 5 or 10 shot mag. Disc. 2013.

This model was POR.

TACTICAL SPG – .264 LBC, 6.5 CSS, 6.5 Grendel (new 2013) or .308 (disc. 2013) cal., AR-15 style, GIO, billet upper and lower receiver, 17 shot mag., 20 in. Krieger stainless match grade contoured barrel with Surefire muzzle brake, Magpul PRS fully adj. stock, free float full length Picatinny forend, ergonomic pistol grip, two-stage trigger, zero headspace match grade black nitride coated bolt carrier group, Black finish, 10 1/2 lbs.

| MSR $3,695 | $3,150 | $2,750 | $2,365 | $2,140 | $1,735 | $1,425 | $1,100 | |

Add $154 for flip-up foresight with integral gas block.

Add $129 for flip-up rear sight assembly.

TACTICAL SVR (SPECIAL VARMINT RIFLE) – .204 Ruger or .223 Rem. cal., AR-15 style, 24 in. full profile heavy match grade stainless steel barrel with target crown plain muzzle, free float forend, 20 shot mag., flat-top Picatinny rail, A2 style fixed or Magpul adj. stock, ergonomic custom grip, adj. trigger, Black or Green finish is standard, Custom Camo finishes are optional, 10 1/2 lbs.

| MSR $3,195 | $2,725 | $2,375 | $2,050 | $1,850 | $1,500 | $1,225 | $950 | |

Add $95 for titanium or chrome match bolt carrier.

Add $185 for Picatinny machined forend.

Add $249 for Magpul adj. stock.

	MSR	100%	98%	95%	90%	80%	70%	60%	*Last MSR*

TACTICAL SOLUTIONS

Current rifle and components manufacturer located in Boise, ID. Dealer sales.

RIFLES: SEMI-AUTO

Tactical Solutions makes a Pac-Lite barrel assembly for the Ruger Mark and .22/.45 Series pistol frame and conversion units for both pistols and AR-15 style rifles. Please contact the manufacturer directly for additional information, availability, and current pricing (see Trademark Index).

X-RING RIFLE – .22 LR cal., 16 1/2 in. standard or threaded barrel, 10 shot mag., choice of Black, OD Green, Ghillie Green or Ghillie Tan Hogue overmolded or Slate, Forest, Crimson or Royal Vantage laminate stock, extended mag. release, Ruger trigger group, 4.3 - 5.1 lbs.

MSR $850	$725	$625	$550	$495	$400	$325	$250

Add $50 for threaded barrel or $150 for Vantage stock.

TACTICAL WEAPONS

Current law enforcement/military division of FNH USA, located in McLean, VA.

Tactical Weapons currently manufactures machine guns only for law enforcement/military.

TACTICAL WEAPONS SOLUTIONS

Current manufacturer located in Apopka, FL.

Tactical Weapons Solutions manufactures and sells a variety of fine quality AR-15 rifles as well as AR-15 pistols and survival supplies. Please contact the company directly for more information on all their parts, accessories, and services (see Trademark Index).

PISTOLS: SEMI-AUTO

MODEL P01 – 5.56 NATO cal., GIO, chromemoly steel barrel with A2 flash hider, forged upper and lower receivers, extended feed ramps, aluminum pistol length handguard, pistol buffer tube, forged "F" front sight base with bayonet lug, ambidextrous rear sling mount, 6.6 lbs.

MSR $1,050	$950	$825	$725	$650	$525	$425	$350

* Model P02 – 5.56 NATO cal., GIO, similar to Model P01, except features pistol length quad rail.

MSR $1,100	$975	$850	$750	$675	$550	$450	$350

MODEL P03 – 5.56 NATO cal., GIO, chromemoly steel barrel, CQB compensator, forged upper and lower receiver, extended feed ramps, carbine length quad rail, pistol buffer tube, forged "F" front sight base with bayonet lug, ambidextrous rear sling mount, 7 lbs.

MSR $1,330	$1,195	$1,050	$900	$815	$650	$550	$425

MODEL P04 – 5.56 NATO cal., GIO, 7 1/2 in. chromemoly barrel with CQB compensator, forged lower and forged M4 upper receivers, Magpul MBUS front and rear flip up sights, extended feed ramps, carbine length quad rail, pistol buffer tube, ambidextrous sling mount, extractor upgrade with Viton O-ring, Black finish, 7 lbs.

MSR $1,400	$1,250	$1,095	$950	$850	$700	$575	$450

RISK TAKERS STANDARD CQB – 5.56 NATO cal., similar to Model P04, except includes Risk Takers logos, 7 lbs.

MSR $1,202	$1,075	$950	$800	$725	$595	$485	$375

* Risk Takers CQB – 5.56 NATO cal., similar to Risk Takers Standard CQB, except includes Troy Medieval flash hider, Ergo Super tactical grip, Nib trigger, hammer, disconnect, FDE finish.

MSR $1,604	$1,425	$1,250	$1,075	$975	$785	$650	$525

RIFLES: SEMI-AUTO

MODEL 01 – 5.56 NATO cal., GIO, chromemoly steel barrel with A2 flash hider, forged upper and lower receiver, extended feed ramps, two piece handguard with Delta assembly, 6-position adj. stock, receiver extension tube, forged "F" front sight base with bayonet lug, ambidextrous rear sling mount, extractor upgrade with Viton O-Ring, 6 1/2 lbs.

MSR $880	$795	$695	$595	$535	$435	$350	$275

Subtract $80 for El-Model 01 without extractor upgrade with Viton O-Ring.

* Model 02 – 5.56 NATO cal., GIO, similar to Model 01, except features two-piece quad rail, 6.8 lbs.

MSR $900	$810	$710	$610	$550	$450	$375	$285

* Model 03 – 5.56 NATO cal., GIO, similar to Model 01, except features free floating quad rail, low profile or single rail gas block, 6.7 lbs.

MSR $1,000	$900	$795	$675	$610	$495	$400	$325

MSR	100%	98%	95%	90%	80%	70%	60%	Last MSR

MODEL 4 ALPHA – 5.56 NATO cal., GIO, 16 in. chromemoly barrel with flash hider, extended feed ramps, forged lower and forged M4 upper receivers, extractor upgrade w/Viton O-ring, free float quad rail, rec. extension tube, ambidextrous rear sling mount, nickel boron trigger, hammer, and disconnector, upgraded front and rear sights, 6-pos. adj. stock, pistol grip, Black finish, 6 1/2 lbs.

| MSR $1,425 | $1,275 | $1,115 | $950 | $875 | $700 | $575 | $450 | |

* **Model 5 Elite** – 5.56 NATO cal., similar to Model 4 Alpha, except includes nickel boron barrel extension, Bravo Co. "Gunfighter" charging handle, and upgraded trigger and hammer pins.

| MSR $1,800 | $1,625 | $1,425 | $1,225 | $1,100 | $895 | $750 | $600 | |

MODEL 06 MOE – 5.56 NATO cal., chromemoly barrel with A2 flash hider, forged lower and forged M4 upper receivers, extended feed ramps, forged front sight base w/bayonet lug, ambidextrous rear sling mount, Magpul MOE handguard, buttstock, and pistol grip, Magpul MBUS rear flip-up sight, Black finish, 6.4 lbs.

| MSR $950 | $850 | $750 | $650 | $575 | $475 | $385 | $300 | |

MODEL 7 LOADED – 5.56 NATO cal., GIO, chromemoly barrel with A2 flash hider, extended feed ramps, forged lower and forged M4 upper receivers, two piece quad rail with Delta assembly, 6-position adj. stock, receiver extension tube, ambidextrous rear sling mount, forged front sight base with bayonet lug, black finish, extractor upgrade with Viton O-ring, includes 5mW green laser, 90 Lumen tactical flashlight, 6x32 scope, 5-position foldable foregrip, and tactical bipod, 6 1/2 lbs.

| MSR $1,251 | $1,125 | $985 | $850 | $775 | $625 | $500 | $400 | |

MODEL 08/MODEL 09/MODEL 10/MODEL 11 – 5.56 NATO cal., GIO, chromemoly barrel with A2 flash hider, extended feed ramps, forged lower and forged M4 upper receivers, two piece quad rail with Delta assembly, 6-position adj. stock, receiver extension tube, ambidextrous rear sling mount, forged front sight base with bayonet lug, extractor upgrade with Viton O-ring, Cerakote FDE (Model 08), OD Green (Model 09), Pink (Model 10), or MultiCam camo (Model 11) finish, 6.8 lbs.

| MSR $990 | $890 | $775 | $675 | $600 | $500 | $400 | $325 | |

MODEL 12/MODEL 14/MODEL 16/MODEL 18 – 5.56 NATO cal., GIO, chromemoly barrel with A2 flash hider, extended feed ramps, forged lower and forged M4 upper receivers, two piece quad rail with Delta assembly, 6-position adj. stock, receiver extension tube, ambidextrous rear sling mount, forged front sight base with bayonet lug, extractor upgrade with Viton O-ring, free floating quad rail, low profile or single rail gas block, Cerakote MultiCam (Model 12), Digital ACU (Model 14), Digital Desert (Model 16), or Reaper (Model 18) finish, 6.7 lbs.

| MSR $1,120 | $1,000 | $875 | $750 | $675 | $550 | $450 | $350 | |

MODEL 13/MODEL 15/MODEL 17/MODEL 19/MODEL 20 – .56 NATO cal., GIO, chromemoly barrel with A2 flash hider, extended feed ramps, forged lower and forged M4 upper receivers, two piece quad rail with Delta assembly, 6-position adj. stock, receiver extension tube, ambidextrous rear sling mount, forged front sight base with bayonet lug, extractor upgrade with Viton O-ring, Digital ACU (Model 13), Desert Digital (Model 15), Pink (Model 10), Reaper (Model 17), Muddy Girl (Model 19), or MultiCam Pink (Model 20) finish, 6.8 lbs.

| MSR $990 | $890 | $775 | $675 | $600 | $500 | $400 | $325 | |

.308 INTIMIDATOR – .308 Win. cal., GIO, 16 in. chromemoly steel barrel, fixed stock, pistol grip, oversized trigger guard, DPMS style upper receiver, black finish.

| MSR $2,350 | $2,100 | $1,850 | $1,575 | $1,425 | $1,150 | $950 | $750 | |

TALON ORDNANCE

Current semi-auto rifle manufacturer located in Richland, MS.

RIFLES: SEMI-AUTO

TM4-A1 – .223 Rem. cal., GIO, hard coat anodized flat-top upper, lower receiver, and charging handle, aluminum lower receiver extension, 16 in. chromemoly vanadium hammer forged steel barrel with removable Eagle Claw flash hider, Magpul aluminum enhanced trigger guard, 6-position retractable buttstock with rubber butt pad, G10 pistol grip, low profile gas block, M4 feed ramps, 30 shot stainless steel mag., Class 2 hard coat anodized finish, includes case, 7 1/2 lbs. New 2014.

| MSR $2,695 | $2,425 | $2,125 | $1,825 | $1,650 | $1,350 | $1,095 | $850 | |

Add $500 for special Mississippi edition package.

TAR-HUNT CUSTOM RIFLES, INC.

Current custom rifled shotgun manufacturer established in 1990, and located in Bloomsburg, PA. Dealer and consumer direct sales.

In addition to rifles and shotguns, Tar-Hunt also builds custom XP-100 pistols on a customer supplied action. Contact the company directly for a price quotation (see Trademark Index).

MSR	100%	98%	95%	90%	80%	70%	60%	Last MSR

SHOTGUNS: BOLT ACTION

Add $110 for left-hand action on all current models, $300 for high gloss metal, $495 for nickel, $250 for Jewell trigger, and $110 for dipped camouflage stock finish.

RSG-TACTICAL (SNIPER) MODEL – 12 ga. only, similar to RSG-12, except has M-86 McMillan fiberglass black tactical stock with Pachmayr Decelerator pad and heavy barrel. Mfg. 1992-98.

	$1,495	$1,250	$995	$875	$750	$700	$650	$1,595

Add $150 for Bipod.

TAURUS INTERNATIONAL MFG., INC.

Currently manufactured by Taurus Forjas S.A., located in Porto Alegre, Brazil. Currently imported by Taurus International Mfg., Inc. located in Miami, FL since 1982. Beginning 2007, Taurus Tactical, a separate entity, was created for law enforcement/military sales and service. Distributor sales only.

During late 2012, Taurus Holdings purchased an exclusive global distribution agreement with Diamondback Firearms, LLC. Taurus will assume all sales and marketing efforts of the Diamondback branded products from its Miami office.

All Taurus products are known for their innovative design, quality construction, and proven value, and are backed by a lifetime repair policy.

Taurus order number nomenclature is as follows: the first digit followed by a dash refers to type (1 = pistol, 2 = revolvers, 3 = longuns, 4 = Magazines/Accessories, 5 = grips, and 10 = scope mount bases), the next 2 or 3 digits refer to model number, the next digit refers to type of hammer (0 = exposed, 1 = concealed), the next digit refers to barrel length (w/o fractions), the last digit refers to finish (1 = blue, 9 = stainless), and the suffix at the end refers to special features (T = total titanium, H = case hardened, M = matte finish, PLY = polymer, UL = Ultra-Lite, C = ported (compensation), G = gold accent, PRL = mother-of-pearl grips, R = rosewood grips, NS = night sights, MG = magnesium, and FO = fiber optic). Hence, 2-454089M refers to a Model 454 Raging Bull revolver in .454 Casull cal. with an exposed hammer and a 8 3/8 in. barrel in matte stainless finish.

PISTOLS: SEMI-AUTO

From 1990-92, certain models became available with a Laser Aim LA1 sighting system that included mounts, rings (in matching finish), a 110 volt AC recharging unit, a 9 volt DC field charger, and a high impact custom case.

Taurus incorporated their keyed Taurus security system on most models during 2000, except the PT-22 and PT-25, and this is now available with all models. When the security system is engaged (via a keyed button on the bottom of rear grip strap), the pistol cannot be fired, cocked, or disassembled, and the gun's manual safety cannot be disengaged. This security key also works for the revolvers.

Recent variations that are CA approved are not broken out separately, as pricing is usually the same as the standard model.

Add approx. $30 for the Deluxe Shooter's Pack option (includes extra mag. and custom case) on the 92, 99, 100, and 101 Series (disc. 2000).

PT-24/7 – 9mm Para., .40 S&W, or .45 ACP (new 2005) cal., DAO, SFO, large black polymer frame with blued steel or satin stainless steel slide, 4 in. barrel with 3-dot sights, grips have Ribber grip overlays, 10, 12 (.45 ACP cal.), 15 (.40 S&W cal.), or 17 (9mm Para. cal.) shot mag., built-in Picatinny rail system on bottom of frame, includes 3 safeties, 27 1/2 oz. Mfg. late 2004-2005.

	$450	$395	$345	$295	$260	$225	$195	$578

Add $16 for stainless steel.

PT-24/7 PRO FULL SIZE – 9mm Para., .40 S&W, or .45 ACP cal., SA first shot, and follows continually in SA model, SFO, large black polymer frame with blued steel, Duo Tone (new 2009), titanium (9mm Para. cal. only), or satin stainless steel slide, 4 in. barrel with Heinie front and Slant Pro rear sight, Ribber grips (.45 ACP cal.) or Ribber overmold grips (grip inlays), 10, 12 (.45 ACP cal.), 15 (.40 S&W cal.), or 17 (9mm Para. cal.) shot mag., built-in Picatinny rail system on bottom of frame, includes 3 safeties, 27.2 oz. Mfg. 2006-2010.

	$415	$350	$310	$280	$240	$210	$185	$498

Add $16 for stainless steel or $188 for titanium.

This model uses a SA trigger mechanism. However, if a cartridge does not fire, a DA feature allows the shooter a second firing pin strike via the DA trigger pull. If the cartridge still does not fire, then extraction by slide operation will insert a fresh round while reverting to the SA model automatically.

* **PT-24/7 Pro Long Slide** – similar to Full Size 24/7-Pro, except has 5.2 in. barrel, also available in .38 Super cal. (new 2010), similar mag. capacities, Tenifer finish new 2010, 29.1 oz. Mfg. 2006-2010.

	$445	$385	$340	$295	$260	$225	$195	$530

Add $15 for stainless steel. Add $31 for Tenifer finish (new 2010). Add $197 for Tenifer finish with night sights (.40 S&W cal. only, new 2010).

MSR	100%	98%	95%	90%	80%	70%	60%	Last MSR

* PT-24/7 Pro Compact – similar to Full Size 24/7-Pro, except has 3 1/3 in. barrel, similar mag. capacities. Mfg. 2006-2010.

	$415	$350	$310	$280	$240	$210	$185	*$498*

Add $16 for stainless steel or $188 for titanium.

PT-24/7 G2 – 9mm Para., .40 S&W, or .45 ACP cal., advanced DA/SA trigger system, SFO, 4.2 in. barrel, large black polymer frame, horizontally grooved grips with metallic inserts and 3 interchangeable backstraps, ambidextrous thumb rests, matte blue or stainless steel slide, Strike Two trigger with safety, ambidextrous manual decocker latch and safety, fixed front and low-profile adj. rear sight, vertical loaded chamber indicator, built-in Picatinny rail system on bottom of frame, 10, 12 (.45 ACP cal. only), 15 (.40 S&W cal. only) or 17 (9mm Para. only) shot mag., 28 oz. New 2011.

MSR $528	$435	$385	$340	$295	$260	$225	$195	

Add $15 for stainless steel.

* PT-24/7 G2 Compact – similar to PT-24/7 G2, except has 3 1/2 in. barrel, 27 oz. New 2011.

MSR $528	$435	$385	$340	$295	$260	$225	$195	

Add $15 for stainless steel.

PT-24/7 OSS – 9mm Para., .40 S&W, or .45 ACP cal., similar operating system as PT-24/7 Pro Full Size, including SA/DA trigger system, choice of tan or black frame, 5 1/4 in. match grade barrel, Novak sights, lower frame Picatinny rail, 10, 12, 15, or 17 shot mag., ambidextrous decocking safety, black Tenifer steel or stainless (new 2009) slide with front and rear serrations, approx. 32 oz. Mfg. 2007-2010.

	$475	$415	$370	$325	$285	$240	$210	*$623*

Add $63 for Novak Lo-Mount night sights.

Add $18 for matte finished stainless steel slide (new 2009).

PT-38S – .38 Super cal., 4 1/4 in. barrel, DA/SA utilizes Model PT-945 alloy frame, choice of blue, stainless steel, or stainless/gold finishes, 3-dot fixed sights, 10 shot mag., checkered rubber (standard) or smooth faux mother-of-pearl grips, 30 oz. Mfg. 2005-2010.

	$525	$480	$425	$375	$325	$280	$230	*$695*

Add $16 for stainless steel slide.

Add $48 for stainless steel slide, gold accents, and faux mother-of-pearl grips.

PT-58 HC PLUS – .380 ACP cal., medium frame, similar to PT-58, except has 19 shot mag., ambidextrous safety, fixed sights, 18.7 oz. Mfg. 2006-2010.

	$495	$450	$395	$350	$295	$260	$220	*$664*

Add $16 for stainless steel slide.

PT-92(AF) – 9mm Para. cal., DA/SA, design similar to Beretta Model 92 SB-F, exposed hammer, ambidextrous safety, 5 in. barrel, current mfg. has frame accessory rail in front of trigger guard, 10 (C/B 1994), 15*, or 17 (new late 2004) shot mag., smooth Brazilian walnut (disc.) or checkered rubber (new 1999) grips, blue or nickel (disc.) finish, fixed or night (mfg. 2000-2004) sights, loaded chamber indicator, Taurus Security System, 34 oz.

MSR $638	$540	$490	$430	$375	$325	$280	$230	

Add $40 for satin nickel finish (disc. 1994).

Add $415 for Laser Aim Sight (disc. 1991).

Add $78 for night sights (disc. 2004).

Add $266 for blue or stainless conversion kit to convert 9mm Para. to .22 LR (mfg. 1999-2004).

* PT-92SS (Stainless Steel) – similar to PT-92AF, except is combat matte (new 2006, high cap. mag. only) or regular stainless steel. New 1992.

MSR $653	$550	$495	$450	$395	$350	$295	$245	

Add $78 for night sights (disc. 2004).

* PT-92AFC – compact variation of the Model PT-92AF, 4 in. barrel, 10 (C/B 1994) or 13* shot mag., fixed sights. Disc. 1996.

	$395	$345	$300	$260	$220	$195	$175	*$449*

Add $38 for satin nickel finish (disc. 1993).

* PT-92AFC (Stainless Steel) – similar to PT-92AFC, except stainless steel. Mfg. 1993-96.

	$425	$360	$315	$280	$240	$210	$185	*$493*

PT-99 (AF) – 9mm Para. cal., similar to Model PT-92AF, except has adj. rear sight, 10 or 17 shot mag., 34 oz. Disc. 2011.

	$495	$450	$395	$350	$295	$260	$220	*$617*

Add $45 for satin nickel finish (disc. 1994).

Add $266 for blue or stainless conversion kit to convert 9mm Para. to .22 LR (mfg. 1999-2004) or .40 S&W (mfg. 2000-2004).

This action is similar to the Beretta Model 92SB-F.

MSR	100%	98%	95%	90%	80%	70%	60%	Last MSR

* PT-99SS (Stainless Steel) – similar to PT-99, except is fabricated from stainless steel. Mfg. 1992-2011.

	$495	$450	$395	$350	$295	$260	$220	$633

PT-100 – .40 S&W cal., DA/SA, large frame, 5 in. barrel, 10 (C/B 1994), 11* (reintroduced late 2004) shot mag., safeties include ambidextrous manual, hammer drop, inertia firing pin, and chamber loaded indicator, choice of blue, satin nickel (disc. 1994), or stainless steel finish, accessory rail, smooth Brazilian hard wood (disc.) or rubber grips, 34 oz. Mfg. 1992-97, reintroduced 2000. Disc. 2012.

	$495	$450	$395	$350	$295	$260	$220	$641

Add $40 for satin nickel finish (disc. 1994).
Add $78 for night sights (mfg. 2000-2004).
Add $266 for blue or stainless conversion kit to convert .40 S&W to .22 LR cal. (disc. 2004).

* PT-100SS (Stainless Steel) – .40 S&W cal., similar to PT-100, except is fabricated from stainless steel, and 16 shot mag. Mfg. 1992-96, reintroduced 2000-2013.

	$515	$460	$400	$350	$295	$260	$220	$668

Add $78 for night sights (disc. 2005).

PT-101 – .40 S&W cal., similar to PT-100, except has adj. rear sight., 10 or 11 shot mag., 34 oz. Mfg. 1992-96, reintroduced 2000-2011.

	$495	$450	$395	$350	$295	$260	$220	$617

Add $266 for blue or stainless conversion kit to convert .40 S&W to .22 LR cal. (disc. 2004).
Add $45 for satin nickel finish (disc. 1994).

* PT-101SS (Stainless Steel) – similar to PT-101, except is stainless steel. Mfg. 1992-96, reintroduced 2000-2011.

	$495	$450	$395	$350	$295	$260	$220	$633

PT-111 MILLENNIUM – 9mm Para. cal., DAO, SFO, 3 1/4 in. barrel with fixed 3-dot sights, black polymer frame with steel slide, striker fired, 10 shot mag. with push-button release, 18.7 oz. Mfg. 1998-2004.

	$375	$310	$265	$220	$200	$180	$165	$422

Add $78 for night sights (new 2000).
Add $47 for pearl or burl walnut grips (limited mfg. 2003).

* PT-111 Millennium Stainless – similar to Model PT-111, except has stainless steel slide. Mfg. 1998-2004.

	$385	$335	$295	$260	$220	$195	$175	$438

Add $78 for night sights (new 2000).
Add $46 for pearl or burl walnut grips (limited mfg. 2003).

* PT-111 Millennium Titanium – similar to Model PT-111, except has titanium slide and night or 3-dot (new 2004) sights. Mfg. 2000-2004.

	$435	$385	$340	$295	$260	$225	$195	$508

Add $78 for night sights.

PT-111 MILLENNIUM PRO – 9mm Para. cal., SA/DA trigger, SFO, 10 or 12 (new late 2004) shot mag., blue steel frame, current mfg. has Heinie Straight 8 sights, improved ergonomics, Posi-Traction slide serrations, recessed magazine release, manual safety lever, trigger block mechanism, firing pin block, and lightweight frame, 18.7 oz. Mfg. 2003-2012.

	$375	$310	$265	$220	$200	$180	$165	$467

Add $78 for night sights (disc. 2004).

* PT-111 Millennium Pro Stainless – similar to Model PT-111 Millennium Pro, except has stainless steel slide. Mfg. 2003-2012.

	$395	$330	$285	$260	$210	$170	$135	$483

Add $78 for night sights (mfg. 2004).

* PT-111 Ti Millennium Pro Titanium – similar to Model PT-111 Millennium Pro, except has titanium slide and 3 dot sights, 16 oz. Mfg. 2005-2011.

	$525	$480	$425	$375	$325	$280	$230	$655

PT-138 MILLENNIUM PRO – .380 ACP cal., similar to Model PT-138 Millennium, SFO, 10 or 12 shot (new 2005) mag., SA/DA trigger, current mfg. has Heinie Straight 8 sights, improved ergonomics, Posi-Traction slide serrations, recessed magazine release, manual safety lever, trigger block mechanism, firing pin block, and lightweight frame, 18.7 oz. Mfg. 2003, reintroduced 2005-2011.

	$375	$310	$265	$220	$200	$180	$165	$467

Add $78 for night sights (disc. 2003).

* PT-138 Millennium Pro Stainless – similar to Model PT-138 Millennium Pro, except has stainless steel slide. Mfg. 2003, reintroduced 2005-2011.

	$395	$345	$300	$260	$220	$195	$175	$483

MSR	100%	98%	95%	90%	80%	70%	60%	Last MSR

PT-140 MILLENNIUM – .40 S&W cal., DAO, SFO, 3 1/4 in. barrel, black polymer frame, manual safety, 10 shot mag., fixed 3-dot sights, blue steel slide, 18.7 oz. Mfg. 1999-2004.

| | $375 | $310 | $265 | $220 | $200 | $180 | $165 | $461 |

Add $78 for night sights (new 2000).
Add $47 for pearl or burl walnut grips (mfg. 2003).

* PT-140 Millennium Stainless – similar to Model PT-140, except has stainless steel slide. Mfg. 1999-2004.

| | $380 | $335 | $295 | $260 | $220 | $195 | $175 | $476 |

Add $78 for night sights (new 2000).
Add $46 for pearl or burl walnut grips (mfg. 2003).

PT-140 MILLENNIUM PRO – .40 S&W cal., similar to Model PT-140 Millennium, except has SA/DA trigger, current mfg. has Heinie Straight 8 sights, improved ergonomics, Posi-Traction slide serrations, recessed magazine release, manual safety lever, trigger block mechanism, firing pin block, and lightweight frame, 23 1/2 oz. Mfg. 2003-2012.

| | $395 | $330 | $285 | $260 | $210 | $170 | $135 | $483 |

Add $78 for night sights (disc. 2004).

* PT-140 Millennium Pro Stainless – similar to Model PT-140 Millennium Pro, except has stainless steel slide. Mfg. 2003-2012.

| | $415 | $350 | $310 | $280 | $240 | $210 | $185 | $498 |

Add $78 for night sights (disc. 2004).

PT-145 MILLENNIUM – .45 ACP cal., otherwise similar to Model PT-140 Millennium, 23 oz. Mfg. 2000-2003.

| | $400 | $350 | $310 | $280 | $240 | $210 | $185 | $484 |

Add $79 for night sights (new 2000).

* PT-145 Millennium Stainless – similar to Model PT-140, except has stainless steel slide. Mfg. 1999-2003.

| | $400 | $350 | $310 | $280 | $240 | $210 | $185 | $500 |

Add $78 for night sights (new 2000).

PT-145 MILLENNIUM PRO – .45 ACP cal., similar to Model PT-145 Millennium, except has SA/DA trigger, current mfg. has Heinie Straight 8 sights, improved ergonomics, Posi-Traction slide serrations, recessed magazine release, manual safety lever, trigger block mechanism, firing pin block, and lightweight frame, 22.2 oz. Mfg. 2003-2012.

| | $395 | $345 | $300 | $260 | $220 | $195 | $175 | $483 |

Add $78 for night sights (disc. 2004).

* PT-145 Millennium Pro Stainless – similar to Model PT-145 Millennium Pro, except has stainless steel slide. Mfg. 2003-2013.

| | $415 | $350 | $310 | $280 | $240 | $210 | $185 | $498 |

Add $78 for night sights (mfg. 2000-2004).

PT-400 – .400 Cor-Bon cal., similar to Model PT-940, except has 4 1/4 in. ported barrel and 8 shot mag., 29 1/2 oz. Mfg. 1999 only.

| | $415 | $350 | $310 | $280 | $240 | $210 | $185 | $523 |

* PT-400 Stainless – similar to Model PT-400, except has stainless steel slide. Mfg. 1999 only.

| | $415 | $350 | $310 | $280 | $240 | $210 | $185 | $539 |

PT-609/609TI-PRO – 9mm Para. cal., DA/SA, 3 1/4 in. barrel with titanium slide, fixed sights, black polymer grips, lower rail on frame, 13 shot mag., 19.7 oz. Mfg. 2007-2010.

| | $535 | $490 | $430 | $375 | $325 | $280 | $230 | $670 |

PT-638 PRO COMPACT – .380 ACP cal., SA target style trigger with trigger safety, 3.2 in. barrel, low mount sights with adj. rear, 15 shot mag., ambidextrous manual safety, loaded chamber indicator, blue or matte stainless slide, black polymer frame with Memory Pad, 28 oz. Mfg. 2011 only.

| | $395 | $345 | $300 | $260 | $220 | $195 | $175 | $483 |

Add $15 for matte stainless steel slide.

PT-709 SLIM – 9mm Para. cal., SA (disc.) or DA/SA trigger (current mfg.), 3 in. barrel, 7 shot mag., blue finish, black polymer frame with grip texturing, compact frame, 3 dot sights, loaded chamber indicator, advanced "Strike Two" trigger system, Taurus Security System, 19 oz. Mfg. late 2008-2012, reintroduced 2014.

| MSR $404 | $350 | $300 | $260 | $220 | $200 | $180 | $165 | |

Add $14 for Bulldog Case (mfg. 2010-2011).

* PT-709 Slim Stainless – 9mm Para. cal., similar to Model 709, except has matte finished stainless steel slide, 19 oz. New late 2008.

| MSR $504 | $425 | $360 | $315 | $280 | $240 | $210 | $185 | |

Add $15 for Bulldog Case (new 2010).

MSR	100%	98%	95%	90%	80%	70%	60%	Last MSR

PT-709 G2 SLIM – 9mm Para. cal., sub-compact frame, 7 or 9 (extended) shot mag., 3.2 in. barrel with low profile adj. rear sights, loaded chamber indicator, black polymer frame and blue or matte stainless slide, 19.4 oz. Limited mfg. 2011 only.

	$395	$345	$300	$260	$220	$195	$175	$483

* **PT-709 G2 Slim Stainless** – similar to PT-709 G2 Slim, except has matte finished stainless steel slide. Limited mfg. 2011 only.

	$415	$350	$310	$280	$240	$210	$185	$498

PT-745 COMPACT MILLENNIUM PRO – .45 ACP cal., SA/DA, SFO, compact variation of Millennium Pro with 3 1/4 in. barrel, Heinie Straight 8 sights, 6 shot mag. with finger extension, matte blue steel slide, loaded chamber indicator, black polymer grip frame, Desert Tan grips were added 2006 (disc.), 20.8 oz. Mfg. 2005-2012.

	$395	$345	$300	$260	$220	$195	$175	$483

* **PT-745 Compact Millenium Pro Stainless** – similar to PT-745 Compact Millennium Pro, except has stainless steel slide. Mfg. 2005-2012.

	$415	$350	$310	$280	$240	$210	$185	$498

PT-809 – 9mm Para. cal., similar design to the PT-24/7 OSS, 4 in. barrel, DA/SA with Strike Two capability, SFO, Novak sights, 17 shot mag., external hammer, loaded chamber indicator, blue or stainless (disc. 2012), front and rear slide serrations, lower Picatinny rail, ambidextrous 2-position safety and decocker, ambidextrous mag. release, extended grip, small, medium, and large interchangeable backstraps, double stack magazines, unique takedown levers, Taurus Security System, 30.2 oz. New 2007.

MSR $487	$395	$345	$300	$260	$220	$195	$175	

Add $15 for stainless steel slide (disc. 2012).
Add $188 for .22 LR conversion kit (10 shot mag., mfg. 2011 only).

* **PT-809 Compact** – 9mm Para. cal., 3.5 in. barrel, 3 dot fixed sights, polymer grips with metallic inserts, loaded chamber indicator, ambidextrous mag. release, "Strike Two" trigger, external hammer, shortened grip frame, Taurus Security system, 24.7 oz. New 2011.

MSR $487	$395	$345	$300	$260	$220	$195	$175	

Add $15 for stainless steel slide (disc. 2012).

PT-840 – .40 S&W cal., similar design to the PT-24/7 OSS, 4 in. barrel, DA/SA with Strike Two capability, Novak sights, 15 shot mag., matte blue or matte stainless slide (disc. 2012), front and rear slide serrations, lower frame Picatinny rail, ambidextrous 3-position safety and decocker, ambidextrous mag. release, extended grip, small, medium, and large interchangeable backstraps, external hammer, double stack magazines, Taurus Security System, approx. 30 oz. New 2008.

MSR $487	$395	$345	$300	$260	$220	$195	$175	

Add $15 for stainless steel slide (disc. 2012).
Add $188 for .22 LR conversion kit (10 shot mag., mfg. 2011 only).

* **PT-840 Compact** – .40 S&W cal., 3.5 in. barrel, 3 dot sights, polymer grips with metallic inserts, loaded chamber indicator, ambidextrous mag. release, "Strike Two" trigger, shortened grip frame, external hammer, 24.7 oz. New 2011.

MSR $487	$395	$345	$300	$260	$220	$195	$175	

Add $16 for stainless steel slide (disc. 2012).

PT-845 – .45 ACP cal., similar design to the PT-24/7 OSS, 4 in. barrel, DA/SA with Strike Two capability, SFO, Novak sights, 12 shot mag., blue or stainless (disc.), front and rear slide serrations, lower frame Picatinny rail, ambidextrous 3-position safety and decocker, ambidextrous mag. release, extended grip, small, medium, and large interchangeable backstraps, external hammer, double stack magazines, takedown lever, approx. 30 oz. New 2008.

MSR $487	$395	$345	$300	$260	$220	$195	$175	

Add $15 for stainless steel slide (disc. 2012).
Add $188 for .22 LR conversion kit (10 shot mag., mfg. 2011 only).

PT-908 – 9mm Para. cal., compact version of the PT-92 with 3.8 in. barrel, DA/SA, 8 shot mag., fixed sights, blue or nickel finish. Mfg. 1993-1997.

	$360	$300	$260	$220	$200	$180	$165	$435

* **PT-908D SS (Stainless Steel)** – similar to Model PT-908, except is stainless steel. Mfg. 1993-97.

	$385	$335	$295	$260	$220	$195	$175	$473

PT-909 – 9mm Para. cal., DA/SA, 4 in. barrel, lower frame Picatinny rail, 10 or 17 shot mag., blue finish, fixed rear sight, alloy medium frame with steel slide, checkered rubber grips, 28.2 oz. Mfg. 2006-2010.

	$500	$450	$395	$350	$295	$260	$220	$648

Add $16 for stainless steel slide.

MSR	100%	98%	95%	90%	80%	70%	60%	Last MSR

PT-911 COMPACT – 9mm Para. cal., DA/SA, 4 in. barrel, 10 or 15 (new late 2004) shot mag., checkered rubber grips, fixed sights, 28.2 oz. Mfg. 1997-2010.

| | $500 | $450 | $395 | $350 | $295 | $260 | $220 | $648 |

Add $79 for night sights (disc. 2004).

* PT-911 Compact SS (Stainless Steel) – stainless variation of the PT-911 Compact. Disc. 2010.

| | $530 | $480 | $425 | $375 | $325 | $280 | $230 | $664 |

Add $78 for night sights (disc. 2004).

* PT-911 Compact Deluxe – choice of blue/gold finish or stainless steel with gold, rosewood, or mother-of-pearl grips. Mfg. 2000-2010.

| | $550 | $495 | $450 | $395 | $350 | $295 | $245 | $702 |

Add $15 for stainless steel with gold or faux mother-of-pearl grips.

PT-917 COMPACT PLUS – 9mm Para. cal., DA/SA, 4 in. barrel with fixed sights, rubber grips, 19 shot mag., medium frame, blue finish or stainless steel, 31.8 oz. Mfg. 2007-2010.

| | $500 | $450 | $395 | $350 | $295 | $260 | $220 | $609 |

Add $18 for stainless steel.

PT-938 COMPACT – .380 ACP cal., DA/SA, 3 3/4 in. barrel, ambidextrous safety, 10 or 15 (new late 2004) shot mag., blue finish with alloy frame and steel slide, rubber grips, fixed sights, 34 oz. Mfg. 1997-2005.

| | $410 | $350 | $310 | $280 | $240 | $210 | $185 | $516 |

* PT-938 Compact SS (Stainless Steel) – stainless slide variation of the PT-938 Compact with matte stainless finish.

| | $420 | $360 | $315 | $280 | $240 | $210 | $185 | $531 |

PT-940 – .40 S&W cal., compact version of the PT-100 with 3 5/8 in. barrel, DA/SA, 10 shot mag., fixed sights, 28.2 oz. Mfg. 1996-2010.

| | $500 | $450 | $395 | $350 | $295 | $260 | $220 | $648 |

Add $79 for night sights (disc. 2004).

* PT-940 SS (Stainless Steel) – similar to PT-940, except is stainless steel. Mfg. 1996-2010.

| | $530 | $480 | $425 | $375 | $325 | $280 | $230 | $664 |

Add $80 for night sights (disc. 2009).

PT-945 – .45 ACP cal., DA/SA, 4 1/4 in. ported (mfg. 1997-2003) or unported barrel, 8 shot single stack mag., ambidextrous 3 position safety, chamber loaded indicator, 3-dot sights, 29 1/2 oz. Mfg. 1995-2010.

| | $560 | $495 | $450 | $395 | $350 | $295 | $245 | $695 |

Add $78 for night sights (disc. 2004).
Add $39 for ported barrel (disc. 2003).

* PT-945 SS (Stainless Steel) – stainless steel variation of the PT-945. Mfg. 1995-2010.

| | $575 | $510 | $455 | $395 | $350 | $295 | $245 | $711 |

Add $78 for night sights (disc. 2004).
Add $39 for ported barrel (disc. 2003).

PT-957 – .357 SIG cal., compact model with 3 5/8 in. ported (available only with night sights or in 957 Deluxe beginning 2002) or non-ported (new 2002) barrel and slide, DA/SA, 10 shot mag., ambidextrous 3-position safety, blue finish, checkered rubber grips, fixed sights, 28 oz. Mfg. 1999-2003.

| | $425 | $360 | $315 | $280 | $240 | $210 | $185 | $523 |

Add $90 for night sights.
Add $40 for ported barrel (disc. 2002).

* PT-957 SS (Stainless Steel) – stainless steel variation of the PT-957. Mfg. 1999-2003.

| | $430 | $385 | $340 | $295 | $260 | $225 | $195 | $539 |

Add $40 for ported (disc. 2001) barrel, or $130 for ported barrel and night sights (disc. 2003).

PT-1911 – .38 Super (mfg. 2006-2011), 9mm Para. (new 2006), .40 S&W (mfg. 2006-2010) or .45 ACP cal., SA, 5 in. barrel, choice of Heinie front and rear sights or Picatinny rail, 8 (.40 S&W or .45 ACP) or 9 (.38 Super or 9mm Para.) shot mag., blue or Duo-tone (new 2008) finish, choice of steel or aluminum (new 2008) frame with steel slide, checkered diamond pattern or bull's head wood grips, bobbed hammer, front and rear serrations on slide, accurized hand tuned action, 32 oz. New mid-2005.

| MSR $729 | $595 | $550 | $480 | $415 | $365 | $315 | $265 | |

Add $116 for Picatinny rail (.45 ACP cal. only).
Add $147 for bull's head grips (.45 ACP cal. only).
Add $168 for Duo-Tone finish (.45 ACP cal. only), not available with Picatinny rail.
Add approx. $75 for aluminum frame (disc. 2011).

MSR	100%	98%	95%	90%	80%	70%	60%	Last MSR

* PT-1911 Compact – .45 ACP cal., only, similar to PT-1911, except has 4 1/4 in. barrel, 6 shot mag. Mfg. 2006 only.

	$490	$430	$365	$335	$270	$220	$170	$599

Add $20 for stainless steel slide.

* PT-1911 Stainless – 9mm Para. or .45 ACP cal., similar to PT-1911, except has matte stainless steel frame and slide (mirror finished beginning 2008).

MSR $907	$775	$675	$595	$525	$450	$395	$330	

Add $38 for lower frame Picatinny rail.
Add $68 for bull's head grips.
Subtract $81 for 9mm Para cal.

PT-1911B SERIES – .38 Super (1911B-38, disc.), 9mm Para. (1911B-9), or .45 ACP (1911BHC-12) cal., 5 in. barrel, SA, blue, stainless, 9, 11, or 12 shot mag., with or w/o Novak night sights (disc. 2010), Heinie sights became standard 2011, 38-40 oz. Mfg. mid-2009-2011.

	$535	$490	$430	$375	$325	$280	$230	$677

Add $103 for stainless steel. Add $17 for 11 shot mag. Add $79 for .45 ACP with 12 shot mag. Add $63 for Novak night sights. Add $93 for Hi-Polish with bull's head walnut grips. Add $16 for pearl grips.

PT-2011 DT INTEGRAL – .380 ACP or 9mm Para cal., DA/SA with trigger safety, SFO, 3.2 in. barrel, 11 (.380 ACP), 13 or 15 (.380 ACP) shot mag., aluminum frame with black polymer grips, loaded chamber indicator, matte black metal finish, removable back straps, adj. rear sight, 21 or 24 oz. Mfg. 2012 only.

	$475	$415	$370	$325	$285	$240	$210	$572

* PT-2011 DT Integral Stainless – similar to PT-2011 DT Integral, except has stainless steel slide. Mfg. 2012 only.

	$485	$425	$375	$325	$285	$240	$210	$588

PT-2011 DT HYBRID – 9mm Para or .40 S&W cal., DA/SA with trigger safety, SFO, 3.2 in. barrel, 11 (.40 S&W) or 13 (9mm Para) shot mag., black polymer lower frame with steel upper frame and slide, loaded chamber indicator, matte black metal finish, removable back straps, adj. rear sight, 24 oz. Mfg. 2012-2013.

	$490	$425	$375	$325	$285	$240	$210	$589

* PT-2011 DT Hybrid Stainless – similar to PT-2011 DT Hybrid, except has stainless upper frame and slide. Mfg. 2012-2013.

	$500	$450	$395	$350	$295	$260	$220	$605

PT-2045 – .45 ACP cal., SFO, 4.2 in. barrel, blue or stainless, 12 shot mag., checkered polymer grips, with or w/o Novak night sights, approx. 32 oz. Limited mfg. 2009 only.

	$450	$395	$345	$295	$260	$225	$195	$561

Add $16 for stainless steel. Add $62 for night sights.

REVOLVERS: RECENT PRODUCTION

From 1990-1992, certain models became available with a Laser Aim LA1 sighting system that included mounts, rings (in matching finish), a 110 volt AC recharging unit, a 9 volt DC field charger, and a high impact custom case.

The following Taurus revolvers have been listed in numerical order. All currently manufactured revolvers listed are rated for +P ammunition.

Tracker model nomenclature refers to a heavy contoured barrel with full shroud, porting, and with or w/o VR.

All currently manufactured Taurus revolvers are equipped with the patented Taurus Security System, introduced in 1998, which utilizes an integral key lock on the back of the hammer, locking the action.

Add approx. $45 for scope base mount on currently produced models that offer this option.
Add $31 for carrying case on Raging Bull & Raging Hornet Models listed (disc. 2006).

MODEL 45-410 "THE JUDGE" (44-TEN TRACKER) – .45 LC/.410 shotshell cal., 2 1/2 or 3 (new 2008) in. chamber, SA/DA, 5 shot, 2 1/2 (disc.), 3 (new 2007), or 6 1/2 (not available in 3 in. chamber) in. barrel, blue or stainless, fiber optic front sight, Ribber grips, compact frame, 29 or 32 oz. New 2006.

MSR $608	$500	$450	$395	$350	$295	$260	$220	

Add $45 for 3 or 6 1/2 (new 2013) in. cylinder.
Add $39 for 2 1/2 in. cylinder with ported barrel and accessory rail (mfg. 2010-2012).
Add $156 for Crimson Trace laser grips (mfg. 2010-2012).

During late 2007, this model's nomenclature changed to the Model 45-410 Judge.

* Model 45-410 The Judge Stainless (44-Ten Tracker Stainless) – similar to Model 45-410, except is matte stainless steel, 29, 32, or 36.8 (3 in. chamber) oz. New 2006.

MSR $653	$550	$495	$450	$395	$350	$295	$245	

Add $48 for 3 in. cylinder.
Add $31 for 2 1/2 in. cylinder with ported barrel and accessory rail (mfg. 2010-2012).
Add $157 for Crimson Trace laser grips (mfg. 2010-2012).

MSR	100%	98%	95%	90%	80%	70%	60%	Last MSR

* ***Model 45-410 The Judge Ultra-Lite*** – similar to Model 45-410 Judge, 2 1/2 in. barrel, except has alloy frame, choice of blued steel or stainless steel cylinder, not available in 3 in. cylinder, 22.4 oz. Mfg. 2008-2011.

| | $575 | $510 | $455 | $395 | $350 | $295 | $245 | *$648* |

Add $32 for stainless steel barrel and cylinder. Add $313 for Crimson Trace laser grips (new 2010).

MODEL 45-410 "THE JUDGE" PUBLIC DEFENDER

– .45/.410 shotshell, 2 in. barrel, similar to original Judge, except only available with 2 1/2 in. chamber, blue or matte stainless, steel or titanium cylinder, reduced profile hammer, Ribber grips, 28.2 oz. New mid-2009.

| MSR $607 | $500 | $450 | $395 | $350 | $295 | $260 | $220 | |

Add $46 for stainless steel cylinder or $78 for titanium cylinder (disc. 2011).
Add $47 for pink Ribber grips (mfg. 2010-2011) or $82 for pink Ribber grips and Bulldog Case (mfg. 2010-2011).

* ***Model 45-410 "The Judge" Public Defender Ultra-Lite*** – similar to Model 45-410 The Judge Public Defender, except has ultra-lite aluminum frame and choice of blue steel or stainless, 2 1/2 in. cylinder, 20.7 oz. Mfg. 2011 only.

| | $575 | $510 | $455 | $395 | $350 | $295 | $245 | *$648* |

Add $32 for stainless steel barrel and cylinder.

* ***Model 45-410 "The Judge" Public Defender Polymer*** – similar to Model 45-410 The Judge Public Defender, except has black light-weight polymer frame, choice of 2 1/2 in. blue (disc. 2011) or stainless cylinder, 27 oz. New 2011.

| MSR $653 | $550 | $495 | $450 | $395 | $350 | $295 | $245 | |

Subtract approx. 10% for blue cylinder (disc. 2011).

* ***Model 45-410FS Polymer*** – .45 LC/.410 bore, features polymer frame with blued steel cylinder, 2 1/2 in. chamber, 23 oz. New 2013.

| MSR $515 | $425 | $360 | $315 | $280 | $240 | $210 | $185 | |

MODEL 513 RAGING JUDGE MAGNUM

– interchangeably shoots .454 Casull, .45 LC, or .410 ga., 3 in. non-fluted cylinder, large frame, 6 shot, SA/DA, 3 (non-ported) or 6 1/2 (VR) in. barrel with Hi-Viz fiber optic front sight, rubber grips with cushion inserts and red "Raging Bull" backstrap, blue finish, 60.6 or 72.7 oz. Mfg. 2011-2013.

| | $850 | $750 | $650 | $550 | $475 | $420 | $350 | *$1,012* |

* ***Model 513 Raging Judge Magnum SS*** – similar to Model 513 Raging Judge Magnum, except is matte stainless steel.

| MSR $1,038 | $895 | $775 | $675 | $565 | $485 | $430 | $360 | |

MODEL 513 RAGING JUDGE MAGNUM ULTRA-LITE

– .45 LC cal./.410 bore with 3 in. cylinder, SA/DA, 7 shot, 3 or 6 1/2 in. barrel with high vis. fiber optic front sights, features Ultra-Lite frame, blue finish, rubber grips with cushion inserts, 41.4 or 47.2 oz. Mfg. 2011-2012.

| | $825 | $735 | $630 | $540 | $465 | $410 | $340 | *$983* |

* ***Model 513 Raging Judge Magnum Ultra-Lite SS*** – similar to Model 513 Raging Judge Magnum Ultra-Lite, except is matte stainless steel. Mfg. 2011-2012.

| | $885 | $775 | $675 | $565 | $485 | $430 | $360 | *$1,030* |

MODEL 605

– 9mm Para. or .357 Mag. cal., small frame, 5 shot, 2 in. unported (new 2002), 2 1/4 (disc. 2005), or 3 (mfg. 1996-98, reintroduced 2006-disc.) in. barrel, blue steel, 4 port compensated barrel (2 1/4 in. only) with fixed sights, exposed or concealed (Model 605CH, mfg. 1997-2005, 2 1/4 in. barrel) hammer, full barrel shroud, oversized finger grooved rubber grips, 24 1/2 oz. New 1995.

| MSR $456 | $350 | $300 | $260 | $220 | $200 | $180 | $165 | |

Add $16 for ported barrel (disc. 2003).
Add $303 for Crimson Trace laser grips (disc. 2011).

* ***Model 605 SS (Stainless Steel)*** – 9mm Para. or .357 Mag. cal., stainless variation of the Model 605.

| MSR $502 | $385 | $335 | $295 | $260 | $220 | $195 | $175 | |

Add $16 for ported barrel (disc. 2003).
Add $303 for Crimson Trace laser grips (mfg. 2008-2011).

* ***Model 605T Titanium*** – similar to Model 605, except is titanium with shadow grey finish. Mfg. 2005-2006.

| | $535 | $490 | $430 | $375 | $325 | $280 | $230 | *$625* |

* ***Model 605PLYB2/Protector Ply*** – .357 Mag. cal., small frame, 5 shot, features lightweight polymer frame, Ribber grips, blued or stainless cylinder assembly, ambidextrous thumb safety, 1 or 2 in. barrel with VR in high vis. fiber optic front sight, 19 3/4 oz. New 2011.

| MSR $456 | $350 | $300 | $260 | $220 | $200 | $180 | $165 | |

Add $15 for stainless steel cylinder (new 2012).

MSR	100%	98%	95%	90%	80%	70%	60%	Last MSR

MODEL 608 – .357 Mag. cal., large frame, 8 shot, 3 (mfg. 1997-98), 4, 6 1/2 (VR), or 8 3/8 (VR, new 1997) in. barrel with integral compensator, rubber finger grooves, exposed or concealed (mfg. 1997-2010, 3 in. barrel) hammer, adj. sights, 44-56 oz. Mfg. 1996-2004.

	$355	$300	$260	$220	$200	$180	$165	*$469*

Add $15 for 6.5 or 8 3/8 in. VR ported barrel.

* ***Model 608SS (Stainless Steel)*** – .357 Mag. cal., matte stainless variation of the Model 608, 3 (disc.), 4, 6 1/2, or 8 3/8 (disc. 2012) in. VR barrel, 51 or 56 oz. New 1996.

MSR $688	$525	$480	$425	$375	$325	$280	$230	

MODEL 617 – .357 Mag. cal., medium frame, 7 shot, double action, 2 in. regular or ported (disc.) barrel, fixed sights, exposed or concealed (Model 617CH, disc. 2005) hammer, rubber (disc. 2006) or Ribber (new 2007) grips, 28.3 oz. Mfg. 1998-2012.

	$415	$350	$310	$280	$240	$210	$185	*$508*

Add $15 for ported barrel (disc. 2003).

* ***Model 617SS (Stainless Steel)*** – .357 Mag. cal., similar to Model 617, except is polished (disc. 2007) or matte stainless steel. New 1998.

MSR $560	$450	$395	$345	$295	$260	$225	$195	

Add $15 for ported barrel (disc. 2003).

* ***Model 617 ULT*** – similar to Model 617, except is 5 shot, aluminum alloy receiver and titanium cylinder, matte stainless finish, 2 in. regular or ported barrel, soft rubber grips. Mfg. 2001-2002.

	$455	$395	$345	$295	$260	$225	$195	*$530*

Add $15 for ported barrel.

MODEL 669 – similar to Model 66 except has fully shrouded 4 or 6 in. barrel, blue finish, 37 oz. Disc. 1998.

	$285	$250	$215	$185	$170	$155	$145	*$344*

Add $10 for VR barrel (mfg. 1989-1992).
Add $400 for Laser Aim Sight (offered 1990-1992).
Add $19 for compensated (669CP) barrel (new 1993).

MODEL 689 – similar to Model 669, except has VR. Disc. 1998.

	$300	$260	$220	$185	$170	$155	$145	*$358*

Add $390 for Laser Aim Sight (mfg. 1990-91 only).

MODEL 817 ULTRA-LITE – .38 Spl.+P cal., medium frame, 7 shot, 2 in. ported (disc. 2002) or unported solid rib barrel, soft rubber (disc. 2006) or Ribber (new 2007) grips, bright blue finish, 21 oz. Mfg. 1999-2012.

	$400	$350	$310	$280	$240	$210	$185	*$508*

Add $20 for ported barrel (disc. 2002).

* ***Model 817 Ultra-Lite Stainless*** – similar to Model 817 Ultra-Lite, except is matte stainless steel. Mfg. 1999-2012.

	$425	$360	$315	$280	$240	$210	$185	*$555*

Add $20 for ported barrel (disc. 2003).

RIFLES: SEMI-AUTO

CARBINE CT G2 SERIES – 9mm Para. (Model CT9G2L), .40 S&W (Model CT40G2M), or .45 ACP (Model GT45G2M) cal., tactical design featuring hybrid aluminum/polymer frame with steel reinforcement, 10 (.45 ACP cal), 15 (.40 S&W cal.), or 34 (9mm Para. cal) shot mag., 16 in. barrel, fixed black polymer pistol grip skeletonized stock, ribbed polymer forearm with lower Picatinny rail, flat-top aluminum upper receiver with built-in full length Picatinny rail, fixed front and adj. rear sights, 9 1/4 lbs. Mfg. 2011.

Retail pricing was not established on this model.

TAVOR

Current trademark manufactured by IWI US, Inc., located in Harrisburg, PA.

RIFLES: SEMI-AUTO

Conversion kits are available in 9mm Para. or 5.45x39mm. Please contact the importer directly for pricing (see Trademark Index).

TAVOR SAR – 5.56 NATO cal., bullpup design, non-lubricated long stroke GPO, right or left hand action, 16 1/2 or 18 in. chrome lined barrel, matte black, OD Green (new 2014), or Flat Dark Earth finish, flat-top with full Picatinny rail, optional bayonet lug, 30 shot mag., short rail forward, accepts AR-15/M16 style magazines, approx. 8 lbs.

MSR $1,999	$1,700	$1,495	$1,275	$1,150	$935	$765	$595	

Add $600 for SAR IDF Model with Mepro-21 reflex sight affixed to barrel.

MSR	100%	98%	95%	90%	80%	70%	60%	Last MSR

TAYLOR'S & CO., INC.

Current importer and distributor established during 1988, and located in Winchester, VA.

Taylor's & Co. is an Uberti importer and distributor of both black powder and firearms reproductions, in addition to being the exclusive U.S. distributor for Armi Sport, located in Brescia, Italy. Taylor's is also a distributor for Bond Arms - please refer to the Bond Arms section.

For more information and up-to-date pricing regarding current Taylor's & Co., Inc. black powder models, please refer to the *Blue Book of Modern Black Powder Arms* by John Allen. This book features information, complete pricing, and reference guides.

Black Powder Revolvers - Reproductions & Replicas and *Black Powder Long Arms & Pistols - Reproductions & Replicas* by Dennis Adler are also invaluable sources for most black powder reproductions and replicas, and include hundreds of color images on most popular makes/models, provide manufacturer/trademark histories, and up-to-date information on related items/accessories for black powder shooting - www.bluebookofgunvalues.com.

PISTOLS: SEMI-AUTO

1911 TACTICAL – .45 ACP cal., 3 5/8 (Compact Carry) or 5 in. barrel, 7 or 8 shot mag., combat hammer, skeletonized trigger, ambidextrous safety, extended beavertail, Picatinny underrail, parkerized finish, checkered walnut grips. Importation began 2013.

| MSR $570 | $475 | $415 | $350 | $325 | $260 | $215 | $165 | |

Add $15 for Compact Carry.

1911 .22 – .22 LR cal., 5 in. barrel, SA, black frame with black or olive green slide, checkered wood grips, 10 shot mag., mfg. by Chiappa. Mfg. 2011-2013.

| | $250 | $225 | $195 | $175 | $140 | $115 | $90 | *$300* |

Add $79 for black slide (disc. 2012).
Add $65 for target model (disc. 2012).

M4 TACTICAL SERIES – .22 LR cal., GIO, 6 in. solid steel barrel, 10 or 28 shot mag., fire control group, dust cover, adj. sights, pseudo flash hider, bayonet lug, forward assist, and bolt release, quad rail capable forearm, includes two mags. Imported 2011-2012.

| | $350 | $315 | $275 | $235 | $200 | $180 | $165 | *$419* |

RIFLES: SEMI-AUTO

M4 22 – .22 LR cal., GIO, 16 in. solid steel barrel, 10 or 28 shot mag., fire control group, dust cover, adj. sights, pseudo flash hider, bayonet lug, forward assist, and bolt release, quad rail capable forearm, includes two mags, 5 1/2 lbs. Mfg. 2011-2012.

| | $350 | $295 | $260 | $230 | $200 | $180 | $165 | *$419* |

TECHNO ARMS (PTY) LIMITED

Previous manufacturer located in Johannesburg, S. Africa circa 1994-1996. Previously imported by Vulcans Forge, Inc. located in Foxboro, MA.

SHOTGUNS: SLIDE ACTION

MAG-7 SLIDE ACTION SHOTGUN – 12 ga. (60mm chamber length), 5 shot detachable mag. (in pistol grip), 14, 16, 18, or 20 in. barrel, straight grip or pistol grip stock, matte finish, 8 lbs. Imported 1995-96.

| | $795 | $675 | $625 | $550 | $500 | $450 | $400 | *$875* |

TEMPLAR CUSTOM, LLC

Current custom AR-15 rifle and component manufacturer located in Apex, NC since 2008.

RIFLES: SEMI-AUTO

MCWS (MULTI-CALIBER WEAPONS SYSTEM) – .223 Rem./5.56 NATO (.223 Wylde chamber), 6.5 Grendel, and .50 Beowulf cal., GIO, 16 in. stainless steel button rifled barrel (.50 Beowulf), 16 in. chromemoly steel button rifled barrel (5.56 NATO), 16 in. stainless steel button rifled barrel (6.5 Grendel), all quick change barrels with stainless WCI muzzle brakes, forged lower and matched upper receiver, Magpul ACS stock, Ergo ambi grip, Geissele SSA trigger, PRI low pro witness sights, 14 in. Templar Fastrail system includes 14 in. handguard, swivel sling stud, one case hardened black oxide barrel tool and allen wrench, multi-caliber cleaning kit, choice of hard or soft case, Desert Snake Duracoat finish.

| MSR $2,899 | $2,600 | $2,275 | $1,950 | $1,775 | $1,425 | $1,175 | $925 | |

Add $450 for cut rifle barrel upgrade.
Add $400 for MCWS 3 caliber kit.

MSR	100%	98%	95%	90%	80%	70%	60%	Last MSR

TEMPLAR CUSTOM SPR (SPECIAL PURPOSE RIFLE) – .223 Rem./5.56 NATO (.223 Wylde chamber) cal., GIO, 16 in. chromemoly steel medium contour barrel with A2 flash hider, forged upper and lower receiver, steel bolt carrier, 12 1/2 in. Templar FastRail, Magpul ACS or MOE stock, Ergo Ambi grip, A2 front sight assembly, other options available on this model.

MSR $2,449	$2,200	$1,925	$1,650	$1,500	$1,225	$1,000	$800	

Add $550 for single point cut rifle stainless steel barrel.

TEMPLAR CUSTOM STANDARD RIFLE – .223 Rem./5.56 NATO (.223 Wylde chamber) cal., GIO, 16 in. chromemoly steel medium contour barrel with A2 flash hider, forged lower and upper receiver, steel bolt carrier, 12 1/2 in. Templar FastRail, Magpul ACS or MOE stock, Ergo Ambi grip, A2 front sight assembly.

MSR $2,249	$2,025	$1,775	$1,525	$1,375	$1,115	$910	$710	

TEMPLAR TACTICAL ARMS LLC

Current AR-15 manufacturer located in Bozeman, MT since 2008.

RIFLES: SEMI-AUTO

TTA MARK 12 RIFLE – 5.56 NATO/.223 Rem. cal., GIO, 18 in. SPR profile match barrel, billet upper and lower receivers, carbon fiber full floating forend with Picatinny rails on bottom and both sides, full length Swan Sleeve Picatinny rail, front and rear flip-up iron sights, Magpul MOE or Magpul ACS buttstock.

Consumer may customize this rifle to individual specifications. Base MSR is $2,150-$2,450.

TTA 15 TACTICAL – 5.56 NATO/.223 Rem. or 6.8 SPC cal., GIO, 16 in. match barrel, billet upper and lower receivers, front and rear flip-up sights, choice of 10 or 12 in. Daniel Defense full floating rail, collapsible stock, custom models feature single stage trigger, Magpul grip, and Magpul ACS stock.

Consumer may customize this rifle to individual specifications. Base MSR is $1,700-$2,000.

TEMPLAR TACTICAL FIREARMS

Current AR-15 style rifle and suppressor manufacturer located in Spring, TX.

RIFLES: SEMI-AUTO

SENESCHAL PRECISION RIFLE – 6.5 Creedmoor or .308 Win. Mag. cal., Defiance Action, free floated match grade Bartlien barrel, stainless steel receiver, McMillan A3-5 fully adj. tactical stock, vertical pistol grip, adj. comb, tapered forend, adj. spacer system, Anschutz Rail, M-16 type extractor, Badger Tactical bolt knob, matte Cerakote in Patriot Brown or Coyote Tan.

MSR $5,250	$4,725	$4,150	$3,550	$3,225	$2,600	$2,125	$1,750	

Current MSR is for a base model only. Many other calibers, barrels, options, and finishes are available - custom build lead times are 6-8 months.

SERGEANT LONG RANGE HUNTING RIFLE – .308 Win. Mag. cal., Rem. 700 action, free floated medium contour threaded barrel, Tempar Tactical drop bottom magazine, oversized tactical bolt knob, Bell & Carlson Medalist A2 stock, glass bedded in Marine Tex, custom stock texturing, custom Cerakote finish.

MSR $3,400	$3,050	$2,675	$2,300	$2,075	$1,675	$1,375	$1,125	

Current MSR is for a base model only. Many other calibers, barrels, options, and finishes are available - custom build lead times are 6-8 months.

THOMPSON

Current trademark of pistols and carbines manufactured by Auto Ordnance located in Worcester, MA, and corporate offices in Blauvelt, NY. Auto Ordnance became a division of Kahr Arms in 1999. Dealer and distributor sales.

Auto-Ordnance Corp. manufactures an exact reproduction of the original 1927 Thompson sub-machine gun. They are currently available from Kahr Arms in semi-auto only since production ceased on fully automatic variations (Model 1928 and M1) in 1986 (mfg. 1975-1986 including 609 M1s). All current models utilize the Thompson trademark, are manufactured in the U.S., and come with a lifetime warranty.

CARBINES: SEMI-AUTO

The Auto-Ordnance Thompson replicas listed below are currently supplied with a 15, 20, or 30 shot stick mag. Tommy Guns are not currently legal in CA or CT.

Add the following for currently manufactured Thompson 1921 A-1 models:

Add $70 for 20 or 30 shot stick mag.

Add $68 for 10 shot stick mag.

Add $193 for 10 shot drum mag. (they resemble the older 50 shot L-type drum) - new 1994.

Add $299 for 50* shot drum mag. or $577 for 100* shot drum mag. (mfg. 1990-93, reintroduced 2006).

Add $221 for factory violin case or $204 for hard case.

MSR	100%	98%	95%	90%	80%	70%	60%	Last MSR

1927 A3 - .22 CAL. – .22 LR cal., 16 or 18 in. finned barrel with compensator, alloy frame and receiver, fixed or detachable walnut stock, pistol grip, and forearm pistol grip, 7 lbs. Disc. 1994.

	$995	$875	$750	$650	$550	$500	$450	*$510*

1927 A5 PISTOL/CARBINE – .45 ACP cal., 13 in. finned barrel, alloy construction, overall length 26 in., 10 (C/B 1994) shot mag., 7 lbs. Disc. 1994.

	$1,050	$925	$825	$750	$650	$600	$500	*$765*

THOMPSON M1 CARBINE (.45 ACP CAL.) – .45 ACP cal., combat model, 16 1/2 in. smooth barrel w/o compensator, 30 shot original surplus mag., side-cocking lever, matte black finish, walnut stock, pistol grip, and grooved horizontal forearm, current mfg. will not accept drum mags., 11 1/2 lbs. New 1986.

MSR $1,334	$1,175	$1,050	$900	$775	$650	$550	$450	

* **Thompson M1-C Lightweight** – similar to M1 Carbine, except receiver is made of a lightweight alloy, current mfg. accepts drum mags., 9 1/2 lbs. Mfg. 2001-2002, reintroduced 2005.

MSR $1,206	$1,075	$925	$825	$725	$625	$525	$425	

During 2006, this model incorporated a large machined radius on the bottom of the receiver to improve magazine insertion.

THOMPSON 1927 A-1 DELUXE CARBINE – 10mm (mfg. 1991-93) or .45 ACP cal., 16 1/2 in. finned barrel with compensator, includes one 30 shot original surplus mag., current mfg. accepts drum mags., solid steel construction, matte black finish, adj. rear sight, walnut stock, pistol grip, and finger grooved forearm grip, 13 lbs.

MSR $1,420	$1,100	$975	$800	$675	$550	$495	$450	

Add $433 for detachable buttstock and horizontal foregrip (new 2007).

During 2006, design changes included a more authentic spherical cocking knob, improved frame to receiver fit, and a large machined radius at the bottom of the receiver to help with magazine insertion.

* **Thompson 1927 A-1C Lightweight Deluxe** – .45 ACP cal., similar to 1927 A-1 Deluxe, except receiver made of a lightweight alloy, currently shipped with 30 shot stick mag. (where legal), current mfg. accepts drum mags., 9 1/2 lbs. New 1984.

MSR $1,286	$1,075	$950	$800	$700	$600	$500	$425	

Add $413 for 100 shot drum mag.

* **Thompson 1927 A-1 Presentation Walnut Carbine** – .45 ACP cal., similar to 1927 A-1 Deluxe, except has presentation grade walnut buttstock, pistol grip, and foregrip, supplied with plastic case. Limited mfg. 2003.

	$850	$675	$525	$425	$350	$325	$295	*$1,121*

* **Thompson 1927 A-1 Deluxe .22 LR Cal.** – .22 LR cal., very limited mfg., 30 shot mag. standard.

	$1,100	$995	$925	$800	$700	$650	$575	

THOMPSON 1927 A-1 COMMANDO – .45 ACP cal., 16 1/2 in. finned barrel with compensator, 30 shot mag., black finished stock and forearm, parkerized metal, black nylon sling, 13 lbs. New 1997.

MSR $1,393	$1,095	$975	$800	$675	$550	$495	$450	

During 2006, this model incorporated a spherical cocking knob.

THOMPSON SBR – .45 ACP cal., 10 1/2 in. finned barrel, closed bolt, blue metal finish, pistol grip forearm, 30 shot mag., 12 lbs. New 2004.

MSR $2,053	$1,825	$1,600	$1,375	$1,150	$975	$850	$725	

Add $501 for detachable buttstock and horizontal foregrip (new 2007).

This carbine model may only be shipped from the factory to an NFA Class II manufacturer or NFA Class III dealer.

THOMPSON M1 SBR – .45 ACP cal., 10 1/2 in. barrel, closed bolt, blue metal finish, regular forearm, 30 shot mag., 12 lbs. New 2004.

MSR $1,970	$1,750	$1,500	$1,300	$1,125	$925	$800	$700	

This carbine model may only be shipped from the factory to an NFA Class II manufacturer or NFA Class III dealer.

PISTOLS: SEMI-AUTO

1911 THOMPSON CUSTOM – .45 ACP cal., stainless steel or aluminum (Lightweight model, mfg. 2005-2007) construction, Series 80 design, 5 in. barrel, SA, Thompson bullet logo on left side of double serrated slide, 7 shot mag., grip safety, checkered laminate grips with medallion, skeletonized trigger, combat hammer, low profile sights, 31 1/2 (Lightweight) or 39 oz. Mfg. 2004-2013.

	$695	$575	$485	$415	$350	$300	$275	*$813*

MSR	100%	98%	95%	90%	80%	70%	60%	Last MSR

THOMPSON 1927 A-1 DELUXE – .45 ACP cal., SA, blowback design, 10 1/2 in. finned barrel, grooved walnut forearm with sling swivel, blade front sight, adj. rear sight, 10 or 30 shot mag., also accepts 50 shot drum, 30 shot stick, 10 shot stick, and 100 shot drum magazines, approx. 6 lbs. New 2008.

    MSR $1,284 $1,050 $875 $775 $675 $575 $475 $425

    Add $93 for 50 shot mag. or $259 for 100 shot drum mag.

This model is marked "Model of 1927A-1" and "Thompson Semi-Automatic Carbine" on the left side and Auto-Ordnance Corporation on the right side.

THOMPSON/CENTER ARMS CO., INC.

Current manufacturer established during 1967, and located in Springfield, MA. Previously located in Rochester, NH. Distributor and dealer sales.

On Dec. 18, 2006 Smith & Wesson holding corp. announced that it purchased Thompson Center Arms Co., Inc. During late 2010, Smith & Wesson moved their production to its Springfield, MA facility.

Thompson/Center also has created a custom shop to enable customers to create custom pistols, rifles, shotguns, and muzzleloaders. Please contact the factory for availability and an individualized quotation.

Please refer to the *Blue Book of Modern Black Powder Arms* by John Allen (also online) for more information and prices on Thompson/Center's lineup of modern black powder models.

Black Powder Revolvers - Reproductions & Replicas and *Black Powder Long Arms & Pistols - Reproductions & Replicas* by Dennis Adler are also invaluable sources for most black powder reproductions and replicas, and include hundreds of color images on most popular makes/models, provide manufacturer/trademark histories, and up-to-date information on related items/accessories for black powder shooting - www.bluebookofgunvalues.com.

RIFLES: BOLT ACTION

A recall has been issued for all Venture rifles manufactured prior to October 28, 2011. To determine if your rifle is affected, please visit Smith & Wesson's website: www.smith-wesson.com or call 1-800-713-0356.

ICON PRECISION HUNTER – .204 Ruger, .223 Rem., .22-250 Rem., .243 Win., 6.5 Creedmoor (mfg. 2010-2011), or .308 Win. cal., 22 in. heavy fluted barrel with 5R button rifling, fat bolt design with tactical style handle, classic varminter style brown synthetic stock with cheekpiece and beavertail forend, detachable 3 shot mag. with single shot adapter, Picatinny rail, adj. trigger, two position safety, sling swivel studs, 8 lbs. Mfg. 2009-2012.

                  $900 $775 $675 $575 $475 $425 $350   *$1,019*

ICON WARLORD – .308 Win. or .338 Lapua cal., 5 or 10 shot mag., hand lapped stainless steel fluted barrel, carbon fiber tactical style stock with adj. cheekpiece, available in OD Green, Flat Black, or Desert Sand, Weather Shield finish on all metal, adj. trigger, Picatinny rail, tactical bolt handle, 12 3/4 - 13 3/4 lbs. Mfg. 2010-2011.

                  $3,000 $2,600 $2,200 $1,800 $1,500 $1,250 $1,125   *$3,499*

THOR

Current trademark manufactured by Thor Global Defense Group, located in Van Buren, AR. Distributed by Knesek Guns, located in Van Buren, AR.

PISTOLS: SEMI-AUTO

THOR 1911 SERIES – .45 ACP cal., 4 1/4 (Carry) or 5 in. (Tactical) barrel, SA, carbon steel frame, matte black finish, GI night sights, mfg. in partnership with Guncrafter Industries. Disc. 2013.

                  $2,750 $2,400 $2,065 $1,875 $1,515 $1,240 $965   *$3,250*

    Add $205 for Carry Model.

STEVEN SEAGAL LIMITED EDITION 1911A1 – black finish, white grips. New 2014.

    MSR $935 $795 $695 $595 $540 $435 $360 $275

RIFLES: BOLT ACTION

THOR M375 – .375 CheyTac cal., advanced long range interdiction system, 30 in. fluted match grade Krieger barrel with removable muzzle brake, 7 shot box mag., 10 in. top rail, carry handle, right or left hand action, fully adj. hardened aluminum stock with sliding mechanism and adj. monopod, 26 lbs.

    MSR $12,600 $10,700 $9,375 $8,025 $7,275 $5,895 $4,825 $3,750

THOR TR375 – .375 CheyTac cal., similar to M375 Model, except has 29 inch stainless steel barrel and McMillan A5 stock. New 2014.

    MSR $8,999 $7,650 $6,695 $5,750 $5,200 $4,200 $3,450 $2,675

MSR	100%	98%	95%	90%	80%	70%	60%	Last MSR

THOR M408 – .408 Cheytac cal., 29 in. fluted barrel, 7 shot mag., no sights, fully adj. aluminum modular stock, M-1913 Picatinny rail, integral bipod, muzzle brake, polymer pistol grip, advanced long range interdiction system, 27 lbs.

| MSR $12,600 | $10,700 | $9,375 | $8,025 | $7,275 | $5,895 | $4,825 | $3,750 | |

THOR XM408 – .408 Cheytac cal., 30 in. fluted match grade barrel with removable muzzle brake, 5 or 7 shot detachable box mag., 10 in. Mil-Std 1913 upper rail, CNC machined receiver and bolt, adj. hardened aluminum stock with sliding mechanism, adj. mono-pod, black or camo finish, optional advanced shroud assembly, approx. 26 lbs. Disc. 2013.

| | $5,850 | $5,300 | $4,850 | $4,350 | $3,900 | $3,250 | $2,650 | *$5,999* |

Add $6,000 for advanced shroud assembly.

THOR TR408 – .408 Cheytac cal., 29 in. fluted stainless steel barrel, fluted bolt with tactical bolt knob, Huber Concepts trigger, Harris HBRS bipod, McMillan A5 stock, 7 shot mag., beavertail forearm.

| MSR $8,999 | $7,650 | $6,695 | $5,750 | $5,200 | $4,200 | $3,450 | $2,675 | |

THOR TRLA 300 – .300 Win. Mag. cal., lightweight aluminum chassis with folding stock, Surefire SOCOM muzzle brake, Huber Concepts trigger, Harris HBRS bipod.

| MSR $5,167 | $4,395 | $3,850 | $3,295 | $2,995 | $2,400 | $1,975 | $1,550 | |

Add $479 for HS Precision chassis.
Add $815 for McMillan A3-5 stock.
Add $1,598 for Cadex chassis.

THOR TRMA338 – .338 Lapua cal., 20 in. barrel, 416R stainless steel action, Surefire muzzle brake, Huber Concepts trigger, lightweight aluminum chassis with folding stock, Harris bipod, one piece bolt, plunger ejector, mini-16 extractor, Picatinny scope rail, accept AI/AW magazines.

| MSR $5,167 | $4,395 | $3,850 | $3,295 | $2,995 | $2,400 | $1,975 | $1,550 | |

THOR TRSA SERIES – .300 Blackout or .308 Win. cal., 16 1/2 (.300 Blackout cal. only), 20 or 24 in. threaded or unthreaded barrel, lightweight aluminum chassis with folding stock, Surefire SOCOM muzzle brake, Huber Concepts trigger, Harris HBRS bipod.

| MSR $5,167 | $4,395 | $3,850 | $3,295 | $2,995 | $2,400 | $1,975 | $1,550 | |

Add $200 for .300 Blackout cal.
Add $479 for HS Precision chassis.
Add $815 for McMillan A3-5 stock.
Add $1,598 for Cadex chassis.

THOR LRIM 338 LM – .338 Lapua cal., 27 in. fluted stainless steel barrel, 416R stainless steel action, Surefire muzzle brake, Huber Concepts trigger, lightweight aluminum chassis with folding stock, adj. monopod, 10 in. rail, 24 lbs. New 2014.

| MSR $12,600 | $10,700 | $9,375 | $8,025 | $7,275 | $5,895 | $4,825 | $3,750 | |

RIFLES: SEMI-AUTO

THOR TR-15 – 5.56 NATO cal., GPO, 16.1 or 18 (DMR Model) in. barrel, 30 shot mag., detachable carry handle, M4 handguard, variety of Cerakote custom finishes available, with or w/o flash hider and muzzle brake, collapsible Mil-spec stock, F marked front sight post, flat-top upper receiver, optional THOR rail system.

| MSR $1,250 | $1,125 | $985 | $850 | $775 | $625 | $500 | $395 | |

Add $250 for THOR rail system.
Add $760 for 18 in. barrel.

Thor Global Defense Group also offers the Thor TR-15 Series in a variety of short barreled rifle configurations for military/law enforcement.

* ***Thor TR-15 CQB Carbine*** – 5.56 NATO cal., GPO, 16.1 in. barrel with Noveske KX3 flash suppressor, 30 shot mag., detachable carry handle, Daniel Defense Omega X12 OFSP quad rail, Troy folding rear battle sight, Magpul MIAD grip, Vltor E-Mod stock, Knight's Armament rear sling swivel mount, dark earth Cerakote finish. New 2014.

| MSR $2,350 | $2,125 | $1,850 | $1,595 | $1,450 | $1,175 | $950 | $750 | |

THUNDER-FIVE

Previous trademark manufactured by MIL Inc., located in Piney Flats, TN. Previous company name was Holston Enterprises, Inc. Previously manufactured by Mil, Inc. located in Piney Flats, TN. Previously distributed by C.L. Reedy & Associates, Inc. located in Jonesborough, TN.

REVOLVERS

While previously advertised as the Spectre Five (not mfg.), this firearm was re-named the Thunder-Five.

MSR	100%	98%	95%	90%	80%	70%	60%	Last MSR

THUNDER-FIVE – .45 LC cal./.410 bore with 3 in. chamber or .45-70 Govt. cal. (mfg. 1994-98), single or double action, unique 5 shot revolver design permits shooting .45 LC or .410 bore shotshells interchangeably, 2 in. rifled barrel, phosphate finish, external ambidextrous hammer block safety, internal transfer bar safety, combat sights, hammer, trigger, and trigger guard, Pachmayr grips, padded plastic carrying case, 48 oz., serialization started at 1,101. Mfg. 1992-circa 2007.

	$495	$450	$400	$375	$350	$325	$300	*$545*

Sub-caliber sleeve inserts were available until 1998 for 9mm Para., .357 Mag./.38 Spl., and .38 Super cals.

THUREON DEFENSE

Current manufacturer located in New Holstein, WI.

PISTOLS: SEMI-AUTO

THUREON SA PISTOL – 9mm Para. or .45 ACP cal., same operating system as the SA Carbine. New 2012.

MSR $1,019	$875	$765	$650	$595	$480	$400	$325	

THUREON GA PISTOL – 9mm Para., 357 SIG, .40 S&W, 10mm Auto, or .45 ACP cal., similar to Thureon SA pistol. New 2012.

MSR $1,069	$975	$855	$725	$665	$535	$440	$350	

RIFLES: SEMI-AUTO

Add $15 for M4 telescoping buttstock.
Add $35 for laser/tactical light mount.
Add $75 for open sights nested in sight rail.

THUREON SA CARBINE – 9mm Para. or .45 ACP cal., blowback action, 32 shot mag. (modified Uzi or Colt SMG mag.), AR-15 trigger components, integral Picatinny rail, closed bolt, aluminum upper and lower receivers, adj. buttstock, black finish, approx. 6 1/2 lbs.

MSR $1,143	$1,025	$900	$775	$700	$575	$475	$375	

THUREON GA CARBINE – 9mm Para., .357 SIG, .40 S&W, 10mm Auto, or .45 ACP cal., similar to Thureon SA Carbine, except uses Glock magazines. New 2012.

MSR $959	$875	$775	$650	$600	$475	$400	$325	

Add $40 for 10mm or .357 SIG cal.

TIKKA

Current trademark imported by Beretta U.S.A. Corp., located in Accokeek, MD. Previously imported until 2000 by Stoeger Industries, located in Wayne, NJ. Tikka rifles are currently manufactured by Sako, Ltd. located in Riihimäki, Finland. Previously manufactured by Oy Tikkakoski Ab, of Tikkakoski, Finland (pre-1989).

During 2000, Tikka was purchased by Beretta Holding of Italy. All currently produced Tikkas are imported by Beretta U.S.A. Corp., located in Accokeek, MD.

Also see listings under Ithaca combination guns and bolt action rifles for older models.

RIFLES: BOLT ACTION

About 3,000 rifles sold under the Tikka name have been recalled following catastrophic failures, but a small number of guns sold in the American market remain in the hands of consumers who have apparently not heard about the recall. A weakness in the stainless steel used to manufacture rifles during 2003-2004 has led to ruptured barrels. Consumers are urged to contact the Tikka Recall Center at 800-503-8869 with their rifle's serial number to find out if their firearm is affected.

* **T3 Scout CTR** – .223 Rem. or .308 Win. cal., 20 in. heavy barrel w/o sights, black synthetic stock with built in Monte Carlo cheekpiece, 5 or 6 shot mag., Picatinny rail on receiver. Mfg. 2010-2012.

	$825	$725	$625	$525	$425	$365	$330	*$950*

* **T3 Super Varmint** – .22-250 Rem., .223 Rem., or .308 Win. cal., 23 3/8 in. heavy stainless barrel, 3 or 4 shot mag., laminated synthetic stock with adj. comb, Picatinny rail, extra swivel stud, adj. trigger. Imported 2005-2007.

	$1,250	$1,000	$800	$695	$585	$485	$415	*$1,425*

* **T3 Tactical** – .223 Rem. or .308 Win. cal., T3 action, 20 or 24 (disc. 2007) in. free floating match grade barrel with protected threaded muzzle, 5 shot mag., black synthetic stock with adj. comb, wide forearm, Picatinny rail, 7 1/4 lbs. Importation began 2004.

MSR $1,775	$1,550	$1,225	$1,050	$875	$750	$650	$550	

TIPPMAN ARMS CO.

Previous manufacturer located in Fort Wayne, IN.

Tippman Arms manufactured 1/2 scale semi-auto working models of famous machine guns. All models were available with an optional hardwood case, extra ammo cans, and other accessories. Mfg. 1986-1987 only.

MSR	100%	98%	95%	90%	80%	70%	60%	Last MSR

RIFLES: REPRODUCTIONS, SEMI-AUTO

MODEL 1919 A-4 – .22 LR cal. only, copy of Browning 1919 A-4 Model, belt fed, closed bolt operation, 11 in. barrel, tripod, 10 lbs.

	100%	98%	95%	90%	80%	70%	60%	Last MSR
	$4,750	$4,300	$3,950	$3,600	$3,250	$2,850	$2,350	*$1,325*

MODEL 1917 – .22 LR cal. only, copy of Browning M1917, watercooled, belt fed, closed bolt operation, 11 in. barrel, tripod, 10 lbs.

	100%	98%	95%	90%	80%	70%	60%	Last MSR
	$6,375	$6,000	$5,500	$5,000	$4,350	$3,750	$3,250	*$1,830*

MODEL .50 HB – .22 WMR cal. only, copy of Browning .50 cal. machine gun, belt fed, closed bolt operation, 18 1/4 in. barrel, tripod, 13 lbs.

	100%	98%	95%	90%	80%	70%	60%	Last MSR
	$6,625	$6,400	$5,950	$5,400	$4,950	$4,500	$4,000	*$1,929*

TOMAHAWK

Current trademark of shotguns manufactured by M&U, located in Konya, Turkey. No current U.S. importation.

M&U manufactures a complete line of hunting and tactical style shotguns under the Tomahawk trademark, including semi-auto, slide action, O/U, SxS, and single barrel configurations. Currently, these guns have had little or no importation into the U.S. Please contact the company directly for more information, including pricing and domestic availability (see Trademark Index).

TORNADO

Currently manufactured by AseTekno located in Helsinki, Finland.

RIFLES: BOLT ACTION

TORNADO MODEL – .338 Lapua Mag. cal., unique straight line design with free floating barrel, 5 shot mag., pistol grip assembly is part of frame, limited importation into the U.S.

The factory should be contacted direcly regarding domestic availability and pricing (see Trademark Index).

TRACKINGPOINT

Current bolt action rifle manufacturer established late 2011 and located in Pflugerville, TX, previously located in Austin, TX.

RIFLES: BOLT ACTION

1000-338T (XS1) – .338 Lapua cal., features TrackingPoint's XactSystem with internal scope software and integrated guided trigger and tag button, 27 in. Krieger barrel with AAC Blackout 90T muzzle brake, matte black finish, Surgeon Rifles XL action, box mag., Accuracy International AX chassis system with detachable rails, Harris bipod with LaRue quick detach mount, includes hardshell case and 200 rounds of ammo.
Current MSR on this model is $27,500.

1000-300T (XS2) – .300 Win. Mag. cal., 24 in. Krieger barrel with AAC Blackout 90T muzzle brake, matte black finish, Surgeon Rifles XL long action, Accuracy International AX chassis system with detachable rails, Harris bipod with LaRue quick detach mount, features TrackingPoint's XactSystem with internal scope software and integrated guided trigger and tab button, includes 200 rounds of ammo.
Current MSR on this model is $25,000.

1000-300H (XS3) – .300 Win. Mag. cal., 22 in. Krieger threaded barrel with thread protector, matte black finish, Surgeon Rifles XL long action, McMillan A5 stock, Harris bipod with LaRue quick detach mount, features TrackingPoint's XactSystem with internal scope software and integrated guided trigger, includes 200 rounds of ammo.
Current MSR on this model is $22,500.

1000-338H (XS4) – .338 Lapua cal., similar to 1000-338T, except has McMillan stock and fluted barrel. New 2014.
Current MSR on this model is $27,500.

750-300H – .300 Win. Mag., features similar network tracking scope, guided trigger, and track button in trigger guard as 1000 Series, 26 in. fluted stainless steel barrel, 3 shot, McMillan A5 stock, Harris bipod Larue quick-detach mount, 12 lbs. New mid-2014.
Current MSR on this model is $9,995.

750-308H – .308 Win. Mag. cal., features same optics and Tracking system as 1000 Series, 26 in. fluted stainless steel barrel, 4 shot, Bell & Carlson stock with Harris bipod and Larue quick detach mount, 12 lbs. New mid-2014.
Current MSR on this model is $9,995.

750-7MMH – 7mm Rem. cal., similar optics and tracking system with integrated track button in trigger guard as 1000 Series, 26 in. fluted stainless steel barrel, 3 shot, Bell & Carlson stock, 12 lbs. New mid-2014.
Current MSR on this model is $9,995.

MSR	100%	98%	95%	90%	80%	70%	60%	Last MSR

RIFLES: SEMI-AUTO

AR 300 – .300 AAC Blackout cal., carbine gas system, long range precision guided firearm features TrackingPoint Networked optics, 16 in. S2W profile chromemoly vanadium steel cold hammer forged barrel with Daniel Defense flash suppressor, 30 shot Magpul PMag., mil-spec lower receiver with enhanced flared mag. well and rear receiver QD swivel attachment point, upper receiver with indexing marks and M4 feed ramps, 12 in. Daniel Defense modular float rail, Daniel Defense low profile gas block, TrackingPoint AR Series buttstock, includes integrated Network tracking scope, guided trigger, and Tag Track Xact (tag button), includes cleaning kit, three batteries and chargers, 7.8 lbs. New late 2014.

   Current MSR on this model is $11,995.

   The networked tracking scope streams video to Android and iOS smart phones and tablets. Wind speed is the only data you'll manually input to the scope, using a toggle button.

AR 556 – 5.56 NATO cal., similar to AR 300, except features mid-length gas system, 7.8 lbs. New late 2014.
   Current MSR on this model is $10,995.

AR 762 – 7.62 NATO cal., 16 in. S2W profile barrel with flash suppressor, low profile gas block, carbine gas system, lower receiver with multiple QD swivel attachment points, upper receiver with indexing marks, two 20 shot PMag. mags., Picatinny rail with rail segments, TrackingPoint AR Series buttstock, includes integrated Network tracking scope, guided trigger, and Tag Track Xact (tag button), cleaning kit, three batteries, and chargers, 8.8 lbs. New late 2014.

   Current MSR on this model is $13,995.

   The networked tracking scope streams video to Android and iOS smart phones and tablets. Wind speed is the only data you'll manually input to the scope, using a toggle button.

TRANSFORMATIONAL DEFENSE INDUSTRIES, INC.

Previous name of a manufacturer of civilian and law enforcement firearms 2008-late 2010 and located in Virginia Beach, VA.

Transformational Defense Industries, Inc. was part of the Gamma Applied Visions Group SA. On Sept. 1, 2010, the company name was changed to Kriss USA. Please refer to the Kriss listing for current information.

TRISTAR SPORTING ARMS, LTD.

Current importer established in 1994, and located in N. Kansas City, MO. Distributor and dealer sales.

PISTOLS: SEMI-AUTO

The following semi-auto pistol variations are manufactured by Canik55 in Turkey.

C-100 – 9mm Para. and .40 S&W cal., DA/SA, 10 (9mm), 11 (.40 S&W) or 15 (9mm Para.) shot mag., 3.7 in. barrel, steel slide, rear snag-free dovetail sights and fixed blade front sight, black polycoat or chrome finish, black polymer checkered grips, includes two magazines and hard plastic case, 1.53-1.63 lbs. New 2013.

MSR $459	$385	$340	$300	$275	$250	$225	$200	

   Add $20 for chrome finish.

T-100 – 9mm Para. cal., DA/SA, 15 shot mag., 3.7 in. barrel, black polymer grips, rear snag-free dovetail and fixed blade front sights, Black Cerakote, Titanium Cerakote (new 2014), or chrome finish, includes black plastic case, 1.64 lbs. New 2013.

MSR $459	$385	$340	$300	$275	$250	$225	$200	

   Add $20 for chrome or Titanium Cerakote (new 2014) finish.

L-120 – 9mm Para. cal., DA/SA, 4.7 in. barrel, black polymer grips, steel slide, alloy frame, rear snag-free dovetail and fixed blade front sights, Black Cerakote or chrome finish, 17 shot mag., includes black plastic case and extra mag., 1.75 lbs. New 2013.

MSR $459	$385	$340	$300	$275	$250	$225	$200	

   Add $20 for chrome finish.

P-120 – 9mm Para. cal., DA/SA, 17 shot mag., 4.7 in. barrel, steel slide, alloy frame, black polymer grips, rear snag-free dovetail and fixed blade front sights, Black Cerakote or chrome finish, includes two mags., gun lock, cleaning kit, and black plastic carrying case, 1.87 lbs. New 2013.

MSR $489	$415	$350	$325	$295	$250	$225	$200	

   Add $20 for chrome finish.

S-120 – 9mm Para. cal., DA/SA, 17 shot mag., 4.7 in. barrel, steel frame, steel slide, black polymer grips, rear snag-free dovetail and fixed blade front sights, Black Cerakote or chrome finish, includes extra mag. and black plastic case, 2.26 lbs. New 2013.

MSR $469	$400	$345	$315	$285	$250	$225	$200	

   Add $30 for chrome finish.

MSR	100%	98%	95%	90%	80%	70%	60%	Last MSR

T-120 – 9mm Para. cal., DA/SA, full size, 17 shot mag., steel alloy frame, steel slide, 4.7 in. barrel, rail under barrel for laser or flashlight mount, scalloped ridges on slide for better grip, black polymer grips, rear snag-free dovetail and fixed blade front sights, Black Cerakote, Desert Sand Cerakote (new 2014), Titanium Cerakote (new 2014), or chrome finish, 1.88 lbs. New 2013.

MSR $469	$400	$345	$315	$285	$250	$225	$200	

Add $30 for Desert Sand Cerakote (new 2014), Titanium Cerakote (new 2014), or chrome finish.

TP-9C – 9mm Para. cal., DA/SA, SFO, 10 shot mag., 3 1/2 in. barrel, polymer, 1.39 lbs. Mfg. 2013 only.

	$400	$345	$315	$285	$250	$225	$200	*$469*

SHOTGUNS: SEMI-AUTO

Shim kits and fiber optic sights became standard on all hunting models (except Setter) beginning 2011.

PHANTOM SERIES – 12 ga. only, 3 or 3 1/2 (Phantom Field/Synthetic Mag. only) in. chamber, various VR (except Phantom HP) barrel lengths with choke tubes, available in Field (blue metal finish, gold accents, and checkered walnut stock and forearm), Synthetic (black non-glare matte metal and flat black synthetic stock and forearm), or HP (home security with open sights, matte finished metal, and synthetic stock and forearm), 6 lbs. 13 oz.-7 lbs. 6 oz. Italian mfg., limited importation 2001-2002.

	$385	$350	$315	$285	$265	$245	$225	*$425*

Subtract $44 for Phantom Synthetic.
Add $74 for 3 1/2 in. Mag. (Field).
Add $44 for Mag. Synthetic.

* ***TSA Black 3-1/2 In.*** – similar to TSA Camo 3-1/2 in., except 26 or 28 in. barrel, metal is flat black and black finished stock and forearm, 7.4 lbs. New 2012.

MSR $639	$550	$495	$450	$400	$350	$325	$295	

VIPER G2 SERIES – 12, 20, or 28 (wood stock or silver only) ga., 2 3/4 or 3 in. chamber, gas operated, 24, 26 or 28 in. barrel, choke tubes, 5 shot mag., G2 action became standard 2010, configurations include wood, synthetic, camo, and silver, brass bead front sight, mag. cut off, vent. rib with matted sight plane, choice of wood, black synthetic, camo, or carbon fiber pistol grip (disc. 2009) stock, approx. 5.7 - 6.9 lbs. Importation began 2007.

* ***Viper G2 Camo*** – 12 or 20 ga., 3 in. chamber, 24, 26, or 28 in. VR barrel with 3 choke tubes, features 100% Realtree Advantage Timber or Realtree Max-4 (28 in. only) camo finish, 6.2-6.9 lbs. New 2012.

MSR $609	$515	$450	$365	$315	$275	$235	$185	

Add $60 for left-hand action (28 in. barrel only).

* ***Viper G2 Youth Camo*** – 12 (disc.) or 20 ga., 3 in. chamber, 24, 26 (disc) or 28 (disc.) in. barrel, G2 action became standard during 2010, similar to Viper Series, except has 100% Mossy Oak Duck Blind (disc.), 100% Realtree Advantage Timber camo coverage, soft touch stock/forearm finish became standard 2011, 5.7 lbs. New 2008.

MSR $609	$515	$450	$365	$315	$275	$235	$185	

Add $16 for Viper G2 TW (Turkey/Waterfowl) Model with 12 or 20 ga., 24 or 28 in. barrel (disc.).

VIPER G2 TACTICAL – 12 ga., 20 in. barrel, matte black finish, blade front sight, 5 shot mag., cylinder choke, swivel studs, 6 1/2 lbs. Mfg. 2010-2012.

	$395	$350	$300	$265	$235	$200	$175	*$444*

RAPTOR A-TAC – 12 ga., 3 in. chamber, gas operated, 20 in. barrel with extended choke, fixed pistol grip synthetic stock, Picatinny rail, swivel studs, tactical style operating handle, bridge front sight with fiber optic bead, 7 lbs. New 2013.

MSR $439	$375	$325	$295	$265	$235	$200	$185	

TEC12 – 12 ga., 3 in. chamber, capable of operating in pump or semi-auto mode by the turn of a dial, inertia rotary bolt action, 20 or 28 (mfg. 2013 only) in. barrel with choke tubes, external ported cyl. choke, black synthetic stock with rubber fixed pistol grip plus one set of military sling swivels and swivel studs, matte black finish, Picatinny rail, ghost ring sight and raised front bridge sight with fiber optic bead, 7 lbs. New 2013.

MSR $689	$585	$525	$450	$395	$365	$335	$295	

SHOTGUNS: SLIDE ACTION

COBRA SERIES – 12 ga. only, 3 in. chamber, various barrel lengths, includes 1-3 choke tubes. Importation began 2007.

* ***Cobra Field Black*** – 12 ga., 3 in. chamber, 24 (Turkey configuration with fixed pistol grip stock), 26, or 28 in. barrel, 3 choke tubes, fiber optic front sight, extended forearm, swivel studs, matte black finish, 6 1/2 lbs.

MSR $349	$285	$250	$225	$200	$185	$175	$165	

Add $50 for 24 in. barrel with fixed pistol grip stock (Turkey configuration).

MSR	100%	98%	95%	90%	80%	70%	60%	Last MSR

* **Cobra Field Camo** – 12 ga., 3 in. chamber, 24 (Turkey configuration with fixed pistol grip stock), 26, or 28 in. barrel, 3 choke tubes, fiber optic front sight, extended forearm, swivel studs, camo finish, 6.5-6.9 lbs. New 2012.

MSR $429 $360 $315 $275 $250 $225 $200 $185

Add $60 for 24 in. barrel with fixed pistol grip stock (Turkey configuration).

* **Cobra Force** – 12 ga. only, 3 in. chamber, 18 1/2 (new 2014) or 20 (disc. 2013) in. barrel, fixed pistol grip stock with soft rubber grip, 2 choke tubes, Picatinny rail on top of receiver, fiber optic bridge front sight, rear sight, swivel studs, matte black finish, 6.6 lbs.

MSR $399 $335 $295 $260 $240 $220 $200 $185

* **Cobra Tactical** – 12 ga., 3 in. chamber, 18 1/2 (new 2014) or 20 (disc. 2013) in. barrel, spring-loaded forearm, faux extended mag tube, 1 choke tube, blade front sight, Black synthetic stock, swivel studs, 6.3 lbs.

MSR $319 $275 $235 $215 $190 $175 $160 $150

TROMIX CORPORATION

Previous firearms manufacturer established in 1999, and located in Inola, OK. Previously located in Broken Arrow, OK.

Tromix currently offers conversions for Saiga shotguns, as well as accessories and modifications. Please contact the company directly for its current services and conversion pricing (see Trademark Index).

RIFLES: SEMI-AUTO

Tromix manufactured AR-15 style rifles until 2008. Tromix lower receivers bear no caliber designation. Serialization was TR-0001-0405.

The models listed were also available with many custom options.

TR-15 SLEDGEHAMMER – .44 Rem. Mag. (disc. 2001), .440 Cor-Bon Mag., .458 SOCOM, .475 Tremor, or .50 AE cal., GIO, 16 3/4 in. barrel, other lengths and weights available by custom order. Mfg. 1999-2006.

   $1,175 $975 $850 $775 $700 $650 $600   *$1,350*

TR-15 TACKHAMMER – various cals., GIO, 24 in. bull barrel, other lengths and weights were available by custom order. Mfg. 1999-2006.

   $1,175 $975 $850 $775 $700 $650 $600   *$1,350*

SHOTGUNS

Tromix manufactures Class II short barrel shotguns based on the Saiga model. Please contact the company directly for more information (see Trademark Index).

TROY DEFENSE

Current firearms manufacturer located in West Springfield, MA.

Troy Defense, created in 2012, is the firearms division of Troy Industries. Troy is well-known for its high quality accessories, including sights and rails. Troy Defense offers a complete line of AR-15 style rifles for military and law enforcement, as well as some models for the civilian marketplace. A wide variety of options and accessories are available. Please contact the company directly for more information, including pricing and availability (see Trademark Index).

TRUVELO ARMOURY

Current manufacturer located in Midrand, South Africa. Truvelo Armoury is a division of Truvelo Manufacturers (Pty) Ltd. No current U.S. importation.

Truvelo Armoury manufactures a variety of barrels (.22 to 40mm cal.) and firearms, including the 12 ga. Neostead shotgun, the BXP 9mmP Tactical pistol, custom built hunting and sporting rifles, and military sniper rifles in 7.62x51 NATO, .338 Lapua, 12.7x99mm, 14.5x114mm, 20x82mm, and 20x110mm cals. Truvelo also manufactures the Raptor Infantry rifle and carbine in 5.56 NATO cal. Please contact the factory directly for more information, including delivery time and availability (see Trademark Index).

U SECTION

U.S. GENERAL TECHNOLOGIES, INC.

Previous manufacturer located in S. San Francisco, CA circa 1994-96.

MSR	100%	98%	95%	90%	80%	70%	60%	Last MSR

RIFLES: SEMI-AUTO

P-50 SEMI-AUTO – .50 BMG cal., includes 10 shot detachable mag., folding bipod, muzzle brake, matte black finish. Mfg. 1995-96.

	100%	98%	95%	90%	80%	70%	60%	Last MSR
	$5,600	$4,950	$4,475	$3,975	$3,500	$3,050	$2,600	*$5,995*

U.S. MACHINE GUN ARMORY LLC

Current rifle manufacturer established in the late 1990s and located in Sandy, UT. Previous company name was Practical Defense International.

RIFLES: SEMI-AUTO

U.S. Machine Gun Armory LLC also manufactures the MGA SAW line of military machine guns for military and law enforcement.

MGA MK46/48 MC – 5.56 NATO, 5.45x39mm, 6.8mm SPC, or .308 Win. cal., belt fed, closed bolt rifle, utilizes standard H&K G3 style trigger pack, adj. tactical style stock, vertical pistol grip, carry handle, Picatinny top rail, MK48 Model has tripod mount and MOD 1 bipod as standard, Desert Tan finish. New 2014.

MSR $11,998	$10,800	$9,450	$8,100	$7,350	$5,950	$4,875	$3,775	

Add $3,670 for MK48 configuration.

U.S. ORDNANCE

Current manufacturer and distributor located in Reno, NV. Commercial sales through Desert Ordnance, located in Sparks, NV.

U.S. Ordnance is licensed by Saco Defense to be the exclusive manufacturer and distributor for the M60 Series machine gun and spare parts.

RIFLES: SEMI-AUTO

U.S. Ordnance manufactures semi-auto reproductions (BATFE approved) of the M-60/M-60E3 (MSR is POR), M60E4/Mk43 (MSR $12,500-$13,000, new 2004). Previous models included the .303 Vickers (MSR was $4,500 w/o tripod), Browning M-1919 (last MSR was $1,995), and the M-1919A4 (last MSR was $2,095). These belt-fed variations are machined to military specifications, and have a 5 year warranty. Please contact the distributor directly for more information, including pricing and availability (see Trademark Index).

USAS 12

Previous trademark manufactured by International Ordnance Corporation located in Nashville, TN circa 1992-95. Previously manufactured (1990-91) by Ramo Mfg., Inc. located in Nashville, TN. Previously distributed by Kiesler's Wholesale located in Jeffersonville, IN until 1994. Originally designed and previously distributed in the U.S. by Gilbert Equipment Co., Inc. located in Mobile, AL. Previously manufactured under license by Daewoo Precision Industries, Ltd. located in South Korea.

SHOTGUNS: SEMI-AUTO

USAS 12 – 12 ga. only, gas operated action available in either semi or fully auto versions, 18 1/4 in. cylinder bore barrel, closed bolt, synthetic stock, pistol grip, and forearm, carrying handle, 10 round box or 20 round drum mag., 2 3/4 in. chamber only, parkerized finish, 12 lbs. Mfg. 1987-1995.

	100%	98%	95%	90%	80%	70%	60%	Last MSR
	$1,500	$1,250	$1,050	$925	$850	$750	$650	*$995*

Add $300-$500 for extra 20 shot drum magazine (banned by the BATFE).

Values above are for a semi-auto model. This model is currently classified as a destructive device and necessary federal NFA Class III transfer paperwork must accompany a sale.

UMAREX SPORTWAFFEN GmbH & Co. KG.

Current firearms, airguns, air soft, and signal pistol manufacturer established in 1972 as Uma Mayer Ussfeller GmbH, with headquarters located in Arnsberg, Germany.

Initially, the company manufactured tear gas and signal pistols for eastern bloc countries, and then started producing air rifles. After acquiring Reck Sportwaffen Fabrick Karl Arndt, the company was reorganized under the Umarex name.

Umarex purchased Walther during 1993, and also manufactures ammunition, optics, and accessories. During 2006,

MSR	100%	98%	95%	90%	80%	70%	60%	Last MSR

Umarex purchased Hämmerli, and production equipment was moved from Lenzburg, Switzerland to Ulm, Germany. During mid-2006, Umarex purchased RUAG Ammotec USA Inc., and moved the company to Fort Smith, AR, and the company's name was changed to Umarex USA. During 2008, Colt Industries licensed Umarex to manufacture the Colt AR-15 in .22 LR cal. During 2009, H&K licensed Umarex to manufacture replicas in .22 LR cal. During 2011, Colt Industries licensed Umarex to manufacture a Govt. 1911-A1 Model in .22 LR cal. In late 2011, IWI licensed Umarex to manufacture a .22 LR copy of the UZI carbine and pistol. These guns are being imported exclusively by Umarex USA located in Fort Smith, AR. During late 2012, Umarex and Carl Walther GmbH Sportwaffen announced the formation of Walther Arms, Inc. to import, sell, and market all Walther products in the U.S. beginning Jan. 1, 2013, except the P22 and PK380 models.

Please refer to the Colt, H&K, Hämmerli, Regent (trademark only), UZI, and Walther listings for information and values on currently imported firearms. For more information on currently manufactured (beginning circa 1984) Umarex airguns, including many major U.S. trademark mfg. under license, please refer to the *Blue Book of Airguns* by Dr. Robert Beeman & John Allen (also online).

UNERTL ORDNANCE COMPANY, INC.

Previous manufacturer circa 2004-2006 and located in Las Vegas, NV.

Unertl Ordnance Company manufactured a .45 ACP cal. semi-auto pistol in various configurations, including MEU (SOC) $2,795 last MSR, UCCP $2,195 last MSR, and the DLX $2,195 last MSR. The company also manufactured the UPR bolt action sniper rifle in .308 Win. cal. Last MSR was $5,900.

UNIQUE-ALPINE

Current manufacturer established in 2002 and located in Bavaria, Germany, with manufacturing sites in Germany and Switzerland. No current U.S. importation.

RIFLES: BOLT ACTION

TPG-1/TPG-2/TPG-3 A1/A4 (TACTICAL PRECISION GEWEHR) – various cals. (TPG-1/TPG-2), TPG3 -A1 is chambered in .308 Win., .300 Win. Mag., or .338 Lapua Mag. cal., 20, 24, or 26 in. match grade free floating fluted barrel with muzzle brake, 8 or 10 shot mag., full length Picatinny rail, modular interchangeable rifle system allows for transfer from single shot to magazine fed rifle, tactical adj. and detachable (TPG3-A1 or TPG3-A4) stock available in right hand or Universal configuration and a variety of colors and camo, adj. palm rest, accessory rails. 15 lbs. (TPG-3 A1).

A wide variety of options are available on these models. Please contact the company directly for more information, including options, pricing, and U.S. availability (see Trademark Index).

UNIVERSAL FIREARMS

Previous manufacturer 1958-1987 and located in Hialeah, FL. Previous company name was Bullseye Gunworks, located in Miami, FL. The company moved to Hialeah, FL in 1958 and began as Universal Firearms.

Universal Firearms M1 carbines were manufactured and assembled at the company's facility in Hialeah starting in the late 1950s. The carbines of the 1960s were mfg. with available surplus GI parts on a receiver subcontracted to Repp Steel Co. of Buffalo, NY. The carbines of the 1970s were mfg. with commercially manufactured parts due to a shortage of GI surplus. In 1983, the company was purchased by Iver Johnson Arms of Jacksonville, AR, but remained a separate division as Universal Firearms in Hialeah until closed and liquidated by Iver Johnson Arms in 1987.

PISTOLS: SEMI-AUTO

MODEL 3000 ENFORCER PISTOL – .30 Carbine cal., walnut stock, 11 1/4 in. barrel, 17 3/4 in. overall, 15 and 30 shot. Mfg. 1964-83. Also see listing under Iver Johnson.

	100%	98%	95%	90%	80%	70%	60%
Blue finish	$450	$375	$325	$275	$235	$200	$185
Nickel-plated	$500	$425	$350	$295	$250	$235	$220
Gold-plated	$500	$425	$350	$275	$250	$225	$200
Stainless	$600	$550	$450	$350	$275	$225	$195

Add $50 for Teflon-S finish.

RIFLES: SEMI-AUTO, CARBINES

1000 MILITARY – .30 Carbine cal., "G.I." copy, 18 in. barrel, satin blue finish, birch stock. Disc.

	100%	98%	95%	90%	80%	70%	60%
	$375	$325	$275	$235	$200	$180	$170

MODEL 1003 – 16, 18, or 20 in. barrel, .30 M1 copy, blue finish, adj. sight, birch stock, 5 1/2 lbs. Also see listing under Iver Johnson.

	100%	98%	95%	90%	80%	70%	60%	Last MSR
	$375	$325	$275	$235	$200	$180	$170	*$203*

* ***Model 1010*** – nickel finish, disc.

	100%	98%	95%	90%	80%	70%	60%
	$425	$375	$325	$275	$235	$200	$180

MSR	100%	98%	95%	90%	80%	70%	60%	Last MSR

* **Model 1015** – gold electroplated, disc.

Add $45 for 4X scope.

| | $425 | $375 | $325 | $275 | $235 | $200 | $180 | |

1005 DELUXE – .30 Carbine cal., custom Monte Carlo walnut stock, high polish blue, oil finish on wood.

| | $425 | $365 | $325 | $275 | $235 | $200 | $180 | |

1006 STAINLESS – .30 Carbine cal., stainless steel construction, birch stock, 18 in. barrel, 6 lbs.

| | $475 | $425 | $375 | $325 | $275 | $235 | $200 | $234 |

1020 TEFLON – .30 Carbine cal., Dupont Teflon-S finish on metal parts, black or grey color, Monte Carlo stock.

| | $425 | $375 | $325 | $275 | $235 | $200 | $180 | |

1025 FERRET A – .256 Win. Mag. cal., M1 Action, 18 in. barrel, satin blue finish, birch stock, 5 1/2 lbs.

| | $400 | $350 | $300 | $265 | $235 | $200 | $175 | $219 |

2200 LEATHERNECK – .22 LR cal., blowback action, 18 in. barrel, birch stock, satin blue finish, 5 1/2 lbs.

| | $350 | $300 | $250 | $215 | $185 | $170 | $160 | |

5000 PARATROOPER – .30 Carbine cal., metal folding extension or walnut stock, 16 or 18 in. barrel.

| | $550 | $475 | $400 | $350 | $295 | $250 | $225 | $234 |

5006 PARATROOPER STAINLESS – similar to 5000, only stainless with 18 in. barrel only.

| | $650 | $575 | $500 | $425 | $350 | $285 | $250 | $281 |

1981 COMMEMORATIVE CARBINE – .30 Carbine cal., "G.I Military" model, cased with accessories. Mfg. for 40th Anniversary 1941-1981.

| | $700 | $625 | $550 | $475 | $400 | $325 | $275 | |

USA TACTICAL FIREARMS

Current manufacturer located in Statesville, NC.

USA Tactical Firearms currently manufactures rifles, parts, and components for the AR-15 market. They also offer training classes. Please contact the company directly for more information on all their products and services (see Trademark Index).

RIFLES: SEMI-AUTO

MODEL USA-15 PACKAGE A – .223 Rem./5.56 NATO cal., GIO, 16 in. M4 barrel, pinned and welded muzzle brake, multi-caliber lower receiver, flat-top upper receiver with removable carry handle, A2 front sight, SST, carbine length Picatinny handguard with covers, standard 6-position stock with buttpad, Sniper pistol grip, 10 shot mag., includes black hard case.

| MSR $1,499 | $1,350 | $1,175 | $1,025 | $925 | $750 | $625 | $500 | |

* **Model USA-15 Package B** – .223 Rem./5.56 NATO cal., similar to Package A, except features 16 in. H-Bar barrel.

| MSR $1,649 | $1,475 | $1,300 | $1,100 | $1,000 | $825 | $675 | $525 | |

* **Model USA-15 Package C** – .223 Rem./5.56 NATO cal., similar to Package A, except features single rail gas block with flip-up front sight.

| MSR $1,539 | $1,375 | $1,200 | $1,025 | $950 | $750 | $625 | $500 | |

MODEL USA-15 PACKAGE D – 7.62x39mm cal., GIO, 16 in. H-Bar barrel, pinned and welded muzzle brake, flat-top upper receiver with removable carry handle, A2 front sight, SST, carbine length Picatinny handguard with covers, standard 6-position stock with buttpad, Sniper pistol grip, 10 shot mag., includes black hard case.

| MSR $1,688 | $1,525 | $1,350 | $1,150 | $1,050 | $850 | $675 | $550 | |

USELTON ARMS INC

Current manufacturer located in Franklin, TN. Previously located in Madison, TN.

PISTOLS: SEMI-AUTO, SINGLE ACTION

Beginning 2014, all pistols come standard with 3-dot Novak front and rear sights, front and rear cocking serrations, high ride beavertail grip safety, ceramic coated stainless steel parts, brushed polished bead blast, G10 black grips with medallions, classic solid or 3-hole trigger, 25 LPI front and rear checkering, one magazine, and soft case.

Damascus slides are POR on all models.

Add $70 for Frag (black, dark earth), or Alumagrip (laser logo engraved) grips.

Add $120 for adj. compact night sights or $130 for compact sights.

MIL-SPEC – .45 ACP cal., 5 in. barrel, black or blued slide, Government match frame, Armor coat finish.

| MSR $2,299 | $1,950 | $1,700 | $1,475 | $1,325 | $1,075 | $875 | $685 | |

Add $600 for integrated aluminum (IA) model with stainless steel slide, or $800 for IA slide.

MSR	100%	98%	95%	90%	80%	70%	60%	Last MSR

COMPACT CLASSIC OFFICER – .45 ACP cal., 3 1/2 in. barrel, 7 shot mag., diamond checkered rosewood grips, beaver tail grip safety, 32 oz. Disc. 2011.

	$2,850	$2,500	$2,150	$1,950	$1,575	$1,275	$1,000	$3,150

COMPACT CLASSIC – .45 ACP cal., 3 1/2 in. barrel, 7 shot mag., available in black finish with stainless steel slide, all stainless, or blue finish with stainless slide, with or w/o Bobtail, approx. 32 oz. Disc. 2013.

	$2,375	$2,050	$1,775	$1,615	$1,300	$1,075	$825	$2,800

* **Compact Classic Companion** – similar to Compact Classic, except is available in .357 SIG or .40 S&W cal., 32 oz.

	$2,375	$2,050	$1,775	$1,615	$1,300	$1,075	$825	$2,800

COMPACT MATCH – .45 ACP cal., 3 1/2 in. match grade barrel, stainless steel or integrated aluminum frame and stainless steel slide, Armor coat finish. New 2014.

MSR $2,799	$2,375	$2,075	$1,775	$1,625	$1,300	$1,075	$825	

Add $600 for integrated aluminum frame and stainless steel slide.

CARRY CLASSIC – .45 ACP cal., stainless steel frame, black slide, smooth Uselton grips, 4 1/4 in. barrel, skeletonized hammer and trigger, Novak low profile sights, checkered front strap, 7 shot mag., 34 oz.

	$2,295	$2,000	$1,725	$1,550	$1,250	$1,050	$800	$2,700

CLASSIC NATIONAL MATCH – .45 ACP cal., Commander (4 1/4 in. barrel) or Government (5 in. barrel) style frame, 8 shot mag., Cerakote/blue finish, various grip styles available, checkered front strap, stainless steel or integrated aluminum (IA) frame, combat hammer, beavertail grip safety, 40 oz.

MSR $2,599	$2,200	$1,925	$1,650	$1,495	$1,200	$995	$775	

Add $200 for Commander Match.

Add $800 for IA Commander Match or $1,100 for IA Government Match.

TACTICAL – .45 ACP cal., Compact (3 1/2 in. barrel), Commander (4 1/4 in. barrel), or Government (5 in. barrel), Cerakote finish, 8 shot mag., skeletonized trigger, combat hammer, stainless steel or integrated aluminum (IA) frame, G10 grips, beavertail grip safety, Novak low profile sights, Picatinny rail, brushed stainless and UA Armor coat finish, 44 oz.

MSR $2,699	$2,295	$2,000	$1,725	$1,550	$1,250	$1,050	$800	

Add $200 for Commander or Compact frame.

Add $800 for IA frame with stainless steel slide, or $900 for IA frame and IA slide.

MATCH CLASSIC BOBTAIL – .45 ACP cal., 4 1/4 in. barrel, Bobtail stainless steel frame and polished stainless steel slide, 8 shot, extended safety, combat hammer, skeletonized trigger, checkered metal mainspring housing, 35 oz.

	$2,425	$2,125	$1,815	$1,650	$1,325	$1,095	$850	$2,840

DOUBLE STACK RACE GUN – .38 Super, 9mm Para., .40 S&W, or .357 SIG cal., stainless steel slide, double stack mag.

	$2,725	$2,395	$2,050	$1,850	$1,500	$1,225	$950	$3,200

TAC RAIL – .45 ACP cal., 5 in. barrel, 8 shot mag., stainless steel or Cerakote finish, available in Black Maxx, Custom Cote 1, Custom Cote 2, or Custom Cote 3 configurations, accessory under rail, approx. 44 oz.

	$2,375	$2,050	$1,775	$1,615	$1,300	$1,075	$825	$2,800

Add $100 for Cerakote finish.

100 YEAR ANNIVERSARY 1911 LIMITED EDITION – .45 ACP cal., Officer or Government Model frame, case colored frame, mirror polished slide with fire blue accents, G10 grips, special laser engraving, limited to 100 of each type, match sets also available.

	$3,150	$2,750	$2,375	$2,150	$1,725	$1,425	$1,100	$3,700

Add $300 for Government Model.

RIFLES: BOLT ACTION

WARRIOR MOUNTAIN LITE – 7.82/.308 Warbird cal., Warrior Mountain Lite action (new 2013), 26 in. medium contour stainless steel barrel with six flutes and removable muzzle brake, M16 extractor, Black carbon Kevlar or high grade walnut stock, drilled and tapped for scope mounts, other options are available, 6 lbs. 14 oz.

MSR $3,900	$3,500	$3,075	$2,625	$2,375	$1,925	$1,575	$1,225	

Walnut stock is POR.

Add $490 for armor coat finish on barrel and action.

* **Predator Mountain Lite** – .220 Swift cal., similar to Warrior Mountain Lite, except features 24 in. stainless steel barrel.

MSR $3,900	$3,500	$3,075	$2,625	$2,375	$1,925	$1,575	$1,225	

Add for walnut stock - POR.

MSR	100%	98%	95%	90%	80%	70%	60%	Last MSR

* **Raptor Mountain Lite** – .270 Win. cal., similar to Warrior Mountain Lite, except features 24 in. stainless steel barrel.

| MSR $3,900 | $3,500 | $3,075 | $2,625 | $2,375 | $1,925 | $1,575 | $1,225 | |

Add for walnut stock - POR.

* **Stalker Mountain Lite** – 7mm Rem. Mag. cal., otherwise similar to Warrior Mountain Lite.

| MSR $3,900 | $3,500 | $3,075 | $2,625 | $2,375 | $1,925 | $1,575 | $1,225 | |

Add for walnut stock - POR.

* **Stealth Mountain Lite** – .300 Win. Mag. cal., otherwise similar to Warrior Mountain Lite.

| MSR $3,900 | $3,500 | $3,075 | $2,625 | $2,375 | $1,925 | $1,575 | $1,225 | |

Add for walnut stock - POR.

WARRIOR LITE TACTICAL LONG RANGE – 7.82/.308 Warbird Lazzeroni cal., 26 in. stainless steel button rifled and fluted barrel with removable muzzle brake, one-piece helical cut bolt, carbon Kevlar stock, 5 shot mag., Black matte finish, 10 1/2 lbs.

| MSR $5,400 | $4,850 | $4,250 | $3,650 | $3,300 | $2,675 | $2,175 | $1,700 | |

RIFLES: SEMI-AUTO

BLACK WIDOW A3 MODEL – 5.56 NATO/.223 Rem. cal., GPO, 16 in. barrel with door jammer flash suppressor, round counter mag., adj. sight, Magpul CTR 6-position stock, quad rail with front grip, Flat Dark Earth finish.

| MSR $3,200 | $2,875 | $2,500 | $2,150 | $1,950 | $1,575 | $1,295 | $1,000 | |

* **Black Widow A4 Model** – 7.62 NATO/.308 Win. cal., features 18 in. barrel with door jammer flash suppressor, otherwise similar to Black Widow A3 Model.

| | $2,350 | $2,050 | $1,775 | $1,600 | $1,300 | $1,050 | $825 | *$2,600* |

UTAS

Current shotgun manufacturer located in Antalya, Turkey. Currently imported by UTAS-USA, located in Des Plaines, IL.

SHOTGUNS: SLIDE ACTION

UTS-15 – 12 ga., 3 in. chamber, 18 1/2 in. barrel threaded for Beretta -style choke tubes, bullpup configuration with pistol grip, unique design utilizes two 7 shot alternately feeding or selectable mag tubes with selector switch, 100% polymer receiver, top Picatinny rail, no sights, choice of black (UTS-15), Hunting Camo (UTS-15 Hunting), Desert Camo (UTS-15 Desert), or corrosion resistant Marine finish (UTS-15 Marine), 28 1/2 in. OAL, 6.9 lbs. Mfg. by UTAS in Turkey beginning late 2012.

| MSR $1,400 | $1,275 | $1,100 | $975 | $875 | $775 | $675 | $575 | |

UZI

Current trademark manufactured by Israel Weapon Industries (IWI, previously called Israel Military Industries) and Umarex Sportwaffen GmbH (.22 cal. pistols/rifles only). Semi-auto pistols are currently imported begining 2013 by IWI US, Inc., located in Harrisburg, PA. .22 cal. Uzi pistols and rifles are currently imported by Umarex USA, located in Fort Smith, AR. Uzi America, a partnership between IMI and Mossberg, is currently importing a 9mm Para. and .40 S&W cal. submachine gun carbine built on the mini-Uzi receiver for the law enforcement market. During 1996-1998, Mossberg imported the Uzi Eagle pistols. These models were imported by UZI America, Inc., subsidiary of O.F. Mossberg & Sons, Inc. Previously imported by Action Arms, Ltd., located in Philadelphia, PA until 1994.

Serial number prefixes used on Uzi Firearms are as follows: "SA" on all 9mm Para. semi-auto carbines Models A and B; "45 SA" on all .45 ACP Model B carbines; "41 SA" on all .41 AE Model B carbines; "MC" on all 9mm Para. (only cal. made) semi-auto mini-carbines; "UP" on 9mm Para. semi-auto Uzi pistols, except Eagle Series pistols; and "45 UP" on all .45 semi-auto Uzi pistols (disc. 1989). There are also prototypes or experimental Uzis with either "AA" or "AAL" prefixes - these are rare and will command premiums over values listed below.

CARBINES/RIFLES: SEMI-AUTO

CARBINE MODEL A – 9mm Para. or .45 ACP (very rare) cal., semi-auto, 16.1 in. barrel, parkerized finish, 25 shot mag., mfg. by IMI 1980-1983 and ser. range is SA01,001-SA037,000.

| | $1,650 | $1,475 | $1,325 | $1,125 | $975 | $875 | $750 | |

Approx. 100 Model As were mfg. with a nickel finish. These are rare and command considerable premiums over values listed above.

CARBINE MODEL B – 9mm Para., .41 Action Express (new 1987), or .45 ACP (new 1987) cal., semi-auto carbine, 16.1 in. barrel, baked enamel black finish over phosphated (parkerized) base finish, 16 (.45 ACP), 20 (.41 AE) or 25

MSR	100%	98%	95%	90%	80%	70%	60%	Last MSR

(9mm Para.) shot mag., metal folding stock, includes molded case and carrying sling, 8.4 lbs. Mfg. 1983 - until Federal legislation disc. importation 1989 and ser. range is SA037,001-SA073,544.

| | $1,500 | $1,325 | $1,200 | $1,000 | $950 | $850 | $750 | *$698* |

Subtract approx. $150 for .41 AE or .45 ACP cal.
Add $150 for .22 LR cal. conversion kit (new 1987).
Add $215 for .45 ACP to 9mm Para./.41 AE conversion kit.
Add $150 for 9mm Para. to .41 AE (or vice-versa) conversion kit.
Add $215 for 9mm Para. to .45 ACP conversion kit.

MINI CARBINE – 9mm Para. cal., similar to Carbine except has 19 3/4 in. barrel, 20 shot mag., swing-away metal stock, scaled down version of the regular carbine, 7.2 lbs. New 1987. Federal legislation disc. importation 1989.

| | $2,375 | $2,175 | $1,850 | $1,600 | $1,350 | $1,150 | $995 | *$698* |

UZI RIFLE – .22 LR cal., patterned after the Uzi Carbine Model B, 17.9 in. barrel with faux suppressor, blowback semi-auto action, features metal receiver, folding stock, traditional Uzi handguard, hidden Picatinny rail, adj. front and rear sights, grip safety, 10 or 20 shot mag., black finish, 7.7 lbs. Importation by Umarex began 2012.

| MSR $599 | $525 | $450 | $400 | $360 | $310 | $280 | $260 | |

PISTOLS: SEMI-AUTO

UZI PISTOL – 9mm Para. or .45 ACP cal. (disc.), 4 1/2 in. barrel, SA, parkerized finish, 10 (.45 ACP) or 20 (9mm Para.) shot mag., supplied with molded carrying case, sight adj. key and mag. loading tool, 3.8 lbs. Importation disc. 1993.

| | $1,000 | $875 | $795 | $750 | $700 | $650 | $600 | *$695* |

Add $285 for .45 ACP to 9mm Para./.41 AE conversion kit.
Add $100 for 9mm Para. to .41 AE conversion kit.
Add approx. 30%-40% for two-line slide marking "45 ACP Model 45".

UZI .22 CAL. PISTOL – .22 LR cal., patterned after the Uzi centerfire pistol, blowback semi-auto action, 5 in. barrel with muzzle brake slots on top, black metal receiver, lower Picatinny rail, adj. sights, grip safety, 20 shot mag., 3.9 lbs. Importation by Umarex USA began 2012.

| MSR $499 | $440 | $385 | $340 | $300 | $275 | $250 | $225 | |

UZI EAGLE SERIES – 9mm Para., .40 S&W, or .45 ACP cal., DA/SA, various configurations, matte finish with black synthetic grips, 10 shot mag. Mfg. 1997-1998.

* **Uzi Eagle Series Full-Size** – 9mm Para. or .40 S&W cal., 4.4 in. barrel, steel construction, decocking feature, tritium night sights, polygonal rifling. Imported 1997-98.

| | $485 | $440 | $400 | $365 | $335 | $330 | $275 | *$535* |

* **Uzi Eagle Series Short Slide** – 9mm Para., .40 S&W, or .45 ACP cal., similar to Full-Size Eagle, except has 3.7 in. barrel. Imported 1997-98.

| | $485 | $440 | $400 | $365 | $335 | $330 | $275 | *$535* |

Add $31 for .45 ACP cal.

* **Uzi Eagle Series Compact** – 9mm Para. or .40 S&W cal., available in double action with decocking or double action only, 3 1/2 in. barrel. Imported 1997-98.

| | $485 | $440 | $400 | $365 | $335 | $330 | $275 | *$535* |

* **Uzi Eagle Series Polymer Compact** – 9mm Para. or .40 S&W cal., similar to Compact Eagle, except has compact polymer frame. Imported 1997-98.

| | $485 | $440 | $400 | $365 | $335 | $330 | $275 | *$535* |

UZI PRO PISTOL – 9mm Para cal., blowback operation, closed bolt, 4 1/2 in. mil-spec cold hammer forged CrMoV barrel, SA, matte black finish, includes 20 and 25 shot mag., polymer pistol grip lower, firing pin block, thumb operated manual safety, approx. 3 2/3 lbs. Importation began 2013.

| MSR $1,099 | $950 | $825 | $700 | $600 | $525 | $450 | $400 | |

V SECTION

VM HY-TECH LLC

Previous rifle manufacturer located in Phoenix, AZ.

MSR	100%	98%	95%	90%	80%	70%	60%	Last MSR

RIFLES

VM15 – .223 Rem. or 9mm Para. cal., AR-15 style, semi-auto, unique side charging on left side of receiver operated by folding lever allowing easy replacement of scopes, 16, 20, or 24 in. fluted and ported Wilson barrel, aluminum free-floating handguard, forged lower receiver, A-2 style buttstock with pistol grip, black finish. Mfg. 2002-2009.

	100%	98%	95%	90%	80%	70%	60%	Last MSR
	$800	$750	$675	$600	$550	$500	$400	$865

Add $34 for side-charging loading (new 2005).
Add $310 for 9mm Para. cal.

VM-50 – .50 BMG cal., single shot, 18, 22, 30, or 36 in. Lothar Walther barrel with muzzle brake, aluminum stock, includes bipod, black finish, 22-29 lbs. Mfg. 2004-2009.

	100%	98%	95%	90%	80%	70%	60%	Last MSR
	$2,300	$2,000	$1,775	$1,600	$1,475	$1,350	$1,225	$2,299

Add $40 - $120 for 22-36 in. barrel.

VALKYRIE ARMS LTD.

Current manufacturer located in Olympia, WA. Dealer sales.

Valkyrie Arms Ltd. manufactures custom suppressors made to order. Previously, Valkyrie Arms manufactured the DeLisle 2000, Browning M1919-SA and the DeLisle Sporter Carbine.

PISTOLS: SEMI-AUTO

M3A1 GREASE GUN – faithful reproduction of the original using USGI parts, 8 in. barrel, new and improved design.

MSR $1,450	$1,400	$1,225	$1,050	$950	$775	$625	$500

STEN MKII – modified AR-15 parts, one piece S-7 tool, similar to original, semi-gloss baked on "Gun-Koat 2300" finish.

MSR $1,250	$1,050	$925	$795	$715	$580	$475	$375

RIFLES: SEMI-AUTO

M3A1 GREASE GUN – faithful reproduction using USGI parts, new and improved design, 16 1/2 in. barrel, collapsible stock.

MSR $1,550	$1,300	$1,125	$950	$850	$675	$550	$425

STEN MKII CARBINE – modified AR-15 parts, one piece S-7 tool, similar to original, semi-gloss baked on "Gun-Koat 2300" finish.

MSR $1,450	$1,300	$1,125	$950	$835	$700	$575	$450

DELISLE COMMANDO CARBINE – reproduction of WWII original, uncheckered wood stock and forearm, parkerized finish, sling swivels, optional dummy suppressor.

MSR $2,495	$2,125	$1,850	$1,595	$1,450	$1,175	$950	$750

VALMET, INC.

Previous manufacturer located in Jyvaskyla, Finland. Previously imported by Stoeger Industries, Inc. located in South Hackensack, NJ.

The Valmet line was discontinued in 1989 and replaced by Tikka (please refer to the Tikka section in this text) in 1990.

RIFLES: SEMI-AUTO

Magazines for the following models are a major consideration when purchasing a Valmet semi-auto rifle, and prices can run anywhere from $85 (.223 Rem.) up to $250 (.308 Win.). Model 76 .308 mags. will function in a Model 78, but not vice versa.

M-62S TACTICAL DESIGN RIFLE – 7.62x39 Russian, semi-auto version of Finnish M-62, 15 or 30 shot mag., 16 5/8 in. barrel, gas operated, rotary bolt, adj. rear sight, tube steel or wood stock. Mfg. 1962-disc.

	100%	98%	95%	90%	80%	70%	60%
	$2,500	$2,250	$1,750	$1,500	$1,250	$1,000	$900

Add approx. $200 for tube stock.

M-71S – similar to M-62S, except .223 Rem. cal., stamped metal receiver, reinforced resin or wood stock.

	100%	98%	95%	90%	80%	70%	60%
	$1,650	$1,450	$1,325	$1,175	$975	$875	$775

MODEL 76 – .223 Rem., 7.62x39mm, or .308 Win. cal., gas operated semi-auto tactical design rifle, 16 3/4 in. or 20 1/2 (.308 only) in. barrel, 15 or 30 (7.62x39mm only) shot mag., parkerized finish. Federal legislation disc. importation 1989.

	100%	98%	95%	90%	80%	70%	60%	Last MSR
Plastic Stock	$1,500	$1,250	$1,100	$900	$800	$700	$600	
Wood Stock	$1,700	$1,300	$1,100	$900	$800	$700	$600	$740

MSR	100%	98%	95%	90%	80%	70%	60%	Last MSR

Add approx. 10% for folding stock.
Add 100% for 7.62x39mm cal. with wood stock.
Add 20% for wood stock in .308 Win. cal.

MODEL 78 – .223 Rem., 7.62x39mm, or .308 Win. cal., similar to Model 76, except has 24 1/2 in. barrel, wood stock and forearm, and barrel bipod, 11 lbs. New 1987. Federal legislation disc. importation 1989.

	100%	98%	95%	90%	80%	70%	60%	Last MSR
	$1,750	$1,525	$1,375	$1,175	$950	$825	$700	$1,060

Add 10% for 7.62x39mm cal.

MODEL 82 BULLPUP – .223 Rem. cal., limited importation.

	100%	98%	95%	90%	80%	70%	60%
	$1,675	$1,425	$1,200	$995	$775	$650	$525

VALOR ARMS

Curent rifle manufacturer established in 1997 and located in Akron, OH.

CARBINES: SEMI-AUTO

OVR-16 – various cals. including 5.56 NATO and 6.5 Grendel, AR-15 style, GIO, 16.1 in. barrel, 30 shot mag., black Valorite coated stainless steel, single stage match trigger, six or eight (includes ambi-sling adapter) position adj. stock, rifle length forearm, free floating quad rail standard, flat-top receiver with Picatinny rail continuing into quad rail, ergonomic soft rubber grip with battery storage, with or w/o sight package, approx. 8 lbs.

Base price on this model starts at $2,350.
Add $200 for iron sight package.
Add $300 for .264 LBC-AR cal.
Add $700 for Designated Marksmen Rifle (DMR).

VALTRO

Current trademark established during 1988 manufactured by Italian Arms and located in Collebeato, Brescia, Italy. Currently imported by Valtro USA, located in Hayward, CA. Previously located in San Rafael, CA.

Valtro manufactures both excellent quality slide action and semi-auto shotguns, in addition to a very high quality semi-auto pistol, and a variety of signal pistols. Currently Valtro USA is importing only semi-auto pistols. Please contact them directly for more information and availability (see Trademark Index listing).

PISTOLS: SEMI-AUTO

1998 A1 .45 ACP – .45 ACP cal., forged National Match frame and slide, 5 in. barrel, SA, deluxe wood grips, 8 shot mag., ambidextrous safety, blue finish, flat checkered mainspring housing, front and rear slide serrations, beveled mag. well, speed trigger, 40 oz., lifetime guarantee. Very limited importation.

	100%	98%	95%	90%	80%	70%	60%
	$5,500	$5,200	$4,950	$4,650	$4,250	$3,850	$3,500

SHOTGUNS: SLIDE ACTION

TACTICAL 98 SHOTGUN – 12 ga. only, 18 1/2 or 20 in. barrel featuring MMC ghost ring sights and integral muzzle brake, 5 shot mag., internal chokes, receiver sidesaddle holds 6 exposed rounds, pistol grip or standard stock, matte black finish, lightweight. Imported 1998 - disc.

	100%	98%	95%	90%	80%	70%	60%
	$790	$630	$525	$475	$425	$400	$360

PM5 – 12 ga., 20 in. barrel, 7 shot mag., black synthetic stock with matte black finish, available with or w/o ghost ring sights, optional folding stock. Limited importation.

	100%	98%	95%	90%	80%	70%	60%
	$995	$900	$800	$725	$650	$575	$500

VAN DYKE RIFLE DESIGNS

Current rifle manufacturer located in Plainville, KS.

RIFLES: BOLT ACTION

Van Dyke Rifle Designs manufactures bolt action rifles in a variety of configurations, with many options available. Prices listed represent base rifles w/o optics or available options. Please contact the company directly for more information on the variety of available options for each rifle, as well as custom made rifles (see Trademark Index).

DECISION MAKER – .308 Win. cal., 25 in. Shilen stainless steel match grade barrel, teflon coated Earth Tan desert camo finish, A-4 McMillan tactical stock with saddle cheekpiece, three baffle muzzle brake.

MSR $3,425	100%	98%	95%	90%	80%	70%	60%
	$3,085	$2,700	$2,315	$2,095	$1,695	$1,395	$1,075

TACTICAL ELIMINATOR SUPER MAGNUM – .338 Lapua cal., Shilen match grade barrel, advanced muzzle brake, designed for extreme distance, wide variety of options available.

Base price on this model is POR.

MSR	100%	98%	95%	90%	80%	70%	60%	Last MSR

M24 SUPER MAGNUM – .338 Lapua cal., 28 1/2 or 30 in. Shilen stainless steel free floating barrel, custom chamber dimension, aluminum bedding block, many options available, including rail systems, optics, muzzle brakes, trigger types and stock.

Base price on this model is POR.

REAPER CUSTOM SNIPER – various cals., Shilen stainless steel barrel, Reaper stock design includes aluminum bedding block, three-way adj. buttpad, adj. cheekpiece, long or short action, various options available.

| MSR $3,495 | $3,150 | $2,750 | $2,350 | $2,150 | $1,725 | $1,425 | $1,100 | |

AI TACTICAL ELIMINATOR I/II – .308 Win. cal., Rem. 700 short action, 22 (Eliminator I) or 24 (Eliminator II) in. Shilen stainless steel match barrel, black matte Teflon finish, multibaffled muzzle brake, Accuracy International stock with adj. cheekpiece and adj. LOP, 5 or 10 shot mag., five sling attachments.

| MSR $3,725 | $3,360 | $2,950 | $2,525 | $2,285 | $1,850 | $1,525 | $1,175 | |

Subtract $30 for Eliminator II.

* **AI Tactical Eliminator III** – similar to Eliminator I & II, except has Rem. long action, Magnum calibers, longer barrel length.

| MSR $3,775 | $3,400 | $2,975 | $2,550 | $2,325 | $1,875 | $1,525 | $1,195 | |

DISTANCE DOMINATOR I/II – various cals., Rem. 700 long action, 26 in. Shilen stainless steel barrel (I) or match grade barrel with heavy varmint benchrest contour (II), muzzle brake, H-S Precision heavy Kevlar tactical stock, adj. LOP, variety of options, including floorplate, detachable box mag., and optics.

| MSR $3,580 | $3,225 | $2,820 | $2,425 | $2,200 | $1,775 | $1,450 | $1,125 | |

Subtract $90 for Distance Dominator II.

RANGEMASTER SERIES – various cals., designed for long range target shooting.

* **Rangemaster I** – M70 short action, controlled round push feed, Shilen stainless steel match grade free floating barrel, glass pillar bedded A4 McMillan tactical stock, adj. cheekpiece, adj. spacer system, sling swivels, deep forend, various finishes.

| MSR $3,450 | $3,100 | $2,710 | $2,325 | $2,125 | $1,700 | $1,400 | $1,075 | |

* **Rangemaster II** – M70 short action, controlled round push feed, 24 in. Shilen stainless steel match grade heavy varmint barrel, stainless bead blast natural texture finish, muzzle brake, A2 McMillan tactical stock, vertical pistol grip, extra high comb, tapered forend, adj. cheekpiece, various finish and available optics.

| MSR $3,475 | $3,125 | $2,735 | $2,350 | $2,125 | $1,725 | $1,400 | $1,100 | |

* **Rangemaster III** – Rem. 700 long action, 26 in. Shilen stainless steel match grade light varmint benchrest contour barrel, triple baffle muzzle brake, bead blast natural stainless color with Teflon silver matte finish, box mag., A3 McMillan lightweight tactical stock, adj. cheekpiece, adj. spacer system, vertical pistol grip, various options available.

| MSR $3,375 | $3,050 | $2,675 | $2,285 | $2,075 | $1,675 | $1,375 | $1,075 | |

* **Rangemaster IV** – similar to Rangemaster III, 30 in. Shilen stainless steel barrel, A5 McMillan tactical stock, wider beavertail forend, adj. cheekpiece, Teflon OD green finish, double baffle semi-box muzzle brake, box mag., various options available.

| MSR $3,575 | $3,225 | $2,825 | $2,425 | $2,200 | $1,775 | $1,450 | $1,125 | |

DISINTEGRATOR – various varmint cals., Rem. 700 short action, based on the Anschütz Silhouette design, 26 in. stainless steel light varmint match grade barrel, Teflon black matte finish, H-S Precision black/grey web stock, double baffle muzzle brake, blind mag., two sling swivels, various options and optics available.

| MSR $2,795 | $2,525 | $2,225 | $1,900 | $1,725 | $1,395 | $1,125 | $885 | |

LONG RANGE HUNTER – various cals., Rem. 700 long action, 26 in. Shilen stainless steel sporter weight barrel, McMillan BDL style stock, Magna Port muzzle brake, bolt sleeved, glass pillar bedded, various optical options.

| MSR $3,095 | $2,785 | $2,435 | $2,100 | $1,895 | $1,525 | $1,250 | $975 | |

VECTOR ARMS, INC.

Current tactical rifle, pistol, and parts manufacturer located in N. Salt Lake, UT.

PISTOLS: SEMI-AUTO

Currently, Vector Arms is offering Uzi pistols with a 5 year warranty.

UZI STYLE PISTOL – 9mm Para or .45 ACP cal., full size copy of Uzi pistol, parkerized or stainless steel finish, ported barrel, back plate sling swivel.

| MSR $900 | $800 | $700 | $600 | $550 | $475 | $425 | $375 | |

Add $59 for .45 ACP cal.

Add $295 for stainless steel.

MSR	100%	98%	95%	90%	80%	70%	60%	*Last MSR*

MINI UZI STYLE PISTOL – 9mm Para. cal. only, parkerized finish or stainless steel, scaled down size.

| MSR $1,299 | $1,175 | $1,030 | $875 | $800 | $675 | $550 | $450 | |

Add $100 for stainless steel.

V-51 PISTOL – .308 Win. cal., 9 in. barrel, gun-coating, flash hider, butt cap, sling swivel, SEF metal lower.

| MSR $1,429 | $1,275 | $1,125 | $950 | $875 | $700 | $575 | $475 | |

V-52 PISTOL – 7.62x39mm cal., 9 in. barrel, butt with sling swivel, flash hider and SUO lower, powder coated, 75 shot drum mag. or 30 shot clip mag. Disc. 2012.

| | $1,450 | $1,275 | $1,095 | $985 | $800 | $650 | $510 | *$1,699* |

V-53 PISTOL – .308 Win. cal., 9 in. barrel, gun-coating, flash hider, butt cap, sling swivel, SUO polymer lower.

| MSR $1,429 | $1,275 | $1,125 | $950 | $875 | $700 | $575 | $475 | |

V-94/V-94S PISTOL – 9mm Para. cal., 5.9 (V94S) or 9 in. barrel, SUO lower, flash hider, butt cap, sling swivel

| MSR $2,299 | $1,950 | $1,700 | $1,465 | $1,325 | $1,075 | $880 | $685 | |

Add $100 for V-94S.

RIFLES: SEMI-AUTO

Currently, Vector is offering AK-47 style and Uzi SBR rifles, including a wide variety of parts, accessories, and ammunition. Please contact the company directly for more information on these rifles, including availability and options (see Trademark Index).

Until 2009, Vector Arms offered the following semi-auto tactical style rifles: V-53 (semi-auto version of the HK53 - $1,350 last MSR), V51 (semi-auto version of the HK-91, $1,024 last MSR). Vector also offered the RPD (drum or belt fed - $1,999 last MSR).

UZI STYLE RIFLE – 9mm Para. or .45 ACP cal., parkerized finish or stainless steel, fixed, folding, or side fold stock.

| MSR $900 | $800 | $700 | $600 | $550 | $475 | $425 | $375 | |

Add $295 for stainless steel.

MINI UZI STYLE RIFLE – 9mm Para. or .45 ACP cal., parkerized finish or stainless steel, fixed, folding, or side fold stock, scaled down frame.

| MSR $1,299 | $1,175 | $1,030 | $875 | $800 | $675 | $550 | $450 | |

Add $100 for stainless steel.

UZI STYLE SBR – 9mm Para. cal. only, parkerized finish, short barrel rifle configuration.

| MSR $1,000 | $900 | $79=75 | $675 | $600 | $525 | $450 | $395 | |

AK47 STYLE RIFLE – 7.62x39mm cal., AK47 style with stamped receiver and fixed or under folder wood or polymer stock.

| MSR $895 | $800 | $700 | $600 | $550 | $475 | $425 | $395 | |

V-93 RIFLE – .223 Rem. cal., semi-auto version of the HK33, fixed or collapsible stock.

| MSR $1,229 | $1,100 | $975 | $850 | $750 | $650 | $550 | $450 | |

Add $200 for collapsible stock.

V-94 RIFLE – 9mm Para. cal., 16 in. barrel, SUO lower, no flash hider.

| MSR $2,299 | $1,950 | $1,700 | $1,465 | $1,325 | $1,075 | $880 | $685 | |

VEKTOR

Current trademark established during 1953 as part of LEW (Lyttelton Engineering Work). In 1995, Vektor became a separate division of Denel of South Africa.

Vektor has manufactured a wide variety of firearms configurations, including semi-auto pistols, bolt action and slide action rifles, as well as military arms for South African law enforcement for quite some time. Currently, the company does not make any civilian small arms.

PISTOLS: SEMI-AUTO

All Vektor pistols feature polygonal rifling, excluding the Z88.

MODEL CP1 – 9mm Para. cal., 4 in. barrel, compact model with unique aesthetics and ergonomic design allowing no buttons or levers on exterior surfaces, hammerless, striker firing system, black or nickel finished slide, 10 shot mag., approx. 25 1/2 oz. Imported 1999-2000.

| | $440 | $400 | $360 | $330 | $300 | $280 | $260 | *$480* |

Add $20 for nickel slide finish.

This model was recalled due to design problems.

MODEL Z88 – 9mm Para. cal., double action, patterned after the M92 Beretta, 5 in. barrel, steel construction, black synthetic grips, 10 shot mag., 35 oz. Importation began 1999.

| | $550 | $495 | $450 | $400 | $360 | $330 | $295 | *$620* |

MSR	100%	98%	95%	90%	80%	70%	60%	Last MSR

MODEL SP1 – 9mm Para. cal., double action, 5 in. barrel with polygonal rifling, wraparound checkered synthetic grips, matte blue or normal black finish, 2.2. lbs. Importation began 1999.

| | $535 | $485 | $445 | $395 | $360 | $330 | $295 | $600 |

Add $30 for natural anodized or nickel finish.
Add $230 for Sport Pistol with compensated barrel.

* **Model SP1 Compact (General's Model)** – similar to Model SP1, except is compact variation with 4 in. barrel, 25.4 oz. Importation began 1999.

| | $575 | $510 | $460 | $410 | $360 | $330 | $295 | $650 |

* **Model SP1 Sport Pistol/Tuned** – similar to Model SP1, except is available with tuned action or target pistol features. Importation began 1999.

| | $1,050 | $900 | $775 | $650 | $525 | $400 | $350 | $1,200 |

Add $100 for Target Pistol with dual color finish.

MODEL SP2 – .40 S&W cal., otherwise similar to Model SP1. Importation began in 1999.

| | $575 | $510 | $460 | $410 | $360 | $330 | $295 | $650 |

Add $190 for 9mm Para. conversion kit.

* **Model SP2 Compact (General's Model)** – similar to Model SP2, except is compact variation. Importation began 1999.

| | $575 | $510 | $460 | $410 | $360 | $330 | $295 | $650 |

* **Model SP2 Competition** – competition variation of the Model SP2 featuring 5 7/8 in. barrel, additional magazine guide, enlarged safety levers and mag. catch, and straight trigger, 35 oz. Importation began 2000.

| | $850 | $775 | $675 | $575 | $510 | $460 | $395 | $1,000 |

STOCK GUN – 9mm Para. cal., normal black finish. Importation began 2000.

| | $850 | $775 | $675 | $575 | $510 | $460 | $395 | $1,000 |

ULTRA MODEL – 9mm Para. or .40 S&W (new 2000) cal., top-of-the-line double action with most performance features, optional Lynx (disc. 1999) or Tasco (new 2000) scope. Importation began 1999.

| | $1,950 | $1,700 | $1,500 | $1,300 | $1,100 | $900 | $700 | $2,150 |

Subtract $150 if w/o Tasco scope.

RIFLES: SLIDE ACTION

H5 – .223 Rem. cal., 18 or 22 in. barrel, rotating bolt, uncheckered forearm and thumb-hole stock with pad, includes 4X scope with long eye relief, 9 lbs., 7 oz.-10 1/4 lbs. Imported 2000-disc.

| | $775 | $650 | $575 | $510 | $460 | $410 | $350 | $850 |

VEPR

Current trademark manufactured by Molot JSC (Vyatskie Polyany Machine Building Factory) located in Russia. Currently imported beginning 2014 by I.O., Inc., located in Palm Bay, FL, and beginning 2013 by Molot USA, located in Walnut Creek, CA. Previously imported by ZDF Import/Export, Inc., located in Salt Lake City, UT. Previously imported during 2004 by European American Armory, located in Sharps, FL.

RIFLES: SEMI-AUTO

VEPR HUNTER (VEPR II) CARBINE/RIFLE – .223 Rem., .270 Win. (new 2004), .30-06 (new 2004), .308 Win., or 7.62x39mm (new 2001) cal., features Vepr.'s semi-auto action, 16 (.223 Rem. or 7.62x39mm cal.), 20 1/2 (carbine, .308 Win. only, disc.), 21.6 or 23 1/4 (disc.) in. barrel with adj. rear sight, scope mount rail built into receiver top, standard or optional thumbhole checkered walnut stock with recoil pad and forend, paddle mag. release, 5 or 10 shot mag., approx 8.6 lbs.

| MSR $550 | $550 | $495 | $440 | $395 | $365 | $335 | $300 | |

SUPER VEPR – .308 Win. cal., thumbhole stock. Limited importation 2001-2007.

| | $950 | $850 | $750 | $650 | $550 | $475 | $400 | |

VEPR IV – 5.56 NATO cal., matte black finish, 23.3 in. heavy chrome lined barrel with US-made muzzle brake, 30 shot detachable mag., adj. rear sight, original RK clubfoot foldable stock, bipod, pistol grip. Importation began 2014.

| MSR $1,400 | $1,250 | $1,095 | $950 | $850 | $700 | $575 | $450 | |

SHOTGUNS: SEMI-AUTO

VEPR 12 – 12 ga., AK-47 design, various configurations and barrel lengths, two lever safety, folding tube stock with recoil pad, pistol grip, 5 or 8 shot mag, approx. 8 1/2 lbs. New 2011.

| MSR $1,350 | $1,200 | $1,050 | $900 | $825 | $675 | $550 | $425 | |

MSR		100%	98%	95%	90%	80%	70%	60%	*Last MSR*

VICTOR ARMS CORPORATION

Previous manufacturer located in Houston, TX.

Victor Arms Corporation manufactured limited quantities of a .22 LR upper unit for the AR-15. The V22 and its .22 LR cal. magazine replaced the standard .223 upper assembly/magazine. Additionally, a complete protoype gun was also manufactured.

VIGILANCE RIFLES

Current rifle manufacturer located in Chino Valley, AZ beginning 2012. Previously located in Banning, and Redlands, CA.

RIFLES: BOLT ACTION

MODEL 12 WINDRUNNER – .223 Rem. or .308 Win. cal., all steel construction, 4 shot detachable mag., collapsible stock with adjustable cheekpiece and monopod, heavy recoil pad, bipod, Picatinny rail, matte black finish, Savage Accutrigger, includes drag bag. New late 2013.

MSR $2,975		$2,675	$2,450	$2,000	$1,825	$1,475	$1,200	$950

Add $499 for optional pivoting bipod mount.

RIFLES: SEMI-AUTO

VR1 – .338 Lapua, .375 Cheytac, .408 Cheytac, or .505 Gibbs (disc. 2012) cal., gas operated, stainless steel upper receiver, bull barrel, titanium muzzle brake, premium wood stock in a variety of colors or synthetic tactical stock, two-stage trigger, detachable 5 shot mag., many options available, weights vary according to configuration.

MSR $10,000		$8,995	$8,200	$7,500	$6,750	$6,000	$5,500	$4,995

VIPER

Current trademark imported by Tristar, located in North Kansas City, MO. Please refer to the Tristar section.

VLTOR WEAPON SYSTEMS

Current manufacturer of AR-15 style rifles, receivers, parts, and related accessories located in Tucson, AZ.

CARBINES: SEMI-AUTO

TS3 CARBINE – 5.56 NATO cal., AR-15 style, GIO, 16 1/4 in. barrel with muzzle brake, flat-top Vltor receiver with full length Picatinny rail, 30 shot mag., Geissele high speed National Match trigger, flip up combat sights, collapsible stock, quad rail, black finish, approx. 7 1/2 lbs. Mfg. 2011-2013.

		$2,275	$2,000	$1,800	$1,600	$1,400	$1,200	$995	*$2,495*

XVI DEFENDER – 5.56 NATO cal., GIO, 16 in. M4 barrel with A1 flash hider, Vltor buffer, Keymod handguard, mid-length gas tube, flip up front and Diamond Head rear sights, Picatinny rail, Bravo Co. charging handle, standard trigger, Vltor IMOD stock, Tango Down pistol grip, Black, Foliage Green, or FDE finish. New 2014.

MSR $1,560		$1,400	$1,225	$1,050	$950	$770	$630	$490

XVI WARRIOR – 5.56 NATO cal., GIO, 16 in. chrome lined barrel with flash hider, 15 in. KeyMod system handguard, mid-length gas tube, Diamond Head sights, Picatinny rail, Bravo Co. charging handle, Geissele DMR trigger, Vltor EMOD stock, Tango Down pistol grip, Black finish. New 2014.

MSR $2,360		$2,100	$1,840	$1,575	$1,430	$1,155	$945	$735

VOLKMANN PRECISION, LLC

Current pistol manufacturer established in 2007 and located in Littleton, CO. Previously located in Lakewood, CO until 2011. Consumer direct sales through FFL.

Volkmann Precision LLC was founded by Luke Volkmann, formerly a pistolsmith for Ed Brown Products. In 2011, the company name changed from Volkmann Custom Inc. to Volkmann Precision, LLC.

PISTOLS: SEMI-AUTO

All pistols are hand built, and a variety of options are available. Please contact the company directly (see Trademark Index).

Add $100 for ambidextrous safety. Add $250 for custom finish. Add $300 for engraving. Add $250 for custom serial number.

COMBAT CUSTOM – .45 ACP cal., 5 in. barrel, SA, full size frame, 7 or 8 shot mag., black Rockote or blue finish, fixed tritium night sights, 25 LPI checkering.

MSR $3,095		$2,650	$2,325	$2,000	$1,800	$1,475	$1,200	$1,000

MSR	100%	98%	95%	90%	80%	70%	60%	Last MSR

COMBAT CARRY – .45 ACP cal., 4 1/4 in. barrel, SA, 7 or 8 shot mag., Commander size frame and slide with Ed Brown Bobtail mainspring housing, Rockote black, OD green, titanium blue, or desert tan finish, fixed tritium night sights, 25 LPI checkering.

MSR $3,195	$2,725	$2,385	$2,050	$1,850	$1,500	$1,225	$1,025	

CLINT SMITH COMBAT SPECIAL – .45 ACP cal., SA, Clint Smith inspired and designed 1911 style, 7 or 8 shot mag., carbon or stainless steel frame, Rockote finish, Heine Ledge combat sights, gold dot front post sights, tactical accessory rail, lanyard loop mainspring, short match trigger and safety, 34-38 oz. New 2012.

MSR $3,595	$3,050	$2,675	$2,300	$2,075	$1,675	$1,375	$1,100	

VOLQUARTSEN CUSTOM (LTD.)

Current pistol/rifle customizer and manufacturer established in 1974 and located in Carroll, IA. Dealer sales.

RIFLES: SEMI-AUTO

Current Volquartsen stock configurations include: Laminated Lightweight Thumbhole Stock, Laminated Thumbhole Silhouette Stock, Laminated Sporter Stock, Signature Series Bastogne Walnut Stock, VX-5000 Stock, McMillan Fiberglass Thumbhole Stock, McMillan Fiberglass Sporter Stock, or Hogue Overmolded Stock. Laminated stocks are available in Brown, Blue, Gray, Green, Orange, Pink, Yellow, Red, Turquoise, or Brown/Grey. Base prices listed represent standard Hogue synthetic stock.

Beginning 2014, rifles have been organized by actions and barrel combinations - Ultralite, Superlite, Lightweight, Stainless, Deluxe, IF-5, or SF-1. Previously, the nomenclature for these guns were the Standard Models listed in different calibers.

Add $120 for Hogue Overmolded Stock (Black or OD Green).
Add $250 for Laminated Sporter Stock.
Add $350 for Laminated Lightweight Thumbhole or Laminated Thumbhole Silhouette stocks.
Add $450 for VX-5000 stock.
Add $650 for McMillan Fiberglass Sporter or McMillan fiberglass Thumbhole stock.
Add $800 for Signature Series Bastogne Walnut stock.

EVOLUTION MODEL – .204 Ruger or .223 Rem. cal., gas operated, stainless steel receiver, trigger guard, and bolt, integral machined Picatinny rail on receiver top, brown laminate stock with extended Monte Carlo cheekpiece, 20 or 24 (.204 Ruger only) in. standard barrel, 10 shot AR-15 style mag., 11 1/2 lbs. New 2005.

MSR $2,483	$2,125	$1,950	$1,700	$1,475	$1,225	$1,000	$850	

Add $226 for camo (now avail. only as part of camo package w/scope), disc. 2011.
Add $1,271 for Evolution Camo package with scope.

VOLUNTEER ENTERPRISES

Previous manufacturer located in Knoxville, TN.

Volunteer Enterprises became Commando Arms after 1978.

CARBINES

COMMANDO MARK III CARBINE – .45 ACP cal., semi-auto, blowback action, 16 1/2 in. barrel, aperture sight, stock styled after the Auto-Ordnance "Tommy Gun." Mfg. 1969-1976.

	$750	$675	$625	$565	$525	$475	$425	

Add 10% for vertical grip.

COMMANDO MARK 9 – similar to Mark III in 9mm Para. cal.

	$675	$625	$565	$525	$475	$425	$375	

Add 10% for vertical grip.

VULCAN ARMAMENT, INC.

Previous rifle manufacturer 1991-circa 2013 and located in Inver Grove Heights, MN. Previously located in South St. Paul, MN.

Vulcan Armament specialized in tactical style firearms and offered a complete line of parts and accessories.

CARBINES/RIFLES: SEMI-AUTO

Vulcan Armament made a wide variety of AR-15 styled semi-auto carbines and rifles, including configurations for military and law enforcement.

All rifles included sling, manual, cleaning kit, Vulcan knife, and hard case.

Add $20-$25 for removable carry handle.

V15 9MM CARBINE SERIES – 9mm Para. cal., GIO, 16 in. chromemoly vanadium steel barrel with threaded muzzle, A2 front sight bases with bayonet lug, all parts manganese phosphate finished, M4 contour, M4 length handguard, full heat shield, A2 upper receiver or A3 flat-top receiver, carry handle, adj. sights, Picatinny rail, black anodized hard

MSR	100%	98%	95%	90%	80%	70%	60%	Last MSR

coat finish, forward assist, hinged ejection port cover, six position adj. buttstock, removable flash hider, accepts Sten magazines, 6 1/2 lbs. Disc. 2012.

	$775	$685	$585	$525	$425	$350	$275	*$860*

V15 DISPATCHER SERIES – .223 Rem. cal., GIO, 16 in. chromemoly vanadium steel barrel with threaded muzzle, gas block mounted under the handguard, A2 flash hider, A2 front sight bases, bayonet lug, fixed A2 stock, A2 or A3 flat-top upper receiver, black hard coat anodized finish, 6 1/2 lbs.

	$850	$750	$650	$575	$475	$385	$300	*$999*

V15 M4 CARBINE SERIES – .223 Rem. cal., GIO, 16 in. chromemoly vanadium steel button rifled barrel with threaded muzzle, A2 flash hider, A2 front sight bases, bayonet lug, A2 or A3 flat-top upper reciever, black hard coat anodized finish, M4 length handguard with full heat shields, six position M4 buttstock, 6.4lbs.

	$850	$750	$650	$575	$475	$385	$300	*$999*

V15 POLYMER SERIES – .223 Rem. cal., GIO, 16 or 20 in. chromemoly vanadium steel button rifled H-Bar barrel with threaded muzzle, all parts manganese phosphate finished, A2 flash hider, A2 sight bases, bayonet lug, six position M4 buttstock, Picatinny rail, A2 or A3 polymer receiver, forward assist, hinged ejection port cover. Disc. 2012.

	$625	$550	$475	$425	$350	$280	$225	*$700*

V15 TARGET RIFLE – .223 Rem. cal., GIO, 20 in. chromemoly vanadium steel threaded button rifled heavy barrel, A2 flash hider, all parts manganese phosphate finished, rifle length handguard, full heat shield, A2 or A3 flat-top upper receiver, Picatinny rail, black hard coat anodized finish, fixed A2 buttstock, removable flash hider, aluminum spacer, trap door buttplate.

	$850	$750	$650	$575	$475	$385	$300	*$999*

V15 VARMINATOR SERIES – .223 Rem. cal., GIO, 16 (new 2013), 20 or 24 in. stainless steel bull barrel, full length aluminum handguard, hard coat anodized finish, aluminum gas block, four Picatinny rails, forged A3 upper receiver, forward assist, hinged ejection port cover, fixed A2 buttstock, aluminum spacer, trap door buttplate, 9-9.2 lbs.

	$850	$750	$650	$575	$475	$385	$300	*$999*

V15 200 SERIES – 7.62x39mm cal., GIO, 16 in. chromemoly vanadium steel threaded barrel, A2 flash hider, A2 front sight bases, bayonet lug, all parts manganese phosphate finished, M4 length handguard, full heat shields, forged A2 or A3 flat-top upper receiver, forward assist, hinged ejection port, six position buttstock, 6.4 lbs.

	$950	$825	$715	$650	$525	$425	$325	*$1,100*

* V15 200 Piston Series – .223 Rem. cal., similar to V15 200 Series, except has proprietary short stroke GPO.

	$1,075	$940	$800	$725	$595	$485	$375	*$1,250*

V15 202 MODULAR CARBINE – .223 Rem. cal., GIO, 16 in. chromemoly vanadium steel threaded barrel, A2 flash hider, all parts manganese phosphate finished, A3 flat-top upper receiver, four Picatinny rails, black hard coat anodized finish, forward assist, hinged ejection port cover, modular handguard, low profile aircraft aluminum gas block, six position buttstock, 6 1/2 lbs.

	$835	$725	$625	$575	$450	$375	$295	*$925*

V18 SERIES – .223 Rem. cal., short stroke GPO, 16 1/2 or 20 in. chrome lined barrel, copy of the AR-180, machined gas block, front sight base, Picatinny rail, A2 flash hider, FAL style handguard, ambidextrous charging handle, carbon fiber lower, AR pistol grip, polymer FAL stock, rubber buttpad, aluminum recoil plate, last round hold open, 6.8 lbs.

	$750	$650	$565	$510	$415	$340	$265	*$889*

V73 SERIES – 7.62x39mm, 223 Rem., or .308 Win. cal., GIO, copy of Israeli Galil, 100% part interchangeability, including mags. and accessories, machined monoblock receiver, skeletonized black tactical stock, available in AR, ARM, SAR, and Micro configurations. Disc. 2012.

	$1,395	$1,220	$1,050	$950	$765	$630	$495	*$1,550*

Add $300 for .308 Win. cal.
Add $100 for ARM model with top carry handle.
Add $449 for SAR or Micro configuration.

RIFLES: BOLT ACTION

All rifles included manual, bipod, removable muzzle brake, gun lock, Vulcan knife, cleaning rod and brush, and scope rail.

V50 SERIES – .50 BMG cal., single shot, 60 degree bolt throw, capable of hits at ranges exceeding one mile, scope mounting rail, standard Mauser pattern trigger, thick recoil pad, "Shark Fin" muzzle brake, available in SS-100 (30 in. barrel, brown laminated thumbhole wood stock, disc. 2012), SS-200 (36 in. barrel, grey laminated thumbhole wood stock), SS-300 (30 in. barrel, retractable black tactical stock, disc. 2012) or the SS-400 Bullpup (30 in. barrel, bullpup stock).

	$1,725	$1,525	$1,295	$1,175	$950	$775	$600	*$1,900*

Add $300 for SS-400 Bullpup.

W SECTION

WAFFEN HIENDLMAYER

Current manufacturer located in Eggenfelden, Germany. No current U.S. importation.

Klaus Hiendlmayer specializes in custom guns and engraving, and manufactures a version of the SIG 550 sniper rifle and prices range from €1,999-€2,750. Please contact the company directly for more information, including domestic availability (see Trademark Index).

WALTHER

Current manufacturer established in 1886, and currently located in Ulm, Germany 1953 to date. Sport and Defense models are currently imported by Walther Arms, Inc. located in Fort Smith, AR. Previously imported, distributed, and manufactured (Models PPK and PPK/S only) by Smith & Wesson circa 2002-2012, and located in Springfield, MA. Walther target pistols and target rifles are distributed by Champions Choice located in La Vergne, TN. All target, competition and service pistols are also currently imported, distributed, and factory serviced by Earl's Repair Service, Inc., located in Tewksbury, MA since 1984, and in Pearisburg, VA beginning 2012. Previously imported and distributed 1998-2001 by Walther USA LLC, located in Springfield, MA, and by Interarms located in Alexandria, VA circa 1962-1999. Previously manufactured in Zella-Mehlis, Germany 1886 to 1945. Walther was sold to Umarex Sportwaffen GmbH circa 1994, and company headquarters are located in Arnsberg, Germany. Smith & Wesson was the primary distributor for most Walther firearms and accessories in the United States from 2002-2012. During 2012, Carl Walther GmbH Sportwaffen and Umarex announced the formation of Walther Arms, Inc. located in Fort Smith, AR to import, sell, and market all Walther products in the U.S. beginning Jan. 1, 2013.

The calibers listed in the Walther Pistol sections are listed in American caliber designations. The German metric conversion is as follows: .22 LR - 5.6mm, .25 ACP - 6.35mm, .32 ACP - 7.65mm, and .380 ACP - 9mm kurz. The metric caliber designations in most cases will be indicated on the left slide legend for German mfg. pistols listed in the Walther section.

For more information and current pricing on both new and used Walther airguns, please refer to the *Blue Book of Airguns* by Dr. Robert Beeman & John Allen (also online).

MSR	100%	98%	95%	90%	80%	70%	60%	*Last MSR*

PISTOLS: SEMI-AUTO, POST-WAR

Smith & Wesson has placed a recall on all Walther PPK and PPK/S pistols manufactured by Smith & Wesson from March 21, 2002-Feb. 3, 2009. Ser. no. ranges subject to this recall are as follows: 0010BAB-9999BAB, 0000BAC-9999BAC, 0000BAD-9999BAD, 0000BAE-999BAE, 0000BAF-9999BAF, 0000BAH-9999BAH, 00000BAJ-9999BAJ, 0000BAK-9999BAK, 0000BAL-5313BAL, 0000BAM-1320BAM, 0000LTD-0499LTD, 0001PPK-1500PPK, 0026REP-0219REP, and 0001WLE-0459WLE. Smith & Wesson has advised all owners to discontinue usage and return the pistol to S&W for free repair. Please contact S&W directly for more information (see Trademark Index).

MODEL PPQ – 9mm Para. or .40 S&W cal., SFO, synthetic frame with steel slide, 4 (.40 S&W cal. only), or 4.1 (threaded barrel available on first edition only) in. barrel, 12 (.40 S&W cal. only), 15, or 17 shot mag., black finish, textured synthetic grips, night sights (first edition only) or adj. front and rear sights, Quick Defense Trigger, 24 1/2 oz. Mfg. 2011-2012.

	100%	98%	95%	90%	80%	70%	60%	Last MSR
	$525	$450	$415	$365	$325	$295	$275	*$600*

Add $300 for first edition model.

MODEL PPQ M2 – 9mm Para. or .40 S&W cal., SFO, appearance and most features similar to Model PPQ, except 4 (9mm Para. only), 4.1 (.40 S&W cal.), 4.6 (threaded, 9mm Para.), or 5 in. barrel, 11, 15, or 17 shot mag., ambidextrous mag. release button, low profile combat sights, 24 oz. New 2013.

MSR $649	$550	$470	$425	$375	$325	$295	$275	

Add $100 for 5 in. barrel.
Add $50 for PPQ M2 Navy SD variation with 4.6 in. threaded barrel.

MODEL PPX M1 – 9mm Para. or .40 S&W cal., hammer fired action, DAO, 4 or 4.6 (PPX SD) in. barrel, low profile 3 dot sights, lower Picatinny rail, checkered trigger guard, ergonomic textured synthetic grips, ambidextrous slide stop, bobbed hammer, polymer frame with steel or stainless steel slide, 14 or 16 shot mag., 27.2 oz. Manufactured in Ulm, Germany. New 2013.

MSR $449	$395	$350	$315	$285	$260	$240	$220	

Add $50 for stainless steel slide.

MODEL P88 & VARIATIONS – 9mm Para. or 9x21mm cal., double action, alloy frame, 4 in. barrel, 15 shot button release mag., fully ambidextrous, decocking lever, matte finish, adj. rear sight, internal safeties, plastic grips, 31 1/2 oz. Mfg. 1987-93.

	$1,100	$925	$750	$600	$500	$450	$400	*$1,129*

P88 cutaways were also mfg. in small quantities for instructional use. Current pricing for a mint specimen is approx. $2,000.

MSR	100%	98%	95%	90%	80%	70%	60%	*Last MSR*

* ***Model P88 Compact*** – 9mm Para. or 9x21mm cal., 3.93 in. barrel, 14* (disc.) or 10 (C/B 1994) shot mag., 29 oz. Imported 1993-2003.

	$975	$800	$650	$550	$500	$475	$450	*$900*

Add 25% for 14 shot mag.

* ***Model P88 Champion*** – 9mm Para. only, 6 in. barrel, SA only, 14* shot mag., 30.9 oz. Very limited mfg. 1992-disc.

	$3,000	$1,850	$1,500	$1,250	$995	$775	$625	

* ***Model P88 Competition*** – similar to P88 Champion, except has 4 in. barrel, SA only, 14* shot mag., 28.2 oz. Very limited mfg. 1992-disc.

	$2,400	$1,500	$1,250	$995	$775	$625	$550	

P99 & VARIATIONS – 9mm Para., 9x21mm (limited importation 1996), or .40 S&W (new 1999) cal., SFO, 4 (9mm Para.) or 4.1 (.40 S&W) in. barrel, polymer frame, 10, 12 (.40 S&W cal. only), 15, or 16 (9mm Para. cal. only, disc. 2006) shot mag., standard, anti-stress (traditional double action, AS Model, new 2004), or quick action (QA, allowing consistent SA trigger performance) trigger, decocking, and internal striker safeties, cocking and loaded chamber indicators, choice of matte black, QPQ (mfg. 1999-2003) finished (silver colored) slide, or titanium coated (mfg. 2003-2006) finish, ambidextrous mag. release, ergonomic black, desert tan (disc. 2008), or green (Military model, new 1999) synthetic grip with interchangeable backstrap, adj. rear sight, 25 oz. Importation began 1995.

MSR $629	$545	$485	$435	$375	$315	$275	$250	

Add $140 for tritium sight set with green 3-dot system (.40 S&W only), or $109 for white 3-dot metal sights (disc. 2011).
Add $260 for night sight kit (mfg. 2010-2011).
Add $31 for titanium finish (disc. 2006).
Add $125 for 9x21mm cal. (disc.).
Engraved P99s were also available in the following configurations in 9mm Para. cal. only - Grade I Arabesque ($3,700 last MSR), Grade II Goldline ($4,200 last MSR), Grade III Arabesque w/gold ($4,660 last MSR).

* ***P99 Compact*** – 9mm Para. or .40 S&W cal., SFO, 3 1/2 in. barrel, 8 (.40 S&W cal.) or 10 shot mag. with finger extension, available in QA, AS, or DAO (disc. 2006), Weaver rail, compact frame, blue finish only, 20 oz. New 2004.

MSR $629	$545	$485	$435	$375	$315	$275	$250	

P990 – similar to P99, SFO, except is double action only, features Walther's constant pull trigger system, black, QPQ slide finish, or Military Model (green), 25 oz. Mfg. 1998-2003.

	$550	$475	$425	$385	$350	$325	$295	*$644*

RIFLES: DISC.

MODEL WA-2000 – .300 Win. Mag. (55 mfg., standard) or .308 Win. (92 mfg., optional) cal., ultra-deluxe semi-auto, 25.6 in. barrel, 5 or 6 shot mag., optional extras include aluminum case, spare mags., integral bipod, adj. tools and leather sling, regular or night vision scope, special order only, 16 3/4 lbs. Disc. 1988.

	$36,000	$32,000	$29,000	$27,000	$25,000	$22,500	$20,000	

A 7.5 Swiss cal. conversion kit was also optional on this model.

RIFLES: CURRENT/RECENT MFG.

Except for the G22 and GSP rifles, the following models are available from Champion's Choice.

MODEL G22 SEMI-AUTO – .22 LR cal., bullpup design, 20 in. barrel, 10 shot mag., fire control and mag. integrated in rear of stock, black synthetic, carbon fiber, or camo (disc. 2006) thumbhole stock, adj. sliding sights, right or left-hand controls and ejection, blue or military green finish, Weaver style rails on rear sight/carry handle, lower forearm, and on front right mount, approx. 6 lbs. Mfg. 2004-2011.

	$435	$380	$330	$290	$250	$225	$195	*$509*

Add $39 for scope or $67 for laser or $102 for red-dot sights (disc. 2009).
Add $56 for carbon fiber stock (disc. 2007) or $50 for camo stock (disc. 2006).

WEATHERBY

Current trademark manufactured and imported by Weatherby located Paso Robles, CA since 2006. Previously located in Atascadero, CA 1995-2006, and in South Gate, CA, 1945-1995. Weatherby began manufacturing rifles in the U.S. during early 1995. Dealer and distributor sales.

Weatherby is an importer and manufacturer of long arms. Earlier production was from Germany and Italy, and German mfg. is usually what is collectible. Rifles are currently produced in the U.S., while O/U shotguns are made in Italy and semi-autos are mfg. in Turkey.

Weatherby is well-known for their high-velocity proprietary rifle calibers.

Weatherby offers a research authentication service for Weatherby firearms. The cost is $50 per serial number ($75 for

MSR	100%	98%	95%	90%	80%	70%	60%	Last MSR

custom rifles, $100 for special editions and commemoratives), and includes a certificate signed by Roy Weatherby Jr. and company historian Dean Rumbaugh. Please contact the company directly for more information regarding this service (see Trademark Index).

Early Weatherby rifles used a Mathieu Arms action in the 1950s - primarily since it was available in left-hand action. Right-handed actions were normally mfg. from the FN Mauser type.

RIFLES: BOLT ACTION, MARK V SERIES

Pre-Mark V production started in 1945 and ended in 1961. Initially, rifles were customized from customer supplied guns, and this ended circa 1949. Between 1949-1963, Weatherby manufactured rifles in Southgate from FN Mauser actions in various cals., including the .257, .270, 7mm, .300, and .375 Wby. Mag. cals. From 1955-1959, Southgate also manufactured guns using the Mathieu left-hand action. Additionally, Schultz & Larson from Denmark was subcontracted to make rifles in .378 Wby. Mag. circa 1955-1962. Between 1956-1962, Southgate manufactured a .460 Wby. Mag. cal. using the Brevex Magnum action. Sako of Finland was also subcontracted circa 1957-1961 to produce rifles using a FN Mauser action. Initial Mark V production began in Southgate circa 1958-1959. During 1959-1973, J.P. Sauer of W. Germany was subcontracted to make the Mark V in a variety of calibers up to .460 Wby. Mag. These earlier pre-Mark V rifles will have a 20%-30% premium, depending on original condition and caliber.

In 1992, 24 in. barrels were disc. on most calibers of .300 or greater (including Models Mark V Deluxe, Fibermark, Lazermark, and Euromark). The Mark V action has also been manufactured in Japan.

All recently manufactured Weatherby Magnums in .30-378, .338-378, .378, .416, and .460 cal. are equipped with an Accubrake.

TRR (THREAT RESPONSE RIFLE) – .223 Rem., .308 Win., .300 Win. Mag. (disc. 2002), .300 Wby. Mag. (disc. 2002), .30-378 Wby. Mag. (disc. 2002), or .338-.378 Wby. Mag. (disc. 2002) cal., 22 in. barrel, 5 shot mag., Mark V action with black finished metal and black hybrid composite stock, various barrel lengths, optional Picatinny style ring and base system, 8 1/2-10 1/2 lbs. Mfg. 2002-2005.

	100%	98%	95%	90%	80%	70%	60%	Last MSR
	$1,400	$1,225	$1,050	$950	$770	$630	$490	$1,737

Add $52 for .300 Win. Mag. or .300 Wby. Mag. cals. (disc. 2002).
Add $208 for .30-378 Wby. Mag. or .338-378 Wby. Mag. cals. (disc. 2002).

TRR RC (RANGE CERTIFIED) – .300 Win. Mag., .300 Wby. Mag., .30-378 Wby. Mag., .338 Lapua Mag. (new 2012), or .338-378 Wby. Mag. cal., 26 in. Kreiger barrel with Accubrake, adj. trigger, 2 shot mag., laminated stock with T-6 aluminum bedding system with three position buttstock, includes Leupold 4.5-14x50 LRT M1 scope (disc. 2012), Talley ring rail, bipod, and hard case, 9 1/4 lbs. New 2010.

MSR	100%	98%	95%	90%	80%	70%	60%	
MSR $4,200	$3,575	$3,050	$2,575	$2,250	$1,900	$1,650	$1,375	

Add approx. $1,700 for TRR Package including Leupold scope, ring rail, bipod, and hard case (disc. 2012).

RIFLES: BOLT ACTION, CUSTOM SHOP

TRCM (THREAT RESPONSE CUSTOM MAGNUM) – .300 Win. Mag., .300 Wby. Mag., .30-378 Wby. Mag., or .338-.378 Wby. Mag. cal., Mark V action with ergonomic, fully adjustable composite stock, black finished metal, various barrel lengths, optional Picatinny style ring and base system. Mfg. 2002-2009.

	100%	98%	95%	90%	80%	70%	60%	Last MSR
	$2,325	$2,035	$1,745	$1,580	$1,280	$1,045	$815	$2,899

Add $270 for .30-378 Wby. Mag. or .338-378 Wby. Mag. cals.
Add $499 for desert camo stock and titanium nitride coating.

TRR CUSTOM MAGNUM – .300 Win. Mag., .300 Wby. Mag., .30-378 Wby. Mag., .338 Lapua Mag. (new 2012), or .338-378 Wby. Mag. cals., 26 (disc. 2013) or 28 in. barrel with Accubrake, fully adj. black tactical stock, adj. trigger, w/o sights, approx. 9 lbs. New 2011.

MSR	100%	98%	95%	90%	80%	70%	60%	
MSR $2,800	$2,375	$2,000	$1,700	$1,475	$1,275	$1,100	$900	

Add $200 for .30-378 Wby. Mag., .338 Lapua Mag. (new 2012) or .338-378 Wby. Mag. with 28 in. barrel and Accubrake.

RIFLES: BOLT ACTION, VANGUARD SERIES I

The Vanguard Series 1 rifles were discontinued in 2011. All guns were shipped with a factory three shot target, guaranteeing 1.5 in. accuracy at 100 yards.

VANGUARD SUB-MOA – same cals. as Vanguard Synthetic, matte finished steel or stainless steel action and 24 in. barrel, choice of light tan or charcoal Monte Carlo Fiberguard stock with Pachmayr Decelerator pad, no sights, guaranteed to shoot a three shot .99 in. group at 100 yards, 3 or 5 shot mag., 7 3/4 lbs. Mfg. 2005-2011.

	100%	98%	95%	90%	80%	70%	60%	Last MSR
	$865	$750	$650	$580	$475	$385	$300	$1,019

Add $31 for WSM cals.
Add $150 for stainless steel action/barrel (disc. 2009).

* **Vanguard Sub-MOA TR** – .223 Rem. or .308 Win. cal., 22 in. contoured barrel with recessed target crown, 5 shot mag., laminated Monte Carlo composite stock with beavertail forearm and Pachmayr Decelerator pad, three swivel studs, adj. trigger, guaranteed to shoot 3-shoot group of .99 in. or less with factory or premium ammo, 8 3/4 lbs. Mfg. 2010-2011.

	100%	98%	95%	90%	80%	70%	60%	Last MSR
	$875	$750	$640	$580	$470	$385	$300	$1,016

MSR	100%	98%	95%	90%	80%	70%	60%	Last MSR

* Vanguard Sub-MOA TRR Package – .300 Win. Mag., .300 Wby. Mag., .30-378 Wby. Mag., or .338-378 Wby. Mag. cal., 28 in. barrel with Accubrake, adj. trigger, laminated stock with T-6 aluminum bedding system with three position buttstock, includes Leupold 4.5-14x50 LRT M1 scope, Talley ring rail, bipod, and hard case. Mfg. 2010 only.

| | $3,350 | $2,975 | $2,550 | $2,200 | $1,875 | $1,550 | $1,300 | $3,999 |

VANGUARD SUB-MOA VARMINT – .204 Ruger (mfg. 2007-2010), .22-250 Rem., .223 Rem., or .308 Win. cal., features hand laminated composite stock with oversized vented forend and CNC machined aluminum bedding plate, Pachmayr decelerator pad, three sling swivels, 22 in. barrel, 5 shot mag., 8 1/4 lbs. Mfg. 2006-2011.

| | $925 | $800 | $700 | $600 | $500 | $425 | $375 | $1,101 |

Add $59 for .204 Ruger cal. (disc. 2010).

RIFLES: BOLT ACTION, VANGUARD SERIES 2

Weatherby discontinued its Vanguard Series 1 in 2011, and released the Vanguard Series 2 in 2012. Differences on the Series 2 include a creep-free, match quality, two-stage trigger, 3-position safety, and Griptonite synthetic stock with special inserts and palm swell (select models). All Series 2 Vanguards come with a Sub-MOA accuracy guarantee.

VANGUARD SERIES 2 TRR RC – .223 Rem. or .308 Win. cal., 22 in. barrel with recessed target crown, hand laminated Monte Carlo composite stock with aluminum bedding plate, beavertail forend, Pachmayr Decelerator recoil pad, includes factory-shot target certified and signed by Ed Weatherby and special RC engraved floorplate, 8 3/4 lbs. New 2012.

| MSR $1,199 | $1,025 | $875 | $750 | $625 | $525 | $425 | $350 | |

SHOTGUNS: SEMI-AUTO

Beginning 2008, all semi-autos are manufactured in Turkey. Previous manufacture was by ITI of Italy until 2007, and utilized the IMC choke system (integral multi-choke), which allows interchangeability with Briley choke tubes.

Add $359 for interchangeable SAS rifled 22 in. slug barrel (mfg. 2004-2007).

SA-459 TR – 12 or 20 ga., 3 in. chamber, 18 1/2 in. ported barrel, 5 shot mag., tactical configuration with black synthetic pistol grip stock and forearm, includes ghost ring rear sight on Picatinny receiver rail, M-16 front sight, oversized bolt handle, approx. 7 lbs. New 2011.

| MSR $699 | $625 | $550 | $495 | $425 | $350 | $295 | $250 | |

SHOTGUNS: SLIDE ACTION

PA-08 KNOXX HD – 12 ga., 3 in. chamber, 18 in. barrel with fixed IC choke, features black synthetic Knoxx SpecOps adj. stock with pistol grip, extended mag. (5 shot capacity), 7 lbs., mfg. in Turkey. Mfg. 2008.

| | $425 | $370 | $320 | $290 | $235 | $190 | $150 | $499 |

PA-08 TR – 12 or 20 (new 2013) ga., 3 in. chamber, 19 in. barrel with fixed cylinder choke and bladed white dot front sight, matte black finish, black synthetic stock and forearm, crossbolt trigger guard safety, 5 shot mag., dual action slide bars, 6 3/4 lbs. New 2011.

| MSR $399 | $350 | $310 | $270 | $240 | $210 | $180 | $160 | |

Add $20 for TR accessory rail that attaches to screw-on magazine end cap.

PA-459 HOME DEFENSE – 12 ga. only, 3 in. chamber, 19 in. barrel, black synthetic stock and forearm. Mfg. 2010 only.

| | $350 | $305 | $265 | $240 | $195 | $160 | $125 | $469 |

PA-459 TR – 12 or 20 (new 2013) ga. only, 3 in. chamber, 19 in. ported removeable cylinder choke tube, M-16 style fiber optic front sight, black synthetic grooved pistol grip stock and forearm, alloy receiver with integral Picatinny rail and adj. ghost ring sight, 13 1/2 in. LOP, 5 shot mag., matte black metalwork, 6 1/2 lbs. New 2011.

| MSR $499 | $425 | $375 | $335 | $295 | $265 | $235 | $210 | |

* PA-459 Digital TR – 12 ga. only, otherwise similar to PA-459 TR, except has green/tan digital camo pattern on stock (not pistol grip) and forearm. New 2011.

| MSR $549 | $450 | $395 | $350 | $295 | $265 | $235 | $210 | |

WEAVER ARMS CORPORATION

Previous manufacturer located in Escondido, CA circa 1984-1990.

CARBINES

NIGHTHAWK CARBINE – 9mm Para. cal., semi-auto design carbine, fires from closed bolt, 16.1 in. barrel, retractable shoulder stock, 25, 32, 40, or 50 shot mag. (interchangeable with Uzi), ambidextrous safety, parkerized finish, 6 1/2 lbs. Mfg. 1987-90.

| | $675 | $600 | $525 | $450 | $375 | $325 | $300 | $575 |

MSR	100%	98%	95%	90%	80%	70%	60%	Last MSR

PISTOLS: SEMI-AUTO

NIGHTHAWK PISTOL – 9mm Para. cal., closed bolt semi-auto, 10 or 12 in. barrel, alloy upper receiver, ambidextrous safety, black finish, 5 lbs. Mfg. 1987-90.

	100%	98%	95%	90%	80%	70%	60%	Last MSR
	$800	$700	$625	$550	$475	$425	$350	$475

WEBLEY & SCOTT AG (LIMITED)

Current trademark of firearms manufactured in Turkey and airguns manufactured in England with headquarters located in Luzern, Switzerland beginning 2010. Currently imported beginning mid-2013 by Centurion International, located in Reno, NV. Previously imported mid-2011-mid-2013 by Webley & Scott USA, located in Reno, NV. Previously located in West Midlands, England, with history dating back to 1790, and Birmingham, England. SxS shotguns were previously imported and distributed late 2007-2008 by Legacy Sports International, located in Reno, NV.

Webley & Scott is one the oldest names in the UK gun industry, being able to trace its origins back to 1790 when William Davies started making bullet moulds in his small factory in Birmingham, England. In this early period Birmingham flourished as the greatest manufacturing centre of firearms in the world. Yet the only official proof house was in London, then in 1813 the world famous Birmingham Proof House was established by an Act of Parliament.

For more information and current pricing on both new and used Webley & Scott airguns, please refer to the *Blue Book of Airguns* by Dr. Robert Beeman & John Allen (also online).

SHOTGUNS: CURRENT MFG.

Currently, Webley & Scott has a line of private label shotguns manufactured for them in Turkey by Komando Av Sa. Tic. Ltd. Sti.

MODEL 600 DELUXE TACTICAL SLIDE ACTION – 12 ga., 3 in. chamber, 20 in. chrome lined barrel, matte blue receiver, 5 shot, black polymer tactical stock with pistol grip and extra ammo storage, fiber optic bridge, heat shield, top Picatinny rail, spring loaded extended forend, swivel studs, rubber recoil pad, 6.6 lbs.

MSR $450	100%	98%	95%	90%	80%	70%	60%
	$375	$275	$250	$200	$175	$150	$125

MODEL 612P20T TACTICAL SLIDE ACTION – 12 ga., 3 in. chamber, 20 in. chrome lined barrel, matte blue receiver, 5 shot, black polymer tactical stock with pistol grip, fiber optic bridge, heat shield, top Picatinny rail, spring loaded extended forend, swivel studs, rubber recoil pad, 6.6 lbs.

MSR $400	100%	98%	95%	90%	80%	70%	60%
	$340	$300	$250	$225	$185	$150	$125

WESSON FIREARMS CO. INC.

Previous manufacturer located in Palmer, MA 1992-95. Previously located in Monson, MA until 1992. In late 1990, ownership of Dan Wesson Arms changed (within the family), and the new company was renamed Wesson Firearms Co., Inc.

REVOLVERS: DOUBLE ACTION

As a guideline, the following information is provided on Wesson Firearms frames. The smallest frames are Models 738P and 38P. Small frame models include 22, 722, 22M, 722M, 32, 732, 322, 7322, 8-2, 708, 9-2, 709, 14-2, 714, 15-2, and 715-2. Large frames include 41, 741, 44, 744, 45, and 745. SuperMag frame models include 40, 740, 375 (disc.), 414 (new 1995), 7414 (new 1995), 445, and 7445. Small frames are sideplate design, while large frames are solid frame construction. Dan Wesson revolvers were mfg. with solid rib barrels as standard equipment.

MODEL 11 – .357 Mag. cal., 6 shot, 2 1/2, 4, or 6 in. interchangeable barrels, fixed sights, blue, interchangeable grips, exposed barrel nut. Mfg. 1970-71 only.

	100%	98%	95%	90%	80%	70%	60%
	$450	$395	$340	$305	$250	$205	$160

Add $60 per extra barrel.

MODEL 12 – similar to Model 11, with adj. sights. Mfg. 1970-71 only.

	100%	98%	95%	90%	80%	70%	60%
	$500	$440	$375	$340	$275	$225	$175

MODEL 14 (1970s Mfg.) – similar to Model 11, with recessed barrel nut. Mfg. 1971-75.

	100%	98%	95%	90%	80%	70%	60%
	$500	$440	$375	$340	$275	$225	$175

MODEL 15 (1970s Mfg.) – similar to Model 14, with adj. sights. Mfg. 1971-75.

	100%	98%	95%	90%	80%	70%	60%
	$500	$440	$375	$340	$275	$225	$175

MODEL 9 (1970s Mfg.) – similar to Model 15, except .38 Spl. cal. Mfg. 1971-75.

	100%	98%	95%	90%	80%	70%	60%
	$450	$395	$340	$305	$250	$205	$160

MODEL 38P – .38+P cal., 5 shot, 6 1/2 in. barrel, fixed sights, wood or rubber grips, 24.6 oz. Mfg. 1992-93.

	100%	98%	95%	90%	80%	70%	60%	Last MSR
	$450	$395	$340	$305	$250	$205	$160	$285

MODEL 14 – .357 Mag. cal., 2 1/2, 4, 6, or 8 (disc. 1994) in. interchangeable barrels, fixed sights, blue. Mfg. 1975-95.

	100%	98%	95%	90%	80%	70%	60%	Last MSR
	$450	$395	$340	$305	$250	$205	$160	$274

Add approx. $7 for each additional barrel length.

MSR	100%	98%	95%	90%	80%	70%	60%	Last MSR

MODEL 8 – similar to Model 14, except .38 Spl. cal. Disc. 1995.

	$450	$395	$340	$305	$250	$205	$160	$274

Add approx. $6 for each additional barrel length.

MODEL 15 – similar to Model 14, except adj. sights, available with 2, 4, 6, 8, 10, 12, or 15 in. barrels. Disc. 1995.

MODEL 15 GOLD SERIES – .357 Mag. cal., 6 or 8 in. VR heavy slotted barrel, "Gold" stamped shroud with Dan Wesson signature, smoother action (8 lb. double action pull), 18kt. gold-plated trigger, white triangle rear sight with orange-dot Patridge front sight, exotic hardwood grips. Mfg. 1989-94.

	$650	$570	$490	$440	$360	$295	$230	$544

MODEL 9 – similar to Model 15, except .38 Spl. cal. Use same add-ons as in Model 15. Disc. 1995.

	$550	$480	$415	$375	$305	$250	$195	$346

This model was also available in a Pistol Pac - same specifications and values as the Model 15 Pistol Pac.

MODEL 41 – .41 Mag. cal., double action, 6 shot, 4, 6, 8, or 10 in. barrel VR. Disc. 1995.

	$650	$570	$490	$440	$360	$295	$230	$447

Add approx. $20 for heavy barrel shroud, approx. $15 for each additional barrel length.

MODEL 45 – .45 LC cal., 4, 6, 8, or 10 in. VR barrel, same frame as Model 44V, blue finish. Mfg. 1988-95.

	$550	$480	$415	$375	$305	$250	$195	$447

Add $20 for VR heavy barrel shroud, approx. $15 for each additional barrel length.

MODEL 45 PIN GUN – .45 ACP cal., competition pin gun model with 5 in. vent. or heavy vent. barrel configuration, blue steel, two stage Taylor forcing cone, 54 oz. Mfg. 1993-95.

	$650	$570	$490	$440	$360	$295	$230	$654

Add $9 for VR heavy shroud barrel.

REVOLVERS: STAINLESS STEEL

Models 722, 722M, 709, 715, 732, 7322, 741V, 744V, and 745V were available in a pistol pack including 2 1/2, 4, 6, and 8 in. solid rib barrel assemblies, extra grip, 4 additional sight blades, and fitted carrying case. Last published retail prices were $712 and $785 for the standard and stainless steel models, respectively. VR or full shroud barrels were optional and were approx. priced $103 and $210, respectively.

MODEL 708 – .38 Spl. cal., similar to Model 8. Add approx. $6 for each additional barrel length. Disc. 1995.

	$450	$395	$340	$305	$250	$205	$160	$319

* **Model 708 Action Cup/PPC** – .38 Spl. cal., extra heavy shrouded 6 in. bull barrel with removable underweight, Hogue Gripper grips, mounted Tasco Pro Point II on Action Cup, Aristocrat sights on PPC. Mfg. 1992 only.

	$750	$655	$565	$510	$415	$340	$265	$857

Add $56 for Action Cup Model with Tasco Scope.

MODEL 709 – .38 Spl. cal., target revolver, adj. sights. Also available in special order 10, 12 (disc.), or 15 (disc.) in. barrel lengths. Disc. 1995.

	$450	$395	$340	$305	$250	$205	$160	$376

Add approx. $10 for each additional longer barrel length, approx. $19 for VR, approx. $56 for heavy VR.

MODEL 714 (INTERCHANGEABLE OR FIXED) – .357 Mag. cal., fixed sight Service Model with 2 1/2, 4, or 6 in. barrel, brushed stainless steel. Mfg. 1993-95.

	$450	$395	$340	$305	$250	$205	$160	$319

Add approx. $6 for 4 or 6 in. barrel.
Subtract $6 for fixed barrel (2 1/2 or 4 in. barrel only).

* **Model 714 Action Cup/PPC** – .357 Mag. cal., extra heavy shrouded 6 in. bull barrel with removable underweight, Hogue Gripper grips, mounted Tasco Pro Point II on Action Cup, Aristocrat sights on PPC. Mfg. 1992 only.

	$750	$655	$565	$510	$415	$340	$265	$857

Add $56 for Action Cup Model with Tasco Scope.

MODEL 715 INTERCHANGEABLE – .357 Mag. cal., 2 1/2, 4, 6, 8, or 10 in. barrel with adj. rear sight, brushed stainless steel. Mfg. 1993-95.

	$450	$395	$340	$305	$250	$205	$160	$376

Add approx. $10 for each additional longer barrel length, approx. $19 for VR, approx. $56 for heavy VR.

* **Model 715 Fixed Target** – .357 Mag. cal., 3, 4, 5, or 6 in. fixed barrel, adj. rear sight. Mfg. 1993-95.

	$450	$395	$340	$305	$250	$205	$160	$345

Add approx. $70 for compensated barrel (4, 5, or 6 in. - new 1994).

MSR	100%	98%	95%	90%	80%	70%	60%	Last MSR

MODEL 732 – .32 H&R Mag. cal., similar to Model 32, except is stainless steel. Mfg. 1986-95.

| | $550 | $480 | $415 | $375 | $305 | $250 | $195 | *$400* |

Add $22 for VR barrel shroud (Model 732-V), $53 for VR heavy barrel shroud (Model 732-VH), approx. $9 for each additional barrel length over 2 1/2 in.

MODEL 738P – .38 +P cal., 5 shot, 6 1/2 in. barrel, fixed sights, wood or rubber grips, 24.6 oz. Mfg. 1992-95.

| | $450 | $395 | $340 | $305 | $250 | $205 | $160 | *$340* |

MODEL 741V – .41 Mag. cal., similar to Model 41V. Disc. 1995.

| | $650 | $570 | $490 | $440 | $360 | $295 | $230 | *$524* |

Add approx. $20 for heavy VR, approx. $13 for each barrel length over 4 in.

MODEL 744V – .44 Mag. cal., similar to Model 44V. Disc. 1995. - limited mfg.

| | $650 | $570 | $490 | $440 | $360 | $295 | $230 | *$524* |

Add approx. $20 for heavy VR, $13 for each barrel length over 4 in.

* Model 744V Target Fixed Barrel – .44 Mag. cal., 4, 5, 6, or 8 in. barrel, brushed stainless steel. Mfg. 1994-95.

| | $600 | $525 | $450 | $410 | $330 | $270 | $210 | *$493* |

Add approx. $4 for each barrel length over 3 in.

MODEL 745V – .45 LC cal., similar to Model 45, except in stainless steel. Disc. 1995.

| | $650 | $570 | $490 | $440 | $360 | $295 | $230 | *$524* |

Add $20 for heavy full shroud VR barrels, $13 for each additional barrel length.

MODEL .45 PIN GUN – .45 ACP cal., similar to Model 45 Pin Gun, except is stainless steel. Mfg. 1993-95.

| | $650 | $570 | $490 | $440 | $360 | $295 | $230 | *$713* |

Add $49 for VR heavy rib shroud.

SUPER RAM SILHOUETTE – .357 Max., .414 Super Mag., or .44 Mag. cal., silhouette variation featuring modified Iron Sight Gun Works rear sight, Allen Taylor throated barrel, factory trigger job, 4 lbs. Mfg. 1995 only.

| | $850 | $745 | $640 | $580 | $470 | $385 | $300 | *$807* |

Add $43 for .414 Super Mag. cal.

HUNTER SERIES – .357 Super Mag., .41 Mag., .44 Mag., or .445 Super Mag. cal., 7 1/2 in. barrel with heavy shroud, Hogue rubber finger grooved and wood presentation grips, choice of Gunworks iron sights or w/o sights with Burris base and rings, non-fluted cylinder, with or w/o compensator, approx. 4 lbs. Mfg. 1994-95.

| | $850 | $745 | $640 | $580 | $470 | $385 | $300 | *$849* |

Add $32 for compensated barrel.
Add $32 for scope mounts (w/o sights).

WILD WEST GUNS

Current custom gunsmith and manufacturer established in 1992 and located in Anchorage, AK and in Las Vegas, NV beginning 2013. Dealer and consumer direct sales.

Wild West Guns offers firearms engraving by Guild Engraver Jim White. Please contact the company directly for a price quotation.

RIFLES: LEVER ACTION

RIFLE – various cals., big loop lever, bear proof ejector, ghost ring rear sight, fiber optic front sight with cut hood, straight grip walnut stock, hand fitted max recoil pad, stainless steel. New 2013.

| MSR $1,899 | $1,700 | $1,500 | $1,300 | $1,075 | $950 | $800 | $675 | |

WILDEY, INC.

Previous manufacturer located in Warren, CT 2000-circa 2011. Previously located in New Milford, CT until 1999.

Originally, the company was named Wildey Firearms Co., Inc. located in Cheshire, CT. At that time, serialization of pistols was 45-0000. When Wildey, Inc. bought the company out of bankruptcy from the old shareholders, there had been approximately 800 pistols mfg. To distinguish the old company from the present company, the serial range was changed to 09-0000 (only 633 pistols with the 09 prefix were produced). These guns had the Cheshire, CT address. Pistols produced by Wildey, Inc., New Milford, CT are serial numbered with 4 digits (no numerical prefix).

CARBINES: SEMI-AUTO

WILDEY CARBINE – .44 Auto Mag., .45 Wildey Mag., .45 Win. Mag., or .475 Wildey Mag. cal., features 18 in. barrel with forearm and detachable skeleton walnut stock, polished or matte stainless steel. Mfg. 2003-2011.

| | $2,700 | $2,225 | $1,750 | $1,500 | $1,235 | $1,030 | $855 | *$3,110* |

Add $237 for matte stainless steel finish.

MSR	100%	98%	95%	90%	80%	70%	60%	Last MSR

PISTOLS: SEMI-AUTO

Add $585-$1,950 per interchangeable barrel assembly, depending on barrel length and finish.

WILDEY AUTO PISTOL – .45 Win. Mag., .45 Wildey Mag., or .475 Wildey Mag., gas operated, 5, 6, 7, 8, 10, or 14 in. VR barrel, SA, selective single shot or semi-auto, 3 lug rotary bolt, fixed barrel (interchangeable), polished stainless steel construction, 7 shot, double action, adj. sights, smooth or checkered wood grips, designed to fire proprietary new cartridges specifically for this gun including the .45 Win. Mag. cal., 64 oz. with 5 in. barrel.
Add $560-$1,148 per interchangeable barrel.

* ***Wildey Survivor Model*** – .357 Mag., .44 Auto Mag. (new 2003), .45 Win. Mag., 45 Wildey Mag., or .475 Wildey Mag. cal., 5, 6, 7, 8, 10, 12, 14 (new 2000), or 18 (new 2003) in. VR barrel, polished stainless steel finish. Mfg. 1990-2011.

	$1,375	$1,025	$800	$665	$560	$465	$410	$1,571

Add $26 - $125 for 5 in. - 12 in. barrel, depending on length, and $1,206 for 18 in. silhouette model.
Add $26 for .45 Wildey Mag. or .475 Wildey Mag. cal.

The .475 Wildey cal. is derived from a factory cartridge.

* ***Wildey Survivor Guardsman*** – similar to Survivor Model, except has squared-off trigger guard, same options apply to this model as for the Survivor model. Mfg. 1990-2011.

	$1,375	$1,025	$800	$665	$560	$465	$410	$1,571

* ***Wildey Hunter Guardsman*** – similar to Hunter Model, except has squared-off trigger guard, same options apply to this model as for the Hunter model. Mfg. 1990-2011.

	$1,575	$1,225	$950	$810	$670	$565	$475	$1,829

Add $100 for 12 in. barrel.
Add $625 for 14 in. barrel.
Add $1,175 for 18 in. silhouette barrel.

WILDEY AUTO PISTOL OLDER MFG. – .475 Wildey Mag. cal. was available in 8 or 10 in. barrel only.

* ***Older Wildey Serial Nos. 1-200.***

	$1,900	$1,700	$1,550	$1,365	$1,125	$950	$775	$2,180

Add $20 for 8 or 10 in. barrel.

* ***Older Wildey Serial Nos. 201-400.***

	$1,750	$1,550	$1,400	$1,235	$1,000	$870	$700	$1,980

Add $20 for 8 or 10 in. barrel.

* ***Older Wildey Serial Nos. 401-600.***

	$1,650	$1,375	$1,250	$1,100	$895	$785	$630	$1,780

Add $20 for 8 or 10 in. barrel.

* ***Older Wildey Serial Nos. 601-800.***

	$1,450	$1,200	$1,000	$885	$715	$610	$515	$1,580

Add $20 for 8 or 10 in. barrel.

* ***Older Wildey Serial Nos. 801-1,000.***

	$1,100	$925	$800	$695	$585	$485	$415	$1,275

Add $25 for 8 or 10 in. barrel.

* ***Older Wildey Serial Nos. 1,001-2,489.***

	$1,025	$850	$750	$640	$535	$450	$390	$1,175

Add $20 for 8 or 10 in. barrel.

WILKINSON ARMS

Previous trademark established circa 1996 and manufactured by Ray Wilkinson circa 1996-1998 (limited production), and by Northwest Arms located in Parma, ID circa 2000-2005.

CARBINES

LINDA CARBINE – 9mm Para. cal., 16 3/16 in. barrel, aluminum receiver, pre-ban configuration (limited supplies), fixed tubular stock with wood pad, vent. barrel shroud, aperture rear sight, small wooden forearm, 18 or 31 shot mag., beginning 2002, this model came standard with many accessories, 7 lbs. Mfg. circa 1996-2005.

	$1,295	$1,075	$850	$725	$600	$500	$425	$1,800

Only 2,200 Linda Carbines were marked "Luger Carbine" on the receiver. The last 1,500 distributed by Northwest Arms include a longer stock, and matched bolt and barrel (Rockwell 57).

MSR	100%	98%	95%	90%	80%	70%	60%	*Last MSR*

TERRY CARBINE – 9mm Para. cal., blowback semi-auto action, 31 shot mag., 16 3/16 in. barrel, closed breech, adj. sights, 7 lbs. Disc.

With black P.V.C. stock	$475	$395	$325	$295	$260	$230	$200	
With maple stock	$625	$525	$400	$350	$340	$325	$300	

WILSON COMBAT

Current firearms manufacturer, customizer, and supplier of custom firearms parts and accessories established in 1978, and located in Berryville, AR.

PISTOLS: SEMI-AUTO, SINGLE ACTION

Prices reflect .45 ACP cal. base model w/o upgrades. A wide variety of options are available - contact the company directly for pricing. Add $110 for 9mm Para, .38 Super, or .40 S&W cal. or $225 for 10mm cal. on most models.

CONTEMPORARY CLASSIC CENTENNIAL – .45 ACP cal., 100th anniversary of the 1911, full size carbon steel frame and slide, 5 in. carbon match grade barrel and bushing, 8 shot mag., Turnbull charcoal blue finish, French walnut double diamond grips, beavertail grip safety, contoured mag well, lanyard loop mainspring housing, 30 LPI high cut checkered front gripstrap, "1911-2011" engraving, battlesight with gold bead front sight, tactical thumb safety, top and rear slide serrations, special serial numbers (JMB001-JMB100) includes walnut presentation box, 45 oz. Limited edition of 100 mfg. during 2011.

	100%	98%	95%	90%	80%	70%	60%	*Last MSR*
	$3,550	$3,150	$2,725	$2,350	$1,950	$1,650	$1,350	*$3,995*

CLASSIC SUPERGRADE – 9mm Para., 10mm, .38 Super, .40 S&W, or .45 ACP cal., full size stainless steel frame, 5 in. stainless match grade barrel and bushing, carbon steel slide, blue finish, 30 LPI high cut checkered front strap, top and rear slide serrations, Lo-Mount adj. rear sight, improved ramp front sight, ambidextrous safety, Speed-Chute mag well, cocobolo double diamond grips, beavertail grip safety, full length guide rod, each gun hand built. Limited mfg.

MSR $5,195	$4,675	$4,225	$3,750	$3,150	$2,650	$2,200	$1,700	

TACTICAL SUPERGRADE – 9mm Para., 10mm (disc. 2011), .38 Super, .40 S&W (disc. 2011), or .45 ACP cal., full size stainless steel frame, 5 in. stainless match grade barrel and bushing, carbon steel slide, blue finish, 30 LPI high cut checkered front strap, top and rear slide serrations, ambidextrous safety, Speed-Chute mag well, G10 starburst grips, beavertail grip safety, battlesight with white outline tritium front sight.

MSR $5,045	$4,550	$4,125	$3,700	$3,100	$2,600	$2,100	$1,650	

Add $105 for .38 Super or 9mm Para. cal.

* ***Tactical Supergrade Professional*** – 9mm Para., .38 Super, or .45 ACP cal., carbon steel frame, 4 in. stainless match grade cone barrel, carbon steel slide, 8 shot mag., blue finish, 30 LPI high cut checkered front strap, top and rear slide serrations, ambidextrous thumb safety, Speed-Chute mag well, G10 starburst grips, beavertail grip safety, battlesight with white outline tritium front sight, full length guide rod and reverse plug, 44.8 oz. New 2010.

MSR $5,045	$4,550	$4,125	$3,700	$3,100	$2,600	$2,100	$1,650	

Add $105 for .38 Super or 9mm Para. cal.

* ***Tactical Supergrade Compact*** – 9mm Para., .38 Super, or .45 ACP cal., compact carbon steel frame, 4 in. stainless match grade cone barrel, carbon steel slide, blue finish, 30 LPI high cut checkered front strap, top and rear slide serrations, ambidextrous thumb safety, Speed-Chute mag well, G10 starburst grips, beavertail grip safety, battlesight with white outline tritium front sight, full length guide rod and reverse plug.

MSR $5,045	$4,550	$4,125	$3,700	$3,100	$2,600	$2,100	$1,650	

ULTRALIGHT CARRY – 9mm Para., .38 Super, or .45 ACP cal., full size aluminum round butt frame, 5 in. stainless match grade barrel and bushing, flush cut and crowned, carbon steel slide, blue finish, 30 LPI high cut checkered front strap, top and rear slide serrations, tactical thumb safety, contoured mag well, G10 starburst grips, beavertail grip safety and hammer, battlesight with fiber optic front sight, countersunk slide stop.

MSR $3,650	$3,350	$2,950	$2,550	$2,150	$1,825	$1,525	$1,225	

* ***Ultralight Carry Compact*** – 9mm Para., .38 Super, or .45 ACP cal., similar to Ultralight Carry, except has compact frame and 4 in. fluted barrel.

MSR $3,650	$3,350	$2,950	$2,550	$2,150	$1,825	$1,525	$1,225	

* ***Ultralight Carry Sentinel*** – 9mm Para. cal., Sentinel aluminum round butt frame, 3 1/2 in. stainless match grade cone fluted barrel, 8 shot mag., carbon steel slide, blue finish, 30 LPI high cut checkered front strap, top and rear slide serrations, tactical thumb safety, contoured mag well, G10 starburst grips, beavertail grip safety and hammer, battlesight with fiber optic front sight, shortened rounded mag. release, countersunk slide stop, approx. 31 oz.

MSR $3,875	$3,500	$3,100	$2,650	$2,225	$1,875	$1,575	$1,275	

MSR	100%	98%	95%	90%	80%	70%	60%	Last MSR

CARRY COMP COMPACT – 9mm Para. (disc. 2011), .38 Super, or .45 ACP cal., full size stainless steel, lightweight aluminum, or carbon steel frame, 4 1/2 in. compensated match grade barrel, green, black, tan, or grey Amor-Tuff finish, high ride beavertail grip safety, Diamondwood grips, combat tactical sight system 30 LPI front strap checkering, skeletonized ultra light hammer.

MSR $3,765	$3,425	$3,025	$2,600	$2,175	$1,850	$1,550	$1,250	

Add $165 for Carry Comp Compact Lightweight (disc. 2012).

* **Carry Comp Professional** – 9mm Para. (disc. 2011), .38 Super, or .45 ACP cal., similar to Carry Comp, except has compact frame that is 1/2 in. shorter. Disc. 2012.

	$3,425	$3,025	$2,600	$2,175	$1,850	$1,550	$1,250	$3,765

Add $165 for Carry Comp Professional Lightweight.

X-TAC – .45 ACP cal., full size carbon steel frame, 8 shot mag., 5 in. stainless match grade barrel and bushing, carbon steel slide, parkerized finish, X-Tac front strap/mainspring housing, X-Tac rear cocking serrations, tactical thumb safety, contoured mag well, G10 starburst grips, beavertail grip safety, battlesight with fiber optic front sight, 46.2 oz.

MSR $2,760	$2,495	$2,100	$1,800	$1,550	$1,225	$1,050	$925	

Add $25 for X-Tac Compact with smaller frame.

CQB – 9mm Para., .38 Super, .40 S&W (new 2012), 10mm (new 2012), or .45 ACP cal., full size aluminum round butt frame, 5 in. stainless match grade barrel and bushing, flush cut and crowned, carbon steel slide, blue finish, 30 LPI high cut checkered front strap, top and rear slide serrations, tactical thumb safety, contoured mag well, G10 starburst grips, beavertail grip safety and hammer, battlesight with fiber optic front sight, countersunk slide stop.

MSR $2,865	$2,575	$2,150	$1,825	$1,550	$1,225	$1,050	$925	

* **CQB Elite** – 9mm Para., 10mm, .38 Super, .40 S&W, or .45 ACP cal., full size carbon steel frame, 5 in. stainless match grade barrel and bushing, carbon steel slide, blue finish, 30 LPI high cut checkered front strap, top and rear slide serrations, tactical thumb safety, Speed-Chute mag well with lanyard loop, G10 diagonal flat bottom grips, beavertail grip safety, battlesight with fiber optic front sight.

MSR $3,425	$3,100	$2,700	$2,400	$2,000	$1,700	$1,400	$1,150	

* **CQB Tactical LE Light-Rail** – 9mm Para., 10mm, .38 Super, .40 S&W, or .45 ACP cal., full size carbon steel frame, 5 in. stainless match grade bull barrel, carbon steel slide, blue finish, integral light rail, 30 LPI high cut checkered front strap, top and rear slide serrations, tactical thumb safety, Speed-Chute mag well with lanyard loop, G10 diagonal flat bottom grips, beavertail grip safety, battlesight with fiber optic front sight.

MSR $3,115	$2,700	$2,300	$2,000	$1,750	$1,450	$1,200	$1,050	

* **CQB Light-Rail** – 9mm Para., 10mm, .38 Super, .40 S&W, or .45 ACP cal., full size aluminum frame, 5 in. stainless match grade barrel and bushing, carbon steel slide, blue finish, integral light rail, 30 LPI high cut checkered front strap, top and rear slide serrations, tactical thumb safety, contoured mag well, G10 starburst grips, beavertail grip safety, battlesight with fiber optic front sight. Disc. 2012.

	$2,625	$2,225	$1,950	$1,700	$1,400	$1,175	$1,025	$3,005

* **CQB Lightweight/Light-Rail Lightweight** – 9mm Para., 10mm, .38 Super, .40 S&W, or .45 ACP cal., full size aluminum frame, 5 in. stainless match grade barrel and bushing, carbon steel slide, blue finish, with or w/o integral light rail, 30 LPI high cut checkered front strap, top and rear slide serrations, tactical thumb safety, contoured mag well, G10 starburst grips, beavertail grip safety, battlesight with fiber optic front sight, weighs 14% less than steel model.

MSR $3,030	$2,650	$2,225	$1,950	$1,700	$1,400	$1,175	$1,125	

Add $115 for light rail.

» **CQB Light-Rail Lightweight Professional** – 9mm Para., .38 Super or .45 ACP cal., similar to CQB Light-Rail Lightweight, except has professional size aluminum frame and 4 in. stainless match grade cone barrel.

MSR $3,205	$2,775	$2,350	$2,025	$1,775	$1,475	$1,225	$1,075	

» **CQB Light-Rail Lightweight Compact** – 9mm Para., .38 Super (disc. 2011) or .45 ACP cal., compact aluminum round butt frame, 4 in. stainless match grade cone barrel, carbon steel slide, blue finish, integral light rail, 30 LPI high cut checkered front strap, top and rear slide serrations, tactical thumb safety, contoured mag well, G10 starburst grips, high ride beavertail grip safety, battlesight with fiber optic front sight, weighs 14% less than steel model.

MSR $3,280	$2,825	$2,375	$2,050	$1,800	$1,500	$1,200	$1,125	

* **CQB Compact** – 9mm Para., .38 Super or .45 ACP cal., compact carbon steel frame, 4 in. stainless match grade cone barrel, carbon steel slide, blue finish, 30 LPI high cut checkered front strap, top and rear slide serrations, tactical thumb safety, contoured mag well, G10 starburst grips, high ride beavertail grip safety, battlesight with fiber optic front sight.

MSR $2,890	$2,575	$2,150	$1,850	$1,575	$1,250	$1,075	$950	

Add $205 for CQB Compact Lightweight.

MSR	100%	98%	95%	90%	80%	70%	60%	Last MSR

PROFESSIONAL – 9mm Para., .38 Super, 40 S&W (disc. 2011), or .45 ACP cal., professional size carbon steel frame, 4 in. stainless match grade cone barrel, carbon steel slide, blue finish, 30 LPI high cut checkered front strap, top and rear slide serrations, tactical thumb safety, contoured mag well, G10 starburst grips, high ride beavertail grip safety, battlesight with fiber optic front sight.

| MSR $2,920 | $2,475 | $2,175 | $1,850 | $1,685 | $1,350 | $1,125 | $975 | |

* ***Professional Lightweight*** – 9mm Para., .38 Super or .45 ACP cal., similar to Professional, except has lightweight aluminum frame.

| MSR $3,090 | $2,625 | $2,300 | $1,975 | $1,785 | $1,450 | $1,175 | $1,000 | |

CLASSIC – 9mm Para., 10mm, .38 Super, 40 S&W, or .45 ACP cal., full size carbon steel frame, 5 in. stainless match grade barrel and bushing, carbon steel slide, two-tone finish, 30 LPI high cut checkered front strap, rear slide serrations, tactical thumb safety, contoured mag well, cocobolo double diamond grips, high ride beavertail grip safety, Lo-Mount adj. rear sight with improved ramp front sight.

| MSR $3,030 | $2,575 | $2,250 | $1,975 | $1,750 | $1,450 | $1,175 | $1,000 | |

PROTECTOR – 9mm Para., 10mm, .38 Super, 40 S&W, or .45 ACP cal., full size carbon steel frame, 5 in. stainless match grade barrel and bushing, carbon steel slide, two-tone finish, 30 LPI high cut checkered front strap, front and rear slide serrations, tactical thumb safety, contoured mag well, G10 starburst grips, high ride beavertail grip safety, battlesight with fiber optic front sight.

| MSR $2,920 | $2,475 | $2,175 | $1,850 | $1,685 | $1,350 | $1,125 | $975 | |

TACTICAL ELITE – 9mm Para., 10mm, .38 Super, 40 S&W, or .45 ACP cal., full size carbon steel frame, 5 in. stainless match grade heavy flanged cone barrel, carbon steel slide, blue finish, 30 LPI high cut checkered front strap, front and rear slide serrations, ambidextrous thumb safety, Speed-Chute mag well, G10 starburst grips, high ride beavertail grip safety, battlesight with fiber optic front sight.

| MSR $3,650 | $3,350 | $2,950 | $2,550 | $2,150 | $1,825 | $1,525 | $1,225 | |

Add $165 for Tactical Elite Lightweight.

ELITE PROFESSIONAL – 9mm Para., .38 Super or .45 ACP cal., professional size carbon steel frame, 4 in. stainless match grade heavy flanged cone barrel, carbon steel slide, blue finish, 30 LPI high cut checkered front strap, rear slide serrations, ambidextrous thumb safety, Speed-Chute mag well, G10 diagonal flat bottom grips, high ride beavertail grip safety, battlesight with fiber optic front sight.

| MSR $3,650 | $3,350 | $2,950 | $2,550 | $2,150 | $1,825 | $1,525 | $1,225 | |

Add $165 for Elite Professional Lightweight.

STEALTH (S.D.S.) – 9mm Para., .38 Super, .40 S&W (disc. 2011) or .45 ACP cal., compact carbon steel frame, 4 in. stainless match grade heavy flanged cone barrel, carbon steel slide, blue finish, 30 LPI high cut checkered front strap, rear slide serrations, ambidextrous thumb safety, contoured mag well, G10 starburst grips, high ride beavertail grip safety, battlesight with fiber optic front sight, full length guide rod with reverse plug.

| MSR $3,535 | $3,225 | $2,875 | $2,500 | $2,100 | $1,775 | $1,475 | $1,175 | |

Add $280 for Stealth Lightweight.

SENTINEL – 9mm Para. cal., carbon steel frame that is 1/2 in. shorter than compact, 3 1/2 in. stainless match grade cone barrel, 8 shot mag., carbon steel slide, blue finish, 30 LPI high cut checkered front strap, rear slide serrations, tactical thumb safety, contoured mag well, G10 slimline grips, high ride beavertail grip safety, battlesight with fiber optic front sight, full length guide rod with reverse plug, approx. 32 oz.

| MSR $3,310 | $2,850 | $2,375 | $2,050 | $1,800 | $1,500 | $1,225 | $1,125 | |

Add $115 for Sentinel Lightweight.

* ***Sentinel Compact*** – 9mm Para. cal., similar to Sentinel, except has carbon steel compact frame. Mfg. 2012.

| | $2,800 | $2,375 | $2,050 | $1,800 | $1,500 | $1,250 | $1,075 | $3,255 |

Add $170 for Sentinel Compact Lightweight.

* ***Sentinel Professional*** – 9mm Para. cal., similar to Sentinel, except has professional size carbon steel frame. Mfg. 2012.

| | $2,850 | $2,375 | $2,050 | $1,800 | $1,500 | $1,225 | $1,125 | $3,310 |

Add $115 for Sentinel Professional Lightweight.

MS. SENTINEL – 9mm Para. cal., aluminum frame that is 1/2 in. shorter than compact, 3 1/2 in. stainless match grade cone fluted barrel, 8 shot mag., carbon steel slide, blue finish, 30 LPI high cut checkered front strap, rear slide serrations, tactical thumb safety, contoured mag well, cocobolo starburst grips, concealment Bullet Proof beavertail grip safety and hammer, Bullet Proof shortened/rounded mag. release, battlesight with fiber optic front sight, countersunk slide stop, heavy machine chamfer on bottom of slide, full length guide rod with reverse plug, approx. 31 oz.

| MSR $3,875 | $3,500 | $3,100 | $2,650 | $2,225 | $1,875 | $1,575 | $1,275 | |

MSR	100%	98%	95%	90%	80%	70%	60%	Last MSR

SUPER SENTINEL – .38 Super cal., 8 shot mag., 3.6 in. match grade barrel, carbon steel slide, Sentinel aluminum frame, 30 LPI high cut checkered front strap, High Ride Bullet Proof beavertail grip safety, Bullet Proof thumb safety, contoured mag well, G10 slimline grips, fiber optic front sight, full length guide rod with reverse plug, 25.2 oz. New 2012.

| MSR $3,875 | $3,500 | $3,100 | $2,650 | $2,225 | $1,875 | $1,575 | $1,275 | |

BILL WILSON CARRY PISTOL – 45 ACP cal., compact carbon steel round butt frame, 4 in. stainless match grade cone barrel, 7 shot mag., carbon steel slide, blue finish, 30 LPI high cut checkered front strap, rear slide serrations, tactical thumb safety, contoured mag well, G10 starburst grips, high ride beavertail grip safety, battlesight with fiber optic front sight, countersunk slide stop, full length guide rod with reverse plug, approx. 39 oz.

| MSR $3,205 | $2,775 | $2,350 | $2,025 | $1,775 | $1,475 | $1,275 | $1,075 | |

SPEC-OPS 9 – 9mm Para. cal., 4 1/4 in. stainless steel match grade barrel, mid-size polymer frame with fully machined stainless steel rail insert, 16 shot mag., blue finish, 20 LPI checkered frontstap, concealment Bullet Proof beavertail grip safety and Spec-Ops ultralight hammer, tactical thumb safety, starburst grip pattern with textured grip radiuses, countersunk slide stop, contoured mag well, 30 LPI slide top serrations, Spec-Ops Lo-Profile rear sight, inline dovetail improved ramp fiber optic front sight, 37 oz.

| MSR $2,285 | $2,000 | $1,750 | $1,525 | $1,300 | $1,100 | $900 | $775 | |

HUNTER – 10mm or .460 Rowland cal., 5 1/2 single port compensated barrel with fully supported chamber, full size carbon steel frame with carbon steel slide, 30 LPI high cut checkered frontstrap, tactical thumb safety, contoured mag well, high ride beavertail grip safety, Crimson Trace laser grips, countersunk slide stop, full length guide rod with reverse plug, approx. 40 oz.

| MSR $4,100 | $3,650 | $3,150 | $2,750 | $2,350 | $1,875 | $1,550 | $1,350 | |

RIFLES

All rifles come standard with nylon tactical case.

A variety of accessories are available for additional cost - please contact the company directly for more information on available options (see Trademark Index).

UT-15 URBAN TACTICAL CARBINE – .223 Rem. cal., GIO, 16 1/4 in. fluted match grade barrel with muzzle brake, aluminum flat-top upper and lower receiver, quad rail free float aluminum handguard, black, green, tan or gray anodized finish, 20 shot mag., single stage trigger, ERGO pistol grip, six position collapsible stock, 6.9 lbs. Disc. 2011.

| | $1,825 | $1,650 | $1,450 | $1,250 | $1,050 | $875 | $675 | *$2,025* |

M4 TACTICAL CARBINE – .223 Rem. cal., GIO, 16 1/4 in. fluted match grade barrel with muzzle brake, aluminum flat-top upper and lower receiver, quad rail free float aluminum handguard, black, green, tan or gray anodized finish, 20 shot mag., single stage trigger, ERGO pistol grip, six position collapsible stock, 6.9 lbs. Disc. 2011.

| | $1,825 | $1,650 | $1,450 | $1,250 | $1,050 | $875 | $675 | *$2,000* |

SPR SPECIAL PURPOSE RIFLE – 5.56 NATO cal., GIO, 18 in. barrel, lo-profile gas block, forged flat-top upper and lower receiver, quad rail free float aluminum handguard, black, green, tan or gray anodized finish, 20 shot mag., single stage trigger, ERGO pistol grip, A2 fixed buttstock, 6.9 lbs.

| MSR $2,450 | $2,250 | $1,850 | $1,675 | $1,350 | $1,100 | $875 | $750 | |

SS-15 SUPER SNIPER RIFLE – .223 Rem./5.56 NATO (.223 Wylde chamber new 2012) cal., GIO, 20 in. fluted heavy match grade stainless steel barrel with muzzle brake, aluminum flat-top upper and lower receiver, aluminum free float handguard, black, green, tan or gray anodized finish, 20 shot mag., single stage trigger, ERGO pistol grip, fixed A2 stock, 8.7 lbs.

| MSR $2,225 | $1,995 | $1,725 | $1,550 | $1,250 | $1,050 | $850 | $750 | |

RECON TACTICAL – 5.56 NATO, .300 Blackout, 6.8SPC, or 7.62x40 WT cal., GIO, 16, 18, or 20 (7.62x40 WT cal. only) in. medium weight stainless steel barrel, lo-profile gas block, quad rail, flash hider, 15 shot mag., Magpul CTR buttstock with MOE pistol grip and tactical trigger guard, black, green, tan, or grey finish, single stage trigger, 7 1/2 lbs.

| MSR $2,300 | $2,050 | $1,750 | $1,575 | $1,275 | $1,050 | $850 | $750 | |

Add $50 for fluted barrel.
Add $300 for 6.8 SPC or 7.62x40 WT cal.

TACTICAL LIGHTWEIGHT – 5.56 NATO, 6.8 SPCII, or 7.62x40 WT cal., GIO, 16.2, 18 (7.62x40 WT cal. only), or 20 (7.62x40 WT cal. only) in. match grade barrel, lo-profile gas block, Picatinny rail, ERGO pistol grip, tactical trigger guard, two-stage trigger, black Armor-Tuff finish, 20 shot mag., adj. black synthetic Rogers/Wilson Super-Stoc buttstock. New 2012.

| MSR $2,250 | $2,025 | $1,750 | $1,550 | $1,250 | $1,050 | $850 | $750 | |

Add $300 for 6.8 SPCII cal.

SHOTGUNS

Please refer to Scattergun Technologies for complete listing of shotguns and accessories.

MSR	100%	98%	95%	90%	80%	70%	60%	Last MSR

WINCHESTER

Current trademark established in 1866 in New Haven, CT. Currently manufactured by Miroku of Japan since circa 1992, Herstal, Belgium (O/U shotguns since 2004), and in Columbia, SC (Model 70 only beginning 2008). Previously manufactured in New Haven, CT, 1866-2006, and by U.S. Repeating Arms from 1981-2006 through a licensing agreement from Olin Corp. to manufacture shotguns and rifles domestically using the Winchester Trademark. Corporate offices are located in Morgan, UT. Olin Corp. previously manufactured shotguns and rifles bearing the Winchester Hallmark at the Olin Kodensha Plant (closed 1989) located in Tochigi, Japan, Cobourg, Ontario, Canada, and also in European countries. In 1992, U.S. Repeating Arms was acquired by GIAT located in France. In late 1997, the Walloon region of Belgium acquired controlling interest of both Browning and U.S. Repeating Arms.

For more information and current pricing on both new and used Winchester airguns and current black powder models, please refer to the *Blue Book of Airguns* by Dr. Robert D. Beeman & John B. Allen, and the *Blue Book of Modern Black Powder Arms* by John Allen (also online).

In addition to the models listed within this section, Winchester also offered various models/variations that were available only at the annual SHOT SHOW beginning 2004. More research is underway to identify these models, in addition to their original MSRs (if listed).

RIFLES: SEMI-AUTO

MODEL SX-AB – .308 Win. cal., 20 in. heavy barrel w/o sights, fully adj. stock with textured pistol grip and forearm, includes three interchangeable cheekpieces, 10 shot detachable mag., Picatinny bottom rail on forearm, 100% Mossy Oak Brush camo coverage, 10 lbs. Approx. 2,000 mfg. during 2009 only.

	100%	98%	95%	90%	80%	70%	60%	Last MSR
	$1,150	$1,000	$900	$800	$700	$600	$550	$1,379

RIFLES: BOLT ACTION - MODEL 70, 1964-2006 MFG.

Beginning 1994, Winchester began using the Classic nomenclature to indicate those models featuring a pre-1964 style action with controlled round feeding.

U.S. Repeating Arms closed its New Haven, CT manufacturing facility on March 31, 2006, and an auction was held on Sept. 27-28, 2006, selling the production equipment and related assets.

WSM cals. will bring an approx. 10% premium, and WSSM cals. will bring an approx. 15% premiums on most of the following models, if in 95%+ condition.

MODEL 70 STEALTH – .22-250 Rem., .223 Rem., .308 Win. cal., push-feed action, 26 in. heavy barrel w/o sights, non-glare matte metal finish, Accu-Block black synthetic stock with full length aluminum bedding block, 5 or 6 shot mag., 10 3/4 lbs. Mfg. 1999-2003.

	100%	98%	95%	90%	80%	70%	60%	Last MSR
	$850	$700	$650	$600	$550	$500	$450	$800

MODEL 70 STEALTH II – .22-250 Rem., .223 WSSM, .243 WSSM, .25 WSSM, or .308 Win. cal., push-feed action, 26 in. heavy barrel w/o sights, matte blue finish, redesigned black synthetic stock with aluminum pillar bedding, 3 or 5 shot mag., 10 lbs. Mfg. 2004-2006.

	100%	98%	95%	90%	80%	70%	60%	Last MSR
	$750	$600	$500	$425	$375	$325	$300	$886

Add 10% for WSSM cals.

RIFLES: BOLT ACTION - POST 1964 MODEL 70 CUSTOM GRADES

* **Model 70 Classic Custom Grade Sharpshooter I/II** – .22-250 Rem. (new 1993), .223 Rem. (mfg. 1993-94), .30-06, .308 Win., or .300 Win. Mag. cal., specially designed McMillan A-2 (disc. 1995) or H-S Precision heavy target stock, Schneider (disc. 1995) or H-S Precision (new 1996) 24 (.308 Win. cal. only) or 26 in. stainless steel barrel, choice of blue or grey finish starting 1996. Mfg. 1992-1998.

	100%	98%	95%	90%	80%	70%	60%	Last MSR
	$1,950	$1,500	$1,050	$900	$850	$750	$675	$1,994

Subtract $100 if without stainless barrel (pre-1995).

This model was designated the Sharpshooter II in 1996 (features H-S Precision stock and stainless steel barrel).

This model was also available in left-hand action beginning 1998 (.30-06 and .330 Win. Mag. cals. only).

* **Model 70 Classic Custom Grade Sporting Sharpshooter I/II** – .270 Win. (disc. 1994), 7mm STW, or .300 Win. Mag. cal., 1/2-minute of angle sporting version of the Custom Sharpshooter, custom shop only, Sharpshooter II became standard in 1996. Mfg. 1993-98.

	100%	98%	95%	90%	80%	70%	60%	Last MSR
	$1,875	$1,425	$1,000	$875	$825	$750	$675	$1,875

This model was also available in left-hand action in 1998.

* **Model 70 Classic Custom Grade Sporting Sharpshooter** – .220 Swift cal., 26 in. Schneider barrel, controlled round feeding, available with either McMillan A-2 or Sporting synthetic (disc. 1994) stock. Mfg. 1994-95 only.

	100%	98%	95%	90%	80%	70%	60%	Last MSR
	$1,950	$1,525	$1,200	$975	$850	$750	$650	$1,814

MSR	100%	98%	95%	90%	80%	70%	60%	Last MSR

Shotguns: Post-1964, Semi-Auto

Winchester introduced WinChokes in 1969.

* ***Super X2 2 3/4 in. Magnum Field Practical MK I*** – 12 ga., similar to Super X2 Practical MKII, except is 2 3/4 in. chamber, has regular TruGlo iron sights, and does not have Dura-Touch, cylinder bore Invector choke standard, 8 lbs. Mfg. 2003-2007.

	$960	$800	$675	$575	$500	$465	$435	$1,116

* ***Super X2 3 in. Magnum Field Practical MK II*** – 12 ga., home defense configuration featuring black composite stock and forearm, black metal finish, 22 in. barrel with Invector choke system and removable LPA ghost ring sights, 8 shot extended mag., includes sling swivels, Dura-Touch armor coated composite finish became standard during 2003, 8 lbs. Mfg. 2002-2006.

	$1,075	$885	$715	$635	$550	$495	$440	$1,287

Subtract 10% if w/o Dura-Touch finished stock and forearm.

SX3 (SUPER X3) SPORTING – 12 ga. only, 2 3/4 in. chamber, 28, 30, or 32 in. ported VR barrel with 5 extended choke tubes and TruGlo front sight, checkered adj. comb walnut stock and forearm, Active Valve gas system, gun metal grey receiver finish, Pachmayr Decelerator recoil pad, approx. 7 1/2 lbs., includes red ABS hard case with Winchester logo. New 2011.

MSR $1,700	$1,450	$1,175	$1,000	$875	$750	$625	$550	

This model was originally featured as a 2010 SHOT Show Special.

SHOTGUNS: SLIDE ACTION, 1964-CURRENT

Winchester introduced WinChokes in 1969.

U.S. Repeating Arms closed its New Haven, CT manufacturing facility on March 31, 2006. There may be some speculation on recently manufactured Model 1300 shotguns. All Model 1300 last MSRs listed are from the Winchester 2006 price sheet.

MODEL 1200 POLICE STAINLESS – 12 ga. only, 18 in. barrel, 7 shot mag. Disc.

	$250	$195	$165	$125	$105	$90	$75	

MODEL 1200 DEFENDER – 12 ga. only, 18 in. cylinder bore barrel, 7 shot mag., 6 lbs. Disc.

	$250	$200	$180	$155	$140	$125	$110	

MODEL 1300 CAMP DEFENDER – 12 ga. only, 3 in. chamber, 8 shot mag., 22 in. barrel with rifle sights and WinChoke, choice of black synthetic (disc. 2000) or hardwood (new 2001) stock and forearm, matte metal finish, 6 7/8 lbs. Mfg. 1999-2004.

	$300	$230	$180	$150	$125	$110	$100	$392

MODEL 1300 DEFENDER – 12 or 20 (disc. 1996, reintroduced 2001) ga., 3 in. chamber, available in Police (disc. 1989), Practical (new 2005), Marine, and Defender variations, 18 or 24 (mfg. 1994-98) in. cyl. bore barrel, 5 (disc. 1998), 7 (disc. 1998), or 8 shot mag., matte metal finish, choice of hardwood (disc. 2001), composite (matte finish), or pistol grip (matte finish, 12 ga. only) stock, TruGlo sights became standard 1999, 5 3/4 - 7 lbs. Disc. 2006.

	$270	$210	$160	$130	$110	$95	$85	$341

Add $13 for short pistol grip and full length stocks.

Add approx. $100 for Combo Package (includes extra 28 in. VR barrel - disc. 1998).

* ***Model 1300 Defender NRA*** – 12 or 20 ga., 18 in. barrel with removable TruGlo fiber optic front sight, composite stock, 8 shot mag., features NRA medallion on pistol grip, also available in 12 ga. combo with pistol grip stock, 6 1/4 - 6 1/2 lbs. Limited mfg. 2006.

	$285	$215	$175	$140	$120	$110	$95	$364

Add $13 for combo with pistol grip and full length stock.

* ***Model 1300 Defender Practical*** – 12 ga. only, 3 in. chamber, 8 shot mag., 22 in. barrel with TruGlo adj. open sights, designed for practical shooting events, black synthetic stock and forearm. Mfg. 2005.

	$300	$230	$170	$145	$125	$110	$100	$392

» **Model 1300 Defender Practical NRA** – 12 ga. only, 3 in. chamber, 8 shot mag., 22 in. barrel with TruGlo sights, black synthetic stock and forearm, Winchoke system, adj. open sights, NRA logo grip cap, 6 1/2 lbs. Limited mfg. 2006.

	$315	$240	$180	$150	$130	$110	$100	$414

* ***Model 1300 Defender Stainless Coastal Marine*** – 12 ga. only, 18 in. cyl. bore stainless steel barrel and mag. tube, a Sandstrom 9A phosphate coating was released late 1989 to give long lasting corrosion protection to all receiver and internal working parts, Dura-Touch armor coating stock treatment added 2004, 6 shot mag., synthetic pistol grip (disc. 2001) or full black stock configuration, approx. 6 3/8 lbs. Mfg. 2002-2005.

	$465	$380	$275	$225	$195	$165	$140	$575

MSR	100%	98%	95%	90%	80%	70%	60%	Last MSR

»**Model 1300 Defender Stainless Coastal Marine NRA** – 12 ga. only, 18 in. nickel plated stainless steel barrel, anodized aluminum alloy receiver and plated parts for corrosion resistance, Dura-Touch Armor coating on composite stock, 7 shot mag., sling swivel studs, removable TruGlo fiber optic front sight, 6 1/2 lbs. Limited mfg. 2006.

	$480	$390	$280	$230	$200	$165	$140	*$598*

* *Model 1300 Lady Defender* – 20 ga. only, 3 in. chamber, choice of synthetic regular or pistol grip stock, 4 (disc. 1996) or 7 shot mag., 18 in. cyl. bore barrel (new 1996), 5 3/8 lbs. Disc. 1998.

	$235	$190	$150	$120	$105	$90	$80	*$290*

SPEED PUMP DEFENDER – 12 ga., 3 in. chamber, side ejection, 5 shot mag., features 18 in. plain barrel with fixed cylinder choke, black composite stock with non-glare finish and ribbed forearm. Mfg. by Miroku during 2008.

	$240	$210	$190	$170	$150	$135	$120	*$299*

SXP (SUPER X PUMP) DEFENDER – 12 ga., 3 in. chamber, 18 in. fixed cylinder bore barrel, non-glare metal finish, 5 shot mag., deep groove forearm, black composite pistol grip stock, 6 1/4 lbs. New 2009.

MSR $350	$295	$265	$230	$200	$175	$150	$125	

SXP (SUPER X PUMP) MARINE DEFENDER – 12 ga., 3 in. chamber, 18 in. barrel with Invector Plus cylinder choke tube, black synthetic stock with textured gripping surfaces, Inflex technology recoil pad, non-glare matte black alloy drilled and tapped receiver with hard chrome barrel and mag. tube, tactical ribbed forearm, includes both brass bead and TruGlo fiber optic front sights, drop out trigger, crossbolt safety, 4-lug rotary bolt, 6 1/4 lbs. New 2013.

MSR $400	$350	$315	$285	$250	$220	$195	$175	

WINDHAM WEAPONRY

Current manufacturer of AR-15 style rifles, receivers, parts, barrels, and related accessories established in 2011, and located in Windham, ME.

Windham Weaponry is located in the former Bushmaster Manufacturing plant in Windham, ME.

CARBINES/RIFLES: SEMI-AUTO

Windham Weaponry also makes several variations of the SBR (Short Barreled Rifle) for military/law enforcement. All Windham rifles and carbines carry a lifetime transferable warranty.

CDI CARBINE – .223 Rem. cal., GIO, 16 in. M4 chrome lined barrel with Vortex flash suppressor, 30 shot mag., flat-top upper receiver, aluminum forged lower receiver, hardcoat black anodized finish, steel bolt, Magpul MOE six position telescoping buttstock with pistol grip, Diamondhead free float forend, Magpul AFG angled foregrip, machined aluminum trigger guard, Diamondhead flip up front and rear sights, manual safety, includes black sling and hard plastic case, 7 lbs.

MSR $1,680	$1,495	$1,275	$1,150	$925	$750	$600	$500	

MPC CARBINE – .223 Rem. cal., GIO, 16 in. M4 chrome lined barrel with A2 flash suppressor, 30 shot mag., M4A4 flat-top upper receiver with detachable carry handle, aluminum forged lower receiver, hardcoat black anodized finish, steel bolt, six position telescoping buttstock with A2 pistol grip, M4 double heat shield handguards, machined aluminum trigger guard, adj. dual aperture rear sight, adj. square post front sight, manual safety, includes black sling and hard plastic case, 6.9 lbs.

MSR $1,086	$975	$850	$750	$600	$500	$450	$395	

* *MPC-RF Carbine* – .223 Rem. cal., similar to MPC Carbine, except does not have carry handle, includes Diamondhead rear flip up sight. New mid-2013.

MSR $1,086	$975	$850	$750	$600	$500	$450	$395	

Add $125 for tactical quad rail handguard (MPC-RF MFT Model).

SRC CARBINE – .223 Rem. cal., GIO, 16 in. M4 chrome lined barrel with A2 flash suppressor, 30 shot mag., M4A4 flat-top upper receiver with Picatinny rail, aluminum forged lower receiver, hardcoat black, True Timber Snowfall (new 2014), or TimberTec camo (new 2014) anodized finish, steel bolt, six position telescoping buttstock with A2 pistol grip, M4 double heat shield handguards, machined aluminum trigger guard, no sights, manual safety, includes black sling and hard plastic case, 6.3 lbs.

MSR $1,040	$950	$825	$725	$600	$500	$450	$395	

Add $120 for True Timber Snowfall (new 2014), or TimberTec camo (new 2014).

* *SRC .308 Carbine* – .308 Win. cal., GIO, 16 1/2 in. medium profile chrome lined barrel with A2 flash suppressor, 20 shot Magpul PMag., M4A4 flat-top upper receiver, aluminum forged lower receiver, hardcoat black anodized finish, steel bolt, mid-length tapered heat shielded handguards, six position telescoping buttstock, Hogue overmolded beavertail pistol grip, integral trigger guard, 7 1/2 lbs. New 2014.

MSR $1,413	$1,250	$1,050	$900	$800	$700	$600	$475	

MSR	100%	98%	95%	90%	80%	70%	60%	Last MSR

HBC CARBINE – .223 Rem. cal., GIO, 16 in. heavy profile chrome lined barrel with A2 flash suppressor, 30 shot mag., M4A4 flat-top upper receiver with detachable carry handle, aluminum forged lower receiver, hardcoat black anodized finish, steel bolt, six position telescoping buttstock with A2 pistol grip, M4 double heat shield handguards, machined aluminum trigger guard, adj. dual aperture rear sight, adj. square post front sight, manual safety, includes black sling and hard plastic case, 7 1/2 lbs.

MSR $1,096	$985	$850	$750	$600	$500	$450	$395	

VEX-SS RIFLE – .223 Rem. cal., GIO, 20 in. matte finished fluted stainless steel barrel, 5 shot mag., M4A4 flat-top upper receiver, optics riser blocks, aluminum forged lower receiver, hardcoat black or Snow Camo anodized finish, steel bolt, skeleton stock with Hogue rubber pistol grip, knurled vented aluminum free floating forend with sling swivel, machined aluminum trigger guard, no sights, manual safety, includes black sling and hard plastic case, 8.2 lbs.

MSR $1,295	$1,150	$975	$875	$750	$650	$550	$450	

Add $175 for Snow Camo finish.

CARBON FIBER CARBINE – .223 Rem. cal., GIO, 16 in. M4 profile chrome lined barrel with A2 flash suppressor, 30 shot mag., M4A4 flat-top upper receiver with molded Picatinny rail, molded carbon fiber composite receiver, matte black finish, steel bolt, six position telescoping buttstock with A2 pistol grip, M4 double heat shield handguards, integral molded carbon fiber trigger guard, no sights, manual safety, includes black sling and hard plastic case, 5.6 lbs.

MSR $958	$875	$750	$650	$550	$500	$450	$395	

WISEMAN, BILL AND CO.

Current custom rifle and action manufacturer established in 1980 and located in College Station, TX.

Bill Wiseman also manufactures top quality actions and test barrels used throughout the firearms industry. Additionally, Wiseman/McMillan manufactures rifle barrels and custom stocks. He also performs many gunsmithing services to customer supplied rifles. Please contact the company directly for more information on these products (see Trademark Index).

RIFLES: BOLT ACTION

Add 11% excise tax to prices shown for new manufacture. Some models listed have very limited production.

TSR TACTICAL (OLDER MFG.) – .300 Win. Mag., .308 Win., or .338 Lapua Mag. cal., 5 shot detachable mag., or standard floorplate, synthetic stock with adj. cheekpiece, stainless steel fluted barrel with integral muzzle brake, guaranteed 1/2 MOA accuracy. Mfg. 1996-2003.

	$2,795	$2,200	$1,700	$1,500	$1,235	$1,030	$855	$2,795

Add $195 for fluted barrel.
Add $195 for muzzle brake.
Add $150 for 3 position safety.

TSR TACTICAL (NEW MFG.) – various cals., various barrel lengths with or w/o muzzle brake, receiver features integral Picatinny rail, Certa metal coating, adj. black composite Hogue stock (2 options available), detachable mag., guaranteed 1/4 MOA accuracy. New 2011.

The base MSR on this model is $3,850.

Tactical actions are available separately - the short action has an MSR of $850, and the long action has an MSR of $1,925.

X-Y-Z SECTIONS

XN ARMS INDUSTRY AND TRADE CO.

Current tactical semi-auto shotgun manufacturer located in Istanbul, Turkey. No current U.S. importation.

MSR	100%	98%	95%	90%	80%	70%	60%	Last MSR

SHOTGUNS: SEMI-AUTO

EKSEN MKE 1919 – 12 ga. only, 2 3/4 in. chamber, gas operated, AR-15 style design in either black finish or 100% camo coverage, 19 in. barrel with muzzle brake, 5 shot detachable mag., ribbed handguard with A2 front post sight and detachable carrying handle, 6 1/2 lbs. New 2012.

Please contact the manufacturer directly for U.S. availability and pricing on this model (see Trademark Index).

XTREME MACHINING

Current rifle manufacturer located in Drifting, PA. Previously located in Grassflat, PA. Previously distributed until 2012 by American Tactical Imports, located in Rochester, NY.

RIFLES: BOLT ACTION

.338 XTREME – .338 Xtreme cal., single shot (black or tan only) or repeater (5 or 7 shot detachable mag.) action, choice of laminated wood target, aluminum tactical, or McMillan A-5 stock, stainless steel receiver and 30 in. fluted barrel with 42-port muzzle brake, Picatinny rails, black, tan, or green finish, approx. 15 1/2 lbs.

MSR $4,678	$4,150	$3,850	$3,500	$3,000	$2,750	$2,250	$1,750

Add $414 for repeater.

.338 XTREME M100 SERIES – .338 Xtreme cal., 26 (black finish only) or 30 in. fluted barrel, M100 side folding custom stock, full length Weaver rail, 7 shot detachable box mag., available in black, tan, desert mirage, or AM tiger stripe finish. New 2011.

MSR $6,199	$5,750	$4,995	$4,300	$3,850	$3,150	$2,600	$2,000

.50 BMG – .50 BMG cal., single shot or repeater, available in light gun, heavy gun, or unlimited gun configurations, 34 in. stainless steel barrel with specially designed muzzle brake, Rifle Basix trigger, aluminum steel Picatinny-style scope mounting rails, Sako-style extractor, removable plunger ejector, choice of aluminum or laminated wood stocks with forend up to 8 in. wide, options include barrel lengths, fluting, and custom stock dimensions.

Current MSR for Light Gun is $5,500, Heavy Gun is $6,000, and Unlimited Gun is P.O.R.

RIFLES: SEMI-AUTO

Xtreme Machining currently manufactures AR-15 style rifles in 5.56 NATO and .223 Rem. cals. Current models include Basic XR-15, and Enhanced XR-15. Base prices start at $1,650. They also manufacture an AK-47 design model. Please contact the company directly for more information on these models including options, availability, and pricing (see Trademark Index).

YANKEE HILL MACHINE CO., INC. (YHM)

Current manufacturer of AR-15 style rifles, receivers, parts, suppressors, and related accessories established in 1951, and located in Florence, MA. Consumer direct and dealer sales.

CARBINES/RIFLES: SEMI-AUTO

YHM manufactures a complete line of AR-15 style tactical rifles and carbines, as well as upper receivers and a wide variety of accessories. Please contact the company directly for more information about available options and dealer listings (see Trademark Index).

BLACK DIAMOND CARBINE – 5.56 NATO, 7.62x39mm (mfg. 2011-2013), .300 Blackout (new 2014), or 6.8 SPC (new 2010) cal., GIO, 16 in. chromemoly vanadium steel threaded barrel, Diamond fluting, Phantom flash hider, 30 shot mag., black anodized finish, aluminum lower and flat-top upper receiver, mil spec bolt carrier assembly, forward assist, carbine length Diamond handguard, free floating continuous top Picatinny rail, flip up tower front and rear sights, 6 position adj. carbine stock, standard A2 grip, 6.7 lbs.

MSR $1,472	$1,295	$1,100	$1,000	$825	$675	$525	$450

Add $80 for 6.8 SPC, .300 Blackout (new 2014) or 7.62x39mm (disc. 2013) cal.

BLACK DIAMOND SPECTER CARBINE – 5.56 NATO, 7.62x39mm (mfg. 2011-2013), .300 Blackout (new 2014), or 6.8 SPC (new 2010) cal., GIO, similar to Black Diamond Carbine, except features Specter length Diamond handguard, 6.9 lbs.

MSR $1,498	$1,315	$1,100	$1,000	$825	$675	$525	$450

Add $81 for 6.8 SPC, .300 Blackout (new 2014), or 7.62x39mm (disc. 2013) cal.

BLACK DIAMOND SPECTER XL CARBINE – 5.56 NATO, 7.62x39mm (mfg. 2011-2013), .300 Blackout (new 2014), or 6.8 SPC (new 2010) cal., GIO, similar to Black Diamond Specter Carbine, except has Specter XL length Diamond handguard, approx. 7 lbs.

MSR $1,525	$1,350	$1,150	$1,050	$850	$695	$550	$475

Add $54 for 6.8 SPC, .300 Blackout (new 2014) or 7.62x39mm (disc. 2013) cal.

MSR	100%	98%	95%	90%	80%	70%	60%	Last MSR

BLACK DIAMOND RIFLE – 5.56 NATO, 7.62x39mm (mfg. 2011-2013), or 6.8 SPC cal., GIO, 20 in. chromemoly vanadium steel barrel, 30 shot mag., black anodized finish, aluminum lower and flat-top upper receiver, mil spec bolt carrier assembly, forward assist, rifle length Diamond handguard, Picatinny rail risers, A2 fixed stock, A2 pistol grip, single rail gas block, two mini-risers, 8 lbs.

| MSR $1,445 | $1,275 | $1,085 | $975 | $800 | $650 | $500 | $425 | |

Add $53 for 6.8 SPC or 7.62x39mm (disc. 2013) cal.

CUSTOMIZABLE CARBINE – 5.56 NATO, 7.62x39mm (new 2011), or 6.8 SPC (new 2010) cal., GIO, 16 in. chromemoly vanadium steel barrel, black anodized finish, aluminum lower and flat-top upper receiver, mil spec bolt carrier assembly, forward assist, Phantom flash hider, carbine length customizable handguard, adj. carbine stock, flip up front tower sight and flip up rear sight, 6.3 lbs. Disc. 2013.

| | $1,295 | $1,100 | $1,000 | $825 | $675 | $525 | $450 | $1,472 |

Add $54 for 6.8 SPC or 7.62x39mm cal.

CUSTOMIZABLE RIFLE – 5.56 NATO, 7.62x39mm (new 2011), or 6.8 SPC (new 2011) cal., GIO, 20 in. chromemoly vanadium steel barrel, black anodized finish, aluminum lower and flat-top upper receiver, mil spec bolt carrier assembly, forward assist, rifle length customizable handguard, 12 in. Co-Witness rail, fixed A2 stock, single rail gas block, two mini-risers, 8 lbs. Disc. 2013.

| | $1,275 | $1,085 | $975 | $800 | $650 | $500 | $425 | $1,445 |

Add $53 for 6.8 SPC or 7.62x39mm cal.

DESERT ENFORCER – 5.56 NATO cal., GIO, 16 in. threaded barrel with 6 grooves and Diamond fluting, YHM Annihilator flash hider, E-Z Pull takedown pins, forged aluminum lower and flat-top A3 upper, Gen. 2 PMag., TJ Competition Series rifle length handguard with top Picatinny rail, Quick Deploy Sights, Magpul 6-pos. adj. stock, Magpul MOE pistol grip, Desert Earth finish with contrast of Black parts, 7.1 lbs. New 2014.

| MSR $1,950 | $1,750 | $1,575 | $1,350 | $1,150 | $950 | $825 | $650 | |

ENTRY LEVEL CARBINE – 5.56 NATO, 7.62x39mm (mfg. 2011-2013), .300 Blackout (new 2014), or 6.8 SPC (new 2010) cal., GIO, 16 in. chromemoly vanadium steel threaded barrel, YHM Phantom flash hider, 30 shot mag., black anodized finish, aluminum lower and flat-top upper receiver, mil spec bolt carrier assembly, forward assist, carbine length handguard, 6-pos. adj. carbine stock, A2 pistol grip, single rail gas block, 6.4 lbs.

| MSR $1,284 | $1,095 | $975 | $875 | $700 | $575 | $450 | $395 | |

Add $54 for 6.8 SPC, .300 Blackout (new 2014), or 7.62x39mm (disc. 2013) cal.

ENTRY LEVEL RIFLE – 5.56 NATO, 7.62x39mm (mfg. 2011-2013), or 6.8 SPC (new 2011) cal., GIO, 20 in. chromemoly vanadium steel non-fluted barrel, 30 shot mag., black anodized finish, aluminum lower and flat-top upper receiver, mil spec bolt carrier assembly, forward assist, rifle length tube handguard, fixed A2 stock, A2 pistol grip, single rail gas block, two mini-risers, 8 lbs.

| MSR $1,311 | $1,125 | $985 | $895 | $725 | $600 | $475 | $425 | |

Add $43 for 6.8 SPC or 7.62x39mm (disc. 2013) cal.

HUNT READY CARBINE – 5.56 NATO, 7.62x39mm (disc. 2013), .300 Blackout (new 2014), or 6.8 SPC cal., GIO, 16 in. steel threaded and fluted barrel with YHM-28-5C2 Flash Hider, forged aluminum flat-top upper and lower receiver, low profile gas block, 5 shot mag., vented round customizable forearm, two 3 in. modular rails, bolt carrier assembly, forward assist, adj. carbine buttstock, standard pistol grip, matte black or 100% Realtree AP camo finish, includes Bushnell Banner 3-9x40mm camo scope with Circle-X reticule, Grovetec deluxe padded camo sling. New 2012.

| MSR $1,531 | $1,335 | $1,125 | $1,000 | $825 | $675 | $525 | $450 | |

Add $53 for 6.8 SPC, .300 Blackout (new 2014), or 7.62x39mm (disc. 2013) cal.

HUNT READY RIFLE – 5.56 NATO, 7.62x39mm (disc. 2013), or 6.8 SPC cal., GIO, 20 in. free floating steel barrel, diamond fluting, forged aluminum flat-top upper and lower receiver, low profile gas block, 5 shot mag., A2 Trapdoor buttstock, vented round customizable forearm, bolt carrier assembly, forward assist, matte black or 100% Realtree AP camo finish, includes Bushnell Banner 3-9x40mm camo scope with Circle-X reticule, Grovetec deluxe padded camo sling. New 2012.

| MSR $1,563 | $1,350 | $1,175 | $1,000 | $825 | $675 | $525 | $450 | |

Add $42 for 6.8 SPC or 7.62x39mm (disc. 2013) cal.

LIGHTWEIGHT CARBINE – 5.56 NATO, 7.62x39mm (new 2011), or 6.8 SPC (new 2010) cal., GIO, 16 in. chromemoly vanadium steel barrel, black anodized finish, aluminum lower and flat-top upper receiver, mil spec bolt carrier assembly, forward assist, Phantom flash hider, carbine length lightweight handguard, adj. carbine stock, forearm endcap, flip up tower front sight, flip up rear sight, 6.7 lbs. Disc. 2013.

| | $1,275 | $1,085 | $975 | $800 | $650 | $500 | $425 | $1,445 |

Add $80 for 6.8 SPC or 7.62x39mm cal.

MSR		100%	98%	95%	90%	80%	70%	60%	Last MSR

LIGHTWEIGHT RIFLE – 5.56 NATO, 7.62x39mm (new 2011), or 6.8 SPC (new 2011) cal., GIO, 20 in. chromemoly vanadium steel barrel, black anodized finish, aluminum lower and flat-top upper receiver, mil spec bolt carrier assembly, forward assist, rifle length lightweight handguard, fixed A2 stock, single rail gas block, two mini-risers, 8 lbs. Disc. 2013.

		$1,275	$1,085	$975	$800	$650	$500	$425	*$1,445*

Add $53 for 6.8 SPC or 7.62x39mm cal.

MODEL 57 – 5.56 NATO, 6.8 SPC, or .300 Blackout cal., GIO, 16 in. threaded barrel with fluting, mid-length top rail aluminum handguard (SLR Slant Series), Quick Deploy Sight System, two 30 shot Gen. 2 Black PMags., E-Z Pull takedown pins, Magpul 6-pos. adj. stock, Magpul MOE pistol grip, YHM Slant Comp/Brake, oversized magwell, aluminum flat-top A3 upper receiver, tactical charging handle, Matte Black finish. New 2014.

MSR $2,195		$1,950	$1,725	$1,475	$1,350	$1,075	$895	$695	

Add $70 for 6.8 SPC or .300 Blackout cal.

SLR SMOOTH SPECTER – 5.56 NATO, 6.8 SPC, or .300 Blackout cal., GIO, 16 in. threaded barrel with Diamond fluting, Phantom flash hider, Quick Deploy Sight System, mid-length free floating handguard with continuous top Picatinny rail, EZ Pull takedown pins, 30 shot mag., forged alum. lower and flat-top A3 upper receiver, 6-pos. adj. carbine stock, A2 pistol grip, Matte Black finish.

MSR $1,700		$1,525	$1,325	$1,150	$1,050	$850	$685	$550	

Add $81 for 6.8 SPC or .300 Blackout cal.

* **SLR Quad Specter** – 5.56 NATO, 6.8 SPC, or .300 Blackout cal., GIO, similar to SLR Smooth Specter, except has mid-length quad rail handguard, 7.3 lbs.

MSR $1,700		$1,525	$1,325	$1,150	$1,050	$850	$685	$550	

Add $81 for 6.8 SPC or .300 Blackout cal.

SLR SMOOTH SPECTER XL – 5.56 NATO, 6.8 SPC, or .300 Blackout cal., GIO, 16 in. threaded barrel with rifling grooves and Diamond fluting, Phantom flash hider, alum. rifle length free floating customizeable handguard with continuous top Picatinny rail, 30 shot mag., Quick Deploy Sight System, EZ Pull takedown pins, forged alum. lower and flat-top A3 upper receiver, 6-pos. adj. carbine stock, A2 pistol grip, Matte Black finish, 7.1 lbs.

MSR $1,725		$1,550	$1,350	$1,175	$1,050	$850	$700	$550	

Add $81 for 6.8 SPC or .300 Blackout cal.

* **SLR Quad Specter XL** – 5.56 NATO, 6.8 SPC, or .300 Blackout cal., GIO, similar to SLR Specter XL, except features mid-length quad rail handguard, 7.4 lbs.

MSR $1,725		$1,550	$1,350	$1,175	$1,050	$850	$700	$550	

Add $81 for 6.8 SPC or .300 Blackout cal.

SMOOTH CARBINE – 5.56 NATO, 7.62x39mm (mfg. 2011-2013), .300 Blackout (new 2014), or 6.8 SPC (new 2010) cal., GIO, 16 in. chromemoly vanadium steel threaded barrel, Diamond fluting, Phantom flash hider, 30 shot mag., oversized magwell, black anodized finish, aluminum lower and flat-top upper receiver, mil spec bolt carrier assembly, forward assist, carbine length smooth handguard, 6-pos. adj. carbine stock, A2 pistol grip, flip up front tower sight and flip up rear sight, 6.8 lbs.

MSR $1,472		$1,295	$1,100	$1,000	$825	$675	$525	$450	

Add $53 for 6.8 SPC, .300 Blackout (new 2014), or 7.62x39mm (disc. 2013) cal.

SMOOTH RIFLE – 5.56 NATO, 7.62x39mm (new 2011), or 6.8 SPC (new 2011) cal., GIO, 20 in. chromemoly vanadium steel barrel, black anodized finish, aluminum lower and flat-top upper receiver, mil spec bolt carrier assembly, forward assist, rifle length smooth handguard, fixed A2 stock, single rail gas block, forearm endcap, two mini-risers, 8 lbs.

MSR $1,445		$1,275	$1,085	$975	$800	$650	$500	$425	

Add $54 for 6.8 SPC or 7.62x39mm cal.

SPECTER LIGHTWEIGHT CARBINE – 5.56 NATO, 7.62x39mm (new 2011), or 6.8 SPC (new 2010) cal., GIO, 16 in. chromemoly vanadium steel barrel, black anodized finish, aluminum lower and flat-top upper receiver, mil spec bolt carrier assembly, forward assist, Phantom flash hider, Specter length lightweight handguard, adj. carbine stock, forearm endcap, flip up front and rear sights, low profile gas block, 6.9 lbs. Disc. 2013.

		$1,315	$1,100	$1,000	$825	$675	$525	$450	*$1,498*

Add $54 for 6.8 SPC or 7.62x39mm cal.

SPECTER XL LIGHTWEIGHT CARBINE – 5.56 NATO, 7.62x39mm (new 2011), or 6.8 SPC (new 2010) cal., GIO, similar to Specter Lightweight Carbine, except has XL length lightweight handguard, 7.1 lbs. Disc. 2013.

		$1,350	$1,150	$1,050	$850	$695	$550	$475	*$1,525*

Add $54 for 6.8 SPC or 7.62x39mm cal.

OD GREEN SLR SPECTER SMOOTH CARBINE – 5.56 NATO cal., GIO, 16 in. steel threaded barrel with grooves and Diamond fluting, YHM Phantom 5C2 flash hider, forward assist, YHM SLR-Smooth mid-length handguard, Magpul Gen 2 Black PMag., forged aluminum upper and lower receiver, Q.D.S. Sight System, Ergo ambidextrous pistol grip, Ergo Ti-7 six position adj. stock, OD Green Cerakote finish, 6.9 lbs. New mid-2013.

MSR $1,950		$1,750	$1,575	$1,350	$1,150	$950	$825	$650	

MSR	100%	98%	95%	90%	80%	70%	60%	Last MSR

SPORTSMAN SCOUT CARBINE – 5.56 NATO, 7.62x39mm, or 6.8 SPC cal., GIO, 16 in. free floating steel barrel with Phantom 5C2 flash hider, diamond fluting, aluminum lower and flat-top upper receiver with Picatinny rail, 100% Realtree AP camo coverage, forward assist, low profile gas block, M4 telescoping buttstock, includes two 3 in. modular rails, Specter length customizable handguard, forearm endcap. Mfg. 2011-2013.

	$1,195	$1,000	$900	$725	$600	$475	$425	$1,391

Add $54 for 6.8 SPC or 7.62x39mm cal.

SPORTSMAN SERIES RIFLE – 5.56 NATO, 7.62x39mm, or 6.8 SPC cal., GIO, 20 in. free floating steel barrel, diamond fluting, aluminum lower and flat-top upper receiver with Picatinny rail, 100% Realtree AP camo coverage, forward assist, low profile gas block, A2 trapdoor buttstock, includes two 3 in. modular rails, rifle length customizable handguard, forearm endcap. Mfg. 2011-2013.

	$1,275	$1,085	$975	$800	$650	$500	$425	$1,445

Add $96 for 6.8 SPC or 7.62x39mm cal.

TODD JARRETT COMPETITION SERIES CARBINE – 5.56 NATO or 6.8mm cal., GIO, 16 in. chrome-lined threaded barrel, fluted with YHM's signature "Diamond Flute" and Phantom 5C2 flash Hider, 30 shot mag., free floating forearm, available with rifle, mid-length, or carbine length handguard, ergonomic pistol grip, padded ACE stock, Q.D.S. flip up front and rear sights, EZ Pull Takedown Pins, forged aluminum lower and flat-top "T" marked upper with Picatinny rail, low profile gas block, forearm end cap, matte black finish. New mid-2013.

MSR $2,007	$1,800	$1,575	$1,350	$1,225	$1,000	$825	$650	

Z-M WEAPONS

Current rifle manufacturer and pistol components maker located in Richmond, VT. Previously located in Bernardston, MA. Dealer and consumer direct sales.

PISTOLS: SEMI-AUTO

STRIKE PISTOL – .38 Super, .40 S&W, or .45 ACP cal., several configurations available, with or without compensator. Limited mfg. 1997-2000.

	$2,375	$1,825	$1,700	$1,400	$1,150	$995	$750	$2,695

RIFLES: SEMI-AUTO

LR 300 & VARIATIONS – .223 Rem. cal., modified gas system using AR-15 style action, features pivoting skeletal metal stock, 16 1/4 in. barrel, flat-top receiver, matte finish, aluminum or Nylatron handguard, 7.2 lbs. New 1997.

MSR $2,208	$2,100	$1,800	$1,550	$1,300	$1,100	$900	$750	

Add $23 for Nylatron handguard.
Add $50 for Military/Law Enforcement model.
Add $75 for Military/Law Enforcement model with Nylatron handguard.

ZVI

Current manufacturer located in Prague, Czech Republic. No current U.S. importation.

ZVI manufactures the Kevin line of small frame .380 ACP cal. semi-auto pistols. ZVI also manufactures the Falcon, a .50 BMG bolt action repeater (2 shot mag.). Currently, these guns do not have any U.S. importation. Please contact the company directly for more information, including pricing and U.S. availability (see Trademark Index).

ZASTAVA ARMS

Current manufacturer established in 1853, and located in Serbia. Currently, certain models are imported by Century International Arms, located in Fairfax, VT. Please refer to C section. Some models were imported by EAA, located in Rockledge, FL, and please refer to EAA in the E section. Remington previously imported certain models until 2009, as well as KBI until 2005. Previously distributed by Advanced Weapons Technologies, located in Athens, Greece, and by Nationwide Sports Distributors, located in Southampton, PA. Previously imported by T.D. Arms, followed by Brno U.S.A., circa 1990.

Zastava Arms makes a wide variety of quality pistols, rifles, and sporting shotguns. Zastava Arms was subcontracted by Remington Arms Co. to make certain bolt action rifle models.

HANDGUNS: SEMI-AUTO

MODEL CZ99 – 9mm Para. or .40 S&W cal., DA/SA, 15 shot, 4 1/4 in. barrel, short recoil, choice of various finishes, SIG locking system, hammer drop safety, ambidextrous controls, 3-dot Tritium sighting system, alloy frame, firing pin block, loaded chamber indicator, squared-off trigger guard, checkered dark grey polymer grips, 32 oz.

	$550	$400	$375	$330	$300	$285	$265	$495

While a Z9 was advertised, it was never commercially imported. All guns were CZ99 or CZ40.

MSR	100%	98%	95%	90%	80%	70%	60%	*Last MSR*

Zastava CZ99 configurations (with finishes) included matte blue with synthetic grips (500 imported), commercial blue with synthetic grips (750 imported), military "painted finish" with synthetic grips (1,000 imported), matte blue finish with checkered wood grips (115 imported), high polish blue with checkered grips (115 imported), and military "painted finish" with wood grips (2 prototypes only).

MODEL CZ999 SCORPION – 9mm Para. cal., similar to CZ99, except has indicator for the last three rounds in the magazine, fire selector for pistol and revolver mode.

Please refer to the Skorpion listing in the S section for current information on this model. This pistol was imported by K.B.I. as the ZDA model.

MODEL CZ40 – .40 S&W cal., 55 prototypes were imported for testing, but most had a feeding problem due to improper magazine design, mag. design changes were planned, but were cancelled due to the Serbian/Croatian war. **Suggested retail was $495.**

MODEL CZ70 – 9mm Para. cal., SA, Tokarev style, no slide safety, blue finish, limited importation.

	100%	98%	95%	90%	80%	70%	60%
	$1,000	$850	$775	$675	$575	$510	$460

MODEL M88 – 9mm Para. or .40 S&W cal., SA, 6 or 8 shot mag., 3.6 in. barrel, blue finish, compact frame, military version, not recent import, 28 oz.

	100%	98%	95%	90%	80%	70%	60%
	$600	$525	$465	$415	$360	$330	$295

ZELENY SPORT s.r.o.

Current manufacturer located in the Czech Republic. No current U.S. importation.

RIFLES: SEMI-AUTO

Zeleny Sport manufactures a AK-47 design Model 96 Beryl semi-auto in .223 Rem. cal., the company also makes a Works 11 Series with fixed wood, fixed synthetic, or folding stock. Please contact the company directly for possible U.S. importation, availability, and pricing (see Trademark Index).

ZOMBIE DEFENSE

Current custom manufacturer located in Henrico, VA since 2009.

RIFLES: SEMI-AUTO

Zombie Defense builds custom rifles on the AR-15 platform to the customer's specifications using their own unique custom lower receivers. Current models with base MSRs include: Entry Level Z4 - $775, Z4 .300 Blackout - $850, Z4 6.8 SPC - $850, and Z4 18 in. SPR - $950. Please contact the company directly for more information including options, pricing, and availability (see Trademark Index).

NOTES

TACTICAL FIREARMS TRADEMARK INDEX

We can guarantee you that no informational source has a more accurate firearms industry Trademark Index than what you are about to [rea]d. Remember, this invaluable section is also available online at no charge, so you can get the most recent contact information any time, [an]y where, with internet access, and it is updated quarterly as things change. Why guess when you can be sure?

The following listings of domestic and international tactical firearms manufacturers, trademarks, importers, distributors, factory repair [cen]ters, and parts companies are the most complete and up-to-date ever published. Even more so than in the last edition, you will note [ad]ditions and substantial changes regarding website and email listings – this may be your best way of obtaining up-to-date model and [pri]cing information directly from some current manufacturers, importers, and/or distributors who don't post retail pricing. When online [wit]h the various company websites, it's not a bad idea to look at the date of the last web update, as this will tell you how current the online [inf]ormation really is.

[F]or a complete listing of companies and contact information for airguns and modern black powder reproduction industries, please refer to [the] respective Trademark Indexes in the *Blue Book of Modern Black Powder Arms* and the *Blue Book of Airguns*. These Trademark Indexes [are] available online at no charge (www.bluebookofgunvalues.com).

[I]f parts are needed for older, discontinued makes and models, it is recommended you contact either Numrich Gun Parts Corp. located [in] West Hurley, NY, or Jack First, Inc. located in Rapid City, SD for domestic availability and prices. For current manufacturers, it is [re]commended that you contact an authorized warranty repair center or stocking gun shop, unless a company/trademark has an additional [ser]vice/parts listing. In Canada, please refer to the Bowmac Gunpar Inc. listing.

[H]undreds of hours have been spent in this database, and we feel that this information is the most reliable source material available to [con]tact these companies/individuals. However, if you feel that you have something to add or find an error, we would like to know about it. [Sim]ply contact us at: cassandraf@bluebookinc.com.

[D]uring the course of the year, the Trademark Index is constantly updated as more information becomes available. Please visit www. [blu]ebookofgunvalues.com for the most current database (available free of charge).

[I]f you should require additional assistance in "tracking" any of the current companies listed in this publication (or perhaps, current [co]mpanies that are not listed), please contact us and we will try to help you regarding these specific requests. Again, the most up-to-date [Tra]demark Index for the firearms, black powder reproductions, tactical, and airguns industries will be posted on our [we]bsite: www.bluebookofgunvalues.com. We hope you appreciate this service – no one else in the industry has anything like it.

[2]VETS ARMS CO, LLC
[P].O. Box 1639
[E]ufaula, OK 74432
[W]ebsite: www.2VetsArms.com
[E]mail: Sales@2VetsArms.com

[A].M.S.D. (ADVANCED MILITARY SYSTEM [DE]SIGN)
[Fa]ctory
[P].O. Box 487
[V]ernier/Geneva CH-1214 SWITZERLAND
[F]ax No.: 011-41-223497691
[W]ebsite: www.amsd.ch
[E]mail: sales@amsd.ch

[C]57LLC (57 Center LLC)
[?]525 152nd Ave NE
[R]edmond, WA 98052
[P]hone No.: 888-900-5728
[F]ax No.: 888-900-5728
[W]ebsite: www.57center.com

[A]-7 INDUSTRIES L.L.C.
[Pl]ease refer to Armalite, Inc. listing.

[A]WC SYSTEMS TECHNOLOGY, LLC
[2]3606 N. 19th Ave
[S]uite 10
[P]hoenix, AZ 85085
[P]hone No.: 623-780-1050
[T]oll Free: 800-401-7269
[F]ax No.: 623-780-2967
[W]ebsite: www.awcsilencers.com

[A]CCURACY INTERNATIONAL LTD.
[U.]S. Office
[F]redericksburg, VA
[E]mail: aina@accuracyinternational.us
[Di]stributor – Tac Pro Shooting Center
[3]5100 North State Hwy. 108
[M]ingus, TX 76463-6405
[P]hone No.: 254-968-3112
[F]ax No.: 254-968-5857
[W]ebsite: www.tacproshootingcenter.com

Distributor – Mile High Shooting Accessories
14178 Lexington Circle
Broomfield, CO 80023
Phone No.: 303-255-9999
Fax No.: 303-254-6572
Website: www.milehighshooting.com
Distributor – SRT Supply
4450 60th Ave. N.
St. Petersburg, FL 33714
Phone No.: 727-526-5451
Website: www.srtsupply.com
Factory – ACCURACY INTERNATIONAL LTD.
P.O. Box 81, Portsmouth
Hampshire, U.K. PO3 5SJ
Fax No.: 011-44-23-9269-1852
Website: www.accuracyinternational.com
Email: ai@accuracyinternational.org

ACCURATE ARMS RIFLES LLC
Phone No.: 205-345-0036
Website: www.accuratearmsinc.com
Email: ricky@accuratearmsinc.com

ACCURATE TOOL & MANUFACTURING
1108 South Broadway Unit A
Lexington, KY 40504
Phone No.: 859-231-6453
Fax No.: 859-233-0636
Website: www.accuratearmory.com
Email: kpitts@accuratearmory.com

ADAMS ARMS
612 Florida Ave
Palm Harbor, FL 34683
Toll Free: 877-461-2572
Phone No.: 727-853-0550
Fax No.: 727-853-0551
Website: www.adamsarms.net
Email: sales@adamsarms.net

ADCOR DEFENSE
234 South Haven Street
Baltimore, MD 21224
Phone No.: 888-612-3267
Website: www.adcordefense.com
Email: sales@adcordefense.com

ADEQ FIREARMS COMPANY
4921 W. Cypress Street
Tampa, FL 33607
Phone No.: 813-636-5077
Fax No.: 813-281-8925
Website: www.adeqfirearms.com

ADVANCED ARMAMENT CORP.
2408 Tech Center Parkway
Suite 150
Lawrenceville, GA 30043
Phone No.: 770-925-9988
Website: www.advanced-armament.com
Email: salesinfo@advanced-armament.com

AIM SURPLUS
3801 Lefferson Rd.
Middletown, OH 45044
Phone No.: 888-748-5252
Fax No: 513-424-9960
Website: www.aimsurplus.com
Email: sales@aimsurplus.com

ALASKA MAGNUM AR'S
3875 Geist Road
Suite E PMB453
Fairbanks, AK 99709
Phone No.: 907-835-4868
Website: www.alaskamagnumars.com

ALBERTA TACTICAL RIFLE SUPPLY
#6, 2016 25th Ave. NE
Calgary, Alberta, CANADA T2E 6Z4
Phone No.: 403-277-7786
Fax No.: 403-277-7181
Website: www.albertatacticalrifle.com
Email: info@albertatacticalrifle.com

ALEXANDER ARMS LLC
U.S. Army - Radford Arsenal
P.O. Box 1
Radford, VA 24143
Phone No.: 540-639-8356
Fax No.: 540-639-8353
Website: www.alexanderarms.com
Email: support@alexanderarms.com

ALL STAR TACTICAL LLC
1249 Ridgeway Ave., Ste. N
Rochester, NY 14615
Phone No.: 585-324-0345
Website: www.allstartactical.com
Email: info@allstartactical.com

ALPHARMS
Please refer to Leader Arms Technology listing.

AMBUSH FIREARMS
101 War Fighter Way
Black Creek, GA 31308
Phone No.: 855-262-8742
Website: www.ambushfirearms.com

AMERICAN CLASSIC
Importer - please refer to Eagle Imports listing.
Website: www.americanclassic1911.com
Email: info@americanclassic1911.com

AMERICAN GUNSMITHING ASSOCIATION
800 Connecticut Ave.
P.O. Box 5656
Norwalk, CT 06856-5656
Phone No.: 800-241-7484

AMERICAN PRECISION ARMS
55 Lyle Field Rd.
Jefferson, GA 30549
Phone No.: 706-367-8881
Website: www.americanprecisionarms.com

AMERICAN SPIRIT ARMS
16001 N. Greenway Hayden Loop, Suite B
Scottsdale, AZ 85260
Phone No.: 480-367-9540
Fax No.: 480-367-9541
Website: www.americanspiritarms.com
Email: rifles@americanspiritarms.com

AMERICAN TACTICAL IMPORTS
231 Deming Way
Summerville, SC 29483
Phone No.: 800-290-0065
Fax No.: 585-328-4168
Website: www.americantactical.us

AM-TAC PRECISION
4577 W. Chinden Blvd.
Garden City, ID 83714
Phone No.: 208-906-0585
Fax No.: 208-904-3887
Website: www.am-tac.com

ANDERSON MANUFACTURING
1743 Anderson Blvd.
Hebron, KY 41048
Phone No.: 859-689-4085
Fax No.: 859-689-4110
Website: www.andersonrifles.com
Email: sales@ATDMachineshop.com

ANZIO IRONWORKS
1905 16th Street North
St. Petersburg, FL 33704
Phone No.: 727-895-2019
Fax No.: 727-827-4728
Website: www.anzioironworks.com
Email: anzioshop@hotmail.com

ARES DEFENSE SYSTEMS, INC.
P.O. Box 120789
Melbourne, FL 32912
Phone No.: 321-242-8410
Website: www.aresdefense.com
Email: sales@aresdefense.com

ARIZONA ARMORY
Phoenix, AZ
Fax No.: 602-252-5477
Website: www.azarmory.net
Email: azarmory@msn.com

ARMALITE, INC.
P.O. Box 299
Geneseo, IL 61254
Phone No.: 800-336-0184
Fax No.: 309-944-6949
Website: www.ArmaLite.com
Email: info@armalite.com

ARMAMENT TECHNOLOGY
(Repair only - no current mfg.)
3045 Robie St., Suite 113
Halifax, N.S. CANADA B3K 4P6
Phone No.: 902-454-6384
Fax No.: 902-454-4641
Website: www.armament.com

ARMS ROOM LLC
19048 East Colonial Dr.
Orlando, FL 32820
Phone No.: 407-282-3803
Fax No.: 407-282-1165
Website: www.ArmsRoom.com
Email: service@armsroom.com

ARMS LLC
Oregon
Phone No.: 503-789-8578
Website: www.customfirearmsllc.com
Email: LarryMartin@myway.com

ARMS TECH LTD.
5025 N. Central Ave., Ste. 459
Phoenix, AZ 85012
Phone No.: 623-936-1510
Fax No.: 623-936-0361
Website: www.armstechltd.com

ARMSCOR (ARMS CORPORATION OF THE PHILIPPINES)
Importer & Distributor - Armscor Precision International
150 N. Smart Way
Pahrump, NV 89060
Phone No.: 775-537-1444
Fax No.: 775-537-1446
Website: www.rockislandarmory.com
Email: armscor@armscor.net
Factory office - Arms Corp. of the Philippines
Armscor Avenue, Fortune
Marikina City 1800, PHILIPPINES
Phone No.: 632-941-6243
Fax No.: 632-942-0682
Website: www.armscor.com.ph
Email: info@armscor.com.ph
Executive office - Arms Corp. of the Philippines
6th Floor, Strat 100 Bldg., Emerald Ave.
Ortigas Center, Pasig City, 1600 PHILIPPINES
Fax No.: 632-634-3906
Email: squires@cnl.net

ARSENAL, BULGARIA
Importer - please refer to Arsenal Inc. listing.
Factory - Arsenal 2000 JSCo.
100, Rozova Dolina St.
6100 Kazanlack, BULGARIA
Fax No.: 011-359-431-50001
Website: www.arsenal2000-bg.com
Email: arsenal2000@arsenal2000.com

ARSENAL FIREARMS
Importer – please refer to EAA Corp. listing.
Factory
Gardone, ITALY
Website: www.arsenalfirearms.com

ARSENAL INC.
3395 S. Jones Blvd. #331
Las Vegas, NV 89146
Phone No.: 702-643-2220
Fax No.: 702-643-8860
Website: www.arsenalinc.com
Email: customerservice@arsenalinc.com

ARSENAL USA LLC
Please refer to Armory USA LLC listing.

ASHBURY PRECISION ORDNANCE
P.O. Box 8024
Charlottesville, VA 22906-8024
Phone No.: 434-296-8600
Fax No.: 434-296-9260
Website: www.Ashburyprecisionordnance.com
Email: info@Ashburyprecisionordnance.com

ASTRA ARMS S.A.
Case Postale 103
1951 Sion SWITZERLAND
Fax No.: 011-41-027-322-3707
Website: www.astra-arms.ch
Email: astra@astra-arms.ch

AUTO-ORDNANCE CORP.
Please refer to the Kahr Arms listing.
Website: www.auto-ordnance.com
Website: www.tommygun.com
Website: www.tommygunshop.com

AZTEK ARMS
1641 W. Alvey Drive #1
Mapleton, UT 84664
Phone No.: 801-704-9760
Fax No.: 801-704-9759
Website: www.aztekarms.com
Email: info@aztekarms.com

BAER, LES
Please refer to the Les Baer Custom listing.

BWE FIREARMS
Longwood, FL
Phone No.: 407-592-3975
Website: www.bwefirearms.com
Email: Richard@bwefirearms.com

BAIKAL
Importer – please refer to US Sporting Goods listing.
Baikal Factory
Izhevsky Mekhanichesky Zavod
8, Promyshlennaya str.
Izhevsk, 426063 RUSSIA
Fax No.: 011-95-007-341-2665830
Website: www.baikalinc.ru
Email: worldlinks@baikalinc.ru

BARNES PRECISION MACHINE, INC.
1434 Farrington Road
Apex, NC 27523
Phone No.: 919-362-6805
Fax No.: 919-362-5752
Website: www.barnesprecision.com
Email: info@barnesprecision.com

BARRETT FIREARMS MANUFACTURING, INC.
P.O. Box 1077
Murfreesboro, TN 37133
Phone No.: 615-896-2938
Fax No.: 615-896-7313
Website: www.barrett.net
Email: mail@barrett.net

TLE RIFLE COMPANY
056 Hercules Ave.
ouston, TX 77058
one No: 281-777-0316
x No.: 866-804-3049
ebsite: www.battleriflecompany.com
nail: info@battleriflecompany.com

NELLI
orter - Benelli USA
7603 Indian Head Highway
ccokeek, MD 20607-2501
hone No.: 800-264-4962
ax No.: 301-283-6988
ebsite: www.benelliusa.com
tol/Airgun Importer - please refer to Larry's
ns listing.
rranty Repair Address - Benelli USA
01 Eighth Street
ocomoke, MD 21851
ctory - Benelli Armi S.p.A.
ia della Stazione, 50
61029 Urbino (PU) ITALY
ax No.: 011-39-0722-307-207
ebsite: www.benelli.it

RETTA, PIETRO
porter - Beretta U.S.A. Corp
7601 Beretta Drive
ccokeek, MD 20607
hone No.: 301-283-2191
ax No.: 301-283-0189
ebsite: www.berettausa.com
ctory - Fabbrica d'Armi Pietro Beretta S.p.A
ia Pietro Beretta 18
5063 Gardone Val Trompia
rescia, ITALY
ax No.: 011-39-30-834-1421
ebsite: www.beretta.it

RSA
porter - please refer to Eagle Imports listing.
ebsite: www.bersa.com
mail:info@bersa.com
ctory - Bersa S.A.
astillo 312
1704) Ramos Mejia, ARGENTINA
ax No.: 011-54-1-656-2093

ACK DAWN INDUSTRIES
511 N. Ohio
edalia, MO 65308
hone No.: 660-851-0907
ax No.: 660-851-0207
ebsite: www.blackdawnguns.com

ACK FORGE
hone No.: 407-737-7222
ebsite: www.blackforgeweapons.com

ACK RAIN ORDNANCE, INC.
.O. Box 1111
eosho, MO 64850
hone No.: 417-456-1920
oll Free: 888-836-2620
ax No.: 417-451-2811
ebsite: www.blackrainordnance.com
mail: info@blackrainordnance.com

ACK RIFLE COMPANY LLC
5140 SE 82nd Drive, Ste. 350
ackamas, OR 97015
oll Free: 888-566-1405
ebsite: www.blackriflecompany.com

ACK WEAPONS ARMORY
645 E. Broadway Blvd.
ucson, AZ 85711
hone No.: 866-779-2268
ebsite: www.blackweaponsarmory.com

BLACKHEART INTERNATIONAL LLC
21150 Barbour County Hwy.
Philippi, WV 26416
Phone No.: 304-457-1280
Fax No.: 304-457-1281
Website: www.bhiarms.com

BLACKOPS TECHNOLOGIES
196 Sunrise Creek Loop
Suite 55
Columbia Falls, MT 59912
Website: www.blackopsprecision.com

BLASER
Importer & Distributor - Blaser USA, Inc.
403 East Ramsey, Ste. 301
San Antonio, TX 78216
Phone No.: 210-377-2527
Fax No.: 210-377-2533
Website: www.blaser-usa.com
Factory - Blaser Jagdwaffen GmbH
Ziegelstadel 1
D-88316 Isny im Allgau, GERMANY
Fax No.: 011-49-75-62702-43
Website: www.blaser.de

BLUEGRASS ARMORY
Good Times Outdoors
4600 West Highway 326
Ocala, FL 34482
Phone No.: 352-401-9070
Fax No.: 352-401-9667
Website: www.bluegrassarmory.com
Email: support@bluegrassarmory.com

BOBCAT WEAPONS INC.
Please refer to Red Rock Arms listing.

BOWMAC GUNPAR INC.
Canadian Parts Supplier
69 Iber Rd., Unit 101
Stittsville, Ontario CANADA K2S 1E7
Phone No.: 800-668-2509
Phone No.: 613-831-8548
Fax No.: 613-831-0530

BRAVO COMPANY MFG., INC.
P.O. Box 361
Hartland, WI 53029
Phone No.: 877-272-8626
Fax No.: 262-367-0989
Website: www.bravocompanymfg.com
Email: info@bravocompanyusa.com

BRILEY MANUFACTURING INC.
1230 Lumpkin Rd.
Houston, TX 77043
Phone No.: 713-932-6995 (Technical)
Phone No.: 800-331-5718 (Orders only)
Fax No.: 713-932-1043
Website: www.briley.com

BROWNING
Administrative Headquarters
One Browning Place
Morgan, UT 84050-9326
Phone No.: 801-876-2711
Product Service: 800-333-3288
Fax No.: 801-876-3331
Website: www.browning.com
Website: www.browningint.com
Custom Shop U.S. Representative
Mr. Ron McGhie
Email: ronm@browning.com

Browning Parts and Service
3005 Arnold Tenbrook Rd.
Arnold, MO 63010-9406
Phone No.: 800-322-4626
Fax No.: 636-287-9751
*Historical Research (Browning Arms Co. marked
guns only)*
Browning Historian
One Browning Place
Morgan, UT 84050-9326
Fax No.: 801-876-3331
Website: www.browning.com

BRÜGGER & THOMET
Importer - please refer to DSA listing.
Factory
Zelglistrasse 10
CH-3608 Thun, SWITZERLAND
Fax No.: 011-41-33-334-6701
Website: www.bt-ag.ch

BUEHLER CUSTOM SPORTING ARMS
P.O. Box 4096
Medford, OR 97501
Phone No.: 541-664-9109
Website: www.customsportingarms.com
Email: info@customsportingarms.com

BUL LTD.
Importer – M1911 Parts Only
All America Sales, Inc.
8884 Hwy. 62 West
Piggot, AR 72454
Phone No.: 870-544-2809
Fax: 870-544-2695
Factory - Bul Transmark Ltd.
10 Rival Street
Tel-Aviv 67778, ISRAEL
Fax No.: 011-972-3-687-4853
Website: www.bultransmark.com
Email: info@bultransmark.com

BUMAR
Exclusive Distributor – Beryl ASG
Al. Jana Pawla LL nr 11,
00-828 Warszawa, POLAND
Phone No.: 011-48-22-311-2512
Fax No.: 011-48-22-311-2659
Website: www.bumar.com
Email: bumar@bumar.com

BUSHMASTER FIREARMS INTERNATIONAL
Part of Freedom Group - Headquarters
PO Box 556
Madison, NC 27025
Phone No.: 800-883-6229
Fax No.: 207-892-8068
Website: www.bushmaster.com
Email: info@bushmaster.com

CMMG, INC.
P.O. Box 369
Fayette, MO 65248
Phone No.: 660-248-2293
Fax No.: 660-248-2290
Website: www.cmmginc.com
Email: sales@cmmginc.com

C Z (CESKA ZBROJOVKA)
Firearms & Airguns Importer - CZ-USA
P.O. Box 171073
Kansas City, KS 66117-0073
Phone No.: 913-321-1811
Toll Free No.: 800-955-4486
Fax No.: 913-321-2251
Website: www.cz-usa.com
Email: info@cz-usa.com
Website: www.safariclassics.com
(custom rifles only)

Administration Offices - Ceska Zbrojovka
Svatopluka Cecha 1283
CZ-68827 Uhersky Brod CZECH REPUBLIC
Fax No.: 011-420-63363-3811
Website: www.czub.cz
Email: info@czub.cz

CZ (STRAKONICE)
Factory - LUVO Prague Ltd.
Rejskova 7
120 00 Praha 2 CZECH REPUBLIC
Fax No.: 011-420-222-562-238
Website: www.luvo.cz
Email: luvo@iol.cz

CABELAS INC.
One Cabela Dr.
Sidney, NE 69160
Phone No.: 800-237-4444
Fax No.: 800-496-6329
website: www.cabelas.com

CALICO LIGHT WEAPON SYSTEMS
924 N. Freemont Lane
Cornelius, OR 97113
Phone No.: 503-649-3010
Toll free: 888-442-2542
Fax No.: 503-649-3831
Website: www.calicolightweaponsystems.com

CANIK55
Importer - Please refer to Tristar listing.
Factory - Samsub Domestic Defense and Industry
Corporation
Organize Sanayi Bölgesi
No: 28 Kutlukent/SAMSUN TURKEY
Fax No.: 011-90-362-266-6671
Website: www.canik55.com
Email: samsun@canik55.com

CARACAL
Importer – Caracal USA
2530 Morgan Road
Bessemer, AL 35022
Phone No.: 205-417-8644
Fax No.: 205-417-8647
Website: www.caracalusa.com
Email: info@caracalusa.com
Distributor (Italy only) – please refer to Fratelli
Tanfoglio listing.
Factory
Tawazun Industrial Park
Sweihan
P.O. Box 94499
Abu Dhabi, UNITED ARAB EMIRATES
Tel: 011-971-2-5854441
Fax: 011-971-2-5854445
Website: www.caracal.ae
Email: info@caracal.ae

CASPIAN ARMS, LTD.
75 Cal Foster Dr.
Wolcott, VT 05680
Phone No.: 802-472-6454
Fax No.: 802-472-6709
Website: www.caspianarms.com
Email: info@caspianarms.com

CENTURY INTERNATIONAL ARMS, INC.
430 South Congress Ave., Ste. 1
Delray Beach, FL 33445
Phone No.: 800-527-1252
Phone No.: 561-265-4530
Fax No.: 561-265-4520
Website: www.centuryarms.com
Email: support@centuryarms.com

CHARLES DALY (2011-PRESENT)
Importer – please refer to Samco Global Arms, Inc.
(SGAI)
Website: www.charlesdaly-us.com
Email: orders@charlesdaly-us.com

CHATTAHOOCHEE GUN WORKS LLC
9th Ave., P.O. Box 2361
Phenix City, AL 36867
Phone No.: 334-408-2616
Fax No.: 334-408-2609
Website: www.c-gw.com
Email: service@cgunworks.com

CHEYTAC LLC
541 Hazel Ave.
Nashville, GA 31639
Phone No.: 855-243-9822
Website: www.cheytac.com

CHIAPPA FIREARMS LTD.
U.S. Office
1414 Stanley Ave.
Dayton, OH 47404
Phone No.: 937-835-4894
Fax No.: 888-705-4570
Website: www.chiappafirearms.com
Email: info@chiappafirearms.com

CHRISTIAN ARMORY WORKS
Rock Spring, GA
Phone No.: 423-290-1799
Website: www.christianarmoryworks.com
Email: christianarmoryworks@gmail.com

CHRISTENSEN ARMS
550 North Cemetery Rd.
Gunnison, UT 84634
Phone No.: 435-528-7999
Fax No.: 435-528-5773
Website: www.christensenarms.com
Email: sales@christensenarms.com

CITADEL
Please refer to Legacy Sports listing.

CLARK CUSTOM GUNS, INC.
336 Shootout Lane
Princeton, LA 71067
Phone No.: 318-949-9884
Fax No.: 318-949-9829
website: www.clarkcustomguns.com
Email: ccgweb@shreve.net

COBB MANUFACTURING, INC.
Please refer to Bushmaster listing.

CODY FIREARMS MUSEUM
720 Sheridan Ave.
Cody, WY 82414
Historical Research Phone No.: 307-578-4031
Website: www.centerofthewest.org

COLT
Colt's Manufacturing Company LLC
P.O. Box 1868
Hartford, CT 06144-1868
Phone No.: 800-962-COLT
Fax No.: 860-244-1449
Website: www.coltsmfg.com
Colt Defense LLC (Law Enforcement & Rifles)
P.O. Box 118
Hartford, CT 06141
Phone No.: 860-232-4489
Fax No.: 860-244-1442
Website: www.colt.com
AR-15 Rifles, .22 LR cal. only - please refer to
Umarex USA listing.

Historical Research - Colt Archive Properties LL
P.O. Box 1868
Hartford, CT 01644-1868
If mailing in a request, make sure the proper
research fee is enclosed (please refer to
appropriate Colt section for current fees and rela
information).

COMMANDO ARMS
Komando Av San. Tic. Ltd. Sti.
Hisarici Mah. Ahmet Toprak Cad. No. 9
Balikesir, TURKEY
Fax No.: 011-90-266-243-4764
Website: www.commando-arms.com
Email: info@commando-arms.com

COMPETITIVE EDGE GUNWORKS LLC
17154 CR 180
Bogard, MO 64622
Phone No.: 660-731-5124
Fax No.: 660-731-5091
Website: www.competiveedgegunworks.com

CONTROLLED CHAOS ARMS
8401 Hwy. S52 North
Baxter, IA 50028
Phone No.: 515-344-4443
Website: www.controlledchaosarms.com

CORE 15 RIFLE SYSTEMS
Good Time Outdoors, Inc.
4600 West Highway 326
Ocala, FL 34482
Phone No.: 352-401-9070
Fax No.: 352-401-9667
Website: www.core15rifles.com
Email: sales@core15rifles.com

CORONADO ARMS
450 S. Porter Road
Dixon, CA 95620
Phone No.: 707-678-2864
Fax No.: 707-678-3542
Website: www.coronadoarms.com
Email: sales@coronadoarms.com

CROSS CANYON ARMS
2020 South Painter Lane
West Haven, UT 84401
Phone No: 801-731-0172
Website: www.crosscanyonarms.com

CRUSADER WEAPONRY
5323 S. Baker Street
Murray, UT 84107
Phone No.: 801-808-6439
Website: www.crusaderweaponry.com

CZECHPOINT, INC.
P.O. Box 9207
Knoxville, TN 37940
Phone No.: 865-247-0184
Fax No.: 865-247-0185
Website: www.czechpoint-usa.com
Email: dan.brown@czechpoint-usa.com

D&L SPORTS, INC.
P.O. Box 4843
Chino Valley, AZ 86323
Phone No.: 928-636-1726
Fax No.: 928-636-1757
Website: www.dlsports.com

D.A.R. (DYNAMICS ARMS RESEARCH) GmbH
Thanhofer Straße 111
D-08115 Lichtentanne, GERMANY
Phone No.: 011-49-375-21094780
Website: www.dar-germany.com
Email: info@dar-germany.com

MS FIREARMS
312 12th Street SE
St. Cloud, MN 56304
Phone No.: 320-258-4448
Toll Free: 800-578-3767
Fax No.: 320-258-4449
Website: www.dpmsinc.com
Email: dpms@dpmsinc.com

A, INC.
P.O. Box 370
Barrington, IL 60011
Phone No.: 847-277-7258
Fax No.: 847-277-7259
Website: www.dsarms.com
Email: customerservice@dsarms.com

EWOO
o current commercial importation.

ANIEL DEFENSE
101 Warfighter Way
Black Creek, GA 31308
Phone No.: 866-554-4867
Phone No.: 912-964-4238
Fax No.: 912-851-3248
Website: www.danieldefense.com

AUDSONS ARMOURY
Industrial Estate, Kohat Road
Peshawar, 25210 PAKISTAN
Fax No.: 011-92-91-276059
Web site: www.daudsons.org
Email: info@daudsons.org

AVIDSON'S
6100 Wilkinson Dr.
Prescott, AZ 86301-6162
Phone No.: 800-367-4867
Fax No.: 928-776-0344
Website: www.galleryofguns.com

EL-TON, INCORPORATED
330 Aviation Parkway
Elizabethtown, NC 28337
Phone No.: 910-645-2172
Fax No.: 910-645-2244
Website: www.del-ton.com
Email: sales@del-ton.com

ERYA HUNTING ARMS
Factory
Üzümlü, Beyşehir
Konya, TURKEY
Distributor -Societe Fayoumi
Salim Salam Blvd.
Fayoumi Bldg.
Beirut, LEBANON
Phone No.: 011-90-332-524-6034
Fax No.: 011-90-332-524-6214
Website: www.deryasilah.com.tr
Website: www.societefayoumi.com
Email: deryasilah@hotmail.com

ESERT ORDNANCE
300 Sydney Drive
McCarran, NV 89434
Phone No.: 775-343-1330
Fax No.: 775-313-9852
Website: www.desertord.com
Email: questions@desertord.com

ESERT TECH (DESERT TACTICAL ARMS)
1995 W. Alexander Street
West Valley City, UT 84119
Phone No.: 801-975-7272
Fax No.: 801-908-6425
Website: www.deserttech.com

DETONICS DEFENSE TECHNOLOGIES, LLC
609 South Breese Street
Millstadt, IL 62260
Phone No.: 618-476-3200
Fax No.: 618-476-3226
Website: www.detonics.ws
Email: contactus@detonics.ws

DEZ TACTICAL ARMS, INC.
WI
Phone No.: 608-547-9034
Website: www.deztacticalarms.com
Email: info@deztacticalarms.com

DLASK ARMS CORP.
16 7167 Vantage Way
British Columbia, V46 1K7 CANADA
Phone No.: 604-952-0837
Website: www.dlaskarms.com

DOLPHIN GUN COMPANY
Southwold, Station Road, Donington on Bain
Lincolnshire LN11 9TR U.K.
Phone No.: 011-44-01507343898
Website: www.dolphinguncompany.co.uk

DOUBLESTAR CORPORATION
P.O. Box 430
Winchester, KY 40392
Phone No.: 888-736-7725
Fax No.: 859-745-4638
Website: www.jtfoc.com
Email: doug@star15.com

DRULOV
Factory – PPK s.r.o.
Dukelska 451
01 Holice, CZECH REPUBLIC
Phone No.:011-420-739-043-139
Website: www.zbrojovkaholice.cz
Email: info@zbrojovkaholice.cz

E.D.M. ARMS
2410 West 350 North
Hurricane, UT 84737
Phone No.: 435-635-5233
Fax No.: 435-635-5258
Website: www.edmarms.com
Email: sales@edmarms.com

E.M.F. COMPANY
1900 E. Warner Ave., Suite 1-D
Santa Ana, CA 92705
Phone No.: 949-261-6611
Fax No.: 949-756-0133
Website: www.emf-company.com
Email: sales@emf-company.com

EAGLE ARMS
Please refer to Armalite listing.

EAGLE IMPORTS, INC.
1750 Brielle Ave., Unit B-1
Wanamassa, NJ 07712
Phone No.: 732-493-0302
Fax No.: 732-493-0301
Website: www.eagleimportsinc.com
Email: info@bersa.com

EAST RIDGE GUN COMPANY, INC.
6319 5th Ave.
Bancroft, WI 54921
Phone No.: 715-366-2006
Website: www.statearms.com
Email: eastrdge@uniontel.net

ED BROWN PRODUCTS, INC.
P.O. Box 492
Perry, MO 63462
Phone No.: 573-565-3261
Fax No.: 573-565-2791
Website: www.edbrown.com
Email: edbrown@edbrown.com

EDWARD ARMS COMPANY
3020 N. 44th Street
Phoenix, AZ 85018
Phone No.: 602-456-9833
Website: www.edwardarms.com
Email: info@edwardarms.com

ENTRÉPRISE ARMS INC.
15509 Arrow Hwy
Irwindale CA 91706-2002
Phone No.: 626-962-8712
Fax No.: 626-962-4692
Website: www.entreprise.com

ESCORT
Importer - please refer to Legacy Sports
International listing.
Factory - Hatsan Arms Company
Izmir - Ankara Karayolu 28. km. No. 289
Kemalpasa 35170, İzmir - TURKEY
Fax No.: 011-90-232-878-9102-878-9723
Website: www.hatsan.com.tr
Email: info@hatsan.com.tr

EUROPEAN AMERICAN ARMORY CORP.
P.O. Box 560746
Rockledge, FL 32959
Phone No.: 321-639-4842
Fax No.: 321-639-7006
Website: www.eaacorp.com
Email: eaacorp@eaacorp.com

EVOLUTION USA
P.O. Box 154
White Bird, ID 83554
Phone No.: 208-983-9208
Fax No. 208-983-0944
Website: www.evo-rifles.com
Email: info@evo-rifles.com

EXCEL INDUSTRIES, INC.
1601 Fremont Ct.
Ontario, CA 91761
Phone No.: 909-947-4867
Fax No.: 909-947-0100
Website: www.excelarms.com
Email: excelind@verizon.net

F&D DEFENSE
2405 Lifehaus Industrial Dr. Suite 101
New Braunfels, TX 78130
Phone No.: 405-380-4346
Fax No.: 214-451-6380
Website: www.fd-defense.com
Email: info@fd-defense.com

FEG
Factory - FEGARMY
1095 Budapest, Soroksari ut 158
Levelcim: H-1440 Budapest Pf. 6 HUNGARY
Fax No.: 011-361-280-6669

FMK
P.O. Box 1358
Placentia, CA 92871
Phone No.: 714-630-0658
Fax No.: 714-630-0664
Website: www.fmkfirearms.com

FMR
3 rue Michelet
93500 Pantin FRANCE
Website: www.fmr-unique.com
Email: stephane-rolin@orange.fr

FNH USA
P.O. Box 697
McLean, VA 22101
Phone No.: 703-288-1292
Fax No.: 703-288-1730
Website: www.fnhusa.com
Email: info@fnhusa.com
Military Only
P.O. Box 896
McLean, VA 22101
Phone No.: 703-288-3500
Fax No.: 703-288-4505
Factory - F.N. Herstal S.A.
Voie de Liege, 33
Herstal, BELGIUM B4040
Fax No.: 011-324-240-8679
Website: www.fnherstal.com

FABARM S.p.A.
Importer – Fabarm USA
700 Lake Street
Cambridge, MD 21613
Phone No.: 410-901-1260
Website: www.fabarmusa.com
Factory - Fabbrica Breciana Armi
Via Averolda 31, Zona Industriale
I-25039 Travagliato, Brescia ITALY
Fax No.: 011-39-030-686-3684
Website: www.fabarm.com

FABRIQUE NATIONALE
Factory - Browning S.A.
Fabrique Nationale Herstal SA
Parc Industriel des Hauts Sarts
3me Ave. 25
B-4040 Herstal, BELGIUM
Fax No.: 011-32-42-40-5212

FABRYKA BRONI LUCZNIK – RADOM SP. ZO.O.
Imorter - please refer to I.O., Inc.
Ul. 1905 Roku 1/9
26-600 Radom, POLAND
Phone No.: 011-48-48-380-3122
Website: www.fabrykabroni.pl

FAXON FIREARMS
11101 Adwood Drive
Cincinnati, OH 45240
Phone No.: 513-674-2580
Website: www.faxonfirearms.com

FEATHER USA
600 Oak Avenue
P.O. Box 247
Eaton, CO 80615
Phone No.: 800-519-0485
Fax No.: 970-206-1958
Website: www.featherusa.com
Email: featherawi@aol.com

FIERCE FIREARMS, LLC
321 South Main Street
P.O. Box 1045
Gunnison, UT 84634
Phone No.: 435-528-5080
Website: www.fiercearms.com
Email: info@fiercearms.com

FIREARMS INTERNATIONAL INC.
5200 Mitchelldale, Suite E-17
Houston, TX 77092
Phone No.: 713-462-4200
Fax No.: 713-681-5665
Website: www.highstandard.com
Email: info@highstandard.com

FIREBIRD PRECISION
P.O. Box 855
Mountainair, NM 87036
Phone No.: 505-847-0108
Website: www.firebirdprecision.com

FORT SOE SIA
Factory - Science Industrial Association Fort of the
Ministry of Internal Affairs of Ukraine
27, 600-letiya str.
Vinnitsa 21027 UKRAINE
Fax No.: 011-380-432-468-016-461-002
Website: www.fort.vn.ua
Email: siafort@ukr.net

FRANCHI, LUIGI
Importer - please refer to Benelli USA listing.
Website: www.franchiusa.com
Factory - Franchi, Luigi, S.p.A.
via Artigiani 1
I-25063 Gardone, VT (Brescia) ITALY
Fax No.: 011-039-030-8341-899
Website: www.franchi.com
Email: info@franchi.com

FRANKLIN ARMORY
305 Vineyard Town Center #220
Morgan Hill, CA 95037
Phone No.: 408-779-7560
Fax No.: 408-782-1200
Website: www.franklinarmory.com
Email: info@franklinarmory.com

FULTON ARMORY
8725 Bollman Place Suite #1
Savage, MD 20763
Phone No.: 301-490-9485
Fax No.: 301-490-9547
Website: www.fulton-armory.com

GA PRECISION
1141 Swift Street
N. Kansas City, MO 64116
Phone No.: 816-221-1844
Website: www.gaprecision.net

G.A.R. ARMS
P.O. Box 1193
Fairacres, NM 88033
Phone No.: 575-647-9703
Fax No.: 575-541-9056
Website: www.gar-arms.com

GWACS ARMORY
907 S. Detroit Ave
6th Floor
Tulsa, OK 74120
Website: www.gwacsarmory.com
Email: sales@gwacsarmory.com

GALIL
No current U.S. importation - semi-auto rifle
configuration was banned April, 1998.
Israel Weapon Industries Ltd.
P.O Box 63 Ramat Hashron
47100 ISRAEL
Website: www.israel-weapon.com
Email: info@israel-weapon.com

GERMAN SPORT GUNS GmbH
Importer - please refer to American Tactical
Imports listing.
Oesterweg 21
Ense-Höingen, D-59469 GERMANY
Fax No.: 011-49-2938-97837-130
Website: www.gsg-5.de

GIBBS RIFLE CO.
Please refer to Navy Arms listing.

GIRSAN MACHINE & LIGHT WEAPON INDUSTR
COMPANY
Factory
Batlama Deresi Mevkii Sunta Sokak No. 19
Giresun, TURKEY
Fax No.: 011-90-454-215-3928
Website: www.yavuz16.com
Email: satis@yavuz16.com

GLOCK, INC.
Importer
6000 Highlands Pkwy.
Smyrna, GA 30082
Fax No.: 770-433-8719
Website: www.US.Glock.com
Factory - Glock Ges.m.b.H.
Nelkengasse 3, POB 9
A-2232 Deutsch-Wagram AUSTRIA
Fax No.: 011-43-2247-90300312
Website: www.glock.com

GSI (GUN SOUTH INC.)
Please refer to Merkel USA listing.

G.U. INC.
Please refer to SKB Shotguns listing.

THE GUN ROOM CO., LLC
Please refer to Noreen Firearms LLC listing.

GUNCRAFTER INDUSTRIES
171 Madison 1510
Huntsville, AR 72740
Phone No.: 479-665-2466
Website: www.guncrafterindustries.com

GUNSMOKE
9690 W. 44th Ave
Wheat Ridge, CO 80033
Phone No.: 303-456-4545
Website: www.gunsmokeguns.com
Email: info@gunsmokeguns.com

GUNSMOKE ENTERPRISES
P.O. Box 2537
Okeechobee, FL 34973
Phone No.: 863-763-1582
Fax No.: 863-357-3737
Website: www.gunsmokeenterprises.net

H-S PRECISION, INC.
1301 Turbine Dr.
Rapid City, SD 57703
Phone No.: 605-341-3006
Fax No.: 605-342-8964
Website: www.hsprecision.com

HAGELBERG ARMS DESIGN
DENMARK
Website: www.frans-hagelber.dk
Email: info@franshagelber.dk

HATCHER GUN COMPANY
76650 Road 342
Elsie, NE 69134
Phone No.: 308-228-2454
Fax No.: 308-228-2522
Website: www.hatchergun.com
Email: th@hatchergun.com

TSAN ARMS COMPANY
*porter - please refer to Legacy Sports
ernational LLC listing.*
mir-Ankara Karayolu 28.km. No. 289
emalpasa 35170 Izmir TURKEY
ax No.: 011-90-232-878-9102
ebsite: www.hatsan.com.tr
mail: info@hatsan.com.tr

CKLER & KOCH, INC.
porter – H&K USA
575 Transport Blvd.
olumbus, GA 31907
hone No.: 706-568-1906
ax No.: 706-568-9151
ebsite: www.hk-usa.com
ctory - Heckler & Koch GmbH
lte Steige 7
.O. Box 1329
-78722 Oberndorf Neckar GERMANY
ax No.: 011-49-7423-792350
ebsite: www.heckler-koch.com

AD DOWN PRODUCTS
031 Fambrough Court, Suite 300
allas, GA 30770
hone No.: 770-485-7015
ax No.: 770-421-6345
ebsite: www.hdrifles.co

NRY REPEATING ARMS COMPANY
9 East 1st Street
ayonne, NJ 07002
hone No.: 201-858-4400
ax No.: 201-858-4435
ebsite: www.henry-guns.com
mail: info@henryrepeating.com

RA ARMS
iegelhüttenweg 5
riefenstein D-97855 GERMANY
ax No.: 011-49-0939-878723
ebsite: www.hera-arms.com
mail: info@hera-arms.de

ENDLMAYER, KLAUS
ease refer to Waffen Hiendlmayer listing.

-POINT FIREARMS
S. Marketer - MKS Supply, Inc.
611-A North Dixie Drive
ayton, OH 45414
hone No.: 877-425-4867
ax No.: 937-454-0503
ebsite: www.hi-pointFirearms.com
mail: mkshpoint@aol.com

GH STANDARD MANUFACTURING CO.
751 Mitchelldale, Ste. B-11
ouston, TX 77092
hone No.: 713-462-4200
ax No.: 713-681-5665
ebsite: www.highstandard.com
mail: info@highstandard.com

GAN MANUFACTURING LLC
Glendale, AZ 85301
Phone No.: 623-463-1939
Fax No.: 623-463-1941
Website: www.hoganguns.com

USTON ARMORY
13335 Murphy Rd., Suite B
Stafford, TX 77477
Phone No.: 281-289-4867
Website: www.HoustonArmory.com
Email: info@HoustonArmory.com

HOULDING PRECISION FIREARMS
2980 Falcon Drive
Madera, CA 93637
Phone No.: 559-675-9922
Website: www.houldingfirearms.com
Email: info@houldingfirearms.com

HOWA
Importer - please refer to Legacy Sports listing.

HULDRA ARMS
Mfg. – please refer to Adams Arms listing.
Distributor – Fleet Farm stores
Service
512 Laurel Street
P.O. Box 5055
Brainerd, MN 56401
Phone No.: 218-829-3521
Website: www.huldraarms.com
Email: service@huldraarms.com

I.O. INC.
2144 Franklin Drive NE
Palm Bay, FL 32905
Phone No.: 321-499-3819
Fax No.: 321-499-3822
Website: www.ioinc.us
Email: info@ioinc.us

ISSC HANDELSGESELLSCHAFT
Importer – please refer to Legacy Sports listing.
Factory
Hannesgrub 3
A-4910 Ried/Innkreis AUSTRIA
Fax: 011-43-7752-21271
Website: www.issc.at
Email: issc@inext.at

INTEGRITY ARMS & SURVIVAL
1450 Greensboro Hwy.
Watkinsville, GA 30677
Phone No.: 678-883-AR15
Website: www.customar15.net

INTERARMS ARSENAL
Please refer to High Standard listing.

INTERSTATE ARMS CORP.
6 Dunham Road
Billerica, MA 01821
Phone No.: 800-243-3006
Phone No.: 978-667-7060
Fax No.: 978-671-0023
Website: www.interstatearms.com

IRON BRIGADE ARMORY
100 Radcliffe Circle
Jacksonville, NC 28546
Phone No.: 910-455-3834
Fax No.: 910-346-1134
Website: www.deathfromafar.com

IRON RIDGE ARMS CO.
1110 Delaware Ave.
Suite A
Longmount, CO 80501
Phone No.: 303-772-4365
Fax No.: 303-772-6204
Website: www.ironridgeguns.com
Email: tech@ironridgeguns.com

ISRAEL WEAPON INDUSTRIES LTD. (I.W.I.)
Importer –IWI US, Inc. (centerfire firearms)
P.O. Box 12607
Harrisburg, PA 17112
Phone No.: 717-695-2081
Website: www.iwi.us
Importer – Please refer to Umarex USA listing.

ITHACA GUN COMPANY
420 N. Warpole St.
Upper Sandusky, OH 43351
Phone No.: 877-648-4222
Fax No.: 419-294-3230
Web site: www.ithacagun.com

IVER JOHNSON ARMS, INC.
1840 Baldwin Street, Unit 10
Rockledge, FL 32955
Phone No.: 321-636-3377
Fax No.: 321-632-7745
Website: www.iverjohnsonarms.com

J.B. CUSTOM INC.
16335 Lima Rd., Bldg. #5
Huntertown, IN 46748
Phone No.: 260-338-1894
Fax No.: 260-338-1585
Website: www.jbcustom.com
Email: jbcjim@gmail.com

J.L.D. ENTERPRISES, INC.
Please refer to PTR Industries listing.

JP ENTERPRISES, INC.
P.O Box 378
Hugo, MN 55038
Phone No.: 651-426-9196
Fax No.: 651-426-2472
Website: www.jprifles.com
Email: service@jprifles.com

J R CARBINES, LLC
Please refer to Just Right Carbines listing.

JACK FIRST, INC.
Gun Parts/Accessories/Service
1201 Turbine Dr.
Rapid City, SD 57703
Phone No.: 605-343-9544
Fax No.: 605-343-9420
Website: www.jackfirstgun.com

JAMES RIVER ARMORY
3601 Commerce Drive
Suite 110
Halethorpe, MD 21227
Phone No.: 410-242-6991
Website: www.jamesriverarmory.com
Email: jamesriverarmory@gmail.com

JARD, INC.
3149 Nest Ave.
Sheldon, IA 51201
Phone No.: 712-324-7409
Website: www.jardinc.com
Email: jardusa@live.com

JARRETT RIFLES, INC.
383 Brown Road
Jackson, SC 29831
Phone No.: 803-471-3616
Fax No.: 803-471-9246
Website: www.jarrettrifles.com

JUST RIGHT CARBINES
231 Saltonstall Street
Canandaigua, NY 14424
Phone No.: 585-396-1551
Fax No.: 585-394-1523
Website: www.justrightcarbines.com

K-VAR CORP.
4001 S. Decatur Blvd. #37383
Las Vegas, NV 89103
Phone No.: 702-364-8880
Fax No.: 702-307-2303
Website: www.k-var.com

KAHR ARMS
130 Goddard Memorial Dr.
Worcester, MA 01603
Phone No.: 508-795-3919
Fax No.: 508-795-7046
Website: www.kahr.com
Website: www.kahrshop.com

KEL-TEC CNC INDUSTRIES, INC.
P.O Box 236009
Cocoa, FL 32923
Phone No.: 321-631-0068
Fax No.: 321-631-1169
Website: www.keltecweapons.com
Email: ktcustserv@kel-tec-cnc.com

KEPPELER TECHNISCHE ENTWICKLUNG GmbH
Friedrich-Reinhardt Strasse 4
D-74427 Fichtenberg, GERMANY
Fax No.: 011-49-07971-91-1243
Website: www.keppeler-te.de
Email: info@keppeler-te.de

KIMBER
Corporate Offices - Kimber Mfg., Inc.
555 Taxter Road, Suite 235
Elmsford, NY 10523
Phone No.: 888-243-4522
Fax No.: 406-758-2223
Website: www.kimberamerica.com
Email: info@kimberamerica.com

KING'S ARSENAL
1110 Hwy. 80 E
Abilene, TX 79601
Phone No.: 325-669-5064
Website: www.kingsarsenal.com

KNESEK GUNS INC.
1204 Knesek Lane
Van Buren, AR 72956
Phone No.: 479-474-1680
Fax No.: 479-471-0377
Website: www.knesekguns.com
Email: sales@knesekguns.com

KNIGHT'S ARMAMENT COMPANY
701 Columbia Blvd.
Titusville, FL 32780
Phone No.: 321-607-9900
Website: www.knightarmco.com

KORSTOG
Mfg. – please refer to Adams Arms listing.
Exclusive U.S. Retailer – Fleet Farm stores
Service
512 Laurel Street
P.O. Box 5055
Brainerd, MN 56401
Phone No.: 218-829-3521
Website: www.korstog.com
Email: info@korstog.com

KRISS SYSTEMS SA
Importer/US Factory – Kriss USA
P.O. Box 8928
Virginia Beach, VA 23450
Phone No.: 757-821-1089
Fax No.: 757-821-1094
Website: www.kriss-tdi.com

Factory
Ch. De la Vuarpilliere 35 1260 Nyon
SWITZERLAND
Phone No.: 011-41-22-363-7820
Fax No.: 011-41-22-363-7821

LRB ARMS
96 Cherry Lane
Floral Park, NY 11001
Phone No.: 516-327-9061
Website: www.lrbarms.com

LWRC INTERNATIONAL, LLC
815 Chesapeake Dr.
Cambridge, MD 21613
Phone No.: 410-901-1348
Fax No.: 410-228-1775
Website: www.lwrci.com

LANCER SYSTEMS
7566 Morris Court
Suite 300
Allentown, PA 18106
Phone No: 610-973-2600
Website: www.lancer-systems.com

LARUE TACTICAL
850 Country Road 177
Leander, TX 78641
Phone No.: 512-259-1585
Website: www.laruetactical.com

LAUER CUSTOM WEAPONRY
3601 129th Street
Chippewa Falls, WI 54729
Toll-Free: 800-830-6677
Website: www.lauerweaponry.com

LAZZERONI ARMS COMPANY
P.O. Box 26696
Tucson, AZ 85726-6696
Phone No.: 888-492-7247
Fax No.: 520-624-4250
Website: www.lazzeroni.com
Email: arms@lazzeroni.com

LEGACY SPORTS INTERNATIONAL LLC
4750 Longley Lane, Ste. 209
Reno, NV 89502
Phone No.: 800-553-4229
Fax No.: 800-786-6555
Website: www.legacysports.com

LEGION FIREARMS
1901 Ramcon Drive
Temple, TX 76504
Toll Free : 855-453-4466

LEITNER-WISE DEFENSE
Parts and Accessories only
P.O. Box 25097
Alexandria, VA 22313
Phone No.: 703-209-0556
Fax No.: 703-548-1427
Website: www.leitner-wise.com
Email: info@leitner-wise.com

LES BAER CUSTOM, INC.
1804 Iowa Drive
LeClaire, IA 52753
Phone No.: 563-289-2126
Fax No.: 563-289-2132
Website: www.lesbaer.com
Email: info@lesbaer.com

LEW HORTON DISTRIBUTING CO.
Distributor Only
P.O. Box 5023
Westboro, MA 01581
Toll Free: 800-446-7866
Fax No.: 508-366-5332
Website: www.lewhorton.com
Email: questions@lewhorton.com

LEWIS MACHINE & TOOL COMPANY (LMT)
1305 11th Street West
Milan, IL 61264
Phone No.: 309-787-7151
Fax No.: 309-787-2636
Website: www.lmtdefense.com

LIBERTY ARMS INTERNATIONAL LLC
3505C Houston Hwy.
Victoria, TX 77901
Phone No.: 361-788-3147
Website: www.libertyarmsusa.com
Email: depot@libertyarmsusa.com

LONE STAR TACTICAL SUPPLY
21515 Hufsmith-Kohrville Road
Tomball, TX 77375
Phone No.: 832-454-7549
Website: www.lonestartacticalsupply.com

LOSOK CUSTOM ARMS
314 Willow Run Lane
Delaware, OH 43015
Phone No.: 740-363-8437

LUSA USA
1575 Hooksett Road, Ste. 3
Hooksett, NH 03106
Phone No.: 902-922-1515
Website: www.lusausa.com

M+M, INC.
Colorado Gun Sales
PO Box 639
East Lake, CO 80614
Phone No.: 866-926-5419
Fax No.: 888-236-2619
Website: www.cogunsales.com
Email: website@cogunsales.com

MG ARMS, INC.
6030 Treaschwig Road
Spring, TX 77373
Phone No.: 281-821-8282
Fax No.: 281-821-6387
Website: www.mgarmsinc.com
Email: mgarms@swbell.net

MGI
1168 Main Street
P.O. Box 138
Old Town, ME 04468
Phone No.: 207-817-3280
Fax No.: 207-817-3283
Website: www.mgimilitary.com
Email: mgi@mgimilitary.com

MKE
Factory
06330 Tandogan, Ankara TURKEY
Fax No.: 011-90-312-222-2241
Website: www.mkek.gov.tr

MKS SUPPLY, INC.
8611-A North Dixie Drive
Dayton, OH 45414
Phone No.:937-454-0363
Fax No.: 937-454-0503
Website: www.mkssupply.com

MC ARMORY
0549 Mennies Lane
ark, IL 61340
hone No.: 815 – 339 – 2226
ebsite: www.MMCArmory.com
mail: customerservice@MMCArmory.com

DUFFEE ARMS
252 Eaton Circle
estminster, CO 80003
hone No.: 303-325-3219
ax No.: 866-687-6633
ebsite: www.mcduffeearms.com
mail: info@mcduffeearms.com

GNUM RESEARCH, INC.
ase refer to Kahr Arms listing.
ctory (Except for Baby Eagle Series)
2602 33rd Ave SW
llager, MN 56473
hone No.: 508-635-4273
ax No.: 508-795-7046
ebsite: www.magnumresearch.com
mail: info@magnumresearch.com

RLIN FIREARMS COMPANY
.O. Box 1781
adison, NC 27025
hone No.: 203-239-5621
un Service No.: 800-544-8892
epairs: 800-544-8892
ebsite: www.marlinfirearms.com

ARSTAR CANADA
.R. #1, Vankleek Hill
ntario, CANADA K0B 1R0
hone No.: 888-744-0066
ax No.: 613-678-2359
ebsite: www.marstar.ca

ASTERPIECE ARMS
.O. Box 67
omer, GA 30629
hone No.: 866-803-0000
ax No.: 770-832-3495
ebsite: www.masterpiecearms.com
mail: darah@masterpiecearms.com

ATCH GRADE ARMS & AMMUNITION
ease refer to MG Arms, Inc. listing.

AUNZ MATCH RIFLES LLC
.O. Box 104
aumee, OH 43537
hone No.: 419-832-2512
ebsite: www.maunzmatchrifles.com
mail: maunzmatchrifles@yahoo.com

AVERICK ARMS, INC.
ease refer to Mossberg listing.

AWHINNEY, CHUCK
ctory - Please refer to Riflecraft listing.
350 Carter Street
aker City, OR 97814
ebsite: www.chuckmawhinney.com
mail: cmawhinney@eoni.com

AXIMUS ARMS, LLC
226-C Lakeview Drive
ranklin, TN 37067
hone No.: 615-595-9777
ebsite: www.maximusarms.com

CCANN INDUSTRIES LLC
.O. Box 641
panaway, WA 98387
hone No. 253-537-6919
ax No. 253-537-6993
ebsite: www.mccannindustries.com
mail: info@mccannindustries.com

McMILLAN FIREARMS MANUFACTURING, LLC
1638 W. Knudsen Dr. Suite 101
Phoenix, AZ 85027
Phone No.: 623-582-9635
Fax No.: 623-581-3825
Website: www.mcmillanusa.com

METROARMS CORPORATION
Distributor – please refer to Eagle Imports, Inc. listing.
Website: www.metroarms.com

MICOR DEFENSE, INC.
P.O. Box 2175
Decatur, AL 35602
Phone No.: 256-560-0770
Fax No.: 256-341-0002
Website: www.micordefense.com
Email: orders@micordefense.com

MICROTECH SMALL ARMS RESEARCH, INC.
(MSAR)
300 Chesnut Street
Bradford, PA 16701
Phone No.: 814-363-9260
Fax No.: 814-362-7068
Website: www.msarinc.com

MILLER PRECISION ARMS
3816 Hwy. 40
Columbia Falls, MT 59912
Phone No.: 406-892-2149
Website: www.MillerPrecisionArms.com

MILTAC INDUSTRIES, LLC
P.O. Box 982
Boise, ID 83701
Phone No.: 866-587-7130
Website: www.miltacindustries.com

MITCHELL'S MAUSERS
P.O. Box 9295
Fountain Valley, CA 92728 -9295
Phone No.: 800-274-4124
Fax No.: 714-848-7208
Website: www.mauser.org
Email: customerservice@mauser.org

MOLOT
Please refer to Vepr. listings.

MOSSBERG
O.F. Mossberg & Sons, Inc.
7 Grasso Ave., P.O. Box 497
North Haven, CT 06473-9844
Phone No.: 203-230-5300
Fax No.: 203-230-5420
Factory Service Center - OFM Service Department
Eagle Pass Industrial Park
Industrial Blvd.
Eagle Pass, TX 78853
Phone No.: 800-989-4867
Website: www.mossberg.com
Email: service@mossberg.com

MOWHAWK ARMORY
995 Mowhawk Creek Rd.
Midway, TN 37809
Phone No.: 423-335-6528
Website: www.mohawkarmory.com

NAVY ARMS CO.
219 Lawn St.
Martinsburg, WV 25401
Phone No.: 304-262-9870
Fax No.: 304-262-1658
Website: www.navyarms.com
Email: info@navyarms.com

NEMESIS ARMS
1090 5th Street, Ste. 110
Calimesa, CA 92320
Phone No.: 909-446-1111
Fax No.: 909-446-1109
Website: www.nemesisarms.com

NEMO ARMS
3582 Hwy 93 S.
Kalispell, MT 59901
Phone No.: 406-752-NEMO
Website: www.nemoarms.com
Email: info@nemoarms.com

NESIKA
1310 Industry Road
Sturgis, SD 57785
Phone No.: 605-347-4686
Website: www.nesikafirearms.com
Email: info@nesikafirearms.com

NEWTOWN FIREARMS
103 Main Street
Placerville, CA 95667
Phone No.: 530-626-9945
Fax No.: 530-644-6684
Website: www.newtown-firearms.com

NIGHTHAWK CUSTOM
1306 W. Trimble Ave.
Berryville, AR 72616-4632
Phone No.: 877-268-4867
Fax No.: 870-423-4230
Website: www.nighthawkcustom.com
Email: info@nighthawkcustom.com

NOREEN FIREARMS LLC
351 Floss Flats Rd., Ste. A
Belgrade, MT 59714
Phone No.: 406-388-2200
Fax No.: 406-388-6500
Website: www.onlylongrange.com

NORINCO
European Distributor – Norconia GmbH
Zeppelinstrabe 3
D-97228 Rottendorf, GERMANY
Phone No.: 01149-0903-1405
Factory - China North Industries Corporation
12A Guang An Men Nan Jie
Beijing 100053 CHINA
Fax No.: 011-86-10-63540398
Website: www.norinco.com
Email: norinco@norinco.com.cn

NORTHERN COMPETITION
P.O. Box 44697
Racine, WI 53404-4697
Phone No.: 262-639-5955
Website: www.northerncompetition.com
Email: productsales@northerncompetition.com

NOSLER, INC.
107 SW Columbia St.
Bend, OR 97709
Phone No.: 800-285-3701
Fax No.: 800-766-7537
Website: www.nosler.com
Email: catalog@nosler.com

NOVESKE RIFLEWORKS LLC
P.O. Box 607
Grants Pass, OR 97528
Phone No.: 541-479-6117
Fax No.: 541-479-2555
Website: www.shopnoveske.com

NUMRICH GUN PARTS CORP.
Parts supplier only
226 Williams Lane
P.O. Box 299
W. Hurley, NY 12491
Phone No.: 866-686-7424
Fax No.: 877-486-7278
Website: www.e-gunparts.com
Email: info@gunpartscorp.com

OBERLAND ARMS
Am Hundert 3
D-82386 Huglfing GERMANY
Fax No.: 011-49-8802914-751
Website: www.oberlandarms.com
Email: info@oberlandarms.com

OHIO ORDNANCE WORKS, INC.
P.O. Box 687
Chardon, OH 44024
Phone No.: 440-285-3481
Fax No.: 440-286-8571
Website: www.ohioordnanceworks.com
Email: oow@oowinc.com

OLYMPIC ARMS, INC.
624 Old Pacific Hwy. SE
Olympia, WA 98513
Phone No.: 800-228-3471
Fax No.: 360-491-3447
Website: www.olyarms.com
Email: info@olyarms.com

OMNI
Please refer to E.D.M. Arms listing.

ONLY LONG RANGE
Please refer to Noreen Firearms LLC listing.

ORSIS
14/8 Pod'emnaya Street
Moscow, RUSSIA 109052
Phone No.: 011-7-495-647-8866
Email: order@orsis.com

PGW DEFENCE TECHNOLOGIES
Importer – Leroy's Big Valley Gun Works
527 2nd Ave. N.
Glasgow, MT 59230
Phone No.: 406-228-4867
Email: leroygun@nemontel.net
Factory
#6-59 Scurfield Blvd.
Winnipeg, Manitoba, CANADA R3Y1V2
Phone No. 204-487-7325
Fax No.: 204-231-8566
Website: www.pgwdti.com

PTR INDUSTRIES
U.S. Representative - Vincent Pestilli & Associates
193 Sam Brown Hill Rd.
Brownfield, ME 04010
Phone No.: 207-935-3603
Fax No.: 207-935-3996
Email: vapame@fairpoint.net
Factory - PTR INDUSTRIES
101 Cool Springs Dr.
Aynor, SC 29511
Phone No.: 855-676-1776
Website: www.PTR91.com
Email: sales@ptr91.com

PALMETTO STATE ARMORY
3760 Fernandina Road
Columbia, SC 29210
Website: www.palmettostatearmory.com
Email: info@palmettostatearmory.com

PALMETTO STATE DEFENSE, LLC
1514 S. Hwy 14, Unit B
Greer, SC 29650
Phone No.: 864-469-9875
Website: www.palmettostatedefense.com
Email: sales@palmettostatedefense.com

PARA USA INC.
10620 Southern Loop Blvd.
Pineville, NC 28134-7381
Phone No.: 704-930-7600
Fax No.: 704-930-7601
Website: www.para-usa.com
Email: contact@para-usa.com

PATRIOT ORDNANCE FACTORY (POF)
23011 N. 16th Lane
Phoenix, AZ 85027
Phone No.: 623-561-9572
Fax No.: 623-321-1680
Website: www.pof-usa.com
Email: sales@pof-usa.com

PIONEER ARMS CORP.
Importer - please refer to I.O. listing.
Factory
1905 Roku 1/9 Street
26-612 Radom, POLAND
Fax No.: 011-48-383-0776
Website: www.pioneer-pac.com
Email: contact@pioneer-pac.com

PISTOL DYNAMICS
2510 Kirby Ave. NE
Palm Bay, FL 32905
Phone No: 321-733-1266
Website: www.pistoldynamics.com
Email: info@pistoldynamics.com

PRECISION FIREARMS
74 Dupont Rd., Ste. A
Martinsburg, WV 25404
Phone No.: 240-217-6875
Fax No.: 480-287-8094
Website: www.precisionfirearms.com
Website: www.pf15.com
Email: pf15@pf15.com

PRECISION REFLEX, INC.
710 Streine Drive
New Bremen, OH 45869
Phone No.: 419-629-2603
Fax No.: 419-629-2173
Website: www.precisionreflex.com
Email: info@precisionreflex.com

Predator Custom Shop
3539 Papermill Drive
Knoxville, TN 37909
Phone No.: 865-521-0625
Fax No.: 865-521-0624
Website: www.predatorcustomshop.com
Email: sales@predatorcustomshop.com

PREDATOR TACTICAL LLC
Tempe, AZ
Phone No.: 602-652-2864
Fax No.: 602-492-9987
Website: www.predatortactical.com

PRIMARY WEAPONS SYSTEMS
800 E. Citation Court, Ste. E
Boise, ID 83716
Phone No.: 208-344-5217
Fax No.: 208-344-5395
Website: www.primaryweapons.com

PROARMS ARMORY s.r.o.
Tousenska 431
250 81 Nehvizdy
CZECH REPUBLIC
Phone No.: 011-420-326-997-345
Website: www.proarms-armory.com
Email: info@proarms-armory.com

PROOF RESEARCH
Columbia Falls, MT
Phone No.: 406-756-9290
Website: www.proofresearch.com
Email: proofinfo@proofresearch.com

PUMA RIFLES
Importer - please refer to Legacy Sports International, LLC listing.

QUALITY PARTS CO.
Please refer to Bushmaster Firearms, Inc. listing.

R GUNS
140 N. Western Ave
Carpentersville, IL 60110
Phone No.: 847-428-3569
Website: www.rguns.net
Email: rguns@rguns.net

RAAC
677 S. Cardinal Lane
Scottsburg, IN 47170
Phone No.: 877-752-2894
Website: www.raacfirearms.com
Email: info@raacfirearms.com

R.I.P. TACTICAL
Utah
Phone No.: 435-590-6036
Website: www.rip-tactical.com

RND MANUFACTURING
14399 Mead Street
Longmont, CO 80504
Phone/Fax No.: 970-535-4458
Website: www.rndrifles.com
Email: info@rndrifles.com

RPA INTERNATIONAL LTD.
P.O. Box 441
Tonbridge, Kent, U.K. TN9 9DZ
Fax No.: 011-44-8458803232
Website: www.rpainternational.co.uk
Email: custom@rpainternational.co.uk

RWC GROUP LLC
911 William Leigh Drive
Tullytown, PA 19007
Phone No.: 866-611-9576
Fax No.: 215-949-9191
Website: www.rwcgroupllc.com
Email: info@rwcgroupllc.com

RED ROCK ARMS
P.O. Box 21017
Mesa, AZ 85277
Phone No.: 480-832-0844
Fax No.: 206-350-5274
Website: www.redrockarms.com
Email: info@redrockarms.com

RED X ARMS
Phone No.: 320-424-1362
Website: www.redxarms.com
Email: sales@redxarms.com

REGENT
Importer – please refer to Umarex USA listing.

...MINGTON ARMS CO., INC.
...nsumer Services
...70 Remington Drive
...O. Box 700
...adison, NC 27025-0700
...hone No.: 800-243-9700
...ax No.: 336-548-7801
...ebsite: www.remington.com
...mail: info@remington.com
...epairs
...4 Hoefler Ave.
...ion, NY 13357
...hone No.: 800-243-9700
...ax No.: 336-548-7801

...HINO ARMS
...212 Central Industrial Drive
...t. Louis, MO 63110
...hone No.: 855-25-RHINO
...ebsite: www.rhinoarms.com

...FLES, INC.
...580 Leal Rd.
...leasanton, TX 78064
...hone No.: 830-569-2055
...ax No.: 830-569-2297
...ebsite: www.riflesinc.com
...mail: info@riflesinc.com

...FLECRAFT LTD.
...8G Speedwell Way
...order Valley Industrial Estate
...harleston, Norfolk, IP20 9EH, U.K.
...ebsite: www.riflecraft.co.uk

...OBAR COMPANIES, INC.
...1438 N. 7th Avenue, Ste. B
...hoenix, AZ 85027
...hone No.: 623-581-2648
...ax No.: 623-582-0059
...ebsite: www.robarguns.com
...mail: info@robarguns.com

...OBINSON ARMAMENT CO.
...925 W. 100 N, Ste. A
...N. Salt Lake City, UT 84116-0776
...hone No.: 801-355-0401
...ebsite: www.robarm.com
...mail: sales@robarm.com

...OCK ISLAND ARMORY
...lease refer to Armscor listing.

...OCK RIVER ARMS, INC.
...1042 Cleveland Road
...Colona, IL 61241
...hone No.: 309-792-5780
...ax No.: 309-792-5781
...ebsite: www.rockriverarms.com
...mail: info@rockriverarms.com

...OCKY MOUNTAIN ARMS, INC.
...1813 Sunset Place, Unit D
...Longmont, CO 80501
...hone No.: 800-375-0846
...ax No.: 303-678-8766
...ebsite: www.bearcoat.com

...OHRBAUGH FIREARMS CORP.
...P.O. Box 785
...Bayport, NY 11705
...hone No.: 800-803-2233
...hone No.: 631-242-3175
...ax No.: 631-242-3183
...ebsite: www.rohrbaughfirearms.com

...USSIAN AMERICAN ARMORY COMPANY
...lease refer to RAAC listing.

S.W.A.T. FIREARMS
6585 East I-30
Campbell, TX 75422
Phone No.: 855-862-SWAT (7928)
Website: www.swatfirearms.com

SI DEFENSE
2902 Highway 93 North
Kalispell, MT 59901
Phone No.: 406-752-4253
Fax No.: 406-755-1302
Website: www.si-defense.com
Email: sales@si-defense.com

SOG ARMORY
11707 S. Sam Houston Pkwy. W., Unit R
Houston, TX 77031
Phone No.: 281-568-5685
Fax No.: 281-568-9191
Website: www.sogarmory.com
Email: sog@sogarmory.com

SRM ARMS
Exclusive Distributor
GSA Direct LLC
802 W. Bannock St. Ste 700
Boise, ID 83702
Phone No.: 208-424-3141
Fax No.: 208-248-1111
Factory
4375A W. McMillan Rd.
Meridian, ID 83646
Phone No.: 888-269-1885
Website: www.srmarms.com
Email: order@srmarms.com

SSK INDUSTRIES
590 Woodvue Lane
Wintersville, OH 43953
Phone No.: 740-264-0176
Fax No.: 740-264-2257
Website: www.sskindustries.com
Email: info@sskindustries.com

STI INTERNATIONAL
114 Halmar Cove
Georgetown, TX 78628
Phone No.: 800-959-8201
Fax No.: 512-819-0465
Website: www.stiguns.com
Email: sales@stiguns.com

SADLAK INDUSTRIES LLC
Nadeau Industrial Park
712 Bread and Milk Street, Unit 7
Coventry, CT 06238
Phone No.: 860-742-0227
Fax No.: 860-742-4244
Website: www.sadlak.com
Email: sales@sadlak.com

SAFETY HARBOR FIREARMS, INC.
P.O. Box 563
Safety Harbor, FL 34695-0563
Phone No.: 727-726-2500
Fax No.: 727-797-6134
Website: www.safetyharborfirearms.com
Email: sales@safetyharborfirearms.com

SAIGA
Exclusive Distributor – please refer to RWC Group LLC listing.
Importer – please refer to U.S. Sporting Goods listing.
Importer – please refer to RAAC (Russian American Armory Company) listing.
Importer – please refer to K-VAR Corp. listing.

SAKO LTD.
Importer (USA) - please refer to Beretta USA listing.
Factory - Sako, Limited
P.O. Box 149
FI-11101 Riihimaki, FINLAND
Fax No.: 011-358-19-720446
Website: www.sako.fi
Email: export@sako.fi

SAMCO GLOBAL ARMS, INC.
6995 N.W. 43rd St.
Miami, FL 33166
Toll Free: 800-554-1618
Phone No.: 305-593-9782
Fax No.: 305-593-1014
Website: www.samcoglobal.com
Email: samco@samcoglobal.com

SAN SWISS ARMS AG
Industrieplatz 1, Postbox 1071
Neuhausen am Rheinfall
CH-8212 SWITZERLAND
Fax No.: 011-41-052-674-6418
Website: www.swissarms.ch
Email: info@swissarms.ch

SARCO INC.
323 Union Street
Stirling, NJ 07980
Phone No.: 908-647-3800
Fax No.: 908-647-9413
Website: www.sarcoinc.com
Email: sarcopa@sarcoinc.com
Parts Only
50 Hilton Ste.
Easton, PA 18042
Phone No. 610-250-3960

SARSILMAZ
Importer - please refer to US Sporting Goods Inc. (shotguns)
Importer - please refer to European American Armory
Factory
Nargileci Sk. Sarsilmaz is Merkezi No.: 4
Mercan 34116, Istanbul, TURKEY
Fax No.: 011-90212-51119-99
Website: www.sarsilmaz.com

SAUER, J.P. & SOHN
Importer – Sauer USA, Inc.
403 East Ramsey, Ste. 301
San Antonio, TX 78216
Phone No.: 210-377-2527
Fax No.: 210-377-2533
Website: www.sauer-usa.com
Factory - J.P. Sauer & Sohn GmbH
Ziegelstadel 20
88316 Isny im Allgau, GERMANY
Fax No.: 011-49-7562-97554-801
Website: www.sauer-waffen.de
Email: info@sauer.de

SAVAGE ARMS, INC.
Sales & Marketing
118 Mountain Road
Suffield, CT 06078
Phone No.: 855-493-6962
Fax No.: 860-668-2168
Parts & Service – SAVAGE ARMS, INC.
100 Springdale Road
Westfield, MA 01085
Phone No.: 413-568-7001
Fax No.: 413-562-7764
Website: www.savagearms.com

Older Savage Arms Historical Research
Mr. John Callahan
P.O. Box 82
Southampton, MA 01073
$30.00/gun research fee, $25.00 per gun for
Models 1895, 1899, and 99 rifles.

SCATTERGUN TECHNOLOGIES INC.
Please refer to Wilson Combat listing.

SCHMEISSER GmbH
*Importer – please refer to American Tactical
Imports listing.*
Adolf-Dembach-Strasse 4
D-47829 Krefeld
GERMANY
Phone No.: 011-49-2151-457810
Fax No.: 011-49-2151-45781-45
Website: www.schmeisser-germany.de
Email: info@schmeisser-germany.de

SCHUETZEN PISTOL WORKS, INC.
Please refer to Olympic Arms listing.

SCHWABEN ARMS GmbH
Neckartal 95
D-78628, Rottweil, GERMANY
Fax No.: 011-49-0741-9429218
Website: www.schwabenarmsgmbh.de
Email: schwabenarmsgmbh@web.de

SCORPION TACTICAL
P.O. Box 1989
Leander, TX 78646
Phone No.: 512-637-9570
Fax No.: 512-637-9571
Website: www.scorpion-tactical.com
Email: info@scorpion-tactical.com

SEEKINS PRECISION
1708 6th Ave North Ste D
Lewiston, ID 83501
Phone No.: 208-743-3400
Website: www.seekinsprecision.com
Email: sales@seekinsprecision.com

SENNI ARMS CO.
Ste. 243/15 Albert Ave.
Broadbeach, Queensland, AUSTRALIA 4218
Fax No.: 011-07-5597-3655
Website: www.senniarms.com

SERBU FIREARMS, INC.
6001 Johns Rd., Ste. 144
Tampa, FL 33634
Phone/Fax No.: 813-243-8899
Website: www.serbu.com

SERO LTD.
1106 Feher Str. 10 3/A
Budapest, HUNGARY
Fax No.: 011-36-1433-2182
Website: www.sero.hu
Email: info@sero.hu

**SHOOTERS ARMS MANUFACTURING
INCORPORATED**
*Importer - please refer to Century International
Arms listing.*
Factory
National Highway, Wireless
Mandaue City, Cebu, PHILIPPINES
Fax No.: 011-6032-346-2331
Website: www.shootersarms.com.ph
Email: rhonedeleon@yahoo.com

SIG SAUER
18 Industrial Park Drive
Exeter, NH 03833
Phone No.: 603-772-2302
Fax No.: 603-772-9082
Customer Service Phone No.: 603-772-2302
Customer Service Fax No.: 603-772-4795
Law Enforcement Phone No.: 603-772-2302
Law Enforcement Fax No.: 603-772-1481
Website: www.sigarms.com
*Factory - SIG - Schweizerische Industrie-
Gesellschaft*
Industrieplatz , CH-8212
Neuhausen am Rheinfall, SWITZERLAND
Fax No.: 011-41-153-216-601

SIONICS WEAPON SYSTEMS
5118 E. Prima Street
Tucson, AZ 85712
Phone No.: 520-441-1260
Fax No.: 520-844-8329
Website: www.sionicsweaponsystems.com
Email: sales@sionicsweaponssystems.com

SISK RIFLES LLC
400 County Road 2340
Dayton, TX 77535
Phone No.: 936-258-4984
Website: www.siskguns.com

SKORPION
Please refer to Czechpoint, Inc. listing.

SMITH & WESSON
2100 Roosevelt Avenue
P.O. Box 2208
Springfield, MA 01104
Phone No.: 800-331-0852
Website: www.smith-wesson.com
Service email only: qa@smith-wesson.com
Smith & Wesson Research
Attn: Mr. Roy Jinks, S&W Historian
P.O. Box 2208
Springfield, MA 01102-2208
Phone No.: 413-747-3223 (8am-5pm)

SOUTHERN GUN COMPANY
UNITED KINGDOM
Phone No.: 011-44-1208-851074
Fax No.: 011-44-1208-850860
Website: www.southern-gun.co.uk

SPARTAN GUN WORKS
Please refer to the Remington listing.

SPARTAN PRECISION RIFLES
1065 Shary Circle, Ste. E
Concord, CA 84518
Phone No.: 510-755-5293
Website: www.spartanrifles.com

SPECIAL WEAPONS INC.
Warranty service & repair for Special Weapons LLC
Website: www.tacticalweapons.com

SPECIALIZED DYNAMICS
925 N. California Street
Chandler, AZ 85225
Phone No.: 602-425-7500
Website: www.specializeddynamics.com
Email: info@specializeddynamics.com

SPECIALIZED TACTICAL SYSTEMS
2743 N. Parkland Blvd.
Pleasant View, UT 84404
Phone No.: 801-648-7004
Fax No.: 801-648-7357
Website: www.specializedtactical.com

SPHINX SYSTEMS LTD.
Importer – please refer to Kriss USA listing
Factory
Gsteigstrasse 12
CH-3800 Matten Interlaken SWITZERLAND
Fax No.: 011-41-033-821-1006
Website: www.sphinxarms.com
Email: info@sphinxarms.com

SPIDER FIREARMS
2005-B Murcott Dr.
St. Cloud, FL 34771-5826
Phone No.: 407-957-3617
Fax No.: 407-957-0296
Website: www.ferret50.com
Email: info@ferret50.com

SPIKE'S TACTICAL LLC
2036 Apex Ct.
Apopka, FL 32703
Phone No.: 407-928-2666
Fax No.: 866-283-2215
Website: www.spikestactical.com
Email: sales@spikestactical.com

SPORT-SYSTEME DITTRICH
North American Importer – Wolverine Supplies
Box 729 Virden
R0M 2C0 Manitoba CANADA
Website: www.wolverinesupplies.com
Factory – SPORT-SYSTEME DITTRICH
Burghaiger Weg 20a
D-95326 Kulmbach, GERMANY
Fax No.: 011-49-09221-8213758
Website: www.ssd-weapon.com

SPRINGFIELD ARMORY
Springfield Inc.
420 W. Main St.
Geneseo, IL 61254
Phone No.: 309-944-5631
Phone No.: 800-680-6866
Fax No.: 309-944-3676
Website: www.springfield-armory.com
Email: sales@springfield-armory.com
Custom Shop Email: customshop@springfield-
armory.com

STAG ARMS
515 John Downey Dr.
New Britain, CT 06051
Phone No.: 860-229-9994
Fax No.: 860-229-3738
Website: www.stagarms.com
Email: sales@stagarms.com

STERLING ARSENAL
201 Davis Drive
Unit FF
Sterling, VA 20164
Phone No.: 571-926-8705
Website: www.sterlingarsenal.com
Email: support@sterlingarsenal.com

STEYR ARMS (STEYR MANNLICHER)
2530 Morgan Road
Bessemer, AL 35022
Phone No.: 205-417-8644
Fax No.: 205-417-8647
Website: www.steyrarms.com
Website: www.steyrarms.com
Factory - Steyr Mannlicher A.G. & Co. KG
Ramingtal 46
Kleinraming A-4442 AUSTRIA
Fax No.: 01143-7252-78621
Website: www.steyr-mannlicher.com
Email: office@steyr-mannlicher.com

OEGER INDUSTRIES
7601 Indian Head Hwy.
ccokeek, MD 20607-2501
Phone No.: 301-283-6981
oll Free: 800-264-4962
ax No.: 301-283-6988
Website: www.stoegerindustries.com

ONER RIFLE
ctory - please refer to Knight's Manufacturing
. listing.

RATEGIC ARMORY CORPS, LLC
ease refer to Surgeon Rifles listing.

URM, RUGER & CO., INC.
adquarters
Lacey Place
outhport, CT 06490
Phone No.: 203-259-7843
ax No.: 203-256-3367
Website: www.ruger.com
rvice Center for Pistols, PC4 & PC9 Carbines
00 Ruger Road
Prescott, AZ 86301-6181
Phone No.: 928-778-6555
ax No.: 928-778-6633
Website: www.ruger-firearms.com
*rvice Center for Revolvers, Long Guns & Ruger
ate of Manufacture*
11 Sunapee Street
ewport, NH 03773
Phone No.: 603-865-2442
ax No.: 603-863-6165

PERIOR ARMS
36 Weaver Blvd.
Wapello, IA 52653
Phone No.: 319-523-2016
ax No.: 319-527-0188
Website: www.superiorarms.com
Email: sales@superiorarms.com

URGEON RIFLES, INC.
48955 Moccasin Trail Road
Prague, OK 74864
Phone No.: 405-567-0183
Fax No.: 405-567-0250
Website: www.surgeonrifles.com
Email: info@surgeonrifles.com

INTERNATIONAL
P.O. Box 787
Louisville, TN 37777
Phone No.: 865-977-9707
Fax No.: 865-977-9728
Website: www.tnguns.com
Email: sales@tnguns.com

NW INC.
P.O. Box 311
Vernonia, OR 97064
Phone No.: 503-429-5001
Fax No.: 503-429-3505
Website: www.tnwfirearms.com
Email: tnwcorp@aol.com

ACTICAL ARMS MANUFACTURING, INC.
Huntersville, NC 28070
Phone No.: 704-200-2533
Fax No.: 978-215-8804
Website: www.tacticalarmsmfr.com

ACTICAL ARMZ
4451 E. Farm Road 132
Springfield, MO 65802
Phone No.: 417-893-0486
Website: www.tacticalarmz.com
Email: info@tacticalarmz.com

TACTICAL RIFLES
38439 5th Ave. #186
Zephryhills, FL 33542
Phone No.: 352-999-0599
Website: www.tacticalrifles.net
Email: info@tacticalrifles.net

TACTICAL SOLUTIONS
2772 S. Victory View Way
Boise, ID 83709
Phone No.: 866-333-9901
Fax No.: 208-333-9909
Website: www.tacticalsol.com

TACTICAL WEAPONS
Please refer to FNH USA listing.

TACTICAL WEAPONS SOLUTIONS
2578 Clark Street
Apopka, FL 32703
Phone No.: 407-730-6567
Website: www.twsarms.com
Email: info@twsarms.com

TALO DISTRIBUTORS, INC.
120 Pleasant St.
Framingham, MA 01701
Phone No.: 508-872-9242
Website: www.taloinc.com

TALON ORDNANCE
106 Business Park Dr.
Ridgeland, MS 39157
Phone No.: 601-345-8678
Website: www.talonordnance.com
Email: contact@Talonordnance.com

TAR-HUNT CUSTOM RIFLES, INC.
101 Dogtown Rd.
Bloomsburg, PA 17815-7544
Phone No.: 570-784-6368
Fax No.: 507-389-9150
Website: www.tarhunt.com
Email: sales@tarhunt.com

TAURUS INTERNATIONAL MANUFACTURING INC.
16175 NW 49th Ave.
Miami, FL 33014-6314
Phone No.: 305-624-1115
Fax No.: 305-623-7506
Website: www.taurususa.com

TAVOR
Importer – IWI US, Inc.
P.O. Box 126707
Harrisburg, PA 17112
Website: www.iwi.us
Email: info@iwi.us

TAYLOR'S & CO.
304 Lenoir Dr.
Winchester, VA 22603
Phone No.: 540-722-2017
Fax No.: 540-722-2018
website: www.taylorsfirearms.com
Email: info@taylorsfirearms.com

TEMPLAR CUSTOM, LLC
P.O. Box 15
Apex, NC 27502
Phone No.: 877-878-2334
Website: www.templarcustom.com

TEMPLAR TACTICAL ARMS LLC
26 Shawnee Way, Suite A
Bozeman, MT 59715
Phone No.: 406-579-4612
Fax No.: 406-585-1215
Website: www.templartacticalarms.com

TEMPLAR TACTICAL FIREARMS
P.O. Box 131595
Spring, TX 77393-1595
Phone No.: 936-271-4867
Fax No.: 936-271-6652
Website: www.templartacticalfirearms.com

THOMPSON
Please refer to the Kahr Arms listings.
Website: www.tommygun.com
Website: www.tommygunshop.com

THOMPSON/CENTER ARMS CO., INC.
400 North Main Street
Rochester, NH 03867
Customer Service Phone No.: 603-332-2333
Repair Only Phone No.: 866-730-1614
Fax No.: 603-30-8614
Website: www.tcarms.com
Email: tca@tcarms.com
Custom Shop - Fox Ridge Outfitters
P.O. Box 1700
Rochester, NH 03866
Phone No.: 800-243-4570

THOR GLOBAL DEFENSE GROUP
1206 Knesek Lane
Van Buren, AR 72956
Phone No.: 479-474-3434
Fax No.: 479-262-6925
Website: www.thorgdg.com

THUREON DEFENSE
2118 Wisconsin Ave.
P.O. Box 173
New Holstein, WI 53061
Phone No.: 920-898-5859
Fax No.: 920-898-5868
Website: www.thureondefense.com
Email: info@thureondefense.com

TIKKA
Importer - please refer to Beretta U.S.A. Corp. listing.
Factory - please refer to Sako listing.
Website: www.tikka.fi

TORNADO
Factory - AseTekno OY
Pälkäneentie 18/PL 94
FIN-00511 Helsinki, FINLAND
Fax No.: 011-358-9-753-6463
Website: www.asetekno.fi
Email: jaakko.vottonen@asetekno.fi

TRACKINGPOINT
3813 Helios Way, Suite 290
Pflugerville, TX 78660
Phone No.: 512-354-2114
Website: www.tracking-point.com

TRANSFORMATIONAL DEFENSE INDUSTRIES, INC.
Please refer to Kriss USA listing.

TRISTAR SPORTING ARMS LTD.
1816 Linn St.
N. Kansas City, MO 64116
Phone No.: 816-421-1400
Fax No.: 816-421-4182
Website: www.tristarsportingarms.com
Email: tsaservice@tristarsportingarms.com

TROMIX CORPORATION
20039 E. 600 Road
Inola, OK 74036
Phone No.: 918-543-3456
Fax No.: 918-543-2920
Website: www.tromix.com
Email: rumore@tromix.com

TROY DEFENSE
A division of Troy Industries
West Springfield, MA 01089
Phone No.: 866-788-6412
Fax No.: 413-383-0339
Website: www.troyind.com
Website: www.troydefense.com

TRUVELO MANUFACTURERS (PTY) LTD.
Factory - Truvelo Armoury
P.O. Box 14189
Lyttelton 0140 SOUTH AFRICA
Fax No.: 011-27-11-203-1848
Website: www.truvelo.co.za
Email: armoury@truvelo.co.za

U.S. ARMAMENT CORP.
Distributor - MGE Wholesale
3415 Grape Road
Mishawaka, IN 46545
Fax No.: 574-255-2542
Website: www.mgewholesale.com

U.S. MACHINE GUN ARMORY LLC
1914 East 9400 South
Sandy, UT 84093
Phone No.: 801-839-4683
Website: www.machinegunarmory.com
Email: sales@machinegunarmory.com

U.S. ORDNANCE
*Commercial Distributor - see Desert Ordnance
listing.*

U.S. SPORTING GOODS
P.O. Box 560746
Rockledge, FL 32956
Phone No.: 321-639-4842
Fax No.: 321-639-7006
Website: www.ussginc.com
Email: ussg@eaacorp.com

UMAREX SPORTWAFFEN GmbH & CO. KG
Importer - Colt AR-15 .22 LR only & Airguns
Umarex USA (Rimfire firearms)
7700 Chad Colley Blvd.
Ft. Smith, AR 72916
Phone No.: 479-646-4210
Fax No.: 479-646-4206
Website: www.umarexusa.com
Headquarters and Factory
Donnerfeld 2
D-59757 Arnsberg GERMANY
Fax No.: 011-49-2932-638224
Website: www.umarex.de

UNIQUE-ALPINE
Postfach 15 55
D-85435 Erding Bavaria GERMANY
Fax No.: 011-49-08122-9797-230
Website: www.unique-alpine.org
Email: info@unique-alpine.com

USA TACTICAL FIREARMS
933 Meacham Road
Statesville, NC 28677
Phone No.: 704-872-5150
Fax No.: 704-872-5122
Website: www.usatf.us

USELTON ARMS INC.
390 Southwinds Dr.
Franklin, TN 37064
Phone No.: 615-595-2255
Fax No.: 615-595-2254
Website: www.useltonarms.com

UTAS
Importer - UTAS USA
1247 Rand Road
Des Plaines, IL 60016
Phone No.: 847-768-1011
Fax No.: 847-768-1001
Website: www.utas-usa.com
Factory - UTAS Makine, Ltd.
Caglayan Mah., 2020 Sok. Uğur Apt.
No.:9/1 07230, Antalya, TURKEY
Fax No.: 011-90-242-323-6676
Website: www.utasturk.com

UZI
Importer - IWI US, Inc.
P.O. Box 126707
Harrisburg, PA 17112
Website: www.iwi.us
Email: info@iwi.us

VALKYRIE ARMS LTD.
120 State Ave. NE, No. 381
Olympia, WA 98501
Phone/Fax No.: 360-482-4036
Website: www.valkyriearms.com
Email: info@valkyriearms.com

VALOR ARMS
2812 Riverview Road
Akron, OH 44313
Phone No.: 330-962-8269
Website: www.valorarms.us
Email: valorarms@gmail.com

VALTRO
Importer - Valtro USA
P.O. Box 56384
Hayward, CA 94545-6384
Phone No.: 510-489-8477
Website: www.valtrousa.com
Factory - Italian Arms Srl
Via de Gasperi 26/C,
25060 Collebeato (BS), ITALY
Fax No.: 39-030-2512545

VAN DYKE RIFLE DESIGNS
2324 17 RD
Plainville, KS 67663
Phone No.: 785-434-7577
Fax No.: 785-434-7517
Website: www.vandykerifles.com
Email: vandykerifles@yahoo.com

VECTOR ARMS INC.
270 West 500 North
N. Salt Lake, UT 84054
Phone No.: 801-295-1917
Fax No.: 801-295-9316
Website: www.vectorarms.com
Email: sales.vectorarms@gmail.com

VEPR. RIFLES
Importer - Molot USA
P.O. Box 30664
Walnut Creek, CA
Phone No.: 775-200-1678
Website: www.molot-usa.com
Factory - MOLOT JSC
Vyatskie Polyany Machine Building Plant
135 Lenin St., Vyatski Polyany
RUS-612960 Kirov Region, RUSSIA
Fax No.: 011-007-83334-61832

VIGILANCE RIFLES
3795 N. Hwy 89 Ste. E
Chino Valley, AZ 86323
Phone No.: 877-884-4336
Website: www.vigilancerifles.com
Email: affedm@aol.com

VIPER
Please refer to Tristar listing.

VLTOR WEAPON SYSTEM
3735 N. Romero Road
Tucson, AZ 85705
Phone No.: 520-408-1944
Fax No.: 520-293-8807
Website: www.vltor.com
Email: sales@vltor.com

VOLKMANN PRECISION LLC
11160 S. Deer Creek Rd.
Littleton, CO 80127
Phone No.: 303-884-8654
Website: www.volkmannprecision.com
Email: volkmannprecision @yahoo.com

VOLQUARTSEN CUSTOM
P.O. Box 397
24276 240th St.
Carroll, IA 51401
Phone No.: 712-792-4238
Fax No.: 712-792-2542
Website: www.volquartsen.com
Email: info@volquartsen.com

WAFFEN HIENDLMAYER GmbH
Landshuter Strasse 59
D-84307 Eggenfelden GERMANY
Fax No.: 011-49-8721-6451
website: www.waffen-hiendlmayer.de
Email: mail@waffen-hiendlmayer.de

WALTHER
Importer - Walther Arms, Inc.
7700 Chad Colley Boulevard
Fort Smith, AR 72916
Phone No.: 479-242-8500
Website: www.waltherams.com
*Target pistol & rifle importer - please refer to
Champion's Choice Inc. listing.*
*GSP/rifle conversion kits & factory repair station
– Repair - Earl's Repair Service, Inc.*
2414 Pulaski-Giles Turnpike (Rt. #100)
Pearisburg, VA 24131
Phone No.: 540-921-0184
Fax No.: 540-921-0183
Website: www.carlwalther.com
Email: info@carlwalther.com
German Company Headquarters (Umarex)
Carl Walther Sportwaffen GmbH
Donnerfeld 2
D-59757 Arnsberg GERMANY
Fax No.: 011-49-29-32-638149
Website: www.carl-walther.de
Email: sales@carl-walther.de
Factory - Carl Walther, GmbH Sportwaffenfabrik
Postfach 4325
D-89033 Ulm/Donau, GERMANY
Fax No.: 011-49-731-1539170

WEATHERBY
1605 Commerce Way
Paso Robles, CA 93446
Technical Support: 805-227-2600
Service/Warranty: 800-227-2023
Fax No.: 805-237-0427
Website: www.weatherby.com

DAN WESSON FIREARMS
Distributor - please refer to CZ-USA listing.
Factory
5169 Highway 12 South
Norwich, NY 13815
Phone No.: 607-336-1174
Fax No.: 607-336-2730
Website: www.danwessonfirearms.com

LD WEST GUNS, LLC.
100 Homer Drive
nchorage, AK 99518
hone No.: 800-992-4570
ax No.: 907-344-4005
vada Location
225 Wynn Road
as Vegas, NV 89118
hone No.: 702-798-4570
ax No.: 702-895-9850
Jebsite: www.wildwestguns.com
mail: Alaska@wildwestguns.com
mail: vegas@wildwestguns.com

LSON COMBAT
234 CR 719
.O. Box 578
erryville, AR 72616-0578
hone No.: 800-955-4856
ax No.: 870-545-3310
Jebsite: www.wilsoncombat.com

NCHESTER - REPEATING ARMS
dministrative Offices
75 Winchester Avenue
Jorgan, UT 84050-9333
ustomer Service Phone No.: 800-333-3288
arts & Service Phone No.: 800-945-1392
ax No.: 801-876-3737
Jebsite: www.winchesterguns.com
inchester Parts and Service
005 Arnold Tenbrook Rd.
rnold, MO 63010-9406
hone No.: 800-322-4626
ax No.: 636-287-9751

WINDHAM WEAPONRY
999 Roosevelt Trail
Windham, ME 04062
Phone No.: 855-808-1888
Fax No.: 207-893-1632
Website: www.windhamweaponry.com

XN ARMS INDUSTRY AND TRADE CO.
Hamidiye Mah. K. Sanayi Sitesi Sok. No. 21
42700 Beysehir/Konya TURKEY
Fax No.: 011-90-332-512-1099
Website: www.xnarms.com
Email: info@xnarms.com

XTREME MACHINING
6506 Kylertown Drifting Hwy.
Drifting, PA 16834
Phone No.: 814-345-6290
Fax No.: 814-345-6292
Website: www.xtrememachining.biz
Email: xtrememachining@gmail.com

YANKEE HILL MACHINE CO., INC.
20 Ladd Ave., Ste. 1
Florence, MA 01062
Phone No.: 877-892-6533
Fax No.: 413-586-1326
Website: www.yhm.net

Z-M WEAPONS
1958 Wes White Hill Road
Richmond, VT 05477
Phone No.: 802-777-8964
Fax No.: 802-434-7426
Website: www.zmweapons.com
Email: zm@zmweapons.com

ZASTAVA ARMS
Importer - please refer to Century listing.
Importer - please refer to European American Armory listing.
Importer – please refer to USSG listing.
Factory
Trg Topolivaca 4
34000 Kragujevac, SERBIA
Fax No.: 011-381-034-323683
Website: www.zastava-arms.co.rs

ZBROJOVKA BRNO
Please refer to the CZ USA listing.

ZELENY SPORT s.r.o.
Slatina 116
56601 Vysoke Myto, CZECH REPUBLIC
Website: www.zelenysport.cz

ZOMBIE DEFENSE
8736 Landmark Road
Henrico, VA 23228
Phone No.: 804-972-3991
Fax No.: 804-716-1012
Website: www.zombie-defense.com
Email: info@zombie-defense.com

AMMUNITION TRADEMARK INDEX

AAA ARMS & AMMO
14717 Industrial Road
Omaha, NE 68144
www.aaa-ammo.com

ALS TECHNOLOGIES, INC.
1103 Central Blvd.
Bull Shoals, AR 72619
www.lesslethal.com

ALEXANDER ARMS
US Army, Radford Arsenal
P.O. Box 1
Radford, VA 24143
www.alexanderarms.com

ALLIANCE ARMAMENT
1077 Mt. Gilead Road
Boonville, IN 47601
www.alliancearmament.com

ARMAS Y CARTUCHOS DEL SUR S.L.
Ctra. HU-4403 Km. 1,200
Alosno (Huelva), E-21520
SPAIN
www.delsur.es

ARMS CORPORATION OF THE PHILIPPINES
6th Floor, Strata 100 Bldg.
Emerald Avenue
Ortigas Center
Pasig City, 1600
PHILIPPINES
www.armscor.com.ph

ATLANTA ARMS AND AMMO
721 Vine Circle
Social Circle, GA 30025
www.atlantaarmsandammo.com

AZOT
1 Rdultovskogo Square
Krasnozavodsk 141321
RUSSIA
www.azot-patron.ru

BARNES BULLETS
P.O. Box 620
Monda, UT 84645
www.barnesbullets.com

BARNAUL MACHINE TOOL PLANT
28 Kulagina St.
Barnaul 656002
RUSSIA
www.ab.ru/~stanok

BASCHIERI & PELLAGRI S.P.A.
Via frullo 26
Marano di Castenaso (BO) I-40055
ITALY
www.bascheri-pellagri.com

BITTEROOT VALLEY AMMO & COMPONENTS
3616 Eastside Highway
Stevensville, MT 59870
www.bvac-ammo.com

BLACK HILLS AMMUNITION
P.O. Box 3090
Rapid City, SD 57709-3090
www.black-hills.com

BORNAGHI S.R.L.
Via dei Livelli Snc
24047 Treviglio (Bg)
ITALY
www.bornaghi.it

BRENNEKE GMBH
Postfach 1646
30837 Langenhagen
GERMANY
www.brenneke.de

BUFFALO BORE AMMUNITION
www.buffalobore.com

BUMAR SP. Z.O.O.
ZPS Pionki
Ul. Zakladowa 7
26-670 Pionki
POLAND
www.bumar.com

CARTUCHOS SAGA S.A.
Caparrella, s/n
25192 Lleida
SPAIN
www.saga.es

CCC AMMO
1713 Meridian Court
Conroe, TX 77301
www.cccammo.com

CCI AMMUNITION
2299 Snake River Ave.
Lewiston, ID 83501
www.cci-ammunition.com

CESARONI TECHNOLOGY INCORPORATED
P.O. Box 246
2561 Stouffville Rd.
Gormley, Ontario L0H 1G0
CANADA
www.cesaronitech.com

CHEDDITE FRANCE S.A.
Route de Lyon, 99/Box 112
Bourg-Les-Valence, F-26500
FRANCE
www.cheddite.com

CHEDDITE ITALY
Via del Giaggiolo 189
Livorno, I-5700
ITALY
www.chedditeITALY.com

CHEYTAC, LLC
303 Sunset Drive, P.O. Box 822
Arco, ID 83213
www.cheytac.com

CLEVER MIRAGE S.R.L.
Via A. De Legnago No. 9
37141 Ponte Florio Montorio (VR)
ITALY
www.clevervr.com

COMPANHIA BRASILEIRA DE CARTUCHOS
Av. Humberto de Campos, 3220 CEP
09426-900 Guapituba Ribeiro Pires/SP
BRAZIL
www.cbc.com.br

CONCHO CARTRIDGE COMPANY, INC.
P.O. Box 1430
San Angelo, TX 76902
www.conchocartridge.com

CONLEY PRECISION CARTRIDGE CO.
207 E. Oak Av.
Como, MS 38619
www.cpcartridge.com

COR-BON/GLASER
1311 Industry Rd.
Sturgis, SD 57785
www.corbon.com

CUSTOM CARTRIDGE, INC.
5878 Hollister Av.
Goleta, CA 93117
www.customcartridge.com

DDUPLEKS LTD.
Brivibas Gatve 197
Riga, LV-1039
LATVIA
www.ddupleks.lv

DESERT TECH (DESERT TACTICAL ARMS)
1995 W. Alexander Street
West Valley City, UT 84119
Phone No.: 801-975-7272
Fax No.: 801-908-6425
Website: www.deserttech.com

DOUBLE TAP AMMUNITION
646 S. Main St., #333
Cedar City, UT 84720
www.doubletapammo.com

DYNAMIC RESEARCH TECH.
405 N. Lyon Street
Grant City, MO 64456
www.drtammo.com

ELEY LIMITED
Selco Way
Minworth Industrial Estate
Sutton, Coldfield
West Midlands B76 1BA
ENGLAND
www.eleyammunition.com

ELEY HAWK LTD.
Selco Way, First Ave.
Minworth Industrial Estate
Sutton Coldfield
West Midlands B76 1BA
ENGLAND
www.eleyhawk.com

ELITE ENTERPRISES INC. DBA ELITE AMMUNITION
P.O. Box 639
Harvard, IL 60033
www.eliteammunition.net

ENGEL BALLISTIC RESEARCH, INC.
544 Alum Creek Road, Unit A
Smithville, TX 78957
www.ebr-inc.net

ENVIRON-METAL INC.
1307 Clark Mill Rd.
Sweet Home, OR 97386
www.hevishot.com

STATE CARTRIDGE, INC.
900 Ehlen Dr.
Anoka, MN 55303
www.estatecartridge.com

XTREME SHOCK USA
Rt. 2, Box 304-N
Clintwood, VA 24228
www.extremeshockusa.com

AM - PIONKI LLC
Ul. Zakladowa 7
Pionki PL-26-670
POLAND
www.fam-pionki.pl

FEDERAL PREMIUM AMMUNITION
900 Ehlen Dr.
Anoka, MN 55303
www.federalpremium.com

FIOCCHI USA
6930 N. Fremont Rd.
Ozark, MO 65721
www.fiocchiusa.com

&L CALIBERS LTD
P.O. Box 22198
Nicosia, 1518
CYPRUS
www.victorycom.com

GAMEBORE CARTRIDGE CO. LTD.
Great Union St.
GB-Hull HU9 1AR
U.K.
www.gamebore.com

GARRETT'S CARTRIDGE, INC.
1004 Long Road
Centralia, WA 98531
www.garrettcartridges.com

GEORGIA ARMS
P.O. Box 238
15 Industrial Court E.
Villa Rica, GA 30180
www.georgia-arms.com

GOEX INC.
P.O. Box 659
Doyline, LA 71023
www.goexpowder.com

GRIZZLY CARTRIDGE CO.
See Rintoul Enterprises, LLC

GYTTORP AB
Malmvagen 1
Nora, SE-71330
SWEDEN
www.gyttorp.com

HS MUNITIONS, INC.
4406 Rathbun Lane
Stevensville, MT 59870
www.thehuntingshack.com

HORNADY MANUFACTURING CO.
P.O. Box 1848
Grand Island, NE 68802
www.hornady.com

HULL CARTRIDGE CO. LTD.
Bontoft Ave., National Ave.
Hull, U.K.
www.hullcartridge.co.uk

IGMAN D.D.
Donje Polje 42
88400 Konjic
Bosnia-Herzegovina
www.igman.co.ba

IMPALA EUROPA
Dr. Karl Renner Str. 2b
Guntramsdorf A-2353
AUSTRIA
www.impalabullets.at

INDUSTRIAS TECNOS S.A. DE C.V.
Km. 6 carretera Cuernavaca a Tepoztlan
Cuernavaca, Mor. Mexico C.P. 62000
www.itecnos.com.mx

INTERNATIONAL CARTRIDGE CORP.
2273 Route 310
Reynoldsville, PA 15851
www.internationalcartridge.com

ISRAEL MILITARY INDUSTRIES LTD (IMI)
Ramat Hasharon 47100
ISRAEL
www.imi-israel.com

JSC NOVOSIBIRSK LVE PLANT
(JSC Novosibirsk Cartridge Plant)
Stantsionnaya 30A
Novosibirsk 630108
RUSSIA
www.lveplant.ru

JAMES CALHOON
4343 U.S. Hwy. 87
Havre, MT 59501
www.jamescalhoon.com

JAMISON INTERNATIONAL V LLC
3551 Mayer Av.
Sturgis, SD 57785

KENT CARTRIDGE
P.O. Box 849
Kearneysville, WV 25430
www.kentgamebore.com

KRASNOZAVODSK CHEMICAL FACTORY
Moscow Region
Krasnovavodsk RUSS-141321
RUSSIA
www.khz-record.ru

KYNAMCO LTD.
The Old Railway Station, Station Road
Mildenhall, Suffolk IP28 7DT
U.K.
www.kynochammunition.co.uk

KYRGIAS M.G. S.A.
1 klm. Neochorouda turn
Neochorouda Thessaloniki, GR-54500
GREECE

LAZZERONI ARMS COMPANY
P.O. Box 26696
Tucson, AZ 85726
www.lazzeroni.com

LIGHTFIELD AMMUNITION CORP.
P.O. Box 162
Adelphia, NJ 07710
www.lightfieldslugs.com

LYALVALE EXPRESS LTD.
Express Estate
Fisherwick Nr. Whittington
Lichfield WS13 8XA
ENGLAND
www.lyalvaleexpress.com

MFS 2000 INC.
Magyar Loszergyarto ZRt.
3332 Sirok, Pf. 9
HUNGARY
www.mfs2000.hu

MAGSAFE AMMO, INC.
4700 So. U.S. Hwy. 17-92
Casselberry, FL 32707
www.magsafeonline.com

MAGTECH AMMUNITION
248 Apollo Dr. #180
Lino Lakes, MN 55014
www.magtechammunition.com

MAST TECHNOLOGY INC.
P.O. Box 1026
Blue Springs, MO 64013
www.masttechnology.com

MASTERCAST BULLET COMPANY
292 Anderson Road
Enon Valley, PA 16120
www.mastercast.net

MAXAM OUTDOORS S.A.
Avenida del Partenon, 16 bajo
Madrid, E-28042
SPAIN
www.ueec.es

MESKO S.A.
Zaklady Metalowe
Ul. Legionow 122
Skarzysko-Kamienna PL-26111
POLAND

METALLWERK ELISENHUTTE GMBH NASSAU (MEN)
10 Elisenhutte
Nassau/Lahn D-56377
GERMANY
Men-info@elisenhuette.de
www.elisenhuette.de

NAMMO LAPUA OY
P.O. Box 5
Lapua FIN-62101
FINLAND
www.lapua.com

NIKE FIOCCHI SPORTING AMMUNITION LTD.
Lajos Street 78
H-1036 Budapest
HUNGARY
www.nike-fiocchi.hu

NITRO AMMUNITION COMPANY
7560 Newkirk road
Mountain Grove, MO 65711
www.nitrocompany.com

NITRON S.A.
Zaklady Tworzyw Sztucznych
Krupski Mlyn PL-42693
POLAND

NOBEL SPORT S. A.
57 Rue Pierre Charron
Paris F-75181
FRANCE
www.nobelsport.fr

NOBEL SPORT ESPANA S.A.
Apartado 428
Villacil (Leon), E-24080
SPAIN
www.excopesa.com/nobel

NOBEL SPORT ITALIA S.R.L.
Via di Palazzetto 7/11
San Giuliano (PI) I-56017
ITALY
www.nobelsport.it

NORMA PRECISION AB
Jagargatan
SE-67040 Amotfors
SWEDEN
www.norma.cc

NOSLER, INC.
107 SW Columbia St.
Bend, OR 97702
www.nosler.com

OJSC "THE TULA CARTRIDGE WORKS"
47-b Marata
Tula, 300004
RUSSIA
www.wolfammo.ru

OLD WESTERN SCOUNGER/ NAVY ARMS
219 Lawn St.
Martinsburg, WV 25401
www.ows-ammunition.com

P. GAVRIELIDES LTD
P.O. Box 40217,6302
Larnaka, CYPRUS
www.olympia.com.cy

PINNACLE AMMUNITION
111 W. Port Plaza #600
St. Louis, MO 63146
www.pinnacleammo.com

POLYSHOK, INC.
2702 Woodmere Drive
Panama City, FL 32405
www.polyshok.com

POLYWAD, INC.
P.O. Box 396
Roberta, GA 31078
www.polywad.com

POONGSAN METALS CORP. (PMC)
Keuk Dong Bldg.
60-1 Chungmuro
Chung-ku
Seoul 100-705
KOREA
www.poongsan.co.kr
www.pmcammo.com

PRECISION CARTRIDGE, INC.
940 Georgiana St.
Hobart, IN 46342

PRECISION DELTA CORPORATION
P.O. Box 128
Ruleville, MS 38771
www.precisiondelta.com

PRETORIA METAL PRESSINGS (PMP)
Div. of Denel Ltd.
Private Bag X334
Pretoria, 0001
REPUBLIC OF SOUTH AFRICA

PRVI PARTIZAN
Milosa Obrenovica 2
Uzice YU-31000
SERBIA
www.privipartizan.com

QUALITY CARTRIDGE
P.O. Box 445
Hollywood, MD 20636
www.qual-cart.com

RBCD PERFORMANCE PLUS
1538 SE Military Drive, Suite 206
San Antonio, TX 78214
www.rbcd.net

REMINGTON ARMS CO.
P.O. Box 700
Madison, NC 27025
www.remington.com

RINTOUL ENTERPRISES, LLC
Grizzly Cartridge Co.
30201 Carmel Road
P.O. Box 1466
Rainier, OR 97048
www.grizzlycartridge.com

RUAG USA
5402 East Diana St.
Tampa, FL 33610
www.ruag-usa.com

RUAG AMMOTEC AG (RWS, NORMA, DYNAMIT NOBEL, HIRTENBERGER, GECO, ROTTWEIL, SWISS MATCH)
Uttigenstrasse 67
CH-3602 Thun
SWITZERLAND
www.ruag.com

SBR AMMUNITION
1118 Glynn Park Rd.
Brunswick, GA 31525
www.sbrammunition.com

SNC TECHNOLOGIES
5 Montee des Arsenaux
Le Gardeur Quebec J5Z 2P4
CANADA
www.snctec.com

SAGE CONTROL ORDNANCE
3391 E. Eberhardt St.
Oscoda, MI 48750
www.sageinternationalltd.com

SCHARCH MFG. INC.
10325 County Road 120
Salida, CO 81201

SELLIER & BELLOT JSC
Licicka 667
Vlasim CZ-25813
CZECH REPUBLIC
www.sellier-bellot.cz

SILVER STATE ARMORY
P.O. Box 962
Packwood, WA 98361
www.ssarmory.com

SOTIRIOS NAFPLIOTIS A.B.E.E.
P.O. Box 8- Eleon
Thiva, GR-32200
GREECE

SPEER
2299 Snake River Ave.
Lewiston, ID 83501
www.speer-bullets.com.

SRC ARMS(SHARPS RIFLE CO)
1195 U.S. Hwy 20-26-87
Glenrock, WY 82637
Website: **www.srcarms.com**
Phone No.: 877-256-4794

SUPERIOR AMMUNITION, INC.
20788 Mossy Oak Place
Sturgis, SD 57785
www.superiorammo.com

SUPERIOR BALLISTICS, INC.
c/o Mic McPherson
10725 Road 24.4 Loop
Cortez, CO 81321
www.superiorballistics.com

SWIFT BULLET COMPANY
201 Main Street
Quinter, KS 67752
www.swiftbullets.com

TTI ARMORY
14884 Heritagecrest Way
Bluffdale, UT 84065
www.ttiarmory.com

TEN-X AMMUNITION
5650 Arrow Highway
Montclair, CA 91763
www.tenxammo.com

THIFAN INDUSTRIE S.A.R.L.
275 Rue de Malitorne, B.P. 61
18230 St. Doulchard
FRANCE
www.sauvestre.com

TRUST EIBARRES S.A.
Murrategui 9 (Azitain)
Apartado 32
Eibar ES-20600
SPAIN
www.trust-eibarres.com

UEE CARTUCHERIA DEPORTIVA S.A.
Avda. del Partenon, 16 bajo
28042 Madrid - Espana
SPAIN
www.ueec.es

ULTRAMAX AMMUNITION
2112 Elk Vale Rd.
Rapid City, SD 57701
www.ultramaxammunition.com

ULYANOVSK MACHINERY PLANT SUE, PA
2 Metallistov St.
Ulyanovsk RUSS-32007
RUSSIA
www.ulmash.narod.ru

WEATHERBY, INC.
1605 Commerce Way
Paso Robles, CA 93446
www.weatherby.com

WINCHESTER DIV.
Olin Corp.
Shamrock St.
East Alton, IL 62024
www.winchester.com

WOLF PERFORMANCE AMMUNITION
P.O. Box 757
Placentia, CA 92871
www.wolfammo.com

YAVASCALAR A.S.
Ataturk Mah. Badirma Cad N 49
Balikesir, TR-10100
TURKEY
www.yavascalar.com

ZERO AMMUNITION CO. INC
P.O. box 1188
Cullman, AL 35056
www.zerobullets.com

The following listings represent manufacturers and companies which specialize in making optics, magazines, upper and lower receivers, stocks, forends/forearms, slides, iron sights, trigger groups, weapon lights, laser sights, accessory rails, metal finishes, slings, and other accessories which enhance the functionality of tactical firearms.

STAR FIREARMS
Billet aluminum revolver speedloaders for 9mm, 327 Mag., .38/.357 Mag. (5,6,7, and 8 shot), 410/.45 Judge, .44 Spl./Mag., .45 Colt, .454 Casull, .460 & .500 S&W.
1666 N. Sheridan Road
Zion, IL 60099
Website: www.5starfirearms.com
Phone No.: 847-731-7808
Fax No.: 847-731-7899

A.R.M.S. INC.
Mounting systems for day optics, night vision, thermal imagers, lasers, and lights, detachable iron sights.
230 West Center St
West Bridgewater, MA 02379
Website: www.armsmounts.com
Phone No.: 508-584-7816
Fax No.: 508-588-8045

ACCUSHOT B&T INDUSTRIES, LLC
Atlas bipods, monopods.
P.O. Box 771071
Wichita, KS 67277
Website: www.accu-shot.com
Phone No.: 316-721-3222
Fax No.: 316-721-1021

ACE LTD. USA
Modular folding stocks, sling mounts, vertical foregrips.
P.O. Box 430
Winchester, KY 40391
Website: www.riflestocks.com
Phone No.: 859-745-1757
Fax No.: 859-745-4638

ACT-MAG SRL
Pistol and rifle magazines.
Via Sardegna, 5/F I-25069
Villa Carcina, Brescia Italy
Website: www.act-mag.com
Phone No.: 011-390308980035
Fax No.: 011-390308988833

ADAMS ARMS
AR15 retrofit gas piston systems.
255 Hedden Ct
Palm Harbor, FL 34681
Website: www.arisfix.com
Phone No.: 727-853-0550
Fax No.: 727-353-0551

ADAMS INDUSTRIES, INC.
Night vision and thermal imaging products.
P.O. Box 641413
Los Angeles, CA 90064
Website: www.adamsindustries.com
Phone No.: 310-472-3017

ADCO ARMS CO., INC.
Riflescopes, and red dot sights.
4 Draper Street
Woburn, MA 01801
Website: www.adcosales.com
Phone No.: 781-935-1799
Fax No.: 781-935-1011

ADDAX, INC.
AR15 gas piston upper assemblies.
9600 Cozycroft Av, Suite B
Chatsworth, CA 91311
Phone No.: 818-886-5008
Fax No.: 818-886-5007

ADVANCED ARMAMENT CORPORATION
Suppressors, flash hiders, muzzle brakes, compensators, and adaptors.
1434 Hillcrest Rd
Norcross, GA 30093 USA
Website: www.advanced-armament.com
Phone No.:770-925-9988
Fax No.: 770-925-9989

ADVANCED TECHNOLOGY INTERNATIONAL
Injection-molded synthetic gunstocks and accessories.
W60 N171 Cardinal Ave.
Cedarburg, WI 53012
Website: www.atigunstocks.com
Phone No.: 800-925-2522
Fax No.: 414-464-3112

ADVANTAGE TACTICAL SIGHT
"Pyramid Sight Picture" adjustable metallic sights for handguns, rifles, and shotguns.
Wrentech Industries, LLC
7 Avenida Vista Grande B-7, Suite 510
Santa Fe, NM 87508
Website: www.advantagetactical.com
Phone No.: 505-466-1811
Fax No.: 505-466-4735

AE LIGHT
HID and LED lights.
Allsman Enterprises, LLC
P.O. Box 1869
Rogue River, OR 97537
Website: www.aelight.com
Phone No.: 541-471-8988
Fax No.: 888-252-1473

AIMPOINT, INC.
Electro-optical red dot sights.
14103 Mariah Ct
Chantilly, VA 20151
Website: www.aimpoint.com
Phone No.: 703-263-9795
Fax No.: 703-263-9463

AIMSHOT
Laser and red dot sights, weapon lights, and mounting systems.
340 Dewpoint Lane
Alpharetta, GA 30022
Website: www.aimshot.com
Phone No.: 770-840-8039
Fax No.: 770-840-0269

AIM SPORTS, INC.
Tactical optics, lasers, muzzle brakes, bipods.
5095 Walnut Grove Av.
San Gabriel, CA 91776
Website: www.aimsportsinc.com
Phone No.: 626-286-0600
Fax No.: 626-286-5095

AIMTECH MOUNT SYSTEMS
Scope mounting systems for handguns, shotguns, and rifles.
P.O. Box 223
Thomasville, GA 31799
Website: www.aimtech-mounts.com
Phone No.: 229-226-4313
Fax No.: 229-227-0222

AJAX CUSTOM GRIPS, INC.
American made weapon grips.
9130 Viscount Row
Dallas, TX 75247
Website: www.ajaxgrips.com
Phone No.: 214-630-8893
Fax No.: 214-630-4942

AKER INTERNATIONAL INC
Holsters
2248 Main Street, Suite 6
Chula Vista, CA 91911
Website: www.akerleather.com
Phone No.: 619-423-5182

ALL STAR TACTICAL
AR-15 parts, accessories, and tools.
1249 Ridgeway Ave.
Rochester, NY 14615
Phone No.: 585-324-0345
Website: www.allstartactical.com
Email: info@allstartactical.com

ALESSI HOLSTERS
247 Cayuga Road, Suite 911r
Buffalo, NY 14225
Website: www.alessigunholsters.com
Phone No.: 716-932-7497

ALOT ENTERPRISE CO. LTD.
Optics
1503 Eastwood Center
5 A Kung Ngam Village Road
Shaukeiwan, Hong Kong
Website: www.alothk.com
Phone No.: +852 25199728

ALTAMONT COMPANY
Pistol grips and rifle stocks.
901 North Church Street
P.O. Box 309
Thomasboro, IL 61878
Website: www.altamontco.com
Phone No.: 217-643-3125
Fax No.: 217-643-7973

ALUMAGRIPS
Ultra high quality handgun grips.
2851 North 34th Place
Mesa, AZ 85213
Phone No.: 602-690-5459
Fax No.: 480-807-3955

AMEGA RANGES, INC.
Picatinny rail systems for Mini-14, M14, M1 Garand, M1 Carbine rifles, and Remington 870 shotguns, and tactical weapon light mounts.
6355 Stinson #202
Plano, TX 75093
Website: www.amegaranges.com
Phone No.: 888-347-0200

AMELON COATINGS, LLC
Micro Slick permanent lubricating firearm component coating.
227 Mount Olive Road
Amherst, VA 24521
Website: www.ameloncoatings.com
Phone No.: 434-946-5157
Fax No.: 434-946-5159

AMERICAN BODY ARMOR
13386 International Parkway
Jacksonville, FL 32218
Website: www.safariland.com
Phone No.: 904-741-5400

AMERICAN DEFENSE MFG.
Mounting solutions, firearms.
2525 S. 162nd Street
New Berlin, WI 53151
Website: www.adm-mfg.com
Phone No.: 262-780-9831

AMERICAN RIFLE COMPANY
Bolt actions, scope rings and mounts.
4433 Russell Road, Suite 103
Mukilteo, WA 98275
Website: www.americanrifle.com
Phone No.: 206-226-4387

AMERICAN SPIRIT ARMS
AR15 style uppers, lowers, barrels, parts ans accessories.
16001 North Greenway-Hayden Loop, Suite A
Scottsdale, AZ 85260
Website: www.americanspiritarms.com
Phone No.: 480-367-9540
Fax No.: 480-367-9541

AMERICAN TACTICAL INC.
Tactical equipment and accessories.
231 Deming Way
Summerville, SC 29483
Website: www.americantactical.us
Phone No.: 800-290-0065

AMERICAN TECHNOLOGIES NETWORK, CORP.
Night vision and thermal imaging systems, tactical lights.
1341 San Mateo Ave
South San Francisco, CA 94080
Website: www.atncorp.com
Phone No.: 650-989-5100
Fax No.: 650-875-0129

AMERIGLO
Tritium self-luminous sights for pistols, rifles, and shotguns.
5579-B Chamblee Dunwoody Road, Suite 214
Atlanta, GA 30338
Website: www.ameriglo.com
Phone No.: 770-390-0554
Fax No.: 770-390-9781

AMMUNITION STORAGE COMPONENTS
150 Production Court
New Britain, CT 06051
Phone No.: 860-225-3548

AM-TAC PRECISION
See Trademark Index

ANZIO IRONWORKS CORP.
See Trademark Index

APRESYS INC.
Optics
4th Floor 11 Building #1528 East Zhuanxing Road
Shanghai, China 201108
Website: www.apresys.com
Phone No.: +8621 609 13188

AR57/57CENTER
5.7x28mm caliber uppers for AR15 style rifles.
8525 152nd Avenue NE
Redmond, WA 98052
Website: www.57center.com
Phone No.: 888-900-5728

AREA51 PRODUCTS
Tactical weapon accessories.
Taylor, AL 36301
Website: www.area51tactical.com
Phone No.: 908-686-1383
Fax No.: 908-845-0316

ARES DEFENSE SYSTEMS, INC.
See Trademark Index

ARMAMENT DYNAMICS INDUSTRIES LLC
AR15 ambidextrous charging handle.
10903 W. 84th Place
Arvada, CO 80005-5219
Phone No.: 303-868-6314

ARMAMENT TECHNOLOGY, INC.
ELCAN Optical Technologies sighting systems and related equipment.
3045 Robie Street, Suite 113
Halifax, Nova Scotia, B3K4P6 Canada
Website: www.armament.com
Phone No.: 902-454-6384
Fax No.: 902-454-4641

ARMASIGHT INC.
Night vision, thermal imaging, and laser devices.
815 Dubuque Av.
San Francisco, CA 94080
Website: www.armasight.com
Phone No.: 480-907-6950

ARMATAC INDUSTRIES INC.
150 round capacity dual drum "SAW-MAG"; 78 round capacity dual drum "SAW-LITE" AR15/M16 magazines.
P.O. Box 340
Lyndhurst, VA 22952
Website: www.armatac.com
Phone No.: 540-943-6735
Fax No.: 540-943-6735

ARMORSHIELD USA LLC
Body armor & helmets
30 ArmorShield Drive
Stearns, KY 42647
Website: www.armorshield.net
Phone No.: 606-376-4449

ARMORWORKS & ATV CORP.
Body, vehicle & aircraft armor
305 North 54th Street
Chandler, AZ 85226
Website: www.armorworks.com
Phone No.: 480-598-5700

ARMS TECH, LTD.
Suppressors
5025 North Central Avenue, Suite 459
Phoenix, AZ 85012
Website: www.armstechltd.com
Phone No.: 602-272-9045
Fax No.: 602-272-1922

ARMYTEK OPTOELECTRONICS INC.
Flashlights & related accessories
57 Vandervoort Drive
Richmond Hill, Ontario, Canada L4E0C7
Website: www.armytek.com
Phone No.: 647-407-0111

ARREDONDO ACCESSORIES
AR15 and handgun action shooting/3 gun competition accessories.
2984-F First Street
La Verne, CA 91750
Website: arredondoaccessories.com
Phone No.: 909-596-9597
Fax No.: 909-596-3496

ASE UTRA
S Series, jet-Z, Northstar, and DUAL suppressors
Rahkeentie 6
80100 Joensuu, Finland
Website: www.aseutra.fi
Phone No.: 010 4238810
Fax No.: 013 227347

ASHBURY INTERNATIONAL GROUP INC.
Mfr. of SABER FORSST modular rifle chassis, electro-optical weapon mounts, TACT3 field tripod.
P.O. Box 8024
Charlottesville, VA 22906
Website: www.AshburyPrecisionOrdnance.com

ASP, INC.
Weapon lights.
2511 East Capitol Dr
Appleton, WI 54911
Website: www.asp-usa.com
Phone No.: 920-735-6242
Fax No.: 920-735-6245

ATK LAW ENFORCEMENT
Tactical optics and firearm accessories.
2299 Snake River Avenue
Lewiston, ID 83501
Website: www.atk.com
Phone No.: 208-746-2351
Fax No.: 208-798-3392

ATK SECURITY
900 Ehlen Drive
Anoka, MN 55303
Website: www.atk.com
Phone No.: 800-322-2342

ATK SPORTING
900 Ehlen Drive
Anoka, MN 55303
Website: www.atk.com
Phone No.: 800-322-2342

ATN
See AMERICAN TECHNOLOGIES NETWORK, CORP.

ATS, INC. (ADVANCED TRAINING SYSTEMS)
Live fire shooting ranges
4524 Highway 61 North
St. Paul, MN 55110
Phone No.: 651.429.8091
Website: www.atsusa.biz
Email: info@atsusa.biz

WC SYSTEMS TECHNOLOGY
.22 to .50 BMG caliber suppressors for pistols, submachine guns, and rifles.
1515 West Deer Valley Road, Suite A-105
Phoenix, AZ 85027
Website: www.awcsystech.com
Phone No.: 623-780-1050
Fax No.: 623-780-2967

ADGER BARRELS, INC.
Cut-rifled and hand-lapped target-grade barrels.
8330 196 Avenue, P.O. Box 417
Bristol, WI 53104
Website: www.badgerbarrelsinc.com
Phone No.: 262-857-6950
Fax No.: 262-857-6988

ADGER ORDNANCE
Military grade rifle actions, mounting systems, rails, and scope rings.
1209 Swift Street
North Kansas City, MO 64116
Website: www.badgerordance.com
Phone No.: 816-421-4958
Fax No.: 816-421-4958

ARNES PRECISION MACHINE, INC.
AR15 style receivers, parts, and accessories.
2276 Farmington Road
Apex, NC 27523
Website: www.barnesprecision.com
Phone No.: 919-362-6805
Fax No.: 919-362-5752

ARSKA OPTICS
Riflescopes and accessories.
1721 Wright Avenue
La Verne, CA 91750
Website: www.barska.com
Phone No.: 909-445-8168
Fax No.: 909-445-8169

ATTLE ARMS DEVELOPMENT, INC.
AR10/AR15 ambidextrous safety levers.
P.O. Box 92742
Henderson, NV 89009
Website: www.battlearmsdevelopment.com
Phone No.: 702-508-8625
Fax No.: 702-948-4472

BATTLECOMP ENTERPRISES, LLC
Battlecomp tactical compensators and Midnight Mounts.
101 Hickey Blvd., Suite A455
South San Francisco, CA 94080
Website: www.battlecomp.com
Phone No.: 650-678-0778

BCI DEFENSE
Suppressors.
545 N. Bowen Av.
Bremen, IN 46506
Website: www.bcidefense.com
Phone No.: 574-331-0358

BEAMSHOT-QUARTON USA, INC.
Laser sighting systems.
5805 Callaghan Road, Suite 102
San Antonio, TX 78228
Website: www.beamshot.com
Phone No.: 210-735-0280
Fax No.: 210-735-1326

BELL AND CARLSON, INC.
Hand-laminated fiberglass, carbon fiber, and aramid fiber rifle and shotgun stocks and accessories.
101 Allen Road
Dodge City, KS 67801
Website: www.bellandcarlson.com
Phone No.: 620-225-6688
Fax No.: 620-225-9095

B.E. MEYERS & CO.
"OWL" night vision scopes, "GLARE" non-lethal lasers, "IZLID" targeting/illuminating lasers.
14540 NE. 91st St.
Redmond, WA 98052
Website: www.bemeyers.com
Phone No.: 425-881-6648
Fax No.: 425-867-1759

BERGARA BARRELS
Barrels, scope mount systems, and rifle slings.
5988 Peachtree Corners East
Norcross, GA 30071
Website: www.bergarabarrels.com
Phone No.: 770-449-4687
Fax No.: 770-242-8546

BETA COMPANY, THE
"BETA C-MAG" dual drum magazines.
2137 B Flintstone Drive
Tucker, GA 30084
Website: www.betaco.com
Phone No.: 800-669-2382
Fax No.: 770-270-0559

BIRCHWOOD CASEY, LLC
Shooting and gun care products
7887 Fuller Road, Suite 100
Eden Prairie, MN 55344
Toll Free: 800-Shoot-N-C (746-6862)
Fax: 952-388-6718
Website: www.birchwoodcasey.com
Email: customerservice@birchwoodcasey.com

BIRDSONG MANUFACTURING LLC
AR-15 platforms, weapons components and suppressors
1437 Monterey Road
Florence, MS 39073
Website: www.birdsongmfg.com
Phone No.: 601-398-1125

BKL TECHNOLOGIES INC.
Scope mounts
P.O. Box 2478
Fort Worth, TX 76113
Website: www.bkltech.com
Phone No.: 817-451-8966

BLACK WEAPONS ARMORY
See Trademark Index

BLACKHAWK PRODUCTS GROUP
Rifle and shotgun stocks, slings, tactical accessories.
6160 Commander Parkway
Norfolk, VA 23502
Website: www.blackhawk.com
Phone No.: 800-694-5263
Fax No.: 757-436-3088

BLACKTHORNE PRODUCTS, LLC
AR-15, AK47 and Galil parts and accessories
P.O. Box 2441
Inver Grove Heights, MN 55076
Website: www.blackthorneproducts.com
Phone No.: 952-232-5832
Fax No.: 912-964-7701

BLUE FORCE GEAR INC.
Vickers Combat Applications Sling and weapon accessories.
P.O. Box 853
Pooler, GA 31322
Website: www.blueforcegear.com
Phone No.: 877-430-2583

BOYDS GUNSTOCK INDUSTRIES, INC.
Walnut and birch laminate replacement stocks.
25376 403rd Ave
Mitchell, SD 57301
Website: www.boydsgunstocks.com
Phone No.: 605-996-5011
Fax No.: 605-996-9878

BRESSER-EXPLORE SCIENTIFIC
Optics
621 Madison
Springdale, AR 72762
Website: www.bresser.com
Phone No.: 479-419-5871

BRILEY MANUFACTURING, INC.
1911 style pistol accessories.
1230 Lumpkin Road
Houston, TX 77043
Phone No.: 713-932-6995
Fax No.: 713-932-1043

BRITE-STRIKE TECHNOLOGIES, INC.
Tactical weapon lights.
26 Wapping Road, Jones River Industrial Park
Kingston, MA 02364
Website: www.brite-strike.com
Phone No.: 781-585-5509
Fax No.: 781-585-5332

BROWNELLS MIL/LE SUPPLY GROUP
Worldwide distributor of armorer's tools, accessories, and OEM parts.
200 South Front Street
Montezuma, IA 50171
Website: www.brownells.com
Phone No.: 641-623-5401
Fax No.: 641-623-3896

BSA OPTICS
Riflescopes and red dot sights.
3911 Southwest 47th Avenue, Suite 914
Ft. Lauderdale, FL 33314
Website: www.bsaoptics.com
Phone No.: 954-581-2144
Fax No.: 954-581-3165

B-SQUARE
Rings, bases, rail mounting systems.
13387 International Pkwy
Jacksonville, FL 32218
Phone No.: 904-741-5400
Fax No.: 904-741-5404

BUFFER TECHNOLOGIES
Recoil buffers for rifles and pistols.
P.O. Box 105047
Jefferson City, MO 65110
Website: www.buffertech.com
Phone No.: 573-634-8529
Fax No.: 573-634-8522

BULLDOG BARRELS, LLC
OEM barrel blanks and finished barrels.
106 Isabella Street, 4 North Shore Center Suite 110
Pittsburgh, PA 15212
Website: www.bulldogbarrels.com
Phone No.: 412-322-2747
Fax No.: 412-322-1912

BURRIS COMPANY, INC.
Riflescopes, red dot sights, rings, and bases.
331 East 8th Street
Greeley, CO 80631
Website: www.burrisoptics.com
Phone No.: 970-356-1670
Fax No.: 970-356-8702

BUSHNELL OUTDOOR PRODUCTS
Riflescopes, red dot sights.
9200 Cody Street
Overland Park, KS 66214
Website: www.unclemikesle.com
Phone No.: 913-752-3400
Fax No.: 913-752-3550

BUTLER CREEK CORP.
Magazines, replacement barrels, and stocks.
9200 Cody Street
Overland Park, KS 66214
Website: www.butlercreek.com
Phone No.: 913-752-3400
Fax No.: 913-752-3550

BUTTON SLING, INC.
Single point shooting slings.
2913 Northwest 5th Street
Blue Springs, MO 64014
Website: www.buttonsling.com
Phone No.: 816-419-8100
Fax No.: 816-224-4040

C PRODUCTS, LLC
AR platform rifle magazines.
30 Elmwood Court
Newington, CT 06111
Website: www.cproductsllc.com
Phone No.: 860-953-5007
Fax No.: 860-953-0601

CADEX INC/CADEX DEFENSE
Rifle stocks, scope mounts, other mission essential accessories.
755 Avenue Montrichard
Saint-Jean-Sur-Richelieu
Quebec J2X 5K8 CANADA
Website: www.cadexdefense.com
Phone No.: 450-348-6774

CALIFORNIA COMPETITION WORKS
AR-15 accessories & parts
P.O. Box 4821
Culver City, CA 90232
Website: www.demooner.com
Phone No.: 310-895-0736

CAMMENGA COMPANY, LLC
Rifle magazines, AR15 rifle parts.
2011 Bailey Street
Dearborn, MI 48124
Website: www.cammenga.com
Phone No.: 616-392-7999
Fax No.: 616-392-9432

CARL ZEISS OPTRONICS GMBH
Optronic and optical sighting systems.
Gloelstr 3-5
Wetzlar, 35576 GERMANY
Website: www.zeiss.com/optronics
Phone No.: 011 4964414040
Fax No.: 044 49644140510

CAROLINA PRECISION ARMS LLC
Suppressors.
2725 N. Church St.
Rocky Mount, NC 27804
Phone No.: 252-904-0721

CASPIAN ARMS, LTD.
1911 pistol components, replacement slides for Glock pistols.
75 Cal Foster Drive
Wolcott, VT 05680
Website: www.caspianarms.com
Phone No.: 802-472-6454
Fax No.: 802-472-6709

CCF RACE FRAMES, LLC
Replacement frames for the Glock pistols in aluminum, stainless steel, and titanium alloys.
P.O. Box 29009
Richmond, VA 23242
Website: www.ccfraceframes.com
Phone No.: 804-622-4277
Fax No.: 804-740-9599

CENTURY INTERNATIONAL ARMS, INC.
Importer of firearms parts and accessories.
430 South Congress Drive, Suite 1
Delray Beach, FL 33445
Website: www.centuryarms.com
Phone No.: 561-265-4500
Fax No.: 561-265-4520

CERAKOTE
See NIC INDUSTRIES, INC.

CHAMPION TRAPS & TARGETS
Clay andinteractive targets
1 ATK Way
Anoka, MN 55303
Phone Number: 800-831-0850
Website: www.championtarget.com

CHECK-MATE INDUSTRIES, INC.
1911, Beretta 92, M-14, and other firearm magazines.
777 Mount Av.
Wyandanch, NY 11798
Website: www.checkmateindustries.com
Phone No.: 631-491-1777
Fax No.: 631-491-1745

CHIP MCCORMICK CUSTOM, LLC
Extra-capacity 1911 pistol magazines, AR-15 match and tactical trigger groups.
105 Sky King Drive
Spicewood, TX 78669
Website: www.cmcmags.com
Phone No.: 830-798-2863
Fax No.: 830-693-4975

CHOATE MACHINE & TOOL
Polymer fixed and folding stocks, and accessories for rifles and shotguns.
116 Lovers Lane
Bald Knob, AR 72010
Website: www.riflestock.com
Phone No.: 501-724-6193
Fax No.: 501-724-5873

CHRISTIE'S PRODUCTS
Collapsible stocks and accessories for Ruger 10/22 rifles, AR15 type titanium firing pins, left-handed AR15 .22 LR conversion kit.
404 Bolivia Blvd.
Bradenton, FL 34207
Website: www.1022central.com
Phone No.: 440-413-0031

CJ WEAPONS ACCESSORIES
Military rifle slings and buttstock cleaning kits.
317 Danielle Court
Jefferson City, MO 65109
Website: www.cjweapons.com
Phone No.: 573-634-7292
Fax No.: 573-634-2355

CMC TRIGGERS CORP.
Drop-in AR platform triggers.
5597 Oak St.
Fort Worth, TX 76140
Website: www.cmctriggers.com
Phone No.: 817-563-6611

CMMG, INC.
AR15 gas piston kits, .22 LR conversion kits, receivers, parts and accessories.
620 County Road 18
Fayette, MO 65248
Website: www.cmmginc.com
Phone No.: 660-248-2293
Fax No.: 660-248-2290

C-MORE SYSTEMS
Tubeless ultra-light and miniature red dot sights.
680-D Industrial Road
Warrenton, VA 20186
Website: www.cmore.com
Phone No.: 540-347-4683
Fax No.: 703-361-5881

C.O. ARMS
1911 style pistol concealed carry parts.
5599 Old Millington Road
Millington, TN 38053
Website: www.coarmsusa.com
Phone No.: 206-888-2899

COATING TECHNOLOGIES INC
NP3/NP3 Plus electroless nickel-phosphorus firearm coating.
21438 North 7th Av.
Phoenix, AZ 85027
Website: www.coatingtechnologiesinc.com
Phone No.: 623-581-2648
Fax No.: 623-581-5397

COMBAT SHOOTING AND TACTICS/CSAT
AR15/M16 rear sight aperture, CSAT glass breaking tool.
3615 Press Road
Nacogdoches, TX 75964
Website: combatshootingandtactics.com
Phone No.: 936-559-1605
Fax No.: 936-569-6840

COMMAND ARMS ACCESSORIES (CAA)
See EMA TACTICAL
Stocks, grips, rails, slings, sights, laser and weapon light mounts, shotgun forends, bipods, Glock and Uzi accessories, pistol/carbine conversions.

CONETROL SCOPE MOUNTS
Rings, bases.
Hwy 123 South
Seguin, TX 78155 USA
Website: www.conetrol.com

COUNTERSNIPER MILITARY OPTICAL
INSIGHTS CORP.
Variable power scopes, 1-12x30,
4-16x44, 4-50x75, and other optical innovations.
2231 W. Sunset
Springfield, MO 65807
Website: www.countersniperoptics.com
Phone No.: 800-883-9444

CRIMSON TRACE CORPORATION
Grip-integrated laser sighting systems.
9780 Southwest Freeman Drive
Wilsonville, OR 97070 USA
Website: www.crimsontrace.com
Phone No.: 503-783-5333
Fax No.: 503-783-5334

CUSTOM METAL PRODUCTS, LLC
Full range product line of steel shooting targets
5781 Westwood Dr
Weldon Spring, MO 63304
Phone Number: 636-329-0142
Fax Number: 636-329-8937
Website: www.custommetalprod.com

CYLINDER & SLIDE, INC.
Custom handgun parts and accessories.
245 East 4th Street
Fremont, NE 68025
Website: www.cylinder-slide.com
Phone No.: 402-721-4277
Fax No.: 402-721-0263

D&H TACTICAL
AR10/AR15/M16 magazines and accessories.
510 S. Worthington St.
Oconomowoc, WI 53066
Website: www.dh-tactical.com
Phone No.: 262-569-1960

D.S.A., INC.
Accessories for AR15 and FAL rifles, B&T rail
systems.
27 West 990 Industrial Avenue,
P.O. Box 370
Lake Barrington, IL 60011
Website: www.dsarms.com
Phone No.: 847-277-7258
Fax No.: 847-277-7263

DANIEL DEFENSE, INC.
Military small arms upgrade parts, integrated
weapon rail systems.
6002 Commerce Boulevard, Suite 109
Savannah, GA 31408
Website: www.danieldefense.com
Phone No.: 912-851-3225
Fax No.: 912-964-3247

DANISH GUNTECH I/S
Rifle actions and Hagelberg brand suppressors.
Sverigesgade 6
DK-7430 Ikast
Denmark
Website: www.danishguntech.dk

DARK HORSE ARMS
See JOHN'S GUNS

DASAN
1911 and Glock parts, AR rifle parts.
13071 Rosecrans Av.
Santa Fe Springs, CA 90670
Website: www.dasanusa.com
Phone No.: 562-483-6837

DELORME
Communications satellite professional mapping
solutions
2 DeLorme Drive
Yarmouth, ME 04096
Website: www.delorme.com
Phone No.: 207-846-7000

DEL-TON, INC.
AR15 style rifle parts and accessories.
330 Aviation Way
Elizabeth Town, NC 28337
Website: www.del-ton.com
Phone No.: 910-645-2172
Fax No.: 910-645-2244

DESERT TECH
See Trademark Index

DIAMONDHEAD USA, INC.
M4/AR15 style accessories, "Diamondhead" back-
up iron sights.
44 Allston Av.
West Springfield, MA 01089
Website: www.Diamondhead-USA.com
Phone No.: 413-739-6970
Fax No.: 413-739-6973

DIPOL
Night vision scopes, IR and IR Laser illuminators.
115A, Lugo St.
Vitebsk, 210033
Republic of Belarus
Website: www.dipol.biz
Phone No.: +375 212 261 242
Fax No.: +375 212 261 414

DNZ PRODUCTS, LLC
Billet aluminum one-piece rings/base scope
mounts.
2710 Wilkins Drive
Sanford, NC 27330
Website: www.dnzproducts.com
Phone No.: 919-777-9608
Fax No.: 919-777-9609

DO-ALL OUTDOORS, LLC
Targeting systems and outdoor accessories
216 19th Ave. North
Nashville, TN 37203
Phone Number: 615-269-4889
Fax Number: 615-269-4434
Website: www.doalloutdoors.com
Email: customerservice@doalloutdoors.com

DOCTER OPTIC
Riflescopes, red dot sights.
7661 Commerce Lane
Trussville, AL 35173
Website: www.merkel-usa.com
Phone No.: 205-655-8299
Fax No.: 205-655-7078

DOMINION ARMS/RAUCH TACTICAL
Polymer magazines for SIG 550 rifles, M14 and
VZ58 rifle upgrade components.
250 H Street, Suite 226
Blaine, WA 98230
Website: www.domarms.com
Website: www.rauchtactical.com
Phone No.: 877-829-1050
Fax No.: 866-606-2743

DOUBLESTAR CORPORATION
AR-15 parts and accessories
P.O. Box 430
Winchester, KY 40392
Phone No.: 888-736-7725
Fax No.: 859-745-4638
Website: www.jtfoc.com
Email: doug@star15.com

DREADNAUGHT INDUSTRIES LLC
Parts assembler.
1648 Palo Alto Drive
Van Ormy, TX 78073
Phone No.: 210-601-8149
Website: www.dreadnaught-industries.com

DUOSTOCK DESIGNS, INC.
Rifle stocks for CQB weapons.
P.O. Box 32
Welling, OK 74471
Website: www.duostock.com
Phone No.: 866-386-7865
Fax No.: 918-431-3182

DUMMIES UNLIMITED, INC.
Scenario based training equipment
2435 Pine Street
Pomona, CA 91767
Phone Number: 909-392-7502
Fax Number: 909-392-7510
Website: www.dummiesunlimited.com

DURASIGHT SCOPE MOUNTING SYSTEMS
Scope mounts and rings for center-fire rifles.
5988 Peachtree Corners East
Norcross, GA 30071
Website: www.durasight.com
Phone No.: 770-449-4687
Fax No.: 770-242-8546

EAGLE GRIPS, INC.
Handgun grips.
460 Randy Road
Carol Stream, IL 60188
Website: www.eaglegrips.com
Phone No.: 630-260-0400
Fax No.: 630-260-0486

EAGLE INDUSTRIES
Sling, holsters, & tactical gear
1000 Biltmore Drive
Fenton, MO 64026
Website: www.eagleindustries.com
Phone No.: 888-343-7547

EBERLESTOCK USA LLC
Rifle stocks/chassis.
P.O. Box 862
Boise, ID 83701
Website: www.eberlestock.com
Phone No.: 208-424-5081

ED BROWN PRODUCTS, INC.
1911 style pistol parts.
P.O. Box 492
Perry, MO 63462
Website: www.edbrown.com
Phone No.: 573-565-3261
Fax No.: 573-565-2791

EDWARDS RECOIL REDUCER
Mechanical recoil reduction devices.
1300 Seabright Drive
Annapolis, MD 21409
Website: www.edwardsrecoilreducer.com

ELCAN OPTICAL TECHNOLOGIES
Riflescopes and other military grade optics.
1601 North Plano Road
Richardson, TX 75081
Website: www.elcan.com
Phone No.: 972-344-8077
Fax No.: 972-344-8260

ELITA ARMS AND AMMUNITION
Parts and accessories for AR-15 style rifles and carbines.
1901 Liberty Drive
Thomasville, NC 27360
Phone No.: 336-847-4406
Website: www.elitearmsandammunition.com

ELITE IRON, LLC
Standard and custom caliber suppressors.
1345 Thunders Trail Bldg. D
Potomac, MT 59823
Website: www.eliteiron.net
Phone No.: 406-244-0234
Fax No.: 406-244-0135

ELITE SURVIVAL SYSTEMS
Cases, bags, holsters, and tactical gear
310 West 12th Street
P.O. Box 245
Washington, MO 63090
Website: www.elitesurvival.com
Phone No.: 636-390-8360

ELITE TACTICAL ADVANTAGE
Entry and tactical shotgun rails, oversize safety and charging handle for Mossberg shotguns.
Website: www.elitetacticaladvantage.com
Phone No.: 888-317-8523

ELZETTA DESIGN, LLC
LED weapon lights and accessories.
P.O. Box 54364
Lexington, KY 40555
Website: www.elzetta.com
Phone No.: 859-707-7471
Fax No.: 859-918-0465

ELYSIUM ARMS/WATKINS TOOL
Rifle barrels and firearm components.
P.O. box 429
101 Bacon St.
Raton, NM 87740
Phone No.: 575-445-0100

EMA TACTICAL
.223 CountDown magazine, rail systems, stocks, grips, slings, and scope mounts.
1208 Branagan Drive
Tullytown, PA 19007
Website: www.ematactical.com
Phone No.: 215-949-9944
Fax No.: 215-949-9191

ENIDINE
See ITT ENIDINE INC.

ERGO GRIP
See FALCON INDUSTRIES
AR15 style pistol and forward grips, stocks, mounts, and rails; 1911 style pistol grips, shotgun tri-rail forends.

E.R. SHAW/SMALL ARMS MFG.
Firearm barrels.
5312 Thoms Run Rd.
Bridgeville, PA 15017
Website: www.ershawbarrels.com

EXTREMEBEAM TACTICAL
High-output weatherproof military weapon lights.
2275 Huntington Drive, Suite 872
San Marino, CA 91108
Website: www.extremebeamtactical.com
Phone No.: 626-372-5898
Fax No.: 626-609-0640

FAB DEFENSE
Tactical equipment for military, police, and self-defense weapons.
43 Yakov Olamy Street
Moshav Mishmar Hashiva, Israel 50297
Website: www.fab-defense.com
Phone No.: 011 972039603399
Fax No.: 011 972039603312

FAILZERO
EXO Technology coatings for firearm accessories and parts.
7825 Southwest Ellipse Way
Stuart, FL 34997
Phone No.: 772-223-6699
Fax No.: 772-223-9996

FALCON INDUSTRIES
Ergonomically designed tactical weapon grips and accessories.
P.O. Box 1459
Moriarty, NM 87305
Website: www.ergogrips.net
Phone No.: 505-281-3783
Fax No.: 505-281-3991

FAXON FIREARMS
ARAK-21 gas piston upper receivers, barrels, and parts for AR-15 style rifles.
11101 Adwood Drive
Cincinnati, OH 45240
Website: www.faxonfirearms.com
Phone No.: 513-674-2580

FDI/FREED DESIGNS, INC.
Pateneted XGRIP adaptors which allow full-size pistol magazines to be used in compact pistols.
P.O. Box 1231
Ojai, CA 93024
Website: www.x-grips.com
Phone No.: 805-814-0668

F.J. FEDDERSEN, INC.
.22 through .50 BMG barrels.
7501 Corporate Park Drive
Loudon, TN 37774
Website: www.1022rifle.com

FLIR SYSTEMS, INC.
Electro-optical and infrared imaging systems.
27700 SW. Parkway Av.
Wilsonville, OR 97070
Website: www.flir.com/gs
Phone No.: 503-498-3547/3149
Fax No.: 503-684-5452

FTS TECHNOLOGIES, LTD
Fulcrum Target Systems
711 South Carson Street, Suite 4
Carson City, NV 89701
Phone Number: 775-238-3282
Website: www.fulcrumtargetsystems.com

GEISSELE AUTOMATICS, LLC
National Match and combat replacement trigger
1920 West Marshall Street
Norristown, PA 19403
Website: www.ar15triggers.com
Phone No.: 610-272-2060
Fax No.: 610-272-2069

GEMTECH
OSHA-safe sound suppressors in most defense calibers.
P.O. Box 140618
Boise, ID 83714
Website: www.gem-tech.com
Phone No.: 208-939-7222

G&G
Optical mounting systems and tactical weapon accessories.
3602 East 42nd Stravenue
Tucson, AZ 85713
Website: www.gggaz.com
Phone No.: 520-748-7167
Fax No.: 520-748-7583

G. RECKNAGEL E.K.
Tactical mounts
Landwehr 4
Bergrheinfeld, GERMANY 97493
Website: www.recknagel.de
Phone No.: 011-49972184366

GARMIN USA
Maps & related devices
1200 East 151st Street
Olathe, KS 66062
Website: www.garmin.com
Phone No.: 913-397-8200

GLOCKSTORE
Custom Glock pistol parts.
4585 Murphy Canyon Road
San Diego, CA 92123
Website: www.glockstore.com
Phone No.: 858-569-4000
Fax No.: 858-569-0505

GRAUER SYSTEMS
IGRS - integrated grip rail system for AR15 style rifles.
303 5th Avenue, Suite 1502
New York, NY 10016
Website: www.grauersystems.com
Phone No.: 202-436-9980

GRIFFIN ARMAMENT
Mil/LE/civilian suppressors.
128 Elm St, Unit D
Dousman, WI 53118
Website: www.griffinarmament.com
Phone No.: 262-501-8447

GROVETEC U.S., INC.
Slings, ammo carriers, sling swivel sets for rifles and shotguns.
P.O. Box 220060
Milwaukie, OR 97269-0060
Website: www.grovtec.com
Phone No.: 503-557-4689
Fax No.: 503-557-4936

GUNTECH USA
AR15/AK47/Saiga parts and accessories.
7850 E. Evans Rd. #105
Scottsdale, AZ 85260
Website: www.guntechusa.com
Phone No.: 480-478-4517

GWACS ARMORY
See Trademark Index

H-S PRECISION, INC.
Synthetic stocks, detachable rifle magazines, rifle accessories.
1301 Turbine Drive
Rapid City, SD 57703
Website: www.hsprecision.com
Phone No.: 605-341-3006
Fax No.: 605-342-8964

HARRIS ENGINEERING, INC.
Bipods and adaptors for attaching bipods.
999 Broadway
Barlow, KY 42024
Phone No.: 270-334-3633
Fax No.: 270-334-3000

HAWKE SPORT OPTICS, LLC
Rifle and shotgun scopes.
6015 Highview Drive, Suite G
Fort Wayne, IN 46818
Website: www.hawkeoptics.com
Phone No.: 877-429-5347
Fax No.: 260-918-3443

HAERING GMBH
Support live fire training in varied environments
Phone Number: 49 (6163) 9347-0
Fax Number: 49 (6163) 9347-50
Website: www.haeringtargets.com
Email: info@haering-gmbh.de

HEAD DOWN PRODUCTS
Distributor – please refer to American Tactical Imports listing.
Uppers, rails, muzzle brakes, & related parts
4031 Fambrough Court, Suite 300
Powder Springs, GA 30127
Phone No.: 770-485-7015
Fax No.: 770-421-6345
Website: www.hdrifles.co

HEINIE SPECIALTY PRODUCTS
Pistol sights (low profile, tritium night, tactical), parts, and accessories.
301 Oak Street
Quincy, IL 62301
Website: www.heinie.com
Phone No.: 217-228-9500

HELLFIGHTER TACTICAL LIGHTING SYSTEMS
Weapon-mounted tactical lights.
2231 West Sunset
Springfield, MO 65807
Website: www.HellFighterLights.com
Phone No.: 417-883-9444
Fax No.: 417-883-8636

HENNING SHOP
Barrels & gun parts
1629 Atwood Street
P.O. Box 6648
Longmont, CO 80501
Website: www.henningshop.com
Phone No.: 303-834-8289

HERA ARMS GMBH
Military, law enforcement, and sporting weapon accessories.
Ziegelhuettenweg 5
Triefenstein, GERMANY 97855
Website: www.hera-qarms.com
Phone No.: 011 499395878724
Fax No.: 011 499395878723

HI LUX INC.
Leatherwood scopes.
3135 Kashiwa Street
Torrance, CA 90505
Website: www.hi-luxoptics.com
Phone No.: 310-257-8142

HIVIZ SHOOTING SYSTEMS
Fiber-optic firearm sights, recoil pads.
North Pass, Ltd.
1941 Health Parkway, Suite 1
Fort Collins, CO 80524
Website: www.hivizsights.com
Phone No.: 970-407-0426
Fax No.: 970-416-1208

HKS PRODUCTS INC.
Revolver speedloaders and magazine loaders.
7841 Foundation Drive
Florence, KY 41042
Website: www.hksspeedloaders.com
Phone No.: 800-354-9814

HOGUE, INC.
Synthetic handgun, rifle, and shotgun grips and stocks, recoil pads, sling swivels, AR15/M16 accessories.
550 Linne Road
Paso Robles, CA 93447
Website: www.hogueinc.com
Phone No.: 805-239-1440
Fax No.: 805-239-2553

HOPLITE SYSTEMS
Precision firearm components.
14000 NW 58th Court
Miami Lakes, FL 33014
Website: marktwoarms.com
Phone No.: 305-889-3280

HORUS VISION, LLC
Long range and CQB riflescopes.
659 Huntington Avenue
San Bruno, CA 94066
Website: www.horusvision.com
Phone No.: 650-588-8862; 650-583-5471
Fax No.: 650-588-6264

HOT SHOT TACTICAL
Lights, packs, & tactical gear
121 Interpark Boulevard #706
San Antonio, TX 78216
Website: www.hotshottactical.com
Phone No.: 855-357-2327

HOULDING PRECISION FIREARMS
AR15 style weapon components.
2980 Falcon Drive
Madera, CA 93637
Website: www.houldingfirearms.com
Phone No.: 559-675-9922

HOUSTON ARMORY
See Trademark Index

HUBER CONCEPTS
Two-stage tactical triggers.
Website: www.huberconcepts.com
Phone No.: 820-821-8841

HUNTER COMPANY INC
Holsters & accessories
3300 West 71st Avenue
Westminster, CO 80030
Website: www.huntercompany.com
Phone No.: 303-427-4626
Fax No.: 650-588-6264

HYPERBEAM
Riflescopes, night vision scopes.
1504 Sheepshead Bay Road, Suite 300
Brooklyn, NY 11236
Website: www.nightdetective.com
Phone No.: 718-272-1776
Fax No.: 718-272-1797

IHC, INC.
All types of aluminum color and graphic anodizing.
12400 Burt Road
Detroit, MI 48228
Website: www.ihccorp.com
Phone No.: 313-535-3210
Fax No.: 313-535-3220

INSIGHT TECHNOLOGY
Tactical lasers and illuminators.
9 Akira Way
Londonderry, NH 03053
Website: www.insighttechgear.com
Phone No.: 877-744-4802
Fax No.: 603-668-1084

INTENSITY OPTICS
Riflescopes.
Onalaska Operations
P.O. Box 39
Onalaska, WI 54650
Website: www.intensityoptics.com
Phone No.: 800-635-7656

IOR S.A.
Rifle scopes, red dot sights, night vision scopes, and mounts.
4 Bucovina St.
030393 Bucharest, ROMANIA
website: www.ior.ro
Phone No.: +40 21 324 42 61
Fax No.: +40 21 324 45 12

ITAC DEFENSE, INC.
Slings, vertical foregrips, rear diopter back-up iron sights, red dot and laser sights, front/rear sights for SIG 522 rifle.
189 Lafayette Road
North Hampton, NH 03862
Website: www.itacdefense.com
Phone No.: 866-964-4822
Fax No.: 866-965-4822

ITT ENIDINE INC.
AR15/M4 style rifle hydraulic rate/recoil reduction buffers.
7 Centre Drive
Orchard Park, NY 14127
Website: www.enidine-defense.com
Phone No.: 716-662-1900
Fax No.: 716-662-1909

ITT NIGHT VISION
Generation III night vision sights.
7635 Plantation Road
Roanoke, VA 24019
Website: www.nightvision.com
Phone No.: 540-563-0371
Fax No.: 540-366-9015

JAE - J. ALLEN ENTERPRISES, INC.
Precision synthetic tactical stocks for M1A/M14
and Remington 700 rifles.
21520-G Yorba Linda Blvd. #175
Yorba Linda, CA 92887
Website: www.jae100.com
Phone No.: 714-693-3523
Fax No.: 714-692-3547

JAPAN OPTICS, LTD.
Riflescopes (formerly HAKKO).
2-11-29, Ukima, Kita-ku
Tokyo, 115-0051 Japan
Website: www.japanoptics.co.jp
Phone No.: 011 81359146680
Fax No.: 011 81353922232

JOHN MASEN COMPANY, INC.
Mini 14 and AR-15 accessories, shotgun stocks.
1305 Jelmak Street
Grand Prairie, TX 75050
Website: www.johnmasen.com
Phone No.: 972-790-0521
Fax No.: 972-970-3691

JOHN'S GUNS
Suppressors for military, law enforcement and
civilian applications.
Dark Horse Arms Company
1041 FM 1274
Coleman, TX 76834
Website: www.darkhorsearms.com
Phone No.: 325-382-4885
Fax No.: 325-382-4887

JONATHAN ARTHUR CIENER, INC.
.22 LR conversion units/kits for centerfire
handguns and rifles.
8700 Commerce Street
Cape Canaveral, FL 32920
Website: www.22lrconversions.com
Phone No.: 321-868-2200
Fax No.: 321-868-2201

JP ENTERPRISES, INC.
JPoint red dot sight, optics mounts, rifle
accessories.
P.O. Box 378
Hugo, MN 55038
Website: www.jprifles.com
Phone No.: 651-426-9196
Fax No.: 651-426-2472

KAHLES USA
Firearm scopes.
3911 SW. 47th Av., Suite 914
Fort Lauderdale, FL 33314
Website: www.kahlesusa.com
Phone No.: 954-581-5822
Fax No.: 954–581-3165

KDF INC
Scopes and muzzle brakes.
2485 State Highway 46 North
Seguin, TX 78155
Website: www.kdfguns.com
Phone No.: 830-379-8141

KELBLY'S INC.
Rifle stocks, tactical scopes and rings, triggers.
7222 Dalton Fox Lake Road
North Lawrence, OH 44666
Website: www.kelbly.com
Phone No.: 330-683-4674

KFS INDUSTRIES
Bipods and mounting adaptors, adjustable sights
for 1911 style pistols.
875 Wharton Drive Southwest, P.O. Box 44405
Atlanta, GA 30336
Website: www.versapod.com
Phone No.: 404-691-7611
Fax No.: 404-505-8445

KG INDUSTRIES, LLC
High performance firearm finishes.
16790 US Highway 63 South, Building 2
Hayward, WI 54843
Website: www.kgcoatings.com
Phone No.: 715-934-3566
Fax No.: 715-934-3570

KICK-EEZ PRODUCTS
Sorbothane recoil pads.
1819 Schurman Way, Suite 106
Woodland, WA 98674
Website: www.kickeezproducts.com
Phone No.: 360-225-9701
Fax No.: 360-225-9702

KINETIC RESEARCH GROUP
Modular stocks and components for long range/
sniper rifles.
22348 Duff Lane
Middleton, ID 83644
Website: www.kineticresearchgroup.com
Phone No.: 720-234-1145

KLEEN-BORE INC.
Comprehensive line of gun care products
13386 International Parkway
Jacksonville, FL 32218
Phone Number: 800-347-1200
Fax Number: 800-366-1669
Website: www.kleen-bore.com

KNIGHTS MANUFACTURING COMPANY
Suppressors in popular calibers, night vision
scopes.
701 Columbia Boulevard
Titusville, FL 32780
Website: www.knightarmco.com
Phone No.: 321-607-9900
Fax No.: 321-383-2143

KNS PRECISION, INC.
AR15/M16 receivers, parts and accessories; iron
sights.
112 Marschall Creek Road
Fredericksburg, TX 78624
Website: www.knsprecisioninc.com
Phone No.: 830-997-0000
Fax No.: 830-997-1443

KONUS CORP USA
Optics
7530 NW 79th Street
Miami, FL 33166
Website: www.konususa.com
Phone No.: 305-884-7618

KREBS GUNSMITHING
SIG and AK pattern rifle accessories.
1000 N. Rand Road
Wauconcla, IL 60084
Phone No.: 847-487-7776

KRIEGER BARRELS, INC.
Precision single-point, cut-rifled barrels in caliber
ranging from .17 cal. through 4 Bore.
2024 Mayfield Road
Richfield, WI 53076
Website: www.kriegerbarrels.com
Phone No.: 262-628-8558
Fax No.: 262-628-8748

KRUGER OPTICS INC.
251 West Barclay Drive
P.O. Box 532
Sisters, OR 97759
Website: www.krugeroptical.com
Phone No.: 541-549-0770

KURZZEIT USA
Bullet speed chronographs, trigger systems
3267 Valley Crest Way
Forest Grove, OR 97116
Website: www.mktactical.com
Phone No.: 503-577-6824

K-VAR CORP.
AK style rifle parts and accessories.
3300 South Decatur Boulevard
Suite 10601
Las Vegas, NV 89102
Website: www.k-var.com
Phone No.: 702-364-8880
Fax No.: 702-307-2303

KWIK-SITE COMPANY/IRONSIGHTER COMPANY
Scope mounts, bases, rings, and extension rings.
5555 Treadwell
Wayne, MI 48184
Website: www.kwiksitecorp.com
Phone No.: 734-326-1500
Fax No.: 734-326-4120

L&G WEAPONRY
Customizes, services, and designs AR-15 & M16
style weapons.
Huntington Beach, CA
Website: www.lgweaponry.com
Email: larry@lgweaponry.com
Phone No: 714-840-3772
Fax No.: 714-625-4631

L.P.A. SRL DI GHILARDI
Metalic front and rear sights, sight accessories.
Via Vittorio Alfieri, 26
Gardone, V.T. 25063 Italy
Website: www.lpasights.com
Phone No.: 011 390308911481
Fax No.: 011 390308910951

L-3 COMMUNICATIONS-EOTECH
Holographic red dot weapon sights.
1201 East Ellsworth Road
Ann Arbor, MI 48108
Website: www.l-3com.com/eotech
Phone No.: 734-741-8868
Fax No.: 734-741-8221

3 ELECTRO-OPTICAL SYSTEMS
Gen III night vision and thermal imaging weapon sights.
3414 Herrmann Drive
Garland, TX 75041
Website: www.l3nightvision.com
Phone No.: 972-840-5788
Fax No.: 972-271-2195

LANCER SYSTEMS
L5 translucent magazines and other firearms accessories.
7566 Morris Court, Suite 300
Allentown, PA 18106
Website: www.lancer-systems.com
Phone No.: 610-973-2614
Fax No.: 610-973-2615

LARUE TACTICAL
Quick-detach optical sight mounts, rails, AR15 style weapon handguards.
850 CR 177
Leander, TX 78641
Website: www.laruetactical.com
Phone No.: 512-259-1585
Fax No.: 512-259-1588

LASER AIMING SYSTEMS CORPORATION
Viridian brand green laser sights.
5929 Baker Road, Suite 440
Minnetonka, MN 55345
Website: www.viridiangreenlaser.com
Phone No.: 800-990-9390
Fax No.: 952-224-4097

LASER DEVICES, INC.
Laser sights and lights; rifle/shotgun/submachine gun mounts and rails, weapon lights.
70 Garden Court
2 Harris Court, Suite A-4
Monterey, CA 93940
Website: www.laserdevices.com
Phone No.: 831-373-0701
Fax No.: 831-373-0903

LASER GENETICS OF AMERICA
Laser illuminators.
3721 SW. 47th AV., Suite 305
Fort Lauderdale, FL 33314
Website: www.lasergenetics.com
Phone No.: 954-581-5822
Fax No.: 954-581-3165

LASERLYTE
Laser sights.
101 Airpark Road
Cottonwood, AZ 86326
Website: www.laserlyte.com
Phone No.: 928-649-3201
Fax No.: 928-649-3970

LASERMAX, INC.
Laser sights.
3495 Winston Place Suite B
Rochester, NY 14623
Website: www.lasermax.com
Phone No.: 585-272-5420
Fax No.: 585-272-5427

LAUER CUSTOM WEAPONRY
Firearms suppressors, Duracoat self-lubricating firearms finish.
3601 129th Street
Chippewa Falls, WI 54729
Website: www.lauerweaponry.com
Phone No.: 715-720-6128
Fax No.: 715-723-2950

LAW ENFORCEMENT TARGETS, INC.
Targets and range training products
8802 West 35W Service Dr. NE
Blaine, MN 55449-6740
Phone Number: 888-489-7830
Fax Number: 651-645-5360
Website: www.letargets.com

LEAPERS, INC.
Electro-optical and tactical scopes, rail mounting systems.
32700 Capitol Street
Livonia, MI 48150
Website: www.leapers.com
Phone No.: 734-542-1500
Fax No.: 734-542-7095

LEATHERWOOD/HI-LUX OPTICS
Rifle scopes, auto-ranging trajectory scopes, 30mm tactical scopes.
Hi-Lux, Inc.
3135 Kashiwa Street
Torrance, CA 90505
Website: www.hi-luxoptics.com
Phone No.: 310-257-8142
Fax No.: 310-257-8096

LEGION ARMS, LLC
Rifle and handgun rail and mounting systems.
620 Valley Forge Road, Suite B
Hillsborough, NC 27278
Phone No.: 919-672-8620
Fax No.: 919-883-5265

LEHIGH DEFENSE, LLC
AR style weapon components and accessories.
130 Penn AM Drive, Suite D-1
Quakertown, PA 18951
Website: www.lehighdefense.com

LEICA SPORT OPTICS
Optical sights.
1 Pearl Court, Suite A
Allendale, NJ 07401 USA
Website: www.leica-camera.com/usa
Phone No.: 201-995-0051
Fax No.: 201-955-1686

LEITNER-WISE DEFENSE
Weapon-mounted "Countashot" electronic shot counter.
P.O. Box 25097
Alexandria, VA 22313
Website: www.leitner-wise.com
Phone No.: 703-209-0556

LES BAER CUSTOM, INC.
1911 pistol frames, slides, barrels, sights, grips, scope mounts.
1804 Iowa Drive
Leclaire, IA 52753
Website: www.lesbaer.com
Phone No.: 563-289-2126
Fax No.: 563-289-2132

LEUPOLD & STEVENS, INC.
Tactical optical and electro-optical scopes, rings, and bases.
14400 Northwest Greenbriar Parkway 9700,
P.O. Box 688
Beaverton, OR 97006
Website: www.leupold.com
Phone No.: 503-646-9171
Fax No.: 503-526-1478

LEVELLOK SHOOTING SYSTEMS
Monopods, bipods, and tripods.
105 South 12th Street
Pittsburgh, PA 15203
Website: www.levellok.com
Phone No.: 412-431-5440
Fax No.: 412-488-7608

LEWIS MACHINE & TOOL
Tactical weapon accessories.
1305 11th Street West
Milan, IL 61264
Website: www.lewismachine.net
Phone No.: 309-787-7151
Fax No.: 309-787-7193

LIMBSAVER
LimbSaver recoil pads.
50 West Rose Nye Way
Shelton, WA 98584 USA
Website: www.limbsaver.com
Phone No.: 360-427-6031
Fax No.: 360-427-4025

LINE OF FIRE, LLC
TEGS grip system, 3.2.1. Slings.
3200 Danville Blvd., Suite 220
Alamo, CA 94507
Website: www.loftactical.com
Phone No.: 323-899-3016
Fax No.: 562-424-1562

LONE STAR TACTICAL
See Trademark Index

LONE WOLF DISTRIBUTORS, INC.
Glock pistol accessories.
57 Shepard Road, P.O. Box 3549
Oldtown, ID 83822 USA
Website: www.lonewolfdist.com
Phone No.: 208-437-0612
Fax No.: 208-437-1098

LRB ARMS
M14 and AR15 receivers.
96 Cherry Lane
Floral Park, NY 11001 USA
Website: www.lrbarms.com
Phone No.: 516-327-9061
Fax No.: 516-327-0246

LUCID
HD7 red dot sight.
235 Fairway Drive
Riverton, WY 82501
Website: www.my lucidgear.com
Phone No.: 307-840-2160

LUNA OPTICS, INC.
Night vision riflescopes.
54 Columbus Avenue
Staten Island, NY 10304
Website: www.lunaoptics.com
Phone No.; 718-556-5862
Fax No.: 718-556-5869

LWRC INTERNATIONAL, LLC
Tactical firearm accessories.
815 Chesapeake Drive
Cambridge, MD 21613
Website: www.lwrci.com
Phone No.: 410-901-1348
Fax No.: 410-228-1799

LYMAN PRODUCTS CORP.
Lyman sights; Pachmayr synthetic grips, stocks, recoil pads, and sights; Uni-Dot fiber optic sights; and TacStar weapon lights, shotgun grips/shell carriers/magazine extensions, AR style rifle grips and accessories.
475 Smith Street
Middletown, CT 06457
Website: www.lymanproducts.com
Phone No.: 860-632-2020
Fax No.: 860-632-1699

MAG-NA-PORT INTERNATIONAL INC.
Handgun, shotgun, and rifle barrel porting/muzzle brakes.
41302 Executive Drive
Harrison Twp, MI 48045
Website: www.magnaport.com
Phone No.: 586-469-6727
Fax No.: 586-469-0425

MAGPUL INDUSTRIES CORP.
Fully adjustable buttstocks, magazines, grips, rail covers, and sights for AR15 and other tactical weapons.
P.O. Box 17697
Boulder, CO 80308
Website: www.magpul.com
Phone No.: 303-828-3460
Fax No.: 303-828-3469

MAJESTIC ARMS, LTD.
Ruger rimfire rifle and pistol parts, Aluma-lite 10/22 and 77/22 barrels.
101A Ellis St.
Staten Island, NY 10307
Website: www.majesticarms.com
Phone No.: 718-356-6765
Fax No.: 718-356-6835

MAKO GROUP
Tactical weapon accessories.
170-20 Central Ave.
Farmingdale, NY 11735
Website: www.themakogroup.com
Phone No.: 631-880-3396
Fax No.: 631-880-3397

MANNERS COMPOSITE STOCKS
Carbon fiber and fiber glass gunstocks.
1209 Swift
North Kansas City, MO 64116
Website: www.mannersstock.com
Phone No.: 816-283-3334

MANTA / MANTARAILS
Manta railguards and wire management systems, heat shield "suppressor sleeves".
326 Pearl St. NE
New Philadelphia, OH 44663
Website: www.manta.us
Phone No.: 330-308-6360

MARVEL PRECISION LLC
.22 LR conversions for 1911 style pistols, and associated scope mount ribs, sights, parts, and compensators.
2464 South 54th Road, Suite 2
Firth, NE 68358
Website: www.marvelprecision.com
Phone No.: 800-295-1987
Fax No.: 402-791-2246

MASTERPIECE ARMS
.22 LR/WMR, 5.7x28, 9mm, .45 ACP, 5.56 and .308 suppressors.
4904 Hwy. 98
P.O. Box 67
Comer, GA 30629
Website: www.masterpiecearms.com
Phone No.: 866-803-0000

MATECH, INC.
Back-up iron sights.
510 Naylor Mill Road
Salisbury, MD 21801
Website: www.matech.net
Phone No.: 410-548-1627
Fax No.: 410-548-1628

MCCANN INDUSTRIES LLC
AR-15 parts and accessories
P.O. Box 641
Spanaway, WA 98387
Phone No. 253-537-6919
Fax No. 253-537-6993
Website: www.mccannindustries.com
Email: info@mccannindustries.com

MCMILLAN FIBERGLASS STOCKS
Fiberglass rifle stocks.
1638 West Knudsen Drive, Suite A
Phoenix, AZ 85027
Website: www.mcmillanusa.com
Phone No.: 623-582-9635
Fax No.: 623-581-3825

MEC-GAR SRL
Handgun and rifle magazines.
Via Mandolossa, 102/a
Gussago, Brescia, 25064 Italy
Website: www.mec-gar.it
Phone No.: 011-390303735413
Fax No.: 011-390303733687

MEGA ARMS LLC
AR-15 style upper and lower receivers, rails, and accessories.
5323 Joppa St. SW
Tumwater, WA 98512
Website: mega-arms.com
Phone No.: 877-857-5372

MEGGITT TRAINING SYSTEMS
Supplier of integrated live fire and simulation weapons training systems
296 Brogdon Road
Suwanee, GA, 30024
Phone Number: 678-288-1090
Website: www.meggitttrainingsystems.com

MEOPTA USA, INC.
Riflescopes.
50 Davids Drive
Hauppauge, NY 11788
Website: www.meopta.com
Phone No.: 631-436-5900
Fax No.: 631-436-5920

MEPROLIGHT/KIMBER
Tritium night sights and red dot reflex sights.
2590 Montana Hwy 35, Suite B
Kalispell, MT 59901
Website: www.kimberamerica.com
Phone No.: 406-758-2222
Fax No.: 406-758-2223

MEPROLIGHT, LTD.
Electro-optical and optical sights and devices.
58 Hazait Street, Or-Akiva Industrial Park
Or-Akiva, 30600 Israel
Website: www.meprolight.com
Phone No.: 011-97246244111
Fax No.: 011-97246244123

MESA TACTICAL
Telescoping stock systems, shell carriers, rails, and sling loops for tactical shotguns.
1760 Monrovia Ave, Suite A14
Costa Mesa, CA 92627
Website: www.mesatactical.com
Phone No.: 949-642-3337
Fax No.: 949-642-3339

MEYERS & CO.
See B.E. MEYERS & CO.

MFI
Rails, risers, scope mounts, and accessories for tactical weapons.
563 San Miguel
Liberty, KY 42539
Website: www.mfiap.com
Phone No.: 606-787-0022
Fax No.: 606-787-0059

MGI
AR-15/M-4/M-16 lower receivers, 90 round magazines, and parts.
102 Cottage Street
Bangor, ME 04401
Website: www.MGImilitary.com
Phone No.: 207-945-5441
Fax No.: 207-945-4010

MGM TARGETS/MIKE GIBSON MANUFACTURING
Manufacturer of AR Steel Targets
17891 Karcher Rd.
Caldwell, ID 83607
Phone Number: 208-454-0555
Fax Number: 208-454-0666
Website: mgmtargets.com

MICOR INDUSTRIES, INC.
Flash suppressors.
1314 A State Docks Road
Decatur, AL 356601
Website: www.micorind.com
Phone No.: 256-560-0770
Fax No.: 256-341-0002

MICRO SLICK
See AMELON COATINGS, LLC

MIDWAYUSA, INC.
Shooting and gun care products
5875 West Van Horn Tavern Rd.
Columbia, MO 65203-9274
Phone Number: 800-243-3220
Fax Number: 800-992-8312
Website: www.midwayusa.com

MIDWEST INDUSTRIES, INC.
Tactical rifle accessories.
828 Philip Drive, Suite 2
Waukesha, WI 53186
Website: www.midwestindustriesinc.com
Phone No.: 262-896-6780
Fax No.: 262-896-6756

...LLETT SIGHTS
...actical scopes, red dot sights, metallic sights,
...ngs, and bases.
...200 Cody
...Overland Park, KS 66214
Website: www.millettsights.com
Phone No.: 913-752-3400
Fax No.: 913-752-3550

...SSION FIRST TACTICAL
...actical rifle accessories.
...80 Haunted Lane
Bensalem, PA 19020
Phone No.: 267-803-1517
Fax No.: 267-803-1002

...ODULAR DRIVEN TECHNOLOGIES
...AC21 and LSS chassis systems for Rem. 700,
...avage, and Tikka T3 rifles.
...3022 Evans Road, #103
Chilliwack, British Columbia
V2R5R8 Canada
Website: www.mdttac.com
Phone No.: 604-210-0016

...OROVISION NIGHT VISION, INC.
...aw enforcement and commercial night vision
...ptical sights.
P.O. Box 342
Dana Point, CA 92629
Website: www.morovision.com
Phone No.: 949-488-3855
Fax No.: 949-488-3361

...OUNTING SOLUTIONS PLUS
...Muzzelite, LightLink, SightLink, and Glock Pistol
...Fiber Optic Sight.
10655 Southwest 185 Terrace
Miami, FL 33157
Website: www.mountsplus.com
Phone No.: 305-253-8393
Fax No.: 305-232-1247

...URRAYS GUNS
...Replacement SKS firing pin kit, Yugoslav SKS gas valve.
12696 FM 2127
Bowie, TX 76230
Website: www.murraysguns.com
Phone No.: 940-928-002
Fax No.: 800-836-7579

...VISION OPTICS LLC
Night vision and thermal optics.
220 Reservoir St., Suite 26
Needham, MA 02494
Website: www.nvisionoptics.com
Phone No.: 781-505-8360

...ECG LTD. / NEW ENGLAND CUSTOM GUN
...ERVICE, LTD.
...Rifle and shotgun iron sights, sling swivels, recoil
...pads, and scope mounts.
741 Main St.
Claremont, NH 03743
Website: newenglandcustomgun.com
Phone No.: 603-287-4836
Fax No.: 603-287-4832

...EW CENTURY NCSTAR, INC.
...Firearms accessories, optics including precision
...rifle and pistol scopes, and red dot sights.
10302 Olney Street
El Monte, CA 91731
Website: www.ncstar.com
Phone No.: 626-575-1518
Fax No.: 626-575-2478

NEWCON OPTIK
Electro-optical products, night vision rifle scopes.
105 Sparks Ave
Toronto, ON M2H 2S5 Canada
Website: www.newcon-optik.com
Phone No.: 416-663-6963
Fax No.: 416-663-9065

NIC INDUSTRIES, INC.
Liquid ceramic coating developed to withstand the
most extreme conditions.
7050 Sixth Street
White City, OR 97503
Website: www.nicindustries.com
Phone No.: 541-826-1922
Fax No.: 541-830-6518

NIGHTFORCE OPTICS
Nightforce precision rifle scopes.
Lightforce USA, Inc.
1040 Hazen Lane
Orofino, ID 83544
Website: www.nightforceoptics.com
Phone No.: 208-476-9814
Fax No.: 208-476-9817

NIGHT OPTICS USA, INC.
Commercial, law enforcement, and military
thermal/night vision systems.
15182 Triton Lane, Suite 101
Huntington Beach, CA 92649
Website: www.nightoptics.com
Phone No.: 714-899-4475
Fax No.: 714-899-4448

NIGHT OWL OPTICS/BOUNTY HUNTER
Night vision and infrared scopes.
1465-H Henry Brennan
El Paso, TX 79936
Website: www.nightowloptics.com
Phone No.: 915-633-8354
Fax No.: 915-633-8529

NITESIGHT LTD.
NiteSite converts a conventional scope into a
night vision sight.
Unit 13, West Lane
Full Sutton Airfield
York, North Yorkshire, YO41 1HS
UNITE KINGDOM
Website: www.nitesite.co.uk
Phone No.: 44-0-1759-377235

NIGHT VISION DEPOT
Night vision weapon sights and accessories.
P.O. Box 3415
Allentown, PA 18106
Website: www.nvdepot.com
Phone No.: 610-395-9743
Fax No.: 610-395-9744

NIGHT VISION SYSTEMS
Night vision, thermal imaging, combat
identification, and lasers.
542 Kemmerer Lane
Allentown, PA 18104
Website: www.nightvisionsystems.com
Phone No.: 610-391-9101
Fax No.: 610-391-9220

NIKON, INC.
Riflescopes.
1300 Walt Whitman Road
Melville, NY 11747
Website: www.nikonhunting.com
Phone No.: 631-547-4200
Fax No.: 631-547-4040

NITREX OPTICS
Riflescopes.
Weaver/ATK Commercial Products
N5549 County Trunk Z
Onalaska, WI 54650
Website: www.nitrexoptics.com
Phone No: 800-635-7656
Fax No.: 763-323-3890

NIVISYS INDUSTRIES, LLC
Night vision weapon sights, and related laser
aiming and illumination systems.
400 South Clark Drive, Suite 105
Tempe, AZ 85281
Website: www.nivisys.com
Phone No.: 480-970-3222
Fax No.: 480-970-3555

NODAK SPUD LLC
AKM receivers and fire control parts, AR lowers,
Picatinny rails, flash hiders, Benelli 1014/M4
extended mag tubes.
7683 Washington Ave. S.
Edina, MN 55439
Website: www.nodakspud.com
Phone No.: 952-942-1909
Fax No.: 952-942-1912

NORGON, LLC
AR15/M16 ambidextrous magazine catch.
7518 K Fullerton Road
Springfield, VA 22153
Website: www.norgon.com
Phone No.: 703-455-0997
Fax No.: 703-569-6411

NOVAK DESIGNS, INC.
Handgun sights ("LoMount", "Mega Dot"), 1911
extended safety lever, Picatinny rail, and
magazines.
P.O. Box 4045
1206 30th Street
Parkersburg, WV 26104
Website: www.novaksights.com
Phone No.: 304-485-9295
Fax No.: 304-428-22676

OBERLAND ARMS OHG
Flash suppressors and compensators for tactical
rifles.
Frank Satzinger & Matthias Hainich
Am Hundert 3
82386 Huglfing - GERMANY
Website: www.oberlandarms.com
Phone No.: 49 08802914750
Fax No.: 49 08802914751

OSPREY DEFENSE, LLC
AR15 style gas piston conversion kits.
6112 33rd Street E, Unit #104
Bradenton, FL 34203
Website: www.gaspiston.com
Phone No.: 941-322-26561
Fax No.: 941-322-2562

OSPREY INTERNATIONAL, INC.
Laser sights, holographic sights, and daytime riflescopes.
25 Hawks Farm Road
White, GA 30184
Website: www.osprey-optics.com
Phone No.: 770-387-2751
Fax No.: 770-387-0114

PACHMAYR
See LYMAN PRODUCTS CORP

PALMETTO STATE ARMORY
AR15 rifle accessories.
3670 Fernandina Road
Columbia, SC 29210
Website: www.palmettostatearmory.com
Phone No.: 803-724-6950

PARKER-HALE
Scope mounts, bipods, suppressors, and barrels.
Bedford Road
Petersfield, Hampshire, GU32 3XA
United Kingdom
Website: www.parker-hale.co.uk
Phone No.: 011 441730268011
Fax No.: 011 441730260074

PATRIOT ORDNANCE FACTORY
Gas piston weapon systems and uppers, precision sniper stocks, AR rifle magazines, AR rails/ forends, and flash hiders.
23623 North 67 Ave
Glendale, AZ 85310
Website: www.pof-usa.com
Phone No.: 623-561-9572
Fax No.: 623-321-1680

PEARCE GRIP
Replacement grips for firearms.
P.O. Box 40367
Fort Worth, TX 76140
Website: www.pearcegrip.com
Phone No.: 817-568-9704
Fax No.: 817-568-9707

PENTAGONLIGHT
Tactical weapon light systems.
151 Mitchell Ave
San Francisco, CA 94080
Website: www.pentagonlight.com
Phone No.: 650-877-1555
Fax No.: 650-877-9555

PENTAX IMAGING COMPANY
Riflescopes.
600 12th Street, Suite 300
Golden, CO 80401
Website: www.pentaxsportoptics.com
Phone No.: 303-799-8000
Fax No.: 303-460-1628

PHOEBUS TACTICAL FLASHLIGHTS
LED tactical flashlights.
2800 Third Street
San Francisco, CA 94107
Website: www.phoebus.com
Phone No.: 415-550-0770
Fax No.: 415-550-2655

PHOENIX TACTICAL
"Pod Claw" bipod feet, Harris bipod rail adaptors, DLG lighted scope level indicator.
1016 W. Poplar Av., Suite 106-320
Collierville, TN 38017
Website: www.phoenixtactical.com
Phone No.: 901-289-1110
Fax No.: 901-854-0633

PHOENIX TECHNOLOGY LTD.
Kicklite stocks and accessories
P.O. Box 249
Burgaw, NC 28425
Website: www.kicklitestocks.com
Phone No.: 877-774-1867

POINT TECH, INC.
1911 type pistol barrels, frames, and slides, Glock barrels, Beretta barrels, Mauser barrels, AR16/M16 barrels, and .50 caliber barrels.
160 Gregg Street, Suite 1
Lodi, NJ 07644
Phone No.: 201-368-0711
Fax No.: 201-368-0133

PRECISION BARRELS
Rifle barrels
Website: www.precisionbarrels.com
Phone No.: 615-461-7688

PRECISION FIREARMS
AR15 upper receivers.
74 Dupont Road, Suite A
Martinsburg, WV 25404
Website: www.precisionfirearms.com

PRECISION REFLEX, INC.
Custom built AR uppers, rings, bases, carbon fiber forearms, shotgun mounts, charging handles, and auxiliary iron sights.
710 Streine Drive,
P.O. Box 95
New Bremen, OH 45869
Website: www.pri-mounts.com
Phone No.: 419-629-2603
Fax No.: 419-629-2173

PREMIER RETICLES
Tactical riflescopes, scout scopes, owner of patented Gen 2 Mildot reticle.
175 Commonwealth Court
Winchester, VA 22602
Phone No.: 540-868-2044
Fax No.: 540-868-2045

PRIMARY WEAPONS SYSTEMS
AR15 receivers, parts, quad rails, Ruger 10/22 trigger groups and barrels.
800 East Citation Court, Suite C
Boise, ID 83716
Website: www.primaryweapons.com
Phone No.: 208-344-5217
Fax No.: 208-344-5395

PRO-DEFENSE
Picatinny rail mounted pepper spray.
3512 Sunny Lane
P.O. Box 3065
Columbia Falls, MT 59912
Website: www.Pro-Defense.com
Phone No.: 406-892-3060

PROMAG INDUSTRIES, INC.
Rifle and pistol magazines, scope rings, mounts, shotgun stocks, tactical rifle and pistol accessory
10654 South Garfield Ave
South Gate, CA 90280
Website: www.promagindustries.com
Phone No.: 562-861-9554
Fax No.: 562-861-6377

PSI, LLC
LPA adjustable pistol sights, tactical shotgun sights, ACT-MAG/PSI and Novak pistol magazine
2 Klarides Village Drive, Suite 336
Seymour, CT 06483
Website: www.precisionsalesintl.com
Phone No.: 203-262-6484
Fax No.: 203-262-6562

PULSAR
Thermal, Gen 2, Gen 3, and digital night vision.
2201 Heritage Parkway
Mansfield, TX 76063
Website: www.pulsarnv.com
Phone No.: 817-225-0310

QUAKE INDUSTRIES, INC.
Sling swivels, tactical attachments, and parts.
5988 Peachtree Corners East
Norcross, GA 30071
Website: www.quakeinc.com
Phone No.: 770-449-4687
Fax No.: 770-242-8546

QUICKSILVER MANUFACTURING,LLC
Ultralight titanium rifle suppressors.
1373 E. 3700 N.
Buhl, ID 83316
Website: www.qsmsilencers.com
Fax No.: 208-543-0913

R GUNS
See Trademark Index

RCI - XRAIL
High capacity shotgun magazines.
3825 E. Calumet St., Suite 400-173
Appleton, WI 54915
Website: www.XRAILbyRCI.com
Phone No.: 920-585-6534

R & D PRECISION
Oversize bolt handle knobs, replacement ambidextrous latch for Badger M5 detachable bo. magazine system.
942 S. Dodsworth Av.
Glendora, CA 91740
Website: www.rdprecision.net
Phone No.: 626-806-4389

RAINIER ARMS, LLC
Tactical rail systems, barrels, receivers, buffers, gas blocks, flash suppressors, bolt carriers, and enhanced trigger guards.
3802 N. Auburn Way, Suite 305
Auburn, WA 98002
Website: www.rainierarms.com
Phone No.: 877-556-4867
Fax No.: 253-218-2998

RAMLINE
Synthetic gunstocks.
Onalaska Operations
P.O. Box 39
Onalaska, WI 54650
Website: www.atk.com
Phone No.: 800-635-7656

RANCH PRODUCTS
Scope mounts and other specialty gun parts.
P.O. Box 145
Malinta, OH 43535
Website: www.ranchproducts.com
Phone No.: 419-966-2881
Fax No.: 313-565-8536

REDRING USA LLC
Optical shotgun sight.
100 Mill Plain Road
Danbury, CT 06811
Website: www.redringusa.com
Phone No.: 203-546-3511

RESET INC.
Picatinny riser rail with integral battery pack and contacts for central power supply of weapon accessories - RIPR/Rifle Integrated Power Rail.
49 Strathearn Place
Simi Valley, CA 93065
Website: www.reset-inc.com
Phone No.: 805-584-4900
Fax No.: 805-583-2900

RESCOMP HANDGUN TECHNOLOGIES
Compensators and mounts for all 1911 style pistols as well as AR-15, AK and Galil rifles; magazines for STI and Para Ordnance style hi-cap pistols.
P.O. Box 11786
Queenswood, 186 South Africa
Website: www.crspeed.co.za
Phone No.: 011 27123334768
Fax No.: 011 27123332112

RIVERBANK ARMORY
Coded oilers, type one bands, flip sights and other parts for M1 carbines and M1 Garands.
P.O. Box 85
Riverbank, CA 95367
Website: www.riverbankarmory.com
Phone No.: 209-869-5576

ROBAR COMPANIES, INC.
Polymer frame pistol grip reductions and texturizing, and NP3/NP3 Plus, Roguard, black oxide, electroless nickel, stainless steel blackening, phosphating/parkerizing, and Polymax camouflage firearm finishes.
21438 North 7th Av., Suite B
Phoenix, AZ 85027
Website: www.robarguns.com
Phone No.: 623-581-2648
Fax No.: 623-582-0059

ROCK RIVER ARMS, INC.
Parts and accessories for .223, 9mm, .458 Socom, 6.8 SPC, and .308 rifles.
1042 Cleveland Road
Colona, IL 61241
Website: www.rockriverarms.com
Phone No.: 309-792-5780
Fax No.: 309-792-5781

ROTH CONCEPT INNOVATIONS, LLC
High capacity "XRAIL" shotgun magazine tube extension system.
3825 E. Calumet St., Suite 400-173
Appleton, WI 54915
Website: www.XRAILBYRCI.com
Phone No.: 920-585-6534
Fax No.: 920-731-6660

ROYAL ARMS INTERNATIONAL INC.

Tactical accessories for shotguns and AR15 rifles, billet AR lower receivers.
1300 Graves Av.
Oxnard, CA 93030
Website: www.royalarms.com
Phone No.: 805-288-5250

S&K SCOPE MOUNTS
"Insta Mount" no drill/no tap scope mounting bases for ex-military rifles.
70 Swede Hollow Road
Sugar Grove, PA 16350
Website: www.scopemounts.com
Phone No.: 800-578-9862
Fax No.: 814-489-7730

S.W.A.T. FIREARMS
AR15 receivers.
6585 I-30 East
Campbell, TX 75422
Website: www.swatfirearms.com
Phone No.: 903-862-2408

SADLAK INDUSTRIES LLC
M-1A and M-14 parts, scope mounts, and accessories.
Nadeau Industrial Park
712 Bread & Milk Street, #7
Coventry, CT 06238
Website: www.sadlak.com
Phone No.: 860-742-0227

SAGE ORDNANCE SYSTEMS GROUP
EBR Aluminum Chassis Stock for M14 rifles, and accessories for law enforcement/military weapons.
3455 Kings Corner Road
Oscoda, MI 48750
Website: www.sageinternationalltd.com
Phone No.: 989-739-7000
Fax No.: 989-739-7098

SALT RIVER TACTICAL, LLC
Support items for Combloc and Soviet-era weapons systems.
P.O. Box 20397
Mesa, AZ 85277
Website: www.saltrivertactical.com
Phone No.: 480-656-2683

SAMSON MFG. CORPORATION
Rail systems and other tactical accessories.
4 Forge Street
Keene, NH 03431
Website: www.samson-mfg.com
Phone No.: 888-665-4370
Fax No.: 413-665-1163

SCHERER SUPPLIES, INC.
High capacity magazines for Glock pistols.
205 Four Mile Creek Road
Tazewell, TN 37879
Phone No.: 423-733-2615
Fax No.: 423-733-2073

SCHMIDT & BENDER GMBH
High precision rifle scopes for military and law enforcement.
Am Grossacker 42
Biebertal, Hessen, 35444 GERMANY
Website: www.schmidtbender.com
Phone No.: 011 496409811570
Fax No.: 011 496409811511

SEEKINS PRECISION
See Trademark Index

SHEPHERD ENTERPRISES, INC.
Riflescopes with integral range finder, bullet drop compensator, and patented dual reticle system.
P.O. Box 189
Waterloo, NE 68069
Website: www.shepherdscopes.com
Phone No.: 402-779-2424
Fax No.: 402-779-4010

SHERLUK MARKETING
M-16/AR-15 parts and accessories.
P.O. Box 156
Delta, OH 43615
Website: www.sherluk.com
Phone No.: 419-923-8011
Fax No.: 419-923-812

SHIELD FIREARMS & SIGHTS LTD.
Combat proven red dot sights.
P.O. Box 7633
Bridport, Dorset DT6 9DW
UNITED KINGDOM
Website: www.shieldpsd.com
Phone No.: 44-1297-678233

SHOOTERS RIDGE
Bi-pods, Picatinny rail adaptors, rings, and bases.
N5549 County Trunk Z
Onalaska, WI 54650
Website: www.shootersridge.com
Phone No.: 800-635-7656
Fax No.: 763-323-3890

SI DEFENSE, INC.
AR15 style rifle parts.
2902 Hwy 93 North
Kalispell, MT 59901
Website: www.si-defense.com
Phone No.: 406-752-4253
Fax No.: 406-752-4082

SIERRA PRECISION RIFLES
Tactical rifle components and accessories.
24927 Bonanza Drive
Mi Wuk, CA 95346
Website: www.spaceguns.com
Phone No.: 209-586-6071
Fax No.: 209-586-6555

SIGHTMARK
Riflescopes, laser sights, red dot sights, night vision sights, and weapon lights.
201 Regency Parkway
Mansfield, TX 76063
Website: www.sightmark.com
Phone No.: 817-394-0310
Fax No.: 817-394-1628

SIGHTRON, INC.
Tactical and mil-dot scopes, and red dot sights.
100 Jeffrey Way, Suite A
Youngsville, NC 27596
Website: www.sightron.com
Phone No.: 919-562-3000
Fax No.: 919-556-0157

SILENCERCO, LLC
Suppressors.
5511 South 6055 West
West Valley City, UT 84118
Website: www.silencerco.com
Phone No.: 801-973-2023
Fax No.: 801-973-2032

SIMMONS
Rifle, shotgun, and handgun scopes.
9200 Cody Street
Overland Park, KS 66214
Phone No.: 913-782-3131
Fax No.: 913-782-4189

SLIDE FIRE SOLUTIONS
Bump fire stocks.
751 FM 2408
Moran, TX 76464
Website: www.slidefire.com
Phone No.: 325-945-3800

SOG ARMORY, INC.
AR upper and lower receivers, M4 carbine stocks.
11707 South Sam Houston Parkway West, Suite R
Houston, TX 77031
Website: www.sogarmory.com
Phone No.: 281-568-5685
Fax No.: 285-568-9191

SPA-DEFENSE
Night vision systems, laser systems, tactical/law enforcement equipment.
3400 NW. 9th AV., Suite 1104
Fort Lauderdale, FL 33309
Website: www.spa-defense.com
Phone No.: 954-568-7690
Fax No.: 954-630-4159

SPEEDFEED, INC.
Synthetic shotgun stocks/forends.
13386 International Parkway
Jacksonville, FL 32218
Website: www.safariland.com
Phone No.: 800-347-1200

SPHINX SYSTEMS, LTD.
Importer - See Kriss USA listing.
Suppressors, special mounts, parts.
Gstiegstrasse 12
Matten, Switzerland 3800
Website: www.sphinxarms.com
Phone No.: 011 41338211005
Fax No.: 011 41338211006

SPUHR AB
Scope and night vision rings/bases, tilting mounting bases, weapon light mounts, Harris bipod conversion.
Box 10
SE-24732 Dalby
Sweden
Website: www.spuhr.com
Phone No.: 46 0733926770
Fax No.: 46 046200575

SRT ARMS
Suppressors.
522 Finnie Flat Road, Suite E
PMB 138
Camp Verde, AZ 86322
Website: www.srtarms.com

STONEY POINT PRODUCTS, INC.
Monopods, bipods, quadrapods, weapon accessories.
9200 Cody
Overland Park, KS 66214
Website: www.stoneypoint.com
Phone No.: 913-752-3400
Fax No.: 913-752-3550

STRIKE INDUSTRIES
AR15, AK, Glock, and 1911 accessories.
P.O. Box 38137
Santa Ana, CA 92799
Website: www.strikeindustries.com

STURM, RUGER & CO., INC.
Integrated OEM laser device
Headquarters
1 Lacey Place
Southport, CT06490
Phone No.: 203-259-7843
Fax No.: 203-256-3367
Website: www.ruger.com
Service Center for Pistols, PC4 & PC9 Carbines
200 Ruger Road
Prescott, AZ86301-6181
Phone No.: 928-778-6555
Fax No.: 928-778-6633
Website: www.ruger-firearms.com
Service Center for Revolvers, Long Guns & Ruger Date of Manufacture
411 Sunapee Street
Newport, NH03773
Phone No.: 603-865-2442
Fax No.: 603-863-6165

SUMMIT NIGHT VISION GROUP, INC.
Night vision, thermal, and day optics.
1845 Summit Av., Suite 403
Plano, TX 75074
Website: mwww.summitnightvision.com
Phone No.: 800-985-7684

SUN DEVIL MANUFACTURING, LLC
Billet aluminum AR15 components and accessories; hard anodizing, ceramic coating, and nickel teflon finishing.
663 West Second Avenue, Suite 16
Mesa, AZ 85210
Website: www.sundevilmfg.com
Phone No.: 480-833-9876
Fax No.: 480-833-9509

SUNNY HILL ENTERPRISES INC.
Trigger guard assemblies, scope rings, and stainless steel trigger guards for Rem. 700s.
W1015 County HHH
Chilton, WI 53014
Website: www.sunny-hill.com
Phone No.: 920-898-4707

SUN OPTICS USA
Scopes, dot sights, scope mounts, and accessories.
P.O. Box 2225
Burleson, TX 76097
Website: www.sunopticsusa.com
Phone No.: 817-783-6001
Fax No.: 817-783-6553

SUREFIRE, LLC
Weapon lights and mounts.
18300 Mount Baldy Circle
Fountain Valley, CA 92708
Website: www.surefire.com
Phone No.: 714-545-9444
Fax No.: 714-545-9537

SWAROVSKI OPTIK NORTH AMERICA
Riflescopes and accessories.
2 Slater Road
Cranston, RI 02920
Website: www.swarovskioptik.com
Phone No.: 401-734-1800
Fax No.: 401-734-5888

SWR MANUFACTURING, LLC
.22, 9mm, .45 ACP, 5.56mm, and .30 caliber suppressors.
P.O. Box 841
Pickens, SC 29761
Website: www.swrmfg.com
Phone No.: 864-850-3579
Fax No.: 864-751-2823

TACM III, INC.
Tactical weapon lights and mounts.
2300 Commerce Park Drive, Suite 7
Palm Bay, FL 32905
Website: www.tacm3.com
Phone No.: 321-726-0644
Fax No.: 321-726-0645

TACSTAR
See LYMAN PRODUCTS CORP.

TACTICAL ARMZ
Suppressors.
4451 E Farm Road 132
Springfield, MO 65802
Website: www.tacticalarmz.com
Phone No.: 417-893-0486

TACTICAL INNOVATIONS, INC.
AR15 receivers, .223 suppressors.
345 Sunrise Road
Bonners Ferry, ID 83805
Website: www.tacticalinc.com
Phone No.: 208-267-1585
Fax No.: 208-267-1597

TACTICAL NIGHT VISION CO.
Night vision systems and accessories.
25612 Barton road, #328
Loma Linda, CA 92354
Website: www.tnvc.com
Phone No.: 909-796-7000
Fax No.: 909-478-9133

TACTICAL SOLUTIONS
Suppressors.
2772 S. Victory View Way
Boise, ID 83709
Website: www.tacticalsol.com
Phone No.: 866-333-9901

TACTICAL WEAPONS SOLUTIONS
See Trademark Index

TALLEY MANUFACTURING, INC.
Rings, bases, custom gun parts, and accessories.
9183 Old No. 6 Highway
P.O. Box 369
Santee, SC 29142
Website: www.talleyrings
Phone No.: 803-854-5700
Fax No.: 803-854-9315

TANGENT THETA INCORPORATED
Rifle scopes.
60B Otter Lake Court
Halifax, Nova Scotia B3S 1L9
CANADA
Website: www.tangenttheta.com
Phone No.: 902-876-2935

TANGODOWN, INC.
Mil-spec tactical weapon accessories.
4720 North La Cholla Blvd., Suite 180
Tucson, AZ 85705
Website: www.tangodown.com
Phone No.: 520-888-3376
Fax No.: 520-888-3787

TANNERITE® SPORTS LLC
Patented Binary Exploding Targets
36366 Valley Road
Pleasant Hill, Oregon 97455
Phone Number: 541-744-1406
Fax Number: 541-744-1384
Website: www.tannerite.com/

TAPCO, INC.
Synthetic stocks and forends, slings, high capacity magazines, slings, and U.S. "922r" compliance parts.
P.O. Box 2408
Kennesaw, GA 30156
Website: www.tapco.com
Phone No.: 770-425-1280
Fax No.: 770-425-1510

TASCO
Riflescopes.
9200 Cody
Overland Park, KS 66214
Website: www.tasco.com
Phone No.: 913-752-3400
Fax No.: 913-752-3550

T.A.S., LTD.
Unique single dot miniature pistol and long gun sights.
1 Eilat Street
P.O. Box 84
Tiberias, Israel 14100
Phone No.: 011 972507983433
Fax No.: 011 972467722985

TDI ARMS
Camouflage firearms finish, tactical weapon accessories.
2441 Dakota Craft
Rapid City, SD 57701
Phone No.: 605-415-4910

TEMPCO MANUFACTURING COMPANY, INC.
Firearm magazines, receivers, and other stamped and machined components.
2475 Hwy. 55
St. Paul, MN 55120
Website: www.tempcomfg.com

TEMPLAR CUSTOM, LLC
Barrels, Suppressors, Muzzle brakes.
P.O. Box 15
Apex, NC 27502
Phone No.: 877-878-2334
Website: www.templarcustom.com

TENEBRAEX, A DIVISION OF ARMAMENT TECHNOLOGY INC.
Anti-reflection devices, scope covers, and weapon sight polarizers.
3045 Robie Street, Suite 113
Halifax, B3K 4P6 Canada
Website: www.tenebraex.com
Phone No.: 902-454-6384

THERMOLD DESIGN & DEVELOPMENT
Zytel high capacity magazines.
115 Perimeter Center Place NE., Suite 150
Atlanta, GA 30346
Website: www.thermoldmagazines.com
Phone No.: 877-548-4062
Fax No.: 866-523-1653

THOMPSON MACHINE
Suppressors.
172 Center Street
Panacea, FL 32346
Website: www.ThompsonMachine.net
Phone No.: 850-766-4197

TIMNEY MANUFACTURING, INC.
Replacement triggers for rifles and Rem. 870 shotguns.
3940 West Clarendon Avenue
Phoenix, AZ 85019
Website: www.timneytriggers.com
Phone No.: 602-274-2999
Fax No.: 602-241-0361

TRIJICON, INC.
Night sights, red dot sights, riflescopes, night vision and thermal imaging systems.
49385 Shafer Avenue
P.O. Box 930059
Wixom, MI 48393
Website: www.trijicon.com
Phone No.: 248-960-7700
Fax No.: 248-960-7725

TRIPLE K MANUFACTURING COMPANY, INC.
Pistol, rifle, and shotgun magazines.
2222 Commercial Street
San Diego, CA 92113
Website: www.triplek.com
Phone No.: 619-232-2066
Fax No.: 619-232-7675

TROY INDUSTRIES, INC.
Small arms components and accessories, complete weapon upgrades.
126 Myron Street
West Springfield, MA 01089
Website: www.troyind.com
Phone No.: 413-788-4288
Fax No.: 413-383-0339

TRUGLO, INC.
Tritium fiber-optic aiming systems, red dot sights, riflescopes.
710 Presidential Drive
Richardson, TX 75081
Website: www.truglo.com
Phone No.: 972-774-0300
Fax No.: 972-774-0323

ULTIMAK
Rails, accessories, optics mounts, grips, rings, and stocks for AK, Saiga, AR, M14, Mini 14/30 and M1 rifles.
2216 S. Main, Suite B2
Moscow, ID 83843
Website: www.ultimak.com
Phone No.: 208-883-4734
Fax No.: 208-882-3896

ULTRA DOT DISTRIBUTION
Red dot, micro dot, and fiber optic sights.
6304 Riverside Drive
P.O. Box 362
Yankeetown, FL 34498
Website: www.ultradotusa.com
Phone No.: 352-447-2255
Fax No.: 352-447-2266

UNI-DOT
See LYMAN PRODUCTS CORP

URBAN-E.R.T. SLINGS, LLC
Custom weapon slings.
P.O. Box 429
Clayton, IN 46118
Website: www.urbanertslings.com
Phone No.: 317-223-6509
Fax No.: 317-539-2585

US NIGHT VISION CORPORATION
Night vision and laser sights.
1376 Lead Hill Blvd., Suite 190
Roseville, CA 95661
Website: www.usnightvision.com
Phone No.: 916-788-1110
Fax No.: 916-788-1113

U.S. OPTICS, INC.
Riflescopes, mounting systems, custom scopes, lenses, and mounts.
150 Arovista Circle
Brea, CA 92821
Website: www.usoptics.com
Phone No.: 714-582-1956
Fax No.: 714-582-1959

VALDADA OPTICS
European tactical, precision, and long range riflescopes.
P.O. Box 270095
Littleton, CO 80127
Website: www.valdada.com
Phone No.: 303-979-4578
Fax No.: 303-979-0256

VANG COMP SYSTEMS
Barrels, magazine tube extensions, oversized safeties, and sights for tactical shotguns.
400 West Butterfield Road
Chino Valley, AZ 86323
Website: www.vangcomp.com
Phone No.: 928-636-8455
Fax No.: 928-636-1538

VICKERS
See BLUE FORCE GEAR, INC.

VIKING TACTICS, INC.
AR15/M16 parts and accessories, slings, sights, and mounts.
Fayetteville, NC 28306
Website: www.vikingtactics.com
Phone No.: 910-987-5983
Fax No.: 910-565-3710

VIRIDIAN
See LASER AIMING SYSTEMS CORPORATION.

VLTOR WEAPON SYSTEMS
Modular buttstocks, and components and accessories for AR15/M16/AK rifles.
3735 North Romero Road
Tucson, AZ 85705
Website; www.vltor.com
Phone No.: 520-408-1944
Fax No.: 520-293-8807

VORTEX OPTICS
Red dot sights, riflescopes, rings and mounts.
2120 West Greenview Drive, Suite 4
Middleton, WI 53562
Website: www.vortextactical.com
Phone No.: 800-426-0048
Fax No.: 608-662-7454

WARNE MANUFACTURING COMPANY
Scope rings and mounts.
9057 SE Jannsen Road
Clackamas, OR 97015
Website: www.warnescopemounts.com
Phone No.: 503-657-5590
Fax No.: 503-657-5695

WEAVER OPTICS
Mounting systems, riflescopes, red dot sights.
N5549 County Trunk Z
Onalaska, WI 54650
Website: www.weaveroptics.com
Phone No.: 800-635-7656
Fax No.: 763-323-3890

WILCOX INDUSTRIES CORP.
*Night vision mounting systems, weapon video
display, thermal sights, tail cap switches, AK-SC,
M4, and MP-7 rail systems, Rapid Acquisition
Aiming Module (RAAM).*
25 Piscataqua Drive
Newington, NH 03801
Website: www.wilcoxind.com
Phone No.: 603-431-1331
Fax No.: 603-431-1221

WILLIAMS GUN SIGHT COMPANY
*Pistol, rifle, and shotgun fiber optic sights, scope
mounts, open sights, receiver sights, shotgun
sights, sling swivels, and tactical rifle muzzle
brakes .*
7389 Lapeer Road
Davison, MI 48423
Website: www.williamsgunsight.com
Phone No.: 810-653-2131
Fax No.: 810-658-2140

WILLIAMS TRIGGER SPECIALTIES
*Sniper grade trigger upgrades for most semi-auto
rifles.*
111 SE Second Street
Atwood, IL 61913
Website: www.williamstriggers.com
Phone No.: 217-578-3026

WMD GUNS LLC
*AR15 parts, bolt carriers, and .22 LR
conversion kits.*
3070 SE Dominica Terrace
Stuart, FL 34997
Website: www.wmdguns.com
Phone No.: 772-324-9915

WRENTECH INDUSTRIES LLC
Mfr. of the Advantage Tactical Sight.
7 Avenida Vista Grande B-7
PMB #510
Santa Fe, NM 87508
Website: www.advantagetactical.com

XGRIP
See FDI/FREED DESIGNS, INC.

X PRODUCTS
*High capacity magazines and firearm
accessories.*
14838 NW Fawnlily Drive
Portland, OR 97229
website: www.xproducts.com

XRAIL
See ROTH CONCEPT INNOVATIONS, LLC.

XS SIGHT SYSTEMS, INC.
*XS 24/7 tritium night sights for handguns, rifles,
and shotguns; tactical sights for AR15/M16/HK
rifles, and mounting systems.*
2401 Ludelle Street
Fort Worth, TX 76105
Website: www.xssights.com
Phone No.: 817-536-0136
Fax No.: 817-536-3517

YANKEE HILL MACHINE CO., INC.
*Rail systems, forearms, flip-up sights, rifle and
pistol suppressors, flash suppressors,
compensators, and forward grips.*
20 Ladd Av, Suite 1
Florence, MA 01062
Website: www.yhm.net
Phone No.: 413-584-1400
Fax No.: 413-586-1326

YUKON ADVANCED OPTICS
Riflescopes and night visions optics.
201 Regency Parkway
Mansfield, TX 76063
Website: www.yukonopticsusa.com
Phone No.: 817-225-0310
Fax No.: 817-394-1628

ZEL CUSTOM/TACTILITE
*Bolt-action uppers for AR style rifles in .338
Lapua, .416 Barrett, and .50 BMG calibers.*
11419 Challenger Av
Odessa, FL 33556
Website: www.zelcustom.com
Phone No.: 303-880-8701
Fax No.: 303-353-1473

ZEV TECHNOLOGIES, INC.
Drop-in components for Glocks.
1051 Yarnell Place
Oxnard, CA 93033
Website: www.glockworx.com

BATFE GUIDE

A listing has been provided below of Field Division offices for the BATFE. You are encouraged to contact them if you have any questions regarding the legality of any weapons or their interpretation of existing laws and regulations. Remember, ignorance is no excuse when it involves Federal firearms regulations and laws. Although these various offices may not be able to help you with state, city, county, or local firearms regulations and laws, their job is to assist you on a Federal level.

S. Department of Justice
reau of Alcohol, Tobacco,
rearms and Explosives:
ebsite: www.atf.gov

lanta Field Division
00 Century Parkway Suite 300
lanta, Georgia 30345
one No.: (404) 417-2600
x: (404) 417-2601
nail: AtlantaDiv@atf.gov

ltimore Field Division
Hopkins Plaza, 5th Floor
ltimore, Maryland 21201
one No.: (443) 965-2000
x: (443) 965-2001
nail: BaltimoreDiv@atf.gov

ston Field Division
Causeway Street, Suite 791
ston, Massachusetts 02222
one No.: (617) 557-1200
x: (617) 557-1201
nail: BostonDiv@atf.gov

harlotte Field Division
01 Carmel Road, Suite 200
harlotte, North Carolina 28226
one No.: (704) 716-1800
x (704) 716-1801
nail: CharlotteDiv@atf.gov

hicago Field Division
5 West Van Buren Street,
ite 600
hicago, Illinois 60607
hone No.: (312) 846-7200
x: (312) 846-7201
mail: ChicagoDiv@atf.gov

olumbus Field Division
30 West Street, Suite 400
olumbus, Ohio 43215
hone No.: (614) 827-8400
x: (614) 827-8401
mail: ColumbusDiv@atf.gov

allas Field Division
114 Commerce Street, Room 303
allas, TX 75242
hone No.: (469) 227-4300
ax: (469) 227-4330
mail: DallasDiv@atf.gov

enver Field Division
50 17th Street, Suite 1800
enver, Colorado 80202 USA
hone No.: (303) 575-7600
ax (303) 575-7601
enverDiv@atf.gov

Detroit Field Division
1155 Brewery Park Boulevard,
Suite 300
Detroit, Michigan 48207
Phone No.: (313) 202-3400
Fax: (313) 202-3445
Email: DetroitDiv@atf.gov

Houston Field Division
5825 N. Sam Houston Pkwy, Suite 300
Houston, Texas 77086 USA
Phone No.: (281) 716-8200
Fax (281) 716-8219
HoustonDiv@atf.gov

Kansas City Field Division
2600 Grand Avenue, Suite 200
Kansas City, Missouri 64108
Phone No.: (816) 559-0700
Fax: (816) 559-0701
Email: KansasCityDiv@atf.gov

Los Angeles Field Division
550 North Brand Avenue
8th Floor
Glendale, California 91203
Phone No.: (818) 265-2500
Fax: (818) 265-2501
Email: LosAngelesDiv@atf.gov

Louisville Field Division
600 Dr. Martin Luther King Jr. Place, Suite 322
Louisville, KY 40202
Phone No.: (502) 753-3400
Fax: (502) 753-3401
Email: LouisDiv@atf.gov

Miami Field Division
11410 NW 20 Street, Suite 201
Miami, FL 33172
Phone No.: (305) 597-4800
Fax: 305-597-4801
Email: MiamiDiv@atf.gov

Nashville Field Division
5300 Maryland Way, Suite 200
Brentwood, Tennessee 37027
Phone No.: (615) 565-1400
Fax: 615-565-1401
Email: NashDiv@atf.gov

Newark Field Division
1 Garret Mountain Plaza Suite 500
Woodland Park, New Jersey 07424
Phone No.: (973) 413-1179
Fax: (973) 413-1190
Email: NJDivision@atf.gov

New Orlearns
One Galleria Boulevard Suite 1700
Metairie, Louisiana 70001
Phone No.: (504) 841-7000
Fax: (504) 841-7039
Email: NewOrleansDiv@atf.gov

New York Field Division
Financial Square
32 Old Slip
Suite 3500
New York, New York 10005 USA
Phone No.: (646) 335-9000
Fax (646) 335-9001
NYDiv@atf.gov

Philadelphia Field Division
The Curtis Center
601 Walnut Street, Suite 1000E
Philadelphia, Pennsylvania 19106
Phone No.: (215) 446-7800
Fax: (215) 446-7811
Email: PhilDiv@atf.gov

Phoenix Field Division
201 E. Washington Street, Suite 940
Phoenix, Arizona 85004
Phone No.: (602) 776-5400
Fax: (602) 776-5429
Email: PhoenixDiv@atf.gov

San Francisco Field Division
5601 Arnold Road, Suite 400
Dublin, California 94568
Phone No.: (925) 557-2800
Fax: (925) 557-2805
Email: SanFranciscoDiv@atf.gov

Seattle Field Division
915 2nd Avenue, Room 790
Seattle, Washington 98174
Phone No.: (206) 389-5800
Fax: (206) 389-5829
Email: SeattleDiv@atf.gov

St. Paul Field Division
30 East Seventh Street , Suite 1900
St. Paul, Minnesota 55101
Phone No.: (651) 726-0200
Fax: (651) 726-0201
Email: StPaulDiv@atf.gov

Tampa Field Division
400 North Tampa Street
Suite 2100
Tampa, Florida 33602
Phone No.: (813) 202-7300
Fax: (813) 202-7301
Email: TampaDiv@atf.gov

Washington Field Division
1401 H. Street NW, Suite 900
Washington, District of Columbia 20226
Phone No.: (202) 648-8010
Fax: (202) 648-8001
Email: WashDiv@atf.gov

INDEX

#

A